Book Three of the Corpus Tibullianum:

Introduction, Text, Translation and Commentary

By

Robert Maltby

Pierides
Studies in Greek and Latin Literature

Volume X

Series Editors:
Philip Hardie, Stratis Kyriakidis,
Antonis K. Petrides

Pierides

Volume I
Stratis Kyriakidis
Catalogues of Proper Names in Latin Epic Poetry:
Lucretius – Virgil – Ovid

Volume II
Antonis K. Petrides and Sophia Papaioannou (eds)
New Perspectives on Postclassical Comedy

Volume III
Myrto Garani and David Konstan (eds)
The Philosophizing Muse:
The Influence of Greek Philosophy on Roman Poetry

Volume IV
Sophia Papaioannou (ed.)
Terence and Interpretation

Volume V
Stephen Harrison (ed.)
Characterisation in Apuleius' Metamorphoses
Nine Studies

Volume VI
Stratis Kyriakidis (ed.)
Libera Fama: An Endless Journey

Volume VII
Vayos Liapis, Maria Pavlou, Antonis K. Petrides (eds)
Debating with the Eumenides:
Aspects of the Reception of Greek Tragedy in Modern Greece

Volume VIII
Consuelo Ruiz-Montero (ed.)
Aspects of Orality and Greek Literature in the Roman Empire

Volume IX
Sophia Papaioannou and Chrysanthe Demetriou (eds)
Plautus' Erudite Comedy:
New Insights into the Work of a doctus poeta

Book Three of the Corpus Tibullianum:

Introduction, Text, Translation and Commentary

By

Robert Maltby

Cambridge
Scholars
Publishing

Book Three of the Corpus Tibullianum:
Introduction, Text, Translation and Commentary

By Robert Maltby

This book first published 2021

Cambridge Scholars Publishing

Lady Stephenson Library, Newcastle upon Tyne, NE6 2PA, UK

British Library Cataloguing in Publication Data
A catalogue record for this book is available from the British Library

Copyright © 2021 by Robert Maltby

All rights for this book reserved. No part of this book may be reproduced, stored in a retrieval system, or transmitted, in any form or by any means, electronic, mechanical, photocopying, recording or otherwise, without the prior permission of the copyright owner.

ISBN (10): 1-5275-6823-7
ISBN (13): 978-1-5275-6823-5

For Stratis and Eleni

Contents

Preface ix

Corporis Tibulliani Codicum Manuscriptorum Sigla 1

TEXT AND TRANSLATION *Corporis Tibulliani Liber Tertius* 3

Prolegomena 80

General Introduction 84

1. The Structure and Origins of [Tibullus] 3 84
   1.1. The traditional view: multiple authorship 84
   1.2. The arguments for unitary authorship 86
   1.3. A unifying intertext: Ovid *Metamorphoses* 7.661-882 90

2. The Author's Masks and the Book's sections 94
   2.1 The Author's Masks 94
   2.2 The Book's Sections 96
      2.2.1 *Lygdamus* 3.1-6 96
      2.2.2 Poem 3.7, the *Laudes Messallae* (*Panegyricus Messallae*) .. 100
      2.2.3 The *Sulpicia Cycle*: poems 3.8-12 102
      2.2.4 The *Sulpicia* poems 3.13-18 104
      2.2.5 The Closural Poems 3.19 and 20 110

3. The Characters of Book 3: Significant Names and their Past 111
   3.1 Lygdamus 111
   3.2 Neaera 118
   3.3 Valerius Messalla Corvinus 120
   3.4 Cerinthus 123
   3.5 Sulpicia 126

4. The Manuscript Tradition of [Tibullus] 3 128

5. Concluding Remarks 129

Commentary 130
   Poem 3.1 130
   Poem 3.2 159
   Poem 3.3 177
   Poem 3.4 200
   Poem 3.5 274
   Poem 3.6 298
   Poem 3.7 337
   Poem 3.8 436
   Poem 3.9 456
   Poem 3.10 473
   Poem 3.11 487
   Poem 3.12 499
   Poem 3.13 508
   Poem 3.14 519
   Poem 3.15 524
   Poem 3.16 526
   Poem 3.17 530
   Poem 3.18 533
   Poem 3.19 536
   Poem 3.20 553
   Epitaph of Tibullus attributed to Domitius Marsus 556
   Life of Tibullus 559

Appendix 563

Bibliography 572

Index 1 (General Index) 599

Index 2 (Index of Latin and Greek Words) 609

Index 3 (Index Locorum) 618

PREFACE

Work on this volume began over ten years ago. Its aim was to provide the first complete text, translation and commentary in English on the third book of the *Corpus Tibullianum*. It is natural that over such a long period one's ideas on the work should change. I started with the commonly accepted view that this was the work of several different authors, but as I became more deeply acquainted with the book it became clear to me that profound links and resonances between the different sections made the concept of a single author for the whole work a more likely possibility. It is hoped that this volume will help to highlight the literary sophistication often denied to this work and to open a debate on questions of authorship, structure and aesthetic value.

The text for this volume was established by a new collation of all the manuscripts listed in the *sigla*. I acknowledge a huge debt of gratitude to the staff of numerous libraries over Europe who have provided me with access to the original manuscripts or to photographs on-line.

Numerous friends and colleagues have helped me over this book's long period of gestation. The publishing team has provided patient and professional support at all times. I am particularly grateful to Barrie Hall for his help and advice on the establishment of the text and for his detailed comments on earlier versions of this book. His unfailing eye for detail saved me from committing a number of errors and his sound judgement has served to improve the volume in many ways. My thanks also go to Tony Woodman for reading and improving a number of sections and, in particular, for his detailed comments on the *Messalla Panegyric*. I owe a debt to Stephen Heyworth for inviting me to speak at his Oxford seminar on [Tibullus] 3 in 2016 at which I benefitted from discussions on the topic with a number of scholars, including Laurel Fulkerson, who had just completed her own commentary on the elegies of the Tibullan Appendix. I owe a similar debt to other colleagues who have invited me to share my views on this subject at conferences or invited lectures, the feedback from which has enriched this volume considerably, namely: Niklas Holzberg (University of Munich - on two occasions), Anna Chahoud and Boris Kayachev (Trinity College Dublin), Tristan Franklinos and Laurel Fulkerson

(University of Oxford), Anke Walter (University of Newcastle), Charilaos Michalopoulos (University of Thrace, Komotini), Athanassios Vergados (University of Newcastle). I am grateful to Philip Hardie who read a final version of the manuscript and provided help and support at all times. Boris Kayachev, a former doctoral student of mine, read through and commented on the manuscript at a late stage and I am grateful to him for his many sensible suggestions. Last but not least, my friends Stratis Kyriakidis and Eleni Kyriakidou read through the book in its final stages of completion, encouraged me in my speculations about authorship and gave advice on a number of literary issues. In grateful recognition of their hard work on the detailed preparation of the manuscript and their help and support over the years with this and many other projects the present volume is dedicated to them. For such errors, misprints and omissions as remain I alone am responsible.

Robert Maltby
St. Margaret's Bay
Kent
August 2020

CORPORIS TIBULLIANI
CODICVM MANVSCRIPTORVM SIGLA

A	Mediolanensis Ambrosianus R 26 sup., a. 1375
B	Parisinus latinus 7989, a. 1423
C	Carpentoractensis Bibl. municip. Inguimbertine 361 (L357), c. 1440-1450
D	Berolinensis Diez B. Sant. 39b, a. 1463
E	Berolinensis Diez B. Sant. 21, ante 1463
F	Fragmentum Cuiacianum, aetatis incertae
F (*Plant.*)	lectiones Scaligeri ex fragmento Cuiaciano in mg. ed. Plant. 1569 scriptae
F (*Cast.*)	lectiones Scaligeri ex fragmento Cuiaciano in Castigationibus 1577 scriptae
G	Guelferbytanus Aug. 82, 6, saec. XV
H	Hamburgensis Bibl. publ. et uniu. scrin. 139, saec. XV
J	Londiniensis Egerton 3027, a. 1467
K	Oxoniensis Bodl. Canon. class. lat. 33, a. 1450
L	Londiniensis Harley 2574, a. 1460
M	Mediolanensis Braidensis AD XII 37 No. 2, a. 1450
N	Oxoniensis Bodl. lat. class. d. 5 (30059), a. 1421

O	Vaticanus Ottobonianus latinus 1202, a. 1426
P	Vaticanus Palatinus latinus 1652, c. 1445-1460
p	Vaticanus Palatinus latinus 1707, saec. XV
Q	Caesaraugustanus Bibl. Del Real Seminario de San Carlos A-5-9 (9377), a. 1469
R	Parisinus latinus 8018, c. 1464-1465
S	Vaticanus latinus 2794, a. 1434
T	Vindobonensis latinus 224, c. 1450-1470
V	Vaticanus latinus 3270, a. 1420
v	Venetus Marcianus lat. 12.153 (4453), c. 1460-1470
W	Londiniensis Harley 4059, saec. XV
X	Parisinus latinus 8233, a. 1465
Y	Eboracensis Heinsii deperditus, a. 1425

Excerpta et Florilegia

Exc. Fris.   Excerpta Frisingensia, Monacensis clm 6292, saec. XI (in.)

Flor. Ven.   Florilegium Venetum, Marcianus latinus Z 497 (1811), saec. XI (ex.)

Flor. Gall.   Florilegium Gallicum Parisinus latinus 7647, saec. XIII; Parisinus latinus 17903, saec. XIII

His etiam compendiis utor

A+	A cum plerisque codicibus
codd.	omnes quos noui codices

Corporis Tibvlliani

Liber Tertivs

I-VI ELEGIAE
(IN PERSONA LYGDAMI)

I

Martis Romani festae uenere Kalendae
   (exoriens nostris hic fuit annus auis)
et uaga nunc certa discurrunt undique pompa
   perque uias urbis munera perque domos.
dicite, Pierides, quonam donetur honore   5
   seu mea seu fallor cara Neaera tamen.
'carmine formosae pretio capiuntur auarae:
   gaudeat, ut digna est, uersibus illa tuis.
lutea sed niueum inuoluat membrana libellum
   pumex et canas tondeat ante comas   10
summaque praetexat tenuis fastigia charta
   indicet ut nomen littera rubra tuum
atque extra geminas pingantur cornua frontes:
   sic etenim comptum mittere oportet opus.'

7 *Flor. Gall.*

I 2 hinc Q, *Scaliger, Broukhusius*   **7-14** *Musis dederunt editores plurimi a Mureto. sequor*   **7** auari *Flor.Gall.*   **8** tuis *Muretus*: meis *codd.*: nouis *Postgate*   **10** pumex et G^{pc}, *Muretus*: pumicet et A+: pumice que et C Q   arte E W   **11** praetexat G H S: protexit A+: protexat N   charta *Becker*: cartae A+: carta D   **12** rubra *Némethy*: facta *codd.*: picta *Liuineius*   tuum A+: meum C   **13** extra *Hall*: inter *codd.*: intra *Blümner*   geminae *Wunderlich*

Book Three of the Corpus Tibullianum: 5
Introduction, Text, Translation and Commentary

1-6 ELEGIES (IN THE MASK OF LYGDAMUS)

Poem 1

The festive Calends of Roman Mars have come – this was New Year for our ancestors – and wandering gifts run about on all sides in fixed procession through the streets and houses of the city. Tell me, Pierian Muses, with what gift should my Neaera (or, if I am mistaken, at least dear Neaera) be honoured.

'Beautiful women are taken by poetry, greedy ones by cash: let her rejoice, as she deserves, in your verses. But let saffron parchment wrap the snowy papyrus, and first let pumice shave off its white hairs **[10]**. Let a small label border its topmost edge, to make known your name with red inscription, and let the horns projecting from the two sides be painted. This is how one should send a polished work.'

per uos auctores huius mihi carminis oro 15
    Castaliamque umbram Pieriosque lacus,
ite domum cultumque illi donate libellum,
    sicut erit: nullus defluat inde color.
illa mihi referat sit nostri mutua cura
    an minor an toto pectore deciderim. 20
sed primum meritam larga donate salute
    atque haec submisso dicite uerba sono:
'haec tibi uir quondam nunc frater, casta Neaera,
    mittit et accipias munera parua rogat
teque suis iurat caram magis esse medullis, 25
    siue sibi coniunx siue futura soror.
sed potius coniunx: huius spem nominis illi
    auferet extincto pallida Ditis aqua.'

16 *Flor. Ven.*

15 per uos B[pc] C G N: paruos A+: peruos V   **16** umbram *Flor.Ven.*, G[ac] O: umbrosam A+: undam G[pc]   lacos *Flor.Ven.*   **19** mihi referat B C: mihi referet A+: referte mihi *O.Skutsch*   sit nostri *Lee*: si nostri A+: nostri si C N S   cura C, *Lee*: cura est A+   **20** an maneam G, *Baehrens*   **21** meritam G V[pc]: meritum A+: nymphen C: nympham P longa P   **26** sibi B G O V[pc] : tibi A+

I beg you as inspirers of this work of mine, by Castalian shade and Pierian spring, go to her house and give her this stylish book, just as you will find it: let it lose none of its colour. Let her tell me whether her love is equal to mine, or smaller, or whether I have fallen completely from her heart [20]. But first, as she deserves, wish her the best of health and speak these word in a low voice:

'Chaste Neaera, this small gift your former husband, now your brother, sends and asks you to receive, and he swears that you are dearer to him than his innermost being, whether you will be his wife or his sister, but rather his wife: hope of this name the pale waters of Dis will take from him at death.'

II

Qui primus caram iuueni carumque puellae
    eripuit iuuenem, ferreus ille fuit.
durus et ille fuit qui tantum ferre dolorem
    uiuere et erepta coniuge qui potuit.
non ego firmus in hoc, non haec patientia nostro   5
    ingenio: frangit fortia corda dolor.
nec mihi uera loqui pudor est uitaeque fateri
    tot mala perpessae taedia nata meae.
ergo cum tenuem fuero mutatus in umbram
    candidaque ossa supra nigra fauilla teget,   10
ante meum ueniat longos incompta capillos
    et fleat ante meum maesta Neaera rogum.
sed ueniat carae matris comitata dolore:
    maereat haec genero, maereat illa uiro.
praefatae ante meos manes animamque recentem   15
    perfusaeque pias ante liquore manus,
pars quae sola mei superabit corporis, ossa
    incinctae nigra candida ueste legant.
et primum annoso spargant collecta Lyaeo,
    mox etiam niueo fundere lacte parent,   20
post haec carbaseis umorem tollere uelis
    atque in marmorea ponere sicca domo.
illic quas mittit diues Panchaia merces
    Eoique Arabes diues et Assyria
et nostri memores lacrimae fundantur eodem: 25
    sic ego componi uersus in ossa uelim.
sed tristem mortis demonstret littera causam
    atque haec in celebri carmina fronte notet:
LYGDAMVS HIC SITVS EST. DOLOR HVIC ET CVRA NEAERAE
    CONIVGIS EREPTAE CAVSA PERIRE FVIT.   30

1-2 *Exc.Fris.* 6 *Flor.Gall.*

II 1 carumque A+, *Exc. Fris.*: carumue C N P   5 patiemur ex aequo *Petreius 'ex antiquis'. ed. pr. mai. 1472*   7 est B N V^{pc}: om. A+   9 ergo cum A+: ergo ego cum V^2: o ego cum *Hall*   8 taedia nata A+: taedia nota G V^{pc}: tot superesse C, *Ald. 1502*: tot superasse Q   9 ergo ego cum V^{pc} 10 super B G   12 casta C Q   15 recentem *Bach*: rogatae A+ G^{pc}: precatae Y^{pc}: togatae G^{ac}: uocatam *uel* rogatam *Cartault*   18 legant H, *Muretus*: legent A+   19 spargant *Muretus*: spargent *codd.*   21 uelis *tres Vossiani apud Huschke*: uentis A+   23 illic A+: illinc C Q: illuc *Passerat*   24 pinguis C Q   29 cura G^{pc}: cara G^{ac}: causa A+   Neaerae *Muretus*: neaera A+

Poem 2

Iron-hearted was that man who first snatched from a youth his dear girl or from a girl her dear youth. And unfeeling too was he who could bear such pain and live on with his wife snatched away. I am not strong enough for that, such endurance is not in my nature; pain breaks strong hearts. I am not ashamed to speak the truth and confess that I have become tired of a life which has suffered so many wrongs.

Therefore, when I am changed into an insubstantial shade and black ash covers my white bones over **[10]**, may grieving Neaera come, her long hair unkempt, and weep before my pyre. But may she come in the company of her dear mother's grief; the one mourning her son-in-law, the other her husband.

Having first addressed my ghost and recently departed spirit and cleansed with water their dutiful hands, wrapped in black let them gather my white bones, the only part of my body to remain, and first, when gathered, sprinkle them with vintage wine, and next prepare to pour over them snow-white milk also **[20]**, then to remove the moisture with linen cloths and place them dry in their marble home. There let the wares that rich Panchaia and the Arabs of the East and rich Assyria send be poured over them together with tears in memory of me. That is how I would wish to be laid to rest when turned to bones.

But let an inscription show the sad cause of my death and mark this epitaph on the frequented side: LYGDAMUS IS BURIED HERE. GRIEF AND LOVE FOR NEAERA, THE WIFE SNATCHED FROM HIM, CAUSED HIS DEATH **[30]**.

III

Quid prodest caelum uotis inplesse Neaera,
    blandaque cum multa tura dedisse prece,
non ut marmorei prodirem e limine tecti
    insignis clara conspicuusque domo
aut ut multa mei renouarent iugera tauri   5
    et magnas messes terra benigna daret,
sed tecum ut longae sociarem gaudia uitae,
    inque tuo caderet nostra senecta sinu,
tunc cum permenso defunctus tempore lucis
    nudus Lethaea cogerer ire rate?   10
nam graue quid prodest pondus mihi diuitis auri
    aruaque si findant pinguia mille boues?
quidue domus prodest Phrygiis innixa columnis,
    Taenare, siue tuis, siue, Caryste, tuis
et nemora in domibus sacros imitantia lucos   15
    aurataeque trabes marmoreumque solum?
quidue in Erythraeo legitur quae litore concha
    tinctaque Sidonio murice lana iuuat,
et quae praeterea populus miratur? in illis
    inuidia est. falso plurima uulgus amat.   20
non opibus mentes hominum curaeque leuantur,
    nam Fortuna sua tempora lege regit.

11-13 *Flor.Gall.*   **16-22** *Flor.Gall.*   **21-2** *Exc.Fris.*

III 1 flammis C Q   **2** tulisse B   **3** marmoreo C Q   **7** sociarem G H: sociarent A+   **9** permensae E   **11** quid prodesse potest pondus graue *Flor.Gall.*   **13** subnixa C Q   **14** Caryste *editores*: thariste A+: cariste G: carista C   **17** Erythraeo *editores*: erit(h)reo A+: eritheo *Flor. Gall.*, C   legitur quae *Flor.Gall.*, G O: legiturque in A+   **20** inuidia est *Flor. Gall.*, G[pc]: inuida quae A+   **21** hominum *Exc. Fris.*, *Flor.Gall.*, G V[pc]: homini A+   **22** nam A+: nec *Exc.Fris.*   regit *Flor.Gall.*, G: gerit *Exc.Fris.*, A+

Poem 3

What good does it do, Neaera, to fill heaven with vows and offer pleasing incense with many a prayer, not that I might come forth from the door of a marble mansion, admired and distinguished for my illustrious house, or that my oxen should renew my many acres and that the bountiful earth should give great harvests, but that I should share with you the joys of a long life and that my old age should fall in your embrace then when I have completed my allotted span of light and am forced to depart naked on Lethe's boat [10]?

What good to me is a heavy mass of precious gold and a thousand oxen ploughing my rich fields? Or what good is a house supported on Phrygian pillars, or on yours, Taenarus, or on yours, Carystos, and woods in the house imitating sacred groves, and gilded beams and a marble floor? Or what use are the shells gathered on the Red Sea's shores and wool dyed in purple from Sidon and whatever else the people admire? In them lies envy. The crowd loves most things falsely [20]. It is not wealth that lightens the minds and cares of men; Fortune with her own law rules the times.

sit mihi paupertas tecum iucunda, Neaera,
   et sine te regum munera nulla uolo.
o niueam quae te poterit mihi reddere lucem,   25
   o mihi felicem terque quaterque diem.
at si pro dulci reditu quaecumque uouentur
   audiat auersa non meus aure deus,
nec me regna iuuant nec Lydius aurifer amnis
   nec quas terrarum sustinet orbis opes.   30
haec alii cupiant. liceat mihi paupere cultu
   securo cara coniuge posse frui.
adsis et timidis faueas, Saturnia, uotis
   et faueas concha, Cypria, uecta tua.
quod si fata negant reditum tristesque sorores   35
   stamina quae ducunt quaeque futura canunt,
me uocet in uastos amnes nigramque paludem
   Ditis et ignauam luridus Orcus aquam.

24 *Flor.Ven.*   **26** *Flor.Ven.*   **29** *Exc.Fris.*, *Flor.Gall.*, *Flor.Ven.*   **30-32** *Flor.Gall.*   **38** *Exc.Fris.*

23 sed mihi Y   **24** at *Flor.Ven.*, C D G N   **25** poterit quae te C Q   **27** reditu dulci G   **28** auersa C O: aduersa A+   **29** non me *Flor.Gall.*, C G   iuuent G   **31** capiant C Q   **32** securo uitae munere *Flor.Gall.*   **35** quod *Hall, coll.* Ou. *Met.* 10.38, 633: aut A+: at G² *Vat. Pal. lat.* 910   **36** canunt *Heinsius*: neunt *codd.*   **38** Ditis et ignauam ... aquam *Heinsius*: diues in ignaua...aqua *codd.*

Let me have poverty with you, Neaera -that would be sweet - and without you I want no royal gifts. O bright the day that can bring you back to me! Oh three and four times happy for me will be that day. But if whatever vows are made for your sweet return a god not favourable to me should hear with ears averted, then neither kingdoms can help me, nor Lydia's gold-bearing river, nor all the wealth the earth's globe bears **[30]**. Let others wish for these things, if only I with simple life and free from care be allowed to enjoy my dear wife.

Be present, Saturn's daughter, and grant my fearful prayers; grant them, Lady of Cyprus, voyaging on your seashell. But if the Fates and the sad sisters who spin their threads and sing the future forbid her return, then let pale Orcus call me to the desolate streams, black swamp and stagnant waters of Dis.

IV

Di meliora ferant nec sint mihi somnia uera
    quae tulit hesterna pessima nocte quies.
ite procul, uani, falsumque auertite, uisus,
    desinite in nobis quaerere uelle fidem.
diui uera monent, uenturae nuntia sortis;   5
    uera monent Tuscis exta probata uiris:
somnia fallaci ludunt temeraria nocte
    et pauidas mentes falsa timere iubent.
et natum in curas hominum genus omina noctis
    farre pio placant et saliente sale.   10

7-8 *Exc.Fris., Flor.Gall.*

IV 1 insomnia D P   **2** hesterna A+: externa C D M N Q S: extrema J^{ac} pessima A+: pexima B N T^{ac}: proxima C L Q W   **3-4** *post 16 Postgate*   **3** uani A B C^{pc} G J^{pc} K L M O P p S^{pc} V^{ac} v: uarii J^{ac}: uanum D E H N S^{ac} T V^{pc} X Y   uisus *Bolle, Lee*: uisum *codd.*   **4** nobis *Guietus*: uotis *codd.*   **5** diuae vera monent, uenturi nuntia, sortes *Antolín*   **9** at G^{pc}, *Muretus*   natum in curas C J^{pc} K S^{pc} T v W: natum maturas A^{ac} B O S^{ac} V: natum naturas A^{pc}: natum in curam L^{ac}: uanum in curam pnatum in matura M: uatum metuens D: uanum uentura E G J^{ac} L^{pc} N P V^{ul} X Y^{pc}: uarium uentura H Y^{ac} omina A+: omnia D E H J M O P p T X

Poem 4

May the gods bring better things, and may the dreams that sleep at its worst brought me last night be untrue. Away with you, empty visions, and turn aside your falsehood. Cease wishing to search in me for credibility. The gods give true warnings, messages of our coming fate; entrails tested by Tuscan men give true warnings. Random dreams delude in the deceptive night and bid fearful minds conceive false terrors; and the human race, born for cares, expiates the night omens with sacred spelt and leaping salt **[10]**.

et tamen, utcumque est, siue illi uera moneri
 mendaci somno credere siue uolent,
efficiat uanos noctis Lucina timores
 et frustra inmeritum pertimuisse uelit,
si mea nec turpi mens est obnoxia facto 15
 nec laesit magnos inpia lingua deos.
iam nox aetherium nigris emensa quadrigis
 mundum caeruleo lauerat amne rotas
nec me sopierat menti deus utilis aegrae
 Somnus (sollicitas deficit ante domos). 20
tandem, cum summo Phoebus prospexit ab ortu,
 pressit languentis lumina sera quies.
hic iuuenis casta redimitus tempora lauro
 est uisus nostra ponere sede pedem.
non uidit quicquam formosius ulla priorum 25
 aetas, humanum nec fuit illud opus.
intonsi crines longa ceruice fluebant
 stillabat Syrio myrrea rore coma.
candor erat qualem praefert Latonia Luna,
 et color in niueo corpore purpureus, 30
ut iuueni primum uirgo deducta marito
 inficitur teneras ore rubente genas,
et cum contexunt amarantis alba puellae
 lilia et autumno candida mala rubent.

19. *Flor.Gall.*, *Exc.Fris*.

11 utrumque D E J^{ac} N^{ac} S   illis *Dissen*   monenti C D E G^{pc} P v W
12 uolent A+: uelint B C D E v^{2}: solent *Postgate*   **14** pertimuisse A^{pc}+: pertinuisse A^{ac} : pretimuisse T   **17** aetherium G: etethereum A+ emensa D V^{pc}: emersa A+: dimensa G: demensa N S   **19** sopor utilis aegrae est *Flor.Gall.*   **25** uidit *Heyne*: illo *codd.*   **26** humanum nec fuit illud opus *Heyne*: humanum nec uidet illud opus *codd.*: heroum nec tulit ulla domus *Lachmann*: humanum nec tulit ille decus *Baehrens*: humanum nec uidet ulla domus *Postgate*: aut hominum nunc uidet ulla domus *Cartault*   **28** Syrio *Scaliger*: t(h)yrio *codd.*   myrrea G^{pc}: mirthea A+ : myrtea G^{ac} **33** aut cum *Puccius*

Nevertheless, however it is, whether they wish to receive true warnings or to believe in deceptive sleep, may Lucina render vain the terrors of the night and may it be her will that in my innocence my fear was groundless, provided my mind is not guilty of any shameful deed and my tongue has not offended with impiety the great gods.

Night in her black chariot had already traversed the heavenly sky and had washed her wheels in Ocean's blue stream, but Sleep, the god who helps the ailing mind, had brought me no rest – he fails before troubled homes [20]. Finally, when Phoebus looked forth from the top of his rising, late sleep closed my tired eyes.

Then a youth, his brows wreathed in chaste laurel, appeared in my dream to set foot in my home. No previous age of men saw anything more beautiful than he, nor was that a human work of art. His unshorn locks flowed down his slender neck and his myrrh-scented hair dripped with Syrian dew. His radiance was such as Latona's daughter the Moon displays, and rosy was the colour on his snow-white body [30], as a maiden first escorted to her young husband with blushing face dyes her tender cheeks, and as when girls entwine amaranthus with white lilies and as shining apples grow red in autumn.

ima uidebatur talis alludere palla   35
    namque haec in nitido corpore uestis erat.
artis opus rarae, fulgens testudine et auro
    pendebat laeua garrula parte lyra.
hanc primum ueniens plectro modulatus eburno
    felices cantus ore sonante dedit.   40
sed postquam fuerant digiti cum uoce locuti,
    edidit haec dulci tristia uerba modo:
'salue, cura deum: casto nam rite poetae
    Phoebusque et Bacchus Pieridesque fauent.
sed proles Semelae Bacchus doctaeque sorores   45
    dicere non norunt quid ferat hora sequens:
at mihi fatorum leges aeuique futuri
    euentura pater posse uidere dedit.
quare ego quae dicam non fallax, accipe, uates
    quodque deus uero Cynthius ore feram.   50
tantum cara tibi quantum nec filia matri,
    quantum nec cupido bella puella uiro,
pro qua sollicitas caelestia numina uotis,
    quae tibi securos non sinit ire dies
et cum te fusco Somnus uelauit amictu,   55
    uanum nocturnis fallit imaginibus,
carminibus celebrata tuis formosa Neaera
    alterius mauult esse puella uiri
diuersasque tuis agitat mens inpia curas,
    nec gaudet casta nupta Neaera domo.   60

35 alludere *Cyllenius ex cod., def. Allen (CR 20* [*1906*] *456*): illudere *codd.*
41 loquti A   **42** dulci tristia *Bernensis 527, Broukhusius*: tristi dulcia
A+   modo] sono D E T   **45** semel(a)e A J^{ac} M N^{pc} O^{ac} S T V Y :
semeles B C D E H K J^{pc} N^{ac} L O^{pc} P p v W X: semelis G   **47** aeuiique
A+ J^{pc} G^{pc}: cuique B M V: cuicumque J^{ac} **48** dedit ... pater L M
49 *dicam Voss, Tränkle*: dico *codd.*   **50** quodque P: quidque A+:
quodue C: quamque *Postgate*   feram *Broukhusius*: ferat A+: fauet C:
ferar *Havet*   **59** tuis *Lipsius*: suas A+: suis *Muretus*   anxia C   **60**
neaera G^{pc}: nerea A+: neera G^{ac} H

The hem of his cloak seemed to play about his ankles (for this was the garment on his shining body). A work of rare art, gleaming with tortoiseshell and gold, a melodious lyre hung on his left side. This he played when first he came with an ivory plectrum and gave forth auspicious songs from his tuneful lips **[40]**. But after his fingers and voice had spoken together he sweetly pronounced these sad words:

"Hail, beloved of the gods; for Phoebus, Bacchus and the Pierides rightly favour the pure poet. But Bacchus, offspring of Semele, and the learned sisters know not how to tell what the next hour will bring. But my father gave me the ability to see the laws of fate and the events of the future age. Therefore accept what I say as no false prophet, and what I, the Cynthian god, utter from my truthful lips **[50]**.

She who is as dear to you as no daughter ever was to her mother, no pretty girl to her passionate lover, for whom you importune the heavenly powers with prayers, who does not allow your days to pass in peace and, when Sleep has veiled you in his dusky robe, deceives you in your naivety with nocturnal visions, beautiful Neaera, celebrated in your songs, prefers to be another man's girl. Her wicked mind concerns itself with cares that are the opposite of yours, and as a wife Neaera takes no joy in her chaste home **[60]**.

a crudele genus nec fidum femina nomen,
   a pereat, didicit fallere si qua uirum.
sed flecti poterit; mens est mutabilis illis:
   tu modo cum multa bracchia tende prece.
saeuus Amor docuit ualidos temptare labores,   65
   saeuus Amor docuit uerbera posse pati.
me quondam Admeti niueas pauisse iuuencas
   non est in uanum fabula ficta iocum.
tunc ego nec cithara poteram gaudere sonora
   nec similes chordis reddere uoce sonos,   70
sed perlucenti cantum meditabar auena,
   ille ego Latonae filius atque Iouis.
nescis quid sit amor, iuuenis, si ferre recusas
   inmitem dominam coniugiumque ferum.
ergo ne dubita blandas adhibere querelas;   75
   uincuntur molli pectora dura prece.
quod si uera canunt sacris oracula templis,
   haec illi nostro nomine dicta refer:
"Hoc tibi coniugium promittit Delius ipse;
   felix hoc, alium desine uelle uirum.'"   80

63 *Flor.Gall.*   **65** *ab hoc uersu incipit* F   **66** *Exc.Fris.*   **76** *Flor.Ven.*

63 illis *Flor.Gall.* A+: illi B G   **64** prece G H V^{mg}: fide A+   **65** saeuus ... labores F(*Cast. et Plant.*) T^{ac}, *om.* A, *alii alia suppl.* flere nec ante pedes pudeat dominamque uocare G (*Pontanus*): saeuus Amor docuit dominae fera (uera p) uerba minantis B C D E H J L M N O (*Aurispa*) P p S T^{pc} v W X (*Puccius*): te uictum placidumque tuae monstrate puellae V *ima pag. qui uersus deinde deletus est*   **66** posse A+: saeua F(*Cast. et Plant.*)   **67** niueas ... iuuencas A+: niueos ... iuuencos C^{pc} J^{pc} L M S^{pc}: niueo ... iuuenco v^{pc} **71** perlucenti A+: polucenti N S: perluenti J^{pc}: permulcenti *Huschke*   cantus C L J^{pc} M W   **80** hoc F(*Cast.*): ac A+: at p

O cruel race, o faithless the name of woman. O death to her who has learned to deceive her man.

But she can be swayed; their minds are changeable. Simply stretch out your arms to her with many a prayer. Fierce Love has taught us to attempt tough labours, fierce Love has taught us to bear the lash. That I once pastured the snow-white heifers of Admetus is no myth invented as an idle joke. Then I could take no joy in the singing lyre, nor with my voice utter sounds to fit its strings **[70]**, but I practised my song on a translucent oat-stalk, I the son of Latona and of Jove. You do not know what love is, young man, if you refuse to bear a ruthless mistress and a cruel marriage. Therefore do not hesitate to use flattering complaints. Hard hearts are won over by gentle prayer. But if in holy temples the oracles sing true, then pass on to her these words in my name: "This marriage Delian Apollo in person promises to you; be happy in this and cease to wish for another husband **[80]**."

dixit, et ignauus defluxit corpore somnus.
    a ego ne possim tanta uidere mala.
nec tibi crediderim uotis contraria uota
    nec tantum crimen pectore inesse tuo.
nam te nec uasti genuerunt aequora ponti   85
    nec flammam uoluens ore Chimaera fero
nec canis anguina redimitus terga caterua,
    cui tres sunt linguae tergeminumque caput,
Scyllaque uirgineam canibus succincta figuram,
    nec te conceptam saeua leaena tulit   90
barbara nec Scythiae tellus horrendaue Syrtis,
    sed culta et duris non habitanda domus
et longe ante alias omnes mitissima mater
    isque pater quo non alter amabilior.
haec deus in melius crudelia somnia uertat   95
    et iubeat tepidos inrita ferre Notos.

86 *Flor.Ven.*

---

86   fero *Flor. Ven.*, A+: suo H   **87** canis anguina *Postgate*: consanguinea A B C H K M O T^{ac} V^{ac} v: canis anguinea D E G J L N P p S T^{pc} V^{pc} W X   **89** scyllaue *Heyne ex Bernensi* succincta C^{pc} F(*Plant.*): submixta A+: subnixa C: comitata D E   **96** inrita Q S^{ul}: impia A+: itrita L

Thus he spoke and lazy sleep slipped from my body. Ah, may I not see such great evils! I could not believe that you harbour wishes contrary to mine, nor that so great a crime lies in your heart. For neither the expanse of the vast ocean brought you forth, nor the Chimera rolling flame from her fierce mouth, nor the dog with its back covered in a throng of snakes, who has three tongues and a triple head, or Scylla, whose virgin form is girdled by dogs; nor did a fierce lioness conceive and bear you **[90]**, nor the barbarian land of Scythia, nor the dread Syrtis, but a cultured house, not to be dwelt in by the hard of heart, and a mother far milder than all others, and a father than whom no other is more lovable. May god change these cruel dreams for the better and order the warm South winds to carry them off unfulfilled.

V

Vos tenet Etruscis manat quae fontibus unda,
   unda sub aestiuum non adeunda Canem,
nunc autem sacris Baiarum proxima lymphis
   cum se purpureo uere remittit humus.
at mihi Persephone nigram denuntiat horam: 5
   inmerito iuueni parce nocere, dea.
non ego temptaui nulli temeranda uirorum
   audax laudandae sacra docere deae.
nec mea mortiferis infecit pocula sucis
   dextera nec cuiquam trita uenena dedit.   10
nec nos sacrilegos templis admouimus ignes,
   nec cor sollicitant facta nefanda meum,
nec nos insanae meditantes iurgia mentis
   inpia in aduersos soluimus ora deos.
et nondum cani nigros laesere capillos,   15
   nec uenit tardo curua senecta pede.
natalem primo nostrum uidere parentes,
   cum cecidit fato consul uterque pari.
quid fraudare iuuat uitem crescentibus uuis
   et modo nata mala uellere poma manu?   20

12 *Flor.Gall.* **15-16** *Flor.Gall.* **16** *Flor.Ven.* **19-20** *Flor.Gall., Exc.Fris.*

V 1 uos G^{mg} V^{pc}: nos A+   **3** proxima *Scioppius*: maxima A+   **7** uirorum D^{mg} J^{pc} *Scaliger* (*ex cod.*): deorum A+: piorum *exc. Colotii*: reorum *Sandbach*   **8** laudandae] celandae *Heinsius*: uelandae *Hall* sacra docere] cernere sacra *Vossius*: noscere sacra *Heyne*: sacra uidere *Erath*: discere sacra *Hall*   **10** trita F(*Cast.*): certa A+: taetra G^{pc} **11** sacrilegos G T Y: sacrilegis A+: sacrilegi H S^{pc} admouimus ignes T^{pc}: amouimus ignes T^{ac}: admouimus aegros C M P Y: amouimus aegros A+   **12** facta] pectus *Flor.Gall.*: furta *Baehrens*   meum] reum *Flor.Gall.*   **13** meditantes M: meditantis A+   **15** saepe quidem *Flor.Gall.*   **16** tardo A+ *Flor.Ven.*: tacito *Flor.Gall.*: tarda L

Poem 5

You are detained by the waves that flow from the Etruscan springs, waves not to be visited at the time of the summer Dog-star, but which now are second only to the sacred waters of Baiae, when the earth loosens itself in bright-coloured spring. But for me Persephone announces the dark hour.

O goddess, do not harm an innocent youth. I have not rashly sought to make known the rites of the goddess who must be praised – rites which no man's presence should defile. My hand has not infected cups with deadly juices nor given anyone pounded poison [10]. I have not set sacrilegious flames to temples, nor do unspeakable crimes trouble my heart. Nor, framing curses in an unsound mind, have I opened my impious mouth against unfavourable gods. Nor yet has my black hair been spoilt by white, nor has bent old age arrived on slow foot. My parents saw my birthday for the first time when both consuls fell by the same fate. Why does it please you to rob the vine of its growing grapes or with evil hand to pluck the new-born fruit [20]?

parcite, pallentes undas quicumque tenetis
    duraque sortiti tertia regna dei.
Elysios olim liceat cognoscere campos
    Lethaeamque ratem Cimmeriosque lacus,
cum mea rugosa pallebunt ora senecta   25
    et referam pueris tempora prisca senex.
atque utinam uano nequiquam terrear aestu.
    languent ter quinos sed mea membra dies.
at uobis Tuscae celebrantur numina lymphae,
    et facilis lenta pellitur unda manu,   30
uiuite felices, memores et uiuite nostri,
    siue erimus seu nos fata fuisse uelint.
interea nigras pecudes promittite Diti
    et niuei lactis pocula mixta mero.

25 *Flor.Ven.*   **31** *Flor.Ven.*

27 nequiquam *Postgate*: necquiquam A+: necquicquam E L M O P p S torrear H N *ed. pr. min. 1472*   **28** sed A+: iam C N S v^{pc} W   **29** at G N V^{pc} Y: atque A+: et CHL   uobis G S: nobis A+: mihi P p flumina *Heinsius*   **32** uolent H, *unus Statii*

Spare me, whatever gods possess the pallid waters and hold as their lot the harsh third kingdom. May I one day be allowed to know the Elysian fields, Lethe's boat and the Cimmerian lakes, when my face grows pale with wrinkled age and as an old man I tell boys of times gone by.

Would that I was frightened in vain by an ineffectual fever, but for thrice five days my limbs have lost their strength. But you venerate the deities of the Tuscan stream and with leisurely hand part the yielding waves **[30]**. Live happily and live remembering me, whether I live or whether the fates wish me to die. Meanwhile promise black sheep to Dis and cups of snow-white milk together with neat wine.

VI

Candide Liber, ades - sic sit tibi mystica uitis
    semper, sic hedera tempora uincta feras -
aufer et ipse meum patera medicante dolorem:
    saepe tuo cecidit munere uictus Amor.
care puer, madeant generoso pocula Baccho,   5
    et nobis prona funde Falerna manu.
ite procul durum curae genus, ite labores:
    fulserit hic niueis Delius alitibus.
uos modo proposito dulces faueatis amici,
    neue neget quisquam me duce se comitem,   10
aut si quis uini certamen mite recusat
    fallat eum tecto cara puella dolo.
ille facit mites animos deus ille ferocem
    contudit et dominae misit in arbitrium.

2 *Exc.Fris.* **7** *Flor.Gall.* **13** *Flor.Gall.*

VI 1 uitis] uictis A O V^{ac} **2** sic edera semper C H L p   tempora] cornua *Statius*   geras G H   **3** patera medicante *Waardenburg*: pariter medicando *codd.*: patera medicare *Birt*: pariles medicate *Postgate*   **7** curae durum *Flor.Gall.*   **8** fulserit C F^{pc} G^{pc} P S T V^{pc} W: pulserit A+: fulxerit G M   delius] Euhius *Baehrens*: Idalis *Postgate*   **11** aut] at H: quod *Hall*   **13** mites *Lipsius*: dites *Flor.Gall.*, A+   feroces *Flor.Gall.*, G

Poem 6

Bright Liber, come near; so may the mystic vine be yours forever, so may your brow be wreathed in ivy. Take away my sorrow in person with your healing cup. Often has Love fallen defeated by your gift.

Dear boy, let the cups be soaked with good wine and pour us Falernian with down-turned hand.

Go far away, harsh race of cares; away with you, troubles. Here may the Delian shine with bright birds of omen.

Only, sweet friends, approve my intention and let no one refuse to keep me company as I lead **[10]**. But if anyone refuses the mild contest of wine, may his dear girl deceive him with well-hidden treachery.

That god makes minds gentle; he crushes the arrogant and sends him under the command of a mistress.

Armenias tigres et fuluas ille leaenas 15
   uicit et indomitis mollia corda dedit.
haec Amor et maiora ualet; sed poscite Bacchi
   munera. quem uestrum pocula sicca iuuant?
conuenit ex aequo nec toruus Liber in illis
   qui se quique una uina iocosa colunt. 20
conuenit iratus nimium nimiumque seueris:
   qui timet irati numina magna bibat.
quales his poenas qualis quantusque minetur,
   Cadmeae matris praeda cruenta docet.
sed procul a nobis hic sit timor illaque siqua est, 25
   quid ualeat laesi sentiat ira dei.
quid precor a demens? uenti temeraria uota
   aeriae et nubes diripienda ferant.
quamuis nulla mei superest tibi cura, Neaera,
   sis felix et sint candida fata tua. 30
at nos securae reddamus tempora mensae:
   uenit post multas una serena dies.

16 *Flor.Gall.*

15 armenias G H: armenas A+: armeniasque L M: armeniosque p   **17** ualet *unus Statii*: uolet A+   **19** illis A+: illo Y: illos *ed. Ald. 1502*   **21** conuenit S^{ac}: non uenit A+: nam uenit C: iam uenit J^{pc} P^{pc} p S^{pc} W : quom uenit H   seueris *Liuineius*: seuerus A+: securus C^{ac}: seueros *Lachmann*   **23** qualis quantusque F (*Cast. et Plant.*): deus hic quantumque A+: deus hic quantasque C M W: deus hic quaecumque G V^{mg} **25** illaque A+: iraque *Huschke*   **26** sentiat A+: sentiet C G N S^{ac} V X   ira A+: illa *Huschke*   **30** fata A+: facta D E M L Y: uota H   **32** multas A+: multos C H J L M S^{pc} W: nimbos *Santen*: maestas *Baehrens*: pluuias *Housman*

He conquers Armenian tigers and tawny lionesses and bestows gentle hearts upon the untamed. These things and more can Love achieve.

But ask for Bacchus' gifts. Which of you finds pleasure in dry cups? Liber meets on equal terms and is not hostile to those who revere him and, along with him, merry wine [20]. But he meets the austere with anger beyond measure. He who fears the great god's anger, let him drink. With what punishments he threatens them, in what manner and with what strength, we learn from the bloody victim of the Cadmean mother.

But let such fear be far from us, and, if anger there be on the part of the injured god, let *her* feel its force. Ah, what am I praying for in my madness? May the winds and the airy clouds carry off such rash wishes and tear them apart. Although you no longer have any care for me, Neaera, may you be happy and may your fate be bright [30].

But let us devote our time to the carefree table; after many days one unclouded day has come.

ei mihi, difficile est imitari gaudia falsa,
    difficile est tristi fingere mente iocum,
nec bene mendaci risus componitur ore,   35
    nec bene sollicitis ebria uerba sonant.
quid queror infelix? turpes discedite curae:
    odit Lenaeus tristia uerba pater.
Cnosia, Theseae quondam periuria linguae
    fleuisti ignoto sola relicta mari: 40
sic cecinit pro te doctus, Minoi, Catullus
    ingrati referens inpia facta uiri.
uos ego nunc moneo: felix quicumque dolore
    alterius disces posse cauere tuo.
nec uos aut capiant pendentia bracchia collo   45
    aut fallat blanda sordida lingua prece.
etsi perque suos fallax iurauit ocellos
    Iunonemque suam perque suam Venerem,
nulla fides inerit: periuria ridet amantum
    Iuppiter et uentos inrita ferre iubet.   50
ergo quid totiens fallacis uerba puellae
    conqueror? ite a me, seria uerba, precor.
quam uellem tecum longas requiescere noctes
    et tecum longos peruigilare dies,
perfida nec merito nobis inimica merenti,   55
    perfida, sed quamuis perfida, cara tamen.

33-6 *Flor.Gall.*, *Exc.Fris.*   **43-4** *Flor.Gall.*, *Exc.Fris.*   **45-6** *Flor.Gall.*   **52** *Exc.Fris.*, *Flor.Ven.*

33 *nou. eleg. inc. codd.*   ei N^{pc} O: si A+: sic E: hei C D G^{pc} H J$^{mg.}$ M P S T v W X: heu *Flor. Gall.*, p: et *Exc.Fris.*   mihi] quam *Flor.Gall.*   **35** nec *Exc.Fris.*, A+: non *Flor.Gall.*   **36** nec *Exc.Fris.*, A+: non *Flor.Gall.*   **39** Cnosia *Kenney* (*ad Ou. Art. 1.293*): Gnosia *codd.*   **41** sic] sed M   Minoi] Minoe C M N P^{ac} S^{ac} **44** disces *Exc.Fris.*, A+ : didicit *Flor. Gall.*: discis G v^{pc} W   cauere F(*Plant.*) *Flor.Gall.*, *Exc.Fris.*: carere A+   tuo *Exc.Fris.*, A+.: suum *Flor.Gall.*: tuos F(*Plant.*): tuum *Baehrens*   **45** ne *Flor.Gall.* J^{pc} M   decipiant *Flor.Gall.*   **46** aut fallat] nec capiat *Flor.Gall.*   sordida] subdola *Heinsius*   prece *Flor.Gall.*: fide *codd.*   **51** quid *ed. Romana 1475*: qui *codd.*   **53** *nou. eleg. inc.* G   **55** inimica] nec amica T, *exc. Pocchi, ed. Veneta 1475*

Alas it is difficult to feign joy which is insincere; it is difficult to fake merriment when one's mind is sad. Laughter is not well contrived on a lying face, nor do drunken words sound well on anxious lips.

Why do I complain in my wretchedness? Be off, shameful cares. Father Lenaeus hates sad words. You, Cnossian maid, abandoned and alone in an unknown sea, once wept at the perjuries of Theseus' tongue **[40]**. Thus for you, daughter of Minos, learned Catullus sang, recalling the impious acts of a thankless husband. Now I give you warning: happy are you who learn from another's distress to be able to avoid your own. Let not arms clinging around your neck deceive you, nor be tricked by a mean tongue's flattering prayer. Even if she treacherously swears by her own eyes, her own Juno and her own Venus, there will be no truth in her. Jupiter laughs at the perjuries of lovers and orders the winds to carry them off unfulfilled **[50]**. So why do I so often complain of my deceitful girl's words? Away from me, I pray, you serious words.

How I could wish to rest long nights with you and to spend with you long waking days; faithless girl, an enemy to me against my just deserts, faithless, but, though faithless, dear nevertheless.

Naida Bacchus amat. cessas, o lente minister?
  temperet annosum Marcia lympha merum.
non ego, si fugit nostrae conuiuia mensae
  ignotum cupiens uana puella torum, 60
sollicitus repetam tota suspiria nocte.
  tu, puer, i, liquidum fortius adde merum.
iamdudum Syrio madefactus tempora nardo
  debueram sertis inplicuisse comas.

58 marcia S^{ac}: martia A+   **59** fugit A^{ac} O: fugiet A^{pc} B G J N T V^{ac} X: fugiat D E L P p v   **62** i F (*Cast. et Plant.*): et A+   **63** Syrio *Lipsius*: tyrio A+: thirio N: tyria B D: **64** *post hunc uersum in omnibus codd. sequitur nullo intervallo III 18, quod suo loco iterum traditur in codd. exceptis* G J

Bacchus loves Nais. Why delay, o slow servant? Let Marcian water temper the vintage wine. If a fickle girl flees the hospitality of my table, yearning for a stranger's bed **[60]**, I will not anxiously sigh the whole night long. Go on, boy, add more boldly the clear neat wine. Long since should I have soaked my brows in Syrian nard and entwined my hair with garlands.

LAVDES MESSALLAE
(IN PERSONA TIBVLLI)

VII

Te, Messalla, canam, quamquam me cognita uirtus
terret ut infirmae ualeant subsistere uires.
incipiam tamen ac meritas si carmina laudes
deficiant humilis tantis sim conditor actis
nec tua praeter te chartis intexere quisquam   5
facta queat dictis ut non maiora supersint,
est nobis uoluisse satis. nec munera parua
respueris: etiam Phoebo gratissima dona
Cres tulit, et cunctis Baccho iucundior hospes
Icarus, ut puro testantur sidera caelo   10
Erigoneque Canisque, neget ne longior aetas.
quin etiam Alcides, deus ascensurus Olympum,
laeta Molorceis posuit uestigia tectis
paruaque caelestes placauit mica nec illis
semper inaurato taurus cadit hostia cornu.   15
hic quoque sit gratus paruus labor, ut tibi possim
inde alios aliosque memor componere uersus.
alter dicat opus magni mirabile mundi,
qualis in inmenso desederit aere tellus,
qualis et in curuum pontus confluxerit orbem,   20

1 me G^{pc}: mea A+: tua G^{ac} M^{sscr} **2** nequeant F (*Cast. et Plant.*)   **3** ac G^{pc}: a A+: at F (*Plant.*)   meritas G^{pc}: meritis A+: meritae *Tränkle*   **5** te praeter *Wittianus Broukhusii deperditus*, cf. 3.19.3 *infra*   **10** puro H V^{pc}: pura A+: primo G: puero M: pulchro T^{mg} **11** ne G H N^{pc}: *om.* A+   **13** Molorceis *Morgan* (1992): Molorcheis *codd.*   tectis *Muretus*: terris *codd.*   **14** placauit G^{pc}: pacauit A+: peccauit D M   **18** dicat opus A^{pc} B G V: dictat opus A^{ac} +: opus dicat G   **19** desederit A+ F (*Plant.*): descenderit D E H L P p Y   **20** defluxerit C D E H M W

Poem 7 THE PRAISES OF MESSALLA (IN THE MASK OF TIBULLUS)

Messalla, I will sing of you, though your known valour makes me afraid that my feeble powers may not be strong enough to bear its weight. Nevertheless, I shall begin, and, if my songs should not be equal to the praise you deserve, and I should be but a humble chronicler of such great deeds and no one but you could interweave his pages with your achievements so that more than what was told should not remain unspoken, it is enough that I have wished to try. You will not despise my small gifts. Even Phoebus found the gifts a Cretan brought most acceptable, and Icarus was a more cordial host to Bacchus than all others, as Erigone and the Dog Star bear witness in the clear heaven **[10]**, lest future generations deny it. And Alcides also, about to ascend as a god to Olympus, happily set foot in the house of Molorcus, and a small grain of salt has pleased the heaven-dwellers, nor does a bull with gilded horns always fall as a sacrifice to them. May this small work of mine be pleasing too, so that remembering this in future I may be able to compose for you more and more verses. Let another tell of the wonderful workings of the great universe, how the Earth sank down in the immeasurable Air, and how Ocean flowed round the curving globe **[20]**,

ut uagus e terris qui surgere nititur aer
huic et contextus passim fluat igneus aether,
pendentique super claudantur ut omnia caelo.
at quodcumque meae poterunt audere Camenae,
seu tibi par poterunt seu (quod spes abnuit) ultra   25
siue minus (certeque canent minus), omne uouemus
hoc tibi, nec tanto careat mihi carmine charta.
nam quamquam antiquae gentis superant tibi laudes,
non tua maiorum contenta est gloria fama,
nec quaeris quid quaque index sub imagine dicat,   30
sed generis priscos contendis uincere honores,
quam tibi maiores maius decus ipse futuris.
at tua non titulus capiet sub nomine facta,
aeterno sed erunt tibi magna uolumina uersu,
conuenientque tuas cupidi componere laudes   35
undique quique canent uincto pede quique soluto.
quis potior, certamen erit. sim uictor in illis,
ut nostrum tantis inscribam nomen in actis.
nam quis te maiora gerit castrisue foroue?
nec tamen hic aut hic tibi laus maiorue minorue,   40

28-9 *Flor.Gall.*   **31-2** *Flor.Gall.*   **39-47** *Flor.Gall.*

21 ut *Heinsius*: et *codd.*   qui *Heyne*: qua *codd.*   **22** huic G M p: hinc A+: hic C T   et contextus A+: ut contextus *exc. Colotii et Pocchi*: circumtextus *Heinsius*: ut praetextus *Postgate*   **24** at G: et A+   **26** uouemus A+ F (*Cast. et Plant.*): mouemus B L P   **27** carmine A+F (*Cast. et Plant.*): nomine G J   **28-29** ordine 29-28 habet *Flor. Gall.* **28** quamuis antiquae superent praeconia gentis *Flor. Gall.*   **30** quaque F (*Cast. et Plant.*): qua A+   index F (*Cast. et Plant.*): iudex A+   **31** uincere sed priscos generis contendis honores *Flor.Gall.*   **36** uincto G: iuncto A+   **37** quis A+: qui F (*Cast. et Plant.*)   potior N^{pc}: potius A+   **39-47** ordine 45-47, 39-44 habent *Flor. Gall.*, G   **39** nam quis te F (*Cast. et Plant.*): nec quisquam *Flor.Gall.* G: nam quique tibi A+   castrisue *Flor.Gall.*: cartis ne A V X: chartisue C G H O P T: cartisue B D E J M N p S W   **40** hic aut hic tibi F (*Cast. et Plant.*) G N^{pc} p S T: haec aut haec tibi *Flor.Gall.*: hic aut tibi A+

and how the wandering Air which strives to rise above the earth and the fiery Ether interwoven with it flow in all directions and how everything is enclosed by the heaven hanging above. But whatever my Muses will be able to dare, whether they can achieve the same as you or even more (which hope refuses), or less (and certainly they will sing less), I vow it all to you, lest my pages lack so great a theme. For although the praises of your ancient family abound, your glory is not content with the fame of your ancestors, nor do you ask what the inscription under each mask says **[30]**, but you strive to outdo the ancient renown of your race, yourself a greater honour to your descendants than your ancestors were to you. But no label beneath your name will suffice for your deeds, but you will have huge volumes of immortal verse and from all sides will come men eager to compose your praises, both those who sing in verse and those who will in prose. There will be a competition to see who is best. May I be victor among them, so that I may inscribe my name on such great deeds.

For who does greater deeds than you in camp or forum? Neither here nor there is your praise greater or less **[40]**,

iusta pari premitur ueluti cum pondere libra
prona nec hac plus parte sedet nec surgit ab illa,
qualis inaequatum si quando onus urget utrimque
instabilis natat alterno depressior orbe.
nam seu diuersi fremat inconstantia uulgi,   45
non alius sedare queat, seu iudicis ira
sit placanda, tuis poterit mitescere uerbis.
non Pylos aut Ithace tantos genuisse feruntur
Nestora uel paruae magnum decus urbis Vlixem,
uixerit ille senex quamuis dum terna per orbem   50
saecula fertilibus Titan decurreret horis,
ille per ignotas audax errauerit urbes
qua maris extremis tellus includitur undis.
nam Ciconumque manus aduersis reppulit armis,
nec ualuit lotos captos auertere cursus,   55
cessit et Aetnaeae Neptunius incola rupis
uicta Maroneo foedatus lumina Baccho.
uexit et Aeolios placidum per Nerea uentos,
incultos adiit Laestrygonas Antiphatemque
nobilis Artacie gelida quos irrigat unda.   60

42 post **44** *Postgate*   **43** sed magis aequatum *Flor.Gall.*   **46** nemo magis *Flor.Gall.*   **55** nec S *Brixianus Quirin. A VII 7*: non A+   lotos F (*Cast. et Plant.*): ciclops A+   captos F (*Cast. et Plant.*): c(o)eptos C D E H J^{pc} K L M N^{pc} O P p T v: certos W: tectos S: tempus A B J^{ac} G N^{ac} V X   auertere C E K L M O P p T V v: uertere A D J: conuertere G H N P S X: aduertere B W   **56** et G V^{2}: *om.* A N S V   **60** artacie C N V: artacre A+   gelida *Broukhusius*: gelidos *codd.*   erigit F (*Cast. et Plant.*)

as, when a true balance is loaded with equal weights, it does not sink lower on one side or rise higher on the other as it does when an unequal burden weighs down each side and it floats uneasily with each scale going down alternately.

For if the fickle crowd should roar in discord, no other could calm it. If a judge's anger is to be placated, it will be able to be soothed by your words. Neither Pylos nor Ithaca is said to have produced men so great in Nestor or Ulysses, the great glory of a small town, although the former lived into old age while Titan ran round his orbit **[50]** with his fruitful seasons for three generations, and the latter wandered boldly through unknown cities, where the land is enclosed by the sea's most distant waves.

For he repelled the bands of Ciconians with opposing arms, nor could the lotus turn him from his chosen course, and the son of Neptune who dwells on Etna's rock yielded, maimed in his eye overcome by Maronian Bacchus. He bore the Aeolian winds over calm Nereus' sea. He approached the savage Laestrygonians and Antiphates, watered by the icy wave of famed Artacie **[60]**.

solum nec doctae uerterunt pocula Circes,
quamuis illa foret Solis genus, apta uel herbis
aptaque uel cantu ueteres mutare figuras.
Cimmerion etiam obscuras accessit ad arces
quis numquam candente dies apparuit ortu,   65
seu supra terras Phoebus seu curreret infra.
uidit ut inferno Plutonis subdita regno
magna deum proles leuibus discurreret umbris,
praeteriitque cita Sirenum litora puppi.
illum inter geminae nantem confinia mortis   70
nec Scyllae saeuo conterruit impetus ore,
cum canibus rabidas inter fera serperet undas,
nec uiolenta suo consumpsit more Charybdis,
uel si sublimis fluctu consurgeret imo
uel si interrupto nudaret gurgite pontum.   75
non uiolata uagi sileantur pascua Solis,
non amor et fecunda Atlantidos arua Calypsus,
finis et erroris miseri Phaeacia tellus.
atque haec seu nostras inter sunt cognita terras,
fabula siue nouum dedit his erroribus orbem,   80

63 aptaque uel *codd.*: uel magico *non male Tränkle*: captas uel *Baehrens*: uel cantu uictas *Postgate*   **64** cim(m)erion G H V: cymerion A+   **67** ut A B J K N^{pc} O P p S V v X: et C D E G^2 H K L M N^{ac} T W   **68** ius diceret *Postgate*   umbris G^{pc} H: undis A+   **70** inter geminae F (*Cast. et Plant.*): tergeminae A^{pc} +: terminae A^{ac} N S^{ac} V^{ac} nantem G V^{pc}: nautem A+   **71** ore F (*Cast. et Plant.*): orbe A+   **72** rapidas C E p W X fera G^{pc}: freta A+   **74** alto *Hall*   **73** more B: in ore A+   **75** pontum A^{pc}+ : puntum A^{ac}: fundum *Cartault*   **77** calypsus G^{pc} p T: calipsos A+   **78** erroris F (*Plant.*):errorum A+   miseri A+ F (*Plant.*): misero *ed. Ald. 1515*   **79** edita *Hall*

He alone was not transformed by learned Circe's potions, although she was daughter of the Sun, and skilled with herbs and skilled with song to change former shapes. He even drew near to the dark citadels of the Cimmerians, for whom day never appeared with bright rising, whether Phoebus ran above the earth or below it. He saw how, subject to the infernal rule of Pluto, the great offspring of the gods wandered with insubstantial shades and in his swift ship he passed the Sirens' shores. As he sailed between the confines of a double death **[70]**, he was not terrified by the attack of Scylla's savage mouth, as she crept out, wild with her dogs amid the surging waves, nor did violent Charybdis devour him as was her wont, whether she rose on high with her deepest billow, or whether she laid bare the sea-bed with a gulf in her waters. The violation of the wandering Sun's pastures should not be kept silent, nor the love of Atlas' daughter, Calypso, and her rich fields, nor the end of his sad wanderings, the land of Phaeacia. But whether these things were experienced among our lands, or whether legend created a new world for these wanderings **[80]**,

sit labor illius tua dum facundia maior.
iam te non alius belli tenet aptius artes,
qua deceat tutam castris praeducere fossam,
qualiter aduersos hosti defigere ceruos,
quemue locum ducto melius sit claudere uallo   85
fontibus ut dulces erumpat terra liquores
ut facilisque tuis aditus sit et arduus hosti,
laudis ut assiduo uigeat certamine miles
quis tardamue sudem melius celeremue sagittam
iecerit aut lento perfregerit obuia pilo   90
aut quis equum celeremque arto compescere freno
possit et effusas tardo permittere habenas,
inque uicem modo derecto contendere passu
seu libeat curuo breuius conuertere gyro;
quis parma seu dextra uelit seu laeua tueri,   95
siue hac siue illac ueniat grauis impetus hastae,
aptior, aut signata cita loca tangere funda.
iam simul audacis ueniant certamina Martis
aduersisque parent acies concurrere signis,
tunc tibi non desit faciem componere pugnae,   100

82-105 *Flor.Gall.* **95** *Exc.Fris.*

82 iam *exc. Pucci Broukhusius*: nam *Flor.Gall.* A+   artes B G N O p: arces *Flor.Gall.* P: artos A+ V(-th-) X: artem v   **84** ceruos *ed. Rom. 1475*: neruos *Flor.Gall.* B C D E G H J K L M P p S T V v W X: uernos A N O   **86** fontis *Cartault*   ubi G^{pc}, *Cartault*   **87** stabulisque *Flor. Gall.*   **88** ut *Flor.Gall.*: et A+   **89** melius tardamue sudem *Flor. Gall.*   **90** miserit *Flor. Gall.*   **91** aut quis *Flor.Gall.* C J L M v^{ac}: et quis A B H K N p S^{ac} T V v^{pc} W X Y: at quis D E O P S^{pc}: ecquis G   celeremque *Ayrmann*: celeremue A+: celerem ne G: celerem ut L   **94** breuius A+: melius D E H M S^{ul} Y^{pc}: leuius W Y^{ac} conuertere *Crusius*: contendere *codd.*   **96** ueniat grauis *Flor. Gall.* F (*Plant.*): grandis uenit A+: ueniat grandis v   **97** aptior *Francken*: amplior *Flor.Gall.* A+ F (*Plant.*): amplius J H N X   ut F (*Plant.*)   **98** audacis] aduersi Flor.Gall.   ueniant *Flor. Gall.*: uenient A+

let his be the greater hardship and yours the greater eloquence.

Next, no one but you has a surer mastery of the arts of war: where one should draw a protective trench for the camp; how one should drive in stakes to stop the enemy; what position is best to surround with an enclosing rampart, so that the earth can cause sweet water to break forth from springs and so that access is easy for your men and hard for the enemy; how the soldier thrives on unceasing competition for praise, who is best at throwing a slow stake or a swift arrow or at breaking through the opposition with a flexible javelin **[90]**, or who can control a swift horse with a tight bridle and let the reins fly loose for a slow one and in turn now gallop in a straight line or, if he pleases, turn more tightly in a curving circle; who can more skilfully protect either right or left with a shield as he will, if the weight of the spear's onset comes from this side or that, or hit a marked target with a swift sling-shot. Next, as soon as the battles of daring Mars arrive, and the lines prepare to close with opposing standards, then you do not fail to form the order of battle **[100]**,

seu sit opus quadratum acies consistat in agmen
rectus ut aequatis decurrat frontibus ordo,
seu libeat duplicem seiunctim cernere Martem
dexter uti laeuum teneat dextrumque sinister
miles sitque duplex gemini uictoria casus.   105
at non per dubias errant mea carmina laudes,
nam bellis experta cano. testis mihi uictae
fortis Iapydiae miles, testis quoque fallax
Pannonius gelidas passim disiectus in Alpes,
testis Arupinis et pauper natus in aruis,   110
quem si quis uideat uetus ut non fregerit aetas
terna minus Pyliae miretur saecula famae.
namque senex longae peragit dum tempora uitae,   112a
centum fecundos Titan renouauerit annos,
ipse tamen uelox celerem super edere corpus
audet equum ualidisque sedet moderator habenis.   115
te duce non alias conuersus Dalmata tergum
libera Romanae subiecit colla catenae.
nec tamen his contentus eris: maiora peractis
instant, compertum est ueracibus ut mihi signis

102 ut *Flor.Gall.* F (*Plant.*) T: in A+   **103** seiunctim *Salmasius*: seu uinctum *Flor.Gall.* p X: seu iunctum A+   **104** dexter uti *Flor.Gall.* F (*Plant.*): dexteraque ut A+   **108** iapidiae A^{pc} D G J^{pc} M S^{ul}: iapigiae A^{ac}+   **110** arupinis F (*Cast. et Plant.*) G^{pc}: et arpinis A+: et alpinis G^{ac} HP S^{ul} aruis *ed. princ. quarta* (*Bartoliniana*) *Venetiis 1472*: armis *codd.*   **112a** *om.* D E H J L M P v   tempora uitae *Vossius*: saecula famae A+: saecula uitae C^{pc} **113** renouauerit K T^{pc}: renouauerat C D E H J M N O P p S^{pc} v W X Y: renouerat A B V T^{ac}: reuocauerat G S^{ac} **115** audet] gaudet E *Heinsius*   **116** Dalmata tergum *Heyne:* terga domator *codd.*: terga domatus *Liuineius*: terga salassus *Baehrens* whether the line needs to be drawn up in a square column so that the dressed rank runs with a levelled front, or, if it pleases you to fight a double battle on separate fronts so that your right flank may hold their left and your left flank their right, and the outcome of the double hazard should be a double victory.

But my verses do not stray among unattested praises; for I sing of things proven in war. A witness for me is the brave soldier of defeated Iapydia, a witness also the treacherous Pannonian, scattered on all sides towards the frozen Alps; a witness too the poor man born in Arupium's fields **[110]**: if one saw how old age has failed to break him, one would marvel less at the three generations of the Pylian legend. For while the old man completes his long life's span, the Titan may have renewed a hundred fruitful years, yet unaided he dares to fling his agile body upon a swift horse and when seated masters him with tight rein. Under your leadership the Dalmatian, who never before turned his back, bowed his free neck beneath a Roman chain. But you will not be content with these deeds: feats greater than those achieved draw near, as I have found out through truthful signs

quis Amythaonius nequeat certare Melampus. 120
nam modo fulgentem Tyrio subtegmine uestem
indueras oriente die duce fertilis anni,
splendidior liquidis cum Sol caput extulit undis
et fera discordes tenuerunt flamina uenti,
curua nec adsuetos egerunt flumina cursus, 125
quin rapidum placidis etiam mare constitit undis
nulla nec aerias uolucris perlabitur auras
nec quadrupes densas depascitur aspera siluas
quin largita tuis sit muta silentia uotis.
Iuppiter ipse leui uectus per inania curru 130
adfuit et caelo uicinum liquit Olympum
intentaque tuis precibus se praebuit aure
cunctaque ueraci capite adnuit. additus aris
laetior eluxit structos super ignis aceruos.
quin hortante deo magnis insistere rebus 135
incipe: non idem tibi sint aliisque triumphi.
non te uicino remorabitur obuia Marte
Gallia nec latis audax Hispania terris
nec fera Theraeo tellus obsessa colono,

127 nulla D E L M S^{pc}: ulla A+: nullas O   **129** sit *Huschke*: sunt *codd.* muta G^{pc}: multa A+   **131** liquit A^{pc} G p W: linquit A^{ac}+   **134** laetior A+: lectior S: purior C D E G^{pc} L^{ac} M p S^{ul} v   **136** non T: nunc A+: nec C   sint P: sunt A+   **139** theraeo G^{pc} : te tereo A O W: tetereo F (*Plant.*) H J L M N O S T V v X Y^{ac}: tetero B: nec tereo K: tereo Y^{pc}: tartareo C D E T^{mg}: threicio G^{ac}: tyrreneo P: detereo p which Amythaon's son Melampus could not challenge **[120]**.

For you had just put on the robe that shone with Tyrian weave, as the day dawned that leads the fruitful year, when a brighter Sun raised his head from the liquid waves, and battling winds held in check their wild blasts, and the winding rivers did not move in their accustomed courses. Why, even the raging sea stood still with waves at peace, and no bird glided through the air above, no rough four-footed beast grazed the dense woodlands that did not lavish still silence on your vows. Jupiter himself, riding through the void on his light chariot **[130]**, was present and left Olympus that neighbours heaven. He gave himself over to your vows with attentive ear and granted them all with truthful nod. Then on the altar flames shone more happily above the heaped offerings.

With the encouragement of the god, begin to press on to great achievements. Let not Triumphs be the same for you as for others. Gaul confronting you with war close at hand will not delay you, nor bold Spain with its broad territory, nor the wild land occupied by the Theraean settlers,

nec qua uel Nilus uel regia lympha Choaspes 140
profluit aut rapidus Cyri dementia Gyndes
+creteis ardet aut unda caristia+ campis,
nec qua regna uago Tomyris finiuit Araxe,
inpia nec saeuis celebrans conuiuia mensis
ultima uicinus Phoebo tenet arua Padaeus 145
quaque Hebrus Tanaisque Getas rigat atque Magynos.
quid moror? Oceanus ponto qua continet orbem,
nulla tibi aduersis regio sese offeret armis.
te manet inuictus Romano Marte Britannus
teque interiecto mundi pars altera sole. 150
nam circumfuso consistit in aere tellus
et quinque in partes toto disponitur orbe.
atque duae gelido uastantur frigore semper:
illic et densa tellus absconditur umbra,
et nulla incepto prolabitur unda liquore, 155
sed durata riget densam in glaciemque niuemque,
quippe ubi non umquam Titan super egerit ortus.
at media est Phoebi semper subiecta calori,
seu propior terris aestiuum fertur in orbem
seu celer hibernas properat decurrere luces: 160

149 *Flor.Ven.*

140 choaspes G: dyaspes (diaspes) A+ F (*Cast. et Plant.*)   **141** gyndes *ed. Vicentina 1481*: cydnus A+: cidnus D F (*Plant.*)   **142** cret(h)eis ardet aut unda caristia A+: ardet arectais aut unda perhospita F (*Cast. et Plant.*): aret (*iam Lachmannus*) araccaeis aut unda oroatia (*uel* Copratia) *Postgate*   **143** tomyris G²: tamyris A+ G^{ac}   **146** magynos F (*Plant.*): maginos A+: mosynos *Broukhusius ex codd.*   **155** prolabitur *Tränkle*: perlabitur *codd.*   liquore] tenore *Postgate* nor where the Nile or the royal waters of the Choaspes flow **[140]**, or where the rushing Gyndes, that maddened Cyrus, +...+ nor where the realm of Tomyris is bounded by the winding Araxes, nor where the Padaean, celebrating impious feasts on savage tables, as neighbour to Phoebus, holds his distant lands, and where the Hebrus and the Tanais water the Getae and the Magyni. Why stop? Where Ocean circles the globe with its sea, no region will meet you with opposing arms. There remains for you the Briton, unbeaten by Roman arms, and the other part of the world separated from us by the sun **[150]**.

For the earth rests surrounded by air, and its whole sphere is divided into five parts. And two are forever ravaged by icy cold; there the earth is hidden in dense shade, and when liquid has begun to form no water flows forth, but it stiffens solid into dense ice and snow, since there the Titan never makes his rising. But the middle region always lies beneath the heat of Phoebus, whether he is carried closer to the earth in his summer orbit, or whether he swiftly hastens to run through the winter days **[160]**.

non igitur presso tellus exsurgit aratro,
nec frugem segetes praebent neque pabula terrae;
non illic colit arua deus Bacchusue Ceresue
nulla nec exustas habitant animalia partes.
fertilis hanc inter posita est interque rigentes 165
nostraque et huic aduersa solo pars altera nostro,
quas similis utrimque tenens uicinia caeli
temperat, alter et alterius uires necat aer.
hinc placidus nobis per tempora uertitur annus,
hinc et colla iugo didicit submittere taurus 170
et lenta excelsos uitis conscendere ramos,
tondeturque seges maturos annua partus,
et ferro tellus pontus confinditur aere,
quin etiam structis exsurgunt oppida muris.
ergo ubi praeclaros poscent tua facta triumphos, 175
solus utroque idem diceris magnus in orbe.
non ego sum satis ad tantae praeconia laudis,
ipse mihi non si praescribat carmina Phoebus.
est tibi qui possit magnis se accingere rebus
Valgius: aeterno propior non alter Homero. 180

161 igitur F (*Plant.*): ergo A+   **164** nulla A+: ulla H   **165** rigentes A[ac] C F (*Plant. ut uid.*) P: rigentem A[pc]+   **167** quas utrimque tenens similis *Broukhusius ex codd.*   utrimque C G[pc] S: utrique A+   **168** alter] alteram F (*Plant.*)   necat *Vossius*: negat *codd.*   **169** uertitur A[mg]+: *om.* A: labitur E L[ac] M O P p S v   **170** hinc G H V: huic A+   **171** l(a)eta G H J[ac] M V XY   **173** confinditur G[pc]: confunditur A+: conscinditur G[ul]: confoditur W   **174** exsurgunt G H: exurgitat A+   **175** praeclaros A+ F (*Plant.*): per claros *Scaliger*   poscent A+: possent W: ierint F (*Cast. et Plant.*): noscent *uel* scierint *Postgate*

So there the land does not rise in ridges when the plough is pressed upon it, neither do cornfields produce grain nor the land pasture. There no god cultivates the land, whether Bacchus or Ceres. No animals inhabit these burnt regions. Between this and the frozen parts is placed a fertile region, ours and another which is opposite our land. These similar parts the sky near them holds in on either side and tempers, with one air destroying the other's force. Hence for us the year turns equably through its seasons, hence also the bull has learnt to place his neck beneath the yoke **[170]** and the pliant vine to climb the lofty branches, and each year the cornfield is shorn of its ripe harvest, and the earth is ploughed with iron and the sea with bronze; yes, and towns too rise up with their walls built high. Therefore, when your deeds demand their famous triumphs, you alone will be said to be great in either world.

I am not equal to the heralding of praise so great, not even if Phoebus himself were to dictate to me the song. In Valgius you have one who can gird himself for the telling of great achievements; no other comes nearer to deathless Homer **[180]**.

languida non noster peragit labor otia, quamuis
Fortuna, ut mos est illi, me aduersa fatiget.
nam mihi, cum magnis opibus domus alta niteret,
cui fuerant flaui ditantes ordine sulci
horrea fecundas ad deficientia messes,   185
cuique pecus denso pascebant agmine colles
(et domino satis et nimium furique lupoque),
nunc desiderium superest; nam cura nouatur
cum memor anteactos semper dolor admonet annos.
sed licet asperiora cadant spolierque relictis,   190
non te deficient nostrae memorare Camenae.
nec solum tibi Pierii tribuentur honores:
pro te uel rapidas ausim maris ire per undas,
aduersis hiberna licet tumeant freta uentis;
pro te uel densis solus subsistere turmis   195
uel paruum Aetnaeae corpus committere flammae.
sum quodcumque, tuum est. nostri si paruula cura
sit tibi - quantalibet, si sit modo - non mihi regna

181 non A+: nec *Heyne*   **184** ordine sulci] horrea culmi *Heinsius*
185 fecundas ad deficientia messes F (*Cast. et Plant.*): fecundis indeficientia mensis A+   **189** anteactos *Scaliger* (*ex libris*): accitos C J L p T v W: accitus A+   **190** relictis H: relictus A+   **193** ausi F (*Plant.*)   **195** obsistere E^{ac} L M S W   **196** paruum *codd.*: pronum *Burmannus*   **197** quodcumque GH: quidcunque A+   **198** sit modo: sint modo (*ut uid.*) F (*Plant.*)

My labour does not pass its time in idle leisure, though Fortune, as is her wont, wearies me with her enmity. For though once my lofty house shone with great riches and I had rows of golden furrows enriching my granaries so that they were insufficient to hold the fruitful harvest, and the hills fed my herds in close-packed ranks (enough for their master and more than enough for thief or wolf), now a sense of loss remains; for care is renewed when sorrow, remembering, ever reminds me of years gone by.

But even if worse should befall, and I should be stripped of what remains **[190]**, my Muses will not fail to tell of you. Nor shall Pierian honours alone be offered to you. For you I would dare to cross the devouring waves of the sea, though the wintry waters should swell with adverse winds; for you I would face alone massed ranks of cavalry, or consign my feeble body to the fires of Aetna. Whatever I am is yours. If you should have some small care for me – however small, provided only that there is some – not the kingdom

Lydia, non magni potior sit fama Gylippi,
posse Meleteas nec mallem uincere chartas.   200
quod tibi si uersus noster, totusue minusue,
uel bene sit notus, summo uel inerret in ore,
nulla mihi statuent finem te fata canendi.
quin etiam mea tunc tumulus cum texerit ossa,
seu matura dies celerem properat mihi mortem,   205
longa manet seu uita, tamen, mutata figura
seu me finget equum rigidos percurrere campos
doctum, seu tardi pecoris sim gloria taurus,
siue ego per liquidum uolucris uehar aera pennis,
quandocumque hominem me longa receperit aetas,   210
inceptis de te subtexam carmina chartis.

199 magni A+: gnati T   gy(i)lippi A+: Philippi *quidam apud Cyllenium*
200 nec G H O V^{pc}: *om.* A+ : non T   uincere F (*Cast. et Plant.*):
mittere A+: tangere T^{mg} **202** summo uel] summo F *ut. uid.*   **203**
statuent G^{pc} v^{pc}: statuunt A+   **204** tunc tumulus cum texerit] cum
tumulus contexerit *Puccius*   **205** celerem *Scaliger*: fato *codd.*: fati
Huscke (*coll. Ou. Her. 1.114*)   **206** figura A+ : figuram C G^{pc} L O P p
Scaliger (*ex F, ut uid.*)   **207** uirides *Cornelissen*   **210**
quandocumque F (*Plant et Cast.*): inqu(a)ecunque A^{ac} H T V v W:
inquencumque A^{pc}+

of Lydia nor the fame of great Gylippus would please me more, nor would I prefer to be able to outdo the writings of Meletean Homer **[200]**.

But if my verse, in whole or part, should either be well known to you or should simply brush your lips in passing, no Fates will set bounds for my singing of you. Not even then when the tomb shall cover my bones, whether an early day hastens my swift death, or whether a long life remains, nevertheless, whether a changed shape should turn me into a horse, trained to run over hard plains, or whether I am a bull, pride of the slow herd, or whether as a bird I fly on wings through the liquid air, whenever the long ages receive me back as a man **[210]**, I will weave songs to add to the pages I have begun about you.

VIII-XII DE SVLPICIA ELEGIAE
(IN PERSONA POETAE SINE NOMINE)

VIII

Sulpicia est tibi culta tuis, Mars magne, Kalendis:
    spectatum e caelo, si sapis, ipse ueni.
hoc Venus ignoscet. at tu, uiolente, caueto
    ne tibi miranti turpiter arma cadant.
illius ex oculis, cum uult exurere diuos,   5
    accendit geminas lampadas acer Amor.
illam, quidquid agit, quoquo uestigia mouit,
    componit furtim subsequiturque decor.
seu soluit crines, fusis decet esse capillis;
    seu compsit, comptis est ueneranda comis.   10
urit, seu Tyria uoluit procedere palla;
    urit, seu niuea candida ueste uenit.
talis in aeterno felix Vertumnus Olympo
    mille habet ornatus, mille decenter habet.
sola puellarum digna est cui mollia caris   15
    uellera det sucis bis madefacta Tyros
possideatque metit quicquid bene olentibus aruis
    cultor odoratae diues Arabs segetis
et quascumque niger Rubro de litore gemmas
    proximus Eois colligit Indus aquis.   20
hanc uos, Pierides, festis cantate Kalendis,
    et testudinea Phoebe superbe lyra.
hoc sollemne sacrum multos celebretur in annos;
    dignior est uestro nulla puella choro.

3-4 *Exc. Fris.*   **13** *Exc.Fris.*

VIII 6 lampades C E H L M P p T   **14** habet E G^{pc} J K M N^{pc} O^{pc} P p S T v: hunc A B G^{ac} H N ^{ac} O^{ac} V X   **23** celebretur L v: hoc sumet A+: haec sumet H V^{pc}: hoc sumat G^{pc}: hoc firmet S: consummet *Scaliger* (*ex libris*): celebrate *per Heyne*   **24** nostro C O P p v^{pc} choro G^{pc} W X: thoro A+

8-12 ELEGIES ABOUT SULPICIA (IN THE MASK OF AN ANONYMOUS POET)

Poem 8

Sulpicia is adorned for you, great Mars, on your Kalends. Come yourself, if you are wise, from heaven to see her. Venus will pardon this. But you, violent one, take care your arms do not shamefully fall to the ground as you wonder. From her eyes, when he wishes to enflame the gods, fierce Love lights his twin torches. Whatever she does, wherever she turns her steps, grace adorns her and secretly follows in her train. If she loosens her hair, her flowing locks become her; if she combs it, her combed tresses are adorable **[10]**. She enflames the heart if she chooses to appear in a Tyrian robe; she enflames it if she arrives shining in a snow-white gown.

Just so, happy Vertumnus on everlasting Olympus has a thousand outfits and wears the thousand with grace.

Alone of girls she is worthy to receive from Tyre soft wool twice bathed in costly dye, and to possess whatever the rich Arabian cultivator of a perfumed crop harvests from his sweet-smelling fields, and whatever pearls the swarthy Indian, close by the Eoan waters, collects from the Red Sea's shore **[20]**.

Sing of her, you Pierides, on the festal Kalends, and you also, Phoebus, proud of your tortoise-shell lyre. Let this solemn rite be celebrated for many a year; no girl is more worthy of your chorus.

IX

Parce meo iuueni, seu quis bona pascua campi
    seu colis umbrosi deuia montis aper,
nec tibi sit duros acuisse in proelia dentes:
    incolumem custos hunc mihi seruet Amor.
sed procul abducit uenandi Delia cura.   5
    o pereant siluae deficiantque canes.
quis furor est, quae mens, densos indagine colles
    claudentem teneras laedere uelle manus?
quidue iuuat furtim latebras intrare ferarum
    candidaque hamatis crura notare rubis?   10
sed tamen, ut tecum liceat, Cerinthe, uagari,
    ipsa ego per montes retia torta feram,
ipsa ego uelocis quaeram uestigia cerui
    et demam celeri ferrea uincla cani.
tunc mihi, tunc placeant siluae si, lux mea, tecum   15
    arguar ante ipsas concubuisse plagas.
tunc ueniat licet ad casses, inlaesus abibit,
    ne Veneris cupidae gaudia turbet, aper.
nunc sine me sit nulla Venus, sed lege Dianae,
    caste puer, casta retia tange manu;   20
et quaecumque meo furtim subrepit amori
    incidat in saeuas diripienda feras.
at tu uenandi studium concede parenti
    et celer in nostros ipse recurre sinus.

10 *Exc. Fris.*

IX 3 proelia F (*Cast. et Plant.*): pectore A+: pectora Y   *post* 4 *uersus duo uel plures excidisse uedentur Postgate*   **18** ne G S^{ul} V^{mg}: da A+: nec W   **19** nunc *Broukhusius*: tunc A+   **20** tende B G   **21** et A+: at *Scaliger* (*ex libris*)   subrepit A+: surrepet J, *Heinsius*

Poem 9

Spare my young man, wild boar, whether you haunt the good pastures of the plain or the lonely places of the shady mountain, and let it be no care of yours to sharpen your hard tusks for battle; may Love, his guardian, keep him safe for me.

But the Delian maid leads him far away with a passion for hunting. O may woods die out and hounds fail. What madness is this? What sense is there in wishing to harm soft hands by closing off tree-clad hills with encircling nets? What pleasure is there in entering the lairs of wild beasts by stealth and scratching your white legs with barbed brambles **[10]**.

But, Cerinthus, if I could be allowed to roam with you, I myself would carry the twisted nets through the mountains; I myself would search out the tracks of the fleet-footed stag and release the swift hounds from their iron chains. Then, o then, the woods would please me, if, my light, I could be said to have lain with you before the very traps. Then, though the wild boar come to the nets, he will go away unharmed, so as not to disturb the joys of eager Venus.

But now, without me, let there be no Venus, but according to Diana's law, chaste boy, touch the nets with chaste hands **[20]**. And whatever girl steals upon my love by stealth, let her fall among wild beasts and be torn to pieces.

But leave the pursuit of hunting to your father, and you yourself run back quickly to my embrace.

X

Huc ades et tenerae morbos expelle puellae,
    huc ades, intonsa Phoebe superbe coma.
crede mihi, propera, nec te iam, Phoebe, pigebit
    formosae medicas applicuisse manus.
effice ne macies pallentes occupet artus,   5
    neu notet informis candida membra color,
et quodcumque mali est et quicquid triste timemus
    in pelagus rapidis euehat amnis aquis.
sancte, ueni tecumque feras quicumque sapores,
    quicumque et cantus corpora fessa leuant,   10
neu iuuenem torque metuit qui fata puellae
    uotaque pro domina uix numeranda facit.
interdum uouet, interdum quod langueat illa
    dicit in aeternos aspera uerba deos.
pone metum, Cerinthe; deus non laedit amantes.   15
    tu modo semper ama: salua puella tibi est.
nil opus est fletu: lacrimis erit aptius uti   21
    si quando fuerit tristior illa tibi.   22
at nunc tota tua est, te solum candida secum   17
    cogitat, et frustra credula turba sedet.
Phoebe, faue: laus magna tibi tribuetur in uno
    corpore seruato restituisse duos.   20
iam celeber iam laetus eris, cum debita reddet   23
    certatim sanctis laetus uterque focis.
tunc te felicem dicet pia turba deorum,   25
    optabunt artes et sibi quisque tuas.

X   3 te iam A+: iam te C H   L M S^{ac} v W   **6** candida *ed. Rom. 1475*: pallida A+: tabida *Guietus*   **8** rapidis G V: rabidis A+   **13** uouet A+: mouet A^{ac} O P S^{ac} W   **21-22** *post* **16** *colloc. ed. Ald.1515*   **17** at G V: ac A+   **24** laetus A+: gratus *Martinon*:lotus *Broukhusius*: tutus *Cyllenius*: sospes *Heinsius*

Poem 10

Come here and drive out disease from a tender girl; come here, Phoebus, proud of your unshorn hair. Believe me, hurry, Phoebus, and you will never regret placing your healing hands on a beautiful girl. See to it that no wasting falls upon her pallid limbs, and let no disfiguring colour mark her fair body; and whatever ill there is, whatever sadness we fear, let the river with its rushing waters carry it out to the sea.

Holy one, come, and with you bring whatever juices, whatever incantations relieve tired bodies **[10]**. Do not torture the youth who fears for the fate of his girl and makes innumerable vows for his mistress. Sometimes he vows, sometimes he speaks harsh words against the eternal gods because she grows weak.

Set aside your fear, Cerinthus. God does not harm lovers. Simply love her forever and your girl is safe **[16]**. There is no need for weeping; it will be more fitting to use tears if ever she is harsh with you **[21, 22]**. But now she is all yours; of you alone does the lovely girl think in her heart; and the credulous crowd sits by her in vain.

Phoebus, be favourable; great praise will be given you if in saving one body you restore two lives **[20]**. Then you will be famous, then you will be glad, when each in turn will happily vie to repay their debts at your sacred altar. Then the pious company of the gods will call you fortunate, and each will desire your skills for himself.

XI

Qui mihi te, Cerinthe, dies dedit, hic mihi sanctus
    atque inter festos semper habendus erit.
te nascente nouum Parcae cecinere puellis
    seruitium et dederunt regna superba tibi.
uror ego ante alias; iuuat hoc, Cerinthe, quod uror,   5
    si tibi de nobis mutuus ignis adest.
mutuus adsit amor, per te dulcissima furta
    perque tuos oculos per Geniumque rogo.
magne Geni, cape tura libens uotisque faueto,
    si modo cum de me cogitat ille calet.   10
quod si forte alios iam nunc suspiret amores,
    tunc precor infidos, sancte, relinque focos.
nec tu sis iniusta, Venus: uel seruiat aeque
    uinctus uterque tibi uel mea uincla leua.
sed potius ualida teneamur uterque catena,   15
    nulla queat posthac quam soluisse dies.
optat idem iuuenis quod nos, sed tectius optat,
    nam pudet hic illum dicere uerba palam.
at tu, Natalis, quoniam deus omnia sentis,
    adnue. quid refert clamne palamne roget?   20

XI 1 qui mihi *Scaliger (ex libris)*: est qui *codd.*   **4** dederunt G: dederant A+   **6** de nobis B: ne de nobis A+: ne de uobis O   **7** te per J^{ac} G N p T   **9** magne *Scaliger (ex libris)*: mane *codd.*   **10** calet *Muretus*: ualet A+: uolet F (*Cast. et Plant.*)   **11** suspirat C E G^{pc} J M N S v^2 W   **16** quam *ed. Ald. 1502*: om. A B M V: quae O S: nos C E G H K L N P p T V^{sscr} X Y: nulla W: hanc *Rossbach*   soluisse A+: exsoluisse B: disoluisse M   **17** tectius *Puccius, Muretus*: tutius A+: citius W   **18** hic A B O P V^{ac} X: hoc M: haec C E G H J K L N p S T V^{pc} v W   **20** refert G: referet A+   clamne palamne *Muretus*: clamue palamue A+

Poem 11

This day that gave you to me, Cerinthus, shall be sacred for me and always to be held among the festivals. When you were born the Fates sang of a new slavery for girls and gave you a proud dominion. I burn more than others; it pleases me, Cerinthus, that I burn, provided a mutual fire for me enflames you. May you feel like love for me, I beg you, by our thefts most sweet, by your eyes and by your Genius.

Great Genius, take the incense gladly and look favourably on my prayers, if only he grows hot at the thought of me [10]. But if now by chance he should sigh after another love, then I pray, holy one, leave his faithless hearth.

And you, Venus, be not unjust; either let both of us, equally bound, be your slaves, or release me from my chains. But rather let us both be held by a strong chain which no day to come can break. My young man wishes for the same as I, but he wishes more secretly; for he is ashamed to speak out openly here [20].

But you, Birthday Spirit, since as a god you know all things, grant our prayer. What matter if he should ask openly or in secret?

XII

Natalis Iuno, sanctos cape turis aceruos,
　quos tibi dat tenera docta puella manu.
lota tibi est hodie, tibi se laetissima compsit,
　staret ut ante tuos conspicienda focos.
illa quidem ornandi causas tibi, diua, relegat,　　　　5
　est tamen occulte cui placuisse uelit.
at tu, sancta, faue, neu quis diuellat amantes,
　sed iuueni, quaeso, mutua uincla para.
sic bene compones. ullae non ille puellae
　seruire aut cuiquam dignior illa uiro.　　　　10
nec possit cupidos uigilans deprendere custos,
　fallendique uias mille ministret amor.
adnue purpureaque ueni perlucida palla:
　ter tibi fit libo ter, dea casta, mero.
praecipit et natae mater studiosa quid optet:　　　　15
　illa aliud tacita iam sua mente rogat.
uritur ut celeres urunt altaria flammae,
　nec liceat quamuis sana fuisse uelit.
sis Iuno grata ac ueniet cum proximus annus
　hic idem uotis iam uetus extet amor.　　　　20

XII 3 lota *ed. Plant. 1569 in mg.*: tota A+　　**5** ornandi G: orandi A+
7 neu quis *Scaliger* (*ex libris*) G^{pc}: ne nos A+　　**9** ullae A+: ulli
Colbertinus　　**10** cuiquam G^{pc}: cuidam A+　　**13** purpureaque G^{pc}:
purpurea A+: perlucida $G^{ras.}$　　**14** fit G^{pc} J^{pc} S W^{pc}: sit C E H K M N P p
S^{ul} T^{pc} W^{ac}: sic A B G^{ac} J^{ac} O T^{ac} V X: sis *Scaliger*　　**15** quid *Broukhusius
ex exc. Lipsii*: quod A+ optet G^{pc} H: optat A+　　**16** sua A+ : sibi E^{pc} G
p: tua *Baehrens*　　**19** sis F *Gruppe*: sit G^{pc}: si A+　　Iuno *Gruppe*: iuueni
A+　　grata ac *Lipsius, Gruppe*: grata A+　　ueniet A+: adueniet: G^{pc} Y
20 extet G^{ac}: esset A+: adsit C E J^{pc} L M P p S T^{ac} W: ut sit G^{pc} v

Poem 12

Birthday Juno, accept the holy heaps of incense which a learned girl offers you with soft hand. Today she has bathed for you and for you has most joyfully adorned herself, so that she can stand for all to see before your altar. She does indeed attribute the reason for her adornment to you, goddess; but there is someone she secretly wishes to please.

But you, holy one, show favour and let no one tear lovers apart, but, I beg you, prepare mutual chains for the young man. In that way you will match them well. Let him not more fittingly serve another girl, nor she another man **[10]**. Let no vigilant guard surprise them in their passion, but let love provide a thousand ways for his deception. Grant my prayer and come shining in a purple robe. Three times an offering of cake is made to you and three times, chaste goddess, of wine.

The caring mother prescribes to her daughter what she should pray for; but she, now her own mistress, asks silently for something else. She burns as the swift flames burn the altar offerings and, although she could be cured, she would not wish it. Be favourable, Juno and, when next year comes, may this same love, now of long standing, live on through these vows **[20]**.

XIII-XVIII CARMINA
(IN PERSONA SVLPICIAE)

XIII

Tandem uenit amor qualem texisse pudore
    quam nudasse alicui sit mihi fama magis.
exorata meis illum Cytherea Camenis
    attulit in nostrum deposuitque sinum.
        exsoluit promissa Venus. mea gaudia narret   5
    dicetur si quis non habuisse sua.
non ego signatis quicquam mandare tabellis
    ne legat id nemo quam meus ante uelim,
sed peccasse iuuat: uultus componere famae
    taedet. cum digno digna fuisse ferar.   10

XIV

Inuisus natalis adest qui rure molesto
    et sine Cerintho tristis agendus erit.
dulcius urbe quid est? an uilla sit apta puellae
    atque Arretino frigidus amnis agro?
iam, nimium Messalla mei studiose, quiescas.   5
    non tempestiuae saepe, propinque, uiae.
hic animum sensusque meos abducta relinquo,
    arbitrio quamuis non sinis esse meo.

XIII 1 *bis scriptus in A* pudore A (*posteriore loco*) B G J V v^{pc} X: pudori A (*priore loco*) C E H K L M N O P p S T v^{ac} W   **2** quam] et *Wittianus Broukhusii deperditus*: at *Scaliger*   fama] cura *Heyne*   magis] minor *Broukhusius*   **6** sua F (*Cast.*) G^{pc}: suam A+: suum G^{ac} **8** ne G *ed. Plant.1569*: me A+   nemo G^{pc}: uenio A+   quam meus G: quoniam meus A+

XIV 3 puellis H   **4** arretino GJ: aretino A+: eretino G^2 (*in mg.*), *exc. Pocchi*: Reatino *Huschke*   amnis A+: Arnus *Heinsius*: annus *Scaliger*, *Huschke*   **6** non D E: neu A+: heu V^{pc} **8** arbitrii ... mei *Broukhusius* (*ex libris*) *Heinsius*   quamuis non A+: quoniam non G: quin tu me *Heyne*   quamuis] quam uis *Statius*   sinit *Statius*

13-18 POEMS (IN THE MASK OF SULPICIA)

Poem 13

At last a love has come which it would disgrace me more to hide out of shame than to reveal to anyone. Cytherea, won over by my Muses, brought him here and placed him in my arms. Venus has fulfilled her promise. Let that man tell of my joys who will be said to have none of his own. I would not wish to entrust anything to sealed tablets, so that no one could read it before my man. But it pleases me to have sinned. I am tired of putting on a mask for reputation's sake. Let me be said, as a worthy woman, to have been with a man worthy of her **[10]**.

Poem 14

The hateful birthday is at hand which must be spent in sadness, without Cerinthus, in the loathsome countryside. What is sweeter than the city? Would a country villa and the cold river in the Arretian fields be suitable for a girl? Now, Messalla, be at rest; you worry too much about me. Journeys, kinsman, are often ill-timed. If I am carried off, I leave my heart and senses here, although you do not allow me mastery over my own life.

XV

Scis iter ex animo sublatum triste puellae?
    natali Romae iam licet esse suo.
omnibus ille dies nobis natalis agatur,
    qui necopinanti nunc tibi forte uenit.

XVI

Gratum est securus multum quod iam tibi de me
    permittis, subito ne male inepta cadam.
sit tibi cura togae potior pressumque quasillo
    scortum quam Serui filia Sulpicia.
solliciti sunt pro nobis quibus illa dolori est   5
    ne cedam ignoto maxima causa toro.

XVII

Estne tibi, Cerinthe, tuae pia cura puellae,
    quod mea nunc uexat corpora fessa calor?
a, ego non aliter tristes euincere morbos
    optarim quam te si quoque uelle putem.
at mihi quid prosit morbos euincere, si tu   5
    nostra potes lento pectore ferre mala?

XV 2 iam licet F (*Cast. et Plant.*): non sinet A+   suo *ed. Ald. 1502*: tuo A+ F (*Cast. et Plant.*): meo *Huschke*   **3** dies] bonis *Housmann*   nobis] annis *Postgate*   natalis A+: genialis *ed. Vicentina a.* 1481: tam laetus *Baehrens, Postgate*   **4** qui A+: quod *Drenckhahn*: quam *Baehrens, Postgate*   necopinanti A+: necopinata *Heyne*   forte A+: sorte *Heyne*

XVI 1 tibi H Y: mihi A+   **2** permittis A+: promittis *Heinsius*   **3** sit] si *Heinsius*   togae] toga est *Heinsius*   **5** dolori est A+: doloris *Haupt, Rigler*   **6** ne C E P S: nec A+   cedam *Statius*: credam *codd.*   causa A+ *Scaliger* (*ex libris*): cura E^{pc} G^{pc}

XVII 1 pia cura *Broukhusius*: placitura *codd.*   **2** quod A+: quid L S^{ac}: qui B C E^{pc} P T W   **3** a] ha A+ J^{ac}: ah J^{pc} V   **4** si A B G J^{pc} N V^{ac} X: sic C E H J^{ac} K M P p S T V^{pc} v: sit O   **5** at *Scaliger* (*ex libris*) Y: ha A+   si G^{pc} V^{pc}: quid A+: quod G   **6** lento *Scaliger* (*ex libris*) V^{pc}: laeto A+

Poem 15

Do you know the sad journey is lifted from your girl's heart? Now she can be at Rome for her birthday. Let that day which now comes unexpectedly to you by chance be celebrated as a birthday by us all.

Poem 16

I am grateful that in your lack of concern you allow yourself much leeway in my regard, so that I do not suddenly fall into disgrace in my complete folly. Let your love for a toga and for a strumpet weighed down by a wool-basket be preferable in your eyes to Sulpicia, daughter of Servius. Those are worried for me to whom it is the greatest source of pain that I should submit to an ignoble bed-fellow.

Poem 17

Cerinthus, do you have any tender care for your girl, now that a fever afflicts my tired body? Ah, I would choose to conquer sad disease only if I thought that you too wished it. But what good would it do me to conquer disease, if you can bear my sufferings with an unfeeling heart?

XVIII

Ne tibi sim, mea lux, aeque iam feruida cura
   ac uideor paucos ante fuisse dies,
si quicquam tota commisi stulta iuuenta
   cuius me fatear paenituisse magis
hesterna quam te solum quod nocte reliqui,   5
   ardorem cupiens dissimulare meum.

ELEGIA
(IN PERSONA TIBVLLI)

XIX

Nulla tuum nobis subducet femina lectum:
   hoc primum iuncta est foedere nostra Venus.
tu mihi sola places, nec iam te praeter in urbe
   formosa est oculis ulla puella meis.
atque utinam posses uni mihi bella uideri.   5
   displiceas aliis: sic ego tutus ero.
nil opus inuidia est. procul absit gloria uulgi.
   qui sapit in tacito gaudeat ille sinu.
sic ego secretis possim bene uiuere siluis,

XVIII   *hoc loco om.* B. *cum priore coniunctum est in ceteris codd. praeterea post* **VI** *traditur in omnibus codd. exceptis* G J L v

priore loco (post 3.6.64): **1** ne A+: nec B C E K L P W X   sim *non nisi posteriore loco traditur*: sit A B E H K M N O P p S T V W X: sed C iam *non nisi posteriore loco traditur*: tum A B: tam C E H K M N O P p S T V W X   **2** ac A+ : ut E p: at O P   uideor A+ : uideo C K P p paucos uidear B   **3** commisi tota C   **4** fateor E M p X   pernituisse X   **5** externa N S   solam H L T

posteriore loco (hic): **1** ne M O S T V^{pc}: nec A B C E G H J K L N P p V^{ac} v W X   sim A+: sit C J N O P p V^{sscr}: sum K   iam] tam C P   **2** uideor A (*ut uidetur*) G H L T: uidear B M v: uideas E J K N O P p S V W X: uideo C   **3** toto K   **4** fateor T   **5** externa M   solam N T   quod] cum K

XIX 3 mihi B V^{pc}: modo A+   **5** possis E *Heinsius*   **8** ille D E: ipse A+   **9** possim E: possum A+

Poem 18

Let me no more, my light, be so fervently loved by you as I seemed to have been a few days ago, if I have in my folly committed anything in the whole of my youth of which I should confess I am more ashamed than that I left you alone last night, wishing to hide my passion.

AN ELEGY (IN THE MASK OF TIBULLUS)

Poem 19

No woman shall steal from me your bed: with this agreement we first joined our love-tie. You alone are pleasing to me, and now no girl in the city save you is beautiful in my eyes.

Would that you could seem pretty to me alone! May you displease the others; then I will be safe. There is no need for envy. Away with the boasting of the common crowd. Let the wise man quietly keep his joy to himself.

Thus I could live well in secret woods,

> qua nulla humano sit uia trita pede. 10
> tu mihi curarum requies, tu nocte uel atra
> lumen et in solis tu mihi turba locis.
> nunc licet e caelo mittatur amica Tibullo,
> mittetur frustra deficietque Venus.
> hoc tibi sancta tuae Iunonis numina iuro, 15
> quae sola ante alios est mihi magna deos.
> quid facio demens? heu heu mea pignora cedo.
> iuraui stulte. proderat iste timor.
> nunc tu fortis eris, nunc tu me audacius ures.
> hoc peperit misero garrula lingua malum. 20
> iam facias quodcumque uoles tuus usque manebo
> nec fugiam notae seruitium dominae,
> sed Veneris sanctae considam uinctus ad aras:
> haec notat iniustos supplicibusque fauet.

15 hoc A+: haec F G H J L N p V X: nec C W Y   **16** mihi *Scaliger* (*ex libris*): tibi *codd.*   **17** heu heu *codd.*: eheu *Baehrens*   cedo S *Scaliger* (*ex libris*): credo A+: cede L W.   **18** proderat *Scaliger* (*ex libris*): prodeat *codd.*   **21** iam facias *L. Mueller*: iam faciam *codd.*   **22** notae V^{pc}: noto A+   **23** considam G H: confidam A+: concidam X   **24** haec G H V^{pc}: nec A where no path is trodden by human foot **[10]**. You are my rest from cares, you my light in the dark night, you my crowd in lonely places.

Now though a girl be sent down from heaven for Tibullus, she will be sent in vain and love will fail. This I swear to you by your Juno's holy power, who alone for me above the other gods is great.

What am I doing in my madness? Alas, I let go my pledges. I was foolish to swear. That fear of yours was my gain. Now you will be strong, now you will burn me more boldly. This trouble my chattering tongue has brought me in my misery **[20]**.

Now, do what you will, I will remain yours forever, nor shall I flee servitude to a mistress I know, but I shall sit in chains at holy Venus's altars. She brands the unjust and favours suppliants.

AD RVMOREM CARMEN
(IN PERSONA TIBVLLI)

XX

Rumor ait crebro nostram peccare puellam:
    nunc ego me surdis auribus esse uelim.
crimina non haec sunt nostro sine facta dolore:
    quid miserum torques, rumor acerbe? tace.

2 *Exc. Fris.*

EPITAPHIVM TIBVLLI

Te quoque Vergilio comitem non aequa, Tibulle,
    Mors iuuenem campos misit ad Elysios,
ne foret aut elegis molles qui fleret amores
    aut caneret forti regia bella pede.

post eleg. XX explicit lib iv scriptus Florentie MCCCCLXV (X)
explicit lib III (B)
finis (G)
finis Albii Tibulli poetae liber explicit (N)

    XX 2 me A+: te *Exc. Fris.*   **3** crimina A+: carmina C J M P T W Y: iacta *Pontanus*

Epitaphium exstat in F *et al. D.Marso tribuit* F. *Epitaphium post Vitam afferunt* P p T

A POEM TO RUMOUR (IN THE MASK OF TIBULLUS)

Poem 20

Rumour says that my girl is often unfaithful. Now I wish I had deaf ears. These accusations are not made without pain to me. Cruel rumour, why torture me in my misery? Be silent.

TIBULLUS'S EPITAPH

Unfair death sent you also, Tibullus, in your youth as Virgil's comrade to the Elysian Fields, so that there should be no one to weep of soft love in elegiacs or to sing of royal battles in heroic metre.

VITA TIBVLLI

Albius Tibullus, eques Romanus, insignis forma cultuque corporis obseruabilis, ante alios Coruinum Messallam oratorem dilexit, cuius etiam contubernalis Aquitanico bello militaribus donis donatus est. hic multorum iudicio principem inter elegiographos optinet locum. epistolae quoque eius amatoriae, quamquam breues, omnino subtiles sunt. obiit adulescens, ut indicat
epigramma supra scriptum.

Vita non legitur in C E F J

1 romanus (Ro.) P: regalis A+: regius V^{pc} **2** oratorem *ed. Ven. 1475*: originem A+   **3** aquitanico *Vat. lat. 2794*: equitanico A+   **5** *post* locum *add.* N sunt qui Propertium malint (*ex Quint. Inst.*); *add* S Ouidius utroque lasciuior sicut asperior Gallus (*ex Quint. Inst.*)   **6** subtiles *Rostagni*: utiles A+: non inutiles T v   **7** supra scriptum H: superscriptum A+: supra inscriptum N: superius epitaphium X: epitaphium subscriptum P: epigramma infra scriptum p: eius epitaphium legimus T   *post finem add.* P sub teneris annis tenerorum scriptor amorum / decedens dura hac ecce Tibullus humo

THE LIFE OF TIBULLUS

Albius Tibullus, Roman knight, noted for his good looks and remarkable for his personal adornment, above others loved the orator, Messalla Corvinus, as whose aide in the Aquitanian war he was awarded military decorations. In the opinion of many he holds first place among the writers of elegy. His amatory letters, also, although short, are extremely subtle. He died young, as the epigram written above shows.

PROLEGOMENA

Over the ten years I have been working on this commentary my views on the work have changed. Starting from the idea that the book's separate sections (*Lygdamus* **1-6**[1], *Praises of Messalla* **7**, *Sulpicia Cycle* **8-12**, *Sulpicia* **13-18** and two concluding poems **19-20**) were written at different times and by different people before being arranged into a book by an unknown editor [as set out in Maltby (2010)], I have now come round to the less orthodox conclusion that a single author could be behind the whole composition. The structure of the book, in which the *Praises of Messalla* takes centre stage, dividing two sets of elegiac poems, one concerning Lygdamus and Neaera, the other Sulpicia and Cerinthus, with poems **19** and **20** providing closure for the whole work, first persuaded me to start thinking along the lines of a unitary composition.

As I opened myself up to this possibility, a number of important intertexts presented themselves, which had relevance to more than one section of the book and seemed to act as important unifying texts. First I will argue (see section 3.1) that Horace *Epode* 15 provides the inspiration for Lygdamus' affair with Neaera, with Lygdamus suffering the fate predicted for his rival by Horace (*Epod.* 15.23 *eheu translatos alio maerebis amores*); this rival's interest in Pythagorean reincarnation (*Epod.* 15.21) connects him further with the author of the *Praises of Messalla* (**7.204-211**) and the search for a relationship based on *mutuus amor* connects (*Epode* 15.10) with *Lygdamus* (**1.19**) and with the *Sulpicia Cycle* (**11.6** and **11.7** in the voice of Sulpicia and **12.8** in the voice of an unnamed objective observer, referred to in earlier scholarship as the *amicus Sulpiciae*). The story of Cephalus and Procris in Ovid (*Met.* 7.661-862) will be seen to provide a second important unifying text (details in section 1.3). Further echoes between the Cephalus and Procris story are found scattered throughout the rest of our book, including in the *Praises of Messalla* , the *Sulpicia Cycle* and the *Sulpicia* poems. Important themes of disguise, change, fidelity, truth and falsehood pervade Ovid's account and the poems of **book 3**. Even the structure of the Cephalus episode, with its inset tragic narrative on hunting the monster of Thebes (*Met.* 7.759-792) in central position, is imitated by the central position of the hexameter

---

[1] Poem and line numbers in bold refer to passages from [Tib.] 3 throughout.

Praises of Messalla in our book. A further series of intertexts linking the various sections of our book is provided by those poems of Propertius (3.6, 4.7 and 4.8) in which Lygdamus appears as a slave of Propertius (details in section 3.1). In Prop. 3.6 Lygdamus is asked by Propertius to deliver a message to the estranged Cynthia just as the Muses are asked to take a message to the estranged Neaera by Lygdamus in *Lygdamus* **1**. The theme of *mutuus amor* at Prop. 3.6.39, as we saw above, has connections throughout the elegiac poems of **book 3**. Cynthia's accusation that Propertius has taken up with a rival of low status (Prop. 3.6.21-34) has its counterpart in the *Sulpicia* poems, with a similar complaint about Cerinthus developed in *Sulp.* **16**. Further links between this poem and poems **19** and **20** (Prop. 3.6.34, cf. **19.13-14** and Prop. 3.6.8, cf. **20.2**) discussed in section 3.1 suggest a sustained engagement by our unitary author throughout the book. In Prop. 4.7 the ex-prostitute Chloris who has become mistress of Propertius' household weighs down with wool baskets *quasillis* (Prop. 4.7.41-42) those slaves who praise the dead Cynthia. The only other occurrence of this word in extant Roman poetry is at *Sulp.* **16.3** in a description of Cerinthus' new low-class mistress. Finally in Prop. 4.8 Lygdamus is in charge of the wine at a party arranged by Propertius, suggesting perhaps the symposium theme of *Lygd.* **6**, and his status as a slave is emphasised (4.8.69, 4.8.79-80), suggesting the appropriateness of his concern with themes of *seruitium amoris* in **book 3**. Intertextual engagement with other poets, which provides structural coherence to the collection, includes that with Tibullus, Catullus and Callimachus.

The structural similarities between the arrangement of **book 3** as a whole and the first book of Tibullus are set out in section 1.1 while section 1.2 discusses the role of Catullan echoes in the opening and closing of the *Lygdamus* group (in **1** and **6**), in the beginning of the *Praises of Messalla* **7** and in the final poems of our collection **19** and **20**. Finally Callimachean themes and poetics (see section 2.2.1) form another strong link between the *Lygdamus* poems, the *Laudes Messallae* and the concluding poems.

At a thematic level two strong ideas pervade and unify the collection. The first of these is the theme of change as suggested by the reference to Vertumnus strategically placed at the beginning of the second (*Sulpician*) half of the collection in the first poem of the *Sulpicia Cycle*, where Sulpicia is compared with Vertumnus: **8.13-14** *talis in aeterno felix Vertumnus Olympo / mille habet ornatus, mille decenter habet*. The god whose name was thought by the Romans to be derived from his changing shapes, disguises and even gender is emblematic of the stance taken up in the collection by our unitary author who in the course of the work puts on various masks to explore love and love elegy from various angles. This author appears first as Lygdamus, then as a young Tibullus (unnamed) who is the author of the *Laudes Messallae*, next as the *anonymous poet* who explores the affair of Sulpicia and Cerinthus from the point of view of a concerned but detached observer **8-12**, himself impersonating Sulpicia in poems **9** and **11**, and, with a change of gender, as the mistress Sulpicia herself in poems **13-18**, before returning in **19** to the mask of Tibullus (this time named) in a concluding closural poem, and, as it seems, also in the closural epigram 20. This unifying Vertumnan theme is picked up in the closural **19** by references to Ovid's account of Vertumnus' wooing of Pomona (*Met.* 14.641ff.) in lines **4**, **8**, and **12** of that poem (see commentary ad loc.). On the importance of themes of change in Augustan poetry and their relation with Vertumnus, especially in Prop. 4.2, see Hardie (1992) 74-75.

The fact that the Vertumnan comparison in **8** applies specifically to the character Sulpicia may suggest that our unitary author was a woman. Questions of style and language exclude the possibility that the 'historical' Sulpicia, niece of Messalla, could have been this author (see section 3.5), but a woman of high status, writing say in the late first century, would have good reason to obscure her true identity.

Whatever the gender of the author, the god Vertumnus, with his strong Propertian associations in Prop. 4.2, provides a perfect mythological paradigm for a work which investigates change in all its aspects, seeing love from male and female viewpoints, and incorporating in the *Praises of Messalla* (**7.204-211**) the Pythagorean theory of transmigration of souls. Both these Vertumnan themes were, as we have seen, prefigured in the important intertext Hor. *Epod.* 15 in line 21 *nec te Pythagorae fallunt arcana renati* and line 23 *translatos alio ... amores*. Our author had a good precedent for writing poems in different voices and from different viewpoints, both male and female, in the *Heroides* of Ovid and in the Propertian poems 4.3 (Arethusa), 4.7 (Cynthia's ghost) and 4.11 (Cornelia).

The stylistic variety of the single book which contains not only elegy but also a panegyric in hexameters and smaller scale epigrammatic works in the voice of Sulpicia (**13-18**), which in form look forward to the closural **20**, can be paralleled by that which characterises Catullus' book as we now have it.

The second unifying theme is that of revelation and secrecy. It is argued in section 3.1 that a possible etymology of the name Lygdamus could connect it with making public one's sorrow, an apt function for an elegiac poet reflected in his epitaph imagined at **2.27-28** and in the statement at **2.7** about his willingness to reveal the truth concerning his affair. The theme of revealing and concealing is one that dominates the whole collection, not just the *Lygd.* poems, and could be used as evidence that the *Lygdamus* poet was in fact the author of the whole book, writing under different masks. It is a theme that dominates the *Sulpicia* poems, which begin with the tension between hiding and revealing one's love (**13.1-2**). In **18** Sulpicia is shown to regret leaving Cerinthus out of a desire to keep her passion secret (**18.5-6**), by the time of poem **13**, which is dramatically later than poem **18**, Sulpicia is presented as having decided to remove her mask (**13.9-10**) and reveal her love (**13.5-6**). In poem **19**, by contrast, in the mask of Tibullus the poet regrets his open confessions of love to his mistress (**19.20**) and wishes to withdraw from society (**19.9-10**) and to keep his love to himself (**19.8**). This theme comes to its climax in the closural epigram **20** in which the final word *tace* (**20.4**) seeks total silence. On the invalidation of the name Lygdamus and its etymological significance as a closural feature of poems **19** and **20** see section 1.2 below.

Finally the name Neaera, which, as suggested in section 3.2, may be a bilingual pun on Greek *nea* 'new' and Latin *era* 'mistress', reflects the idea that Neaera will be the subject of a different kind of elegy, centered upon a failing marriage of a couple of equal status. By the penultimate poem of the collection the mistress – no matter how she is called– has become 'known' **19.22** to her lover *notae ... dominae,* which also invalidates her name, and the names Lygdamus and Neaera are replaced by those of 'Tibullus' and his unnamed mistress. This turning of the tables probably reflects a similar reversal between Tibullus books one and two, where the openness of the Delia poems – as her name denotes – in one is replaced by the darker and more secretive Nemesis poems in two. Book three as a whole shows a movement from openness to secrecy and silence, a thematic which lends unity and development to the whole collection.

These, then, are the main considerations which over the years have led me to accept a unitary theory of authorship for **book 3** of the corpus.

GENERAL INTRODUCTION

1. The Structure and Origins of [Tibullus] 3

1.1 The traditional view: multiple authorship

Book 3 of the *Corpus Tibullianum* consists of 20 poems. All of these except the first six, which are by an author who calls himself Lygdamus and writes about his relationship with a certain Neaera, are associated with Tibullus' patron Messalla. So poem **7**, the *Laudes Messallae* or the *Panegyricus Messallae*, is a eulogy of Messalla composed, ostensibly to celebrate the great man's entry on the consulship in 31 BC, by an author who, without naming himself, impersonates a young Tibullus. Poems **8-12** the *Sulpicia Cycle*, are spoken either by an author who does not name himself (**8, 10, 12**) or are put by him in the mouth of Sulpicia herself (**9** and **11**) and celebrate the affair of Sulpicia, presented as a relation of Messalla, with a young man who is given the pseudonym Cerinthus. Poems **13-18** are shorter epigrams, of a different style from **8-12** and written by an author who calls himself/herself Sulpicia. The author of poem **19** names himself as Tibullus (**19.13**), but the poem's relatively short length and its probable adaptations of Propertius and Ovid suggest that it is the work of a pseudo-Tibullus. The final four-line epigram, poem **20**, is carefully constructed and worthy of Tibullus himself, but likely to be post-Tibullan in view of echoes from Prop. 4 and Ov. *Am*. 3.

The arrangement of the whole collection into a single book shows great skill. Holzberg [(2001) 98-109] has argued for correspondences between **book 3** and the structure of Tibullus' first book, with the Neaera poems of *Lygd*. **1-6** being based on the Delia poems of Tib. 1.1-6, and the *Laudes Messallae* of **7** being the equivalent of Tib.'s description of Messalla's Aquitanian triumph in 1.7. The comments by a third party on the affair of Cerinthus and Sulpicia have parallels with Tib.'s treatment of the Marathus/Pholoe affair in Tib. 1.8 and 9 and the birthday poems which occur in both the *Sulpicia Cycle* and the *Sulpicia* poems (**11, 12, 14, 15**) are influenced by the birthday poem to Cornutus at Tib. 2.2. Furthermore there are internal correspondences between the *Lygdamus* poems, the *Sulpicia Cycle* and the *Sulpicia* poems, as well as between *Lygd*. **1** and the *Laudes Messallae* (see below). Because of its clear associations with the work of Tibullus and the naming of Tibullus in **19** this book could eventually have been added to the genuine two books of Tibullus at the latest by the second half of the fourth century AD, since Ausonius and Avienus echo the poems of the first two books along with **7** and **19**.[2] The fact that the *Lygdamus* poems are not connected with Messalla or (overtly) with Tibullus led Renaissance scholars to split **book 3** unnecessarily into two books, with their **book 3** consisting of the *Lygd.* poems **1-6** and their **book 4** consisting of the remaining poems **7-20**.

In an earlier paper[3] I suggested that a close connection with Messalla Corvinus himself was unlikely, since all the poems with the possible exception of **13-18** (*Sulpicia* poems) appear on stylistic and metrical grounds to have been composed after Messalla's death in AD 8. Given the associations with Messalla discussed above, I argued that the book was put together in its final form by descendants of Messalla, perhaps in the late first or early second century AD, around the time of L. Valerius Catullus Messallinus in AD 96, a prominent member of the family in the Flavian period. This Messallinus was a dangerous sycophant and *delator* under Domitian [Tac. *Agr.* 45.1 with Woodman (2014) 316-317 ad loc.; Juv. 4.113-116; Plin. *Epist.* 4.22.5-6], a man with whom it would certainly pay to curry favour. The paper suggested dates for the separate sections of this book as follows: *Lygdamus* no earlier than the late nineties AD; the *Laudes Messallae* the end of the first or beginning of the second century AD, the newest part of the collection; the *Sulpicia Cycle* early first century AD, before *Lygdamus* and the *Laudes Messallae* and shortly after the death of Ovid in AD 17; *Sulpicia* the end of the first century BC, the oldest part of the collection; poem **19** first century AD, after late Ovid; **20** early first century AD, after Propertius 4. I now believe that to propose separate dates for the composition of the different sections of the book was methodologically flawed. As has recently been pointed out by Fulkerson [(2017) 36], developing a point made in passing by Maltby [(2010) 327], the huge amount of Latin poetry that has disappeared makes such chronological distinctions and the grounds of lexical and metrical anomalies an uncertain science and even when two passages from different poets seem to be clearly related to one another it is often difficult to ascertain with certainty which came first. During the writing of this commentary, I have become aware (as made clear in the Prolegomena

---

[2] Auson. *Eph.* 3.72 echoes Tib. 1.1.59; *Techn.* 3.2 echoes Tib. 2.6.19-20; *Epigr.* 54.1 echoes *Laud. Mess.* [Tib.] 3.7.121; *Epigr.* 88-3-4 echoes [Tib.] 3.19.5-6. Avien *Arat.* 399-400 echoes both Tib. 2.1.47-48 and *Laud. Mess.* [Tib.] 3.7.172.
[3] Maltby (2010).

above) of close connections between the different sections, as traditionally recognised, that is **1-6**, **7**, **8-12**, **13-18**, **19-20**, and though I still believe in a post-Ovidian and probably Flavian date of composition for the whole book I am now coming round to the view that only a unitary author could have given the shape and meaning I have recognised in the book as a whole.

1.2 The arguments for unitary authorship

Holzberg (1998) made a case for the whole book being composed by a single author, whom he calls Pseudo-Tibullus. As we saw above (p. 84), he considered the form of the whole book to be based on the construction of Tibullus' first book of elegies. Lygdamus' mention of a birth date in the central couplet of poem **5** (**5.17-18**), which echoes that of Ovid's reference to his own birth date at *Trist.* 4.10.5-6 (see section 2.2.1 and 2.2.2 below) makes Holzberg's view that the author of **book 3** consistently poses as Tibullus difficult to accept. In fact Holzberg himself [(1998) 181] sees this couplet as a 'large fly in the ointment', casting doubt on the theory of Lygdamus as a Tibullan impersonator. However, the clear and detailed connections between the different groups of poems which make up the book are difficult to reconcile with a theory of a separate author for each section. A full list of references to the links between the different sections of the work are to be found in Index 1 under 'links'. The degree of editing required to bring about these correspondences by a final editor, putting together the work of a number of different poets into a single coherent collection, would seem to stretch our credibility. These could perhaps be accounted for by positing a single author adopting varying masks or *personae* in the different sections of the book. Thus echoes of Catullus 1.1 in poem **1**, with its theme of the gift of a book of poems, its reference to these as a *libellum* (**1.9** and **17**) in the same line-end position as Catullus' *libellum* in Cat. 1.1 and 1.9, and the possible echo of Ovid's birth date in his own *sphragis* at **5.17-18**, simply serve to set the poems of **book 3** and their author in the time of the practitioners of the golden age of Roman elegy. Like Catullus, however, our author will not restrict himself/herself to a single genre of poetry. The Catullan reference from poem **1** is picked up at the end of the *Lygdamus* group in **6.41** with its naming of Catullus as a poetic predecessor for the Theseus and Ariadne story.

Not only does the naming of Catullus in **6.41** provide the *Lygdamus* group with a satisfying ring-structure but it could also pave the way, with its mention of Catullus' most famous hexameter poem, to a change of tack in poem **7**, in which the same author who had named himself/herself as

Lygdamus in poems **1-6** now takes up the role of a young Tibullus in a hexameter panegyric addressed to his future patron Messalla. This is a poem for which Catullus' poem 66, a translation of Callimachus' *Coma Berenices*, provides a significant intertext, see poem **7** with **headnote, 9-11n.** and **18n.** Another important link between the programmatic poem **1** of the *Lygdamus* group and the opening of the *Laudes Messallae* is the emphasis in both on Callimachean poetics and literary imagery. These are signalled by the theme of a dialogue between Lygdamus and the Muses, beginning with *dicite Pierides* (**1.5**) and continuing to the end of the poem. This type of dialogue was introduced into poetry in the first two books of Callimachus' *Aetia* (see **1 headnote**) and through it the author associates himself at the beginning of his work with Callimachean poetics and, implicitly, with his elegiac predecessor Propertius, who styles himself as the Roman Callimachus (Prop. 4.1A.64). The name Lygdamus had after all, as we have mentioned (see Prolegomena above) and shall discuss in more detail below (section 3.1), occurred as a slave name in Prop. 3.6, 4.7 and 4.8. Callimachean themes and poetics, however, have a broader relevance to Roman elegy in general, see Hunter (2006), and our author as Lygdamus marks his allegiance to this type of poetics by a number of other metapoetic pointers spread throughout his programmatic poem **1** (see *libellum* in **9** and **17**; *tenuis* in **11**; *comptum* in **14** and *cultum* in **18** with **nn.** ad loc.). Perhaps the most important phrase in this context is *munera parua* with reference to his own modest gift of poetry in **24**, a phrase which is repeated with reference to the panegyricist's gift of poetry to Messalla in **7.7**. In fact the opening 17 lines of the *Laudes Messallae* emphasise in a similar way Callimachean principles and serve to link that poem with the *Lygdamus* group and to anchor the *Laudes Messallae* into the genre of Callimachean epinician (see **7 headnote**). Important Callimachean pointers in the opening of the *Laud. Mess.* include the following, on which see **nn.** in the commentary ad loc: *humilis* in **4** with reference to the poet's modest literary merit; *munera parua* in **7**, linking the poem with **1.24**, and emphasising the Callimachean ideal of a small work, perfectly crafted (Call. *Aet.* fr. 1.5-6 Pf.), with the idea repeated again in the reference to *paruus labor* at **7.16**, with its Callimachean use of *labor* = Gk. πόνος (e.g. Call. *Ep.* 6.1-2) with reference to the craft that goes into polishing a literary work; this Callimachean character of the opening of the *Laudes Messallae* is continued in **10-13** in the reference to the Callimachean myths of Erigone and Molorcus, with their epinician associations (see **7 headnote** and **7.10-13nn.**). Similar references to Callimachean poetics mark the opening of the *Sulpicia Cycle*, see **8 headnote** and **1n.** *candida,* **10n.** *compta* and **12n.** *candida* and are picked up in the closural poem **19** with its emphasis on the absence of the *uulgus* and its *inuidia* and retreat to trackless places (see **19 headnote, 6n., 7n., 9n., 10n.**). This concluding poem also emphasises the importance, stressed in poems **1**, **6** and **7**, of Catullus as a predecessor; see **19 headnote, 4n., 5n., 21n., 22n., 23n**. In fact Catullus and his interest in the Callimachean poetics of the *Aetia* can be seen as a unifying structural feature running through the whole of **book 3**. In re-iterating key Callimachean elements at important points in the collection, often in conjunction with Catullan echoes, in poems **1**, **7**, **8**, and **19**, the author seems to be following a principle adopted by Catullus, who, as Wiseman [(1985) 183] argues, marked the opening of each of his 'original' three books (**1-10, 61-64**, and **65-116**) by references to Callimachus' *Aetia*. One should add that the final poem of Catullus' 'last' book is marked, like poem **19**, by its Callimachean content, in that Catullus there claims he has been unable to send any Callimachean poems (Cat. 116. 2 *carmina ... Battiadae*) to mollify his critic Gellius.

Not only does the last *Lygdamus* poem **6** seem to prepare the way for poem **7**, but the end of poem **7** with its discussion at **206-211** of the Pythagorean theory of transmigration of souls, introduced by *mutata figura* (**206**), could arguably be said to prepare the way for the second half of the book in which the author takes up a number of different masks, an anonymous poet on the affair of Sulpicia and Cerinthus (in **8,-12**), Sulpicia (in **13-18**) and Tibullus (in **19**). If we include Lygdamus in **1-6** and the young Tibullus in **7** as further masks, it becomes clear that this theme of changing identity could be seen as a motif which unifies the whole collection. This would explain, as discussed in the Prolegomena above, the key importance of the comparison between Sulpicia and Vertumnus, the god of change par excellence, in central position in poem **8** at the start of the *Sulpicia Cycle*: **13-14** *talis in aeterno felix Vertumnus Olympo / mille habet ornatus, mille decenter habet*.

There are clear thematic similarities, as we should expect, between the *Sulpicia Cycle* **8-12** and the *Sulpicia* poems **13-18**, since both deal with the affair of Sulpicia and Cerinthus, In particular the theme of the illness of Sulpicia at *Sulpicia Cycle* **10** is taken up again at **17** and the birthday theme of **11** (Cerinthus' birthday) and **12** (Sulpicia's birthday) appears again in **14** and **15** (Sulpicia's birthday). These thematic connections are confirmed by two striking verbal reminiscences, namely *lux mea* (an endearment used earlier by Catullus of Lesbia at Cat. 68A 132 and 140) of Cerinthus at *Sulpicia Cycle* **9.15** (in Sulpicia's voice) and *mea lux* of Cerinthus in the *Sulpicia* poems at **18.1** and *corpora fessa* (a phrase used of the failing Ariadne at Cat. 64.189) of the sick Sulpicia at **10.10** and **17.2**.

More controversially perhaps, the *Lygdamus* poems have correspondences with those of the *Sulpicia Cycle* and the *Sulpicia* poems. So both poems **1** and **8** take as their setting the Matronalia festival, celebrated on the Kalends of March, originally an occasion for giving gifts to married women: **1.1** *Martis Romani festae uenere Kalendae* is paralleled in the opening of *Sulpicia Cycle* **8.1** *Sulpicia est tibi culta tuis, Mars magne, Kalendis*. Lygdamus certainly considers Neaera as an estranged wife (cf. **1.26-27**) and Sulpicia in **8.1** could possibly be considered to be married to the Cerinthus, whose love-affair with her prior to a marriage is the subject of the remaining *Sulpicia* poems. In both the mention of the war god Mars comes as something of a surprise at the beginning of a book of elegies, just as had Ovid's epic-sounding *arma graui numero* which opens his first book of *Amores* [Cf. also *Fast.* 3.1-2]. At a more detailed level *Lygd.* **1.8** *gaudeat, ut digna est, uersibus illa tuis,* which may have Gallan connections,[4] looks forward to *digna* used of Sulpicia at **8.24** *dignior est uestro* (i.e. *Pieridum*) *nulla puella choro,* **8.15** *sola puellarum digna est* (sc. to be given luxurious goods), and **13.10** (Sulpicia of her relationship with Cerinthus, in a possible echo of a marriage formula) *cum digno digna fuisse ferar*. Similarly the *cultum ... libellum* that Lygdamus is to send Neaera at **1.17** *ite domum cultumque illi donate libellum* may recall **8.1** *Sulpicia est tibi culta ... Mars magne...* where *Sulpicia* could refer not only to the person but also to the name of a group of poems about her, as with *Cynthia* referring to Propertius' first book of poems about Cynthia at Prop. 2.24.1-2 *sic loqueris, cum sis iam noto fabula libro / et tua sit toto Cynthia lecta foro*?[5]

Poems **19** and **20** are not mere afterthoughts, appended to the end of the collection, as some have argued. Rather they are clearly conceived as a closural pair, providing a meaningful conclusion for the whole book. This is clearly seen in their recapitulation of Catullan and Callimachean themes which, as we saw above (cf. also **19 headnote**), have an important structural role to play in unifying the whole collection. Poem **19** also has significant echoes of the wooing of Pomona by Vertumnus at Ov. *Met.*14.641 (see **19 headnote** and **3-4n.**, **8n.** and **12n.**). In this way it picks

---

[4] Gallus fr. 2 6-7 (Courtney = 145.6-7 Hollis) *tandem fecerunt c[ar]mina Musae / quae possem domina deicere digna mea.*
[5] See Fulkerson (2017) 224.

up the theme of Vertumnus as god of disguise and change which has been a leitmotiv throughout the book (see **8 headnote** and **8.13-14n.**).

Another important intertext which serves as a unifying reference throughout the book is the story of Cephalus and Procris at Ov. *Met.* 7.661-862 (see section 3.1 below), which has an important role to play in both **19** (see **headnote, 2n. 11-12n., 13-14n.**) and **20** (see **20.3n.**), a powerful argument for the unity of the whole book and for the integration in it of these two closural poems.

The names Lygdamus and Neaera from the opening poems **1-6**, whose significance we shall discuss below (sections 3.1 and 3.2), of course are not mentioned in the final poems, where our author at **19.13**, assumes the name and mask of Tibullus. However the associations of Neaera's name as a 'new mistress' (*nea-era*) are now seen to be inappropriate for a mistress whose failings have become too well known (**19.22** *notae ... dominae*, cf. Cat. 72.5 of Lesbia, *nunc te cognoui*). Furthermore, the unsuitability of Lygdamus as 'publisher of grief' (see below section 3.1) is hinted at in **19.20** with its reference to the evil such garrulity brings about *hoc peperit misero garrula lingua malum*. The author has learnt to turn a deaf ear **20.2** *surdis auribus* to the gossip from which the Lygdamus and Sulpicia *personae* had suffered and the book ends with a satisfactorily closural order to rumour to 'be quiet' **20.4** *tace*.

1.3 A unifying intertext: Ovid *Metamorphoses* 7.661-862

Philip Hardie [(2012) 212-238], in an important essay on "Virgil's Catullan Plots", shows how the overall architecture of the *Aeneid* was influenced by the author's awareness of recurrent patterns in the work of Catullus as a whole and compares this with the way in which other important intertexts such as Apollonius of Rhodes' *Argonautica* and Euripides' *Bacchae* may be taken as keys to a reading of the plot of the *Aeneid* as a whole. I discuss in section 3 below the way in which certain intertexts link various sections of **[Tib.] 3**; so Hor. *Epod.* 15 links the *Lygdamus* poems with the *Laud*es *Messallae* and the Propertius poems in which Lygdamus is mentioned, 3.6, 4.7 and 4.8 can throw light on our interpretation not only of the *Lygd.* poems **1-6**, but also of those relating to *Sulpicia* **8-18**. One important intertext however stands apart from these in its apparent influence on the themes and structure of the whole of **book 3** and this is Ovid's story of the doomed marriage of Cephalus and Procris.

The story related to Phocus, son of Aeacus, by Cephalus at the end of book 7 of Ovid's *Metamorphoses*, about how jealousy ruined his happy marriage with Procris and led eventually to his killing her in a hunting accident, has such a plethora of correspondences with all parts of **[Tib.] 3** that it lends weight to arguments in favour of a unitary author for the whole of the collection. A shorter version of the myth, which Ovid uses as an exemplum of the dangers of jealousy in his advice to women occurs at *Ars* 3.683-746, but seems to have been less influential on our text. On the difficulty of establishing the relative chronology of the two Ovidian versions see Gibson (2003) 42-43. In the *Met.* version, after some preliminary scene setting (7.661-686), Cephalus tells Phocus how shortly after his happy marriage to Procris he was approached while out hunting by the goddess Aurora who attempted to seduce him (687-704). He rejected her advances on the grounds that he was in love with his new wife. The goddess sent him home with a warning that he would regret his marriage (705-713). Cephalus took the warning to refer to his wife's possible infidelity and, adopting a disguise provided by Aurora, he entered his home and attempted to seduce Procris with the offer of gifts (714-740). She eventually gave way, and Cephalus revealed himself and denounced her faithfulness. After a period of separation in which Procris retreated to the mountains to hunt there was a reconciliation to mark which she gave her husband a hunting dog and a javelin (741-758). At the centre of the narrative (759-792) is inserted Cephalus' description, in more tragic style, of the events that took place in Thebes after the slaying of the Sphinx by Oedipus. A new monster had been sent against the city and Cephalus had joined in the hunt with the hound and javelin his wife had given him. The episode ends with a metamorphosis in which his hound and the beast are turned to stone in the course of the hunt. In the second part of the narrative Cephalus tells Phocus how, after their reconciliation, the married couple lived a happy life of reciprocated love (793-803). He used to hunt alone in the woods protected only by his javelin (804-808). When tired he used to call on the breeze, *aura*, to come and refresh him, but a passer-by took the name Aura to be that of a nymph and reported his supposed unfaithfulness to Procris, who was smitten with grief, but determined to find out for herself whether the report was true (809-834). She followed Cephalus on his hunt and heard him calling to Aura, whom she mistook for a nymph. Cephalus, hearing a rustling in the trees, threw his javelin at the sound and unwittingly wounded his wife. While she was dying he was able to explain to her the mistake about the name *aura*. He had to live with the guilt of the death he had caused, but Procris seemed to die happy in the knowledge that she had not been deceived by her husband (835-862).

A number of detailed verbal echoes between Ovid's narrative and various sections of **[Tib.] 3** suggest a clear connection between the two works. Of key importance are Ovidian echoes in the opening poem **1** and the closing two poems **19** and **20**, suggesting that Ovid's narrative influenced the structure of **book 3** as a whole. Like Lygdamus and Neaera, the pair were initially happily married (*Met.* 7.799: **1.26-27** *coniuge /coniunx*), a *mutua cura* existed between them (*Met.* 7.800: **1.19**), and the wife was dearer to the husband than his own body (*Met.* 7.847 *corpus ... meo mihi carius*: **1.25** *teque suis iurat caram magis esse medullis*). This poem is taken up again in **19** where the lover there (who impersonates Tibullus) refers to his relationship as a *foedus* (**19.2** *iuncta est foedere nostra Venus*) as Procris does at *Met.* 7.852 *per nostri foedera lecti* echoing Cephalus' reference to their first union at *Met.* 7.710 *primaque deserti referebam foedera lecti*. Both lovers swear that no girl sent from heaven would separate them *Met.* 7.802-803 *nec me quae caperet, non si Venus ipsa ueniret / ulla erat*: **19.13-14** *nunc licet e caelo mittatur amica Tibullo, / mittetur frustra deficietque Venus*, in a sentence in which the *mutua cura* echoed in **1.19** had occurred. Cephalus' words to *aura*/*Aura* at *Met.* 7.817-819 *tu mihi magna uoluptas / ... tu me reficisque fouesque, / tu facis ut siluas ut amem loca sola* are echoed in the words to the mistress at **19.11-12** *tu mihi curarum requies, tu nocte uel atra / lumen, et in solis tu mihi turba locis*. Finally, the false rumour of Cephalus' unfaithfulness caused Procris pain *Met.* 7.825-827 *Procrin adit linguaque refert audita susurra. / credula res amor est: subito conlapsa dolore, / ... cecidit* just as rumours of his mistress' unfaithfulness caused the author pain in the final poem of the collection **20.3** *crimina non haec sunt nostro sine facta dolore*; for *crimina* in this context, cf. *Met.* 7.824 *criminis extemplo ficti temerarius index*.

There are clear signs in the echo of the same intertext in the opening and closing poems of our **[Tib.] 3**, brought out especially in *Met.* 7.800-804, a sentence taken up in both **1** and **19**, that a single author lay behind the construction of the whole work. These echoes are not restricted to the opening and closing poems, but are scattered throughout the work, occurring in all sections, including the *Laudes Messallae*. Any single case could be fortuitous but the cumulative effect of the correspondences is striking: *Met.* 7.689 *coniugis amissae* see **2.4n., 2.30n.**; 7.691-692 *si uiuere nobis / fata diu dederint* see *Laudes Messallae* **7.206n.**; 7.692 *coniuge cara* see **3.32n.**; 7.697 *dignior ipsa rapi* see **8.24n.**; 7.698 *hanc mihi iunxit amor* see **19.2n.**; 7.698 *felix dicebar* see **4.80n.**; 7.705 *liceat mihi uera referre* see **2.7n.**; 7.722 *immutat ... meam ... figuram* see **7.206**; 7.724-725 *culpa domus ipsa carebat / castaque signa dabat* see **4.60n.**;

7.726 *aditus per mille dolos ... factus* see **8.14n., 12.12n.**; 7.733 *decor fuerit ... dolor ipse decebat* see **8.8n., 8.14n.**; 7.736 *mea gaudia* see **9.18n., 13.5n.**; 7.742 *perfida* see **3.6.5n.**; 7.766 *indagine cinximus agros* see **9.7-8n.**; 7.814 *intres ... sinus ... nostros* see **13.4n.**; 7.855 (*per*) *causam mihi mortis amorem* see **2.27n.**

More striking, perhaps, than the verbal echoes are the thematic and structural similarities. The Vertumnus theme of perpetual change and disguise (see commentary on poem **8 headnote** and **8.13-14n.**) which is central to [**Tib.**] **3** (see section 1.2 above) is reflected in Aurora's disguise of Cephalus at *Met.* 7.721-722, the metamorphosis of the hunting dog and beast into stone at 7.790-791 and more generally in the treatment of the fidelity theme, with its alteration of faithful love and jealousy. Cephalus, the faithful husband, first being tested by Aurora and then testing Procris, and Procris, the faithful wife, eventually testing Cephalus, and dying in the attempt. The dangers of *Rumor* with which our collection ends (**19**) has its origins in the false report of Cephalus' infidelity at *Met.* 7.824-825, and underpins a deep concern in both authors with questions of openness and secrecy, hiding and revealing. Finally the theme of the dangers posed to a relationship by hunting, central to the Ovidian account, are given a whole poem to themselves at *Sulpicia Cycle* **9**. At a structural level it is possible that the inset passage in tragic style on the hunting of the Theban monster (*Met.* 7.759-792), occurring at exactly the half-way point of the Cephalus narration (*Met.* 7.661-862), could have inspired the author of [**Tib.**] **3** to place his/her hexameter panegyric on Messalla, poem **7**, at the mid point of his collection. It may be significant that both this tragic inset and the panegyric end with themes of metamorphosis (*Met.* 7.790-791 and *Laudes Messallae* **7.206-211**). The way in which Cephalus' suspicions of Procris are mirrored later in Ovid's account by Procris' suspicions of Cephalus, are perhaps reflected in the move from Lygdamus' love in the first half of [**Tib.**] **3** to that of Sulpicia in the second. At a more speculative level the mention of Cephalus' *coitusque nouos thalamosque recentes* (*Met.* 7.709) could have contributed to the appropriateness of author's choice of the name Neaera for Lygdamus' mistress (a bilingual pun = 'new mistress', see section 3.2 below), and the repetition of words suggesting complaint and sorrow at *Met.* 7.711 (*querellas*), 720 (*doleam*), 731 *(dolebat)*, 796 (*doloris*), 826 (*dolore*) could have suggested Lygdamus' own name (see section 3.1 below).

2 The Author's Masks and the Book's Sections

2.1 The Author's Masks

At *Sulpicia Cycle* **8.13-14**, marking the beginning of the second, Sulpician, half of the book after the central *Laudes Messallae* of **7**, the god Vertumnus is compared to Sulpicia in his possession of a thousand appropriate outfits or disguises (*ornatus*): *talis in aeterno felix Vertumnus Olympo / mille habet ornatus, mille decenter habet*. This is one of the few mythological *exempla* in the work and is clearly meant to draw attention to the theme of change which dominates the whole work (see **8 headnote, 8.13-14n., 19 headnote, 19.3-4n., 8n.** and **12n.**). This theme is exemplified most clearly by the adoption of what can best be described as different 'masks', in the different sections into which the work has traditionally been divided, by the unitary author, male or female, of the whole book (henceforth referred to as 'the author'). These masks allow our unitary poet to explore the theme of love and love poetry from different viewpoints in each section:

1. In elegies **1-6** (s)he names himself/herself as Lygdamus (**2.29**). In taking his name from Propertius (Prop. poems 3.6, 4.7, 4.8), his date of birth (**5.17-18**) from Ovid (*Trist.* 4.10.5-6), and the theme of the elegist's death and funeral (**2.9-30**) from Tibullus (Tib. 1.1.59-68, 3.5-10) and Propertius (Prop. 1.17.19-24, 2.13.17-58, 3.16.21-30) the poet sets himself/herself firmly in the era of the golden age of elegy. However, by discussing the problems of married love Lygdamus takes elegy in a new direction little explored by his Augustan predecessors, except for Ovid in the *Tristia*. The poems in this mask will be referred to as *Lygd.*

2 In poem **7**, the *Laudes Messallae*, inspired by Tibullus' poem 1.7 on the triumph of his patron Messalla over Aquitania in 28 BC, the author does not name himself/herself, but apparently takes on the mask of a young Tibullus, applying to Messalla for patronage (see Peirano 2012, 132-148). This assumed identity is made almost certain by our author's reference to his family's poverty (**7.183-189**) in terms very reminiscent of those of Tibullus (Tib. 1.1.33-4). The poem praises Messalla on the occasion of his consulship in 31 BC. The change in metre to hexameters and the change in genre to panegyric allow the poet to explore, using the conventions of another genre, another facet of the poet's life, his relationship with hs patron. The poem in this mask will be referred to as *Laud. Mess.*

3. In poems **8-12** the author adopts the mask of a sympathetic observer who comments upon the affair of Sulpicia and Cerinthus, characters who, like Tibullus, are to be thought of as connected with the circle of Messalla. This observer, who is not named, was traditionally referred to as the *amicus Sulpiciae,* a term rejected in the current commentary as tending to give a spurious biographical reality to what is clearly an imaginary figure. Poems in the observer's own voice (**8, 10, 12**), alternate with two poems of the same length and style, written in the voice of Sulpicia (**9** and **11**). Our author here undertakes an ambitious double impersonation, playing the role of the unnamed observer speaking in the voice of Sulpicia. The role of this section is to allow our poet to explore elegy from the point of view of a poet detached from the affair he observes. Again the inspiration is Tibullan, taking its lead from Tibullus' comments on the affair of Marathus and Pholoe in poems 1.8 and 1.9. The direct speech of Marathus to Pholoe included in Tib. 8.55-66 could well have provided the inspiration for the speeches given to Sulpicia in poems 9 and 11. This group is carefully constructed with its alternation of male and female voices and its unity of style. It will be referred to for convenience as the *Sulpicia Cycle.*

4. In a distinct group of shorter poems, **13-18**, the author takes on the mask of Sulpicia (self-named at **16.4**), in which an introductory poem **13** introduces a group of short epistolary epigrams, addressed to Messalla (**14**) and Cerinthus (**15-18**). Here the author explores the subject of love from the female point of view and varies his/her style to suit the type of language appropriate for a female writer. As with the change of genre in poem **7** to panegyric, the change in genre here from elegy (in **8-12**) to epigram serves to underline our unitary poet's new perspective. Again the setting is the circle of Messalla, his relatives and associates. The poems in this mask will be referred to as the *Sulpicia* poems.

5. In the first of two related closural poems, **19** and **20**, the author names himself/herself as Tibullus (**19.13**) and thus emphasises the connections with Tibullus and his patron Messalla's circle which have dominated the whole book. Whereas the Lygdamus poems had dealt with the problems of married love, this elegy, in the mask of Tibullus, returns to the more traditional subject of the elegiac lover and his mistress. In rejecting openness in favour of secrecy the elegy reverses the themes of the Lygdamus and Sulpicia elegies. Again the inspiration for this reversal is Tibullan, where the dark secrecy of the Nemesis poems of book two reverses the bright openness of the Delia poems of his first book (see Maltby 2004).

6. The mask of the final epigram 20 is not identified. However, the emphasis on the mistress' unfaithfulness and the suffering of the lover reflects the traditional elegiac content of poem 19, and the same Tibullan mask is probably the one intended here also. The themes of secrecy and revelation which had dominated the whole work are brought to a satisfactory closure by the order to rumour in the last word of the poem to be quiet *tace*.

The verse epitaph and short prose life of Tibullus which are found at the end of **book 3** in most manuscripts have traditionally been thought of as added later as a conclusion to the three books of Tibullus. The epitaph was attributed to a contemporary of Tibullus, Domitius Marsus, by Scaliger in the 1570s on the evidence of a now lost fragmentary manuscript, the *Fragmentum Cuiacianum* and the life was thought to derive from Suetonius' now lost lives of the poets. Such pieces from Domitius Marsus and from the much later Suetonius (mid-first century AD) could well have been placed in their position at the end of **book 3** to emphasise its Tibullan associations. However, the evidence for neither attribution is secure and both pieces could have been added by a learned editor of the books or indeed by our author of **book 3**, who now comes out of his/her masks and pays tribute to the poet who inspired his/her work, Tibullus. This transition from the masked author to an author speaking in his/her own persona could be marked by the phrase *te quoque* with which the epitaph begins, a significant transitional marker in Virgil (see **headnote** to *Epitaph* below). There follows a more detailed discussion of the mask adopted in each of the book's sections in turn.

2.2. The Book's Sections

2.2.1 *Lygdamus* 3.1-6

The earliest modern commentators on **book 3** of the *Corpus Tibullianum* from Scaliger (1577) to Heyne (1777) never questioned its Tibullan authorship and saw in Lygdamus a pseudonym for the young Tibullus. The first scholar to distinguish between the poems of books 1 and 2 as genuinely Tibullan and those of **book 3** as falsely attributed to him was J. H. Voss in 1786.[6] Voss saw important differences between Tibullus and Lygdamus in style, criticising Lygdamus as an unskilful imitator of Tibullus. Furthermore he argued that Tibullus never used a pseudonym for himself but only for his mistresses, Delia and Nemesis, and that Ovid, in

---

[6] In *Musenalmanach* (Hamburg 1786 80ff.), see N-A n. 7 for full details.

his poem on the death of Tibullus, *Am.* 3.9, while speaking of Delia and Nemesis, makes no mention of Neaera, the mistress addressed in the *Lygdamus* poems. A further problem with the identification of Lygdamus with Tibullus was the couplet on Lygdamus' birth, **5.17-18** *natalem primo nostrum uidere parentes / cum cecidit fato consul uterque pari* which is almost identical with Ovid's reference to his own birth in the year 43 BC, when both consuls, Hirtius and Pansa, were killed at the battle of Mutina: *Trist.* 4.10.5-6 *editus hic ego sum nec non, ut tempora noris, / cum cecidit fato consul uterque pari*. Tibullus cannot have been born in the same year as Ovid, since Ovid implies he was younger than Tibullus at *Trist.* 4.10.51-52, and a birth date of 43 BC would make Tibullus only 12 when he took part in Messalla's Aquitanian campaign (31 BC) mentioned in Tib. 1.7. Voss concluded that Lygdamus was a Greek freedman born in the same year as Ovid.

Once it was accepted that Tibullus and Lygdamus could not be the same person, various attempts were made to identify the writer behind the pseudonym:[7] Oebeke (1831) suggested Cassius Parmensis, a poet mentioned by Horace *Epist.* 1.14.3 as inferior to Tibullus. This involves moving the birth date mentioned in **5.17-18** back to 83 BC, another year in which both consuls died; Haase (1837) proposed Lucius Valerius Messallinus, Messalla's second son; Gruppe (1838) and a number of others were in favour of the young Ovid; Doncieux (1888) suggested Ovid's elder brother;[8] Kneppers (1904) proposed Marcus Valerius Messalla Messallinus, Messalla's eldest son; Wagenvoort (1917) suggested Servius Sulpicius, cousin of Sulpicia, a thesis revised and expanded upon by Butrica (1993). Most of these suggestions account for similarities between *Lygdamus* and late Ovidian work by seeing Ovid as the imitator.

In fact, the couplet on the birth date appears rather to be an example of our author's borrowing from Ovid. While such a reference fits well into its context of the *sphragis* at the end of *Tristia* 4, it is less at home in the argument of poem **5**, where the poet is simply making the point that he is too young to die. The mention of the birth date could then be a learned reference to Ovid by a post-Ovidian imitator, which should not be taken at face value. Another approach suggested by Hagen (1954) and taken up by Lee (1958-1959) and Axelson (1960b) is that the birth year referred to by

---

[7] For a full discussion of these see N-A 6-16.
[8] Since he was born a year before Ovid (*Trist.* 4.10.9-10), this involves taking *Lygd.* **5.17-18** as a reference to his first birthday.

our author, speaking as Lygdamus, could be the next year in which both consuls died, namely AD 69, in the January of which year the *consules ordinarii* Servius Galba and Titus Vinnius were both assassinated. If then the reference to himself as *iuuenis* at **5.6** is to be taken at face value the composition date of the poem would fall in the late first or early second century AD. In fact, as Lygdamus is a fiction, our author can give him any birth date he pleases and a date linking him with Ovid simply adds to the impression he wishes to give of writing in the golden age of elegy.

The present commentary has revealed not only echoes of the earlier elegists, but also of poets of the Flavian era including Senecan tragedy, *Culex*, *Ciris*, Valerius Flaccus, Silius, Statius, and, especially, Martial. In many of these cases similarities between these poets and the *Lygd.* poems suggest that, as with **5.17-18**, our author was the imitator.[9] So, in **5.19-20** the couplet about cheating the vine of its new fruit: *quid fraudare iuuat uitem crescentibus uuis / et modo nata mala uellere poma manu*? alludes to Ov. *Am.* 2.14.23-24 *quid plenam fraudas uitem crescentibus uuis / pomaque crudeli uellis acerba manu*? The reference to tearing away unripe fruit makes more sense in the context of Ovid's mistress's abortion than it does with reference to killing the youthful Lygdamus. Often, however, priority is impossible to prove and the fact that the work of many poets has simply not survived means that the use of apparent echoes can never be used as secure evidence for chronology. On the whole the stylistic evidence points to a Flavian date of composition and this conclusion is not invalidated by the metrical evidence on *Lygdamus* which I have discussed in detail elsewhere.[10]

If we are correct in our assumption of a late, possibly Flavian, date for the *Lygdamus* poems, then their content can be seen as an attempt to move the genre of elegy on from the traditional stance of a well-to-do elegiac lover describing his affair with a lower-class mistress to the description of the breakdown of a relationship of love and marriage between social equals. The theme of marriage is approached for the first time in earlier elegy in Ovid's *Tristia* as we will see below. In poem **1** Lygdamus sends on the Kalends of March a gift of poems to Neaera who was once but no longer appears to be his *coniunx*. In the second poem he imagines his death brought about by the loss of his *coniunx* (**2.4**) and his funeral attended nevertheless by Neaera and her mother, who will weep

---

[9] See **1.9-14n.**, **6.21**, **6.57** (Martial); **1.15-16n.**, **5.1n.**, **5.24n.** (*Culex*); **4.35**, **6.13-17** (*Ciris*); **6.12**, **6.16** (Silius Italicus).
[10] Maltby (2010) 328.

for her son-in-law (*gener* **2.14**). Poem **3** expresses a wish for a simple life in the company of a dear wife (*cara coniuge* **3.32**), or, failing that, death. Apollo appears to Lygdamus in poem **4** and informs him that Neaera prefers to be the mistress of another man (*alterius ... puella uiri* **4.58**) than to accept the marriage (*coniugium* **4.79**) with Lygdamus promised by Apollo. In the following poem **5** Lygdamus lies sick in Rome and there is no mention of Neaera. In the final poem **6** the break-up between Lygdamus and Neaera is presented as final (*nulla mei superest tibi cura, Neaera* **6.29**) and Lygdamus attempts to drown his sorrows in a symposium with his friends. Although these six poems in no way give a chronologically linear account of his affair with Neaera, a clear indication of the fact that they were intended to be read in the order in which they occur in our collection is provided by the close connections between the endings and beginnings of consecutive poems, a technique he learned from Tibullus; see Maltby (2002) 49-50. So the theme of the poet's death at the end of **1** links neatly with the theme of the poet's funeral which is the subject of the poem **2**; the address to Neaera at the end of **2** is picked up by the address to Neaera in the first line of **3**; the apotropaic *di meliora ferant* at the opening of **4** links with the end of **3** by warding off the evil associations of the wish for death expressed in its final couplet; the mention of *mixta mero* in **5.34** leads smoothly into the mention of the wine-god Liber with which the sixth poem opens (more on these links in the commentary in **2.1n., 3.3-4n., 6.1n., 6.3n.**)

Our author presents Lygdamus as consistently referring to Neaera as his *coniunx* (**1.26-27; 2.4, 30; 3.32**), a term suggesting marriage, or at least betrothal,[11] and never applied to the mistress by the other elegists, although Ovid does use it of his own wife in *Tristia* 1.2.37, 1.3.79, 82, 1.6.26, 3.3.15, 55, 3.4b.53, 59, 3.8.10, 3.11.15, 4.3.35, 4.3.72, 4.10.74, 5.1.39 and 5.14.2. Lygdamus is made to describe himself as Neaera's *uir* (**1.23, 2.14**) and her mother's *gener* ('son-in-law', **2.14**), and Apollo in poem **4** refers to Neaera as Lygdamus' *nupta* and to their relationship as a *coniugium* (**4.74, 79**). Although Catullus had seen his affair with Lesbia in terms of a *foedus amoris* (Cat. 76.3, 87.3, 109.6), which had similarities with a formal marriage, and although Ovid speaks of his own wife in the *Tristia*, no elegist used marriage terminology with relation to his mistress so consistently as our author in the mask of Lygdamus. Coming late in the elegiac tradition, our author turns elegy in a largely new and unexpected direction.

---

[11] Cf. Turnus' use of the term *coniunx praerepta* of his former betrothed Lavinia at Virg. *Aen.* 9.138.

Another innovative aspect of the unitary author's work is the fact that the name of Lygdamus, presented as a poet, is obviously a pseudonym (a point already made by Voss). In Catullus and the earlier elegists it was the mistress who was designated by a pseudonym, Catullus' Lesbia, Tibullus' Delia and Nemesis, Propertius' Cynthia and Ovid's Corinna, while the poet retained his own name. 'Lygdamus' was a contemporary slave-name in Rome, attested in inscriptions and in Propertius (in 3.6, 4.7 and 4.8). If this name was intended to suggest a connection with Propertius, it could be taken, along with a birth date reminiscent of that of Ovid at **5.17-18**, and the Tibullan themes of the sickness of the poet (poem **5**, cf. Tib. 1.3) and the drowning of love's sorrows in wine (poem **6**, cf. Tib.1.2) as part of an attempt by the author to associate himself/herself closely with all three of his/her great predecessors in the genre. For more on the literary and etymological associations of the names Lygdamus and Neaera see sections 3.1 and 3.2 below.

2.2.2. Poem 3.7, the *Laudes Messallae* (*Panegyricus Messallae*)

Despite the fact that this poem differs in metre, length and genre from the rest of the collection, it is clear that it is a well-integrated part of the whole book, functioning as a central fulcrum between the elegiacs concerning the love affairs of Lygdamus and Neaera **1-6** and of Sulpicia and Cerinthus **8-18**, with the final poems **19** and **20** acting as a closural pair for the whole book. In my view the central positioning of poem **7** is motivated by a desire to emphasise the importance of Tibullus and his patron, Messalla, to the book as a whole. This emphasis is further strengthened by the naming of Messalla in the *Sulpicia* poems at **14.5** and our author's self-naming as 'Tibullus' in the closural poem **19.13**. The emphasis given to this poem by its central positioning and its relation to the poems that precede and follow argue strongly that it was integral to our author's conception of his/her whole undertaking. This is not a separate genre piece simply attached to a collection of otherwise unrelated poems.

This panegyric in hexameters, purports to be written for Messalla on his entry to the consulship with Octavian on 1 January 31 BC (**7.118-190**), an event that went unmentioned by the genuine Tibullus, whose work records only Messalla's Eastern command of 30-29 BC (poem 1.3) and his governorship of Aquitania 28-27 BC (poem 1.7). On the importance of Tib. 1.7, celebrating Messalla' triumph over Aquitania in September 27 BC, as an inspiration for poem **7** of **book 3** see section 3.3 below and **7 headnote** in the commentary. In the *Laudes* the entry to the consulship in January 31 BC is the latest event mentioned in the poem, which omits even Messalla's part in the battle of Actium in September of the same year. The terms in which the author mentions the reduction in his ancestral property (182-190) recall lines of the genuine Tibullus on the same subject (Tib. 1.1.19-22, 33-42) and suggest that the writer is posing as a young Tibullus; so, recently, Peirano (2012) 144-148.[12] However, the writer of the poem nowhere refers to himself by name. The title *Laudes Messallae* is attested in the main manuscript tradition (A+), while the now more commonly used *Panegyricus Messallae* is reported by Scaliger to have been the title in the Fragmentum Cuiacianum (F). The position of this poem in the book would make it parallel to Tibullus' birthday poem for Messalla 1.7, just as the *Lygdamus* **1-6** could be seen as parallel to the six Delia poems which open Tib.'s first book. On metrical and stylistic grounds this hexameter poem could not have been written in the time of Tibullus, but may come, like the *Lygd.* poems, which I suggest were by the same author, from the late first or early second century AD, written perhaps at the suggestion of one of Messalla's descendants, Catullus Messallinus.[13] Echoes of Manilius put the poem certainly after AD 20,[14] and echoes of Statius, Pliny the Younger and Juvenal suggest a much later date.[15] As Peirano [(2012) 120-122] has argued, the poem, like *Catalepton* 9 and *Ciris*, both addressed to Messalla,[16] is part of a pseudo-biographical tradition that serves to fill in details of his role as a literary patron of the immediately pre-Augustan period. The only historical facts mentioned in our poem are in lines **106-118** which list the races Messalla is supposed to have overcome on an Illyrian campaign. Again, no such campaign is mentioned by Tibullus or by anyone else in relation to Messalla (although it is possible that Octavian, unmentioned in the poem as he is also in Tib. books 1 and 2, could have led such a campaign in 35-33 BC). The

---

[12] The idea was initially suggested by Heyne (1777); cf. also Hartung (1880), Ehrengruber (1889-1899), Tränkle 172-184, Maltby (2010) 329.
[13] See Maltby (2010) 329-331, Tränkle 182-184, some of whose findings are criticised in Butrica (1992) and Luck (1994), and also De Luca (2009) 9-12.
[14] See **nn.** on **41, 152** and cf. e.g. the Manilian use of *Phoebus* for the sun at 1.175, 186, 198, 311, and *passim*.
[15] On Statian echoes see **nn. 1, 31, 36, 70, 96, 144, 200**; on Plin. *Epist.* see **nn. 161** and **179**; on Juvenal see **nn. 32** and **111**.
[16] On *Catalepton* 9 and Messalla see Peirano (2012) 120-132; on *Ciris* and Messalla see Peirano (2012) 173-188. For *Laudes Messallae* and *Catalepton* 9 see **nn.** on **4, 5-6, 25, 27, 32, 48-49, 53, 135-176, 193-195, 211** and cf. Rostagni (1959), Miguet (1980) 257-262, Schoonhoven (1983) 1702-1706, Papke (1986); for *Laudes Messallae* and *Ciris* see **nn.** on **5-6, 34, 124, 125, 197, 200, 202, 209, 211**.

projected military exploits against Britain mentioned in **150** would be compatible with Octavian's unfulfilled intentions in this sphere,[17] but they could equally well relate to Flavian propaganda.[18] The poem may have been influenced by the only other surviving poem of this type written in Latin before the end of the first century AD, namely the *Laus Pisonis*, addressed to the conspirator Calpurnius Piso of AD 65,[19] but composed possibly as early as the AD 40s. Both these poems go back to a tradition of encomium in Greek poetry that began with Simonides, Pindar and Bacchylides and continued into the Hellenistic period with Callimachus and Theocritus.[20] On the importance in particular of the Callimachean epinician tradition on **[Tib.] 3.7** see the **headnote** to that poem in the commentary and section 3.3 below. In Latin the first verse panegyric, the *Panegyricus Augusti* by Varus, has not survived. This was followed by the *Laus Pisonis* and the lost *Laudes Neronis* of Lucan. At the end of the first century comes Statius' *Laudes Crispini* (*Silu.* 5.2), perhaps closely followed by the *Laudes Messallae*. There is then a gap in production until the encomiastic works of Claudian in the fourth century. A parallel development of encomiastic literature in prose led to the discussion of the genre in the rhetorical handbooks. Numerous references in the commentary show that the author of the *Laudes Messallae* was well aware of the rules laid out in this rhetorical tradition.[21]

2.2.3 The *Sulpicia Cycle*: poems 3.8-12

These five poems, in which our author, as in the *Laudes Messallae,* does not give himself/herself a name, form a tightly constructed group, with alternating male (**8, 10,** 12) and female (**9, 11**) speakers, known traditionally as the *Sulpicia Cycle*. Their subject is the love of Sulpicia for a certain Cerinthus. In poems **8, 10** and **12** our author speaks in the mask of an unnamed objective observer of the affair. It is possible that internal hints in these poems, echoing the works of a poet now lost to us, could, rather like the echoes of Tibullus in the *Laud. Mess.*, have suggested to our

---

[17] Hor. *Carm.* 3.5.1-3, Cassius Dio 49.38.2.
[18] See Momigliano (1950) 41-42, Evans (2003).
[19] On links with the *Laus Pisonis* see commentary on **7, 28-32, 34, 37, 39, 45-47, 46-47, 48-49, 175, 178, 180** and see Salvatore (1949), La Penna (1991).
[20] Cf. Callimachus fr. 54-59 Pf. (victory of Berenice II in the Nemean chariot race) and Theocr. *Id.* 16 (for Hiero of Syracuse) and *Id.* 17 (for Ptolemy Philadelphus).
[21] *Rhet. Alex.* n.118-134; *Rhet. Her.* **nn. 5-6, 17, 28-32, 135-176**; Cic. *Part. Or.* **nn. 28-32, 118-134,** Men. Rhet. **nn. 28-32, 39, 48-49, 89-97, 106-117, 118-134, 196** and see further Papke (1986) 123-134, Tränkle 175, De Luca (2009) 15-16.

author's original audience a particular name for this mask, but with the loss of so much Latin poetry these hints are no longer recoverable by us. In poems **9** and **11** our unitary author impersonates the *observer* speaking in the voice of Sulpicia. The model for such role playing in which a female is presented as speaking in her own voice could perhaps have been Arethusa in Propertius 4.3, Cornelia in Propertius 4.11 and the heroines of Ovid's *Heroides*. This group also has its roots in Tibullan elegy. In Tib. 1. poems 8 and 9 Tibullus takes up the role of the observer of an affair between Marathus and Pholoe and in 1.8.55-66 the boy Marathus is given a speech in his own voice. The *Sulpicia Cycle* treats similar themes to those found in what purport to be the *Sulpicia* poems themselves (**13-18**), but differs considerably from them metrically, stylistically and lexically.[22] This need not imply a different author for both, but simply that the author of the so-called *Sulpicia* poems **13-18** was attempting to write in the style of letters composed by a woman (see section 3.5 below). The poems of the *Sulpicia Cycle* are very similar in size (24, 24, 26, 20 and 20 lines respectively) and are in line with poem **19** at 24 lines. They are shorter than those of *Lygdamus* (28, 30, 38, 96, 34, 64, average 48 lines) and the genuine Tibullus (book 1 average 80, book 2 average 72). The author's use of long periods (e.g. **8.15-20**) and of paired synonyms (e.g. **8.9, 10.5-6, 11.6-7, 14-15**) puts him/her closer to the author of poems **1-6** (with whom I would argue (s)he is identical) than to the earlier elegists.

The *Sulpicia Cycle* is carefully constructed, with Sulpicia's adorning herself for Mars in the **first poem (8)** and for Juno in the **last (12)**, and both poems end with a wish for the annual repetition of the festivals described, both of which, the Matronalia of Mars and the birthday festival of Juno, are concerned in part with the renewal of amatory vows. These two addresses, to Mars in the first and Juno in the last poem, are balanced by the address to Apollo in the central poem **10**. A link with the *Lygdamus* elegies is provided by the opening theme of the Matronalia, the festival of Mars, which opens both groups (see section 1.2 above). The theme of the second poem is Cerinthus' absence at the hunt. Spoken in the voice of Sulpicia it is reminiscent of Phaedra's letter to Hippolytus in Ovid *Heroides* 4. In poem **10** Apollo is addressed on the occasion of Sulpicia's illness (a theme found also in poem **17** on her own illness, and common in

---

[22] On differences between the *Sulpicia Cycle* (**8-12**) and the *Sulpicia* poems (**13-18**) in metre, lexicon and style see Santirocco (1979) 235-237, Hinds (1987) 44, Lowe (1988) 197-205, Hubbard (2004) 189-192 and Maltby (2010) 331-334.

earlier elegy[23]) and Cerinthus is assured by him of his mistress's love. Poem **11** forms a pair with **12**. The first, in the voice of Sulpicia, is a congratulation of Cerinthus on his birthday and the second, in the voice of the unnamed observer, is a congratulation of Sulpicia on her birthday. Both poems use the same birthday theme as Sulpicia in poems **14** and **15**, and belong to the elegiac tradition of the *genethliakon* as seen in Tib. 1.7 and 2.2 and in Prop. 3.10. These thematic similarities with the *Sulpicia* poems are confirmed by two striking verbal similarities, namely *lux mea* of Cerinthus at **9.15** and **18.1** and *corpora fessa* at **10.10** and **17.2**. The alternation of male and female voices in this section may owe something to the amoebaean exchanges of pastoral.

2.2.4 The *Sulpicia* poems: 3.13-18

Immediately after the *Sulpicia Cycle* in the collection come the poems traditionally attributed to Sulpicia herself, but better described as poems in the mask of Sulpicia, **13-18**. Four of the six poems are addressed to a certain Cerinthus, the object of Sulpicia's love, already mentioned in the *Sulpicia Cycle*. This could possibly be a pseudonym for the Cornutus addressed by Tibullus in poem 2.3 of the *Corpus*, on the occasion of his birthday and betrothal. However other interpretations are more likely; on Cerinthus and its literary and etymological background see section 3.4 below. The poet in the mask of Sulpicia would thus be continuing the elegiac tradition by which the poet uses his own name but refers to the object of his love by a pseudonym. Here our author as poetess uses what is to be taken as her own name (Sulpicia) for herself, but uses a pseudonym for her male lover, Cerinthus.

    The content of the poems reveals a familiarity with the conventional themes of Roman elegy, though in scale they have more in common with epigram. The first poem, **13**, has no addressee, but expresses Sulpicia's joy at the consummation of her love with a worthy partner, a fact that she has no intention of keeping secret out of considerations of shame and propriety. Parallels for this theme of successful love in elegy are to be found in Prop. 2.14 and Ov. *Am.* 2.12. The next two poems, **14** and **15**, of eight and four lines respectively, deal with the theme of Sulpicia's birthday. In **14**, addressed to Messalla, she complains that his invitation to her to spend it at his country estate will deprive her of the company of Cerinthus, who will remain in town, while **15**, addressed to Cerinthus,

---

[23] Tib. 1.5.9ff., Prop. 2.9.25ff, 2.28, Ov. *Am.* 2.13 (on Corinna's abortion), *Her.* 20, 21, *Ars* 2.315ff.

reveals that the plan has been abandoned and she will, after all, be able to spend her birthday with Cerinthus and her friends in Rome. The birthday theme connects these poems with the *genethliakon* for Cornutus in Tib. 2.2, and with other elegiac birthday poems such as Tib. 1.7 (for Messalla), and Prop. 3.10 (for his mistress). The theme of the separation of lovers found in **15** is another common elegiac topos: in Tib. 1.3 the poet is separated from Delia by his absence in Corcyra, where he has fallen sick while accompanying Messalla on a mission abroad; in Tib. 2.3 the poet's mistress Nemesis is held in the country while Tibullus remains in Rome. The effect of the two birthday poems **14** and **15** taken together resembles that of Propertius 1.8A and 8B in which Cynthia threatens in 8A to depart for Illyria, but in 8B actually remains in Rome. But perhaps a more important inspiration, since it leaves what appear to be verbal echoes in this and other poems of Sulpicia, is Ov. *Am.* 2.16, in which Ovid is away in his native Sulmo, but finds no solace in the countryside there, because of the absence of his mistress (presumably left behind in Rome). Poems **16** and **17** introduce stresses into the relationship. Poem **16** expresses jealousy at the fact that Cerinthus has been unfaithful to her with a *scortum*, loaded down with a wool basket, *quasillum*; both are prosaic words unsuited to elegy. The links between this poem, *Lygdamus* and Prop. 4.7 are discussed below in section 3.1. Jealousy constitutes perhaps the most consistent trait of the earlier elegists, Tibullus, Propertius and Ovid, and is so pervasive that no particular poems need to be singled out as parallels. The theme of illness in poem **17** is found in all three earlier elegists, but in all cases except Tib. 1.3 it is the mistress rather than the poet who is ill; so Delia's illness in Tib. 1.5, Cynthia's in Propertius 2.28 and Corinna's abortion in Ov. *Amores* 2.13. The final poem in the group, poem **18** has no real parallel in the elegists: Sulpicia excuses herself for leaving Cerinthus in haste the previous evening, for fear of revealing the strength of her passion. This forms a neat link back to the first poem of the group (**13**) in which she has made the decision to reveal her passion to the world. Although the themes of these poems can all be paralleled in the earlier elegists, particularly from Tibullus, Propertius and early Ovid, the way in which they are expressed differs considerably from their treatment in elegy. The whole emphasis is placed not on the events themselves, but on the analysis of the emotions they arouse in the author. We learn very little about Cerinthus (apart from his affair with a slave girl), but a lot about the emotions felt by Sulpicia. In poem **13** the emphasis is on the conflict between preserving one's good name and the desire to make public a love which is worthy of both partners. In the final poem **18** it was shame which had the upper hand, but in the opening poem **13**, which some see as representing a situation later in the imagined narrative than poem **18**, the joy of public revelation has won through. The birthday poems express her sadness at the prospect of being separated from Cerinthus on her birthday, and the fact that her heart will remain in Rome with him. There is nothing about Cerinthus' feelings. In **16** Cerinthus' lack of concern for her and the fact that she may fall into some folly is contrasted with the concern felt for her by others of her friends. And the central interest of the poem on her illness, **17**, is how this will affect Cerinthus' attitude towards her.

This emphasis on emotional self-analysis by the author is of course not absent from the elegists, but in Tibullus and Propertius it tends to be integrated within the narrative, whereas in Ovid its role recedes, for the most part, before a more witty and detached treatment of conventional themes. The obvious fact that the longest of these poems is only ten lines should be a clear warning that we should not take them to be elegies or even *elegidia*, as they are sometimes called, but that their true genre is that of epigram. One only has to think of the self-analysis of Catullus 85 *odi et amo*, or Cat. 75 a longer four-line version of the same theme, to see that this is the genre to which the poems in the mask of Sulpicia belong. The difference in style between these poems and those of the *Sulpicia Cycle* and the *Lygdamus* poems is not to be accounted for by the different sections being written by different authors, but rather by a unitary author suiting his/her style to his/her different masks. Here, under the mask of Sulpicia, the author attempts to ape the style of a female aristocrat. The tradition of the amateur Roman aristocrat dabbling in epigram goes right back to the last half of the second century BC, with the poems of Valerius Aedituus, Porcius Licinus and Quintus Lutatius Catulus, inspired by Hellenistic epigram but written in a style and language that was purely Roman, including a greater emphasis on the analysis of emotion. It is not suggested here that the *Sulpicia* poems contain specific echoes from these writers, but simply that they provide a generic context, illustrated later by the epigrams of Catullus, within which these poems can best be understood and evaluated. Again the adoption by Catullus of different styles in different sections of his work is an important model. Apparent infelicities in *Sulpicia*'s style, obscure syntax, and a strange lexical mix of colloquial and archaic elements, earlier explained as female Latin or as the passionate, but ultimately flawed, efforts of an inexperienced amateur, have to be re-assessed in the light of this generic re-assignment.

It is quite striking how many of the so-called elegiac themes of these five short *Sulpicia* poems are anticipated in our meagre remains of early epigram. So, *cura,* used of love in **17.1** and **18.1**, can be found in the first epigram of Valerius Aedituus (fr. 1.1 Courtney). The theme of love's fire *calor* at **17.2** (where it is combined with the notion of a fever, for which *calor* is the technical term) and *ardorem* at **18.6** can be paralleled with the theme of *ignis Veneris* in Valerius Aedituus (fr. 2.5 Courtney) and Porcius Licinus (fr. 7.2-4 Courtney). Finally the conceit in **14.7** that the heart of the lover can be parted from its owner to reside with the beloved can be paralleled from Lutatius Catulus (fr. 1 Courtney). It is clear that our poet as *Sulpicia* is not echoing these epigrams directly: the phrase *pia cura* at **17.1**, for example, comes from Ov. *Am.* 2.16.47; *calor* in **17.2** is a medical word, not found in elegy or epigram; the normal word for erotic fire in *Sulpicia* is *ardor* (**18.6**), frequent in Propertius and Ovid, rather than *ignis*. Nevertheless it remains clear that in his/her guise as *Sulpicia* the author has chosen a range of themes, a psychological focus, and a scale of expression which is appropriate for the genre of epigram. This influence is reflected also at the syntactical level, where the proliferation of dependent infinitives in poem **13** is very reminiscent of the type of structures we find in the epigrams of Catullus, as Cat. 73, for example, illustrates. Another feature of the syntax of the *Sulpicia* poems, seen in poem **18**, namely the fact that this whole poem consists of a single sentence, is also paralleled, as Lyne [(2007) 365] has pointed out, by the structure of several Catullan epigrams: Cat. 75, 81, 82, 96, 102, 103. Other features, which Lyne, for example, rightly categorises as idiosyncratic to the *Sulpicia* poems, are more at home in epigram than elegy: these include the plethora of subordinate clauses and metrically convenient infinitives; a liking for the comparative expressions *quam ... magis* in **13.2**, *potior ... / ... quam* in **16.3-4**, and *aliter ... / ... quam* in **17.3-4**; jussive subjunctives in all poems except **17**; the *quod* noun-clause in **16.1-2**, **17.2** and **18.5-6** and the focussing *iam* or *nunc* in every poem except **13**. Once the poems are identified as epigrams it is easier to explain the fact that the language is less elevated than that of elegy, and is often close to the polite conversational style of the upper classes, to be found, for example, in the letters of Cicero. So in **13.10** *esse cum aliquo* as a euphemism for having sex with someone is frequent in Plautus, and is seen as a somewhat old-fashioned expression by Varro, although it occurs later in Cicero and Ovid. In **14.5** *studiosus* + gen. in the sense of 'worried about' can be paralleled in Cicero's letters. And *quiescas* 'relax' is found in Horace's *Sermones*. In **15.4** *necopinans* 'against one's expectation', is found in Terence and Lucretius, as well as Cicero's letters, but not in elegy. Poem **16**, with its bitter accusation of unfaithfulness with a slave-girl on Cerinthus' part, is the poem most characterised by colloquial, and, in this case, almost vulgar features. In **16.1** *gratum est quod* 'I'm glad that' a polite thanking formula, here used ironically, is again frequent in Cicero's letters, but not elsewhere in Augustan prose or verse, with the exception of Ov. *Her.* 16.13; in **16.1-2** *sibi permittere aliquid de* 'to allow oneself freedom over something' belongs to this same conversational register, occurring in Cicero's letters and then once in Ovid's *Heroides*; in **16.2** the intensifying *male* in *male inepta* is a colloquial feature, as at Cat. 10.33 *insulsa male* and Hor. *Serm.* 1.3.45 *male parvus* and 1.4.66 *rauci male*; in **16.3** *quasillus* is a prose word for a wool basket, denoting low-class slave work; it occurs in elegy elsewhere only at Prop. 4.7.41-42, while poetry and prose prefer the Greek loan word *calathus*; in **16.4** *scortum* again a low-style word for *meretrix* 'a prostitute'; it is not found elsewhere in elegy but occurs in Plautus (frequently) and Terence, as well as in Cat. 6.5, Hor. *Carm.* 2.11.21, and *Epist.* 1.8.24. Finally the syntax of **18.1-3** *ne tibi sim...si* follows, as Lyne has argued [(2007) 365], a colloquial structure, for which parallels are most frequent in Cicero's letters. It would be impossible to assemble such a collection of colloquial and prosaic features from forty consecutive lines of elegy. In verse, apart from comedy, only the epigrams of Catullus and perhaps the *Sermones* of Horace would provide such a number. This colloquial tone of the *Sulpicia* poems distinguishes them from the poems of the *Sulpicia Cycle* **8-12**, which are closer in style to traditional elegy and may well reflect an attempt on the part of a unitary author to make a show of his/her abilities in varying his/her style in accordance with the mask (s)he assumes.

Finally, literary allusions are less frequent in the *Sulpicia* poems than in the *Sulpicia Cycle*; however, Alison Keith (1997) demonstrates convincingly that the Dido episode in Virg. *Aen.* 4 establishes an important precedent for Sulpicia's love affair, especially in poem **13**. The struggle between *pudor* 'shame' and preserving one's good name and the dangers of *fama* 'evil reputation' or 'rumour' are of course central to the Dido episode as they are to *Sulpicia*, especially in **13** and **18**. The use of *Cytherea* for Venus in **13.3** is not found in Latin poetry until the 20s BC, occurring at Hor. *Carm.* 3.12.4, Prop. 2.14.25 and no fewer than six times in the *Aeneid*. One of these six occasions is at *Aen.* 1.657 where Venus Cytherea tells Cupid to sit in Dido's lap, disguised as Ascanius, to inspire her with love for Aeneas. This reference is clearly picked up, as Keith [(1997) 302] points out, in **13.4** *in nostrum deposuitque sinum*. To back up Keith's Virgilian echo here I would point to the fact that *Camenae* in the same line, the old Italian name for the goddesses of song in Livius Andronicus and Naevius, which dropped out of Latin poetry to be replaced by *Musae* from the time of Ennius, was not re-introduced until Virgil's *Eclogues*, where it makes a single appearance at *Ecl.* 3.59. Horace in

Serm. 1.10.44-5 makes an elegant reference to the fact that it was Virgil who re-introduced *Camenae*. They occur in Hor. *Carm.* and *Epist.* and in Ov. *Fast., Met.* and *Pont.*, but not elsewhere in elegy. In my view the *Sulpicia* author uses them here to emphasise the Virgilian background to the poem.

The only other possible literary reference in the *Sulpicia* poems is *pia cura* at **17.1**. Unfortunately this reading is not attested in our best manuscripts, but is a late Renaissance conjecture. However, it fits the context well and may be correct. The phrase comes from Ovid *Am.* 2.16.47 and this poem also provides a clue to the origin of *non tempestiuae uiae* in **14.6**. In Ovid the phrase *pia cura* is addressed to Corinna, left in Rome while he is absent in the country at Sulmo, whereas in Sulpicia it comes in a question to Cerinthus, asking if he has any real concern for her illness. *Cura* had been used in a similar context by Virgil in *Ecl.* 7.40. Here in 3.17.1 *pia cura* suggests something deeper and more committed than the simple *cura* 'love' of 3.16.3 and recalls the *pietas* of Catullus' affair with Lesbia as seen, for example in Catullus 76. One of the peculiarities of Ov. *Am.* 2.16 is the repetition in the space of four lines 15-18 of the Tibullan phrase *longas uias* in a curse on the inventors of travel. Tibullus had used the phrase in a similar context at 1.3.36 and of his own unwilling travels to war in 1.1.26. The Ovidian repetition and its Tibullan ancestry would have perhaps stuck in our author's mind in a poem which foresees her own absence in the country on her birthday, separated from her love, and it could well have been this that led to the expression in line **6** *non tempestiuae saepe, propinque, viae*. Further support for the idea that this Ovidian poem was in our poet's mind in **14** comes in line **7** where the phrase *hic animum sensusque meos abducta relinquo* seems to reverse the idea contained in Ovid's couplet at *Am.* 2.16.11-12 where Love's flame is absent, but the *ardor* it inspires is present in his heart. In Sulpicia's case she may be absent in the country but her mind and senses remain behind with her lover.

For a rejection of the theory that the author of the *Sulpicia* poems was in fact a niece of Messalla named Sulpicia, and for the more likely possibility that they were in fact written by a skilled impersonator, either male or, perhaps more likely, female, the author of the whole collection, see Prolegomena above and section 3.5 below.

2.2.5 The Closural Poems 3.19 and 20

The role of poems **19** and **20** as closural poems, well-integrated into the structure of the whole book has been discussed above (section 1.2, p. 89-90). There attention was drawn to their recapitulation of structurally important Catullan and Callimachean ideas, the Vertumnan theme of change, and the Cephalus and Procris episode in Ov. *Met.* 7.661-862, an importvant intertext binding together the whole of **book 3**. Furthermore deliberate echoes in **19** of the opening *Lygdamus* poem **1**, as set out in Gen. Intro., section 1.3, *Lygd.* **1 headnote** and **19 headnote** provide a neat ring-structure for the whole collection. At **19.13**, in a final change of mask after the *Sulpicia* poems, the author names himself/herself as Tibullus and this impersonation lends emphasis to the Tibullan associations of the whole book. These associations, as we saw above (p. 96), are underlined further by the attachment of the Tibullan epitaph and *Vita* after the end of the collection. In length, language, style and literary echoes from Propertius and Ovid poem **19** has more in common with the elegies of the *Sulpicia Cycle* than with those of the real Tibullus and so must be considered as the work of a Tibullus *personatus* (see **19 headnote**). Our proposed unitary author, having posed as a young Tibullus in the *Laudes Messallae* (**7**) without actually naming himself/herself as such now openly adopts the mask of his/her admired predecessor. The author of the elegant final epigram **20** does not name himself/herself. Perhaps we are to assume it is written in the same Tibullan mask as **19**. Be that as it may, its post-Tibullan and post-Ovidian features (as set out in **20 headnote**) are typical again of our proposed unitary author. Poems **19** and **20** are further linked by the theme of jealousy (esp. **19.5-6, 20.1-2**) which had also played a key role in the Cephalus and Procris intertext. Poem **20**'s central concern with *rumor* provides a suitable conclusion for a collection whose focus on questions of openness and secrecy is one of its key characteristics. The desire to publicise the sorrows of one's love had been foreshadowed in *Lygd.* **2.7** *nec mihi uera loqui pudor est* as also in **2.27-28** (see Gen. Intro., section 3.1 p. 113 below). The theme dominates the *Sulpicia* poems which begin with a discussion of the tension between hiding and revealing one's love. In **18.5-6** Sulpicia regrets leaving Cerinthus out of a desire to keep her passion secret, but by the time of the dramatically later **13.5-6** and **9-10** she has decided to remove her mask and reveal her passion. In our closural poem **19**, by contrast, Tibullus *personatus* regrets his open confessions of love to his mistress (**19.20**) and wishes to withdraw to the woods (**19.9-10**) where he can keep his love to himself (**19.18**). There may be a parallel here to the movement in the first two Tibullan books from the bright openness of the Delia poems in book one to the dark secrecy of the

Nemesis poems in book two. This theme of secrecy comes to its climax in poem **20** in which the final word *tace* (**20.4**) seeks total silence.

The book as a whole then shows a movement from Lygdaman openness to Tibullan secrecy and silence and from the new kind of elegy presented in Lygdamus' love for his estranged wife Neaera (on the significance of whose name see Gen. Intro., section 3.2 below) to a traditional Tibullan form of elegy in **19** and **20** involving servitude to a well-known mistress *notae seruitium dominae* (**19.22**). This thematic, which brings unity and development to the whole book, is thus neatly underscored in the concluding two poems and provides a further argument in favour of a single unitary author for the whole book.

3. The Characters of Book 3: Significant Names and their Past

3.1 Lygdamus

LYGDAMVS HIC SITVS EST. DOLOR HVIC ET CVRA NEAERAE
CONIVGIS EREPTAE CAVSA PERIRE FVIT.
(**2.29-30**)

Our author presents Lygdamus naming himself only once. This is in the imagined epitaph at the end of poem **2** in the six-poem cycle on the love of Lygdamus and Neaera (**1-6**). As with the two cases where Tibullus gives his name, that is Tib. 1.3.55-56: *hic iacet immiti consumptus morte Tibullus / Messallam terra dum sequiturque mari* and Tib. 1.9.83-84 *hanc tibi* (sc. *Veneri*) *fallaci resolutus amore Tibullus / dedicat et grata sis dea mente rogat*, it is mentioned in a context (epitaph or dedication) where inscriptional elegiacs would be expected in real life. For the reasons given below, connected with the 'speaking' nature of the name, Lygdamus was chosen by our author as a pseudonym. Other elegists speak of themselves using their real names, Tibullus, Propertius and Ovid, and reserve pseudonyms for their mistresses Delia, Nemesis, Cynthia, Corinna. In the case of Lygdamus and Neaera (on which see sections 3.1 and 3.2) both names appear to be pseudonyms. The Greek name Lygdamus is not found in Greek mythology or Greek literature, but occurs on inscriptions in Rome as the name of freedmen: see Knox (2018) 139 n. 14 and Hutchinson (2006) 178 at *CIL* VI 5327.2, 21744, IX 816, X 1403g., 8059, XV 1418, 1419, *Inscr. It.* III (I) 286. In Greek it occurs (in the form

Lygdamis) only in inscriptions from south Italy, e.g. *L'Anneé Épigraphique* (1994) no. 367b, with further examples in Fraser and Matthews (1987-) III.A s.v. In Latin literature it occurs as the name of Propertius' slave in Prop. 3.6, 4.7 and 4.8. The choice of a slave or freedman name as a pseudonym, suggesting lowly origins and the composition of humble poetry, is shared with Cerinthus, the object of Sulpicia's love in poems **9, 10, 11, 14**, and **17** [see (c) below]. Bickel (1960) and N-A 21 suggest that our author could have adopted the name of Propertius' slave in order to associate himself with the elegiac theme of the 'slavery of love', *seruitium amoris*. Certainly this theme has an important role to play in the *Lygdamus* poems (see **4.66n., 4.73n., 4.74n., 6.14n.**), as it does also in the *Sulpicia Cycle* (see **10.12n., 11.3-4n., 11.13-14n., 12.10n.**), the *Sulpicia* poems (see **16.4n.**), and in the final poem **19**, where the author refers to himself/herself as Tibullus (see **19.15n., 19.22n., 19.23n., 19.24n.**). If, as I suggest, the same author is responsible for the whole book, this association of Lygdamus with *seruitium* may serve as a theme connecting the different elegiac groups.

Etymologically the name may be related to the Greek λύγδος 'white marble' and the adj. λύγδινος 'marble-white', 'luminous', a suggestion first made by Dissen (1835) xxxi. Such an association could serve to link Lygdamus with 'Albius' Tibullus, an important model for the *Lygdamus* poems, the *Laud. Mess.* **7**, the final poem **19** and for the structure of **[Tib.] 3** as a whole [see Booth and Maltby (2005) 128], as well as with Tib.'s patron Messalla Corvinus, the subject of poem **7** [see Booth and Maltby (2005) 126-128 and n. 28]. Such an etymology could lie behind Lygdamus' mention of his *candida ossa* in his funeral description at **2.10** and **2.17-18**. Another possibility for this 'paleness' connection is the characteristic pallor of the elegiac lover (see N-A 21).

The ancients did not believe in a single etymology for each name, but saw multiple etymological explanations as elucidating the multiple characteristics of the object named. A second Greek derivation of Lygdamus could be from the adverb λύγδην 'with sobs', connected with the verb λύζω 'to sob' and the noun λυγμός 'a sob'. This suggestion was first made by Ehrwald [(1889) 6], cf. Schol. et Gloss in Nicand. 81b.2 λύγδην ἀντὶ κατὰ λυγμόν and Schol. in Soph. *OC* 1621.1 (= Suda, *Lambda* 767.1, 789.5) λύγδην λύζοντες. In this connection it may be significant that the word *dolor* in line **29** of the epitaph quoted above occurs mid-verse, between the two names Lygdamus and Neaera. The separation of the names in the verse mirrors the separation of the characters in the elegiac narrative and the *dolor* that results takes up the emphatic central position.

The word *dolor* recurs frequently elsewhere in *Lygd.* (**2.3, 2.6, 2.13, 6.3, 6.43**) and may well have been associated with his one element of his name. Elegy was, of course, associated etymologically with lamentation, see *LALE* 202-202 s.v. *elegeus, elegia, elegiacus*, making the name appropriate for an elegiac poet, see Heyworth and Morwood (2011) 147. The second element of Lygdamus' name, δᾶμος 'people' (Doric for δῆμος) could also be etymologically significant for the construction of his persona. The publication of his verse represents the theme of 'making public' his elegiac sufferings. This theme is brought out in the couplet immediately before the epitaph quoted above:

2.27-28:   sed <u>tristem</u> mortis <u>demonstret</u> littera causam
             atque haec in <u>celebri</u> carmina fronte <u>notet</u>.

Here *tristem* refers to the first 'elegiac' element of his name (picked up in **29** by *dolor*), while *demonstret, celebri ... fronte* and *notet* underline his desire to make public his experiences. This desire had already been foreshadowed in **2.7** *nec mihi uera loqui pudor est*. This contrast between revelation and secrecy is one that, as we have seen in the Prolegomena above, dominates the whole collection, not just the *Lygdamus* poems.

Four important intertexts appear to have contributed to the construction of Lygdamus' character in poems **1-6**: Horace *Epode* 15, where Horace loses a faithless Neaera to a rival, and the three poems of Propertius in which Lygdamus appears as Propertius' slave, Prop. 3.6, 4.7 and 4.8. These texts are set out in the Appendix.

To deal first with Horace *Epode* 15 [Appendix 1(a)]: In his important (1998) paper suggesting a single authorship for the whole of **[Tib.] 3**, Holzberg hides away in n. 43 the important suggestion that Lygdamus wanted to create the impression that he was the man who stole Horace's girl from him in this poem (confusingly referred to in Holzberg's note as *Epode* 14), the rich rival addressed in 17-20, and that his elegies relate to his suffering the consequences that Horace had predicted in 23-24, namely that Neaera would reject him in turn. Lygdamus is not named in this poem, but Neaera, of course, is (11) and a number of verbal echoes between this poem and *Lygdamus* group suggest that our author wished to assume the mask of Horace's rival. Both Horace and Lygdamus make the mistake of wishing for a permanent and marriage-like relationship with a faithless Neaera, whose name connects her with the world of the *hetaira* (see 2 below). At *Epode* 15.10 Neaera had sworn falsely to Horace that their love would be mutual *fore hunc amorem mutuum*. As a result he threatens to look elsewhere for a love that is *parem* (14). It is a similar relationship of mutual love that Lygdamus in the opening poem wishes to have with Neaera: **1.19** *illa mihi referat sit nostri mutua cura*. On the importance of this concept of *mutuus amor* in the context of marriage songs and writing on marriage see L. C. Watson [(2003) 465 and n. 38] with more examples from both Latin and Greek *epithalamia*. In fact our author goes further than Horace by presenting Lygdamus' failed relationship with Neaera as having been one of *coniugium* 'marriage', or at least 'betrothal': Neaera is described as *coniunx* at **1.26**, **1.27**, **2.4**, **2.30**, **3.32**, their relationship as *coniugium* by Apollo at **4.74** and **4.79**; Lygdamus refers to himself as the son-in-law *genero* of Neaera's mother and as the *uiro* 'husband' of Neaera at **2.14**. This concept of *mutuus amor* is not restricted in **[Tib.] 3** to the Lygdamus' relationship with Neaera, but is also applied in Sulpicia's voice at **11.6** and **11.7** and in the voice of the unnamed observer at **12.8** to relationship she hopes for with Cerinthus. Furthermore the terms in which Neaera's false oath is described at *Epode* 15.3 *magnorum numen laesura deorum* is echoed in Lygdamus' claim to be innocent of perjury at **4.16** *nec laesit magnos inpia lingua deos*. Of course it is not Lygdamus who is guilty of such false oaths, but, as in Horace's poem, his mistress Neaera (described as *fallacis ... puellae* in **6.51** and *perfida* in **6.55** and **6.56**). The peaceful description of the night scene in *Epode* 15.1-2, which provides the setting for Neaera's false oath, is echoed in Lygdamus' description of the night scene **4.17-18** which precedes the revelation to him by Apollo of his own Neaera's perfidy. If Lygdamus is to be thought of as a rich character, as his projected deluxe funeral at **2.9-30** suggests [see Büchner (1965) 68, 72, 74 and Holzberg (1998) 180], this would again tie in with his impersonation of Horace's rich rival (*Epod.* 15.19-20). It would give added point to Lygdamus' rejection of wealth in favour of love in **3**, especially as one of the riches rejected by Lygdamus there at **3.29** is the gold of the Lydian river Pactolus *Lydius aurifer amnis*, ascribed to Horace's rival at *Epod.* 15.20 *tibique Pactolus fluat*. The fact that such Lydian riches *Lydia / regna* are also rejected by the author of the *Laud. Mess.* (**7.198-199**) in favour of regard from his patron, suggests a possible identification between Lygdamus and the author of that poem. This possibility is made even stronger by the fact that Horace's rival at *Epod.* 15.21 is said to be an expert in Pythagorean reincarnation, a theme developed by the author of the *Laud. Mess.* at the end of his poem **7.206-210**. Could Lygdamus, the poet of *dolor*, have seen in *Epod.* 15.16 *si certus intrarit dolor* the opportunity to take up the role of Horace's rival in his own Neaera poems and give a literary embodiment to Horace's threat at *Epode* 15.23 *translatos alio maerebis amores*? Change and impermanence is to become a major theme not just of the *Lygd.* poems but of **[Tib.] 3** as a whole.

The poems of Propertius in which Lygdamus is named as Propertius' slave (Prop. 3.6, 4.7, 4.8) must clearly be of significance for our author, as they are the only other context in which this name is mentioned in extant Roman literature. The connection with Propertius and the importance of the *seruitium amoris* theme in his works may have influenced our author in his/her choice of pseudonym. The poems in question have links not only with the *Lygd.* **1-6**, but also with other poems in **[Tib.] 3**, suggesting again a single author for the whole work.

In Prop. 3.6 [Appendix 1(b)] Lygdamus is named no fewer than seven times. The poem begins by Prop. interrogating Lygdamus on how Cynthia was behaving when he visited her house. The description of her household by Lygdamus contains direct speech from Cynthia 19-34. It is clear from Lygdamus' report that the pair have been separated, that Cynthia suspects Prop. of being bewitched by another woman, and that the separation is affecting her badly. Prop. instructs Lygdamus to go back to Cynthia with a message of reconciliation, which, if achieved will earn Lygdamus his freedom. Prop.'s use of Lygdamus as a messenger to effect a reconciliation with his mistress exactly mirrors Lygdamus' use of the Muses in this role in poem **1 (15-28)**. The use of direct speech in this message **23-28** echoes Cynthia's direct speech in Lygdamus' message at Prop. 3.6.19-34, and may have inspired the poems in **[Tib.] 3** in which Sulpicia is made to speak in her own voice **(9, 11, 13-18)**. This use of direct speech in elegy is characteristic of Prop., either as whole poems – 1.16 a door, 4.2 Vertumnus (an important character for **[Tib.] 3**, see **8.13-14**), 4.11 (the dead Cornelia) – or as parts of poems, as when Cynthia speaks here, at 1.3.35-46, 2.29.31-38 and 4.7.13-94, and Horus speaks at 4.1B.71-150. In addition to these general similarities there are more significant verbal echoes. The importance of the concept of *mutuus amor* to Lygdamus' relationship with Neaera was mentioned above in connection with Hor. *Epode* 15. At **1.19** he asks Neaera to report back to him via the Muses *sit nostri mutua cura*, but this idea also forms part of Prop.'s message to Cynthia via Lygdamus at Prop. 3.6.39 *me quoque consimili impositum torrerier igni*. The line may also have influenced the wish expressed in Sulpicia's voice at **11.5-6** that Cerinthus should burn with an equal flame to her own: *iuuat hoc, Cerinthe, quod uror, / si tibi de nobis mutuus ignis adest.* Cynthia's mention of her dreams of Prop.'s unfaithfulness at 3.6.31 *si non uana cadunt mea somnia* is turned by Lygdamus at **4.1** into a wish that his dreams concerning Neaera's unfaithfulness should not prove to be true *nec sint mihi somnia uera*. Prop.'s question to Lygdamus about Cynthia's tears and dishevelled hair as a sign of her feelings for him at Prop. 3.6.9 *sic illam incomptis uidisti flere capillis* are echoed in Lygdamus' wish for Neaera to show her feelings for him at his funeral: **2.11-12** *ueniat longos incompta capillos / et fleat ante meum maesta Neaera rogum*. As we saw with *mutuus ignis* (**11.6**) discussed above, the influence of this poem on [**Tib.**] **3** extends well beyond the poems **1-6** themselves. Cynthia's complaint at Prop. 3.6.21-34 that Prop. has been replaced in her affections by a woman of low status becomes the theme at [**Tib.**] **3.16** of Sulpicia's complaint about Cerinthus. However, whereas Cynthia uses a euphemism for the prostitute she suspects at Prop. 3.6.21-22 *ille potest nullo miseram me linquere facto, / et qualem nolo dicere habere domi*?, Sulpicia spells out in no uncertain terms, using the word *scortum*, the status of her rival Sulpicia **16.3-4** *sit tibi cura togae potior pressumque quasillo / scortum*. The rare term *quasillum* incidentally occurs elsewhere in verse only in another of Prop.'s Lygdamus poems, namely Prop. 4.7.41. The punishment Cynthia wishes upon Prop., namely that of impotence, Prop. 3.6.34 *noctibus illorum dormiet ipsa Venus*, is turned by the author of **19.13-14** into an oath of fidelity: *nunc licet e caelo mittatur amica Tibullo, / mittetur frustra deficietque Venus*. The 'ears held poised' *suspensis auribus* at Prop. 3.6.8 with which Prop. will drink in Lygdamus' news of Cynthia's sorrow at his departure is intentionally contrasted with the *surdis auribus* with which the author of the final epigram in [**Tib.**] **3**, at **20.2** wishes to be deaf to news of his mistress's infidelity. Finally, the promise of freedom offered to Lygdamus by Propertius at 3.6.41-42 in recompense for effecting a reconciliation may have inspired our author to present Lygdamus in the character of a rich freedman. Any single one of these correspondences could, of course, be put down to coincidence, but their cumulative effect points to a sustained engagement with Prop. 3.6, not only in the *Lygd.* poems proper (**1-6**) but also in [**Tib.**] **3** overall, again providing possible evidence for a unitary author for this collection.

The next Propertian poem in which the slave Lygdamus is named is 4.7 [Appendix 1(c)]. Here at 35-46 Cynthia's ghost, in direct speech, threatens Lygdamus with branding for poisoning the wine that killed her. The slave girl Nomas, who mixed the poison is also threatened, and those that speak in Cynthia's favour, Petale and Lalage, suffer at the hands of Chloris, an ex-prostitute who now holds sway in Prop.'s house, probably the same unsuitable partner mentioned in 3.6.22. In this poem, as in 4.8.37-38 where Lygdamus is in charge of the wine at a party organised by Prop., it is clear that one of Lygdamus' duties in Prop.'s household was to dispense the wine, an important link perhaps with poem **6**, where Lygdamus presides over a symposium. As with the name Lygdamus, all the slave names mentioned in this poem are attested in inscriptions; see Hutchinson (2006) 178. Indeed Petale is attested in an epitaph [*AE* (1929) 20, n.73] for a *lectrix Sulpiciae*. This slave, whose job was that of a reader to her mistress, has been associated with the Sulpicia of **[Tib.] 3** by Carcopino (1929) and more recently by Hauser [(2016) 156-167] and others, but the metre and linguistic archaisms it contains seem to date it to a period somewhat earlier than that of the elegists Tibullus, Propertius and Ovid, and certainly, in my view, earlier than that of the author of **[Tib.] 3**. The closest link between Prop. 4.7 and the *Sulpicia* poems, as mentioned above, is the reference to the ex-prostitute, Chloris (4.7.39 *quae modo per uiles inspecta est publica noctes*), who has become mistress of Propertius' household (perhaps identical with the rival of Cynthia mentioned at Prop. 3.6.22 *et qualem nolo dicere habere* [sc. *Propertium*] *domi*), and weighs down with extra wool the baskets (*quasillis*) of those slaves who praise Cynthia (4.7.41-42). There seems to be a possible model here for the prostitute rival mentioned by Sulpicia in **16.3-4**, who herself is described as weighed down by such baskets *pressumque quasillo / scortum*. This rival in Propertius has now become rich and brushes the ground with her gold-hemmed cloak, an image which seems to have been borrowed by our author at **4.35** where it is applied to the long cloak worn by Apollo in his dream appearance to Lygdamus: *ima uidebatur talis illudere palla*. Any slave girl who is too talkative *garrula* (Prop. 4.7.42) about Cynthia's beauty, will suffer at Chloris' hands, just as the *garrula lingua* of the author of **[Tib.] 3.19.20** causes him suffering at the hands of his mistress.

The last of the Propertian poems to mention Lygdamus is 4.8 [see Appendix 1(d)]. Here, back in a time before Cynthia's death, Lygdamus assists Prop. at his party with Phyllis and Teia, where his job is to be in charge of the wine (4.8.37-38), an idea, as suggested above, which may have led to our author developing Lygdamus' symposium theme in poem **6**. When Cynthia arrives back mid-party and threatens Lygdamus, the slave appeals to Prop.'s genius to save him [4.8.69 (sc. *Lygdamus*) *eruitur, geniumque meum prostratus adorat*], as Sulpicia had appealed to Cerinthus' Genius in *Sulpicia Cycle* **11.8** *perque tuos oculos per Geniumque rogo*, herself taking on the role of a slave of love. The slave shackles which Cynthia demands for Lygdamus at 4.8.79-80, perhaps suggested to our author that Lygdamus would be an appropriate name for a poet concerned with the theme of *seruitium amoris*; these *uincla* are further echoed in the shackles of love that Sulpicia and her observer demand for her and Cerinthus at *Sulpicia Cycle* **11.14** and **12.8**. Again, as in Prop. 3.6.19-34, mention of Lygdamus is associated with direct speech from Cynthia (4.8.73-80), a possible inspiration, as we have said, for the *Sulpicia* poems in **[Tib.] 3** and Lygdamus' association with elegy could here be reflected in Cynthia's words at 4.8.79 *Lygdamus in primis, omnis mihi causa querelae*, an idea taken up perhaps in Lygdamus' epitaph, with which this section began *Lygd.* **2.29-30** DOLOR HVIC ET CVRA NEAERAE / ... CAVSA PERIRE FVIT.

Not all these similarities with earlier literature may be equally convincing, but the aim of this section has been to illustrate that the origins of the Lygdamus mask are to be found not in real life but in the literature of the Augustan period. Even the *sphragis* at the mid-point of *Lygdamus* **5** at **17-18** *natalem primo nostrum uidere parentes / cum cecidit fato consul uterque pari*, apparently giving his date of birth, need not be taken at face value. The fact that its wording echoes Ovid's line about his own date in 43 BC at *Trist.* 4.10.6 *cum cecidit fato consul uterque pari* need not suggest an actual date of birth of 43 BC for Lygdamus, or even the later date of AD 69 (which would suit better his possibly Flavian style), but simply serves to present the poet(ess) as a contemporary of the great elegists in the mask (s)he is adopting for the composition of his/her book (see commentary on *Lygd.* **5.17-18** below). This is all literary artistry in which earlier poetry and not real-life chronology has the key role to play. Finally it is significant that links with earlier poems concerning characters called Lygdamus are not restricted to the *Lygdamus* poems themselves, poems **1-6**, but are also found in the other poems of **book 3**, suggesting a unitary author for the whole work.

3.2 Neaera

The object of Lygdamus' devotion, Neaera, described in terms of an estranged wife (**1.23**, **2.29**, **4.60**), is mentioned in all the *Lygdamus* poems (**1-6**), apart from poem **5**, on Lygdamus' illness, which can in part be seen as a sickness of love, caused by his problems with Neaera. In the opening poem, where Lygdamus is still hoping for a reconciliation, she is described as *cara* (**1.6**) and *casta* (**1.23**); in poem **2** she is imagined as being *maesta* (**2.12**) at his funeral; in poem **3** he addresses her in connection with the theme of rejecting riches in favour of a life of love with her (**3.1**, **3.23**); in **4**, as Apollo reveals the truth of her deception to Lygdamus, she is mentioned as preferring another man (**4.57-58**) and as rejecting her home and married status (**4.60**). In the final symposiastic poem **6**, he addresses her in **29-30** with the realisation that she has deserted him, but nevertheless wishes her a happy fate *candida fata* (perhaps a play on the etymology of his own name, see 3.1 above).

As we saw in the discussion of *Epode* 15 above, the name Neaera had always suggested untrustworthy girls. A hetaira of this name is the target of [Dem.] *Or.* 59 and a wife named Neaera seduces her husband's friend in Parthenius *Erotika Pathemata* 18. Elsewhere in Greek literature the name is applied to several relatively innocent nymphs (see *RE* XVI 2104, including the mother of Phaethusa and Lampetie in Hom. *Od.* 12.133), as well as to characters in comedy (Timocles fr. 25-26 and Philemon fr. 49 Kassel-Austin). In Latin literature the name always has associations of infidelity. It occurs first in a comedy by Licinius Imbrex (fr. 1.1 Ribbeck$^{2-3}$ 1898, 39-40 from Gell. 13.23.16), where the name connotes a girl of loose morals [see Appendix 2(a)]. In Virg. *Ecl.* 3.3-5 Neaera is a girl whose affections are fought over by two shepherds [Appendix 2(b)]. At Hor. *Carm.* 3.14.21-24 she is a hired singing-girl invited by Hor. to his symposium [Appendix 2(c)] and at *Epode* 15.11 [Appendix 2(d)], as we have seen above, she is named as Horace's faithless mistress. Finally in Ov. *Am.* 3.6.27-28 [Appendix 2(e)] she is a beautiful nymph who ravages the river Xanthus. By the time of Prudentius the term *neaera* is used as a common noun to denote a prostitute. On the associations of the name with faithless women see further Postgate [(1914) 121-122], Ullman [(1915) 29], Paoli (1953), Herter [(1957) 1169], Clausen [(1994) 93 on Virg. *Ecl.* 3], Lightfoot [(1999) 490 on Parthenius *Erotika Pathemata* 18.1], L. C. Watson [(2003) 472 on Hor. *Epode* 15.11], and N-R [(2004) 189 on Hor. *Carm.* 3.14.21], who also connect the name with the Greek word for 'young', contrasting with the grey-haired Horace (25 *albescens ... capillus*). A noticeable echo of Horace's *Carm.* 3.14.22 may be found in the reference to Apollo's myrrh-scented locks at **4.28** *stillabat Syrio myrrea rore coma*. L. C. Watson [(2003) 466 on Hor. *Epode* 15] suggests that by investing his relationship with the faithless Neaera with the characteristics of marriage Horace may have intended to put his audience in mind of Archilochus' Neoboule. Whether or not our author intended a connection with Archilochus' Neoboule, (s)he clearly wished to follow Horace in choosing for a mistress described in terms of a wife or betrothed a name which suggests the very opposite of a faithful bride.

The relationship described between Lygdamus and Neaera is different from that of traditional elegy [Fulkerson (2017) 29] and this difference could be reflected in the name Neaera, by means of a bilingual pun on Greek *nea* 'new' and Latin *era* 'mistress'. Neaera will be a new kind of elegiac mistress. For a closural reversal of the significance of this name in **19** with its reference at **19.22** to the mistress as *notae dominae* see section 1.2 above.

The elegiac 'story' begins when the relationship, described, as we saw above, in terms of a marriage, is already at an end, and illustrates Lygdamus' growing awareness of this fact, starting with optimism in the opening poem that the relationship could be revived, through attempts at persuasion in poems **2** and **3**, to the final realisation in **4** through Apollo's appearance to him in a dream that Neaera has been unfaithful, a fact which Lygdamus finally comes to accept in **6**. The Greek pseudonyms Lygdamus and Neaera are, as we have seen, full of significance derived from their earlier literary associations and perhaps reflect Propertius' use of the Greek pseudonyms Arethusa and Lycotas in 4.3, where a Roman wife writes to her husband abroad on military service. Elsewhere Greek pseudonyms are used for Roman characters in elegy by Tibullus (Marathus in 1.4 and 1.8, Pholoe in 1.8) and by Prop. (Panthus in 2.21, Demophoon in 2.22a and Lynceus in 2.34) and, in **[Tib.] 3** in the name of Sulpicia's lover, Cerinthus.

3.3 Valerius Messalla Corvinus

Apart from passing mentions of the poets Catullus (**6.41**), Valgius (**7.180**) and Tibullus (**19.13**), Messalla is the only historical character mentioned in the collection, The evidence of his real life activities is relatively plentiful, and yet hardly any of this finds its way into the panegyric addressed to him in **7**.

Marcus Valerius Messalla Corvinus was a member of the old and distinguished gens Valeria. He was born in 64 BC and died in AD 8. Like his contemporary Horace and many of his class he went off to Athens to complete his education, where he developed a lifelong interest in Greek bucolic poetry and philosophy. He probably arrived there in 45 BC but returned immediately to Rome on the assassination of Caesar in 43 BC. Again, like Horace, he fought on the side of Cassius and the liberators at Philippi[24] and later transferred his allegiance to Antony. He was subsequently one of the first aristocrats to cross over from Antony to Octavian, a move he had made by 40 BC. He is known to have fought for Octavian in the Sicilian war of 36 BC against Sextus Pompey.[25] In the

---

[24] Plutarch *Brutus* 40-42, 45.
[25] Appian *Bell. Ciu.* 5.102-113; cf. Tansey (2007).

months leading up to Actium in 31 BC he wrote propaganda against Antony and was rewarded with the religious post of augur and subsequently became co-consul with Octavian in 31 BC. At the battle of Actium he had an important command in charge of a naval squadron under Agrippa. After Actium came two foreign commands (celebrated by Tibullus in poems 1.3 and 1.7) the chronological order of which is disputed, but probably an Eastern command in Syria and Egypt came first in 30-29 BC (the background to Tib. 1.3) followed by a governorship in Gaul 28-27 BC, where he won a triumph over the Aquitanians celebrated on 25 Sept. 27 BC (Tib. 1.7. 1-12, *Fasti Capitolini CIL* I² p. 180). He spent part of the spoils of his victory on the repair of some of the Via Latina (as recorded in Tibullus 1.7.57-62). In 26-25 BC we hear of him resigning his office of *praefectus urbi* City Prefect, as being incompatible with his republican ideals (Hier. *Chron. a. Abr.* 1991 *inciuilem potestatem esse contestans*). At some stage before 20 BC Messalla took on another important religious post, this time as an Arval Brother, and in 19 BC his son Messallinus was elected to the prestigious board of *decemuiri sacris faciundis* in charge of the Sibylline books (celebrated in Tibullus 2.5). After Tibullus' early death in late 19 BC or early 18 BC Messalla went on to become *curator aquarum* in 11 BC and it was he whom the senate chose, perhaps on account of his more independent political stance, to propose the title of *pater patriae* to Augustus in 2 BC. This then was the career of an independent-minded politician, but one who strongly supported the Augustan regime, and was involved at the highest levels in imperial policy, especially where it concerned religious and moral revival, and these concerns are reflected in the work of Tibullus.

In artistic circles he was the most important literary patron after Maecenas. His circle included Tibullus and the young Ovid (*Pont.* 2.3.77-78, *Trist.* 4.4a.27-30), as well as perhaps his niece Sulpicia, and possibly the historian and literary publisher Cornutus, whose birthday and forthcoming marriage is celebrated in Tib. 2.2. Messalla himself wrote memoires, philosophical and grammatical works (for example, a book on the letter 's')[26] and we hear from [Virg.] *Catalepton* 9, a poem in elegiacs purportedly written by a young Virgil in praise of Messalla (40), that he also wrote bucolic poetry in Greek in the manner of Theocritus, which, it is claimed, influenced Virgil's poetry, presumably the *Eclogues* [see Appendix 3(a)].[27] He was a noted orator with a keen interest in Latin

---

[26] *GRF* 505-507.
[27] On this interpretation of *Catalepton* 9.13 see Peirano (2012) 124 and n. 23.

language (Cic. *Ad Brut.* 23.1, Sen. *Contr.* 2.4.8, Quint. *Inst.* 10.1.113, Tac. *Dial.* 18.2).

His importance for our **book 3** is based firstly on the fact that the central poem **7** *Laudes Messallae* is addressed to him by our author who assumes the guise of the young Tibullus, and secondly on his family connection with Sulpicia, whose affair with Cerinthus dominates the second part of the **book 3 (8-18)**. In fact the only two poems in book **3** which make specific mention of Messalla by name are poem **7**, purportedly addressed to Messalla on the occasion of his joint consulship with Octavian in 31 BC, and poem **14**, one of the *Sulpicia* poems, in which Sulpicia represented as complaining that her kinsman, Messalla, is inviting her, against her will, to spend her birthday with him at his country estate when she would prefer to stay in Rome with her lover Cerinthus. As discussed in section 3.5 below it is perhaps unlikely that the author of the *Sulpicia* poems **(13-18)** was actually a niece of Messalla named Sulpicia, but such a pretence would lend a certain unity to the collection as a whole, which seems to be the product of a later, possibly Flavian, pseudepigraphic tradition.[28] The influence of Tib. 1.7, however, is more thorough-going and for this reason I print it in full in Appendix 3(b). Tib.'s elegiac epinicion has more Callimachean echoes than any other poem in Tibullus [see Appendix 3(c)]. This Tibullan concern for the work of his Greek predecessor is reflected in the emphasis placed on Callimachean poetics and mythology found in the opening of *Laud. Mess.* **7**, discussed in the **headnote** to that poem, a feature which also serves to link it with the opening of the *Lygd.* group (see section 2.2.1 above). Key thematic and structural correspondences between the *Laud. Mess.* and Tib. 1.7 depend essentially on Tib.'s Callimachean approach to his theme in that poem. As discussed in **7 headnote** this Callimachean epinician technique had also been seen earlier in the brief panegyric to Octavian embodied in the prologue to Virgil's *Georgics* 1.24-42. The description of Messalla's triumph in Tib. 1.7.5-8 is just as generic in character and lacking in detail as the description of Messalla's installation as consul at *Laud. Mess.* **7.118-134**. The way in which Tib. describes Messalla's activities in the Gaul (1.7.7-9) and in the East (1.7.13-22) by giving simply a list of mountains, rivers and geographical areas that witnessed his activities reflects the account of Messalla's Illyrian campaign in *Laud. Mess.* **7.106-117**, which consists simply of a list of tribes conquered. No specific military action is described in either account. The long central

---

[28] For further information on the historical Messalla Corvinus see Hammer (1925), Hanslik (1955), Valvo (1983), Syme (1986) 200-206.

section of Tib. 1.7 on the role of Osiris as inventor of agriculture, wine and song and his association with Bacchus (Tib. 1.7.22-48), performs the role of the central mythological section in Greek epinicia and is reflected in the *Laud. Mess.* in his mythological *exempla* of Ikarios and Erigone as well as Molorcus (both Callimachean topics) in **7.10-13**, and the digression on the contents of the *Odyssey* at **7.54-81**. The geographical discussion of the Nile and its unknown sources in Tib. 1.7.23-26 has its parallel in the panegyricist's longer digression on the five zones of the earth **7.151-174** (perhaps influenced by a work of Callimachus' pupil, Eratosthenes). Even the prediction of Messalla's future victories at **7.135-150**, beginning, like Messalla's real victories at Tib. 1.7.3 with Gaul, echoes the way in which Messalla's achievements in Tib.'s poem are first expressed as predictions of the *Parcae* at Tib. 1.7.1-4.

A number of verbal echoes underline the above thematic similarities between the two poems. So the anaphora of *testis* in the account of Messalla's Illyrian victories at **7.106-111** echo the anaphora of the same word used by Tibullus in his account of the places that witnessed Messalla's victories at Tib. 1.7.9-11. Its use in both passages may reflect Callimachus statement at fr. 612 Pf. ἀμάρτυρον οὐδὲν ἀείδω ['I sing of nothing unwitnessed']. Finally, the reference to the flowing Nile in relation to Messalla's future foreign conquests at **7.140-141** echoes its mention in the culmination of Messalla's Eastern campaign as described by Tib. 1.7.21-22. As we have seen in the case of Lygdamus and Neaera the influence of previous literary treatments is what is key to the picture of Messalla reflected in poem 7. In this case the treatment of his main literary predecessor, Tibullus, far outweighs any concern for the real-life details of Messalla's career.

3.4 Cerinthus

The name of Sulpicia's lover occurs six times in our collection, five of which are vocative addresses (*Sulpicia Cycle* **9.11**, **10.15**, **11.1**, **11.5** and *Sulpicia* poems **17.1**) and once in the abl. *sine Cerintho* in the *Sulpicia* poems **14.2**. Like Lygdamus the name is Greek, restricted on Greek inscriptions mainly to Italy [see Fraser and Matthews (1987-), s.v.] and occurring in Latin inscriptions mostly as a slave name (*ThLL Onom.* s.v.). Fulkerson [(2017) 31] points to one funerary inscription of a higher status Cerinthus connected to the same gens Valeria as Messalla (*CIL* VI 6.4.3 39011 for L. Valerius Cerinthus). In Greek literature it occurs as a name in Theognis 1.891.4, and as a place in Euboea in Hom. *Il.* 2.538. Like Lygdamus the name is probably a pseudonym.

Etymologically the name has been connected with the Greek *κήρινθος* 'bee bread', a mixture of pollen and honey made by bees to feed their young; Aristotle *HA* 623b23, Plin. *Nat.* 11.17.2 – see Davies (1973). The connection between bees and poetry is widespread in Apolline poetics [Thomas (2011) 113, on Hor. *Carm.* 4.2.27-32] and so a substance used for feeding bees is a good name for a character providing our author with material for his/her poetry. Roessel [(1990) 243-245] takes this idea further by suggesting that the connection between beeswax *κηρός* and Cerinthus' name could be connected with the wax tablets with which Sulpicia communicated with him, with Cerinthus again providing the medium for her epistolary epigrams.

A further suggestion by Knox [(2018) 152] would associate the pallor of beeswax with the common image of the pallor of the lover. At Virg. *Georg.* 4.62-63 the poet recommends sprinkling the herb *cerintha* 'honeywort' to attract bees: *huc tu iussos adsperge sapores, / trita melisphylla et cerinthae ignobile gramen*. The plant, obviously connected with the Greek *κήρινθος*, occurs only here and at Plin. *Nat.* 21.70. Servius ad loc. comments on *ignobile gramen*: *uile, ubique nascens*. The suggestion could be that the status of Cerinthus, as an inspirer of verse, is lower than that of the poetess Sulpicia, cf. *Sulpicia* poems **16.5-6** *solliciti sunt pro nobis quibus illa dolori est / ne cedam **ignoto** maxima causa toro*. It may be significant that Virg. applies the same adj. to himself in the *sphragis* at the end of the *Georgics*: 4.566 *studiis florentem **ignobilis** oti*, though in Virgil the emphasis is on the quiet life and anonymity of the scholarly poet, see Kyriakidis (2002) 284.

Hints in the poems about his social status are confusing. His interest in hunting (*Sulpicia Cycle* **9**) is a characteristic of the Roman elite; however, Sulpicia taunts him, as we have seen, at **16.5-6** with being of lower status, perhaps meaning only that he is not as noble as the Servii Sulpicii. Unlike Lygdamus, Cerinthus is not himself a poet, but simply a recipient of love poems from Sulpicia. In this sense the pseudonym, like Tib.'s Marathus (another Greek plant-derived name), would suggest Cerinthus belonged to the tradition of the *puer delicatus*, a low-status, effeminised character, who is the object of erotic attention, in this case, unusually, from a woman. If we accept that he is a literary creation, based, as was the case with Lygdamus and Neaera, on earlier Roman poetry, then these apparent inconsistencies can be better explained. As always in this collection we are dealing with a character who originates not in real life, but in poetry. The two literary sources for Cerinthus are a low class *puer delicatus* in Horace *Serm.* 1.2.80-82 [Appendix 4(a)] and a noble prospective husband (Cornutus) in Tib. 2.2 and 2.3 [Appendix 4(b)]. The apparent inconsistencies concerning the exact status of Cerinthus arise from the amalgam of these two characters. Both poems have clear textual links with the Cerinthus poems and clearly contributed to the establishment of his character. In *Serm.* 1.2.80-82 Horace advises the effeminate Cerinthus, who prides himself on his own beauty, that he should seek as a partner a readily available, toga-clad prostitute rather than a rich matrona. The situation is clearly the same as in *Sulpicia* **16.3-4** *sit tibi cura togae potior pressumque quasillo / scortum quam Serui filia Sulpicia*, where Sulpicia accuses Cerinthus of being more interested in a toga-clad slave-girl rather than in herself. The discussion of *quasillis* at Prop. 4.7.41 at 3.1 above (on Lygdamus, p. 117) shows that this passage also owes something to Propertius' slave-girl mistress in that poem. The Horatian parallel here, suggesting a low class Cerinthus with interests in a slave as a mistress in preference to the noble Sulpicia can be seen as a reversal of the Lygdamus-Neaera relationship in which Lygdamus looks for a respectable marriage arrangement with a character whose name suggests a low class prostitute. This is just the kind of miss-matching that Horace in his Ode addressed to Albius Tibullus (1.33) sees as the essence of elegiac love poetry: Hor. *Carm.* 1.33.10-12 *sic uisum Veneri, cui placet imparis / formas atque animos sub iuga aenea / saeuo mittere cum ioco*.

This identification with Horace's *puer delicatus* is then complicated by the suggestion, first made by Gruppe [(1838) 27], that Cerinthus is to be identified with Cornutus, the addressee of Tib. 2.2 and 2.3 [Appendix 4(b)] whose birthday and forthcoming marriage are the subject of Tib. 2.2. The Cornutus referred to there was probably M. Caecilius Cornutus (*CIL* VI 32338), a member, with Messalla, of the Arval college, (or possibly his son *CIL* VI 2023a). I would not argue, with Hubbard (2004), that Cornutus and Cerinthus are the same person under different names, but rather that Tib.'s poem about Cornutus influences some aspects of the character of Cerinthus as presented in our poems. First, the names are metrically equivalent, share the same C R N T consonants and could provide an example of a bilingual pun (Greek *keras* and Latin *cornu*). Second, as pointed out by Hubbard (2004), numerous verbal echoes connect Tib.'s poem with those about Cerinthus. So the conjugal chains of Tib. 2.2.18-19 are echoed in **11.13-16**; the nod of the Genius at 2.2.9-10 is echoed in **11.20** and **12.13**; the offering of cake and wine to the Genius at 2.2.8 is echoed in **12.14** with *libo* and *mero* in the same *sedes*. The influence of Tib. 2.2 is not restricted to the birthday poems: the sweet-smelling Arabian herbs of 2.2.3-4 are those worthy to be offered to Sulpicia at the Matronalia in **8.17-18** and the gems from India and the Red Sea to be rejected in favour of love at 2.15-16 are a worthy gift for Sulpicia at **8.19-20**. Other echoes between Tib.'s birthday poem and the *Sulpicia* poems will be pointed out in the commentary. Our Cerinthus is not to be identified either with the Horatian Cerinthus or with the Tibullan Cornutus, but these poems clearly contribute to the construction of his character, and its inconsistencies, just as Horace *Epode* 15 and poems 3.6, 4.7 and 4.8 of Propertius contribute to the construction of Lygdamus.

3.5 Sulpicia

Clues in the poems have been used to create a real identity for this character. At **14.5-6** she addresses Messalla in a familiar tone *iam, nimium Messalla mei studiose, quiescas. / non tempestiuae saepe, propinque, uiae* (although the text of the second line here is uncertain) and at **16.4** she refers to herself as *Serui filia Sulpicia*. From this Haupt [(1871) 32-34] first suggested that she could be the daughter of Messalla's sister Valeria and Servius Sulpicius Rufus, the son of the great jurist and friend of Cicero (cf. Cic. *Fam.* 4.3.4, 4.4.5, 13.27.4). This Servius is mentioned by Hor. *Serm.* 1.10.85-86 and may be the author of erotic poetry mentioned by Ovid (*Trist.* 2.441-442); see further Syme (1986) 205-206, Hollis (2007) 427-428. Both Holzberg [(1998) 184] and Hubbard [(2004) 178-179] reject this hypothesis and see Sulpicia as an invented character. In Holzberg's case he argues that the affair between Cerinthus and Sulpicia could have been inspired by the birthday/marriage poem to Cornutus (Tib. 2.2) with our poet filling in the missing information about whom Cornutus married and the background to his affair. In this sense there would be a parallel with *Laud. Mess.* which, as Peirano (2012) argues, was meant to fill in the gap in Tibullus' early career, before he wrote the Delia and Nemesis poems and while he was approaching Messalla as a patron. Hubbard (2004) makes the equally telling point that the content of the *Sulpicia* poems with their frank discussion of her affair, her refusal to think of her reputation and her cavalier attitude towards her mother and uncle could hardly have been published if she were indeed the daughter of a noble family writing at the time of the events described. However, an impersonator, writing perhaps decades after her death, need have no such compunction. Whether or not Sulpicia, the daughter of Servius, existed in real life, the name and its possible connection with Messalla would have recommended itself to one working on such a literary pseudepigraphic project. As we have seen above, both Propertius in book 4 and Ovid in his *Heroides* had pointed the way for male poets adopting a female persona. The difference in style between those poems placed in Sulpicia's mouth by the unnamed observer in the *Sulpicia Cycle* (**9** and **11**) and *Sulpicia*'s poems in the form of letters **14-18** (with their prefatory poem **13**) could again have been produced intentionally by our author, male or female, who had learned the lesson of Ov. *Ars* 3.479-482 [Appendix 5(a)] where girls were taught how to write letters using a polite conversational style avoiding unusual words and expressions. Again this could be a Catullan feature of his work. For Catullus consciously deciding to write in different ways for distinctive artistic reasons see Ross (1969) 174, Solodow (1989) 319, Fain (2008) 57-61 and Feeney (2012) 47 and nn. 89 and 90. Our author would also have had before him/her the example in Prop. 3.23.11-16 [Appendix 5(b)] of the type of letter that would have been sent to him by Cynthia; see further Holzberg (1998) 187-188, Hooper (1975) 121. There are verbal echoes in the *Sulpicia* poems of Cynthia's letter at **13.7** *non ... signatis ... tabellis* (= Prop. 3.23.4 *qui non signatas iussit habere fidem*), **13.7** *mandare tabellis* (= Prop. 3.23.11).

On the evidence of Martial 10.35 and 10.38 [Appendix 5 (c)] about a writer named Sulpicia who composed poems about her love for her husband Calenus, it is possible that the name Sulpicia suggested an archetypal faithful wife (contrasting with the faithless Cerinthus) and that our author's use of this name could have referred to this specific type of poetry; so Fulkerson [(2017) 34]. Martial's Sulpicia is mentioned later in marriage contexts at Ausonius *Cento Nuptialis* 10.9-10 (Prete) and Sidonius Apollinaris 9.261-262 (an epithalamium). In fact Hermann [(1951) 3-16] went as far as to suggest that Martial's Sulpicia may have invented ours. If **[Tib.] 3** is the work of a single author and if certain characteristics of the *Lygdamus* poems and the *Laud. Mess.* are indeed Flavian, as many suggest, then the composition date of our *Sulpicia* poems and Martial 10.35 and 10.38 could be very similar. There can be no certainty about any of this. Impersonation of a Sulpicia from the Augustan age would lend coherence to our book with its constant engagement with the work of Tibullus, Propertius and Ovd and such a thesis should perhaps be preferred to that of a reference to Martial's Sulpicia. The authorship by a 'real' Sulpicia, niece of Messalla, seems highly unlikely. Possible echoes of Ov. *Ars* would argue against it, and certainly the attribution to a real-life person from the Augustan period would go against the pseudepigraphic type of literary fiction which seems to dominate the rest of the collection. As it is, the adoption by our author of a Sulpician mask from the period of the great elegists lends an air of authenticity to his pseudoepigraphic project.

4. The manuscript tradition of [Tibullus] 3

The manuscript tradition of **book 3** is that of the *Corpus Tibullianum* as a whole, since all complete manuscripts transmit this book along with books 1 and 2. I have described this tradition in detail elsewhere[29] and so will not repeat the information here. I have viewed in person all the manuscripts listed in the *sigla*. The principles used in establishing the text are the following:

- The oldest evidence for the text comes from three collections of medieval florilegia, the Excerpta Frisingensia (Exc. Fris.) from the end of the tenth or the beginning of the eleventh century, the Florilegium Venetum (Flor. Ven.) from the late eleventh century and the Florilegium Gallicum (Flor. Gall.) from the thirteenth century. Although these are disfigured in places by adaptation they are cited wherever they are available.

- The oldest complete manuscript is the Ambrosianus (A) from 1375. There is no evidence that any of the complete manuscripts later than A is independent of A. If A is the sole source for these later manuscripts it has to be assumed that, until or unless a detailed examination of all Tibullan manuscripts can prove otherwise, anything new and worthy of note in them is a conjecture. A is our most important manuscript and its readings are cited throughout.

- Later manuscripts are adduced only when they are correcting the errors of A, and then only the earliest witnesses to the correction are cited.

- Noteworthy readings from later manuscripts, along with modern conjectures, are cited only when thought to be worthy of consideration.

- An important source of readings in **book 3** is the Fragmentum Cuiacianum, a mutilated codex beginning at **4.65**, now lost, but belonging once to Jacques Cujas (1522-1590) and seen by Scaliger in 1571-1572. Scaliger preserved some of its readings in the margins of his Plantin edition of 1569 and/or in his *Castigationes* of 1577. These readings, whose status and importance remain the

---

[29] Maltby (2002) 21-23; cf. also the important discussions by Rouse and Reeve (1983) and Luck (1988) v-xix.

subject of debate, are reported in full, either as F Plant. (for those found in the Plantin margins), F Cast. (for those found in the *Castigationes*), or F Plant. et Cast. (for those found in both).

5. Concluding Remarks

The various sections of this collection display marked differences in style, content and metre, which have led many, including myself in the past, to conclude that they were composed by different authors and then put together as a book by a final editor. However, the connections between the sections discussed in the Prolegomena and 1.2 above as well as the important intertexts discussed in 1.3 and section 3, all of which have significant links with more than one part of the book, argue in favour of a single author for the whole work. A unifying theme running through the book is that of change and of a multiplicity of view-points, which I would now trace back to the inspiration of a single author, but which gives the impression, intentionally I believe, of multiple authorship. Inspired perhaps by the pseudepigraphic works of the writers of the *Appendix Vergiliana* and the *Laus Pisonis* the author adopts a series of different masks in the different sections of his book and the importance of this theme of change can be seen in the central comparison between Sulpicia and Vertumnus, the god of changing appearances, at the start of the Sulpicia series of poems at **8.13-14**; in the importance attributed to the Pythagorean theory of migration of souls, with its reference to the author's multiple reincarnations in different forms at **7.201-211**; and in the alternation of male and female viewpoints in the elegiac sections **1-6, 8-12, 13-18** and **19-20**. The fact that no one questioned the attribution of this book to Tibullus between the time it was added to the two genuine Tibullus books in the second half of the fourth century AD until the nineteenth bears unequivocal witness to the quality of the poetry it contains.

COMMENTARY

Poem 1

The elegy serves as an apt introduction to the *Lygdamus* group (**1-6**) as a whole. It consists of a dialogue between Lygdamus and the Muses concerning the gift he should send to his beloved Neaera on the occasion of the Matronalia. Neaera is described in lines **26-27** as having been Lygdamus' *coniunx*, a term never applied to a mistress in the earlier elegies of Tib. and Prop. or in Ov. *Am.*, *Ars* and *Rem*. Where the term is used in elegy it refers specifically to a 'wife', implying marriage, or at least betrothal, between social equals. It is Ovid in his exile poetry who is the first elegist to address and dedicate poems to his wife, see **26n.** below. This change in tone could have been occasioned by the fact that his earlier elegies, and particularly the *Ars*, had been the cause of his exile. After Ovid's exile Roman love poetry could never be the same again. Certainly in the case of the *Lygd.* poems it is made clear from the outset that the relationship described between Lygdamus and Neaera is going to be different from that between the well-to-do elegiac poet and his usually lower class mistress, which had characterised traditional Latin love elegy until the time of Ovid's exile. This change may be reflected in the pseudonym for the mistress, *Neaera*, a bilingual pun on Gk. *nea* 'new' and Latin *era* 'mistress' (see Gen. Intro., section 3.2). Here the Greek pseudonyms Lygdamus and Neaera are used for a Roman married couple, just as Propertius had used the pseudonyms Lycotas and Arethusa in the letter from a Roman wife to her husband abroad on military service in elegy 4.3. Elsewhere Greek pseudonyms are used for Roman characters in elegy by Tib. (Marathus in 1.4 and 1.8, Pholoe in 1.8) and by Prop. (Panthus in 2.21, Demophoon in 2.22A and Lynceus in 2.34).

The technique of a question and answer dialogue between the poet and the Muses was first introduced into poetry by Callimachus in the first two books of the *Aetia*, where, according to Kennedy [(1989) 202], it was borrowed from the language of scholarship. Kyriakidis [(1998) 171] discusses this phenomenon in the evocation of Erato at the opening of book seven of the *Aeneid* as alluding programmatically to Callimachean poetics and it is difficult to escape the conclusion that the theme plays a similar programmatic role in the opening poem of the *Lygdamus* group (**1-**

6). The unitary author of the whole book thus associates himself at the beginning of the work with Callimachean poetics and, implicitly, with his elegiac predecessor, Propertius, the Roman Callimachus (Prop. 4.1A.64). For other Callimachean/ neoteric metapoetic markers in this opening poem see **9-14n.** below and cf. *dicite Pierides* **5**, *libellum* **9**, *tenuis* **11**, *comptum* **14**, *Castaliamque umbram Pieriosque lacus* **16**, *cultum* **17**, *munera parua* **24** below with notes. For a detailed discussion of Callimachean influence on programmatic Latin poetry see Hopkinson (1989) 98-101. In the past not all critics have been willing to accept the presence of such Callimachean features in the present poem, see **9-14n.** below. Both the Callimachean metapoetic pointers and Callimachean programmatic material (derived from Virgil's *Georgics*) link this poem closely with the opening of the *Laud. Mess.*, see Gen. Intro., section 1.2 and cf. **15-16n.** on *Castaliamque umbram Pieriosque lacus* below, **7 headnote**, **7.4** *humilis*, **7.7** *munera parua*, **7.9-11n.**, **12-13n.** and **7.15-16n.** on *paruus labor*. There are also verbal and thematic links with the poem which begins the *Sulpicia Cycle* **8**, for which see **1n.** below. The *Lygd.* poems, then, do not constitute a separate and unrelated part of **[Tib.] 3**, but are well integrated into the structure of the book as a whole and thus provide an argument in favour of a unitary author for the whole collection (see Gen. Intro., section 1.2).

The poem is carefully constructed of four balanced sections of 6 – 8 – 8 – 6 lines respectively. Their content may be summarised as follows:

1-6 Lygdamus asks the Muses what gift he should send to honour his love, Neaera, on the occasion of the Matronalia.

7-14 The Muses advise him to please her with a beautifully finished papyrus roll of his own poems.

15-22 Lygdamus asks the Muses to deliver the volume personally to her house and to report back her reaction, having wished her good health and addressed her in the following terms:

23-28 "Your former husband and present friend begs you accept this gift with the hope that you will be his wife, rather than his friend; a hope that will go with him to the grave."

The use of the dialogue form with no scene setting is unusual in Latin elegy, but does have parallels in earlier Greek (e.g. Sappho fr.114, 137, 140a *PLF*) and Roman lyric (e.g. Hor. *Carm.* 3.9), Hellenistic epigram (e.g. *AP* 5.46 Philodemus [=20 Sider], 5.101, 12.155); Catullus 67 (conversation with a door) and the satires of Horace and Persius. Ovid ends his *Fasti* with a dialogue with the *Pierides* (*Fast.* 6.799-811), in which Clio acts as their spokeswoman in reply to the poet's questions, with a short scenic parenthesis at 801. The closest parallels to the present poem are found in the epigrams of Martial. In Martial 3.20, which has no scene setting, the poet asks his Muse to tell him what his friend Canius is doing, and she reports back the answer that he is laughing (*ridet*). In epigram 8.3, which does contain a scene-setting parenthesis, Martial asks his Muse, Thalia, whether he should continue to write after completing seven books of poems and she tells him to proceed with his work as before. Perhaps the closest in theme is epigram 10.20 in which Martial asks Thalia to deliver a book of his poems to the younger Pliny, telling her how to reach his house and pointing out the best time to call. Finally in 12.11 Martial asks his Muse to visit Parthenius with a request that he should deliver a book of Martial's epigrams to the Emperor. The theme of sending the gift of a book at a festival had occurred earlier in Catullus 14, in that case on the occasion of the Saturnalia, but prior to Martial and the present poem the poet sending the book never addressed the Muses. The question of priority between Martial and **[Tib.] 3** is difficult to establish, but it is more likely that our author is taking this theme from Martial, than that Martial would use our author's idea in four separate poems.

The content of the *libellus* (**9**) that Lygdamus is invited to send has been much discussed. It should clearly consist, as in Mart. 10.20 and 12.11, of a collection of the poet's own verses (*uersibus ...tuis* **8**). The question is whether, as N-A 93 suggests, on the model of Catullus 1 and the opening poem of the *Sulpicia Cycle* **8.21-24**, the volume is thought of as containing the group of poems it introduces (i.e. **1-6**), or whether it refers to some other unspecified collection of the poet's work (of the type mentioned at **4.57**). Tränkle 65-66 is probably correct in favouring the latter option, since poem **5** contains no mention of Neaera at all and in poem **6**, she is rejected on the grounds that she has betrayed Lygdamus with another lover. Such poems would hardly honour his mistress in the terms envisaged in **5** and **8** or achieve the hoped-for rapprochement and reconciliation of **1.23-28**. A significant intertext for poem **1**, and one which links it with the final two poems of the whole book **19** and **20,** is the story of Cephalus and Procris, as related by Cephalus at the end of Ov. *Met.* 7.796-862, where the happy marriage of the pair is destroyed by an untrue rumour that Cephalus was having an affair with a nymph named Aura (see Gen. Intro., section 1.3). Like Lygdamus and Neaera the pair were initially happily married (*Met.* 7.799: *Lygd.* **1.26-27** *coniuge/coniunx*), a *mutua cura* existed between them (*Met.* 7.800: *Lygd.* **1.19**), and the wife was dearer to the husband than his own body (*Met.* 7.847 *corpus ... meo mihi carius*: *Lygd.* **1.25** *teque suis iurat caram magis esse medullis*). This poem is taken up again in poem **19** where the lover there (who impersonates Tibullus) refers to his relationship as a *foedus* (**19.2** *iuncta est foedere nostra Venus*) as Procris does at *Met.* 7. 852 *per nostri foedera lecti*), both lovers swear that no girl sent from heaven would separate them: *Met.* 7.802-803 *nec me quae caperet, non si Venus ipsa ueniret, / ulla erat*, **19.13-14** *nunc licet e caelo mittatur amica Tibullo, / mittetur frustra deficietque Venus* and Cephalus' words to Aura at *Met.* 7.817-819 *tu mihi magna uoluptas / ... tu me reficisque fouesque, / tu facis ut siluas, ut amem loca sola* are echoed in the words to the mistress at **19.11-12** *tu mihi curarum requies, tu nocte uel atra / lumen et in solis tu mihi turba locis*. Finally, the false rumour of Cephalus' unfaithfulness caused Procris pain *Met.*7.825-827 *Procrin adit linguaque refert audita susurra. / credula res amor est; subito conlapsa dolore / ... cecidit* just as rumours of his mitress' unfaithfulness caused the author pain in the final poem of the collection **20.3** *crimina non haec sunt nostro sine facta dolore*. There are clear signs in the echo of the same intertext in the opening and closing poems of **[Tib.] 3** that a single author lay behind the construction of the whole work. Another important intertext behind this and *Lygd.*'s other Neaera poems is Hor. *Epod.* 15 (see Gen. Intro., section 3.1). Here Horace rejects a faithless Neaera, who had sworn to him that their love would be mutual (10, cf. **19n.** below) and subsequently left him for a rich rival. Numerous echoes of this poem elsewhere in *Lygd.* (see **3 headnote, 3.29, 4.16, 6.47-49, 6.53**) suggests he may have put on the mask of Horace's rival for her affections, who, as Horace had predicted (*Epod.* 15.23-24), suffers the same deceit and rejection at her hands that Horace had experienced. Both Horace and Lygdamus make the mistake of wishing for a permanent and marriage-like relationship with a faithless Neaera, whose name connects her with the world of the *hetaira*.

The term the poet/author or our poet/author is used throughout the commentary from now on to refer to the unitary author posited for the whole book and not to the individual characters (such as Lygdamus, Sulpicia and her observer, Tibullus) that this author assumes in the various sections of the work. Since we cannot know whether this unitary author was male or female, masculine pronouns will now be used by default throughout to designate this author.

1-4: The feast described here as celebrated on 1 March is the Matronalia 'Feast of the Married Women'; see Weinstock *RE* 14.2 (1930) 2306-2309, Gagé (1963) 66-80, Scullard (1981) 87, Heyworth (2019) 115-116. Originally it marked the anniversary of the foundation in 375 BC of the temple of Juno Lucina, the patron goddess of women in labour; see Ov. *Fast.* 3.245-248; *Fast. Praen.*; Paul. Fest. 131 L.; *Schol. Juv.* 9.53, Latte *RE* 13.2 (1927) 1648-1651. Lygdamus invokes the aid of Juno Lucina at **4.13** and Juno appears as the tutelary goddess of women in *Lygd.* **6.48**, *Sulpicia Cycle* **12.1** and in **19.15**. Another tradition tells that the festival was introduced by Romulus to honour married women in commemoration of the peace which the Sabine women established between their Roman husbands and their Sabine fathers (Ov. *Fast.* 3.229-232; Plut. *Rom.* 21.1). It was traditionally a day on which Roman husbands gave gifts to their wives (Suet. *Vesp.* 19; Tert. *Idol.* 14; Pomp. *Dig.* 24.1.31.8), although married women may also have received gifts from other relatives (e.g. from their daughters, cf. Plaut. *Mil.* 691). It was clearly still a festival restricted to married women in the late first century BC as Hor. *Carm.* 3.8.1 *Martiis caelebs quid agam Kalendis* attests, cf. Porph. ad loc. *Kalendae autem Martiae hodieque matronarum dies festus est*. Such a context would be a very suitable occasion for a gift from Lygdamus to his estranged wife. However, the scene described at **3-4** suggests that by the time of this poem's composition the giving of gifts at this feast had been extended from married women to include women in general, especially mistresses; hence the need for slaves running from all directions to join a gift-bearing procession. Long before the time of Vespasian it is clear that this transformation had taken place. Suet. *Vesp.* 19.1 describes the Kalends of March as a female equivalent of the Saturnalia, with women receiving gifts on the Matronalia, just as men did on the Saturnalia. Martial makes fun of this practice in 5.84.10-12 where he jokes about returning to his mistress, Galla, on the Kalends of March, the gifts she had failed to give him on the Saturnalia. At Mart. 9.90.13-18 the association of the Matronalia with Venus, rather than Juno, points to this change in the nature of the festival, further evidence for which is to be found at Juv. 9.53 and Tert. *Idol.* 14.6. The fact that the *Sulpicia Cycle* begins with a reference to the same festival can hardly be co-incidental: **8.1** *Sulpicia est tibi culta tuis, Mars magne, Kalendis*. It is possible that there too, the festival was particularly suited to Sulpicia as a married woman, see **8 headnote** and **8.1n.** on *Sulpicia est tibi culta*. On other links between **1.1** and **8** see **8 headnote** and below **1n.** *festae uenere Kalendae*.

1   Martis Romani: as father of Romulus through his rape of Ilia (described in Tib. 2.5.51-54), Mars was seen as the father of the Roman race (cf. Cic. *Diu*. 1.20; Vell. 2.131.1; Fest. 198-2000 L.; Serv. auct. *Aen.* 3.35). As war god, it is difficult to see why he should be associated with the married women's festival. This is the very question Ovid asks Mars at *Fast.* 3.169-170. In reply Mars suggests this is either because the Sabine matrons *Oebaliae matres* put an end to martial war *Martia bella* (*Fast.* 3.229-232) or because mothers in general celebrate his day to commemorate his making Ilia a mother (*Fast.* 3.233-234). In any case the mention of the war god Mars is remarkable as first word in a book of elegies and perhaps recalls the epic-sounding opening of Ovid's *Amores*: *arma graui numero uiolentaque bella parabam / edere*, cf. Fulkerson (2017) 77. Similarly, the first of the *Sulpicia* poems (**13**) echoes a poem from the end of the *Amores* 3.14 (see *Sulpicia* **13 headnote**), perhaps suggesting Ovidian influence in the overall structure of **[Tib.] 3**. Mars is of course addressed in the opening of the *Sulpicia Cycle* **8.1**, the first of a number of similarities between these two poems, see *festae uenere Kalendae* **n.** below. The presence of *Martia ... classica* at the beginning of the opening poem of Tib.'s book 1 (Tib. 1.1.4) may also be relevant here. The combination of *Romanus* with *Mars* is found elsewhere only in *Laud. Mess.* **7.149**, where *Mars* is used metonymically for war: *inuictus Romano Marte Britannus*; for the line-opening here cf. Manil. 4.718 *Martia Romanis urbis pater induit ora*.

Martis ... Kalendae: this particular formulation is found at Ov. *Fast.* 3.135-136, Mart. 9.90.15. More normal with *Kalendae* was the genitive of the month's name *Kalendae Martii* or the adjective in agreement *Kalendae Martiae* (which would not scan); see *ThLL* 7(2).756.76-757.10.

festae uenere Kalendae: echoes the hexameter ending at Hor. *Serm.* 1.3.87 *tristes misero uenere Kalendae*, but reverses the association. What for Horace was an ill-starred day, when debts fell due, becomes for Lygdamus a festive occasion. The adjective / noun combination *festae ... Kalendae* occurs again in the opening poem of the *Sulpicia Cycle* at **8.21** *festis ... Kalendis*. This poem displays a number of other similarities to the present elegy. It opens with an address to Mars on the occasion of Matronalia, celebrated on the Kalends of March (**8.1**); Cerinthus, addressing the Muses, opts for them to sing of her every year (**8.21-24**); apart from the echo of *festae ... Kalendae* there is also an echo of *digna est* at **8** in *digna est* at **8.15** and *dignior est* at **8.24** and possibly of *uenere* here in *ueni* (**8.2**) – see below. See further **8 headnote**.

uenere: this metrically convenient alternative to the third person plural form *-erunt* is the only form found in *Lygd*. (**1.1** *uenere*, **5.15** *laesere*, **5.17**

uidere), apart from the contracted *norunt* at **4.46**. Tibullus himself has eight instances of *-ere* as opposed to four of *-erunt* (see Smith on Tib. 1.5.47). The *-ere* form had an archaic or poetic flavour which meant it was more common in epic and elegy than in other genres; see H-Sz 404, 720, Thomas [(2011) 110 on Hor. *Carm.* 4.2.14-15] for the greater frequency or *-ere* across all works in Horace, and Woodman [(2014) 134-135] for its role as an archaising mannerism in historiographical prose. The verb *uenio* is connected etymologically with Venus (see *Sulpicia Cycle* **8.2n.**) and may contain a suggestion here of the affair between Mars and Venus (see **8.3n.**); the occurrence of the verb at the opening of the present poem may serve to link it with the address to Mars *ipse ueni* in the first poem of the *Sulpicia Cycle* (**8.2**) and the opening of the *Sulpicia* poems (**13.1**) *tandem uenit amor*. In both these later poems the connection with Venus is made explicit: **8.2-3** *ipse ueni. / hoc Venus ignoscet* and **13.1-5** *tandem uenit amor ... / exsoluit promissa Venus*.

Kalendae: originally the first day of the lunar month (from *calo* 'to announce', see *LALE* 321), the term remained in use for the first day of the month even after the introduction of the Julian solar calendar in 45 BC.

2 exoriens nostris hic fuit annus auis: the primitive calendar of Romulus consisted of ten lunar months (Ov. *Fast.* 1. 27-28), beginning with March (Atta *Com.* 18ff. R.; Varro *Ling.* 6.33; Ov. *Fast.* 1.39, 3.135-136; Fest. 136 L.). Even after Numa added the months of January and February (Ov. *Fast.* 1.43-44), March remained the first month until, in the year 153 BC, the ceremony in which the new consuls took up office was moved to 1 January (Cassiod. *Chron. Min.* II 130) and this became the first day of the civil calendar. The line is a learned excursus reflecting our author's antiquarian interests.

exoriens ... annus: 'New Year'. The participle would be more appropriate with *dies*; see *ThLL* 5(2).1572.63-76. The extension of its use to *annus* is unparalleled, apart from Isid. *Nat.* 4.2 *a Martio, quia ex ipso anni exorientis ordinem seruauerunt antiqui*, which, as Tränkle 67 suggests, may be a reminiscence of the present passage. Both here and in *Sulpicia Cycle* **8** the New Year associations of the Matronalia make it an appropriate time to begin a new group of poems.

nostris ... auis: the phrase shows that Lygdamus conceives of himself as a Roman citizen; see Fulkerson (2017) 28. The internal rhyme between the two halves of the pentameter is a characteristic feature of the style of the elegists, occurring in 21% of Tibullus' pentameters and 18% of those of *Lygd.*; see Platnauer 49.

hic: this reading of the A+ makes good sense and need not be changed to *hinc*, read in some later manuscripts and adopted by Broukhusius on the model of Ov. *Fast.* 3.145 *nec mihi parua fides, annos hinc* (sc. *a Marte*) *isse priores*. What works well with *Mars* as an antecedent is less convincing with *Martis Kalendae.*

auis: the literal meaning in prose is 'grandfathers', but here it is used in the poetic sense of 'forebears', a meaning restricted mainly to the higher genres, e.g. Virg. *Aen.* 7.56; Val. Fl. 6.518; Stat. *Theb.* 5.670, but not exclusively so, cf. Tib. 2.1.2; Ov. *Her.* 16.176; Mart. 7.47.2, 72.4.

3-4 The distich represents the hectic confusion of presents being rushed through the streets and houses of the city. There is a pointed contrast between *uaga* 'from all directions' and *certa ... pompa* 'in a fixed procession'. Individual servants rushing from all directions eventually join a continuous stream.

uaga ... discurrunt: also at Mart. 4.78.3 *discurris tota uagus urbe* (of a scurrying old man), 8.33.15 *nec uaga tam tenui discurrit aranea tela*. The phrase suggests hectic running to and fro.

uaga ... discurrunt ... / ... munera: the gifts themselves appear to run, perhaps suggesting the slaves doing the carrying are hidden beneath them. The same idea is found in Tertullian's description of the Matronalia at *Idol.* 14.6 *munera commeant et strenae*. The verb *discurro* 'to run about hapazardly', occurs again at *Laud. Mess.* **7.68**. It is found three times in Ovid (*Rem.* 443, *Met.* 14.419, *Fast.* 2.285), but is absent from Tib. and Prop. The placement of the adj. and its accompanying noun in adjacent lines of the couplet is rare in *Lygd.*, cf. **2.1-2** *carum ... / ... iuuenem*, **17-18** *ossa / ... candida*, **4.17-18** *aetherium ... / mundum*, **25-26** *ulla ... / aetas*, **33-34** *alba ... / lilia*, **5.9-10** *mea ... / dextera*, **6.43-44** *dolore / ... tuo/*.

pompa: the Greek loan word (< πομπή) is found in Latin from Plaut. onwards. It is absent from Tib., but occurs twice in Prop. and no fewer than 23 times in Ov.

perque uias urbis ... perque domos: N-A 102 sees the presents carried through the city streets, *per uias*, as intended for mistresses and those carried through houses *per domos*, as intended for wives. It may simply be that the formula suggests ubiquity, as in Virg. *Aen.* 2.364-365 *plurima* *perque uias sternuntur inertia passim / corpora perque domos*, which our author seems to have in mind here. In either case, the pentameter certainly reflects a widening of the original Matronalia, to include gifts for all women. Its first half *perque uias urbis* corresponds word for word with the opening of the hexameter at Ov. *Fast.* 2.553, describing a procession of ghosts.

-que ... / -que : doubling of *-que* is stylistically elevated and not found in Classical prose. Although probably a native idiom inherited from Indo-European it had become obsolete before the time of Ennius, who revived it in Latin on the model of Homeric τε ... τε; see Skutsch (1985) 338-339 on Enn. *Ann.* 170. In Plautus it is restricted mainly to high-sounding contexts; see Christenson (2000) 136-137 on *Amph.* 7. In later poetry it is used more frequently, often to recall Homer [see Wills (1996) 372-377], and occurs most commonly in epic, e.g. Ennius, Virgil, Lucan, Statius, and Valerius Flaccus; see Zissos [(2008) 169 on 1.150] for its particular frequency in that author. Its use here seems to be derived directly from Virg. *Aen.* 2.364-365 (quoted above). In the *Lygdamus* poems it occurs again at **1.16, 3.16, 26, 5.24, 6.47-48**; also in *Laud. Mess.* **7.11, 36, 156, 187**. Full statistics are given in Smith (1913) 192-193; cf. Maltby (2002) 134, McKeown II 152-153, N-A 103, H-Sz 515, K-S II 2.236. Here the figure adds to the ceremonial tone of the passage, as with the double *perque* at Tib. 1.4.25-26.

5 dicite, Pierides: the same hexameter opening at Virg. *Ecl.* 8.63; Ov. *Fast.* 2.269, 6.799. The author puts the traditional epic motif of the invocation to the Muses to a new use: the Muses are to advise Lygdamus what present to give to Neaera. On this dialogue with the Muses and its literary associations with the first two books of Callimachus' *Aetia* see the **headnote** to this poem above. Questions to the Muses have a literary pedigree going back to Homer *Il.* 2.484-492, where Homer asks the Muses to tell him who were the leaders at Troy, introducing the catalogue of ships; at the beginning of the *Aeneid* Virgil asks the Muse to tell him the cause of Juno's anger against Aeneas, *Aen.* 1.8 *Musa, mihi causas memora*, and *dicite Pierides* at Ov. *Fast.* 2.269 marks the first address to the Muses in this work, introducing the discussion of the origins of the Lupercalia; see Robinson (2011) 209-210 ad loc. Our author as Lygdamus uses this topos in a different way by asking them what gift he should bestow on Neaera; see Maltby [(2010) 321] on links with Cat. 1.1 (who asks to whom his new book should be given, see **9-14n.** below) and Melager *AP* 4.1.1 (where the Muses are asked where they will bring their fruits and garlands of poetry). Pierides is not used of the Muses in Homer, but occurs first in Greek at Hes. *Scut.* 206 and in Latin at Lucr. 1.926 (= 4.1). Hesiod addresses the Pierides in the opening line of the *Works and Days* and in Lucretius the *auia Pieridum* are connected with new poetic ground in contrast with Helicon, which is associated with Homer (3.1037-1038) and Ennius (1.117-119); see Kyriakidis (2016) 113-114 and n.16. In Virgil references to the Pierides are restricted to the *Eclogues*. In view of their opening words at **7-8** in which those women who are captured through poetry *carmine* are contrasted with those who are captured by cash *pretio*, the author's designation of the Muses here may have been influenced by Tib. 1.4.61-62 *Pierides, pueri, doctos et amate poetas, / aurea nec superent munera Pieridas*. The designation *Pierides* comes from their association with the area of Pieria, north of Olympus, where, according to Hes. *Theog.* 53f. (with West ad loc.), the Muses were born. A different tradition is preserved in Ov. *Met.* 5.294-317, 663-678 according to which the Muses took the name after defeating the original Pierides (daughters of Pieros of Macedonia) in a singing contest. On the role of the Pierides in Tibullus and the *Lygdamus* poems see Lieberg (1980). The Muses are never addressed as *Musae* in **[Tib.] 3**, but only as *Pierides* (*Lygd.* **1.5, 4.44** and *Sulpicia Cycle* **8.21**) or *Camenae* (*Laud. Mess.* **7.24, 191**, *Sulpicia* poems **13.3**).

quonam donetur honore: for the combination of *donare* and *honos* cf. *Ciris* 269 *sceptri donauit honore*. In an address to the Muses the honour conferred is likely to be through a gift of poetry.

6 seu mea seu fallor cara Neaera tamen: there must be a clear echo of this line in the last poem of *Lygd.* at **6.56** *perfida, sed quamuis perfida, cara tamen* (with reference to Neaera). While here in the first poem there is uncertainty about Neaera's fidelity, by the time we reach the last poem, and particularly after Apollo's warning to the poet at **4.51-60**, her infidelity is certain. The meaning of the present line is ambiguous. First, is *fallor* passive 'I am deceived (by her)' or middle 'I deceive myself'? In view of the epithet *casta Neaera* at **23**, the second alternative would seem preferable, though the author could be playing with the ambiguity, as had Ovid in Juno's words at *Met.* 1.607-608 *aut ego fallor / aut ego laedor*. On the ambiguities of *fallor* in elegy see Pichon 141-142. Second, what is the syntax of the double *seu*? The phrase could be taken to mean *uel mea, uel, si fallor, tamen cara Neaera* 'either my, or, if I am mistaken, nevertheless dear Neaera' in which case *mea* and *cara* are contrasted. This would involve the first *seu* being a disjunctive conjunction and the second standing for *uel si*. Both N-A 106 and Tränkle 68 prefer to interpret *siue mea est, siue fallor, pariter cara Neaera* 'whether she is mine, or whether

I am mistaken, in either case dear Neaera' in which case *mea* and *fallor* are contrasted, with a slight anacoluthon. In my view the use of *tamen* with *cara* makes the first interpretation more plausible, hence my translation "my Neaera (or, if I am mistaken, at least dear Neaera)."

fallor: the theme of women's trickery is common in the *Lygd.* poems, cf. also **4.56, 62, 6.12, 46**. The form *fallor* (often followed by *an*) is characteristic of Ovid, see Robinson (2011) 514 on Ov. *Fast.* 2.853 and cf. *Am.* 1.6.49, 3.1.34, 12.7, *Fast.* 1.515, 5.549, *Met.* 13.641, *Trist.*1.2.107, *Pont.* 2.8.21.

cara: the epithet is used occasionally of the mistress in elegy, e.g. Tib. 1.2.95, Prop. 2.8.1, but is extremely rare, whereas it is used commonly in the *Lygd.* poems of Neaera, also at **1.25, 3.32, 4.51, 6.12, 6.56**. This could be another indication that the couple were married, see especially **3.32** *cara coniuge*. In fact *cara* (mostly in the superlative *carissima*) is frequently applied to wives on Roman epitaphs; see Treggiari (1991) 231, Nielson (1997) 185-193 and, on the non-erotic character of the adj., Dickey (2002) 136. Ovid uses *cara* of his own wife at *Trist.* 3.11.15, 5.1.39, *Pont.* 1.2.50, 1.8.32. If they were married, then Lygdamus would risk prosecution under the *Lex Iulia de maritandis ordinibus* if he did nothing about her apparent adultery – but this would perhaps be to take a too strictly biographical approach to the elegy. Interestingly the adj. *carus* comes from the same PIE root *kah₂ros 'dear' as the English word 'whore'.

Neaera: Like Tib.'s Delia, Neaera is mentioned in the opening poem of the collection, but, unlike Prop.'s Cynthia, not as the first word. On the name and its significance see Gen. Intro., section 3.2 and see **23n.** below.

tamen: only 3% of pentameter endings in the three elegists are made up of adverbs, conjunctions, numerals and adjectives, the majority 80% being accounted for by nouns and verbs and the remaining 17% by pronouns, see Platnauer 40-48. The only examples of the first group in *Lygdamus* are *tamen* here and, in a deliberate echo, at **6.56** (see **n.** ad loc.), *purpureus* at **4.30** and adjectival *sequens* at **4.46**.

7-14 In **5-6** Lygdamus has asked a question of the Muses and at **7-14** we would expect their reply and this is confirmed by *nomen ... tuum* at **12**. The problem is that the manuscript reading *uersibus ... meis* at **8** would give this line to Lygdamus. One solution would be [with N-A (108-110) following Ehrwald (1901) 572-578, Schuster (1930) 151 and Lieberg

(1980) 138-142] to have the Muses speak **7**, the poet **8** and the Muses **9-14**. However, the division of the distich **7-8** between two speakers would be unusual. A preferable solution, adopted by editors since Muretus, is to emend *meis* at **8** to *tuis*, and so attribute the whole of **7-14** to the Muses. A similar confusion of *tua* and *mea* occurs at **7.1**. Postgate's suggestion of *nouis* for *meis* at **8** would achieve the same effect, as the fact that the author of these poems is meant is made clear later in 12.

7 carmine: poetry, through which the poet seeks access to his mistress, cf. Tib. 2.4.19 *ad dominam faciles aditus per carmina quaero*. A secondary meaning of 'charms', 'spells' with which to bewitch the mistress may also be present, as often in elegy; see Sharrock (1994) 50-86, Ingleheart (2010) 66 on Ov. *Trist*. 2.4, Fulkerson (2017) 6. The contrast *carmine / pretio* is a common elegiac theme, cf. Tib. 1.4.61-62 quoted on **5** above.

formosae ... auarae: the two groups are not mutually exclusive. On the contrary, it is a commonplace of elegy that beautiful mistresses are greedy; cf. Tib. 2.4.35-36 *heu quicumque dedit formam caelestis auarae, / quale bonum multis attulit ille malis*. The opposition simply serves Lygdamus' immediate purpose in **7-8** of flattering his mistress, through the Muses' address, by alluding not only to her beauty but also to her good taste as a *docta puella* in preferring poetry to riches. This would be particularly appropriate if the rival who has stolen her from him (**1.6, 23, 26-28, 2.1-4, 29-30**) is a *diues amator*. The adjective *formosus* is common in pastoral and elegy, but rare in epic (e.g. Virg. *Ecl*. 16, *Georg*. 1, *Aen*. 0), and so stands mid-way between the colloquial *bellus* (see **4.52n.**) and the more elevated *pulcher*. For the statistics see N-A 110-111; cf. Axelson (1945) 60-61, McKeown II 111-112 on *Am*. 1.5.11, Monteil (1964) 23-60, 71-109, Ernout (1947) 64-67, P. Watson (1985) 439-441. For its use in the context of asking for gifts, cf. Ov. *Am*. 1.10.47 *parcite, formosae, pretium pro nocte pacisci*. For the connotations of sexual attraction in *formosus*, as opposed to moral or physical beauty in *pulcher*, see Fordyce on Cat. 86 (headnote), McKeown III 204 (on *Am*. 2.10.7-8) and N-A ad loc. The adj. is applied specifically to Neaera by Apollo at **4.57** below.

pretio: contrasted with *carmine*, see above. The poet, in contrast to the *diues amator*, should not be asked to provide rich presents, cf. Ov. *Ars* 3.551 *a doctis pretium scelus est sperare poetis* (with Gibson 316 ad loc.) on the contemptuous tone of *pretium*, suggesting a commercial relationship with a prostitute. A similar diatribe against girls asking for gifts from poets instead of from rich lovers occurs at Ov. *Am*. 1.10. For a more positive view of amatory gift-exchange, in this case in Plautus, see Zagagi (1987) 131.

capiuntur: 'captivated, seduced', an example of the language of *militia amoris*; see Pichon 98-9 and cf. Prop. 1.1.1 *Cynthia prima suis miserum me cepit ocellis*.

8 ut digna est: 'as she deserves'. Neaera's beauty justifies her celebration in verse, cf. Ov. *Ars* 3.535 *nos facimus placitae late praeconia formae*. The adj. *dignus* may have had associations with Gallus cf. fr. 2.6-7 (Courtney = 145.6-7 Hollis) ... *tandem fecerunt c[ar]mina Musae / quae possem domina deicere digna mea*. Its use here links the opening Lygdamus poem with the *Sulpicia Cycle* **8.24** *dignior est uestro* (i.e. *Pieridum*) *nulla puella choro*, **8.15** *digna est*, **12.10** (sc. *non*) *cuiquam dignior illa uiro* and the opening *Sulpicia* poem, **13.10** *cum digno digna* (see **nn.** ad loc.), where programmatic Gallan associations could also have been active; see further Hinds (1983). For the possible connection between the adj. *dignus* and marriage partners see *Sulpicia Cycle* **8.15n.** and *Sulpicia* poems **13.10n.**; another hint here perhaps at the married status of Lygdamus and Neaera.

tuis: a conjecture for the *meis*, which would not fit the assignment of this line to the Muses and betrays some uncertainty about the speaker. Postgate's suggestion of *nouis* would fit the Callimachean context, but has no manuscript support.

9-14 The Muses specify that Lygdamus' gift of poems should consist of a luxury edition. Catullus had first made use of the theme of the appearance of the poetry book in the opening poem of his collection (Cat. 1.1-2 *cui dono lepidum nouum libellum / arida modo pumice expolitum*?). At Cat. 22.6-8 the poor quality of Suffenus' verse is contrasted with the luxury editions in which it is produced ... *chartae regiae, noui libri, / noui umbilici, lora rubra, membranae, / derecta plumbo, et pumice omnia aequata*. On connections between the physicality of the book and the qualities of the poems it contains see the discussion in Feeney [(2012) 35] with further bibliography in his n.34. A more detailed description occurs in the opening lines of Ovid's first book of exile poems (*Trist*. 1.1.5-14):

> *nec te purpureo uelent uaccinia fuco –*   5
> *non est conueniens luctibus ille color –*
> *nec titulus minio, nec cedro charta notetur,*
> *candida nec nigra cornua fronte geras.*

> *felices ornent haec instrumenta libellos:*
> *fortunae memorem te decet esse meae.*   10
> *nec fragili geminae poliantur pumice frontes,*
> *hirsutus passis sed uideare comis.*
> *neue liturarum pudeat; qui uiderit illas,*
> *de lacrimis factas sentiet esse meis.*

["Let not your cover be dyed purple by the juice of berries – that colour is not suitable for grief – let not your title be distinguished with vermillion and your paper with cedar oil, have no white bosses on your dark edges. Such decorations should adorn books of good omen; you should be mindful of my fate. Let not your two edges be polished with brittle pumice, so you appear with locks rough and unkempt. Be not ashamed of blots; he who sees them will feel they were made by my tears."]

For a parallel reading of these two texts see Somerville (2006). Here Ovid's book is to be plain and unadorned, to suit the fortune of its exiled author; see Williams (1992). By contrast, Martial 3.2.7-11 describes a smarter book to be sent as a present to Faustus

> *cedro nunc licet ambules perunctus*
> *et frontis gemino decens honore*
> *pictis luxurieris umbilicis,*
> *et te purpurea delicata uelet,*   10
> *et cocco rubeat superbus index.*

["Now you may walk anointed with cedar oil, and your edges handsome with twin decoration you may luxuriate with painted bosses and delicate purple should cover you and your proud title should shine red with vermillion."]

and briefly repeats the theme of the book with a purple outer covering in the opening of the eleventh book: Mart. 11.1.1-2:

> *Quo tu, quo, liber otiose, tendis*
> *cultus Sidone non cotidiana?*

["Where, where are you going, holiday book, clothed in purple not of everyday?"]

The poetic description has a number of points in common with that of Ovid, which it reverses, and it seems likely that he is taking *Trist.* 1.1.5-14 as his model. What is being described in all the examples above is not a modern book (known as a *codex*) but a papyrus roll. The most frequently used rolls were wound round a wood or bone *umbilicus* (Cat. 22.7; Mart. 3.2.8). The *umbilicus* had projecting ends, often painted, called *cornua* (Ov. *Trist.* 1.1.8; Mart. 11.107.1; *Lygd.* **1.13** see **13n.** below). The back of the papyrus could be treated with cedar oil (Ov. *Trist.* 3.1.13; Mart. 3.2.7) to protect it from termites, perfume it and give it a yellowish colour. The edges of the papyrus were smoothed by being rubbed down by pumice stone Cat. 1.2, 22.8; *Lygd.* **1.10**. The name of the author and title were affixed in red letters on a label (Ov. *Trist.* 1.1.7; Mart. 3.2.11; *Lygd.* **1.12**). The roll could have a leather/parchment cover, *membrana* **9**, here coloured yellow *lutea,* but more commonly purple (Ov. *Trist.* 1.1.5; Mart. 3.2.10, 11.1.2), with painted ribbons or straps to tie it up *lora rubra* (Cat. 22.7). On Roman book production see further Kenney (1982) *CHCL* II 15-22. With the neoterics the polishing and smoothing of the papyrus roll became a metaphor for the 'polished' nature of the poetry it contained: Cat. 1.1-2, on which see Copley (1951), Elder (1966), Cairns (1969), Levine (1969), Hubbard (1983); cf. Prop. 3.1.8 *exactus tenui pumice uersus eat*; Hor. *Epist.* 1.20.1-2 ... *liber* .../... *pumice mundus*; Mart. 1.117.16 *rasum pumice*. The adjective *leuis* at Cinna fr. 11.3 (Courtney = 13. 3 Hollis) *leuis in aridulo maluae descripta libello,* in the description of a copy of Aratus' *Phaenomena* written on mallow bark, may have a similar metapoetic function. Conversely, lack of physical embellishment may suggest lack of poetic finish, e.g. Mart. 4.10.1-2 *dum nouus est nec adhuc rasa mihi fronte libellus, / pagina dum tangi non bene sicca timet,* 8.72.1-2 *nondum murice cultus asperoque / morsu pumicis aridi politus* with Schöffel (2002) 604 ad loc. Parca [(1986) 461-474] and Williams [(1992) 178-189] suggest that in our poem the terms *libellum* **9**, *comptum* **14** and *cultum* **17** may have neoteric overtones of small scale, polished verse and both accept Postgate's conjecture of *nouis* at **8** to back up their argument. Others, for example Pieri (1982) 57-59 and N-A 114-115, argue against seeing any such literary associations here at this late date, but the examples from Mart. above seems to refute their view. The detailed physical description of the book, they argue, contains no metapoetic element but simply serves to show that the poet should spare no effort to make it attractive to his estranged wife. A reference to the refined character of the poetry, however, would serve to increase the worth of the proposed gift and to flatter Neaera as a *docta puella* with good literary taste and in my view a metapoetic meaning seems likely here; see **headnote** above on Callimachean metapoetic pointers and cf. *libellum* **n.** below.

9 lutea ... membrana: the leather/parchment book covering, as discussed in the note above, was usually purple. Only the present passage mentions yellow *lutea*; the present line is perhaps at the root of Isid. *Etym.* 6.11.4 *membrana ... aut candida aut lutea aut purpurea*. The reason the Muses recommend yellow here could be that Lygdamus is trying to renew his marriage with Neaera and yellow was the colour of the bride's veil in the Roman marriage ceremony (Plin. *Nat.* 21.46). The combination of the two colours *lutea ... niueum* here could echo the same colour combination in Catullus' description of Hymenaeus in the wedding hymn 61.9-10 *huc ueni, niueo gerens / luteum pede soccum*, or it could simply be an example of Lygdamus' characteristic love of such colour combinations; cf. **2.10** *candida ... nigra*, **18** *nigra candida*, **4.30** *niueo ... purpureus*, **33-34** *alba ... candida ... rubent*, **5.4-5** *purpureo ... nigram*, **15** *cani nigros*.

lutea sed: for the postponement of particles in elegy, a feature introduced into Latin poetry by the neoterics on the model of Alexandrian Greek writers, see Norden (1927) 402-403, Marouzeau (1949) 70-91, 105-108, Ross (1969) 67-69, Platnauer 93-96 and Maltby (1999) 384-387. The first example of postponed *sed* is Cat. 51.9. There are three examples in Tib. 1.7.46, 8.63, 2.4.3, one further example in *Lygd.* **5.28** (to fourth position) and one in at *Laud. Mess.* **7.34**. For postponed *nec* in *Lygd.* see **4.91n.**, and cf. also **6.19, 55**. For postponed *et* see **10n.** below.

niueum: papyrus was produced in varying levels of brightness, the highest quality, as here, having the whitest colour, cf. Plin. *Nat.* 13.78 *spectatur in chartis tenuitas, densitas, candor, leuor*. For the poetic *color* of the term *niueus* see McKeown III 18 (on *Am.* 2.1.23-24).

libellum: need not imply a small book, but is an affective diminutive, suggesting a modest, unpretentious volume, usually of verse, as in Cat. 1.1 and 1.8; Ov. *Am. Epigr.* 1, 1; Stat. *Silu.* 1 *Praef.;* Mart. 1 *Praef.*; see further Diggle (1980) 401-419. Like *tenuis* **11**, *comptum* **14**, and *cultum* **18** the word in this context may have neoteric associations. Its repetition at the line end here and in line **17** may echo the line-end repetitions of the word in lines 1 and 8 of Catullus' first poem where the same neoteric associations are present. Such line-end repetition of *libellus* does not guarantee a link, as it is found elsewhere e.g. at Hor. *Serm.* 1.4.66 and 71; Ov. *Trist.* 1.7.19 and 33, 2.545 and 549 and *Dirae* 26 and 34, but a thematic connection seems likely. For Catullus as a named poetic predecessor see **6.41n.** below.

10 pumex et: a humanist correction for *pumicet et* of the manuscripts, which would leave *membrana* as the subject. For this use of pumice stone to smooth the edges of the papyrus and for its possible metapoetic associations see **9-14n.** above and cf. Prop. 3.1.8 quoted on **11-12n.** below. For the postponed *et* see **9n.** above on postponed *sed*. Mankin [(1995) 54-55 on Hor. *Epod*. 1.12] argues that postponed *et* is used *metri gratia* (at least in Horace) and is not necessarily a neoteric feature, but Mayer [(2012) 65 on Hor. *Carm.* 1.2.9] argues for the postposition of *et* as a Greek Hellenistic feature comparing postponed καί at Callimachus *Aetia* 1, fr. 1.15 (Pf.).

canas tondeat ante comas: the personification of the roll with its 'hair' fits better into the context of Ov. *Trist*. 1.1.11-12, quoted in **9-14n.** above, than it does here and so suggests that our author is imitating Ovid. In contrast with the poetry roll here, Apollo, the god of poetry, is known for his unshorn (*intonsus*) locks, see Tib. 1.4.38, 2.3.12, 2.5.121; *Lygd*. **4.27**, *Sulpicia Cycle* **10.2**. On *comae* and other words for hair in *Lygd*. see **2.11n.** For the *iunctura* of *cana* + *coma* in the same *sedes* see Tib. 1.2.94, 1.6.86; Prop. 4.9.52 and elsewhere in the line at Prop. 2.18.18; Sen. *Troad.* 184, *Phoen.* 440, *Oed.* 555; Mart. 4.53.3-4.

11-12 The reference is to the fixing of a label (*index /titulus*) to the top of the roll, on which was written the author's name or title of the work in red letters; see **9-14n.** above and cf. Ov. *Trist.* 1.1.7; Mart. 3.2.11 (quoted there). There are considerable problems with the manuscript readings *praetexit* (**11**), *chartae* (**11**) and *facta* (**12**) in this couplet. In **11** the humanist correction *praetexat*, jussive subjunctive, has generally been accepted. If *chartae* (gen.) were kept in **11**, it would have to refer to the whole roll and be dependent on *summa ... fastigia* 'the topmost edge of the slender roll' with *littera* (**12**) the subject of *praetexat* 'form the border'. Again the humanist correction *charta* in the sense of 'label' improves the sense, as it is this small (*tenuis*) label that should adorn the roll's topmost edge. The adj. *tenuis* itself in **11**, like *libellum* **9**, **17**, *comptum* **14**, *cultum* **17** and *munera parua* **24**, is an emphatic metapoetic sign, in this case the equivalent of the Callimachean λεπταλέος (*Aetia* 1 fr. 1.24 Pf.) indicating a small and well-wrought work cf. Virg. *Ecl.* 1.2, 6.8 (with Clausen 175); Prop. 3.1.5 *carmen tenuastis*, 3.1.8 *tenui pumice*; Ov. *Am.* 1.2.7, 3.1.9, see further Thomas (1988) 191-192 on Virg. *Georg.* 2.180, Brink (1982) on Hor. *Epist.* 2.1.225, Harrison (2007) 72, Heyworth (2019) 169 on Ov. *Fast.* 3.429-434. Finally *facta* in **12** looks like an empty filler. Here Némethy's conjecture *rubra* (like Livineius' *picta*) has the advantage of referring to the well-attested use of a red-painted label.

11 summaque ... fastigia: the combination originates in Virg. *Aen.* 1.342, 2.758, then Ov. *Met.* 2.3; Manil. 2.813, 4.254; Germ. *Arat.* 478.

12 littera: 'inscription' see **2.27n.** *littera* below.

13 extra geminas pingantur cornua frontes: what is meant by the terms *cornua* and *frontes* in this context? There are only three occurrences of the term *cornua* in relation to books: Ov. *Trist.* 1.1.8 *candida nec nigra cornua fronte geras*; Mart. 11.107.1-3 *explicitum nobis usque ad sua cornua librum / et quasi perlectum, Septiciane, refers. / omnia legisti* and *Lygd.* 1.13. The Martial example shows the term being used in a similar way to *umbilicus* to mark the end of the book, cf. Mart. 4.89.1-2 *ohe, iam satis est, ohe, libelle. / iam peruenimus usque ad umbilicos*. The *umbilicus* was a stick of wood or bone around which the roll was wound. All three occurrences of *cornua* are in elegy, where the metre precludes the use of the term *umbilicus* itself. The *umbilicus*, like the *cornua* here, could be coloured in a luxury edition, cf. Mart. 3.2.9 *pictis luxurietis umbilicis*. The *cornua*, then, probably refer to the thickened or bent ends of the *umbilicus*, projecting from the roll and preventing the roll from slipping off. As for the *frontes* it appears from Ov. *Trist.* 1.1.11 *nec fragili geminae poliantur pumice frontes* that these must refer to the right and left edges of the roll [so *CHCL* II 31, Ingleheart (2010) 227 on Ov. *Trist.* 2.241-242] rather than to its ends [as others, e.g. Luck (1977) on *Trist.* 1.1.8, argue], since they appear to have been on view when the roll was properly wound and so were smoothed by pumice, and, at least in *Trist.* 1.1.8, coloured black. In *Trist.* 1.1.8 the *cornua* project from the sides of the roll as from a forehead, *fronte*, of a bull, a metaphor brought out clearly in Ovid's use of the verb *geras*. See further on these two terms Blümner (1916) 436-437 and Possanza (1994). I adopt the conjecture of J. B. Hall of *extra* for the MSS reading *inter* as the *cornua* would 'project from' rather than 'stand between' their *frontes*. Wunderlich reads *geminae* for *geminas* thus avoiding this difficulty by placing the painted (as in Ovid *Trist.* 1.1.8) *frontes* between the *cornua*, but on the whole better sense can be made by reading *extra*. For the phrase *cornua frontes*, cf. Virg. *Georg.* 4.299 *cornua fronte* followed by *geminae nares* in the next line and *Culex* 16 *cornua fronte* in a passage which could well have influenced our author here see **15-16n.** below. The combination *geminas ... frontes* occurs in the same *sedes* at Ov. *Fast.* 1.135 and *Trist.* 1.1.11 (quoted above).

14 etenim: 'for indeed'. The only occurrence of this particle in the *Corp. Tib.* It is very rare in poetry, except in Lucretius, and is avoided completely by Catullus, Tibullus, Lucan and Martial; see Axelson (1945)

123 n.15 and full statistics in N-A 125. Normally in initial position, it occurs in second position in verse from Lucretius and in prose from Sen. *Epist.* 95.45; see *ThLL* 5(2).917.14-23.

comptum: the term can be used, like *cultus* **17**, of style in the sense 'polished', 'elegant' (Quint. *Inst.* 8.3.42), but also of personal appearance, particularly with regard to arranging the hair, cf. *Sulpicia Cycle* **8.9-10** *seu soluit crines ... / seu compsit, comptis est ueneranda comis*, an association aided by a supposed etymological connection between *comptus* and *coma*, cf. Isid. *Etym.* 10.56 *comtus a coma dictus, quod sit formosus capillis*. The image from **10** above of trimming the book's hair *tondeat ... comas* with its metapoetic connotations may still be active here. For the metapoetical associations of *comptus* see *Sulpicia Cycle* **8.10n.** and **12.3n.** with reference to Sulpicia's polished verse.

oportet: rare in poetry [Axelson (1945) 13-14], but common, according to *ThLL* 9(2).737.34-52 in proverbs and so appropriate for the sententious tone of the Muses here.

opus: for its use of a literary work of art see Ingleheart (2010) 274 on Ov. *Trist.* 2.327-328 and *ibid.* 290 on 355-356, Robinson (2011) 60 on Ov. *Fast.* 2.4, *OLD opus* 9c. Like *labor* (Gk. πόνος) of *Laud. Mess.* **7.16** it suggests the painstaking labour that goes into producing a polished (*comptum*) work.

15-16 per... / Castaliamque umbram Pieriosque lacus: it was common from the early period in imprecations for the preposition *per* to be separated from the noun it governed, e.g. Plaut. *Bacch.* 905-906 *per te, ere, obsecro / deos immortales* with later verse examples at Virg. *Aen.* 4.314, 12.56-60; Tib. 1.5.7-8; Ov. *Her.*10.73, *Fast.* 2.841 etc. The length of the separation here between *per* and *Castaliam*, however, at six words, is unparalleled. *Pace* Fulkerson [(2017) 82 ad loc.] *uos auctores* here is object of *oro* and not governed by *per*, so Lygdamus does not beseech the Muses in their own name.

auctores ... carminis: the Muses, referring back to *Pierides* in **5**. They are addressed as the inspirers of his poetry. The phrase *carminis auctor* occurs first at Tib. 2.4.13 *carminis auctor Apollo* and, as there, is normally reserved for Apollo (cf. Germ. *Arat.* 2; *Culex* 12; *Aetna* 4). At Ov. *Fast.* 6.709 Minerva uses the phrase of herself: *sum tamen inuentrix auctorque ego carminis huius*.

Castaliamque umbram Pieriosque lacus: the poet calls upon the Muses in the name of two specific sites of poetic inspiration: the shade of the Castalian spring on Mount Parnassus and the Pierian spring near the birth place of the Muses (see **5n.** above). For the listing of deities' attributes and associations in prayers see McKeown III 283 (on *Am.* 2.13.11-12). For the association of *Castalius* and *Pierius* cf. *Culex* 17-18 (quoted below); Sil. 11.481-482 *sic tunc Pierius bellis durata uirorum / pectora Castalio frangebat carmine Teuthras*; Stat. *Silu.* 5.5.2-4 ... *Castaliae uocalibus undis / inuisus Phoeboque grauis. quae uestra, sorores, / orgia, Pieriae, quas incestauimus aras*? At Pindar *Paean* 6.6-9 the poet describes himself as the prophet of the Pierides and watches the dancing nymphs by the Castalian stream. The Castalian spring according to Pausanias 10.8.9 was named from a local woman Kastalia, or man Kastalios, or from Kastalia, daughter of Achelous. A scholion on Statius tells how it was named after a girl from Delphi who, being pursued by Apollo, threw herself into the spring and became its nymph: Schol. Stat. *Theb.* 1.698 *Castaliae: ubi quondam uirgo Castalia fuit. quam cum Apollo amaret et uim uellet inferre in fontem se praecipitauit*. In Greek poetry this spring is sacred to Apollo and the nymphs, but these nymphs are not associated specifically with the Muses (Eur. *Ion* 94ff., *Phoen.* 222-225). Theocritus' address at *Id.* 7.148, a poem set in Cos, to the 'Castalian nymphs, who haunt the steeps of Parnassus' is seen by Gow ad loc. as unlikely to refer to the Muses. However, the questions they are asked on the type of wine Chiron served to Heracles and Odysseus served to Polyphemus certainly suggest a detailed knowledge of poetry. It is possible (see Thomas on Virg. *Georg.* 3.292-293) that the Castalian spring could have had programmatic significance in Alexandrian poetry, perhaps in a lost work of Callimachus. If so, this use of Callimachean programmatic material derived from Virgil's *Georgics* would link the opening of the *Lygd.* group with the opening of the *Laud. Mess.*, see **7 headnote, 7.9-11n., 12-13n., 15-16n.** Such a connection would be further strengthened by the use of Callimachean metapoetic pointers in both: see *tenuis* **11**, *comptum* **14**, *cultum* **18** and *munera parua* **24** here and cf. *humilis* **7.4**, *munera parua* **7.7** and *paruus labor* **7.16** in the *Laud. Mess.* In Latin verse the spring is mainly associated with Apollo as inspirer of poetry. From Virg. *Georg.* 3.291-293 *sed me Parnasi deserta per ardua dulcis / raptat amor; iuuat ire iugis, qua nulla priorum / Castaliam molli deuertitur orbita cliuo* onwards it replaced Hippocrene on Helicon as the source of poetic inspiration, so Hor. *Carm.* 3.4.61; Ov. *Am.* 1.15.35-36 *mihi flauus Apollo / pocula Castalia plena ministret aqua*; *Culex* 12 (quoted below)]. Propertius appears to mix up the two locations in the poem on his own

150   Commentary

poetic initiation 3.3: so 3.3.1 *Heliconis in umbra*, but 3.3.13 *me Castalia speculans ex arbore Phoebus*. The adjective *Castalius* there, however, may mean nothing more than 'belonging to Apollo'. Certainly the description of the grotto of the Muses later in Propertius' poem at 27-38 is thought of as being on Helicon as the reference to Hippocrene in *Gorgoneo ... lacu* 32 shows. Unambiguous cases of association between the Muses and the Castalian spring are late, beginning with Mart. 4.14.1 *Sili, Castalidum decus sororum*, 7.12.10 *per ... Castalium ... gregem* and, later, Auson. 399.3 (Green) *Paule, Camenarum celeberrime Castaliarum alumne*. Shade provided by the Castalian grove is referred to at Sen. *Oed.* 712-713 *... Castalium nemus / umbram Sidonio praebuit hospiti.*

Castaliamque umbram: the phrase is perhaps influenced by a combination of Prop. 3.3.1 and 3.3.13 (quoted above). It probably refers to the shade provided by a wood of laurel trees, which grew around the Castalian spring, cf. *ex arbore* in Prop. 3.3.13 and Sen. *Oed.* 712-713 (quoted above). Alternatively it could refer to the shady cave from which the spring flowed, cf. Prop. 3.3.27 *hic erat affixis uiridis spelunca lapillis*; Ov. *Met.* 3.14 *Castalio ... antro*.

Pieriosque lacus: cf. *Culex* 18 *Pierii laticis* (quoted below). Probably a reference to the Pimplean spring in Pieria, associated with the Muses since Hesiod (*Op.* 1, *Theog.* 1). The exceptional use of *lacus* for 'spring' [see ThLL 7(2). 862.40-52] is perhaps influenced by Prop. 3.3.32 *Gorgoneo ... lacu* (of the spring of Hippocrene). It occurs again only at Stat. *Theb.* 8.175-176 *lacusque / Castalii*. Both Némethy and Tränkle ad loc. point to the similarity between the present passage and *Culex* 12-19:

> *Phoebus erit nostri princeps et <u>carminis auctor</u>*
> *et recinente lyra fautor, siue educat illum*
> *Arna Chimaeraeo Xanthi perfusa liquore,*
> *seu decus Asteriae, seu qua Parnasia rupes*   15
> *hinc atque hinc patula praepandit cornua fronte,*
> *<u>Castaliaeque</u> sonans liquido pede labitur unda.*
> *quare, <u>Pierii</u> laticis decus, <u>ite</u> sorores*
> *Naides, et celebrate deum plaudente chorea.*

["Phoebus will be my guide and the author of my song and inspirer with accompanying lyre, whether Arna nurtured him bathed in the Chimaera's stream of Xanthus, or the glory of Asteria, or the place where the Parnasian rock with broad brow spreads his horns this way and that and the echoing waters of Castalia glide on their flowing course. Therefore come forth, sister Naiads, glory of the Pierian spring and celebrate the god in a dance of praise."]

The fact that the elements *auctores ... carminis* (**15**) / *carminis auctor* (*Culex* 12), *Castaliamque umbram* (**16**) / *Castaliaeque ... unda* (*Culex* 17), *Pieriosque lacus* (**16**) / *Pierii laticis* (*Culex* 18) and *ite* (**17**) / *ite* (*Culex* 18) occur in the same order in both poems suggests that one is dependent on the other. Since in this passage *carminis auctor* refers traditionally to Apollo and not to the Muses and since *ite* in *Culex* has the more natural reference in the context, that the Naiads should go and praise Apollo, as compared with the rather unusual request in our poem that they should go and deliver a book to Neaera, it seems probable, as Tränkle suggests, that the *Culex* passage came first. For a further example of the influence of the *Culex* on [**Tib. 3**] see **5.24n.**, below. Another possibility here is that both passages are dependent on a lost poem of Gallus, so Kennedy (1982) 382-385.

que ... que: see **3-4n.** above.

17 ite domum: an unusual request to be addressed to the Muses. It sounds initially like a brusque dismissal 'go home', perhaps influenced by Tib. 2.4.15 *ite procul, Musae,* until the pronoun *illi* makes it clear that he wishes them to go to Neaera's house. Even so, the peremptory address to the Muses to act as simple messengers (a role fulfilled by a slave named Lygdamus at Prop. 3.6) sounds somewhat tactless. Perhaps, as Lieberg suggests [(1980) 139], the poet is thinking of the effect such prestigious messengers would have on Neaera and her reception of his book. Perhaps one should see in *ite domum* a possible allusion to the last line of the *Eclogues*: 10.77 *ite domum saturae, uenit Hesperus, ite capellae,* in the context of the closural address to the Pierides (10.72) at the end of the book (10.70-77). Lygdamus' book has now been completed and is ready to be delivered to his mistress, making a similar closural reference appropriate paradoxically in his opening poem. For similar closural material in opening poems see *Sulpicia* poems **13.1-2n.** on *tandem uenit amor* with bibliography.

cultumque ... libellum: the adjective has the same associations as *comptum* (**14**), 'elegant', 'polished', but with emphasis on appearance as well as the content, cf. Mart. 8.72.1-3 *nondum murice cultus asperoque / morsu pumicis aridi politus / Arcanum properas sequi, libelle,* 11.1.1-2 *quo tu, quo, liber otiose, tendis / cultus Sidone non cotidiana*? There is again an echo of the opening of the *Sulpicia Cycle* **8.1**, where the phrase

Sulpicia est tibi culta has similar metapoetic connotations, with *Sulpicia ... culta* standing not only for the person 'adorned' for Mars, but also for an 'elegant' book of poems about her, see *Sulpicia Cycle* **8.1n.** For the repetition of *libellum* at the verse end here and at **9** with its echoes of Cat. 1.1 see **9n.** above.

18 sicut erit: nullus defluat inde color: referring back to the yellow parchment cover and the white papyrus of **9**. As with *cultum ... libellum* the term *color* can also have rhetorical implications, in this case referring to lively literary composition, see *Lygd.* **4.30n.** and *Sulpicia Cycle* **10.6n.** The use of *defluere* in the sense of *euanescere* is rare and late. It is used by our author of sleep leaving Lygdamus' body at **4.81** *defluxit corpore somnus* and by Pliny *Nat.* 13.7 of scent evaporating: *celerrime is* (sc. *odor*) *euanescit atque defluit*. Lygdamus' attitude to the Muses remains rather high-handed: they should take care the book they are to deliver arrives in the same state (*sicut erit*) in which they receive it. The future tense (*erit*) simply implies that he has not yet handed the volume over to them.

19-20 The meaning of the couplet seems clear. Lygdamus wishes to ascertain whether Neaera's love (*cura*) for him is as great as his for her (*mutua*), or less (*minor*), or whether he has been forgotten by her altogether (*toto pectore deciderim*). It is related to the theme of sending a letter to ascertain the mistress's feelings at Ov. *Ars* 1.455-456 *ergo eat et blandis peraretur littera uerbis, / exploretque animos, primaque temptet iter*. In Prop. 3.6 Prop. sends his slave Lygdamus to Cynthia with this task. However, the form of the couplet as presented by A+ (*illa mihi referet si nostri mutua cura est / an minor an toto pectore deciderim*) presents a number of difficulties: (1) the future *referet* has been judged unacceptable, as Lygdamus cannot be certain that Neaera will reply (even though sometimes a future indicative can be used to express a strong wish); (2) disjunctive questions introduced by *si ... an ... an* are extremely rare and, with the exception of three disputed passages in Celsus (*Praef.* 36, 3.18.22, 3.21.8), occur only in Christian texts from the late fourth century and Gregory of Tours (e.g. *Hist. Franc.* 6.22), though disjunctive *an ... an* is more common (e.g. Virg. *Aen.* 10.681-683; Ov. *Met.* 10.254-255 and see K-S II 2.528c); (3) the mixture of moods within the indirect questions (*est ... deciderim*), which is unusual, but not unparalleled (e.g. Prop. 3.5.26-28 *quis ... temperet ... / qua uenit ... qua decidit; unde ... / ... redit*). The first objection can be met by reading, as I do, *referat* (attested in some later manuscripts): 'let her tell me' (verbally, presumably through the intermediary of the Muses). The second and third objections can be met by accepting Guy Lee's conjecture [(1958-1959) 21] of *sit nostri ...*

cura in **19**, which Lee himself admits in his discussion may be unnecessary, even though it would cure the syntax; see further Maltby (2010) 325.

19 mutua cura: significantly for the status of the relationship between Lygdamus and Neaera the phrase is used in the context of married couples by Ovid at *Fast.* 2.729-730 *ecquid in officio torus est socialis? et ecquid / coniugibus nostris mutua cura sumus?* and, more significantly (see **headnote** above) *Met.* 7.799-800 *coniuge eram felix, felix erat illa marito. / mutua cura duos et amor socialis habebat* (of Cephalus and Procris). Echoes from this *Met.* episode in the final two poems of **[Tib.] 3**, namely in **19** and **20** are discussed in the Gen. Intro., section 1.3 and the **headnote** above, suggesting that they are used as a structural device by a unitary author providing a ring-structure for the whole collection. For *mutua cura* in other contexts cf. Ov. *Fast.* 2.64 (to Augustus) *sit superis ... mutua cura tui*, Mart. 10.13 (20).9 (to his friend Manius) *si tibi mens eadem, si nostri mutua cura est*. The second half of Martial's line, where the indicative *est* is quite regular, is identical to the transmitted version of **1.19**, which could have been influenced by it. For other examples of the possible influence of Martial in this poem see **headnote** above. The erotic motif of 'reciprocated love', ἴσος Ἔρως / *mutuus amor* occurs in the context of marriage or betrothal at Hom. *Od.* 6.183-184 (Odysseus to Nausicaa); Pind. *Ol.* 7.6; Theocr. *Id.* 18. 51-52 (epithalamium for Helen); its occurrences in Greek New Comedy are discussed by Leo (1912) 145; in Latin it is found from Plaut. *Cist.* 191-3 and Ter. *Eun.* 91-92 on, e.g. Cat. 45.20 *mutuis animis amant amantur* (of Acme and Septimius; a poem which also speaks of *medullis* at 16, cf. **25n.** below), 62.57 *par conubium* in a marriage hymn, 64.336 (the *concordia* of Peleus and Thetis); Tib. 1.2.65, 1.6.76; Ov. *Am.* 2.3.2, 2.10.29, 3.6.87; Stat. *Silu.* 5.1.43-44; Mart. 4.13.7; *Sulpicia Cycle* **11.6, 7, 12.8** (all of Cernithus' love for Sulpicia). On the importance of this concept in the context of marriage songs and writing on marriage see L. C. Watson [(2003) 465 and n. 38] on *amorem mutuum* at Hor. *Epod.* 15.10, with more examples from both Latin and Greek *epithalamia*. Horace's Neaera in that poem had sworn falsely that there love would be mutual, and Horace has to look elsewhere for a partner who is *parem* (*Epod.* 15.14). Both Horace there and Lygdamus here make the mistake of looking for a permanent marriage-like relationship with a woman whose name suggests the world of the *hetaira*. For *cura* = 'love' as a technical term in Roman love poetry from Plautus (*Epid.* 135) on, see Pichon 120. Skutsch (1956) and Ross [(1975) 68-69], on the strength of Virg. *Ecl.* 10.22 *tua cura Lycoris*, argue that for the elegists it would have had a particular association with Gallus.

20 minor: common in combination with *cura* in both prose (e.g. Cic. *Am.* 43.7, *Off.* 1.141, *Fam.* 6.2.1, 7.10.2; Liv. 6.27.10, 39.27.3) and verse (e.g. Hor. *Serm.* 2.4.85; Virg. *Aen.* 5.803-804; Ov. *Pont.* 1.2.74 *haec est caelesti pectore cura minor*).

toto pectore deciderim: the metaphor 'to fall from the heart' in the sense of 'to be forgotten' goes back to Homer, e.g. *Il.* 23.595 ἐκ θυμοῦ πεσέειν. The normal phrase in Latin is *excidere animo* (e.g. Virg. *Aen.* 1.25-26 *necdum etiam causae irarum saeuique dolores / exciderant animo*; Ov. *Her.* 20.188, *exciderant animo foedera lecta tuo*) or just *excidere* (e.g. Cic. *Fam.* 5.13 *quae cogitatio cum mihi non omnino excidisset*; Ov. *Her.* 2.105 *utque tibi excidimus, nullam puto Phyllida nosti*). The choice of *decidere* for *excidere* here is for metrical reasons to avoid synaloepha. For the replacement of *animo* by the more poetic *pectore*, cf. Ov. *Pont.* 2.4.23-24 *non ego, si biberes securae pocula Lethes, / excidere haec credam pectore posse tuo* and for the emphatic *toto pectore*, cf. Cat. 66.24-25 *ut tibi nunc toto pectore sollicitae / sensibus ereptis mens excidit*, with further examples from Virg. and Ov. in Pichon 228-229 and Fulkerson (2017) 91 ad loc.

21-22 Commentators compare Stat. *Silu.* 4.4.10-11 where a letter to Victorius Marcellus is asked first to greet the recipient and then to pass on a message in verse: *cui primum solito uulgi de more salutem, / mox inclusa modis haec reddere uerba memento*. Martial at 12.11.1 similarly asks a Muse to greet his friend Parthenius: *Parthenio dic, Musa, tuo nostroque salutem* and to pass on a request, 12.11.6 *tradat ut ipse duci carmina nostra roga* (see **headnote** to this poem above). For the construction of *donare* here + acc. + abl. 'to honour someone with something', cf. Cat. 101.3 *ut te postremo donarem munere mortis* and for the abl., cf. **5** above (*quonam donetur honore*). Here *meritam larga donate salute* meaning literally 'honour her as she deserves with effusive greeting' is a poetic variation on the formulaic epistolary phrase *plurimam salutem dicere* (cf. Cic. *Att.* 6.8.5, 14.21.4, 16.7.8 etc.).

submisso ... sono: 'in a low voice', a variant on the more common *submissa uoce* (e.g. Cic. *Flac.* 66; Ov. *Met.* 7.90; Mart. 8.75.11). The Muses are to adopt the humble tone of voice of suppliants. For *submissus* in contexts of supplication, cf. Ov. *Met.* 5.234-235 *sed tamen os timidum uultusque in marmore supplex / submissaeque manus faciesque obnoxia mansit*, *Pont.* 3.1.149-150 *... submissaque terra / ... bracchia tende*. For *sonus* = *uox*, cf. Prop. 4.1A.58; Ov. *Am.* 3.1.64, *Met.* 3.401, *Fast.* 2.119 with Robinson (2011) 142 ad loc.

23-28 These lines contain the message the Muses are to pass on word for word from Lygdamus to Neaera when they deliver his book to her. In this sense the Muses are asked to fulfil the traditional elegiac go-between role of the slave, as we saw (**17n.** above) with Lygdamus in Prop. 3.6, or of the lena.

23 uir quondam nunc frater: to be taken closely with **26** *siue sibi coniunx siue futura soror*. The terms *uir* and *coniunx* must refer to a relationship between husband and wife, while *frater* and *soror* refer simply to one of friendship; see Adams (2016) 260-261. In **23** Lygdamus states he was once (*quondam*) Neaera's husband, but is now simply her friend. For the attachment of temporal adverbs to nouns cf. Virg. *Aen.* 1.198 *neque enim ignari sumus ante malorum* (cf. Gk. τῶν πρὶν κακῶν); Prop. 2.28.61 *diuae nunc, ante iuuencae* and see K-S II 1.218 and Jocelyn (1969) 210 on Enn. *Trag.* 33. In **26** the reference is to two possibilities in the future; Neaera could either be his wife or his friend. In the final couplet a preference for the former is expressed. For examples of *frater* in the sense of friend, cf. Petr. 9.3.4 *iste frater seu comes*, Tab. Vind. II 310 *Chrauttius Veldeio suo fratri contubernali antiquo plurimam salutem* and see *ThLL* 6(1).1256.23-69. At Mart. 2.4.3 *fratrem te uocat et soror uocatur* the poet satirises an incestuous relationship between mother and son who conceal their real relationship beneath the innocently affectionate terms *frater* and *soror*.

casta Neaera: although the couple no longer live as man and wife, the adjective *casta* suggests that, at least in Lygdamus' view, Neaera has not become involved with another man. For *casta* in the specialised sense of true to one man cf. Tib. 1.3.83, 6.67, 75 and see Pichon 101, *ThLL* 3.566.54-567.68 and, in the context of marriage, Ingleheart (2010) 262 on Ov. *Trist.* 2.307-308. Contrast Apollo's words at **4.60**, after Lygdamus is informed of Neaera's adultery: *nec gaudet casta nupta Neaera domo*. There could be some irony in the use of the adj. here, as the name Neaera is applied elsewhere in Latin literature to faithless women, cf. Virg. *Ecl.* 3.3-4 ... *ipse Neaeram / dum fouet ac ne me sibi praeferat illa ueretur*; Hor. *Epod.* 15.23 *eheu, translatos alio maerebis amores* (sc. *Neaerae*); Ov. *Am.* 3.6.28 *cum rapuit uultus, Xanthe, Neaera tuos*.

24 accipias ... rogat: parataxis of this kind with *rogo* occurs mainly in Early Latin, e.g. Plaut. *Most.* 680 *roga circumducat*, *Pers.* 634 *rogarat ... diceret*. In the Classical period it is found mostly in colloquial contexts, such as Cicero's letters e.g. *Att.* 4.14.2 *rogo ... nos quam primum reuisas*, although Caesar uses it at *BG* 1.20.5 *rogat finem orandi faciat*. In elegy, apart from here, it occurs in Ov. *Am.* 1.4.51 *uir bibat usque roga* and probably belongs to the educated colloquial register; for further occurrences outside elegy see K-S II 1.228-9, Adams (2016) 248, Hallaaho (2009) 81-85.

munera parua: a self-deprecatory diminutive, probably intentionally echoed at *Laud. Mess.* **7.7-8** *est nobis uoluisse satis. nec munera parua / respueris.* For the Callimachean implications see *Laud. Mess.* **7.7n., 16n.** and cf. Call. *Aetia* fr. 1.5 Pf. ἔπος δ' ἐπὶ τυτθὸν ἑλ[ίσσω ["I roll forth a tale on the small scale"]. The adj. is frequently used in programmatic passages on small scale in elegy and lyric, cf. Hor. *Epist.* 2.1.257-258, *Carm.* 4.2.31-32, 15.3; Prop. 3.3.18, 4.1A.58; Ov. *Trist.* 2.332. The *iunctura* occurs also at Hor. *Carm.* 1.28.3-4 and Ov. *Fast.* 2.533-535 (offerings to the dead); Ov. *Ars* 2.256 *porrige Fortunae munera parua die* (small present to the beloved).

25 A hyperbolic expression of affection in which Neaera is said to be dearer to Lygdamus than his innermost marrow. The normal comparison is with life itself, e.g. Cic. *Fam.* 14.7.1 *Tulliolam quae nobis nostra uita dulcior est*; Virg. *Aen.* 5.724-725 *nate mihi uita ... / care magis*, or with the eyes, e.g. Cat. 104.2 *ambobus mihi quae carior est oculis.* In an important intertext at Ov. *Met.* 7.847 the mistress's body is said to be dearer to the lover than his own (see Gen. Intro., above, p. 92). The *medullae* are often used by the elegists and others as the seat of the emotions, including love; cf. Cat. 45.16 [sc. *amoris*] *ignis mollibus ardet medullis* (Acme to Septimius); Cic. *Tusc.* 4.24; Lucr. 3.250; Hor. *Epod.* 5.37, *Epist.* 1.10.28; Prop. 2.12.17; further references in *ThLL* 8.600.68-601.32, Pease (1935) 143-144 on Virg. *Aen.* 4.66, Mankin (1995) 121 and L.C. Watson (2003) 214 on Hor. *Epod.* 5.37. The nearest parallel to their use in the present context is the comparison with *uiscera* at Maecenas fr. 3.1-2 (Courtney = 186.1-2 Hollis) *ni te uisceribus meis, Horati, / plus iam diligo.*

suis: for the free use of the reflexive pronoun, cf. *Lygd.* **6.19** *nec toruus Liber in illis, / qui se quique una uina iocosa colunt.*

caram magis: replaces the regular comparative *cariorem* here for metrical reasons, as at Cat. 62.58 and Virg. *Aen.* 5.725 quoted above. This analytic comparative is absent from Tibullus, but is relatively frequent in Ovid (35). In late Latin and Romance it replaces the synthetic form, see Woelfflin (1897), Maltby (2016). On the epithet *cara* applied specifically to wives see **6n.** above.

26 siue ... siue: this form is found in the *Tibullan Corpus* only in *Lygd.* and the *Laud. Mess.* Tibullus uses only *seu*.

coniunx: a more elevated alternative to *uxor* (which is found in Tib. 1.9.54, 1.10.42 and 2.2.11 but never in **[Tib.] 3**) in the sense of 'wife'; see Axelson (1945) 57-58, Adams (1972) 252-253, P. Watson (1985) 431-432. The term *coniunx* is found only in *Lygd.* in **[Tib.] 3**, always with reference to Neaera: **1.26, 27, 2.4, 30, 3.32**. On the husband and wife relationship between Lygdamus and Neaera, see Gen. Intro., section 2.2.1 and **headnote** above. In an important intertext at Ov. *Met.* 7.799 (Gen. Intro., section 1.3 and **headnote** above) Cephalus refers to his relationship with Procris as one of man and wife *coniuge eram felix, felix erat illa marito*. Neither *coniunx* nor *uxor* is applied to the beloved in the other elegists, except in Ovid's exile poetry (see below). In Greek poetry the expression of erotic feelings of a husband for a wife are extremely rare; examples in Sider [(1997) 90 on Philodemus *AP* 5.4.5 (=7.5 Sider)], where he argues that the poet addresses Xantho as his wife (ἄκοιτις). The traditional Roman elegiac relationship is one of the poet/ lover and his mistress, who is normally referred to either by name or as *puella* or *domina*. In *Lygd.* the author uses the less respectful *puella* in reference to Neaera only in the bitter poem of rejection **6.51** and **60**. Tib. uses *coniunx* of Delia's husband at 1.2.43, 6.15, of Delia as the wife of a rich rival at 1.6.33 and of the wife of a certain Titius in 1.4.74, as well as the noun *coniugium* of Cornutus' forthcoming marriage in 2.2.18. Prop. uses *coniunx* as 'husband' or 'wife' in the case of mythological couples at 1.15.15, 21, 19.7, 2.6.23, 2.8.29, 28.33, 48 and of contemporary Roman couples at 3.12.16, 23, 3.22.42, 4.3.49 and *coniugium* of mythical characters at 2.9.5 and of contemporaries at 3.11.31, 4.11.11, 87. Ovid mentions his own wife in connection with a visit to a festival of Juno in Falerii at *Am.* 3.13.1 and uses the term *coniunx* frequently of mythological couples. It is not until Ovid's exile poetry that the author's wife, *coniunx,* comes to play a central role. In *Tristia* the following poems are addressed to her: 1.6, 3.3, 4.3, 5.2, 5.5, 5.11 and 5.14; occasional references to her occur at 1.2.37-44, 1.3.17-18, 41-46, 63-64, 79-102, 3.4b.7-16, 3.8.7-10, 3.11.15-16, 4.6.45-46, 4.8.5-12, 4.10.73-74, 5.1.39-40; see Michalopoulos (2016) 103-104 on 5.14.1-6, 11-14 and 41-42. At *Pont.* 3.1 addresses to his faithful wife found at 3.1.43-48 and 57-66 are discussed in Michalopoulos (2016) 100-103. On the role of Ovid's wife in the exile poetry see further Tissol (2014) 103-104. On marriage taking on the characteristics of passionate love, particularly where some separation or threat to the relationship is involved, see Hutchinson (2006) 100, in his headnote to Prop. 4.3, where he compares Cic. *Fam.* 14.2.2-3, written from exile to his wife Tullia.

soror: on the meaning of the term here, see **23n**. above and cf. *OLD soror* 1d. For its use as an affectionate address rather than a kinship term see Dickey (2002) 125.

27-28 Only death will take from Lygdamus the hope of Neaera's being called his *coniunx*. For the concept of death washing away the pains of love Büchner [(1965) 28] sees a connection with Gallus as reflected in Prop. 2.34.91-92 *et modo formosa quam multa Lycoride Gallus / mortuus inferna uulnera lauit aqua*. N-A ad loc. sees in the couplet a reference to the proverb *dum spiro spero* (see Otto 329-330 s.v. *spero*), as reflected e.g. in Fronto *Epist*. 2.7.19 *si tantisper dum spirat, paulisper sperabit*.

spem nominis: for the phrase cf. Cic. *Phil*. 14.28.7; Liv. 5.45.4; Vell. 2.103.1; Plin. *Pan*. 26.4.1. It may be significant, as N-A points out (ad loc.), that *sperata* was used as an alternative for *pacta* or *desponsata* of a betrothed woman, cf. Non. 706 L. *uirgo, priusquam petatur, sperata dicitur ... dehinc promissa, dicta uel pacta uel sponsa dici potest*. In Lygdamus' case, however, the force of *uir quondam* in **23** suggests that the *sperata* in this case was not a *uirgo* but a former wife. On *speratus* as an affectionate form of address in general see Adams (2016) 261 and on *spes* (with *mea* or other possessive) as an affectionate form of address for anyone except a lover see Dickey (2002) 360.

pallida Ditis aqua: the reference is to the water of the river Lethe, which, when drunk by the dead, brought oblivion of their former life. It was common in Latin poetry from Ennius on for the underworld itself [e.g. Enn. Trag. xxxiv *pallida Leti ... loca*, with Jocelyn (1967) 255 ad loc.] or for the ghosts in the underworld [e.g. Tib. 1.10.38 *pallida turba*] to be referred to as pale. The extension of this epithet to the waters of the underworld is a later development: cf. *Culex* 333 *pallentes ... lacus et squalida Tartara*; Sil. 9.250-251 *pallenti laetus in unda / laxabat sedem uenturis portitor umbris*; *Lygd*. **5.21** *pallentes undas*. A similar verse ending, *Ditis aquas*, occurs at Mart. 9.29.2.

Ditis: a name of Hades, god of the underworld, implying, like its Greek counterpart Pluto, the boundless riches that death brings to himself. The god was introduced into the Roman state cult in 249 BC as an equivalent of the Greek Pluto, cf. Enn. *Var*. 78 *Pluto Latine est Dis pater, alii Orcum uocant*; Cic. *Nat. Deor.* 266 and see Jocelyn (1967) 331, Latte (1960) 246-248, and *LALE* s.v. *Dis* for further references.

Poem 2

The mention of the poet's death at the end of the first poem links neatly with the funeral theme of the second. Verbal echoes between the end of poem 1 and the beginning of poem 2 (*caram* **1.25, 2.1**; *coniunx* **1.26, 27**; *coniuge* **2.4**) further link the two elegies in a technique reminiscent of Tibullus; see e.g. Maltby (2002) 417 on Tib. 2.4.1-6, and Gen. Intro., section 2.2.1 above. Since Neaera has been stolen from him by a rival, Lygdamus has become weary of life and looks forward to his death, presumably through suicide, though this is not stated explicitly, **1-8**. The same theme of the loss of a mistress, followed by the poet's wish for death forms the basis of Prop. 2.8, but there his death does not procure a reconciliation, but rather Cynthia will persecute his ghost (2.8.19-20) and his death will be followed by hers (2.8.25-28). *Lygd.*'s introductory section is followed in the body of the poem, **9-30**, by a detailed description of his future funeral, attended by Neaera and her mother and culminating in an epitaph in which his death is linked with the loss of his wife. This imagined funeral presupposes that through his death Lygdamus will regain the affection of his mistress. At a rhetorical level the death threat serves as an instrument of emotional blackmail, showing the dire consequences of a final break-up with Neaera, while at the same time it serves as a striking declaration of the poet's never-failing love. The fantasy of the poet's funeral, attended by a caring and affectionate mistress, is a favourite theme with Tibullus (1.1.59-68, 3.5-10) and Propertius (1.17.19-24, 2.13.17-58 with epitaph at 35-36, 3.16.21-30), and is touched on again in passing at *Lygd.* **3.8**. A Hellenistic parallel is provided by [Theocr.] *Id.* 23.16-48 in which an *erastes* hangs himself at the door of his unresponsive *eromenos*, again providing, as here (**29-30**), his own epitaph. For death fantasies in elegy see Müller (1952) 38-42. On funerals in Roman elegy see Houghton (2011) and for the theme of suicide in the genre see Hill (2004) 91-104.

The contents may be analysed as follows:

1-8 Lygdmus finds the man who separates lover hard-hearted; he cannot bear such separation and wishes for suicide.

9-14 He requests that Neaera and her mother should attend his funeral.

15-26 He gives instructions for his funeral and the disposal of his bones.

27-30 He dictates the wording for his epitaph: Lygdamus died of love for Neaera who was stolen from him.

1-8 The opening of the poem is rich in literary reminiscences from earlier Augustan poetry. It takes the form of a priamel in which the harshness of others (either active, in parting lovers, **1-2**, or passive, in enduring separation, **3-4**) is contrasted with the poet's own sensitivity and desire for death if he is separated from his wife (**5-8**). The theme of the 'first inventor' (πρῶτος εὑρετής), with which it begins, contains clear echoes of Tib. 1.10.1-2 *quis fuit horrendos primus qui protulit enses? / quam ferus et uere ferreus ille fuit*, while the syntactical structure of the opening of the priamel *qui primus ... / eripuit ... ferreus ille fuit. / durus et ille fuit, qui ... / ... potuit* resembles Virg. *Georg.* 2.490-493 *felix, qui potuit rerum cognoscere causas / ... / ... / fortunatus et ille, deos qui nouit agrestes*. On the form and history of the literary priamel, literally 'preamble', which contrasts the poet's own preferences with a list of rejected possibilities, see Race (1982); Williams (1968) 66, N-H on Hor. *Carm*.1.1 (headnote pp. 1-3), N-A 148 and Maltby (2002) 117. It has a long literary history stretching back to Homer *Il.* 9.378-391 and occurs frequently in the Roman elegists (Tib. 1.1.1-6; Prop. 1.12.15-20; Ov. *Ars* 3.121-122). On the theme of the 'first inventor', which goes back to the invention of the arts by Prometheus in [Aesch.] *Prom.* 7-8, see further Kleingünther (1933), N-H on Hor. *Carm.* 1.3.12, Fedeli on Prop. 1.17.13-14, Mynors on Virg. *Georg.* 4.281ff. and N-A 148-149. It is particularly common in Tib., occurring at 1.4.59-60, 1.7.19f., 29f., 1.10.1f., 45f., 2.1.37f., and usually involves the invention of some unwanted or pernicious object (e.g. the sword) or action (e.g. sailing).

1-2 The couplet seems to be influenced by Prop. 2.8.1 *eripitur nobis iam pridem cara puella*, in which the poet's thoughts turn to death in his sorrow at the snatching away of his mistress by a rival; see **headnote** above and **4n.** below. The verb *eripio*, repeated at **4** *erepta coniuge* (cf. Prop. 2.8.29 *abrepta ... coniuge*) and **30** *coniugis ereptae*, is found from Plautus on in the sense of 'snatching' or 'stealing' a girl from a rival, e.g. Plaut. *Merc.* 972-973 *haud aequom ... / adulescenti amanti amicam eripere, Mil.* 814 *eripiam ego hodie concubinam militi*. A more immediate model for our author here as *Lygd.* is perhaps Catullus, who uses the verb of rivals 'stealing' Lesbia from him at 77.4, 5 and 82.3; see further examples at **4n.** below.

Qui primus: as a verse opening also at Lucr. 3.2; Hor. *Carm.* 4.4.41, *Serm.* 1.6.83; Ov. *Her.* 13.94; Manil. 4.207; Colum. *Rust.* 10.435 and cf. especially, in a similar context of castigating an offender against love, Ov. *Am.* 2.3.3-4 *qui primus pueris genitalia membra recidit, / uulnera quae fecit, debuit ipse pati*.

primus: this word often acts as a marker for etymological word-play in Tibullus, see Cairns (1996) 14-24. Its occurrence at Tib. 1.10.1 hints at plays there on *ferrum* from *ferre* and *ferus* see Maltby (2002) 341 on Tib 1.10.1-6 and *LALE* 230 s.v. *ferus* and cf. *Lygd.* **4.74** with **n.** below. Here the *ferrum / ferre* connection is again hinted at in the close proximity of *ferreus* (**2**) and *ferre* (**3**) and shows the author's awareness of the etymological content of his model. The masculine form *primus* need not suggest that the person who steals the girl or the boy is a man, but may simply be a generalising masculine.

caram: recalls *caram* at **1.25** and so links the general statement here more closely with Lygdamus' own position. On the connotations of the adj. see **1.6n.** On its use in the context of stealing a beloved mistress cf. Prop. 2.8.1 (quoted above).

iuueni ... puellae: used commonly in elegy to refer to the male and female beloved respectively, see Pichon 180 (on *iuuenis*) and 245 (on *puella*), and cf. Tib. 2.1.76 *ad iuuenem tenebris sola puella uenit*.

carumque: for the use of *-que* introducing an alternative in the sense of *-ue* (disjunctive instead of copulative) see Löfstedt (1911) 200-201. This is mainly a late and colloquial feature, but examples are found in Classical verse, cf. Lucr. 5.985 *spumigeri suis aduentu ualidique leonis*. For the repetition *caram ... carumque* see Wills (1996) 277-278

ferreus ille fuit: same pentameter ending at Tib. 1.10.2. The same phrase opens a hexameter at Tib. 1.2.67. For *ferreus* denoting insensitivity in elegy, see Pichon 146 and cf. Tib. 2.3.2; Prop. 2.8.12 (of the mistress); Ov. *Am.* 1.6.27 (with McKeown II 139), 2.19.4. N-A ad loc. quotes as a Greek precursor Aristoph. *Acharn.* 491 σιδηροῦς τ' ἀνήρ (a man of iron); cf. also metaphorical uses at [Aesch.] *Prom.* 242 σιδηρόφρων (iron-minded); Eur. *Med.* 1279-1280 σίδαρος (of iron); Enn. *Trag.* 109 Jocelyn *quasi aut ferrum aut lapis*.

fuit: gnomic perfect, see **3-4n.** below.

3 durus: frequent in elegy in the sense of 'hard', 'unfeeling', 'insensitive to love', see Maltby (2002) 142 on Tib. 1.1.56; Leonotti (1990), Pichon 136. It is particularly common in *Lygd.*, cf. **4.76, 92; 5.22; 6.7**.

tantum ferre dolorem: the same hexameter ending occurs at Val. Fl. 1.766 *potui quae tantum ferre dolorem;* see Zissos ad loc. and Nordera [(1969) 56] on the influence on this line of Virg. *Aen.* 4.419-420 (Dido to

Anna) *hunc ego si potui tantum sperare dolorem / et perferre, soror, potero*. However, given the frequency of *ferre* (or compound) with *dolorem* (*-es*) at the verse end, e.g. Lucr. 3.990; Virg. *Aen*. 6.464 (Aeneas to Dido in the underworld) *hunc tantum tibi me discessu ferre dolorem*, 9.426 *perferre dolorem*; Maxim. 3.39 *ferre dolores*, the similarity with Val. Fl. here could be simple coincidence. For the sense cf. Ov. *Met*. 14.716-717 *non tulit impatiens longi tormenta doloris / Iphis*, where the sorrows of love turn Iphis to suicide. The adjective *impatiens* there corresponds to *non haec patientia* in **5** here. For *dolor* with reference to the anguish of love, particularly in contexts of separation from the beloved, see Pichon 132-133 and for its association with Lygdamus' name see Gen. Intro., section 3.1.

ferre: on the possible etymological play with *ferreus* **2**, see **1-2n.** *primus* above.

3-4 fuit ... / ... potuit: gnomic perfects in a statement of general principle, as with *fuit* **2** above.

4 uiuere et: on the rare elision at the end of the inf. see Smith on Tib. 1.2.72 and Fulkerson (2017) 97. For the theme of living without the object of one's love cf. Plaut. *Pseud*. 94-95 *profecto nullo pacto possum uiuere / si illa a me abalienatur atque abducitur*; Cat. 68.84 (of Laodamia after the loss of Protesilaus) *posset ut abrupto uiuere coniugio*.

erepta coniuge: echoes *coniunx* at **1.26** and **27** above, and looks forward to *CONIVGIS EREPTAE* in the epitaph with which this elegy ends (**30**); the phrase could be based on the description of Orestes' reaction to the loss of his wife Hermione at Virg. *Aen*. 3.330-331 *ereptae magno flammatus amore / coniugis*; cf. also Cat. 68.106-107 (Laodamia's loss of Protesilaus) *ereptum est uita dulcius atque anima / coniugium*; Prop. 2.8.29 (loss of Briseis) *ille etiam abrepta desertus coniuge Achilles*; Virg. *Aen*. 2.738 *erepta Creusa*, 9.138 (Turnus' loss of Lavinia) *coniuge praerepta*; Ov. *Met*. 5.10 (Phineus of Andromeda) *en adsum praereptae coniugis ultor*, *Met*. 7.688-689 (Cephalus of Procris – an important intertext for the whole book, see Gen. Intro., section 1.3) *tactus ... dolore / coniugis amissae*. A close intertext is Prop. 2.8, which begins with the stealing of his *puella* 2.8.1 *eripitur nobis iam pridem cara puella* and, like **7-8** here, abruptly introduces the theme of his own death at 2.8.17-18 *sic igitur prima moriere aetate, Properti; / sed morere: interitu gaudeat illa tuo*; see **headnote** above. On the implications of *coniuge* for the married relationship between Lygdamus and Neaera and possible influence of

Ovid's exile poetry, with its addresses to his wife see **1.26n**. above. On *erepta* see **30n**. below. For the resumption of *eripuit* **2** in *erepta* **4** see Wills (1996) 315 and cf. **8.10n**. below.

5-8 Each couplet in this second part of the priamel contrasts Lygdamus' reaction at having his love snatched away with that of the heartless man in **3-4**. So *durus* in **3** is contrasted with *non ... firmus ... non ... patientia* in **5** and *ferre dolorem* in **3** with *frangit ... dolor* in **6**; similarly *uiuere ... potui* in **4** is contrasted with *uitae ... taedia* in **7-8**.

5-6 The two short clauses with anaphora of *non* and the verb 'to be' suppressed, followed by the proverbial statement *frangit ... dolor* lend the couplet an elevated tone, which is added to by the archaic use of *ingenium* in the sense of 'character' and the high-style, poetic *cor*. For *ingenium* and *firmus* in a similar context of firmness of resolve, cf. Plaut. *Asin.* 944 *nec quisquam est tam ingenio duro nec tam firmo pectore*.

non ego: a characteristic opening for the figure of *auersio*, favoured by our author as *Lygd.*, cf. **5.7**, **6.59** and see the full discussion below at **5.7-14n.**

firmus: describing a lover's resolve, cf. Ov. *Ars* 2.340 *si bene nutrieris, tempore firmus erit* (a new lover must be spoilt, but eventually he will gain confidence), *Rem.* 697 *qui silet est firmus* in a context of *discidium* from the mistress, see further Pichon 149.

patientia: 'endurance', for its use in elegy see Pichon 227. In the sense of putting up with a wife's sexual misdemeanours the term was recognised in law (cf. *Dig.* 14.4.1.3, 48.5.30 *Praef.* 4; Sen. *Contr.* 2.7.1 and see McKeown III 431-433 on *Am.* 2.19.57 and 59-60). The word occurs here only in the *Lygd.* group and is rare in poetry: Horace (2), Ovid (9), Lucan (6), Sil. (1), and Mart. (1). For the combination with *ingenium* cf. Ov. *Trist.* 5.12.31 *contudit ingenium patientia longa malorum*.

nostro / ingenio: dative, with *est* understood after *patientia* 'there is not this patience in my character'.

frangit fortia corda dolor: a *sententia* or proverbial expression. These were common in Latin of all periods, e.g. Ter. *Phorm.* 203 *fortis fortuna adiuuat*, Virg. *Ecl*.10.69 *omnia uincit amor*, but become more frequent from Ovid onwards.

fortia corda: the collocation occurs first in Virg. *Aen.* 5.729 *lectos iuuenes, fortissima corda*; cf. Ov. *Trist.* 3.3.57 *extenua forti mala corde ferendo*; Val. Fl. 1.315-316 *fortia languent / corda partum*; Sil. 10.518-519 *cui fortia ... / ... caluerunt corda*.

7 nec mihi uera loqui pudor est: a reminiscence of Tib. 1.6.31 *nec me iam dicere uera pudebit*. For *pudor est* + inf. as a poetic equivalent of *pudet* cf. Prop. 3.13.20 *pudor est non licuisse mori* and see Shackleton Bailey (1956) 304; the usage is characteristically Ovidian (*Ars* 3.203, *Rem.* 359 *multa ... pudor est mihi dicere*, *Met.* 14.18, *Fast.* 1.205, 5.532 *pudor est ulteriora loqui*). Sulpicia discusses the *pudor* involved in revealing her affair in the opening poem of *Sulpicia* group, namely **13.1**, no such shame prevents Lygdamus from revealing his suicidal feelings, or the possible cause of his future death (see **27-28n.** below). Such free speech is the sign of a free man, whereas denial of free speech was the sign of a slave; see Woodman (2014) 81 on Tac. *Agr.* 2.2. At the end of the collection **19.20** the poet sees the dangers of his *garrula lingua* and accepts his slavery to love **21-24**. For the centrality of themes of revealing and hiding to the whole collection see Prolegomena p. 83 and Gen. Intro., pp. 96, 113, 114 above and *Sulpicia Cycle* **8.8n.** *furtim subsequiturque* below. On elegiac *pudor* see further Pichon 242-244. For *uera dicere* etc. in the context of revealing unwelcome truths, cf. Cephalus' words at Ov. *Met.* 7.704-705 (admitting he prefers the love of Procris to that of the goddess Aurora) *liceat mihi uera referre / pace deae* and see Gen. Intro., section 1.3.

7-8 uitaeque ... / ... taedia: the phrase *taedia uitae* is often used in verse in contexts of suicide, as here. So at Ov. *Met.* 10.482, Myrrha, ashamed at her incestuous relationship with her father, is described as *inter mortisque metus et taedia uitae* and at *Met.*10.624-625 Atalanta describes Hippolytus' wish to race against her as effectively suicidal *intereat, quoniam tot caede procorum / admonitus non est agiturque in taedia uitae*; further examples can be found at *Pont.* 1.9.31, *Nux* 159; Stat. *Theb.* 7.464; *CLE* 1430.3. The word *taedia* occurs first in verse at Virg. *Georg.* 4.332 and, as at Tib. 1.4.16 and Prop. 1.2.32, is the only form usable in dactylic verse; see McKeown III 419 on *Am.* 2.19.25-26. In prose *taedium uitae* is used in the same suicidal context as here, e.g. Nep. ex. fr. 2 P.; Liv. fr. 60; Sen. *Suas.* 6.17; Plin. *Nat.* 7.186.

uitaeque ... / tot mala perpessae: cf. Sil. 2.620 *rabie cladum perpessaeque ultima uitae*. For *mala* of sufferings in love in elegy, see Pichon 195 and cf. Tib. 2.6.19 in a similarly suicidal context: *iam mala finissem leto*. For *tot mala* in this context at the line opening cf. Prop. 3.15.20; Ov. *Trist.*

3.11.59. The verb *perpetior* is not found elsewhere in the *Corp. Tib.*, but cf. Prop. 2.26B.35 *omnia perpetiar*; Ov. *Am.* 1.13.25 *omnia perpeterer*, *Her.* 20.83 *omnia perpetiar* in all of which the emphasis is on the lover's excessive suffering.

9-30 For the elegiac predecessors to the theme of the poet's own funeral and for its overall function in the poem, see the **headnote** above. Our poet takes from Tib. 1.1.59-68 the weeping of the mistress and her dishevelled hair and from Tib. 1.3.5-10 the detailed description of the collection of the bones, the *ossilegium*, and the presence of other female relatives, the poet's mother and sister in Tibullus' case, and his mother-in-law in the case of Lygdamus. From Propertius 2.13.17-36 come the introductory particles *ergo cum* (**9**), cf. Prop. 2.13.17 *quandocumque igitur*, the detailed instructions for the burial (**11-22**), cf. Prop. 2.13.19-32, and the final focus on the tomb and its epitaph (**23-30**), cf. Prop. 2.13.33-36. The epitaph had also occurred earlier in Tib. 1.3.55-56. On a different treatment of the theme of the poet's death in reaction to the loss of his mistress cf. Prop. 2.8.17-28, discussed in the **headnote** above.

9 ergo: the causal connection is unclear. If Lygdamus' suicide was caused by his separation from Neaera, why should she be present at his funeral? Possibly Lygdamus is suggesting that the separation was against her will, or possibly he thinks that his suicide will bring about a change of mind. The particle *ergo* is not found in genuine Tibullus, but occurs frequently in Ovid (58). *Lygd.*'s three examples are all in initial position in the hexameter (also at **4.75**, **6.51**) and all have long *-o*, which is the norm in the elegiac poets (except for Ov. *Her.* 5.59 and *Trist.* 1.1.87). The shortening of the final *-o* is characteristic of post-Ovidian poetry; the long *-o* in *Lygd.* cannot be used as an argument for his chronology, but probably just reflects the influence of Ovid. J. B. Hall suggests reading *o ego* as a means of avoiding the problems posed by the causal connective *ergo*.

cum tenuem fuero mutatus in umbram: cf. Calvus fr. 15 (Courtney = 27 Hollis) *cum iam fulua cinis fuero*. For *mutatus* in this context, cf. Ov. *Trist.* 3.3.83 *quamuis in cinerem corpus mutauerit ignis*. The phrase *mutatus in umbram* here looks forward to *uersus in ossa* at **26** below and forms part of the theme of change which runs through the collection, cf. *mutare figuras* at *Laud Mess.* **7.63** and *mutate figura* at **7.206** and see further **26n.** below.

tenuem ... in umbram: for *tenuis umbra* of the spirits of the dead, cf. Virg. *Georg.* 4.472 *umbrae ibant tenues*. For *tenuis* with *umbra* in other senses, see Prop. 2.12.20, 3.9.29; Ov. *Ars* 3.723; *Met.* 6.62. For the possible metapoetic significance of *tenuis* here with reference to an 'elegiac' ghost, see *Lygd.* **1.11n.**

fuero mutatus: for this form of the future perfect, cf. Ov. *Her.* 11.120 *nec mater fuero dicta*, and, closer to the present context, *Ibis* 141 *tum quoque, cum fuero uacuas delapsa in auras*.

10 candidaque ossa ... nigra fauilla: such colour contrasts are a characteristic of the *Lygd.* poems; see **1.9n.** above. For the possibility that *candidus* here may refer to Lygdamus' name (derived from *lygdos,* a white Parian marble) see Luck (1959) 95, Holzberg (1998) 180 and Gen. Intro., section 3.1, just as Tibullus plays on his own *nomen* Albius at 1.3.93-94 and 1.7.58 see Booth and Maltby (2005) 124-128 and *Lygd.* **3.3n.** below. The adjective is applied to his bones at **18** below (there contrasted with *nigra ... ueste*), and occurs in all five times in his poems (**2.10, 18, 4.34, 6.1, 30**). The term *fauilla* refers to the light, sooty ashes of the body, as opposed to the *cineres* or burnt remains of the rest of the pyre; see *ThLL* 6(1).380.37-43 and cf. Plin. *Nat.* 19.19 *corporis fauillam ab reliquo separant cinere*. For *nigra fauilla* cf. Ov. *Met.* 6.325, *Fast.* 2.523; Colum. *Rust.* 10.354. For the reference to *ossa* by poets speaking their own burial (as at **17** and **26** below and *Laud. Mess.* **7.204**), cf. Virg. *Ecl.* 10.33 (of Gallus); Tib. 1.3.6, 1.3.54; Prop. 1.17.22; Ov. *Trist.* 3.3.76.

supra: the adverb is the reading of A+ and seems to offer acceptable sense here: the settling black ash covers the bones 'from above'. As the form is rare in poetry, (though cf. *Laud. Mess.* **7.66** *seu supra terras Phoebus seu curreret infra*), most editors print *super* attested in B and G and take it in tmesis with *teget*. The form *supertegere* is found in Colum. *Rust.* 9.14.14 and Apul. *Met.* 11.14, though not in tmesis.

11-14 The description of the poet's own funeral, as well as recalling the passages from Tibullus and Propertius mentioned in the **headnote** and **9-30n.** above, also brings to mind the opening of Ovid's elegy on Tibullus' death at *Am.* 3.9.1-4 *Memnona si mater, mater plorauit Achillem, / et tangunt magnas tristia fata deas, / flebilis indignos, Elegia, solue capillos. / a, nimis ex uero nunc tibi nomen erit* and serves as an indication of our author's poetic allegiance to Tibullus. Just as the name Lygdamus (see **29** below) links him with Propertius and the wording of his birth date at **5.17-18** connects him with Ovid (see Gen. Intro., section 3.1), so here the poet expresses his proximity to Tibullus. In this way our author highlights his role as the successor to the three great elegists of the past.

11-12 ante meum ... / ... ante meum ... rogum: Tränkle 85 retains this reading of the MSS, but suspects the repetition of *ante meum* before the noun *rogum* and the use of *ante* in two senses, directional in the first instance and locative in the second. He suggests replacing its first occurrence by *ante urbem* on the grounds that burials in Rome had to take place outside the city limits; cf. Cic. *Leg.* 2.35.58 *hominem mortuum in urbe ne sepelito neue urito* and see Toynbee (1971) 48-49. The phrase *ante urbem* occurs in this context at Virg. *Aen.* 3.302 and Ov. *Met.* 13.687. The advantage of the text as it stands, however, is, as N-A 165 points out, that it reproduces through its tortuous syntax the charged emotion of its content.

ueniat ... / ... fleat: the first in a series of optative subjunctives, running from *ueniat* here down to *uelim* in **26** and expressing Lygdamus' wishes for his funeral.

longos incompta capillos: cf. Tib. 1.3.8 (of his sister) *et fleat effusis ante sepulcra comis*. Unbound hair was a sign of grief at funerals, cf. Tib. 1.1.67-68 *solutis / crinibus*, and of women's grief in general, cf. Prop. 3.6.9 *sic illam incomptis uidisti flere capillis*? (Prop. asks Lygdamus if this was how Cynthia reacted to his break with her), Prop. 1.15.11 (Calypso's sadness at the departure of Ulysses); Ov. *Fast.* 3.470 (Ariadne complaining of Bacchus' infidelity). For *longos ... capillos* as an accusative of respect, cf. Delia's appearance to Tibullus at Tib. 1.3.91 *longos turbata capillos* and for *incompta* in this context, cf. Ov. *Met.* 4.261 *nudis incompta capillis* of the grief of the nymph Clytie. The author in the *Lygdamus* poems uses three words for hair: *crinis* of Apollo's hair in **4.27** is thought to be the most elevated (see McKeown II 19 on Ov. *Am.* 1.1.11-12, and Fedeli on Prop. 1.2.1), but it is combined there with *coma* **4.28**, which is also found at **1.10** and **6.64**; *capillus* is found here of Neaera's hair and at **5.15** of Lygdamus' own hair. Full statistics on the distribution of *capillus, coma* and *crinis* in *ThLL* 3.314.25, Axelson (1945) 51, Bréguet (1946) 197-207, and Thomas (2011) 202 on Hor. *Carm.* 4.9.13-14 for their use in Horace and Virgil.

fleat ante meum ... rogum: recalls the description by Tibullus of the funeral of a faithful mistress at Tib. 2.4.46 *ardentem flebitur ante rogum*. The term *rogus* refers strictly to the burning funeral pyre, cf. Serv. *Aen.*

11.185 '*pyra*' *est lignorum congeries;* '*rogus*' *cum iam ardere coeperit;* '*bustum*' *uero iam exustum uocatur.*

maesta: the adjective is more poetic than *tristis* according to *ThLL* 8.46.4-29. and McKeown II 100 on Ov. *Am.*1.4.61. It refers not only to grief (picked up by *maereat* in **14**) but also to the dishevelled appearance occasioned by grief *ThLL* 8.49.35-42.

13 sed ueniat: picks up and repeats *ante meum ueniat* ... / ... *rogum* from **11-12**. For *sed* introducing new or explanatory material, with repetition of the idea elaborated on, cf. Tib. 2.5.5-7 *ipse* ... / ...*ueni,* / *sed nitidus pulcherque ueni* and see K-S II 2.77.

matris comitata dolore: the metonymy of abstract for concrete 'accompanied by her mother's grief' for 'accompanied by her grieving mother' is relatively common in poetry, cf. Tib. 1.2.11 *mala si qua tibi dixit dementia nostra* ('my madness' for 'I being mad'); Prop. 1.3.46 *illa fuit lacrimis ultima cura meis* ('for my tears' for 'for me crying'), *Lygd.* **3.8** *inque tuo caderet nostra senecta sinu* ('my old age' for 'I as an old man'). Particularly close to the present line is Stat. *Ach.* 2.23 *lacrimis comitata sororum*. The presence of female relatives at the funeral in addition to the beloved is taken from Tib. 1.3.5-9 (sister, and mother), but whereas Tib. speaks of his own mother, Lygdamus speaks of the mother of Neaera. He has a Tibullan precedent for flattering the mother of the beloved in the description of Delia's mother as *aurea* ... *anus* at Tib.1.6.58, but here the mention is given added significance in his wish to stress the nature of his relationship with Neaera as one of marriage (see **4.93n.**), a point emphasised in **14** by the use of the terms *genero* and *uiro*.

14 maereat ... genero, maereat ... uiro: an emphatic statement of the way Lygdamus conceives of his married relationship with Neaera. For parallel half-lines of this kind as a frequent feature of the style of Ovid and Propertius, e.g. Prop. 1.12.20 *Cynthia prima fuit; Cynthia finis erit*, see Wills (1996) 414-415. The normal construction of *maereo* is with an accusative object, e.g. Hor. *Epod.* 15.23 *translatos alio maerebis amores*. The intransitive use with causal ablative is found in prose from Cicero (e.g. *Tusc.* 1.30 *nemo maeret suo incommodo*) and in verse from Virg. *Georg.* 3.518 *maerentem ... fraterna morte iuuencum*, cf. Ov. *Trist.* 1.3.23 *femina uirque meo, pueri quoque, funere maerent*. Elsewhere the ablative always denotes a thing rather than a person, as here, and even in the transitive use a personal object is rare, though cf. Hor. *Epist.* 1.14.7

fratrem maerentis. Explanations of *genero* and *uiro* as datives must be rejected.

15-25 These lines contain a most detailed description of the ceremony of *ossilegium* in which the bones of the corpse are collected after cremation, sprinkled with wine, dried and placed with sweet-smelling spices in an urn, which is then set in a sepulchre. A series of temporal particles make the chronological sequence clear: *ante* in **15** describes the initial preparatory prayer to propitiate the spirit of the dead before picking up the bones and *ante* in **16** the washing of the hands prior to the ceremony. In **19** *primum* marks the beginning of the ceremony itself, the collection and sprinkling of the bones with wine, followed in **20** (*mox*) by the pouring of milk. After this (*post haec*) **21** the bones are dried in linen cloth and **22** placed in a marble urn, to which spices **23-24** are added, along with the tears of the mourners **25**.

15 praefatae ante: refers to a preparatory prayer to secure the good-will of the spirit of the departed before touching the bones. A good parallel is to be found at Virg. *Aen*. 11.301 *praefatus diuos solio rex infit ab alto*. This prayer, which takes place after the cremation of the body, is distinct from the *conclamatio*, or calling the dead man by name, which took place immediately after the death to ensure he is really dead, for which cf. Virg. *Aen*. 3.303-304 *Andromache manisque uocabat / Hectoreum ad tumulum* and see Toynbee (1971) 44. The pleonastic expression *praefatae ante* is characteristic of our author in the *Lygdamus* poems, cf. **4.47-48** *aeuique futuri / euentura,* **4.93** *longe ante alias omnes mitissima,* **5.27** *uano nequiquam.*

manes animamque recentem: the reading *recentem* is a conjecture for the meaningless *rogatae* of the manuscripts. With reference to the spirit of a man who had died young the adjective is found in Ov. *Met*. 8.488-489 *uos modo fraterni manes animaeque recentes / officium sentite meum*, who may have been our poet's model here. The terms *manes* and *anima* are virtually synonymous and, in addition to *Met*. 8.488, occur in conjunction at Hor. *Serm*. 1.8.28-29 *ut inde / manis elicerent, animas responsa daturas* and Sil. 13.395 *excire ... manes animasque suorum.*

16 perfusaeque pias ante liquore manus: ritual purification by water was necessary as a preparation for any religious ceremony, cf. Tib. 2.1.13-14 *casta placent superis: pura cum ueste uenite / et manibus puris sumite fontis aquam*; Ov. *Fast*. 5.435 *manus puras fontana perluit unda*. The collocation *pia manus* is found in Virg. *Aen*. 3.42, 4.517; Val. Fl. 2.600

and elsewhere in poetry. The adjective here is proleptic; the hands are made pious through the ritual washing, or possibly, so N-A 169 ad loc., through fulfilling an obligation of piety by picking up the bones.

17-18 The couplet describes the ritual act of *ossilegium*, the gathering of the bones after cremation; cf. Tib. 1.3.5-6 *mater / quae legat in maestos ossa perusta sinus*; Prop. 2.24B.50 *uix uenit extremo qui legat ossa die*, 4.1B.127 *ossaque legisti non illa aetate legenda*. On this ancient rite, both Greek and Roman, see Blümner (1911) 487, *RE* 18.2 (1942) 1599-1602 (Rohde), Vahlen (1908) II 491-497, Toynbee (1971) 50.

17 pars quae sola mei superabit corporis, ossa: the poet here uses in a more down-to-earth context a wording applied earlier to poetic fame: Hor. *Carm.* 3.30.6-7 *non omnis moriar, multaque pars mei / uitabit Libitinam*, Ov. *Am.* 1.15.41-42 *ergo etiam cum me supremus adederit ignis, / uiuam, parsque mei multa superstes erit.*, *Met.* 15.875-876 *parte tamen meliore mei super alta perennis / astra ferar*. For *corpus* referring metaphorically to a body of work see **7.176n.** and cf. **10.20n.** Our author can hardly be unaware of these earlier literary contexts and so would seem to suggest that in his case only Lygdamus' bones, not his poetry, will survive. N-A 171 may be correct in suggesting that the author is influenced by the language of epitaphs, e.g. *CLE* 14.2 *quoius corporis reliquiae quod superant sunt in hoc panario*, 1247.1 *quod superest homini, requiescunt dulciter ossa*. For the inversion *pars quae* for *quae pars* see K-S II 2.291-292.

17-18 ossa / incinctae: a rare example of hiatus over the line break.

18 incinctae nigra ... ueste: 'wrapped in black'. For the use of black clothing at funerals cf. Prop. 4.7.27-28 *denique quis nostro curuum te funere uidit? / atram quis lacrimis incaluisse togam?*; Ov. *Met.* 8.448 *auratis mutauit uestibus atras* and see Woodman and Martin (1996) 86 on Tac. *Ann.* 3.2.2 *atrata plebes*. There need be no suggestion in *incinctus* that the robes are untied or unfastened, as suggested by Postgate (1922) 127, Némethy 41 and others. Although it was common for religious ceremonies to require nothing bound or tied, there is no evidence that this applied to the *ossilegium*.

nigra candida: for the black/white colour contrast, perhaps hinting at Lygdamus' name, see **10n.** above.

legant: as with *spargant* in **19**, this is a necessary correction by Muretus for the forms *legent* and *spargent* transmitted by the manuscripts.

19 annoso spargant collecta Lyaeo: the sprinkling of wine on the ashes or collected bones is commonly referred to in Roman poetry, cf. Virg. *Aen.* 6.227 *reliquias uino ... lauere*; Prop. 4.7.34 *fracto busta piare cado* and see Toynbee (1971) 50. The metonymic use of *Lyaeus* (lit. 'the liberator', a cult title of Dionysus/Bacchus) is attested from Hor. *Epod.* 9.37-38 *curam metumque Caesaris rerum iuuat / dulci Lyaeo soluere*, with its play in *soluere* on the meaning of *Lyaeus*. The title *Lyaeus* occurs first in Latin at Enn. *Trag.* 120-121 Jocelyn *his erat in ore Bromius, his Bacchus pater, / illis Lyaeus* and is found here only in the *Corp. Tib.* For the many names of Bacchus/Dionysus cf. Ov. *Met.* 4.11-17 *turaque dant Bacchumque uocant Bromiumque Lyaeumque / ignigenamque satumque iterum solumque bimatrem; / additur his Nyseus indetonsusque Thyoneus / et cum Lenaeo genialis consitor uuae / Nycteliusque Eleleusque parens et Iacchus et Euhan, / et quae praeterea per Graias plurima gentes nomina, / Liber, habes.* The use of the adjective *annosus* of old vintage wine occurs first in Ov. *Ars* 2.418 *annoso ... mero* (a phrase borrowed by our author at **6.58**).

collecta: refers back to *legant* (**18**), a rhetorical feature known as *deriuatio*. Normally a compound verb is picked up by its simple form, e.g. Ov. *Met.* 9.504 *componar, positae*, but in *collecta* here the prefix preserves its full meaning of 'gathered together'. A similar repetition of *ponere* (**22**) in *componi* (**26**) occurs below.

20 niueo ... lacte: the phrase *niueum lac* appears first in Virg. *Ecl.* 2.20, with later examples at Ov. *Fast.* 4.151 Sen. *Oed.* 495 and *Lygd.* **5.34**. This is the only place in which reference is made to the use of milk in the *ossilegium*. At Stat. *Theb.* 6.211-212 *spumantesque mero paterae uerguntur et atri / sanguinis et rapti gratissima cymbia lactis*, the wine, blood and milk are poured as an offering onto the pyre, probably reflecting Greek funeral practice.

21-22 After the bones have been sprinkled with wine and milk they are dried before being placed in the urn. This is our only reference to such a practice.

carbaseis ... uelis: Lygdamus wishes his bones to be dried with the finest linen cloth. *carbasus* is a fine type of linen (see Serv. *Aen.* 3.357). *uelis* here is a reading found in some later manuscripts in place of *uentis* of A+. This use of *uela* in the sense of cloth is very rare, cf. Ov. *Am.* 1.14.6 (with McKeown II 366 ad loc.), Plin. *Nat.* 35.150 and *Ciris* 35 (where there is a play on the sense 'sail') and see *OLD uelum* 5. The collocation *carbasea uela*, however, occurs at Cic. *Verr.* 2.5.30, 80 and Marcian. *Dig.* 39.4.16.7, passages which support the reading here. Defenders of the majority reading *uentis* rely on the phrase *uentus textilis* 'woven wind' at Petr. 55.6.15 (which occurs also, according to N-A 177, at Publ. Syr. 17), but this seems to be a Petronian invention, and there is no evidence that *uentus* has any currency in the sense of cloth.

umorem tollere: cf. Lucr. 6.506-507 *umor / tollitur in nubis*, 627-628 *tollere nubes / umorem*.

in marmorea ... domo: the reference is to a marble burial urn. The use of *domus* of a burial urn is found in literature only here, but at [Ov.] *Epiced. Drusi* 73-74 *claudite iam Parcae*, ... / *sepulcrum*; *plus iusto iam domus ista patet* it is used of a sepulchre. It occurs more commonly in these contexts on grave inscriptions of the late Republic and early Empire, e.g. *CLE* 55.1-2 *heus oculo errante quei aspicis leti / domus, morare gressum*, especially in the phrase *domus aeterna* (e.g. *CLE* 434.15), a usage reflected in Petr. 71.7 *ualde ... falsum est uiuo quidem domos cultas esse, non curari eas, ubi diutius nobis habitandum est*. Cf. Sen. *Epist.* 60.4 quoted in **3.3n** below. On the possible significance of *marmoreus* in *Lygd.* and on the connection between his marble tomb here and his marble dwelling in the following poem see **3.3n.** and Gen. Intro., sections 2.2.1 and 3.1.

ponere: see **26n.** *componi* below.

23-25 For the mixing of expensive perfumes and aromatic spices with the bones before the closing of the tomb cf. Tib. 1.3.7 *soror, Assyrios cineri quae dedat odores* and Ov. *Trist.* 3.3.69 (*ossa*) *cum foliis et amomi puluere misce*. For the double offering of spices and tears, cf. Ov. *Fast.* 3.561 *mixta ... lacrimis unguenta, Pont.* 1.9.53 *diluit et lacrimis maerens unguenta profusis*. The syntax of the passage is harsh as both *merces* and *lacrimae* are the subject of the same verb *fundantur*, and the two different local adverbs *illic* and *eodem* have the same reference (*in marmorea domo*). In the long periphrasis describing the provenance of the spices both *Panchaia* and *Assyria* are given the same epithet, *diues*.

23 mittit: for this poetic use in the sense of 'export', cf. Virg. *Georg.* 1.56-57 *nonne uides, croceos ut Tmolus odores / India mittit ebur, molles sua tura Sabaei*; Tib. 2.2.3-4 *odores / quos tener e terra diuite mittit Arabs*; Hor. *Epod.* 5.22; Prop. 3.13.5; Ov. *Ars* 3.213.

diues Panchaia: a mythical spice-bearing Island in the Indian Ocean, where Euhemerus (whose *Historia Sacra* had been translated into Latin by

Ennius) places his Utopia (*FGrHist* 63). It is mentioned as a source of incense in Latin by Lucr. 2.417 *ara ... Panchaeos exhalat ... odores*; Virg. *Georg.* 2.139 *turiferis Panchaia pinguis harenis*, 4.379 *Panchaeis adolescunt ignibus arae*; Ov. *Met.* 10.307-309 *sit diues amomo / ... / ... Panchaia tellus*; *Culex* 87 *Panchaica tura* and in later authors. Miller [(1969) 103] identifies Virgil's *Panchaia* with the real island of Socotra, situated at the end of the Horn of Africa, which produced most of the incense used in Rome. The adjective *diues* is applied to *Panchaia* at *Met.* 10.307-309, quoted above.

24 Eoique Arabes: 'Arabs of the East', cf. Virg. *Georg.* 2.115 *Eoasque domos Arabum*. The adjective *Eoos*, derived from the Greek word for 'dawn', simply means 'eastern' (as seen from Rome) and does not specify any particular area of Arabia, cf. *Sulpicia Cycle* **8.20** below. The main spice exported from Arabia, especially from the Roman province of *Arabia Felix*, was incense; cf. Plaut. *Truc.* 539-540 *ex Arabia tibi / attuli tus*; Tib. 2.2.3-4 quoted above; Ov. *Fast.* 4.569 *turilegos Arabas*; Stat. *Theb.* 1.263 *turis Eoi*; Mart. 3.65.6 *Eoo ture*; *Sulpicia Cycle* **8.18n**. below, and see Plin. *Nat.* 12.51 and Miller (1969) 101-105.

diues et Assyria: Syria was rich in aromatic spices, cf. Cat. 68.144 *Assyrio ... odore*; Virg. *Ecl.* 4.25 *Assyrium uulgo nascetur amomum*; Hor. *Carm.* 2.11.16-17 *Assyriaque nardo / ... uncti*; Mart. 8.77.3 *Assyrio ... amomo*. For *diues* of a people or region rich in spices, cf. *diues Arabs* at *Sulpicia Cycle* **8.18** below. Roman poets preferred the adjective *Assyrius* to *Syrius*, but the noun *Assyria* (unlike the noun *Syria*) is found only here in verse. In prose it occurs first (and frequently) in the Elder Pliny, e.g. *Nat.* 5.66, 6.121 etc.

diues: the epithet has come under suspicion, as it repeats *diues* applied to *Panchaia* in **23**. Two more recent manuscripts suggest *pinguis* here, an epithet appropriate for a rich spice producing region and applied to *Panchaia* at Virg. *Georg.* 2.139 quoted on **23n**. above. In fact our author does not avoid repetitions of this kind, cf. **3.33-34** *faueas ... / et faueas*, and it is probably better to retain the reading of A+.

25 nostri memores lacrimae: for the use of *memor* referring to abstract objects and for its dependent genitive (the norm in Classical Latin after verbs of remembering and forgetting and their related adjectives) cf. Hor. *Carm.* 3.11.51-52 *nostri memorem sepulcro / scalpe querelam*. For the phrase *memores ... nostri* see **5.31n**. In real life wine or water was poured on the ashes after cremation; for the substitution of tears by the poets cf.

Hor. *Carm.* 2.6.22-24 *ibi tu calentem / debita sparges lacrima fauillam / uatis amici* with N-H on 23.

26 sic: refers to the instructions for his burial contained in **11-25**.

sic ego: for this phrase at the opening of the line in elegy, see **19.9n.** below.

componi: 'to be laid to rest'. The verb refers to the collecting together of the ashes and bones and their placing in the funeral urn cf. Prop. 2.24B.35 *tu mea* (sc. *ossa*) *compones*. As with *legant / ... collecta* in **18-19** above, our author repeats here in compound form the simple verb *ponere* used above in **22**, see **19n**. *collecta*. As with *collecta* above, *componi* here retains some of its original meaning of 'placed together'. For the use of the simple *ponere* in this context, as at **22** above, cf. Prop. 1.17.22 *molliter et tenera poneret ossa rosa*, Ov. *Fast.* 5.480 *positis iusta feruntur auis*. The phrase *componi uersus* cannot here mean 'for verses to be composed' (cf. *Laud. Mess.* **7.17** below), an alternative meaning suggested by Fulkerson [(2017) 110], since the short 'u' of *uersus* prevents such an interpretation, although the collocation is striking.

uersus in ossa: syntactically parallel to *mutatus in umbram* above (**9**). The phrase is a variation on the more commonly occurring *uersus in cinerem(-es)* in this context; cf. *CLE* 1038.5 and see *ThLL* 3.1073.3-7. There is perhaps a hint in the use of *uersus* here of the theme of change which runs through the whole collection and is reflected in the central position of the ever-changing god Vertumnus (derived from *uerto* see *LALE* 639) at **8.13-14**. The same theme of change combined with that of the poet's death is found at the end of **7** (**204-207**) *mea tunc tumulus cum texerit ossa/ ... / ... mutata figura / seu me finget equum etc.* on which see **7.206-210n.** below. See further **2.9n., 7.63n., 8 headnote, 8.13-14n.**

uelim: optative in sense, see **11-12n.** *ueniat .../ ... fleat* above.

27-30 Lygdamus' final request concerning his funeral is that an inscription should mark his grave, on the most frequented side, facing the road, giving the cause of his death, love for a wife who has been snatched away from him. The literary use of the epitaph has its roots in Hellenistic pastoral (e.g. [Theocr.] *Id.* 23.47-48) and the epitaph for Daphnis at Virg. *Ecl.* 5.43-44 has its model in the dying words of Daphnis at Theocr. *Id.* 1.120-121. Elegy shares its elegiac metre with real funerary epigrams, so the use of literary epitaphs in Latin elegy is natural. Its first occurrence is Tib. 1.3.55-56, where the poet imagines the epitaph to be placed on his tomb if he dies abroad accompanying his patron Messalla on a mission. Subsequent examples occur at Prop. 2.13.35-36, 4.7.85-86; Ov. *Am.* 2.6.61-62 (with McKeown III 144 ad loc.), *Her.* 2.147-148, 7.195-196, 14.129-130, *Fast.* 3.549-550, *Trist.* 3.3.73-76; see further Schmidt (1985), Ramsby (2007), Maltby (2011) 91, with nn. 20 and 21 there.

27-28 The emphasis in this couplet through *tristem ... causam*, and *demonstret, celebri ... fronte*, and *notet* on making Lygdamus' 'grief' 'public' picks up one interpretation of the first and second elements of the name Lygdamus which occurs in the epitaph below, see **29n.** and Gen. Intro., section 3.1.

27 tristem mortis ... causam: the cause of death was frequently given on funerary inscriptions; see Lattimore (1942) 142-158. Our author's model for an erotic cause of death is probably Dido's epitaph at Ov. *Her.* 7.195-196 *praebuit Aeneas et causam mortis et ensem*; / *ipsa sua Dido concidit usa manu* (repeated at Ov. *Fast.* 3.549-550). The link with Dido reinforces the threat of suicide at **8**, and Dido's belief in her married relationship with Aeneas echoes Lygdamus' insistence on his relationship with Neaera as one of marriage (emphasised at **4** and **14** above). Another important intertext for the theme of love being the cause of death in a married context is the oath of the dying Procris to her husband Cephalus at Ov. *Met.* 7.854-855 (*sc. oro*) *per si quid merui de te bene perque manentem / nunc quoque cum pereo, causam mihi mortis, amorem*. On the importance of this text as a model for the themes and structure of **[Tib.] 3** as a whole see Gen. Intro., section 1.3. The phrase *mortis causa* is frequent elsewhere in Ovid (*Her.* 18.200, *Ars* 3.40, *Met.* 7.855, 10.380, *Pont.* 1.2.15, 4.6.11, 7.12, *Ibis* 318, cf. *Her.* 2.148 *necis causam praebuit*). For *tristis* applied to *causa* in the sense of a tragic reason for Medea and Procne to murder their children cf. Ov. *Am.* 2.14.31-32 *sed tristibus utraque causis / iactura socii sanguinis ulta uirum*. Also relevant may be Propertius' account of how Cynthia is the 'cause' of all his moods: Prop. 1.11.25-26 *seu tristis ueniam seu contra laetus amicis, / quidquid ero, dicam 'Cynthia causa fuit'*.

demonstret: common in prose, but rare in verse [outside comedy: Plaut. (10); Ter. (2)]; elsewhere only Cat. 55.2; Prop. 3.16.15; Sil 16.223; Stat. *Theb.* 10.603, 12.220, *Ach.* 1.582; Phaedr. *Fab. Aes.* 3.15.19, *Fab. App.* 7.16, 28.9; see *ThLL* 5(1).503.55-56 and Axelson (1945) 69.

littera: 'inscription', collective singular, as at **1.12** above, cf. Ov. *Met.* 11.706, *Culex* 411-412 quoted on **28n.** below and see *ThLL* 7(2).1528.5-36.

28 in celebri ... fronte: Lygdamus wishes the inscription to be carved on the front of the tomb stone, facing the busy road. For *frons* in this context cf. *Culex* 411-412 *fronte locatur / elogium, tacita firmat quod littera uoce*. Cynthia wished her epitaph to be read by travellers in this way at Prop. 4.7.83-84 *hic carmen media dignum me scribe columna, / sed breue, quod currens uector ab urbe legat*. By contrast, Propertius wanted his tomb to be hidden from the road, Prop. 3.16.25-26 *di faciant mea ne terra locet ossa frequenti / qua facit assiduo tramite uulgus iter*. The adjective *celeber* is here used in the sense of 'busy', 'much frequented' which is frequent in Ovid (27), e.g. *Ars* 1.97 *sic ruit ad celebres cultissima femina ludos*, but rare elsewhere in verse, where the sense 'famous', 'celebrated' is more common, see **10.23** below.

carmina: the term is commonly applied to funerary inscriptions, see McKeown III 144 on *Am*. 2.6.59-60, *ThLL* 3.465.74ff. and the long list of parallels given by N-A here ad loc.

29-30 The epitaph provides the poem with a ring structure, with *dolor* **29** recalling *dolorem* **3** and *dolor* **6**, *coniugis ereptae* **30** echoing *erepta coniuge* **4** and *perire* **30** looking back to *uiuere* **4** and *uitae ... / ... taedia* in **7-8**. A number of the themes in the epitaph reflect ideas found on real funerary inscriptions, such as the formula *hic situs est* with the name, and the mention of the *causa mortis* (cf. **27n.**).

29 LYGDAMVS ... NEAERAE: the line is carefully constructed with a proper name at each end, separated by *dolor* in central position. This is the only place where the author mentions his name. On the name Lygdamus see Gen. Intro., section 3.1. Especially relevant here is its connection with *dolor* (through the connection of its first element with the adverb λύγδην 'sobbing'), and its connection with 'making public' δημόσιος through its second element δᾶμος / δῆμος, see **27-28n.** above. In Propertius, Lygdamus had occurred as the name of a slave of Cynthia's in 3.6 and, apparently, of a slave of Propertius himself in 4.7 and 4.8; see further Hutchinson [(2006) 178] for occurrences of the name in real life at *CIL* VI 5327.2, 21744, XV 1418-1419. Elegiac inscriptions are a common context for self-naming in elegy, cf. Tib. 1.3.55, 9.83, Prop. 2.14.27, Ov. *Am*. 1.11.27, 2.13.25, *Ars* 2.744, 3.812.

LYGDAMVS HIC SITVS EST: a common formula on real funerary inscriptions, often abbreviated to *H.S.E*, cf. *CLE* 461 *Suetrius Hermes hic situs est*. In literature it is found from Ennius, e.g. Enn. *Var*. 19 *hic est ille situs*, cf. Ov. *Met*. 2.327 *hic situs est Phaethon*.

DOLOR ... ET CVRA: a common collocation in the context of love-sickness, see McKeown III 207 on *Am*. 2.10.11-12 and cf. Tib. 1.5.37-38 *saepe ego temptaui curas depellere uino, / at dolor in lacrimas uerterat omne merum*; Prop. 2.25.1 *Cynthia, nata meo pulcherrima cura dolori*; Ov. *Met*. 10.75 (of Orpheus at the loss of Eurydice) *cura dolorque animi lacrimaeque alimenta fuere*. Here, as often in elegy, *cura* combines the senses of 'passion for' and 'worry over'. The reading *cura* occurs as a correction in a late MS for *causa* of A+, which has clearly crept in from **30**.

NEAERAE: objective genitive.

30 CONIVGIS EREPTAE: echoes *erepta coniuge* at **4** above. In both places the phrase suggests that his separation from Neaera was not due to her own free will, but rather the result of the violence of a rival who stole her away. For the combination of *dolor* with the theme of the lost wife, cf. Ov. *Met*. 7.688-689 quoted on **3** above with **n.** ad loc. The idea could be seen as a reversal of the common funerary motif that death snatches away a loved one, on which see Thomas (2011) 111 on Hor. *Carm*. 4.2.21; cf. Hor. *Epist*. 1.14.6-8.

CAVSA PERIRE: for the common mention of the *causa mortis* on funeral inscriptions see **27n.** above. For love as the cause of death cf. the epitaph Propertius imagines Maecenas speaking as he passes the poet's grave: Prop. 2.1.78 *huic misero fatum dura puella fuit*. The verb *perire* is used frequently of dying for love from Plautus *Poen*. 96 on and is frequent in this sense in elegy, see Pichon 230. The use of the infinitive after nouns such as *causa* in place of a genitive gerund is unusual in the Classical period, though cf. Virg. *Aen*. 10.90 *quae causa fuit consurgere in arma*? It becomes more common in later Latin, perhaps through Greek influence, e.g. Lucan 5.463-464 *Hapso gestare carinas / causa palus*; see further K-S II 1.744, H-Sz 351.

Poem 3

Just as the beginning of poem **2** contains verbal echoes of the end of poem **1**, so here the opening address to Neaera in **1** echoes the mention of Neaera in the final couplet of poem **2**, and the phrase *marmorea ... domo* in **2.22**, describing the marble burial urn, is picked up here in **3** by the mention of a real house of marble *marmorei ...tecti* (cf. *domo* **4**) rejected by Lygdamus. The long opening sentence ends at **9-10** with a reference to the poet's death, a theme touched upon at the end of poem **1**, central to poem **2**, and repeated at the end of poem **3**. Thematically, then, the elegy is well integrated with what has gone before. At its heart is a wish for the return of Neaera and for a continuation of married life together until death in old age. Closely connected with this wish is a very Tibullan rejection of wealth in favour of a simple life dedicated to love (cf. especially Tib. 1.1 and cf. Prop. 1.14 on the advantages of love over wealth). This theme of 'love not wealth' is expressed in three successive priamels; see Race (1982) 130:

1-10 What use is praying to heaven not for riches but for a long life together with Neaera?

11-22 What use are gold, land, a rich house, jewels and purple? The common crowd loves these things, but they cannot ease the cares caused by Fortune's laws.

23-32 Poverty would be acceptable provided Neaera would return, but if the gods refuse this wish no riches could help. Let others wish for them.

33-38 The poem ends with a prayer to Juno and Venus to grant his wish for Neaera's return and the admission that, if the Fates forbid this, death would be preferable.

The theme of the rejection of wealth, ψόγος πλούτου, is a common one in ancient literature, cf. Archil. 19 West; Theogn. 83-86, 227-232, 523-524; Anacr. 16 *PMG*; Aristoph. *Plut.* 558-561; Epicur. *Ep.* 3.130; Philodemus *AP* 5.120.1 (=27.1 Sider); Lucr. 2.20-61; Hor. *Serm.* 1.1.38-119, *Epod.* 1.25-34, *Carm.* 2.18 with N-H 287-292; Sen. *Epist.* 90.41; as at Theogn. 1155-1156 οὐκ ἔραμαι πλουτεῖν οὐδ' εὔχομαι, ἀλλά μοι εἴη / ζῆν ἀπὸ τῶν ὀλίγων μηδὲν ἔχοντι κακόν ["I do not desire riches, nor pray for them, but may it be my lot to live on a little with no misfortune"] and Tib. 1.1.5, wealth is rejected here in favour of the elegiac ideal of poverty (*paupertas* **23**) and, as in Hor. *Carm.* 2.12.21 (with further examples in N-H ad loc.) and Tib. 2.2.13-16, in favour of a life devoted to love (**7-8, 23-28**). For criticism of wealth and luxury in Roman poetry of the first century BC generally see Williams (1968) 578-619, and for its importance in the elegists see Newlands (1980).

An important intertext for the present poem (as for other Lygdamus poems concerned with Neaera, see **1 headnote, 1.19n., 3.29n. 4.16, 6.47-49, 6.53**) seems to be Hor. *Epod.* 15 in which a rich rival has stolen Horace's Neaera from him, cf. esp. *Epod.* 15.17-24 *et tu, quicumque es felicior atque meo nunc / superbus incedis malo, / sis pecore et multa* *diues tellure licebit / tibique Pactolus fluat,/ nec te Pythagorae fallant arcana renati, / formaque uincas Nirea, / eheu translatos alio maerebis amores. / ast ego uicissim risero* (see Gen. Intro., section 3.1). Holzberg [(1998) 180 n. 43] suggests Lygdamus wanted to create the impression that he was the man who stole Horace's girl from him and was suffering the consequences Horace had predicted. The mention of this man's interest in Pythagorean re-incarnation (*Epod.* 15.21) may serve to connect him with the author of the *Laud. Mess.* (**7.206-210**) and so provide a possible argument for identifying Lygdamus with the *Laud. Mess.* poet. If Lygdamus is to be thought of as a rich character, as his projected deluxe funeral at **2.9-30** suggests [see Büchner (1965) 68, 72, 74 and Holzberg (1998) 180], this would give added point here to his rejection of riches in favour of love, especially as one of the riches rejected here (**20** and by our author in *Laud. Mess.* **7.199**) includes the gold of the river Pactolus, ascribed to Horace's rival at *Epod.* 15.20.

1 Quid prodest ... ?: anaphora involving this phrase (also at **11, 13** and varied at **18-19** with *quid ... / ... iuuat*?) binds together the opening half of the poem **1-22** and lends rhetorical weight to Lygdamus' rejection of the goals of the common crowd. For this combination of *prodesse* and *iuuare* in philosophical and rhetorical contexts cf. Cic. *Fin.* 2.5 *bonum ... quid prodesset aut quid iuuaret*; Hor. *AP* 333 *aut prodesse uolunt aut delectare poetae*, where Brink ad loc. compares for *prodesse* the Greek ὠφελεῖν in similar contexts. For *quid prodest*?, either together or separated, cf. Tib. 1.2.77-78, 1.8.9; Prop. 1.9.9 Ov. *Her.* 21.133, *Met.* 2.589; Sen. *Ben.* fr. 14 Haase; Lucan 1.669; Quint. *Decl. Mai.* 13.2; Mart. 7.12.5 and for the use of this and similar phrases in elegy see Pichon 241.

caelum uotis inplesse: *caelum* 'heaven' the home of the gods stands here by metonymy for the gods themselves, cf. Ov. *Am.* 3.3.41-42 *quid queror et toto facio conuicia caelo? / di quoque habent oculos, di quoque pectus habent*; Serv. *Aen.* 8.64 *caelo: ... pro his qui in caelo sunt*. The term *uotis* here refers to vows to make an offering to the gods in return for a favour granted. For *inpleo* 'fill' in this context, cf. Virg. *Aen.* 9.480 *caelum ... questibus implet* (Val. Fl. 6.726); Ov. *Met.* 7.428 *muneribusque deos implet*. The verb *inpleo* is not found in Tib. or Prop., but is frequent in Ov. (26). For the use of a perfect inf. here for metrical convenience, in place of the present, see Platnauer 109-112 and Maltby (2002) 132-133 on Tib. 1.1.29-30. It is possible, however, as Tränkle 92 and N-A 197 suggest, that the inf. could be taken as a real past, implying that Lygdamus' vows had been made in vain.

Neaera: see the **headnote** above on the link this address forms with the end of the previous poem.

2 blandaque cum multa tura dedisse prece: the adj. *blanda* here combines the ideas of 'pleasing' and 'persuasive'. It had been applied to *tus* at Prop. 4.6.5 *date et blandi mihi turis honores*, but is more common with *preces* (e.g. in an amatory context at Ov. *Met.* 10.642). The phrase *tura dedisse* had occurred in the same metrical *sedes* and in a similar context at Tib. 1.8.70 *nec prodest sanctis tura dedisse focis*. For *multa prece* cf. Hor. *Epist.* 1.13.18, *Carm.* 4.5.33; Sen. *Medea* 846.

tura: an aromatic resin from the sap of a tree, imported at great expense from Arabia and Africa, and used by the Romans as incense in religious rites., cf., in a birthday context, **11.9, 12.1**.

3 marmorei ... e limine tecti: Lygdamus rejects the prestige associated with a luxurious marble mansion, cf. Hor. *Carm.* 3.1.45-46 *cur inuidendis postibus et nouo / sublime ritu moliar atrium?*, *Epod.* 1.29-30 *neque ut superni uilla candens Tusculi / Circaea tangat moenia.* There may be an intentional contrast here with the marble funerary urn *marmorea ... domo* mentioned in **2.22**. Similar plays on marble dwellings for the living and the dead are found at Sen. *Epist.* 60.4 *sic in domo sunt, quomodo in conditiuo. horum licet in limine ipso nomen marmori inscribas, mortem suam antecesserunt* and Petr. 71.1 (quoted in **2.21-22** *marmorea ... domo* above). Marble was associated with excess, cf. Cic. *Parad.* 13 *marmoreis tectis ebore et auro fulgentibus*. The adj. is absent from Tib., but occurs three times in the *Lygd.* poems (**2.22, 3.3, 16**), where its relative frequency suggests perhaps an oblique reference to Lygdamus' own name, derived from *lygdos*, a white Parian marble, cf. **2.10n.** and Gen. Intro., section 3.1. For the adj. in collocation with *limen*, cf. Hor. *Epist.* 1.18.73 *intra marmoreum uenerandi limen amici*; *Ciris* 222 *marmoreo ... in limine*. The hexameter ending *limine tecti* occurs in Ov. *Met.* 5.43, 14.254, *Fast.* 1.137, *Ibis* 613. For the theme of the rejection of urban luxury cf. Lucr. 2.20-36; Virg. *Georg.* 2. 461-466 and see Griffin (1976) and Griffin (1985) 1-29.

prodirem: describes the ceremonial exit of the master from his house, cf. *OLD prodeo* 1b and see Varro *Ling.* 7.81 *qui exit in uestibulum, quod est ante domum, prodire et procedere dicitur.* Cf. the haughty gait of Horace's rival for Neaera at *Epod.* 15.18 (quoted in the introduction above).

4 insignis ... conspicuusque: the tautology is typical of the *Lygd.* poems, see examples listed in **2.15n. praefatae ante**. The adj. *conspicuus* occurs thirteen times in Ovid. Elsewhere it is rare in verse (e.g. Hor. *Carm.* 3.16.19; Sen. *Thy.* 126; Lucan 4.170) and avoided by Tib. in favour of the verbal adj. *conspiciendus* 1.2.70, 2.3.52; see further McKeown III 231 (on Ov. *Am.* 2.11.3-4). On the postponement of *-que* to this position, attached to a quadrisyllabic adjective, cf. Ov. *Trist.* 2.532 *exiguasque*, 4.1.40 *immemoremque* and see Platnauer 91.

clara ... domo: more likely to be used in the physical sense of 'resplendent house', as in Hor. *Carm.* 2.12.8 *fulgens ... domus*, repeating the idea of *marmorei ... tecti* in **3**, rather than 'noble family' as at Ov. *Her.* 17.52 *clara satis domus haec nobilitate sua*.

5-6 After his rejection of the life of the rich city *patronus* in **3-4**, Lygdamus goes on here to reject the life of the prosperous land-owner.

5 An example of the so-called *uersus aureus*, favoured by Catullus and the neoteric poets under the influence of Greek Alexandrian verse, see Wilkinson (1963) 215-216, Ross (1969) 132ff. Here the two adjectives and their respective nouns are arranged in the order *abab* around the central verb *renouarent*. The same arrangement is found in Ov. *Am.* 1.3.9 *nec meus innumeris renouatur campus aratris*, which probably influenced the present line; cf. *Laud. Mess.* **7.13n.** below.

multa ... iugera: echoes *iugera multa* at Tib. 1.1.2 (and argues in favour of this reading there in preference to A's *iugera magna*) in the same context of the rejection of wealth; also at Tib. 2.3.42 and (of the sea) Ov. *Pont.* 4.9.86.

renouarent: a technical term, favoured by Ovid, for the renewal of land, usually by ploughing, cf. *Am.* 1.3.9 quoted above (with McKeown II 67 ad loc.) and see *OLD renouo* 1d. For the use of oxen in this context, cf. Ov. *Met.* 15.125 *quibus* (sc. *bubus*) *totiens durum renouauerat aruum*.

6 magnas messes: for the collocation cf. Plaut. *Most.* 159 *messis magna*.

terra benigna: the phrase occurs in the same *sedes* at Tib. 1.3.62 *floret odoratis terra benigna rosis*. In both cases the meaning of the adj. is 'fertile', in its strict etymological sense from *bene* + *gigno* (see *LALE* 78), as at Ov. *Am.* 1.10.56 *benignus ager*. For the opposite, cf. Virg. *Georg.* 2.179 *collesque maligni*; see further *ThLL* 2.1904.22-46 and Maltby (1999b) 247.

7-10 The two couplets of lifestyles rejected by *Lygd.* in **3-6** are balanced by two couplets describing his ideal of a long life of love with a faithful partner lasting until death in old age. As N-A 205 points out, although the idea of dying in the presence of one's mistress is common in descriptions of elegiac love (e.g. Tib. 1.1.59 *te spectem, suprema mihi cum uenerit hora*; Ov. *Am.* 1.3.17-18 *tecum, quos dederint annos mihi fila sororum, / uiuere contingat teque dolente mori*) the idea of growing old together with the beloved is a theme more often associated with marriage, e.g. Tib. 2.2.19-20 (describing the chains of love binding Cornutus with his wife) *uincula quae maneant semper, dum tarda senectus / inducat rugas inficiatque comas*; Ov. *Trist.* 4.8.11-12 *inque sinu dominae* (referring to his wife) *... / securus ... consenuisse*. This is an aspect of his relationship with Neaera that Lygdamus is always anxious to emphasise, cf. **2.13n**. By contrast, traditional elegy, influenced by the figure of the *senex amator* from new comedy (as in Plaut. *Asin., Bacch., Cas., Cist., Merc.*, and *Stich.*) often sees old age as an inappropriate time for love (e.g. Tib. 1.1.71-72, 1.2.92-98, 1.9.73-74; Ov. *Am.* 1.9.4 *turpe senilis amor*), although Prop. at 2.25.9-10 declares his love for Cynthia will last into old age.

7-8 For the sentiment, cf. Plaut. *Cist.* 243 (of a potential bride) *quae esset aetatem exactura mecum in matrimonio*, Hor. *Carm.* 3.9.24 *tecum uiuere amem, tecum obeam libens*; Ov. *Am.* 1.3.17-18 (quoted above) with further examples in McKeown II 71 ad loc.

7 longae ... uitae: the phrase occurs in the same metrical *sedes* at Virg. *Ecl.* 4.53; *Nux* 152; Lucan 1.457, 8.625; Juv.10.275; *Laud. Mess.* **7.112a.**

sociarem gaudia: for *gaudia* in erotic poetry and elegy as a technical term referring to the joys of sexual intercourse, cf. *Sulpicia Cycle* **9.18** and see Pichon 159, Maltby (2002) on Tib. 1.5.39-40 and 2.1.12, Brown (1987) on Lucr. 4.1106 and Adams (1982) 197-198. In combination with *sociarem* here the reference is to the sharing of sexual pleasure, cf. Tib. 1.1.69 *iugamus amores*.

8 inque tuo ... sinu: for *inque* as a line opening, followed by some form of *sinus* cf. Prop. 3.4.15; Ov. *Am.* 2.15.14, *Her.* 13.78, 20.48, *Ars* 2.458, *Met.* 4.596, 6.338, 9.338, 10.558, 13.426, *Fast.* 3.218, *Trist.* 4.1.98, 4.8.11 (quoted above on **7-10**); Manil. 4.597; Sil. 4.34; Stat. *Silu.* 1.4.10; Mart. 2.26.2.

caderet: the verb is normally used of dying (falling) in battle, see *ThLL* 3.23.9-24.58, but as Dissen points out ad loc. it is particularly suited to death in infirm old age. Elsewhere in elegy the simple *cado*, as opposed to the compound *occido*, in the sense of 'die' occurs only at Prop. 2.28.42 *uiuam, si uiuet; si cadet illa, cadam*.

nostra senecta: metonymy for *ego senex*. Other examples occur at Hor. *Carm*. 2.6.6 *meae sedes ... senectae*; Virg. *Aen*. 11.165-166 *sors ista senectae / debita erat nostrae*; Prop. 3.19.15; Sen. *Herc. F*. 1249; Stat. *Theb*. 4.536; Ciris 287 *nostrae ... inimice senectae*, 314 *o sola meae uiuendi causa senectae*. For abstract for concrete metonymy of this kind in the *Lygd*. poems see **2.13n**. While Tib. uses both *senectus*, the norm in Classical prose, at 2.2.19 to avoid hiatus, and the mainly poetic *senecta* (1.4.31, 1.6.77, 1.8.42, 1.10.40), our poet in *Lygd*. uses *senecta* only; here, **3.8, 5.16, 25**.

9 permenso defunctus tempore lucis: for *Lygd.*'s love of pleonastic expressions of this kind and a list of examples see **2.15n**. The participle *permensus* in a passive meaning occurs before Apuleius only at Colum. *Rust*. 3.13.13 *sic permensum et perlibratum opus in similitudinem ueruacti semper procedit*. For *defungi* in the context of bringing one's life to a close cf. Virg. *Georg*. 4.475 (= *Aen*. 6.306) *defunctaque corpora uita*; Ov. *Her*.14.125-126 *defunctaque uita / corpora*; Sen. *Epist*. 99.10 *qui cito uita defungitur*, and, with *tempus* as object Hor. *Epist*. 2.1.21-22 *nisi quae terris semota suisque / temporibus defuncta uidet*. For *lux* as an equivalent to *uita* (avoided here because of *gaudia uitae* in 7) cf. Virg. *Aen*. 12.873-874 *qua tibi lucem / arte morer?* with Tarrant (2012) 313-314 ad loc. for Homeric, Greek tragic and Lucretian parallels.

10 nudus Lethaea cogerer ire rate?: close in expression to Prop. 3.5.14 *nudus at inferna, stulte, uehere rate*; on the Propertian text see Fedeli (1985) 184 and Heyworth (2007a) 301. As there, *nudus* implies bereft of all worldly riches, cf. Sil. 5.267 *nudum Tartarea portabit nauita cymba*. The reference in *rate* is to the boat of Charon, which ferries the shades of the dead across the Acheron. *Lethaeus* (found first at Cat. 65.5 *Lethaeo gurgite*) refers generally to the underworld, without specific reference to the river Lethe, as at Hor. *Carm*. 4.7.27-28 *Lethaea ... / uincula* and Tib. 1.3.80 *Lethaeas ... aquas*. Our author uses the combination with *ratis* again at **5.24**. On the formation and use of such adjectives in place of genitive nouns see Löfstedt (1942) 107-124.

11-19 nam graue quid prodest ... populus miratur?: the introductory *nam* suggests this section functions as an explanation for the opening question *quid prodest caelum uotis inplesse?* In fact it acts simply as an amplification of the rejection of wealth in **3-6**. It consists of three separate questions introduced by *quid prodest?* (**11**), *quidue ... prodest?* (**13**) and *quidue* (sc. *prodest*)? (**17**), each describing various examples of wealth admired by the general populace (**19**) but rejected by the poet.

11-12 Gold and land are commonly combined in traditional descriptions of wealth: e.g. Pind. *Nem.* 8.37-38 χρυσὸν εὔχονται, πεδίον δ' ἕτεροι / ἀπέραντον ["some pray for gold, others for land without limit"]; Hor. *Serm.* 1.2.13 *diues agris, diues positis in faenore nummis*; Tib. 1.1.1-2 *diuitias alius fuluo sibi congerat auro / et teneat culti iugera multa soli*; Prop. 3.5.3-5 *nec tamen inuiso uictus mihi carpitur auro / ... / nec mihi mille iugis Campania pinguis aratur*; Sen. *Troad.* 1019-1021 *remouete multo / diuites auro, remouete centum / rura qui scindunt opulenta bubus*. Particularly relevant here are the possessions in land and the gold of Pactolus ascribed to the rich rival for Horace's Neaera at Hor. *Epod.* 15.19-20 (quoted in the **headnote** above).

11 graue ... pondus: the collocation occurs elsewhere in verse at Hor. *Epod.* 4.17-18; Ov. *Her.* 21.170, *Met.* 7.118; Manil. 1.286; Phaedrus *Fab. Aes.* 2.6.10; Sen. *Troad.* 491; Stat. *Theb.* 1.212-213; Mart. 5.65.9.

pondus ... diuitis auri: the expression is Tibullan, cf. Tib. 1.9.31-32 *nullo te diuitis auri / pondere ... uendere uelle fidem*, 1.10.7 *diuitis hoc uitium est auri*. The phrase *diuitis auri* at the line end occurs also at Manil. 5.16 and *Laus Pis.* 219.

12 aruaque ... pinguia: for the rejection of rich agricultural wealth, cf. Hor. *Serm.* 1.1.49-51 *uel dic quid referat ... / ... iugera centum an / mille aret?*, *Epod.* 1.25-28 *non ut iuuencis inligata pluribus / aratra nitantur mea, / pecusue Calabris ante sidus feruidum / Lucana mutet pascuis*. The adj. *pinguis* denoting fertility is characteristic of Virgil's *Georgics* where it occurs over 20 times (applied to soil at 1.64, 105; 2.92, 139, 184, 203, 248, 274; 4.118), see Thomas (1988) I 70 on *Georg.* 1.8; in elegy, cf. Cat. 68.110 *siccare emulsa pingue palude solum*; Tib. 2.3.6 *uersarem ualido pingue bidente solum*; Prop. 3.5.5 *Campania pinguis*. For the *iunctura* with *arua* in verse cf. Virg. *Ecl.* 5.33; Hor. *Carm.* 3.4.15-16; Val. Fl. 7.607-608 *pinguia Nili / fertilis arua*. Horace's rival at *Epod.* 15.19 was *pecore et multa diues tellure* as well as rich in the gold of the river Pactolus, rejected by Lygdamus at **29** below, see **n.** ad loc. On his possible connection with Lygdamus, see **headnote** and Gen. Intro., section 3.1 above.

si findant: for the replacement of a subject noun (*pondus*) in the first half of the question by a *si* clause in the second Tränkle [ad loc.] compares Stat. *Silu.* 5.3.41-43 ... *nam Sicanii non mitius halat / aura croci, dites nec si tibi rara Sabaei / cinnama, odoratas nec Arabs decerpsit aristas*. For *findere* used of ploughing cf. Hor. *Carm.* 1.1.11-12 *patrios findere sarculo / agros*; Ov. *Her.* 12.94 *solidam iusso uomere findis humum*, *Ars* 2.671 *uomere findite terras*.

mille boues: for *mille* as an indefinitely large number, cf. Virg. *Ecl.* 2.21 *mille meae Siculis errant in montibus agnae*; Hor. *Serm.* 1.1.51 (quoted above), *Epod.* 4.13; *Sulpicia Cycle* **8.14, 12.12**; it is particularly common in Tib., cf. 1.3.50, 2.3.44, 4.60. Its use in the current line was probably inspired by Prop. 3.5.5 *nec mihi mille iugis Campania pinguis aratur*.

13-16 The rejection of a luxurious mansion with its marble colonnades **13-14**, extensive wooded grounds **15**, gold-panelled ceilings and marble floor **16** serves as an elaboration of the *marmoreum tectum* of **3** above. The main inspiration seems to be Prop. 3.2.11-13 *quod non Taenariis domus est mihi fulta columnis, / nec camera auratas inter eburna trabes, / nec mea Phaeacas aequant pomaria siluas*, though the theme is common in earlier Roman poetry, e.g. Lucr. 2.24-28; Virg. *Georg.* 2.458-467; Hor. *Carm.* 2.15.14-16 18.1-6, 3.1.45-46 (quoted on **3n.** above), *Epod.* 1.29-30 (quoted on **3n.** above); Tib. 2.3.35-46.

13 Phrygiis innixa columnis: Phrygian marble from the town of Synnada in Phrygia was violet with white streaks (so-called Pavonazzetto) and is mentioned first as a luxury item by Horace: *Carm.* 3.1.41-43 *quodsi dolentem nec Phrygius lapis / ... / delenit*. Coloured marble columns surrounded the inner court of a well-to-do Roman house, in which trees and shrubs (as described in **15**) were grown, cf. Hor. *Epist.* 1.10.22 *nempe inter uarias nutritur silua columnas*. For the hexameter ending *innixa columnis* cf. Ov. *Pont.* 3.2.49; Stat. *Silu.* 4.2.38. The verb is not found elsewhere in the *Corp. Tib.*

14 Taenare, siue tuis, siue, Caryste, tuis: Taenarus was a peninsula on the Southern end of the Peloponnese which produced marbles of various colours, black (Plin. *Nat.* 36.135, 158), yellowish (Sext. Emp. *Pyrrh. Hyp.* 130), and a reddish type (Plin. *Nat.* 36.158). Columns made from this marble are mentioned at Prop. 3.2.11 (quoted on **13-16n.** above). Marble from Carystos, at the South East end of Euboea, had green and white stripes (so-called Cipollino). We learn from Nepos (ex. fr. 24 P) that Caesar's chief architect, Mamurra, was the first to have marble-faced walls and columns of Carystian marble in his private house. The mention of various types of marble becomes characteristic of poetry of the Flavian period, so Mart. 6.42.11-13 (Laconian, Phrygian and Libyan), 9.75.7-9 (Carystian, Phrygian, Numidian, Laconian); Stat. *Silu.* 1.2.148-149 (Libyan, Phrygian, Laconian), 1.5.34 (Thasian, Carystian, Numidian, Phrygian), 2.2.85-93 (Lybian, Phrygian, Laconian, Numidian, Thasian, Chian, Carystian), 4.2.26-29 (Lybian, Ilian, Chian, Etrucan). Some critics use this as an argument for a late Flavian date for this poem, e.g. Axelson (1960b) 291-292, N-A 215; more sceptical Tränkle 96.

15 nemora in domibus sacros imitantia lucos: Horace twice mentions groves of trees growing between columns in the courtyards of well-to-do mansions: *Carm.* 3.10.5-6 *nemus / inter pulchra satum tecta* (with further parallels in N-R 144 ad loc.) and *Epist.*1.10.22 quoted on **13** above. The word *nemus* belonged originally to the sacral language and referred to a grove of trees belonging to a deity, see Jocelyn (1967) 352 on Enn. *Trag.* 208 Jocelyn *in nemore Pelio*. Sacred groves were typically densely planted and shady, as they remained uncut.

16 aurataeque trabes: for gilded roof-beams as a sign of luxury, cf. Enn. *Trag.* 90-91 Jocelyn, of the house of Priam, *tectis caelatis laqueatis, / auro ebore instructam* (sc. *domum*) *regifice*, with Jocelyn (1967) 249 ad loc.; Hor. *Carm.* 2.18.1-2 *non ebur neque aureum / mea renidet in domo lacunar* (with N-H 293); Prop. 3.2.12 (quoted on **13-16** above; Virg. *Aen.* 2.448 *auratas trabes, ueterum decora illa parentum*; Ov. *Met.* 15.672 (quoted below); Sen. *Thy.* 347 *auro nitidae trabes*, 646-647 *immane tectum, cuius auratas trabes / ... columnae nobiles ... ferunt*; Stat. *Silu.* 1.3.35-37 *auratasne trabes ... / ... / mirer*.

marmoreumque solum: the phrase perhaps comes from Ov. *Met.* 15.672 *marmoreumque solum fastigiaque aurea* (of the temple of Asclepius), which also combines marble flooring with a gilded roof, as does Cic. *Parad.* 49 *aurata tecta in uillis et sola marmorea*.

-que ... -que: see **1.3-4n**.

17-18 The list of rejected riches closes with two examples of luxury items from the East: pearls and purple dye. These figure frequently in earlier elegy as the types of gifts the poor poet is unable to provide for his avaricious mistress, e.g. Tib. 2.4.27-30; Prop. 3.13.5-8. Sulpicia is said to be worthy of them at *Sulpicia Cycle* **8.15-20**.

17 in Erythraeo ... litore: refers to an area more extensive than the Red Sea, including the Persian Gulf, Red Sea and the north-westerly part of the Indian Ocean. The designation *Erythraeus* for this area, as opposed to *Ruber* (e.g. *Rubro ...mari* Tib. 2.4.30; *Rubris ... aequoribus* Prop.1.14.12; *Rubro ... salo* Prop. 3.13.6; *Rubro de litore, Sulpicia Cycle* **8.19**) is late and appears first in the Flavian era, e.g. Plin. *Nat.* 12.70; Stat. *Silu.* 4.6.18, *Theb.* 7.566; Mart. 5.37.4 etc. (7 times in all). Axelson [(1960b) 291-292] uses this as evidence for a Flavian dating for *Lygdamus*, followed by Tränkle 97 and N-A 222-223. The use of the earlier form in the *Sulpicia Cycle* tells us nothing about the date of that section (which I claim is the same as the rest of the book), where it could be a reminiscence of earlier literary uses. In fact Tacitus, writing in AD 97, uses the phrase *in rubro mare* at *Agric.* 12.6.

concha: for this metonymic use, denoting not the oyster shell but the pearl within it cf. Varro. *Men.* 382; Tib. 2.4.30 *e Rubro lucida concha mari*; Prop. 1.8B.39 *non Indis flectere conchis*, 3.13.6; Ov. *Am.* 2.11.13, *Ars* 3.124, *Met.* 10.260 and see further examples at *ThLL* 4.28.41-47. Pearls from this area were considered particularly valuable, cf. Plin. *Nat.* 9.106-124.

18 tinctaque Sidonio murice lana: the reference is to wool dyed with expensive Tyrian purple, produced from the excretions a marine mollusc (*murex*). On the dye manufacture process see Plin. *Nat.* 9.125-141. Sidon is a Phoenician coastal city near Tyre and the adj. *Sidonius* can be used to mean from Tyre, especially where the reference is to purple [e.g. at Hor. *Epist.* 1.10.26; Prop. 2.16B.55 (*Sidonia uestis*); Ov. *Trist.* 4.2.27; *Ciris* 387, Stat. *Silu.* 5.1.225] or, more generally, Phoenician (e.g. *Sidonia Dido* in Virg. *Aen.* 1.446, 613 etc.). For earlier references to the use of purple dye as a symptom of decadence, cf. Lucr. 2.34ff., 501f., 4.1127, 5.1423f., 1427f.; Virg. *Ecl.* 4.42-45, *Georg.* 2.465; Hor. *Carm.* 3.1.42 (quoted on **21-22** below); Tib. 2.4.28 *et niueam Tyrio murice tingit ouem*; Ov. *Ars* 3.170 *nec te* (sc. *requiro*), *quae Tyrio murice, lana, rubes*. For *tinctaque* at the opening of the pentameter, cf. Ov. *Her.* 20.236, *Pont.* 3.1.26, 3.3.106.

19-20 For the sense of the distich with its Stoic polemic against the false opinions and lack of taste of the common people in its admiration and envy compare Cleanthes fr. 4 (Powell) μὴ πρὸς δόξαν ὅρα, ἐθέλων σοφὸς αἶψα γενέσθαι, / μηδὲ φοβοῦ πολλῶν ἄκριτον καὶ ἀναιδέα βάξιν. / οὐ γὰρ πλῆθος ἔχει συνετὴν κρίσιν, οὔτε δικαίαν / οὔτε καλήν, ὀλίγοις δὲ παρ᾽ ἀνδράσι τοῦτό κεν εὕροις ["Do not gaze after glory, wishing to become suddenly wise, nor should you fear the uncritical and shameless rumours of the many. For the multitude have no judgement which is prudent, just or good, a thing you can find in few men"], Plutarch *Mor.* 44B ὁ γὰρ φιλόσοφος λόγος τὸ μὲν ἐξ ἀπορίας καὶ ἀγνοίας θαῦμα καὶ θάμβος ἐξαιρεῖ γνώσει καὶ ἱστορίᾳ τῆς περὶ ἕκαστον αἰτίας ["Philosophical discourse with the knowledge and the investigation of the cause of each thing takes away the admiration and the amazement owed to perplexity and ignorance"] and Sen. *De Vita Beata* (*Dial.* 7) 2.4 *quam magnus mirantium, tam magnus inuidentium populus est ... ista quae spectantur, ad quae consistitur, quae alter alteri stupens monstrat, foris nitent, introrsus misera sunt* and see further Thom (2005) 133-135, Kyriakidis (2016) 142. However, rejection of popular values has a long tradition in Roman poetry, e.g. Lucil. 588f. M.; Cat. 95.7f. Hor. *Serm.* 1.4.71ff., 1.10.73ff., *Carm.* 1.1.29ff., 2.16.39ff. 3.1.1ff., *Epist.* 1.19.37ff., 1.20.4f., 2.1.64f.; Prop. 2.13.13f.; Ov. *Am.* 1.15.35; Manil. 2.137ff.; *Catal.* 9.61ff. esp. 64 *pingui nil mihi cum populo*; *Ciris* 2; [**Tib.**] **3.19.7**, and is probably Callimachean in origin, cf. Call. *Aetia* 1 fr. 1.25ff.Pf., *Epig.* 28.1ff. Pf. [esp. 4, σικχαίνω πάντα τὰ δημόσια ["I hate all popular things"], the inspiration of Hor. *Carm.* 3.1.1 *odi profanum uulgus et arceo*; see further Thomas (2011) 2-4, *Sulpicia Cycle* **10.18n.**, and **19.7n.**

in illis / inuidia est: for the short concluding statement after the enumeration of rejected luxuries cf. Tib. 2.4.31 *haec fecere malas.* The connection between *inuidia* and the preferences of the *populus* is again reminiscent of Callimachus, cf. Envy's words at *Hymn* 2 (to Apollo) 106 οὐκ ἄγαμαι τὸν ἀοιδὸν ὃς οὐδ᾽ ὅσα πόντος ἀείδει ["I do not admire the poet who does not sing as much as the sea"] and Apollo's reply at 108-112 Ἀσσυρίου ποταμοῖο μέγας ῥόος, ἀλλὰ τὰ πολλὰ / λύματα γῆς καὶ πολλὸν ἐφ᾽ ὕδατι συρφετὸν ἕλκει. /Δηοῖ δ᾽οὐκ ἀπὸ παντὸς ὕδωρ φορέουσι Μέλισσαι, /ἀλλ᾽ ἥτις καθαρή τε καὶ ἀχράαντος ἀνέρπει / πίδακος ἐξ ἱερῆς ὀλίγη λιβὰς ἄκρον ἄωτον. ["Great is the stream of the Assyrian river, but it carries in its waters much filth of the earth and much rubbish. And the Bees do not carry water to Dio from everywhere, but only from that small stream which clear and undefiled trickles from a holy fountain, the purest of waters"] and cf. Call. *Epig.* 21.4 Pf.; Prop. 3.1.21; Ov. *Am.* 1.15.1, *Rem.* 361-398. See further **19.7n.** below. As the adverb *falso* (**20**) suggests, *inuidia* here implies not only 'envy' but also 'lack of vision' according to its two etymologies, one in which the *in-* is intensive [Isid. *Etym.* 10.134 *inuidus dictus ab intuendo felicitatem alterius*; cf. Hardie [(2012a) 168] and the other in which it is privative (Prisc. *GL* 3.268.30 *inuideo tibi,* *quasi non uidens tibi fio*). The theme is picked up by Sen. *Dial.* 7.2.4 *quam magnus mirantium tam magnus inuidentium populus est.*

falso plurima uulgus amat: the adverb *falso* 'falsely' is rare in Latin poetry, except in Ovid, who has eight examples in all (absent from Tib. and Prop.). For the expression cf. Ov. *Am.* 1.15.35 *uilia miretur uulgus.* The *inuidia* of the *uulgus* occurs again later in the book at **19.7**, where the envy appears to be amatory.

21-22 Each line of the distich contains a commonplace of popular philosophy. Wealth cannot lighten men's cares **(21)** and Fortune rules human affairs **(22)**. Both ideas occur commonly in Latin poetry, especially Horace. For the first cf. Hor. *Carm.* 2.16.9-12 *non enim gazae neque consularis / submouet lictor miseros tumultus / mentis et curas laqueata circum / tecta uolantes,* 3.1.37-46 ...*sed Timor et Minae / scandunt eodem quo dominus, neque / decedit aerata triremi et / post equitem sedet atra cura. / quod si dolentem nec Phrygius lapis / nec purpurarum sidere clarior / delenit usus nec Falerna / uitis Achaemeniumque costum, / cur inuidendis postibus et nouo / sublime ritu moliar atrium*?, *Epist.* 1.2.47-49 *non domus et fundus, non aeris aceruus et auri / aegroto domini deduxit corpore febris, / non animo curas*; also Varro *Men.* 36.1-3 *non fit thensauris, non auro pectus solutum*; / *non demunt animis curas ac religiones / Persarum montes, non atria diuitis Crassi.* For the second cf. Virg. *Ecl.* 9.5 *quoniam fors omnia uersat*; also Tib. 1.5.70 *uersatur celeri Fors leuis orbe rotae* [the 'wheel of fortune', on which see Maltby (2002) 259 ad loc. and Maltby (2004) 103-122], Hor. *Carm.* 1.34.14-16 ... *hinc apicem rapax / Fortuna cum stridore acuto / sustulit, hic posuisse gaudet,* 1.35.1-4 (an Ode dedicated to *Fortuna*) *o diua gratum quae regis Antium / praesens uel imo tollere de gradu / mortale corpus uel superbos / uertere funeribus triumphos*, and see further examples in Otto 142-143 s.v. *Fortuna* and McKeown III 271 (on *Am.* 2.12.15-16).

leuantur: 'are lightened' with *mentes* in the sense of 'troubled minds' being taken almost as an equivalent to *curae.* Alternatively (so Tränkle and N-A ad loc.) the verb could be used zeugmatically in a slightly different sense with *mentes* (= 'free' as in Lucr. 2.365 *animum curaque leuare*) and with *curae* (= 'relieve' as in Cat. 2.10 *tristis animi leuare curas*).

sua ... lege regit: on the rule of fortune cf. the subtitle to Plutarch *de Fortuna* τύχη τὰ θνητῶν πράγματ' οὐκ εὐβουλία ["Fortune, not good sense (rules) human affairs"], a sentiment translated by Cicero and attributed to

Theophrastus *Callisthenes* at *Tusc.* 5.25 *uitam regit fortuna, non sapientia*; Manil. 1.56 *in quas fortunae leges quaeque hora ualeret*.

23-24 The rejection of wealth in favour of a modest life of love is a key theme of Tibullus' Delia elegies of the first book: e.g. Tib. 1.1.5 *me mea paupertas uitae traducat inerti*, and *passim*, 1.2.77-78 *quid Tyrio recubare toro sine amore secundo / prodest, cum fletu nox uigilanda uenit*? The theme of love being preferable to wealth occurs also at Tib. 1.8.33-34 (quoted below), and 2.2.10-16. It is common in Hellenistic poetry (e.g. Call. *Aet.* 3 fr. 75.44-48 Pf., Theocr. *Id.* 8.53-56) and in the love poetry of Horace (e.g. *Carm.* 2.12.21-28, 3.9.1-4) and Propertius (e.g. 1.8B.33-36, 1.14).

sit: the subjunctive expresses a wished for ideal, which can only come to pass with Neaera's agreement.

mihi: for the emphatic pronoun at the end of the priamel see N-H on Hor. *Carm.* 1.1.29 and cf. Hor. *Carm.* 1.7.10; Tib. 1.1.5.

paupertas: not true poverty, for which the terms would be *inopia* or *egestas*, but a relative term with positive moral overtones, suggesting modest means and lack of luxury, cf. Serv. *Georg.* 1.146 *peior est egestas quam paupertas; paupertas enim honesta esse potest*. The *paupertas* of the poet is a conventional feature of both Hellenistic (Theocr. *Id.* 16) and Augustan poetry (Hor. *Carm.* 2.18.9-10 with N-H's note on 10, 3.29.14, *Epist.* 2.2.51f.; Tib. 1.1.5 with Maltby (2002) 120-121 ad loc.; Prop. 1.8B.39-40; Ov. *Am.* 1.3.9-10 with McKeown II 66-67 ad loc.). On the theme of *paupertas* in Tib. see Schuster (1968) 81-84, Cairns (1979) 20f., Mutschler (1985) 41 n. 20, 216-212, Holzberg (1998) 178-179.

iucunda: normally used to describe the pleasant aspects of the lover's life (see Pichon 176-177) the adj. is striking here in combination with *paupertas*. It is rare in high-style verse outside Lucr. (5) and, from its frequency in Cat. (15), Ross [(1969) 76-80] argues that its use in elegy [Tib. (2), Prop. (6), Ov. (12)] is due to neoteric influence.

sine te: probably influenced by *sine amore secundo* in a similar context at Tib. 1.2.77 (quoted in full above), but as N-H 307 point out on Hor. *Carm.* 1.26.9-10 *nil sine te* (referring to a Muse) *mei / prosunt honores* the phrase is common in hymns and other religious contexts, cf. Cat. 61.61-62 *nil potest sine te Venus / ... commodi capere*, so that the effect here could be to suggest for Neaera a semi-divine status.

Book Three of the Corpus Tibullianum: 191
Introduction, Text, Translation and Commentary

regum munera nulla uolo: perhaps influenced by the pentameter in Tib. 1.8.33-34 *huic tu candentes umero subpone lacertos / et regum magnae despiciantur opes*; similar sentiments occur in Prop. 1.14, e.g. 15-16 *nam quis diuitiis aduerso gaudet Amore? / nulla mihi tristi praemia sint Venere* and 23-24 *quae* (sc. *Venus*) *mihi dum placata aderit, non Lyda uerebor / regna uel Alcinoi munera despicere*, the second of which may also have influenced our author's wording here.

25-26 The double accusative of exclamation introduced by the interjection *o* marks an emotional climax. It becomes clear that the return of Neaera is the central focus of *Lygd.*'s poem.

25 niueam ... lucem: lucky or happy days (or nights) were thought of as 'bright', 'shining'. The adjective *niueam* here (lit. = 'snow white') in the sense of happy or lucky (*OLD niueus* 2d) is a variation on *candidus*, used more frequently in this context, (*OLD candidus* 7), cf. Cat. 8.3 *fulsere quondam candidi tibi soles*; Tib. 1.3.93-94 *... hunc illum nobis Aurora nitentem / Luciferum roseis candida portet equis*; Prop. 2.15.1 (quoted above); Ov. *Her.* 16.320 *candidior medio nox erit illa die*. This symbolism was reflected in the use of white stones to mark lucky days, e.g. Cat. 68.147-148 *quare illud satis est, si nobis is datur unis / quem lapide illa diem candidiore notat*; Plin. *Epist.* 6.11.3 *o diem ... laetum notandumque mihi candidissimo calculo*. The metonymic use of *lux* for *dies* is common in Latin poetry of all periods from Acc. *Trag.* 37 onwards, cf. Cat. 107.6 *o lucem candidiore nota*; Tib. 2.1.5 *luce sacra*.

26 o mihi felicem terque quaterque diem: a variation on the traditional μακαρισμός or praise of the happy man, for which the classical model was Hom. *Od.* 5.306 τρισμάκαρες Δαναοὶ καὶ τετράκις οἳ τότ' ὄλοντο / Τροίῃ ἐν εὐρείῃ ["three and four times blessed were the Greeks who died then in the broad lands of Troy"], rendered into Latin by Virgil in *Aen.* 1.94-96 as *o terque quaterque beati / quis ... / contigit oppetere*. On the Semitic background for the augmentation by one (e.g. 'three and four', 'four and five' etc.) see West (2011) 86 on Hom. *Il.* 1.128 τριπλῇ τετραπλῇ τ' ἀποτίσσομεν and cf. West (1997) 259-260. For μακαρισμός in love poetry, where it retains a certain solemnity, cf. Tib. 1.10.63-64 *quater ille beatus, / quo tenera irato flere puella potest* with Maltby (2002) 356-357; Hor. *Carm.* 1.13.17-18 *felices ter et amplius / quos irrupta tenet copula* with N-H 177; Prop. 3.12.15 *ter quater in casta felix, o Postume, Galla* with Fedeli 403; Ov. *Am.* 2.5.9 *felix, qui quod amat defendere fortiter audet* with McKeown III 88, *Lygd.* **6.43-44** below and see further Dirichlet (1914). For the dative of advantage (here *mihi*) with *felix* see *ThLL*

6(1).440.29-30. For the combination *felix dies* cf. Ter. *Andr.* 956 *o faustum et felicem diem*; Virg. *Georg.* 1.276-277; *Aetna* 636; *Ciris* 27; *Laus Pis.* 159; Sen. *Troad.* 470.

que- ... que-: see **1.3-4n.**

27 pro dulci reditu quaecumque uouentur: refers, like *reddere* in **25**, to the return of Neaera to her relationship with Lygdamus. For the phrase *dulcis reditus* cf. Hor. *Epod.* 16.35-36 *haec et quae poterunt reditus abscindere dulces / eamus omnis exsecrata ciuitas*. The formulation is used in Homer with reference to sweet a return to the native land, so *Od.* 11.100, νόστον ... μελιηδέα, 22.323 νόστοιο ... γλυκεροῖο and cf. Archilochus fr. 8.2 West. The term *uouentur* picks up the theme of vows *uotis* (**1**) with which the poem opened. As N-A 236-237 suggests, the author could be alluding here to one of the traditional themes of the *propemptikon* or 'send off' poem, namely a final prayer for the safe return of one setting out on a dangerous journey; see Cairns (1972) 160-163, Maltby (2002) 184, and cf. Menander Rhetor (3.399.1ff. Sp.).

28 audiat auersa non meus aure deus: the possible negative reaction of the god to Lygdamus' prayers is indicated in two ways. First he would listen to them with ears averted *auersa ... aure* and second he would be unfavourable to Lygdamus' *non meus*. For the first, cf. Liv. 24.26.10 *auersis auribus animisque cum conclamassent ne tempus tereretur* and see *ThLL* 2.1510.67-72. For the possessive adj. (*meus* here) applied to gods in the sense of 'favourable', 'propitious' cf. Virg. *Aen.* 2.396 *uadimus inmixti Danais haud numine nostro*; Ov. *Her.* 12.84 *sed mihi tam faciles unde meosque deos*? and see *ThLL* 8.918.8-20. In general the sense of the phrase is the opposite of Prop. 1.1.31 *quibus facili deus annuit aure.* On the use of *audio* of gods hearing and granting a prayer see Thomas (2011) on Hor. *Carm.* 4.13.1-2 and *ThLL* 2.1289.83-1290.34. On gods 'hearing' a prayer as a traditional theme in IE poetry see West (2007) 316-317.

29 regna: either 'kingdoms' in general, conventionally rejected in favour of love, cf. Plaut. *Curc.* 211 *siquidem hercle mihi regnum detur, numquam id potius persequar*; Prop. 1.8B.32 (*Cynthia*) *sine me dulcia regna negat*, 1.14.23-24 *quae* (sc. *Venus*) *mihi dum placata aderit, non ulla* (*Lyda* Markland) *uerebor / regna uel Alcinoi munera despicere*, or, more likely, as Tränkle argues ad loc., a specific reference to the kingdom of Croesus. *Lydius ... amnis* later in the line refers to the gold-bearing river Pactolus, which flows through Lydia in Asia Minor, formerly the kingdom of Croesus. Tränkle, comparing *regna Lydia* at *Laud. Mess.* **7.198-199** *non*

30 For the hyperbolic rejection of all the world's wealth in favour of love, cf. Ov. *Met.* 7.59-60 (Medea) *quemque ego cum rebus, quas totus possidet orbis, / Aesoniden mutasse uelim.*

31-32 The couplet summarises Lygdamus' prayer, making use of terminology with clear Tibullan echoes. In structure with its pleonastic *liceat ... posse* and the pentameter ending *posse frui* it is close to Ov. *Her.* 20 (Acontius to Cydippe).71-72 *quamlibet accuses et sis irata licebit, / irata liceat dum mihi posse frui.*

31 alii ... mihi: for this traditional expression of the contrast between the wishes of others and the poet's ideal, cf. Tib. 1.1.1-5 *alius ... me* with Maltby (2002) 117-118 ad loc. and see Bréguet (1962). The same theme recurs in the *Lygd.* poems at **5.1-5** *uos ... mihi.*

paupere cultu: the same hexameter ending occurs at Tib. 1.10.19 in the context of the simple faith of ancient times: *tunc melius tenuere fidem, cum paupere cultu / stabat in exigua ligneus aede deus.* Here the emphasis is on simplicity of lifestyle (see **23n.** on *paupertas* above), but the same moral overtones apply, including in both cases a carefree family life; Tib. 1.10.39-42 and *Lygd.* **3.32.**

32 securo: 'free from care' (see *LALE* 555 and cf. Serv. *auct. Aen.* 2.374 *securus sine cura*), a key concept in Tibullus, see Wimmel [(1968) 196 n. 45], including both freedom from material (Tib. 1.1.77-78) and physical (Tib. 1.10.10) worries as well as from amatory concerns about the faithfulness of one's wife or mistress (Tib. 1.1.48; Ov. *Am.* 2.19.37 *formosae nimium secure puellae*; see Pichon 260). It recurs in the amatory sense at *Lygd.* **4.54** and **6.31** and in Sulpicia's criticism of Cerinthus at *Sulpicia* poems **16.1.**

cara coniuge: the adjective *carus* is commonly applied to *coniunx*, both in its feminine (Virg. *Aen.* 4.91; Ov. *Met.* 7.692, and of his own wife at *Trist.* 3.4b.7, *Pont.* 1.8.32) and its masculine (Virg. *Aen.* 8.377; Ov. *Met.* 9.382; *CLE* 542.7, 965.7, 998.1) forms cf. **1.6n.** above. On the significance of *coniuge* for the relationship between Lygdamus and Neaera here see **1.26n.** and Gen. Intro., section 2.2.1. The phrase is used in the Cephalus narrative, an important intertext for the whole book, at Ov. *Met.* 7.692-693 *hoc me cum coniuge cara / perdidit* (see Gen. Intro., section 1.3).

frui: common of the enjoyment of sexual relations from Early Latin onwards, cf. Plaut. *Asin.* 917-918 ... *ut sinat / sese alternas cum illo noctes hac frui*; Ter. *Phorm.* 165 *ut mihi liceat tam diu quod amo frui*; Tib. 1.5.17

fruitur nunc alter amore; Ov. *Her.* 20.72 quoted on **31-32n.** above and see Pichon 156 and Adams (1982) 198.

33-34 Lygdamus appeals to two goddesses to look favourably upon his prayers: first Juno (*Saturnia*), goddess of marriage and married women and second Venus (*Cypria*), goddess of love. The two goddesses had worked together to bring about the union of Dido and Aeneas in the fourth book of the *Aeneid* and their association here serves to emphasise that what Lygdamus is praying for is the return of married love. They occur together in a similar context at Stat. *Silu.* 2.7.84 where the Muse Calliope promises Lucan a wife *qualem blanda Venus daretque Iuno.* Juno is described as *pronuba* 'the one who accompanies the bride' at the 'marriage' of Dido and Aeneas in the cave at *Aen.* 4.166-168 ... *prima et tellus et pronuba Iuno / dant signum*; *fulsere ignes et conscius aether / conubiis* and cf. Serv. ad loc. *et pronuba Iuno: quae nubentibus praeest.* Hera, her Greek counterpart, had the title of Ἥρα Ζυγία ["Hera of the marriage yoke"], and Latin equivalents of this are found in Festus' comments on *Iuno Iuga* at Paul. Fest. 92 L. *ara Iunonis Iugae, quam putabant matrimonia iungere* and *Iuno Cinxia* at Paul. Fest. 55 L. *Cinxiae Iunonis nomen sanctum habebatur in nuptis.*

adsis: the ritual verb used in appeals for the appearance of a deity, cf. Tib. 1.1.37 *adsitis diui*, 2.2.5 *Genius adsit*; **[Tib.] 3. Lygd. 6.1** *candide Liber, ades, Sulpicia Cycle* **10.1-2** *huc ades ... / huc ades ... Phoebe* and see Robinson (2011) 68 on Ov. *Fast.* 2.17 and Jocelyn (1969) 199 on Enn. *Trag.* 23, who compares the augural prayer quoted by Serv. *Aen.* 8.72 *adesto Tiberine cum tuis undis.*

timidis ... uotis: the phrase occurs first in Ovid, in the same metrical *sedes* at *Pont.* 2.8.51 *adnuite o timidis, mitissima numina, uotis*; cf. also *Met.* 9. 546 *cogor opemque tuam timidis exposcere uotis.*

faueas ... / ... faueas: another ritual verb, like *adsis*, common in appeals to deities for their help or good will, cf. Tib. 2.5.1 *Phoebe, faue*; **[Tib.] 3. Lygd. 4.44** and see *Sulpicia Cycle* **11.9n.** below.

Saturnia: 'daughter of Saturn' used as an epithet for Juno from Enn. *Ann.* 54 Sk. *Iuno Saturnia* onwards; at *Ann.* 445 Sk. *Saturnia* is used alone in an address to Juno as here. It is common in Virgil's *Aeneid* (16), always in the same position in the hexameter as here, and in Ovid's *Met.* (13). Here, as in Virgil, it may carry with it associations of the innocent golden age of

196   Commentary

Saturn, as described by Tib. 1.3.35-48, 10.9-24, with its implications of religious simplicity and respect for marriage and family life.

concha, Cypria, uecta tua: a reference to Venus, invoked here as goddess of love. Venus was early assimilated to the Greek goddess Aphrodite, who was said to have been born from the foam of the sea on the island of Cyprus (cf. *LALE* 41 *Aphrodite* and Ov. *Met*. 4.538). The epithet *Cypria* is found in verse of Venus only here, but its mention with reference to Venus by both Festus (Paul. Fest. 45 L. *Cypria Venus, quod ei primum in Cypro insula templum sit constitutum*) and Servius (on *Aen.* 5.760 *VENERI IDALIAE: Cypriae*) suggests it may have occurred in earlier Latin verse. Similar epithets for Aphrodite in Greek are frequent, cf. Κυπρία itself at Pind. *Ol*. 1.75, as well as in Homer; and elsewhere Κύπρις, Κυπρογενής and Κυπρογένεια. The shell is mentioned first as an attribute of Venus in Latin at Plaut. *Rud*. 704 where Venus is said to have been born from a shell. The motif of Venus riding on a shell, as here, is rarer: Stat. *Silu.* 1.2.117-118 *haec et caeruleis mecum consurgere digna / fluctibus, et nostra potuit considere concha*, 3.4.5 ... *inque sua ducet* (sc. *Cytherea*) *super aequora concha*; Paul. Fest. 45 L. *Cytherea Venus ab urbe Cythera, in quam primum deuecta esse dicitur concha*. The shell had also been an attribute of Aphrodite in Greek literature, e.g. Call. *Epig.* 5 Pf. where Arsinoe makes her an offering of a shell, and for riding on a shell cf. Lucian. *Dial. marin.* 15.3 τὴν Ἀφροδίτην δύο Τρίτωνες ἔφερον ἐπὶ κόγχης κατακειμένην ["two Tritons carried Aphrodite lying on a shell"]. In the plastic arts Aphrodite is occasionally represented as standing or sitting on a shell from the fourth century BC on, see *LIMC* II (1984), Aphrodite, 1011-1117 and 1183-1188. The best example of this motif in Roman art is the first century AD fresco in the Casa della Venere in conchiglia in Pompeii; see Andreae (1977) plate 73.

35-38 The pathos of the ending is heightened by the repetition in negative form of the conditional clause of **27-30**. There he had stated that if Neaera returned to him he would reject wealth. Here he states that if the fates forbid Neaera's return to him he would choose death. The ending powerfully echoes the theme of death as a result of love's sorrow, which had been central to his second elegy.

35 quod si fata negant reditum: this phrase is close in form and content to Ov. *Met.* 10.38-39 *quod si fata negant ueniam pro coniuge, certum est / nolle redire mihi; leto gaudete duorum*. J. B. Hall suggests emending *aut si* or *at si* of the manuscripts here to *quod si*. A similar formula, again with reference to a wife, occurs at *Met*. 10. 633-634 ... *quod si felicior essem /*

Book Three of the Corpus Tibullianum: 197
Introduction, Text, Translation and Commentary

nec mihi coniugium fata importuna negarent. Phrases of the type *fata negant* (cf. also Ov. *Met.* 13.132; Sen. *Troad.* 511; Sil. 1.107) and *fata sinunt* (e.g. Virg. *Aen.* 1.18; Tib. 1.1.69) attest the common idea of the participation of the fates in human destiny; see further **5.32** *seu nos fata fuisse uelint* with commentary ad loc.

tristesque sorores: the *Parcae*. Originally a single Roman goddess of birth, the three *Parcae* were later assimilated to the three Greek Μοῖραι, deities in charge of human destiny, especially the time of an individual's birth and death; see further **11.3n.** below; Thomas (2011) 70 on Hor. *Carm. Saec.* 25-36, Fraenkel on Aesch. *Ag.* 1535f. In Greek the sisters were named Atropos, Clotho and Lachesis (Hes. *Theog.* 904-906). In Rome of the late Republic, the three *Parcae*, represented in the forum by three statues often referred to as the *tria Fata* (Gell. 3.16.9f.), presided over birth, marriage and death, and their power, like that of fate, was greater than that of the gods, who could not overturn human destiny once the sisters had spun it, cf. Tib. 1.7.1-2 *hanc cecinere diem Parcae fatalia nentes / stamina non ulli dissoluenda deo*. If the *Parcae* had decreed that Neaera should not be returned to Lygdamus, then Juno and Venus would have been powerless to do anything about it. Like the Muses, the *Parcae* are referred to as sisters, first with the addition of the number three (e.g. Hor. *Carm.* 2.3.15-16 *sororum / fila trium*; Prop. 2.13.44 *iussisset saeuis de tribus una soror*; Ov. *Met.* 15.808-809 *sororum / tecta trium*) to distinguish them from the nine Muses, and then, as with *tristes* here and at Stat. *Theb.* 5.274, with an epithet emphasising their sinister nature: *immites* Prop. 4.11.13; *durae* Sen. *Herc. F.*, 181, Sil. 1.281; *nigrae* Stat. *Theb.* 6.376, *Silu.* 3.3.21. For *tristis* in the sense of 'grim', cf. Virg. *Aen.* 2.337 *tristis Erinys*. For the combination of the *Parcae* with *fata*, as here, cf. Stat. *Ach.* 1.255 *nil humiles Parcas terrenaque fata uererer*.

36 stamina ... ducunt: refers to the act of spinning, literally pulling (*ducunt*) the threads (*stamina*) from the allotted weight of wool; cf. Tib. 1.6.78 *ducit inops tremula stamina torta manu* and, with reference to the *Parcae* spinning fate, cf. Cat. 64.311-314; Tib. 1.7.1-2 (quoted above); Ov. *Trist.* 5.3.25-26 (quoted below); Juv. 12.65; Mart. 6.58.7-8 *si mihi lanificae ducunt non pulla sorores / stamina nec surdus uox habet ista deos*. For a detailed description of this spinning technique see Forbes (1964) 149f. It involved drawing off yarn from wool held on a distaff in the left hand onto a spindle which was hung from the right hand and kept constantly spinning, as described most clearly in Cat. 64.311-314; see further Maltby (1999) 244.

canunt: a conjecture by Heinsius for the reading *neunt* of A+. The form *neunt* for *nent* is attested elsewhere, according to N-A ad loc., only in the *Vetus Latina* versions of *Matth.* 6.28 and *Luc.* 12.27 and is unlikely in a writer as careful as our author. It would also simply repeat the physical act of spinning presented in the first half of the pentameter, while the reference to singing would add a new element common in poetic representations of the fates prophesying in song while spinning, e.g. Cat. 64.306-310; Tib. 1.7.1-2 (quoted above); Ov. *Trist.* 5.3.25-26 ... *hanc legem nentes fatalia Parcae / stamina ... cecinere tibi*, *CLE* 1141.16 (late C2 AD), describing the Parcae, *quae uitam pensant quaeque futura canunt* contains perhaps an echo of the original ending of our author's line. For the common practice of singing while spinning or weaving cf. Virg. *Georg.* 1.293-294 *interea longum cantu solata laborem / arguto coniunx percurrit pectine telas* with Mynors ad loc.

37-38 The couplet, whose pentameter in the transmitted text presents considerable difficulties, has as its main aim to highlight the dark and frightening vastness of the underworld which would await him as an inevitable consequence of a separation from Neaera. In content it recalls the final couplet of *Lygd.* **1.27-28**.

37 me uocet: the verb is often used in connection with the call of imminent death, e.g. *CLE* 2075.1-2 ... *nam curua senectus / te rapit et Ditis ianua nigra uocat*; especially frequent in the phrase *fata uocant*: Virg. *Georg.* 4.495-496 *crudelia retro / fata uocant, Aen.* 6.147 *si te fata uocant*, 10.471-472 *etiam sua Turnum / fata uocant*, 11.96-97 *horrida belli / fata uocant*; Ov. *Her.* 6.28, 7.1; Sen. *Herc. F.* 396; Sil. 4.508.

uastos amnes: *uastus* is used in connection with the waters of the underworld also at Lucr. 1.115 *an tenebros Orci uisat uastasque lacunas*; *Culex* 374 *uastum Phlegethonta*; *Eleg. in Maec.* 1.6 *in uastos ... lacus*; it implies vastness and emptiness, as at *Lygd.* **4.85** *uasti ... aequora ponti*, and is applied to various aspects of Hades, e.g. Enn. *Trag.* 152 Jocelyn *inferum uastos specus*; Ov. *Met.* 10.30 *per Chaos hoc ingens uastique silentia regni*; Sen. *Herc. F.* 666 *ingens uorago faucibus uastis patet*.

nigramque paludem: for the *iunctura* cf. Sen. *Thy.* 665-666 *fons ... nigra piger / haeret palude*; Sil. 13.571-573 *Acheron ... / ... / descendit nigra lentus per stagna palude*. The reference here is to the proverbially black waters of the Styx, cf. Virg. *Georg.* 1.243 *Styx atra*; Ov. *Met.* 11.500 *Stygia modo nigrior unda*, a characteristic they share with those of the infernal river Cocytus, e.g. Hor. *Carm.* 2.14.17-18 *uisendus ater flumine* *languido / Cocytus errans*; Virg. *Aen.* 6.132 *Cocytus sinu labens ... atro.* Darkness was one of the terrors of hell, cf. Lucr. 3.1011 *Cerberus et Furiae iam uero et lucis egestas*; Hor. *Carm.* 1.4.16 *iam te premet nox*; Sen. *Epist.* 24.18 *nemo tam puer est ut Cerberum timeat et tenebras* and the adj. *niger* was applied to anything connected with death, e.g. Tib. 1.3.4-5 *Mors nigra ... / ... Mors atra*, with Maltby (2002) 187 ad. loc.; Virg. *Aen.* 6.134-135 *nigra uidere / Tartara*; Ov. *Her.* 2.72 *nigri regia caeca dei*; **[Tib.]** 3. Lygd. **2.18** *nigra ... ueste*, **5.5** *nigram ... horam*, **5.33** *nigras pecudes*; see André (1949) 51 and cf. Serv. *Aen.* 6.272 *hoc et uidemus et tractatur ab Epicuris, rebus tollere noctem colorum uarietatem: unde etiam apud inferos omnia nigra esse dicuntur.*

38 A+ here reads *diues in ignaua luridus Orcus aqua* which would involve an unusual asyndetic accumulation of adjectives *diues ... luridus* and a problematic *in* + abl. *in ignaua ... aqua*. This reading is defended by Schuster [(1968) 153-154], who takes *Diues ... Orcus* as a single unit equivalent to *Dis Pater*. This unit would then be capable of further adjectival qualification as at **3.29** *Lydius aurifer amnis*, **4.5-6** *uenturae nuntia sortis*; / ... *Tuscis exta probata* and **5.22** *duraque ... tertia regna dei*. Otherwise such accumulation would be rare, if not unparalleled; cf. **8.19-20** ... *niger* ... */ proximus Eois ... Indus aquis*. Further problems are caused by the phrase *in ignaua ... aqua*. If *in* + abl. here is dependent on *diues*, meaning 'rich in' as at Ov. *Met.* 5.302 *diues in aruis*, this would be unusual both in its syntax (the normal construction would be with a simple genitive or ablative, see *OLD diues* 3) and in its meaning since the wealth of Hades (Pluto) usually consists in agricultural produce which he sends up from the underworld for mortals. If, on the other hand, *in* + abl. is local it would be awkward after *in* + acc. in **37** and would add nothing new to the hexameter. For these reasons many editors accept the necessity for emendation here, and I print the suggestion of N. Heinsius *Ditis et ignauam luridus Orcus aquam*. For the combination *-que ... et* in *nigramque paludem / ... et ignauam ... aquam* cf. **2.24** *Eoique Arabes diues et Assyria* and **4.44** *Phoebusque et Bacchus*. For the three-element phrase in **37-38** *in uastos amnes nigramque paludem / ... et ignauam ... aquam* Tränkle compares in a similar context **5.23-24** *Elysios olim liceat cognoscere campos / Lethaeamque ratem Cimmeriosque lacus*. For the reference to the waters of *Dis* cf. *Culex* 372-373 *Ditis opacos / ... lacus*; Stat. *Theb.* 7.782-783 *atraque Ditis / flumina*; Mart. 9.29.2 *ad infernas ... Ditis aquas*; Lygd. **1.28** *pallida Ditis aqua*.

Ditis: see **1.27-28n**. The god's name is connected with riches and summarises the poem's theme of the uselessness of riches, which are a characteristic only of death.

ignauam ... aquam: the rivers and marshes of Hades are traditionally slow-running or stagnant: Pind. fr. 130 βληχροὶ δνοφερᾶς νυκτὸς ποταμοί ["the sluggish rivers of dark night"]; Hor. *Carm.* 2.14.17-18 *ater flumine languido / Cocytus errans*; Prop. 4.11.15 *uada lenta Acherontis*; Ov. *Met.* 4.434 *Styx nebulas exhalat iners*; Sen. *Herc. F.* 686 *palus inertis foeda Cocyti iacet*; Sil. 13.572-573 *Acheron ... / ... descendit nigra lentus per stagna palude.*

luridus Orcus: for the *iunctura* cf. Hor. *Carm.* 3.4.74-75 *... partus fulmine luridum / missos ad Orcum.* The adj. refers to the yellow pallor of corpses (*ThLL* 7.2.1862.2-3) and by metonymy to things causing such pallor. For the identification of Orcus with Dis cf. Enn. *Var.* 78 *Pluto Latine est Dis pater, alii Orcum uocant* and see *Lygd.* **1.27-28n.** above. It can denote either the place (Hades) or its personal ruler, see further N-H on Hor. *Carm.* 2.18.30. Although *Orcus* is well attested in high-style poetry (Lucr. 3, Hor. 10, Virg. 10) it is rare in elegy, occurring only here and at Prop. 3.19.27.

Poem 4

In this, the longest and most ambitious of *Lygd.* elegies, Lygdamus relates a dream which has deeply disturbed him. In the dream Apollo has appeared to him in his role of Citharoedus, the lyre-playing protector of poets, and has informed him that Neaera prefers to be another man's girl *alterius mauult esse puella uiri* (**58**). An important intertext for Apollo's warning here must be Apollo's warning to Gallus of his mistress Lycoris' infidelity at Virg. *Ecl.* 10.21-23 *uenit Apollo / 'Galle, quid insanis?' inquit. 'tua cura Lycoris / perque niues alium perque horrida castra secuta est.'*

The contents may be analysed as follows:

1-16 Lygdamus' reaction to the dream, contrasting his belief in oracles and haruspicy with his doubt in the veracity of dreams, and wishing that in this case, in particular, its contents may prove to be untrue.

17-81 The central section taken up with a description of the dream.

17-22 The time of its occurrence, towards dawn after an initial sleepless night, is related in epic style.

23-42 Description of the androgynous appearance of Apollo Citharoedus.

43-50 The speech of Apollo begins opens with an assurance of his favour and of the truth of what he will say.

51-60 He goes on to reveal that Neaera prefers a relationship with another man to a faithful marriage.

61-62 Apollo curses women who trick their husbands.

63-76 He advises Lygdamus to bear his sufferings and to attempt to bring Neaera round by prayer and supplication, using his own service to his lover Admetus as an example.

79-80 The speech ends with a message Lygdamus should give Neaera from Apollo. She should abandon her new lover and accept the marriage with Lygdamus that the god has promised.

81-96 The final sixteen lines balance the opening sixteen, giving again Lygdamus' reaction to the dream: in this case his assurance that Neaera cannot be as heartless as Apollo describes her, especially as she comes from such gentle and loveable parents (**93-94**).

The final couplet (**95-96**), asking the god to change the dream for the better, closely echoes the opening couplet, thus lending the poem a neat ring-structure.

The poem has been criticised by earlier commentators for its long-windedness and internal inconsistencies, a view perhaps summed up best in Heyne's comment: *otiosa rerum ac uerborum copia laborare uidetur totum carmen*. Two factors may have contributed to this impression. First some of the inconsistency could be intended to reflect the poet's emotional turmoil. His statement at **7-8** that dreams, in contrast to oracles and haruspicy, give false predictions, is only wishful thinking, as his prayers at **1-2**, **13-14** and **95-96** for this dream to prove untrue show. Apollo's assurance that his warnings are true (**49-50**) is apparently undermined by the fact that it is delivered in a dream, but that dream takes place at dawn (**17-22**), a time at which dreams are traditionally supposed to be true. Apollo's dream is rejected out of hand (**82, 95-96**) although in addition to the warning about Neaera's unfaithfulness (**58**) it contains advice on how she can be won back (**63-74**) and a statement that his marriage to Neaera was promised him by Apollo. The second factor, which may have contributed to the idea of the poem's long-windedness, is the fact that our author is aiming at a higher poetic style, reminiscent of Tibullus in 2.5, where the Sibylline oracles on Aeneas' flight from Troy to Italy at 2.5.18ff. allow Tibullus to raise the tone of his elegy to approach that of Virgilian epic. So the author here, although his theme is by no means as lofty, aspires to a similarly elevated stylistic level, for example with the chronological periphrasis to denote dawn at **17-22**, the epic similes for Apollo's pale and pink complexion at **29-34** and the long ekphrasis on the appearance of the god at **23-38**. This description, with its emphasis on Apollo's pale complexion, long flowing locks and long cloak, and his lyre, which he played with an ivory plectrum goes back ultimately to the description of Apollo in Call. *Hymn* 2.32-42. However it has a closer model in Tibullus' description of Apollo at 2.5.1-10, on the introduction of Messalla's son Messalinus into the priestly college of the *quindecimuiri sacris faciundis*. Tibullus there seems to have in mind the statue of Apollo Citharoedus by Scopas (fourth century BC) which Augustus had placed in his new temple of Apollo on the Palatine.

The general theme of a dream giving advice on love is perhaps Ovidian in its inspiration. The normal role of Apollo is to give advice not on love but on the type of poetry to write. This is true in Call. *Aetia* prologue fr. 1.21ff. Pf. where his advice is followed by a dream in which Callimachus is sanctified by the Muses on Mt. Helicon. Prop. 3.3 makes the warning from Apollo to Propertius part of a dream in which he is encouraged by Apollo and the Muses to keep to love-elegy. Three further Propertian dreams involving Cynthia attest the importance of the dream topos in elegy, but have no input from Apollo. So at 2.26A he dreams that Cynthia is drowning at sea and confesses her unfaithfulness to him; at 3.10.1-4 the Muses remind Propertius in a dawn dream that it is his mistress's birthday and at 4.7 Cynthia's ghost appears to Propertius in a dream shortly after her death complaining of his lack of care at her funeral. In Tib. 1.4 advice on love (in this case of boys) is given not by Apollo in a dream but by a statue of the god Priapus. The only poem in which Apollo gives advice on love, rather than on poetry, is at Ov. *Ars* 2.493-510 where the god appears to Ovid as he is performing his poem and sings verse of general advice to lovers to the accompaniment of his lyre. At *Am.* 3.5 Ovid recounts an allegorical dream about the infidelity of his mistress, but this does not involve any divine appearance. In this it is rather like Hero's dream at *Her.* 19.193-202 in which a dying dolphin warns her of the dangers faced by her lover Leander. At *Rem.* 555-576 it is *Amor Lethaeus* who appears to Ovid in a dream and gives general advice to lovers on ridding themselves of their passion. Finally at *Pont.* 3.3 Amor appears to Ovid in a dream and advises him to give up hope of any pardon from Augustus. Here the lengthy setting of the dream and detailed description of Amor before he speaks may have influenced this poem, even though it differs in the content of the advice given. Perhaps closer in content is the warning by Apollo to Gallus that his mistress Lycoris has followed a rival on his campaigns abroad at Virg. *Ecl.* 10.21-23 quoted in para **1** above (cf. Apollo's words to Lygdamus at **57-58** below with commentary ad loc.). For other possible Gallan touches in Apollo's intervention see **51-52n.** and **56n.** below.

1 Di meliora ferant: an apotropaic formula, cf. Hofmann [(1926) 31], warding off evil, in this case the dream mentioned in the second half of the line. Before this becomes clear the formula could be thought of as linking with the end of the previous elegy, warding off the evil associations of the wish for death in its final couplet. The phrase is a variation on expressions of the type *di monuerint meliora* (Pacuv. *Trag.* 112); *di meliora faxint* (Plaut. *Poen.* 1400); *di meliora uelint* (Ov. *Met.* 7.37); *di melius faxint* (Plaut. *Merc.* 285) and *di melius faciant* (Plaut. *Bacch.* 626a, *Cas.* 813, *Pseud.* 315), often abbreviated to *di meliora* (e.g. Cic. *Phil.* 8.9.9, 10.5.3; *Sen.* 47.6) or, in Ovid, *di melius* (*Am.* 2.7.19, *Her.* 3.125, 17.30, *Ars* 2.388, *Rem.* 439, *Met.* 9.497, *Ibis* 2). Here the verb *ferant* corresponds to *tulit* in the pentameter.

nec sint mihi somnia uera: a negative after a jussive subjunctive is regularly introduced by *nec,* see K-S II 1.193 and cf. Hor. *Carm.* 2.11.3-4 *remittas / quaerere nec trepides.* On true and false dreams and the different gates of sleep through which they arrive see Hom. *Od.* 19.562-567; Virg. *Aen.* 6.893-901. True dreams are those whose content comes to pass, cf. Ov. *Her.* 19.196 *somnia quo cerni tempore uera solent.* The opposite are *somnia uana* or *inania*, false dreams, e.g. Prop. 3.6.31 (Cynthia to Lygdamus) *si non uana canunt mea somnia, Lygdame.* For the wish that the content of the dream should not be realised cf. Ov. *Met.* 9.474-475 *me miseram, tacitae quid uult sibi noctis imago?/ quam nolim rata sit. cur haec ego somnia uidi?* of the incestuous dreams of Byblis concerning her brother Caunus. This is a passage which our author may have had in mind here, since it also foreshadows the doubt in dreams expressed by Lygdamus below, see **7-10n.**

2 quae tulit hesterna ... nocte: the phrase is close in structure to Tib. 2.1.12 *cui tulit hesterna gaudia nocte Venus.* The combination *hesterna ...*

nocte also occurs at Prop. 2.29A.1 *hesterna ... cum potus nocte uagarer*; Mart. 1.27.1; *Sulpicia* poems **18.5** below, and cf. also Ov. *Her.* 19 (Hero to Leander) 72 *nocte sed hesterna* and 193 *nec minus hesternae confundor imagine noctis*. The reading *externa* of some MSS makes no sense, while *extrema* found in J, was favoured by Scaliger and some later editors who interpreted it as 'at the end of the night', see **17-22** below, a time when dreams were supposed to be truest, cf. Ov. *Her.* 19.195-196 *namque sub aurora iam dormitante lucerna / somnia quo cerni tempore uera solent*. The phrase *extrema nocte* in the sense of 'at the end of the night' is attested at Cic. *Arat.* 82; Varro *Ling.* 8.63; Manil. 5.698; Lucan 5.734, Val.-Fl. 5.140.

pessima: better taken with *somnia* than with *quies*, thus producing the balanced pair *meliora ferant / tulit ... pessima*. For the idea of bad dreams cf. Tib. 1.5.13-14 *ipse procuraui ne possent saeua nocere / somnia*, 2.6.37 *ne tibi neglecti mittant mala somnia manes*.

quies: see **22n.** *sera quies* below.

3 The majority of MSS have *uani* and all have *uisum*. The problem with the vocative *uani* is that it must refer to *somni* in a *constructio ad sensum* picking up *somnia*, but this would create an unacceptable ambiguity given the presence of *di* (**1**). One solution would be to read *uanum* with the later MSS 'away with you (dreams) and turn away a vane and false vision', but this would leave *ite procul* without its usual vocative, as e.g. in Tib. 1.1.75-76 *... uos, signa tubaeque, / ite procul, cupidis uulnera ferte uiris*, 2.4.15 and 20 *ite procul, Musae*; Prop. 4.6.9 *ite procul, fraudes*; Mart. 14.47,1 *ite procul, iuuenes*; **[Tib.] 3.** *Lygd.* **6.7** *ite procul durum curae genus*. A better approach is that proposed by Lee [(1974) 57 following Bolle (1872)] who changes *uisum* to *uisus* 'away with you empty visions, and turn aside your falsehood', which is the reading adopted here. For *falsum* in the sense of falsehood, cf. Lucr. 4.764 *nec possunt falsum ueris conuincere rebus*.

ite procul: originally a liturgical phrase, used to expel all those who would pollute a religious site or ritual, cf. Call. *Hymn* 2.2 ἑκάς, ἑκάς ὅστις ἀλιτρός ["away, away whoever is sinful"]; Tib. 2.1.11-12 *uos quoque abesse procul iubeo, discedat ab aris, / cui tulit hesterna gaudia nocte Venus*; Ov. *Met.* 2.464 *i procul hinc ... nec sacros pollue fontis, Fast.* 2.623 *procul hinc, procul impius esto*, with Robinson (2011) 396 ad loc. It becomes a general formula of rejection in the Augustan and later poets, as the examples above show.

uani ... uisus: for the *iunctura* cf. Lucan 3.38 *quid ... uani terremur imagine uisus?* The adj. implies 'empty' in the sense of 'delusive', while *uisus* refers specifically to a supernatural vision, as here of the god Apollo.

4 in nobis quaerere uelle fidem: *in nobis* is Guietus' conjecture for the meaningless *in uotis* of the MSS. For *quaerere fidem* in the sense of 'search for my belief (in you)', cf. Ov. *Ars* 1.612 *haec tibi quaeratur qualibet arte fides* 'you must search for her belief (sc. in your role as a lover) by any device'. For the prohibition *desinite ... uelle*, cf. *desine uelle* at **80** below.

5-10 Lygdamus contrasts true messages given by the gods' oracles and the inspection of entrails (**5-6**) with delusive dreams which trick credulous humans (**7-10**).

5-6 uera monent: the same phraseology occurs at Tib. 2.4.51 *uera quidem moneo*; Ov. *Met.* 13.775-776 *... sic frustra uera monentem / spernit* (of Polyphemus mocking the seer Telemus), and Stat. *Theb.* 8.333-334 *... caeloque et uera monentibus aris / concilies* (sc. *me*) (Thiodamas, addressing the shade of the seer Amphiaraus).

uenturae nuntia sortis: I take this phrase with Lee as being in apposition to *uera* of the first half of the hexameter: literally 'the gods warn of true things, things announcing our coming fate.' *nuntia* is best construed as a n. pl. adj. rather than a noun 'messages', since *nuntium* is rare in this sense. For the gen. with adjectival *nuntius* cf. Virg. *Aen.* 8.548-550 *... pars cetera prona / fertur aqua ... / nuntia uentura Ascanio rerumque patrisque*; Ov. *Met.* 5.549 *foedaque fit uolucris, uenturi nuntia luctus*. Others take the phrase as proleptic, looking forward to *exta* in **6**, in which case *nuntia* would again be adjectival, as at Tib. 2.1.25-26 *... uiden ut felicibus extis / significet placidos nuntia fibra deos*. The second explanation would involve an awkward enjambement and a lack of balance between the two sources of prophecy, the gods and haruspicy (divination by inspection of entrails). For *uenturae ... sortis* cf. Virg. *Aen.* 10.501 *nescia mens hominum fati sortisque futurae*.

Tuscis ... uiris: the inspection of entrails as a form of prophecy was the speciality of *haruspices* who came originally from Etruria, cf. Cic. *Fam.* 6.6.3 *disciplina Tusca*; Liv. 5.15.11 *disciplina Etrusca*. On *Tuscus* and *Etruscus* in the *Lygd.* group see **5.1n.** on *Etruscis ... fontibus*.

exta: probably a shortened form of **exsecta*, the parts 'cut out' from a sacrificed animal. The main organ used was the liver, but also the heart, lungs and gall bladder were inspected. Here the term *fibra* (literally 'fibre', 'filament') is avoided, as used of entrails, e.g., by Tib. 1.8.3 *conscia fibra deorum*, 2.1.26 *nuntia fibra*; Prop. 4.1B.104 *fibra locuta deos*, and Ovid (8), but *exta* also occurs in the earlier elegists at Tib. 2.5.14 and Prop. 4.1A.24 and is more frequent than *fibra* in Ovid (20).

probata: this seems to be a technical term for the 'examination' of the organs, whose size, shape, colour and markings were thought to convey prophetic information, cf. Serv. *Georg.* 2.194 *reddi...dicebantur exta, cum probata et elixa arae superponebantur*.

7-8 In contrast to the true warnings sent by gods and derived from haruspicy, dreams simply delude men's minds. The falseness of dreams, especially those emanating from the gate of ivory, is a commonplace of ancient literature: Hom. *Od.* 19.564-565; Plaut. *Merc.* 225-226 *miris modis di ludos faciunt hominibus / mirisque exemplis somnia in somnis danunt*; Lucr. 5.62-63 *sed simulacra solere in somnis fallere mentem, / cernere cum uideamur eum quem uita reliquit*; Hor. *Carm.* 3.27.39-42 (Europa) *an uitiis carentem / ludit imago / uana, quae porta fugiens eburna, / somnium ducit?*; Virg. *Aen.* 6.896 *sed falsa ad caelum mittunt insomnia Manes*, 10.642 *aut quae sopitos deludunt somnia sensus*; Petr. 128.6.1-2 *nocte sopifera ueluti cum somnia ludunt / errantes oculos*, fr. 30.1 *somnia, quae mentes ludunt uolitantibus umbris*; Sen. *Dial.* 1.6.3 *animos inanes uelut longo fallacique somnio lusi*; Sil. 8.641 *ludificante etiam terroris imagine somnos*. After his dream in *Am.* 3.5 Ovid questions whether such visions contain any truth: *Am.* 3.5.31-32 *dic age, nocturnae, quicumque es, imaginis augur, / si quid habent ueri, uisa quid ista ferant*.

somnia ... temeraria: 'chance dreams'; the adj. is used here in the sense of 'fortuitous', see *OLD temerarius* 1, rather than the more common meaning of 'rash, thoughtless' *OLD temerarius* 3, as at **6.27**. The word is avoided by Horace, Virgil and Tibullus, and occurs once only in Propertius at 2.8.13, but is frequent in Ovid (33).

fallaci ... nocte: the darkness of night is deceptive, cf. Ov. *Ars* 1.245-246 *hic tu fallaci nimium ne crede lucernae: / iudicio formae noxque merumque nocent*.

ludunt: 'delude, deceive', commonly applied to dreams, cf. Hor. *Carm.* 3.27.40; Petr. 128.6.1; Sen. *Dial.* 1.6.3, all quoted above.

pauidas mentes: the collocation is found first at Lucr. 6.51 *mortales, pauidis cum pendent mentibus saepe*, and then only in post-Augustan

Latin, see *ThLL* 10.815.51-54 and cf. Petr. 89.1.17 *mentisque pauidae gaudium lacrimas habent*; Sen. *Phaed.* 636 *pauidae mentis exaudi preces*, 1082 ... *pauida sonipedes mente exciti.*

9 The text of this line is corrupt. I adopt the reading *natum in curas* found in a number of later MSS for the meaningless *natum maturas* of A+. Other later MSS offer *uanum uentura*. No completely satisfactory solution has been found, but *natum in curas* provides a possibility which would not disrupt the required sense of the couplet, namely men's expiation of dreams by offerings of spelt and salt.

natum in curas: describes the wretched condition of mortals, modelled perhaps on the Homeric οἰζυροῖσι βροτοῖσι and δειλοῖσι βροτοῖσι ("wretched mortals, miserable mortals"). Other equivalents found in earlier Latin didactic and epic would be *mortalibus aegris* at Lucr. 6.1; Virg. *Georg.* 1.237, *Aen.* 2.268, 10.274, 12.850 or *miseris mortalibus* at Lucr. 5.944; Virg. *Georg.* 3.66, *Aen.* 11.182. This would be the only occurrence of such a phrase in elegy. For *natus in* + acc. cf. Liv. 30.28.11 *uelut fatalem eum ducem in exitium suum natum horrebant*; Sen. *Epist.* 120.14 *et sit in hoc natum hominem, ut uita defungeretur.*

hominum genus: the phrase occurs only here in elegy. It is first attested in verse in Lucr. 3.307, 5.1430, followed by Virg. *Aen.* 1.743; Val.-Fl. (2); Plin. *Paneg.* (3), and Sil. (3) etc. and in prose in Cicero (5); one occurrence each in Columella, Curtius, Mela, and Plin. *Nat.*, then Sen. *Dial.* (2) and Quint. (5). Like *natum in curas* it is an elevated circumlocution.

omina: used of dreams also at Ov. *Her.* 9.39-40 (Deianira) *me pecudum fibrae simulacraque inania somni / ominaque arcana nocte petita mouent* and Lucan 7.21-22 *siue per ambages solitas contraria uisis / uaticinata quies magni tulit omina planctus.*

10 farre pio: *far* was emmer wheat (*triticum dicoccum*), the standard grain of the early Romans (cf. Ov. *Fast.* 2.519f.), later replaced by wheat of the type *triticum durum* whose husk was easier to remove; see Moritz (1958) xxiiff. In a mixture with salt known as *mola salsa* the *far* was used in religious offerings, being sprinkled on the altar or on the head of the sacrificial victim (cf. *immolatio, immolare*). For *far pium* with reference to *mola salsa* cf. Serv. *Ecl.* 8.82 *sparge molam: far et salem. (add. auct.) hoc nomen de sacris tractum est: far enim pium, id est mola casta, salsa*. Its use to expiate dreams, often in combination with incense is mentioned by

Plaut. *Amph.* 738-740 ... *somnium narrat tibi.* / *sed, mulier, postquam experrecta es, te prodigali Ioui* / *aut mola salsa hodie aut ture comprecatum oportuit*; Tib. 1.5.13-14 *ipse procuraui ne possent saeua nocere* / *somnia ter sancta* (*salsa* Muretus) *deueneranda mola*; Mart. 7.54.1-6 *semper mane mihi de me mera somnia narras* ...; 5 *consumpsi salsasque molas et turis aceruos*; / *decreuere greges dum cadit agna frequens.*

placant: an unusual word in the context, where one would expect a word meaning 'expiate' (e.g. *purgant*) rather than 'placate'. The reason seems to be that for the wording of the pentameter our author is influenced by Hor. *Carm.* 3.23.19-20 (*immunis manus*) *molliuit auersos Penates* / *fare pio et saliente mica* where the meaning 'placate' *molliuit* is required. The plural *placant* is a *constructio ad sensum* after the singular subject *hominum genus* equivalent to the plural *homines*, cf. **10.26n.** below for examples with *quisque*.

saliente sale: Our author takes the picture of the salt 'dancing' in the hot flames from Horace (quoted above), but his substitution of *sale* for *mica* aims at an alliteration which his model had avoided, perhaps to bring out the popular etymology of *sal* 'salt' from *salire* 'to leap', see *LALE* 539 and cf. Isid. *Etym.* 16.2.3 *sal quidem dictum putant quod in igne exiliat.*

11-16 Whatever men will choose to believe regarding true and false prophecies, Lygdamus prays that Lucina render his night terrors groundless, provided he has not offended the gods in word or deed.

11-12 I print the text of A which seems to offer adequate sense. In **5-8** Lygdamus had contrasted the gods (**5**) and haruspicy (**6**) which give true prophecies with dreams (**7-8**) which are deceptive. The *siue ... siue* clauses here (**11-12**) present two possibilities arising from this introductory section (**5-8**). Thus *uera moneri* (**11**) relates back to the true prophecies of **5-6** and contrasts with *mendaci somno credere* (**12**) which refers back to the false prophecies of dreams in **7-8**.

illi: 'they', nom. pl., i.e. 'men', looking back to *hominum genus* (**9**). Dissen (followed by Tränkle ad loc.), feeling that the subject could be understood without the pronoun, conjectures *illis* instrumental, referring to *exta* (**6**).

moneri: N-A (where?), following some of the later MSS, prints *monenti* to give two contrasting terms agreeing with *somno*, *uera monenti* 'true' and *mendaci* 'false'. As explained above, in my view A's text presents no insuperable difficulties and can be retained.

mendaci somno: for the collocation, cf. Ov. *Her.* 13.107 *aucupor in lecto mendaces caelibe somnos*, of Laodamia dreaming of her absent husband.

uolent: 'will wish to' future with indefinite reference. Postgate (followed by Tränkle and N-A) finds the future awkward in this context and conjectures *solent*.

13-14 Lucina is an odd goddess to invoke in connection with a dream. Her usual role, often under the title of Juno Lucina, was as the goddess who presided over childbirth (cf. Plaut. *Aul.* 692, *Truc.* 476; Ter. *And.* 473, *Ad.* 487 etc.). Her name was connected etymologically with *lux* (see *LALE* 348), as she brought new-born infants into the light of day (cf. Varro *Ling.* 5.69; Ov. *Fast.* 3.255; Porph. Hor. *Carm.* 3.22.2-3 *ideo Lucinam appellamus, quod lucem nascentibus tribuat*). However, she is never associated with light in general, for example, as a goddess of daybreak, who could be appealed to to put an end to night's terrors, as Cynthia appeals to Vesta at Prop. 2.29B.27-28. In view of the content of Lygdamus' dream here, the warning that Neaera is being unfaithful (cf. **58** below), it could be that Lucina is being invoked as guardian of the marriage bed, as in Sen. *Medea* 1-2 *di coniugales tuque genialis tori, / Lucina, custos*. In this context it could be significant that the festival of Juno Lucina was the *Matronalia* held annually on the first of March, which had provided the background for the opening elegy of the *Lygd.* group, where Neaera's possible unfaithfulness (**1.23-28**) was also a theme. A new temple to Juno Lucina had been dedicated on the Esquiline by AD 8, see Boyle (2003) 246-247 and cf. Ov. *Fast.* 2.55-66. The goddess is frequently depicted in mythology as reacting angrily to Jove's infidelities, see Ingleheart (2010) 253 on Ov. *Trist.* 2.291-292. However, even in the opening of Seneca's *Medea*, Lucina's association with the children of the marriage is to the fore. Her children have an important role to play in Medea's revenge, but children play no part in Lygdamus' relationship with Neaera. Other associations of Lucina could, then, be relevant. Perhaps due to Greek influence Lucina is later associated with Artemis/Diana (cf. Cat. 34.13-16; Cic. *Nat. Deor.* 2.68 with Pease ad loc.), who herself had three facets as the moon in heaven (Lucina), Artemis on earth (Diana) and Hecate in the underworld, cf. Serv. *auct. Aen.* 4.511 *non nulli eandem Lucinam, Dianam, Hecaten appellant, ideo quia uni deae tres adsignant potestates nascendi, ualendi, moriendi*. For the epithet *Lucina* applied to Diana, see Virg. *Ecl.* 4.10; Hor. *Carm. Saec.* 13-16. Hecate presided over magic and witchcraft (cf. Hor. *Serm.* 1.8.33; Tib. 1.2.54), and in Greek was associated with the sending of dreams (Eur. *Hel.* 569-570), though there are no parallels for this in Latin literature. It may be significant, however, that it is Diana whom Atalanta asks to supress her evil dreams at Stat. *Theb.* 9.626-627 *preme dira malorum / signa*. For more on Juno Lucina and her association with Diana see Thomas (2011) 67-68 on Hor. *Carm. Saec.* 15-16.

13 efficiat uanos noctis ... timores: 'may she render vain terrors of the night'; for the distinction between 'true' and 'vain' fears, cf. Liv. 41.23.18 *donec ad certum redigatur, uanusne hic timor noster an uerus fuerit*; Sen. *Oed.* 700-701 *qui pauet uanos metus, / ueros meretur*; Val. Fl. 8.408-409 *sed miser ut uanos, ueros ita saepe timores / uersat amor*. For *uani timores* cf. [Ov.] *Halieut.* 50 *aut uani quatiunt semper lymphata timores*. The singular is especially common in Liv.: 2.63.4 *perfusis uano timore Romanis*, 3.3.3, 26.3.6, 35.31.7, 38.28.8.

14 frustra inmeritum: on the unusual elision see Platnauer 75.

pertimuisse: except for comedy, Plaut. (5), Ter. (1), and Ovid (19), this verb is restricted mainly to prose, especially Cicero. Five of Ovid's nineteen examples occur in the same form, *pertimuisse*, and verse position as here. Elsewhere in poetry it is found only at *Ciris* 82 and Mart. 6.43.8 *nec longas pertimuisse uias*, in the same *sedes* as here and in a phrase reminiscent of Tib., e.g. 1.3.36 *tellus in longas est patefacta uias*.

14-16 Lygdamus prays that Lucina should wish that in his innocence (*immeritum*) his fear was groundless (*frustra*), provided he has not offended the gods. The idea that the suffering caused by his dream was undeserved, since he has not sinned against the gods, echoes a similar situation at Tib. 1.2.81-88 in which Tib. asks whether the suffering caused him by Delia's being closely guarded by her husband could be put down to impious behaviour on his part against Venus and the gods:

> *num Veneris magnae uiolaui numina uerbo,*
> * et mea nunc poenas inpia lingua luit?*   82
> *num feror incestus sedes adiisse deorum*
> * sertaque de sanctis deripuisse focis?*
> *non ego, si merui, dubitem procumbere templis*   85
> * et dare sacratis oscula liminibus,*
> *non ego tellurem genibus perrepere supplex*
> * et miserum sancto tundere poste caput.*

["Has any word of mine violated the majesty of mighty Venus and is my impious tongue now paying the price? Can I be accused of profanely approaching the seats of the gods and of snatching garlands from their holy hearths? If guilty, I would not hesitate to fall prostrate before their temples and bestow kisses upon their sacred thresholds, to crawl the earth on my knees as a suppliant and to beat my wretched head against their holy door."]

Various verbal and thematic echoes show that our author has this passage in mind: *inpia lingua* **16**, also at Tib. 82 in the same metrical *sedes*; *inmeritum* **14**, cf. *si merui* at Tib. 85; *magnos ...deos* **16**, cf. *Veneris magnae* at Tib. 81. Whereas Tib. agrees, if he is guilty *si merui* (85), to do penance (85-88), no such agreement is found here since he claims to be innocent of any crime *immeritum* (**14**). In this case the *si* clause, taken from his model, does not quite fit the new context after *immeritum*, where a causal clause 'since my mind is not guilty' would have been more natural. In a similar passage at **5.6-14** the adj. *inmerito* is followed not by a conditional but by a series of negative statements *non ego temptaui* (**7**) ... *nec* (**9**) ... *nec* (**11**) ... *nec* (**13**).

15-16 Lucina's aid is dependent on Lygdamus' being innocent of sacrilege in either deed (*facto* **15**) or word (*lingua* **16**). The same distinction between evil acts and blasphemy is drawn in Lygdamus' *auersio* at **5.7-14** below, with the acts being listed in **7-12** and blasphemy in **13-14**.

15 turpi ... facto: cf. **5.12** *nec cor sollicitant facta nefanda meum* below. For the dative after *obnoxia*, cf. Sall. *Cat.* 52.21 *animus ... neque delicto neque lubidini obnoxius.* For the combination *turpe factum* cf. Cic. *Caec.* 8 *ex facto quidem turpi*, De Inu. 2.77 *cum de facto turpi aliquo... fateatur*; Sall. *Iug.* 85.31 *causas turpium factorum saepe extitisse*; Sen. *Contr.* 9.2.16 *factum ipsum turpe est.*

16 laesit: the technical term for offending the gods, often in the phrase *numen laedere*, e.g. Hor. *Epod.* 15.3 *magnorum numen laesura deorum* of the faithless Neaera, on which see L. C. Watson (2003) 467-468, Tib. 1.3.79 *et Danai proles, Veneris quod numina laesit*, 1.9.6; Virg. *Aen.* 1.8, 2.183; Prop. 2.15.48; Lucan 7.848, **[Tib.] 3.** *Lygd.* **6.26** (of Neaera) *quid ualeat laesi sentiat ira dei.* The irony here is that it is not Lygdamus but Neaera (as becomes clear later at **6.51, 55, 56**) who has sworn falsely, just as Horace's Neaera had. The combination with *magnos ... deos* suggests a definite echo of Hor. *Epod.* 15. On the possibility that Lygdamus presents himself as the rich rival of Hor. for Neaera's affections, addressed in that poem, see Gen. Intro., section 2.2.1, **1 headnote**, **1.19n.**, **3 headnote**, **3.29n.**, **6.47-49n.**, **6.53n.**

magnos ... deos: *magnus* is a common epithet for the gods, expressing their strength and power, cf. Enn. *Ann.* 6.190; Hor. *Epod.* 15.3 (quoted on *laesit* above); Tib. 1.2.81 *num Veneris magnae uiolaui numina uerbo*; Virg. *Aen.* 3.12, 8.679; **[Tib.] 3** *Sulpicia Cycle* **8.1** *Mars magne* below and for the phrase *magnos ... deos*, often in the same *sedes*, cf. Hor. *Serm.* 1.7.33; Prop. 2.34.46; Ov. *Am.* 3.7.45-46, *Her.* 12.34, 21.238, *Fast.* 5.38, *Trist.* 2.22, 184, 5.9.12, *Pont.* 1.6.26, 2.9.35, 3.1.162; Manil. 1.422-423; *Ibis* 94; [Ov.] *Epiced. Drusi* 130; Sil. 4.731; Mart. 2.91.2; Serv. *Aen.* 3.12 connects the *magni di* either with the *penates* or with specific Roman gods: '*penatibus et magnis dis*': *Varro quidem unum esse dicit penates et magnos deos; nam et in basi scribebatur 'magnis dis'. potest tamen hoc pro honore dici; nam dii magni sunt Iuppiter, Iuno, Minerva, Mercurius*: more details in N-A 280-282 ad loc. and Bömer on Ov. *Met.* 1.170.

inpia lingua: cf. Apul. *Met.* 11.23 on the tongue's *noxam ... impiae loquacitatis*; contrast the *garrula lingua* of our author (as Tibullus) at **19.20**, who had sworn faithfulness to his mistress truthfully but to his own detriment.

17-24 Lygdamus passes abruptly on to describe, in a circumlocution worthy of epic, the time, around dawn, at which he finally fell asleep and had his dream of Apollo. The poetic model here seems to be Ov. *Her.* 19.191-200 (Hero to Leander):

> *Sed mihi, caeruleas quotiens obuertor ad undas*
>   *nescio quo pauidum frigore pectus hebet.*
> *nec minus hesternae confundor imagine noctis,*
>   *quamuis est sacris illa piata meis.*
> *namque sub aurora, iam dormitante lucerna,*   195
>   *somnia quo cerni tempore uera solent,*
> *stamina de digitis cecidere sopore remissis,*
>   *collaque puluino nostra ferenda dedi.*
> *hic ego uentosas nantem delphina per undas*
>   *cernere non dubia sum mihi uisa fide.*   200

["But, as often as I turn my face towards the blue waves, my fearful breast is numbed by some chill. Nor am I less perturbed by last night's dream, although its threat has been expiated by my sacrifice. For just before dawn, when the lamp was already dying down, at a time when true dreams are wont to be seen, the threads fell from my fingers relaxed by sleep and I lay my head upon the pillow in rest. There in no uncertain vision I seemed to see a dolphin swimming through the wind-swept waves."]

What is made clear in Ovid (196) and remains unspoken in *Lygd.* is that dawn is the time when true dreams appear, cf. Hor. *Serm.* 1.10.33 *post mediam noctem ... cum somnia uera*; Tert. *Anima* 48.1 *certiora et collatiora somniari affirmant sub extremis noctibus.* This underlying fact adds to the ambiguity of Lygdamus' reaction to the dream and his belief in its veracity, see **headnote** above. The brief indications of time in Ovid *sub aurora* and *iam dormitante lucerna* (195) are expanded into circumlocutions worthy of epic with **17-18** describing the end of night, equivalent to *iam dormitante lucerna* and **21** describing the first light of dawn equivalent to *sub aurora*.

17-18 The image of night's chariot does not occur in Homer but is common in Greek poetry thereafter, occurring first at Aesch. *Choeph.* 660-661 *νυκτὸς ἅρμα ...* / *σκοτεινόν* ["the black chariot of night"] and fr. 69.5-6 R. *μελανίππου.../...νυκτός* ["of black-horsed night"]; cf. Eur. *Ion* 1150-1151 *μελάμπελος δὲ Νὺξ ἀσείρωτον ζυγοῖς / ὄχημ' ἔπαλλεν* ["Night, robed in black, was making her chariot drawn by a yoked pair with no traces, swing forward"]. Its first occurrence in Latin is at Enn. *Trag.* 96-97 Jocelyn *<sacra nox> quae caua caeli / signitenentibus conficis bigis.* In elegy night's horses are mentioned at Tib. 2.1.87 *iam Nox iungit equos* and Ov. *Am.* 1.13.40 *lente currite, Noctis equi.* Chronological periphrases of this type begin as high-style features of early tragedy and epic but are later adopted by the neoterics, see Tränkle (1960) 24. As at Hor. *Epod.* 15.1-2 *nox erat et caelo fulgebat Luna sereno / inter minora sidera*, an important intertext for the Neaera poems (see **16n.** above), the calmness of the nocturnal setting, particularly frequent in amatory contexts [see L. C. Watson (2003) 466, Harrison (2007) 127], contrasts with the violent emotions to be released by Apollo's speech at **42-80** below.

aetherium ... / mundum: a circumlocution for 'the heavens', found also at *Culex* 102 and Sen. *Phaed.* 333-334.

nigris ... quadrigis: This is the first reference we have to night's four-horse chariot; previous poets had spoken of only two: so Eur. *Ion* 1150; Enn. *Trag.* 97 Jocelyn (quoted above); Virg. *Aen.* 5.721; *Culex* 202. Whereas night's horses are appropriately black, those of dawn are pink: whether they form two-horse chariot as at Virg. *Aen.*7.26 (*roseis ... bigis*) or a four-horse chariot as at *Aen.* 6.535 (*roseis ... quadrigis*).

emensa: for *emetiri* in the sense of 'measure out', 'cover a distance' see *ThLL* 5(2).481.73-482.7 and cf. Liv. 27.43.2 *totam ferme longitudinem Italiae emensi essent*; Virg. *Aen*. 11.244 *iter emensi* and Ov. *Fast*. 1.544 *emensus longi clauiger orbis iter*; Manil. 2.836 *emenso qui condit sidera mundo*.

caeruleo lauerat amne rotas: for the image of night washing her chariot in the sea cf. the sun washing his chariot at Virg. *Georg*. 3.359 *Oceani rubro lauit aequore currum* and Tib. 2.5.60 (quoted below). The idea of the Ocean as a river is Homeric, cf. Ὠκεανὸς ποταμός ["river Ocean"] at *Il*. 14.245 and *Od*. 11.639. It occurs earlier in Latin at Virg. *Georg*. 4.233 *Oceani ... amnis* and Tib. 2.5.60 *Solis anhelantes abluit amnis equos*. For *caeruleus* or *caerulus* as an epithet of the sea cf. Ov. *Her*.19.191 quoted on **17-24** above, and Serv. *Aen*. 7.198 on '*per uada caerula*': *caerulum est uiride cum nigro, ut est mare*. For its use with *amnis* cf. Virg. *Aen*. 8.64 *caeruleus Thybris, caelo gratissimus amnis* and Stat. *Silu*. 1.5.51 *caerulus amnis*.

19-20 Night is coming to an end, but Lygdamus has not yet managed to sleep. For the well-known figure in which all the world is asleep except the miserable lover, see Ap. Rhod. 3.744ff.; Theocr. *Id*. 2.38ff.; Virg. *Aen*. 4.522ff. For insomnia as a classic symptom of love in elegy see Tib. 2.4.11, with Maltby (2002) 419-420; Ov. *Am*. 1.2.1-4 with McKeown II 34-5, *Ars* 1.735-736 with Hollis, and cf. Prop. 1.1.33 *nam me nostra Venus noctes exercet amaras*, 2.17.3-4 *desertus amaras / expleui noctes*, 4.3.29 *at mihi cum noctes induxit uesper amaras*; Ov. *Rem*. 585-586 *tristior idcirco nox est quam tempora Phoebi: / quae releuet luctus, turba sodalis abest*, *Her*. 12.169 *non mihi grata dies*; *noctes uigilantur amarae*. Worry about Neaera is clearly what is keeping him awake, cf. **55-56** below and see **6.59-61** where Lygdamus declares he will no longer lose sleep over a faithless girl.

menti ... aegrae: N-A's statement that this is the only known occurrence of the phrase *mens aegra* is incorrect; cf. Liv. 2.42.10 *accessere ad aegras iam omnium mentes prodigia caelestia*; Ov. *Trist*. 3.8.25 *seu uitiant artus aegrae contagia mentis*, *Pont*. 1.6.15 *tecum tunc aberant aegrae solacia mentis*; [Ov.] *Epiced. Drusi* 395 *qui dolor et menti lenissimus influit aegrae*; Stat. *Silu*. 2.6.56-75 *non mente fidelior aegra / sperauit ... redictus Eumaeus*; Sil. 3.131-132 *aegramque leuare / attonitis mentem curis*, 8.118 *quis aegram mentem ... leuaret*. Again love is at the root of Lygdamus' diseased mind. For the common elegiac motif of love as a disease, see La Penna (1951) 206-207, Grassman (1966) 94ff., Maltby (2002) 399-400 on

Tib. 2.3.13-14 and cf. Prop. 3.24.17f. with Fedeli and Ov. *Am.* 1.10.9-10 with McKeown II 287, *Rem.* 109-110.

deus utilis: for *utilis* + dat. in the sense of 'useful, helpful in the case of...' see *OLD utilis* 4. For the phrase cf. Ov. *Fast.* 3.173 (*Mars*) *deus utilis armis*, where *armis* could, however, be taken as an instrumental ablative; see Heyworth (2019) 117.

Somnus: the personification of *Somnus* / Ὕπνος goes back to Homer (e.g. *Il.* 14.233ff., 16.454) and Sleep appears in the retinue of Night at Tib. 2.1.89-90. In particular our author could have been influenced by the detailed description of personified Sleep at Ov. *Met.* 11.592-645, a passage in which Iris addresses Sleep as (11.624) *pax animi, quem cura fugit*.

sollicitas: the adjective is used commonly in Ovid of worry caused by love: *Am.* 1.15.38 *a sollicito multus amante legar*, *Her.* 1.12 *res est solliciti plena timoris amor*, 18.196 *aut mors solliciti finis amoris erit*, *Rem.* 557 *o qui sollicitos modo das, modo demis amores*. Given Virg. *Ecl.* 10.6 *sollicitos Galli dicamus amores*, its origin may be Gallan where the prime reference is to the composition of elegy. It is used again of Lygdamus' mind in this context at **6.36** where sympotic themes are said to be unsuitable for those with elegiac worries and **6.61** where elegiac worries are rejected in favour of sympotic themes; see further Pichon 265.

deficit: Sleep 'fails' to perform his normal duty of restoring afflicted minds when faced with homes troubled by love.

21 summo ... ab ortu: taken literally as 'from the top of his rising' the phrase has caused commentators some difficulty as it would imply a time towards noon, which would be inconsistent with **17-18** which suggests early dawn. Given the likely influence of Ov. *Fast.* 3.361 *ortus erat summo tantummodo margine Phoebus* 'scarcely had Phoebus risen with his topmost rim' the meaning here must be 'when Phoebus looked out from the upper edge of his disk', as correctly seen by Heyne ad loc. who translates 'als Phoebus mit dem obersten Rand der aufgehenden Scheibe hervorschaute'. For *ortus* as the disk of the rising sun, cf. *Laud. Mess.* **7.65-66** *... numquam candente dies apparuit ortu, / seu supra terras Phoebus seu curreret infra*. For *summo ... ortu* in the sense of 'early dawn', cf. also Gell. 2.1.2 *stare solitus Socrates dicitur ... a summo ortu ad solem alterum orientem* '... from early dawn until the next rising of the sun'. Here *ab* is probably spatial 'from' rather than instrumental 'with', though both are possible.

216   Commentary

Phoebus: this epithet is used in **book 3** of both the sun, as here, and of Apollo (sun: **7.66, 145, 158**; Apollo **4.44, 7.8, 178, 8.22, 10.2, 3, 19**) and the same is true in Ovid [sun: (35); Apollo (93)]. In Greek the epithet Phoebus was used of Apollo from Hom. *Il.* 1.43 on. The sun god Helios and Apollo were separate gods in Greek cult and Fontenrose (1940) argues that the two were kept separate even in Roman poetry. However, although the Greek Helios is never associated with Apollo and his functions in Greek poetry, Apollo is associated with the sun, cf. *Hom. Hymn Apollo* 3.441-442 (see **29n.** below) and Eur. *Phaeth.* 224-225 (with **7.66n.**). However this may be, the sun here in his role of Phoebus ('the shining one') prepares the way for the appearance of Apollo (described as *Phoebus* at **44** below) in Lygdamus' dream in his role of Citharoedus, the god of music and poetry (**23-44**) and as god of prophecy (**47-50**).

prospexit: with a heavenly body as subject also at Lucan 10.434-435 *Lucifer a Casia prospexit rupe diemque / misit.*

ab ortu: a common hexameter ending in Ovid: *Her.* 16.143, *Met.* 2.112, 6.49, 15.619, *Trist.* 1.2.27, 5.8.25, *Pont.* 1.4.29, 3.1.127; also at Hor. *Epist.* 2.2.185; Manil. 4.591; Germanicus *Arat.* 340; *Il. Lat.* 867; Sil. 4.113.

22 pressit: a common image of sleep 'pressing down' the eyelids, cf. Prop. 1.10.7 *quamuis labentes premeret mihi somnus ocellos*; [Sen.] *Oct.* 116-117 *membra cum soluit quies / et fessa fletu lumina oppressit sopor.*

languentis: here 'tired' through lack of sleep, cf. Val. Fl. 4.388 *languentia lumina somno.*

lumina: a common metonymy for 'eyes' in Latin poetry from Catullus on, including all three elegists, cf. Val. Fl. 4.388 quoted above.

sera quies: a high-style phrase, occurring also at Stat. *Theb.* 3.392-393 *animosaque pectora laxet / sera quies*, cf. Virg. *Aen.* 8.30 ... *seramque dedit per membra quietem.* The noun *quies* occurs only in this poem (also at line **2** above) in the whole of the Tibullan Corpus. It occurs 6 times in Propertius and is relatively frequent in Ovid (28), especially in *Met.*: *Her.* (2), *Am.* (1), *Ars* (2), *Met.* (13), *Fast.* (5), *Trist.* (2), *Pont.* (2), *Ibis* (1).

23-42 There follows a detailed description of the god Apollo as he appears to Lygdamus in his dream. The god is not immediately named, but his identity is revealed gradually, by the mention first of his sacred plant, the laurel (**23**), then of his unshorn locks (**27**), and finally of his lyre (**37-38**), before the god's own use of the epithet *Cynthius* (**50**) makes his identity certain. The description of Apollo is based partly on the description of Apollo Citharoedus in the opening of Tibullus 2.5.1-10. This in turn could have taken its inspiration from the statue of Apollo Citharoedus by Scopas (fourth century BC), which Augustus had placed in his new Palatine temple of Apollo, dedicated in October 28 BC (cf. *Res Gestae* 19; Suet. *Aug.* 29), also described by Propertius at 2.31.5-6 *hic equidem Phoebo uisus mihi pulchrior ipso, / marmoreus tacita carmen hiare lyra* and 15-16 *deinde inter matrem deus ipse interque sororem / Pythius in longa carmina ueste sonat.* Other literary influences could have been *Hom. Hymn Herm.* 4.499-501 (with Vergados on 153, 499 and O. Thomas on 145-154):

κίθαριν δὲ λαβὼν ἐπ' ἀριστερὰ χειρὸς
Λητοῦς ἀγλαὸς υἱός, ἄναξ ἑκάεργος Ἀπόλλων,
πλήκτρῳ ἐπειρήτιζε κατὰ μένος.

["when the glorious son of Leto, the far-shooting lord Apollo, took the lyre in his left hand, he tried it vigorously with the plectrum."]

also Callimachus' description in his *Hymn to Apollo* 2.32-42, or Ovid's description of Apollo in his musical competition with Pan at *Met.* 11.165-171:

ille caput flauum lauro Parnaside uinctus   165
uerrit humum Tyrio saturata murice palla
distinctamque fidem gemmis et dentibus Indis
sustinet a laeua, tenuit manus altera plectrum;
artificis status ipse fuit. tum stamina docto
pollice sollicitat, quorum dulcedine captus   170
Pana iubet Tmolus citharae submittere cannas.

["Apollo with his golden head wreathed with the laurel of Parnasus swept the ground with his cloak dyed with Tyrian purple and he held in his left hand his lyre distinguished with gems and Indian ivory, while his right hand held the plectrum. His very pose was that of an artist. Then with expert thumb he plucked the strings and Tmolus, charmed by their sweetness, ordered Pan to lower his reeds before the lyre."]

see also Ovid's description of Narcissus, who compares himself specifically with Bacchus and Apollo (421) in *Met.* 3.420-423:

spectat humi positus geminum, sua lumina, sidus   420
et dignos Baccho, dignos et Apolline crines

218   Commentary

> *impubesque genas et eburnea colla decusque*
> *oris et in niueo mixtum candore ruborem.*

["Lying on the ground he gazes at his eyes, twin stars, and at his hair worthy of Bacchus and worthy of Apollo and at his smooth cheeks and ivory neck, the glory of his face, and the rosy blush mixed with snowy white."]

and 482-485:

> *pectora traxerunt roseum percussa ruborem,*
> *non aliter quam poma solent, quae candida parte,*
> *parte rubent, aut ut uariis solet uua racemis*
> *ducere purpureum nondum matura colorem.*   485

["His breast, when struck, takes on a rosy glow, just as apples are accustomed to do which are pale in some parts and red in others, or as grapes with different coloured clusters are wont to take on a purple colour when not yet ripe."]

Cf. also Prop.'s description of Bacchus at 3.17.31-32:

> *leuis odorato ceruix manabit oliuo,*
> *et feries nudos ueste fluente pedes.*

["Your smooth neck will stream with perfumed olive oil and you will brush your bare feet with your flowing robe."]

23 hic: here temporal 'then', cf. *ThLL* 6(3).2766.3-32, as in his model Ov. *Her.* 19.199-200 (quoted above on **17-24**) *hic ego ... delphina ... / cernere ... sum ... uisa*, where *hic* refers back to *sub auroram* (195).

iuuenis: Apollo is characterised by his eternal beauty and youth, cf. Call. *Hymn.* 2.36 καὶ μὲν ἀεὶ καλὸς καὶ ἀεὶ νέος ["always beautiful and always young"]; Mart. 4.45.7 (addressed to Apollo) *perpetuo sic flore mices*.

casta redimitus tempora lauro: influenced by Virgil's description of King Anius, priest of Apollo at *Aen.* 3.81 *uittis et sacra redimitus tempora lauro* and of Tibullus' description of Apollo at 2.5.5 *ipse triumphali deuinctus tempora lauro*. The combination *casta ... lauro* occurs only here. The epithet *casta* alludes to the myth of Daphne (Ov. *Met.* 1.452-567) who was transformed into a laurel tree by her father Peneus to prevent her being raped by Apollo. The god then adopted the laurel tree as his favourite symbol (*Met.* 1.557-559). Its evergreen leaves made it an appropriate plant for the ever-youthful Apollo, and it became the symbol of prophecy and poetry, both of which were inspired by the god. The most common epithet for the plant is *sacra* as at *Aen.* 3.81 (above), cf. also Hor. *Carm.* 3.4.18-19; Tib. 2.5.63; Virg. *Aen.* 7.59-60; Lucan 1.287. The phrase *redimitus tempora* + abl. occurs first in Virgil at *Georg.* 1.349 and *Aen.* 3.81, then Ov. *Met.* 14.654; Sen. *Oed.* 430; Val. Fl. 1.278. For *tempora lauro* as a hexameter ending cf. Virg. *Aen.* 3.81, 5.246, 539; [Ov.] *Epiced. Drusi* 459; Val. Fl. 4.334; Claud. *Carm. Min. app.* 2.19, varied at Ov. *Am.* 2.12.1 with *tempora laurus* (see McKeown III 265 ad loc.).

24 est uisus: the passive of *uideo* was used to introduce dream appearances in Latin from Plautus on, either of the thing dreamed e.g. Plaut. *Mil.* 389 *arguere in somnis me meus familiaris uisust*; Enn. *Ann.* 3 Sk. ... *uisus Homerus adesse poeta*; Hor. *Serm.* 1.10.32-33 ... *Quirinus / post mediam noctem uisus, cum somnia uera*; Virg. *Aen.* 2.270-271 *in somnis... ante oculos maestissimus Hector / uisus adesse mihi*; Prop. 4.7.3 *Cynthia namque meo uisa est incumbere fulcro*; Ov. *Fast.* 3.639-640 *nox erat: ante torum uisa est adstare sororis / ... Dido*, or of the person dreaming e.g. Enn. *Trag.* 50-51 Jocelyn *parere se ardentem facem / uisa est in somnis*, with Jocelyn (1969) 223 ad loc.; Prop. 3.3.1 *uisus eram molli recubans Heliconis in umbra*; Ov. *Her.* 19.200 (*delphina*) *cernere non dubia sum mihi uisa fide*.

nostra ... sede: in comparison with *domus* the word carries with it the emotional connotations of '(ancestral) home' rather than simply 'house', cf. Tib. 1.10.18 (of the Lares) *sic ueteris sedes incoluistis aui*, and 2.4.53 *quin etiam sedes iubeat si uendere auitas*.

ponere ... pedem: can be used without any indication of place simply to mean 'to step', so Lucr. 4.318-319 (of reflections in the mirror) *pedemque / ponere nobiscum credas*; Varro *Ling.* 9.10.5 *pedes male ponere*; Tib. 1.2.19-20 *illa* (sc. *Venus*) *docet ... / ... pedem nullo ponere posse sono*; Sen. *Epist.* 110.7 *nec ob hoc ... circumspectius pedem ponere*, or, as here, 'to set foot (in a place)', e.g. Plaut. *Rud.* 489-490 ... *quae numquam pedem / uoluisti in nauem cum Hercule una imponere*; Prop. 2.32.48 *hic posuit nostra nuper in urbe pedem*; Ov. *Met.* 3.114 ... *imoque pedes in margine ponunt*. For the possible metapoetic associations of *pedem* ('metrical foot') see Ingleheart (2010) 73 on Ov. *Trist.* 2.16 and Fulkerson (2017) 144 ad loc.; Apollo is about to introduce his verse into Lygdamus' dwelling. For Apollo as the god of Callimachean poetry, see Robinson (2011) 201 on Ov. *Fast.* 2.248.

25-26 The distich has come down in a mutilated form. The underlying idea seems to be that the beauty of Apollo in his vision surpassed all mortal measure. The reading of all MSS is: *non illo quicquam formosius ulla priorum / aetas, humanum nec uidet illud opus*. As it stands the first part of the phrase up to *aetas* has no verb, and the second has no subject. Lachmann's re-writing of the pentameter *aetas, heroum nec tulit ulla domus* would provide a single verb *tulit* for both clauses and the whole sentence builds to a climax from past ages to the more distant time of heroes. For *tulit* in this context commentators compare Prop. 1.4.7 *et quascumque tulit formosi temporis aetas*. However, Lachmann's re-writing of the pentameter is considerably different from the transmitted text. Nearer to the original is Heyne's *non uidit quicquam formosius ulla priorum / aetas, humanum nec fuit illud opus* on which he comments '*opus humanum* h. homine natus, ut *opus* saepe, *illud* pro *ille* propter *opus. vidit* vero primo versu extrusum erat a glossa *illo*'. This explains how *uidit* could have been replaced by *illo* in **25** and why *illud* replaces the expected *ille* in **26**. But there is perhaps more in *humanum ... opus* than Heyne had seen. *opus* is often applied to a work of art, either a work of literature as at **1.14** above, or to the plastic arts, in particular sculpture, see *OLD opus* 9b and examples quoted at **26n.** below. One of our author's main sources for the description of Apollo is Tib. 2.5.1-10, based on Scopas' sculpture of the god in Augustus' new temple complex; Propertius commenting on the same sculpture declares that it was fairer than the god himself: 2.31.5 *hic equidem Phoebo uisus mihi pulchrior ipso*. The author here, in characteristic manner, reverses this idea: the vision of the god Apollo was more beautiful than a mere human statue *humanum ... opus*. It is possible to see in the distich a variation on the theme from IE poetry 'there never were such men before and never will be again' on which see M.L. West (2007) 104.

25 formosius: the adj. is used of Apollo at Virg. *Ecl.* 4.56-57 *quamuis ... pater adsit / ... Lino formosus Apollo* and Tib. 2.3.11 *pauit et Admeti tauros formosus Apollo*; cf. ἀεὶ καλός ("always beautiful") at Call. *Hymn* 2.36 (quoted on **23** above) and *pulcher* at Virg. *Aen.* 3.119 *taurum Neptuno, taurum tibi, pulcher Apollo*. For outstanding beauty as an attribute of gods and deified mortals, cf. *pulcher et humano maior* of the deified Romulus at Ov. *Fast.* 2.503, with further examples in Robinson (2011) 316 ad loc.

priorum: 'ancestors', cf. Virg. *Aen.* 3.693-694 *nomen dixere priores / Ortygiam* and see *OLD prior* 3b.

26 humanum ... opus: 'a work of human construction'. The combination *humanum opus* occurs also at Cic. *De Orat*. 2.76; Sen. *Suas*. 6.5; Plin. *Nat*. 10.94, 27.2. For *opus* of a statue, cf. Ov. *Met*. 4. 673-675 ... *nisi quod leuis aura capillos / mouerat* ... / *marmoreum ratus esset opus*; Mela 2.42 *delubrum ... simulacro quod Phidiae opus est ... nobile*. For supernatural visions, especially those of gods, being larger than mortal, cf. Ov. *Fast*. 2.503 quoted in **25n.** above; Virg. *Aen*. 2.772-773, with Austin ad loc., (Creusa's ghost), 6.49-50 (the Sibyl); Ov. *Met*. 9.269-270 (Hercules becoming a god), *Fast*. 6.539-540 (Carmenta).

27 intonsi crines: flowing locks, as a sign of eternal youth, are a characteristic of Apollo from Homer on, cf. *Il*. 20.39 *Φοῖβος ἀκερσεκόμης* ("Phoebus with unshorn hair"). It is a feature he shares with Bacchus, Tib. 1.4.37-38 *solis aeterna est Baccho Phoeboque iuuentas, / nam decet intonsus crinis utrumque deum*, Ov. *Am*. 1.14.31-32, *Met*. 3.421. Other examples of *intonsus* with reference to Apollo's hair are found at Hor. *Carm*. 1.21.2 with N-H, *Epod*. 15.9 where Neaera swears falsely by them, see L. C. Watson (2003) 471 ad loc.; Prop. 3.13.52 with Fedeli; Tib. 1.4.38, 2.3.12, 5.121; Ov. *Met*. 1.564, 12. 585, *Trist*. 3.1.60; Stat. *Silu*. 3.4.8 and **[Tib.] 3** *Sulpicia Cycle* **10.2** below. On *crines* as a rare and elevated word for hair in Latin poetry, see **2.11n.** above.

longa ceruice: the adj. *longus* here means 'slim', slender'. This is the only use of *ceruix* in the *Corp. Tib.*; Tib. himself uses only *collum* (6). The phrase *longa ceruix* is used by Ovid of Aesacus, when transformed into a sea bird (*mergus*) at *Met*. 11.793 *longa manet ceruix, caput est a corpore longe*. Elsewhere the phrase is used mainly of cattle (Varro *Rust*. 2.5.7, 2.9.4; Colum. *Rust*. 6.1.3) or horses (Cic. *Arat*. 34.385; Germ. *Arat*. 213, 510; Colum. *Rust*. 6.29.2) and once in Pliny of a type of onion (*Nat*. 19.107).

fluebant: used of his mistress's flowing hair by Prop. 2.3.13 *nec de more comae per leuia colla fluentes* and of Apollo's locks by Virg. *Aen*. 4.147-148 *mollique fluentem / fronde premit crinem*.

28 stillabat Syrio myrrea rore coma: already in Call. *Hymn*. 2.38 Apollo's hair distils fragrant perfume on the ground: *αἱ δὲ κόμαι θυόεντα πέδῳ λείβουσιν ἔλαια* ["his locks distil fragrant oil upon the ground"], but in that case the aromatic essence is that of panacea (39-41). The adj. *myrrea* here is a correction found in some later MSS for A's *myrtea*, which is applied to garlands, but never to the hair itself, e.g Tib. 1.3.66 *et gerit insigni myrtea serta coma*. For *myrreus* (*murreus*) applied to hair, cf.

Hor. *Carm.* 3.14. 22 of a certain Neaera *murreum nodo cohibere crinem*, where the meaning is more likely to be 'scented with myrrh' (so ps.-Acro ad loc.), rather than 'myrrh-coloured' as suggested by Porphyrio ad loc.: *colorem myrrheum in crinibus hodieque dicunt, qui medius est inter flauum et nigrum*. Myrrh is an aromatic resin obtained from a thorny shrub associated by the ancients with Arabia, and hair perfumed with myrrh was often, as probably here, seen as a sign of eastern effeminacy, cf. Virg. *Aen.* 12.97-100 (Turnus on the oriental Aeneas) ... *da sternere corpus / loricamque manu ualida lacerare reuolsam / semiuiri Phrygis et foedare in puluere crinis / uibratos calido ferro murraque madentis*, with Tarrant (2012) 116 ad loc.; Ov. *Met.* 5.52-53 (on the Indian Attis) ... *ornabant aurata monilia collum / et madidos murra curuum crinale capillos*; Sen. *Herc. Oet.* 376 (of Hercules serving Omphale) *hirtam Sabaea marcidus myrrha comam*. For *stillo* + abl. 'to drip with (a liquid)' see *OLD stillo* 2 and for the expression cf. Tib. 1.7.51 (of Messalla's Genius) *illius et nitido stillent unguenta capillo*, 2.2.7 (of Cornutus' Genius) *illius puro destillent tempora nardo*; Ov. *Her.* 21.161 *stillant unguenta capillis* (of Hymen).

Syrio ... rore: The adj. *Syrio* is a conjecture for *Tyrio* of the MSS, which is applied mainly to purple dye. *Syrius* and its higher-style equivalent *Assyrius* (e.g. Tib. 1.3.7) were used by the ancients as conventional epithets for perfumes from the East in general (not specifically from Syria), cf. *Syrio ... nardo* at **6.63** below and see N-H on Hor. *Carm.* 2.7.8 and 2.11.16. The original meaning of *ros* is 'dew', but from Cicero on it was widened to cover other liquids such as water, milk and blood; its extension to perfumes, as here, is relatively late, see *OLD ros* 2d and cf. Stat. *Theb.* 12.138-9 *arcanis roribus artus / ambrosiaeque rigat sucis*, Apul. *Met.* 10.22 *labias ... modicas ambroseo rore purpurantes*.

coma: on words for hair see **2.11n.**

29-34 Although the passage refers at a surface level to Apollo's youthful complexion, many of the terms contained within it also have rhetorical or metapoetic functions, reflecting Apollo's role as a god of poetry: so **29** *candor* (clarity of style, Quint. *Inst.* 10.1.101); **30** *color* (rhetorical colouring, Cic. *de Orat.* 2.54; Quint. *Inst.* 10.6.5); **30** *purpureus* (rhetorical 'purple patch' Hor. *AP* 15); **31** *deducta* ('finely woven' of a literary work, Hor. *Epist.* 2.1.225 *tenui deducta poemata filo*); **33** *contexunt* ('weave', 'compose' of a speech or literary work, Quint. *Inst.* 10.6.2). For *deduco* in particular as a well known metapoetic term from weaving applied to the composition of a poem with Callimachean associations of finely wrought work see Reitzenstein (1931) 49-51, Ross (1975) 19, 26, Fedeli (1980) on

Prop. 1.16.41, Thomas (1988) 40 on Virg. Georg. 3.11, Hinds (1998) 54, Kyriakidis (1998) 97, n. 65 and Cucchiarelli (2012) 328 on Virg. *Ecl.* 6.5. It contains no implication of 'drawing down' Apollo from epic themes to a lower genre as suggested by Fulkerson (2017) 149 ad loc.

29 candor erat qualem praefert Latonia Luna: the noun *candor* here refers both to the 'radiance' of Apollo as 'sun', see **21n. Phoebus** above (and cf. *Hom. Hymn Apollo* 3.441-442) and to his 'beauty'. The term applies equally in both senses to his twin sister, Diana, the moon. Both were children of Latona (Gk. Leto). The noun comes from the same root as Skt. *candra* which means both 'shining' and 'moon'. The comparison of radiant beauty with the brightness of the full moon has a long literary history going back to Sappho fr. 96.6-8 *PLF* (where a girl's beauty is said to eclipse that of her companions as the moon's brightness eclipses that of the stars) and the *Hom. Hymn Aphrodite* 5.89-90 where her tender breast shines like the moon. In Latin the comparison is taken up first by Horace in *Carm.* 2.5.18-20 *Chloris albo sic umero nitens / ut pura nocturno renidet / luna mari*. A pale complexion was considered a sign of beauty (*ThLL* 3.247.34-73), both female, see Pichon 98 and cf. *candida puella* at Cat. 13.4, 35. 8 (with Fordyce); Ov. *Am.* 1.5.10, 7.40 with McKeown on both, II 110 and 184, 3.3.5, 3.7.8, and male, cf. Hor. *Epod.* 3.9 *Iasonem praeter omnes candidum* (Porph. ad loc.: *candoris nomine et Vergilius in significatione pulchritudinis semper utitur*); Virg. *Ecl.* 5.56-57 *candidus ... / ... Daphnis* (Serv. *auct.*ad loc.: *saepe ... candidum pro puchro ponit*). Whiteness of complexion is often attributed to deities, so Ov. *Her.* 18.61 *dea candida* (of the moon), *Fast.* 1.637 *candida* (of Concordia), 3.772 *candide Bacche*; **[Tib.] 3.** *Lygd.* **6.1** *candide Liber*, especially to Apollo, cf. Hor. *Carm.* 1.2.31-32 *nube candentes umeros amictus, / augur Apollo*; Virg. *Aen.* 8.720 *candentis ... Phoebi*; *Catal.* 9.1 *niueo ... Phoebo*; Val. Fl. 3.481 *Phoebus candentior*. The comparison of Apollo's *candor* to that of the moon here, however, is strange, since the moon's brightness actually came from the sun, and so should have been less than his. Perhaps the simile serves to undermine to a certain extent Apollo's clarity as a seer, an idea further enforced by the adj. *Latonia* applied to the moon, connected with the Greek λανθάνω (*Et. Magn.* s.v. Λητώ) and Latin *lateo* 'to hide', cf. Fulg. *Virg. cont.* p. 104.13 *a latitando ... unde et Latona dicta est Luna quod nunc superna celet, nunc inferiora, nunc uniformis latet*. Could there be a suggestion here that Apollo's prophecy may not reveal the full truth? A further association of *candor*, like *color* in **30**, is that it can be used as a positive rhetorical term referring to clear composition in relation to Apollo's poetic activity, see **8.6n.**

praefert: the verb is generally used with *ore* or *uultu* to describe the display of an expression on the face, e.g. Curt. 6.9.1 *procedit uultu praeferens dolorem*. The fact that it is sometimes used of giving a false impression, as at Tac. *Ann.* 13.45.11 *modestiam praeferre et lasciuia uti*, may hint here at the moon's use of borrowed light (cf. Cat. 34.15-16 *notho es / ... lumine Luna*). There is some irony here in the fact that the moon's brightness is actually borrowed from the sun, Apollo; see above *candor erat* **29n.**

Latonia Luna: the patronymic *Latonius, -a* is shared by Apollo and Diana as twin children of Latona by Jupiter, cf. Cat. 34.5-6 *o Latonia, maximi / magna progenies Iouis*. The Roman goddess Luna was assimilated to Diana-Artemis as the light of the moon, one of the three facets of Diana Triformis, cf. Cat. 34.16 *tu* (sc. *Diana*) *... Triuia et notho es dicta lumine Luna*. On the possible implications of the rare *Latonia* see above and cf. *Latonae filius* of Apollo at **72** below.

30 et color in niueo corpore purpureus: a rosy complexion, consisting of a blend of white and red, is seen as an ideal for both men and women from Hellenistic times on, cf. Ov. *Am.* 3.3.5-6 *candida candorem roseo suffusa rubore / ante fuit – niueo lucet in ore rubor*; also Prop. 2.3.9-12 (of Cynthia) *nec me tam facies, quamuis sit candida, cepit / (lilia non domina sunt magis alba mea), / ut Maeotica nix minio si certet Hibero, / utque rosae puro lacte natant folia* with Enk on 11-12, who gives a number of Hellenistic Greek parallels, which almost all refer to the faces of *ephebi*. Heyworth here [(2007a) 121] deletes 11-12, perhaps correctly, as an intrusion. More examples are provided by Mulder on Stat. *Theb.* 2.231 *candida purpureum fusae super ora pudorem* and see further Blümner (1899) 157-158. For the combination *niueo ... purpureus* cf. Stat. *Ach.* 1.161-162 (on the face of a young bride) *niueo natat ignis in ore / purpureus*. The colour contrast perhaps goes back originally to Hom. *Il.* 4.141-147 where the staining of ivory with purple acts as a metaphor for the blood on Menelaus' wound, an image picked up by Virgil in his description of Lavinia's blush at *Aen.* 12.67-68 *Indum sanguineo ueluti uiolauerit ostro / si quis ebur* (see **31-34n.** below). The closest parallel here in both language and content is Ovid's description of Narcissus' beauty at *Met.* 3.423 *in niueo mixtum candore ruborem*. As N-A points out ad loc., when this ideal is applied to boys, they are always *pueri delicati*, e.g. Stat. *Silu.* 2.1.41 (on the dead Glaucias, the favourite of Atedius Melior) *o ubi purpureo suffusus sanguine candor*. As with *candor* **29**, *color* can have positive associations in rhetorical theory, see **1.18n., 10.6n.**

in niueo corpore: for this *iunctura* cf. Ov. *Am.* 3.2.42 *sordide de niueo corpore puluis abi*; [Ov.] *Halieut.* 131 *et nigrum niueo portans in corpore uirus*; Sen. *Medea* 61 *niuei femina corporis*. For *niueus* of a pale complexion, cf. Prop. 2.13.53 *niueum ... Adonin*; Ov. *Am.* 3.3.6 (quoted above); and, of Apollo, *Catal.* 9.1 *niueo Phoebo*; see further Otto 244 on the proverbial whiteness of snow. The adj. is particularly frequent in Catullus' longer poems (e.g. 64.364, of the limbs of the sacrificed Polyxena, 63.8, of the hands of the emasculated Attis) and was perhaps a feature of Alexandrian style, see Clausen (1994) on Virg. *Ecl.* 6.53 and Maltby (2002) 219 on Tib. 1.4.12.

purpureus: when used of a person's complexion the stress is on the sheen rather than on the colour = 'radiant', 'glowing', as a sign of youth and vitality, see *OLD purpureus* 3.b and cf. Virg. *Aen.* 11.818-819 (on the death of Camilla) *labitur exsanguis ... / ... purpureus quondam color ora reliquit*; Sen. *Phaed.* 375-376 *non idem uigor, / non ora tinguens nitida purpureus rubor*, Stat. *Silu.* 2.1.41 (quoted above). The combination *purpureus color* in verse is found in Tib. 1.4.29; Hor. *Carm.* 2.5.12; Virg. *Aen.* 11.819; Ov. *Met.* 3.485, 4.127, 10.213, 14.393 and *Dirae* 21. On the unusual use of the adj. *purpureus* as a pentameter line ending see **1.6n.** *tamen*.

31-34 Similes for radiant complexions and for blushes have a long literary history. For Greek examples see Kost on Musaeus p. 55f. In Latin the author's main exemplars are Virg. *Aen.* 12.67-69 (Lavinia's blush in the presence of Turnus):

> *Indum sanguineo ueluti uiolauerit ostro*
> *si quis ebur, aut mixta rubent ubi lilia multa*
> *alba rosa, talis uirgo dabat ore colores.*

["As when one stains Indian ivory with crimson dye, or as when white lilies blush with many a rose, such were the colours the maiden showed on her face."]

and Ov. *Am.* 2.5.33-37 (his mistress's blush, when accused of adultery):

> *at illi*
> *conscia purpureus uenit in ora pudor,*
> *quale coloratum Tithoni coniuge caelum*
> *subrubet, aut sponso uisa puella nouo;*
> *quale rosae fulgent inter sua lilia mixtae.*

["But a blush of shame came upon her guilty face, like the sky growing red with the tint of Tithonus' bride, like a bride seen by her new husband, like roses gleaming red when mixed among lilies."]

On Lavinia's blush and its literary history see Cairns (2005) and Tarrant (2012) 106-107 on Virg. *Aen.* 12.67-69. On its possible relevance here see Lyne (1983) 60. The blush of the young bride on her wedding night mentioned by Sappho 112 *PLF*, has a parallel in the description of Medea falling in love with Jason in Ap. Rhod. *Arg.* 3.297-298 ἁπαλὰς δὲ μετετρωπᾶτο παρειάς / ἐς χλόον, ἄλλοτ' ἔρευθος, ἀκηδείῃσι νόοιο ["and the colour of her soft cheeks went and came, now pale, now red, in her soul's distraction"] and became conventional in wedding songs in Latin, cf. Cat. 61.185-188 *uxor in thalamo tibi est, / ore floridulo nitens, / alba parthenice uelut / luteumue papauer*. Further examples of the red-white contrast applied to girls in love and brides occur at Stat. *Silu.* 1.2.244-245 (Lavinia again) *non talis niueos strinxit Lauinia uultus / cum Turno spectante rubet*, also *Ach.* 1.161-162 (quoted above in **30n.**), *Theb.* 2.231.

31 iuueni ... uirgo ... marito: the emphasis is on the youth and inexperience of the newly married couple. *iuueni marito* stresses the youth of the groom and replaces the normal term *nouus maritus* (used in Plaut. *Cas.* 782, 859; Ter. *Ad.* 938; Cat. 61.54-55; Varro *Rust.* 2.4.9 etc.), while *uirgo*, also attested for 'bride' at Ov. *Met.* 12.216, stresses the bride's virginity and inexperience and replaces the normal term *noua nupta* (used in Plaut. *Cas.* 782, 881; Ter. *Ad.* 751; Cat. 61.91, 66.15; Varro *Rust.* 2.4.9; Ov. *Her.* 13.139, *Met.* 7.394, 10.462, 12.223, *Fast.* 3.689; Mart. 3.93.26 etc.). The term *virgo* which defines a woman's social status as a young unmarried female is rare in elegy, where the more emotionally charged *puella* predominates; on the semantic difference between the two terms see P. Watson (1983) and (1985) 433-434.

deducta marito: the verb *deducere* describes the leading of the new bride in procession to the house of her husband, see *ThLL* 5(1).272.80-273.16 and cf. Plaut. *Cas.* 472, 881; Caes. *BG* 5.14.5; Cat. 68.143; Ov. *Met.* 10.462; Stat. *Theb.* 8.235. The term *maritus* 'legally married husband' occurs only here in the *Corp. Tib.* The same hexameter ending is found at Ov. *Fast.* 4.153 *cum primum cupido Venus est deducta marito*. On the metapoetic associations of *deducta* see **29-34n.** above.

32 inficitur teneras ore rubente genas: 'dyes her tender cheeks with blushing face', cf. the bride at Cat. 61.186 *ore floridulo nitens*. The verb *inficio* in the sense 'dye' is normally used in the active, e.g. Hor. *Epod.*

7.15 *albus ora pallor inficit*, and, closer to the present context; Lucan 5.214f. *rubor ... inficit ora liuentisque genas*; occasionally in the passive, e.g. Manil. 5.666 *inficiturque suo permixtus sanguine pontus*; but only here in the middle with retained accusative. The dying metaphor brings out more clearly the intertext with Hom. *Il.* 4.141-147 and Virg. *Aen.* 12.67-68 (quoted on **4.30** above). For *ore rubente* cf. Mart. 5.2.7 *ore non rubenti*.

teneras ... genas: cf. Ap. Rhod. *Arg.* 3.297 ἁπαλὰς ... παρειὰς (quoted above on **31-34n.**). The phrase is particularly common in love-elegy, most frequently in the same case and metrical *sedes* as here, e.g. Tib. 1.4.14; Ov. *Am.* 2.5.46, 6.4, *Ars* 1.532, 2.452, 3.568.

33-34 et cum contexunt amarantis alba puellae / lilia: Our author replaces the usual red-white combination of roses and lilies, cf. Virg. *Aen.* 12.67-68; Ov. *Am.* 2.5.37 (quoted on **31-34** above), and Prop. 2.3.10-12 (quoted on **30** above) with amaranth and lilies. The amaranth flower, originally from India, comes in several different colours, but in view of the red-white contrast required by the context the poet must here be referring to the crimson variety. The Greek etymology of the name means 'unfading', a feature mentioned by Colum. *Rust.* 10.175 *Aeacii flores immortalesque amaranti* and Plin. *Nat.* 21.47 *summa naturae eius in nomine est, appellati, quoniam non marcescat*, see *LALE* 27. This would make the plant appropriate for Apollo, known for his everlasting youth (cf. Call. *Hymn.* 2.36, quoted on **23** above). Mention of the plant is rare in verse, apart from Colum. *Rust.* 10.175 only Ov. *Fast.* 4.439 and *Culex* 406. The poet could have had the *Fasti* passage in mind, where the mention of the flowers picked by Persephone's girl companions in Henna (439 *has, hyacinthe, tenes; illas, amarante, moraris*) is followed three lines later by the mention of white lilies gathered by Persephone herself: 442 *ipsa crocos tenues liliaque alba legit*. The mention of *puellae* here further suggests our author may have had this Ovidian passage in mind.

contexunt: 'entwine', rare in poetry until the post-classical period, but cf. Lucr. 3.695; Cat. 64.292; Virg. *Aen.* 2.112 and see further *ThLL* 4.691.39-693.79.

alba ... / lilia: for the proverbial whiteness of lilies, apart from the passages mentioned above, cf. Mart. 1.115.2-3 *candidior puella ... / ... lilio* and see Otto 193. For the *iunctura* with *alba*, cf. Virg. *Georg.* 4.130-131; Prop. 2.3.10; Ov. *Fast.* 4.442; Petr. 127.9.

34 et autumno candida mala rubent: the third simile for Apollo's rosy complexion (cf. **30n.** above) is taken from the colour of apples as they ripen from pale to red in autumn. Two Ovidian passages lie behind this choice. First the myth of Narcissus, already used in the description of Apollo's beauty at *Met.* 3.482-485 (quoted on **23-42n.** above). Here our author has combined the two images of apples and grapes ripening into the single image of apples. The second passage is Ovid's description of Hermaphroditus' blush at hearing the Naiad Salmacis' declaration of love for him at *Met.* 4.329-332:

> *Nais ab his tacuit. pueri rubor ora notauit*
> (*nescit enim quid amor*), *sed et erubuisse decebat.*   330
> *hic color aprica pendentibus arbore pomis*
> *aut ebori tincto est ...*

["On this the Naiad fell silent. A blush coloured the boy's face (for he did not know what love was), but even his blush became him. Such a colour have apples hanging from a sunny tree or dyed ivory."]

The possibility that the author had this second passage in mind is made more likely in view of his use of the phrase *nescis quid sit amor* at **73** below (alluding to Ovid's *nescit enim quid amor* at 330).

candida ... rubent: cf. Ov. *Met.* 3.483-484 ... *quae candida parte, / parte rubent* (quoted in full on **23-42n.** above).

mala: the word denotes initially 'apple' and then by extension 'fruit' in general. It is less elevated than *pomum*, which the poet uses at **5.20** to avoid confusion with the adj. *malus*.

35 ima uidebatur talis alludere palla: the long cloak (*palla*, Greek πέπλος) was part of Apollo's costume as Citharoedus. It is alluded to in Tib.'s invocation to Apollo at 2.5.7-8 *sed nitidus pulcherque ueni: nunc indue uestem / sepositam, longas nunc bene pecte comas* and is mentioned specifically in two passages of Ovid: *Am.* 1.8.59 *ipse deus uatum palla spectabilis aurea* and *Met.* 11.166 *uerrit humum Tyrio saturata murice palla* (where mention of his lyre follows in both). The cloak is usually golden rather than purple as at *Met.* 11.166 (so Call. *Hymn.* 2.32; *Rhet. Her.* 4.60; *Ciris* 151; Curt. 3.3.18; Stat. *Ach.* 1.262, *Theb.* 7.38-39). Two statues of Apollo with cloak and lyre are mentioned by Propertius in the portico of Apollo on the Palatine: Prop. 2.31.5-6 and 16 *Pythius in longa carmina ueste sonat*, and for others see *LIMC* II, 1984 s.v. Apollo. For the *palla* as the traditional garb of the poet see McKeown II 233 on Ov. *Am.*

1.8.59-60 and Robinson (2011) on Ov. *Fast.* 2.107 (of Arion). The image of the hem of the *palla* 'playing' with the god's heels seems to be original to our author, but cf. the gold cloak of Prop.'s new mistress Chloris, now in charge of a household of which the slave Lygdamus is part, at Prop. 4.7.40 *haec nunc aurata cyclade signat humum*.

ima ... palla: i.e. the hem of the cloak.

uidebatur: the passive of *uideo* is common in the representation of dreams, see **24n.** above on *est uisus*.

talis alludere: the image of a cloak touching the feet occurs in Tib. 1.7.46 (of Osiris) *fusa sed ad teneros lutea palla pedes*; Prop. 3.17.32 (of Bacchus) *feries nudos ueste fluente pedes*; Val. Fl. 1.385 (of Apollo's son, the seer Mopsus) *palla imos ferit alba pedes*. The nearest parallel for the use of *alludere* here is *Ciris* 144 *suspensam gaudens in corpore ludere uestem*. The verb *alludere* here was proposed by Cyllenius for *illudere* of the manuscripts, since *illudere* never means 'play with' but always 'make fun of'. By contrast *alludere* is used for the playful contact of waves from Cat. 64.66-67 *omnia quae toto delapsa a corpore passim / ipsius ante pedes fluctus salis alludebat* on, cf. Ov. *Met.* 4.342-343 *... in alludentibus undis / summa pedum taloque tenus uestigia tinguit*; Sen. *Oed.* 266-267 *per te, pater Neptune, qui fluctu breui / utrimque nostro geminus alludis solo*; Stat. *Theb.* 9.336 (of Europa) *... extremis alludunt aequora plantis*. At Sen. *Thy.* 156-157 this usage is extended to the action of fruit-laden branches 'brushing against' the open mouth of Tantalus: *et curuata suis fetibus ac tremens / alludit patulis arbor hiatibus*. It is to this extended sense of intermittent 'brushing' that the contact of the hem with the heels in this passage belongs.

palla: a long cloak reaching down to the feet, which was the normal garment for married women in Rome. In connection with deities and heroes it emphasises their divine (and often foreign) origins, so Tib. 1.7.46 (quoted above – Osiris); Prop. 3.17.32 (Bacchus); Virg. *Aen.* 1.404 (Venus); Ov. *Her.* 21.164 (Hymenaeus), *Fast.* 2.107 (Arion), *Met.* 6.705 (Boreas); Val. Fl. 3.718 (Jason); Stat. *Theb.* 7.45 (Hermes), 11.400 and 12.312 (Polynices). As a male garment in Rome it was worn by foreigners (especially Greeks), actors, singers, poets, lyre-players and seers. It probably also carried with it associations of effeminacy, cf. Prop. 4.9.47 (Hercules as a female slave dressed in a *Sidonia palla*).

36 namque haec in nitido corpore uestis erat: *namque* is a reinforced form of the explicative particle *nam* = 'for indeed'. It is relatively rare in the elegists, Tib. (2), Prop. (9), Ov. never in *Am*. but (5) in *Her.*; frequent in Virg. *Aen*. (37) and Ov. *Met*. (22). It often introduces a clause in parenthesis, as here: e.g. Virg. *Georg*. 4.487 *pone sequens* (*namque hanc dederat Proserpina legem*); Ov. *Her*. 18.55 *nox erat incipiens – namque est meminisse uoluptas*, *Met*. 14.841 *o dea – namque mihi nec quae sis dicere promptum est*.

in nitido corpore: the original meaning of *nitidus* was 'bright', 'shining', a suitable epithet for the sun god Phoebus Apollo (see **29n.** above). When linked with *corpus*, as here, it refers to the radiance of bodily beauty, cf. Tib. 2.5.7 (addressed to Apollo) *nitidus pulcherque ueni*. For the *iunctura* cf. Sen. *Phaed*. 378 *tenerque nitidi corporis cecidit decor*. N-A ad loc. 323-324 questions how Lygdamus can see the god's body, as it is covered in the robe, and suggests that the *palla* was of transparent silk. But this seems an over-literal approach since Apollo's appearance was traditionally understood to be 'bright'.

37 artis opus rarae: 'a work of rare art', in apposition to *lyra* (**38**), with the two elements framing the couplet. For *opus* as a work of art see **25-26n.** and **26n.** above. For *ars* as 'artistic skill', cf. Virg. *Aen*. 1.639 *arte laboratae uestes*. The phrase *artis opus* is mainly Ovidian, cf. *Met*. 13.289-90 (of the arms of Achilles) *caelestia dona, / artis opus tantae*; also at *Ars* 1.266, 2.14, , *Met*. 8.159, 13.390, *Fast*. 1.268, 6.662; Val. Max. 9.2.9; Mart. *Spect*. 16.2, 6.13.2. The adj. *rarus* here means 'rare', 'oustanding', 'remarkable', see *OLD rarus* 6 and cf. *Cynthia rara* Prop. 1.8B.42, 17.16 *rara puella*; it is combined with *ars* elsewhere only at Ov. *Am*. 2.4.17 *places raras dotata per artes*, though cf. *Met*. 14.337 *rara quidem facie, sed rarior arte canendi*.

fulgens testudine et auro: his lyre gleaming with tortoiseshell and gold was a sign of the god's opulence. The instrument was invented by Hermes, but given by him to Apollo (*Hom. Hymn Herm.* 4.41-54). For Apollo's golden lyre cf. Hes. *Scut*. 203; Pind. *Pyth*. 1.1, Call. *Hymn* 2.32 (with Williams ad loc.); Prop. 3.3.14; Ov. *Am*. 1.8.60 (with McKeown II 234), *Ars* 2.494, *Met*. 8.15-16. Although tortoiseshell was originally used to make the sound box for the lyre (*Hom. Hymn Herm.* 4.47-54 – see Bömer on Ov. *Fast*. 5.104), the reference here is to the use of tortoiseshell inlay as decoration, cf. Prop. 4.6.32 *testudineae ... lyrae*; **[Tib.] 3.** *Sulpicia Cycle* **8.22** *testudinea Phoebe superbe lyra*. The use of tortoiseshell inlay on furniture and other items is attributed by Pliny to a certain Carbilius

Pollio in the early first century BC (*Nat.* 9.11); examples are mentioned in poetry by, e.g., Virg. *Georg.* 2.463 *nec uarios inhiant pulchra testudine postis*; Ov. *Met.* 2.737-738 *ebore et testudine cultos / ... thalamos*, and, particularly close in phraseology to our line here, Stat. *Silu.* 2.4.11 *domus rutila testudine fulgens*.

38 pendebat ... garrula ... lyra: the initial verb and the rare *garrula* echoes Tib. 2.5.29-30 *pendebatque uagi pastoris in arbore uotum / garrula siluestri fistula sacra deo*, who was the first to apply the adj. to a musical instrument.

pendebat: denotes the resting position of an instrument such as a pipe or lyre, which, when not in use hung from a peg or from the player's belt, cf. Hor. *Carm.* 3.19.20 *cur pendet tacita fistula cum lyra*?

laeua ... parte: locative, on his left side. The expression is somewhat prosaic and suggests the description of a statue rather than of a live figure. The lyre was normally held in the left hand (see Hom. *Hymn Herm.* 4.499 and Ov. *Met.* 11.168 quoted in **23-42n.** above) and the plectrum held in the right.

garrula: 'talkative', an innovation by Tibullus at 2.5.30 (quoted above), for the image of the talking musical instrument, cf. Lucr. 4.981-982 *citharae liquidum carmen chordasque loquentis / auribus accipere*; Hor. *Carm.* 3.11.5 (*testudo*) *nec loquax olim neque grata*. After Tib., the adj. is used in this context here, and at Manil. 5.330 (*tibia*); Mart. 14.54.2 (*sistra*), and 16.9.1 (*anulus* 'a rattle'). At **19.20** below the adj. is used in the more literal sense of a 'talkative' tongue.

39 hanc ... modulatus: 'having played this', i.e. the lyre. The verb is very rare with the acc. of the instrument played, as here, but cf. Claud. *Carm.* 34.15 *modulatus pectine neruos*. The usual construction is with the song as the acc. object and the musical instrument as an instrumental ablative, e.g. Virg. *Ecl.* 10.51 (of Gallus) *carmina pastoris Siculi modulabor auena*; Tib. 2.1.53-54 *est modulatus auena / carmen*; Ov. *Rem.* 181 *pastor inaequali modulatur harundine carmen*.

primum ueniens: 'when first he came', i.e. on his arrival, denoting an action simultaneous with the main verb *dedit* (not previous to it, a usage which becomes common in later Latin). The verb *uenio* is the technical term for the epiphany of a god, see McKeown II 110 on Ov. *Am.* 1.5.9-10 and cf. Virg. *Ecl.* 10.21 (Apollo – in a passage anticipating Apollo's

232   Commentary

intervention here, see **57-58n.** below), 10.24 (Silvanus). 10.26 (Pan); Ov. *Am.* 1.3.1, 13 (Dawn), 3.1.7 (Elegy), 3.1.11 (Tragedy), 3.13.23 (Juno).

plectro ... eburno: the plectrum was a quill-shaped instrument used for plucking the strings of the lyre, cf. Sen. *Troad.* 321 *leui canoram uerberans plectro chelyn*; Stat. *Ach.* 2.157-158 ... *Apollineo quam fila sonantia plectro / cum quaterem*; *Eleg. in Maec.* 1.51 *Actius ipse lyram plectro percussit eburno*. When playing the lyre in this way the plectrum was held in the right hand and the lyre in the left, cf. Ov. *Ars* 3.319-320 *nec plectrum dextra, citharam tenuisse sinistra / nesciat*, *Met.* 11.167-168 *...fidem ... / sustinet a laeua, tenuit manus altera plectrum*. The lyre could also be held in the right hand and its strings plucked with the fingers of the left (Apul. *Flor.* 15 p. 20 Helm), cf. Virg. *Aen.* 6.647 (of Orpheus) *iamque eadem digitis, iam pectine* (i.e. *plectro*) *pulsat eburno*; Stat. *Silu.* 5.5.31-33 ... *nec eburno pollice chordas / pulso, sed incertam digitis errantibus amens / scindo chelyn*. While the plectrum was used in purely instrumental pieces, the fingers were used only to accompany singing. Here Apollo begins with an instrumental introduction **39**, and then goes on to sing **40-41**, before eventually speaking **42**. Similarly, at Ov. *Ars* 2.493-497 Apollo plays the lyre on his first appearance before eventually speaking. While in the Latin tradition Apollo's plectrum is usually of ivory (in addition to *Lygd.* here and *Eleg. in Maec.* 1.51, cf. also Prop. 3.3.25 *dixerat* (sc. *Apollo), et plectro sedem mihi monstrat eburno*, in Greek it was of gold (Pind. *Nem.* 5.24; Eur. *Heracl.* 351; Call. *Hymn.* 2.185).

40 felices cantus: there is a contrast (introduced by *sed* **41**) between Apollo's singing here, which is joyful and elegant (both ideas are contained in *felices*), and the sad words (*tristia uerba* **41**) of his speech to Lygdamus. For *felix* applied to a speech, poem or song in the sense of 'elegant', 'well finished' cf. Quint. *Inst.* 9.4.27 *felicissimus ... sermo est, cui ... rectus ordo ... contigit*. The same term is applied by Ovid to his poems (*carmina*) at *Am.* 2.17.27 and to their subject matter (*materiem*) at *Am.* 1.3.19, with an additional meaning of 'rich', 'fertile', see further Stroh (1971) 137 n. 45.

cantus ... dedit: for this periphrasis for *canere /cantare* cf. Virg. *Aen.* 1.398 *cantusque dedere* (of swans), 9.618 *dat tibia cantum*; Ov. *Fast.* 2.767 *iam dederat cantus* (of a cockerel); Manil. 5.332 *ille dabit cantus*.

ore sonante: for the expression cf. Hor. *Serm.* 1.4.43-44 *os / magna sonaturum*; Virg. *Georg.* 3.294 *magno nunc ore sonandum*, *Aen.* 4.183 *totidem ora sonant*; Ov. *Am.* 3.9.12 *oraque ... sonant*, *Ars* 1.206 *magno ...*

ore sonandus eris. Met. 8.533 *ora sonantia, Fast.* 1.572 *ore sonante* (in the same *sedes*); Sil. 11.579 *sonas ore*; Stat. *Theb.* 6.397 *ora sonant*, 11.533; Mart. 8.50.14 *ore sonat*. The verb is normally used of elevated utterances, examples in Ingleheart (2010) 382-383 on Ov. *Trist.* 2.529-530. On the use of *os* + adj. to indicate stylistic register see further Thomas (1978) and Thomas (2011) 107 on Hor. *Carm.* 4.2.7-8 *profundo / ... ore.*

41 postquam fuerant ... locuti: the use of the pluperfect in place of the perfect indicative after *postquam* is found occasionally in Augustan poetry, e.g. Virg. *Aen.* 11.94; Prop. 4.9.63, but is not generalised until the post-classical period, see K-S II 2.353, H-Sz 598 para. 322a. It is found only here in the *Corp. Tib.*

digiti cum uoce: on this method of plucking the lyre with the hand as an accompaniment to song see **39n.** on *plectro ... eburno*, and cf. Ov. *Met.* 5.112 *... citharam cum uoce moueres.*

42 edidit haec ... uerba: the verb *edo* is used of solemn and formal utterances, often in the context of prophecy, cf. Enn. *Trag.* 58-59 *ibi ex oraculo uoce diuina edidit / Apollo* with Jocelyn (1969) 226 ad loc.; Cic. *Tusc.* 1.116 *oraculo edito, Diu.* 2.115 *cum illa sors edita est ... regi* and see *OLD edo* 6b, 8c. The verb is used in a similar context by Ovid of Faunus making an announcement in a dream to Numa at *Fast.* 4. 664 *edidit a dextro talia uerba toro*. It is common in epic in the form *edere ore*, e.g. Virg. *Aen.* 7.194; Ov. *Met.* 1.637. This phrase is used with humorous effect in elegy by Tib. 1.4.73 *haec mihi, quae canerem Titio, deus* (i.e. *Priapus*) *edidit ore*. The phrase *edere uerba* is used in technical language of formal proclamations, e.g. Paul. *Dig.* 2.13.12 *iubet praetor uerba testamenti edere* and see *ThLL* 5(2).92.13-14. Again it is used by Tib. for humorous effect of the indiscreet words the god allows slaves to utter when drunk 1.9.25-26 *ipse deus tacito permisit saepe ministro / ederet ut multo libera uerba mero*. In the present form *edidit uerba* the phrase is restricted elsewhere in verse to Ovid: *Met.* 5.105-106, 8.754, 14.744-745, *Fast.* 3.470, 4.664, 4.910.

dulci tristia uerba modo: A has *tristi dulcia*, but since Broukhusius the reading *dulci tristia* (which also occurs in some of the *recentiores*) has been preferred, since the content of the message (*uerba*) is indeed sad, even if Apollo tried to soften the manner (*modo*) of its delivery. The phrase *dulcia uerba* at Ov. *Am.* 2.19.17 and *Ars* 2.152 could have influenced A's reading. For *tristia uerba* see **6.38n.** below. For the combination *dulcis /tristis*, which Tarrant on Virg. *Aen.* 12.802 *dulci tristes* describes as a typically elegiac juxtaposition of opposites, cf. also Manil. 4.527; Sil. 6.67. Some MSS read *sono* for *modo*, but this would be more appropriate for song (cf. *ore sonante* **40**) than for speech. On the association of the adj. *tristis* with the elegiac genre see **6.34n.** and the description of Gallus as *tristis* at Virg. *Ecl.* 10.31; cf. Pichon 283-284.

43-80 Direct address by Apollo to Lygdamus. On the literary background of the address by Apollo to Lygdamus see the **headnote** to the poem above.

43-44 The direct address opens with a greeting to the pure poet who rightfully stands under the protection of Apollo, Bacchus and the Muses. The couplet contains multiple echoes of Ov. *Ars* 3, as will become clear in the individual notes below. Ovidian echoes in this passage are discussed by Baligan (1948) 28-29, Axelson (1960) 102-103, Büchner (1965) 506-507, Tränkle 122. Also relevant here is the statement in Call. *Hymn* 2.9 that Apollo appears only to the good: ὠπόλλων οὐ παντὶ φαείνεται, ἀλλ' ὅ τις ἐσθλός ["Apollo does not appear to everyone, but to whoever is good]".

salue: a common form of greeting in Plautus and Terence, but afterwards relatively rare, Cat. (3), Cic. *Epist.* (4), Hor. (1 – *Carm.* 3.2.15), Virg. *Georg.* (1), *Aen.* (4), Ov. *Met.* (5), *Fast.* (1), except in epitaphs, where the dead man addresses a passer-by. Its use in *Aen.* and *Met.* as well as in epitaphs, suggests it was not as colloquial in later Latin poetry as its early Latin usage would imply.

cura deum: see Ov. *Ars* 3.405 *cura deum fuerunt olim regumque poetae* with Gibson ad loc. Cf. also cf. Ov. *Am.* 3.9.17 *at sacri uates et diuum cura uocamur.* The idea of divine protection for poets, of course, goes back earlier than Ovid; cf. Hor. *Carm.* 1.17.13-14 *di me tuentur, dis pietas mea / et Musa cordi est*; Tib. 2.5.113 *nam diuum seruat tutela poetas.* The use of *cura* as an object of solicitous attention occurs first in Virg. *Ecl.* 1.57 *raucae, tua cura, palumbes,* cf. also Tib. 1.9.34 *Bacchi cura Falernus ager.* For *cura deum /deorum* applied to those other than poets, cf. Virg. *Aen.* 3.476 (Anchises); Ov. *Met.* 8.724 (Philemon and Baucis); Stat. *Silu.* 4.2.15 (Domitian); Mart. 1.82.10 (Regulus). For *cura* of the beloved, as the lover's only concern cf. Plaut. *Epid.* 135 *illam amabam olim, nunc iam alia cura impendet pectori*; Virg. *Ecl.* 10.22 *tua cura, Lycoris* (perhaps an echo of Gallus); Ov. *Am.* 1.3.16 *tu mihi ... cura perennis* and see *ThLL* 4.1475.42ff., Pichon 120. There is perhaps an intentional contrast between the poet as *cura deum* here and Neaera's impious concern with *diuersas ... curas* (other love affairs) at **59** below.

casto ... poetae: cf. Cat. 16.5-6 *nam castum esse decet pium poetam / ipsum, uersiculos nihil necesse est.* The adj. implies honesty, simplicity and faithfulness, as well as devotion to his art, as in Ovid's detailed account of the virtues of poets at *Ars* 3.539-550:

> *adde quod insidiae sacris a uatibus absunt,*
>   *et facit ad mores ars quoque nostra suos.*   540
> *nec nos ambitio nec amor nos tangit habendi:*
>   *contempto colitur lectus et umbra foro.*
> *sed facile haeremus ualidoque perurimur aestu*
>   *et nimium certa scimus amare fide.*
> *scilicet ingenium placida mollitur ab arte,*   545
>   *et studio mores conuenienter eunt.*
> *uatibus Aoniis faciles estote, puellae:*
>   *numen inest illis, Pieridesque fauent.*
> *est deus in nobis, et sunt commercia caeli:*
>   *sedibus aetheriis spiritus ille uenit.*   550

["Besides, treachery is absent from sacred bards and our art too moulds us to its character. Neither ambition nor love of gain affect us: we despise the forum and cultivate the couch and shade. But we are easily caught and burn with a strong passion; we know how to love with a loyalty most sure. Indeed our spirit is softened by our gentle art and our manners are suited to our occupation. Girls, be kind to Aonian bards: there is divinity in them, and the Muses show them favour. There is a god in us and we mingle with heaven; that spirit of ours comes from celestial abodes."]

Again a contrast is drawn between the chastity of the poet here and Neaera's rejection of it at **60** below: *nec gaudet casta nupta Neaera domo.*

nam: for the postponement of this causal particle to second position, under the influence of Catullus and the neoterics, see Platnauer 94-95, K-S II 2.113. Apart from *etenim* (1.14) and *namque* (**36** above) *nam* is the only explicative particle used by the author of **book 3** (14) as it is also by Tib. (18). Neither our poet nor Tib. uses *enim* which occurs frequently in Ovid, see Axelson (1945) 122-123.

rite: 'rightly', both from the religious point of view, because of Lygdamus' piety, (according to rite *OLD rite* 1a and b), and from the secular standpoint of what is 'proper' (according to custom *OLD rite* 3) and 'just', 'reasonable' (*OLD rite* 4).

Phoebusque et Bacchus Pieridesque fauent: Ov. *Ars* 3.347-348 *o ita, Phoebe, uelis, ita uos, pia numina uatum, / insignis cornu, Bacche, nouemque deae.* The line ending echoes Ov. *Ars* 3.548 *numen inest illis* (sc. *poetis*) *Pieridesque fauent*. Again there is a precedent in the *Amores* with *Phoebus comitesque nouem uitisque repertor* mentioned as supporters of poets at *Am.* 1.3.11. This group of Apollo, Bacchus and the Muses as gods of poetry is found elsewhere at Call. fr. 191.7-8 Pf.; Prop. 3.2.9-10, 15, 4.6.75-76; *Catal.* 9.59-60; Stat. *Silu.* 1.5.2, 5.1.25-26. The linking of the deities by *-que et ... -que* is unusual, and serves to put Apollo and Bacchus together as a pair which is then linked by the second *-que* with the Muses. For *-que et* as archaic and elevated in Cat., Tib., Hor. and Virg. see H-Sz 515 para. 283b.

Phoebus: for this epithet shared by Apollo and the sun-god, see **21n.** above. The name Apollo is never used in **[Tib.] 3**, as it is in Tib. (2.3.11, 4.13, 5.79), but is replaced by the epithets *Phoebus* (see **21n.** above), *Cynthius* (**4.50**)*, Delius* (**4.79**) and at **72** below by *Latonae filius*.

Bacchus: a name of Dionysus and linked in Rome with the Italic god *Liber Pater* (see **6.1n.** below). As god of wine, inspiration and mystical ecstasy, his association with drama and poetic inspiration goes back to the archaic Greek period; see Privitera (1970). Callimachus associated him with Apollo and the Muses (fr. 191.7-8 Pf.) and made him responsible for poetic inspiration (*Epig.* 7 and 8 Pf.). In Roman poetry, in addition to his association with Apollo and the Muses mentioned above, this theme of Bacchus as an inspirer of poetry is taken up by Hor. *Carm.* 2.19.1-2 with N-H, 9-16, 3.25.1-3, *Epist.* 1.19.1f. (good poets must drink heavily); Prop. 2.30.37f., 3.17 with Fedeli 515; Ov. *Ars* 1.525 with Hollis, 3.714, 789-790, *Trist.* 5.3.1f.

Pierides: on this epithet for the Muses, see **1.5n.** above.

fauent: 'give their favour', used in connection with poets at Ov. *Ars* 3.548 (quoted above), *Fast.* 3.714 *Bacche, faue uati, dum tua festa cano*; Nemes. *Ecl.* 1.5 *uersuque bonus tibi fauit Apollo*.

45-48 Apollo marks himself out from Bacchus and the Muses as being the only patron god of poets who is able to give prophecies. In fact some ancient authors attribute this ability to the Muses (Hes. *Theog.* 66-68) and also to Dionysus (Macr. *Sat.* 1.18), but Apollo is the main prophetic deity.

For Apollo as seer and giver of oracles, cf. Aesch. *Eumen.* 17-18; Call. *Hymn* 2.68-69; Tib. 2.5.11-12 *tu procul euentura uides, tibi deditus augur / scit bene quid fati prouida cantet auis*; Hor. *Carm.* 1.2.32 *augur Apollo* (*Carm. Saec.* 61); Virg. *Aen.* 3.251-252 *quae Phoebo pater omnipotens, mihi Phoebus Apollo / praedixit*, 6.11-12 ... *magnam cui mentem animumque / Delius inspirat uates aperitque futura*; Ov. *Met.* 1.517-518 ... *per me quod eritque fuitque / estque patet*, 3.8 *Phoebi ... oracula*; Stat. *Theb.* 1.705-708 ... *tu doctus iniquas / Parcarum praenosse manus fatumque quod ultra est / et summo placitura Ioui, quid letifer annus, / bella quibus populis, quae mutent sceptra cometae*.

45 proles: an archaism already in Cicero's time, who quotes it among the words (*De Orat.* 3.153) *quibus loco positis grandior atque antiquior oratio saepe uideri solet*. It is used mainly in poetry among the Augustans (Quint. *Inst.* 8.3.26 '*prolem*' *dicendi uersu est ius*), especially of gods and heroes of divine origin, e.g. Tib. 1.3.79 (of the Danaids) *Danai proles* and 1.4.7 (with some humour, of Priapus) *Bacchi ... rustica proles*. Its distribution in Ovid, *Met. / Fast.* (47), other works (7), gives an indication of its elevated tone.

proles Semelae Bacchus: an echo perhaps of Ov. *Met.* 3.520 (*dies*) *qua nouus huc ueniat, proles Semeleia, Liber*. Whereas in Ovid the mention of Bacchus' mother Semele has some point in a prophecy of Teiresias to Pentheus, here in it is a superfluous piece of ornamentation. Ovid's adj. *Semeleia* (also used at Hor. *Carm.* 1.17.22; Ov. *Met.* 5.329, 9. 461, *Ibis* 278; Stat. *Silu.* 1.2.220) would not fit here, but the MSS are divided as to whether he used the Greek (*Semeles*) or Latin (*Semelae*) form of the genitive. The gen. *Semeles* is found at Ov. *Met.* 3.274, 278; Stat. *Theb.* 7.602; Hyg. *Fab.* 167.2, whereas *Semelae* occurs at Hor. *Carm.* 1.19.2; Ov. *Fast.* 6.503 and Hyg. *Fab.* 224.1 (and dat. *Semelae* at Prop. 2.28.27). There is no way of knowing exactly what our poet wrote, but A's *Semelae* would have the advantage of avoiding the homoeoteleuton with *proles*.

doctaeque sorores: referring back to the Muses *Pierides* (**44**). The use of this epithet, commonly found in relation to poets and poetry (cf. **6.41** below), with reference to the Muses goes back to Cat. 65.2 *doctis ... uirginibus*. The phrase *doctae sorores* is Ovidian: *Met.* 5.255, *Fast.* 6.811, *Trist.* 2.13; also at Manil. 2.49; Stat. *Theb.* 9.137; Mart. 1.70.15, 9.42.3. See further Woodman (2012) 133 and n. 12.

46 dicere non norunt quid ferat hora sequens: the content of the pentameter contrasts with the elevated depiction of Bacchus and the Muses in 45. Neither Bacchus, despite his divine lineage, nor the Muses, despite their wisdom, can foretell what even the immediate future will bring.

non norunt: = *nesciunt*. For the phrase, cf. Plaut. *Cas.* 15; Cic. *De Orat.* 3.137, *Tusc.* 1.116, *Fam.* 8.4.2; Ov. *Her.* 6.124 *fallere non norunt*; Mart. 10.2.12. *norunt* is a syncopated form of *nouerunt*.

quid ferat: with expressions of time, cf. Cic. *Fam.* 1.7.6 *quid tempus ferat, tu facillime ... perspicies*; Liv. 3.27.7 *quid quaeque nox aut dies ferat incertum esse*, 45.8.6 *quid uesper ferat, incertum sit*.

hora sequens: 'the next hour', in the sense of the immediate future cf. Sen. *Epist.* 88.16 *numquam te crastina fallet hora*. In contrast with Apollo's extensive prophetic powers *aeui ... futuri* (**47**), Bacchus and the Muses are incapable of even short-term prophecies.

sequens: on the unusual use of adjectival *sequens* at the pentameter line-end see **1.6n**. *tamen* above. For restrictions on the use of present participles at the verse end cf. Serv. *Aen.* 3.300 (*litora liquens*): *notandum sane, finitum esse uersum participio: quod raro apud Latinos est, apud Graecos uitiosissimum*. Participial line-ends never occur in Tib., but are found occasionally in Prop.; e.g. 3.16.24 *sedens*, 3.20.30 *egens*, 4.8.68 *latens*, and in Ov., e.g. *Ars* 3.258 *potens* (cf. Gibson ad loc); see Platnauer 45-47.

47-48 For Zeus' entrusting the art of prophecy to Apollo cf. *Hom. Hymn Herm.* 4.533-538 ["But as for sooth-saying, noble, heaven-born child, of which you ask, it is not lawful for you to learn it, nor for any other of the deathless gods: only the mind of Zeus knows that. I am pledged and have vowed and sworn a strong oath that no other of the eternal gods save I should know the wise-hearted counsel of Zeus"]. The formulation is a combination of Tib. 2.5.11 (of Apollo) *tu procul euentura uides* and Ov. *Met.* 3.336-338 (of Jove's gift of prophecy to Tiresias) *at pater omnipotens ... / ... pro lumine adempto / scire futura dedit*.

at: marks a strong contrast with the previous line: Apollo's knowledge of prophecy is contrasted with the inability of Bacchus and the Muses to predict the near future.

fatorum leges: the law(s) of fate are mentioned from Cic. *Tim.* 43 *imposuit commonstrauitque leges fatales* (= νόμους τε τοὺς εἱμαρμένους, Plut. *Mor.* 573D) onwards. For *lex fati* cf. Virg. *Aen.* 12.819 *nulla fati quod lege tenetur*; Curt. 5.12.11; Manil. 2.149; Sen. *Quaest. Nat.* 2.38.3.

Cases of *lex* (*leges*) *fatorum* are generally later: *Ciris* 199; Sen. *Ag.* 706-7, *Thy.* 74; Sen. *Nat. Quaest.* 1 pr. 3, Lucan 8.568; Serv. *Aen.* 4.696. Compare fortune's law, mentioned at **3.22** with **n**. ad loc. In general fate is what is ordained by the gods (Min. Fel. 36.2 *quod de unoquoque nostrum deus fatus est*, see *LALE* 225) and fortune is what occurs by chance (connected etymologically with *fortuitus*, see *LALE* 241-242).

aeuique futuri / euentura: for this type of pleonasm as a feature of our author's style, see **2.15n.**; here it is caused, in part, by the combination of Tib. 2.5.11 (*euentura*) and Ov. *Met.* 3.338 (*futura*) quoted above. For *aeuum futurum* see Lucr. 3.486 *aeuo priuata futuro*; Ov. *Her.* 4.131 *ista uetus pietas, aeuo moritura futuro*; Apul. *Plat.* 2.20 *praeteriti futurique aeui ultimas partes adtingere*; Tert. *Pud.* 13 *in isto et in futuro aeuo* and cf. Virg. *Aen.* 8.627 *uenturique inscius aeui*. For *euentura* as a noun cf. Cic. *Diu.* 1.29 *nuntiant euentura*; Tib. 2.1.25 *euentura precor* (= [Ov.] *Epiced. Drusi* 415), **2.5.11** (quoted above); Ov. *Pont.* 3.4.113 *di, quorum monitu sumus euentura locuti*.

pater: The idea that Apollo received his prophetic powers from his father Zeus / Jupiter goes back to *Hom. Hymn Herm.* 4.471-472, 534-539 [(translated above), see Vergados on 533-566 and O. Thomas on 471-472, 533, 535] and Aesch. *Eumen.* 19, fr. 86 R.; in Latin cf. Virg. *Aen.* 3.251-252 *quae Phoebo pater omnipotens, mihi Phoebus Apollo / praedixit*. The mention of *pater omnipotens* at Ov. *Met.* 3.336 (quoted above), where it has more point in relation to Tiresias, probably occasioned the reference to Apollo's father here, where such information is less relevant.

posse uidere dedit: a combination of Tib. 2.5.11 *euentura uides* and Ov. *Met.* 3.338 *scire futura dedit*. Other examples of *uidere* in the context of divination are found e.g. at Ov. *Met.* 5.146 *sagax ... uentura uidere*. For *dedit* (= *permisit*) + *posse* + inf. cf. Tib. 1.8.56 *ipse dedit cupidis fallere posse deus*; Ov. *Ars* 2.28 *da mihi posse mori*, *Met.* 11.177 *dat posse moueri*, 12.556-558 *... cui posse figuras / sumere ... / Neptunus dederat* and, closest to the present context, *Met.* 14.843-844 *quem si modo posse uidere / fata semel dederint*.

49-50 The text of A here presents some problems: *quare ego quae dico, non fallax, accipe, uates / quidque deus uero Cynthius ore ferat*. The two lines are virtually parallel in sense, but the change from relative clause *quae dico* (**49**) to indirect question *quidque ... ferat* (**50**) after *accipe* is awkward, as is the change of person in the pentameter (from first to third). Broukhusius' conjecture of *feram* (**50**) and the replacement of *quidque* by *quodque* (**50**), a reading found in the *recentiores*, restores the parallelism between the two clauses, which is further enhanced by Voss's suggestion of *dicam* for *dico* (**49**).

49 quare ego: for the rare elision of final long *-e* before initial short *-e* see Platnauer 74. For the use of the phrase as a hexameter opening cf. Mart. 5.79.5 *quare ego non sudo, qui tecum, Zoile, ceno*? (where *quare* is used in the different sense of *cur*?). The use of the particle *quare* here + imperat. = 'and so' in concluding clauses is characteristic of Propertius (7), cf. 1.5.31-32 *quare ... desine, Galle / quaerere* (also at 1.9.33, 2.16A.7). It is generally rare in Augustan verse and occurs only here in the *Corp. Tib.* In Virgil (6) it is restricted to the formula *quare age / agite* (as it is in the later epic poets Lucan, Valerius Flaccus and Silius Italicus). In Ovid it is used relatively frequently (31), but only in the interrogative sense = *cur*? (as also in Juvenal). Its wider use in Martial in a variety of senses probably reflects its more conversational character.

non fallax: litotes for 'truthful', cf. Cic. *Planc.* 22 *laudanda est ... uicinitas ... non fallax* and, of Apollo, Hom. *Hymn Herm.* 4.462, 545: οὐδ' ἀπατήσω ["and I will not trick you]" (with O. Thomas on 545); Virg. *Aen.* 6.343-344 *dic age. namque mihi, fallax haud ante repertus, / hoc uno responso animum delusit Apollo*, cf. Call. *Hymn* 2.68 ἀεὶ δ' εὔορκος Ἀπόλλων ["Apollo always keeps his oath"]. See further **50n.** *uero ... ore* below.

accipe: this imperat. is commonly used from Plautus onward in the sense of 'hear' with regards to a statement, story or reply, cf. Prop. 4.2.2. (of a statement from the god Vertumnus) *accipe Vertumni signa paterna dei*, 4.8.74 (of a quasi-legal pronouncement from Cynthia) *accipe quae nostrae formula legis erit* and see *OLD accipio* 18.

uates: this title = 'seer' is applied to Apollo in his function as an oracular god first in Virg. *Aen.* 6.12 (cf. Ov. *Ars* 2.496; Sen. *Oed.* 230, 269; Val. Fl. 4.445). From Virgil and Horace on [cf. Virg. *Ecl.* 9.33-34; Hor. *Carm.* 1.1.35 with N-H and see Hauser (2016) 153-154] the term is applied to poets as divinely inspired, see *OLD uates* 2.

50 uero ... ore: of Apollo also at Ov. *Met.* 10.209 *talia dum uero memorantur Apollinis ore*, the probable model for the present line. Cf. also Ov. *Fast.* 1.474 *ore dabat uero carmina plena dei*, 6.426 (of Apollo) *hos non mentito reddidit ore sonos*, *Pont.* 2.7.23 *crede mihi, si sum ueri tibi cognitus oris*. At **5-8** above Lygdamus had stated that while gods give true warnings, dreams deceive. Apollo is a god, but gives his advice in a dream, hence the need for Apollo's double assurance of veracity here: *non fallax* (**49**), *uero ... ore* (**50**).

Cynthius: epithet of Apollo (and his sister Diana) from their birth place at the foot of Mount Cynthus in Delos. The title for Apollo appears first in Hellenistic poetry, e.g. Call. *Hymn.* 4.10, *Aetia* fr. 67.6 Pf. with Harder (2012) ad loc., and is popularised in Latin by Virg. in his Callimachean *Ecl.* 6.3-4 ... *Cynthius aurem / uellit et admonuit* (cf. Serv. ad loc. *Cynthius Apollo a Cyntho monte Deli, in quo natus est*). Clausen [(1976) 245 n.2] sees it as a Callimachean coinage. Its occurrences are rare in comparison with *Cynthia* for his sister; see Hor. *Carm.* 1.21.2 with N-H; Prop. 2.34.80; Ov. *Ars* 2.239, *Fast.* 3.346, 353; *Catal.* 9.60; *Ecl. Einsid.* 1.17; *ThLL Onom.* 2.792.64-81.

feram: a conjectural reading, see **49-50n.** above. For the use of *fero* in the sense 'relate', 'tell' see *OLD fero* 33, *ThLL* 6(1).543.63-544.49, and for this use in the context of divination cf. Virg. *Aen.* 6.82 *uatisque ferunt responsa per auras*; Mela 1.46 *pro responsis ferunt somnia*; Serv. *Aen.* 8.314 *quorum* (sc. *Fauni et Pici*) *etiam responsa ferebantur*.

51-60 Apollo's revelation about Neaera is delivered in a single period consisting of five couplets. Seven of the lines are devoted to Lygdamus and his love for Neaera (he loves her deeply **51-52**, prays to the gods on her behalf **53**, worries about her day and night **54-56**, celebrates her in his poems **57**) while only three are devoted to Neaera and her preference for another man (**58-60**). Suspense is achieved by the delay in the mention of Neaera's conduct, and the disparity in the length of the two sections serves to emphasise the contrast in the behaviour of the two. The basic structure follows that of Cat. 37.11-14 *puella nam mi, quae meo sinu fugit, / amata tantum quantum amabitur nulla, / pro qua mihi sunt magna bella pugnata, / consedit istic* with echoes of *tantum ... quantum* at **51** and *pro qua* at **53**, and the whole passage is full of other Catullan echoes. Periods of this length are rare in elegy, e.g. Prop. 1.2.1-6; Ov. *Her.* 7.157-163, *Trist.* 2.15-18; see further Platnauer 27-33.

51-52 A two-line comparison in which Lygdamus' love for Neaera is said first to be greater than the family relationship between mother and daughter (**51**) and secondly than the sexual relationship between a girl and her eager lover. Catullan models lie behind both ideas, cf. Cat. 72.3-4 *dilexi tum te non tantum ut uulgus amicam / sed pater ut gnatos diligit et generos* (a passage which perhaps owes something to Andromache's words to Hector at Hom. *Il.* 6.429-430 ["Hector, you are my father and my dear mother, you are my brother, you are my strong husband"]) and cf. also Prop. 1.11.21-23 *ei mihi, non maior carae custodia matris / aut sine te uitae cura sit ulla meae. / tu mihi sola domus, tu, Cynthia, sola parentes.* The formulation *tantum ... quantum nec ... quantum nec* also has a Catullan feel to it: cf. 8.5 *amata nobis quantum amabitur nulla*, 37.12 *amata tantum quantum amabitur nulla*, 87.1-2 *nulla potest mulier tantum se dicere amatam / uere, quantum a me Lesbia amata mea est*, and was clearly recognised as such by Martial: 12.59.1-3 *tantum dat tibi Roma basiorum / ... / quantum Lesbia non dedit Catullo*. It may also have had Gallan associations, cf. Virg. *Ecl.* 10.73-74 *Gallo, cuius amor tantum mihi crescit in horas / quantum uere nouo uiridis se subicit alnus* (for further possible Gallan influence on Apollo's speech see **headnote** above and **56n.** and **57-58n.** below). It was clearly at home in conversational prose, e.g. Cic. *Fam.* 9.14.4 *nam cum te semper tantam dilexerim quantum tu intellegere potuisti* (cf. *Att.* 3.15.4). For *tantum ... quantum nec ... nec* cf. Cic. *Amic.* 9.2 *quod mihi tantum tribui dicis, quantum ego nec adgnosco nec postulo*.

cara: used of Neaera also at **1.6, 25, 3.32, 6.56**.

filia matri: parallel to *puella uiro* at the end of the pentameter.

cupido bella puella uiro: for the mimetic enclosure of the beloved by the lover cf. Ov. *Am.*1.9.6 *hos petit in socio bella puella uiro*, 2.5.26 *sed* (sc. *oscula*) *tulerit cupido mollis amica uiro*.

cupido ... uiro: for *cupidus* in the sense of 'eager' or 'ardent' of a lover or husband, cf. Cat. 64. 374 *dedatur cupido iamdudum nupta marito*, 70.3 *dicit, sed mulier cupido quod dicit amanti*. The adj. is made a substantive in Tib. in the sense 'lover', cf. 1.8.56, 74, 9.58, as also at Ov. *Ars* 3.674, [Tib.] 3. *Sulpicia Cycle* **12.11**, see *ThLL* 4.1427.21-24. The phrase *cupido ... uiro* occurs in Ov. *Am.* 2.5.26 (quoted above); *Priap.* 16.6 and in the plural at Ov. *Ars* 3.88 *gaudia nec cupidis uestra negate uiris*.

bella puella: the phrase occurs in this position in the line at Cat. 69.8 *bestia, nec quicum bella puella cubet*, 78.4 *cum puero ut bello bella puella cubet* and Ov. *Am.* 1.9.6 (quoted above), where, as here, it is followed by *uiro*. A diminutive of *bonus*, the adj. *bellus* is colloquial in tone, frequent in Plaut. (27) and Cat. (15); see Ross (1969) 110-111. It is rare in elegy, only Tib. 1.9.71; Ov. *Am.* 1.9.6, our author uses it here and at **19.5**, see also **1.7n**. In the Ovidian passage its use is occasioned by its association with *bellum* (war), while the remaining passages seem to have been influenced by Cat. 8.16 *cui uideberis bella?*, so Tib. 1.9.71 *iuueni cuidam uult bella uideri* and **19.**5 *atque utinam posses uni mihi bella uideri.*

puella uiro: parallels *filia matri* at the end of **51**, cf. *puella uiri* at **58** below. *puella uiro* is a common pentameter ending, especially in Ovid: Prop. 4.3.72; Ov. *Am.* 1.9.6, *Her.* 4.2, *Ars* 1.54, 682, *Rem.* 554, 608, *Trist.* 2.1.284; *Priap.* 16.6; Mart. 7.88.4.

53 A reference back to **3.1-10**, where the prayer was that he should share a long life with Neaera and **3.27-28** where Lygdamus prays for Neaera's return to him.

pro qua ... uotis: 'with prayers for whom'. A *uotum* is a vow to the gods to make a gift or offering to them in return for their granting a favour, see **3.1** and *OLD uotum* 1. In view of **3.27-28** the favour required from the gods by Lygdamus in respect of Neaera is that she should be returned to him. For the construction cf. Ov. *Trist.* 1.9.3 *utinam pro te possint mea uota ualere*; **[Tib.]** 3. *Sulpicia Cycle* **10.12** *uotaque pro domina uix numeranda facit.*

sollicitas ... numina: for *sollicito* in the sense of 'importune' (with requests) see *OLD sollicito* 2b and cf. Ov. *Met.* 9.682-683 *Telethusa maritum / sollicitat precibus* and, with the gods as object; Sen. *Medea* 271 *alia sedens tellure sollicita deos*; Lucan 1.63-65 *nec ... / ... Cirrhaea uelim secreta mouentem / sollicitare deum*; Sil. 6.561-562 *(deos) seris ... / sollicitant precibus.* The phrase is a variation on the more widespread *deos fatigare*, as e.g. at Liv. 27.5.6 *suppliciis uotisque fatigare deos.*

caelestia numina: from its original meaning of 'nod of the head' (*OLD numen* 1), [from the same IE root *neu- as *–nuo* 'to nod (assent)', see De Melo (2019) II 1000] the noun *numen* comes to denote 'divine power' (*OLD numen* 2), and then from Virgil on can be used of the deity itself, as here (*OLD numen* 6), cf. Virg. *Aen.* 1.603 *si qua pios respectant numina.* The phrase *caelestia numina* begins in Livy: 1.21.1 *cum interesse rebus humanis caeleste numen uideretur* (8.6.5 *caeleste numen est*) and in the plural is found mainly in Ovid: *Her.* 20.181 *non boue mactato caelestia numina gaudent, Pont.* 3.6.21 *miseris caelestia numina parcunt*, 4.8.89-90 *tangat ut hoc uotum caelestia ... / numina*; cf. also *Aetna* 339 *placantes etiam caelestia numina ture*; Apul. *Met.* 9.34 *numinum caelestium minis.* On the traditional IE theme of the gods as 'heaven-dwellers' see **7.14n.** below.

54 Again a reference back to poem **3.3**, where Lygdamus had expressed the wish to spend a carefree existence with his wife: **3.31-32** ... *liceat mihi ... / securo cara coniuge posse frui*. Apollo makes it clear that Neaera denies him such a carefree life.

securos ... dies: for the meaning of *securus* in this context, see **3.32n.** above. For its use with *dies*, cf. Plin. *Paneg.* 68.2 *itaque securus tibi et laetus dies exit* and Mart. 5.20.1-2 *si tecum mihi, care Martialis, / securis liceat frui diebus*.

ire dies: the verb *ire* is used regularly for the passing of time = 'go by'. Examples with *dies* are found e.g. at Plaut. *Pseud.* 240 *it dies*; Ov. *Her.* 1.8 *nec quererer tardos ire relicta dies*, *Trist.* 2.142 *nube solet pulsa candidus ire dies*; Sen. *Suas.* 3.1 *nec omnis ex uoto iret dies*, *Epist.* 108.25 *numquam Vergilius ... dies dicit ire, sed fugere* and with other time expressions e.g. at Hor. *Epist.* 2.2.55 *anni ... euntes*; Ov. *Am.* 1.6.24 *tempora noctis eunt*; Sen. *Dial.* 10.16.3 *tarde ire horas queruntur*.

dies: not just time in general here, but days as opposed to nights, which are mentioned in **55-56**.

55 et cum te fusco Somnus uelauit amictu: another chronological periphrasis in epic style, see **17-24n.** and cf. **21** above. The image of sleep wrapping someone in a dark cloak occurs only here, but it is perhaps only a short step from the more common idea of sleep touching or covering the sleeper with its wings, as in Prop. 1.3.45 *dum me iucundis lapsam Sopor impulit alis*; Ov. *Met.* 8.823-824 *lenis adhuc Somnus placidis Erysicthona pennis / mulcebat*, especially when these wings are black as in Tib. 2.1.89-90 *... furuis circumdatus alis / Somnus* and Claud. *Carm.* 5.325 *nigrasque Sopor diffuderat alas*. The dark cloak normally belongs not to Sleep but to Night (e.g. Eur. *Ion* 1150, quoted above **17-18n.**); in Latin verse (typically with *amictu* at the line end, as here) this occurs at Sil. 5.36 *atrae noctis amictu*, 12.613 *terras caeco nox condit amictu*, 15.284 *... nox, atro circumdata corpus amictu*; Stat. *Theb.* 3.415-416 *nox subiit ... / ... nigroque polos inuoluit amictu*. The transfer of this aspect from Night to Sleep could have been facilitated by the fact that Night, like Sleep, can also be pictured with black wings, e.g. Virg. *Aen.* 8.369 *nox ... fuscis tellurem amplectitur alis*. The verse ending *uelauit amictu* could be another Catullan echo (cf. Cat. 64.266 *uelabat amictu*; also at Virg. *Aen.* 8.33) and occurs elsewhere at *Ciris* 250 and *Ecl. Einsid.* 1.47.

56 uanum ... fallit: for the combination and the proleptic use of the adjective = 'deceived' after *fallere*, cf. Ov. *Pont.* 2.9.29 (sc. *Ceres*) *uana laborantis si fallat uota coloni.* For *fallere* of deceptive dreams, cf. Lucr. 5.62 *simulacra solere in somnis fallere mentem.*

imaginibus: illusory nocturnal visions, sent by Neaera to deceive Lygdamus, cf. Hor. *Carm.* 3.27.40-42 *ludit imago / uana quae ... / somnium ducit.* On *imaginibus* as a possible Gallan pentameter ending see Cairns [(2006) 79-80] who quotes Prop. 1.5.24 (addressed to Gallus) *nescit Amor priscis cedere imaginibus* and Prop. 1.20.42 *errorem blandis tardat imaginibus.* See **headnote** above, **51-52n.** and **57-58n.** on other possible Gallan echos in this passage. For *nocturnis ... imaginibus*, cf. *nocturnae ... imagines* at Ov. *Am.* 3.5.31 and 33.

57-58 The inspiration for this couplet has long been recognised as Virg. *Ecl.* 10. 21-23 *... uenit Apollo, / 'Galle, quid insanis?' inquit 'tua cura Lycoris / perque niues alium perque horrida castra secuta est'*, where Apollo warns Gallus that his mistress is following a rival on his campaigns abroad; see Bürger (1903), Marx *RE* 1.1.1326 sv. 'Albius'. Given the other possible Gallan touches in Apollo's intervention here, see **51-52n.** and **56n.** above, the ultimate source may be an account in Gallus' *Amores* of a vision of Apollo and a revelation similar to that related by Lygdamus here.

57 carminibus celebrata tuis formosa Neaera: a reference back to **1.7-8**: *carmine formosae pretio capiuntur auarae: / gaudeat, ut digna est, uersibus illa tuis.* For *carminibus celebrare* cf. Virg. *Aen.* 8.303 *talia carminibus celebrant* and, closer to the present context, Ov. *Am.* 1.10.59-60 *est quoque carminibus meritas celebrare puellas / dos mea*, and, close in sense, Prop. 3.2.17 *fortunata meo si qua es celebrata libello.* Given the probable Gallan theme of the couplet, Ov. *Trist.* 2.445 *non fuit opprobrio celebrasse Lycorida Gallo* must also be an important intertext.

formosa: see **1.7n.**

58 alterius ... uiri: for the wording cf. Ov. *Rem.* 772 *esse quod alterius coeperat illa uiri.* The adj. *alter* becomes almost a technical term for the 'rival' in elegy: Tib. 1.5.17; Prop. 1.3. 36 (in this case female), 2.8.5, 9.2, 21.17, 4.5.40; Ov. *Am.* 2.5.53, although *alius* can sometimes be used, see **80** below and cf. Prop. 2.14.21 and Ov. *Am.* 3.7.80.

puella uiri: for the pentameter ending cf. *puella uiro* at **52** above. On *puella* with reference to Neaera see **6.51-52n.**

59 diuersasque tuis ... curas: the *mutua cura* whose existence Lygdamus questioned in **1.19** has been broken and Neaera's mind pursues love concerns (*curas*) which are different from those of Lygdamus. *tuis* is a conjecture by Lipsius for the empty *suas* of the MSS. For *diuersus* + dative, cf. Hor. *Epist.* 1.18.5 *est huic diuersum uitio uitium*; Ov. *Her.* 18.75 *uel certe non his diuersa*, *Met.* 9.321 *forma est diuersa priori*.

diuersas ... curas: the same combination, but with a different sense, occurs at Virg. *Aen.* 12.487 *diuersaeque uocant animum in contraria curae*.

agitat mens: the phrase first occurs in Virgil in a philosophical passage about the *anima mundi* at *Aen.* 6.726-727 *totamque infusa per artus / mens agitat molem et magno se corpore miscet* and then of mental activity at *Aen.* 9.186-187 *aut pugnam aut aliquid iamdudum inuadere magnum / mens agitat mihi*; cf. Sen. *Medea* 46-47 ... *terris mala / mens intus agitat*; Lucan 6.414-415 ... *cunctos belli praesaga futuri / mens agitat*; Stat. *Theb.* 2.176-177 ... *o quam te parcum in praeconia famae / mens agitat matura tuae*, and in the same metrical *sedes* as here Sil. 13.399 *noscere uenturos agitat mens protinus annos*.

agitat ... curas: for *agito* + acc. in the sense of 'to be occupied with, concerned with' see *OLD agito* 11 and for its use with *curas* cf. Liv. 21.41.16 *nec domesticas solum agitet curas*; Sen. *Herc. F.* 137-138 *labor exoritur durus et omnis / agitat curas*.

mens inpia: refers to the state of mind of a person who fails to fulfil their moral obligations, in this case Neaera's obligations as a married woman *nupta* to Lygdamus. For the phrase cf. Cat. 67.25 *siue quod impia mens caeco flagrabat amore*; Cic. *Harusp.* 26.14 *impia mente*; Curt. 9.3.5 *impias mentes*; [Sen.] *Oct.* 225-226 *impia / mens*.

60 gaudet casta ... domo: the verb *gaudet* should not be taken with *nupta* as a perfect participle (+ *esse* understood) in a Graecising construction as suggested by Tränkle and N-A ad loc. Rather it governs the abl. *casta ... domo* 'married Neaera takes no pleasure in a chaste home'. For *gaudeo* + abl. see *OLD gaudeo* 1b; cf. Hor. *Serm.* 2.1.26 *Castor gaudet equis*.

casta ... domo: a common phrase, attested in poetry from Cat. 64.384, often implying the chaste home of a married couple, e.g. Virg. *Georg.* 2.524 *casta pudicitiam seruat domus* (of the home of the upright farmer); Hor. *Carm.* 4.5.21 (of life under Augustus) *nullis polluitur casta domus stupris*; Prop. 2.6.28 (of an artist's indecent pictures decorating a virtuous home) *et posuit casta turpia uisa domo.* There may also be a reference back to *casto ... poetae* in **43** above. There may also be a contrast with the chaste house of Procris, as discovered by Cephalus, when he arrives in disguise at her home to test his wife's fidelity at Ov. *Met.* 7.724-725 *culpa domus ipsa carebat / castaque signa dabat.* On the importance of this intertext see Gen. Intro., section 1.3.

nupta: like *coniunx* at **1.26, 27, 2.4, 30**, the nominalised participle = 'married woman' (cf. *OLD nubo* 1d.) gives a clear indication of Neaera's married status, cf. *coniugium* at **79** below. It occurs here only in the *Corp. Tib.*, but is frequent in Prop. (8) and Ov. (68, though never in *Amores*), where it often retains its original meaning of 'a new bride' *noua nupta*: cf. Prop. 2.3.54 *mox Amythaonia nupta futura domo*; Ov. *Pont.* 1.2.136 *ille ego de uestra cui data nupta domo est.*

61-62 A general condemnation of women is followed by a curse on the woman who teaches others to cheat their men. The theme of misogyny in ancient literature goes back to the bitter complaints of Agamemnon's ghost against women in *Od.* 11.427 and 456 οὐκέτι πιστὰ γυναιξίν ["there is no longer faith in women"]. At Rome the perfidy of women was proverbial, see Otto 231 and cf. Mercury in Virg. *Aen.* 4.569-570 *uarium et mutabile semper / femina.* In elegy the theme is especially prominent in Propertius: 2.9.31-32 *sed uobis* (sc. *feminis) facile est uerba et componere fraudes: / hoc unum didicit femina semper opus,* 25.22 *credule, nulla diu femina pondus habet,* 3.13.23-24 *hoc genus infidum nuptarum, hic* (i.e. Romae) *nulla puella / nec fida Euadne nec pia Penelope.*

a ... / a: a strongly emotional particle, beloved of the neoterics [Cat. 5 examples; see Ross (1969) 51-53]. For its use in elegy see Kershaw (1980) and (1983). The interjection is common in expressions of cruelty, cf. Tib. 1.10.59-60 *a lapis est ferumque, suam quicumque puellam / uerberat*; Ov. *Trist.* 2.77-78 *a ferus et notis crudelior hostibus hostis, / delicias legit qui tibi cumque meas.* For its confusion in the MSS with *ah* (the only form attested in Plautus and Terence) see Bömer on Ov. *Fast.* 2.45.

crudele genus: the adj. *crudelis* is used in love poetry of those who are insensitive to their lover's feelings, especially, as here, by bringing about a *discidium*: see Pichon 117 and cf. Cat. 64.136 *crudelis ... mentis* (of Theseus); Prop. 1.8A.16 (of Cynthia); Ov. *Her.* 7.182 (Dido to Aeneas) *in me crudelis non potes esse diu,* Ars 1.531 *Thesea crudelem surdas clamabat* (sc. *Ariadne) ad undas, Met.* 3.477-478 *... nec me, crudelis, amantem / desere.* The adj. is used at **95** below of Lygdamus' dream. For the application of *genus* as a class to the 'race' of women, cf. Prop. 3.13.23 *genus infidum nuptarum* (quoted in full above); Virg. *Aen.* 9.141-142 ... *penitus modo non genus omne perosos / femineum*; Sen. *Phaed.* 687 *o scelere uincens omne femineum genus*, 564 *Medea reddet feminas dirum genus*; Val. Fl. 2.230-231 *trahit.../femineum genus.*

nec fidum femina nomen: the use of *nomen* + adj. in apposition to a noun recalls Virg. *Aen.* 7.717 *quosque secans infaustum interluit Allia nomen.* Alternatively, the genitive can be used after *nomen*, e.g. Sen. *Phaed.* 230 *exosus omne feminae nomen fugit.* The adj. *fidus* occurs only here in **[Tib.]** 3. It is preferred in verse to the more prosaic *fidelis* [Tib. *fidus* (3) / *fidelis* (1); Prop. *fidus* (7) / fidelis (3); Ov. *fidus* (47) / *fidelis* (16)]. For the relative distributions in prose see Woodman (2014) 164. For the combination *femina nomen* (with a different sense) cf. Ov. *Her.* 19.164 *sola dedit uastis femina nomen aquis.*

femina: used more commonly than *mulier* in elegy: *femina* Tib. (4), Prop. (17), Ov. (64): *mulier* Tib. (1) (in the religious formula *uir mulierque* at 2.2.2), Prop. (5), Ov. (6). In **[Tib.] 3** *mulier* does not occur and *femina* is found only here and at **19.1**. The disparaging connotations of *mulier* (although appropriate here) perhaps made the word less suitable for verse; see further Axelson (1945) 53-57, Adams (1972), McKeown on Ov. *Am.* 1.10.29-30, *ThLL* 8.1571.50-52.

a pereat: a common curse formula, usually at the line beginning: so Prop. 1.6.12, 17.13; *Copa* 34; cf. *o pereat* Tib. 2.4.27; *a(h) pereant* Prop. 1.11.30, 2.23.12; *a peream* 2.24A.15; Ov. *Ars* 2.272, 3.494, *Fast.* 4.240, 241, *Her.* 19.105; *o pereant,* **[Tib.] 3**. *Sulpicia Cycle* **9.6**; with a varied word order at Tib. 1.1.51 *o quantum est auri pereat.*

didicit fallere: for the expression, cf. Tib. 1.9.37 ... *at non ego fallere doctus*; Ov. *Pont.* 3.3.53 *dic, precor, ecquando didicisti fallere nuptas?*; Stat. *Ach.* 1.361-362 ... *iam mutua iura / fallere transmissae pelago didicere carinae.* The verb *didicit* suggests the type of erotodidaxis traditionally provided by the materialistic procuress or *lena*, a common figure in Mime (e.g. Herodas 1), New Comedy (e.g. Cleareta in Plaut. *Asin.*) and elegy [e.g. Tib. 1.5.47-58, 2.6.43-54; Prop. 4.5 (Acanthis); Ov. *Am.* 1.8, 3.5.40]; see further Hollis 100 on Ov. *Ars* 1. 351-398.

fallere ... uirum: according to Ovid, writing in defence of his own poetry, this was the kind of teaching provided for wives by Tibullus in his elegies: Ov. *Trist.* 2.461-462 *docetque* (sc. *Tibullus*) */ qua nuptae possint fallere ab* *arte uiros*. For the phrase cf. Ov. *Ars* 1.310 *siue uirum mauis fallere, falle uiro*, 3.484 *est uobis uestros fallere cura uiros*. The verb becomes a technical term in elegy for betraying one's faith to a husband or lover by deceiving him with another man; see Pichon 141-142.

si qua: cf. Prop. 1.6.12 *a pereat, si quis lentus amare potest*; normally *quaecumque* would be expected in this construction, cf. *a /o pereat quicumque* at Prop. 1.17.13, 2.33B.27; Tib. 2.4.27.

63-76 After the revelation of Neaera's unfaithfulness and the complaint about female perfidy in general Apollo turns to more positive advice, beginning with the statement (**63**) *sed flecti poterit*; Neaera's mind can be swayed and she can be won back by prayers and faithful service *obsequium*. The section consists of a carefully constructed ring-structure, built around the central mythological exemplum of Apollo's service as a cowherd to his beloved, the mortal Admetus: **63-64** *preces* (supplication), **64-65** *obsequium* (service), **67-72** myth of Apollo and Admetus, **73-74** *obsequium*, **75-76** *preces*.

63 flecti: in an elegiac context the verb refers to changing the mind or breaking the resistance of a scornful lover; see Pichon 150 and cf. Prop. 1.8B.39-40 *hanc ego non auro, non Indis flectere conchis / sed potui blandi carminis obsequio*, 1.19.24 *flectitur assiduis certa puella minis*; Ov. *Her.* 17.91-92 (Helen to Paris) *his ego blanditiis, si peccatura fuissem / flecterer*. Our author's inspiration here may have been Ariadne's words to Theseus at Cat. 64.136-137 *nullane res potuit crudelis flectere mentis / consilium*, as is suggested by the verbal echoes of *crudelis* (in **61**) and *potuit flectere* (in **63**) and by the fact that he mentions reading Catullus' poem at **6.39-42** below.

mutabilis: not here in the sense 'fickle' as at Virg. *Aen.* 4.569-570 quoted on **61-62** above, but rather 'flexible', 'capable of being persuaded', a common meaning in Ovid, cf. *Her.* 7.51 (Dido to Aeneas) *tu quoque cum uentis utinam mutabilis esses*, *Met.* 2.145-146 (Titan to Phaethon) ... *uel si mutabile pectus / est tibi consiliis* ... *utere nostris*, *Fast.* 4.601-602 *sed si forte tibi non est mutabile pectus / statque semel iuncti rumpere uincla tori*. Both *flecti* and *mutabilis* reflect the theme of change which has such an important role to play within the collection as a whole, see Prolegomena pp. 81-82 above.

illis: i.e. women in general.

64 tu modo ... tende: the construction *tu modo* + imperat. is common in commands from Plautus on, e.g. *Mil.* 1123 *tu modo istuc cura*. Its use in didactic verse, where *tu modo* normally opens the line, e.g. Virg. *Georg.* 3.73-74 *tu modo ... / praecipuum ... impende laborem* leads to its use in erotodidactic contexts, as here, e.g. Ov. *Ars* 1.67 *tu modo Pompeia lentus spatiare sub umbra*, 270 *tu modo tende plagas*, 480 *tu modo blanditias fac legat usque tuas*; **[Tib.] 3.** *Sulpicia Cycle* **10.16.** *tu modo semper ama* with **n.** For the scansion of the final syllable of *modo* as short by iambic shortening, see Platnauer 50-51 and cf. **5.20** below.

cum multa ... prece: *prece* here is the reading of some later MSS for *fide* of A. The same confusion is found at **6.46**, where *prece* must be the correct reading. Here the idea of supplication in *prece* fits the context better and forms a ring structure with *prece* in **76**. For the expression, cf. **3.2** *cum multa tura dedisse prece* and for its use in the context of a lover's prayer cf. Ov. *Her.* 7.3 (Dido to Aeneas) *nec quia te nostra sperem prece posse moueri*.

bracchia tende: a stance adopted by mortals in praying to the gods, e.g. Cat. 66.10 (of Berenice) *leuia protendens bracchia*, or by conquered warriors begging for mercy, e.g. Ov. *Met.* 5.175-176 ... *trepidum* (sc. *Echemmona*) *Perseus et inertia frustra / bracchia tendentem Cyllenide confodit harpe*. The gesture is transferred to an erotic context by Ovid at *Her.* 4.153-154 (Phaedra to Hippolytus) *uicta precor genibusque tuis regalia tendo / bracchia*.

65 This line is missing in A. Various humanist supplements are listed in the textual apparatus. I print the text reported by Scaliger to have been in the now lost *Fragmentum Cuiacianum*, which is probably as close as we can get to the original. Quotations from this fragment begin with this line.

saeuus Amor docuit: the half-line comes from Virg. *Ecl.* 8.47-48 with reference to Medea killing her children: *saeuus Amor docuit natorum sanguine matrem / commaculare manus*. The adj. *saeuus* is commonly associated with the cruelty of love e.g. Tib. 1.6.3; Ov. *Am.* 1.1.5, 6.34, 2.10.19; Sen. *Medea* 850 and see Kenney on Apul. *Met.* 4.33.1.4. The epithet is, however, more appropriate in relation to Medea than it is in the current context and Virgil's source was probably Ennius' translation of the opening of Eur.'s *Medea*: Enn. *Trag.* 216 Jocelyn *Medea animo aegro amore saeuo saucia*, where there is no exact equivalent in the Greek. The cruel malice of love in general is illustrated by the frequency of similar epithets in both Greek and Latin literature: e.g. in Greek: ἄγριος (wild) *AP*

5.177 (Meleager); βαρύς (stern) Theocr. *Id.* 3.15; δεινός (terrible) Eur. *Hipp.* 28, *AP* 5.176.1-2 (Meleager); ούλιος (baneful) Simonides *PMG* 575, Theogn. 1231, Ap. Rhod. 3.297, 1078; σχέτλιος (cruel) Ap. Rhod. 4.445, *AP* 5.57 (Meleager); χαλεπός (difficult) Call. fr. 75.49 Pf.; in Latin: *acer* Tib. 2.6.15, Prop. 2.30.9, Virg. *Aen.* 12.392, Ov. *Her.* 4.70, *Pont.* 4.7.40, **[Tib.] 3.** (*Sulpicia Cycle*) **8.6**; *crudelis* Virg. *Ecl.* 10.29; *durus* Virg. *Georg.* 3.259, *Aen.* 6.442; *ferus* Ov. *Am.* 1.2.8, 3.1.20, *Ars* 1.9; *improbus* Virg. *Ecl.* 8.49, *Aen.* 4.412, Prop. 1.1.6; *malus Ciris* 133. Meleager *AP* 5.180 devotes a whole epigram to explaining how the harshness of Eros was to be explained by the fact that his mother Aphrodite was the wife of Hephaestus and the lover of Ares.

docuit: for Love's teaching, cf. Virg. *Ecl.* 8.47-48; Prop. 1.1.5-6 *donec* (sc. *Amor*) *me docuit castas odisse Puellas / improbus et nullo uiuere consilio*; *Ciris* 135-136 *ille* (sc. *Amor*) *etiam Poenos domitare leones / et ualidas docuit uires mansuescere tigris.* Fedeli [67 on Prop. 1.1.5] points to the particular meaning of *docere* in these contexts, which is closer to 'induces' than 'teaches', cf. *ThLL* 5(1).1747.1-70. Whereas *docuit* in our author's model at *Ecl.* 8.47 is aorist in meaning referring to a single action in the past, in *Lygd.* it becomes a generalised gnomic perfect 'teaches people'.

ualidos temptare labores: the adj. suggests the strenuous labours of Hercules, which became proverbial for any difficult task, cf. in an amatory context, Prop. 2.23.7-8 and see Otto 162. A more common epithet in amatory contexts is *durus*: cf. Tib. 1.4.47 *nec te paeniteat duros subiisse labores*; *Ciris* 291 *duros passa labores*. For *temptare labores* as a line-end, cf. Virg. *Aen.* 5.498-499 ... *Acestes / ausus et ipse manu iuuenum temptare laborem.*

labores: used commonly of toil and hardship suffered in military contexts (Enn. *Ann.* 327-328 Sk.; Tib. 1.1.3; Hor. *Serm.* 1.1.5; Liv. 26.13.9; Ov. *Met.* 13.316, *Fast.* 1.302, *Pont.* 1.6.10) and so suggesting here the common elegiac theme of *militia amoris* on which see Spies (1930) and Murgatroyd (1975). The clearest examples of military *labores* applied to lovers occur at Ov. *Am.* 1.9.1ff. *militat omnis amans*, and *Ars* 2.233-250, a passage beginning *militiae species amor est* and mentioning specifically the service of Apollo for Admetus at 239-240. For the term *labor/labores* applied to the hardships endured by lovers, cf. Plaut. *Merc.* 861 (with a detailed list of *labores* at 858-863); Tib. 1.2.33, 4.46; Prop. 2.23.7-8 *labores / Herculis*, 24B.29.

65-66 ualidos temptare labores, / ... uerbera posse pati: the lover must put up with all kinds of hardship *labores* and even, like a slave, suffer blows *uerbera* in the service of his beloved. Parca [(1986) 472] points out that these sufferings have more in common with the Milanion-Atalanta episode at Prop. 1.1.9-16, where the hero's suffering and endurance win the mistress, than with Apollo's demeaning agricultural service for Admetus described in **67-72** here. Certainly our author seems to have had this Propertian poem in mind, as the note on *docuit* above shows, cf. also the *saeuus Amor / improbus* (*Amor*) parallel. The following echoes from the Milanion episode also seem striking: *labores* **65** and Prop. 1.1.9, *saeuus* **65** and *saeuitia* Prop. 1.1.10, *uerbera* **66** and *uulnera ... / saucius* Prop. 1.1.13-14. The Admetus *exemplum* however is more appropriate to the speaker, Apollo, and is mentioned by Ov. *Ars* 2.239-240 in a comparison of the *labores* of soldiers and lovers, cf. note on *labores* above.

66 uerbera posse pati: to suffer a beating, *uerbera*, was a slave punishment, so the phrase here invokes the image of *seruitium amoris* in which the lover acts out the role of slave to his mistress, see Copley (1947), Lyne (1979), Murgatroyd (1981) and cf. Hor *Carm*. 1.33.14 (with N-H); Tib. 1.1.55 with Maltby 141-142, 2.4.1-6; Prop. 1.4.1-4, 2.8.15, 3.6 with introduction by Heyworth and Morwood (2011) 145-146; Ov. *Am*. 1.2.18, 3.5-6 with McKeown II 64-65, 3.11.9-12. On the name Lygdamus, which appears as that of Prop.'s slave in Prop. 3.16, 4.7 and 4.8, as particularly appropriate for one suffering the pains of *seruitium amoris* see Bickel (1960), N-A 21 and see Gen. Intro., section 3.1. For *uerbera* in this context, apparently an innovation of Tibullus, cf. Tib. 1.6.37-38 ... *non saeua recuso / uerbera, detrecto non ego uincla pedum*, 2.3.79-80 *ducite. ad imperium dominae sulcabimus agros: / non ego me uinclis uerberibusque nego*. For the specific connection between slave beatings and the sufferings of a lover, cf Ov. *Her*. 20.77-78 (Acontius to Cydippe) *utque solent famuli, cum uerbera saeua uerentur, / tendere submissas ad tua crura manus*, where *tendere ... manus* recalls *bracchia tende* of **64** above.

67-72 The myth of Apollo's service to Admetus as a cowherd. The myth serves as an example of the *obsequium* and *seruitium* demanded of the lover by *saeuus Amor*. It follows the more detailed account in Tib. 2.3.11-32 in that it makes Apollo's servitude voluntary and motivated by the god's love for the mortal Admetus. The erotic version of the myth is probably a Hellenistic innovation, as earlier poets, e.g. Hesiod fr. 54 M-W, Eur. *Alcest*. 8, Apollodorus 3.10.4, had given punishment by Zeus for

Apollo's slaying of the Cyclopes as the reason for his servitude. On this divine punishment version of the myth and its IE background see West (2007) 148. The erotic version is found in Call. *Hymn.* 2.47-49 (see Williams ad loc.) and may have received a fuller treatment in Rhianus (see fr.10 Powell), cf. also Plut. *Mor.* 761e. This Hellenistic version is hinted at in Virg. *Georg.* 3.1-2 ... *te memorande canemus / pastor ab Amphryso*, where the reference to the location of Apollo's herding duties for Admetus by the Thessalian river Amphrysus is a detail taken from Callimachus' account of the myth at *Hymn.* 2.48. Servius' note on *Georg.* 3.2, however, gives the original version *Apollo, spoliatus diuinitate ob occisos Cyclopas, Admeto regi pauisse armenta dicitur.* In Tib. 2.3.11-32 the myth is more carefully woven into the context, as it illustrates Tib.'s readiness to undertake agricultural labour in order to be near his mistress Nemesis, who has retired to the country. In Tibullus the name Admetus (meaning *indomitus*) corresponds to *inmitem dominam* (**74**) [Peraki-Kyriakidou (2016) 86; cf. Maas (1895) 151]; see below **74**. Between Tib. and [**Tib.**] 3 came Ovid who used the myth as a general illustration of *obsequium* at *Ars* 2.239-241 *Cynthius Admeti uaccas pauisse Pheraei / fertur et in parua delituisse casa: / quod Phoebum decuit, quem non decet*? *exue fastus.* Whereas in Tib. Apollo still attempted to sing (2.3.23) and to play the lyre (2.3.12), although neither consoled him, in our *Lygd.* poem he has abandoned singing and the the lyre for the rustic pipe **69-71**. The herdsman's pipe is mentioned as an attribute of Apollo when guarding cattle in another context by Ovid at *Met.* 2.681-682 ... *onusque fuit baculum siluestre sinistrae, / alterius dispar septenis fistula cannis*, and the replacement of the lyre by the pipe is found in relation to the Admetus story at Sen. *Phaed.* 296-298 *Thessali Phoebus pecoris magister / egit armentum, positoque plectro / impari tauros calamo uocauit* and Stat. *Silu.* 3.3.58 ... *nec erubuit famulantis fistula Phoebi.*

67 quondam: for the use of this adverb to introduce mythological paradigms set in the past, cf. Tib. 1.5.45-46 *talis ad Haemonium Nereis Pelea quondam / uecta est*; Prop. 1.2.17-18 ... *Idae et cupido quondam discordia Phoebo / Eueni ... filia* and see McKeown II 377 on Ov. *Am.* 1.14.33-34 ... *quas* (sc. *comas*) *quondam nuda Dione / pingitur ... sustinuisse.*

Admeti: king of Pherae in Thessaly, cf. Ov. *Ars* 2.239 (quoted on **67-72** above) *Her.* 5.151-152 *uaccas pauisse Pheraeas / fertur* (sc. *Apollo*); Sen. *Herc. F.* 451 *pastor Pheraeos Delius pauit greges.*

niueas ... iuuencas: originally the animals Apollo looked after for Admetus were horses, as one would expect in Thessaly (cf. Hom. *Il.* 2.767; Call. *Hymn.* 2.47). Pindar speaks of sheep (*Pyth.* 9.64) and Euripides of cattle (*Alcest.* 8). Cattle become the rule in Latin versions, though there is some uncertainty as to whether they were cows, as here (also Ov. *Ars* 2.239 *uaccas*, *Her.* 5.151 *uaccas*) or bulls (Sen. *Phaed.* 298 *tauros*); Tib. includes cattle of both sexes: 2.3.11 (*tauros*), 15 (*uaccas*), 21 (*uitulum*). For the phrase *niueas iuuencas* cf. Ov. *Am.* 2.12.25-26, 3.13.13 and, in the masc. *niuei iuuenci* Virg. *Ecl.* 6.46, *Georg.* 1.15. For Ovid's fondness for applying the adj. *niueus* to cattle see Fantham on Ov. *Fast.* 4.825-826.

pauisse: occurs in the same position in the line in Ovid's account of the myth at *Ars* 2.239 and *Her.* 5.151, both quoted above on *Admeti*.

68 non est in uanum fabula ficta iocum: the subject is the inf. clause *me ... pauisse iuuencas*; the fact that Apollo pastured Admetus' heifers 'is no myth invented as an idle joke'. A *fabula ficta* is an invented story; the phrase is common in Cicero, e.g. *Verr.* 2.3.182 *non me fugit ... uetera exempla pro fictis fabulis iam audiri atque haberi*, *Rep.* 2.19 *antiquitas enim recepit fabulas fictas*, *Mil.* 8 etc., cf. Prop. 3.5.45 (of the underworld) *... ficta in miseras descendit fabula gentes*; Phaedr. *Fab. Aes*.1 *pr.* 7 *quod arbores loquantur, non tantum ferae, fictis iocari nos meminerit fabulis*. In Tib.'s account of the Admetus myth the word *fabula* is applied to Apollo himself, both as the subject of a myth and as a 'laughing-stock' 2.3.31 *fabula nunc ille* (sc. *Apollo*) *est*. The phrasing of the line recalls Ov. *Fast.* 3.738 *non habet ingratos fabula nostra iocos*. For the phrase *in iocum conuertere* used of turning a myth into a joke cf. Porph. *Hor. Epod.* 3.9-10 *notam autem historiam* (sc. *Medeae*) *hic in iocum conuertit*.

69-70 Apollo laments that as a herdsman he was unable to sing songs to the accompaniment of the lyre, cf. Tib. 2.3.12 *nec cithara intonsae profueruntue comae*. On the metapoetic implications of the couplet, suggesting that Apollo's situation necessitated a change from lyric to bucolic poetry, see **71n.** below. For the repetition *sonora* / ... *sonos* in consecutive line-ends see Wills (1996) 421-422.

69 sonora: the adj. is used first by Virgil as a learned variant on *canorus* or *sonans* to refer to a full-toned sound; so *Aen.* 1.53 *tempestatesque sonoras*, 12.139 *fluminibusque sonoris*, 12.712 *aere sonoro*, cf. *Culex* 281 *siluaeque sonorae*. It is frequent, again always at the line-end, in Stat.

(11), who has the only other example of its application to the lyre: *Silu.* 1.5.4-5 *ferae ... sonorae / terga.*

70 similes chordis ... sonos: i.e. sounds in tune with the strings of the lyre. For the idea, cf. Hor. *Carm.* 4.9.4 *uerba loquor socianda chordis.* For *similis* + dat. see *OLD similis* 1b and cf. Ov. *Met.* 1.708 *effecisse sonum tenuem similemque querenti.*

reddere uoce sonos: for *uoce reddere* of producing vocal sounds cf. Hor. *Carm.* 4.11.34-35 *... condisce modos, amanda / uoce quos reddas*; Ov. *Fast.* 6.426 *hos non mentito reddidit ore sonos.*

71 The line is clearly inspired by Virg. *Ecl.* 1.2 *siluestrem tenui Musam meditaris auena.* It also suggests a change to the more lowly genre of bucolic poetry, better suited to Apollo's rural situation, echoing Gallus at Virg. *Ecl.* 10.50-51 *ibo et Chalcidico quae sunt mihi condita uersu / carmina pastoris Siculi moderabor auena.*

perlucenti ... auena: the epithet has caused problems for interpreters. Postgate explains *perlucenti* as 'translucent' since the holes in the pipe would let the light through and compares passages such as Plaut. *Rud.* 102 *perlucet ea quam cribrum crebrius* (of a villa with holes in the roof) and Juv. 11.13 *iam perlucente ruina.* Némethy interprets the adj. also in the sense 'translucent', but meaning that the stalk of the pipe was so thin as to allow the light through, connecting it with the epithet *tenui* at Virg. Ecl.1.2 and λεπτός at Eur. *Or.* 146 λεπτοῦ δόνακος ["of a light reed"]. Postgate's suggestion seems more convincing, as it is difficult to imagine a functioning pipe being so thin as to allow the light through. The meaning here could simply be 'bright, shining' *OLD perluceo* 2b, or 'clear' of sound, like Gk. διαυγής, cf. Ov. *Met.* 3.16 *fons sonat ... perlucidus* where *perlucidus ... sonat* could be related both to vision and to sound; cf. Quint. *Inst.* 11.3.154. Of the numerous conjectures suggested by other scholars Huschke's *permulcenti* 'soothing' is worthy of note, cf. Ov. *Met.* 2.683 *dumque amor est curae, dum te tua fistula mulcet.*

meditabar: in the sense of 'work over (a song) in performance' (*OLD meditor* 7) occurs first in Virg. *Ecl.*, cf. 1.2 (quoted above), 6.8 *agrestem tenui meditabor harundine Musam,* 82-83 *omnia quae Phoebo quondam meditante beatus / audiit Eurotas* and later at Ov. *Pont.* 3.4.45, Apul. *Flor.* 17. At **5.13** it occurs in a different sense of 'ponder', 'have in mind' *... insanae meditantes iurgia mentis.*

256   Commentary

auena: literally 'an oaten pipe'. Used first by Virgil, cf. *Ecl.* 1.2 (quoted above), 10.51 *carmina pastoris Siculi modulabor auena* and taken up by Tib. at 2.1.53 *et satur arenti primum est modulatus auena* and by Ovid in the plural = 'pan-pipes' at *Met.* 1.677 *structis cantat auenis* and *Trist.* 5.10.25 *iunctis ... cantat auenis*. Such a slender oaten straw would be impractical as a musical instrument in real life and Virgil may have borrowed the word from an insulting reference by Comatas in Theocr. *Id.* 5.7 to a καλάμας αὐλόν ["oaten straw pipe"]; see Clausen on *Ecl.* 1.2 and cf. the equally contemptuous *stipula* 'straw' at *Ecl.* 3.27 *stridenti miserum stipula disperdere carmen*. In fact ancient rustic pipes, whether single (as here, cf. αὐλός at Theocr. *Id.* 5.7, 6.43, 10.34, *tibia* Virg. *Ecl.* 8.21, 25 etc.), or multiple 'pan pipes' (cf. Gk. σῦριγξ, δόνακες, Lat. *fistula* at Virg. *Ecl.* 2.37, 3.22, 25, 7.24, 8.33, 10.34, *auenae* in Ovid above), were made of hemlock stalks (*cicuta* Lucr. 5.1383; Virg. *Ecl.* 2.36, 5.85), or, more often, marsh reed (Gk. δόνακες, Lat. *harundo* Virg. *Ecl.* 6.8, *calamus* Virg. *Ecl.* 1.10, 2.34, 5.2, 48, 6.69). It is thanks to Virgil that the oaten pipe became part of the later pastoral tradition in both Latin and English, cf. Spenser's 'oaten reed', Shakespeare's 'oaten straw', Milton's 'oaten flute' and Marvell's 'slender oat'.

72 ille ego: a rather grandiloquent form of self introduction, frequent in dactylic poetry, cf. Ov. *Am.* 2.1.2 *ille ego nequitiae Naso poeta meae* (with McKeown III 5), 3.8.23 *ille ego Musarum purus Phoebique sacerdos*, often, as here, implying a loss of former status, see Austin (1968) and cf. [Virg.] *Aen.*1a-1b *ille ego qui quondam gracili modulatus auena / carmen*. In the context of *obsequium amoris* it had occurred at Tib. 1.5.9-10 *ille ego, cum tristi morbo defessa iaceres, / te dicor uotis eripuisse meis* and 6.31-32 *ille ego sum ... / instabat tota cui tua nocte canis*.

Latonae filius atque Iouis: Apollo and his sister Diana were the twin children of Latona by Jupiter, see **29n.** above on *Latonia Luna*. For Apollo as *Latonae filius* cf. Liv. Andron. *Od.* 21.1 *Mercurius cumque eo filius Latonas*; Hor. *Carm.* 4.6.37 *Latonae puerum*; Ov. *Trist.* 5.1.57 *Latonia proles*. Latona was the Latin name for the Greek goddess Leto, see *RE* 12.2148ff. (Fiesel), and cf. Hom. *Il.* 1.9 where Apollo is referred to as Λητοῦς καὶ Διὸς υἱός ("the son of Leto and Zeus"). In Tib.'s version of the Admetus myth Latona laments at Apollo's dishevelled hair: Tib. 2.3.27 *saepe horrere sacros doluit Latona capillos*.

atque Iouis: the only example in the *Lygd.* poems where the second syllable of *atque* is unelided (contrast elided examples at **1.13, 22, 2.22, 28, 5.27**). Such unelided cases of *atque* are rare in elegy in general (only

Book Three of the Corpus Tibullianum: 257
Introduction, Text, Translation and Commentary

19 at most), see Platnauer 78-82 and cf. Butterfield [(2008) 397 n. 33], especially, as here, in the second half of the pentameter. They become more common in post-classical authors such as Martial.

73 nescis quid sit amor: another echo of Virgil's eighth *Eclogue* (cf. **65n.** on the echo of *Ecl*. 8.47 *saeuus amor docuit*); here the model is *Ecl*. 8.43 *nunc* scio, *quid sit amor*. In both cases the reference is to the savagery of love, as the Theocritean model for 8.43 shows: Theocr. *Id.* 3.15 νῦν ἔγνων τὸν Ἔρωτα· βαρὺς θεός ["now I know Love: a difficult god"].

iuuenis. Lygdamus suggests he is a youth at **2.1** and makes it clear in his prayer at **5.6** *inmerito iuueni parce nocere, dea*. For Apollo as *iuuenis* see **23** above.

ferre recusas: the only example of *recuso* in Tib. is in a similar context of *seruitium amoris*: Tib. 1.6.37-38 ... *non saeua recuso / uerbera*. It occurs in **[Tib.]** 3 only here and at **6.11**, and is completely absent from Prop. It is common in Hor. (10), Virg. (13), and Ov. (25). For *ferre + recuso* (in various forms) at the line-end, cf. Hor. *Serm*. 2.7.108 (*recusant*), *Epist*. 2.1.259 (*recusant*), *AP* 39 (*recuset*); Ov. *Met*. 10.171 (*recusat*); Lucan 6.97 (*recusat*); Mart. 10.10.7 (*recusas*).

74 The nouns and adjectives here are carefully arranged in the pattern *a b b a*.

inmitem: originally 'unripe', 'sour' of fruit or wine, see *OLD immitis* 1, e.g. Hor. *Carm*. 2.5.9-10 *tolle cupidinem / immitis uuae*, and then 'harsh', 'savage' of both animate and inanimate objects. It is common in Ov. *Met*. (15), but is rare in elegy [Tib. (3), Prop. (2), Ov. (5) –see Pichon 204], and is used elsewhere of a heartless mistress only in the famous oxymoron of Hor. *Carm*. 1.33.2 (addressed to Albius, i.e. Tibullus) *immitis Glycerae* and at Ov. *Met*. 13.804 (of Galatea) *calcato immitior hydro*. The reference to Neaera here clearly contrasts with that of her mother as *mitissima* at **93** below. For its reference to a husband in the context of *obsequium* cf. [Sen.] *Oct*. 177 *uince obsequendo potius immitem uirum*. For the combination *immitem / ferum* cf. Liv. 23.5.12 *hunc natura et moribus immitem et ferum insuper dux ipse efferauit*; Sen. *Herc. F*. 1280 *monstrum impium saeuumque et immite ac ferum*, Phaed. 272-273 ... *labor est aggredi iuuenem ferum / mentemque ... flectere immitis uiri*.

dominam coniugiumque: *domina* is common in Latin poetry from Catullus on (68.68, 156, cf. *era* at 68.136) to refer to the beloved, especially in elegy, as an expression of *seruitium amoris*, e.g. Tib. 2.3.79

ducite, ad imperium dominae sulcabimus agros, 4.1 *sic mihi seruitium uideo dominamque paratam*; see Pichon 134, Syndikus (2006) 296 n.161. Its use with *coniugium* 'marriage' is unusual, and may recall the use of *domina* as 'wife' and (female) 'head of the household' in colloquial language and inscriptions of the imperial period, as also at Ov. *Trist.* 3.3.23; Petr. 66.5 etc. For the combination of *domina* with *coniunx /coniugium* see Sen. *Ag.* 263 *nec coniugem hoc respicere nec dominam decet*; Quint. *Decl. Mai.* 2.16 *uxor et domina* and for the masculine equivalent, cf. Ov. *Her.* 3.5 (of Achilles) *dominoque uiroque*. Fulkerson [(2017) 171 ad loc.] could be right as seeing this as a conflation of elegiac (*dominam*) and legalistic (*coniugium*) language. For *ferre coniugium*, where the noun verges on a metonymy for 'wife' (*OLD coniugium* 3a), cf. Prop. 4.11.87 *coniugium, pueri, laudate et ferte paternum* with Hutchinson. Lygdamus refers to Neaera as his *coniunx* or 'wife' at **1.26-27, 2.4, 30, 3.32** and Apollo refers to their relationship as a *coniugium* 'marriage' at **79** below; it would be difficult, with N-A 382 on 4.74, to take such specific terminology as referring simply to a 'love relationship'.

coniugiumque ferum: the adj., implying cruelty or overweening pride, may contain an etymological word-play with *ferre* in **73**, see *LALE* 230 s.v. *ferus* and cf. **2.1n.** above *primus* and Maltby [(2002) 341 on Tib. 1.10.1-6] where the same play is found. On the use of the adj. in elegy see Pichon 147.

75-76 A return to the theme of **63-64**. Neaera can be swayed by entreaty. For the importance of flattery (*blanditia*), complaints (*querelae*) and prayers (*preces*) in love, cf. Tib. 1.4.71-72 *blanditiis uult esse locum Venus: illa querellis / supplicibus, miseris fletibus illa fauet*; Prop. 1.1.16 *tantum in amore preces ... ualent*; Ov. *Met.* 3.375-376 *o quotiens uoluit* (sc. *Echo ad Narcissum*) *blandis accedere dictis / et mollis adhibere preces*. For *prece* cf. **64** above.

75 ergo: on the prosody, see **2.9n.**

ergo ne dubita: For the phrase cf. Ov. *Ars* 1.343 *ergo age ne dubita cunctas sperare puellas*. The construction *ne* + imperat. probably sounded archaic by the Augustan period (see McKeown II 195 on Ov. *Am.* 1.7.63-64) and here would lend a certain authority to Apollo's advice. Other examples of *ne dubita* occur at Prop. 2.20.14; Virg. *Aen.* 3.316; Ov. *Am.* 1.7.63, *Ars* 1.343 (quoted above), *Met.* 2.101, 5.335, 9.698, *Fast.* 3.641, 699; Calp. *Ecl.* 3.75. As McKeown points out (loc. cit.) *dubitare* is more common in Ov. (97) than in the other Augustan poets: Hor. (2), Virg. (10), Tib. (1), Prop. (1).

blandas ... querelas: cf. Stat. *Silu.* 2.1.45 *blandis ... querelis*; Mart. 11.70.3-4 *nec te blanditiae nec uerba rudesue querelae / ... mouent.* The reference is to blandishments mixed with entreaty, a combination found at Tib. 1.4.71-72 (quoted on **75-76** above). For *querela* in elegy in a sense nearing prayer or entreaty see Pichon 248. It is relatively frequent in Prop. (11) and Tib. (3), occurs here only in **[Tib.] 3**, and of Ovid's 34 occurrences only one appears in *Am.* (2.6.8), although 19 are found in the other elegiac works. At a metapoetic level *querelae* could refer to elegy, which the ancients associated etymologically with 'complaint', see *LALE* 201-202 s.v. *elegia* and *elegiacus*.

adhibere: perhaps here in the medical sense (appropriate for Apollo) of applying a cure, cf. Cels. 1 pr. 23.2 *neminem putant his adhibere posse remedia*; for its use in an amatory context cf. Ov. *Met.* 3.376 *mollis adhibere preces* (of Echo wishing to address prayers to Narcissus).

76 uincuntur: the image is that of *militia amoris* for which see **65-66n.** above on *labores*. There could be an echo of Virg. *Ecl.* 10.69 *omnia uincit Amor* (again with Gallan associations). The verb occurs again of softening hearts at **6.15-16** with Amor as subject and in combination with *mollis*, as here: *Armenias tigres et fuluas ille leaenas / uicit et indomitis mollia corda dedit*. For the use of the verb in elegy in the sense of 'winning over' a beloved see Pichon 294.

molli ... dura: for the juxtaposition cf. Hor. *Carm.* 4.1.6-7 (sc. *desine*) *flectere mollibus / iam durum imperiis*; Ov. *Am.* 2.1.22 *mollierunt duras lenia uerba fores* and the contrast between *mollia ... uerba* and *duro ore* at *Am.* 1.12.22-24; see Cairns (2006) 232-234. On *mollis* in elegy = 'yielding in love', 'susceptible to love' see Pichon 204-6 and *ThLL* 8.1377.71 and on *mollis* itself as a characteristic of elegy, cf. Virg. *Ecl.* 10.33 (of Gallus) *molliter ossa quiescent* with Clausen 302 ad loc.; Prop. 1.7.19 *mollem ... uersum*, 2.1.2 *mollis ... liber*; Ov. *Trist.* 2.349 *mollia carmina*, *Pont.* 3.4.85 *molles elegi*. On the elegiac meaning of *durus* see **2.3n.** above.

molli ... prece: cf. Ov. *Am.* 2.2.66 *quid precibus nostris mollius esse potest* and *mollis ... preces* at *Met.* 3.376 (quoted on **75-76n.** above).

pectora dura: for the phrase cf. Ov. *Met.* 14.693 and, with *uinco*; Liv. 10.31.12 *quibus nequierunt dura illa pectora uinci*. For the metaphorical use of *pectus* 'spirit' in connection with amorous feelings cf. *Lygd.* **1.20, 4.84.** and see Pichon 229. By contrast *pectus* in Tib. is always used in the physical sense of 'breast' (1.4.12, 6.18, 49, 7.40).

77 An initial statement about the truthfulness of oracles leads into an oracular message (**79-80**), to be delivered to Neaera (**78**), with which Apollo ends his speech. There is some ambiguity in the formulation here. Apollo does not simply state 'my oracles are true', but the particle *quod si* introduces an element of doubt 'but if my oracles are true'; furthermore there is no possessive pronoun such as *mea* or *nostra* to indicate whose oracles are in question.

quod si: 'but if'; although the phrase is common in Cicero *quod si* is not particularly prosaic, or colloquial, as Axelson [(1945) 47-48] points out. It occurs in high-style verse, e.g. Virg. *Aen.* (5), Ov. *Met.* (8) and in elegy, where it is most common in Prop. (21), but also sporadically in Tib. (2), elegiac Ov. (4), and **[Tib.] 3** (3).

uera canunt: recalls *diui uera monent* above (**5**), where the true warnings of gods are contrasted with the deceptive warnings of dreams. Here the oracle comes from a god but occurs in a dream, which again lends ambiguity to its content. For the phrase *uera canunt* cf. Tib. 2.5.63 (the Sibyl) *uera cano*; Ov. *Ars* 1.30 (the poet) *uera canam*, 3.790 (Ovid's Muse) *uera ... canet*; Val. Fl. 2.218 *uera canentem*; Juv. 2.64 *uera ... canentem*. For *cano* in the sense of *uaticinor* 'utter a prophecy' see *ThLL* 3.271.12-272.57 and cf. Prop. 3.6.31 (Cynthia's words to Lygdamus to be reported back to Prop.) *si non uana cadunt mea somnia, Lygdame, testor*, 3.11.3; Ov. *Her.* 21.232 *a Delphis fata canente deo*; Sil. 2.285 *haec ... uates ... canit*, 3.687 *ales ... responsa canebat*; Serv. *Aen.* 8.656 *canebat: quasi praediuinabat, nam canere et dicere et diuinare significat*.

canunt ... oracula: normally *oracula* would be the object rather than the subject of the verb *cano*, e.g. Virg. *Aen.* 3.456-457 *adeas uatem precibusque oracula poscas / ipsa canat*. Here, however, *oracula* refers to the agent or mouthpiece of the divine utterance, see *OLD oraculum* 2 and cf. Ov. *Pont.* 3.1.131 *non semper sacras reddunt oracula sortes*.

sacris ... templis: an unusually rare combination, perhaps because *sacrum /sacra* is normally used substantively = 'religious rites' in contexts where *templum* also appears, but cf. Liv. 1.20.5 *templa sacra*; Stat. *Silu.* 3.1.82 *sacri ... templi*; Serv. *Aen.* 1.446 *sacrum templum*, 4.200 *templa ... sacra*.

78 illi: i.e. to Neaera.

nostro nomine: 'on my behalf', 'in my name'. In this sense the phrase is restricted mainly to prose, cf. Liv. 8.4.8 *bellum nostro nomine cum Paelignis gessimus*; Quint. *Decl. Min.* 260.12 *libet uobiscum loqui nostro nomine*, and is particularly frequent in legal texts, e.g. Gai. *Inst.* 4.81, 153; Iust. *Dig.* 12.1.9.8, 36.1.41.2 etc.

dicta: the term can be used both as a promise, see *OLD dictum* 2, cf. Virg. *Aen.* 8.643 *at tu dictis, Albane, maneres*, and as an oracular or divine response, e.g. Ov. *Fast.* 5.626 *talia fatidici dicta fuisse Iouis*. Both senses are operative here.

refer: 'pass on', 'report', see *OLD refero* 6. Apollo's oracular utterance (**79-80**) is to be reported word for word to Neaera.

79 Apollo promises Neaera marriage with Lygdamus. The difficulty is that this marriage is presented earlier by both Lygdamus and Apollo as already in existence (see **74n.** *coniugium* above). The meaning must be close to 'this is the marriage Apollo promises you' as a continuing pledge. For Apollo's promises of marriage cf. Call. *Aet.* 3 fr.75.26-29 Pf. Δήλῳ δ' ἦν ἐπίδημος, Ἀκόντιον ὁππότε σὴ παῖς / ὤμοσεν, οὐκ ἄλλον, νυμφίον ἐξέμεναι. / ὦ Κήυξ, ἀλλ' ἤν με θέλῃς συμφράδμονα θέσθαι, / ... τελευτήσεις ὅρκια θυγατέρος ["she was at home in Delos when your child (sc. Cydippe) swore that she would have Acontius and no other for bridegroom. But, Ceyx, if you would like to make me your advisor you will fulfil your daughter's oath"], and for his oracular promises in general cf. Hor. *Carm.*1.7.28-29 *certus enim promisit Apollo / ambiguam tellure noua Salamina futuram*.

hoc ... coniugium: i.e. this marriage with Lygdamus, picking up *coniugium* of **74**.

tibi: i.e. Neaera.

Delius: an epithet given to Apollo (cf. *Delia* of his twin sister Diana) from his birth on the island of Delos, cf. **50n.** *Cynthius* above. The adjectival use is attested from the time of Cicero (e.g. *Verr.* 2.1.47), whereas the substantival use occurs first in Ov. where it is restricted to *Met.* (6); only here and at *Lygd.* **6.8** below.

ipse: emphatic, Apollo himself is making this promise in person.

80 felix hoc: *hoc* is a reading introduced by Scaliger from the *Fragmentum Cuiacianum*, for *ac* in A. The pronoun is abl. dependent on *felix* as at Ov.

Met. 6.681 *coniuge felix* (9.333, 10.422, 11.266, 15.482), *Pont.* 4.11.22 *coniugio felix*. For *felix* in the context of a happy marriage cf. also the important intertext Ov. *Met.* 7.698 (Cephalus of his marriage to Procris) *hanc mihi iunxit amor: felix dicebar eramque.*

alium ... uirum: picks up *alterius ... uiri* of **58** above, with reference to Lygdamus' rival.

desine uelle: a poetic variant for the prosaic *noli uelle*; cf. above **4** *desinite ... quaerere uelle*; also Ov. *Am.* 1.10.64 *quod nego poscenti, desine uelle, dabo*. For the use of *uolo* to denote sexual desire in elegy, see Pichon 288 and cf. Ov. *Am.* 2.19.1-2 *si tibi non opus est seruata, stulte, puella, / at mihi fac serues, quo magis ipse uelim*.

81 For sleep disappearing at the end of a dream in which a god speaks cf. the end of the Roman embassy's dream of Aesculapius at Ov. *Met.* 15.663-664 *extemplo cum uoce deus, cum uoce deoque / somnus abit* and the end of Amor's dream-appearance to Ovid at *Pont.* 3.3.93-94 *dixit, et aut ille est tenues dilapsus in auras, / coeperunt sensus aut uigilare mei.*

dixit, et: a common formula at the line opening to mark the end of a speech, mainly in the higher genres, Virg. *Aen.* (13), Ov. *Met.* (12), Stat. *Theb.* (7), but also Prop. (4), Ov. *Her.* (1), *Ars* (3), *Rem.* (1), *Fast.* (7), *Pont.* (1); Mart. (1). It occurs only here in the *Corp. Tib.* The closest parallel here is *dixit, et* at the end of Amor's speech in a dream to Ovid at *Pont.* 3.3.93 quoted above.

ignauus ... somnus: probably influenced by Ovid's description of the cave of Sleep at *Met.* 11.593 *mons cauus, ignaui domus et penetralia Somni*. The epithet is used only twice in *Corp. Tib.,* here and **3.38**.

defluxit corpore: the image of sleep 'flowing out' of the body is a variant on the common (7) Ovidian phrase *somnus abit*. For *defluere* in the sense of *euanescere* see **1.18n.** above on *nullus defluat inde color*.

82 For the first part of the line cf. Tib. 2.4.7 *o ego ne possim tales sentire dolores*, and for the second, Hor. *Serm.* 1.2.68-69 *huic si mutonis uerbis mala tanta uidenti / diceret haec animus.*

a ego: hiatus after monosyllabic interjections is relatively common in elegy, see Platnauer 57 and cf. Tib. 1.3.2 *o utinam* (Prop. 1.3.39, 8A.9, 16.27; Ov. *Am.* 2.9.7, 11.5, 15.9, 3.6.73); Tib. 2.3.5 *o ego*; Prop. 2.33B.31 *o Eurytion*, 4.9.2 *o Erythea*; Ov. *Am.* 2.9.2 *o in corde*; 3.1.16 *o argumenti.*

For the interjection *a* see **61-62n.** above. The phrase *a ego* occurs in elegy only here and at **[Tib.] 3 17.3** (*Sulpicia*).

tanta ... mala: cf. *tantis ... malis* Cat. 65.4 (of his brother's death); Ov. *Trist.* 1.1.48, 3.13.24, 4.1.88 (of the evils of exile), 4.4.38 *tanti ... mali* (of exile itself).

uidere: in the sense of 'see to one's cost', 'face', 'suffer', cf. Ter. *Ad.* 867 *duxi uxorem; quam ibi miseriam uidi*; Hor. *Serm.* 1.2.68 (quoted above); Virg. *Georg.* 2.68 *casus abies uisura marinos*; *Ciris* 247-248 *... indigna laborum / milia uisuram*, 455 *sit satis hoc, tantum solam uidisse malorum*.

83 nec ... credidierim: potential subjunctive with present reference: 'I could not believe'. For its use with acc. + inf., cf. Prop. 1.1.23-24 *tunc ego credidierim uobis et sidera et umbras / posse ... ducere*.

tibi: probably a possessive dative, with *esse* understood from *inesse* in **84**, rather than dependent on *credidierim* like *uobis* in Prop. 1.1.23 (quoted above).

uotis contraria uota: i.e. Neaera's wishes are the opposite of those of Lygdamus, cf. **59** above *diuersasque tuis agitat mens inpia curas*. Like *curas* there, so *uota* here can have specifically erotic connotations, in this case expressing 'desire': see Pichon 300. For the idea cf. Prop. 1.5.9 *quod si forte tuis non est contraria* (sc. *puella*) *uotis*. The phrase *uota contraria* occurs in a different context at Lucan 9.115 *uotaque sollicitis faciens contraria uotis*. For the use of *contrarius* with polyptoton as a feature of epic language, see Wills (1996) 201-202 and cf. Virg. *Aen.* 1.239 *fatis contraria fata rependens*, 4.628-629 *litora litoribus contraria ... / ... arma armis*, 7.293-294 *fatis contraria nostris / fata*; Ov. *Met.* 14.301 *uerba ... contraria uerbis*; Manil. 4.814 *regnis contraria regna*. Our author here offers the only elegiac example.

84 crimen: for the use of this legal term in elegy in contexts of adultery and unfaithfulness, see Pichon 116 and cf. Tib. 1.6.41; Prop. 1.11.30, 2.30.24; Ov. *Am.* 2.5.6, 7.8, 17, *Her.* 17.218 (quoted below); **[Tib.] 3.20.3** etc.

pectore inesse: for *inesse* + abl. without *in* cf. Lucr. 1.590 *maculas generalis corpore inesse*, 3.634-635 *toto sentimus corpore inesse / uitalem sensum*; Prop. 4.9.72 *... uelis libro dexter inesse meo*; Ov. *Am.* 1.14.32 *capiti ... inesse suo*, 3.3.34 *plus animi debet inesse uiris*, 13.8 *numen inesse loco*, and with *crimen* as subject, *Her.* 17.217-218 *ipse mihi* *quotiens iratus 'adultera' dices / oblitus nostro crimen inesse tuum*. The verb *inesse* is common in Ov. (43), but occurs only once each in Tib. (1.6.34) and Prop. (4.9.72) and twice in [**Tib.**] **3** (here and **6.49**).

85-94 A long period of five distichs in which Lygdamus develops the theme that Neaera would be incapable of the hard-heartedness and treachery of which she is accused. He does this initially (**85-91**) by his deployment in negative form of the topos of 'insensitivity'. In this topos the harshness of an individual is ascribed to their descent from wild animals or to their origin in wild regions. So here it is denied that Neaera was born of the wild ocean (**85**), the Chimaera (**86**), Cerberus (**87-88**), Scylla (**89**), a lioness (**90**), or the barbarian lands of Scythia and the Syrtis (**91**). This denial is then supported in the final three lines (**92-94**) by a reference to the cultured and civilised house in which she was born and to the amiable nature of both her parents.

The topos of 'insensitivity' goes back to Homer *Il.* 16.33-35, where Patroclus finds fault with Achilles for not listening to the pleas of the Greeks and claims he was not the son of Peleus and Thetis but of the grey sea and steep cliffs. Later in Eur. *Bacch.* 988-990 the chorus discuss the ancestry of Pentheus in similar terms: "He was not born of woman's blood, but is the offspring of some lioness or of Libyan Gorgons". In Theocr. *Id.* 3.15-16 the topos is applied to the upbringing of Eros, who was brought up in the wild woods and suckled by a lioness, an image extended to an unresponsive boy-lover in [Theocr.] *Id.* 23.19-20 "reared by a lioness, stony-hearted, unworthy of love". The theme appears first in Latin in Cat. 60, where it is applied to a fickle friend or, more likely, to an unresponsive lover: 1-3 *num te leaena montibus Libystinis / aut Scylla latrans infima inguinum parte / tam mente dura procreauit ac taetra*? and in Cat. 64, a poem very much in our author's mind in this elegy, where it is applied by Ariadane to Theseus: 154-157 *quaenam te genuit sola sub rupe leaena, quod mare conceptum spumantibus expulit undis, / quae Syrtis, quae Scylla rapax, quae uasta Charybdis, / talia qui reddis pro dulci praemia uita*? Virgil adopts the Theocritean example on the birth of Eros at *Ecl.* 8.43-45 *nunc scio quid sit Amor: duris in cotibus illum / aut Tmaros aut Rhodope aut extremi Garamantes / nec generis nostri puerum nec sanguinis edunt*, and is inspired by the Homeric Patroclus' example (*Il.* 16.33-35) in the words of Dido to Aeneas at *Aen.* 4.365-367 *nec tibi diua parens generis nec Dardanus auctor, / perfide, sed duris genuit te cautibus horrens / Caucasus Hyrcanaeque admorunt ubera tigres*. The topos becomes particularly frequent in Ovid: *Her.* 7.37-39 (Dido to Aeneas) *te lapis et montes innataque rupibus altis / robora, te saeuae progenuere ferae, / aut mare, quale uides agitari nunc quoque uentis*; 10.131-132 (Ariadne to Theseus) *nec pater est Aegeus, nec tu Pittheidos Aethrae / filius*; *auctores saxa fretumque tui*; *Met.* 7.32-33 (Medea) *hoc ego si patiar, tum me de tigride natam / tum ferrum et scopulos gestare in corde fatebor*; 8.120-125 (Scylla to Minos) *nec genetrix Europa tibi est, sed inhospita Syrtis, / Armeniae tigres Austroque agitata Charybdis. / nec Ioue tu natus, nec mater imagine tauri / ducta tua est ... /... / qui te progenuit, taurus fuit*; 9.613-615 (Byblis of her brother) *neque enim est de tigride natus / nec rigidas silices solidumue in pectore ferrum / aut adamanta gerit nec lac bibit ille leaenae*; *Trist.* 1.8.37-44 *non ego te genitum placida reor urbe Quirini /... /sed scopulis Ponti quos haec habet ora sinistri / inque feris Scythiae Sarmatiaeque iugis; / ... / ... / quaeque tibi quondam tenero ducenda palato / plena dedit nutrix ubera, tigris erat*; 3.11.3-4 *natus es e scopulis et pastus lacte ferina / et dicam silices pectus habere tuum*. After Ovid the topos can be seen applied to Hercules in Sen. *Herc. Oet.* 143-146 *quae cautes Scythiae, quis genuit lapis*? *num Titana ferum te Rhodope tulit, / te praeruptus Athos, te fera Caspia / quae uirgata tibi praebuit ubera*? and to Hannibal at Sil. 1.638-639 *et, quem insana freta aut coetus genuere ferarum, / uidimus Hannibalem*. Our author is perhaps most influenced by Cat. 64, from which he takes the vast ocean (**85**), Scylla (**89**), the lioness (**90**) and the Syrtes (**91**). The mention of Scythia in this context had occurred earlier in Ov. *Trist.* 1.8.40. Two new mythological monsters are added here: Chimaera (**86**) and Cerberus (**87-88**), which are unprecedented elsewhere in this context. It may be significant that the three mythical creatures Chimaera, Cerberus and Scylla mentioned here are the same as the three mentioned by Plato in his examples of fictive composite beasts at *Rep.* 9.588C. Cf. Lucr. 5.890-924 who denies the existence of Centaurs, Scyllas and Chimaeras. For the negative form of the topos here we may compare Tib. 1.1.64 *nec in tenero stat tibi corde silex*; Ov. *Met.* 9.613-615 (quoted above).

85 For the image of the sea giving birth to monstrous beings see Hom. *Il.* 16.34 (Achilles), Cat. 64.156 (Theseus), Ov. *Her.* 7.39 (Aeneas) and Sil. 1.638-639 (Hannibal), all quoted above.

uasti ... ponti: the first use of the adjective *uastus* applied to the sea occurs at Cat. 63.48 *maria uasta*; cf. also Tib. 1.7.19 *maris uastum ... aequor*. For the specific combination with *pontus*, cf. *uastique ... ponti* at Virg. *Georg.* 4.430; Val. Fl. 1.37; Sil. 2.572 and *uasto ... ponto* at Virg. *Aen.* 3.605; Manil. 1.166; Sen. *Med*ea 318-319; Sil. 4.80, 10.321. For *pontus* (also at **7.20, 75, 147, 173**) as a poetic loan-word from Greek, restricted in Horace to *Carm.*, see Mayer (2012) on Hor. *Carm.* 1.12.31.

genuerunt: in the same context at Sil. 1.638 quoted above.

aequora ponti: 'the plains of the sea' a Lucretian phrase; as a hexameter ending at Lucr. 1.8, 2.772, 6.440; Virg. *Georg.* 1.469; Ov. *Met.* 2.872; Manil. 4.649 and as *ponti / aequora* at Lucr. 4.410-411, 5.1000-1001; Manil. 4.678-679. On *Georg.* 1.469 Servius comments *et 'aequora ponti' non sine causa addidit 'ponti' quia sunt et campi aequora*.

86 The inspiration for this line is again Lucretian, cf. Lucr. 2.705 *tum flammam taetro spirantis ore Chimaeras* in a list of mythical monsters whose existence is denied, a point repeated at Lucr. 5.903-906 (quoted below).

flammam uoluens: the expression often refers to the rolling of flames (molten rock, smoke) from an active volcano, cf. Lucr. 6.691 (of Etna) *crassa uoluit caligine fumum*; Virg. *Georg.* 1.472-473 *uidimus ... Aetnam / flammarumque globos liquefactaque uoluere saxa*; *Aetna* 2 (of Etna) *et quae tam fortes uoluant incendia causae*; Stat. *Silu.* 4.4.80 (Vesuvius) *aemula Trinacriis uoluens incendia flammis*.

ore ... fero: cf. Cic. *Arat.* 326 *ore fero Capricornus*; Sil. 4.539, 10.317-318. For the adj. *ferus* cf. **74** above where it describes Lygdamus' marriage.

Chimaera: according to Homer *Il.* 6.179-182 the mythical monster had a lion in front, a snake behind and a she-goat (Gk. χίμαιρα) in the middle. Hesiod (*Theog.* 319f.) states that it was the product of a union between the giant Typhon (whose eyes blazed with fire) and the serpent Echidna. It was killed by Bellerophon, mounted on the winged horse Pegasus. Flame breathing was one of the monster's characteristic features, cf. Pind *Ol.* 13.90 Χίμαιραν πῦρ πνέοισαν ["Chimaera breathing fire"]; Lucr. 2.705 (quoted above), 5.904-906 *qui fieri potuit, triplici cum corpore ut una / prima leo, postrema draco, media ipsa Chimaera / ore foras acrem flaret de corpore flammam?*; Hor. *Carm.* 2.17.13 *Chimaerae spiritus igneae*, 4.2.15-16 *tremendae / flamma Chimaerae*; Virg. *Aen.* 6.288 *flammis ... armata Chimaera*; Ov. *Met.* 9.647-648 *Chimaera ... mediis in partibus ignem, / pectus et ora leae, caudam serpentis habebat*, *Trist.* 4.7.13-14 *esse Chimaeram / a truce quae flammis separet angue leam*. It may be significant that the image of the Chimaera could be applied to *hetaerae*, see N-H on Hor. *Carm.* 1.27.23-24 *uix inligatum te triformi / Pegasus expediet Chimaera*.

87 canis: Cerberus, guard dog of Hades, first mentioned by Hom. *Il.* 8.368 and Hes. *Theog.* 311-312, 771-773. Like Chimaera, Cerberus was the product of a union between Typhon and Echidna (Hes. *Theog.* 311; Hyg. *Fab.* 151.1). Also like the Chimaera it appears in the context of insensitivity ony here.

anguina ... caterua: the adj. *anguina* is Postgate's conjecture for *anguinea* of some of the MSS. Both forms are attested in Latin, but *anguineus* is much rarer (only Ov. *Trist.* 4.7.12; Colum. *Rust.* 2.9.10, 7.10.5; *Il. Lat.* 891). In favour of Postgate's *anguina* is its occurrence, as here in combination with *redimitus*, at Cat. 64.193-194, *Eumenides, quibus anguino redimita capillo / frons*, a poem never far from Lygdamus' thoughts in this elegy. The form *anguinea* in some MSS could have arisen from the false reading *consanguinea* of A. The use of *caterua* for a large group of animals or flock of birds is rare and poetic, e.g. Lucr. 6.1092 *pecudumque cateruis*; Virg. *Aen.* 11.456-457 *cateruae / ... auium* and see *ThLL* 3.609.46-57.

redimitus terga caterua: N-A ad loc.points to the expressive repetition of the *littera canina* (i.e. the letter 'r') with reference to Cerberus as well as the near homoeoteleuton of *terga caterua* to reinforce the effect. For *redimitus* in this context, cf. Cat. 64.193 quoted above. For the dog's back bristling with snakes, cf. Apollod. 2.5.1 κατὰ δὲ τοῦ νώτου παντοίων εἶχεν ὄφεων κεφαλάς ["along his back he had the heads of all kinds of snakes"]. There is no real parallel for this elsewhere in Latin, apart from perhaps the vaguer *angue uillosi canis* at Enn. *Trag.* 415 Jocelyn, while the other Greek parallels given by N-A ad loc. (Eur. *Heracl.* 611; Plato *Rep.* 9.588c) do not in fact mention snakes on the back. Usually the snakes are on the dog's head (mouth, hair or neck), e.g. Hor. *Carm.* 3.11.17-18 *furiale centum / muniant angues caput eius*; Tib. 1.3.71 *tum niger in porta serpentum Cerberus ore / stridet*; Ov. *Her.* 9.94 *Cerberus inplicitis angue minante comis*; Culex 220-221 *Cerberus ... / anguibus hinc atque hinc horrent cui colla reflexis*; Lucan 6.664-665 *... uillosaque colla colubris / Cerberus excutiens*.

88 tres ... linguae tergeminumque caput: Cerberus is often referred to as *tergeminus canis* (Prop. 4.7.52; Ov. *Ars* 3.322, *Trist.* 4.7.16) or *triformis ... canis* Sen. *Herc. Oet.* 1202, where the reference is probably to his three heads. For more specific reference to three heads (mouths, tongues, barks) cf. Cic. *Tusc.* 1.10 *triceps* (Sen. *Oed.* 581); Hor. *Carm.* 2.19.31-32 *trilingui / ore* (3.11.20); Prop. 3.5.43 *tribus ... faucibus*, 3.18.23 *tria ... colla* (Ov. *Met.* 10. 66-67); Virg. *Georg.* 4.483 *tria ... ora* (Ov. *Am.* 3.12.

26, *Met.* 4.450), *Aen.* 6.417 *latratu ... trifauci*; Ov. *Her.* 9.38 *terna... ora* (Stat. *Silu.* 2.1.984), *Met.* 4.451 *tres latratus*, 7.413 *ternis latratibus*, 10.22 *terna ... guttura*; Sen. *Ag.* 14 *trigemina colla*, Herc. F. 785 *terna ...capita*, 796 *ora ... terna*; Sil. 2.551 *forma ... trifauci*, 13.574 *non uno ... ore*; Stat. *Theb.* 7.783 *tergeminos ... hiatus*; see further *RE* 11.271ff.

89 Scylla: a sea monster living in a cave on the coast of Sicily, opposite the lair of another sea monster, Charybdis, who lived on the other side of the straits of Messina off Southern Italy. The two are often mentioned together in Roman poetry, as at *Laud. Mess.* **7.**70-75 below (so also Cat. 64.156; Hor. *AP* 145; Prop. 2.26B.53, 3.12.28; Virg. *Aen.* 3.420-421, 684, 7.302; Ov. *Am.* 2.11.18, *Met.* 7.62-65, 13.730-731, 14.75, *Ibis* 385; Sen. *Medea* 408; Sil. 14.474; Stat. *Silu.* 3.2.85-86). In Homer Odysseus is advised by Circe (*Od.* 12.107-110) to sail between the two, keeping closer to Scylla, who would only take six of his crew (cf. *Od.* 12.245-246), than to Charybdis, who would destroy his whole boat and crew. According to her description at Hom. *Od.* 12.85-100 Scylla has twelve legs, six long necks, each with a beak containing three rows of teeth, capable of snatching sailors from their ships. Roman writers were influenced by later Hellenistic authors who pictured her as a woman from the waist up but girt with a pack of six fierce hounds below, cf. Hyg. *Fab. pr.* 39.2 *Scyllae, quae superiorem partem feminae, inferiorem canis habuit*. The connection between her name Σκύλλη and the Greek for 'dog' or ' puppy' σκύλαξ is already made by Homer at *Od.* 12.85-86, where her voice was only as loud as that of a new-born puppy. In the Roman tradition her howling dogs become more fierce and threatening: Cat. 60.2 *Scylla latrans infima inguinum parte*; Lucr. 5.892-893 *aut rabidis canibus succinctas semimarinis / corporibus Scyllas*; Virg. *Ecl.* 6.74-75 *quid loquar aut Scyllam ... / candida succinctam latrantibus inguina monstris*; Ov. *Her.* 12.123 *aut nos Scylla rapax canibus mersisset edendos*, *Met.* 7.64-65 *... cinctaque saeuis / Scylla rapax canibus Siculo latrare profundo*, 14.59-60 *Scylla uenit mediaque tenus descenderat aluo, / cum sua foedari latrantibus inguina monstris*, *Pont.* 4.10.25 *Scylla feris trunco quod latret ab inguine monstris*; *Culex* 331 *Scylla rapax canibus succincta Molossis*. The detail here serves to connect Scylla with the immediately preceding Cerberus. On Scylla in general see further *RE* III A.1 (1927) 647-659.

uirgineam ... figuram: the phrase is perhaps influenced by Ovid's description of how Scylla had once been a human girl: *Met.* 13.732-734 *illa* (sc. *Scylla) ... / uirginis ora gerens et, si non omnia uates / ficta reliquerunt, aliquo quoque tempore uirgo*. If taken literally *uirgo* helps Lygdamus' argument that Neaera could not have been born from her.

Elsewhere Scylla is referred to as *uirgo* at Ov. *Trist.* 4.7.13; Sen. *Medea* 350; Stat. *Silu.* 3.2.86. The noun *figura* refers to the outward shape or form, like *forma* in Ov. *Met.* 3.607 *uirginea puerum ducit per litora forma*. The accusative is one of respect, dependent on *succincta*.

canibus succincta: the phrase begins with Lucretius (5.892 quoted above) and, as the examples quoted above show, becomes traditional in descriptions of Scylla (cf. Virg. *Ecl.* 6.75; Ov. *Met.* 7.64-65, 13.732; Sen. *Medea* 351; *Culex* 331).

90 Mention of a lioness as progenitor in the 'insensitivity' topos goes back in Greek as far as Eur. *Bacch.* 990, *Medea* 1342 (linked with Scylla at 1343); Theocr. *Id.* 3.15-16; [Theocr.] *Id.* 23.19 (translated above in **85-94n.**). In Latin the combination of a lioness with Scylla in this context occurs first at Cat. 60.1-3 *num te leaena montibus Libystinis / aut Scylla latrans infima inguinum parte / tam mente dura procreauit ac taetra*.

conceptam: cf. Cat. 64.154-155 (Ariadne to Theseus) *quaenam te genuit sola sub rupe leaena, / quod mare conceptum spumantibus expuit undis*?

saeua leaena: for the combination, cf. Virg. *Georg.* 3.245-246 *leaena / saeuior*; Ov. *Met.* 4.102 *lea saeua*; Val. Fl. 6.148 *saeuae ... leaenae*; *Il. Lat.* 396 *saeua leaena*. The form *leaena* (also at **6.15**) based on the Greek λέαινα occurs in poetry from Cat. 60.1 onwards alongside the slightly less frequent *lea* (attested from Lucr. 5.1318). Cat., Virg., Hor. and **[Tib.] 3** at Lygd. here and **6.15** use only *leaena*, whereas Ov. uses both forms [*leaena* (7), *lea* (8)]; see further *ThLL* 7(2).1077.31-52.

tulit: in the sense of *genuit* 'gave birth to', cf. Virg. *Aen.* 12.845-847 *Dirae, / quas et Tartaream Nox intempesta Megaeram / uno eodemque tulit partu*; Sen. *Herc. Oet.* 144 *num Titana ferum te Rhodope tulit* and cf. *OLD fero* 10.

91 Two real geographical places figure finally in the insensitivity topos, barbarous Scythia on the edge of the known world beyond the Pontus Euxinus, and the Syrtes, two sandbanks off the North African coast, which were a proverbial danger to shipping.

barbara ... Scythiae tellus: first used in this context by Ovid, who says that a friend who had turned away from him in exile cannot have been born in civilised Rome, but rather in the wild mountains of Scythia (in contrast to the flat coastal area to which Ovid had been exiled) *Trist.* 1.8.39-40 *scopulis, Ponti quos haec habet ora sinistri / inque feris*

270   Commentary

Scythiae Sarmatiaeque iugis. This is later taken up by Seneca at *Herc. Oet.*
143 (with reference to Hercules) *quae cautes Scythiae, quis genuit lapis*?
The phrase *barbara tellus* is applied to Scythia first by Ovid: *Met.* 7.53 (of
Medea's homeland) and *Trist.* 3.11.7 and 5.2.31 (of his own place of exile
in Tomis) and subsequently at Sen. *Phaed.* 166; [Sen.] *Oct.* 797; Lucan
8.392-393 and Stat. *Silu.* 5.2.46.

nec: for the postponement of this particle as a neoteric feature, beginning
with Catullus, in imitation of Greek Alexandrian practice, see Platnauer
94-95, Norden (1927) on Virg. *Aen.* 6 p. 404 and cf. **6.55**. Cf. **1.9n.** for
postponed *sed.*

horrenda: 'dread', literally 'making the hair stand on end'. Used first by
Cic. *Tusc.* 2.2.12 *nil habet mors quod sit horrendum*, but then mainly
poetic and epic in tone [so Virg. *Georg.* (1), *Aen.* (24); Ov. *Met.* (9), *Fast.*
(2), *Ibis* (1)]; in elegy, apart from here, only in the mock-epic opening of
Tib. 1.10.1 *quis fuit horrendos primus qui protulit enses*? For its use with
reference to the dangers of the sea cf. Virg. *Aen.* 3.559 *hos Helenus
scopulos, haec saxa horrenda canebat*; Manil. 5.192 *horrendumque fretis
in bella lacessere pontum*; Val. Fl. 1.580 *stat rupes horrenda fretis*, 4.606-
607 *horrenda rapax ad litora puppem / uentus agat*. The adj. is applied
only here to the Syrtes, whose epithets elsewhere in verse usually refer to
their treacherous and inhospitable nature: *aestuosas* Hor. *Carm.* 1.22.5;
barbaras, 2.6.3 (*Dirae* 53, Lucan 9.440, 10.477); *exercitatas ... Noto* Hor.
Epod. 9.31; *inhospita* Virg. *Aen.* 4.41 (Ov. *Met.* 8.120); *uadosas* Manil.
4.600 (Lucan 5.484-485); *dubiis* Lucan 9.861; *uastae* Sil. 1.408; *infidae*
Sil. 2.63; *naufraga* Sil. 17.634; *saeuas* Val. Fl. 7.86.

Syrtis: mentioned first by Herodotus 2.32.2 (in the singular) the name is
found in both singular and plural in Latin poetry. It refers to two
dangerous areas of sandbanks off the coast of North Africa between
Cyrene and Carthage. Syrtis occurs in the insensitivity topos first in
Catullus, (Ariadne to Theseus) at 64.156 *quae Syrtis, quae Scylla rapax,
quae uasta Charybdis* (sc. *te genuit*)?, a line echoed in Juno's speech at
Virg. *Aen.* 7.302-303 *quid Syrtis aut Scylla mihi, quid uasta Charybdis /
profuit*? The second occurrence is at Ov. *Met.* 8.120-121 (Scylla, daughter
of Nisus, about Minos) *non genetrix Europa tibi est, sed inhospita Syrtis, /
Armeniae tigres austroque agitata Charybdis*. A variation on the theme, in
which surprise is expressed that Septimius Severus was in fact born in
such a barbarous area and not in Rome occurs at Stat. *Silu.* 4.5.29-30 *tene
in remotis Syrtibus auia / Leptis creauit*?

92-94 After seven lines of examples of insensitivity which are inappropriate in Neaera's case (**85-91**) the particle *sed* marks a change of direction to a three-line description of her civilised home and mild and amiable parents (**92-94**).

92 culta: 'refined', 'civilised', in opposition to *barbara* **91**; cf. Tib. 1.9.74 *senis amplexus culta puella fugit*. The term is applied by Ovid to Tibullus, with reference to his sophisticated style: *culte Tibulle* Ov. *Am*. 1.5.28, 3.9.66 and this is the meaning of *cultus* at **1.17** (of Lygdamus' book of poetry) and **8.1** (of Sulpicia and/or the *Sulpicia Cycle* group of poems about her).

duris: 'unfeeling', 'insensitive', cf. **76** above and see **2.3n**. For its use in the insensitivity topos, cf. Cat. 60.1-3 *num te leaena .../ aut Scylla ... / tam mente dura procreauit*?

habitanda: often found in legal contexts of 'living in' a house, cf. Iust. *Dig*. 7.8.10.2 *illi domus usus fructus habitandi causa*, 19.2.60 *nisi si paratus fuisset locator commodam domum ei ad habitandum dare*.

domus: refers both to the physical building (*OLD domus* 1), as shown by *habitanda*, and also to the 'family', 'inhabitants' of the house (*OLD domus* 6), as shown by *culta*.

93 longe ante alias omnes mitissima: a pleonasm characteristic of our author's style in the *Lygd.* poems – see **2.15n., 4.47-48n., 5.27n.** The comparative or superlative use of *ante* is initially colloquial in tone, cf. Plaut. *Asin*. 858 *ante omnes minimi mortalem preti*; *Cas*. 8 *placere ante alias ueteres fabulas*; *Trin*. 824 *Neptune, tibi ante alios deos gratias ago ... summas*; Balb. ap. Cic. *Att*. 8.15a.2 *quem ante me diligo*. Its use with *alios / -as* then enters more elevated poetry with Virg. *Ecl*. 3.78 *Phyllida amo ante alias*, cf. *Aen*. 3.321 *o felix una ante alias ... uirgo*. A possibly earlier poetic use in Ennius (*Ann*. 625 V) *multum ante alias infelix littera theta* is considered spurious by Skutsch; see *Spur*. 10 Sk.. It is found later at **11.5**, and **19.16**. The use of *longe* reinforcing comparatives and superlatives (in place of earlier *multo*) occurs first in Cat. 64.215 *longe iucundior*, cf. Ov. *Met*. 12.586 *o mihi de fratris longe gratissime natis*. For the combination of *longe* with *ante alios*, cf. Liv. 1.15.8 *longe ante alios acceptissimus*; Ciris 473 *ante alias longe gratissima Delos*. The use of *ante omnes* in this context goes back to Plaut. *Asin*. 858 quoted above. The combination of *ante alios* + *omnes* occurs before here at Virg. *Aen*. 1.347

Pygmalion, scelere ante alios immanior omnis, and with superlative at *Aen.* 4.141 *ipse ante alios pulcherrimus omnis*.

longe: frequent in Lucretius and epic, the adverb is relatively rare in elegy, except in Ovid (29): Tib. only once, in a mock-epic context, 1.5.2 *nunc longe gloria fortis abest*; Prop. (4); **[Tib.] 3** here ony.

mitissima mater: the same hexameter ending is found at Ov. *Met.* 6.118 (of Ceres) *flaua comas frugum mitissima mater*. The epithet is frequently applied to gods, e.g. to Ceres above and to Themis at *Met.* 1.380, as well as to Augustus and other members of the imperial family in Ovid's exile poetry, examples in Ingleheart [(2010) 80] on *Trist.* 2.27, thus adding to its encomiastic force. With its meaning 'mild', 'gentle', the adjective picks up and contrasts with *saeua* in **90** and *inmitem* at **74**. A similar juxtaposition is found at Sen. *Dial.* 5.10.4 *hic intra domum saeuus est, foris mitis*. The theme of praise for the mistress's mother had occurred earlier at **2.13** (see above ad loc.), and goes back originally in elegy to Tibullus 1.6.57-58, 63-66. In both cases it may reflect a thwarted wish for formal *coniugium* with the mistress, which in Tibullus' case did not exist and in the Lygdamus poems was threatened by his wife's unfaithfulness.

94 While praise of the mistress's mother has a precedent in Tibullus, praise of the father is unparalleled in elegy and emphasises Lygdamus' view of his relationship with Neaera as a formal marriage.

is: 'of such a kind', cf. *OLD is* 10 and cf. Cic. *Att.* 7.8.1 *ego is in illum sum quem tu me esse uis*. The pronoun is rare in elegy, occurring in **Tib. 3** only here, **6.12** (*eum*) and **13.8** (*id*): see further Platnauer 116-117, Axelson (1945) 70-71, Austin (1964) on Virg. *Aen.* 2.17, Ingleheart (2010) 140 on Ov. *Trist.* 2.123-124.

quo non alter amabilior: the use of *alter* rather than *alius* is the rule in this kind of negative comparative clause, cf. Hor. *Serm.* 1.5.42 *neque quis me sit deuinctior alter*; Virg. *Aen.* 6.164 *quo non praestantior alter*; Ov. *Trist.* 1.9a.25 *neque enim moderatio alter*.

amabilior: 'more loveable', also as a pentameter ending at Cat. 65.10 *uita frater amabilior*. The adj. occurs frequently in Cicero's letters, but is rare in verse: Plaut. (5), Lucr. (1), Cat. (1), Hor. (8): *Carm.* (5), *Epist.* (3), Ov. (4, *Ars*), **[Tib.] 3** (1), Sil. (1), and may have had a colloquial ring.

95-96 The final couplet takes up the apotropaic opening verses and provides the poem with a clear ring structure.

deus: indeterminate, like *di* in **1** above, *di meliora ferant*.

in melius ... uertat: derived from common apotropaic phrases of the type *di melius* and *di meliora* discussed in **1n**. above. A close parallel is provided by Prop. 1.17.9 *in melius saeuas conuerte querelas*, cf. also Sen. *Phaed*. 408 *conuerte tristes omnium in melius minas*.

crudelia somnia: cf. Ov. *Her*. 10.111 (Ariadne to Theseus) *crudeles somni, quid me tenuistis inertem*?

96: The prayer that the winds should carry away his dream is related to a common proverbial usage in which the winds are asked to bear away certain verbal utterances such as prayers, oaths, threats and entreaties that are to be ignored, see Otto 364-365 s.v. *uentus* 2. It is common in Greek literature (e.g. Hom. *Od*. 8.408-409; Theogn. 1168; Eur. *Trachin*. 419, 454, *Suppl*. 1155; Theocr. *Id*. 22.167), where it occurs as early as Hom. *Od*. 8.408-409 ἔπος δ' εἴ πέρ τι βέβακται / δεινόν, ἄφαρ τὸ φέροιεν ἀναρπάξασαι ἄελλαι ["and if any harsh word has been spoken, may the storm winds instantly snatch it and bear it away"]. The first occurrence in Latin is Cat. 30.9-10 *ac tua dicta Omnia factaque / uentos irrita ferre ... sinis*, who has further examples with broken promises at 64.59 *irrita uentosae linquens promissa procellae*, 142 *quae cuncta aerii discerpunt irrita uenti*, 65.17-18, and 70. 2-3. After Cat. it occurs at Hor. *Carm*. 1.26.1-3 (on which see N-H ad loc.), *Epod*. 11.16; Virg. *Aen*. 9.312-313 with Hardie ad loc., 10.652, 11.795; Tib. 1.4.21-22 *Veneris periuria uenti / irrita per terras et freta summa ferunt*, 5.35-36; Prop. 1.16.34, 2.28A, 4.7.21-22. For its frequent occurrences in Ovid, see McKeown II 84 on *Am*. 1.4.11-12 ... *nec Euris / da mea nec tepidis uerba ferenda Notis*. Two Ovidian passages in particular may have influenced our author here, namely *Am*. 2.8.19-20 *tu, dea, tu iubeas animi periuria puri / Carpathium tepidos per mare ferre Notos* and *Ars* 1.633-634 *Iuppiter ... periuria ridet amantum / et iubet Aeolios irrita ferre Notos*, the second of which is taken up again at **6.49-50** ... *periuria ridet amantum / Iuppiter et uentos irrita ferre iubet*.

Our author's treatment here differs from all these earlier examples, and from his own usage at **6.27-28, 49-50** in that it is not words that the winds are bidden carry away but dreams. A possible explanation for this could be that Lygdamus is thinking of the words and promises that Apollo uttered in the course of the dream at **43-80**. Of course some of these words had negative connotations, particularly those concerning Neaera's faithlessness (**57-60**) and these Lygdamus would rightly wish blown away, but this does not apply to the more reassuring tone of **79-80**. Perhaps Lygdamus is presented here as suggesting his doubts about the fulfilment of Apollo's promise at **79-80**.

tepidos ... Notos: an Ovidian collocation to describe the warm south wind: *Am.* 1.4.12 (quoted above), 1.7.56 *summaque cum tepido stringitur unda Noto*, 2.8.20 (quoted above, in the same position in the pentameter), *Her.* 11.76 *ut quatitur tepido fraxina uirga Noto*. Catullus was the first to apply the adj. *tepidus* to the winds at 64.282 *tepidi ... Fauoni*.

inrita ferre: the phrase occurs first in this context at Cat. 30.10 and then at Ov. *Ars* 1.634; in the *Lygd.* poems here and **6.50** below (all quoted above). *inrita* here is in fact a correction in some later MSS for *impia* of A. Cartault prefers *impia* and sees *inrita* as a *lectio facilior*. In view of the frequency of *inrita* in this context, however, it is likely to be the correct reading here; in addition to the passages quoted above, cf. Cat. 64.142 *discerpunt inrita*; Tib. 1.4.22 *inrita ... ferunt* (Ov. *Am.* 2.16.46); Ov. *Rem.* 286 *inrita ... tulere*, *Trist.* 1.8.35 *abierunt inrita*.

Poem 5

While Lygdamus lies ill at home in Rome, his friends are relaxing at a spa in Etruria. The poem is carefully constructed of two addresses to his absent friends (**1-5**, and **27-34**) enclosing a central address to the gods of the underworld, asking them to spare him (**5-26**). There are clear similarities with Tib. 1.3 where the author is sick in Corcyra, abandoned by his patron and military colleagues, who continue on their journey to the East. However, while Tib.'s thoughts in this situation turn to his mistress Delia back in Rome, in this poem there is no mention of Lygdamus' love for Neaera. In this respect the poem is unique in the *Lygd.* group, but in language, style and metre it is clearly consistent with the rest of our author's *Lygdamus* poems (see Tränkle 137). The elegy perhaps represents a parallel with Tib. 1.4, a lecture on pederastic love by Priapus, concluding with a mention of Tib.'s love for the boy Marathus and the only one of Tib.'s first six poems which does not mention Delia.

The structure of the poem is as follows:

1-5 An opening address to his friends, relaxing at an Etruscan spa, informs them of his closeness to death.

6-26 The body of the poem consists of an address to the gods of the underworld. First he asks Persephone to spare him (*parce* **6**) on the grounds that he has committed no sacrilege deserving the penalty of death (**7-14**) and that he is too young to die (**15-20**). He then repeats this appeal (*parcite* **21**) to unnamed gods of the underworld (**21-26**), asking them that his death should be delayed until old age.

27-34 A concluding address to his friends contrasts his serious illness (**27-28**) with their carefree holiday (**29-30**). He bids them live happily and remember him, whether he lives or dies (**31-32**), and asks them to make sacrifice to the gods of the underworld for his recovery. The final couplet (**33-34**) thus brings together the two sets of addressees, his friends and the gods of the underworld.

While the main inspiration for the poem is clearly Tib. 1.3, another important influence is Martial, who in 4.57 contrasts his own holiday in Baiae with that of Faustinus in Tibur and in 6.43 contrasts holidays in Baiae and Nomentum. Also Prop. 1.11, where Cynthia is on holiday in Baiae and Propertius remains at home, may have played its part. The theme of the poet's illness links the poem with *Sulpicia Cycle* **10** and *Sulpicia* **17** on the illness of Sulpicia. On the theme of illness in elegy see Müller (1952) 58-80, Holzenthal (1967).

1-5 Vos ... mihi: for this contrast see above **3.31n.**

1 tenet: the model is clearly Tib. 1.3.3 *me tenet ignotis aegrum Phaeacia terris*. Here, however, it is the healthy friends who are away from home while the poet suffers at Rome. For this use of *teneo* with locations, cf. also Tib. 2.3.1 *rura meam, Cornute, tenent uillaeque puellam*; Ov. *Am.* 2.11.30 *felix ... quem sua terra tenet*, 16.1 *me Sulmo tenet* with McKeown II 331, *Ars* 2.419-420 *... dea ... / ... quam tenet altus Eryx, Her.* 17.226 *tellus me tenet ista, Trist.* 3.4b.1-2 *tellus ... Vrsae / me tenet, Pont.* 2.8.11 *nec me tenet ultima tellus*; Mart. 4.57.1 *dum nos blanda tenent lasciui stagna Lucrini*.

Etruscis manat quae fontibus unda: the wording is very close to *Culex* 148 *his suberat gelidis manans e fontibus unda*. For an argument in favour of the priority of *Culex* over our author see **1.15-16n.** above.

Etruscis ... fontibus: the reference is to thermal spas of Etruria, a region which covered parts of Liguria and Umbria as well as the northern part of Latium as far as the Tiber. The many thermal spas of this area are mentioned by Strabo 5.2.9 πολλὴ δὲ καὶ τῶν θερμῶν ὑδάτων ἀφθονία κατὰ

276   Commentary

τὴν Τυρρηνίαν, ἃ τῷ πλησίον εἶναι τῆς 'Ρώμης οὐχ ἧττον εὐανδρεῖ τῶν ἐν
Βαΐαις, ἃ διωνόμασται πολὺ πάντων μάλιστα ["there is a great abundance
of thermal waters in Etruria, which, because of their proximity to Rome,
are no less frequented than those in Baiae, which were by far the best
known of all"], and praised by Martial 6.42.1-2 *Etrusci nisi thermulis
lauaris, / illotus morieris, Oppiane*. The adj. *Etruscus* occurs first at Cat.
39.11 and is found here only in the *Corp. Tib.* Its equivalent *Tuscus* (first
in Plaut.) is found at **4.6** and below at **29**. Neither form is found in Tib.
Elsewhere in Augustan poetry the two forms *Etruscus* and *Tuscus* are
equally spread (Hor. 7:4; Virg. 10:8; Prop. 4:4; Ov. 6:14).

manat ... fontibus unda: for *manat unda* with the simple ablative
fontibus, cf. Cat. 65.5-6 *Lethaeo gurgite ... / ... manans ... unda*. The use
of the simple ablative in a spatial sense without preposition is mainly
poetic, occurring occasionally in prose from Livy on, see K-S II 1.361 and
cf. Enn. *Trag.* 50 Jocelyn *mari magno* with Jocelyn ad loc.; Virg. *Georg.*
3.203 *spumas aget ore cruentas*. For the line-end *fontibus unda*, cf. Virg.
Georg. 2.243; Ov. *Met.* 3.27 (*fontibus undas*); Manil. 1.855; Lucan 9.383
(*fontibus undae*); Stat. *Silu.* 1.2.6 (*fontibus undam*); *Culex* 148 *his suberat
gelidis manans a fontibus unda*.

1-2 unda, / unda ... adeunda: for the anadiplosis (repetition of the last
member of a phrase in one line at the beginning of the following phrase in
the next) *unda, / unda*, cf. Theocr. *Id.* 1.29-30 κισσός, / κισσός; Lucr.
2.159-160 *unum, / unum*, 5.298-299 *instant. / instant*; Virg. *Ecl.* 6.19-20
Aegle, / Aegle, 10.71-72 *Gallo, / Gallo*, *Aen.* 10.691-692 *uni / uni*; Mart.
11.80.1-2 *Baias, / Baias*, and for epanalepsis (repetition) of this kind with
nouns in Latin poetry and its Greek background see Wills (1996) 124-173;
for its use in elegy see Platnauer 33-35. This repetition, coupled with the
paronomasia *unda ... adeunda*, reflects the movement of the waves, cf.
Acc. *Trag.* 570 *unda sub undis labunda sonit*. In the present example the
paronomasia may be etymologically motivated, cf. Isid. *Etym.* 13.20.3
quasi ab eundo et redeundo unda uocata. For similar repetitions involving
unda, cf. Hor. *Epist.* 2.2.175-176 *heres / heredem alternis uelut unda
superuenit undam*; Ov. *Met.* 11.496 *undarum incursu grauis unda*, 553
unda uelut uictrix sinuataque despicit undas, 15.181 *ut unda impellitur
unda*, and for its equivalent in Greek, cf. Musaeus 314 κύματι κῦμα
κυλίνδετο ["wave rolled upon wave"]; Eur. *Phrixus* fr. 1.7 κύματι δ' ὡς ἔπι
κῦμα κυλ[ίνδεται ["as wave rolls upon wave"].

sub aestiuum ... Canem: the hot thermal springs were not a good place to
visit in the height of summer, but rather in cooler seasons such as early

spring, as here. Martial makes a similar point about Baiae, preferable to cool Tibur in winter, but not in the heat of summer: 4.57.9-10 *Herculeos colles gelida uos uincite bruma, / nunc Tiburtinis cedite frigoribus*. The rising of the dog-star Sirius in late July was thought to double the sun's heat, see Manil. 5.207-208 *exoritur candens latratque Canicula flammas / et rabit igne suo geminatque incendia solis*. Its intense and destructive power is a commonplace of ancient literature; see Hom. *Il.* 22.26-31; Hes. *Op*. 417 with West; Hor. *Serm*. 1.7.25-26, *Carm*. 1.17.17-18, 3.13.9-10; Tib. 1.1.27, 4.6, 42, 7.21; Prop. 2.28.3-4; Virg. *Georg*. 2.353, 4.452, *Aen*. 10.273-275; Ov. *Am*. 2.16.3-4 with McKeown; Manil. 5.207-208 (quoted above); Plin. *Nat*. 18.270. For the phrase *aestiuum ... Canem* cf. Tib. 1.1.27 *Canis aestiuos ortus*, 4.6 *aestiui tempora sicca Canis* and see also Virg. *Georg*. 2.353 *Canis aestifer*; Colum. *Rust*. 2.20.1 *aestiui sideris* (of the dog-star). The adj. connects Sirius with the burning fever *aestus*, possibly malaria, that the author presents Lygdamus as suffering from in **27-28** below. For *sub* + acc. in a temporal sense of 'at the time of' cf. the expressions *sub lucem, sub noctem, sub uesperum* etc. and see K-S II 1.571.

non adeunda: 'not to be visited'. The phrase occurs in the same position in the pentameter first in Tib. 1.6.22 *sacra Bonae maribus non adeunda Deae* and then frequently in Ovid: *Fast*. 4.496, 5.374, 6.412, 450, *Trist*. 1.4.18, 8.38, 3.1.70, 10.76, *Ibis* 478.

3 autem: this is the only occurrence of the particle in the whole of the *Corp. Tib*. Despite its relative frequency in Virgil [*Georg*. (7), *Aen*. (28)], it retains a strong prosaic flavour and is rare elsewhere in verse: Lucr. (0); Cat. (4); Hor. (3): *AP* (1), *Epist*. (2); Prop. (1); Ov. (7): *Am*. (1), *Her*. (1), *Met*. (5). In Ovid, apart from *Met*. 14.489, it is used only in questions, and even in Virgil its range is restricted to use with certain particles and pronouns, see Axelson (1945) 85-86.

sacris ... lymphis: each stream or river was consecrated to its own nymphs, cf. **29** below *Tuscae ... numina lymphae* and Martial's description of Baiae as the home of Nymphs and Nereids at 4.57.7-8 *... sacri fontes et litora grata ... / Nympharum pariter Nereidumque domus*. The term *lympha* was used by the poets mostly in the context of sacred springs and rivers. Although it came originally from *lumpa*, an Italic word for water (see Fordyce on Cat. 64.254), popular etymology derived the word directly from the Greek νύμφη = 'nymph' and this probably determined its spelling, cf. Varro *Ling*. 7.85; Paul. Fest. 107 L.; Prisc. *GL* 2.36.22, 3.407.2 and see *LALE* 355 s.v *lympha*. For Greek νύμφη = 'water' in Antigonus *AP* 9.406.3, Antiphanes *AP* 9.258, and Plut. *Sept. Sap.* 147f. see N-H on Hor. *Carm.* 2.3.12. The term is found in Tib. at 1.7.12 and 2.1.46 and elsewhere in **[Tib.]** 3 at **5.29** and **6.58**, both in *Lygd.*

Baiarum: a renowned spa resort in antiquity, famous both for its beaches and for its nearby coastal lakes (Lucrine and Avernus) and medicinal hot springs. From the late Republic it earned a reputation also as a fashionable centre for love affairs and erotic pleasure, cf. Prop. 1.11 (*passim*) especially 18 ...*in hac omnis parte ueretur amor*, 27-28 *tu modo quam primum corruptas desere Baias:* / *multis ista dabunt litora discidium*; Ov. *Ars* 1.255-262 with Hollis, which lasted well into the first century AD; cf. Mart. 11.80.1-2 *litus beatae Veneris aureum Baias,* / *Baias superbae blanda dona naturae.*

proxima: this is Scioppius' conjecture for the unintelligible *maxima* of the MSS. The two words are commonly confused in MSS (cf. Lucan 10.408; Vell. 2.127; Just. 14.4.12). For the use of *proximus* + dat. to denote 'second to' in a ranking cf. Virg. *Ecl.* 7.22-23 *proxima Phoebi* / *uersibus ille facit*; Ov. *Met.* 12.398 *pectoraque artificum laudatis proxima signis*. The Etruscan springs would thus be second in rank to those of Baiae, to which Strabo (quoted above) and Martial 6.42.7 *principes ... Baiae* give first place.

4 cum se ... remittit humus: the reference is to the loosening or relaxing of the earth in spring from the rigours of winter. For *remitto* in this context the closest parallel is Ov. *Fast.* 4.126 *uere remissus ager*, but cf. also Lucan 1.17 *bruma rigens ac nescia uere remitti.* For the dissolving of winter into spring cf. Hor. *Carm.* 1.4.1 *soluitur acris hiems grata uice ueris et Fauoni*, 10 (*florem*) *terrae quem ferunt solutae* with N-H ad loc.; Isid. *Nat.* 37.4 (*Fauonius*) *hiemem rigorem gratissima uice relaxat, floresque producit.*

purpureo uere: 'in the bright spring'; the expression comes from Virg. *Ecl.* 9.40 *hic uer purpureum* and goes back ultimately to Pind. *Pyth.* 4.64 φοινικανθέμου ἦρος ἀκμᾷ ["at the hight of purple-flowered spring"]. The brightness comes from the flowers which characterise spring rather than summer in Mediterranean countries, cf. Virg. *Ecl.* 9.40-41 *hic uer purpureum, uarios hic flumina circum* / *fundit humus flores*; Ov. *Fast.* 4.126 *uere nitent terrae*; *Dirae* 21 *purpureo campos quae pingunt uerna colore*; Colum. *Rust.* 10.256-257 *iam uer purpureum, iam uersicoloribus anni* / *fetibus alma parens pingi sua tempora gaudet.* The epithet also suggests 'bright' in the sense of 'happy', in contrast with the 'dark' *atram* *mihi regna / Lydia, non magni potior sit fama Gylippi*, would take *Lydius* here (**29**) ἀπὸ κοινοῦ 'neither the kingdom of Lydia nor its gold-bearing river'. The wealth of Croesus, derived partly from the gold-bearing Pactolus (cf. Strabo 13.4.5, Prop. 3.18.28), was proverbial, see Otto 98-99 and cf. Cat. 115.3 *cur non diuitiis Croesum superare potis sit*?, Cic. *Fin.* 3.45 *ut interit ... in diuitiis Croesi teruncii accessio*. On the general theme of rejection of oriental luxury, for which the archetype is Archil. fr. 19 West, see N-H 423-424 on Hor. *Carm.* 1.38.1 and McKeown II 414-415 on Ov. *Am.* 1.15.33-34.

Lydius aurifer amnis: the adjective *aurifer* applied to the Pactolus may hint at its Greek name Χρυσορρόας (Schol. Aristoph. *Plut.* 287; *Pan. Lat.* 5.14.1; Plin. *Nat.* 5.110; Hyg. *Fab.* 191), derived from the fact that it brought down gold from Mount Tmolus (Herod. 5.101; Strabo 13.4.5) or that Midas washed away his golden touch in it (Ov. *Met.* 11.134-145). According to Strabo (13.1.23, 13.4.5) this phenomenon was no longer observable in the Augustan period, but the river remained proverbial for its provision of gold (e.g. Hor. *Epod.* 15.20; Prop. 1.14.11, 2.26A.23, 3.18.28). Normally the river Pactolus is named in these contexts, but for the circumlocution *Lydius ... amnis* cf. Sil. 1.157-158 *Lydia ... / stagna*. The mention of the river here is probably Hellenistic in inspiration [see L. C. Watson (2003) 459], and is named at Callimachus *Iamb.* 4.106 Pf. (cf. the same author's *On the Rivers in the World* fr. 457ff. Pf.), Antimachus of Colophon (fr. 79 *SH* = 93 Matthews) and Hermesianax (fr. 7, 41-42 Powell). The phrase *Lydia regna* is used in the same context of the rejection of riches (in this case in favour of the care of a patron) is used again by our author at **7.198-199** and so serves perhaps to make a connection between the *Lygdamus* poems and the *Laudes Messallae*. It may be significant for Lygdamus' possible impersonation of Horace's rich rival for Neaera at *Epod.* 15 (see **headnote** above, **1 headnote, 1.19n., 4.16n., 6.47-49n., 6.53n.**, Gen. Intro., section 3.1) that Horace says of the rival's riches *tibi Pactolus fluat* (*Epod.* 15.20). Lygdamus puts love before the riches ascribed to the rival by Horace. The phrase *amnis aurifer* had been used previously by Catullus of the Spanish river Tagus 29.19 *amnis aurifer Tagus*, also proverbial for its gold; see further McKeown II 415-416 on *Am.* 1.15.34 *auriferi ... Tagi. amnis* is the only word for 'river' found in **[Tib.] 3** (**3.29, 3.37, 4.18, 10.8, 14.4**) except for *Laud. Mess.* **7.125** *flumen*. Tib. himself prefers *amnis* (3), but has one use of *flumen* at 2.5.69. *fluuius* is not found anywhere in the *Corp. Tib.*

hour of Lygdamus' death foretold in **5**. For our author's fondness for such colour contrasts see **1.9n**. The fact that the poem is set in the spring and not in the fever-bringing days of late summer suggest to Heyworth [(2018) 76] that Lygdamus' illness may be love-sickness, but for arguments in favour of a physical disease see **27n**. *terrear aestu* below.

5 Persephone: daughter of Demeter and Zeus, Persephone was the wife of Hades and goddess of the underworld. She lived half her life in the underworld and half in the upper world. Her return to the upper world each year corresponded with the return of spring, hence her relevance here. To Lygdamus' friends she symbolises spring's reawakening of life, while to Lygdamus himself she is a harbinger of death. For Persephone in her role of messenger of death, cf. Ov. *Her.* 21.45-46 (Cydippe to Acontius) *ei mihi, coniugii tempus crudelis ad ipsum / Persephone nostras pulsat acerba fores*. She is sometimes represented as cutting off a lock of hair from people about to die, cf. Hor. *Carm.* 1.28.19-20 with N-H 330-331; Virg. *Aen.* 4.698-699 with Pease 532-533; Stat. *Silu.* 2.1.147. This is the only mention of the goddess in the *Corp. Tib.* The Greek form of her name is restricted to poetry in Latin and is attested first in Prop. 2.13.26, 28.47-48 where it is preferred on metrical grounds to the Latinised form Proserpina, used by Virgil and Horace. Ovid makes use of both forms, as the metre demands: *Persephone* 8 [*Her.* (1), *Met.* (2), *Fast.* (5)]; *Proserpina* 5 [*Met.* (4), *Fast.* (1)].

nigram denuntiat horam: a poetic variation on the prose phrase *denuntiare mortem,* e.g. Cels. 2.6.10 *seriorem mortem ... denuntiant*; Sen. *Epist.* 70.11 *cum mortem uis externa denuntiat*. The phrase *nigram ... horam* is used only here to refer to the hour of death, although *hora* occurs elsewhere with various other epithets in this association, e.g. Tib. 1.1.59 *suprema ... hora*; Prop. 2.13.45 *dubiae ... horae*; Virg. *Ecl.* 8.20 *extrema ... hora*; Lucan 9.87 *fatalis ... hora*; Stat. *Silu.* 2.1.54 *grauis ... hora*; especially on epitaphs, e.g. *CLE* 55.7 *hora tristis fatalis,* 367.1 *miserabilis hora,* 389.2 *fatalis ... hora,* 400.3 *grauis ... hora*. For the association of the adj. *niger* with death and dying see Prop. 2.24B.34 *niger ille dies*; see **3.37-38n**. on *nigramque paludem* and cf. **2.18** *nigra ueste,* **5.33** *nigras pecudes*; also cf. *atra dies* at Virg. *Aen.* 6.429, 11.28.

6 inmerito: innocent of any offence against the gods, as made clear in **7-14** below; the same point is made at **4.14**. As an adverb, *immerito* is used in the same emphatic position at the beginning of the pentameter in Tib. 1.6.72 *immerito pronas proripiarque uias.*

iuueni: introduces the second argument in his own defence: he is too young to die, a point expanded in **15-26**. At its widest limits the term *iuuenis* can cover any age between 15 and 45, see Axelson (1948) and *ThLL* 7(2).734.81-735.4.

parce nocere: cf. Prop. 2.5.18 *parce tuis animis, uita, nocere mihi*. This polite form of prohibition (on which see K-S II 1.202) is restricted before Apuleius to verse, except for Liv. 34.32.20 *parce ... fidem ... iactare*, in a speech characterised by colloquialisms. In verse it is attested from Virg. *Ecl.* 3.94 *parcite, oues, nimium procedere* on and is especially frequent in Ovid, see McKeown on *Am.* 1.2.50, Bömer on *Met.* 10.545, Fantham on *Fast.* 4.203-204. Like *desinite ... uelle* at **4.4** and *desine uelle* at **4.80** (with note) the phrase is designed to avoid the prosaic construction *noli(te)* + inf. Some sense of the verb's original meaning of 'spare', as in **21** below, may be present here. Prohibitions with *parce* are particularly common in prayers and other religious contexts, cf. Virg. *Aen.* 3.41-42 *iam parce sepulto / parce pias scelerare manus*, a passage which neatly illustrates the closeness of the two senses of *parce*.

7-14 A series of four distichs backs up his claim of innocence (**6**) by listing the serious crimes he has not committed. The passage seems to be closely dependent on Tib. 1.3.51-52 *parce, pater. timidum non me periuria terrent, / non dicta in sanctos impia uerba deos*. In both cases sacrilege on the part of the poet is rejected as an explanation for an illness. At the verbal level we may compare *parce ... dea* in **6** with *parce, pater* in Tib. 1.3.51 and *nec ... / inpia in aduersos soluimus ora deos* in **13-14** with Tib. 1.3.52 *non dicta in sanctos impia uerba deos*. For *non ego* as a characteristic of the rhetorical figure of *auersio*, found in **2.5** and **6.59**, see Pease on Virg. *Aen.* 4.425-426; McKeown II 141 on Ov. *Am.* 1.6.33-34, III 54 on *Am.* 2.2.63-64 and cf. Quint. *Inst.* 9.2.39 *illa quoque uocatur auersio, quae a proposita quaestione abducit audientem*: '*non ego cum Danais Troianam excindere gentem / Aulide iuraui*' (Virg. *Aen.* 4.425-426). *quod fit et multis et uariis figuris cum aut aliud expectasse nos aut maius aliquid timuisse simulamus aut plus uideri posse ignorantibus*. Three examples from Ovid show particular similarities with our author here:

Am. 2.2.63-64   *non scelus adgredimur, non ad miscenda coimus*
    toxica, non stricto fulminat ense manus.

["We are not entering on crime, we are not coming together to mix poisons, our hand does not flash with drawn sword."]

Pont. 2.2.9-14   non ego concepi, si Pelion Ossa tulisset,
                    clara mea tangi sidera posse manu,
                    nec nos Enceladi dementia castra secuti
                    in rerum dominos mouimus arma deos,
                    nec, quod Tydidae temeraria dextera fecit,
                    numina sunt telis ulla petita meis.

["I never imagined that, if Ossa had supported Pelion, I could touch the bright stars with my hand; nor have I joined the mad camp of Enceladus and waged war against the gods that rule the world; nor, as the rash hand of Tydeus' son did, have I sought with my spear any holy power."]

Pont. 2.9.67-72   non ego caede nocens in Ponti litora ueni,
                     mixtaue sunt nostra dira uenena manu:
                     nec mea subiecta conuicta est gemma tabella
                     mendacem linis inposuisse notam.
                     nec quicquam, quod lege uetor committere, feci:
                     est tamen his grauior noxa fatenda mihi.

["I have not come to Pontus' shores guilty of murder, nor have dread poisons been mixed by my hand; nor has my seal been convicted by a fraudulent tablet of having placed a false mark on its linen binding; nor have I done anything I am forbidden to do by law; nevertheless, I must confess to a greater crime."]

7-8 The distich presents two main problems, one of text and one of interpretation. The textual problem concerns the reading *deorum* of the MSS at the end of the hexameter, which cannot be correct. The question of interpretation concerns the nature of the rites Lygdamus claims not to have defiled. Two possible conjectures are offered for *deorum*, namely Scaliger's *uirorum* and Sandbach's *reorum*. The choice between them depends on the question of the cult concerned. Influenced perhaps by the address to Persephone in **5**, early interpreters opted for a reference to the mysteries of Demeter (*Ceres*) and her daughter Persephone (*Proserpina*) at Eleusis in Greece, on which see Burkert (1985) 276-277, 285-290. Those people, men or women, who betrayed these rituals to non-initiates (cf. *docere* **8**) could be charged with impiety (cf. Hor. *Carm.* 3.2.26-27 ... *qui Cereris sacrum / uolgarit arcanae*; Ov. *Ars* 2.601 *quis Cereris ritus ausit uolgare profanis*). Those in favour of this interpretation take *laudandae ... deae* in **8** as a reference to Homer's and Hesiod's epithet for Persephone ἐπαινή = 'praiseworthy' (e.g. Hom. *Il.* 9.457, *Od.* 10.491; Hes. *Theog.* 768). If this interpretation is correct, Scaliger's *uirorum* would have to refer to people in general (as at Cat. 64.192; Virg. *Georg.* 3.9; Ov. *Met.* 1.286) rather than specifically to men. Sandbach (1952) proposes *reorum* on the grounds that those guilty of crimes could not attend the Eleusinian mysteries (Suet. *Nero* 34). However, when Roman poets refer to these mysteries, as in the case of Horace and Ovid above, the emphasis is on Ceres rather than on Persephone. Most modern interpreters since Heyne, therefore, connect the *sacra* **8** not with the Eleusinian mysteries but rather with the rights of *Bona Dea*, a Roman fertility goddess whose cult was restricted to women. This cult is mentioned by Tib. at 1.6.22 *sacra Bonae maribus non adeunda Deae* in an allusion to a well known scandal in 62 BC when Clodius allegedly attended the rites dressed as a flute-girl (Plut. *Cic.* 28). If, as I believe, this interpretation is correct, Scaliger's *uirorum* would have its natural meaning of 'males' and *laudandae* could be taken as a periphrasis for the goddess's title *Bona*, though Heinsius and Hall prefer to replace the word with alternatives that would emphasise the secret nature of the cult, *celandae* and *uelandae* respectively. There would be a slight problem with *docere* **8** as the prohibition in this case was not in revealing the cult but in seeing or attending it. The conjectures of Voss *cernere sacra* and Erath *sacra uidere* are intended to remove this difficulty, but on the whole the prohibition on revealing rites was so prevalent with all mystery cults that *docere* here can stand.

7 non ego: for this line-beginning as typical of *auersiones* cf. Virg. *Aen.* 4.425, Ov. *Pont.* 2.2.9, 9.67, **[Tib.] 3.** *Lygd.* **2.5, 6.59** and see **7-14n.** above.

temeranda: the verb is used of religious violation or desecration (see *OLD temero* 1 and cf. Paul. Fest. 501 L. *temerare uiolare sacra et contaminare, dictum uidelicet a temeritate*) in verse from Virg. *Aen.* 6.840 *ultus auos Troiae templa et temerata Mineruae* and in prose from Liv. 26.13.13 *sepulcra maiorum temerata*. The verb is absent from Tibullus, Horace and Propertius, but is found 19 times in Ovid, see further McKeown II 211 on *Am.* 1.8.19, III 303 on *Am.* 2.14 17 *temerasset* and Ingleheart (2010) 371 on Ov. *Trist.* 2.503-504. For the related *temerarius* in the context of an *auersio* cf. Ov. *Pont.* 2.2.13 quoted on **7-14n.** above.

8 laudandae ... deae: on the interpretation of this phrase see **7-8n.** above. As argued there, the reference is probably to *Bona Dea*, the title rather than the name, which is unknown, of an Italian goddess, worshipped especially in Rome and Latium (see *OCD*[4] 239). In Rome she had a temple on the Aventine, from which men were prohibited; see Gibson on Ov. *Ars*

3.637-638 and cf. Prop. 4.9.25-26; Ov. *Fast*. 5.153. Her rites were also celebrated in the absence of men by *matronae* in the house of a magistrate under the direction of his wife or mother and attended by the Vestal Virgins (cf. Cic. *Harusp*. 37). No man should defile her rites (**7** *nulli temeranda uirorum*) and to do so, as Clodius had in 62 BC, would be a dangerous (hence *temptaui* **7**) and foolhardy (*audax* **8**) act. See further Wiseman (1974) 130-137.

9-10 Lygdamus denies being guilty of poisoning, a theme occurring in earlier *auersiones* at Ov. *Am*. 2.2.63-64 and *Pont*. 2.9.68 quoted on **7-14n.** above. In **9** the reference is to poisoning (*infecit*) a cup (*pocula*) with a deadly liquid (*mortiferis ... sucis*) and in **10** to the administering of a powdered poison (*trita uenena*). Although earlier commentators see the couplet as referring to a single crime, pouring poison in the cup (**9**) and administering the cup to the victim (**10**), the contrast between liquid poison in **9** and powdered poison in **10** suggests two different methods of poisoning.

9 nec: repeated in anaphora five times in **9-13**, in initial position in all cases except **10** *dextera nec*. For other examples of this type of repetition in Latin verse with positional variation see Wills (1996) 414.

mortiferis ... sucis:. the compound *mortifer* is rare and mainly poetic, e.g. Enn. *Trag*. 314 Jocelyn *mortiferum bellum* (Virg. *Aen*. 6.279) and see *ThLL* 8.1517.72-1518.22. It is absent from Tibullus, occurs once in Propertius in connection with a dead man's bier 3.13.17 *mortifero ... lecto*, and is used in Ovid only in the context of poisoned arrows: *Rem*. 26 (of Cupid) *sed tua mortifero sanguine tela carent*, and *Pont*. 3.1.26 *tinctaque mortifera tabe sagitta madet*. Closest to its use in the present context is Cic. *Tusc*. 1.71 (*Socrates*) *mortiferum illud tenens poculum*, and Sen. *Medea* 717 (quoted below). For *sucus* as the juice of a plant used either as a medicine or as a poison see *OLD sucus* 2a; for its use as a poison cf. Ov. *Her*. 12.181-182 (Medea to Jason) *dum ferrum flammaeque aderunt sucusque ueneni, / hostis Medeae nullus inultus erit*, *Met*. 14.403 *illa* (sc. *Circe*) *nocens spargit uirus sucosque ueneni*, and, in contexts involving *mortifer*; Vitr. 8.3.15 *inueniuntur aquae genera mortifera, quae per maleficum sucum terrae percurrentia recipiunt in se uim uenenatam*; Sen. *Medea* 717-719 *quodcumque gramen flore mortifero uiret, / dirusque tortis sucus in radicibus / causas nocendi gignit*.

infecit pocula: cf. Virg. *Georg*. 2.128 *pocula si quando saeuae infecere nouercae*; for *inficio* in this sense of poison cf. also Ov. *Met*. 3.75-76 *halitus* .../ ... *uitiatas infecit auras* and see *OLD inficio* 4a and *ThLL* 7(1).1413.42-1414.9.

10 dextera: for emphasis on the guilty 'hand' in *auersiones*, cf. Ov. *Am.* 2.2.65 and *Pont.* 2.9.68 quoted above in **7-14n.** and Petr. 133.1.8 quoted in **11n.** below.

trita uenena: the reading *trita* of F is supported by the parallel at Prop. 2.17.14 *sumere et in nostras trita uenena manus*. A's *certa* in the sense of 'effective' is possible, cf. Plin. *Nat.* 27.146 *certiores medicinae*, but unlikely in view of the Propertian passage.

11 This line is severely mangled in the MSS. If A's reading *templis amouimus aegros* contains any truth it would refer to driving the sick from the temples where they had gone to pray for their health. Some editors have retained *amouimus* but changed the last word to *ignes* (Luck) or *aera* (Helm) referring to the theft of sacred fire or sacred bronze objects from the temple. The verb *amouere*, however, in the sense of 'steal', though present in legal texts (e.g. Gai. *Inst.* 3.195; Ulp. *Dig.* 15.1.3), is rare elsewhere in prose and unattested in poetry. I have adopted the humanist correction *sacrilegos ... admouimus ignes*, widely accepted among modern commentators, referring to the crime of setting fire to temples. This crime was considered the height of sacrilege, cf. Stat. *Theb.* 5.685 *templa Iouis – quid enim haud licitum? – ferat impius ignis*. Commentators adopting this reading point to its similarity in wording to Encolpius' prayer to Priapus at Petr. 133.3.6-9 ... *non sanguine tristi / perfusus uenio, non templis impius hostis / admoui dextram, sed inops et rebus egenis / attritus facinus non toto corpore feci*.

sacrilegos: used once in Tib. of a threatened attack on Venus' temple at 2.4.26 *sacrilegas sentiat illa manus*, the adj. is rare elsewhere in poetry (once each in Hor., Prop. and Virg.), except for Ovid (9): *Am.* (1), *Ars* (1), *Rem.* (1), *Met.* (5), *Fast.* (1).

admouimus ignes: a common phrase in relation to 'setting fire' to an object, e.g. Claud. Quadr. fr. 81 P. *ignem admouit*; Ov. *Met.* 8.460-461 ... *taedasque et fragmina poni / imperat et positis inimicos admouet ignes*; Quint. *Decl. Min.* 323.5 (*Alexander*) *ignem sacris postibus ... admouere ausus est*.

12 The verse concludes the specific list of evil deeds from which the poet Lygdamus exonerates himself in **7-11** with a general exoneration from all evil deeds (*facta nefanda*, **12**), before he moves on in **13-14** to verbal offences (*iurgia* ... / *inpia* ... *ora*). For this generic allusion to crime in *auersiones*, aimed at avoiding any omission, cf. *scelus* Ov. *Am.* 2.2.64 and *caede* at *Pont.* 2.9.67 both quoted in **7-14n.** above. The same distinction between sacrilegious acts and blasphemy is made at **4.15-16** above *si mea nec turpi mens est obnoxia facto / nec laesit magnos inpia lingua deos*.

cor: for the heart as the seat of cares or conscience, see *OLD cor* 2b and cf. Varro *Ling.* 6.46 *cura, quod cor urat*; Isid. *Etym.* 11.1.118 *cor ... a cura*.

sollicitant: for *sollicito* with an abstract subject in the sense of 'worry', 'vex', cf. Plaut. *Rud.* 198 *erile scelus me sollicitat* and see *OLD sollicito* 3.

facta nefanda: the *iunctura* is found twice in Ovid: *Her.* 14.16 *hic solet euentus facta nefanda sequi* and *Fast.* 2.850 ... *regis facta nefanda refert*.

13-14 Lygdamus exonerates himself from the crime of blasphemy, a commonly mentioned religious offence in ancient poetry beginning with the blasphemy of Niobe against Leto in Hom. *Il.* 24.607-608. In elegy cf. Tib. 1.2.81-82 *num Veneris magnae uiolaui numina uerbo / et mea nunc poenas inpia lingua luit?*, 3.52 *non dicta in sanctos inpia uerba deos*, 2.6.17-18 ... *tu mihi dira precari / cogis et insana mente nefanda loqui*; Prop. 2.28.9-14 (on Cynthia's blasphemies against Venus, Juno and Pallas); **[Tib.] 3.** *Lygd.* **4.16** *nec laesit magnos inpia lingua deos*, and *Sulpicia Cycle* **10.14** *dicit in aeternos aspera uerba deos*.

13 insanae ... mentis: for the connection between madness and blasphemy, cf. Tib. 2.6.18 *insana mente nefanda loqui* and for reference to madness in *auersiones*, cf. Ov. *Pont.* 2.2.11 quoted in **7-14n.** above. For madness as characteristic of the elegiac lover, from Gallus on, cf. Virg. *Ecl.* 10.22 (spoken by Apollo) *Galle, quid insanis?*, 44-45 (of Gallus) *nunc insanus amor duri me Martis in armis / tela inter media atque aduersos detinet hostes*; also Prop. 1.5.1 (to Gallus) *quid tibi uis, insane? meos sentire furores?* with further examples in Fulkerson (2017) 190 ad loc., cf. Pichon 172-173.

meditantes: in the sense of 'framing' or 'planning' evil cf. Plaut. *Pseud.* 941 *meditati sunt mihi doli docte*; Cic. *Nat. Deor.* 3.71 *scelera meditantes*; Virg. *Ecl.* 5.60-61 *nec lupus insidias pecori nec retia ceruis / ulla dolum meditantur*; Tac. *Ann.* 14.1 *diu meditatum scelus*.

iurgia: only this form of the noun is found in dactylic verse; see *ThLL* 7(2).665.58-59. Its application to blasphemy is unusual; elsewhere in elegy it refers normally to the reproaches of a lover (Pichon 178), e.g. Prop. 1.3.17-18 *non tamen ausus eram dominae turbare quietem, / expertae metuens iurgia saeuitiae*.

14 The line is carefully constructed, with an intricate *abAB* arrangement of the nouns and adjectives.

inpia ... ora: in the context of blasphemy, cf. Tib. 1.2.82 *inpia lingua*, 3.52 *inpia lingua*; **[Tib.] 3**. *Lygd*. **4.16** *inpia lingua* (**13-14n.** above).

aduersos ... deos: 'hostile, unfavourable gods'. A common combination, occurring in the same position in the line at Prop. 1.1.8 *aduersos cogor habere deos*. As there, the *aduersos ... deos* are likely to include the love gods. It could be significant that their mention here immediately after *insanae ... mentis* (**13**) echoes Gallus' words, describing *militia amoris* rather than literal *militia*, at Virg. *Ecl.* 10. 44-45 *insanus amor ... me ... / ... inter ... aduersos detinet hostes* on which see Harrison (2007) 66-68.

soluimus ora: for *soluo* in the sense of giving free rein to sounds and utterances see *OLD soluere* 7. Close to the present context is Ov. *Met.* 3.261 *dum linguam ad iurgia soluit*. The phrase *ora soluere* of opening the mouth in speech occurs in poetry from Ovid on, cf. Ov. *Met.* 1.181 *ora indignantia soluit* (of Jupiter), Sil. 15.455 *cum dulcia soluerat ora*.

15-20 This section is parallel to **7-14** on Lygdamus' innocence and adds a second reason why he should be spared, namely on account of his youth (picking up *inmerito iuueni* **6**). The passage is heavily reliant on Ovidian precedents, as will be made clear in the line-by-line commentary below, and Ovid's priority in all cases is argued for by Lee (1958-59) 17 and Axelson (1960a) 99-95, (1960b) 282. The way in which a number of different Ovidian references are combined in a single passage is a trait characteristic of Flavian epic; see Hardie (1989) and Maltby (2010) 324. The Ovidian colouring is particularly appropriate in a passage whose central couplet **17-18** describes the year of Lygdamus' birth in terms which clearly echo Ovid's description of his own year of birth at *Trist.* 4.10.5-6.

15-16 Two of the characteristics of old age mentioned here, grey hair (**15**) and slow and bent gait (**16**) are mentioned together in Tib. 2.2.19-20 *dum tarda senectus / inducat rugas inficiatque comas* and in Ovid's description of Juno disguising herself as an old woman at *Met.* 3.275-277 *simulauit anum posuitque ad tempora canos / sulcauitque cutem rugis et curua trementi / membra tulit passu; uocem quoque fecit anilem*.

15 cani nigros: the colour contrast is typical of poems **1-6** (cf. **4-5** above *purpureo* ... / ... *nigram* and see **1.9n.**) and in this case has precedents in Prop. 3.5.24 *spaserit et nigras alba senecta comas* and Ov. *Trist.* 4.8.2 *inficit et nigras alba senecta comas*. For *cani* as a noun 'white hairs' see Maltby (2002) 350 on Tib. 1.10.43 *caput candescere canis*. It occurs first in prose at Cic. *Sen.* 18.62 and is rare in verse after its first occurrence in Tib., except in Ovid: *Met.* (8), *Pont.* (1).

nigros ... capillos: for black hair as a sign of youth cf. Hor. *Epist.* 1.7.25-26 *reddes / forte latus nigros angusta fronte capillos*. On the various words for 'hair' in the *Lygd.* poems see **2.11n.** above.

laesere: for this use of *laedo* in the sense of 'disfigure' cf. Tib. 2.3.10 *laederet ... teneras pussula rupta manus*; **[Tib.] 3**. *Sulpicia Cycle* 9.8 *teneras laedere uelle manus?*. Its use of impairing beauty is typically Ovidian; cf. *Am.* 1.7.40 *laesae ... genae*, 10.14 *nunc mentis uitio laesa figura tua est* with McKeown II 288, 14.39 *non te cantatae laeserunt paelicis herbae*, *Ars* 3.207 *praesidium laesae petitote figurae*: see further *ThLL* 7(2).867.68-71 and Pichon 182. As N-A points out (437) the verb is used in a similar context of colour change at Ov. *Ars* 3.704 *pallescunt frondes, quas noua laesit hiems*. For this form of the perfect see **1.1-4 n.** above on *uenere*.

16 The line echoes Ov. *Ars* 2.670 *iam ueniet tacito curua senecta pede*. Here the silent (surreptitious) approach of old age is replaced with a reference to its characteristic slowness. On the priority of Ovid here see Maltby (2010) 323-324.

tardo ... pede: perhaps better taken as an ablative of description with *senecta* rather than instrumental with *uenit* (so Dissen 366). For the *iunctura* cf. Tib. 1.8.48 (of the swift departure of youth) ... *non tardo labitur illa pede*; Ov. *Am.* 2.19.12 (of Corinna bidding a reluctant Ovid depart) *cunctantem tardo iussit abire pede*, *Trist.* 1.3.56 *pes mihi tardus erat*. The adj. *tardus* is more frequently linked with *senectus/a* itself, reflecting the slow walk of the elderly; e.g. Enn. *Trag.* 348 Jocelyn *tarda in senectute*; Tib. 2.2.19 *tarda senectus*, cf. Hor. *Serm.* 2.2.88; Virg. *Aen.* 8.508, 9.610; Ov. *Trist.* 4.8.23; Sen. *Herc. F.* 849; [Sen.] *Oct.* 74; Stat. *Silu.* 3.3.156.

curua senecta: also at Ov. *Ars* 2.670 quoted above and cf. Stat. *Theb.* 4.419 *incurua senecta*. The adj. = 'stooped' refers to the later stages of old age, contrast Juv. 3.26 *dum noua canities, dum prima et recta senectus*. It is applied to an old woman by Prop. 2.18.20 *ipsa anus haud longa curua futura die*, cf. Ov. *Met.* 14.659 *anus ... incurua*; Tac. *Ann.* 1.34 *curuata senio membra*; Apul. *Met.* 4.7 *anum ... curuatam graui senio*. On the form *senecta* here and in **25** below see **3.8n.** above.

17-18 The pentameter echoes word for word the couplet in which Ovid describes the year of his own birth in *Trist.* 4.10.5-6 *editus hic ego sum, nec non, ut tempora noris, / cum cecidit fato consul uterque pari*. In Ovid's case the year was 43 BC in which the consuls A. Hirtius and C. Vibius Pansa both died in the course of the civil war fought at Mutina. On literary grounds it is now generally accepted that the composition of the whole of **[Tib.] 3** is a post-Ovidian, belonging most probably to the Flavian period (see Gen. Intro., section 2.2.1). It may be significant that this Lygdaman *sphragis* occupies the central couplet of the poem. Of course there is no need to take the poet at his word about the birth date of Lygdamus, who is after all a mask, and the couplet could simply be part of a clever presentation of his creations as contemporary with the three main elegists, Tibullus, Propertius and Ovid – see further Gen. Intro., section 2.2.1, *Lygd.* **6.41n.**, Maltby (2010) 324.

17 natalem primo ... uidere: the word *natalem* is ambiguous in that it could mean either (1) the actual day of birth or (2) an anniversary of that day, see *OLD natalis* 2. The adverb *primo* would work better with the second, referring to Lygdamus' first birthday, but a reference to the actual day of birth is more likely because that is what Ovid is talking about in *Trist.* 4.10.5-6. In this case *primo* would be pleonastic, but that would be in line with our author's love of pleonastic expressions elsewhere in poems **1-6**, see **2.15n.**

primo: less common than *primum* as a temporal adverb, but cf. Ov. *Met.* 15.106 and *Pont.* 3.6.45.

uidere: for this form of the perfect cf. **15** above *laesere* and see **1.1-4n.** above on *uenere*.

18 cecidit fato: for *fatum* in the sense of one's 'last day', 'death', see *OLD fatum* 4b. For the expression, in addition to Ov. *Trist.* 4.10.6, cf. Ov. *Trist.* 1.2.53 *fatoue suo ferroue cadentem*; Sen. *Oed.* 780 *aliquisne cecidit regio fato comes?*, 787 *edissere agedum, quo cadat fato parens*; Tac. *Ann.* 1.55.11 *Varus fato et ui Armini cecidit.*

uterque pari: in addition to Ov. *Trist*. 4.10.6 the verse ending is also found at Ov. *Fast*. 5. 704 *et ex causa pugnat uterque pari*, cf. also Ov. *Her*. 19.114 *incitat et morsus error uterque pares*.

19-20 A rhetorical question which likens an early death to the picking of unripe fruit. Again the inspiration is Ovid. In this case a metaphor concerning Corinna's abortion in which the pregnant Corinna is likened to a laden vine and the bitter, un-ripened grapes to the aborted child: *Am*. 2.14.23-24 *quid plenam fraudas uitem crescentibus uuis / pomaque crudeli uellis acerba manu*? The metaphor fits better the context in Ovid, whereas in our passage hereit is difficult to see the point of comparison of the vine, and the image of *modo nata ... poma* appears exaggerated when applied to a young man; see further Maltby (2010) 323. For the comparison between early death and the picking of unripe fruit, cf. the grave inscription of a seven-year-old boy from Naples *IG* 14. 769 = *Epigr. Gr*. 575-6, Kaibel δακρυχαρὴς Πλούτων, οὐ πνεύματα πάντα βρότεια / σοὶ νέμαται; τί τρυγᾷς ὄμφακας ἡλικίης; ["Pluto, you who delight in tears, not all human souls belong to you. Why do you reap the unripe fruit of youth?"] and Cic. *Sen*. 71 *quasi poma ex arboribus, cruda si sunt, ui euelluntur, si matura et cocta, decidunt, sic uitam adulescentibus uis aufert, senibus maturitas*.

19 fraudare: found mainly in prose, except for Ovid (see below) and Martial (7). It refers to depriving someone of what is theirs by right; cf., in addition to Ov. *Am*. 2.14.23 (quoted above in **19-20n.**); Just. *Dig*. 47.11.4. pr. 3 *indignum ... uideri potest impune eam maritum liberis fraudasse*, and, in the context of an early death, Mart. 7.40.5 *occidit illa prior uiridi fraudata iuuenta*. The construction + abl. is found from Cicero on. The verb does not occur in Tib., Prop. or elsewhere in **[Tib.] 3**, but is frequent in Ovid (9): *Am*. (2), *Her*. (1), *Ars* (1), *Met*. (3), *Fast*. (2).

crescentibus uuis: the same line-ending is found in Ov. *Am*. 2.14.23 (quoted above in **19-20n.**). For immature grapes as an image for youth, cf. Hor. *Carm*. 2.5.9-10 (of a girl too young for love) *tolle cupidinem / immitis uuae* with N-H 84-5 ad loc. For *crescentibus* in the same *sedes* in connection with the years of youth, cf. Ov. *Ars* 1.61 *seu caperis primis et adhuc crescentibus annis*; Mart. 1.88.1-2 *Alcime, quem raptum domino crescentibus annis / Labicana ... uelat humus*. The Martial passage suggests the phrase could have been common on epitaphs, cf. Ov. *Met*. 10.23-24 (Orpheus on Euridice) *in quam calcata uenenum / uipera diffudit crescentesque abstulit annos*.

20 modo nata: 'new-born', used of fruit also in the Ovidian model at *Am.* 2.14.25 *sponte fluant matura sua, sine crescere nata* as well as at Mart. 10.94.5-6 *haec igitur media quae sunt modo nata Subura / mittimus autumni cerea poma manu*. For the iambic shortening of *modo* see **4.64n.** above.

mala ... manu: replaces *crudeli ... manu* of the Ovidian model *Am.* 2.14.24. For the phrase, used elsewhere mainly in the context of black magic, cf. Plaut. *Amph.* 605 *huic homini nescio quid est mali mala obiectum manu*, Pers. 313 *ubi qui mala tangit manu*; Petr. 63.7 *illum tetigerat mala manus*.

uellere: the verb, which is often used of pulling out hair or uprooting plants or trees (see *OLD uello* 1 and 2), implies the use of force in plucking the unripe fruit both here and in the Ovidian model *Am.* 2.14.24, cf. Cic. *Sen.* 71 *poma ... cruda si sunt ui euelluntur, si matura et cocta decidunt,* with Powell (1988) 244 ad loc.

poma: also in Ov. *Am.* 2.14.24. Although the word normally applies to orchard fruit from trees (see *OLD pomum* 2b and cf. Cels. 2.18.6 *at ex fructibus surculorum ualentiores uuae. ficus ... quam quae poma proprie nominantur*), the reference here and in Ovid must still be to the grapes mentioned in the preceding hexameter, rather than to unripe apples, as suggested by N-A ad loc..

21 parcite: repeats Lygdamus' prayer for compassion, which in **6** (*parce*) was addressed to Persephone, but now is directed to all the gods of the underworld. The use of this verb, which is characteristic of prayers, is frequent in Tib. (18), of which *parce* (9), *parcite* (4); see further Hellegouarc'h (1989), and, apart from these two occurrences in **5.6** and here **21**, is found again in **9.1**. The alliteration here *parcite pallentes* is typical of the use of the verb elsewhere, particularly in Tib. cf. 1.1.34 *parcite: de magno praeda petenda grege*, 3.51 *parce, pater*, 4.83 *parce, puer*, 8.51 *parce, precor*.

pallentes undas: it was common for adjectives suggesting pallor to be associated with death. For their use with reference to the waters of the underworld, see **1.27-28n.** and cf. *Aetna* 77-79 *... uiderunt ... manes/ atque inter cineres Ditis pallentia regna / ... undasque canentes*. The collocation occurs elsewhere only at Sil. 9.250 *pallenti ... in unda*.

tenetis: 'hold sway over', 'rule', see *OLD teneo* 9b and cf. Virg. *Aen.* 1.139-140 *tenet ille* (sc. *Aeolus*) *immania saxa / uestras, Eure, domos*.

22 duraque sortiti tertia regna dei: to complete the sense of the pentameter we must assume a rare, but not unparalleled, ellipse of *estis* after *sortiti*, cf. Virg. *Aen*. 5.191-192 *nunc illas promite uiris, / nunc animos, quibus in Gaetulis Syrtibus usi* (sc. *estis*). For *sortior* = 'to receive as one's lot' see *OLD sortior* 4 and cf. Cic. *Att*. 1.13.5 *prouincias praetores nondum sortiti sunt*. In verse it occurs mainly in elevated contexts: Virg. *Georg*. (1), *Aen*. (8); Ov. *Met*. (5), *Trist*. (1). The reference is to the distribution by lot of the heavens to Zeus, the sea to Poseidon and the underworld to Hades, after the overthrow of Kronos and the Titans (Hom. *Il*. 15.187-196). For the underworld as the *tertia regna*, cf. Ov. *Fast*. 4.584 (sc. *Persephone*) *nupta Iouis fratri tertia regna tenet* (with Fantham); Sen. *Herc. F*. 609 *si placerent tertiae sortis loca* (with Billerbeck). Similarly, the sea is referred to as *regnum secundum*, e.g. Sen. *Medea* 597-598 *sed furit uinci dominus profundi / regna secunda* (with Costa), *Herc. F*. 599 *et tu, secundo maria qui sceptro regis* (with Billerbeck); Stat. *Silu*. 3.2.14 (sc. *Nereides*) *quis honor et regni cessit fortuna secundi* and see Hollis on Ov. *Met*. 8 595-596 *proxima mundi / regna* and Ingleheart (2010) 91-92 on Ov. *Trist*. 2.53 *per mare, per caelum, per tertia numina iuro*.

duraque ... regna: the kingdom of the underworld is traditionally grim and harsh, cf. Virg. *Aen*. 6.566 *Cnosius haec Rhadamanthus habet durissima regna*, as are its rulers, who refuse to allow their subjects to return to the upper world, cf. Virg. *Aen*. 12.199 *duri ... Ditis*.

23-25 olim liceat ... / ... / cum ... pallebunt: the combination *olim ... cum* with future reference is rare, with examples in Early Latin, e.g Plaut. *Trin*. 523-524 *... olim terra cum proscinditur / in quinto quoque sulco moriuntur boues*; Turp. *Com*. 193 *cum ad te redierit res olim post mortem patris*; Ov. *Trist*. (all in relation to a future return from exile): 2.575-576 *non ut in Ausoniam redeam nisi forsitan olim, / cum longo poenae tempore uictus eris*, 3.8.19-20 *forsitan hoc olim, cum se satiauerit ira, / tum quoque ... rogandus erit*, 4.4.47-48 *forsitan hanc ... finiet olim, / tempore cum fuerit lenior ira, fugam*, and then sporadically in verse in the first century AD, e.g. Calp. *Ecl*. 5.102-103 *has ...conueniet ... olim / promere, cum pecudes extremus clauserit annus*. For the progression *olim ... cum ...* senecta N-A ad loc. compares Prop. 3.5.23-25 *atque ubi iam Venerem grauis interceperit aetas / sparserit et nigras alba senecta comas, / tum mihi naturae libeat perdiscere mores*, a passage echoed above in *cani ... nigros*, see **15n**.

23 Elysios ... campos: based on the Homeric *Ἠλύσιον πεδίον* (the Elysian plain) (*Od.* 4.563) the phrase is used first in Latin literature at Virg. *Georg.* 1.38 *quamuis Elysios miretur Graecia campos*, where it refers to the abode of the blessed after death, and occurs frequently in later Latin epitaphs as the preferred destination for the dead (e.g. *CLE* 522.5, 1165.4, 1200.6, 1515.9, 1970.1-2). Originally it was a *locus amoenus*, above the ground in the West, identified with the Isles of the Blessed (so Hom. *Od.* 4.563 ff.; Hes. *Op.* 167 ff.; cf. Hor. *Epod.* 16.41-42), but later became a separate part of the underworld (see N-H on Hor. *Carm.* 2.13.23 and cf. Virg. *Aen.* 6.540-543, 638ff.). In Homer it was reserved for relatives of the gods, such as Menelaus (cf. Hom. *Od.* 4.561-569). Our author's immediate model here is Tib. 1.3.58 (sc. *me*) *ipsa Venus campos ducet in Elysios*, where Elysium is described as the resting place of dead lovers (Tib. 1.3.57-66), a suitable destination for Lygdamus himself as an innocent poet of love. For the association of the phrase with Tib., cf. Domitius Marsus *Epitaph. Tib.* 2 *Mors iuuenem* (sc. *Tibullum*) *campos misit ad Elysios*; Ov. *Am.* 3.9.60 (on Tib.'s death) *in Elysia ualle Tibullus erit*.

cognoscere: perhaps influenced by *perdiscere* at Prop. 3.5.25 (quoted above), but as Fedeli points out (176) on Prop. 1.6.13 *an mihi sit tanti doctas cognoscere Athenas*, the verb is common in contexts of 'getting to know' a place as a result of visiting: cf. Enn. *Op. Inc.*1 Sk. *Lunae portum, est operae, cognoscite ciues*; Caes. *BG* 4.20.2 *si ... loca portus aditus cognouisset*. Close to the present context of visiting the underworld is Ov. *Met.* 14.111-112 *Elysiasque domos et regna nouissima mundi / me duce cognosces simulacraque cara parentis*.

24 Lethaeamque ratem: cf. **3.10** *Lethaea ... rate* with **n.** ad loc.

Cimmeriosque lacus: the Cimmerians were a semi-mythical people living in an isolated land where the sun never shone (see **7.64-66** below with **nn.** ad loc.). Their connection with the dead is established by Homer at *Od.* 11.14-19 where Odysseus visits their land of darkness to call up the dead and speak with Tiresias. Ovid (*Met.* 11.592-593) locates their land near the home of Sleep, brother of Death. The fact that in the seventh century BC they had a leader called Lygdamis [Hopkinson (1989) 107 on Call. *Aet.* fr. 75.23 Pf.] is probably pure coincidence. According to Lact. *Diu. Inst.* 1.6.7 the adj. goes back in Latin at least as far as Naev. (fr. 18). In later Latin, as here, the adj. came simply to mean *infernus* ('connected with Hades'), without reference to a specific people; cf. *Culex* 231-232 *feror auia carpens, / auia Cimmerios inter distantia lucos* (where *Cimmerios ... lucos* is close in sound to *Cimmerios ... lacus* here); Sil. 12.132 *Cimmerias ...*

domos; Stat. *Silu.* 3.2.92 *Cimmeriumque chaos*. Hinds [(1987b) 36-38] points to frequent verbal plays in Latin on *locus, lucus* and *lacus* and for paronomasia between *lucus* and *lacus* cites Lucr. 5.75 and Ov. *Fast.* 6.755-756, which would argue in favour of an intentional echo here of *Culex* 232. This could be significant for the dating of **[Tib.] 3**, cf. **1.15-16n.** above on another possible echo of *Culex*. The *Culex* can be dated roughly to the mid first century AD and is echoed in Martial, Lucan and Statius from the Flavian period, of whom the latter wrongly attributed it to Virgil; see Maltby (2010) 326-327. For the use of *lacus* of the waters of the underworld, cf. Tib. 1.10.38 *ad obscuros ... lacus*, 2.6.40 *ad infernos ... lacus* etc.; Virg. *Aen.* 6.134 *Stygios ... lacus*; *Culex* 372-373 *Ditis opacos / cogor adire lacus*; see *OLD lacus* 1c.

-que ... -que: see **1.3-4n.** above.

25 rugosa ... senecta: for wrinkles as a symptom of old age cf. Virg. *Aen.* 7.416-417 (sc. *Allecto*) *... in uultus sese transformat anilis / et frontem obscenam rugis arat*; Tib. 2.2.19-20 *dum tarda senectus / inducat rugas inficiatque comas*; Prop. 3.25.14 *... speculo rugas increpitante tibi*; Ov. *Met.* 14.96 *rugis ... anilibus*, 15.232 *rugas ... aniles*, *Fast.* 5.58 *ruga senilis* (*Trist.* 3.7.34, *Pont.* 1.4.2). The adj. *rugosus* occurs first in Lucil. 430 and 557 M.; Valg. Ruf. fr. 1 (Courtney = 165 Hollis), but is rare in Augustan poetry: only Hor. *Epod.* 9.14, *Epist.* 1.18.105; Prop. 4.5.67 (of Acanthis); Ov. *Am.* 1.18.112, *Her.* 5.28, *Met.* 7.626, 8.674, *Fast.* 1.185.

pallebunt ora: for the phrase, cf. Ov. *Met.* 8.465 *saepe metu sceleris pallebant ora futuri*. For the connection between pallor and old age, cf. Sen. *Ben.* 7.27.3 *indignare aegros, deformes, senes pallidos*; Pers. 1.26 *en pallor seniumque*; Val. Fl. 4.490-491 *... pallentia ... / ora senis*.

senecta: for the form see **3.8n.** above. For the rhetorical effect of the line-ending echo of *senecta* (**25**) and *senex* (**26**) see Wills (1996) 421-422.

26 For the formulation of the line, cf. Tib. 1.10.44 (sc.*liceat*) *temporis et prisci facta referre senem*. The fondness of old men for telling tales of the past is true to life and has a long literary history going back to Homer's Nestor (further references in Murgatroyd 290 on Tib. 1.10.43-44 and cf. Tib. 2.5.93-94 quoted below). Unlike the other indications of old age that would make Lygdamus ready to accept death, mentioned in **25**, the telling of tales to children seems to have positive connotations that would weaken his argument, unless we see in *prisca* a reference to an old-fashioned moral piety that is seen as no longer relevant; see Fordyce on Cat. 64.159,

Mankin (1995) 66 on Hor. *Epod.* 2.2 and Maltby 346 on Tib. 1.10.17. For *priscum tempus* see Ov. *Fast.* 1.197; Sil. 4.45.

pueris ... senex: the antithesis is stressed by the positioning of each word emphatically at the end of its hemistich. For the picture of the old man surrounded by affectionate children, in a more positive family context, cf. Tib. 1.7.55-56 (a birthday wish to Messalla) *at tibi succrescat proles, quae facta parentis / augeat et circa stat ueneranda senem*, 2.5.93-94 *nec taedebit auum paruo aduigilare nepoti, / balbaque cum puero dicere uerba senem*. Here the mention of children or grandchildren could suggest the wish for a relationship with Neaera or some other long-term partner that would result in offspring.

27 atque utinam: the particle *atque* adds emphasis to the wish introduced by *utinam*; a common combination in Propertius (9) and Ov. (24): *Am.* (1), *Her.* (2), *Rem.* (2), *Met.* (4), *Fast.* (1), *Trist.* (6), *Pont.* (6), *Ibis* (1), *Nux* (1), but rare in the *Corp. Tib.*, where it is found only here and **19.5.**

uano nequiquam: the pleonasm is characteristic of our author, particularly in the *Lygd.* poems, see **2.15n., 4.47-48n., 93n.** For the combination, cf. Cat. 64.111 (of the Minotaur) *nequiquam uanis iactantem cornua uentis*. For *nequiquam* as a higher style equivalent of *frustra*, see McKeown II 139 on Ov. *Am.* 1.6.27. The adverb is absent from Tib., who uses only *frustra* (5), and 16 of the 18 occurrences in Ovid occur in *Met.*, the other two being *Am.* 1.6.27 and *Fast.* 6.108; elsewhere in elegy only at Prop. 2.4.5 and 3.17.23: see further Axelson (1945) 128 n. 22.

terrear aestu: for *aestus* in the sense of 'fever', see *OLD aestus* 3 and cf. Cic. *Catil.* 1.31 *homines aegri morbo graui, cum aestu febrique iactantur*. Lygdamus wishes his fears were in vain (*nequiquam*) and his fever imaginary (*uano*). The phrase recalls the action of false dreams at **4.8** *et pauidas mentes falsa timere iubent*. The reading *torrear* found in some MSS and printed in the *ed. princ. min.* of 1472 would suggest being burned by the fires of passion as at Sen. *Phaed.* 362 *torretur* (sc. *Phaedra*) *aestu tacito*, but the details of **28** and the mention of the closeness of death in **5** would fit better with the idea of a physical disease, possibly malaria.

28 languent ... membra: the verb is often used in the sense of 'to be weak' as a result of disease, cf. Lucr. 6.1221 *languebant pleraque morbo*; Virg. *Georg.* 4.252 *tristi languebunt corpora morbo*, **[Tib.] 3.** *Sulpicia Cycle* **10.13** and, in the form *languentia* with *membra*, Lucr. 5.1007-1008 *languentia leto / membra* (6.797; Sil. 1.503-504, 10.274, 11.418; Stat. *Theb.* 6.589,); see *ThLL* 7(2) 921.30-36 and *OLD langueo* 1b.

ter quinos ... dies: the circumlocution *ter quinos* for *quindecim* arises from metrical necessity, cf. Manil. 3.576 *ter quinos, Capricorne, dares* (sc. *annos*). The use of the numeral adverb (*ter*) with distributive (*quinos*) is preferred in post-Augustan poetry, while the Augustan poets (and prose of all periods in high-style contexts) prefer a numeral adverb followed by a cardinal number, e.g. Ov. *Trist.* 1.1.117 *ter quinque uolumina*; see further Seibel (1909), H-Sz 214 para. 113a Zusatz. Our poet could be describing a recurrent malarial fever.

sed: for postponed *sed* (usually to second position) see **1.9n**. The placing of the conjunction in fourth position in its clause here is unique in Latin poetry. It emphasises the fact that Lygdamus' fever was real.

29-34 The poem ends with an appeal to the friends addressed in the opening (**1-4**), giving the elegy a clear ring-composition.

29 uobis: dative of agent; common originally only with perfect forms of the passive, its usage is broadened in Augustan poetry to include other forms of the passive, perhaps under Greek influence, cf. Virg. *Aen.* 1.440 *neque cernitur ulli* and see K-S II 1.324-325.

Tuscae: see **1n.** above on *Etruscis ... fontibus*. For the suggestion that *Tuscae ... lymphae* may refer not to a Tuscan spa, but to the river Tiber see Heyworth (2018) 77.

celebrantur: for the use of this verb in the sense of 'to honour', 'venerate' a deity, see *OLD celebro* 4 and cf. Ov. *Fast.* 4.865 *numina, uulgares, Veneris celebrate, puellae*, 6.775 *ite, deam laeti Fortem celebrate, Quirites*.

numina: see **4.53n.**

lymphae: see **3n.** above on *sacris ... lymphis*.

30 A poetic periphrasis describing the action of swimming; the line appears to have been inspired by a combination of Tib. 1.4.12 *hic placidam niueo pectore pellit aquam* and Prop. 1.11.11-12 (of Cynthia in Baiae) *aut teneat clausam tenui Teuthrantis in unda / alternae facilis cedere lympha manu*.

facilis ... unda: i.e water that yields to the swimmer, cf. Prop. 1.11.12 *facilis ... lympha* (quoted above). For the *iunctura* cf. Lucan 1.221-222 *molli tum cetera rumpit / turba uado faciles iam fracti fluminis undas*; Stat. *Silu.* 3.2.84 ... *an facili te praetermiserit unda*.

lenta ... manu: the adj. *lentus* is notoriously polysemic, cf. Fordyce on Cat. 64.183 and Lyne on *Ciris* 504 *lenta ... bracchia*. Here the meaning appears to be 'slow', 'leisurely', cf. *OLD lentus* 4, as at [Sen.] *Oct.* 820 *o lenta nimium militis nostri manus*. The *iunctura* occurs most frequently in Petr. where it refers to a 'gentle' or 'unhurried' motion of the hand: 18.5 *descendentes ab aure capillos meos lenta manu duxit*, 26.5, 138.2.

31 uiuite felices, memores et uiuite nostri: the whole line is reminiscent of Hor. *Carm.* 3.27.13-14 *sis licet felix, ubicumque mauis, / et memor nostri, Galatea, uiuas*. For the repeated *uiuite* in the same *sedes*, cf. Lucil. 275M. *uiuite lurcones, comedones, uiuite uentris*.

uiuite felices: the same line opening is found in Aeneas' farewell to Helen and Andromache at Virg. *Aen.* 3.493 *uiuite felices, quibus est fortuna peracta*. The phrase is common on funerary inscriptions where the dead urge the living to enjoy what is left of their lives, e.g. *CLE* 373.1 *uiuite felices quibus est data uita fruenda*.

memores ... nostri: the phrase is reminiscent of Tib.'s words to his departing patron at 1.3.2 *o utinam memores ipse cohorsque mei*, and Prop.'s words to Cynthia in Baiae at 1.11.5 *nostri cura subit, memores adducere noctes?*, both poems of considerable influence on the present elegy. Such appeals are recommended for prose propemptica by Menander Rhetor (398.26ff. Spengel) ἀξιώσεις αὐτὸν μεμνῆσθαι τῆς πάλαι συνηθείας ["you should expect him to remember your companionship of old"] and are a natural commonplace in partings, cf. Sappho 94.7-8 *PLF* χαίροισ᾽ ἔρχεο κἄμεθεν / μέμναισ᾽ ["depart in joy and remember me"]; Hor. *Carm.* 3.27.14 (quoted above); Ov. *Am.* 2.11.37 *uade memor nostri*, *Her.* 11.125 *uiue memor nostri*, *Met.* 13.380 *este mei memores* (14.730); Juv. 3.318 *ergo uale nostri memor*. On the propempticon tradition see **3.27n.** above. The phrase *nostri memores* occurs earlier **2.25**. On the use of the gen. *nostri* after *memores* see **2.25n.**

32 siue erimus seu ... uelint: for the combination *siue ... seu* cf. Cat. 67.25-26; Prop. 1.8B.44 *siue dies seu nox uenerit*. For the change of mood *erimus ... uelint* in a similar context cf. **7.207-209** *seu ... finget ... / ...seu ... sim ... / siue ... uehar* and see **7.206-210n.**

seu nos fata fuisse uelint: for *fata uolunt* + acc. + inf. cf. Prop. 1.6.30 *hanc me militiam fata subire uolunt*. For the use of the phrase with reference to death cf. Prop. 1.14.14 *dum me fata perire uolent*. For the pregnant sense of the perfect *fui* meaning 'to be dead', cf. Plaut. *Capt.* 516 *nunc illud est quom me fuisse quam esse ... mauelim*; Virg. *Aen.* 2.325-326 *... fuimus Troes, fuit Ilium et ingens / gloria Teucrorum*; Sil. 6.476 *fuit ille*.

33-34: As Tränkle 151 and N-A 456 point out ad loc., it would be normal in the case of illness, as inscriptional evidence shows, to pray and sacrifice not to Dis, god of the underworld, but to the healing gods [such as Asclepius and Hygieia (*Salus*), Valetudo, or, in imperial times, Isis]. In this case the choice of Dis must be motivated by Persephone's threat of death mentioned in **5** above. Offerings of black victims, milk and wine are mentioned elsewhere as appropriate for the gods of the underworld, cf. Ov. *Met.* 7.244-248 (of Medea) *sacra facit cultrosque in guttura uelleris atri / conicit et patulas perfundit sanguine fossas. / tum super inuergens liquidi carchesia uini / alteraque inuergens tepidi carchesia lactis / uerba simul fundit* and Sen. *Oed.* 563-567 *... sanguinem libat focis, / solitasque pecudes urit, et multo specum / saturat cruore. libat et niueum insuper / lactis liquorem: fundit et Bacchum manu / laeua*.

33 interea: 'meanwhile', i.e. while the outcome of his illness is uncertain.

nigras pecudes: while white victims were sacrificed to the gods of the upper world, black victims were appropriate for the gods of the underworld, cf. Serv. *Aen.* 3.118 *ut inferis nigras pecudes, superis albas immolant*. For the *iunctura* cf. Lucr. 3.52-53 *et nigras mactant pecudes et manibus diuis / inferias mittunt*; Virg. *Aen.* 3.120 *nigram Hiemi pecudem*, 5.736 (sc. *Sibylla*) *nigrarum multo pecudum te sanguine ducet*, 6.153 *duc nigras pecudes*; Sil. 13.404-406 *... mactare repostis / mos umbris, inquit, consueta piacula nigras / sub lucem pecudes*. Although *pecudes* can refer to domesticated animals in general, it was used especially of sheep, see *OLD pecus* 1b.

promittite: for the use of this verb in contexts of vows made to gods see *OLD promitto* 2b and cf. *CIL* 1.2231 *uotum quod promeisit ... pro filio*; Juv. 13.233-234 *... Laribus cristam promittere galli / non audent*.

Diti: on this name for Hades see **1.27-28n**.

34 niuei lactis: for the phrase see **2.20n**.

pocula mixta mero: the usual reference for *pocula mixta* is to cups of wine mixed with water, e.g. Ov. *Trist.* 5.3.50 *apponat labris pocula mixta suis*; Mart. 8.39.4 *et Ganymedea pocula mixta manu* and cf. Tib. 2.1.46 *mixtaque securo est sobria lympha mero*. The most obvious meaning here would be that Lygdamus' friends should make an offering of milk 'mixed with' wine. However, in view of the fact that such libations were normally separate ones of milk and wine, as in Ov. *Met.* 7.246-247 and Sen. *Oed.* 558-560 (quoted above in **33-34n.**), Tränkle 151, followed by N-A 457-458, interprets *mixta* in the sense of 'together with', an attenuated meaning found occasionally in Ovid, e.g. *Met.* 8. 674 *hic nux, hic mixta est rugosis carica palmis*. This could well be correct, especially as the wine used in such ceremonies had to be unmixed, see *mero* **n.** below. However, for a mixture of milk with *sapa* (unfermented grape juice boiled down to triple strength) being drunk in a ceremony for Pales see Fantham on Ov. *Fast.* 4.780.

mero: the adj. originally means 'pure', and then, through the ellipse of *uinum*, the word is substantivised in the sense of 'pure wine'. The Romans generally drank wine mixed with water (cf. **6.58** below), but wine for sacrifices had to be 'neat'; cf. Fest. 474.31ff. L. *spurcum uinum est quod sacris adhiberi non licet ... cui aqua admixta est defrutumue, aut igne tactum est, mustumue antequam deferuescat*; Plin. *Nat.* 14.119.

Poem 6

The setting of the final *Lygd.* poem is a symposium in which the poet, at a drinking party with his friends, attempts to drown his sorrows of love in wine. His two main elegiac models are Prop. 3.17, a hymn to Bacchus, which ends with a prayer to be freed from the slavery of love, and Tib. 1.2, which opens (1-6) with the poet asking for neat wine to cure the miseries of his affair with Delia. There may also be some significance in the fact that Propertius' slave Lygdamus is put in charge of the wine *ad cyathos* at Prop.'s party for Phyllis and Teia at Prop. 4.8.37-38 and is accused of poisoning Cynthia's wine at Prop. 4.7.36 (see Gen. Intro., section 2.2.1). The symposium has a long tradition in Greek poetry, going back to Anacr. 356, 396 *PMG* and there is a detailed description of a Greek symposium in Xenophanes fr. 1 West, which contains many of the features found in this poem, such as perfume and garlands (**63-64**), plentiful supplies of wine (**5-6, 62**) and water for mixing (**58**), exhortation to friends to drink (**9-10**), and invocation to Bacchus (**1-4**). In Roman literature symposiastic themes are found in Cat. 27, and, in the context of *carpe diem*, Hor. *Carm.* 2.3.13-

16 and 2.11.13-14. Drowning general sorrows in wine is a topos found already, e.g., in Alcaeus 346.3-4 *PLF*; Theogn. 879-883; cf. Hor. *Carm.* 1.18.4 (with N-H ad loc.), but drowning specifically the sorrows of love in wine (hinted at perhaps in Anacr. 356 *PMG*) is more typical of Hellenistic epigram, cf. *AP* 12.50 (Asclep.), 12.49 (Meleag.) and see Giangrande (1967) 129 n. 1. It was Meleager's epigram 12.49 that influenced Tib. 1.2.1-4 [see Maltby (1995)] and the theme recurrs in Roman elegy at Tib. 1.5.37-38; Prop. 3.17.3-4. In Ovid there is evidence of an older tradition in which wine in moderation acts as an aphrodisiac, *Ars* 1.229-244 [cf. Hom. *Od.* 21.295 (of the Centaurs); Eur. *Bacch.* 773; Ter. *Eun.* 733; Prop. 1.3.14], but taken in excess can lead to impotence: *Rem.* 805-806 *uina parant animum Veneri, nisi plurima sumas, / et stupeant multo corda sepulta mero*. Possible links with Gallan elegy are more apparent in this poem than elsewhere in the *Lygd.* group see **3n.** *patera medicante,* **7n.** *labores* and **8n.** *alitibus,* **35-36n.** *sollicitis.* The choice of a symposiatic theme with which to end this group of poems perhaps reflects an intention on our author's part to move away from elegy towards a type of poetry closer to Horace's *Carmina* and Greek lyric. The contest between Bacchus and Amor with which the poem opens (**1-4**) may suggest at a metapoetic level a contest between lyric and elegy. In certain parts of the poem our author reverts to his elegiac mode, especially in **33-36** and **53-56**, but by the end of the poem **57-64** lyric is in the ascendancy. On the contrast between serious elegy and playful lyric see Ov. *Her.* 15.5-8 quoted in **33-36n.** below and cf. **4n., 13n., 51-52n., 53-56n.** and **57-58n.**; see further the discussions in Fabre Serris (2009) 166-167; also Bessone (2003). On the inclusion of a 'guest' genre within the framework of a 'host' genre in the closural poem of a collection see Conte [(1986) 100-129] and Harrison [(2007) 17 and 59-74] on the inclusion of Gallan elegy within Virgilian pastoral in Virg. *Ecl.* 10.

The structure of the poem is somewhat confused, with sudden changes of mood on the part of the speaker, intended perhaps to reflect the irrational outpourings of a man under the influence of drink:

1-4 Kletic hymn to Bacchus who is asked to appear and help cure the poet's love sufferings with wine.

5-6 Appeal to slave to pour plentiful wine.

7-8 Appeal to cares to disappear.

9-12 Appeal to friends to join him in the drinking.

13-17 The powers of Amor and Bacchus compared.

17-24 A further appeal for his friends to drink, followed by the warning that while Bacchus spares those who honour him he is angry with abstainers.

25-30 A prayer that Bacchus' anger should be deflected on to Neaera is quickly withdrawn. Neaera should be happy, though no longer an object of Lygdamus' care.

31-32 A further appeal for his friends to enjoy the feast with him.

33-36 It is hard to feign happiness when one's thoughts are sad.

37-52 Self-address. Rid yourself of cares and learn from Ariadne's example not to worry about the false oaths of lovers.

53-56 Address to Neaera. Though she is unfaithful, he still loves her.

57 Even Bacchus fell in love.

57-64 Return to the symposium theme. Lygdamus calls for wine, perfume and garlands. He will not spend the night sighing for the absent Neaera.

As often in poems **1-6** (see **2 headnote** and **3 headnote** above and cf. **5.1n.**), a link is formed between the end of the previous elegy, in this case with its last word, *mero* **5.34** and the theme of the present poem, a drinking party, beginning with an address to the god of wine. In addition, the real disease which threatened Lygdamus in **5.27-28** is picked up at the beginning of the present poem **6.3**, with a request for Bacchus to cure his disease of love *aufer ...meum patera medicante dolorem*.

1 Candide Liber: the adj. refers to the god's youthful radiance, cf. Hor. *Carm.* 1.18.11 *candide Bassareu* (with N-H 234 ad loc.); Ov. *Fast.* 3.772 *candide Bacche*; Sen. *Oed.* 508 *candida formosi uenerabimur ora Lyaei*. Further examples of the adj. applied to gods and goddesses are listed at *ThLL* 3.241.36-46 and cf. *candor* applied to Apollo at **4.29** above. *Liber* is another name for Bacchus, found also at **19** below, along with *Lyaeus* (**2.19**) and *Lenaeus* (**6.38**); it means something like 'Liberator', from the liberating effect of wine, cf. references in Maltby *LALE* 337 sv *Liber* and see **2.19n**. Originally an Italic god of nature, he was later associated with Dionysus and became god of vineyard workers and hence Bacchus (see Schur *RE* 13.68ff.).

ades: a regular formular in kletic hymns, calling for a god to appear, e.g. Cat. 62.5 *Hymen ades*; Maecen. 5.1 (Courtney = 188.1 Hollis) *ades ... O Cybebe*; Tib. 1.7.49 *huc ades* (to Osiris /Bacchus); Ov. *Rem.* 704 *Phoebe saluber, ades*; Sen. *Oed.* 405-407 *huc ades ... / ... / ... Bacche, Phaed.* 412 *Hecate triformis ... ades*; **[Tib.] 3**. *Sulpicia Cycle* **10.2** *huc ades ... Phoebe* and see **3.33-34n.** above. On the conventions of the kletic hymn see Menander Rhetor 334.25-336.4; Norden (1913) 143-163, N-H 343-344 on Hor. *Carm.* 1.30, Cairns (1972) 192-196.

1-2 sic sit tibi mystica uitis / ... sic hedera tempora uincta feras: the well-known religious formula, consisting of *sic* + optative subjunctive, following petitions (in the imperative), offering an inducement, usually addressed to deities, is attested first in Latin at Cat. 17.5-7 (addressed in this case to a town) *sic tibi bonus ex tua pons libidine fiat, / ... / munus hoc mihi ... da*; see further Maltby (2002) 216-217 on Tib. 1.4.1-6, McKeown III 284 on Ov. *Am.* 2.13.11-12, Ingleheart (2010) 167 on Ov. *Trist.* 2.159-160, K-S II 1.191. For the two *sic* clauses in anaphora in this context cf. Tib. 2.5.121-122 *adnue*; *sic tibi sint intonsi, Phoebe, capilli, / sic tua perpetuo sit tibi casta soror*. A similarly phrased appeal to Liber to bring help is found at Ov. *Trist.* 5.3.35-36 *fer, bone Liber, opem*: *sic annua degrauet ulmum / uitis et incluso plena sit uua mero*.

sic sit tibi: normally the personal pronoun comes immediately after *sic*, as in Cat. 17.5; Tib. 2.5.121-122 (quoted above). Exceptions are rare: here, Tib. 1.4.1 *sic umbrosa tibi*; Ov. *Met.* 8.857 *sic sit tibi, Trist.* 5.3.35-36 (quoted above) and Petr. 61.2 *sic felicem me uideas*.

mystica uitis: the adj. (a Greek loan-word) is rare, occurring first at Acc. *Trag.* 687-688 *mystica ad dextram uada / praeteruecti* on which Varro *Ling.* 7.19.1 comments *mystica a mysteriis*, and is applied to objects involved in secret cults; so in the context of the Eleusinian mysteries at Virg. *Georg.* 1.166 *mystica uannus Iacchi* and Ov. *Her.* 2.42 *taediferae mystica sacra deae* (of mystic marriage rites). De Melo [(2019) II 920] derives both *mysticus* and *mysterium* from the Greek μύστης ["an initiate of the Eleusinian mysteries"]. Whereas *mysticus* is restricted to poetry, *mysterium* occurs in prose (e.g. Cic. *Tusc.* 1.29). We have no direct evidence of the use of the vine in Bacchic mysteries, but such a practice seems quite probable, cf. Hor. *Carm.* 3.25.18-20 *... dulce periculum est, / o Lenaee, sequi deum / cingentem uiridi tempora pampino*, 4.8.33-4 *ornatus uiridi tempora pampino / Liber*; Ov. *Met.* 6.591-592 (of Procne preparing for the biennial festival of Bacchus) *ritibus instruitur furialiaque* *accipit arma*; / *uite caput tegitur*. Boris Kayachev suggests to me here a possible wordplay between *mysticus* and *mustum* (implied).

2 hedera: ivy was sacred to Bacchus because the nymphs of Nysa covered his cradle in ivy leaves to hide Jupiter and Semele's child from his stepmother, Juno: Ov. *Fast*. 3.767-770 ... *hedera est gratissima Baccho*: / *hoc quoque cur ita sit, dicere nulla mora est*. / *Nysiadas nymphas puerum quaerente nouerca* / *hanc frondem cunis opposuisse ferunt*, on which see Heyworth (2019) 240 ad loc. For his ivy crown cf. Pind. *Ol*. 2.27 παῖδα κισσοφόρον ["ivy bearing child"]; Ov. *Fast*. 6.483 *Bacche, racemiferos hedera redimite capillos*; Sen. *Oed*. 413-416 *te* (sc. *Bacchum*) *decet cingi comam floribus uernis*, / *te caput Tyria cohibere mitra* / *hederaue mollem* / *bacifera religare frontem*. On its supposed efficacy against drunkenness cf. Isid. *Etym*. 17.9.23 *antipharmacum ebrietatis est si qui potus hedera coronetur* and see further Mayer (2012) 59 on Hor. *Carm*. 1.1.29.

tempora uincta feras: for *fero*, in place of the more common *gero* (the reading of G and H), in the sense of 'wear' cf Ov. *Pont*. 2.2.80 (of Augustus as *triumphator*) *tempora Phoebea uirgine nexa tulit*. The phrase *tempora uincta* is not found elsewhere; the normal construction for these expressions is for *tempora* as an internal accusative after *uinctus* and sim.: Tib. 2.5.5 *triumphali deuinctus tempora lauro*; Virg. *Aen*. 5.269 *euincti tempora taenis*, 8.286 *euincti temora ramis*, 12.120 *uerbena tempora uincti*; Ov. *Her*. 6.44 *sertis tempora uinctus*; [Ov.] *Epiced. Drusi* 334 *fronde triumphali tempora uinctus*.

3 The line is transmitted in all MSS as *aufer et ipse meum pariter medicando dolorem*. The short *-o* in *medicando* would be normal in post-Augustan verse, but *pariter* would make the sense very awkward ('appear ... and at the same time take away'). Of the many suggested conjectures two commend themselves in particular: (1) Birt's *patera medicare*, where a new sentence would start with *aufer* and *et* would join the two imperatives *aufer* and *medicare*; (2) Waardenburg's *patera medicante*, which I print, where a delayed *et* would join the two imperatives *ades* and *aufer*, leaving the two *sic* clauses (**1-2**) in parenthesis.

aufer ... dolorem: for *dolor* used specifically of the sorrows of love see **2.3n**. For wine as a cure for such sorrows see **2 headnote** and cf. Tib. 1.2.1 *adde merum uinoque nouos compesce dolores*, 5.37-38 *saepe ego temptaui curas depellere uino*, / *at dolor in lacrimas uerterat omne merum*; Prop. 3.17.3-4 (in a hymn to Bacchus) *tu potes insanae Veneris compescere flatus*, / *curarumque tuo fit medicina mero*. For love as a disease, see Eur. *Hipp.* 35, 283, 394 etc.; Theocr. *Id.* 2.85-90, 11.1ff.; Plaut. *Cist.* 71, *Mil.* 1272; Caecil. *Com.* 262; Cat. 76.25; Tib. 2.3.13-14, 2.5.110 with Maltby; Prop. 2.1.58, 3.24.17f. with Fedeli; Ov. *Am.* 1.10.9-10 with McKeown, *Rem.* 81, 115, La Penna (1951) 207, Grassmann (1966) 94ff., Giangrande (1990) 121-123. For the link with the real disease in **5.27-28** see **5 headnote.**

patera medicante: for *medicare* here of love cf. Nemes. *Ecl.* 2.28 *medicare furores*, an extension of the use of *medicina* applied to remedies for love, which may have begun with Gallus, cf. Virg. *Ecl.* 10.60 *tamquam haec sit nostri medicina furoris*, and becomes especially characteristic of Propertius, e.g. Prop. 1.5.28, 10.18, 2.14.16. For further possible Gallan links in this poem see **7n.** below on *labores*. If the conjectural *patera* is correct, it would be the equivalent here of *pocula*, the term used most commonly in poetry for cups of wine (see **5** below) and medicine e.g. Mart. 9.94.1-2 *Santonica medicata dedit mihi pocula uirga* / ... *Hippocrates*. Normally *patera* refers to a shallow bowl, often of gold or silver, used mostly in libations and sacred rites. The statistics for its use [Virg. *Georg.* (1), *Aen.* (12); Ov. *Met.* (3), *Fast.* (1) and Stat. *Ach.* (1), *Theb.* (2), absent from Virg. *Ecl.*, Ovid's amatory works and Stat. *Silu.*] suggest an elevated word. Its single occurrence elsewhere in elegy at Prop. 4.6.85 *sic noctem patera, sic ducam carmine* is in the context of a drinking party, which could well have influenced the choice of word here.

4 tuo ... munere: i.e. wine, as at **17-18** below, *Bacchi / munera*.

cecidit ... uictus Amor: a military image, Love often falls defeated by wine. For *cado* in military contexts see *ThLL* 3.23.9-24.58. For battles between Amor and Bacchus cf. Ov. *Ars* 1.231-232 *saepe illic positi teneris adducta lacertis / purpureus Bacchi cornua pressit Amor* with Hollis 84; Kenney [(1959) 244-246] discusses the Greek background, and suggests the Ovidian couplet could derive from a painting of Bacchus and Amor wrestling. For *cecidit ... Amor* cf. Cat. 11.21-22 *meum ... amorem / qui illius culpa cecidit*; [Sen.] *Oct.* 564 *quem* (sc. *Amorem*) *si fouere atque alere desistas, cadit*. For *cecidit ... uictus* cf. Val. Fl. 1.300 *ubi uicta graui ceciderunt lumina somno*. For *uictus Amor* cf. Tib. 1.5.60 *donis uincitur omnis amor* (a reversal of Virgil's famous *omnia uincit Amor* at *Ecl.* 10.69); Ov. *Rem.* 260 (also at the line-end) *nec fugiet uiuo sulphure uictus Amor*, 462 *successore nouo uincitur omnis amor*. A second meaning of *cado*, which relates to feelings that wane (Pichon 96, *ThLL* 3.26.43-27.42), is also operative in this passage, as in Cat. 11.21-22; [Sen.] *Oct.* 564 (quoted above) and Prop. 2.3.2 *cecidit spiritus ille tuus*. For the possibly metapoetic relevance of a battle between Bacchus and Amor, representing an attempt on our author's part to move from elegy to lyric, see **headnote** to the poem above and **13n.**, **33-36n.**, **51-52n.**, **53-56n.** and **57-58n.**

5 care puer: the order to a slave boy (Lat. *puer*, Gk. παῖς) to pour wine in abundance is a commonplace of symposiastic poetry, going back in Greek to Anacreon: ... φέρ' ἡμῖν, ὦ παῖ / κελέβην 356 *PMG* ["bring the wine-jar, boy"], ... φέρ' οἶνον, ὦ παῖ 396 *PMG* ["bring wine, boy"]. See further N-H 421 on Hor. *Carm.* 1.38.1-8 and Mankin 179 on Hor. *Epod.* 9.33 and cf. Hipp. fr. 13.2 W.; Alcaeus fr. 362.2 *PLF*; Cat. 27.1; Hor. *Carm.* 1.29.8, 38.1, 2.3.14, 11.18, 3.14.17; Mart. 9.33.1. The phrase *care puer* is attested from Virg. *Aen.* 8.581 (Evander to his departing son) and occurs mainly in poets of the late first century AD: Val. Fl. 4.53; Sil. 4.475, 6.53; Stat. *Silu.* 3.4.60 (of Earinus, cupbearer to Domitian), 5.5.79, *Ach.* 1.252, 237.

madeant ... pocula: the cups should be 'soaked', in other words filled to the brim, the opposite of *pocula sicca* 'dry', i.e. 'empty', cups at **18** below. The verb *madere* and its related adj. *madidus* are used in poetry to suggest drunkenness from Plautus on. Cf. Tib. 2.1.29-30 *non festa luce madere / est rubor*, 2.8 *madeatque mero*, 5.87 *madidus Baccho ... pastor* and for statistics on the mainly poetic use of both words see McKeown II 152 on *Am.* 1.6.56 (*madere*) and II 369 on *Am.* 1.4.11 (*madidus*). The verb is normally applied to persons drinking, but for its use of an inanimate object, as here, cf. Prop. 2.33B.39 *largius effuso madeat tibi mensa Falerno*.

generoso ... Baccho: the use of the adj. to denote 'noble', 'good quality' wine is attested from Hor. *Epist.* 1.15.18 *ad mare cum ueni, generosum et lene requiro*. For its use with the metonymic *Bacchus* in the same metrical *sedes* cf. Ov. *Met.* 4.765 *postquam epulis functi generosi munere Bacchi*. For the metonymy cf. *Bacchi / munera* at **17-18** below.

pocula Baccho: the same line-end is found at Val. Fl. 1.260.

6 prona ... manu: lit. 'with hand facing downwards' (see *OLD pronus* 2d), i.e. 'freely', 'generously'.

funde: 'pour'; although the context here is the secular one of a symposium, the fact that the verb is a technical term, used, like *patera* (**3**), in relation to libations to the gods, lends an added solemnity here, which is in keeping with the religious tone of the opening prayer to Bacchus. For its use in libations cf. Hor. *Carm.* 1.31.1-3 (libation to Apollo) *quid* *dedicatum poscit Apollinem / uates*? *quid orat, de patera nouum / fundens liquorem?* and on its use as a technical term cf. Serv. *Aen.* 6.244 *fundere est supina manu libare, quod fit in sacris supernis.*

Falerna: sc. *uina*. A strong Campanian wine, which improved with age (Varro *Rust*. 1.65, Schöffel 395 on Mart. 8.45.3). Its price was four times that of ordinary wine in a Pompeian *taberna* (cf. *CLE* 931) and it was considered by Pliny to be of the highest quality: *Nat.* 14.62 *nec ulli nunc uino maior auctoritas*. Falernian is the most commonly named wine in elegy (Tib. 1.9.34, 2.1.27; Prop. 2.33B.39, 4.6.73).

7 ite procul: see above **4.3n**. The use of this originally liturgical formula, also found at **25** and **52**, again adds to the religious atmosphere of the symposium, cf. **6n**. *funde* above. For the repetition of *ite* in the first and fifth feet, a feature mainly of pastoral, cf. Virg. *Ecl.* 1.74 *ite meae, felix quondam pecus, ite capellae*, 7.44 *ite domum ... ite iuuenci*, 10.77 *ite domum ... ite capellae*; Calp. *Ecl.* 2.55 *ite procul, sacer est locus, ite profani* and see Wills (1996) 100, 111. The bucolic diaeresis is also a pastoral feature.

durum ... genus: the phrase occurs from Virg. on, always elsewhere in relation to men: Virg. *Georg.* 1.63 *unde homines nati, durum genus, Aen.* 9.603 *durum a stirpe genus*; Liv. 27.48.10 *Ligures durum in armis genus*; Ov. *Met.* 1.414 *inde genus durum sumus experiensque laborum.*

curae: either cares in general or, more likely in the present context, the cares of love. On the function of wine in relieving cares see Mankin (1995) 181 on Hor. *Epod.* 9.37-38 (with a long list of parallels) and Thomas (2011) 235 on Hor. *Carm.* 4.12.19-20, Mayer (2012) 104 on Hor. *Carm.* 1.7.31.

labores: for the various connotations of this word see **4.65-66n**. Like *curae*, it is likely here to refer to the cares of love, for which see Pichon 180. For its use in the context of drinking to relieve one's cares, cf. Hor. *Carm.* 1.7.17-19 *tu sapiens finire memento / tristitiam uitaeque labores / molli, Plance, mero*. Both *curae* and *labores* may, on the evidence of Virg. *Ecl.* 10, have Gallan links: for *cura* cf. *Ecl.* 10.22 *tua cura Lycoris*, on which see Ross (1975) 68-69, and for *labores* cf. *Ecl.* 10.64 *non illum nostri possunt mutare labores*. The same *Eclogue*, dedicated to Gallus, has repeated *ite* (*Ecl.* 10.77 – see on *ite procul* above) and *medicina* applied to the madness of love (*Ecl.* 10.64 see **3n**. *patera medicante*).

8 fulserit: this is a reading of the *recentiores* for the unintelligible *pulserit* of A. For the perfect subjunctive in a jussive sense 'let him shine' see K-S II 1.185. For its use of the sun as a symbol of happiness cf. Cat. 8.3 *fulsere quondam candidi tibi soles*.

niueis ... alitibus: *ales*, like *auis*, can be used metonymically, as here, of an omen (see *OLD ales*² 2). For the use of *niueus* in the sense of 'happy', 'lucky' see **3.25-26n.** on *niueam ... lucem*. On the poetic register and distribution of *niueus*, which is especially frequent in Tib. (5), Virg. (17), Ov. (46) and **[Tib.]** 3 (*Lygd.*) **1-6** (7), see McKeown III 18 on Ov. *Am.* 2.1.24 *reuocant niueos solis euntis equos*. The sun's shining is to be accompanied by good omens. For birds which are not white bringing bad omens cf. Ov. *Am.* 3.12.1-2 *quis fuit ille dies, quo tristia semper amanti / omina non albae concinuistis aues*? On *alitibus* as a polysyllabic pentameter ending with possible Gallan links see Cairns (2006) 173 and cf. Prop. 1.16.46 *et matutinis obstrepit alitibus*.

Delius: on this epithet for Apollo see **4.79n**. Here it functions as a learned variant on *Phoebus* (cf. **4.21**) for Apollo in his role as the sun. For the close links between Bacchus, the poem's addressee and Apollo see **4.44** above with **nn.** ad loc. The use of *fulserit* and *niueis* may contain a play on the god's name < δῆλος 'bright'.

9 uos modo ... faueatis: for the emphatic request with pronoun + *modo* + subjunctive cf. Virg. *Aen.* 2.16o *tu modo promissis maneas*, 7.263-265 *ipse modo Aeneas ... / ... / adueniat* and see **4.64n.** on its equivalent: pronoun + *modo* + imperative.

modo: for the scansion see **4.64n.**

proposito ... faueatis: for the phrase cf. Ov. *Fast.* 1.468 *propositoque faue*; Sen. *Dial.* 2.9.4 *faueamus, obsecro uos, huic proposito*; Plin. *Paneg.* 95.3 *uos modo fauete huic proposito*. The noun *propositum* is rare in verse, except in Ovid 12 (full statistics in N-A 479 ad loc.), and is not found in Virg., Tib. or Prop.

dulces ... amici: the phrase implies a considerable emotional attachment, cf. Cic. *Amic.* 90.5 *eos amicos, qui dulces uideantur*; Hor. *Serm.* 1.3.69, 139-140, *Epist.* 1.7.12; Ov. *Pont.* 1.8.31 *uos animo, dulces, reminiscor, amici*; Pers. 5.23 *Cornute, ... dulcis amice*, amplified in the case of Cat. by the use of a diminutive: 30.2 *iam te nil miseret, dure, tui dulcis amiculi?*

10 neue neget quisquam me duce se comitem: The idea is that none of his friends should fail to follow Lygdamus' lead as master of the drinking party. For the hierarchical juxtaposition of *dux-comes* 'leader-follower' cf. Cat. 63.15 (Attis to the Gallae) *sectam meam exsecutae duce me mihi comites*; Ov. *Her.* 14.106 (of Io) *tu tibi dux comiti, tu comes ipsa duci*.

neue: the use of *neue* (*neu*) to introduce a prohibition after a positive command is poetic and restricted to prayer-style, cf. Hor. *Carm.* 1.2.50-52 *hic ames dici pater atque princeps, / neu sinas Medos equitare inultos, / te duce, Caesar* (with N-H on 51 *neu*). In prose *neue* is always preceded by a negative (K-S II 1.193).

me duce: originally a military image (cf. *te duce* Hor. *Carm.* 1.2.52 quoted above, and *me duce* at Virg. *Aen.* 10.92; Ov. *Am.* 2.12.13 with McKeown III 270 ad loc.), used here of the *magister* or *arbiter bibendi*, the master of ceremonies at a drinking party, who decided the strength and quality of wine, the proportion of water, the number and type of toasts etc., cf. Cat. 27.3 with Fordyce; Cic. *Verr.* 2.5.28; Hor. *Serm.* 2.6.67ff. with Muecke, *Carm.* 1.4.18 *regna uini* with N-H 71, 2.7.25-26 *arbitrum / ... bibendi* with N-H 121, 4.1.31 *nec certare iuuat mero* with Thomas 99.

11 uini certamen mite: the reference is to a drinking competition as referred to at Plin. *Nat.* 36.156 *potores in certamine bibendi* and Cic. *Flacc.* 92 *magnum erat ei certamen propositum ... nam iste unus totam Asiam magnitudine poculorum bibendoque superauit*. Horace mentions such a contest where the forfeit for not drinking enough was to become the master of ceremonies: *Serm.* 2.2.123 *post hoc ludus erat culpa potare magistra*; elsewhere he mentions another drinking party where the mad rules of the *magister bibendi* would not apply: *Serm.* 2.6.68-70 *... solutus / legibus insanis, seu quis capit acria fortis / pocula, seu modicis uuescit laetius*. For the oxymoron *certamen mite*, cf. *seruitium mite* of love's slavery at Prop. 2.20.20. The epithet here simply signifies that wine drinking is a pleasurable activity, especially for those whose pain Bacchus is relieving. For Bacchus himself as *mitis* cf. Ov. *Met.* 11.134 *mite deum numen: Bacchus peccasse fatentem / restituit* and for the association of the adj. with Amor see **13n.** below.

recusat: on the distribution of this verb in poetry, see **4.73n.**

12 fallat ... tecto ... dolo: for the phrasing cf. Sil. 3.233-234 (*Tyria pubes*) *docilis fallendi et nectere tectos / numquam tarda dolos*, the only other occurrence of the phrase *tectus dolus*. For *doli* in the context of infidelity, cf. Tib. 1.9.24 *scit deus occultos qui uetat esse dolos*, 54, *rideat assiduis uxor inulta dolis*; Prop. 4.7.16; Ov. *Am.* 2.19.44; *Dig.* 48.5.13 *ne quis posthac stuprum adulterium facito sciens dolo malo* (referring to Augustus' *Lex Iulia de adulteriis coercendis*) and see Pichon 133. The combination of *fallere* with *dolus* is found earlier at Ter. *And.* 492-493 *itane tandem idoneus / tibi uideor esse quem tam aperte fallere incipias dolis*? and Virg. *Aen.* 1.683-684 *tu faciem illius ... falle dolo*. For the curse threatening a wife's infidelity N-A ad loc. compares *Priap.* 47.3-4 *illius uxor, aut amica, riualem / lasciuiendo languidum precor reddat*; cf. also Tib. 1.9.53-54 *at te qui puerum donis corrumpere es ausus / rideat assiduis uxor inulta dolis*.

eum: on the rarity of this pronoun in elegy, see **4.94n.** *is*.

cara puella: cf. Prop. 2.8.1 *eripitur nobis iam pridem cara puella*; the phrase occurs elsewhere at Tib. 1.2.95; Hor. *Epist.* 1.18.74; Prop. 3.4.15, **[Tib.] 3.** *Lygd.* **2.1, 4.51-52**; Mart. 2.48.6.

13-17 The difficulty here is to identify the god or gods referred to by the triple *ille* in **13** and **15**. The repeated demonstrative is characteristic of the sacral style, when expressing the powers of a god, the so-called 'Er- Stil'; see Norden (1913) 163ff. It would normally refer to the same god; so Virg. *Ecl.* 1.6-9 triple *ille* (referring to the unnamed *deus*); Tib. 1.2.17-22 (with Maltby 160) triple *illa* referring to Venus, 2.1.73-75 triple *hic* referring to Cupid; Hor. *Carm.* 1.21.13 (with N-H 257) double *hic* referring to Apollo; Prop. 1.14.17-19 triple *illa* referring to Venus; Ov. *Am.* 1.6.7-8 (with McKeown II 127) double *ille* referring to Cupid; *Ciris* 135-138 double *ille* referring to Amor. Double *ille* can refer to alternatives, 'the one ... the other', as in **7.50-53** (Nestor and Ulysses), but in that case the two possibilities are clearly named beforehand. If *dites* of A and *Flor. Gall.* is read in **13**, then the first *ille* here could refer to Bacchus on the grounds that he enriches men's souls, cf. Hor. *Epist.* 1.15.18-20 *ad mare cum ueni, generosum et lene requiro / quod curas abigat, quod cum spe diuite manet / in uenas animumque meum*. The second *ille* (**13**) would then refer to Amor, who by contrast crushes the proud and subjects them to a mistress, and the third *ille* (**15**) would revert to Bacchus, contrasted with Amor named in **17** (so N-A 482-483 ad loc.). The problem with this interpretation of a contrast between Bacchus and Amor is that it would require the couplet **15-16** to refer to Bacchus. This is not impossible (see **15n.** *Armenias tigres* below), but seems unlikely in view of the fact that the closely related lines from *Ciris* 135-136 ... *ille etiam Poenos domitare leones / et ualidas docuit uiris mansuescere tigris* clearly refer to Amor. I would therefore accept Lipsius' emendation of *dites* to *mites* in **13**, which would make all the clauses refer to the traditional taming power of love, on which see Lyne [(2007) 32-33], leaving Amor as the subject of the whole passage, in accordance with normal sacral style. Although the poem began with an address to Bacchus, and the audience could expect him to be addressed here (see **13n.** below), that god falls into the background after **5**, and a reference to Amor at **13ff.** is prepared by his mention in **4** and by the amatory content of **12**.

13-14 ferocem / contudit: the adj., like *ferus*, applies to those who rebel against the slavery of love, cf. Tib. 1.5.5-6 *ure ferum et torque, libeat ne dicere quicquam / magnificum posthac*, 2.6.5 *ure, puer* (sc. Amor*)*, *quaeso, tua qui ferus otia liquit*; Prop. 2.3.49-50 *sic primo iuuenes trepidant in amore feroces, / dehinc domiti faciles aequa et iniqua ferunt*; Ov. *Her.* 4.165 (Phaedra to Hippolytus) *flecte feros animos*; see further Pichon 145. The verb *contundere* in the sense of 'crush', 'suppress' belongs to high epic style: cf. Enn. *Ann.* 385-386 Sk. *quae me fortuna fero sic / contudit ... bello*, 520-521 Sk. *uiresque ualentes / contundit crudelis hiems*; Acc. *Trag.* 174 *ferum feroci contundendum imperiost*; Virg. *Aen.* 1.263-264 *populosque feroces / contundet*; Ov. *Ars* 1.12 [*Chiron*] *animos placida contudit arte feros* and, in an erotic context, Prop. 1.1.10 [*Milanion*] *saeuitiam durae contudit Iasidos*.

13 ille ... deus: the identity of the god is not immediately made clear. Initially the god here might be expected to be Bacchus, as he is the god addressed in the opening, but making minds gentle is more appropriate for the gods of love; see **13-17n.** above. The suspicion that the god referred to is Amor is strengthened by the erotic content of **13-14**, while the taming of tigers and lions (**15-16**) could apply to both gods, only with the naming of Amor in **17** does the addressee of the whole section become clear. On this Alexandrian technique of surprising or deceiving the audience see Cairns (1979) 166-167 and Maltby (2002) 241 on Tib. 1.5. The confusion between the two gods is clearly intentional on our author's part and reflects the poem's constant vacillation between elegiac and symposiastic lyric modes – see further **headnote** above, **33-36n., 51-52n., 53-56n., 57-58n.**

mites animos: this conjecture by Lipsius for *dites* of A and *Flor. Gall.* is to be preferred as being more appropriate to the aretalogy of Amor, see **13-17n.** above. For the *iunctura* cf. Ov. *Pont.* 3.2.103 *adde quod est animus semper tibi mitis*. It is particularly characteristic of the younger Seneca: *Dial.* 4.10.5, 15.3, 5.22.4, *Clem.* 1.7.2, 25.1.

14 dominae ... in arbitrium: the reference is to the slavery of the lover to his mistress, *seruitium amoris*, on which see **4.65-66n.** *uerbera posse pati*. For the expression here cf. Tib. 2.3.79 *ad imperium dominae sulcabimus agros*; Prop. 4.1B.143 *illius* (sc. *dominae*) *arbitrio noctem lucemque uidebis*; Ov. *Ars* 1.504 *arbitrio dominae tempora perde tuae*. For *domina* as the regular word for the elegiac mistress see Pichon 134, **10.12, 19.22**; for its use of a wife, see **4.74** above. The noun *arbitrium* in the sense of 'power', 'control' (*OLD arbitrium* 5) is mainly prosaic, cf. Sen. *Dial.* 6.26.3 *ille in alieni percussoris uenit arbitrium*, *Epist.* 83.22 *haec* (sc. *ebrietas*) *contumacissimos et iugum recusantes in alienum egit arbitrium*; in elegy it is rare except in Ovid (16): *Her.* (6), *Ars* (1), *Rem.* (2), *Fast.* (4), *Trist.* (2), *Pont.* (1); otherwise only Prop. 4.1B.143, **[Tib.] 3** here and at *Sulpicia* **14.8**.

15-16 For the motif of love conquering wild animals, cf. Ov. *Fast.* 4.103 *deposita sequitur taurus feritate iuuencam*. For the specific detail of Amor taming lions and tigers cf. the clearly related passage *Ciris* 135-136 quoted in **13-17n.** above. For lions and tigers in a similarly erotic context, see Ov. *Ars* 2.183 *obsequium tigrisque domat Numidasque leones*. Artistic representations show Amor riding lions or driving a chariot pulled by lions, see e.g. *LIMC* III (1986) 260ff., 335ff. and 388, which depicts a chariot race between four Erotes, one of which is drawn by tigers and another by lions.

15 Armenias tigres: Armenian tigresses are mentioned in Latin first by Virg. at *Ecl.* 5.29-30 *Daphnis et Armenias curru subiungere tigris / instituit* and recur at Prop. 1.9.19; Ov. *Am.* 2.14.35, *Met.* 8.121, 15.86. Virgil's epithet Armenian plays on Varro's derivation of *tigris* from the Armenian word for 'swift', see *LALE* 612 *tigris* and cf. Varro *Ling.* 5.100 *tigris ... uocabulum e lingua Armenia: nam ibi et sagitta et quod uehementissimum flumen dicitur Tigris*. For the true derivation of the word from Iranian/Old Persian see De Melo (2019) II 737-738. In *Ecl.* 5.29 Daphnis is acting as the new Bacchus [Peraki-Kyriakidou (2010) 569, 573-574] and, apart from here and *Ciris* 135-136 quoted above, the taming of tigers elsewhere in Latin literature is associated not with Amor, but with Dionysus /Bacchus in his civilising progress from the East: Virg. *Aen.* 6.805 *Liber agens celso Nysae de uertice tigris*; Hor. *Carm.* 3.3.13-14 ... *Bacche pater, tuae / uexere tigres, indocili iugum / collo trahentes*; Ov. *Am.* 1.2.47-8, *Ars* 1.545, 550 (with Hollis), 559, *Met.* 3.668; Sen. *Medea* 84-85, *Phaedra* 755. He is depicted in a chariot drawn by panthers, *LIMC* III (1986) 461 and 463, and is supposed to have discovered tigers in India or Hyrcania (Plin. *Nat.* 8.66; Ov. *Trist.* 5.3.21ff.). The animals were first exhibited in Rome in 11 BC (Plin. *Nat.* 8.65, cf. Pease on Virg. *Aen.* 4.367).

fuluas ... leaenas: cf. Virg. *Georg.* 4.408 *fulua ceruice leaena*. The epithet is used commonly of lions from Lucr. 5.901 *corpora fulua leonum* on. On the form *leaena* see **4.90n**. Unlike **4.90** where the choice of a lioness is required by the argument, here, as often in Latin poetry, the preference for *leaena* over *leo* is purely arbitrary, unless our author wants to stress the cruelty of Neaera (see **25-26** below).

16 indomitis: 'wild', probably still with reference to animals. Close in sense is Sil. 3.288-289 *misceri gregibus Gaetulia sueta ferarum / indomitisque loqui et sedare leonibus iras*. The adj. is often used with reference to unbridled sexual passion, cf. Tib. 2.4.57 ... *ubi indomitis gregibus Venus adflat amores* with Maltby 429 ad loc., 2.1.67-68 *Cupido / natus ... indomitas dicitur inter equas*; Hor. *Epod.* 12.9 *indomitam ... rabiem* with L. C. Watson ad loc., Sen. *Phaed.* 118 *adulter ille, ductor indomiti gregis*. Here there is an obvious etymological play between *dominae* **14** and *indomitis* **16**.

mollia corda dedit: for the expression cf. Juv. 15.131-132 *mollissima corda / humano generi dare se natura fatetur*. The phrase *molle cor* is Ovidian: *Her.* 15.79 *molle meum ... cor est*, *Trist.* 4.10.65-66 *molle Cupidineis nec inexpugnabile telis / cor mihi*, 5.8.28 *molle cor ... habet*, *Pont.* 1.3.32 *confiteor misero molle cor esse mihi*. For *mollitia* as a characteristic of elegy, see **4.76n**.

17 haec Amor et maiora ualet: a prosaic expression, cf. Cic. *Att.* 16.12.1 *sed haec et alia maiora coram*. For a similar statement of the power of love, cf. Prop. 1.10.20 *non nihil egit Amor*.

Amor: with this mention the subject of **13-17** is made clear.

ualet: a reading reported by Ach. Statius and adopted by all editors since for the meaningless *uolet* of A.

sed: marks the contrast brought about by the sudden re-introduction of Bacchus, after the aretalogy of Amor in **13-17**.

17-18 Bacchi / munera: for wine as the gift of Bacchus to men cf. *tuo ... munere* at **4** above. For *Bacchi / munera* in the same *sedes* cf. Virg. *Georg.* 3.526-527 *Massica Bacchi / munera* and for the phrase, which goes back to the Greek δῶρα Διονύσου (Hes. *Op.* 614 etc.), cf. Ov. *Ars* 1.565;

Colum. *Rust.* 10.3; Germ. *Arat.* 91; Manil. 4.204; Stat. *Theb.* 2.101; Sil. 11.285; Mart. 8.68.4.

18 pocula sicca: i.e. 'empty cups', the opposite of *madeant ... pocula* in **5** above. For *siccare* of 'emptying' or 'draining' a cup cf. Hor. *Serm.* 2.6.68 *siccat inaequales calices conuiua*; it can also be used as the opposite of *madere* 'to drink freely' in the sense of 'to be abstemious', cf. Cels. 1.3.14 *debet ... madens siccare, siccus madefacere* and the colloquial English 'to dry out'. For *siccus* in this sense of 'sober', cf. also Hor. *Carm.* 4.5.38-40 *... dicimus integro / sicci mane die, dicimus uuidi, / cum sol Oceano subest.*

19 conuenit: 'comes together with', 'meets'. Like the more common *uenio* in this context, the verb is appropriate for the epiphany of a god, see Fedeli on Prop. 1.10.25 *irritata uenit* and cf. Ov. *Am.* 1.10.33 quoted below.

ex aequo: 'on equal terms'. Liber's attitude to those who honour him is the same as their attitude towards him. *conuenit ex aequo* here contrasts with *conuenit iratus* describing his attitude to the abstemious in **21**. The expression (equivalent to the Greek ἐξ ἴσου) is attested from Afranius 289-290 *quanto facilius ego, qui ex aequo uenio, / adducor ferre humana humanitus* on, but is absent from later verse until Ovid (8): *Am.* (1), *Her.* (2), *Ars* (2), *Met.* (3), see McKeown II 296 on Ov. *Am.* 1.10.33-34 *quae Venus ex aequo uentura est grata duobus, / altera cur illam uendit et alter emit*? Closer to the present sense is Lucan 8.232 *ex aequo me Parthus* (sc. *rex*) *adit* 'the Parthian king approached me on equal terms'.

nec: links *conuenit* with *toruus* (*est*) 'he meets ... and is not hostile towards'.

toruus: 'grim', 'pitiless', 'hostile' occurring first in tragedy, cf. Pacuv. *Trag.* 37 *feroci ingenio, toruus*; applied to a god at Hor. *Carm.* 1.28.17 *toruo ... Marti.* For its use in elegy, see Pichon 282.

Liber: on this name for Bacchus, see **1n.** above.

in illis: 'in respect of those' dependent on *toruus*. For this use of *in* + abl. with words expressing an attitude or behaviour towards a person or group see *OLD in* 41.d and cf. Sall. *Cat.* 52.12 *sint misericordes in furibus aerari* and Prop. 3.19.28 *aequus in hoste fuit.*

20 qui ... quique: for the repetition of the relative, cf. **2.3-4** *qui ... / ... qui,* **3.36** *stamina quae ducunt quaeque futura canunt.*

se: for the free use of the reflexive, in place of the expected *eum*, see **1.25n.** *suis*.

uina iocosa: this combination is foreshadowed by Hor. *Carm.* 3.21.14-16 *tu* (sc. *testa uini*) *sapientium / curas et Arcanum iocoso / consilium retegis Lyaeo*, and 4.15.26 *iocosi munera Liberi*. The plural *uina* is normal in poetry for the nom. and acc. on metrical grounds, whereas the singular forms *uini* (cf. **11** above) and *uino* are regular for the gen. and abl.

colunt: a play on the double meaning of the verb 'to worship' a god (with *se*), cf. *OLD colo*¹ 6a and to 'devote oneself to' an activity (with *uina iocosa*), cf *OLD colo*¹ 7a.

21 The reading of A *non uenit iratus nimium nimiumque seuerus* would simply repeat the point of **19-20** that Bacchus is merciful to those who follow him. It would make more sense if it referred by contrast to Bacchus' attitude to those who slight him. The replacement of *non uenit* by *conuenit*, found in one of the *recentiores* and conjectured independently by Lachmann, would provide a parallelism with **19**, and the emendation of *seuerus* to *seueris*, dependent on *iratus* and referring to the abstemious, would provide a parallel with *in illis* in **19** and an antecedent for *his* in **23**. For the general idea of Bacchus' hostility towards the sober, cf. Hor. *Carm.* 1.18.3 *siccis omnia nam dura deus* (sc. *Bacchus*) *proposuit* ...

iratus ... seueris: the adj. *iratus* is the opposite of *nec toruus* in **19**. For its use with a dative of the person to whom the anger is directed (here *seueris*), cf. Plaut. *Merc.* 923 *mater irata est patri uehementer*. For *seueri* with reference to the sober or abstemious, cf. Cat. 27.5-7 *at uos quos lubet hinc abite, lymphae, / uini pernicies, et ad seueros / migrate*.

nimium nimiumque: for the reduplication of the adv. = 'excessively', cf. Ov. *Her.* 1.41 *o nimium nimiumque oblite tuorum*. At Mart. 8.3.17 *scribant ista graues nimium nimiumque seueri* each *nimium* is attached to a different adj., as they would be here if we accepted the traditional reading. In any case the line-ending *nimiumque seueri* suggests a close connection with the present passage: see Axelson (1960) 292, Wills (1996) 117 n.71 and Maltby (2010) 325-326. Here sense suggests that the reduplicated *nimium* is to be taken with *iratus* rather than with *seueris*.

22 The general advice to drink, now reinforced by the argument of **19-21**, repeats the exhortation of **17-18**.

irati: sc. *dei*, i.e. *Bacchi*.

numina magna: a Virgilian phrase, cf. *Aen.* 2.623 *numina magna deum*, 3.264 *numina magna uocat*, 6.633-634, 697, 7.310-311, which occurs in the same position in the pentameter at Ov. *Am.* 2.8.18 *per Veneris feci numina magna fidem*; cf. also Ov. *Am.* 3.11.47, *Met.* 5.428, 6.315. On *magnus* used of the power and strength of the gods, see **4.16n.** *magnos ... deos* and on *numina* as 'divine power' see **4.53n.** *caelestia numina*.

23-24 The mythological *exemplum* of Pentheus being torn to pieces by his mother Agave and her attendants in a Bacchic frenzy illustrates Bacchus' cruelty towards his enemies. As in Eur.'s *Bacchae* the jovial god becomes a different and far more dangerous entity in his anger. The well-known *exemplum* of the slaughter of Pentheus serves to provide a similar lesson at Ov. *Met.* 4. 429-430 (quoted on **24** below). Whereas the accumulation of interrogative adjectives in the hexameter is prosaic in tone, the periphrasis for Pentheus in the pentameter reflects a more elevated poetic style.

23 The build-up of interrogatives is characteristic of Cicero's rhetorical style, cf. Cic. *Brutus* 297 *hi enim fuerunt certe oratores*; *quanti autem et quales tu uideris*, *De Oratore* 3.85 *uis enim et natura rei, nisi perfecta ante oculos ponitur, qualis et quanta sit intellegi non potest*; see further H-Sz 459-460 (para. 244 d, Zusatz α). In verse the combination *qualis quantusque* occurs in exclamations and relative clauses, rather than interrogative clauses, as here: cf. Virg. *Aen.* 2.591-592 *alma parens* (sc. *Venus*), *confessa deam qualisque uideri / caelicolis et quanta solet*, 3.641-642 *nam qualis quantusque cauo Polyphemus in antro / lanigeras claudit pecudes*; Ov. *Met.* 3.284-285 *quantusque et qualis* (sc. *Iuppiter*) *ab alta / Iunone excipitur*; Val. Fl. 4.603-604 *femineas nec tu ... crede cateruas / sed qualis sed quanta uiris insultat Enyo*: see further Axelson (1960a) 105, Büchner (1965) 505-506, Tränkle 161. The effect here is somewhat bombastic.

his: refers back to *seueris* in **21**.

his poenas ... minetur: for the construction of *minari* + acc. (of thing threatened) + dat. (of person), see *OLD minor*[1] 2a and cf. Plaut. *Pers.* 361 *erus si minatus est malum seruo meo*; Hor. *Carm.* 1.28.25-26 *quodcumque minabitur Eurus / fluctibus Hesperiis*.

24 Allusion to the myth of Pentheus, king of Thebes, who tried to prevent the establishment of the cult of Dionysus in his land. The god punished him by inflicting madness on his mother Agave, daughter of Cadmus, and all the Theban women, who mistook Pentheus, as he spied on their revels from a tree, for a wild beast and tore him to pieces. The story formed the plot of Euripides' *Bacchae* and was re-formed by Ovid in *Met.* 3.511-733.

Cadmeae matris: a reference to Agave, daughter of Cadmus and mother of Pentheus. For the combination cf. Sen. *Oed.* 1006 *Cadmea mater*; *Culex* 111 *Cadmeis Agaue*; Stat. *Theb.* 4.565 *genetrix Cadmeia*. The adj. *Cadme(i)us* is rare in Augustan poetry (only Prop. 1.7.1, 3.13.7), but becomes frequent in the post-Augustan period, especially in Seneca and Statius. In Ovid and earlier poets the form *Cadmeis –idos* predominates (see *ThLL Onom.* 2 C 10.37-69).

praeda cruenta: the same phrase was used by Ovid at *Fast.* 5.178 of Hylas: *ipse fuit Libycae praeda cruenta ferae*, and *praeda* had been applied by Ovid to Pentheus at *Fast.* 3.721 *tu quoque Thebanae mala praeda tacebere matris*. The term *praeda* is appropriate for Pentheus who, like a wild beast, was trapped and killed by his mother and her companions.

docet: the exemplary nature of the Pentheus myth had already been referred to in Ov. *Met.* 4.428-430 ... (*fas est et ab hoste doceri*) / *quidque furor ualeat, Penthea caede satisque / ac super ostendit*.

25-26 The couplet consists of an ἀποπομπή, Lat. *auersio*, in which a danger is warded off and directed by the power of the god invoked towards another, cf. Cat. 63.92-93 *procul a mea tuus sit furor omnis, era* (sc. *Cybele*) *domo: / alios age incitatos, alios age rabidos*; further examples in Fraenkel on Aesch. *Ag.* 1573; N-H on Hor. *Carm.* 1.21.13; and McKeown III 208 on Ov. *Am.* 2.10.15-16. In this case the anger of Bacchus is warded off from Lygdamus and his companions *nobis* (**25**) and is to be felt by an unspecified *illa* (**25**), who is later identified as Neaera (**29**).

25 sed procul: a monosyllable + *procul* is a very common line-opening; examples with *sed* occur at Prop. 4.9.23; Ov. *Met.* 12.359, *Fast.* 2.499; Stat. *Ach.* 1.409, Juv. 12.5 and at **9.5** below.

procul a nobis: cf., in a similar context, *procul a me* at Cat. 63.92 quoted above and Ov. *Fast.* 4.116 *a nobis sit procul iste furor* with Fantham ad loc. For this characteristically sympotic theme cf. **7n.** *ite procul* above and **51-52n.** *ite a me ... precor* below.

illaque: the introduction of the feminine pronoun comes as a surprise here, although its use shows that Lygdamus had been thinking all along of Neaera as the source of his *dolorem* (**3**). Its reference to Neaera is not made clear to the reader until she is named in **29**.

siqua est: 'if any there be', looking forward to *ira* in **26**. Elsewhere in the *Lygd.* group **1-6** our author uses only two- or three-syllable words at the end of the hexameter. This apparent exception is to be explained by that fact that the poet would have pronounced this phrase as two syllables, *siquast*; see Maltby (2010) 328.

26 laesi ... ira dei: the phrase is found in the same *sedes* in two passages of Ovid, *Trist.* 1.5b.40 *ni fuerit laesi mollior ira dei* and *Pont.* 1.4.44 *perstiterit laesi si grauis ira dei*, a clear indication that Ovid is the model here. On the meaning of *laesi* here see **4.16n.** *laesit*. The more common expression is *numen laedere*, e.g. Tib. 1.9.6; Hor. *Epod.* 15.8; Virg. *Aen.* 1.8; Ov. *Am.* 3.3.4.

sentiat: in the sense of 'feel, experience, to one's cost' of the power of a deity see McKeown II 276 on Ov. *Am.* 1.9.39 *Mars quoque deprensus fabrilia uincula sensit*, and cf. Prop. 1.9.21 *pueri totiens arcum sentire medullis*; Ov. *Am.* 1.11.11 *sensisse Cupidinis arcus*, 2.9.11 *nos tua* (sc. *Cupidinis*) *sentimus ... arma*.

27 quid precor a demens?: a similar appeal to reason after an emotional outburst occurs at **[Tib.] 3.19.17** *quid facio, demens*? (an obvious echo at the end of the whole book of the final poem of the *Lygd.* group) and Ov. *Trist.* 5.10.51 *quid loquor a demens*? For *quid precor* at the opening of the hexameter cf. Ov. *Her.* 2.103, Val. Fl. 7.437; and for *a demens* cf. also Virg. *Ecl.* 2.60; Prop. 2.30.1; Ov. *Her.* 21.72, *Pont.* 4.3.29; Sen. *Medea* 930; *Ciris* 185. On the insanity of love as a Gallan characteristic cf. Virg. *Ecl.* 10.22, 44 and see **[Tib.] 3.** *Sulpicia Cycle* **9.7n**. In the struggle between elegiac and symposiastic features which characterises this poem at the generic level, mention of madness shows the elegiac at this stage still have the upper hand.

27-28: On the commonplace of winds being asked to carry away wishes, prayers etc., which can be traced back to Hom. *Od.* 8.408-409, see **4.96n.**, N-H on Hor. *Carm.* 1.26.2 and McKeown II 84 on Ov. *Am.* 1.4.11-12.

uenti ... / aeriae et nubes: for winds and clouds in this context cf. Cat. 30.9-10 ... *tua dicta omnia factaque / uentos irrita ferre ac nebulas aerias sinis* and for winds alone, cf. Cat. 64.142 *quae cuncta aerii discerpunt*

Book Three of the Corpus Tibullianum: 317
Introduction, Text, Translation and Commentary

irrita uenti; Tib. 1.4.21-22 ... *Veneris periuria uenti / irrita ... ferunt*, and **4.96** above and see Tib. 1.5.35-36 and Prop. 4.7.21-22 quoted below and the frequent Ovidian examples quoted by McKeown II 84.

temeraria uota: the adj. here is used in the sense of 'rash' *OLD temerarius* 1, not 'fortuitous' as in **4.7**. For the distribution of *temerarius* in poetry see **4.7-8n.** *somnia ... temeraria*. For *uota* as the object to be blown away cf. Tib. 1.5.35-36 ... *quae nunc Eurusque Notusque / iactat odoratos uota per Armenios*; Ov. *Am.* 2.6.44 *uota procelloso per mare rapta Noto*.

aeriae et: for the elision of final *-ae* before *et*, see Platnauer 77 and cf. Prop. 1.2.17 *Idae et cupido*, 2.1.74 *uitae et morti*.

aeriae ... nubes: for the combination, cf. Virg. *Aen.* 7.704-705 *aeriam ... / urgeri uolucrum ... ad litora nubem*; Sil. 17.341-342 *haec procul aeria speculantem nube sororem / ut uidit*.

diripienda: the verb is used of the action of the winds also at Tib. 1.6.54 *ut hic uentis diripitur ... cinis*; Prop. 4.7.21-22 *cuius fallacia uerba / ... diripuere Noti*; Stat. *Theb.* 5.366-367 *uenti / diripiunt ... fretum*. It occurs in the same *sedes* in a different context at **9.22** below.

29 A deliberate echo in the final poem of the of the question posed in the opening poem, **1.19-20** *sit nostri mutua cura / an minor an toto pectore deciderim*.

quamuis ... superest: the indicative after *quamuis* is avoided in Classical prose, but is common in poetry from Cat. 12.5 and Lucr. 3.403 on. In elegy the indicative is the norm in Propertius and Ovid, but Tib. uses only the subjunctive (1.4.41, 43, 6.67-68, 8.15). The only other occurrence with the indicative in **[Tib.] 3** is *Sulpicia* **14.8**; see further K-S II 2.442-3 para. 5-6, H-Sz 604 para. 326.

mei ... cura: objective genitive 'love for me'. For *cura* = 'love' in elegy see **1.19n.** *mutua cura* and for the possibly Gallan connotations of the word see **7n.** above.

Neaera: with the mention of the name the reference of *illa* **25** is finally made clear. For the combination of *cura* and *Neaera* at the line end, cf. Lygdamus' imagined epitaph at **2.29** ... *dolor ... et cura Neaerae*.

30 sis felix: a common formula for wishing good luck, also at Cat. 100.8; Virg. *Aen.* 1.330; Stat. *Silu.* 2.2.107, *Ach.* 1.386, cf. also Cat. 68.155 *sitis felices;* Hor. *Carm.* 3.27.13-14 *sis licet felix ... / ...Galatea.*

candida fata: for *candidus* in the sense of 'happy', see *OLD candidus* 1c and cf. Cat. 8.3 *candidi tibi soles*; Ov. *Her.* 16.320 *candidior medio nox erit illa die.* The connection with fate occurs elsewhere only in the late works of Ovid: *Trist.* 3.4.34 *fato candidiore frui,* 5.7.4 *candida fortunae pars manet una meae, Pont.* 2.4.30 *pars fati candida nulla mei est.* The accumulation of *-a* sounds in the three last words of the pentameter is striking.

31-32 The central couplet of the poem returns to the opening theme of the symposium.

31 securae: 'free from care' either in love or in other matters, see **3.32n.** *securo* and Pichon 260.

tempora mensae: the same line-ending (but with gen. *mensae*) occurs at Ov. *Pont.* 4.6.47 *utque Thyesteae redeant si tempora mensae.*

mensae: here in the sense of *conuiuium* 'dinner-party', see *OLD mensa* 5.

32 The line is an example of the commonplace proverb in which the fate of man is compared to the changing weather, see Otto 113 and cf. Theocr. *Id.* 4.41-43 θαρσεῖν χρή, φίλε Βάττε· τάχ' αὔριον ἔσετ' ἄμεινον. / ... / χὠ Ζεὺς ἄλλοκα μὲν πέλει αἴθριος, ἄλλοκα δ' ὕει ["be of good cheer, friend Battos; perhaps tomorrow will be better ... Zeus is sometimes sunny, at other times he rains"]; Ov. *Fast.* 1.495-496 *nec fera tempestas toto tamen horret in anno / et tibi, crede mihi, tempora ueris erunt, Trist.* 2.142 *nube solet pulsa candidus ire dies*; Sen. *Epist.* 107. 8-9 *nubilo serena succedunt; turbantur maria cum quieuerunt; flant in uicem uenti ... ad hanc legem animus noster aptandus est*; see further the numerous examples quoted in N-H on Hor. *Carm.* 2.9.1 and Ingleheart (2010) 157 on Ov. *Trist.* 2.142.

post multas una serena dies: the feminine use of *dies* in the plural is unusual (elsewhere in the *Lygd.* group always masc. **4.54, 5.28, 6.54**), although the fem. sing. may be used in verse for metrical convenience, see Fraenkel (1917). Here *multas* must mean *multas non serenas* and takes its gender from *una serena dies.* As the line omits any express reference to cloudy weather, scholars have emended *multas* to *nimbos* (Santen), *maestas* (Baehrens) and *pluuias* (Housman), but adequate sense can be made without emendation. The pointed opposition of *multas una* is characteristic of Lucretius, cf. 3.665-666 ... *et ea ratione sequetur / unam animantem animas habuisse in corpore multas*, 4.603-605 ... *partis in cunctas diuiditur uox / ex aliis aliae quoniam gignuntur, ubi una / dissiluit semel in multas exorta*, 5.95-96 *una dies dabit exitio, multosque per annos / sustentata ruet moles et machina mundi*.

33-36 Despite the exhortation to carefree feasting in **31-32**, Lygdamus' true mood is revealed as one of sadness, in which it is impossible to feign good cheer. The lines are carefully constructed, with repeated *difficile est* in **33-34** and *nec bene* at the opening of **35-36**, and lexical *uariatio* of verbs expressing pretence (*imitari, fingere, componitur*), nouns expressing joy (*gaudia, iocum, risus, ebria uerba*) and adjectives expressing falsity (*falsa, mendaci*) and sadness (*tristi, sollicitis*). After attempting a carefree lyric style our author reverts to a more sombre elegiac mode. On the contrast between the genres of elegy (more suitable for lamentation) and lyric (more suitable for light-hearted subjects), cf. Sappho's words at Ov. *Her.* 15.5-8 *forsitan et quare mea sint alterna requiras / carmina, cum lyricis sim magis apta modis. / flendus amor meus est – elegiae flebile carmen; / non facit ad lacrimas barbitos ulla meas*. On the generic ambiguity of the present poem see **headnote** above and **13n., 35-36n., 51-52n., 53-56n., 57-58n.**

33-34 difficile est ... / difficile est: a clear echo of Cat. 76.13-14 *difficile est longum subito deponere amorem; / difficile est, uerum hoc qua lubet efficias*. Catullus is named at **41** below and was hinted at in poem **1**, see **41n.** below.

33 ei mihi: an exclamation of self-pity, which is absent from prose and belongs mainly to the lower genres of verse, comedy: Plautus (24), Terence (19); elegy: Tib. (2), Prop. (5), Ov. (46). It is especially common in Ovid, where 26 of the 46 occurrences occur in the amatory works; full statistics in McKeown II 149 on Ov. *Am.* 1.6.52, who notes its absence from Classical prose. Its normal position, as here, is at the beginning of the line; see *ThLL* 5.2.300.79-80.

imitari gaudia falsa: cf. Sen. *Oed.* 419, of Bacchus dressed as a girl, *falsos imitatus artus*. The verb is used elsewhere with emotions at Ov. *Rem.* 497 *furores* and Tac. *Ann.* 1.24 *maestitiam*. For the combination *gaudia falsa*, cf. Prop. 1.8B.29 *falsa licet cupidus deponat gaudia Liuor*; Virg. *Aen.* 6.513-514 ... *ut supremam falsa inter gaudia noctem / egerimus, nosti*; Ov. *Her.* 13.108 *dum careo ueris gaudia falsa iuuant*.

34 tristi ... mente: cf. Ov. *Her.* 12.148 *mens mea trisits erat*; *Script. Hist. Aug. Aurel.* 41.6.1 *qui neces infandas tristissima mente concipiunt*; Serv. *Aen.* 6.156 *defixa lumina habens per quod tristitia mentis ostenditur*. To have a disposition which is *tristis* is the characteristic of an elegiac lover, see Harrison (2007) 66 on Virg. *Ecl.* 10.31 *tristis at ille* (of Gallus) and cf. Pichon 283-284. For its possible connection with Lygdamus' name see Gen. Intro., section 3.1. On the later development into an adverbial function of phrases containing adj. + *mente* see **12.16n.** below.

fingere ... iocum: 'to fake merriment', the combination is not found elsewhere, but cf. **4.68** *non est in uanum fabula ficta iocum*. For *iocus* in the sense of 'joking', 'merriment', cf. Cat. 12.2 ... *in ioco atque uino* and cf. **20** above, *uina iocosa*.

35-36 nec bene ... / nec bene: for *nec bene* as a line opening cf. Lucr. 1.49, 2.651; Ov. *Pont.* 3.3.16, 4.10.17; Mart. 10.31.3. The couplet is concerned at a metapoetic level with the incompatibility of lyric sympotic themes with elegiac concerns. By the end of the poem elegy is finally rejected in favour of lyric.

mendaci ... ore: an Ovidian expression, cf. *Am.* 3.3.43-44 ... *numen sine fraude liceret / femina mendaci falleret ore meum*, and, in the same *sedes*, *Met.* 9.322 *quae quia mendaci parientem iuuerat ore*.

componitur: i.e. *fingitur*; cf. **[Tib.] 3**. *Sulpicia* **13.9-10** *uultus componere famae / taedet*; Sen. *Dial.* 12.16 *per ipsum tamen compositum fictumque uultum lacrimae profunduntur*. The theme of disguise and openness runs through the whole **[Tib.] 3** book.

sollicitis: commonly used in elegy of those troubled by love, see **4.20n.** *sollicitas*, quoting the reference at Virg. *Ecl.* 10.5 to Gallus' elegies as *sollicitos ... amores*.

ebria uerba: like *mendaci ... ore* another Ovidian expression, cf., in the same *sedes*, *Fast.* 6.408 *cantat et ad nautas ebria uerba iacit*. The metapoetic reference is to the sympotic themes of lyric, which are incompatible with those troubled by elegiac concerns *sollicitis*. At **61** below the poet declares himself unwilling to continue as an elegiac *sollicitus* and turns finally to the symposiastic themes of lyric at the end of the poem (and of this group) **62-64**. At that stage his 'speaking' name Lygdamus, implying the sorrow of the elegist (see Gen. Intro., section 3.1), ceases to be relevant, and does not occur again in the book.

37 quid queror infelix?: parallel to *quid precor a demens?* in **27**. For the phrase *quid queror?*, always at the beginning of the hexameter, cf. Tib. 1.8.23; Ov. *Am*. 3.3.41, *Her*. 6.17; Stat. *Theb*. 12.336. On the possible metapoetic significance of the phrase, see **51-52n**. below on *quid ... / conqueror?* The use of *infelix* in this line position after *quid* + verb is characteristic of Ovid: *Am*. 3.2.71 *quid facis infelix? Her*. 2.103 *quid precor infelix?*, 14.93 *quid furis infelix?, Ars* 3.735 *quid facis infelix?*, cf. also Mart. 7.64.6 *quid facit infelix?* On the use of *infelix* in elegy, see Pichon 168.

turpes discedite curae: for the use of *discedo* of emotions cf. Liv. 4.52.8 *sollicitudines discessere*; Ov. *Met*. 10.336 *spes interdictae discedite* and see *ThLL* 5(1).1283.77-1284.24. The use of *discedite* in this position in the hexameter is characteristic of Ovid: *Ars* 2.233, *Met*. 1.381, 4.223, 9.509, *Fast*. 4.365; cf. also Virg. *Aen*. 2.644; Lucan 5.357. For *curae* of amatory cares see **1.19n**. *mutua cura*. The use of *turpis* here is unusual and possibly suggests the degrading nature of such *curae*, see Pichon 285-286. For a similar use of the adj. = 'unseemly', 'inappropriate' cf. Hor. *Carm*. 2.20.21-22 *absint inani funere neniae / luctusque turpes*; Sen. *Oed*. 801-802 *turpes metus / depone*.

38 odit ...pater: cf. Virg. *Aen*. 7.327 *odit et ipse pater Pluton*.

Lenaeus ... pater: the phrase is applied to Bacchus only four times elsewhere; in the voc. at Virg. *Georg*. 2.4, 7 and Ov. *Met*. 11.132 and in the acc. at Colum. *Rust*. 10.430. The voc. *Lenaee* alone is found at Virg. *Georg*. 2.529 and Hor. *Carm*. 3.25.19 (on which see N-R 308 ad loc.) and in Greek at *Hymn. Orph*. 50.5, 52.2. The epithet was thought by the ancients to come from the Greek for wine-press ληνός (see *LALE* 333 and cf. Diod. 4.5.1). On the many titles of Bacchus, see **2.19n**. above. The Lenaea was Dionysus' winter festival at Athens, and his female attendants (Bacchants) were known in Greek as Lenae. The term *pater* is often applied to gods and heroes (see Austin on Virg. *Aen*. 4.58) and is frequently used of Bacchus from Enn. *Trag*. 120 Jocelyn on, cf. Hor. *Carm*. 1.18.6, 3.3.13; Tib. 2.3.66; Prop. 3.17.1-2; Virg. *Aen*. 4.58; Ov. *Met*. 13.669.

tristia uerba: the antithesis of *ebria uerba* above (**36**) and equivalent to *seria uerba* below (**52**). Again there could, at the metapoetic level, be a contrast between elegiac *tristia* and the lyric /symposiatic *ebria* genres, which runs through the whole poem. The phrase is used of Apollo's words at **4.42** above, cf. Hor. *AP* 105-106 *tristia maestum / uultum uerba decent*;

Ov. *Trist.* 1.3.80 (of his wife) *miscuit haec lacrimis tristia uerba suis*; and 2.133 *tristibus inuectus uerbis* (of Augustus), the last two punning on the title of Ovid's *Tristia*.

39-42 The myth of Ariadne, daughter of king Minos of Crete, who was abandoned on the shores of Naxos by her faithless lover, Theseus, comes as something of a surprise in the context of a warning **43f.** to his friends about the deceit of women. It has to be taken as an illustration of the faithlessness of lovers in general (cf. **49** *periuria ... amantum*). The choice of myth could also have been influenced by the fact that Bacchus, the addressee of the poem, later came to the aid of the abandoned Ariadne (although no explicit mention is made of this here), as it is hoped he will come to the aid of the abandoned poet here. Also, as Ovid points out at *Ars* 3.31-32, myths of male deception are far more common than those based on female treachery: *saepe uiri fallunt: tenerae non saepe puellae, / paucaque, si quaeras, crimina fraudis habent*. Our author makes explicit reference **(41)** to Catullus' treatment of the myth (Cat. 64.52-264), but verbal echoes of this poem are few: *periuria* (**39**, cf. Cat. 64.135) and *Minoi* (**41**, cf. Cat. 64.60). The influence of Prop. 1.3.1-2 *qualis Thesea iacuit cedente carina / languida desertis Cnosia litoribus* and Ov. *Ars* 3.35-36 *quantum in te, Theseu, uolucres Ariadna marinas / pauit, in ignoto sola relicta loco* is also apparent. The myth of Ariadne's betrayal by Theseus, from which others, usually women, are to learn, belongs to the erotodidaxis of abandoned heroines as used earlier by Prop. 2.21.11-16 (Medea and Calypso) and Ov. *Ars* 3.457-460 (Ariadne and Phyllis).

39 Cnosia: Ariadne is addressed here as the 'girl from Cnossos', the capital of Crete, as at Prop. 1.3.2 quoted above and frequently in verse elsewhere [references in Fulkerson (2017) 212 ad loc.]. For the use of apostrophe to mythological characters as a feature of neoteric narrative style, see Gibson 101 on Ov. *Ars* 3.35-36. The MSS have the form *Gnosia* here, which is generally considered corrupt: see Kenney (1961) on Ov. *Ars* 1.293.

Theseae ... periuria linguae: Theseus' perjury in regard to his treatment of Ariadne was a commonplace of ancient literature, cf. Eur. *Medea* 21ff., 492; Apoll. Rhod. 4.357ff.; Nonn. 47.389; Cat. 64.58-59, 132-135, 148; Ov. *Am.* 1.7.15 with McKeown II 172 ad loc., who contrasts Theseus' fidelity to Pirithous, *Her.* 4.59, 10.76, *Ars* 3.457, *Fast.* 3.461, 473, 497. For specific mention of his *periuria* cf. Cat. 64.135 *immemor* (sc. *Theseu) ah deuota domum periuria portas?*. For *periuria linguae* at the line-end cf. Ov. *Her.* 7.67 *protinus occurrent falsae periuria linguae*, *Met.* 14.98-99 ...

abstulit usum / uerborum et natae dira in periuria linguae. The theme of the *periuria* of false swearing lovers is repeated at **49** below.

quondam: for the use of this adverb to introduce mythological paradigms set in the past see **4.67n**. For the contrast with *nunc* in **43** cf. **1.23** *uir quondam nunc frater*. For its use in relation to Theseus cf. *Aetna* 583-584 *excidit ... quondam tibi, perfide Theseu, / candida sollicito praemittere uela parenti*.

40 fleuisti ignoto: for the elision of long final *-i* before short initial *-i*, see Platnauer 76 and cf. Tib. 1.2.56 *si in*; Prop. 2.6.21 *docuisti impune*, 3.6.39 *consimili impositum*.

ignoto ... mari: in view of the *loci similes* describing the deserted Ariadne this is more likely to be locative ablative after *relicta* than a dative after *fleuisti* as suggested by N-A 504-505 ad loc.; cf. Cat. 64.57 *desertam in sola miseram se cernat harena*, 132-133 *me ... / perfide deserto liquisti in litore*; Prop. 1.3.1-2 *... Thesea iacuit cedente carina / ... desertis Cnosia litoribus*; Ov. *Ars* 3.35-36 *uolucres Ariadna marinas / pauit in ignoto sola relicta loco*. For the *iunctura* cf. Prop. 2.26B.40 *dux erat ignoto missa columba mari*; Sen. *De Ben.* 7.2.5 *et bella in ignoto mari quaereret*. For *ignotus* implying strangeness and desertion cf. Tib. 1.3.3 *me tenet ignotis aegrum Phaeacia terris* and Ov. *Ars* 3.36 (above).

sola relicta: common in this *sedes* in Ovid, see *Ars* 3.36 (of Ariadne, quoted above), *Her.* 7.84 *occidit a duro sola relicta uiro*, *Trist.* 4.3.40 *... morte fores sola relicta mea*; cf. also Prop. 2.24B.46 (of Medea) *et modo seruato sola relicta uiro est*, [Ov.] *Epiced. Drusi* 327 *pignora de Druso sola relicta tenes*.

41 sic: 'in this way' refers back to the account of Ariadne's desertion in **39-40**; this is how Catullus had reported (*referens* **42**) the myth for her benefit (*pro te* **41**).

sic cecinit: for this phrase at the beginning of the line (also followed by *doctus*), cf. Ov. *Fast.* 6.811 *sic cecinit Clio, doctae adsensere sorores*. For *cano* as the technical term for telling a story in verse, cf. Virg. *Aen.* 1.1 *arma uirumque cano* and see *OLD cano* 3.

doctus ... Catullus: the epithet is applied to Catullus first in Ov. *Am.* 3.9.62 *docte Catulle* and then frequently in Martial (1.61.1, 7.99.7, 8.73.8, 14.100.1, 152.1). It is the Latin equivalent of the Greek σοφός, applied to learned poets: see N-H 13 and Mayer (2012) 58-59 on Hor. *Carm.* 1.1.29

and Cairns (1979) 11-12. In Latin elegy the epithet, implying both technical ability and innate wisdom, is used of the poet (e.g. Tib. 1.4.61), his cultured mistress [e.g. Prop. 1.7.11, **[Tib.] 3.** *Sulpicia Cycle* **12.2**) and the Muses [e.g. **[Tib.] 3.** *Lygd.* **4.45**]: see *ThLL* 5(1).1753.80-1754.14, 1757.2-46, 1758.17-45, *OLD doctus* 3, Knox (2006) 133 n.27, Syndikus (2006) 269 n.77. The citing by name of a poetic predecessor in this way, referring to a specific theme treated by him (in this case the desertion of Ariadne by Theseus in Cat. 64) is unusual in elegy. Other elegists, especially Ovid, usually list predecessors in order to place themselves in a poetic tradition (e.g. Ov. *Trist.* 5.1.17-19). The more specific reference here probably serves to present Lygdamus as a post-Catullan poet, but contemporary with the other elegists, as with the suggestion of his possibly Ovidian birth date at **5.17-18**, see **n.** ad loc. The reference here to Catullus in the last poem of the *Lygd.* group probably looks back to the allusion to Cat.'s gift of a *libellum* in the first poem of the collection (see **1.9-14n.**, **1.9n.** above). It may also recall Ovid's mention of Catullus in the last poem of his *Amores*, and look forward to the Catullan echo in the closural poem **19** poem of the collection see **19 headnote**. Mention of Cat.'s hexameter poem 64 on Ariadne here may prepare the way for the move away from elegy to the hexameter *Laud. Mess.* which is to follow, a panegyric which in its introduction alludes to Cat.'s poem 66 on the *Coma Berenices* (see **7 headnote** and **7.9-11n.**).

Minoi: 'daughter of Minos'; the form *Minois* is found in Latin from Cat. 64.60 onwards. The voc. *Minoi* is found only here.

42 ingrati ... uiri: the phrase is applied to Theseus by Ov. *Fast.* 3.462 *quae* (sc. Ariadne) *dedit ingrato fila legenda uiro*. Theseus had failed to show gratitude to Ariadne, who had provided him with the thread which enabled him to find his way out of the labyrinth after killing the Minotaur. The adj. is used in elegy of anyone who does not repay a mistress's devotion, see Pichon 169 and cf. Prop. 1.6.9-10 ... *illa minatur / quae solet ingrato tristis amica uiro*; Ov. *Her.* 12.124 *debuit ingratis Scylla nocere uiris*, *Fast.* 1.621-622 ... *matronaeque destinat omnis / ingratos nulla prole nouare uiros*.

inpia facta: the phrase is first used by Cat. 23.10, 30.4, cf. Lucr. 1.83; Virg. *Aen.* 4.596; *Dirae* 8-9; Ov. *Fast.* 2.38 and, in relation to the Theseus /Ariadne story Ov. *Her.* 10.99-100 (Ariadne to Theseus) *uiueret Androgeos utinam nec facta luisses / impia funeribus, Cecropi terra, tuis*. For the meaning of *inpius* here, see **4.59n.** *mens inpia*.

43 uos ego ... moneo: Lygdamus seems to be adopting the role of *magister amoris*, warning his friends to learn from others' pain in love to avoid such outcomes in their own case. For *moneo* in erotodidactic contexts, cf. Tib. 1.8.69, 2.4.51; Prop. 1.1.35 15.41, 20.51; Ov. *Am.* 2.19.34, *Ars* 1.387, 459, 3.353 etc. For the phrase cf. Juv. 6.629 *uos ego, pupilli, moneo*.

nunc: marks a return to the present after the mythical past of Theseus and Ariadne, introduced by *quondam* in **39**.

43-44 felix quicumque dolore / alterius disces: for the literary theme of μακαρισμός, see **3.26n.** above. The content is similar to Ov. *Ars* 3.455 *discite ab alterius uestris timuisse querellis*, where girls are asked to learn from the complaints of abandoned heroines; cf. also Prop. 2.21.16 *discite desertae non temere esse bonae* and (on the power of women) 3.11.8 *tu nunc exemplo disce timere meo*.

44 posse cauere tuo: the text here is in doubt. A has *carere tuo*, whereas the Fragmentum Cuiacianum has *cauere tuos* and the Excerpta Frisingensia *cauere tuo*. The reading *carere tuo*, although acceptable Latin (for *carere dolore* in Classical prose, see *ThLL* 3.449.60-61), is less well suited to the context here than *cauere tuo*, as the sense 'lack' (*carere*) is not as appropriate to a warning as the sense 'avoid' (*cauere*). The ablative with *cauere*, however, is restricted before the time of Apuleius, to the phrase *malo cauere*, apart from Plaut. *Rud.* 828 *caue ... infortunio*; see *ThLL* 3.633.10-26 (for *cauere* + abl.), and its regular construction is + acc.; see *ThLL* 3.631.39-633.9. (for *cauere* + acc.). Either one must accept the ablative here, as I do, as an early example of what was later to become a more common construction (perhaps influenced by *dolore* in **43**), or, with Baehrens, emend *tuo* to *tuum*.

45 uos: a return to address the friends of **9**, with a warning not to be deceived by women.

capiant: 'captivate', 'seduce', with a hint of *militia amoris*, see **1.7n.** *capiuntur* above.

pendentia bracchia collo: the reference is to throwing the arms around another's neck in an exaggerated show of affection, cf. Ov. *Trist.* 3.5.15 *bracchiaque accepi presso pendentia collo*. For *pendere* in this context cf. Virg. *Georg.* 2.523 *interea dulces pendent circum oscula nati*, *Aen.* 1.715 *ille ubi complexu Aeneae colloque pependit*; Prop. 3.12.22 *pendebit collo Galla pudica tuo*; Sen. *Thy.* 523-524 *uos quoque, senum praesidia, tot* *iuuenes, meo / pendete collo*; Mart. 14.54.1 *si quis plorator collo tibi uernula pendet.* For *pendentia bracchia* cf. Lucan 3.667 *bracchia linquentes Graia pendentia puppe.* The hexameter ending *bracchia collo* occurs first in Cat. 64.332 *leuia substernens robusto bracchia collo* and then becomes frequent in Ovid: *Her.* 16.167, *Met.* 1.762, 3.389, 9.459, 605; cf. also Stat. *Theb.* 5.217 ... *et indigno non soluit bracchia collo.*

46 blanda ... prece: The reading *prece* is found in the Florilegium Gallicum for *fide* of A+. For a similar confusion between *fide* and *prece* see **4.64n.** on *cum multa ... prece.* If *fide* were correct here it would have to have the meaning 'oath', which would be difficult in view of the word's occurrence three lines below **(49)** in the sense 'good faith'. Also, whereas the combination *blanda prece* (Hor. *AP* 395; Sen. *Herc. F.* 1014) and *blandae/ -as preces* (Hor. *Carm.* 4.1.8; Ov. *Her.* 3.30, *Ars* 1.710, *Met.* 10.64; [Ov.] *Epiced. Drusi* 424) is common, the adj. is not found elsewhere in combination with *fides.* The reference must then be to the coaxing pleas of a deceiving mistress.

sordida lingua: *sordidus* here need not refer to greed (as in *OLD sordidus* 8), since this fault is expressly ruled out in Neaera's case at **1.7** above, but must have the wider sense of 'base', 'despicable' (*OLD sordidus* 7), with reference to a tongue guilty of perjury or deceit, as described in **47-48**. There may be a reference here in the last of the *Lygd.* poems to the trouble brought on the poet by the oaths of loyalty his *garrula lingua* swore to his mistress in **19.20** at the end of the whole collection.

47-49 A warning not to trust a woman's false oaths. The unreliability of female oaths is a commonplace of elegy, see Harrison (2007) 127-128 and cf. Cat. 70.3-4; Prop. 2.28.7-8. Hor. *Carm.* 1.33.4 speaks of the mistress's *laesa ... fide* as the essence of Tibullan elegy. Swearing by the eyes is found in Greek from Aeschin. 2.153; Theocr. *Id.* 6.22 (with Gow 123 ad loc.), 24.75, and in Latin from Plaut. *Men.* 1060 (referring to a *meretrix* and her companions) *si uoltis per oculos iurare* on; in connection with a mistress's infidelity it is found at Prop. 1.15.33-36 *tam tibi ne uiles isti uideantur ocelli, / per quos saepe mihi credita perfidia est! / hos tu iurabas, si quid mentita fuisses, / ut tibi suppositis exciderent manibus*; Ov. *Am.* 2.16.43-46 (with McKeown III 362 on 43-44) *at mihi te comitem iuraras usque futurum / per me perque oculos, sidera nostra, tuos: / uerba puellarum, foliis leuiora caducis, / irrita, qua uisum est, uentus et unda ferunt,* 3.3.9-14 *argutos habuit: radiant ut sidus ocelli, / per quos mentita est perfida saepe mihi. / scilicet aeterni falsum iurare puellis / di quoque concedunt, formaque numen habet. / perque suos illam nuper iurasse* *recordor / perque meos oculos: et doluere mihi.* The last of these is close in wording to the present passage, cf. *perfida / fallax, perque suos* in both, *iurasse / iurauit,* and may have provided the model; cf. also **11.8 perque tuos oculos.** Also relevant is Horace's Neaera who swears falsely to him at *Epod.* 15.1-10 that their love will be mutual. On Lygdamus' possible impersonation of Horace's rival for her affections mentioned in that poem see Gen. Intro., section 3.1, **1 headnote, 3 headnote, 3.29n. Lydius aurifer amnis, 4.16n. laesit** above and **53n.** below. Swearing by Juno as their patron goddess was relatively common for women, cf. **19.15** *hoc tibi sancta tuae Iunonis numina iuro*; Petr. 25.4 (Quartilla) *Iunonem meam iratam habeam, si umquam meminerim uirginem fuisse* and the female oath *eiuno* mentioned by Charis. 258.3 B. *edio fidio ...iuratio propria uirorum est, ut feminarum edepol ecastor eiuno.* There is, however, no other reference to women swearing *per ... suam Venerem* 'by their Venus'. Our author could have been influenced by Demophoon's oath by Juno and Venus at Ov. *Her.* 2.39-41 *per Venerem ... / ... / Iunonemque* and had himself addressed this pair of goddesses at **3.33-34** above. For Venus invoked as the patroness of lovers, see N-H 129 on Hor. *Carm.* 2.8.13.

47-48 etsi: 'even if' the conjunction occurs here only in the whole of the *Corp. Tib.* and was avoided in higher poetic registers; elsewhere in elegy (always at the line-opening) Prop. 2.2.16, 19.1; Ov. *Am.* 3.14.50. See H-Sz 671 and cf. Axelson (1945) 88, 123.

perque ... /Iunonemque ... perque: a native feature reintroduced on the model of the Homeric τε ... τε, repeated *-que* belongs to the high-style and is found most commonly in epic, see **1.3-4n.** above. Here, as in Tib. 1.1.33, the figure suggests a prayer formula. For Juno as the main goddess for women's oaths, cf. **19.15** quoted in **47-49n.** above.

fallax: to be taken as an adjectival noun = 'the false woman', rather than predicatively with *iurauit*.

iurauit: some editors emend the manuscript reading here to *iurarit*, in view of the future *inerit* (**49**), but the perfect can be used in contexts of habitual or repeated actions 'even if she (habitually) swears', see K-S II 1.130-131. The same combination of perfect with future in a conditional clause occurs below **59-61** *si fugit ... (non) repetam.*

ocellos: the only occurrence of this diminutive in the *Corp. Tib.,* influenced perhaps here by its use in a similar context of women's oaths at Prop. 1.15.33 and Ov. *Am.* 3.3.9 (both quoted on **47-49** above). The use of this word in amatory contexts is more characteristic of Prop. (18) and Ov. *Am.* (11), *Ars* (3), *Fast.* (1); see further Maltby (1999a) 388.

49 nulla fides inerit: the same hexameter opening occurs at Manil. 4.577 *nulla fides inerit natis.*

fides: on the meaning 'good faith' here see *OLD fides* 6.

inerit: on the distribution of this verb in elegy see **4.84n.**

49-50: On the ancient commonplace that lovers' oaths were ignored by the gods and were carried off by the wind and the waves see Maltby (2002) 221-222 on Tib. 1.4.21-26 and L. C. Watson (2003) 468 on Hor. *Epod.* 15.4. The theme is found first in Hesiod fr. 124 Merkelbach-West, where it is related to Zeus' false oath to Hera that he had not had intercourse with Io, ἐκ τοῦ δ' ὅρκον ἔθηκεν ἀποίνιμον ἀνθρώποισι / νοσφιδίων ἔργων πέρι Κύπριδος ["from then on he made an oath concerning clandestine love affairs un-punishable for men"], and becomes proverbial: cf. Soph. fr. 742 Nauck; Eur. *Medea* 21-23, 160-163, 208-209, 492-498; Plato Phileb. 65c; Call. *Epig.* 25.3-4, *AP* 5.8.5 (Meleager), 5.133.4 (Maecius); Plaut. *Cist.* 472; Cat. 30.10, 64.59, 142, 70.3-4; Tib. 1.4.21-26, 9.1-6; Prop. 2.16B.47-56, 28.5-8; Ov. *Am.* 1.8.85-86, 2.8.19-20 with McKeown II 164 ad loc., 16.45-46 (quoted below). The closest in wording to the present passage, with an identical second half of the hexameter, is Ov. *Ars* 1.633-634 *Iuppiter ex alto periuria ridet amantum / et iubet Aeolios irrita ferre Notos.* There, however, it is male lovers who are encouraged to swear falsely with impunity to attract *puellae*; as often, our author reverses the standard elegiac gender roles. For further parallels see Clausen on Virg. *Ecl.* 3.72-73, 8.19. N-H on Hor. *Carm.* 2.8 *Intro* and 13, Grassmann (1966) 43-45, Skiadas (1975).

periuria ... amantum: cf. **39-42n.** above on *Theseae ... periuria linguae.*

uentos inrita ferre iubet: cf. Ov. *Am.* 2.16.45-46 *uerba puellarum, foliis leuiora caducis, / inrita, qua uisum est, uentus et unda ferunt* with McKeown III 363 ad loc., and, in a different context, **4.96** above *et iubeat tepidos inrita ferre Notos.*

51-52 ergo quid: for this phrase opening the hexameter cf. Mart. 4.87.4, 9.22.16; elsewhere in the line in Martial at 8.76.7 and 11.57.6; Juv. 10.103. For *ergo* in Ovid introducing indignant, often rhetorical, questions, cf. *Am.* 1.4.3, 6.21, 7.11, 2.7.1, 3.2.8, 11.9, 11, and see McKeown II 80 on *Am.* 1.4.3-4 and *ThLL* 5(2).769.1-38.

quid ... / conqueror?: Cf. *quid queror* at **37** above. In both passages Lygdamus questions his role as an elegiac poet. The word 'elegy' was connected etymologically by the ancients with complaint, see *LALE* s.v. *elegia*. In this poem, the final one of this group, the author turns from elegy to symposiastic themes more characteristic of lyric. In view of the mythological theme of **39-42** above, the rhetorical question here may possibly echo the way Ariadne breaks off her complaint at Cat. 64.164 *sed quid ego ignaris nequiquam conqueror auris*? The verb is used of female complaint also at Tib. 1.10.54 and Ov. Met. 9.147 (Deianeira). For *conqueror* opening the verse cf. Lucan 5.491.

fallacis uerba puellae: Lygdamus' Neaera shares with Horace's Neaera at *Epod*. 15.3, the characteristic of swearing falsely, cf. the triple *perfida* applied to her at **55-56** below. As L. C. Watson (2003) 467-468 on Hor. *Epod*. 15.3 points out, the accusations of perjury were the stock in trade of rejected lovers, cf. *AP* 5.175 and 5.178 (Meleager); Tib. 1.9.1-6; Prop. 1.15.33-42; Ov. *Am*. 3.11.21-26 and see Grassman (1966) 43-44. By contrast Lygdamus asserts that he has never sworn falsely (**4.16**), perhaps a reference to the oath he gives at **1.25** that he loves Neaera more than his own heart. Genuine oaths of fidelity to his mistress proves the downfall of the author at **19.15-20**. The repetition here of *fallax* from **47**, and particularly of *uerba* in penultimate position from **36, 38**, also to reappear in **52**, is seen by some (e.g. Tränkle 168 ad loc.) as an example of stylistic weakness, but may not have been felt as such by the ancients, who seem to have had a rather different view of repetition of this kind; see Wills (1996) 473-477. The phrase *fallacis ... puellae* is found at Tib. 1.6.15; cf. *fallat ... puella* at **12** above. When Neaera is described as *puella* it is always in relation to her infidelity: **4.58**, here and **60** below. The term stresses her role as a typical elegiac mistress, but it is not incompatible with her status as a married woman. For *puella* of married women, cf. Ov. *Fast*. 2.810 (of Lucretia), 445, 451, 557 (with Robinson ad loc.).

ite a me .... precor: for the dismissal of care and seriousness as a typical sympotic theme, and for its quasi-liturgical expression, see **7n**. *ite procul* and **25n**. *procul a nobis* above. Again, the rejection of serious topics implies a move away from elegy.

seria uerba: the equivalent of *tristia uerba* in **38** and the opposite of *ebria uerba* in **36**. The *iunctura* is found only here and at Gell. 1.26.7, but for the sense cf. Hor. *AP* 105-107 *tristia maestum / uoltum uerba decent, iratum plena minarum / ludentem lasciua, seuerum seria dictu*.

53-56 The content of these two couplets comes as a sharp contrast to what has immediately preceded, illustrating the inner contradictions in Lygdamus' position. Despite her treachery, and his efforts to free himself from her, Neaera remains dear to him. His move from elegiac to symposiastic poetry has again stalled temporarily (cf. **33-36** with **n.** above), to be finally re-instated in the concluding couplets of the poem **57-64**.

53 quam uellem: common in Cicero (28), but extremely rare in verse outside comedy (Plaut. *Poen.* 1107; Ter. *And.* 326, *Heaut.* 185, *Ad.* 532), occurring in this context only at Mart. 8.72.9 *quam uellem fieri meus libellus* (also at the beginning of the line).

tecum longas requiescere noctes: the phrase marks a return to elegiac themes with its possible echo of Tib.'s opening poem, in which he rejects ancestral riches in favour of nights of love spent with his mistress: 1.1.43-46 *... satis est requiescere lecto / si licet ... / quam iuuat immites uentos audire cubantem / et dominam tenero continuisse sinu*. In view of the fact that our poet as Lygdamus could be impersonating the rich rival to whom Horace lost his Neaera in *Epod.* 15 (see **47-49n.** above) the *adsiduas ... noctes* with Neaera that Horace wishes to deny his rival may be relevant here: *Epod.* 15.13 *non feret* (sc. *Flaccus*) *adsiduas potiori te dare noctes.* For the phrase *longae noctes*, referring to long winter nights of love cf. Cat. 68.81-83 (of Laodamia) *coniugis ante coacta noui dimittere collum / quam ueniens una atque altera rursus hiems / noctibus in longis auidum saturasset amorem.* Elsewhere the phrase is used of the long, lonely nights of the deserted or excluded lover, perhaps hinting at Lygdamus' current loveless state: Hor. *Carm.* 1.25.7-8 *me tuo longas pereunte noctes, / Lydia, dormis?, Epist.* 1.1.20 *ut nox longa quibus mentitur amica*; Prop. 1.12.13-14 *nunc primum longas solus cognoscere noctes / cogor*; Ov. *Am.* 2.19.21-22 *sine me ante tuos proiectum in limine postes / longa pruinosa frigora nocte pati.* For the use of *requiescere* in erotic contexts, implying lovemaking cf. Prop. 1.8B.33-34 *illa uel angusto mecum requiescere lecto / et quocumque modo maluit esse mea*; Ov. *Her.* 5.13 *saepe greges inter requieuimus arbore tecti*, and see Pichon 249.

54 tecum longos peruigilare dies: parallel to *tecum ... noctes* **53**. For the mention of night and day in the context of lovemaking, cf. Plaut. *Asin.* 753 *Philaenium ut secum esset noctes et dies*; Ter. *Eun.* 193 *dies noctesque me ames me desideres*; Ov. *Rem.* 537-538 *i, fruere usque tua, nullo prohibente, puella: / illa tibi noctes auferat, illa dies.* The use of *peruigilare* with *dies* is unparalleled. It is usually applied to being wakeful at night, e.g. Plaut. *Aul.* 72-73 *peruigilat noctes totas ... / ... domi sedet totos dies.* At Cat. 88.1-2 it is used in the context of keeping vigil (lovemaking) without specific reference to night: ... *qui cum matre atque sorore / prurit et abiectis peruigilat tunicis.* Given that *longos dies* could apply to the long hot days of the summer, the reference could be to making love instead of sleeping at siesta time, the theme of Cat. 32 and Ov. *Am.* 1.5.

55 perfida nec merito nobis inimica merenti: a difficult line, meaning literally, 'faithless girl, hostile to me (*nobis*) unjustly, though deserving well', where *nec merito* = 'undeserving', and *merenti* = 'though deserving well (of you)'. The pleonasm is typical of the *Lygd.* group (see **2.15, 4.47-48, 93, 5.27** with **notes** above). The lack of agreement between *nobis* pl. and *merito* and *merenti* sing., though found in Early Latin, e.g. *absente nobis* at Ter. *Eun.* 649 and Afr. *Com.* 6, is unparalleled at this period. The use of *nobis* and *mi* (referred to by N-A ad loc.) at Cat. 107.3-6 *quare hoc est gratum nobis quoque, carius auro, / quod te restituis, Lesbia, mi cupido, / restituis cupido atque insperanti, ipsa refers te / nobis* is not as difficult as the present case, since *cupido atque insperanti* refers back to *mi*, not forward to *nobis* and the two pronouns occur in different clauses. In view of the difficulties here some editors, perhaps correctly, have accepted the emendation *nec amica* for *inimica* found in some recentiores and the Venice edition of 1475, and have interpreted the line to mean 'faithless to me unjustly and a friend (to another) undeservedly.' The other man would be the rival suggested in *ignotum ... torum* at **60** below.

perfida: the adj is commonly applied to the faithless mistress in Prop. 1.11.16, 16.43, 2.5.3, 9.28, 18.19; cf. Tib. 1.8.63, Ov. *Am.* 3.3.1 and see Pichon 231. On the triple repetition of *perfida* in **55-56** see Wills (1996) 70.

56 The formulation of the line, with its rare final *tamen*, recalls **1.6** *seu mea seu fallor cara Neaera tamen.* This echo of the first poem in the last poem of the *Lygd.* group must be deliberate. By this stage it has become clear that Neaera, while still *cara*, is no longer, from Lygdamus' point of view, *mea*.

quamuis perfida: for the use of *quamuis* + adj. cf. Ov. *Met.* 3.494 with Bömer 567 ad loc.

cara; see **1.6n.**

tamen: unusual at the pentameter ending, arguing for a conscious echo of **1.6**; see **1.6n.** *tamen.*

57-58 A return to the appeal of the opening lines, **5-6**, for a slave boy to pour wine. In this case the servant is asked to add water to the wine on the grounds that Bacchus (wine) loves Naias (a water nymph). For the convention in sympotic verse for the servant to be asked to bring both wine and water, see N-H II 176 on Hor. *Carm.* 2.11.19 *restinguet*. The poet returns at the end of his poem to the sympotic mode of the beginning, making a clear break with his earlier elegiac stance of **33-36** and **53-56**.

57 Naida Bacchus amat: Naiads were nymphs of fresh water springs. Their presence in Bacchus' retinue is attested first in Pratin. fr. 1.4 Page, cf. Hor. *Carm.* 3.25.14-15 ... *o Naiadum potens / Baccharumque*. The bald statement here that Bacchus loves a Naiad is simply a metonymic periphrasis for 'wine is best served with water'. For the expression cf. Ov. *Fast.* 2.606 (of Jupiter) *Naida ... uir tuus... amat*. At a metapoetic level the combination of wine and water could represent a combination of sympotic with Callimachean themes. On the Callimachean preference for water drinkers see Heyworth (1994) 63-67. With the exception of Mart. 7.15.2 *effugit dominam Naida numquid Hylas?*, the forms *Naida /Naidas* are regularly found, as here, at the beginning of the line in elegiac and hexameter verse (Ov. *Met.* 6.453, 9.657, *Fast.* 4.231, *Pont.* 4.16.35; Stat. *Silu.* 1.5.6, *Ach.* 1.295, 825; Priap. 33.1). For the use of *amat* here to denote what wine goes well with, cf. Ov. *Fast.* 5.345 *Bacchus amat flores*.

cessas, o lente minister?: a question introduced by *cessas* is used regularly from Plautus on to press someone into action (e.g. Plaut. *Curc.* 672; Ter. *And.* 343; Tib. 2.2.10; Virg. *Aen.* 11.389; Ov. *Fast.* 6.675 and see Tarrant on Sen. *Ag.* 198). For its use, as here, to order a slave to pour wine in the context of a symposium, cf. Mart. 9.93.1 *addere quid cessas, puer, immortale Falernum?*

lente: the slave is slow to perform his function, cf. Mart. 11.36.5-6 *Hypne, quid expectas, piger? immortale Falernum / funde*.

minister: often used of a cup-bearer at a symposium or dinner-party, see *OLD minister* 1 and cf. Cat. 27.1 *minister uetuli puer Falerni*; Val. Fl. 5.694 (of Ganymede) *Phrygius ... minister*; Mart. 10.98.1 *addat cum mihi Caecubum minister*.

58 temperet: 'to blend', *OLD tempero* 6b.

annosum ... merum: also in the same *sedes* at Ov. *Ars* 2.418 *tritaque in annoso flaua pyrethra mero*. For the use of the adj. of old wine cf. **2.19**

annoso ... Lyaeo, Plin. *Nat.* 23.40.10 *condire eo aliud minus annosum* (sc. *uinum*) *insalubre est*.

Marcia lympha: a reference to water from the *Aqua Marcia*, an aqueduct built in 144-140 BC by Q. Marcius Rex and restored by Agrippa in 33 BC (Plin. *Nat.* 36.121). It was famous for its clean, cold water, cf. Plin. *Nat.* 31.41 *clarissima aquarum omnium in toto orbe frigoris salubritatisque palma praeconio urbis Marcia est*, Frontin. *Aqu.* 91.5; Stat. *Silu.* 1.5.26-27. Its water is mentioned twice by Prop. 3.2.14 *Marcius ... liquor* and 3.22.24 *Marcius umor*. On the use of *lympha* = 'water' here, see **5.3n.** *sacris ... lymphis*.

59 non ego: a characteristic opening for the figure of *auersio* in the *Lygd.* group, see **2.5-6n.** and **5.7-14n.**

si fugit: for the combination of habitual perfect 'if she flees' with the future *repetam* (**61**) 'I will not sigh' in a conditional clause cf. **47-49** above *etsi ... iurauit ... nulla fides inerit* with **n.** on *iurauit*. For the use of *fugit* in this context and for the mention of *torum* (cf. **60** below) cf. Ov. *Am.* 2.11.7-8 *ecce fugit notumque torum sociosque Penates / fallacisque uias ire Corinna parat* with McKeown III 233 ad loc. who compares Prop. 1.8B.38.

conuiuia mensae: the same hexameter ending is found at Ov. *Met.* 1.165, 12.222, *Ibis* 431; *Laus Pis.* 153; Mart. 8.39.1. For the use of *mensa* in the context of a symposium see Heyworth (2007b) 182. For *conuiuia* as characteristic of symposiastic poetry, cf. Hor. *Carm.* 1.6.17-19 *nos conuiuia ... / ... / cantamus uacui* (as opposed to epic), and his description of the lyric poet Alcaeus at *Carm.* 1.32.9-10 *Liberum et Musas ... / ... canebat* see Harrison (2007) 173.

60 ignotum ... torum: this phrase, together with *sollicitus* **61**, is clearly related to the couplet at **16.5-6** in the *Sulpicia* group *solliciti sunt pro nobis quibus illa dolori est / ne cedam ignoto maxima cura toro*, the only other place where this adj. is coupled with *torus*. In that poem *ignoto ... toro* relates to sexual relations with a partner of low social status. Here the reference appears to be to the bed of a 'new' lover, as opposed to the familiar *notus /solitus* bed of Lygdamus; for this last sense, cf. Tib. 1.1.44 *solito ... toro* referring to the bed of his accustomed mistress, Delia; Ov. *Am.* 2.11.7, quoted on **59** above; and **19.22** *notae seruitium dominae* 'enslavement to a familiar mistress.'; see below **19 headnote** and ad loc. As well giving a different meaning to *ignoto ... toro* from that found in the

Sulpicia poems (**13-18**), our poet as Lygdamus also refuses to worry about a situation (*non*) *sollicitus* **61**, which is a cause of concern to Sulpicia's friends *solliciti sunt* at **16.5**.

cupiens: elsewhere in the *Corpus* only at **18.6**, perhaps our author in *Sulpicia*'s last poem echoes the last poem of the *Lygd.* group.

uana: 'unreliable', 'untrustworthy', 'fickle'. The adj is used only rarely of persons, see *OLD uanus* 4 and cf. Virg. *Aen.* 1.392 *ni frustra augurium uani docuere parentes*.

puella: see **51-52n.** above.

61 sollicitus: here, as often, used of the worries caused by love, with a strong metapoetic suggestion of Gallan elegy (Virg. *Ecl.* 10.5) see **4.20n.** and **6.35-36n.** *sollicitis* above and cf. N-R 117 on Hor. *Carm.* 3.7.9. For the use of the adj. in **16.5**, see **60n.** above. Whereas at **35-36** above sympotic themes *ebria uerba* **36** were said to be incompatible with those with elegiac concerns *sollicitis*, here, in the final section of the poem, our author turns from elegy *non ego ... sollicitus* **59-61** to the lyric, sympotic themes of **62-64** (cf. **57n.** above). Just as the final poem of Virgil's *Eclogues* expands the genre of pastoral by importing elegiac material from Gallus [on which see Conte (1986) 100-129, Harrison (2007) 17, 59-74], so here at the end of this elegiac group, the author expands the genre by importing lyric/sympotic material.

repetam ... suspiria: literally 'repeat sighs'; the phrase is Ovidian in the sense of 'sigh deeply', 'heave sighs', cf. Ov. *Met.* 2.125 *repetens suspiria dixit*, 13.739 *talibus adloquitur repetens suspiria dictis*.

tota ... nocte: the accusative was initially regular in expressions of extent of time, see K-S II 1.284 and cf. Plaut. *Asin.* 872 *totam noctem stertere*. However, from Catullus on, the ablative takes over this function in prose and verse, especially in phrases with *totus*, which itself expresses duration; see K-S II 1.360, Anmerkung 12 and cf. Cat. 109.5-6 *tota perducere uita / ... foedus amicitiae*. In the elegists *tota nocte* is the rule for expressing 'all night long': Tib. 1.6.32; Prop. 2.14.28, 16.6, 22.24, 23.10, 3.23.16; Ov. *Am.* 1.6.68, 2.9.39. Nevertheless the ancient grammarians persisted in the belief that the accusative was to be preferred: Serv. *Aen.* 1.47 *in istis elocutionibus* (i.e. *Aen.* 1.47-48 *tot annos / bella gero*) *et accusatiuo et ablatiuo utimur. dicimus enim et 'tota nocte legi' et 'totam noctem legi'. honestior tamen elocutio est per accusatiuum*.

62 The third time in the poem that a slave is asked to pour wine, cf. **5-6** and **57** above. Whereas in **57** the wine was to be mixed with water, here it is to be served neat, as Lygdamus' desire to drown his sorrows comes once more to the fore, cf. **5-7** above. At a metapoetic level the change to neat wine could represent a complete move to the symposiastic genre, cf. **35-36n.**, **57n.** and **61n.** above. In Catullus it is argued that the address to a slave to pour 'stronger' or 'more bitter' cups at 27.1-2 *minister uetuli puer Falerni / inger mi calices amariores* introduces a new section within the polymetrics, signalling a change in tone to invective in the following poems; see Wiseman [(1969) 7-8] and Gutzwiller [(2012) 99-100], who points to the ancient metaphorical equation between wine and poetry at Dionys. Chalcus fr. 4 West.

tu, puer, i: this is the reading of the Fragmentum Cuiacianum for the nonsensical *tu puer et* of A+. Some editors suggest the emendation *i puer et*, first proposed by Ach. Statius, on the grounds that *i* reinforcing an imperative is generally followed by a conjunction, e.g. Prop. 3.23.23 *i puer et citus haec aliqua propone columna*. However, Hor. *Epist.* 1.7.71 *nunc i, rem strenuus auge* provides a rare parallel for the reading of F.

puer: commonly used in apostrophes to servants to pour wine, cf. Mart. 9.93.1 *addere quid cessas, puer, immortale Falernum?*, 14.170.2 *deciens adde Falerna, puer* and cf. **5** above.

liquidum ... merum: 'clear neat wine'; the same combination is found at Ov. *Trist.* 2.490 *quaeque, docet, liquido testa sit apta mero* and Mart. 12.60.8-9 *... ut liquidum potet Alauda merum, / turbida sollicito transmittere Caecuba sacco*, where it is explained that Caecuban wine is made clear, *liquidum*, by being strained through a cloth. Other examples of this use of *liquidus* of 'strained' wine at Plaut. *Stich.* 700; Hor. *Epist.* 1.14.34; Ov. *Met.* 13.639.

fortius: more likely to be an adverb with *adde* 'pour more boldly' than an adj. with *merum* 'stronger wine', in view of the fact that the wine is already qualified by the adj. *liquidum*.

adde merum: the same expression in the same context of drowning the sorrows of love is found in the opening of Tib. 1.2.1 (adapted from Meleager *AP* 12.49.1) and also at the verse end in Ov. *Am.* 1.4.52 *dumque bibit, furtim si potes, adde merum*. For *adde* in the context of pouring wine, cf. also Mart. 9.93.1, 14.170.2, both quoted on *puer* above.

63 iamdudum: a common hexameter opening from Virg. *Aen.* 5.27 onwards, e.g. Virg. (3), Hor. (3), Ov. (6), Stat. (9), Val. Fl. (2), Sil. (4). The adv. is rare in elegy and could be closural here; an end to elegy and a move to sympotic poetry is long overdue, cf. Fulkerson (2017) 221 ad loc.

Syrio madefactus tempora nardo: for the meaning of *Syrio* and the MSS corruption into *Tyrio* see **4.28n.** *Syrio ... rore* above. For the custom of anointing the hair with sweet-smelling nard at a drinking party cf. Hor. *Carm.* 2.11.13-17 *cur non ... / ...et rosa / canos odorati capillos, / dum licet, Assyriaque nardo / potamus uncti*? Nard, the oil of the aromatic plant spikenard, was the most prized and expensive of unguents amongst the ancients; see Harrison 142 on Hor. *Carm.* 2.11.16 and cf. Plin. *Nat.* 12.42 *de folio nardi plura dici par est ut principali in unguentis*, who later on 45 distinguishes between Syrian, Indian, Gallic and Cretan nard and says of the Syrian variety *in nostro orbe proxime laudatur Syriacum.* For the hexameter ending *tempora nardo* cf. Tib. 2.2.7 *illius puro destillent tempora nardo*. The reference to *tempora* here at the end of the poem recalls the opening invocation to Bacchus in **2** above: *sic hedera tempora uincta feras*.

madefactus: 'soaked', cf. Ov. *Met.* 12.301... *ipse suo madefactus sanguine fugit.* The related *madeo* and *madidus* are more frequently used of perfumed hair, e.g. Virg. *Aen.* 4.216 *crinem ... madentem*; Ov. *Am.* 1.6.38 *madidis lapsa corona comis.* Again there is an echo of the opening of the poem, *madeant* **5** above.

64 debueram ... inplicuisse: 'I should have entwined'; for the construction, cf. Juv. 3.163 *debuerant olim tenues migrasse Quirites.* For *inplicuisse* in this position in the pentameter, cf. Tib. 1.4.56; Prop. 3.5.20; Ov. *Her.* 2.142.

sertis inplicuisse comas: for the symposiastic custom of entwining flower garlands in the hair, see Hor. *Carm.* 2.11.13-15 quoted in **63n.** above and see the further examples from Hor. *Carm.* and Anacreon in Harrison 142 on Hor. *Carm.* 2.11.14-15. For the use of *inplico* in this context cf. Ov. *Fast.* 5.219-220 *protinus accedunt Charites nectuntque coronas / sertaque caelestes implicitura comas.*

comas: for this and other words for hair in the *Lygd.* group see **2.11-12n.** *longos incompta capillos.* Fulkerson [(2017) 221 ad loc.] points to a possible echo of *comam*, the last word of the last poem in Horace's third book of Odes: *Carm.* 3.30.16 *lauro cinge uolens, Melpomene, comam.*

The Praises of Messalla

Poem 7

The ostensible date for this poem is immediately after Messalla Corvinus' entry upon the consulship on 1 January 31 BC. The contents include a description of the ceremony (**118-134**), an account of Messalla's achievements as an orator (**45-53**), past military achievements in an Illyrian campaign (**106-117**) and vague prophecies concerning his military and civic success in the future (**135-150**). No mention is made of the main event of Messalla's consulship, the battle of Actium, on the second of September, in which Messalla certainly took part. Perhaps the author intends the date of composition to be taken as after the January inauguration but before the battle of the following September. There is also complete silence about Octavian, Messalla's colleague in the consulship, but, as in the works of the genuine Tibullus, the whole emphasis is placed on the patron, Messalla. Similarly, in the historical section of Tacitus' *Agricola* it is the *laudandus* Agricola that plays a central role while the emperor Domitian is not mentioned; see Woodman (2014) 5.

Our poet presents himself as a young man, from a rich family, which, like that of Tibullus, has suffered some losses in its fortunes (**181-189**). It is suggested that financial support from Messalla would be welcome. The date and authorship of the poem have long been a subject of debate. Early critics saw it as the work of a young Tibullus and took its purported date as genuine, but since the time of Heyne a date in the late first century AD, possibly by a poet masquerading as Tibullus, has been broadly accepted. For further details on the style and possible date of composition see Gen. Intro., sections 2.2.2 and 3.3.

Like *Catalepton* 9 which celebrates in elegiacs Messalla as a possible poetic patron for a poet posing as the young Virgil at the time of writing his *Eclogues* [on which see Kayachev (2016b], and like the *Laus Pisonis*, supposedly written by an anonymous young poet in hexameters looking for a patron for his works from a well-known supporter of the arts from the mid first century AD [on which see La Penna (1991)], so the *Laudes Messallae* is written by our poet masquerading as the young Tibullus, searching for a patron at a stage before he had started on the composition of his elegiac books. For verbal and thematic links with the *Laus Pisonis* see **nn. 1, 2, 7, 28-32, 34, 37, 39, 45-47, 46-47, 48-49, 54-78, 92, 107-110, 118-134, 175, 178** and **180** below. For similar links with

338 Commentary

Catalepton 9 see **nn. 2, 4, 5-6, 25, 26-27, 32, 39, 48-49, 53, 112a, 137-146, 178, 180, 193-195, 196, 211**. Peirano [(2012) 132-148] is the first to bring out clearly the nature of these works, not a serious panegyric, but as humorous 'job application letters' [Peirano p. 148] applying to be the poet of a well-known patron, written some time after the events portrayed and serving to fill in a gap in our historical knowledge of the patron-client relationships of such high-profile writers as Virgil and Tibullus. The purpose of these impersonations is to entertain a private audience, perhaps in the case of the *Laudes Messallae*, in the household of Messalla's descendants. They are intended to be humorous and the humour is often at the expense of the poetic persona. As is clear from the inappropriateness of the way many of the traditional elements of panegyric are treated in this poem which has induced many earlier critics to see it as a bad poem [e.g. Bright (1984) 38 n.1], the lack of a clear historical narrative of Messalla's career to date and the omission of certain key elements about his family and achievements (see **nn. 45-47, 106-117, 147** below) the poem's humour depends on its parodic representation of the genre to which it belongs. The often overblown style, inappropriate digressions and irrelevant mythological examples (see **nn. 8-15, 48-49, 54-78, 81, 89-97** below) all have a role to play in the creation of humour within such a rhetorical context. It has been argued, however, by Schrijvers (2006) that the geographical digressions at **52-81, 118-150** and **151-174** may in fact reflect a particular interest of the addressee in Hellenistic geography, a concern also reflected in Tib. 1.7 and *Catalepton* 9. For the rhetorical context itself see the references to Menander Rhetor's advice on panegyric composition discussed in **nn. 28-32, 39, 89-97, 106-117, 118-134, 123, 196** and **197-200** below.

This fictional panegyric addressed to a patron of a previous generation would fit well into the subgenre of epideictic literature concerned with fictional encomia on abstruse subjects such as Gorgias' *Encomium of Helen*; see Peirano (2012) 171 and nn.143-146. Rhetorical exercises of this kind frequently involved characters from recent or not so recent history. In the dangerous conditions of imperial Rome, as described in the introduction to Tacitus' *Agricola*, this type of parodic panegyric would recommend itself as a safe way of approaching the subject without incurring imperial wrath; see Hardie (2012) 274-283. On the problem of free speech in general under the empire see Feeney (1992).

Why a long poem in hexameter should appear at this point in a poetry book otherwise devoted to elegy needs some explanation. However, its connection with Tibullus' patron Messalla, and its position as seventh poem, reflecting the position of Tibullus' celebration of Messalla's Aquitanian triumph of 27 BC in Tib.1.7, would go some way towards explaining it. Its opening concern with Callimachean poetics (echoing poem 1 see **nn. 4, 7, 8-15** below) and Callimachean mythological *exempla* (see **12-13** with **nn.** ad loc.) as well as its use of numerous themes from Latin love elegy (see e.g. **91n., 137n., 197-200n.**) within the framework of a hexameter panegyric also serve to integrate it well into the collection. On the important Hellenistic and Augustan concept of including within a work of one genre elements of those taken from another see Kroll [(1924) 202-224, where it is termed 'Kreuzung der Gattungen'], Rossi (1971) and Harrison [(2007) where it is termed 'generic enrichment']. The unitary author of **book 3** placed this poem in a central position in the collection, between the *Lygdamus* and *Sulpicia* cycles, in order to give it added prominence. As in the *Lygd.* poems, so in this poem he shares some of the characteristics of Horace's rival for Neaera in *Epod.* 15 (see **198-199n., 206-210n.** below and cf. Gen. Intro., section 2.2.1, **1 headnote, 1.19n., 3 headnote, 3.29n., 4.16n., 6.47-49n., 6.53n.**).

On the poem's relation to other Roman panegyric see Roche [(2011) (ed.)] and on the importance of its relationship with Callimachean elegiac epinicia see Cameron [(1995) 480-481]. Like Catullus 66, a translation of Callimachus' *Coma Berenices* ('Lock of Berenice'), the poem illustrates the way in which it is possible to write epinician poetry without becoming too involved in issues of contemporary war and politics; see the discussions of this poem by Du Quesnay (2012) and (2017). In his poem which was the last piece in *Aetia* 4 [see Massimilla (2010) 161], Callimachus side-steps the necessity of celebrating the Syrian war of Ptolemy Euergetes in 246 BC by focussing on the lock vowed by his new queen Berenice for his safe return and *its* ultimate catasterism. Hutchinson [(2012) 49-50] is instructive on the way Ptolemy's military victories are replaced by a description of his conquests in the bedroom (Cat. 66.13-14). Similarly in the *Laus Pisonis* it is the addressee's abilities at a board game that stand in for his military exploits (*Laus Pis.* 190-208). On the importance of Cat. 66 for the catasterisms in Ovid's *Met.* and the way in which these lead the way to the imperial apotheoses of the last two books see Myers (2012) 244-249. The brief panegyric to Octavian embodied in the proem to Virg. *Georg.* 1.24-42 also betrays the influence of Callimachean encomium, especially in its echo in **32** of a line from Callimachus' *Coma Berenices* (= Call. fr. 110.64 Pf.; Cat. 66.64); see Thomas (1988) 73 on *Georg.* 1.24-42 and 74 on *Georg.* 1.32. Virgil's mention of *Erigone* in this context (*Georg.* 1.33) links the proem of *Georgics* (and its Callimachean model) to our poem; see **9-11n.** below and the discussion in Whitcomb (2018). Similarly the mention of *Molorceis ... tectis* in **13** hints at another Callimachean passage connected with Berenice (*SH* fr. 254-269); see **9-11n.** and **12-13n.** below, which also forms part of a Virgilian proem in *Georgics* 3. See further Thomas (1988) 42-43 on *Georg.* 3.19-20 and (2008) 193-195. This Virgilian use of Callimachean epinicion in the context of praise for a patron is also reflected in another key Latin predecessor of the present poem, namely in Tibullus 1.7, celebrating Messalla's Aquitanian triumph of 27 BC. The text is printed in full in Appendix 3(b) and its relation to poem **7** is discussed in the Gen. Intro., section 3.3. This elegy begins with Messalla's birthday, which is also the day of his triumph, and enumerates the location of Messalla's various victories and appointments over the world, ranging from Gaul to Egypt. Mention of Egypt leads into a central hymn to Osiris, who is identified with Dionysus as a bringer of civilisation to mortals. The poem ends back with Messalla's birthday, which is linked with what has gone before by an invitation to Osiris to attend. This elegiac epinicion has more Callimachean echoes than any other poem in Tibullus. The address to the Nile in 27-28 echoes Call. fr. 383.16 Pf. (= *SH* 254.16) from his elegiac epinicion *Victoria Berenices*, and two further passages reflect lines from Callimachus' epinicion to Sosibius, namely 21-22 on the Nile floods = Call. fr. 384.27 Pf. and 23-24 on the source of the Nile = Call. fr. 384.31-32 Pf.

The position of the present poem as seventh in **[Tib.] 3** reflects the position of Tibullus' poem to Messalla as seventh in his first book. Not only, then, does our poem share its position in the book with Tib. 1.7, but it also shares with Tib. 1.7 a clear concern with Callimachean poetics, especially in the myths of Erigone and Molorcus in **11-13**. The influence of Callimachus' pupil Eratosthenes can be seen in the choice of the Erigone myth (see **9-11n.**) and in the digression on the earth's five zones (see **151-174n.**), and this poet too may have influenced Tib. in his discussion of the invention of the viticulture at Tib. 1.7.31-34. Propertius 4.6 addressed to Augustus on the battle of Actium follows this Callimachean tradition of elegiac epinicion; see Cairns (1984) and Cameron (1995) 478-479. The mention of *Cyrenaeas ... aquas* at Prop. 4.6.4 invokes Callimachus. Like the *Coma Berenices* it lacks any real details of the battle which is its central concern. Only Apollo and Cleopatra are named as taking part and most of the battle description concerns its geographical location. A successful epinicion need not be serious [see Sweet (1972)], but following in Callimachus' footsteps can avoid to a large extent the dangerous military and political themes. The pseudo-Virgilian *Catalepton* 9 also praises Messalla on the occasion of his

Aquitanian triumph (3-4) and also flaunts its Callimachean credentials (see 61-64, especially *si adire Cyrenas* 61) in its attempt to marry elegiac encomium with Callimachean poetics. The theme of an addressee's present or future victories and triumphs is also to be seen in Prop. 2.1.27-38 (where Maecenas is associated with Augustus' victories), 2.10.13-18 (a list of Augustus' future battles, including in Britain 17); Ov. *Ars* 1.117-218 (Gaius' Eastern expedition of 1 BC), with its echo in 187-188 of Call. *Hymn* 1 (to Zeus) 55-57 and *Trist.* 4.2 and *Pont.* 4.2 on the successive triumphs of Tiberius. These, when taken in combination with the *Laus Pisonis*, serve to set our poem in its Latin and Callimachean context. Callimachean metapoetic pointers in the opening of the poem, *humilis* **4**, *paruaque ... mica* **14**, *paruus labor* **16** and, in particular, *munera parua* **7**, echoing the same phrase at **1.24** seem like an intentional reference back to such metapoetic vocabulary in the opening poem of the book and so serve to anchor the piece firmly in its place.

The structure of the poem may be analysed as follows:

1-38 Proemium. The author doubts his own literary capabilities, but will vie with other poets to provide an account of Messalla's great achievements.

39-44 Messalla has achieved great things, both in war and in the civil sphere.

45-53 Messalla's achievements as an orator, both in the law courts and before the popular assembly rival those of Odysseus and Nestor.

54-81 Digression. A detailed account of the contents of the Odyssey.

82-105 Messalla's knowledge of military skills.

106-120 His past triumphs in the Illyrian campaign and prediction of future victories.

121-134 Climax of the poem. Description of the day of Messalla's inauguration as consul; nature's reverential silence and the blessing of Jove.

135-150 Prophecies of Messalla's future victories, both near and far, including Britain and the Antipodes.

151-176 Digression. Description of the earth's five zones.

177-180 The author is not as worthy as Valgius to sing of such triumphs.

181-189 His house is not as affluent as it was.

190-200 He will nevertheless continue to sing of Messalla and face any hardship for his sake.

201-211 If his verse meets with Messalla's approval, he will continue to sing of him until his own death and, after death, will add to these songs when reincarnated once more as a man.

The poem displays a clear ring-structure, with a recapitulation at the end of themes from the opening: **177-180** the poet's unworthiness for the task, cf. **1-2**; **201-203** if his verse finds favour with Messalla, he will continue to sing of him in the future, cf. **16-17**.

The theme of loss of former riches (**181-189**) is so reminiscent in language and content of Tibullus 1.1.19-22, 41-43 that it strengthens the impression that our author intends to impersonate Tibullus. Holzberg [(1998) 191 and n. 50] argues persuasively that the *Laud. Mess.* includes items from epic poetry (i.e. the 'Odyssey' at **48ff.**, and the *bella* at **82f.**), and from cosmological didactic (i.e. at **18ff.** cosmology, and at **151ff.** the five zone theory of the earth), since these themes had been specifically rejected by Tib. in his *recusatio* at 2.4.16-18. On this form of 'generic enrichment' in the poem see Harrison (2007) cited above. Despite his own *recusatio*, suggesting Valgius as better equipped for speaking of *magnae res* (**177-180**), our author claims for Tibullus' youth subjects that Tib. had rejected as a mature elegist.

1-2 The opening two lines present a number of problems of text and interpretation. In line **1** *mea* of A+ makes no sense and must be replaced by *tua* or *me*, found as corrections in some later manuscripts. The advantage of *me* is that it provides an object for *terret*. In line **2** the Fragmentum Cuiacianum offers *nequeant* in place of *ualeant*, which would make *ut ... nequeant* a rather awkward concessive clause, with *incipiam* as its main verb. It would also involve a pause after *terret*. If we accept *ualeant*, then the *ut* (= *ne non*) would follow on more naturally from *terret* and the pause would come after *uires*. The reading *ualeant* seems preferable in view of the possible model for this passage at Ov. *Pont.* 3.4, where the poet entrusts to his friend Rufinus the care of a poem he had written on the triumph of Tiberius over the Pannonians and Dalmatians: cf. especially 13 *uiribus infirmi, uestro candore ualemus* and 83-84 *res quoque tanta fuit quantae subsistere summo / Aeneadum uati* *grande fuisset opus*. (For a further echo from the same poem, see **7n.** below). The choice of *ualeant* would also avoid two almost identical concessive clauses, *quamquam ... / terret* and *ut ... nequeant*, following one after the other.

1. Te, Messalla, canam: corresponds to the formula with ἀείσομαι, or ἄρχομ' ἀείδειν or μνήσομ' ἀοιδῆς found at the beginning or at the end of the Homeric Hymns; see Norden (1913) 153, and in Latin cf. Virg. *Georg.* 2.2 *nunc te, Bacche, canam*, 3.1-2 *te quoque, magna Pales, et te memorande canemus / pastor ab Amphryso*; Tib. 1.7.13 *an te, Cydne, canam*; Hor. *Carm.* 1.10.5-6 *te canam ... Iouis ... / nuntium*.

quamquam: only here and at **28** below in the *Corp. Tib.*; elsewhere always *quamuis*.

cognita uirtus: the phrase is found first at Cic. *Font.* 42.4 and *Epist.* fr. 6.3 and in verse, also at the line-end, in Stat. *Theb.* 9.37. The word *uirtus* is absent from Tibullus books 1 and 2, but is discussed in relation to Piso's eloquence at *Laus Pisonis* 97-98 *magna quidem uirtus erat ... / eloquio sanctum modo permulcere senatum*. On the concept in general in Latin see Eisenhut (1973), McDonnell (2006). For the mention of aristocratic *uirtus* on epitaphs cf. *CIL* I² 11 (L. Cornelius Scipio) *is hic situs quei nunquam uictus est uirtutei*. Commenting on Hor. *Carm.* 3.21.11-12 *narratur et prisci Catonis / saepe mero caluisse uirtus* (in an Ode addressed to Messalla) N-R suggest that since Messalla was connected through his wife Calpurnia to the elder Cato, old-fashioned manliness linked with a propensity for drinking could have been a family trait. Such a double-edged compliment would fit well the tone of the whole piece. See further **147n.** below. The specific link between *uirtus* in Hor. *Carm.* 3.21.12 and in the present line is made by Woodman (*forthcoming*) on Hor. *Carm.* 3.21.12n. For the preoccupation with *uirtus* as a feature of the panegyric preface see Woodman (2014) 70-71 on Tac. *Agr.* 1.2.

2. infirmae ... uires: cf. Cic. *Verr.* 2.4.95 *neque uiribus tam infirmis fuit*; Ov. *Pont.* 3.4.13 quoted on **1-2** above. On the theme of the poet's inadequacy in panegyric, cf. Hor. *Carm.* 1.6.9-12 (to Agrippa) *... dum pudor / imbellisque lyrae Musa potens uetat / laudes egregii Caesaris et tuas / culpa deterere ingeni*; Prop. 2.10.5-6 (in **7n.** below); Ov. *Fast.* 2.123 (on Augustus becoming *pater patriae*) *deficit ingenium, maioraque uiribus urgent, Trist.* 2.73-74 (to Augustus) *te celebrant alii quanto decet ore, tuasque / ingenio laudes uberiore canunt*, 529-532 *bella sonant alii ... / ... / inuida me spatio natura coercuit arto, / ingenio uires exiguasque dedit,*

5.11.23-24 *iure igitur laudes, Caesar, pro parte uirili / carmina nostra tuas qualiacumque canunt*; *Catal.* 9-10; *Laus Pisonis* 72-80, where, as here, the author's youth (cf. *Laus Pisonis* 260-261) and inexperience are described as being to blame; see further **3-4nn.** and **5-6** below. For further examples of the topos in panegyric see Woodman (1977) *index* 286 and Woodman (2014) 92-93 on Tac. *Agr.* 3.3. For *uires* in this context of literary skill cf. also Hor. *AP* 39; Ov. *Trist.* 1.5b.12; Manil. 3.1.

ualeant susbsistere: the use of the inf. with *ualeo* is current in verse from Lucr. 1.108-109 *ualerent / ... minis obsistere uatum*.

subsistere: in the same position in the line at Lucr. 1.1079, 2.236 and below at **195**. For its use = 'bear the weight of' in a literary context, see Ov. *Pont.* 3.4.83-84 quoted on **1-2** above; here it is used absolutely = 'bear up', 'suffice', see *OLD* 1d.

3 incipiam: common at the beginning of a new section or theme in didactic and epic; see Lucr. 1.55, 4.54, 6.906; Virg. *Georg.* 1.5; Manil. 1.809 (in the same metrical *sedes*). At *Aen.* 2.13 it is Aeneas (rather than the author) who starts his narration of past events; at Prop. 4.10.1 (on the origin of Jupiter Feretrius) *incipiam* suggests the beginning of a large and ambitious poem. In Greek, cf. the opening line of Aratus *Phaen.*: 'Let us begin with Zeus'. This use of *incipiam* appears only here in the *Corp. Tib.* It looks forward possibly to *inceptis* in the final line of the poem (**211**).

3-4 ac meritas si carmina laudes / deficiant: the copulative *ac* makes better sense here than the adversative *at* of the Fragmentum Cuiacianum. A+ has *a meritis si carmina laudes / deficiant* ('if you were to praise my poem according to its merits, it would prove lacking'), but *pro meritis* rather than *a meritis* would be expected in this context. The reading printed here, found in G[pc], takes *deficiant* as transitive with *meritas ... laudes* as object: 'if my songs should not be equal to the praise you deserve''. For this sense, a common theme in eulogists, cf. Cic. *Marc.* 4 *nullius tantum flumen ingeni, nulla dicendi aut scribendi tanta uis, tantaque copia quae non dicam exornare, sed enarrare, C. Caesar, res tuas gestas possit.* For the transitive use of *deficio* see *OLD deficio* 1 and cf. Virg. *Georg.* 1.290 *noctes lentus non deficit umor.* There is no need, with De Luca 43, to take *deficiant* intransitively with *laudes* as an internal accusative. Tränkle [186-187] conjectures *meritae* for *meritas*, interpreting 'if my songs should not be equal to the praise you desrve', which is perhaps less well suited to the context of the author's fears of inadequacy (**2**).

meritas ... laudes: for the phrase cf. Liv. 7.7.3 *audientibus laudes meritas*, 7.36.9 *meritas Deci laudes*; Sen. *Herc. F.* 829 *magnique meritas Herculis laudes canit.*

si ... / deficiant: this conditional protasis is followed in asyndeton by a further two protaseis (with *si* understood from **3**) linked by *nec*, namely, **4** *humilis tantis sim conditor actis*, on the limits of the poet's own capabilities, and **5-6** *nec ... quisquam / ... queat* on the impossibility of anyone except the addressee himself being able to fulfil the task; the apodosis is provided by *est nobis uoluisse satis* **7**. On this type of asyndeton, in which the second part presents a logical deduction from the first, Tränkle 186 compares, among other examples, Cic. *Phil.* 11.21 *quo bello de dignitate, de libertate, de uita decernamus, si in potestatem quis Antoni uenerit, proposita sint tormenta atque cruciatus*; cf. K-S II 2.159 (para. 178, section 10).

carmina laudes: the same verse ending is found at **106** below; cf. also Virg. *Aen.* 8.287-288 *qui carmine laudes / Herculeas et facta ferunt.*

4. humilis: The first of a number of Callimachean metapoetic reminiscences in the opening of this poem, which recall the Callimachean imagery in the first poem of the *Lygd.* group discussed in poem **1** above and serve to anchor the panegyric in the genre of Callimachean epinicion (see **headnote** above). For the use of the adj. in relation to literary merit cf. Prop. 1.7.21 *tum me non humilem mirabere saepe poetam*; *Catal.* 9.61 *si laudem aspirare humilis* [sc. *possumus*] in his claim to be following Callimachus in his encomiastic aspirations; Petr. 83.8 *ego ... poeta sum ... non humillimi spiritus*. For its use of the Callimachean 'slender style', equivalent to *tenuis* see Lausberg (1998) 1079a and cf. Cic. *Orat.* 76; Isid. *Etym.* 2.17.3. For knowledge of Callimachus in the late first century AD, cf. Mart. 10.4.12 (to Mamurra) *legas Aetia Callimachi* and see Barchiesi (2011) and Cowan (2014). In fact the pro-Callimachean stance taken in the poem may be a reaction to some of the anti-Callimachean rhetoric of the period.

conditor: this literary sense of 'chronicler', 'author' is attested first in late Ovid, e.g. *Trist.* 2.416 *Eubius, inpurae conditor historiae*, 5.1.10 *sumque argumenti conditor ipse mei*, *Pont.* 2.11.2 *Naso, parum faustae ... conditor Artis*; cf. *ThLL* 4.146.70-82. Here the dat. *tantis ... actis* replaces the more common gen. For the phrase *conditor actis* cf. Ovid's use of *condere* with *acta* at *Trist.* 2.335-336 *diuitis ingenii est inmania Caesaris acta / condere, materia ne superetur opus.*

5-6 For the concept that no one could adequately represent the deeds of the man praised except the man himself, cf. Livy's words about Cicero, as reported by Sen. *Suas.* 6.22 *si quis tamen uirtutibus uitia pensarit, uir magnus ac memorabilis fuit et in cuius laudes exequendas Cicerone laudatore opus fuerit.* Feddern ad loc. adds Val. Max. 5.3.4 as another example of this conceit. For Messalla's own skills as an orator, cf. Sen. *Contr.* 2.4.8; Quint. *Inst.* 10.1.113; Tac. *Dial.* 18.2, and see Gen. Intro., section 3.3. The impossibility of celebrating adequately the deeds of the addressee is a topos of panegyric, cf. Isocr. *Paneg.* 13 and is recommended as a theme for the introduction of an epideictic speech at *Rhet. Her.* 3.6.11 *uereri nos, ut illius facta uerbis consequi possimus; ... ipsa facta omnium laudatorum eloquentiam anteire.* It appears again in connection with Messalla at *Catal.* 9.55-56 *non nostrum est tantas, non, inquam, attingere laudes, / quin ausim hoc etiam dicere, uix hominum est.* The theme of the poet's lack of confidence in his own ability occurs again at **37-38, 175-180** and **197-200** and has a key role to play in his impersonation of a young and inexperienced Tibullus; see Peirano (2012) 138-139.

nec tua praeter te: the poet may well have written *nec tua te praeter*, as reported by Broukhusius in one of his now lost *recentiores*. For the anastrophe *te praeter* see **19.3** below.

chartis intexere ... / facta: a similar phrase, addressed to Messalla, is found at *Ciris* 39 (sc. *te uellem*) *naturae rerum magnis intexere chartis*; but there the verb retains some of its original meaning of 'interweave', since the author wishes to 'weave' his patron into the pages of his proposed didactic poem, as the Athenians weave Athena's exploits on the great *peplos* carried in her festival. A similar usage, in this case referring to praise of Maecenas, had occurred at Prop. 2.1.35 *te mea Musa illis semper contexeret armis* (referring to military actions in the civil wars). Closer to the present context are passages such as Liv. 7.2.11 *ridicula intexta uersibus* and Petr. 118.1 *ut quisque ... sensum ... teneriorem uerborum ambitu intexuit.* A similar expression is found below at **211** *inceptis de te subtexam carmina chartis* where the verb suggests adding poems to an existing collection. On the weaving image for the creation of a literary text here and at **211** see Scheidegger-Lämmle [(2015) 190-191], who discusses the implication that the creation of this text is a never-ending task ("Anfang ohne Ende"). The concept of poetry as weaving is an ancient IE poetic theme, see West (2007) 36-38.

facta ... dictis ... maiora: 'deeds greater than those which have been told'. The contrast between words and deeds is a commonplace of Greek and Roman rhetoric, cf. Otto 367 *uerbum* 6.

dictis ut non maiora supersint: another theme recommended for epideictic introductions in *Rhet. Her.* 3.6.12 *uereri ne cum multa dixerimus plura praetereamus*.

maiora supersint: for the hexameter ending cf. *maiora supersunt* at Lucan 4.501, 9.865, Sil. 4.476.

7. est nobis uoluisse satis: cf. Prop. 2.10.5-6 (on his proposed panegyric of Augustus) *quod si deficiant uires, audacia certe / laus erit: in magnis et uoluisse sat est*, on which see Woodman (2014) 93; Ov. *Pont.* 3.4.79 *ut desint uires, tamen est laudanda uoluntas*; *Laus Pis.* 214-215 *quod si digna tua minus est mea pagina laude, / at uoluisse sat est: animum, non carmina iacto*. The phrase may be related to a traditional aphorism, cf. Caecil. *Com.* 290 *fac uelis: perficies*; Hor. *Serm.* 1.9.54-55 ... *uelis tantummodo: quae tua uirtus, / expugnabis*.

munera parua: the first occurrences of the phrase refer to small tributes paid to the dead at Hor. *Carm.* 1.28.3-4 and Ov. *Fast.* 2.534-535. Could the author be hinting, for those in the know, that his addressee is in fact already dead? Given other connections between **1.1** and the present poem, there is probably an echo here of **1.24** on Lygdamus' poetic offering to Neaera: *mittit et accipias munera parua rogat*. On the Callimachean metapoetic implications of the phrase see **1.24n.** and **16n.** on *paruus labor* below and cf. Cat. 95 9-10 in praise of Cinna's *Smyrna* composed on Callimachean principles: *parua mei mihi cordi monumenta <sodalis>, / et populus tumido gaudeat Antimacho*. The phrase could be picked up at the end of the poem in the reference to *paruum ... corpus* at **196** below. On the idea at the beginning of a poem or collection of the book as a gift see Cat. 1.1.1-2 (also combined with Callimachean metapoetic imagery) and **1.5** *quonam donetur honore*. Cf. Lucr. 1.53, *mea dona*.

8-15 The first of a number of digressions in the poem (cf. **54-81, 82-105, 151-174**), in this case a list of mythological and divine figures who did not despise humble gifts. On the role of such digressions in oratory, which could include geographical, historical and mythological matter, see Quint. *Inst.* 4.3.12 and cf. Peirano [(2012) 136-138], on the fact that in the present poem they may betray an element of parody in being over-inflated or irrelevant. In the present passage two of the three myths discussed are attested in Callimachus (see notes below on Icarus and Molorcus), and the third, on a Cretan's gift to Apollo, may be a lost myth from the same source. Again Callimachean references in the beginning of this poem recall those in poem **1**.

8-10 The theme of hospitality provided by a lowly peasant to an unrecognised god or hero in distress is made fashionable by Eratosthenes' *Erigone* (see **9-11n.** below) and Callimachus' *Hecale* where a poor old woman welcomes Theseus, and recurs in Latin poetry for example in Ovid's story of hospitality provided for Ceres by Celeus at *Fast.* 4.507-560 (on which see Fantham on 508), for Jupiter and Mercury by Hyrieus at *Fast.* 5.499-534 and by Baucis and Philemon at *Met.* 8. 629-720; see further Hollis (1990) App. 3 'The hospitality theme', Plantinga (2007) and N-H on Hor. *Carm.* 1.31.15.

8-9 etiam Phoebo ... / Cres tulit: The exact allusion is uncertain. Porph. *Abst.* 2.15ff., as Tränkle 188 points out, has several stories which revolve around the fact that Delphic Apollo preferred the simple offering of a devout poor man, but none of these turn out to be Cretan. C. Barth suggested a reference here to the *Homeric Hymn to Apollo* 3.388ff. in which Apollo chose Cretan merchants for his priests at Delphi. When they had sailed as far as Crisa, on their way to Pylos, Apollo ordered them to offer him only white barley-meal (ἄλφιτα λευκά 509). This they offered, not because they had nothing more valuable, but because the god had ordered it (509); so again the story is not an exact fit for the myth required here. Cameron [(1995) 481] suggests as a candidate the Cretan Karmanor of Tarrha, who purified Apollo and Artemis after the slaying of Pytho at Delphi (Paus. 2.7.7), but, as a demi-god, he would not exactly fit the requirements of the myth here. For the theme of common folk welcoming gods or heroes with their simple hospitality in Hellenistic and Latin poetry see **8-10n.** above.

dona / ... tulit: the phrase *dona ferre* is used commonly in poetry of making offerings from Virg. *Georg.* 3.21-22 *ipse ... / dona feram* on, see *ThLL* 5(1).2017.20-32.

Cres: this nom. sing. form occurs in verse elsewhere only at Sil. 2.93 (also at the opening of the hexameter) and Sil. 14.39; oblique forms are found at Ov. *Am.* 3.10.19 (*Cretes*); Sen. *Phaed.* 815 (*Cretes*); Lucan 4.441 (*Cretas*).

8 respueris: indefinite subjunctive. Outside Lucretius (7), the verb is rare in verse: Hor. (*Epist.*1), Ov. (*Ars, Ibis* 2), Lucan (1), Pers. (1), Sen. *Trag.* (2), Val. Fl. (1), Stat. *Theb.* (2).

gratissima: frequent in this position in the hexameter in Virg. (*Aen.* 4) and Ov. (*Met.* 7, *Fast.* 3). For the combination with *Phoebo* cf. Virg. *Ecl.* 7.61-62 *gratissima* ... / ... *sua laurea Phoebo* (the first of a series of sustained references to this passage, see **12n. Alcides** and **14-15n.** below), 6.11 *nec Phoebo gratior ulla est* (sc. *pagina*).

9-11 The reference is to a myth recounted in a famous elegiac epyllion by Eratosthenes (c. 285-194 BC), *Erigone* (Eratosth. *Cat.* 14 p. 79), now lost, and occurring for the first time in Latin poetry at Virg. *Georg.* 1.33 (see **headnote** above). For Eratosthenes, a pupil of Callimachus, and his importance as the source of all Ovid's star myths see Robinson (2011) 18-19. Eratosthenes may also have been one of the sources for our poet's digression on the five-zone theory of the earth, see **151-174n.** below. The details of the Erigone myth are known to us best through Apollod. 3.14.7; Pausan. 10.38.1; Ov. *Ibis* 609ff.; Hyg. *Astr.* 2.4, *Fab.* 130; Ampel. 2.6 and Serv. auct. *Georg.* 1.33, 2.389. The name of the peasant involved was usually Ikarios (Icarius), so Call. *Aet.* fr. 178.3 Pf.; Nonn. 1.32; Ov. *Am.* 2.16.4, *Fast.* 4.939; Stat. *Silu.* 5.3.76 etc., though in Latin poetry, as here, the form Icarus is found at Prop. 2.33B.29; Ov. *Met.* 10.450, and *Ibis* 609. This peasant had provided hospitality for Bacchus while he was travelling in Attica and by way of thanks the god had given him a vine plant and taught him how to make wine. When later Icarus had given some of his wine to the local shepherds, they got drunk and killed him, thinking they had been poisoned. Icarus' dog, Maira, led his daughter Erigone to the corpse and Erigone hanged herself. Subsequently Bacchus, in some versions through the agency of Jupiter, turned all three to stars: Icarus to Bootes (cf. Virg. *Georg.* 1.229) or Arcturus, a fact implied but not mentioned here, Erigone into Virgo and the dog into the Dog Star, Sirius, *Canis*; cf. Arat. *Phaen.* 327-332; Virg. *Georg.* 1.218, or Canis Minor (*Canicula*) cf. Hyg. *Astr.* 2.4.2-6. The mention of the festival of Ikarios and Erigone at Call. *Aet.* fr. 178.4 Pf. reinforces the Callimachean tone of this opening section. In fact the stories of Erigone here and Molorcus in **11-13** are both connected with Callimachean epinician poetry to his queen Berenice in the third book of the *Aetia* and both are mentioned for the first time in Latin by Virgil in encomia of Octavian in the proems to *Georgics* 1 (33 Erigone) and *Georgics* 3 (19 Molorcus) – see **headnote** above. At *Georg.* 1.32-35 a catasterism of Octavian is envisaged in which as a new star Octavian will be placed between the constellations of Erigone (Virgo) and Chelae ('Claw' = Libra). In Callimachus' *Coma Berenices* as preserved for us in Catullus' translation (Cat. 66), Berenice's lock becomes a constellation on the other side of Erigone, between her and Leo: Cat. 66.65-66 *Virginis et saeui contingens namque Leonis / lumina*; see full discussion in Whitcomb (2018). Similarly the Molorcus episode (see **12-13** below) comes from an inset panel in the aetion of the founding of the Nemean games, part of the *Victoria Berenices* (*SH* fr. 254-269) in which the peasant Molorcus gives hospitality to Hercules in his quest to kill the Nemean lion and ultimately set up the Nemean games. This Callimachean episode is hinted at in Virg. *Georg.* 3.19 where all Greece will leave the river Alpheus (near Olympia) and the groves of Molorcus (=Nemea) to attend the Roman games to be instituted by Virgil in honour of Octavian; see Thomas (2008) 193-195. The author of the *Laud. Mess.*, then, takes his lead from Virgil in using Callimachean epinician material connected with Berenice in the proem to his own encomiastic poem. An important intermediary in this process is Tibullus 1.7, which, as detailed in the **headnote** above and in Gen. Intro., section 3.3, includes direct quotations from Callimachean epinician. Furthermore the connection between Erigone and the introduction of viticulture to mankind, echoes a key theme of the central prayer to Osiris / Bacchus in Tib. 1.7.33-42; see further Hardie (2003) 178-181, Whitcomb (2018) 416.

9 Baccho: this is the only form of the god's name used in the present poem (here and **163** below); for others see **2.19n.**

iucundior: on the poetic distribution of this adj. see **3.23-24n.** Here our author applies to Bacchus' host an adjective that is often applied to the products of Bacchus' viticulture, cf. Tib. 1.7.35, 2.3.63. The ancient etymology of *iucundus* from *iuuare* (Cic. *Fin.* 2.14; Isid. *Orig.* 10.125, *LALE* 315 s.v.) could also be active here.

10 puro ... caelo: for the *iunctura*, referring to a cloudless sky, cf. Lucr. 6.400-401 ... *caelo iacit ... puro / Iuppiter ... fulmen*; Calp. *Ecl.* 1.77-78 (in the same metrical *sedes*) *cernitis ut puro nox iam uicesima caelo / fulgeat*; Lucan 2.723 *in faciem puri redeunt languentia caeli*. For this technical sense of *purus* see *OLD* 6a. The clarity of the nocturnal sky allows the stars to bear witness without impediment, see L. C. Watson (2003) 466 on Hor. *Epod.* 15.1 *caelo fulgebat Luna sereno*.

sidera caelo: the same hexameter ending occurs at Virg. *Georg.* 2.342, *Aen.* 4.578; Ov. *Am.* 2.10.13, *Met.* 13.292; Manil. 1.381, 472, 2.742;

Lucan 4.53, 107; Sil. 2.289, 7.476, 11.461; Stat. *Theb.* 10.145, *Silu.* 5.1.241.

11. Erigoneque: the same line opening occurs at Ov. *Met.* 10.451 *Erigoneque pio sacrata parentis amore.*

-que ... -que: on this solemn formula, see **1.3-4n.** above; elsewhere in *Laud. Mess.* at **36, 156, 187.**

longior: for *longus* referring to a time in the 'distant' future, cf. Cic. *Phil.* 5.1; Prop. 2.18.20; a rare meaning, see *ThLL* 7(2).1641.63-84.

longior aetas: the same line ending occurs at Val. Fl. 6.62; Sil. 4.22; Stat. *Silu.* 5.1.228.

12-13 Reference to a myth found in the opening of Callimachus' third book of the *Aetia* (epinician to Berenice) fr. 54-59 Pf. (*SH* 257-268), in which Hercules, on his expedition to kill the Nemean lion, was given hospitality and rest by a poor peasant Molorkos in Greek, Molorcus in Latin, in his hut; see **9-11n.** above, Hopkinson (1989) 85, Thomas (2008) 193-195; see also Parsons (1977) 43. On the correct spelling *Molorcus*, often corrupted to *Molorchus* in the manuscripts, see Morgan (1992). The story is mentioned in Latin at Nig. Fig. fr. 93 Swoboda; Virg. *Georg.* 3.19 *lucos ... Molorci* (a periphrasis for Nemea), and appears more frequently in Statius and Martial: Stat. *Silu.* 3.1.29 *pauperis arua Molorci*, 4.6.51 *parci domus ... Molorci*; Mart. 4.64.29-30 *credas ... Penates / ... facti modo diuitis Molorci*, 9.43.13 *... quondam placidi conuiua Molorci*, appearing in its fullest form at Stat. *Theb.* 4.160-164 *sacra Cleonaei cogunt uineta Molorci. / gloria nota casae, foribus simulata salignis / hospitis arma dei paruoque ostenditur aruo / robur ubi et laxos qua reclinauerit arcus / ilice, qua cubiti sedeant uestigia terra.*

12 Alcides: a patronymic for Hercules, derived from Alcaeus, father of Amphitryon and grandfather of Hercules. It occurs first in Latin in Virg. *Ecl.* 7.61 *populus Alcidae gratissima*. This is the second of a number of sustained references to this poem here, see **8n. gratissima** and **14-15n.** below. Norden [(1927) on Virg. *Aen.* 6.123] argues it is a neoteric feature derived from Greek Alexandrian poetry. Its first Greek attestation is in Callimachus (*Hymn.* 3.145) and, like the adj. *Molorceis* (**13**) below, it is perhaps used here by the author to give an intentionally Callimachean tone to a myth he encountered in the *Aetia*. The nom. *Hercules* does not scan in hexameters or elegiacs and was generally replaced by alternatives such as *Alcides, clauiger, Oetaeus* and frequently *Tirynthius*; examples in

Robinson (2011) 231 on Ov. *Fast.* 2.305. On the use of a patronymic alone standing for a name see West (2011) on Hom. *Il.* 1.8 and cf. West (2007) 81 for its background in IE poetry.

deus ascensurus Olympum: *deus* here is proleptic 'as a god'. Hercules had been told by the Delphic oracle that he would become an immortal god after the completion of his labours, of which the slaying of the Nemean lion was the first (cf. Apollod. 2.4.12). For the phrase, also at the verse-end, cf. Manil. 1.367 *cuius* (i.e. *Capellae*) *ab uberibus magnum ille* (i.e. *Iuppiter*) *ascendit Olympum*; Sil. 3.671 ... *medius cum sol ascendit Olympum*.

13 An elaborately constructed 'golden line' with two adjectives and two nouns positioned around a central verb, see **3.5n.** in the pattern *abcab*. This structure is common in the *Laud. Mess.*, cf. **38, 57, 76, 112, 117, 124, 125, 144, 155, 164**; cf. also a similar *abcba* structure, called 'silver' by Wilkinson (1963) 216-217, at **19, 73, 102**.

Molorceis ... tectis: a high sounding phrase to describe the humble cottage of a peasant. The adj. occurs here only in Latin, and probably derives from Callimachus' account of the same myth in the *Aetia* (cf. fr. 59.16 Pf. = *SH* fr. 265.16). For the use of an adj. in place of a gen. subst. see **56n.** below. On the spelling *Molorceis* not *Molorcheis* see **12-13n.** above.

posuit uestigia: another elevated phrase, cf., in a mock epic context, Hor. *Serm.* 2.6.101-102 ... *cum ponit uterque / in locuplete domo uestigia*. It is mainly poetic (Cic. *Nat. Deor.* 2.109.5, *Arat.* 4; Lucr. 3.4; Virg. *Georg.* 3.172; Prop. 2.9.452; *Dirae* 113; Ov. *Met.* 2.871, 8.694; Manil. 1.196, 5.653; Sil. 6.397-398), but is found occasionally in high-style prose (Cic. *Fin.* 5.5, *Phil.* 3.31; Quint. *Decl. Mai.* 1.7.11).

14-15 Even a small offering can placate the gods. The couplet is close in sense to Hor. *Carm.* 3.23.17-20 *immunis aram si tetigit manus, / non sumptuosa blandior hostia, / molliuit auersos Penates / farre pio et saliente mica*. As both Tränkle 190 and De Luca 47 point out (ad loc.), the idea, even down to finer details, such as the golden horned bulls, is also to be found later in Porphyry *Abst.* 2.15 (following Theophrastus' Περὶ εὐσεβείας) καὶ μαρτυρεῖ γε ἡ πεῖρα ὅτι χαίρουσι τούτῳ οἱ θεοὶ ἢ τῷ πολυδαπάνῳ. οὐ γὰρ ἄν ποτε τοῦ Θετταλοῦ ἐκείνου τοῦ τοὺς χρυσόκερως βοῦς καὶ τὰς ἑκατόμβας τῷ Πυθίῳ προσάγοντος μᾶλλον ἔφησεν ἡ Πυθία τὸν Ἑρμιονέα κεχαρίσθαι θύσαντα τῶν ψαιστῶν ἐκ τοῦ πηριδίου τοῖς τρισὶ

Book Three of the Corpus Tibullianum: 353
Introduction, Text, Translation and Commentary

δακτύλοις ["Experience also testifies that the gods take more pleasure in this than in sumptuous offerings. For when that Thessalian sacrificed to the Pythian deity oxen with gilt horns, and hecatombs, the Pythian priestess said that the offering of Hermioneus was more pleasing to him, though he had only sacrificed as many barley cakes as he could take with his three fingers out of a little pouch"]. The sacrifice of bulls with golden horns as an example of religious extravagance is also found at Plato *Alc.* 2.149b-c. The same opposition between rich animal sacrifice and poor offerings of grain and salt is found at Stat. *Silu.* 1.4.127-131 *... qua nunc tibi pauper acerra / digna litem? nec si uacuet Meuania ualles / aut praestent niueos Clitumna noualia tauros, / sufficiam. sed saepe deis hos inter honores / caespes et exiguo placuerunt farra salino.* For the idea of a god (in this case Augustus) being pleased by a small offering as well as by the sacrifice of bulls, cf. Ov. *Trist.* 2.75-76 *sed tamen, ut fuso taurorum sanguine centum, / sic capitur minimo turis honore deus.* A modest sacrifice is seen here and in Ovid as analogous to poetry. This analogy of sacrifice with poetry originates with Callimachus *Aetia* 1 fr. 1.21-24 Pf. *καὶ γὰρ ὅτε πρώτιστον ἐμοῖς ἐπὶ δέλτον ἔθηκα / γούνασιν, Ἀπόλλων εἶπεν ὅ μοι Λύκιος· / '... ἀοιδέ, τὸ μὲν θύος ὅττι πάχιστον / θρέψαι, τὴν Μοῦσαν δ' ὠγαθὲ λεπταλέην'* ["For, when I first placed a tablet on my knees, Lycian Apollo said to me: '... poet feed your sacrificial victim to be as fat as possible, but, my friend, keep your Muse slender'"]: cf. Antipater of Sidon (a contemporary of Ovid) *AP* 9.93.2-3 (Let [Piso] receive [my book] favourably, and praise the poet, just as great Zeus is often won over by a little incense), Hor. *Carm.* 4.2.53-60 with Thomas 120-121; Ov. *Pont.* 3.4.79-82, 4.8.39-44. For grain and salt as a primitive offering that predated animal sacrifice, cf. also Ov. *Fast.* 1.337-338 *ante, deos homini quod conciliare ualeret, / far erat et puri lucida mica salis.* A.J. Woodman suggests to me a similarity here with Virg. *Ecl.* 7.29-36:

CORYDON *saetosi caput hoc apri tibi, Delia, paruos*
    et ramosa Micon uiuacis cornua cerui.   30
    si proprium hoc fuerit, leui de marmore tota
    puniceo stabis suras euincta coturno
THYRSIS *sinum lactis et haec te liba, Priape, quotannis*
    exspectare sat est: custos es pauperis horti.
    nunc te marmoreum pro tempore fecimus; at tu,
    si fetura gregem suppleuerit, aureus esto.

A continuing engagement with this *Eclogue* has already been suggested in **8n. gratissima** and **12n. Alcides** above. In Virg. the adj. *paruos* (29) explains etymologically the Greek name Micon (30), see Clausen (1994) 223 ad loc. This play is picked up here by the pun *parua ... mica*. Corydon's offering of a stag's horns *cornua* (30) and Thyrsis' promise of a gold statue *aureus* (36) are picked up in the reference here to the sacrificial bull's *inaurato ... cornu*. A concern with small / large offerings connects the two passages. The names Delia and Priapus in the Eclogue perhaps suggest future Tibullan themes, which would be relevant to a poet impersonating the young Tibullus.

14 paruaque caelestes placauit mica: close in sense and expression is Ovid's description of small offerings to Ceres at *Fast*. 4.409-412 *farra deae micaeque licet salientis honorem / detis ... / ... / parua bonae Cereri, sint modo casta, placent*.

caelestes: cf. *caelestia numina* at **4.53** above. For the IE theme of the gods as 'heaven-dwellers' see West (2007) 120 and cf. Gk. οὐρανίωνες.

placauit: a gnomic perfect, like *molliuit* in Hor. *Carm*. 3.23.19 (quoted above), see H-Sz 318-319.

mica: a grain of salt, cf. *saliente mica* in Hor. *Carm*. 3.23.20 (quoted above). The use without a specifying genitive (e.g. *mica salis*) is unusual [but cf. Ov. *Fast*. 2.24 *torrida cum mica farra* with Robinson (2011) 74 ad loc.] and assumes a knowledge of the Horatian precedent. For the use of *mola salsa*, a mixture of toasted flour and salt in sacrifices see **4.10n**.

15 inaurato ... cornu: the sacrifice of bulls with golden horns is mentioned as early as Homer (*Il*. 10.294, *Od*. 3.384, 426, 437). In Latin it is referred to at Cic. *Diu*. 2.63; Liv. 25.12.13; Virg. *Aen*. 9.627; Ov. *Met*. 7.161-162 and Plin. *Nat*. 33.39. The adj. *inauratus* is found in verse from Enn. *Trag*. 213 Jocelyn on. On the religious extravagance of such offerings see **14-15n**. above.

cadit hostia: for the phrase cf. Virg. *Aen*. 1.334 ... *nostra cadet hostia dextra*; Ov. *Fast*. 1.320 *hostia caelitibus quo feriente cadit*, *Pont*. 3.2.83, Sil. 12.333.

16-17 For the promise of more and better poetry to come in the future cf. *Culex* 8-10 *posterius grauiore sono tibi musa loquetur / nostra, dabunt cum securos mihi tempora fructus / ut tibi digna tuo poliantur carmina sensu*. For more on the 'future works' topos, usually panegyrical in function, see Woodman (2012) 220-222 and (2014) 91-92 on Tac. *Agr.* 3.3. Peirano [(2012) 136] sees this as a possible reference by the impersonator of the young Tibullus to the poetry of the canonical first and second books, already known to his audience, but envisaged here as still to come.

16 paruus labor: *labor* is used to describe a literary work first in Latin at Cic. *Leg.* 1.8 *intellego equidem a me istum laborem iam diu postulari*, cf. Virg. *Ecl.* 10.1 *extremum hunc, Arethusa, mihi concede laborem*, where Clausen [293 ad loc.] points to precedents in the Hellenistic use of πόνος: e.g. Call. *Epig.* 6.1-2 Pf. τοῦ Σαμίου πόνος εἰμὶ δόμῳ ποτὲ θεῖον ἀοιδόν / δεξαμένου ["I am the work of the Samian <sc. Creophylus> who once received the divine bard <sc. Homer> in his house", trnsl. Clausen], Asclepiades *AP* 7.11.1 (= 28.1 G-P) ὁ γλυκὺς Ἠρίννης οὗτος πόνος ["this is the sweet work of Erinna"], a verse inscribed on a volume of Erinna's poems. The use is found also at Hor. *Epod.* 1.15, with Harrison (2007) 110, Prop. 4.1B.139 and becomes frequent in Latin poetry from Ovid on, cf. *Ars* 3.404, *Trist.* 5.9.24 and see *ThLL* 7(2).794.80-795.20, Cairns (1979) 5 n.20, n. 24, Ingleheart (2010) 71 and 271 on Ov. *Trist.* 2.11-12 and 321-322. The term is used in the same sense near the end of the poem, see **181n**. For its use in prose of the care that goes into a composition see Woodman (2018) on Tac. *Ann.* 4.61. The combination with *paruus* produces a strong Callimachean metapoetic signal, cf. fr. 1.5 Pf. ἔπος δ' ἐπὶ τυτθὸν ἑλ[ίσσω ["I roll forth a tale on the small scale"]. The panegyricist does not aspire to epic qualities, but from the beginning expresses a Callimachean preference for a small work perfectly crafted (see **4n**. *humilis* above), cf. Virg. *Georg.* 4.6 *in tenui labor*, where *tenuis*, similar to *paruus*, has the meaning of the Callimachean λεπτός. On Callimachus' preference for small-scale, exquisite work as opposed to grand monumental subjects see Asmis (1995) 162 and n. 56, 171 and n. 73 and cf. *Aetia* fr. 1.24-28, *Epigr.* 8, 27.3-4 and 28. The Callimachean character of the opening had already been foreshadowed in *humilis* **4**, *munera parua* **7** and was continued in the reference in **10-13** to the myths of Erigone and Molorcus, both subjects taken from the *Aetia* of Callimachus. The adjs *paruus* and *paruulus* recur at the end of the poem in *paruum corpus* (**196**) and *paruula cura* (**197**). The use of an adj. with such clear Callimachean literary associations both at the beginning and at the end of the poem is surely intended to mark the Callimachean principles on which it is composed; see further **headnote** above and **200n.** below.

17 inde: temporal 'from this time on', 'in future'.

alios aliosque: the emphatic gemination is common in prose from *Rhet. Her.* 4.54 on. It is rare in verse outside Lucr. (e.g. *1.605*, 813, 2.776, 5.303), but cf. Cat. 68.152; Virg. *Aen.* 10.881; Ov. *Met.* 15.335; Manil. 2.517; Sil. 4.581, 5.494.

componere uersus: the same hexameter ending occurs at Hor. *Serm.* 1.4.8, cf. Prop. 1.7.19 *componere uersum*. For the use of *componere* of poetic production, cf. **35** below and see *ThLL* 3.2125.80-2126.4.

18-27 The lines make up a *recusatio* in which cosmological themes (**18-23**) are rejected in favour of a panegyric in praise of Messalla (**24-27**). The subject of cosmology, the chosen theme of such writers as Aratus, Lucretius and Manilius, is seen by Virgil at *Georg.* 2.475-482 as the highest form of poetic endeavour. At Tib. 2.4.17-18 cosmology occurs in a context of *recusatio*, as here, and, along with epic, is rejected in favour of love poetry, a theme taken up by Prop. at 2.34.51ff. in his advice to Lynceus to abandon astronomical speculation if he wishes to be successful in love. In the present passage the rejection of cosmology involves a digression on rejected cosmological themes (**19-23**), based on the Stoic doctrine of the four elements arranged in ascending order: Earth (**19**), Ocean (**20**), Air (**21**) and Ether (**22-23**). For the theme of *recusatio* in general see Wimmel (1960), Lyne (1995) 31-39 and cf. Callimachus *Aetia* prologue (fr. 1 Pf.) with Hopkinson (1989) 98-101; Virg. *Ecl.* 6.3-5; Prop. 2.1.39-42 and 3.3.15-24 with Fedeli; Ov. *Am.* 1.1, 3.1, *Fast.* 2.125-126 and see N-H (81-82) and Harrison (2007) 170-174 on Hor. *Carm.* 1.6. Despite the *recusatio* here the poet has no qualms about inserting a digression on the philosophical theory of the earth's five zones within the framework of his panegyric perhaps again under the influence of Eratosthenes, see **151-174n.** below. On the inclusion, in ironic form, within a poem of elements rejected in a *recusatio* see Harrison (2007) 171-173; on the inclusion of Homeric themes in Hor. *Carm.* 1.6; see further La Penna (1995) 326.

18 alter: contrasting with *meae ... Camenae* **24**. This is the well-known rhetorical device of the priamel in which the poet's choice (in this case of poetic composition) is contrasted with that of others; see the detailed comments on this form at **2.1-8n.** above. For *alter* in the sense of *alius* here and also at **180** below see *ThLL* 1.1736.4-48. It occurs first in Ovid and is mainly a feature of Late Latin, see H-Sz 208.

dicat: on *dicere* with reference to the composition of high-style poetry, on the analogy of Greek λέγειν, see N-H on Hor. *Carm.* 1.21.1 and McKeown II 12 on Ov. *Am.* 2.1 and cf. Hor. *Serm.* 2.1.11, *Carm.* 1.6.5, 4.9.21, *Epist.*

1.16.26, 19.8; Prop. 1.7.1, 9.9, 2.10.4, 34.62; Ov. *Ars* 1.209, *Rem.* 381, *Met.* 1.1, *Trist.* 2.334, *Pont.* 4.13.23, 16.23.

opus magni mirabile mundi: the phrase is Lucretian in tone. *opus* with reference to the universe occurs first in his work at 5.158 *adlaudabile opus diuom*, cf. *ThLL* 9(2).849.8. The combination *magni ... mundi* occurs no less than seven times in Lucretius: 2.1144, 5.433, 545, 772, 1204, 6.493, 565 (twice in the same *sedes* as here 5.772, 1204), its other occurrences being at Cat. 66.1 (first attestation); Ov. *Met.* 15.67 (same *sedes*), *Trist.* 4.4b.29; Manil. 1.17, 283, 4.776; *Ciris* 7; Stat. *Silu.* 3.3.88. For the whole phrase cf. Manil. 1.247 *hoc opus inmensi constructum corpore mundi*, which also shares the adj. *inmensus* with **19** below.

19-23 qualis ... / qualis ... / ut ... / ... / ... ut ...: the use of indirect questions of this type in discussing cosmology is frequent in Latin poetry from Virg. *Georg.* 2.475-482 on, cf. Tib. 2.4.17-18; Prop. 2.34.51-54.

19 inmenso ... aere: the same *iunctura* is found at Val. Fl. 1.497 *inmens<usque> ratem spectantibus abstulit aer*; cf. Cic. *Nat. Deor.* 1.26 *Anaximenes aera deum statuit ... eumque ... esse ... inmensum*.

in inmenso desederit aere tellus: describes the separation of the elements out of the original chaos, when the earth, due to its weight, sank to the bottom. The only other passage to use *desidere* of this action is *Aetna* 104 *deseditque infima tellus*, which suggests a close connection between the two passages. The normal verb in this context is *subsidere*, as at Ov. *Fast.* 5.13 *pondere terra suo subsedit* and Manil. 1.159 *ultima subsedit glomerato pondere tellus*. For *aere tellus* at the verse end see **151** below and, in the same cosmological context, Ov. *Met.* 1.12.

20 For the earth being surrounded by the sea at the time of creation cf. Ov. *Met.* 1.36-37 *tum freta diffundi rapidisque tumescere uentis / iussit et ambitae circumdare litora terrae.*

et: for postponed particles in elegy, see **1.9n**. *lutea sed* and for postponed *et* see **1.10**. In the present poem *et* is postponed to second position also at **22, 56, 58, 78, 154, 168, 170** and to third position at **110.**

pontus: this Greek loan word (from πόντος) was originally a characteristic of high poetic language, e.g. Enn. *Ann.* 217 Sk.; Acc. *Trag.* 399; Laev. fr. 11.2 Courtney; Cic. *Arat.* 23; Cat. 36.11, 64.179, but then became common in poetry even outside elevated contexts in Lucretius, Virgil,

Propertius and Ovid; see further Tränkle (1960) 40. The word occurs later in the present poem at **75, 147** and **173**.

confluxerit: the verb is used twice in the same cosmological context in Lucretius, not of the sea, but of the solid particles of the earth sinking to the bottom: Lucr. 1.986-987 ... *copia materiai / undique ponderibus solidis confluxet ad imum*, 5.496-497 ... *omnis mundi quasi limus ad imum / confluxit grauis et subsedit funditus ut faex*.

21-22 The reading of A+ here *et uagus e terris qua surgere nititur aer / hinc et contextus passim fluat igneus aether* makes no sense and must be changed. Most editors now take the lines as a double indirect question 'how the wandering air and the fiery ether flow'. This involves changing the initial *et* to *ut* (Heinsius), replacing *qua* (**21**) with the relative *qui* (Heyne), and replacing the meaningless *hinc* (**22**) with *huic* (found in some later manuscripts), to be taken closely with *contextus* (interwoven with it). The striving of the air to leave the earth and its encirclement by fiery ether would both be in line with Stoic cosmological teaching; Tränkle 192 compares Cleanthes' words at Plut. *Aud. Poet.* 11. p. 31 d (= *SVF* I 535) τὸν ἐκ τῆς γῆς ἀναθυμιώμενον ἀέρα ["the air sent up in vapour from the earth"].

22 huic ... contextus: for *contexo* with the dat. in the sense of 'combine', 'interweave with', see *OLD contexo* 3a and cf. Prop. 2.1.35 *te mea Musa illis semper contexeret armis*; Sen. *Contr.* 7.5.7 *epilogum defensioni contexit*.

et: for postponed *et* see **20n.** above.

fluat: the verb is used of the ether also at Lucr. 5.506-507 *nam modice fluere atque uno posse aethera nisu / significat Pontos*. For the simple verb here following the compound *confluxerit* in **20**, see Woodman and Martin (1996) 263 on Tac. *Ann.* 3.29.1 and Woodman (2018) on Tac. *Ann.* 6.31.2.

igneus aether: the same verse ending occurs at Val. Fl. 1.616 (as the end of **23** echoes the end of Val. Fl. 1.617; see below) and Sil. 1.135, and the *iunctura* is also found at Sen. *Quaest. Nat.* 6.16.2; on the fiery nature of ether Tränkle 192 compares Diog. Laert. 7.137 (= *SVF* II 580) ἀνωτάτω ... εἶναι τὸ πῦρ, ὅ δὴ αἰθέρα καλεῖσθαι ["at the very top ... is the fire which is called ether"]. Here the epithet *igneus* obviously alludes to the etymology of *aether* from the Greek verb αἴθω = 'burn' at Serv. auct. *Aen.* 1.394, see *LALE* 16.

Book Three of the Corpus Tibullianum: 359
Introduction, Text, Translation and Commentary

23 On the content of the line Tränkle 192 compares Zeno in Achill. Tat. *Isag. in Arat.* 5 p. 129e (= *SVF* I 115) οὐρανός ἐστιν αἰθέρος τὸ ἔσχατον ... περιέχει ... πάντα πλὴν αὐτοῦ ["heaven is the limit of the ether ... which contains everything except itself"].

pendentique super: the adv. *super* is to be taken closely with *pendenti*, as in Manil. 5.430 *pendebitque super*. A similar adverbial use of *super* is found at Virg. *Aen.* 10.158 *imminet Ida super*.

omnia caelo: for the hexameter endings here and in **22** above, cf. Val. Fl. 1.616-617 ... *uasto pariter ruit igneus aether / cum tonitru piceoque premit nox omnia caelo* (with Zissos ad loc.), where the double echo clearly suggests a connection between the two passages. The ending *omnia caelo* is also found at Virg. *Aen.* 5.790; Lucan 9.543 and Val. Fl. 2.517; cf. in a similar cosmological context Ov. *Met.* 1.5 *ante mare et terras et quod tegit omnia caelum*.

24 The formulation of the verse is very close to Prop. 1.18.29 *et quodcumque meae possunt narrare querelae*.

audere: for the use of this verb, on the model of the Greek τολμᾶν, of ambitious literary projects, see *ThLL* 2.1256.22-30. It is often found in the context of *recusationes*, e.g. Hor. *Serm.* 2.1.10-11 *aude / Caesaris inuicti res dicere*, *Epist.* 2. 1.258-259 *nec meus audit / rem temptare pudor quam uires ferre recusant*, *AP* 10 *quidlibet audendi ... potestas* (with Brink 92 ad loc.); Virg. *Georg.* 1.40 *audacibus adnue coeptis*; Ov. *Am.* 2.1.11 *ausus eram, memini, caelestia dicere bella* (with McKeown III 11 ad loc.), 18.4 *nos et tener ausuros grandia frangit Amor*, *Fast.* 6.22, *Trist.* 2.337, *Pont.* 2.5.28-29, and cf. Prop. 2.10.5-6 *quod si deficiant uires, audacia certe / laus erit*.

Camenae: Roman nymphs, and goddesses of a spring just outside the Roman Porta Capena (Liv. 1.21.3), identified by Liv. Andr. *Od.* 1.1 and Naevius fr. 64.2 with the Muses. They, along with the native Saturnian meter, were replaced in Ennius by the Greek *Musae*, see Skutsch (1985) 649-650 on Enn. *sed. inc.* 487. They are rare in Augustan Latin poetry, except in Horace (*Carm.* 1.12.39, 2.16.38, 3.4.21, 4.6.27, 4.9.8, *Serm.* 1.10.45, *Epist.* 1.1.1, 18.47, 19.5, *AP* 275); elsewhere in Virg. only at *Ecl.* 3.59; in elegy only at Prop. 3.10.1; Ov. *Fast.* 3.275, 4.245, *Pont.* 4.13.13; [**Tib.**] **3.13.3**; cf. also Ov. *Met.* 14.434, 15.482 and line **191** below. Tib. uses only *Musae*, a word never found in [**Tib.**] **3**. See further *ThLL Onomast. Camenae*. Here they are used metonymically = 'poetry'. They were connected etymologically with *carmen* and *cano*, see *LALE* 99 and cf. Paul. Fest. 38 L *Camenae Musae a carminibus sunt dictae, uel quod canunt antiquorum laudes*; so that *canent* (**26**) and *carmine* (**27**) below could be examples of etymological play. See further **13.3n.**

25 tibi par poterunt: Messalla himself was well known for his poetic compositions (see Gen. Intro., section 3.3), and we hear from *Catalepton* 9, which is now generally agreed to have been addressed to Messalla, that he also wrote bucolic poetry in Greek in the manner of Theocritus: *Catal.* 9.13-20:

> *pauca tua in nostras uenerunt carmina chartas,*
>   *carmina cum lingua tum sale Cecropio,*
> *carmina quae Phrygium, saeclis accepta futuris,*
>   *carmina quae Pylium uincere digna senem.*
> *molliter hic uiridi patulae sub tegmine quercus*
>   *Moeris pastores et Meliboeus erant,*
> *dulcia iactantes alterno carmina uersu,*
>   *qualia Trinacriae doctus amat iuuenis.*

["A few of your songs have entered my pages, songs of Attic tongue as well as Attic wit; songs welcome to future ages and worthy to outlive the aged Phrygian [Priam] and the old man of Pylos [sc. Nestor]. Here under the green covering of the spreading oak were the shepherds Moeris and Meliboeus at leisure, bandying in alternate verse sweet songs, such as the learned youth of Sicily [sc. Theocritus] loves."]

26-27 canent ... / ...carmine: for possible etymological play with *Camenae*, see **24n.** above.

omne uouemus / hoc tibi: For *hoc tibi* in a similar context, cf. Cat. 68.149-151 *hoc tibi, quod potui, confectum carmine munus / pro multis, Alii, redditur officiis, / ne uestrum scabra tangat rubigine nomen*, and for the general sentiment cf. Prop. 4.1A.59-60 *sed tamen exiguo quodcumque e pectore riui / fluxerit, hoc patriae seruiet omne meae*; Ov. *Pont.* 4.8.65-66 *siquid adhuc igitur uiui, Germanice, nostro / restat in ingenio, seruiet omne tibi*.

27 carmine charta: the hexameter ending echoes *carmina chartas* at *Catal.* 9.13 quoted above (**25n.**) with reference to Messalla's own poetry and looks forward to *carmina chartis* in the final line of the present poem **211**.

28-32 Praise of the subject's family is a recommended element in a panegyric (cf. Cic. *Part. Or.* 74; Men. Rhet. p. 370.11f. Sp.), and is found in poetry at Theocr. *Id.* 17.13-33 (encomium to Ptolemy); *Laus Pisonis* 2-4; Stat. *Silu.* 5.2.30-60 (*Laudes Crispini*). Such praise usually comes immediately after the introduction, though in the *Laus Pisonis* it is placed right at the beginning. The point that Messalla will seek to excel the glory of his ancestors and will succeed in doing so (**31-32**) is also a traditional element of panegyric, as shown by *Rhet. Her.* 3.7.13 *genus: in laude, quibus maioribus natus sit: si bono genere, parem aut excelsiorem fuisse.* For the general theme of outdoing one's ancestors in glory, cf. *CIL* 1².10.5 (epitaph of P. Cornelius Scipio) *facile facteis superases gloriam maiorum*, Sall. *Iug.* 4.7.

28 quamquam: see **1n.** above.

antiquae gentis: Messalla belonged to the old and distinguished gens Valeria. The same phrase occurs in Propertius' *recusatio* addressed to Maecenas at Prop. 2.1.29 (of a rejected civil war theme) *euersosque focos antiquae gentis Etruscae*. A possible reminiscence of this same poem is mentioned in **5-6n.** *chartis intexere* above. Ovid refers to Messalla's eloquence being the equal of his nobility at *Pont.* 2.3.75-76.

29 gloria: for Messalla's glory in relation to that of his ancestors, cf. Tib. 2.1.33-34 *gentis Aquitanae celeber Messalla triumphis / et magna intonsis gloria uictor auis*. Messalla's Aquitanian triumph of 25 September 27 BC (celebrated in Tib. 1.7), of course, postdates his joint consulship with Octavian in 31 BC, which is the purported occasion of the present poem; see **headnote** above.

30 quaque index sub imagine: the reference is to the inscription under the masks of the ancestors, which gave the name and achievements of each. These masks were found in the atrium of noble houses. The use of *index* in this precise context is unique, although see *OLD index* 3b and cf. Liv. 41.28.8 *tabula in aedes matris Matutae cum indice hoc posita est*; the normal term would be *elogium*, or, as at **33** below, *titulus*. The combination *sub imagine* is very common in this position in the line in hexameter verse, especially in Ovid: Virg. *Aen.* (2), *Aetna* (1), Calp. *Ecl.* (1), Germ. *Arat.* (2), Gratt. (1), Ov. (17), Manil. (4), Sil. (6), Stat. (2).

31 priscos ... honores: for the *iunctura* cf. Virg. *Aen.* 8.339 *... nymphae priscum Carmentis honorem*; Stat. *Ach.* 2.158 *...priscosque uirum mirarer honores*; Sil. 15. 416 *... priscum Tyriis sollemnis honorem.*

contendis uincere: this use of *contendo* + inf. is found mostly in prose; rare verse uses occur elsewhere at Lucr. 4.94; Prop. 1.4.15; Virg. *Aen.* 1.158; Sil. 13.441; Stat. *Theb.* 6.620, *Silu.* 4.8.11; Mart. 10.33.7; cf. *ThLL* 4.663.68-664.13.

32 maiores maius: polyptoton of adjectives is said by Wills [(1996) 230] to be an Ovidian figure, infrequent in the early works, but well established from the *Fasti* on, e.g. *Fast.* 2.287 *ipse deus nudus nudos iubet ire ministros*. The name of the month *Maius* and the noun *maiores* are juxtaposed at Ov. *Fast.* 5.427 *mensis erat Maius, maiorum nomine dictus* (cf. Varro *Ling.* 6.33.6). For repetition of comparative *maior*, cf. Manil. 1.296 *maioremque Helice maior decircinat arcum*; Mart. 9 *praef.* 7 *maiores maiora sonent*. For a similar repetition with reference to Messalla and involving mention of *decus*, see *Catal.* 9.3 *uictor adest magni magnum decus ecce triumphi*.

decus: the metonymic use of *decus* to refer to a person occurs again at **49** below: *paruae magnum decus urbis Vlixem*. It is found in poetry from Plautus on (e.g. *Asin.* 655, 691, 892, *Truc.* 517; Lucr. 3.30; Cat. 64.323) and later becomes restricted mainly to epic; see *ThLL* 5(1).243.6-244.54. For its use in reference to Messalla at *Catal.* 9.3 see above. Horace uses it of his patron Maecenas at *Carm.* 1.1.2, 2.17.4 and 3.16.20.

ipse futuris: for the hexameter ending De Luca [(2009) 55 ad loc.] compares, in a similar context, Juv. 8.74-76: ... *sed te censeri laude tuorum, / Pontice, noluerim sic ut nihil ipse futurae / laudis agas*.

33 The *imagines* of Messalla's ancestors were mentioned in **30**. Here the point is that the inscription (*titulus*) beneath his own image will not be large enough to contain a description of all his achievements.

34 aeterno sed: for postponed *sed* see **1.9n.** above.

aeterno ... magna uolumina uersu: for the use of a noun and adjective pair to 'bracket' a verse in this way, as at Cat. 64.54 *indomitos in corde gerens Ariadna furores*, see Norden [(1927) 391] and Fordyce [(1961) 275], who argues that this and the chiastic arrangement of two nouns and two adjectives, are purely Latin developments, with no precedents in Greek verse. The present verse is close in content to *Laus Pisonis* 248-249 *tu mihi Maecenas tereti cantabere uersu. / possumus aeternae nomen committere famae* and *Ciris* 100 *atque nouum aeterno praetexite honore uolumen.*

aeterno ... uersu: the same combination is found at Lucr. 1.121 *Ennius aeternis exponit uersibus edens*.

magna uolumina: the reference is to large book rolls. For the *iunctura* cf. Cic. *De Orat.* 1.192 *neque ita ... uoluminibus magnis continentur*; Plin. *Nat.* 7.147 *si diligenter aestimentur cuncta, magna sortis humanae reperiantur uolumina*. In verse it is found in the same *sedes*, but with a different meaning, at Ov. *Met.* 15.721 *perque sinus crebros et magna uolumina labens*.

35-36 conuenient ... / undique: the phrase *undique conueniunt* is Ennian (*Ann.* 391 Sk.), and occurs frequently thereafter as a hexameter opening: Lucr. 5.600; Virg. *Aen.* 5.293, 9.720; *Ciris* 452; Sil. 12.485; *Anth. Lat.* 7.11, cf. Juv. 9.131-132 ... *undique ad illos / conuenient*. Its use in Virgil of contending forces coming together, a common context for the phrase in the historical prose of Caesar and Livy, suggests here the fierce competition of writers, coming together to contend for honours in rival *recitationes*, cf. *certamen* at **37** below.

35 conuenient ... cupidi componere laudes: for a similar sentiment, in the context of a *recusatio*, cf. Virg. *Ecl.* 6.6-7 ... *namque super tibi erunt, qui dicere laudes, / Vare, tuas cupiant et tristia condere bella*, and for *cupidus* in a *recusatio* context, in this case of a poet who claims he is willing but not strong enough to compose on higher themes, cf. Hor. *Serm.* 2.1.12-13 ... *cupidum, pater optime, uires / deficiunt*.

cupidi componere: the use of *cupidus* + inf. is attested first at Prop. 1.19.9 *cupidus ... attingere gaudia* and, outside Fronto, is restricted to verse (e.g. Ov. *Met.* 14.215 *cupidusque moriri*; Lucan 7.266 *priuatae cupidus me reddere uitae*), but is rare except in Statius who shows a particular fondness for the construction (*Theb.* 8.43, 728, 10.457, 11.686, *Silu.* 1.2.85, 2.2.11, 4.2.40). On infinitives dependent on adjectives see H-Sz 350-351.

componere laudes: cf. Suet. *Calig.* 20.1.5 *eorundem et laudes componere coactos*.

36 quique ... quique: on double *-que* see **1.3-4n.** and **11n.** above.

quique canent: the verb is more appropriate for verse (*uincto pede*) than for prose (*soluto*), but can refer to a fault in orators who employ a 'sing-song' voice (Cic. *Or.* 27; Plin. *Epist.* 2.14.13) or simply to a fluent and melodious style of delivery, see Woodman (2018) on Tac. *Ann.* 4.61; here the zeugma is not as harsh as it would be in English, cf. Apul. *Flor.* 20 *canit ... Empedocles carmina, Plato dialogos.*

uincto pede ... soluto: although *oratio soluta* is the normal expression for prose (according to Varro *Ling.* 7.2), there is no corresponding *oratio uincta* for verse. Tränkle, however [194 n.2 ad loc.], sees close precedents in Cic. *De Oratore* 3.184 *liberior* (sc. *quam uersus*) *est oratio et plane, ut dicitur, sic est uere soluta, ... ut sine uinculis sibi ipsa moderetur* and Plin. *Epist.* 7.9.14 *metri necessitate deuincti soluta oratione laetamur.* Closest to the present passage is Stat. *Silu.* 2.7.21-22 (on Lucan as a writer of both prose and verse) *qui uos* (sc. *Musas*) *geminas tulit per artes, / et uinctae pede uocis et solutae.* As *uox pede soluta* makes more sense than the awkwardly shortened *pede ... soluo* of the *Laud. Mess.*, Tränkle 195 would give the chronological priority to Statius. For *pes* applied to prose (in the sense of rhythm), as well as to verse (in the sense of metrical foot), cf. Quint. *Inst.* 9.4.19 *quod non eo dico, quia non illud quoque solutum habeat suos quosdam et forsitan difficiliores etiam pedes.* Persius speaks of the same verse/prose distinction in slightly different terms at *Sat.* 1.13 *scribimus inclusi, numeros ille, hic pede liber*, where *pes* refers to verse metre.

37 quis potior ... illis: an element of competition is a common feature of encomiastic verse, cf. *Laus Pisonis* 221-223 *... iuuat, optime, tecum / degere cumque tuis uirtutibus ... / carminibus certare meis.* Here various authors are imagined as offering their panegyrics to Messalla, who then decides which will be published. As Knox [(2018) 149] points out, such rhetorical competitions of the early empire could have provided the context for the present composition.

potior: the comparative is used in place of the superlative perhaps because the author sees his competitors as a single group, or perhaps influenced by the same line-opening at Pers. 2.20 *quis potior iudex ...?* However, the confusion of comparative and superlative could be seen as a feature of Late Latin, see H-Sz 162, Maltby (2016) 359, which occurs again at **85** and **89** (*melius*) and **97** (*aptior*) below.

38 A golden line, see **3.5n.** and **7.13n.** above. The idea is that, as victor, the author would be allowed to publish his poem so that his name would be associated with the great acts of Messalla that it celebrates. For the joint fame of author and honorand see Plin. *Epist.* 5.8.1 (on the writing of history) *mihi pulchrum in primis uidetur ... aliorum ... famam cum sua extendere* and Woodman (2012) 228.

39 castrisue foroue: the division of the addressee's activities into civil and military is recommended for panegyrists at Men. Rhet. 372.25ff. Sp. τὰς ... πράξεις διαιρήσεις δίχα εἴς τε τὰ κατ' εἰρήνην καὶ τὰ κατὰ πόλεμον ["you should arrange the activities separately into peacetime and wartime deeds"]; cf. Vell. 2.113.1 and Tac. *Agr.* 21.1 with Woodman ad loc. Here Messalla's civil achievements are mentioned at **45-81** and his military exploits at **82-117**. The author assigns an almost equal number of lines to each sphere, reflecting equal service in both areas. Whereas at *Catal.* 9.43 Messalla is said to put military before civic duties [(sc. *quid memorem*) *castra foro, te castra urbi praeponere*] in the present poem he is said to be equally good at both (**40ff.**), a sentiment shared with Ov. *Pont.* 2.1.61-62 (of Germanicus) *iuuenum belloque togaque / maxime* and *Laus Pisonis* 158 *hunc fora pacatum, bellantem castra decebunt*; Vell. 2.125.5 (on Junius Blaesus) *uiro nescias utiliore in castris an meliore in toga*; Sil. 6.617 (on Quintus Fabius Maximus) *par ingenium castrisque togaeque*. On the poetic use of *-ue ... -ue*, attested again in the poem at **40, 89, 163,** and **201**, see H-Sz 521.

40 nec ... hic aut hic: 'neither here nor there'. For this use of *hic ... hic* for *hic ... illic* cf. Virg. *Aen.* 1.427-428 *hic portus ... effodiunt, hic alta theatri / fundamenta locant* with further examples at *OLD* 4a. For a similar, though more commonly attested, use of *ille ... ille* for *ille ... hic,* see **50-52n.** below.

maiorue minorue: on *-ue ... -ue* see **39n.** above.

41 iusta ... libra: the *iunctura* is found elsewhere mainly in connection with the constellation Libra, so Manil. 3.305 *Chelarumque fides iustaeque examina Librae*, 433 *donec perueniunt ad iustae sidera Librae*; Lucan 4.58-59 *... aequatis ad iustae pondera Librae / temporibus*; Sen. *Thy.* 858 *iustaeque cadent pondera Librae*, but for its use of scales, as here, cf. Serenus *Med.* 49.915 *tempora discernens quasi iustae pondere librae.*

pari ... pondere: a common combination in technical writings such as Colum. *Rust.*, Plin. *Nat.* and Scrib. Larg.

pondere libra: for this verse ending, see Lucan 4.58; Sen. *Thy.* 858 and Serenus *Med.* 49.915 quoted above and cf. Manil. 4.548 *felix aequato genitus sub pondere Librae*, and *Moretum* 18 *quae bis in octonas excurrit pondere libras.*

42 nec: for postponed particles in elegy, see **1.9n**. *lutea sed. nec* is postponed to second position in the *Laud. Mess.* also at **61, 125, 144, 164**, and to third at **200**.

ab illa: as *hac ... parte* shows, the simple local ablative *illa* would have sufficed and the *ab* is added simply *metri gratia*. Other examples of the addition of a metrically convenient *ab* in the fifth foot occur at Lucr. 5.306 *ab aeuo*; Ov. *Fast.* 1.215 *ab unda* and Lucan 2.86 *ab ira*, all replacing instrumental ablatives.

43 inaequatum: the adj. occurs only here and at Tert. *Spect.* 22.1. On the invention of such new compounds in *in-* in Horace and Augustan poetry, see Brink (1971) 318-319 on Hor. *AP* 285 *intemptatum*.

onus urget: the same phrase is found at Plaut. *Poen.* 857 and Ov. *Fast.* 4.515.

urget utrimque: also at Virg. *Aen.* 7.566 and 11.524.

44 instabilis: opens the hexameter also at Virg. *Georg.* 4.105; Lucan 9.465 and Sil. 14.160.

natat: the use of this verb to describe the oscillation of an object is rare and poetic, see *OLD nato* 4a and cf. Ov. *Ars* 1.516 *nec uagus in laxa pes tibi pelle natet*; Stat. *Theb.* 6.284 *prensatque rotas auriga natantes*, 841-842 *luxuriant artus, effusaque sanguine laxo / membra natant* and Calp. *Ecl.* 6.43 *monilia ... / extrema ceruice natant*.

alterno ... orbe: for the iunctura cf. Stat. *Ach.* 1.395 *et alternum Mauors interfurit orbem*.

depressior: 'lower', cf. Sen. *Quaest. Nat.* 1.3.11 *illo* (sc. *sole*) *enim descendente altior est* (sc. *arcus*), *alto depressior*.

orbe: commonly used of spherical objects, but only here for the round pan of a scale.

45-47 These three lines are the only ones to give any indication of Messalla's civil activities as an orator. The rest of the section on his civil achievements is taken up by a comparison of his oratory with that of Nestor and Odysseus **(48-53)** and by an account of Odysseus' deeds in the *Odyssey* **(54-81)**, which ends with the statement that while Odysseus' hardships were greater Messalla surpassed him in eloquence **(81)**. Furthermore **45-47** are short on historical detail and treat common literary

Book Three of the Corpus Tibullianum: 367
Introduction, Text, Translation and Commentary

topoi. In **45-46** Messalla's oratory is said to be able to pacify the crowd, presumably in the popular assembly, which in reality would have had little importance in his time. Nothing is said of Messalla's better attested influence in the senate. The idea seems rather to be influenced by Virgil's words on an orator's ability to calm an unruly mob at *Aen*. 1.151-153 *tum pietate grauem ac meritis si forte uirum quem / conspexere, silent arrectisque auribus adstant; / ille regit dictis animos et pectora mulcet* (cf. below **46n. sedare**). The mention of Messalla's success as a defence lawyer (**46-47**) is again a commonplace of panegyric, cf. *Laus Pisonis* 43-56. For Messalla's son Messallinus as an heir to his father's eloquence as a lawyer cf. Ov. *Pont*. (to Messallinus) 2.2.49-52 *nunc tibi et eloquii nitor ille domesticus adsit, / quo poteras trepidis utilis esse reis. / uiuit enim in uobis facundi lingua parentis, / et res heredem repperit illa suum*.

45 diuersi ... uulgi: *diuersus* here must mean something like 'inconsistent', 'having different ideas', see *OLD* 6d; for the sense, cf. Curt. 9.1.20 *orta seditio in diuersa consilia diduxerat uulgum*. For the rejection of the common mob as a Callimachean theme see **3.19-20n., 10.17-18n.,** and **19.7n.**

fremat: cf. Acc. *Trag*. 288 *et nonne Argiuos fremere bellum et uelle uim uulgum uides?*; Liv. 26.35.7 (quoted at **46n.** below); Lucan 9.217 *fremit interea discordia uulgi*; Stat. *Theb*. 3.606-607 *ante fores ubi turba ducum uulgique frementis ... / ... clamat*.

inconstantia: mentioned frequently as an attribute of the mob, cf. Cic. *Nat. Deor*. 1.43 *uulgi opiniones, quae in maxima inconstantia ueritatis ... uersantur*, cf. *Dom*. 4; Liv. 29.37.16 and see Otto 378. The noun is rare in poetry, but occurs in the same *sedes* at Ov. *Met*. 13.646; Lucan 5.415; Calp. *Ecl*. 5.45.

46 non alius sedare queat: one would normally expect a comparative in such contexts, cf. **82** below *non alius belli tenet aptius artes*. For *non alius* used to indicate an exceptional quality (also at **82**) see Virg. *Georg*. 4.372, and Hor. *Carm*. 3.7.25 (with N-R ad loc.).

sedare: used of calming a mob also at Cic. *Rep*. 1.65 *putes autem mare ullum aut flammam esse tantam, quam non facilius sit sedare quam effrenatam insolentia multitudinem*; Liv. 26.35.7 *ingens turba fremebant; nec eos sedare consules ... poterant*.

46-47 For the theme of manipulating the judge's emotions in the courtroom, see Peirano (2012) 154 with n.100 and cf. Cic. *De Orat.* 1.53; Quint. *Inst.*6.2; Tac. *Dial.* 31.3 and *Laus Pisonis* 44-48.

ira / sit placanda: cf. Cic. *Harusp.* 63 *nostrae nobis sunt inter nos irae discordiaeque placandae*; Liv. 25.6.18 *ne qua spes ... placandae ciuium irae*; Ov. *Met.* 12.28 *placandam uirginis iram*.

ira / ... poterit mitescere: outside this passage the use of *mitescere* with reference to *ira* is restricted to Ov. *Pont.* 2.7.79 *spes quoque posse mora mitescere principis iram* and 3.3.83 *... mitescet Caesaris ira*.

47 sit ... poterit: on the variation in mood between subjunctive in the protasis and future indicative in the apodosis with *possum* see K-S II 2.394f.

48-49 Messalla's eloquence is compared to that of Nestor and Odysseus. Nestor's eloquence is praised at Hom. *Il.* 1.247-252, 4.293, and that of Odysseus at Hom. *Il.* 2.335 (in the Thersites episode); see also *Il.* 3.221-223 with Schol. ad loc. [νιφάδεσσιν ἐοικότα] ὁ τρόπος μεταφορά· τὸ λευκὸν δὲ τῶν νιφάδων τὴν σαφήνειαν τῶν λόγων δηλοῖ. ["'similar to snow flakes' it is a metaphor: the white colour of the snow-flakes indicates the clarity of his speech"]. As early as Plato *Phaedr.* 261b-c these two names were applied to outstanding orators, in this case to Gorgias. In Rome Nestor and Odysseus are mentioned as models of eloquence by Cic. *Brut.* 40 and Tac. *Dial.* 16.5, and at Ov. *Met.* 13.63 Odysseus is said to outdo Nestor in eloquence. Piso's oratory is compared to theirs, together with that of Menelaus, at *Laus Pisonis* 61-64, and Statius at *Silu.* 5.3.114f. likens his father's oratory to that of Nestor and Odysseus (where, as at *Il.* 3.221-223, Piso's eloquence is illustrated by a storm simile 57-58). At *Catal.* 9.16 Messalla's poetry is said to be worthy to outdo that of ageing Nestor: *carmina quae Pylium uincere digna senem*. The use of famous mythological characters as objects of comparison in panegyric is recommended frequently by Men. Rhet., cf. especially 372.21-25 Sp. and cf. the comparison of Messalla as a warrior with Meleager and Eryx at *Catal.* 9. 6 *magnus ut Oenides utque superbus Eryx*. For such hyperbole is a natural device for panegyric, see Hardie (1986) 256-257 on Anchises' praise of Augustus at Virg. *Aen.* 6.791-805, Helzle (1989) 158-159 on Ov. *Pont.* 4.7 (especially the comparison between Vestalis and Ajax at *Pont.* 4.7.41-42) and Tissol (2014) 16-18 on Ov. *Pont.* 1.7 (especially the comparison of Augustus with Jupiter wielding his thunderbolt at *Pont.* 1.7.45-50).

48 genuisse: the use of the perfect inf. in this position in the line becomes frequent from Tibullus on, e.g. 2.1.41 *docuisse feruntur*; see **3.1n.** The inf. *genuisse* is found in this *sedes* also at Stat. *Silu.* 2.1.81, 87, 3.3.110.

feruntur: an Alexandrian feature, stressing the traditional source of the poet's story, cf. Call. *Hym*n. 5.56 Pf. and see Maltby (2002) 370 on Tib. 2.1.41; Fordyce on Cat. 64.1, Norden (1926) on Virg. *Aen.* 6.14, Horsfall (1990), Hardie (1994) 90-91 on Virg. *Aen.* 9.82, and Tarrant (2012) 307 on Virg. *Aen.* 12.845. This feature was termed an 'Alexandrian footnote' by Ross (1975) 78, cf. Hinds (1998) 1-3, Gale (2012) 200.

49 paruae ... urbis: on the small size of Ithaca, see Hom. *Od.* 4.605f. and 13.243.

decus: for this metonymic use, referring to a person, see **32n.** above.

50-52 ille ... / ... / ille: in place of *ille ... hic* in the sense of 'the former ... the latter'. It occurs occasionally in verse from Ter. *Phorm.* 332 *quia in illis fructus est, in illis opera luditur* on. In Augustan poetry it is found only in Ovid, see *ThLL* 7(1).363.21-27.

50-51 dum terna ... / saecula ... decurreret: cf. **160** below *seu* (sc. *Phoebus*) *celer hibernas properat decurrere luces*.

terna ... / saecula: according to Homer, Nestor is said to have seen three generations (*Il.* 1.250ff., 9.57f., *Od.* 3.245). In Latin the length of his life is often extended to three lives or three hundred years because of the ambiguity in meaning of *saeculum* (see *OLD* 1 'generation', 5 'human life time', 6 'one hundred years'): Laev. fr. 7.13 (Courtney) *trisaeclisenex*; Cic. *Sen.* 31 *tertiam iam hominum aetatem uidebat*; Hor. *Carm.* 2.9.13 *ter aevo functus* (with N-H 146 ad loc.); Prop. 2.13.46 *Nestoris est uisus post tria saecla cinis*; Ov. *Met.* 12.187-188 *uixi / annos bis centum*; *nunc tertia uiuitur aetas*; Manil. 1.764-765 *Pylium ... senecta / insignem triplici*; Juv. 10.248-249 *felix nimirum, qui tot per saecula mortem / distulit* and cf. **112** below *terna minus Pyliae miretur saecula famae*. There are further examples in Tissol (2014) 105 on Ov. *Pont.* 1.4.10 and for the proverbial use of the theme see Otto 1223.

50 orbem: = 'orbit', see **159n.** below.

51 fertilibus ... horis: 'with its fruitful seasons'. For *hora* in the sense of 'season', under the influence of Greek ὥρα, see *OLD hora* (1), 6, *ThLL* 6(3).2964.1-25. The usage is not attested before Horace, cf. *Carm.*

370   Commentary

1.12.15-16 (of Jupiter) *qui mare et terras uariisque mundum / temperet horis*, 3.13.9 *hora Caniculae, Epist.* 1.16.16 *Septembribus horis, AP* 302 *sub uerni temporis horam*. For *fecundus* in this context, referring to the fertility caused by the changing seasons, cf. **113** below *centum fecundos Titan renouauerit annos*.

Titan: here = 'the sun'. In Hesiod *Theog.* 371ff. the sun was the son of Tethys and Hyperion. From Cic. *Arat.* 343 onward Titan is used of the sun itself, see *OLD Titan* 2(a) and the further examples in Fantham (1998) 126 on Ov. *Fast.* 4.180, and Robinson (2011) 104-105 on Ov. *Fast.* 2.73; cf. **113** (quoted above) and **157** below. Ovid's 17 occurences are found in *Her.* (1), *Fast.* (4) and *Met.* (12).

52 The comparison between Messalla and Odysseus has an important role to play in the author's impersonation of the young Tibullus, since in Tib. 1.3 (a poem still to be composed at the dramatic date of the *Laud. Mess.*) likens the author sick in Phaeacia to Odysseus on his wanderings, with Tib.'s return to Delia at the end of the poem being likened to Odysseus' return to the faithful Penelope, see Bright (1971), (1984), Mills (1974) and Maltby (2002) 183, Tib. 1.3 Intro., 185-186 (Tib. 1.3.3n.), 210 (Tib. 1.3.83-89n.). The theme is echoed in Ovid's lament for Tibullus at *Am.* 3.9.47-48 *sed tamen hoc melius, quam si Phaeacia tellus / ignotum uili supposuisset humo*, an indication of how closely the Odyssean comparison was associated with him. For the wanderings of Odysseus cf. Hom. *Od.* 1.1-2 μάλα πολλὰ / πλάγχθη ["he wandered far and wide"] and 3 πολλῶν δ' ἀνθρώπων ἴδεν ἄστεα ["he saw the cities of many men"].

ignotas ... urbes: the phrase is used in connection with Jason's wanderings at Sen. *Medea* 20 *per urbes erret ignotas egens*. The same *iunctura* is found at Manil. 4.512 *sed iuuat ignotas semper transire per urbes*; Stat. *Theb.* 2.397-398 *... uagus ille ... per urbes / ignotas pactae ... succederet aulae*, and in prose at Liv. 5.39.3 and Tac. *Hist.* 3.20.9. The main influence here, as discussed above, is likely to be Tib. 1.3.3 *me tenet ignotis aegrum Phaeacia terris*. For Phaeacia cf. **78n.** below.

53 For the idea of the earth being surrounded by sea cf. Cat. 64.30 *Oceanus ... mari totum qui amplectitur orbem*; Ov. *Her.* 9.13-14 *respice uindicibus pacatum uiribus orbem, / qua latam Nereus caerulus ambit humum*; *Aetna* 94-95 *quacumque inmensus se terrae porrigit orbis / extremique maris curuis incingitur undis*; Sen. *Herc. Oet.* 3-4 *protuli pacem tibi / quacumque Nereus porrigi terras uetat, Phaed.* 1162-1163 *quidquid Oceanus uagis / conplexus undis ultimo fluctu tegit* and see **147-**

148 below *Oceanus ponto qua continet orbem, / nulla tibi aduersis regio sese offeret armis*.

qua: in the sense of *usque eo*, *qua* is found in a similar context at Ov. *Her.* 9.14; **[Tib.] 3.7.148** and Sen. *Herc. Oet.* 4 (*quacumque*) – all quoted above– and *Catal.* 9.4 (of the extent of Messalla's victories) *uictor, qua terrae quaque patent maria*.

maris ... undis: for the phrase *maris unda* cf. Tib. 2.2.16 *... Eoi qua maris unda rubet*, 2.4.10 *naufraga quam uasti tunderet unda maris*; Ov. *Her.* 18.2, *Met.* 4.556, 11.364, 747, *Trist.* 1.2.26, 2.196, 5.10.2; *Culex* 349; *Aetna* 95; Lucan 2.399-400, 2.665, 4.404; [Sen.] *Oct.* 356-357; Stat. *Theb.* 9.379, *Ach.* 1.411; Serenus *Med.* 5.69 and here *Laud. Mess.* **193** below.

extremis tellus: the phrase occurs in the same *sedes* at Prop. 2.10.17 *et si qua extremis tellus se subtrahit oris*. Cf. Cat.'s description of his brother's grave in Troy: 68.100 *detinet extremo terra aliena solo*.

54-78 These verses contain an account, in chronological order, of the wanderings of Odysseus, as narrated by him at the feast of the Phaeacian king Alcinous in Hom. *Od.* 9-12. A similar narration of Odysseus' travels, though not in chronological order, is found at Prop. 3.12.25-36, and brief accounts of Homer's epics also occur at Hor. *Carm.* 1.6.5-9 (*Iliad* and *Odyssey*), *Epist.* 1.2.6-16 (*Iliad*), 17-31 (*Odyssey*); *Priap.* 68.18-20 (*Iliad* and *Odyssey*) and Ov. *Trist.* 2.371-374 (*Iliad*) and 375-380 (*Odyssey*), with further examples in Ingleheart (2010) 300-301 ad loc. Here the digression appears somewhat inept as the account of Odysseus' travels does nothing to back up the argument about his eloquence, which is the point of the comparison between Odysseus and Messalla introduced at **48-49** and recapitulated at **81**; see further Peirano [(2012) 136-137] on the parodic nature of these comparisons and contrast the more positive use of the Ulysses, Menalaus and Nestor at *Laus Pisonis* 61-64. On the ironic inclusion of epic themes in other genres see Harrison (2007) 170-174 on Hor. *Carm.* 1.6.

54-56 Ciconumque ... / nec ... / ... et: a rather awkward combination of *-que ... et* 'both ... and' (for which cf. **3.37-38, 4.44, 7.87, 91-92**) and *nec* 'nor', made more difficult by the fact that each clause has a different subject.

54 Ciconumque manus: the Cicones were a people of Southern Thrace. At Hom. *Od.* 9.36-61 Odysseus tells king Alcinous how he and his men sacked their city of Ismarus, his first port of call after leaving Troy.

372   Commentary

Instead of fleeing quickly after the fight, as Odysseus had ordered, his men lingered on the shore drinking and feasting, and the Cicones of Ismarus, together with their more warlike neighbours, returned to attack them. Many Greeks perished, but Odysseus managed to escape by ship with his surviving comrades. However, on returning home to Ithaca, Odysseus gives Penelope a more favourable account, in which he simply defeated the Cicones: *Od.* 23.310 ἤρξατο δ' ὡς πρῶτον Κίκονας δάμασ' ["he began by telling how first he defeated the Cicones"].

aduersis ... armis: the phrase recurs at **148** below; cf. also Ov. *Trist.* 1.5.39, Val. Fl. 5.689, 6.740, *Il. Lat.* 267.

55 lotos: the visit to the land of the Lotus-eaters is the next episode mentioned in Odysseus' account to Alcinous, *Od.* 9.82-104. Despite the fact that two of his men who had eaten the lotus wished to stay, he was able to bring them back to his ship under compulsion and to resume his voyage.

captos ... cursus: the reading *captos* of F is to be preferred to A's meaningless *tempus* and the reading *coeptos* of many later manuscripts. For *cursum capere* 'to take a course' cf. Acc. *Praetext.* 36-37 ... *nam quod ad dexteram / cepit cursum a laeua signum praepotens* and Plaut. *Bacch.* 325 *tibimet illuc naui capiendumst iter.*

auertere cursus: i.e. *auertere illum a cursu*. For *uertere cursus* at the line end, cf. Virg. *Aen.* 3.146; Manil. 1.525; Lucan 5.574.

56 Hollis [(2007) 350-351] sees in the reference to Odysseus defeating the Neptunian Cyclops in Sicily a possible allusion to Messalla's role in helping defeat Sextus Pompey, described by Horace (*Epod.* 9.7-8) as *Neptunius / dux*, in the same island; see further Mankin (1995) 163-164 and L. C. Watson (2003) 319-320 ad loc.

et: for postponed *et* see **20n.** above.

Aetnaeae ... rupis: i.e. Mt. Etna. For the poetic use of an adj. in place of a gen. subst. cf. *Molorceis* at **13** above and *Neptunius* in the present line. The phenomenon is a feature of Greek Alexandrian verse (cf. **13n.** above) and its use in Latin is discussed by K-S II 1.210, who compares Hor. *Carm.* 2.20.13 *Daedaleo ... Icaro*; Ov. *Met.* 1.678 *Iunonius custos* and Val. Fl. 8.231 *Iunonia Hebe.* The adj. *Aetnaeus* is found in verse from Lucr. 1.722 on.

Aetnaeae Neptunius incola rupis: at Hom. *Od.* 1.71-73 the Cyclops Polyphemus is said to have been the son of Poseidon (hence *Neptunius* here) and the nymph Thoosa. His association with the region of Etna in Sicily is not attested in Greek until Eur. (*Cycl.* 20ff., 130, 298, 366). In Latin he is always placed in the region of Etna (e.g. Cic. *Verr.* 2.5.146; Virg. *Aen.* 3.678, 8.444, 11.263; Ov. *Met.* 13.770, 14.160, *Pont.* 2.2.113; *Culex* 332; Val. Fl. 4.104ff.; Sil. 14.527; Stat. *Theb.* 6.716-718).

57 For the 'golden line' structure see **3.5n.** and **13n.** above.

uicta ... lumina: of eyes closed in sleep the phrase is found first at Tib. 1.2.2 *occupet ut fessi lumina uicta sopor*, cf. Prop. 3.17.42 *hoc ... uince sopore caput* (both with reference to the soporific effects of wine).

Maroneo foedatus... Baccho: cf. Tib. 1.2.3 ... *multo percussum tempora Baccho*. The metonymy of Bacchus for wine is frequent in poetry from Lucr. on, see *ThLL* 2.1665.78-1666.38. The wine is called Maronean because, according to Hom. *Od.* 9.196-201, it had been given to Odysseus by Maro, a priest of Apollo at Ismarus, who, with his wife and child, had been protected by Odysseus during the siege of the town. The wine was later identified with the strong dark wine produced by the city of Maronea in Thrace, cf. Plin. *Nat.* 14.53 *uino antiquissimo claritas Maroneo in Thraciae maritima parte genito, ut auctor est Homerus*.

foedatus: here = 'maimed', 'disfigured', see *OLD foedo* 3 and *ThLL* 4.997.36-45. It is found in this sense in poetry, rarely, from Plaut. *Amph.* 246 *foedant et proterunt hostium copias* and Enn. *Trag.* 399 Jocelyn *ferro foedati iacent* on. For the so-called 'Greek' accusative construction *foedatus lumina* see Courtney (2003-2004).

lumina: for the use of a plural referring to a single eye, cf. Prop. 3.12.26 *tuae ... Polypheme, genae*, where Fedeli [407 ad loc.] compares the plurals in the same context at Eur. *Cycl.* 463 κόραι and 470, 511 ὄμματα.

58 uexit: Odysseus carried with him on his ship the winds which Aeolus had enclosed in a bag, so that they would not hinder his journey home (Hom. *Od.* 10.17ff.).

et: for delayed *et* see **20n.** above.

Aeolios ... uentos: Aeolus was ruler of the winds who lived in the Aeolian islands. For the use of the adj. in place of a gen. subst. see **56n.** above *Aetnaeae ... rupis*, and cf. Virg. *Aen.* 5.791 *Aeoliis ... procellis*.

placidum per Nerea: the metonymy of Nereus for sea occurs in Greek first with Callimachus (*Hymn*. 1.40) and in Latin from Virg. *Aen*. 10.764 on, cf. Ov. *Her*. 9.14. The sea was calm, *placidum*, until Odysseus' comrades released Aeolus' winds from the bag in which he had carried them to aid their sea passage (Hom. *Od*. 10.47). For *placidus* of the sea cf. Virg. *Aen*. 8.96, 10.103; Prop. 1.8A.20; Ov. *Her*. 19.92 *et facias placidum per mare tutus iter*; Manil. 4.285; Tac. *Ann*. 2.23.2.

59-60 The lines are a reworking of the narration to Alcinous in which the companions of Odysseus meet the daughter of the Laestrygonians' king Antiphates at the spring of Artacia: Hom. *Od*. 10.105-108 κούρῃ δὲ ξύμβληντο πρὸ ἄστεος ὑδρευούσῃ, / θυγατέρ' ἰφθίμῃ Λαιστρυγόνος Ἀντιφάταο. / ἡ μὲν ἄρ' ἐς κρήνην κατεβήσετο καλλιρέεθρον / Ἀρτακίην ["they met a girl drawing water before the city, the goodly daughter of Laestrygonian Antiphates, who had come down to the fair-flowing spring of Artaci"].

59 incultos: the Laestrygonians were cannibals, cf. Ov. *Pont*. 2.9.41 *quis non Antiphaten Laestrygona deuouet*?

adiit: 'visited', *OLD* 4a, 6b.

Laestrygonas Antiphatemque: for the line-ending cf. Hom. *Od*. 10.106 quoted above. For the use of a people's name to designate a country cf. Manil. 4.602 *laeua freti caedunt Hispanas aequora gentes* with Housman ad loc.

60 nobilis Artacie: the spring of Artacia is mentioned only here in Latin literature. For *nobilis* applied to a famous spring cf. Hor. *Carm*. 3.13.13 (of *fons Bandusiae*) *fies nobilium tu quoque fontium*; Plin. *Nat*. 18.190.2 *nobilis fons Orgae nomine*.

gelida ... unda: occurs in the same metrical *sedes* at Hor. *Epist*. 1.15.4 ... *gelida cum perluor unda*; for the *iunctura* see Ov. *Met*. 5.433, 15.310, *Trist*. 4.10.3; Manil. 2.941; Lucan 1.582, 2.570, 585; Val. Fl. 5.350; Sil. 10.363, 17.314; Stat. *Theb*. 1.357, 9.447.

irrigat: for its use in this context, cf. Cat. 61.28-30 ... *Aonios specus / nympha quos super irrigat / frigerans Aganippe* ...; Ov. *Met*. 14.633; Sil. 8.368-369 *gelidoque rigantur / Simbruuio*, 9.207 (quoted below); Calp. *Ecl*. 7.68.

irrigat unda: same hexameter ending at Sil. 9.207 *flaua Thybris quas* (sc. *ripas*) *irrigat unda*.

61 solum: Odysseus alone resisted the magic potions of Circe, cf. Hom. *Od.* 10.327 οὐδέ τις ἄλλος ἀνὴρ τάδε φάρμακ' ἀνέτλη ["no other man has withstood these charms"]. On a possible etymological play between *solum* here and *Solis* (**62**) see Michalopoulos (2001) 160.

nec: for postponed *nec* see **42n.** above.

doctae: used only here of Circe, but cf. Ovid's use of the adj. of Medea's magic at *Her.* 12.165 *doctis medicatibus* and *Met.* 9.743-744 *doctis / artibus*. In these contexts the adj. must mean 'expert' *OLD* 2a rather than 'learned'.

pocula Circes: the same verse ending occurs at Nemes. *Cyn.* 44. For mention of Circe's potions cf. also Cic. *Diu. in Caec.* 57; Hor. *Epist.* 1.2.23 (quoted below); Tib. 2.4.45. On the proverbial nature of *pocula Circes* see Otto 84.

Circes: this form of the gen. for Greek names in *-e* occurs occasionally in Cat. and Prop., but becomes common only from Ov. on (e.g. *Circes* at the line end in *Met.* 4.205, 13.968, 14.247). Horace and Virgil use the Latinised *-ae* (e.g. Hor. *Epist.* 1.2.23 *Circae pocula nosti*); see further Norden (1927) on Virg. *Aen.* 6.705.

62 foret: the archaic form [see Woodman (2014) 174], occurs only here and at Tib. 1.10.11 in the *Corp. Tib.*, where its equivalent *esset* is also rare (3). In Prop. *foret* is more common than *esset* (6/4), as it is in Ovid, who makes frequent use of both forms (88/77).

Solis genus: for Circe as the daughter of the Sun see Hom. *Od.* 10.138. In Latin, cf. Virg. *Aen.* 7.10-12 ... *Circaeae raduntur litora terrae / diues inaccessos ubi Solis filia lucos / adsiduo resonat cantu*; Ov. *Met.* 14.10 *Sole satae Circes* ... The noun *genus* in the sense of 'child of' on the model of the Greek γένος, e.g. Eur. *Cycl.* 104 οἶδ' ἄνδρα ..., Σισύφου γένος ["I knew a man ... the child of Sisyphus"], is found in Latin from Cat. 61.2 *Vraniae genus* (of Hymen) and 64.23 *heroes ..., deum genus* on, see *ThLL* 4.1890.68-1891.30.

62-63 apta ... / aptaque... mutare: the construction of *aptus* + inf. is mostly found in poetry, occurring some 12 times in Ovid; see McKeown II 117 on *Am.* 1.5.19-20, K-S II 1.689, *ThLL* 2.33.1-10. For *mutare* in this context see Virg. *Ecl.* 8.70 (quoted below). On the importance of the theme of change in [**Tib.**] 3 overall, see Prolegomena pp. 81-82, **2.9n., 2.26n., 8 headnote, 8.13-14n.** cf. also **206-210n.** below *mutata figura.*

uel herbis / ... uel cantu: in Homer Circe uses magic potions, φάρμακα, to transform Odysseus' men (see *Od.* 10.327 quoted in **61n.** above). However, at *Od.* 10.136, 221 and 254 Homer had mentioned Circe's beautiful song, and her use of song to transform her victims is found in Latin at Virg. *Ecl.* 8.70 *carminibus Circe socios mutauit Vlixi.* Herbs and incantations are often mentioned together as the tools of magic, e.g. Tib. 1.2.53-55, 62, 8.17-20; Virg. *Aen.* 7.757-758; Ov. *Her.* 12.167, *Met.* 4.49, 7.98, 195-196; Gratt. *Cyneg.* 405; Lucan 4.553-555, 6.492.

63 aptaque uel: the expression, with its redundant *-que*, is rather awkward and Tränkle 202 suggests *uel magico*, as *magicus cantus* is a common combination from Gratt. *Cyneg.* 405 to Juv. 6.610. Less convincing are the conjectures by Baehrens and Postgate cited in the apparatus. On the whole it seems best to print the reading of the manuscripts. For *-que uel* at the line opening cf. Stat. *Theb.* 7.352 *armaque uel Tityon uel Delon habentia ...*

ueteres ... figuras: 'their former shapes', cf. Virg. *Aen.* 6.448-449 *iuuenis quondam nunc femina Caeneus / rursus et in ueterem fato reuoluta figuram,* where the adj. is more appropriate as it describes returning to a 'former' shape rather than to changing an original one.

mutare figuras: the same hexameter ending occurs at Ov. *Ibis* 425. See also above **62-63n.**

64 Cimmerion: cf. Hom. *Od.* 11.14-15 ἔνθα δὲ Κιμμερίων ἀνδρῶν δῆμός τε πόλις τε, / ἠέρι καὶ νεφέλῃ κεκαλυμμένοι ["there is the land and the city of the Cimmerians, a people shrouded in mist and cloud"]. For the Cimmerians see **5.24n.** above. The Greek gen. pl. form *-on* = *-ων* occurs in verse only here and Prisc. *Periheg.* 375: *Tegestraeon*; also possibly the conjectural *Chalybon* at Cat. 66.48. It is equally rare in prose, e.g. Plin. *Nat.* 5.28 *Lotophagon*; Quint. *Inst.* 6.3.96 *tetrastichon.*

obscuras ... arces: cf. Hom. *Od.* 11.15 (quoted above) and cf. **65-66n.** below.

accessit: 'reached'.

ad arces: the same hexameter ending occurs at Ov. *Met.* 13.44, 196; Manil. 4.562; Stat. *Theb.* 3.322, 11.358, *Silu.* 3.4.32; Val. Fl. 4.73, 7.562; Sil. 12.44; *Il. Lat.* 66.

65-66: The Cimmerians lived in everlasting night, cf. Hom. *Od.* 11.15-18 ... οὐδέ ποτ' αὐτοὺς / ἠέλιος φαέθων καταδέρκεται ἀκτίνεσσιν, / οὔθ' ὁπότ' ἂν στείχῃσι πρὸς οὐρανὸν ἀστερόεντα, / οὔθ' ὅτ' ἂν ἂψ ἐπὶ γαῖαν ἀπ' οὐρανόθεν προτράπηται ["never does the bright sun look down upon them with his rays, either when he rises to the starry heaven or when he turns again to earth from heaven)"] a close Latin version of which is provided by Ov. *Met.* 11.594-595 *quo numquam radiis oriens mediusue cadensue / Phoebus adire potest*. In *Laud. Mess.* the author replaces the daily rising and setting of the sun by a journey above and below the earth, in the course of which he illuminates both hemispheres in turn. For this Stoic view see *SVF* 2.657 and Lucr. 5.654-655 *aut quia* (sc. *solem*) *sub terras cursum conuertere cogit / uis eadem, supra quae terras pertulit orbem*.

65 quis: an intentional archaism for *quibus* on which see Austin (1971) on Virg. *Aen.* 1.95, found again at **120** below. The form *quibus* never occurs in the *Laud. Mess.*

candente ... ortu: for *ortus* as the disk of the rising sun see **4.21n.** above. The attribute *candens* 'bright' is normally applied to the sun or its synonyms, cf. Enn. *Trag.* 280 Jocelyn; Lucr. 6.1197; Germ. *Arat.* 480; Colum. *Rust.* 6.13.2, 32.1; Plin. *Nat.* 18.277; Val. Fl. 3.481, and see *ThLL* 3.234.54-64.

66 Phoebus: for *Phoebus* as an epithet of the sun god see **4.21n.** and cf. below **145** and **158**; see further Hardie (1986) 355-356 with nn. 64-65. This use is rare until the first century AD, which argues in favour of a later dating for *Laud. Mess.* than its purported date of 31 BC. In Ovid it is restricted mainly to the later works (*Met.* and *Fast.*), but becomes common from Manilius on, especially in later epic and Senecan tragedy. Although in Greece Apollo was identified with the sun from the late fifth century BC on, with the first secure literary attestation at Eur. *Phaeth.* 224-225 [see Diggle (1970) ad loc.], there is no such metonymic use of Phoebus in Greek for the sun.

curreret: the subjunct. is conditional, as with *consurgeret* **74** and *nudaret* **75**.

67-68 The couplet recalls Odysseus' visit to the underworld in the last part of the Homeric *Nekyia* at *Od.* 11.568-631. Various verbal echoes make this Homeric connection clear: so *uidit* (**67**) picks up the repeated first person forms εἶδον, ἴδον, εἰσεῖδον in Odysseus' narrative at *Od.* 11.568, 576, 582, 593 and 630; *magna deum proles* (**68**) recalls the reference to Theseus and Peirithous as θεῶν ἐρικυδέα τέκνα ["the glorious offspring of gods"] at *Od.* 11.631 and *discurreret* (**68**) echoes Circe's description of the flitting shades at *Od.* 10.495 τοὶ δὲ σκιαὶ ἀΐσσουσιν ["but they flit around as shades"].

67 inferno ... regno: occurs in the same *sedes* at Colum. *Rust.* 10.274 *et nunc inferno potitur Proserpina regno*; for the *iunctura* cf. also Sen. *Herc. F.* 956 *inferna nostros regna sensere impetus*.

subdita regno: the same hexameter ending is found at Prop. 1.11.3. For *subditus* = 'subject to' + dat. see *OLD subdo* 4.

68 magna deum proles: for *magna ... proles* in the same *sedes*, and with the same collective sense, cf. *CLE* 251.4 *magna Iouis proles* (of Castor and Pollux).

deum proles: for the expression, cf. Hom. *Od.* 11.631 (quoted on **67-68n.** above), and in Latin Virg. *Aen.* 6.322 *deum certissima proles* (Aeneas); Sen. *Medea* 227 *prolem deum* (the Argonauts); Sil. 11.293 *proles digna deum* (Dardanus).

leuibus ... umbris: for this *iunctura* with reference to the insubstantial shades of the dead cf. Ov. *Fast.* 5.434 *occurrat tacito ne leuis umbra sibi*; Sen. *Oed.* 562-563; [Sen.] *Oct.* 522; Val. Fl. 1.783; *CLE* 2155.4. The abl. is local 'amid the insubstantial shades'; for verbs of motion with local ablative see K-S II 1.350-351.

discurreret: cf. Hom. *Od.* 10.495 (quoted on **67-68n.** above). Postgate [(1901) 158-159] objects to the close proximity of this verb to *curreret* (**66**), but the traditional reading is defended by Tränkle [205 ad loc.], who points to the author's fondness for such repetition elsewhere in the poem at **83-85** (*duco*), **89-91** (*celer*), **96-98** (*uenio*) and **103-105** (*duplex*).

69 For the episode of the Sirens see Hom. *Od.* 12.165-200. Odysseus had himself tied to the mast and his comrades stuffed their ears with wax to avoid being bewitched by their song. The present line is based closely on *Od.* 12.166-167 τόφρα δὲ καρπαλίμως ἐξίκετο νηῦς ἐυεργὴς / νῆσον Σειρήνοιιν ["meanwhile the well-built ship came quickly to the island of the two Sirens"].

cita ... puppi: the combination had occurred earlier at Cat. 64.6 *ausi sunt uada salsa cita decurrere puppi*.

litora puppi: for the line ending cf. Cat. 64.172 *litora puppes*; Cic. *Arat.* 133 *litora puppim* (also at Ov. *Her.* 1.59; Hyg. *Fab.* 14.33.13); Virg. *Aen.* 10.268 *litora puppis*.

70-75 On Scylla and Charybdis see **4.89n.** above. On Odysseus' encounter with them see Hom. *Od.* 12.222-259.

70 The line refers to the narrow passage afforded to sailors between the equally deadly Scylla and Charybdis, for which cf. Virg. *Aen.* 3.684-686 *contra iussa monent Heleni, Scyllam atque Charybdim / (inter utramque uiam leti discrimine paruo) / ni teneant cursus*.

geminae ... confinia mortis: 'the confines of twin death' referring to the dangers posed by Scylla and Charybdis. A variation on this phrase is found at Claud. *Carm. Min.* 27.70-71 (of the Phoenix) *geminae confinia uitae / exiguo medius discrimine separat ignis*, which presupposes the expression *confinia mortis et uitae*, attested from the second century AD onward, cf. *ThLL* 4.217.6-13. For the line ending *confinia mortis*, cf. Stat. *Theb.* 4.615 *et iunctae sentit confinia mortis* (of blind Oedipus' living death).

nantem: used rarely in elevated poetry of a ship's passengers; see *OLD no* 2b, which quotes only Cat. 66.46 and Virg. *Georg.* 4.506 in addition to this passage.

71-72 The author gives no clear picture of Scylla here. In Homer (*Od.* 12.85-92) she yelps like a young puppy, but is an evil monster with twelve legs and six necks and heads. In later literature she is depicted as a young woman, with dogs about her waist and a fish's tail; see further **4.89n.** above. Although the context is completely different, the present couplet shares a number of lexical items with Ovid's comparison of the anger of a woman discovering her husband's adultery with that of a wild-boar at *Ars* 2.373-374 *sed neque fuluus aper media tam saeuus in ira est / fulmineo rabidos cum rotat ore canes*.

71 saeuo ... ore: cf. the Homeric description of the head on each of Scylla's twelve necks with its triple row of deadly teeth at *Od.* 12.91-92 σμερδαλέη κεφαλή, ἐν δὲ τρίστοιχοι ὀδόντες / πυκνοὶ καὶ θαμέες, πλεῖοι μέλανος θανάτοιο ["a frightful head, in it three rows of teeth close and tight-packed, full of dark death"].

72 canibus: the name Scylla was associated etymologically with the Greek σκύλαξ 'young dog, puppy'. For plays on this etymology in Hom. *Od.* 12.85-87, Call. *Hecale* fr. 90.1-2 (Hollis), Lycoph. 45.669 and in Latin at Lucr. 5.892-893 (quoted below), Virg. *Aen.* 3.432, Prop. 4.4.39-40, see Michalopoulos (2001) 157-158. The abl. here is perhaps best taken with *fera* 'wild with her dogs', but a link with *rabidas* or *serperet* cannot be excluded.

rabidas ... undas: a unique collocation. More common would be *rapidas ... undas* found in some later manuscripts, cf. **193** below and Acc. *Trag.* 297; Lucr. 4.421; Cat. 70.4; Ov. *Am.* 1.5.10, 2.4.8 with McKeown III 69 ad loc., 3.6.51, 80, *Met.* 7.6, 9.104, *Ibis* 512; Sil. 4.448; **[Tib.] 3.7.193, 10.8**. However, the sea is often described as mad *insanus* and the sea's *rabies* is mentioned at Val. Fl. 6.355 and Stat. *Silu.* 1.3.21; for *rabidus* in a similar context see Stat. *Silu.* 3.2.84-85 *an facili te praetermiserit unda / Lucani rabida ora maris* (followed by a description of Charybdis and Scylla). The presence of *canibus* in the same line could have influenced the unusual choice of epithet, as Scylla's dogs are described as *rabidis* at Lucr. 5.892-893 *aut rabidis canibus succinctas semimarinis / corporibus Scyllas* and cf. *rabidos ... canes* at Ov. *Ars* 2.374 (quoted on **71-72** above).

serperet: unlike Homer's Scylla whose lower body remains hidden in its cave (*Od.* 12.93), here the monster creeps through (*serperet*) the waves. For this meaning of *serpere*, which need not imply snake-like movements, but simply a stealthy and dangerous creeping, Tränkle [206 ad loc.] compares Cic. *Arat.* 47-48 *est Ales auis ... / quae uolat et serpens geminis secat aera pinnis*, *De Orat.* 2.203 (in a transferred sense) *serpere occulte coepisti*, and Prop. 3.13.64 (of the Trojan horse) *fallacem Troiae serpere ... equum*.

73-75 For the effect of Charybdis alternately sucking in the tide and belching it forth again three times a day, see Hom. *Od.* 12.105-106 τρὶς μὲν γάρ τ' ἀνίησιν ἐπ' ἤματι, τρὶς δ' ἀναροιβδεῖ / δεινόν ["three times a day she belches it forth and three times she sucks it in terribly"], 12.235ff. and in Latin cf. Prop. 2.26B.53-54 *nec umquam / alternante uacans uasta Charybdis aqua*, 3.12.28; Virg *Aen.* 3.420ff.; Ov. *Am.* 2.16.25-26 *non quae submersis ratibus saturata Charybdis / fundit et effusas ore receptat aquas*, *Rem.* 740, *Met.* 7.63, 13.730-731; Sen. *Thy.* 581. For the rationalistic explanation of this effect as caused simply by the turbulence of the sea in the area, see Stat. *Silu.* 3.2.85-86 *num torta Charybdis / fluctuet*.

73 For the *abcba* golden line arrangement of nouns and adjectives see **3.5n., 7.13n.** above and **7.76n.** below.

consumpsit: 'devoured'. The monster 'sucks in' its victims along with the sea water.

74-77 For the sequential pairs at the line-openings (*uel si* ... / *uel si* / *non* .../ *non*) in the structure *aabb* see Wills (1996) 412-413 and 49n.

74 For the water rising to the heavens as Charybdis belches it forth cf. Hom. *Od.* 12.238-239 ὑψόσε δ' ἄχνη / ἄκροισι σκοπέλοισιν ἐπ' ἀμφοτέροισιν ἔπιπτεν ["high overhead the spray fell on the tops of both cliffs"].

75 For the sea-bed being laid bare when Carybdis sucks in the water cf. Hom. *Od.* 12.242-243 ὑπένερθε δὲ γαῖα φάνεσκε / ψάμμῳ κυανέη ["and below the earth appeared, black with sand"]. A similar effect caused by a storm at sea is described by Ov. at *Fast.* 3.591-592 *adsiliunt fluctus, imoque a gurgite pontus / uertitur* and Tac. at *Ann.* 6.33 *pulsoque introrsus freto breuia litorum nudantur.*

interrupto ... gurgite: 'with the gulf in her waters'. The part. *interruptus* is rare in poetry (Acc. *Trag.* 395; Virg. *Aen.* 4.88, 9.239; Lucan 2.213, 9.335).

nudaret ... pontum: for a similar expression, *nudare uada*, cf. Liv. 26.45.8 *septentrio ortus ... nudauerat uada,* 39.30.10 *qua ... uada nudabat amnis.*

gurgite pontum: for the hexameter ending *gurgite pontum* (-*i*, -*o*) cf. Cic. *Progn.* 3.7; Lucr. 5.387; Virg. *Aen.* 11.642; Ov. *Fast.* 3.591 (quoted above); Lucan 5.234, 7.813; Sil. 1.197, 12.117, 440; Stat. *Theb.* 7.143.

76 The reference is to the killing of the Sun's cattle by Odysseus' companions, as described at Hom. *Od.* 12.353-402. The structure of the verse is that of a 'golden line'; see **3.5n.** and **13n.** above.

uagi ... Solis: for the collocation cf. Laev. fr. 32.1 Courtney ... *Sol uagus ... habenas / immitit*; Cat. 64.271 ... *uagi sub limina Solis.*

pascua Solis: cf. Ov. *Met.* 4.214 *axe sub Hesperio sunt pascua Solis equorum.* On *pascua* see further *Sulpicia Cycle* **9.1n.** below.

77 amor: For Calypso's love and care of Odysseus cf. Hom. *Od.* 5.135 τὸν μὲν ἐγὼ φίλεόν τε καὶ ἔτρεφον ["I loved him and looked after him"], 7.256, 12.450.

fecunda ... arua: for the collocation cf. Lucan 9.696-697 *fecundaque nulli / arua*; Manil. 4.824 *et fecunda suis absistunt frugibus arua*. The reference here is to the rich vegetation of Calypso's island of Ogygia; cf. Hom. *Od.* 5.63-73.

Atlantidos: Calypso was the daughter of Atlas, cf. Hom. *Od.* 1.52, 7.245.

Calypsus: for the gen. form cf. Serv. *Aen.* 3.171.1 *ab Ausone, Vlixis et Calypsus filio*; Plin. *Nat.* 3.96.

78 finis ... erroris ... Phaeacia: Odysseus was escorted directly from Phaeacia to his home in Ithaca; see Hom. *Od.* 13.70-95. For the formulation of the line cf. Hor. *Serm.* 1.5.104 *Brundisium ... finis ... uiae*; Serv. *Aen.* 5.85 *septimus ei annus est finis erroris*; Mela 3.107 *operis huius atque Atlantici litoris terminus*.

et: on delayed *et* in see **20n.** above.

erroris miseri: cf. Prop. 1.20.15 *quae miser ignotis error perpessus in oris*.

Phaeacia tellus: the same verse ending occurs at Ov. *Am.* 3.9.47, in an epikedion for Tibullus, echoing the line-end *Phaeacia terris* at Tib. 1.3.3. For the importance of Phaeacia for Tibullan impersonation see **52n.** above.

79-81 The passage is based on the old controversy as to whether the geographical details of Odysseus' travels in the *Odyssey* were based on reality (*cognita* **79**), as most people believed, or on poetic invention (*fabula, nouum* **80**), a view supported by Eratosthenes. This controversy probably has nothing to do with the argument between Aristarchus and Crates (as reported in Sen. *Epist.* 88.7 and Gell. 14.6.3) as to whether Odysseus' wanderings were set in the Mediterranean or in the Atlantic Ocean. The author probably believes in the truth of Odysseus' travels and so gives him the priority in hardship suffered (*labor* **81**) and Messalla the victory in eloquence (*facundia* **81**).

79-80 seu ... / ... siue: for the rare use of these particles in second position cf. Hor. *Epod.* 16.29; Virg. *Aen.* 9.680, 11.779 and see Marouzeau (1949)

83-84. For *seu* postponed to third position in its clause cf. 206 and 207 below.

79 nostras ... terras: occurs in the same *sedes* at Calp. *Ecl.* 4.84 *at mihi, qui nostras praesenti numine terras* and Val. Fl. 7.437 *quid, precor, in nostras uenisti, Thessale, terras*; cf. also Sen. *Herc. Oet.* 1991 *nunc quoque nostras respice terras*.

sunt cognita: had occurred in the same *sedes* at Lucr. 5.1285.

80 nouum ... orbem: for the *iunctura* cf. Ov. *Fast.* 2.175; Manil. 4.268 and in the abl. at [Ov.] *Epiced. Drusi* 314; Juv. 6.11. On the concept of the 'invented world' see Woodman on Vell. 2.46.1.

81 The main reason for the introduction of Odysseus was the comparison with Messalla's eloquence (see **54-78n.** above). The poet, however, did not mention Odysseus' eloquence but concentrated solely on his wanderings and sufferings. In order to bring the argument somewhat laboriously back to its original purpose, Odysseus here is said to excel in sufferings whereas Messalla is said to be paramount in eloquence. Again the parodic nature of the panegyric is apparent.

labor: for emphasis on the hardships suffered by Odysseus in Homer see *Od.*1.4, 9.37-38, 13.6, 23.350-353; Hor. *Epist.*1.2.21-22 *dum sibi dum sociis reditum parat aspera multa / pertulit, aduersis rerum immersabilis undis*.

tua ...facundia maior: perhaps a pointed reference to Ovid's triple use of the line-ending *facundus Vlixes* (*Her.* 3.192, *Ars* 2.123, *Met.* 13.92). However, Ovid speaks of Messalla as *Latiae facundia linguae* at *Pont.* 2.3.75, addressed to Messalla's son, Cotta Maximus, and of Messalla himself as *facundus* at *Pont.* 2.2.51 (addressed to Messalla's eldest son, Messallinus) *uiuit enim in uobis facundi lingua parentis*.

82-117 This section deals with Messalla's military activities, as advertised in **39**. Verses **82-105** are dedicated to his mastery of the various arts of warfare, and are followed by a relatively short section (**106-117**) on specific military successes. In the first part verses **83-97** deal with his preparations for war as a military leader, while **98-105** recount his actual strategic knowledge. The fact that more space is given over to preparation than to technical knowledge reflects Quintilian's words on the orator with adequate judicial knowledge at *Inst.* 12.3.5 *quis enim potius praeparabit ea quae, cum aget, esse in causa uelit? nisi forte imperatorem quis* *idoneum credit in proeliis quidem strenuum et fortem et omnium quae pugna poscit artificem, sed neque dilectus agere nec copias contrahere atque instruere nec prospicere commeatus nec locum capere castris scientem*: *prius est enim certe parare bella quam gerere.* On the use of the 'ideal general' topos in encomia emphasising in the *laudandus* the various virtues and qualities that were outlined in military handbooks see Woodman [(2014) 26 n. 90] (on Agricola) and the index of that work under 'ideal general'.

82 iam: in the sense 'furthermore', 'besides' is to be preferred to the meaningless *nam* of A, which may have been influenced by *nam* introducting new sections at **39, 45, 54** above.

belli ... artes: for the phrase cf. Manil. 1.89 *tum belli pacisque artes commenta uetustas*; Suet. *Tit.* 3.1 *docilitas ad omnes tum belli tum pacis artes*.

tenet: 'has a (mental) grasp of' *OLD* 23.

83 praeducere fossam: for the phrase cf. Lucan 4.45 *munitumque latus laeuo praeducere gyro*, and, in a passage which also has similarities with **84** below, Sil. 10.410 ... *aut fossas instant praeducere muris*; see **84n.**

fossam: possibly a reference to the *legitima fossa*, the broadest and deepest kind of ditch, as described by Veg. *Mil.* 1.24.2 to be dug as a defence around the camp at the time of a fierce enemy attack *ubi uis acrior imminet hostium*.

84 qualiter: interrogative *qualiter*, as here, is rare and restricted mainly to technical prose, see K-S II 2.495 and cf. Cels. 1 pr. 22 *qui prius illa ipsa qualiter eueniant perceperit*; Colum. *Arb.* 7.1 *qualiter faciendum sit, demonstrabimus, Rust.* 1.4.6, 11.3.65; Plin. *Nat.* 13.22. Relative *qualiter*, by contrast is found in verse from Ov. *Am.* onwards.

defigere: of fixing defensive stakes in the ground cf. Front. *Strateg.* 2.3.17 *imperauit ut densos numerososque palos firme in terram defigerent.*

ceruos: a military technical term for forked stakes driven into the ground to hold up an enemy attack. Its use in poetry outside the present passage is restricted to Sil. 10.412-413 *quaque patet campus planis ingressibus hostis, / ceruorum ambustis imitantur cornua ramis*, a passage which also has similarities with **83** above (see **83n.**).

85 Messalla knows the right place in which to pitch a camp. The choice of a suitable camp site was one of the main responsibilities of a good general, see Veg. *Mil.* 1.22, and cf. Liv. 9.17.15 with Oakley, ad loc.; Stat. *Silu.* 5.2.41 (of Vettius Bolanus); Tac. *Agr.* 20.2 and 22.2 (of Agricola) with Woodman 197-198 and 208-209 ad loc.

ducto ... uallo: military terminology for building a rampart, cf. Liv. 31.96.6 *uallo super ripam amnis ducto*; Lucan 6.31 *ducto procul aggere ualli*; Front. *Strateg.* 2.5.26 *ad Isthmon uallo ducto*.

melius: comparative for superlative, cf. **89, 94, 97**.

86 dulces ... liquores: on the necessity for a good source of drinking water at the camp site cf. Veg. *Mil.* 1.22, 3.2, 8. For the phrase *dulces liquores* of water cf. Colum. *Rust.* 9.11.1 *prius respersas dulci liquore*; Phaedr. 4.9.6 *simul rogauit esset an dulcis liquor*; it is also used of liquid honey, cf. Lucr. 1.938 *mellis dulci flauoque liquore*.

erumpat: in this transitive sense of 'allow to break forth' the verb is rare and restricted to elevated poetry; see *ThLL* 5(2).836.72-75 and cf. Cic. *Arat.* 111 *(Canis) aestiferos ualidis erumpit flatibus ignes*; Petr. 124.1.282 has *erumpit furibundo pectore uoces*.

87 Messalla knows how to position the camp in a place which provides easy access for his own men, but which is difficult for the enemy to approach. Commentators compare Veg. *Mil.* 3.8.3 (on the positioning of a permanent camp) *ne sit in abruptis ac deuiis et circumsedentibus aduersariis difficilis praestetur egressus* and 3.8.23 *difficile ... hostis ad ea loca audet accedere, in quibus a fronte et in tergo nouit aduersarios commorari*.

facilis ... aditus: cf., in a military context, *Bell. Alex.* 17.4.5 *facilis nostris aditus dabatur*; Caes. *BG* 3.25.2; Liv. 32.23.7 etc.; in a transferred sense in elegy cf.Tib. 2.4.19 *ad dominam faciles aditus per carmina quaero*. Contrast Hor. *Serm.* 1.9.55-56 *et est qui uinci possit, eoque / difficilis aditus primos habet*. For *facilis* in a quasi technical sense of routes etc. cf. Liv. 27.42.6 *uia nuda ac facili decurrentes* and see *OLD* 4a.

-que ... et: the combination is not found in Cicero or Caesar and was probably archaic in Plautus' time, see Christenson (2000) 136 on Plaut. *Amph.* 5 and cf. **91-92** and **167** below.

aditus ... arduus: cf. Liv. 24.34.15 *arduum aditum instabilemque ingressum praebebat*.

88 The importance of exercising the troops is emphasised by Veg. *Mil.* 3.2 *cum ei laboris consuetudo et in castris sanitatem et in conflictis possit praestare uictoriam*, and Livy praises Scipio Africanus the elder for his attention to this aspect of military life (Liv.26.51.3-8). On military exercises as a means of counteracting the dangers of *otium* see Woodman on Tac. *Agr.* 16.3 *discordia laboratum, cum adsuetus expeditionibus miles otio lasciuiret*.

ut: the interrogative use here, continuing the indirect questions begun with *qua* in **83**, is somewhat awkward coming directly after the consecutive uses in **86** and **87**, but is to be preferred to A's *et* as the theme of military exercise is not connected directly with the positioning of the camp, but opens a new area of Messalla's expertise.

laudis ... certamine: the combination is surprisingly rare, Cic. *Off.* 3.86; Phaedr. 5.5.7; Val. Max. 5.2.9.

assiduo ... certamine: for the combination cf. Tac. *Dial.* 36.3-4 *et assidua senatus aduersus plebem certamina*.

certamine miles: for the line-ending cf. Sil. 5.671 *armatusque iacet seruans certamina miles*. Sil. shows a predilection for *certamine* in this *sedes* (no less than 39 examples, in comparison, e.g., with 10 in the whole of Ovid).

89-97 The indirect questions introduced by *quis* in **89, 91** and **95** are dependent on the idea of competition between the troops contained in *laudis ... certamine* (**88**). It may seem surprising that this nine-line digression on troop exercises has nothing to do directly with Messalla's own military capabilities [see Peirano (2012) 137], but such digressions are recommended in panegyric by Men. Rhet. 373.17ff. Sp. For the types of exercise mentioned cf. Sen. *Epist.* 88.19 *iuuentuti nostrae ... quam maiores nostri rectam exercuerunt hastilia iacere, sudem torquere, equum agitare, arma tractare*.

89 tardamue sudem: the *sudes* was a long wooden pole with which the Roman soldier exercised, cf. Tib. 1.10.65-66 *sed manibus qui saeuus erit, scutumque sudemque / is gerat*; Paul. Fest. 407 L. *sub uineam iacere dicuntur milites, cum astantibus centurionibus iacere coguntur sudes*. Its weight renders it slow (*tardam*) in comparison with the swift arrow.

melius: comparative for superlative, cf. **85, 94, 97**.

celeremue sagittam: *celer* is the most common epithet applied to *sagitta* in verse (cf. Hor. *Carm.* 3.20.9; Virg. *Aen.* 1.187, 5.485, 9.590, 12.394; Ov. *Met.* 5.367, 8.380); this may be based on a supposed etymological link, cf. Isid. *Etym.* 18.8.1 *sagitta a sagaci ictu, id est ueloci ictu, uocata*. For archery practice in the military cf. Suet. *Iul.* 68.3; Veg. *Mil.* 1.15, 2.23.

90 lento ... pilo: the *pilum* 'javelin' was the main throwing weapon of the legionary soldier. The adj. *lentus* refers to its toughness (see *OLD* 2), as shown also in the common combination *lenta hastilia* (Virg. *Aen.* 11.650, 12.489; Ov. *Met.* 8.28; Manil. 5.203), rather than its flexibility, as suggested by Tränkle 210 and De Luca 77 ad loc. For military practice with the *pilum* cf. Liv. 26.51.4; Veg. *Mil.* 2.15.

perfregerit: refers to 'breaking through' a hostile line, see *OLD perfringo* 2.

obuia pilo: for the line-ending cf. Enn. *Ann.* 582 Sk. *pila retunduntur uenientibus obuia pilis*. For the general context cf. Lucan 1.6-7 *infestisque obuia signis / signa pares aquilas et pila minantia pilis*.

91-97 This section is devoted to equestrian exercises: **91-92** regulation of the horse's speed; **93-94** control of the horse's direction; **95-97** fighting from horseback. Riding techniques and horsemanship constituted a common theme in Augustan poetry, cf. Hor. *Carm.* 1.8.5-7, 3.7.25-26, 3.24.54-55; Tib. 1.4.11 (quoted below); Virg. *Georg.* 3.113-122, 190-208, *Aen.* 6.881, 10.882-887; Ov. *Met.* 6.225-226, 12.468. For the importance of learning riding skills in the Augustan youth movement (*collegia iuuenum*) see N-H 108-109 on Hor. *Carm.* 1.8 headnote. For the combination of good horsemanship and skill at arms as items of praise in encomia, see Gibson 256 on Ov. *Ars* 3.383-384 and cf. Pind. *Pyth.* 2.64f.; Virg. *Aen.* 6.880f.; Stat. *Silu.* 4.4.67f.

91-92 -que ... / ... et: for the combination see **87n.** above and **167** below.

91 For the content cf. Tib. 1.4.11 *hic placet angustis quod equum compescit habenis*, The author transfers to his panegyric a theme, ability at horse-riding, that had been used in a different elegiac context (on the attractions of various boys) in Tib. (see **137n., 197-200n.** below on other examples of themes transferred from elegiac contexts). Elsewhere Virg. *Aen.* 1.62-63 (of Aeolus controlling the winds) *qui foedere certo / et* *premere et laxas sciret dare iussus habenas* uses the image in a different context.

equum celerem: contrasting with *tardo* (**92**). *celer* is a common epithet for *equus* in Latin poetry, cf. **114-115** below and Tib. 1.2.72, with Maltby (2002) 174 ad loc. on its connection with the Homeric ὠκέες ἵπποι e.g. *Il.* 8.88, Ov. *Rem.* 788, *Her.* 18.166, *Trist.* 3.10.54, *Pont.* 1.2.80; *Anth. Lat.* 762.54; *CLE* 865.6. The words ὠκύς and *equus* are derived from the same I.E. root *h₁ek = 'speed'. The etymological correspondence between words for 'swift' and words for 'horse' has a long tradition in IE poetry, with parallels in Vedic and Avestan, see West (2007) 465, De Melo (2019) II 1025.

arto ... freno: a tight bridle would hold a swift horse's speed in check. For the *iunctura* cf. Sen. *Phaed.* 1055 *Hippolytus artis continet frenis equos* and, in a metaphorical sense, Sen. *Ben.* 1.14.2 *frenis artioribus reprimam*.

freno: the sing. is rarer than the pl. *frena* or *freni* at all times, but is attested from Cic. fr. poet. 43.4 Morel, and then occasionally in poetry, e.g. Ov. *Her.* 19.12, *Fast.* 6.772, *Trist.* 4.6.24; Sen. *Medea* 792; Lucan 3.269; Val. Fl. 1.424; Sil. 14.571, 16.380.

92 effusas ... habenas: loosening the reins would speed the horse up. For the *iunctura* cf. Liv. 37.20.10 *effusissimis habenis*; Curt. 7.7.35 *effusis habenis euectus*, 9.13, 8.14.6; Front. *Strateg.* 2.5.31; Sil. 1.161, 7.697, 10.261 and see *ThLL* 5(2).218.78.

permittere habenas: cf. also at the verse end, *Laus Pisonis* 51 *permittit habenas*, and *habenis ... permissis* at Sen. *Phaed.* 1006 and Val. Fl. 4.679.

93 derecto ... passu: 'in a direct line'; cf. Caes. *BC* 2.24.4 *directo itinere*; Plin. *Nat.* 4.77 *directo ... cursu*.

contendere: the use of this verb in an absolute sense = 'to hasten' with a modal ablative is rare; it occurs here, and elsewhere only at Apul. *Met.* 11.26.1. *recta, patrium Larem reuisurus ... contendo*; Symph. 211 *aera per medium uolucri contendo meatu*.

94 A reference to the art of turning a horse in a tight circle. On the special skills required for this cf. Hor. *Carm.* 3.7.25 *non alius flectere equum sciens* (with N-R 121 ad loc.) and see Anderson (1961) 98ff. The technical term for this round course was *gyrus*; see *OLD gyrus* 1; cf. Virg. *Georg.*

4.115-117; Prop. 3.14.11; Ov. *Ars* 3.384 *in gyros ire coactus equus* (with Gibson 256 ad loc.); Lucan 1.425; Stat. *Silu.* 4.7.3f. (with Coleman ad loc.), 5 3.139-140 *non totiens uictorem Castora gyro / ... plausere*; Tac. *Germ.* 6.3

seu libeat: = *uel, si libeat* (see *OLD seue* 2); it picks up *modo* (**93**) and represents a unique variation on the common *modo ... modo*.

curuo ... gyro: cf. Coripp. *Ioh.* 1.544-545 *incuruo nec cessat flectere gyro / cornipedem*.

breuius: one of four examples of comparative for superlative in this passage, *melius* (**85, 89**), *breuius* (**94**) and *aptior* (**97**).

conuertere: a conjecture by Crusius for *contendere* of the manuscripts, introduced in error from **93**. For the intransitive use of *conuertere* = 'to turn' cf. Sil. 9.645-646 *... conuertit Varro manuque / cornipedem inflectens ... inquit*.

95 parma: a small round shield used mainly by the lightly armed infantry *uelites*, but also, as here, by the cavalry, cf. Serv. auct. *Aen.* 11.619 *parma ... est equestre scutum*. Lines **95-97**, then, clearly continue the equestrian theme begun in **91**.

96 hac ... illac: this correlation is attested from Plautus on, but is rare in verse (e.g. Lucr. 6.994; Ov. *Her.* 10.83, 20.132, *Met.* 4.360) and, except for here, becomes restricted to prose from the first century AD; see *ThLL* 6(2).2748.77-78.

grauis impetus hastae: the same phrase is found at the end of the hexameter at Stat. *Theb.* 10.545 (sc. *Anthea*) *desuper Ogygiae pepulit grauis impetus hastae*.

97 aptior: this is Francken's conjecture for *amplior* of the manuscripts. *amplior*, which would have to be taken with *impetus*, leaving *grauis* modifying *hastae*, would not provide adequate sense and would leave the infinitives *tueri* (**95**) and *tangere* (**97**) dependent on *possit* understood from **92**. *aptior* would leave *grauis* modifying *impetus* as in Stat. *Theb.* 10.545 (quoted above). It would govern the infinitives *tueri* and *tangere*, a construction found, e.g., at Ov. *Her.* 18.23 *aptior illa quidem placido dare uerbera ponto*. Furthermore, *aptior* is a common line-opening in Ovid (*Her.* 9.64, 14.66, 18.23, *Ars* 1.594, *Trist.* 5.1.17 and 18). For the comparative, cf. **85, 89, 94**.

390   Commentary

signata ... loca: a place marked out as a target; for the phrase cf. Plaut. *Cist*. 696 *locum signat ubi ea excidit* (she is marking the place where she dropped it).

tangere: in the sense of 'hit' with a weapon is rare and poetic. Commentators compare Hor. *Carm*. 3.26.12; Prop. 2.34.60; *Eleg. in Maec*. 1.30; Sen. *Oed*. 135; Stat. *Theb*. 7.579, 11.151.

funda: a leather strap used as a sling, here used of the sling-shot itself, as often in historical prose, but rarely in poetry, cf. Sil. 9.337, 10.151 and see *ThLL* 6(1).1549.10-23. For *funda* (abl.) at the line-end (always in the sense 'sling') cf. Ov. *Met*. 14.825; Val. Fl. 6.193; Stat. *Theb*. 7.338, 8.416.

98-105 The passage treats Messalla's strategic capabilities in battle. Verses **101-102** and **103-105** offer examples of two types of battle line he could be involved in drawing up.

98-99 iam: see **82n**. above.

ueniant: 'arise', 'occur', see *OLD* 15a.

ueniant ... / ... parent: iterative subjunctives, used of repeated actions. The use of the imperfect and pluperfect subjunctives in these contexts, mainly after *cum* or *si*, referring to past actions is attested from Ennius on (see examples in K-S II 2.206-207). The use of the present and perfect subjunctive in iterative contexts is much rarer (see examples in K-S II 2.207-208 Anmerk. 6), and the present, as here, is not attested until Plin. *Nat*. The use of *simul* introducing such a clause is found in Vitr. 1.6.2 *simul ... ceperint*, but its use with the present subjunctive, apart from here, is not attested until the second century AD. The reading *uenient* of A+ in **98** is unlikely in view of *parent* in **99**.

98 certamina Martis: the phrase occurs first at Virg. *Aen*. 12.73 *in duri certamina Martis euntem*, which reproduces ἴω μετὰ μῶλον Ἄρηος ["I enter the turmoil of Ares"] of Hom. *Il*. 16.245, and is repeated at Virg. *Aen*. 12.790. At the line end, as here, the phrase occurs subsequently in Ov. *Met*. 8.20; Sil. 9.136, 15.440, 823, 16.203.

99 aduersis ... concurrere signis: For the phrase cf. Sall. *Cat*. 60.2 *cum infestis signis concurrunt* and see *aduersis ... armis* at **54** above and **148** below. The phrase *aduersis signis* is found in Manilius with the different meaning of opposing stars at 2.410, 471, 578. The line end *concurrere signis* is found also at Coripp. *Ioh*. 3.200 and 6.239.

100-105 on the appropriate deployment of troops in battle as a feature of the 'ideal general' cf. Front. *Strateg.* 2.3 and see Woodman (2014) 268 on Tac. *Agr.* 35.2 *disposuit*, and Oakley on Liv. 9.17.15.

100 tibi non desit ... componere: for impersonal *deesse* with a subjective inf. cf. Sen. *Vit. Beat.* 25.1, *Ben.* 6.7.4; Sil. 6.10. Propertius uses impersonal *deficio* in the same way at 1.8A.23 *nec me deficiet ... rogitare*; see K-S II 2.675.

faciem componere pugnae: the expression is unique in the sense of setting out the order of battle. The normal expression would be *aciem componere* as at Tac. *Germ.* 6.6 *acies per cuneos componitur* and perhaps something like *tum tibi non aciem desit componere pugnae* would have been possible here, were it not for the presence of *acies* in **99** and **101**. The phrase *pugnae facies* elsewhere refers to the appearance of a battle, e.g. Stat. *Theb.* 11.524 *haec pugnae facies. coeunt sine more, sine arte*; Tac. *Agr.* 36.3 *minimeque aequa nostris iam pugnae facies erat*, *Hist.* 2.42.11 *per locos arboribus ac uineis impeditos non una pugnae facies*. It is used in a different sense again at Lucan 4.164 *et faciem pugnae uoltusque inferte minaces*. The phrase brings to mind *uultus componere famae* at [Tib.] 3. *Sulpicia* **13.9** below.

101-102 In view of Cato *Mil.* fr. 10 Jordan *una depugnatio est fronte longa, quadrato exercitu* and Veg. *Mil.* 3.26.18 *quadrata dimicet fronte* the reference here must be to an oblong battle formation (*quadratum acies ... in agmen* **101**) in which a dressed rank (*rectus ... ordo* **102**) of soldiers runs forward (*decurrat* **102**) with a levelled front line (*aequatis ... frontibus*). Elsewhere in prose writers *agmine quadrato* is used not of a battle formation, as here, but of a defensive marching column, e.g. Cic. *Phil.* 2.108, 5.20, 13.18; Hirt. *BG* 8.8.4; Sall. *Iug.* 100.1; Curt. 5.1.19 etc.; Liv. 7.29.6 etc., Sen. *Epist.* 59.7, cf. Serv. auct. *Aen.* 12.121 *quadratum* (sc. *agmen*), *quod inmixtis etiam iumentis incedit*.

101 sit opus ... consistat: the use of *opus est* with a simple subjunctive occurs elsewhere in verse only at Plaut. *Merc.* 1004 *nihil opust resciscat* and Drac. *Romul.* 5.199.

102 For the arrangement of nouns and adjectives around a central verb in an *abcba* structure see **13n.** above.

rectus ... ordo: not found elsewhere in a military context, but for the *iunctura* cf. Hor. *Carm.* 4.15.9-10; Gratt. *Cyneg.* 7-8; Manil. 3.227, 307, 319.

aequatis ... frontibus: cf. Liv. 37.39.9 *tria milia ferme peditum aequata fronte instruxit*; Sil. 16.355, 380.

103-105 The passage refers to a formation in which the army is divided into two wings, so that the left wing attacks the enemy's right wing and the right wing attacks the enemy's left. The wording corresponds in a number of respects to Vegetius' description of the *depugnatio obliqua* at *Mil.* 3.20.6-8 *cum instructae acies ad congressum ueniunt, tunc tu sinistram alam tuam a dextra aduersarii longius separabis, ne uel missibilia ad eam uel sagittae perueniant; dextram autem alam tuam sinistrae alae illius iunges et ibi primum inchoa proelium, ita ut cum equitibus optimis et probatissimis peditibus sinistram partem illius, ad quam te iunxeris, adgrediaris atque circumeas et detrudendo atque supercurrendo ad hostium terga peruenias. quod si semel aduersarios exinde pellere coeperis, accedentibus tuis indubitatam uictoriam consequeris et pars exercitus tui, quam ab hoste submoueris, secura durabit.*

103 seu libeat: see **94n.** above.

seiunctim: a conjecture for *seu iunctum* or *seu uinctum* of the manuscripts. The adverb occurs elsewhere only in very late prose authors (Isid., Leo Magn.) and only in the combination *separatim atque seiunctim*. Nevertheless, it gives better sense than the manuscript readings and is derived from the verb *seiungo* that was common from Cic. and Lucr. on.

cernere: the use of this verb for the compound *decernere* is archaic and restricted to verse, cf. Enn. *Ann.* 185 Sk. *uitam cernamus*. The latest example before the present passage is *cernere ferro* (an Ennian echo) at Virg. *Aen.* 12.709; see further examples at *ThLL* 3.864.66-865.38.

104 uti: like *cernere* (**103**) is archaic in flavour, see Axelson (1945) 129 and Adams (2016) 178. It occurs only here in the *Corp. Tib.*

laeuum ... sinister: for the use of synonyms in such repeated phrases see Wills (1996) 277-278 and cf. *duplex gemini* in **105** below.

105 uictoria casus: the same hexameter ending is found at *Il. Lat.* 388 *laetaque per uarios petitur uictoria casus*. For the phrase cf. Sall. *Iug.* 25.9 *aut ui aut dolis sese casum uictoriae inuenturum*.

106-117 As confirmation of Messalla's military abilities discussed in **82-105** the author cites his victories in Octavian's Illyrian campaign of 35-33

BC, in which we have no independent evidence that Messalla took part. The Iapydes, Pannonians and Arupini named here were in fact the object of Octavian's campaigns, but there is no mention of any specific accomplishment of Messalla in this war. Cassius Dio 49.38.3 mentions Messalla's command against the Salassi in the western Alps at this period (34 BC), but they do not feature in the catalogue. Peirano [(2012) 141-142] notes that Messalla's son, Marcus Valerius Messalla Messallinus, was legate of Illyria in AD 6 and took part in Tiberius' Illyrian triumph of that year (Ov. *Pont.* 2.2.75-92); also that the son is the addressee of some of Ovid's exile poems (*Pont.* 1.7 and 2.2 and the anonymous *Trist.* 4.1 and 4.4), so that the son's activities rather than the historical facts about his father could have inspired our author here. On the Illyrian campaigns of Octavian and Tiberius see further Ingleheart (2010) 216-217 on Ov. *Trist.* 2.225 and on the Tiberian campaign see Abdale (2019). On the historical background of the *Laud. Mess.* in general see Hammer (1925), Lammert (1950), Schoonhaven (1983), Tränkle (1990) 15-21, Maltby (2010) 329. The discussion, in any case, is kept to a very general level and concentrates mainly on geographical details. In adding these our author could be following the advice of Men. Rhet. 373.17ff. Sp., who recommends that a panegyrist should enliven the discussion of military achievements by the insertion of ethnographic details.

106 For the phraseology cf. Ov. *Pont.* 2.2.30 (a poem addressed to Messalla's son) *sed non per placidas it mea puppis aquas.*

at non per dubias errant mea carmina laudes: this phrase reinforced by *nam bellis experta cano* and *testis* **(107)** has clear Callimachean associations, cf. Call. fr. 612 Pf. ἀμάρτυρον οὐδὲν ἀείδω ["I sing of nothing unwitnessed"]. A. J. Woodman suggests seeing in *errant* a possible reference to the wanderings of Gallus which featured in the song of Silenus at Virg. *Ecl.* 6.64 *tum canit errantem Permessi ad flumina Gallum.*

carmina laudes: for the line-ending see **3n.** above.

107-110 testis ... / ... testis ... / ... / testis: for the use of *testis* in such a context, of peoples and geographic areas bearing witness to great deeds, cf. Enn. *Sat.* 6 *FRL*; Cic. *Manil.* 30.1-7, *Verr.* 2.3.149, *Flacc.* 32; Cat. 64.357-362; Hor. *Carm.* 4.4.38-41; Ov. *Her.* 17.195, *Fast.* 2.273-276, 3.707, 4.69, 203-204, 344, 6.765; [Ov.] *Epiced. Drusi* (*Consolatio ad Liuiam*) 385-391, a passage which also shows similarities with **109** below, *Laus Pisonis* 91. The nearest parallel to, and most likely inspiration for, the present passage is provided by Tib. 1.7.9-12, with *testis* at the opening of lines 10 and 11, listing the rivers and geographic regions that witnessed Messalla's victories in Aquitania [see Appendix 3(b) for full text]. The theme had already been present in Greek literature, the most important passage for our purposes being Call. fr. 612 quoted on **106** above; cf. Eur. *Heracl.* 219 Ἑλλὰς πᾶσα τοῦτο μαρτυρεῖ ["all Greece bears witness to this"].

107 bellis experta: refers to the military capabilities of Messalla, discussed in **82-105**, that were proved in the campaigns mentioned in **107-117**. For *experta* in the sense of 'things experienced' see *OLD experior* 5.

108 fortis Iapydiae miles: the Iapydians were an Illyrian-Celtic people living in the north-west of Dalmatia, who were defeated by Octavian in his Illyrian campaign of 35-33 BC. Tränkle [217 ad loc.] relates the adj. *fortis* to Strabo's description of the tribe as ἀρειμάνιοι ["full of warlike frenzy"] at 7.5.4, to Appian's description of part of the people as ἔθνος ἰσχυρόν τε καὶ ἄγριον ["a strong and wild race"] at 3.18.52, and to Cassius Dio's account of their committing suicide when their main city of Metulum was taken by the Romans at 49.35.4.

108-109 fallax / Pannonius: the Pannonians also were an Illyrian-Celtic people, whose wide territory lay south of the Danube (now part of Austria and West Hungary) and bordered in the east on that of the Iapydians. Octavian attacked them in his Illyrian campaign of 35-33 BC and captured their city of Siscia. However, more concentrated campaigning was required in 12-9 BC and AD 6-9 before they were finally defeated and the province of Pannonia was established in AD 9. The final victory over the Pannonians is recorded in [Ov.] *Epiced. Drusi* 390, a verse which recalls **109** here: *summaque dispersi per iuga Pannonii*. For further similarities between this poem and **107** here, see **107-110n.** above. For Tiberius' triumph over the Pannonians in his Illyrian campaign of AD 6-9 see Ov. *Pont.* 2.2.75. The exact reason why the Pannonian is described as *fallax* is disputed. It is possibly because some of them hid in the woods on the arrival of the Romans in 35 BC and from there carried out attacks on small units of Roman troops (Appian 3.22.64); or because the inhabitants of Siscia at first wanted to hand over the city to the Romans and offered hostages, but later closed the doors and put up further resistance (Appian 3.23; Cassius Dio 49.37.2ff.); or finally because during the capture of the city by Octavian they tried to exterminate a Roman garrison that had been left within the walls (Appian 3.24).

109 gelidas passim disiectus in Alpes: a somewhat exaggerated statement. The combination *gelidae Alpes* is found also at Lucan 1.183, 2.535 and Claud. *Paneg. Cons. Hon.* 357. For *passim disiectus* cf., in the same *sedes*, Ov. *Fast.* 3.525 *plebs uenit ac uirides passim disiecta per herbas*.

110 Arupinis ... pauper ... in aruis: The Arupini were a tribe of the Iapydi (Appian 3.16.48). Their main town Arupium was captured and spared by Octavian (Appian 3.16.48). The adj. *pauper* probably refers to the poverty of the land. That of the Iapydi is described by Strabo 7.5.4 as unfruitful, while Cassius Dio 49.36.2 refers to the infertility of the Pannonians' land.

et: for delayed *et* see **20n.** above.

111 uetus ... aetas: for the *iunctura* cf. Hor. *AP* 61 *uerborum uetus interit aetas*; Ov. *Met.* 15.96 *at uetus illa aetas, cui fecimus aurea nomen* and in prose Quint. *Inst.* 12.1.36, *Decl. Min.* 306.11, 314.13; Tac. *Agr.* 2.3.

fregerit aetas: for the idea cf. Lucr. 1.558-559 *infinita aetas ... / quod fregisset adhuc* and Juv. 14.161 (sc. *Romanis*) *fractis aetate*.

112 A 'golden line', see **3.5n.** and **13n.** above.

terna ... saecula: also at **50-51** above, cf. n. ad loc.

Pyliae: Tränkle [218 ad loc.] sees the phrase *terna ... Pyliae ... saecula famae* as an imaginative variation on earlier poetic phrases involving the adj. *Pylius* and referring to the legendary age of Nestor from Ov. *Met.* on: e.g. *Pylii anni* (Ov. *Met.* 15.838, *Pont.* 2.8.41; Stat. *Silu.* 3.4.103), *Pylii dies* (Ov. *Trist.* 5.5.62), *Pylia senecta* (Sil. 15.456; Stat. *Theb.* 5.751; Mart. 8.2.7, 10.38.14), *Pylias aeui metas* (Stat. *Silu.* 5.3.255) and *Pylium aeuum* (Mart. 4.1.3). Tränkle would place our author towards the end of this tradition.

saecula famae: for the line ending cf. *saecula fama* at Ov. *Met.* 15.878 and Lucan 8.74.

112a longae ... uitae: a common combination, see **206** below and cf. Virg. *Ecl.* 4.53; Ov. *Met.* 4.109; *Nux* 159; *Laus Pisonis* 211; Sen. *Herc. F.* 850; Lucan 9.568; Stat. *Silu.* 3.3.203; Juv. 10.295; [**Tib.**] 3. *Lygd.* 3.7; and in the same *sedes* at Lucan 1.457 and 8.625.

tempora uitae: Vossius' conjecture for *saecula fama* of A+, which simply repeats the end of **112**. The verse ending *tempora uitae* is common: Ov. *Met.* 3.469, *Pont.* 3.2.29; *Catal.* 4.1; Manil. 2.893, 850, 3.560; Sen. *Apoc.* 4.1.2, 21; Lucan 9.233; Stat. *Silu.* 5.1.205; Juv. 14.157.

113 On the use of Titan for the sun and on the meaning of *fecundos ... annos*, see **50-51n.** above.

fecundos ... annos: for the combination cf. Ov. *Am.* 3.10.37 *sola fuit Crete fecundo fertilis anno*, *Fast.* 4.671 *fecundior annus*.

renouauerit: future perfect. While the old man of Arpinum is completing his long life, the sun 'will have renewed' a hundred years.

renouauerit annos: an etymological play. The word *annus* was connected etymologically with *renouare* through its supposed derivation from the Greek ἀνανεοῦσθαι 'to renew', see *LALE* s.v. *annus* and Michalopoulos [(2001) 30-31], and cf. Serv. *Aen.* 1.269 *annus ... ἀπὸ τοῦ ἀνανεοῦσθαι* (i.e. 'from renewal') *id est ab innouatione* (Isid. *Etym.* 5.36.2). Similar plays on *annus* and *renouare* occur at Ov. *Met.* 7.177 *non annis renouare tuis*, 9.425 *Anchisae renouare paciscitur annos*.

114-115 For an equally generic description of horsemanship in an encomiastic context cf. Hor. *Carm.* 4.14.21-24 (of Tiberius) with Thomas (2011) 251 ad. loc.

celerem ... / ... equum: see **91n.** above.

114 ipse: 'himself', i.e. 'unaided'.

tamen: i.e. despite his old age.

uelox celerem: the juxtaposition emphasises the speed of both rider and horse. Tränkle [218-219 ad loc.] sees here a reference to the *ars desultoria* in which a rider jumped from one trotting horse to another attached to it. This practice was particularly common in Southern Dalmatia, cf. Val. Fl. 6.161-162 *comitum ... celer mutator equorum / Moesus*.

115 ualidis ... moderator habenis: close in wording to Lucr. 2.1096 *indu manu ualidas potis est moderanter habenas*. For the combination *ualidae habenae* cf. Cic. *De Orat.* 3.116 (= *Trag. Inc.* 126 R) *ualidae legum habenae*; Stat. *Theb.* 10.857 *et ualidas fundae Balearis habenas*.

moderator habenis: the same line ending is found at Ov. *Fast.* 3.593 and *Pont.* 2.5.75; cf. also Lucr. 2.1096 quoted above.

116 te duce: the abl. absol. has an appropriately military flavour, cf. **6.10n.** above; see Hor. *Carm.* 2.7.2 *Bruto militiae duce* with N-H 109 and Harrison (2017) 104 ad loc. and Ov. *Am.* 2.12.13 *me duce* with McKeown III 270 ad. loc.

Dalmata tergum: this is Heyne's conjecture for *terga domator* of the manuscripts. The traditional reading would have to be taken as a proper name, *Domator*, since *domator* as a common noun in the sense 'tamer (of horses)' for the regular *domitor* is not attested elsewhere. However, to name a single Illyrian leader at the end of the passage would come as an anti-climax. Heyne's suggestion has the advantage that the Dalmatians were named by our sources as allies of the Iapydians and Pannonians in the war against Octavian, cf. Liv. *Perioch.* 131; Cassius Dio 51.21.5; Appian 3.25.71ff.

117. On the perfect five-word 'golden line' structure of the verse see **3.5n.** and **13n.** above.

libera ... colla: cf. Virg. *Georg.* 3.167-168 *ubi libera colla / seruitio adsuerint*; Prop. 2.30.8 *et grauis ipse super libera colla sedet*.

subiecit colla catenae: similar phrases are common in the description of one people's subjection to another, e.g. Sen. *Apoc.* 12.3.19-20 *Brigantas dare Romuleis colla catenis / iussit*; Sil. 7.32 *Libycis praebebat colla catenis*. Ov. uses a similar image in his description of Illyria's defeat by Tiberius at *Pont.* 2.2.77-78 *nec dedignata est abiectis Illyris armis / Caesareum famulo uertice ferre pedem*.

colla catenae: the same hexameter ending is found at Sil. 17.630. In fact *colla* with various other cases of *catenae* is a common verse ending, especially in Sil.: *colla catenis* Prop. 2.1.33; [Ov.] *Epiced. Drusi* 273; Sen. *Apoc.* 12.3.19-20; Sil. 6.505, 7.32, 9.634, 11.117 and *colla catena* Sil. 7.72, 8.276; *colla catenas* Ov. *Am.* 2.2.41.

117-118 catenae. / ... contentus: a possible etymological play. On the supposed connection between *catena* and *teneo* see *LALE* s.v *catena* and cf. Porph. Hor. *Epist.* 1.17.55 *catena ... dicta est, quod canem teneat*; Isid. *Etym.* 5.22.9 *catenae ... quod capiendo teneant*. For other poetic plays on this connection, see Michalopoulos (2001) 49-50 and cf. Tib. 2.4.3 ...

teneorque catenis; Hor. *Carm.* 3.11.44-45; Ov. *Met.* 4.175-176; **[Tib.] 3.** *Sulpicia Cycle* **11.15** with **n.** ad loc. below.

118-134 These verses constitute the high point of the poem. They describe the prodigies that took place on the day of Messalla's entry into the consulship on 1 January 31 BC. Again the author follows rhetorical practice, as such descriptions belong to the *amplificatio* or αὔξησις which is an essential part of a eulogy, cf. *Rhet. Alex.* 31 p. 1425 b 36; Men. Rhet. 368.4 Sp.; Cic. *Part. Or.* 71. The insertion of prodigies in such a section is recommended by Cic. *Part. Or.* 73 *adhibenda ... frequentius etiam illa ornamenta rerum siue admirabilia, siue nec opinata siue significata monstris, prodigiis et oraculis, siue quod uidebuntur et de quo agemus cecidisse diuina atque fatalia*, and had already appeared in verse at Pind. *Isth.* 6.49-51 and Theocr. *Id.* 17.71-73. The investiture of new consuls took place on the first day of the year (**122** *oriente die duce fertilis anni*). The new consuls put on the *toga praetexta* (**121** *fulgentem Tyrio subtegmine uestem*) and processed to the Capitol where white bullocks were sacrificed in front of the temple of Jupiter Optimus Maximus (hence the emphasis on Jupiter's presence in **130-133**) and where the *uotorum nuncupatio* took place (**129** *uotis*, **132** *precibus*). Details of these ceremonies are found at Liv. 21.63.7; Ov. *Fast.* 1.75ff., *Pont.* 4.4.27ff.; see further Talbert (1984) 200-216. The theme of the addressee's appointment as consul is also found at *Laus Pisonis* 68-71. The honour would increase his importance as a potential patron. Again this description of the ceremony has no specific details of Messalla's installation but is of a general nature and could have been written at any time after the event. The same is true of Tib.'s description of Messalla's triumph at Tib. 1.7.5-8.

118 maiora peractis: the same verse ending occurs in a similar context at Sil. 8.239 *en numen patrium spondet maiora peractis*. For the idea contained in *maiora peractis / instant*, common in eulogies cf. Stat. *Silu.* 5.2.180 (to Crispinus) *maioraque disce mereri* and Tac. *Agr.* 6.1 *ad maiora nitenti* (with Woodman ad loc.).

120 quis ... certare: for *quis* = *quibus* see **65n.** above. Dative with *certare* is found exclusively in verse from Virg. *Ecl.* 5.8 *montibus in nostris solus tibi certat Amyntas*; see *ThLL* 3.894.50-895.9, 898.29-32. On the dative with verbs of fighting and competing and its relation to comparable Greek constructions, see Fedeli (1980) 190 on Prop. 1.7.3.

Amythaonius ... Melampus: Melampus, son of Amythaon, was a famous seer, already mentioned in Homer (e.g. *Od.* 15.225), and named several times in Latin poetry from Prop. 2.3.51 (always at the line-end) on, often as the son of Amythaon (e.g. Ov. *Met.* 15.325; Stat. *Theb.* 3.452-453). However, the combination *Amythaonius Melampus* occurs elsewhere only at Virg. *Georg.* 3.550 *Amythaoniusque Melampus* where the combination of Greek name and patronymic is typical of Virgil's style; see Thomas 144 ad loc.

121-123 modo ... / ... / ... cum: for *modo* followed by *cum* in this way De Luca [89 ad loc.] compares Sil. 13.744-746 *decimum modo coeperat annum / excessisse puer, nostro cum bella Latinis / concepit iussu.*

121 fulgentem Tyrio subtegmine uestem: shining robes go back to Homer (*Il.* 6.295, those of Hecuba, and *Od.* 15.108, those of Helen). Here the specific reference is to the *toga praetexta*, a toga with a purple hem, which consuls put on for their inauguration on the first day of the year (cf. Ov. *Fast.* 1.81, *Pont.* 4.4.25, 9.26, 42; Stat. *Silu.* 4.1.1, 22). For *Tyrio subtegmine* in the same *sedes*, cf. Stat. *Theb.* 7.656 and for the line-end *subtegmine uestem*, cf. Virg. *Aen.* 3.483 *subtemine uestis*; Val. Fl. 8.234 *ipse suas illi croceo subtegmine uestes*, and especially Auson. *Epig.* 54.1 *Tyrio textam subtegmine uestem.*

122 die duce fertilis anni: for similar extended circumlocutions for January 1 in describing the inauguration of new consuls cf. Ov. *Pont.* 4.4.23-24 *ergo ubi, Iane biceps, longum reseraueris annum / pulsus et a sacro mense December erit*, 9.59-60 *nam tibi finitum summo, Graecine, Decembri / imperium Iani suscipit ille die*; Stat. *Silu.* 4.1.2-3 *Caesaris insignemque aperit Germanicus annum / atque oritur cum sole nouo*, 18-19 *... talem te cernere semper / mense meo tua Roma cupit*; Tränkle [222 ad loc.] compares Claud. *Paneg. Cons. Olybrio et Probino* 6-7 *iam noua germanis uestigia toqueat annus / consulibus, laetique petant exordia menses*, a poem which also has similarities with **123** below, see **n.** ad loc.

duce: for *dux* used metaphorically in similar temporal contexts, cf. Ov. *Fast.* 5.424 *nec tu dux mensum, Iane biformis, eras*; Sen. *Medea* 878 *dux noctis Hesperus.*

fertilis anni: for the line ending cf. Ov. *Am.* 3.10.37 *sola fuit Crete fecundo fertilis anno.* On the meaning of *fertilis anni* see **50-51n.** above.

123 splendidior ... Sol: the idea of the sun shining brighter on the day of the consuls' entry into office is present also in Auson. *Prec. Kal. Ian.* 3-4 *Sol aeterne, ... solito ... illustrior almo / lumine purpureum iubar exere lucis Eoae* and Claud. *Paneg. Cons. Olybrio et Probino* 1f. *Sol, ... sparge* *diem meliore coma* (a passage with similarities to **122** above, see **n**. ad loc.). The image is also found at Hor. *Carm.* 4.5.7-8 ... *gratior it dies / et soles melius nitent* (on the arrival of Augustus) and Mart. 4.1.4 ... *hoc uoltu uel meliore nite* (on the birthday of Domitian). Cf. Men. Rhet. 378.10-12, 21-23, 381.16-18 Sp.

liquidis ... undis: the phrase occurs in the same *sedes* at Ov. *Met.* 11.116; Manil. 5.443; Mart. *Spect.* 26.7 the common *iunctura* is found elsewhere at Cat. 64.2; Virg. *Aen.* 5.859; Ov. *Met.* 1.95, 4.380, 13.535, 15.135, *Fast.* 6.699; Sil. 4.587; Mart. 10.7.3.

caput extulit: occurs in the same *sedes* at Virg. *Ecl.* 1.24, *Georg.* 2.341, 4.352, *Aen.* 1.127 *prospiciens summa placidum caput extulit unda* (Neptune); Ov. *Met.* 3.37, *Fast.* 1.209, 5.637, *Trist.* 1.9b.9; Sil. 7.254-255 *ut, cum turbatis placidum caput extulit undis* (Neptune), 8.250; Stat. *Theb.* 6.108.

124-129 The *topos* of the silence of nature accompanying auspicious events (εὐφημία) such as divine epiphanies or the singing of Orpheus are present in Greek literature from fifth-century Attic tragedy on (see Dodds on Eur. *Bacch.* 1084-1085 divine epiphany) and in Latin from Enn. *Trag.* LXXIII (Jocelyn, with n. ad loc. 296-297), Virg. *Ecl.* 8.3-4 (the songs of Damon and Alphesiboeus). Here it is applied to Messalla's *nuncupatio uotorum*. More references follow in the individual notes below. Very close in content to the present passage (though not necessarily its direct model) is the parody of the theme at Aristoph. *Thesm.* 43-48 (where Agathon's servant asks nature not to disturb his master's poetic inspiration): ἐχέτω δὲ πνοὰς νήνεμος αἰθήρ / κῦμά τε πόντου μὴ κελαδείτω / γλαυκόν, ... / πτηνῶν τε γένη κατακοιμάσθω, / θηρῶν τ' ἀγρίων πόδες ὑλοδρόμων / μὴ λυέσθων ["let the still air hold back its breezes, let the wave of the blue sea not roar ... let the tribes of birds go to sleep, let the feet of the wild forest beasts not be set free"].

124 The calming of the winds on various auspicious occasions is a commonplace in ancient poetry: e.g. Eur. *Bacch.* 1084-1085; Limen. 8; Mesom. *Hymn.* 2.2 (divine epiphany); Aristoph. *Aues* 778 (divine voice); Virg. *Aen.* 10.103 (speech of Jove); Antip. Sid. *AP* 7.8.3; Hor. *Carm.* 1.12.10; Sen. *Medea* 627 (the song of Orpheus); Calp. *Ecl.* 2.16-17 (songs of shepherds). For the structure of the verse as a 'golden line' here and in **125** see **3.5n.** and **13n.** above.

fera ... flamina: cf. Sil. 17.207-208 ... *ceu flamina comprimit Auster / cum fera*.

discordes ... uenti: the same *iunctura* is found at Virg. *Aen*. 10.356; Ov. *Am*. 2.10.9, *Met*. 4.621; Sen. *Medea* 940-941.

flamina uenti: the same verse ending is found at Cic. *Arat*. 100 and *Ciris* 404.

125 For the 'golden line' structure here and at **124** see **3.5n.** and **13n.** above. The verse is perhaps modelled on Virg. *Ecl*. 8.4 *et mutata suos requierunt flumina cursus*, with which it shares the line-end. In Virgil (see Clausen 241 on *Ecl*. 8.4), as in Calp. *Ecl*. 2.15 *et tenuere suos properantia flumina cursus*, rivers stop flowing on the occasion of shepherds' songs. The *topos* is often associated with the song of Orpheus, which causes rivers to halt in their course, e.g Ap. Rhod. 1.26-27; Hor. *Carm*. 1.12.9-10; Prop. 3.2.3-4; *Culex* 117-118, 278; Sen. *Herc. F*. 573, *Medea* 627, *Herc. Oet*. 1036-1039. Given these parallels, the reference here must be to rivers halting or slowing their flow rather than changing their course. The wording of the line recalls the Manilius' account of the Phaethon episode at 1.743-740 *deflexum solito cursu, curuisque quadrigis / monstratas liquisse uias*.

curua ... flumina: the same combination is found also at Virg. *Georg*. 2.11-12, 4.278, cf. Ov. *Met*. 3.342 *flumine curuo*. Here, as with *curuis ... quadrigis* at Manil. 1.743 quoted above, the adj. could mean 'swerving' from their accustomed course. On *flumen* see **3.29n.** above.

nec: for postponed *nec*, see **42n.** above.

adsuetos: for past participles of intransitive verbs used, as here, with passive sense, cf. Tib. 1.5.4 *quam celer assueta uersat ab arte puer* and see further examples at K-S II 1. 96-97.

egerunt ... cursus: for *cursus* (-*um*) *agere* cf. Ov. *Am*. 3.6.95 *agis ... cursus*; Sen. *Apoc* 7; elsewhere it is found mainly in prose, e.g. Sen. *Quaest. Nat*. 3.26.3.

flumina cursus: the same line-end occurs at Virg. *Ecl*. 8.4 (quoted above); *Ciris* 233; Calp. *Ecl*. 2.15 (quoted above).

126 For the stilling of the sea in similar circumstances cf. Aristoph. *Aues* 778 (when a divine voice speaks); Limen. 9-10; Mesom. *Hymn*. 2.2

(divine epiphany); Virg. *Aen.* 10.103 (speech of Jove); Antip. Sid. *AP* 7.8.4 (song of Orpheus).

rapidum ... mare: a common *iunctura*, see **72n.** above on *rabidas ... undas*. The adj. *rapidum* is more likely here than *rabidum*, given the contrast with *constitit* in the same line.

placidis ... undis: a common combination, cf. Ov. *Met.* 13.899; Lucan 1.439, 4.13; Stat. *Theb.* 11.214, *Ach.* 1.57; Mart. 3.67.8.

constitit undis: for the verse ending cf. Ov. *Met.* 9.662 *constitit unda*.

127 For the silence of the birds in a similar context cf. Mesom. *Hymn.* 2.4 (divine epiphany).

nulla nec: double negatives of this kind are attested in Cicero's philosophical works and in Livy and cannot be considered as colloquial; see **13.8n.** below. For *nullus + nec (neque)* in verse cf. **164** below and Virg. *Ecl.* 5.25; Prop. 2.19.5, 3.13.23-24; Nemes. *Ecl.* 2.46.

aerias ... auras: also at Lucr. 1.12, 5.501; Virg. *Aen.* 5.520; Ov. *Met.* 4.700, 10.178, 14.127, cf. Lucr. 4.933 *aeriis ... auris*.

perlabitur auras: for the verse ending, cf. Virg. *Aen.* 7.646 *famae perlabitur aura*. Transitive *perlabitur* with acc. obj. is attested from Lucil. 1278 M; cf. Virg. *Aen.* 1.147 *summas ... perlabitur undas* on which Servius comments ad loc. *perlabitur undas figura est, quod enim nos modo dicimus per praepositionem nomini copulatam.* Other examples at Lucr. 5.764; Manil. 5.419; Stat. *Theb.* 6.1-2; Sil. 3.410; *Il. Lat.* 607-608.

128 quadrupes ... aspera: for the use of *aspera* = 'bristly, shaggy' with *quadrupes* cf. Pac. *Trag.* 2 *quadrupes tardigrada agrestis humilis aspera*.

densas ... siluas: a common combination in both prose and verse, cf. Caes. *BG* 3.21.2; 4.38.3; Cic. *Att.* 12.15.1; Virg. *Georg.* 2.17; Ov. *Met.* 15.488, *Halieut.* 49; Lucan 3.362-363, 6.205; Plin. *Nat.* 5.14; Sen. *Herc. F.* 663; Stat. *Theb.* 2.497.

depascitur ... siluas: for the transitive use of *depascor* cf. (in the same *sedes*) Virg. *Georg.* 3.458 *artus depascitur arida febris* and cf. K-S II 1.292.

aspera siluas: similar verse endings at Virg. *Georg.* 1.152 *aspera silua* (3.384,) Colum. *Rust.* 10.14), *Aen.* 7.505 *aspera siluis*.

129 largita ... sit: this is Huschke's conjecture for *largita sunt* of the manuscripts. It has the advantage of avoiding a rare passive use of *largiri*, of explaining the presents *perlabitur* **127** and *depascitur* **128**, and indicates who lavished silence on Messalla's vows, as is made clear by Dissen's paraphrase (ad loc.) *nulla auis per aura uolat, nulla fera depascitur siluas, quae non tum quieuit et siluit, cum tu uota nuncupabas in Capitolio*.

muta silentia: in view of the fact that this *iunctura* is found also at Ov. *Met.* 4.433, 7.184, 10.53 and Stat. *Theb.* 10.91-92, this reading should be preferred to *multa silentia* of A+. The two words *multus* and *mutus* are often confused in the manuscripts elsewhere (e.g. Lucr. 4.1057, 5.1087; Lucan 5.218; Stat. *Theb.* 11.604).

silentia uotis: the same verse ending is found at Val. Fl. 4.257.

130-134 Jupiter leaves Olympus in his chariot and is present at the sacrifice and *uotorum nuncupatio*, to which he nods approval. The presence of Jupiter is a common theme in poems celebrating consular inauguration, as the ceremony took place before his temple, e.g. Ov. *Pont.* 4.9.31-32 (on the inauguration of Graecinus, at which Ovid would have been present had he not been in exile) *me quoque secreto grates sibi magnus agentem / audisset media qui sedet aede deus*; Stat. *Silu.* 4.1.45-47 (at the end of a poem in which Janus predicts fresh consulships and victories to Domitian) *tunc omnes patuere dei laetoque dederunt / signa polo, longamque tibi, rex magne, iuuentam / annuit atque suos promisit Iuppiter annos*. The *topos* here is related in an exaggeratedly epic tone. For Jupiter (Zeus) attending in person to receive the sacrifices made to him cf. Hom. *Hymn Demeter* 2.27ff.; Cat. 64.87ff.; for his assenting to the proceedings with a nod cf. Hom. *Il.* 1.5.26-27 (quoted in **133n.** below); Cat. 64.204ff.; Virg. *Aen.* 10.115; Stat. *Theb.* 7.3; for Zeus riding in a chariot cf. Hom. *Il.* 8.41ff., 438-439. This last feature would be particularly appropriate here as a statue of Jupiter riding in a *quadriga* chariot adorned the gable of his Capitoline temple (Liv. 10.23.12; Plin. *Nat.* 35.157). Stylistic features such as the *hysteron-proteron* (see **130-131n.**), the phrase *per inania* (see **130n.**) and the use of the verbs *adfuit* and *liquit*, a feature of kletic hymns (see **131n.**), add to the epic colouring of this section.

130-131 The *hysteron-proteron* (Jupiter would have left Olympus before attending Messalla's inauguration) is a Homeric feature (see L-H-S II 2.2. 698-699).

130 Iuppiter ipse: at the line opening also at Virg. *Aen.* 12.725; Calp. *Ecl.* 4.93.

leui ... curru: a common combination from Ovid on: Ov. *Her.* 4.45, *Ars* 1.4, *Met.* 2.150, 5.645, 10.717; Gratt. *Cyneg.* 534; Manil. 5.73; Sen. *Phaed.* 1088.

per inania: common in this *sedes* in elevated poetry (e.g. Ov. *Met.* 2.506; *Culex* 212; Manil. 1.153, 176, 200, 283, 4.590; Lucan 9.107, 473; Sil. 1.97, 4.8, 136, 14.244; Stat. *Theb.* 6.710, 10.533). The singular *per inane* 'through the void' appears frequently in Lucretius; see examples in Robinson (2011) 83 on Ov. *Fast.* 2.41.

131 adfuit ... liquit: the two verbs often occur in kletic hymns, requesting the presence of a deity who is to leave his usual abode, cf. Virg. *Georg.* 1.16-18 *ipse nemus linquens patrium saltusque Lycaei, / Pan, ... / adsis*.

caelo uicinum: emphasising the height of Olympus, here used in its original sense of a mountain rather than as a synonym for 'heaven'. For the phrase cf. Lucr. 6.459 *montis uicina cacumina caelo*; Sen. *Quaest. Nat.* 4.11.5 *arbor ... uicina caelo*; Sen. *Phaed.* 1136-1137 *caelo / ... uicina petit*.

132 On the 'bracketed' structure of this line, enclosed by an adjective and its noun, a purely Latin feature, see Norden (1927) 391 and cf. Fordyce (1961) 275 on its frequency in Cat. 64.

precibus se praebuit: for the phrase cf. Lucr. 2.66 *tu te dictis praebere memento*.

praebuit aure: for the line-ending cf. Hor. *Serm.* 1.1.22 (of Jupiter) *uotis ut praebeat aurem*; Ov. *Met.* 7.821 *uocibus ambiguis deceptam praebuit aurem*.

133 cunctaque ueraci capite adnuit: cf. the words of Zeus at Hom. *Il.* 1.526-527 οὐ ... ἐμὸν παλινάγρετον οὐδ' ἀπατηλὸν / οὐδ' ἀτελεύτητον, ὅ τι κεν κεφαλῇ κατανεύσω ["no word of mine is to be revoked, nor is it false, nor unfulfilled, whatever I nod my head to"]. The first Latin occurrence of *adnuo* in this context is Cat. 64.204-206 where Jupiter assents to Ariadne's prayer for Theseus to be punished. Cf. Virg. *Georg.* 1.40 *audacibus adnue coeptis*. The verb is used twice in the *Sulpicia Cycle* of the assent of other gods: **11.20** (Natalis), **12.13** (Juno). On its etymological connection with *numen* see **4.53n**.

Book Three of the Corpus Tibullianum: 405
Introduction, Text, Translation and Commentary

133-134 additus aris / ... ignis: an elegant expression for lighting the fire on the altar; for the use of *addo* in a similar context cf. Sil. 7.161 *addunt frugiferis inimica incendia ramis*.

134 laetior eluxit: it was a good sign when the flames on the altar leapt high in the air, cf. Virg. *Georg.* 4.385-386; Prop. 3.10.19-20. For this omen in the context of consular inauguration ceremonies cf. Ov. *Pont.* 4.9.53-54 *surgat ad hanc uocem plena pius ignis ab ara, / detque bonum uoto lucidus omen apex*; Stat. *Silu.* 4.1.23-24 *adspicis ut ... altior aris / ignis*.

laetior ... ignis: cf. *Moretum* 90 *laetum consedit ad ignem*.

135-176 The good omens received from Jupiter on the occasion of Messalla's *uotorum nuncupatio* (**130-134**) lead the poet to predict future victories, both within the known world, namely Europe, Africa and Asia (**137-148**), and beyond the Ocean in Britain (**149**) and the Antipodes (**150, 166**). Again there is no relevance to Messalla's actual career. The listing of victories in the known world had been a feature of encomiastic poetry from Pind. *Isth.* 6.22ff. on. The theme of conquests beyond the Ocean began with Alexander the Great (cf. *Rhet. Her.* 4.31) and was later applied to Caesar (Vell. 2.46.1), Messalla (*Catal.* 9.53-54 *nunc aliam ex alia bellando quaerere gentem / uincere et Oceani finibus ulterius*, and here) and Claudius (Sen. *Apoc.* 12.13ff.). The statement **175-176** that Messalla's glory will, in part, be based on conquests beyond the Ocean goes against Cicero's remark (*Somn. Scip.* 20-22) that glory cannot be acquired beyond the known world. Both Cicero (*Somn. Scip.* 21) and the panegyrist here (**151-174**) contain digressions on the five zones of the world, which suggests our author's dependence on, and modification of, the discussion in Cicero. On the relation of this section to Call. *Hymn.* 4.165-170, the unborn Apollo's prophecy of the extent of the future Ptolemy Philadelphos' empire, and to Tib. 1.7.9-22 on Messalla's foreign victories see Hunter (2006) 65-66.

135-136 magnis insistere rebus / incipe: a possible echo of the address to the child in Virg. *Ecl.* 4.48 *adgredere o magnos ... honores* followed later by *incipe* (60). The same eclogue is echoed later in the poem at **205-206**, see **n.** ad loc. below.

135 hortante deo: cf. Pers. 5.21 *tibi nunc hortante Camena*.

magnis ... rebus: the phrase occurs in the same *sedes* at **179** below, *magnis se accingere rebus*.

insistere: for the use of this verb + dat. in the sense of *incumbere* cf. Ov. *Rem.* 315 *profuit adsidue uitiis insistere amicae*, *Pont.* 1.8.53 *ne solitis insistant pectora curis*; this usage occurs most frequently in the poetry of the first century AD, see *ThLL* 7(1).1925.69-1926.4. For the form *insistere* in the same *sedes*, cf. Lucr. 6.836; Virg. *Georg.* 3.114; Ov. *Rem.* 315, *Fast.* 1.507, *Met.* 5.558, 8.52, 15.149; Manil. 2.643, 3.159; Lucan 3.407; Val. Fl. 3.469; Stat. *Theb.* 3.487; Juv. 9.144.

136 incipe: a common verse opening, especially in pastoral. The most relevant reference here is probably to Virg. *Ecl.* 4.60 (see **135-136n.** above), with others at Virg. *Ecl.* 3.58, 4.62, 5.10, 12, 8.21, 25, 10.6; Calp. *Ecl.* 4.78, 5.98; but also in epic (Virg. *Aen.* 9.741; Stat. *Theb.* 1.271, 11.688) and in elegy (Prop. 2.34.43, 3.6.8, 4.1B. 120; Ov. *Am.* 2.16.48, 19.38, 39).

non idem tibi sint aliisque triumphi: the wish is that Messalla's triumphs will differ from those of other men in being won not only in the known world, but also beyond it in Britain and the Antipodes. Cairns [(2006) 411-412] points out that the words *non idem tibi* occur, in a different order, ...*idem tibi, non ego, Visce* in Gallus fr. 2.8 (Courtney = fr. 145.8 Hollis), in a context which probably anticipates the triumph of Caesar.

137-146 Ten lines describe the regions of Europe, Africa and Asia over which Messalla will triumph with little resistance from their inhabitants (**137** *non te ... remorabitur*). Each subsequent place is introduced by the negative *nec* (**138, 139, 140, 143, 144**). This catalogue is framed by the etymologically related *remorabitur* (**137**) and *moror* (**147**). On the use of *mora* and related terms in Ovidian catalogues to undermine their content see Kyriakidis (2007) 159-160. Here the idea that the nations mentioned are easily conquered and offer no resistance to Messalla could at one level be seen as contributing to this undermining effect rather than as increasing Messalla's prestige. At another level, of course, the ease of their forthcoming conquest could be seen as a result of Messalla's martial prowess. Such ambiguities are characteristic of the *Laud. Mess.* overall, and could be intended to reflect the work of a poet early in his career. The rivers of the countries concerned play an important role in this passage, as their images would be displayed in the triumphal procession, cf. Tib. 1.7.11-12; Ov. *Ars* 1.219ff., *Trist.* 4.2.37, 41-42, *Pont.* 2.1.39. The whole passage is inspired by Horace's praise of Augustus' conquests at *Carm.* 4.14.41-52, where rivers play a similarly prominent role, cf. 45-48 *te, fontium qui celat origines, / Nilusque et Hister, te rapidus Tigris, / te beluosus qui remotis / obstrepit Oceanus Britannis* (sc. *audit*). As Hunter has shown [(2006) 65], the broad sweep of countries mentioned from the far west to the far east and the cold north emulates the empire of Osiris-Dionysus as described by Diodorus Siculus 1.2.5 ["I (sc. Osiris) ... campaigned to every country, as far as the uninhabited regions of the Indians and those which lie in the far north, as far as the sources of the river Ister, and back to the other areas as far as Ocean", trnsl. Hunter (2006) 61] which is reflected in a number of Augustan texts including the description of Messalla's travels and victories in Tib. 1.7.9-22 [quoted in Appendix 3(b)] and *Catal.* 9.51-54. At *Carm.* 3.4.29-36 Horace lists the places he would be willing to travel to under the protection of the Muses, including Spain, Scythia, Britain and Assyria; see Powell (2010) 147 and N-R ad loc. Hardie [(2010) 291] sees such lists with their bookish reflection on ethnography as a typical topic of panegyric, perhaps derived form Posidonius and Stoic interests in the influence of the physical environment on character (bibliography in Hardie loc. cit. n.121). For *descriptiones locorum* as an enhancement to panegyric, with the difficulty of the nations and terrains conquered serving to magnify the victories of the *laudandus* see Woodman on Vell. 96.3.

137-138 non te ... remorabitur ... / Gallia: intended perhaps as a prophecy of Messalla's triumph over Aquitania, celebrated in Tib. 1.7, which took place after the purported date of the present poem on 25 September 27 BC. A similar sentiment about Gaul is found in Hor. *Carm.* 4.14.49-50 (addressed to Augustus) *te non pauentis funera Galliae / ... audit*. Cf. *Epist.* 1.5. On the significance of *remorabitur* here and its relation to *quid moror* in **147**, phrase which frame the catalogue of places to be conquered by Messalla, see **137-146n.** above.

137 uicino ... Marte: cf. Sil. 7.41-42 *ac uicino Marte furebat / ad portas bellum*. The line perhaps contains a distant echo of the opening of Tib.' first poem: Tib. 1.1.3-4 *quem labor assiduus uicino terreat hoste / Martia cui somnos classica pulsa fugent*, thus aiding the poet's self-identification as a young Tibullus, cf. **91n.** (on the Tibullan horse riding theme) and **197-200n.**(on the elegiac theme of love versus riches).

138 latis ... terris: the same collocation is found at Cic. *Poet.* fr. 30.9 *omniaque e latis rerum uestigia terris*; Ov. *Met.* 2.307, *Fast.* 5.243; Sil. 5.399.

audax Hispania: so named from the warlike character of its inhabitants, cf. Hor. *Carm.* 4.14 49-50 (of Augustus) *te ... / duraeque tellus audit*

Hiberiae; Lucan 5.265-266 *partem tibi Gallia nostri / eripuit, partem duris Hispania bellis.*

Hispania terris: the same hexameter ending is found at Claud. *Carm. Min.* 30.49.

139 For the formulation of the line cf. *Anth. Lat.* 236.1 *Corsica Phocaico tellus habitanda colono*; Lucan 2.610 *urbs est Dictaeis olim possessa colonis*; Petr. 5.1.10 *seu Lacedaemonio tellus habitanda colono.*

fera ... tellus: cf. Sen. *Herc. F.* 19-20 *fera / Thebana tellus.*

Theraeo ... colono: the reference is to Cyrene, founded around 630 BC by colonists from the island of Thera, cf. Herod. 4.150-158; Pind. *Pyth.* 4.4-23; Sall. *Iug.* 19.3.2 *Cyrene ... colonia Theraeon.* Cyrene is here called *fera* because at the purported date of composition in 31 BC it was in the hands of Cleopatra. Later, in 27 BC, it became a peaceful senatorial province.

obsessa: unusual in the context of peaceful occupation, but cf. Tib. 2.3.41 *praedator cupit inmensos obsidere campos.*

140 For mention of the Nile and Tigris in a similar context with reference to Augustus see Hor. *Carm.* 4.14.46 quoted above on **137-146n.**

regia lympha Choaspes: the Choaspes (modern Karkeh in Iran) is a tributary of the Tigris, on the west bank of which stood the Persian city of Susa. The river is described as *regia* because Cyrus the Great (Herod. 1.188) or the Parthian kings (Plin. *Nat.* 31.35) drank water only from this source, believing in its health-giving properties (on which cf. Curt. 5.2.9). In Greek it was known for this reason as βασιλικὸν ὕδωρ. On the use of *lympha* for water see **5.3n.** above.

141 rapidus Cyri dementia Gyndes: the Gyndes (modern Diyala, originating in Iran as the Sirwana) is another tributary of the Tigris. According to Herod. 1.189ff., Cyrus the Great, in his campaign against Babylon, had this fast flowing (*rapidus*) river diverted into 360 canals as a punishment for the fact that one of his horses had drowned in an attempt to cross it. Seneca (*De Ira* 3.21.1-5) tells the same story with emphasis on Cyrus' *furor*, hence perhaps *dementia* here. For the Tigris itself as *rapidus* cf. Hor. *Carm.* 4.14.46 quoted in **137-146n.** above. The appositional word order is a Hellenistic Greek feature (cf. Hedylus 2.5; Meleager *AP* 5.199 = 31.3-4 G.-P.), attested in Latin from Virg. *Ecl.* 1.57 *raucae, tua cura,* *palumbes* on (further examples, mostly from the *Ecl.* in Clausen 53-54 ad loc.); see further Norden (1927) on Virg. *Aen.* 6.7-8, Skutsch (1956), who sees a Gallan connection, comparing Prop. 3.3.31 *et Veneris dominae uolucres, mea turba, columbae*, and Solodow (1986).

142 The wording and sense of this line have been completely lost in transmission. Both F and A+ have *aut unda* in mid-line, *campis* at the line-end and the form *ardet* at or near the line-opening. Scaliger suggests that a possible context for *ardet* in conjunction with *unda* would be the flaming oil wells of the Middle East, that were well known to the ancients (e.g. Strabo 16.1.4; Plin. *Nat.* 2.235, 237, 35.179). If this is correct *arectais ... campis* of F probably contains a garbled reference to some oil-bearing region. More recently Jeffreys (1994) suggests *Arderriccaeis aut unda ter hospita campis* based on Herod. 1.185. As no adequate solution has yet been offered for this line I have simply obelised.

143 Tomyris was the queen of the Massagetae who had defeated Cyrus when he had invaded her territory by crossing the river Araxes (modern Arax) which marked its border. A detailed account of the battle, in which Cyrus was killed, is found at Herod. 1.205-214. In Latin, where the forms Tomyris and Tamyris occur, accounts of the battle are found at Val. Max. 9.10 (ext.).1 and Ampel. 13.1.

uago: the adj. is used commonly of meandering rivers cf. *uaga flumina* at Hor. *Carm.* 1.34.9; Prop. 2.19.30, 3.11.51; *Dirae* 67; Petr. 122.1.132-133.

144-145 This constitutes the only mention of the Padaei in Latin literature. They were a people of eastern India, who killed and ate their relatives as they became old and frail. The source here appears to be Herodotus, an author the panegyrist seems to have read (cf. **139n., 140n., 141n., 143n.** above). In the present line echoes of Herod. 3.99 are found, with *celebrans conuiuia* corresponding to the Greek κατευωχέονται ["they feast"] and *ultima uicinus Phoebo tenet arua* to πρός ἠῶ οἰκέοντες τούτων ["living to the east of them"].

144 The structure is that of a 'golden line', see **3.5n.** and **13n.** above.

nec: for postponed *nec* see **42n.** above.

saeuis ... conuiuia mensis: for *saeuis ... mensis*, cf. Stat. *Theb.* 1.246-247 (with reference to the flesh of Pelops eaten by Tantalus) *neque enim arcano de pectore fallax / Tantalus et saeuae periit iniuria mensae*, and for the line-end *conuiuia mensis*, cf. Sil. 11.271. The present passage seems to imitate both.

145 ultima ... tenet arua: cf. Virg. *Aen.* 6.477-478 *arua tenebant / ultima*.

uicinus Phoebo: for Phoebus used of the sun, see **66n.** above. For the closeness of India to the sun, cf. Prop. 2.18.11 *ad uicinos cum ... quiesceret* (sc. *Aurora*) *Indos*; Ach. Tat. 4.5.1 *Ἰνδῶν γὰρ ἡ γῆ γείτων ἡλίου* ["the land of the Indians neighbours the sun"]; Ruf. Fest. 10.1 *Eoas partes totumque orientem ac positas sub uicino sole prouincias*. On the general theme see Sall. *Iug.* 18.9 *Gaetuli sub sole magis, haud procul ab ardoribus*.

146 Getas: The Getae did not live along the Hebrus (in modern Greek, Ἕβρος, in Bulgarian, Maritza) or the Tanais (modern Don), but rather north of the Haemus range on either side of the lower Danube (Cass. Dio 67.6.2). On the unreliability of ancient geographical and ethnographic information in general see Woodman (2014) 11-15. Roman poets were vague on the geographical regions north of Thrace and on the Black Sea, cf. e.g. Virg. *Georg.* 4.463 where the Getae and the Hebrus mourn the death of Eurydice and *Georg.* 4.517 where Orpheus crosses the Tanais. For more on the Getae and the threat they posed to Rome during Augustus' principate see Strabo 7.3.11; Dio Chrysost. 36.4; also Hor. *Carm.* 4.15.22 with Powell (2010) 165, 188 and Ov. *Trist.* 2.191 with Ingleheart (2010) 198-199. Their main literary fame was that they were the tribe to whose land Ovid was exiled, cf. Ov. *Pont.* 1.7.1-2, 4.2.1-2.

rigat: for the use of this verb with rivers to indicate an area in which a people lived cf. **59-60** above and Hor. *Carm.* 3.3.48 *qua tumidus rigat arua Nilus*; Sil. 8.368-369 *gelidoque rigantur / Simbruuio*.

Magynos: a people mentioned nowhere else in extant Greek and Latin texts. Various unsatisfactory conjectures mentioning other peoples have been made, but given the general uncertainty about peoples and regions shown in this passage such attempts to emend seem fruitless. For the use of the names of peoples in place of the area in which they lived, see **59-60n.** above.

147 quid moror?: a common line-opening, cf. Virg. *Aen.* 4.325, 6.528; Ov. *Am.* 3.6.77, *Ars* 2.535, *Rem.* 461, *Met.* 8.879, 13.531, *Fast.* 3.249. Ov. *Rem.* 461 *quid moror exemplis, quorum me turba fatigat?* is particularly relevant, since it occurs, as here, in the closing frame of a catalogue, see

Kyriakidis (2007) 157-158, Heyworth (2019) 131 and cf. **137-146n.** above. On the use of the word *mora* referring to a literary 'digression' see Woodman (1975) 284 and cf. **137-146n.** above.

Oceanus ponto qua continet orbem: similar line structure and content at Cat. 64.30 *Oceanus ... mari totum ... amlpectitur orbem*. Of significance here may be Horace's suggestion that those wishing to escape the harsh realities of civil war should escape to the Isles of the Blessed: *Epod.* 16.41 *nos manet Oceanus circumuagus*. The wording also recalls *te manet ... Britannus* at **149** below, see **n.** ad loc. In view of the mention of Messalla's *uirtus* in **1** above, it is interesting that Horace recommends this escape route for those *quibus est uirtus* (*Epod.* 16.39). On the dangers of the Ocean in relation to Britain see Hor. *Carm.* 4.14.47-48 (sc. *audit*) *te beluosus qui remotis / obstrepit Oceanus Britannis*; Tac. *Agr.* 10.2 *septentrionalia eius, nullis contra terris, uasto atque aperto mari pulsantur* and 10.6 *nusquam latius dominari mare* both with Woodman ad loc. For *Oceanus ... continet* cf. Tac. *Germ.* 1.1 *cetera Oceanus ambit, latos sinus et insularum immensia spatia complectens*.

ponto: see **20n.** above.

continet orbem: a similar line-ending is found at Cic. *Arat.* 299 *extremos continet orbis*.

148 For the theme of spontaneous surrender to a conqueror cf. Hor. *Carm.* 4.14.51-52 (addressed to Augustus) *te caede gaudentes Sygambri / compositis uenerantur armis*.

aduersis ... armis: also at **54** above.

sese offeret: the usage is mainly prosaic, e.g. Hirt. *BG* 8.8.42 *telis hostium flammaeque se offerebat*; however, cf. Sen. *Phoen.* 316 *se ... serpenti offeret*.

149 Caesar had reached Britain in his Gallic campaigns of 55-54 BC and Octavian is credited with planning the conquest of Britain in 34 BC, although this seems unlikely, (Cassius Dio 49.38.2) and, more likely, in 27-26 BC (Hor. *Carm.* 3.5.2-4 *praesens diuus habebitur / Augustus adiectis Britannis / imperio*; Cassius Dio 53.22.5, 25.2; cf. also Hor. *Carm.* 1.35.29-30, 4.14.47-48; Prop. 2.1.76, 27.5). Thus Momigliano's (1950) argument that Messalla's participation in a British campaign would suit well the historical situation of 31 BC, since it was not an area that Octavian was reserving for himself, is unconvincing. In any case, Britain remained undefeated until Claudius' conquest as far as the Thames in AD 43. Claudius' conquest cannot however for that reason be taken as a *terminus ante quem* for our poem, since whenever the author wrote it, he is setting it firmly in 31 BC. Even Agricola's complete conquest of Britain in AD 84, Tac. *Agr.* 10.1 *tum primum* (*sc. Britannia*) *perdomita est*, is qualified in Tac. *Hist.* 1.2 *perdomita Britannia et statim missa* so that in AD 97 (the year in which he wrote the *Agricola*) Tacitus could refer to part of Britain still remaining *manent* to be conquered (*Agric.* 11.4 *segnitia cum otio intrauit ... quod Britannorum olim uictis euenit; ceteri manent quales Galli fuerunt*) – see Woodman [(2014) 18-19, 129], and Courtney on Juvenal 2.159-161 and 4.126-127 for Britain continuing as a by-word for a difficult conquest. For Britain as a land beyond the known world cf. Cat. 11.11-12 *ultimosque Britannos*, 29.4 *ultima Britannia*; Virg. *Ecl.* 1.66 *penitus toto diuisos orbe Britannos*; Hor. *Carm.* 1.35.29-30 *ultimos / orbis Britannos*, 4.14.47-48 *remotis / ... Britannis*, possibly Prop. 2.10.17 *et si qua extremis tellus se subtrahit oris* in a list of future Augustan conquests, cf. Syndicus (2006) 266-267, Sen. *Apoc.* 12.13-14 *Britannos ultra noti / litora ponti*; see further Hunter (2006) 51, Woodman on Vell. 46.1 and on Tac. *Agr.* 10.6.

te manet: at the beginning of the line also at Hor. *Epod.* 13.13 (of Achilles) *te manet Assaraci tellus*. There is perhaps also a reminiscence of Hor. *Epod.* 16.41 quoted on **147n.** above. Perhaps less positive here than *non te ... remorabitur* in **137**, the fact that Britain and the Antipodes **(150)** await Messalla does not necessarily imply he will conquer them. For conquering the unknown as a recognised panegyrical motif, see Woodman (2014) 137 on Tac. *Agr.* 10.4 (Agricola's conquest of the Orkneys), Mela 3.39 (Claudius' conquest of Britain) and cf. Vell. 106.1.

inuictus: for the Briton as undefeated cf. Hor. *Epod.* 7.7 *intactus ... Britannus*.

Romano Marte: cf. Enn. *Ann.* 14 Sk. *sub Marte Pelasgo*; Lucan 3.336 *Martis Hiberi*; Stat. *Theb.* 5.173 *Marte sub Odrysio*, 6.609 *Ogygio ... cum Marte*. For the *iunctura* cf. the first words of **1.1** *Martis Romani*.

Britannus: at the line end also at Lucan 4.134.

150 interiecto mundi pars altera sole: cf. **166** *huic aduersa solo pars altera nostro*, which makes it clear that in both cases the reference is to the Antipodes. The phrase *interiecto sole* refers to the hot desert zone between the two temperate zones of the Northern and Southern hemispheres. But *sole* also refers to the 'ecliptic' or circular path of the sun through the heavens during the year, as described at Virg. *Georg.* 1.238-239 *uia secta per ambas* (sc. *zonas temperatas*) */ obliquus qua se signorum uerteret ordo*, cf. *Aen.* 6.796 *extra anni solisque uias*; Stat. *Silu.* 4.3.156 *ultra sidera flammeumque solem*. The use of *mundus* in the sense of *orbis terrarum* occurs first at Virg. *Ecl.* 4.9 *toto surget gens aurea mundo* and becomes common from Horace on; see *ThLL* 8.1637.46-1638.6. The use of *interiacere* is rare in poetry, elsewhere only at Lucr. 3.859, 4.412; Manil. 2.217; Avien. *Arat.* 1348.

mundi pars: cf. Hor. *Carm.* 3.24.36-38 ... *si neque feruidis / pars inclusa caloribus / mundi* and for *pars* as a geographical term see N-H on *Carm.* 1.35.31-32 *Eois timendum / partibus Oceanoque rubro*.

151-174 The poet explains that the globe is divided into five zones, the north and south poles, a middle desert zone and two temperate zones, northern and southern, of which only the temperate northern zone is occupied by the Romans. The digression emphasises the extent of the world and the size of the areas which for climatic reasons cannot be conquered. Of special interest are the lines which describe in detail the poles and the middle zone where again, as in **137-146**, these form a catalogue with each line introduced with a *non, nec, non* and *nulla* (**161-164**). Lines **153-164**, dealing with the two poles and the central desert zone, are concerned with places unworthy of any kind of human exploitation, let alone a military expedition. This leaves an equal number of verses (**165-176**) which describe the temperate zones, the northern half of which roughly corresponds to the Roman Empire (*nostra* **166**). The five zone theory is attested first in verse at Eratosth. *Hermes* fr. 16 Powell and in prose at Aristot. *Meteor.* 2.5 p. 362a32-b 30 Bekker. Posidonius fr. 49 Kidd attributes the theory to Parmenides, Aëtius 3.13.1 to Pythagoras, while the Stoics claim it as their own, cf. Chrysippus *SVF* II 649. In Latin it is found at Varro Atac. fr. 17 (Courtney = fr. 112 Hollis); Cic. *Nat. Deor.* 1.24 with Pease, *Somn. Scip.* 21; Virg. *Georg.* 1.233-251 with Thomas and Mynors; Ov. *Met.* 1.45-51, *Trist.* 2.195-196 with Ingleheart; Plin. *Nat.* 2.172; see further E. Rawson (1985) 265, and bibliography in Hollis (2007) 186. The present passage is perhaps most influenced by Cic. *Somn. Scip.*, see **135-176n.** above. The connection with Eratosthenes via Virg. *Georg.* 1 recalls the background to the Erigone myth at **9-11** above. On the place of such digressions in panegyric cf. Quint. *Inst.* 4.3.12 and on this particular digression see further Peirano (2012) 137 and n. 59.

414   Commentary

151 A close imitation of Ov. *Met.* 1.12 *nec circumfuso pendebat in aere tellus*, cf. also Lucr. 2.602 *aeris in spatio ... pendere*.

consistit: for *consistere* in the sense of *stare* cf. Cic. *De Orat.* 1.261 *neque ... consistens in loco, sed inambulans*; Lucr. 2.332 *in campis consistere fulgor* and see further examples in *OLD consistere* 1a.

aere tellus: the same verse-end occurs at **19** above.

152 The structure of the line is very close to Manil. 1.574 *et quinque in partes aquilonis distat ab orbe*.

quinque in partes: cf. Crates fr. 34a Mette (= Gem. 15.1) ἡ τῆς συμπάσης γῆς ἐπιφάνεια ... διαιρεῖται εἰς ζώνας πέντε ["the surface of the whole earth is divided into five zones"]; Plin. *Nat.* 2.172 *quinque partes quas uocant zonas*.

toto ... orbe: in the same line position also at Virg. *Georg.* 1.511; Prop. 2.32.15; Ov. *Am.* 1.5.8, *Met.* 14.680, 15.177; Lucan 2.280, 3.230, 7.205, 8.129, 275, 391, 10.157; [Ov.] *Epiced. Drusi* 407; Sil. 6.533, 12.92, 13.758; Stat. *Silu.* 3.4.39, *Ach.* 1.231; Mart. 6.64.25.

153-157 A description of the two cold zones of the Arctic and Antarctic. Mention of cold (**153**), and ice and snow (**156-157**), are common in such passages, but mention of darkness (**154**) is rare. However, cf. Plin. *Nat.* 2.172 *perpetua caligo utrobique* (i.e. in both north and south zones) *et alieno molliorum siderum adspectu maligna ac pruina tantum albicans lux*, where the reference is to the faint light of the sun and moon. In the present passage the darkness is attributed to the fact that the sun never shines. This must be something of an exaggeration in view of the fact that the phenomenon of the midnight sun had been known from the time of Pytheas of Marseilles (fourth century BC Greek navigator), cf. Mela 3.57, Plin. *Nat.* 2.186.

153 gelido ... frigore: the *iunctura* is found also at Cic. *Arat.* 59; Ov. *Her.* 15.112, *Fast.* 2.754; Sil. 2.136 (in the same *sedes*); Mart. 8.68.4.

uastantur: the same verb is used of the two cold regions also at Varro Atac. fr. 17.1-2 (Courtney = fr. 112.1-2 Hollis) *ut quinque aetherius zonis accingitur orbis / ac uastant imas hiemes mediamque calores*.

frigore semper: similar verse-ends occur at Lucr. 6.1171 *frigora semper*; Val. Fl. 2.98 *frigida semper*.

Book Three of the Corpus Tibullianum: 415
Introduction, Text, Translation and Commentary

154 et: for postponed *et* see **20n.** above.

densa ... umbra: the same *iunctura* is found at Cat. 65.13; Virg. *Georg.* 1.342; Hor. *Carm.* 1.7.20-21; Ov. *Pont.* 1.8.65; *Culex* 108, 157; Sen. *Medea* 609, *Ag.* 94; Lucan 6.830; Sil. 15.765; Stat. *Silu.* 1.6.87, *Ach.* 1.640.

155-156 For the description of seas and rivers freezing over as a characteristic of Ovid's exile poetry, see Williams (1994) 9-10, Ingleheart (2010) 194 on Ov. *Trist.* 2.196.

155 On the structure of the verse as a 'golden line' see **3.5n.** and **13n.** above.

incepto ... liquore: literally 'when liquid has been started', i.e. when rain begins to fall or possibly when a thaw starts. Usually *incipere* is constructed with the acc. of a noun describing actions, but for the present use cf. **211** below *inceptis ... chartis* (the pages that have been started) and Stat. *Theb.* 4.441-2 *fugit incepto tremebundus ab aruo / agricola* ['the farmer flees in terror the field he has begun (sc. to plough)"]. The expression is unusual and various conjectures to replace *incepto* have been offered including *inriguo* (Shackleton Bailey), *incerto* (Guyet) and *integro* (Watt).

prolabitur: a conjecture by Tränkle for the manuscripts' *perlabitur*. The verb *perlabor* is rare with liquids and generally means 'fly through' as at **127** above *nulla nec aerias uolucris perlabitur auras*. If the poet did write *perlabitur unda* he could perhaps have been influenced by Virg. *Aen.* 1.147 *atque rotis summas leuibus perlabitur undas* (of Neptune in his chariot); but there also the verb means 'glides over' with an acc. obj. For *prolabor* 'flow forth' with a river as subjet cf. Serv. auct. *Georg.* 4.522 *Hebrus ... fluuius ... ex fontibus ... prolabitur* and with waves and water Tränkle compares Avien. *Orb. Terr.* 335 *prolabitur aequoris unda*, 680-681 *aestum / prolabentis aquae*. Less likely perhaps *praelabitur*, for although it is used of a river at Lucan 9.355 *tacitus praelabitur amnis* its meaning of 'flow past' is not appropriate here.

unda: the use of this word for 'water' in general is mainly poetic (see *OLD* 4). In fact the word comes from the same IE root *wedor (probably with oblique stem *udn-) as Greek ὕδωρ, English 'water'.

156 durata ... in glaciemque niuemque: the construction *durare in* is rare and attested first at Ov. *Met.* 7.446-447 *quae* (sc. *ossa Scironis*) *iactata diu fertur durasse uetustas / in scopulos*. On the double *-que* see **1.3-4n.** and cf. **11** above. For its use at the end of the hexameter cf. **187** below.

riget: used in a similar context at Germ. *Arat.* fr. 3.14 (quoted below) and Ov. *Pont.* 2.7.72 *frigore perpetuo Sarmatis ora riget*.

densam ... niuem: cf. Germ. *Arat.* fr. 3.14 *densa niue saepe rigebunt*. The adj. is used in a similar way with *imber* at Virg. *Georg.* 1.333 and Ov. *Am.* 1.9.16.

157 Titan: for the use of *Titan*, as here, to refer to the sun, see **51n.** above.

egerit ortus: for this periphrasis for *ortus sit* cf. Manil. 1.827 *quod nisi* (sc. *cometae*) *uicinos agerent occasibus ortus*.

158-164 A description of the central desert zone which is too hot to support plants or animals. The repeated negatives at the opening of lines **161-164** (*non, nec, non, nulla*) seems to echo the repeated negatives at the opening of lines 8-12 in Ovid's description of chaos in *Met.* 1 (*nec, non, nullus, nec, nec*). Like Ovid's chaos, described (*Met.* 1.8) as *nec quidquam nisi pondus iners*, the central desert zone here is devoid of life.

158 Phoebi: for the use of *Phoebus* = 'the sun' see **66n.** above.

semper: i.e. both in summer and in winter.

159 aestiuum ... orbem: the reference is to the sun's summer orbit. For *orbis* = 'orbit' see *OLD orbis* 15 and cf. *per orbem* at **50** above and Virg. *Georg.* 1.337 *quos ignis caelo Cyllenius erret in orbis*, which makes use of the same *in* + acc. construction as here, describing the direction of the sun's movement. The present verse, then, refers to the summer, just as in **160** *hibernas ... luces* refers to winter.

fertur in orbem: the same hexameter ending occurs at Manil. 1.232; cf. Sil. 8.418 *refertur in orbem*.

160 celer ... properat: cf. **205** *celerem properat... mortem*.

hibernas ... luces: i.e. 'winter days'. For *lux* = 'day' see *OLD lux* 4 and cf. Mart. 6.59.3 *obscuras luces*.

decurrere: the verb is used in the same sense at **51** above *dum terna ... / saecula ... Titan decurreret*.

161-164 Each line in the description begins with a negative (*non, nec, non, nulla*) see **158-164n.**

161 presso ... aratro: the phrase occurs in the same *sedes* at Ov. *Met.* 3.104; Calp. *Ecl.* 4.121; cf. *depresso ... aratro* at Virg. *Georg.* 1.45; Ov. *Met.* 15.618 and *impresso aratro* at Sil. 3.351.

exsurgit: for the image of the clods of earth rising up as a result of ploughing cf. Plin. *Epist.* 5.6.10 *tantis glaebis tenacissimum solum, cum primum prosecatur, adsurgit, ut nono demum sulco perdometur*; a letter which also has similarities with **171** below; see **n.** ad loc.

frugem segetes praebent: cf. *Inc. Trag.* 136 R *segetes largiri fruges.*

praebent ... pabula: cf. Lucr. 1.229 *pabula praebens*, 2.996 *pabula cum praebet*, 5.991; Prop. 3.7.3; Colum. *Rust.* 10.84.

pabula terrae: the same verse-ending is found at Virg. *Georg.* 1.86 and Ov. *Rem.* 249.

163 Bacchusue Ceresue: the originators of wine and corn respectively, cf. Lucr. 5.14-15 *namque Ceres fertur fruges Liberque liquoris / uitigeni laticem mortalibus instituisse*. The two gods are often mentioned together in this and similar contexts: Tib. 2.1.3-4; Ov. *Pont.* 2.9.30-31; Manil. 2.20-21, 2.558, 3.152-153; Val. Fl. 5.215-216; Stat. *Silu.* 4.2.34, *Ach.* 2.101. The idea that these gods themselves cultivate the fields (*colit arua*) is striking and is found elsewhere at Tib. 2.3.63 *Bacche tener, iucundae consitor uuae* and Hor. *Carm.* 4.5.18 *nutrit rura Ceres*. For -*ue ... -ue* see **39n.** above.

164 For the structure of the verse as a 'golden line', see **3.5n.** and **13n.** above.

nulla nec: for the double negative see **127n.** For postponed *nec* see **42n.**

exustas ... partes: for this aspect of the central torrid zone cf. Plin. *Nat.* 2.172 *uerum media terrarum, qua solis orbita est, exusta flammis et cremata comminus uapore torretur.*

habitant animalia: the phrase occurs in the same *sedes* at *Halieut.* 49 *cetera quae densas habitant animalia siluas.*

165-168 The description of the two temperate zones presented here is very close to that offered by Eratosth. *Hermes* fr. 16 (Powell) 15-18 δοιαὶ δ' ἄλλαι ἔασιν ἐναντίαι ἀλλήλῃσι / μεσσηγὺς θέρεός τε καὶ ὑετίου κρυστάλλου, / ἄμφω εὔκρητοί τε καὶ ὄμπνιον ἀλδήσκουσαι / καρπὸν 'Ελευσίνης Δημήτερος ["the two others are opposite one another, between summer heat and rainy cold, both are well-tempered and bring forth the corn of Demeter of Eleusis"]. Cf. also Virg. *Georg.* 1.237-238 *has inter mediamque duae mortalibus aegris / munere concessae diuom*. One of these zones is occupied by the Romans (**166** *nostraque*) and its description (down to **174**) anticipates, again retrospectively from the view-point of a young Tibullus, the description of the Golden Age at Tib. 1.3.35-48.

165 inter ... interque: for this illogical repetition of *inter* see K-S II 1.580. It occurs in prose from Cicero on. In verse it is rare, but cf. Cic. *Arat.* 97-98, 100; Hor. *Serm.* 1.7.11-12, *Epist.* 1.2.12; Prop. 2.31.15; Sil. 11.180.

rigentes: refers to the two cold zones, as at Plin. *Nat.* 2.172 *circa duae tantum inter exustam et rigentes temperantur*.

166 The reference is to the southern temperate zone, as at **150** above *interiecto mundi pars altera sole*.

nostraque ... nostro: for the use of repeated words to frame the line, see Wills (1996) 429-430 and cf. Tib. 1.3.11 *illa ... illi*, 2.1.84 *uoce ... uocet*; [Tib.] **3**. *Sulpicia Cycle* **11.17** *optat ... optat*.

altera nostro: the same verse-end is found at Prop. 1.18.11; cf. Ov. *Met.* 9.146 *altera nostros*, *Pont.* 1.7.57 *altera nostrum*.

167-168 The fertility of the temperate zones rests upon the mixing of the hot and cold elements of the two neighbouring zones.

167 similis: must be taken as nom. with *uicinia*; the final *-is* is lengthened *in arsi*, on which see Winbolt (1903) 200ff.

168 temperat: for the use of the verb in this context cf. Stat. *Silu.* 3.5.83 *quas* (sc. *sedes*) *et mollis hiems et frigida temperat aestas*; and on temperate climates see further Thomas (2009) 3, 11-12, and Woodman (2018) on Tac. *Ann.* 4.55.4 *temperiem caeli*.

et: for postponed *et*, see **20n.** above.

uires necat aer: Tränkle ad loc. compares Lab. *Mim.* 122 (Ribbeck) *ut hedera serpens uires arboreas necat*; cf. Ov. *Rem.* 808 *lenis alit flammas*, *grandior aura necat*; Plin. *Nat.* 31.2 *terras deuorant aquae, flammas necant.*

169-174 The development of agriculture (**170-173**), seafaring (**173**) and the building of towns (**174**) is here connected with the temperate climate and the peaceful alternation of seasons (**169**). Such developments are associated elsewhere either with the natural evolution of human kind (Lucr. 5.925ff.), or with the transition from the age of Saturn to the age of Jove (Tib. 1.3.35-56), or with remnants of the age of Jove on its transition into a new Golden Age, as in Virg. *Ecl.* 4.31-33 *pauca tamen suberunt priscae uestigia fraudis, / quae temptare Thetim ratibus, quae cingere muris / oppida, quae iubeant telluri infindere sulcos.*

169 For the alternation of the seasons being linked with human progress see Ov. *Met.*

1.116-124, where Jove introduces the four seasons after the idyllic weather of the age of Saturn and causes humans to build homes for shelter and undertake agriculture.

placidus ... annus: cf. Stat. *Silu.* 4.3.149-150 *annos perpetua geres iuuenta / quos fertur placidos adisse Nestor.*

per tempora: the phrase is common in the penultimate foot in Manilius (8) and occurs in the same *sedes* as here at Ov. *Am.* 3.13.7; Val. Fl. 6.563; Sil. 9.298.

uertitur annus: the manuscripts are divided here between *uertitur* and *labitur*, both of which are possible. In favour of *uertitur* is the fact that *uertor* is found frequently with *annus*, e.g. Cic. *Quinct.* 40.5 *anno uertente* (the same phrase is found at Cic. *Phil.* 13.22, *Rep.* 6.24, *Nat. Deor.* 2.53.6; Nep. *Ag.* 4.4; Suet. *Calig.* 37.3), Manil. 1.516 *uertentibus annis*, 3.554; Juv. 7.242 *cum se uerterit annus*, whereas *labor* is rare, only Virg. *Georg.* 1.6 *labentem caelo quae ducitis annum*. The verb *uertitur* also has connotation of change, which is an important theme in the collection as a whole.

170 colla iugo ... submittere: for the phrase cf. Manil. 4.142-143 ... *submittit in astris / colla iugumque suis poscit ceruicibus ipse* (sc. *Taurus*); Sen. *Medea* 1023-1024 ... *colla serpentes iugo / summissa praebent*; Sen. *Dial.* 4.31.6 *aspice elephantorum iugo colla summissa.* For bulls submitting their necks to the plough to indicate the origins of agriculture cf. Ov. *Am.* 3.10.13 *prima* (sc. *Ceres*) *iugis tauros supponere* *colla coegit, Fast.* 4.403 *illa* (sc. *Ceres*) *iugo tauros collum praebere coegit.*

171 In the ancient world vines were trained up trees, mostly elms and poplars, see Plin. *Nat.* 14.10ff.

lenta ... uitis: the same *iunctura* is found at Cat. 61.102-103; Virg. *Ecl.* 3.38, 9.42, 10.40, *Georg.* 1.265; Calp. *Ecl.* 3.72.

excelsos ... ramos: the phrase occurs in the same *sedes* at Sil. 5.480; cf. *excelsis ... ramis* at Stat. *Theb.* 9.269.

conscendere: found only here of a vine, but cf. Plin. *Epist.* 5.6.39 *laetissima uitis per omne tectum in culmen nititur et adscendit*, in the same letter echoed in **161** above, see **n.** ad loc.

172 tondetur ... seges: for *tondeo* of cutting corn cf. Virg. *Georg.* 1.71, 1.290 and see *OLD tondeo* 3b and c.

maturos ... partus: internal (or 'Greek') acc. after the passive *tondetur* see *OLD* 3c. The noun *partus* is first used of a harvest from the fields by Prop. 2.15.31 *terra prius falso partu deludet arantes*, see *ThLL* 10(1).542.5-12. For *maturus* in this context cf. *Nux* 93 *maturos numquam licet edere fetus*; Nemes. *Ecl.* 3.39.

annua: used predicatively as at Tib. 2.1.48 *deponit flauas annua terra comas.* Avien. *Arat.* 399-340 *flauos tondentur semina crines / omnia* seems to combine these two passages from the *Corp. Tib.*

173 For the formulation of this reference to agriculture and sailing cf. Ov. *Ars* 2.671 *aut mare remigiis aut uomere findite terras.*

ferro: used here in the sense of *uomere*, cf. Lucil. 1044 M. *inuitam et glaebas subigas proscindere ferro*? and see *ThLL* 6(1).584.45-77.

pontus: see **20n.** above.

confinditur: the use of this compound for *findere* (cf. Ov. *Ars* 2.671 quoted above) is not found elsewhere except in the *notae Tironiae* (cf. *ThLL* 4.213.23-36). It must, however, be preferred to *confunditur* of A+ as that verb would normally mean 'disturb'. Elsewhere in verse the verbs *findere, infindere* and *proscindere* are used regularly of both ploughs cutting through the earth and prows cutting through the sea.

aere: referring to the bronze prow of a ship as at Virg. *Aen.* 1.35.

174 structis ... muris: the same *iunctura* is found at Sil. 14.46-47 ... *structis qui ... / ... ex sese donarunt nomina muris*. For this aspect of civilisation cf. Virg. *Ecl.* 4.32-33 quoted in **169-174n.** above.

oppida muris: the same verse ending is found at Virg. *Aen.* 8 355; Sil. 3.213; *Ecl. Einsid.* 2.27; *Il. Lat.* 876; cf. Lucan 4.224 *oppida muri*.

175 praeclaros poscent: this is A+'s reading, referring to the famous triumphs to be demanded in the future as a result of Messalla's exploits. Although this makes reasonable sense, some editors prefer F's *ierint* and change *praeclaros* to *per claros* (with Scaliger): 'when your deeds have passed through famous triumphs', arguing that only after his triumphs will Messalla's deeds be made known. *poscent* has the advantage of referring to the convention that a victorious general was expected to ask for a triumph (usually with *petere*), e.g. Liv. 10.37.6 *consul cum triumphum ab senatu petisset*; Tac. *Ann.* 4.26.1 *Dolobellae petenti abnuit triumphalia Tiberius*. Keyechev (2020) plausibly conjectures *parient* on the model of *Catal.* 9.58 *ipsa sibi egregium facta decus parient* (of Messalla's achievements).

praeclaros ... triumphos: cf. Cic. *Planc.* 89.14 *clarissimos triumphos*; *Laus Pisonis* 37 *claros uisura triumphos*; Juv. 4.125 *clarique triumphi*.

176 utroque ... in orbe: i.e. in both hemispheres.

magnus: the official title of Pompey. Otherwise it was rarely applied to mortals; only to Caesar at Cat. 11.10 and, on inscriptions [Reynolds (1982) 159-160], and to Octavian /Augustus at Virg. *Georg.* 4.560; Hor. *Serm.* 2.5.64, *Carm.* 1.12.50 (on which see N-H 166 ad loc.).

177-180 For the theme of the poet's own inadequacy to sing the deeds of a great person **(177-178)** see **5-6n.** above and Peirano (2012) 138-139. This and the suggestion of an alternative poet for the task **(179-180)**, in this case Valgius, are both common *topoi* of *recusationes*. On the 'alternative poet' topos see further Woodman (2012) 220-221. On Callimachean influence on Latin *recusationes* via *Aetia* fr. 1 Pf. see Hopkinson (1989) 98-101 and on *recusationes* in general see **18-27n.** above. For the suggestion of an alternative poet, see Hor. *Carm.* 1.6.1-4 with N-H 83 ad loc. and Harrison (2007) 171-173 (Varus shall sing the praises of Agrippa); 2.12.9-12 with N-H 192-193 ad loc. (Maecenas shall praise Caesar's battles in prose); 4.2.33-34 (Iullus Antonius will write Pindaric

Odes); Virg. *Ecl.* 6.6-7 (others will sing the deeds of Alfenus Varus); Prop. 2.34.61-62 (Virgil will sing of Actium and the Trojan War). As Tränkle points out [243 ad loc.] our author's *recusatio* here contradicts his wish in 35-37 to be the victor among those who vie to sing Messalla's praises.

177 praeconia: in verse the word is found mainly in Ovid; in the same *sedes* at *Am.* 3.12.9, *Her.* 16.141, *Ars* 1.623, 3.535, *Met.* 12.573, *Trist.* 4.9.19, 5.1.19; cf. especially *Her.* 17.207 *non ita contemno uolucris praeconia famae, Pont.* 4.8.45 *carmina uestrarum peragunt praeconia laudum* and see also Lucan 1.472, 4.813; Stat. *Theb.* 2.176-177 ... *a quam te parcum in praeconia famae / mens agitat matura tuae.*

praeconia laudis: the same verse-end is found at *CLE* 661.1 (from 395 AD).

178 si praescribat carmina Phoebus: the idea of Apollo dictating verses to a poet goes back to Hom. *Od.* 8.488 ἐδίδαξε ... σέ γ' Ἀπόλλων ["Apollo taught you"]. In Latin cf. Tib. 2.4.14 *carminis auctor Apollo* (also in a passage on Phoebus' inability to help the poet); Prop. 4.1B.133 *tum tibi pauca suo de carmine dictat Apollo*; *Laus Pisonis* 168 (sc. *cantum*) *te credibile est Phoebo didicisse magistro*; *Catal.* 9.59-60 (Apollo, the Muses, Bacchus and Aglaea composed poetry jointly with Messalla). Perhaps an even more important intertext here is Virg. *Ecl.* 6, where Apollo tells Virgil what kind of poetry to write (6.4-5), and at 82-84 dictates the poetry that was later sung by Silenus. The eclogue also contains the verb *praescripsit*, though in a different context, 6.12 *quam sibi quae Vari praescripsit pagina nomen.*

carmina Phoebus: similar verse endings occur at Nemes. *Ecl.* 1.24, 2.54.

179 magnis se accingere rebus: for the construction cf. Virg. *Aen.* 1.210 *illi se praedae accingunt*, and for the content cf. Virg. *Georg.* 3.46-47 *ardentes accingar dicere pugnas / Caesaris.*

180 Valgius: C. Valgius Rufus, born in 65 BC, suffect consul in 12 BC. Horace, at *Serm.* 1.10.81-82, numbers him, along with Valgius' patron Messalla (1.10.85), among those literary friends whose good opinion he desires. For his life and work, see Unger (1848), Courtney (1993) 287, Hollis (2007) 290-291 and Harrison (2017) 118-121. Valgius' fragments include, in prose, rhetorical and grammatical works (*GRF* 482ff.), the translation of a rhetorical manual by his master Apollodorus (Quint. *Inst.* 3.1.18) and an incomplete work on medical plants (Plin. *Nat.* 25.4), and, in verse, elegy frs. 2, 3, 4 (Courtney = frs. 166, 167, 168 Hollis) and bucolic fr. 5 (Courtney = fr. 169 Hollis). There are no epic fragments, but Horace invites him at *Carm.* 2.9.18 to abandon elegy and join in celebrating the triumphs of Augustus [Powell (2010) 148] and this passage may have motivated the mention of Valgius here. If we accept Heyne's conjecture of *Valgi* (for *uulgi* or *dulcis*) at Tib. 1.10.11, Valgius was the addressee of the final poem of Tib.'s first book. The connections with Messalla, and possibly with Tibullus, could have motivated our poet to name Valgius here, but whether he really merits the comparison with Homer is doubtful and there could be some irony in the naming in this context of a poet who may not have been of the first rank. On Horace's calling into question Valgius' suitability for singing of higher themes by his use of adjectives suggesting elegy at the end of *Carm.* 2.9 (22 *minores*, 24 *exiguis*) see Thomas (2011) 15-16.

aeterno ... Homero: the phrase occurs in the same *sedes* at Ov. *Pont.* 2.10.13 (to Macer) *tu canis aeterno quicquid restabat Homero*. For other comparisons with Homer cf. Hor. *Carm.* 1.6.1-2 (of Varius) *scriberis Vario ... / ... Maeonii carminis alite* (this Varius may have written a poem entitled *Laudes Caesaris* which may have influenced the title of the *Laudes Messallae*); *Catal.* 15.2 (of Virgil) *Homero non minor ore fuit*; *Laus Pisonis* 232 (of Virgil) *Maeoniumque senem Romano prouocat ore*. On Homer as inimitable see Vell. 1.5.1-2.

alter: in the sense of *alius* see **18n.** above.

alter Homero: for the verse ending cf. Hor. *Epist.* 2.1.50 *Ennius ... alter Homerus*.

181-182 Despite his inability to fulfil adequately his panegyric duty towards Messalla (**177**) and despite the fact that Fortune is against him (**182**), the author nevertheless continues his poetic efforts (**181** *labor*).

181 languida ... otia: in the same *sedes* also at Claud. *Rapt. Pros.* 1.277. On the poet's need of *otium* in the sense of leisure to write poetry, see Ingleheart (2010) 214-215 and 224-225 on Ov. *Trist.* 2.224 and 2.235 respectively, Robinson (2011) 466 on Ov. *Fast.* 2.723-724 and cf. Cat. 50.1-2; Virg. *Georg.* 4.563-566.

non: most editors emend to *nec* (with Heyne) in order to establish a closer connection with what has gone before. However, *non*, making a new point about continued poetic activity, gives adequate sense here.

peragit ... otia: the phrase is found at Ov. *Met.* 1.99-100 ... *sine militis usu / mollia securae peragebant otia gentes*; Manil. 4.157 *otia ... peragunt in amore*.

labor: on this literary critical term (cf. Greek πόνος) describing the toil that went into writing polished, learned poetry see the discussion at **16n.** above.

182 Fortuna ... me aduersa fatiget: cf. Virg. *Aen.* 6.533 *an quae te fortuna fatigat*?

Fortuna ... aduersa: a common combination from Lucil. 6.237 M.; Pac. *Trag.* 268 on. For *Fortuna* as a goddess, dispenser of different fortunes, see McKeown III 271 on Ov. *Am.* 2.12.15-16.

ut mos est: in hexameter verse also at Lucan 10.126; Juv. 6.329; earlier verse occurrences at Plaut. *Men.* 906, *Truc.* 16, Cat. 9.8.

183-189 The passage recalls Tib. 1.1.19-22 (reduction in livestock) and 41-42 (reduction in corn harvest), in which the poet laments the reduction in his ancestral lands. In particular the close of **187** *furique lupoque* recalls the close of Tib. 1.1.33 *furesque lupique* (see **187n.** below). Such similarity in theme led earlier scholars to identify the author here as a young Tibullus and has convinced such modern authors as Peirano [(2012) 117-172] that its author is a Tibullan impersonator. Our author's mask here is indeed that of a young Tibullus, although he never names himself as such in this poem. The theme of the poet's reduced circumstances is common in other Augustan writers [e.g. Virg. *Ecl.* 1.70-72, 9.2-6; Hor. *Epist.* 2.2.50-51; Prop. 4.1B.128-130 with Heyworth (2007b) 430-431 for further examples], where it is put down to Octavian's land confiscations of 41-40 BC to resettle veterans after the battle of Philippi. These may not have been the cause of Tibullus' reduced circumstances [see Maltby (2002) 40], although the panegyrist here seems to present himself as a victim of them. The theme is found also at *Laus Pis.* 254-255 and may have formed part of the rhetorical conventions of panegyric; see Maltby (2010) 330.

183 opibus domus ... niteret: such shining is often put down to the use of expensive marble in the construction, cf. Horace's *uilla candens* at *Epod.* 1.29, *Carm.* 2.18.1-5 (with N-H nn. ad loc.) *non ebur neque aureum / mea renidet in domo lacunar, / non trabes Hymettiae / premunt columnas ultima recisas / Africa*, and Lucan 10.114 *nec summis crustata domus sectisque nitebat / marmoribus*; Stat. *Silu.* 3.1.78-80 and see **3.13** above.

domus alta: referring to a substantial rich man's dwelling, the phrase occurs in the same *sedes* at Lucr. 2.1110; Virg. *Georg.* 2.461, *Aen.* 10.101, 12.546; Hor. *Serm.* 2.6.114; Sil. 17.475; Stat. *Silu.* 1.2.145.

alta niteret: for the line ending cf. *Il. Lat.* 231.

184-185 cui fuerant flaui ditantes ordine sulci / horrea: the construction is possessive 'I had rows of golden furrows enriching my granaries'. There is no need to take *fuerant* with *ditantes* as a periphrastic verb form = *ditabant*. For the pluperfect in place of the perfect, a frequent feature of Augustan poetry, cf. Tib. 2.5.79; Virg. *Aen.* 5.397, 6.166, 10.613; Prop. 1.11.29; Ov. *Met.* 15.170 and see H-Sz 388.

flaui ... sulci: the combination occurs here only; the reference is to the golden colour of the furrows when filled with corn, cf. Virg. *Ecl.* 4.28 *flauescet campus arista*, *Georg.* 1.316 *flauis ... aruis*.

ordine: either spatial 'in rows' or temporal 'one after the other'. Both are possible; I have translated the spatial option.

185 fecundas ... messes: the *iunctura* is found at *Priap.* 53.3 *magnaque fecundis cum messibus area desit* and Rut. Nam. 1.147. For the use of *fecundus* in the sense of *largus* cf. Varro *Rust.* 3.16.34; Hor. *Epist.* 1.5.19 and see *ThLL* 6(1).420.62-78.

horrea fecundas ad deficientia messes: this is the reading of F as reported by Scaliger. The word order, in which *ad* refers to *fecundas ... messes*, is unusual but not unparalleled. For the separation of prepositions from their substantives in poetry see K-S II 588 (para. 114h), e.g. Virg *Georg.* 1.345 *nouas circum felix eat hostia fruges*; Tib. 1.6.30 *contra quis ferat arma deos*? The usage *deficere + ad =* 'be insufficient for' is found elsewhere only at Sen. *Epist.* 74.32 *nec dignum ad quod mens sana deficiat*, *Nat. Quaest.* 3. *Praef.* 10. *deficiente ad iniurias terra*. The reading *indeficientia* of A+, agreeing with *horrea* and meaning 'not failing' with *fecundas ... messes* as object, would perhaps provide better sense, but the word occurs elsewhere only in Christian Latin prose, e.g. Tert. *adu. Iud.* 14.

186 denso ... agmine: 'in close packed ranks'; the *iunctura* is attested in the same *sedes* at Ov. *Her.* 16.185. Virg. prefers *agmine denso* at the line-end: *Aen.* 2.450, 9.788, 12.422, as do Lucan 10.543, *Laus Pisonis* 38, and Sil. 5.659.

pascebant: I take *colles* here as subject, with *pascebant* in the sense 'fed', 'provided pasture for' as at Virg. *Georg.* 2.198-199 *campum / pascentem niueos herboso flumine cycnos*; Ov. *Fast.* 5.640 *pascebat sparsas utraque ripa boues*.

187 The line, with its ending *furique lupoque*, imitates Tib. 1.1.33-34 in the context of the poet's own *paupertas*: *at uos exiguo pecori, furesque lupique, / parcite: de magno est praeda petenda grege*. On the purpose of this echo in sustaining a story of the fictional Tibullus' early involvement with Messalla, see Peirano (2012) 144-146, 198-199; cf. also Hor. *Epist.* 1.6.45-46 *exilis domus est, ubi non et multa supersunt / et dominum fallunt et prosunt furibus*.

furique lupoque: for the combination of *fur* and *lupus* as agricultural threats, in addition to Tib. 1.1.33, cf. Virg. *Georg.* 3.407-408 *nocturnum stabulis furem incursusque luporum* (sc. *numquam horrebis*). On *-que ... -que* at the line-end see **156n.** above and on *-que ... -que* in general, see **1.3-4n.** above.

188-189 The poet's regret over his loss of wealth contrasts with Tibullus' acceptance of his *paupertas* (Tib. 1.1.41-44 *non ego diuitias patrum fructusque requiro / quos tulit antiquo condita messis auo. / parua seges satis est, satis est requiescere lecto / si licet et solito membra leuare toro*); see further Peirano (2012) 144-145.

188 desiderium superest: cf. Lucr. 3.900-901 ... *nec tibi earum / iam desiderium rerum super insidet una*.

cura nouatur: cf. Ov. *Her.* 1.20 *Tlepolemi leto cura nouata mea est*. The verb is often used of medical conditions re-starting, e.g. Cels. 2.1.6 *uere tamen maxime, quae cum umoris motu nouantur, in metu esse consuerunt*, or of wounds re-opening, e.g. Ov. *Rem.* 729-730 *refricatur amor, uulnusque nouatum / scinditur* (see *OLD* 6b and c), so the phrase here could involve a medical metaphor.

189 memor ... dolor: the *iunctura* occurs also at Avien. *Arat.* 1208 and Auson. *Cupid.* 14.

dolor admonet annos: *admonere* + acc. is rare except with neuter pronouns and adjectives; the only other example is found at Liv. 6.4.6 *admonet ... desiderium usus*.

190 cadant: 'happen', 'befall', see *OLD cado* 16 and cf. Tib. 1.6.85 *haec aliis maledicta cadant*.

191 non ... deficient ... memorare: for the construction *deficio* + inf. = 'cease to', 'fail to' see *OLD deficio* 9C, K-S II 1.674 and cf. Lucr. 1.1040-1041... *ac deficit suppeditare / materies*; Germ. *Arat.* 260 *deficiente oculo distinguere corpora parua*; Sil. 3.111.112 ... *ut scandere tecum / deficiam montes*.

nostrae ... Camenae: see **24n.** above.

memorare Camenae: De Luca ad loc. compares the similar line-ending at Alcuin *Carm.* 1.1090 *nostris memorare Camenis*.

192 Pierii ... honores: for the adj. *Pierius* = 'relating to the Muses' see **1.15-16n.** above. The combination with *honores* is found only here.

tribuentur honores: cf. Vitr. 9 pr. 16 *neque moribus praestantibus ... scriptorum tribuantur honores.*'

193-196 The dangers the author assures he is ready to face for Messalla are similar to those found in declarations of loyalty in *propemptica* or send-off poems, e.g. Hor. *Epod.* 1.11-24 (for Maecenas); Prop. 1.6.1-18 (for Tullus); Ov. *Am.* 2.16.19-39 (for his mistress); see further McKeown III 343-344 on Ov. *Am.* 2.16.19-32, and N-H 96-97 on Hor. *Carm.* 2.6.1 with Harrison (2017) 93-94 (Septimius is prepared to accompany Horace on dangerous journeys). The *topos* probably goes back to Hellenistic Greek poetry and is parodied by Cat. at 11.1-14. The present passage takes from this tradition the dangers of sea-travel (**193-194**) and war (**195**), but lacks the listing of foreign lands to be visited together and ends in bathos by mentioning committing his body to the fires of Aetna (**196**).

pro te uel ... / ... / pro te uel ... /uel: the parallelism is only apparent: the first *uel* (**193**) is adverbial = 'even', the second (**195**) is disjunctive = 'either', picked up (**196**) by *uel* = 'or'.

193-195 The verses recall Messalla's exploits as recorded in *Catal.* 9.47-49 *saepe trucem aduerso perlabi sidere pontum, / saepe mare audendo uincere, saepe hiemem: / saepe etiam densos inmittere corpus in hostes*.

193 rapidas ... undas: see **72n.** above.

ausim: an archaic form avoided in higher stiles of poetry; see figures in McKeown III 67 on Ov. *Am.* 2.4.1; for its use in a similar context, cf. Ov. *Am.* 2.16.21 *cum domina Libycas ausim perrumpere Syrtes*.

maris ... undas: a common combination, especially in Ovid, see **53n.** above.

ire per undas: the same hexameter-ending is found at Tib. 1.4.45; Prop. 2.30.19; Val. Fl. 7.138.

194 aduersis ... uentis: the combination occurs in verse also at Lucil. 10.390 M.; Varro *Men.* 471.1; Virg. *Aen.* 2.416; Ov. *Her.* 6.7, 21, 71; Lucan 9.149.

tumeant freta uentis: cf. Ov. *Met.* 1.36-37 *tum freta diffundi rapidisque tumescere uentis / iussit*. The line-end *freta uentis* occurs also at Ov. *Her.* 18.7.

195 densis ... turmis: cf. *Catal.* 9.49 (quoted above on **193-195n.**). For the *iunctura* cf. *Culex* 248 and, in the same *sedes*, Stat. *Theb.* 4.125.

subsistere: in the sense 'face', 'stand up against' + dat. see *OLD subsisto* 1b.

196 There is bathos in the final thing the poet is willing to do for Messalla, namely to throw his small body into the volcano Aetna; see Peirano (2012) 140. Horace tells us that the poet-philosopher Empedocles undertook such a deed in order to prove himself immortal: *AP* 464-466 *... deus immortalis haberi / dum cupit Empedocles, ardentem frigidus Aetnam / insiluit. sit ius liceatque perire poetis*. The theme recurs in Ov. *Trist.* 5.2b.73-75 *hinc ego dum muter, uel me Zanclaea Charybdis / deuoret aque suis ad Styga mittat aquis, / uel rapidae flammis urar patienter in Aetnae*, where the poet lists drowning at sea and burning in Aetna as preferable to remaining in Tomi.

paruum: many editors obelise, as being poorly motivated, especially in view of *paruula cura* in **197**. However, the emphasis on the poet's weakness and humility is in accord with rhetorical handbooks on encomia (e.g. Men. Rhet. 369.11 Sp.). Just like the claim that he will follow the actions of the incompetent Empedocles, so mention of his small stature would be in keeping with a young and inexperienced Tibullus as impersonated by our poet here. As Peirano [(2012) 140] argues, the adj. actually provides a good transition to the *paruula cura* 'little regard' he requests from Messalla in **197**. There could be an underlying metapoetic reference in *corpus* to the burning of a body of work (see **2.17n.** above, Cic. *Att.* 5.12.4; Vitr. 5 pr.5; Suet. *Gramm.* 6 and *OLD corpus* 16, *ThLL* 4.1020.62-1021.39). Ovid mentions his threat of burning the *Metamorphoses* at *Trist.* 1.1.117-118, 1.7.19-20, 38, 3.14.19-20 and Virgil's biographer (Don. *Vit. Verg.* 147, 153-154) mentions the *Aeneid* being threatened with a similar fate. For *paruus* of a literary work cf. ὀλ]ιγόστιχος at Call. *Aet.* fr. 1.9 [(a poem) of few lines] and cf. *parua munera* at **7** above. The phrase, then, could pick up the Callimachean poetic imagery of the opening of the poem.

Aetnaeae ... flammae: the same combination is found at Ov. *Pont.* 2.10.33 and Arnob. *Nat.* 5.24. For the use of the adj. in place of the gen. subst. see **56n.** above.

corpus committere: found also at Sen. *Epist.* 114.24; Apul. *Met.* 4.11, *CLE* 698.3. Cf. also *immittere corpus in hostes* at *Catal.* 9.49 quoted in **193-195n.** above.

197-200 The panegyrist states he would put however small an amount of care from Messalla above riches (**198-199** *regna / Lydia*), fame (**199** *fama Gylippi*) and literary achievement (**200** *Meleteas ... uincere cartas*). The passage transfers into the realm of panegyric a theme more at home in elegy, namely that love should be valued above any riches; e.g. Cat. 45.21-22; [Tib.] 3. *Lygd.* 3.27-32 (see **198-199n.** below); also Hor. *Carm.* 2.12.21-24 on which see N-H 197 who list other examples, including some, as here, from outside the romantic sphere, for instance, Hor. *Carm.* 3.9.1-4; Tib. 2.2.11-16; Prop. 1.8.33-36. Close to the present context is Hor. *Epod* 1.24-34 where Horace rejects riches in favour of *gratia* from his patron Maecenas. This novel use of an elegiac theme (cf. **91n.** and **137n.** above) could have been motivated by the author's desire to impersonate the young elegist, Tibullus, at a stage in his career when he badly needed the support of a patron such as Messalla. Peirano [(2012) 40-41] sees a possible inspiration for this theme in the way in which Ovid claims to have been supported by Messalla at the beginning of his career, when he still lacked confidence: cf. Ov. *Trist.* 4.4a.29-30 (probably addressed to Messalla's son, Messallinus) *ingeniumque meum - potes hoc meminisse – probabat, / plus etiam quam me iudice dignus eram, Pont.* 2.3.77-78 *primus ut auderem committere carmina famae / inpulit: ingenii dux fuit ille mei.* The passage complies with the recommendation of rhetorical handbooks that humility and expressions of weakness are appropriate for writers of encomia, e.g. Men. Rhet. 369.11 Sp. cf. **196n.** above.

430　　　　　　　　　　　Commentary

197 paruula: the word is found in the same *sedes* at *Ciris* 479; Juv. 6.89, 10.340. The adj. is rare in verse outside comedy until Seneca and Juvenal: Plaut. (14), Ter. (8), Acc. (1), Cat. (1), Lucr. (4), Hor. (3), Virg. (1), Prop. (2), Manil. (1), *Culex* (1), *Ciris* (2), *Moretum* (1), Sen. *trag.* (6), Juv. (5). As with *munera parua* of the author's gift of poetry to Messalla at **7** above, the adj. could carry with it some metapoetical meaning.

198 quantalibet, si sit modo: a parenthetical clause, emphasising the preceding *paruula*, 'however small, provided only there is some'. For *si modo* + subj. as a poetic construction, expressing a wish, see K-S II 2.429 and cf. Prop. 1.18.4 and Tib. 2.4.59.

198-199 regna / Lydia: the kingdom of Lydia, whose river Pactolus flowed with gold, was a symbol of wealth. The riches of its sixth-century king Croesus were proverbial; cf., in an elegiac context, **3.29** *Lydius aurifer amnis* with **n**. ad loc. Both here and in the *Lygd.* poem these riches are rejected in favour of the love of a mistress or a patron. It must be significant that Horace's rich rival for Neaera's affections, whom, it is argued above (Gen. Intro., section 3.1, **1 headnote, 3 headnote, 3.29n. Lydius aurifer amnis, 4.16n. laesit, 6.47-49n., 6.53n.**) Lygdamus could be impersonating in poems **1-6** is described as possessing the riches of the Pactolus: Hor. *Epod.* 15.20 *tibique Pactolus fluat*. In addition, as happens here, he is described as having an interest in Pythagorean re-incarnation (see **206-210n.** below). These two characteristics suggest a link between the *Lygd.* group and *the Laud. Mess.* Holzberg [(1998) 182] sees this use of a Lygdaman elegiac theme as evidence that the author of the *Laud. Mess.*, whose own *recusatio* at **177-180** shows he is more of an elegiac poet than a writer on grand themes, is in fact the same as the Lygdamus poet. We would identify this poet as the unitary author of the whole collection.

199 potior: a technical term of the *sermo amatorius*, usually referring to a favoured rival, a stock-figure in love poetry, see N-R 135 on Hor. *Carm.* 3.9.2-3. Particularly significant for the present passage (cf. **198-199n.** above) is the fact that Horace uses the term of his rich rival for Neaera's affections at *Epod.* 15.13 *non feret adsiduas potiori te dare noctes*.

fama Gylippi: Gylippus was a Spartan general who was sent to protect Syracuse against the Athenian expedition in winter 415/414 BC and inflicted a crushing defeat on the Athenian forces. His name is rarely mentioned in Latin literature: Plin. *Nat.* 1.1.14; Justin (epitome of Pompeius Trogus) 4.4-5; Oros. 2.14 and cf. Justin 4.4.7 (*ab*

Lacedaemoniis) *mittitur Gylippus solus, sed in quo instar omnium auxiliorum erat*. The original Greek source is Thuc. books 6 and 7, which could well have been known to our author; cf. **notes** on his possible knowledge of Herodotus at **139, 140, 141, 143, 144-145** above.

200 Meleteas ... chartas: i.e. the Homeric poems. The river Meles reached the sea near Smyrna (Plin. *Nat.* 5.118.3), one of the towns that claimed to be the birthplace of Homer (cf. Aristotle fr. 76 Rose; Ephor. fr. 1 Jacoby). According to Wilamowitz-Moellendorff (1916) [*Vit. Hom.* p. 25.10, 28.10 etc.], the god of this river was supposed to have been Homer's father. The only other reference to this river in connection with Homer occurs at Stat. *Silu.* 2.7.34, who puts the river Baetis, on which Lucan was born, above it: *Graio nobilior Melete Baetis*. For the use of *chartae* with reference to literary works cf., of Homer, Ov. *Pont.* 4.12.27 *Maeoniis ... chartis*; *Ciris* 62 *Maeoniae ... chartae*, and, of Cicero, Mart. 10.19.17 *Arpinis ... chartis*; cf. **211** below.

uincere: see **205-206n.**

201 quod tibi si: opens the verse also at Ov. *Met.* 13.113. For *quod tibi* in this position cf. Prop. 1.20.2; Ov. *Am.* 1.4.29, 3.10.43, *Her.* 7.43, 118, *Ars* 1.142, 2.108, *Trist.* 3.3.88.

uersus noster: collective singular = 'my poems'.

totusue minusue: cf. *maiorue minorue* at **39** above with **n.** The combination here of the adj. *totus*, used adverbially, and the adverb *minus* is unusual, but not ungrammatical. Heinsius conjectures *minorue* (printed by Luck).

202 summo uel inerret in ore: although *in ore* is normally used of words which are constantly on one's lips (*OLD* 3), its meaning here, as modified by *summo* and *inerret*, seems to be of a cursory reading out loud. The verb *inerrare* in the sense "wander" is rare and late, occurring in Plin Epist (3), Stat. (4) and Apul. (4) etc. One of the Statius passages comes close to the present line. At Stat. *Theb.* 8.643-644 the dying Atys manages to pronounce with cold lips the name of his wife, Ismene: *solum hoc gelidis iam nomen inerrat / faucibus*. At *Ciris* 356-357, this time with the simple verb *errare*, Scylla with failing voice pleads with her father to open peace talks with her lover Minos: *multus inepto / uirginis insolitae sermo nouus errat in ore*. The closeness to our passage here is brought out by the similar verse-ends *inerret in ore / errat in ore*.

summo uel: for the rare delayed disjunctive *uel* cf. Virg. *Georg.* 2.221, 3.204; Tib. 2.4.9; Prop. 4.1.147; Ov. *Am.* 1.7.6.

in ore: common at the verse-end in hexameters (especially in Ov. *Met.*): Lucil. fr. 456 M.; Lucr. 2.339; Hor. *Epist.* 1.15.13; Virg. *Aen.* 9.442, 10.323; Ov. *Her.* 17.15, *Ars* 3.227, *Met.* 5.206, 7.708, 861, 8.801, 9.787, 10.204, 11.544, 562, 12.251; *Ciris* 357; Lucan 7.129; Pers. 3.113; Val. Fl. 6.674; Sil. 8.587; Stat. *Theb.* 8.87, 10, 629, *Silu.* 2.6.22, *Ach.* 1.161; Juv. 14.205.

203 nulla ... fata: as the remaining verses of the poem show, the reference to *fata* includes death.

statuent finem ... canendi: cf. Sil. 7.13-14 ... *finem inter prospera bella / uincendi statuit*.

204-210 On death and change as an important thematic link giving structure to the **[Tib.] 3** collection as a whole, see Prolegomena pp. 81-82, *Lygd.* **2.9n., 2.26n., 6.26n.,** *Sulpicia Cycle* **8 headnote, 8.13-14n.** and cf. **206-210n.** below.

204 tumulus cum texerit ossa: cf. Ov. *Am.* 2.6.59 *ossa tegit tumulus*, *Ars* 2.96 *ossa tegit tellus*, *Met.* 15.55-56 *tumulum, sub quo ... / ossa tegebat humus*.

205-206 A. J. Woodman suggests to me an echo in this couplet of a passage towards the end of Virg. *Ecl.* 4 referring to the deeds of the child who will usher in the new Golden Age: 53-55 *o mihi tum longae maneat pars ultima uitae / spiritus et quantum sat erit tua dicere facta; / non me carminibus uincat* ... *Orpheus*. The words *mihi, longa uita* and *manet* of the present couplet are all represented there. For *carminibus* cf. *carmina* at **211** below and for *uincat* of a literary contest cf. *uincere* at **200** above. The same *Eclogue* had been echoed at **135-136** above. As a celebratory poem on the consulship of Pollio it would have provided an apt model for our poet's composition on Messalla's inauguration as consul.

205 matura dies: here in the sense of an 'early' day on which to die. The *iunctura* is found with a different sense of a 'maturing day' at Lucr. 4.1031 *ubi ipsa dies membris matura creauit*.

celerem properat ... mortem: the transitive use of *properare* is rare, poetic and mostly late, see K-S II 1.95 and cf. Virg. *Aen.* 9.401 ... *pulchram properat per uulnera mortem*; Sen. *Herc. F.* 867 *quid iuuat* *durum properare fatum*?; Sil. 1.225 *prodiga gens animae et properare facillima mortem*. For the phrase *celeris mors* cf. Ov. *Pont*. 4.16.16 *deseruit celeri morte Sabinus opus*. For *celerem properat* cf. **160** *celer hibernas properat ... luces*.

206-210 mutata figura /... receperit aetas: the Pythagorean theory of the transmigration of souls (cf. *Orph*. fr. 338 Bernabé) was present in Latin literature from Enn. *Ann*. 2-11 Sk., where Homer tells Ennius in a dream that his soul had passed via a peacock into Ennius himself. For Pythagoras' own alleged re-incarnations see Thesleff (1965) 172, and for the Pythagorean doctrine on re-incarnation see Philip (1966) 151-171 and L. C. Watson (2003) 476-477. Most relevant here in view of Lygdamus' possible impersonation of Horace's rival for Neaera at Hor. *Epod*. 15 (see Gen. Intro., section 3.1, **1 headnote, 1.19n., 3.29n., 4.16n., 6.47-49n.** and **53n.**) is that the rival's attractions included an interest in this very theory (*Epod*. 15.21 *nec te Pythagorae fallant arcana renati*); this characteristic, together with his Lydian wealth (see **198-199n.** above) serve to link the *Lygd*. group with the *Panegyric*. The most detailed discussion of the re-incarnation theory in Latin verse comes in Ov. *Met*. 15, e.g. 153ff. and 456ff., where migration between men and animals is discussed (see Hardie ad loc.). Virg. *Aen*. 6.735ff. discusses migration from one human life to another. The animal transformations mentioned here evoke other poets' claims to immortality. The transformation into a bird at **209**, for example, recalls not only Homer's peacock but also Horace's transformation into a swan at *Carm*. 2.20.1-5 *non usitata nec tenui ferar / penna biformis per liquidum aethera / uates, neque in terris morabor / longius inuidiasque maior / urbis relinquam*; see further Peirano (2012) 147, Kayachev (2016b) 198-200. For the passage from the future *finget* (**207**) to the present subjunctive *sim* (**208**), *uehar* (**209**) see **5.32n.** above on *siue erimus seu ... uelint*. On the connection with the theme of change which runs through the whole of **[Tib.] 3** see Prolegomena pp. 81-82 and **206n.** above.

206 longa ... uita: a common combination, see **112n.** and **205-206n.** above. For the idea, cf. Cephalus' words at Ov. *Met*. 7.691-692 (an important intertext for the whole book) *si uiuere nobis / fata diu dederint*.

seu: delayed to third position here; see **79-80n.** above.

mutata figura: for the combination cf. Hor. *Carm*. 1.2.41-43 *siue mutata iuuenem figura / ales in terris imitaris almae / filius Maiae*; Calp. *Ecl*. 4.142 *tu quoque mutata seu Iuppiter ipse figura / ... ales*; Claud. *Carm*.

Min. 27.54. For the verse-ending cf. *mutare figuras* at **63** above and Ov. *Ib.* 425; Manil. 1.491. The phrase *mutare figuram* of course provides the leitmotiv for Ovid's *Metamorphoses*, introduced at *Met.* 1.1 in the phrase *mutatas ... formas* (cf. *Met.* 1.547, 7.722, 15.374), an important source for the theory of transmigration of souls, see **206-210n.** above. As in the *Met.*, although forms may change, they nevertheless retain something of their original character, see Barchiesi (2005) 136 ad loc. and Segal's (2005) introduction p. xvii, so that when the poet here returns again as a man **(210)** he will still be able to continue his literary work. On the theme of change as an important motif in **[Tib.] 3** see Prolegomena pp. 81-82, *Lygd.* **2.9n., 2.26n. 6.26n.,** *Laud. Mess.* **204-210** above and **206-210n.,** *Sulpicia Cycle* **8** headnote, **8.13-14n.** In Cephalus' story at Ov. *Met.*7.722 Aurora changes his appearance so that he can test his wife's fidelity: *immutatque meam* (*uideor sensisse*) *figuram*. On the importance of this episode for **[Tib.] 3** as a whole see Gen. Intro., section 1.3.

207-208 seu me finget equum ... / doctum: very close in expression to Hor. *Epist.* 1.2.64-65 *fingit equum tenera docilem ceruice magister / ire, uiam qua monstret eques*.

percurrere ... / doctum: for *doctus* + inf. (mainly poetic) cf. Hor. *Carm. Saec.* 75-76 *doctus ... chorus ... /dicere laudes* (with Thomas 84) and see further examples at *ThLL* 5(1).1738.31-1739.11.

207 rigidos ... campos: perhaps in contrast to *per liquidum... aera* of the bird's flight in **209**. Commentators also compare the contrast between *sola dura* and *aethera altum* at Cat. 63.40 *lustrauit aethera album, sola dura, mare ferum*. The qualification *rigidos* is nevertheless unusual and a number of conjectures have been proposed of which the best is perhaps Conelissen's *uirides*.

percurrere campos: for the line-end cf. *concurrere campo* at Virg. *Aen.* 12.771; also at Prop. 4.10.35; Lucan 7.80, *decurrere campo* at Stat. *Theb.* 7.415, *Silu.* 1.8.25; Juv. 1.19, *currere campis* at Ov. *Met.* 2.662 and *decurrere campis* at Lucan 4.733, 8.224.

208 tardi pecoris: the slow cattle are contrasted with the horse running across the plains in **207**.

pecoris ... gloria taurus: for *gloria* in apposition to an animal cf. Ov. *Am.* 2.6.20 (of Corinna's parrot) *auium gloria*, and especially *Ars* 1.290 (of Pasiphae's bull) *candidus, armenti gloria, taurus erat*.

209 per liquidum ... aera: cf. in a similar context of his transformation into a swan (quoted in full in **206-210n.** above) Hor. *Carm.* 2.20.2 *per liquidum aethera*. The combination *liquidus aer* is relatively common: Virg. *Georg.* 1.404, *Aen.* 6.202; Germ. *Arat.* 569; Ov. *Am.* 2.6.11, *Met.* 4.667, 11.194; Manil. 1.815; Stat. *Theb.* 1.294, 5.524.

uehar: for the use of this verb with relation to flying animals cf. Virg. *Aen.* 7.65 (of bees) *liquidum trans aethera vectae*. The verb may echo the metrically equivalent *ferar* at Hor. *Carm.* 2.20.1 (quoted in **206-210n.** above), cf. Kayachev (2016b) 199.

aera pennis: the same verse-end is found at Ov. *Met.* 7.354, 11.732; Calp. *Ecl.* 2.11; *Il. Lat.* 120; cf. the last line of *Ciris* 541*secat aethera pennis* and see Kayachev (2016b) 199.

210 quandocumque ... aetas: i.e. when, at some distant time in the future, I will regain my human form.

quandocumque: rare in verse and restricted to the opening word: Hor. *Epist.* 1.14.17, 1.16.58; Prop. 2.1.71, 13.17; Ov. *Met.* 6.554, *Trist.* 3.1.57.

hominem me ... receperit: for the use of *recipere* in the context of transmigration of souls cf. Ov. *Met.* 15.158-159 *morte carent animae semperque priore relicta / sede nouis domibus uiuunt habitantque receptae*. For the construction of *recipere* with double accusative cf. Vell. 2.5.3 (sc. *Q. Macedonicus*) *non deterritus proposito, quem moriturum miserat militem, uictorem recepit*.

longa ... aetas: the combination is found elsewhere in verse at Cat. 76.5; Hor. *Serm.* 1.4.132; Ov. *Her.* 5.96, *Fast.* 4.831; Lucan 9.568; [Virg.] *De Ros. Nasc.* 43.

211 inceptis ... subtexam ... chartis: the weaving metaphor at the end of the poem echoes that in lines **5-6** *chartis intexere ... / facta* at its opening (see above **5-6n.**) The wording here recalls Lucr. 6.42 *quo magis inceptum pergam pertexere dictis*. Kayachev [(2016b) 199] sees a conflation of *Ciris* 39 *naturae rerum magnis intexere chartis* and *Ciris* 9 *non tamen absistam coeptum detexere munus*. The verb *subtexere* is used elsewhere only in prose works with the meaning of attaching a sequence to an already existing narrative, e.g. Vell. 1.14.1; Sen. *Contr.* 1 *praef.* 22 and, especially relevant here, Hirtius in *BG* 8.1 of his continuation of Caesar's Gallic narrative. Peirano [(2012) 148] argues that the poet may be hinting at his own impersonation here: he will weave new poems about Messalla

436   Commentary

into the existing Tibullan corpus. For the promise of future song as a closural feature (going back to the end of Hesiod *Theogony* and the *Homeric Hymns*) cf. *canemus* as the last word in Virg. *Ecl.* 6.67 and Hor.*Carm.* 4.15.32 (with Thomas).

carmina chartis: echoes the line-ending *carmine charta* from the opening section of the poem, **27** above; cf. also the line-end *carmine chartas* at *Catal.* 9.13. For a possible echo of *carmina* at Virg. *Ecl.* 4. 55 see **205-206n.** above.

The Sulpicia Cycle 3.8-3.12

Poem 8

On the five poems of the *Sulpicia Cycle* (**8-12**), which deal with Sulpicia and her love for Cerinthus, and on their relation to the *Sulpicia* poems (**13-18**), see Gen. Intro., section 2.2.3.

The content of the first of these poems may be analysed as follows:

1-12 The poem opens with praise of the incomparable beauty of Sulpicia who has adorned herself for the feast of the Matronalia.

13-14 A central couplet compares her varied allurements to the changing appearance of Vertumnus.

15-20 Sulpicia alone is worthy to receive such luxury products of the East as Tyrian purple, sweet-smelling incense and pearls (**15-20**).

21-24 The poem ends with a request for the Muses and Apollo to sing her praises on this occasion for many years to come, for no girl is worthier of their choir (**21-24**).

The central comparison with Vertumnus (**13-14**) divides the poem neatly into two sections, the first (**1-12**) concentrating on Sulpicia's physical beauty, the second (**15-24**) on her worthiness to receive luxury gifts and to be included in the Muses' choir.

That both the *Lygd.* group (**1-6**) and the *Sulpicia Cycle* (**8-12**) open with reference to the same festival, the Matronalia, can be no coincidence; other similarities with poem **1** include the address to the Pierides **21** (cf. **1.5**); the phrase *festis ... Kalendis* **21** (cf. *festae ... Kalendae* **1.1**) and the description of Sulpicia as *digna* **15, 24** (cf. Neaera described as *digna* at

1.8). Such similarities, I have argued in the past [Maltby (2010)], could have been introduced intentionally in his opening elegy by the author of the *Lygd.* poems to align his collection with that of the *Sulpicia Cycle* author here. Similarly I argued that the author of poem **8** could have introduced intentional echoes of *Sulpicia*'s opening poem **13**, (see **1n.** *Mars magne*, **3n.** on Venus, and **15n.**, **24n.** on the adj. *digna* and its relation to **13.10**) and could perhaps be seen as taking up Sulpicia's offer at **13.5-6** for another to tell her story. My present view, already suggested by Holzberg (1998), is that the same author, putting on different masks, is behind all the different sections of the book and so himself responsible for the clear correspondences between the various sections. It can be assumed that the same author who posed as Lygdamus in **1-6**, is now be posing as the unnamed observer, just as he had posed as the young Tibullus in **7** and will in the later poems **9, 11, 13-18** pose as Sulpicia (in **9** and **11** more accurately as the unnamed observer impersonating Sulpicia) and finally as Tibullus in **19** and **20**. Single authorship for the sequence **8-18** had already been proposed by Della Corte (1964).

There are a number of echoes in this poem of Tib. 2.2, a birthday poem for Cornutus, foretelling his forthcoming marriage (see **17-18n. metit, 19-20n. Eois ... aquis**).

For his possible identification with Cerinthus see Gen. Intro., section 3.4 and see especially Holzberg (1998) 183-184 and Hubbard (2004) 183-188. Although Sulpicia elsewhere in the *Sulpicia Cycle* (**8-12**) is depicted as a typical elegiac *puella* (see **10.1, 11, 16, 12.2**) rather than as a married woman and is referred to even in the present poem as *puella* at **15** and **24**, the Matronalia festival with which the poem opens was originally a feast for married women and may be intended to celebrate Sulpicia's marriage to the man referred to in the *Sulpicia Cycle* by the name of Cerinthus. Just as Neaera is to be offered a book of poems on this occasion at **1.15-18**, so Sulpicia is to be sung of at the Matronalia for many years to come by Apollo and the Muses, **21-24**.

That Apollo and the Muses are asked to sing for Sulpicia at the Matronalia hints at her own activities as a poetess, and at her refined literary tastes. The poem contains a number of possible metapoetic references either to her poetic skill or, more likely, to that of the author of the collection; see **1n.** *Sulpicia est tibi culta*, **10n.** *comptis ... comis*, **12n.** *candida*. Again there are parallels with poem **1** where the collection Lygdamus is to send to Neaera is described as a *comptum ... opus* (**1.14**), and similar literary polish is hinted at in **1.10**. The central address to the god Vertumnus here in **13-14** may also have metapoetic significance. At the literary level the god Vertumnus, who often appears in female garb, is like both the character of Sulpicia portrayed by our author as subverting traditional elegiac gender roles, and our unitary author himself, who in poems **9** and **11** (in the voice of the anonymous observer), as well as in **13-18**, impersonates the female Sulpicia (see **1n.** *Sulpicia est tibi culta*). An engagement with gender roles and their reversal is central to the whole of **[Tib.] 3** and echoes a similar concern in the poems of Catullus and in Ovid's *Heroides* and *Amores*, on which see Hutchinson (2012) 75 and Gale (2012) 188 and 208 (on Cat. 68B). Vertumnus may also represent, through his connection with *uertere* 'to turn', the frequent thematic twists and turns that are characteristic not only of the *Sulpicia Cycle* but also of the *Sulpicia* poems **13-18** and the rest of the collection, including the *Lygd.* poems and the *Laus Mess.* (see **2.9n., 26n., 7.63n., 206-207n.**): cf. in this regard Prop. 4.2.47-48 *at mihi, quod formas unus uertebar in omnes, / nomen ab euentu patria lingua dedit* and see **19-20n.** below with its discussion of Prop. 4.2.1-2 *qui mirare meas tot in uno corpore formas, / accipe Vertumni signa paterna dei.* If a single author is putting on different masks in the different sections of **[Tib.] 3** (*Lygd.* **1-6**, Tibullus **7** and **19** and **20**, an anonymous poet in **8-12** and Sulpicia in poems **13-18**) the mention of Vertumnus here in this central position in the collection would be of important metapoetic significance. He represents the Heraclitean principle that all is in flux πάντα ῥεῖ, cf. Hardie (2004) 509 on Ov. *Met.* 15.178 *cuncta fluunt.*

At a thematic level the idea dominates in particular poems **8-18**. For example Sulpicia's fear of hunting in **9.1-10**, modulates into a willingness to hunt in the presence of her lover at **9.11-22**; the fear of disease in **10.1-14** is balanced by the theme that lovers are protected from disease in **10.15-26**. Similarly in the *Sulpicia* poems the proposed birthday in the countryside which will separate her from Cerinthus in **14** is cancelled in **15** where she is free to spend her birthday with her lover in Rome, while her wish to publicise her feelings in **13** reverses her desire to hide them at **18**.

1 Sulpicia: the name appearing first, as at Prop. 1.1.1 *Cynthia prima*, suggests initially that the Sulpicia of **8-12** is going to be a conventional elegiac mistress, celebrated by her poet lover, as were Prop.'s Cynthia and Tib.'s Delia. As becomes clear, however, this Sulpicia is far from conventional. Some of the poems (**9** and **11**) she is presented as speaking in her own voice; her elegiac lover, Cerinthus, has nothing to say at all, and it is he and not the mistress who is referred to by a pseudonym; the poems describing the affair (**8, 10, 12**) are spoken not in the mask of Cerinthus, but in that of a third party, an interested observer; see further Hinds (1987a) 29-31. On the identity of Sulpicia see Gen. Intro., section **3.5**.

Sulpicia est tibi culta: ladies dressed up for the Matronalia, the festival of Juno Lucina, mother of Mars, held on the Kalends of March, but here the poet adds point by saying that Sulpicia is dressing up for Mars himself (as she does for Cerinthus at the festival of Juno in **12.6**). On the festival and its background see **1.1-4n.** above. There is some evidence that at least until well into the Augustan period gifts at this festival were offered only to married women [Tränkle 255] and while this would be appropriate for Lygdamus' Neaera, it may be considered less so for Sulpicia who is described as *puella* throughout the *Sulpicia Cycle* (**8.15, 24, 10.1, 11, 16, 12.2**). However, on the ambiguities of the term *puella*, which can be used of married women and is also applied to Neaera at **4.58, 6.12, 51, 60** see **6.51-52n.** and P. Watson (1983). On the possibility that the Sulpicia as presented in poem **8** could have been a married woman see the **headnote** above. The Matronalia would make a good occasion for a gift of poems (in this case to be sung by Apollo and the Muses **21-24**) as possibly with the gift of a book to Neaera mentioned at **1.5-18**, to mark Sulpicia's marriage. For a possible double meaning in *est tibi culta* 'is adorned for you' but also 'worshipped by you', leading to the quasi-deification of the beloved begun in **10** with *ueneranda* and completed in **21-24** with the mention of her worthiness to be included in the chorus of the Muses, see **nn.** below and Hinds (1987) 33-34. Since there is some evidence that men may have dressed up as women on the Matronalia (see Weinstock *R.E.* s.v. Matronalia), the phrase *est tibi culta* may, as suggested by Hinds [(1987) 46], contain a programmatic hint that the Sulpicia who speaks in the *Cycle* poems **9** and **11** is not the 'real' Sulpicia of the shorter poems **13-18**, but possibly a male poet in female dress. In fact, in the current interpretation of **[Tib.] 3**, the same poet, either male or female, is the author of the whole collection. The introduction of Vertumnus in the emphatically placed central couplet centre **13-14**, a male god of changeability who often appears in female garb, may serve to draw attention to the underlying themes of identity which lie at the heart of the whole collection. A third meaning of *culta* here would link it with **1.17** *cultum ... illi donate libellum*. It refers there with Callimachean metapoetical imagery to the 'polished' book of verse the Muses are asked to deliver to Neaera, but in a physical sense it also alludes to the 'grooming' of the book, whose papyrus has had its hairs shaved off by pumice (**1.10**) to turn it into a *comptum ... opus* (**1.14**). With the adjective *cultum* at **1.17**, then, our author recalls the imagery of the opening line of the present poem where the woman Sulpicia is literally dressed up for Mars at his festival, but at the metapoetical level *culta* could suggest that the book of poems about Sulpicia is going to be 'polished' in a literary sense. It was a common usage in Roman elegy for the name of the mistress to stand for the name of the book about her, with 'Cynthia', for example, at Prop. 2.24A 1-2 *sic loqueris, cum sis iam noto fabula libro / et tua sit toto Cynthia lecta foro*?, standing for Propertius book 1. For *Sulpicia* here as the name of the group of poems **8-12** see Batstone (2018) 103.

Mars magne: on *magnus* as a common epithet for gods see **4.16n.** above. An invocation to the warlike and violent Mars must at first seem inappropriate for the opening of a collection of love elegies, as he belongs more naturally to the world of epic (as emphasised by the mention of *arma* in **4**). Here Mars is usurping the role of Venus, who is appealed to in *Sulpicia*'s opening poem **13.1-5**; see further Hinds (2006) 31. Similarly Ovid asks Mars to disarm, before entering the gentle world of the *Fasti* at *Fast*. 3.1-4 *bellice, depositis clipeo paulisper et hasta, / Mars, ades et nitidas casside solue comas. / forsitan ipse roges quid sit cum Marte poetae: a te qui canitur nomina mensis habet*, and comments later in the poem on Mars as an inappropriate god to preside over the female festival of the Matronalia: *Fast*. 3.169-170 *cum sis officiis, Gradiue, uirilibus aptus, / dic mihi matronae cur tua festa colant*. On this generic uncertainty, which I have argued is shared with the opening of the *Lygd*. poems (**1.1n.** above) see further Hinds (1987) 31-32.

Kalendis: the same verse-ending is found, in the same context, at **1.1** and at **21** below. The word is generally restricted to this position in Latin verse.

2 spectatum ... ipse ueni: recalls Ov. *Ars* 1.99 *spectatum ueniunt, ueniunt spectentur ut ipsae*. For this type of supine of purpose, absent from Tib., Bréguet [(1946) 143] compares Prop. 2.29B.27 *ibat ... narratum*; Ov. *Trist*. 3.7.1 *uade salutatum*, *Met*. 7.805 *uenatum ... ire solebam*.

si sapis: very colloquial in tone, perhaps shockingly so in an address to a god. The phrase is restricted, before elegy, to comedy [Plaut. (15), Ter. (3)] and to Catullus (1) 35.7. At Prop. 2.16A.7 it occurs in advice to Cynthia to fleece her praetor: *quare, si sapis, oblatas ne desere messes*; in Ov. at *Am*. 2.2.9, 3.4.43, *Rem*. 372, 477, *Met*. 14.675 *si sapies* (Vertumnus in disguise to Pomona), *Trist*. 2.13 *si saperem* (with Ingleheart ad loc.); *Copa* (1), Sen. *Epist*. (4), Mart. (7). See further Bréguet (1946) 135-13,

Tränkle (1960) 165. The phrase *qui sapit* at **19.8** below has similar connotations of colloquial conversation concerning love affairs, but, as here, may have more serious philosophical implications, see **n**. ad loc. At **10.9** *sapores* is used in the context of a concoction of healing herbs and may be connected with one of the derivations of Cerinthus' name as healing plant (see **n**. ad loc.).

ipse ueni: the injunction recalls the terminology of the kletic hymn; see **7.131n**. above and cf. Tib. 2.5.6 (to Apollo) *ad tua sacra ueni*; Mart. 8.39.6 *Iuppiter ipse ueni*. Prayers often contain an appeal for the god to 'come'; see West (1966) on Hes. *Theog.* 429 and (2007) 318-320 on the IE background. The verb is used of Mars' arrival at Ov. *Fast.* 5.550 *Mars uenit*. The same pentameter ending, *ipse ueni*, is found at Ov. *Her.* 1.2, 8.24 (encouraging lovers), and Mart. 7.6.10. The verb *ueni* also contains a reference to the opening of the *Sulpicia incipit*-poem **13.1-5** in which the coming of love (**1**) *tandem uenit amor* is associated with Venus (**5**) *exsoluit promissa Venus*, a goddess whose name was associated etymologically with the verb *uenire*, cf. Cic. *Nat. Deor.* 2.69; Lucr. 1.2-7; Ov. *Am.* 3.1.43-44, *Fast.* 4.13-14 and see *LALE* 635, Michalopoulos (2001) 169-170 and Hinds (2006) 17-36, 29-33. Here Venus's role is being usurped by Mars (cf. **1n**. above), as it is by Sulpicia herself later in the poem, see *ueneranda* **10n**. and *uenit* in **12n**.

3 hoc Venus ignoscet: the content is remarkably similar to Prop. 2.28.33 (asking Jupiter to take pity on Cynthia in her illness) *hoc tibi uel poterit coniunx ignoscere Iuno*; cf. also Mart. 5.7.7-8 (a wish that Venus should excuse Mars for the chains with which her jealous husband Vulcan had bound them as lovers) ... *sic Lemniacis lasciua catenis / ignoscat coniunx et patienter amet*. For the theme of Venus' jealousy of Mars, cf. Ov. *Her.* 15.91-92 (on the effects of Sappho's lover Phaon's beauty on Mars): *hunc* (sc. Phaon) *Venus in caelum curru uexisset eburno, / sed uidet et Marti posse placere suo*. This story of Mars and Venus (Ares and Aphrodite) as adulterous lovers is common in ancient literature, occurring first at Hom. *Od.* 8.267-366, with other versions listed by Mayor (1886-9) on Juv. 10.313-314. Another tradition makes Venus to have children with Mars (Hes. *Theog.* 933-937). The use of *ignoscet* emphasises the erotic potential of Venus' divine lover being asked to consider a mortal alternative, see Hinds (1987) 31. Venus will pardon Mars' bestowing of his erotic attention on Sulpicia instead of on Venus herself, and this verb *ignoscet* possibly suggests another etymology of Venus from *uenia* 'pardon', see Serv. auct. *Aen.* 1.720, *LALE* 635, and, on this passage, Hinds (2006) 33. A possible link with *Sulpicia* **13** is the fact that Venus appears also (referred to as *Cytherea*, picked up by Venus in **5**) in the third line of *Sulpicia* opening poem, where she is said to have helped Sulpicia in her affair. In Hes. *Theog.* 933 Aphrodite/Venus is also called Κυθέρεια.

ignoscēt. at: for the lengthening of a short vowel *in arsi* cf. Tib. 1.5.33 *uirūm hunc*, 1.10.13 *trahōr et*, 2.2.5 *Geniūs adsit*; Prop. 1.10.23 *neu si quid petiīt, ingrata* where the vowel was originally long, cf. Fedeli (1980) 261 ad loc. and see Platnauer 59-60.

at tu ... caueto: also at Tib. 1.2.89 (warning a bystander of the wrath of Venus). This is the only case where *at tu* does not occur as first word in the verse in the *Corp. Tib.* Tib. himself has 10 examples, but all the cases in **book 3** occur (always + imperat.) in the *Sulpicia Cycle*: here, **9.23, 11.19, 12.7**. The phrase is common in addresses in comedy [Plaut. (16), Ter. (8)] and perhaps found its way into elegy through Cat. 8.14 *at tu dolebis* and 8.19 *at tu, Catulle ... obdura*. It is common at the opening of the verse in Prop. (12) and Ov. (25) and is found occasionally outside elegy in mid-verse (Hor. *Epist.* 1.7.16; Ov. *Met.* 1.678, 9.299, 10.351, 13.585). The imperative form *caueto* is common at the verse end, e.g. Cat. 50.21; Hor. *Serm.* 1.4.85; Virg. *Ecl.* 9.25; Tib. 1.2.89, 6.17; Ov. *Am.* 1.8.95, *Her.* 13.65, *Ars* 1.591, 3.237, 801, *Rem.* 579, 689; *Dirae* 61; Mart. 6.79.1, 10.72.12, 11.102.7.

uiolente: the vocative occurs also at Ov. *Her.* 3.61 (Achilles), *Met.* 9.121(Nessus), *Ibis* 29; Sen. *Medea* 605; Stat. *Theb.* 2.464; *Il. Lat.* 851. The epithet is applied to Mars elsewhere only at Sen. *Troad.* 185 *Marte uiolento furens*. Here again the violence of Mars is invoked (and undermined, see **4n.** below) where it would have been more appropriate to call upon the erotic *uis* of Venus; see Hinds (2006) 31; on the etymological connection *Venus / uis* see Aug. *Ciu.* 6.9; Isid. *Etym.* 8.11.76 and *LALE* 635.

4 Mars should beware of falling in love. Allowing objects to drop from one's hands in amazement at the sight of the beloved is mentioned elsewhere at Prop. 4.4.21-22 (of Tarpeia) *obstipuit regis facie et regalibus armis*; / *interque oblitas excidit urna manus*, 4.8.53 (of Propertius seeing Cynthia) *pocula mi digitos inter cecidere remissos*; Ov. *Her.* 16.253-254 (of Paris) *dum stupeo uisis* (*nam pocula forte tenebam*) / *tortilis a digitis excidit ansa meis*, *Met.* 14.349-350 (of Circe) *quae simul ac iuuenem uirgultis abdita uidit,* / *obstipuit; cecidere manu quas legerat herbae*. As Michalopoulos [(2006) 221] points out on Ov. *Her.* 16.253-254 such passages may originate in the story that Menelaus, on seeing Helen's breast, dropped his sword, while on the point of killing her: Aristoph. *Lys.* 155-156; Eur. *Andr.* 629-631, *Or.* 1287.

turpiter arma cadant: there could be a reminiscence here of the discarded arms of Mars at the time of his intercourse with Ilia, as described in the Sibyl's prophecy at Tib. 2.5.54 *et* (sc. *uideo*) *cupidi ad ripas arma relicta dei*, and cf. Ovid's reaction to the sight of his mistress at *Am.* 2.5.47 *ut faciem uidi, fortes cecidere lacerti*. Also relevant here must be the opening of Ov. *Fast.* 3.1-8 with its theme of the disarming of Mars. Hinds [(2006) 31 and n. 21] acutely points to a sexual double-entendre in *arma* here as either arms or penis, see Adams [(1982) 17, 21, 224] and cf. Ov. *Am.* 1.9.26; Petr. 130.4; Mart. 6.73.6; Maxim. *Eleg.* 5.77f., which serves to belittle Mars's violence. At the generic level, the suggestion is that Mars is more appropriate for epic (*arma*) than for love elegy, so that he should not become so engrossed in Sulpicia that he forgets his true function, cf. **1n**. *Mars magne* above. For the wording cf. Ov. *Ars* 3.80 (*flos*) *turpiter ipse cadet*; Stat. *Theb.* 5.397 *arma aliena cadunt*. For *turpiter* in the same *sedes* cf. also Prop. 4.6.22; Ov. *Her.* 16.174, *Rem.* 314, 780. For its combination with *cado* cf. Ov. *Ars* 3.79-80 (on taking a lover while there is still time): *carpite florem / qui nisi carptus erit, turpiter ipse cadet*. On a possible reference to *ne male inepta cadam* of Sulpicia at **16.2** below, see **16.2n**. *subito ... ne cadam*.

5-6 The idea of Love lighting twin torches from the eyes of a girl occurs only here in ancient poetry. In Greek epigram the related image of lighting a torch from a lover's inner glow is found at *AP* 9.15 (anon.), and cf. from earlier Latin epigram Porcius Licinus fr. 7 (Courtney) *custodes ouium teneraeque propaginis, agnum, / quaeritis ignem? ite huc; quaeritis? ignis homost. / si digito attigero, incendam siluam simul omnem, / omne pecus flammast, omnia quae uideo*. For a lover's eyes compared to fire which enflames the beholder cf. *AP* 5.96 (Meleager) ἰξὸν ἔχεις τὸ φίλημα, τὰ δ' ὄμματα, Τιμάριον, πῦρ· / ἢν ἐσίδῃς, καίεις· ἢν δὲ θίγῃς, δέδεκας ["Timarion, your kiss is bird-lime, your eyes are fire; if you look at me, you burn me; if you touch me, you have me bound"], Ov. *Her.* 20.55-56 (Acontius to Cydippe) *tu facis hoc oculique tui, quibus ignea cedunt / sidera, qui flammae causa fuere meae*. At Prop. 2.3.14 the mistress's eyes are compared to stars and torches: *non oculi, geminae, sidera nostra, faces* and Daphne's eyes are likened to stars by her lover Apollo at Ov. *Met.* 1.498-499 ... *uidet igne micantes / sideribus similes oculos*. The language of the couplet contains a number of stylistically elevated features: *exurere* in the transferred sense of arousing passion [*OLD exuro* 4b and Bréguet (1946) 147], *diuos* for *deos*, *geminas* for *duo* and the loan-word *lampadas*, not found elsewhere in the *Corp. Tib.* or Prop., but occurring 8 times in Ov.; more details in **6n.** below.

5 exurere: in the same *sedes* at Prop. 3.8.7 *tu minitare oculos subiecta exurere flamma*; Virg. *Aen.* 1.39, 9.115; Manil. 4.247; Sil. 15.537. The compound here has the same sense as the simple *urit* at **11** and **12** below.

diuos: enforces the suggestion of Sulpicia as an object of erotic attraction for the god Mars.

6 The line is close in diction to Ovid's description of Ceres lighting pines for torches at *Fast.* 4.493 *illic accendit geminas pro lampade pinus*.

geminas: of eyes at Prop. 2.3.14 quoted in **5-6n.** above. On the use of the adj. *geminus* in the sense of 'two' [Tib. (0), Prop. (5), Ov. (61), **[Tib.]** 3.1-6 (1)] see Bréguet (1946) 181-183.

lampadas: a rare loan-word, occurring in comedy and then restricted mainly to elevated contexts: Plaut. *Cas.* 796, 840, *Men.* 841; Ter. *Ad.* 907; Acc. *Trag.* 331, 670; Lucr. 2.25 and importantly in a context of succession and change at 2.78-79: *inque breui spatio mutantur saecla animantum / et quasi cursores uitai lampada tradunt*; Virg. *Aen.* 3.637, 4.6, 6.587, 7.148, 9.535; Ov. *Her.* 12.138, 14.25, *Rem.* 552, *Fast.* 4.493, 5.160, *Met.* 4.403, 12.247, *Pont.* 3.3.60; Manil. 1.846; Lucan 3.15, 6.135, 10.249; Stat. *Silu.* 5.4.9.

acer Amor: the phrase occurs earlier at Tib. 2.6.15, see Maltby (2002) 471 ad loc. The epithet, applied to Amor also at Prop. 2.30.9; Virg. *Aen.* 12.392; Ov. *Her.* 4.70, *Pont.* 4.7.40, reflects the cruelty of a god who delights in human suffering, see **4.65n.** above and McKeown II 43 on Ov. *Am.* 1.2.17-18 and cf. Theogn. 1231; Call. fr. 79.45 Pf.; Virg. *Ecl.* 8.49-50, 10.29-30; Tib. 1.8.7.

7-14 Whatever she does, she is beautiful. For a variation on the common theme in ancient erotic poetry, especially Ovid, of the multiple attractions of the beloved, see e.g. Ov. *Am.* 2.5.43-44 *spectabat terram – terram spectare decebat, / maesta erat in uultu – maesta decenter erat, Her.* 4.79-84 (Phaedra on Hippolytus), *Met.* 8.25-27 (Scylla on Minos) *seu caput abdiderat cristata casside pennis, / in galea formosus erat; seu sumpserat aere / fulgentem clipeum, clipeum sumpsisse decebat* with Hollis 39 on 24ff.n., and compare the advice given to prospective suitors at *Ars* 2.297-306 *siue erit in Tyriis, Tyrios laudabis amictus; / siue erit in Cois, Coa decere puta. / aurata est: ipso tibi sit pretiosior auro; / gausapa si sumpsit,* *gausapa sumpta proba. / astiterit tunicata, 'moues incendia' clama, / sed timida, caueat frigora, uoce roga. / compositum discrimen erit: discrimina lauda; / torserit igne comam: torte capille, place. / bracchia saltantis, uocem mirare canentis, / et, quod desierit, uerba querentis habe*, cf. also Prop. 2.1.5-16 and *AP* 5.260 (Paulus Silentiarius). The idea that whatever she wears Sulpicia is beautiful is perhaps in dialogue with Tib.'s slightly different argument addressed to Marathus in the eighth poem of his first book that dressing up cannot improve beauty, Tib. 1.8.13-16 *frustra iam uestes, frustra mutantur amictus / ansaque compressos colligat arta pedes. / illa placet, quamuis inculto uenerit ore / nec nitidum tarda compserit arte caput.*

7 quidquid agit: cf. Mart. 1.68.1-2 *quidquid agit Rufus, nihil est nisi Naeuia Rufo. / si gaudet, si flet, si tacet, hanc loquitur.* Cf. in a similar context Prop. 2.1.15-16 *seu quicquid fecit, siue est quodcumque locuta, / maxima de nihilo nascitur historia.* The pronoun is absent from Tib., but is common in Prop. (6) and Ov. (28). The combination with *quoquo*, like the combination of *quodcumque* and *quidquid* in **10.7**, is prosaic. In both cases these prosaic phrases are juxtaposed with more grandiose features, so *uestigia mouit* here and the Greek loan-word *pelagus* at **10.8**.

quoquo: here only in elegy.

uestigia mouit: a high-style phrase, cf. **7.13** *posuit uestigia* and, closer in wording, but in a military context Liv. 44.26.11 *nusquam ... Gallos longius uestigium moturos* as also at Curt. 10.2.13. For *uestigia* in the sense 'feet' [Cat. (1), Tib. (0), Prop. (2), Ov. *Fast.* (1), *Met.* (9)] see Bréguet (1946) 183-184.

8 componit: used elsewhere of female adornment by Ov. at *Am.* 2.17.10 (Corinna looking in the mirror) *nec nisi compositam se prius illa uidet*, and *Met.* 4.317-319 (Salmacis seeing Hermaphroditus) *nec tamen ante adiit ... / quam se composuit, quam circumspexit amictus, / et finxit uultum, et meruit formosa uideri*, see *ThLL* 3.2114.25-48, *OLD compono* 5c. Given the possibility that *Sulpicia* in **1** could have a secondary meaning of a book of poems about Sulpicia (see **1n.** above), it would be impossible to exclude a metapoetic meaning for *illam .../ componit* in the present couplet as 'compose a book about her', cf. *OLD compono* 8 'to compose, write'.

furtim subsequiturque: the adv. is most probably to be taken with *subsequitur*, cf. Ov. *Her.* 20.131 *subsequor ancillam furtim famulumque*;

[Tib.] 3.9.21 (below) *et quaecumque meo furtim subrepit amori.* Surprisingly close to our passage in this and other respects is Quint. 1.11.19 *neque enim gestum oratoris componi ad similitudinem saltationis uolo sed subesse aliquid ex hac exercitatione puerili unde nos non id agentes furtim decor discentibus traditus prosequitur.* The adverb *furtim* is used most commonly in elegy of secret love-making, cf. Tib. 1.2.10 etc., and see Pichon 158. In fact the theme of secrecy/openness pervades the second half of [Tib.] 3: with *furtim* at **8.8**, **9.9**, **9.21**, *furta* at **11.7** (cf. Cat. 68.136), *tectius* **11.17**, *palam* **11.18**, *clamne palamne* **11.20**, *occulte* **12.6**, *texisse* ... / ... *nudasse* **13.1-2**, and *signatus* ... *tabellis* **13.7** and *dissimulare* **18.6**. The theme continues in **19.8** with *in tacito* ... *sinu* and **19.9** with *secretis* ... *siluis*. The verb *subsequi* is rare in Augustan verse: apart from Ov. *Her.* 20.131 only *Her.* 4.40, *Pont.* 2.7.3, *Met.* 3.17; Manil. 1.669 *subsequiturque suo solem uaga Delia curru* and three cases of *subsequiturque* in the same *sedes* as here at Ov. *Am.* 3.13.30, *Fast.* 2.336 and 4.528. For *-que* added to the second element of its clause, a common occurrence in Tibullan and Ovidian pentameters cf. Tib. 1.1.40 *pocula de facili composuitque luto* with Maltby (2002) 136 ad loc. and see Platnauer 91.

decor: recalls *decebat* and *decenter* in Ov. *Am.* 2.5.43-44 (quoted on **7-14n.** above) and looks forward to *decenter* of Vertumnus at **14** below. As at Prop. 1.4.13 *motis decor artubus*, the reference is to 'grace' or 'beauty', cf. Quint. 1.11.19 (quoted above). Here the noun is almost personified as subject of *componit*, acting like a maid or attendant beautifying her mistress (or an elegant poet writing about her); cf. the more daring personification at Stat. *Theb.* 2.287-288 *non Decor Idaliusque puer, sed Luctus et Irae / et Dolor et tota pressit Discordia dextra.*

9-12 seu ... uenit: for the repeated *seu* clauses in this context cf. Ov. *Ars* 2.297-298 and *Met.* 8.25-27 both quoted on **7-14n.** above, Prop. 2.1.5-16 and 3.43-44 quoted below on **11-12n.** McKeown [III 70 on Ov. *Am.* 2.4.11-12] comments on the frequency of this construction in the cataloguing of feminine charms in Ovid (more than 30 examples). Wills [(1996) 412] discusses the symmetry of anaphora within couplets, and changing repeated words between couplets *seu* ... */ seu* ... */ urit* ... */ urit*, which emphasise the binary nature of the elegiac metre. Smith [491 ad loc.] notes the chiastic arrangement of informal (indoor) and formal (outdoor) hair and dress: **9** informal (loose) hair, **10** formal (set) hair, **11** formal (purple) dress, **12** informal (white) dress.

9 soluit crines: not here as a sign of grief, as often elsewhere (see **2.11-12n.** and cf. Prop. 4.6.31), but simply an informal loose hairstyle, as opposed to the formal set style *comptis ... comis* of **10**. For loose *crines* and formal *coma* used in a similar contrast in connection with Apollo's hair cf. Tib. 2.3.25-26 *quisquis inornatumque caput crinesque solutos / aspiceret, Phoebi quaereret ille comam*. On the attractions of different hairstyles see Ov. *Ars* 3.133-168, and for attractive hair colours see Ov. *Am.* 2.4.41-43 and *AP* 5.26.1-3 (anon.). In fact elegy has something of an obsession with the hair of attractive women, cf. Prop. 2.1.7-8; Ov. *Am.* 1.1.20, 1.5.10, 1.14, *Ars* 3.141 and *Trist.* 2.527 (with Ingleheart ad loc.). Contrast, however, Tib. 1.8.9-10 to Marathus *quid tibi nunc molles prodest coluisse capillos / saepeque mutatas disposuisse comas*, cf. **7-14n.** above. On the various synonyms for hair used here *crines, capillis* (**9**), *comis* (**10**), see **2.11-12n.** and Bréguet (1946) 197-207.

fusis ... capillis: cf. Ov. *Met.* 9.90 *fusis utrimque capillis*. For the attraction of loose hair cf. Tib. 1.8.15-16 *illa placet, quamuis inculto uenerit ore / nec nitidum tarda compserit arte caput*; Prop. 2.1.7-8 *seu uidi ad frontem sparsos errare capillos, / gaudet laudatis ire superba comis*; Ov. *Ars* 3.153 *et neglecta decet multas coma*, 783-784 *nec tibi turpe puta crinem ... / soluere, et effusis colla reflecte comis*.

decet: looks back to Sulpicia's *decor* (**8**) and forward to *decenter* of Vertumnus (**14**).

10 compsit, comptis: this resumption of a verb by a participle is a favourite device of Ovid; Wills [(1996) 323-325] quotes over 125 examples. In the *Corp. Tib.* it is found at Tib. 1.4.53-54, 9.28-30, 2.3.14b-c, 6.11; [Tib.] 3. *Lygd.*2.1-4 (cf. **2.3n.** above).

comptis ... comis: cf. Ov. *Am.* 1.1.20 *aut longas compta puella comas* (with McKeown II 23 ad loc.), *Her.* 21.88 *comuntur nostrae matre iubente comae*, *Pont.* 3.3.16 *nec bene dispositas comptus ut ante comas*. In all these cases, as McKeown II 23 suggests, an etymological play may be intended, see *LALE* 144 *coma* and cf. Isid. *Etym.* 10.56 *comptus a coma dictus*. On the equal merits of loose and braided hair cf. Ov. *Ars* 3.141-143 *alterius crines umero iactentur utroque / ... / altera succinctae religetur more Dianae*. For criticism of ornate hairstyles in women cf. Prop. 1.2.1 *quid iuuat ornato procedere, uita, capillo*? As with *Sulpicia est ...culta* in **1**, there may be a suggestion in *comptis ... comis* of literary polish (cf. **1n.** above, **1.10n.** on *pumex et canas tondeat ante comas*, the description of Lygdamus' own work as *comptum ... opus* at **1.14** and *se ... compsit* of

Sulpicia at **12.3** with **n.** ad loc.) On the arrangement of hair and its association with literary merit see further Zetzel (1996) 73-81 and Gibson on Ov. *Ars* 3.133, 135.

ueneranda: the word is found in the same *sedes* at Tib. 1.7.56 (of Messalla's offspring) ... *at circa stet ueneranda senem*. It is rarely used of women, though cf. Plin. *Epist.* 7.19.7 (of Fannia, the formidable sixty-year-old widow of Helvidius Priscus) *minus amabilis quam ueneranda*. Often associated with divinities (e.g. Sen. *Phaed.* 1149 *Pallas Actaeae ueneranda genti*), here it prepares the way for the comparison between Sulpicia and the god Vertumnus in **13-14** below and for the quasi-deification of Sulpicia at **21-24** below. For the deification of the mistress, originating with Catullus in Roman literature, see Lieberg (1962). More specifically, as a possible partner for Mars (see **2n.** and **3n.** above), Sulpicia could here be usurping the divine role of Venus. Hinds [(2006) 12] discusses the possibility of an etymological connection between *ueneror* and Venus here and at Prop. 3.5.1 *pacis Amor deus est; pacem ueneramur amantes* (an etymology favoured by modern philologists but not extant in ancient grammarians). Certainly *uenit* at **12** below makes a clearer link between Sulpicia and Venus (see **2n.** above).

11-12 urit ... / urit: for the common image of love as a fire see **5-6n.** above, Pichon 301, Gow on Theocr. 7.55, Pease on Virg. *Aen.* 4.2 and McKeown II 27 on its programmatic use in Ov. *Am.* 1.1.25-26; for the repeated *urit* cf. Hor. *Carm.* 1.19.5-7 *urit me Glycerae nitor / ... / urit grata proteruitas* (with N-H 240 5n.), and Prop. 2.3.43-44 *siue illam Hesperiis siue illam ostendet Eois, / uret et Eoos, uret et Hesperios*. For repeated *urit seu* in line-initial position as an example of so-called expanded gemination see Wills [(1996) 177 9n.] who quotes examples with other verbs and conjunctions at Virg. *Aen.* 8.628-630; Ov. *Her.* 12.178-179 and Stat. *Silu.* 1.2.85-87. Bréguet [(1946) 151-153] points out that forms of the verb *uro* always occur in emphatic line positions and are always repeated in the *Sulpicia Cycle* either in consecutive verses, as here, or in the same verse, as at **11.5** and **12.17**. Cf. emphatic *ures* at the line-end in **19.19**.

palla / ... ueste: for the modal ablative of clothes worn, see K-S I 1.408 and cf. Cic. *Verr.* 2.5.86 *hoc istum uestitu permulti uiderant*; Tac. *Hist.* 2.4.36 *seruili habitu euadere*.

11 Tyria ... procedere palla: the long *palla* was worn by Roman women when they went out in public, an activity suggested also here by *procedere*, a verb used of women stepping out in their finery, cf. Prop. 1.2.1 (to Cynthia) *quid iuuat ornato procedere, uita, capillo?*; Ov. *Ars* 3.165 *femina procedit densissima crinibus emptis*. But the fact that the *palla* was also worn by gods (e.g. Osiris at Tib. 1.7.46-47 with his *lutea palla* and *Tyriae uestes*), by Apollo in his role as citharoedus (see **4.35n.** above), and by Juno (in **12.13** below), may also suggest Sulpicia's divine (cf. **10n.** above *ueneranda*) and poetic (cf. **1n., 10n., 12n.** and **21-22** below) associations. Here the *palla* was dyed with expensive Tyrian purple, the luxury product mentioned again at **16** below (see **15-16n.** for more details). Ovid mentions clothes dyed in this colour as suitable for a mistress and worthy of praise from her lover at *Ars* 2.297-298 (quoted in **7-14n.** above). A special coloured *palla* of this kind may have been associated with dressing up for the festival of Juno Lucina mentioned in the opening couplet, cf. the girls dressing up for a festival of Juno at Ov. *Am.* 3.13.26 *et tegit auratos palla superba pedes*.

12 niuea candida ueste: for the juxtaposition of the two adjectives cf. Tib. 2.5.38 *et niueae candidus agnus ouis*; Ov. *Fast.* 1.186 *et data sub niueo candida mella cado*.

For *niuea ueste*, cf. Ov. *Met.* 10.432 (of the matrons at the festival of Ceres) *niuea uelatae corpora ueste*. For *candida* denoting the mistress's shining beauty, cf. Prop. 2.1.5 *siue illam Cois fulgentem incedere cogis*. As with *culta* **1** and *comptis* **10** there could also be a literary dimension to the adj. *candidus*, which is used by Cic. at *Orator* 53 of the clear and elegant style of the Atticists *puro quasi et candido genere dicendi* and, more significantly for Sulpicia, by Quintilian of Messalla's style: *Inst.* 10.1.113 *Messalla nitidus et candidus*, cf. Ov. *Pont.* 2.2.49 (addressed to Messalla's son with reference to his father's style) *nunc tibi et eloquii nitor ille domesticus adsit*. For the importance of *candor* and related imagery in Tibullus in connection with Messalla's style see Booth and Maltby (2005). In the present context such imagery would prepare the way for Sulpicia's association with Apollo (whose *candor* is mentioned by our author at **4.29**) and the Muses at the end of the poem **21-24** and the fact that, like Messalla, Sulpicia is worthy to be included in the Muses' choir, see **24n.** below.

uenit: on the way in which this verb links Sulpicia with Venus see **2n.** and **10n.** (on *ueneranda*) above.

13-14 On the central position of the comparison with Vertumnus in this poem, on the role of this couplet as a hinge round which the two parts of the poem **1-12** and **15-24** turn, and on the significance of the god for both the *Sulpicia Cycle* and the *Sulpicia* poems and, indeed, for the **[Tib.] 3** as a whole, see the introduction above. Vertumnus was supposedly an Etruscan god (see Varro *Ling.* 5.46 *deus princeps Etruriae* and Prop. 4.2.3 *Tuscus ego, et Tuscis orior*), who had a temple on the Aventine and a statue in the Vicus Tuscus, where shopkeepers made frequent offerings to him (Prop. 4.2.13ff.). Propertius dedicates a whole poem, 4.2, to his speaking statue and Ovid tells of his love for Pomona (*Met.* 14.622-771). These two main sources both derive his functions from the supposed derivation of his name from the verb *uertere* (his 'turning' into different shapes): Prop. 4.2.21-22 *opportuna mea est cunctis natura figuris: / in quamcumque uoles uerte, decorus ero*; Ov. *Met.* 14.684-685 *adde quod est iuuenis, quod naturale decoris / munus habet formasque apte fingetur in omnes*. The name Vertumnus is actually connected with the Etruscan family name Vertimna, see De Melo (2019) II 689. He is an apt deity for a collection of poems characterised by ever changing authorial voices and perspectives; see further Hardie (1992) 74-75. The fact that Vertumnus is named in line **13** of a 24 line poem here, just as 'Tibullus' is named in line **13** of a **24** line poem in **19** must be significant. As often Vertumnus signals the beginning of a new undertaking. Here he marks the beginning of the *Sulpicia* poems **8-18**. The naming of Tibullus in the same position in **19**, recalls the naming of Vertumnus here and marks a move to closure after the end of the Sulpicia episode.

13 talis: introduces a mythological comparison, a function the word has nowhere else in **[Tib.] 3**, but cf. Tib. 1.5.45-46 *talis ... / uecta est frenato caerula pisce Thetis*; Prop. 1.3.1-8 *qualis ... / ... Cnosia ... / talis ... / Cynthia*; Ov. *Am.* 1.10.5-7 *qualis Amymone ... / ... / talis eras*.

in aeterno ... Olympo: only here is Vertumnus promoted to the status of an Olympian god. For the expression cf. Tib. 1.6.83-84 *hanc Venus ex alto flentem sublimis Olympo / spectat*. The adj. *aeternus* is used with *Olympus* only here, although it is use of the gods in the phrase *aeternos ... deos* at Tib. 2.3.30; Ov. *Rem.* 688, *Fast.* 3.804, 4.954, 6.322, and **10.14** below. In relation to Vertumnus the mention of his presence in eternal Olympus perhaps serves to underline the philosophical point that what is always in movement is eternal, Cic. *Tusc.* 1.53 *quod semper mouetur aeternum est*.

felix Vertumnus: for this epithet denied to Vertumnus cf. Ov. *Met.* 14.641-642 *... sed enim superabat amando / hos* (sc. *Satyros et Panes*) *quoque Vertumnus neque erat felicior illis*.

14 mille ... mille: cf. Ov. *Rem.* 526 *mille mali species, mille salutis erunt,* *Met.* 8.628-629 *mille domos adiere locum requiemque petentes, / mille domos clausere serae.* On the symmetrical structure of the pentameter see McKeown III 101 on Ov. *Am.* 2.5.43-44, where the pentameter *maesta erat in uultu, maesta decenter erat* is close to the present line, and Wills (1996) 414-418.

decenter: occurs in the same *sedes* and in a similar context at Ov. *Am.* 2.5.44 (quoted above). The adverb is linked with Vertumnus also at Prop. 4.2.45-46 (Vertumnus' statue speaking) *nec flos ullus hiat pratis, quin ille decenter / impositus fronti langueat ante meae* and cf. *decorus ero* at Prop. 4.2.22 (quoted above) and *decoris / munus* at Ov. *Met.* 14.684-685 (quoted above). Cairns [(2006) 284 and n. 161] argues that all these instances are derived from Prop. 4.2. In the present context the adverb looks back to Sulpicia's *decor* at **8** above (see **8n.** and cf. **9n.** *decet*) and connects Sulpicia's grace with that of Vertumnus.

15-20 Sulpicia alone is worthy to receive the luxury items from the East mentioned in these three consecutive distichs: purple wool from Tyre (**15-16**), spices from Arabia (**17-18**) and pearls from the Indian Ocean (**19-20**). Such gifts were those to be expected by a traditional elegiac *puella* from her *diues amator*, cf. e.g. Tib. 2.3.53-62 on the gifts demanded by Nemesis and promised her by him. The normal stance of the elegiac lover is to deprecate such greed on the part of the *puella* (e.g. Tib. 2.4.27-30). As Fulkerson [(2017) 233 on **8.17-18**] acutely remarks, the difference in this case is that the narrator not being Sulpicia's lover, will not have to provide the gifts he thinks she deserves. The narrator's position resembles rather that of the traditional *lena*, who encourages her charge to get the best possible bargain from her lover; cf. Tib. 1.5.47-48 and see Myers (1996).

15 sola ... digna est: the adj. *digna* applied to Neaera at *Lygd.* **1.8** as the worthy recipient of Lygdamus' verses provides another link between *Lygd.* **1** and *Sulpicia Cycle* **1** where Sulpicia is said to be the only girl worthy of having luxury gifts bestowed on her and at **24** where Sulpicia is said to be worthy of being sung of by the choir of Apollo and the Muses (also named as Pierides **8.21** as in **1.5**. This adj. applied to Sulpicia in the *Sulpicia Cycle* (**8-12**), has its correspondence in the opening poem in *Sulpicia* poems at **13.10** where she says of her relationship with Cerinthus *cum digno digna fuisse ferar.* Cf. its use in her birthday poem at **12.10** (*non*) *cuiquam dignior illa uiro.* Ultimately the word may have had associations with Gallan elegy, cf. fr. 2.6-7 (Courtney = 145.6-7 Hollis) ... *tandem fecerunt c[ar]mina Musae / quae possem domina deicere digna mea*, see

452   Commentary

1.8n. above. Significantly for Sulpicia's marital status here and of that of Lygdamus and Neaera in **1.8** the adj. is often used in the context of well-suited marriage partners, cf. Virg. *Aen* 7.389-390 (Amata says Bacchus alone is worthy to marry Lavinia) *euhoe Bacche fremens, solum te uirgine dignum / uociferans*; Ov. *Trist.* 2.162 *nisi te, nullo coniuge digna fuit*, *Pont.* 3.1.118 *sola est caelesti digna reperta toro*; [Sen.] *Oct.* 544 (Nero of Poppaea) *dignamque thalamis coniugem inueni meis*; see further **13.10n.** with Hubbard [(2004) 185], who suggests the adj. could have played a part in the Roman marriage ceremony.

15-16 Tyrian purple had already been hinted at in **11** above. The Phoenician city of Tyre exported wool twice dyed (*bis madefacta* **16**) in the purple extracted from the shellfish *murex*, see **3.18n.** above, and cf. Hor. *Epod.* 12.21 with L. C. Watson (2003) 413, *Carm.* 2.16.35-37; Ov. *Ars* 3.170, *Fast.* 2.107 with Robinson (2011) 128 ad loc. For its manufacture see Pease on Virg. *Aen.* 4.262 [Reinhold (1970)] and cf. Plin. *Nat.* 9.124-135. According to Nepos fr. 27.3 (= Plin. *Nat.* 9.137) it was an extremely expensive luxury item: *dibapha Tyria, quae in libras denariis mille non poterat emi.* The echo of Arion's garb at Ov. *Fast.* 2.107 *induerat Tyrio bis tinctam murice pallam*, like *palla* in **11** above, may again hint at Sulpicia's poetic prowess, as well as at the wealth and influence of her family, on which see in the *Sulpicia* group **16.4** below.

mollia ... / uellera: cf. Cat. 64.318-319 *... candentis mollia lanae / uellera*; Tib. 2.1.62 *molle ... uellus*; Stat. *Theb.* 2.681 *mollia ... delambit uellera*.

sucis: for *sucus* 'juice' of dye, cf. Ov. *Met.* 6.222-223 *Tyrio ... rubentia suco / terga* with reference to a purple-dyed covering on a horse's back. At **5.9** the word is used of a poisonous herbal concoction.

bis madefacta: cf. Ov. *Fast.* 2.107 *Tyrio bis tinctam murice pallam* and for *madefacta* cf. Sil. 11.40-41 *madefacta ueneno / Assyrio ... uestis*.

17 possideatque: = *et quae possideat*; for the omission of the second relative Tränkle compares Virg. *Aen.* 9.593-594 *cui Remulo cognomen erat, Turnique minorem / germanam nuper thalamo sociatus habebat* and Tib. 1.8.31-32 *carior est auro iuuenis cui leuia fulgent / ora nec amplexus aspera barba terit.*

17-18 metit ... / ... segetis: Arabia was famous for its export of costly scented spices and incense, cf. Tib. 2.2.3-4 *urantur odores / quos tener e terra diuite mittit Arabs*; Mela 3.79 *Arabia ... cinnami et turis aliorumque* *odorum maxime ferax* and see **2.24n.** above. On the theme of Arab riches in Horace, see Powell (2010) 162-163.

metit: *metere, messis* and *messor* are used of spices and incense at Stat. *Silu.* 3.3.34-35 *tu messes Cilicumque Arabumque superbas / merge rogis* and Plin. *Nat.* 12.54 *cum incidant eas arbores* (sc. *turis*) *aut metant*; Mart. 3.65.5 *messor Arabs* and see Heyworth (2007b) 347 on Prop. 3.13.8. The verb is found only here in the whole *Corpus Tibullianum*. There may be a sound play on *mittit* in this context at Tib. 2.2.3-4 quoted above, cf. **2.23**.

bene olentibus aruis / ... odoratae ... segetis: the pleonasm emphasises the most striking aspect of the scented Arabian exports. For *bene olens* cf. (of flowers) Virg. *Ecl.* 2.48 *bene olentis anethi*; *Copa* 35 *bene olentia serta*, and (of incense) Ov. *Med. Fac. Fem.* 91 *bene olentibus ... myrrhis*. For *odoratus* in this context cf. Prop. 3.13.8 *cinnamon et culti messor odoris Arabs*; Stat. *Silu.* 5.3.43 *odoratas nec Arabs decerpsit aristas*, and for *seges* with reference to these products cf. Sen. *Herc. F.* 909-911 *... quidquid Indorum seges ... / Arabesque odoris quidquid arboribus legunt / conferte in aras*, and Stat. *Silu.* 5.1.212 *Indorum ... seges*.

diues Arabs: also at Sen. *Herc. Oet.* 793 (sc. *quod*) *diues Sabaeis colligit truncis Arabs* and compare the use of *diues Panchaia* and *diues ... Assyria* in combination with the *Eoi ... Arabes* at **2.23-24** above.

19-20 niger ... / ... Indus: also at Mart. 7.30.4 *nauigat a rubris et niger Indus aquis*, 10.17.5 *quicquid Erythraea niger inuenit Indus in alga*; the plural occurs at Ov. *Ars* 1.53 *Andromedan Perseus nigris portarit ab Indis*. Cf. *decolor Indus* at Prop. 4.3.10 (quoted below); Ov. *Ars* 3.130 and *Trist.* 5.3.24. The Indians' dark colour was regularly attributed to their closeness to the sun, see Tib. 2.3.59; Sen. *Medea* 484, *Oed.* 122-123; Plin. *Nat.* 6.70.

Rubro de litore: on the areas covered by this designation, which are wider than the modern Red Sea, see **3.17n.** *Erythraeo ... litore* above. The use of *Ruber* for *Erythraeus* here has suggested to some that the present poem is earlier than that of the *Lygd.* group, but the phrase *in rubro mare* is used in the late first century AD by Tacitus (see discussion on **3.17** *in Erythraeo ... litore* above). For the combination *Rubrum litus* cf. Virg. *Aen.* 8.686 *uictor ab ... litore rubro*.

gemmas: 'pearls' here, rather than 'rubies' (as at Sen. *Thy.* 372); see *ThLL* 6(2).1755.76-80 and cf. Tib. 2.2.15 (quoted below); Prop. 1.14.12 *et legitur Rubris gemma sub aequoribus*; **[Tib.] 3.3.17** *quidue in Erythraeo* *legitur quae litore concha* and Mart. 8.28.14 *cedet Erythraeis eruta gemma uadis*. Plin. *Nat*. 9.106 cites the Indian Ocean and the Arabian Gulf as the best source of pearls.

Eois ... aquis: identical with *Rubro de litore* as is suggested by a comparison with Tib. 2.2.15-16 (to Cornutus) *nec tibi gemmarum quidquid felicibus Indis / nascitur Eoi qua maris unda rubet*. This is a significant intertext for those who associate Sulpicia's Cerinthus with the Cornutus in Tib. 2.2. The phrase occurs in the same *sedes* at Ov. *Fast*. 6.474 *et uigil Eois Lucifer exit aquis*, *Pont*. 2.5.50 *qualis ab Eois Lucifer ortus aquis*; cf. also Prop. 4.3.10 *ustus et Eoa decolor Indus aqua* and Apul. *Flor*. 6.11 *Eois regnator aquis*; see further Bréguet (1946) 217-218.

21-24 That Apollo and the Muses are asked to sing for Sulpicia at the Matronalia hints at her own activities as a poetess. For Apollo and the Muses as protectors of poets see **4.43-44n.** *cura deum* above. The veneration Sulpicia is to receive in their songs suggests she has achieved the divine status already hinted at in *ueneranda* (**10**) and in her comparison with Vertumnus (**13-14**) above. That this gift of song is to be repeated annually (**23-24**) suggests possibly a ceremony to mark the anniversary of her wedding since the Matronalia was originally a feast for married women (see **1.1-4n.** above). Like the gift of poems made on the same occasion to Neaera in **1.15-28**, the reference here could be to the presentation to Sulpicia of the current cycle of poems **[Tib.] 3.8-12**.

21 Pierides: the Muses, see **1.5n.** above. Here they are asked to do what the poet is actually doing, namely to sing of Sulpicia at the Matronalia.

festis ... Kalendis: echoes *tuis ... Kalendis* in **1** above. The phrase *festae ... Kalendae* opens *Lygd*. **1**. This, together with the mention of *Pierides* at **1.5**, suggests an intended correspondence between the two poems.

22 testudinea Phoebe superbe lyra: recalls the vision of Apollo at **4.37-38** above: *fulgens testudine et auro / pendebat laeua garrula parte lyra*. For Apollo's tortoiseshell lyre see **4.37n.** above. For *testudinea ... lyra* in the same *sedes*, again with reference to Apollo, cf. Prop. 4.6.32 *testudineae carmen inerme lyrae*.

Phoebe superbe: refers not to his proud character but to his splendid appearance, cf. **10.2** below: *huc ades, intonsa Phoebe superbe coma*. The similarity between these two lines cannot be fortuitous; Apollo is asked to honour Sulpicia here in his role of god of poetry, whereas at **10.2** he is asked to cure her in his role as god of healing. Bréguet [(1946) 172-177] discusses the use of the adj. *superbus* in elegy and concludes that while all three examples in the *Sulpicia Cycle* (**8.22, 10.2, 11.4**) have positive connotations, Tib. has only the negative sense 'proud' (1.8.77, 9.80, 2.5.46); of 13 occurrences in Prop. only one, 2.1.8 *gaudet laudatis ire superba comis*, is in the positive sense and in Ov. 10 out of 23 examples can be taken as positive. The address to *Phoebe superbe* at the end of the poem balances that to *Mars magne* in the opening line, emphasising the divine favour deserved by Sulpicia.

23 sollemne sacrum: a solemn rite, also at Liv. 21.63.8, 39.18.8; Sen. *Troad.* 778, *Medea* 797-798, *Phaed.* 424, *Quaest. Nat.* 4a.2.7; Suet. *Aug.* 94.4. Here the reference must be to the Matronalia referred to in the opening line.

multos ... in annos: in the same *sedes* at Ov. *Ars* 1.425, *Fast.* 5.33; *Eleg. in Maec.* 1.117; Lucan 1.668. Cf. the address to Messalla's birthday spirit in the last couplet of Tib. 1.7. 63 *at tu, Natalis, multos celebrande per annos*, referring to an annually recurring birthday celebration and see **12.19n.** below.

celebretur: I print a reading found in two later manuscripts, which gives adequate sense. The readings of A+, *hoc* (*haec*) *sumet* (*sumat*), with *sumere* in the sense of *accipere*, cannot be paralleled. Conjectures have been offered (see app. crit.) of which the best is probably Heyne's *celebrate per*. The sense in any case is clear; the sacred celebration of Sulpicia in song (*choro* **24**) by Apollo and the Muses should be repeated annually at the Matronalia for many years to come. It is unknown whether choral singing played any part in this ceremony in real life.

24 dignior: see **15n.** above; here perhaps a reminiscence of Sulpicia's *cum digno digna fuisse ferar* at **13.10** below. Hinds [(1987) 34] sees a deliberate ambiguity in this line, at a surface level 'no girl is worthier to be sung by the choir of the Muses' but also 'no girl is worthier to be included in the choir of the Muses' with the second meaning functioning as an introduction to poem **9** in which Sulpicia is made to speak in her own voice. In *Catalepton* 9.8 Messalla is described as worthy to enter the choir of the Muses *sanctos dignus inire choros*. Cf. Hor. *Carm.* 4.3.13-15 *Romae principis urbium / dignatur suboles inter amabiles / uatum ponere me choros*. All three passages probably go back to the honouring of Gallus by the choir of Phoebus in the song of Silenus at Virg. *Ecl.* 6.66 *utque uiro Phoebi chorus adsurrexerit omnis*. For the Gallan associations of *dignior* see **15n.** above.

Poem 9

I take this elegy to be spoken in the mask of the anonymous poet of **8**, now adopting the voice of Sulpicia on the occasion of Cerinthus' absence at the hunt. There is a good Tibullan precedent for an observer of another's affair to introduce direct speech from one of the partners involved in Tib. 1.8. Here Tibullus, commenting on the affair of Marathus and Pholoe, introduces a direct speech by Marathus at 1.8.55-66. However, Parker (1994) and Fabre-Serris (2009) argue that poems **9** and **11** were actually composed by a 'real' Sulpicia (niece of Messalla Corvinus) herself and Hallet (2002) sees the whole of **8-18** as compositions by this Sulpicia. Fabre-Serris (2009) discusses similarities between this poem, Propertius' proposed hunting trip at Prop. 2.19.17-26 and Ov. *Her.* 4 and finds possible Gallan echoes in all three. She sees both **9** and **11** as Sulpician compositions, which predate Ovid's *Heroides*, while Hinds (1987) argues both are written by the anonymous poet, whom he refers to as the *amicus* (author of **8, 10,** and **12**) and imitate Ovid. Whereas in **8**, according to Hinds, the *amicus* had cast Sulpicia in the role of Venus (see **8.10n.** above), in the present poem Sulpicia is made to continue this pose and, ostensibly speaking in her own voice, casts Cerinthus in the role of Adonis. Dronke (2003) supports the Cerinthus – Adonis parallel, but takes the poem to be a composition of the 'real' Sulpicia. For arguments against Sulpicia being the author of these two poems, based mainly on their length and style in comparison with the *Sulpicia* poems **13-18**, see Hubbard (2004) 189-192. My own view is that there would be nothing to prevent a single author of the whole book from adopting a different style in the poems **8-12** (including those, **9** and **11**, in which he takes on the role of the anonymous observer speaking in Sulpicia's voice) from that adopted in the shorter, more emotionally charged, elegies in which he himself takes on the mask of Sulpicia, **13-18**. All the poems of **[Tib.] 3** are in my view the work of the same unitary author. The difference in style between **9** and **11** and **13-18** may be intended to draw attention to the author's versatility in being able to impersonate the anonymous poet speaking in Sulpicia's voice in **9** and **11** and to speak himself as Sulpicia in **13-18**, see Gen. Intro., sections 2.2.3 and 2.2.4 above.

1-4 The poem opens with a mock epic address in the voice of Sulpicia to a boar, asking it to spare her young man and praying for the god of Love to keep him safe on the hunt.

5-10 She curses woods and hunting dogs and blames Diana, the goddess of hunting, for leading Cerinthus into danger .

Book Three of the Corpus Tibullianum: 457
Introduction, Text, Translation and Commentary

11-18 Yet, despite its dangers, she would accompany him on the hunt, if occasion arose, and would willingly lay with him by the snares.

19-22 As it is, Cerinthus should remain chaste in her absence, and any other girl who approaches him should be torn to shreds by wild beasts.

23-24 The poem ends with an appeal for him to leave hunting to his father and return quickly to her embrace.

Important intertexts are Ov. *Her.* 4 (Phaedra to Hippolytus), Ov.*Met.* 7.796-862 (discussed below), *Met* 10. 503-739 the myth of Venus and Adonis and the *Phaedra* of Euripides and Seneca. There may also be echoes, especially in the last couplet, of Hor. *Carm* 1.23 addressed to the young Chloe suggesting it is time for her to leave her mother for a lover. There are clear signs throughout the poem that Gallus is an important influence, see **nn. 3, 5, 7-10, 8, 12,** and **16**, but the loss of his work makes this difficult to pin down. Gallus' treatment of the hunting theme, as reflected e.g. in Virg. *Ecl.* 10. 55-60 and in the myth of Milanion (which may have played a role in his *Amores*, as reflected in Prop. 1.1.9-16) is clearly in our poet's mind. Whereas in Gallus and elsewhere in elegy (see **7-10n.**) hunting is seen as a cure for, or distraction from, love, in the case of Cerinthus absence at the hunt poses a threat to his relationship with Sulpicia. A key intertext of a different order of importance is the story of Cephalus and Procris at Ov. *Met.* 7.796-862, where hunting proves disastrous to a relationship. This poem, which is echoed also at the beginning and end of the whole collection clearly seems to have exerted an influence not only on the present poem but also on the structure and themes of the whole of **[Tib.] 3**, see Gen. Intro., section 1.3, **1 headnote, 19 headnote, 20 headnote** and below **15n. placeant siluae** and **16n. arguar**. On the topos of love as a form of hunting in elegy see Murgatroyd (1984), Bréguet (1946) 294-304 and, for the theme in general, see Davis (1983). A good account of real-life hunting in the ancient world is to be found in Anderson (1985). Like the treatment of the mistress's disease in poem **10**, so the treatment of hunting here takes literally a theme which elsewhere in elegy is taken metaphorically. An important intertext for this procedure is perhaps Virg. *Ecl.* 10.44-49 where Gallus contrasts his metaphorical *militia amoris* (44-45) with Lycoris' absence with his rival on an actual military campaign, see Harrison (2007) 66-67.

The poem exemplifies the twists and turns inspired by the Vertumnus theme introduced at **8.13-14** (see **n.** ad loc. and the **8 headnote**). In the first half of the poem (**1-10**) Sulpicia rejects hunting and its associated dangers, but, as in **poem 8**, a central couplet (**11-12**) serves to change the poem's direction and Sulpicia is willing to take part in hunting provided she can be with her lover (**11-22** and see **n**. below on *retia torta*). This change of perspective is emphasised by the contrast between *pereant siluae* (**6**) and *placeant siluae* (**15**). There is also a change of focus on the boar who in **4** is asked to leave her lover unharmed (*incolumem*), but who himself in **17** will go away unharmed *inlaesus abibit* and on the role of Delia (Diana) who in **5** leads her lover away to the hunt, but in **19** provides him with an exemplum of chastity while he is there. In the opening couplet an apparent prayer introduced by the traditional *seu ... seu* turns out to be an address to a boar, and the apparent *locus amoenus* setting of **1-2** with its *bona pascua* and *colis umbrosi deuia*, the traditional setting for the appearance of a god, emerges instead as the haunt of a dangerous hunting opponent.

1-2 The opening couplet, with its imperative *parce* and mention of favourite haunts *seu ... bona pascua ... / seu colis ... deuia montis*, seems to herald a hymnic address (as with the openings of **8** and **10**), possibly to Apollo or Diana, until the idea is deflated by the final word *aper* in **2**, see Hinds (1987a) 34. For *parce* as a ritual word in prayers see Hor. *Carm.* 2.19.7-8 *parce, Liber / parce* with N-H ad loc. and cf. **5.6** and **21**.

Parce meo ... seu quis ... / seu colis: for the syntactical and metrical structure cf. Tib. 1.2.17-18 *illa fauet seu quis ... / seu*, 10.21-22 *hic placatus erat seu quis ... / seu*. The use of the imperative with *si quis* and a second person verb, as here, is a characteristic of Ovidian syntax, avoided by the other elegists, cf. Ov. *Am.* 1.7.1-2 *adde manus in uincla ... / ... si quis amicus ades*, *Rem.* 613 *si quis amas, nec uis, facito contagia uites*, *Fast.* 1.631 *si quis amas ueteres usus, adsiste precanti*, *Trist.* 1.7.1 *si quis habes nostri similes ... uultus, / deme ... hederas*. An earlier example occurs in a prayer at Hor. *Carm.* 3.27.50-51 *... o deorum / siquis haec audis*. For repeated *seu / siue* in prayers listing all the possible names, locations and powers of the deity addressed, see Robinson [(2011) 414] on Ov. *Fast.* 2.641-644 (address to Terminus) who provides further examples.

1 Parce meo iuueni: the opening of the hexameter recalls Venus' words to Adonis in similar circumstances at Ov. *Met.* 10.545 *parce meo, iuuenis, temerarius esse periclo* and continues the link between Sulpicia and Venus established in poem **8** above; see Dronke (2003). The relevance of this myth becomes more apparent in **11-18** where Sulpicia expresses the wish to take part in the hunt to be with her lover, Cerinthus. The fact that in the case of Adonis the boar did not spare his victim heightens the tension at the start of our poem. Fabre-Serris [(2009) 162] sees in *parce* here a connection with Phaedra's letter to Hipppolytus Ov. *Her.* 4, which ends with a series of prayers to Hippolytus containing various forms of the verb *parcere* at 162 *et mihi si non uis parcere, parce meis* and 167 *per Venerem, parcas, oro*, and in which Phaedra asks Amor to spare her lover 148 *qui mihi nunc saeuit, sic tibi parcat Amor*. In the same poem Phaedra names the wild boar as one of the dangers of hunting that will not prevent her from joining her lover Ov. *Her.* 4.103-104 *ipsa comes ueniam, nec me latebrosa mouebunt / saxa neque obliquo dente timendus aper*. For hunting as an entertainment restricted to the upper classes of Roman society see Hor. *Epist.* 1.18.40ff., Lyne [(2007) 346] and cf. Griffin [(1985) 7] on this type of hunting as a Hellenistic importation; for its popularity with city-dwellers, see Men. *Dysc.* 41-42; Virg. *Ecl.* 2.29, 10.55-57 (Gallus plans a boar hunt, see **5n.** below), Hor. *Epod.* 2.29-36.

bona pascua: *bonitas* seems common in agricultural contexts of good quality land (*OLD bonitas* 2a), e.g. Lucr. 5.1247 *inducti terrae bonitate*; Caes. *BG* 1.28.4 *propter bonitatem agrorum*. For the adj. applied to land cf. Varro *Rust.* 1.7.10 *bonis pratis*, 1.9.1 *terra ... bona aut non bona*. The noun *pascuum* is rare in elegy (Prop. 4.9.20; Ov. *Fast.* 1.244, 4.476); used of the Sun's pastures at Ov. *Met.* 4.214 and **[Tib.] 3.7.76**, it is otherwise mainly prosaic.

pascua campi: not attested elsewhere, but cf. the frequent *aequora campi* in Enn., e.g. *Ann.* 124 Sk. and *campi per ... prata* at Enn. *Ann.* 537 Sk.

2 colis umbrosi deuia montis: cf. Prop. 2.19.2 *laetor quod sine me deuia rura coles*.

Propertius there expresses himself as happy that Cynthia will be in the country, since he sees the urban setting as the main focus for erotic intrigue; in the country she will be safe from the attentions of his rivals: Prop. 2.19.3 *nullus erit castis iuuenis corruptor in agris*. By contrast in **19-22** below Sulpicia expresses her fear of rivals even in the country setting. The verb *colis* preserves the ambiguity about the addressee, since it applies not only to animals and their haunts (*OLD* 1) but also to gods and their habitations (*OLD* 2), an observation I owe to A. J. Woodman. For the phrase *umbrosi ... montis* cf. Apul. *Met.* 4.6 *mons horridus siluestribus frondibus umbrosus*; Plin. *Nat.* 12.47 *in montibus umbrosis ... florens*; *Il. Lat.* 654 *umbrosisque simul consedit montibus Idae*. For *deuia* + gen. *montis* on the model of such phrases as Enn. *Ann.* 264 Sk. *caeli uasta,* cf. Lucan 4.161 *terrarum in deuia*, 8.209 *in deuia mundi*; Stat.

Theb. 5.248-249 ... *deuia uastae / urbis*, 6.454 *deuia campi* (9.877). For *deuia* in a hunting context, cf. Ov. *Met.* 3.146 (of Actaeon's hunting companions – a dangerous precedent) *per deuia lustra uagantes*. For the *locus deuius* as a suitable place for the appearance of a god, see Michalopoulos [(2006) 137] on Ov. *Her.* 16.53-54 *est locus ... / deuius*, on the location of Mercury's appearance there to Paris. Here the last word *aper* undermines these expectations of a divine addressee. For thickly wooded country as the typical haunt of the wild boar cf. Xen. *Cyneg.* 10.6; Ov. *Met.* 8.334-338. There may be an echo here of Chloe like a fawn following her fearful mother through the *montibus auiis* in Hor. *Carm.* 1.23.2.

montis aper: cf. Virg. *Ecl.* 5.76 *dum iuga montis aper ... amabit*.

3 nec tibi sit duros acuisse ... dentes: the line-opening echoes Prop. 1.20.13-14 *ne tibi sit duros montes et frigida saxa / ... semper adire lacus* (addressed to the poet Gallus), in a warning that he should not lose his boyfriend to the wood nymphs. For the elegiac association of *durus*, implying the rejection of love and elegiac values, see **2.3n.** above. Here Cerinthus' boar hunting could prove an obstacle to his love for Sulpicia, hence Sulpicia's appeal to Amor (**4**) to keep him safe. For the construction, perhaps characteristic of Gallus, *nec* + *sit* + dat. pronoun + inf. of an action it should not be one's part to take on cf. Prop. 1.20.13-14 above and Virg. *Ecl.* 10.46 *nec sit mihi credere tantum*; again the context of the *Eclogue* is Gallan. Gallus' military service (like Cerinthus' hunting) keeps him from his mistress, and he does not wish to believe that she has travelled to the Alps with a rival (*Ecl.* 10.46-48 quoted below on *duros acuisse ... dentes*). In the same *Eclogue* Gallus plans a boar hunt (10.55-57) to distract himself from the loss of his mistress, cf. **1n.** above and **7-10n.** below. The same construction, with dative pronoun + *sit* + inf., is found at Tib. 1.6.24 *tunc mihi non oculis sit timuisse meis*; cf. the further examples quoted in Fedeli (1980) 466 on Prop. 1.20.13 and (1985) 147 on Prop. 3.3.41-42.

duros acuisse ... dentes: for boars sharpening their tusks on rocks and trees see Hom. *Il.* 11.416, 13.474-475; Plin. *Nat.* 18.2. For the use of *acuo / exacuo* in this context cf. Virg. *Georg.* 3.255 *ipse ruit dentesque Sabellicus exacuit sus*; Sen. *Phaed.* 346-347 *tunc uulnificos acuit dentes / aper, Dial.* 3.1.6 *spumant apris ora, dentes acuuntur adtritu*. The wild-boar was a dangerous animal, see Sen. *Phaedra* 29-30 (Hippolytus) *hic uersatur, metus agricolis / uulnere multo iam notus aper*. For the combination *duros ... dentes* cf. Lucr. 5.1064 (of Molossian hounds) *ricta* *fremunt duros nudantia dentes*; Virg. *Georg.* 2.378-379 ... *durique uenenum / dentis.* For the elegiac associations of *durus* see above. Of particular significance in the present context is Gallus' use of *dura* of Lycoris, who abandons Gallus to travel abroad, just as Cerinthus here could be seen as abandoning Sulpicia in favour of the hunt. The passage is worth quoting in full, as it has a number of correspondences with the present poem: *Ecl.* 10.46-48 *tu procul a patria – nec sit mihi credere tantum / Alpinas, a dura, niues et frigora Rheni / me sine sola uides.* On *procul* in this *sedes* see **5n.**, and on *nec ... tantum* see **2.3n.** above.

4 incolumem custos ... seruet: cf. Hor. *Serm.* 1.4.118-119 *dum custodis eges, uitam famamque tueri / incolumem possum.*

custos ... Amor: normally the role of the *custos* is to prevent access to the mistress (cf. **12.11-12** with **n.** ad loc. where the role of Love is to find a way round such obstructions). When Love himself is the mistress' guardian this usually bodes ill for the potential lover: cf. Tib. 1.6.51-52 *parcite, quam custodit Amor, uiolare puellam, / ne pigeat magno post tetigisse malo* and Prop. 2.30.7-9 *semper Amor supra caput ... instat ... / ... / excubat ille acer custos*. Here Sulpicia may be thinking of Love's role as keeping Cerinthus safe not only from wild animals but also from the approaches of other *puellae* cf. **21-22** below.

mihi seruet Amor: the line-end echoes Tib. 1.6.76 *mutuus absenti te mihi seruet amor.*

5 sed procul: for the line-opening see **6.25n.** above.

procul abducit: for the theme of hunting keeping a lover apart from his mistress cf. Hor. *Carm.* 1.1.25-26 *manet sub Ioue frigido / uenator tenerae coniugis immemor.* For *procul* in this *sedes* and its Gallan associations at Virg. *Ecl.* 10.46 see **3n.** above on *duros acuisse ... dentes.* The use of *abducit* here must bring to mind *abducta* of Sulpicia, taken off to the country by Messalla at **14.7**. There she is to be taken off against her will, but here Cerinthus is willingly abducted; see Batstone (2018) 104-105. This is a good illustration of the way similar themes are treated in contrasting manners with regard to Cerinthus and Sulpicia in the two groups of **8-12** and **13-18**.

uenandi ... cura: here *cura* is instrumental ablative with *uenandi* 'with zeal for hunting'. For the use of *cura* + gen. expressing 'eagerness', 'passion', 'zeal' for a thing or activity see *OLD cura* 6. The noun perhaps suggests the elegiac use of *cura* as 'the object of love' i.e. the mistress (e.g. Apollo to Gallus at Virg. *Ecl.* 10.22 *tua cura Lycoris*), which should be Cerinthus' real concern. It is possible that the use of *cura* in this sense was characteristic of Gallus, thus deepening the Gallan associations of the poem, on which see **3n.** above. The phrase *uenandi cura* (nom.) occurs also at Manil. 5.204 *et quaecumque solet uenandi poscere cura*. Other genitive gerunds are found in the *Sulpicia Cycle* at **23** below *uenandi*, **12.5** *ornandi*, and **12** *fallendi*; for their distribution in the other elegists see Bréguet (1946) 144-145.

Delia: i.e. Diana, goddess of hunting. Neither Tib. (for obvious reasons) nor Prop. use this epithet for Diana, but it occurs first in Virg. *Ecl.* 7.29, where she is offered a wild boar as a sacrifice (in *Ecl.* 3.67 Delia is probably just a girl's name, like Tib.'s Delia). It goes on to be used in Hor. at *Carm.* 4.6.33 and Ov. at *Her.* 4.40, 20.95, *Fast.* 5.537 and *Met.* 5.639. The title serves to connect Diana with her brother Apollo, both born in Delos. The cult title *Δήλιος* is used in Greek of Apollo (e.g. Call. *Hymn* 4.269), but *Δηλία* is never used of Artemis; see further Clausen (1994) 223 on *Ecl.* 7.29 and Cucchiarelli (2012) 389 ad loc. The context of the *Her.* 4 passage (Phaedra to Hippolytus) is similar to that of the present poem in that Phaedra is willing to devote herself to the goddess of hunting in order to be with Hippolytus: 4.39-42 *iam mihi prima dea est arcu praesignis adunco / Delia; iudicium subsequor ipsa tuum. / in nemus ire libet pressisque in retia ceruis / hortari celeris per iuga summa canes*; see further Bréguet (1946) 236-238, Fabre-Serris (2009) 158. The name must, of course, bring to mind Tibullus' Delia, with whom that poet wishes to live in a rustic idyll (e.g. Tib. 1.2.73, 1.5.21); by contrast here the town is the location for love and the country divides the lovers.

6 o pereant siluae: a common curse formula, usually at the opening of the verse; for a list of examples see **4.61-62n.** *a pereat* above. Contrast *tunc placeant siluae* at **15** below and on this change of focus see the **headnote** above. Again there may be an echo of Chloe's *uano / ... siluae metu* in Hor. *Carm.* 1.23.3-4. At **19.9** below the secluded woods provide an idealised setting for the poet's love, away from the envy of the urban mob.

deficiantque canes: for *deficio* as a synonym for *pereo*, see *OLD deficio* 6 and cf. Ov. *Pont.* 2.7.80 *uiuere ne nolim deficiamque cauet*; Sil. 14.495 of the death of birds in a plague and Plin. *Nat.* 10.37, also of races of birds becoming extinct. The form *deficiantque* is found in the same *sedes* at Tib. 2.5.86 *deficiantque lacus*; cf. also Tib. 1.4.82 *deficiunt artes, deficiuntque doli*, **[Tib.] 3.19.14** *mittetur frustra deficietque Venus*.

canes: for the use of dogs to hunt boar see Xen. *Cyneg.* 10.6; Gratt. *Cyneg.* 150-153.

7-10 For the lover facing the dangers of the hunt cf. also Prop. 1.1.12 (of Milanion's courtship of the huntress Atalanta) *ibat et hirsutas ille ferire feras* with Fedeli [(1980) 72 ad loc.], who argues for a common Alexandrian source. At Virg. *Ecl.* 10.55-60 Gallus will range over Maenalus in pursuit of fierce boars in the hope of assuaging his love for Lycoris (see **3n.** above), while Propertius at 2.19.17-26 will devote himself to hunting during Cynthia's absence from Rome. Similarly hunting is recommended as a cure for love in Ov. *Rem.* 199-206. Here hunting is seen by Sulpicia simply as a potentially dangerous interlude in her affair with Cerinthus. For the dangers posed by hunting to a married relationship the story of Cephalus and Procris at Ov. *Met.* 7.804-830 was probably in our author's mind here, see Gen. Intro., section 1.3 and **headnote** above.

7 quis furor est, quae mens: for the line-opening cf. Tib. 1.10.33 *quis furor est atram bellis arcessere mortem*?; Ov. *Ars* 3.172 *quis furor est census corpore ferre suos*? and, especially, *Am.* 3.14.7 *quis furor est quae nocte latent in luce fateri*. For the sentiment in connection with hunting cf. Phaedra's soliloquy at Sen. *Phaed.* 112 *quid furens saltus amas*? The phrase *quis furor* occurs frequently elsewhere at the beginning of the line, e.g. Ov. *Met.* 3.531; Petr. 108.14.1; Val. Fl. 7.36; Sil. 15.33; Stat. *Theb.* 2.213, 11.329. Normally in elegy *furor* refers to the madness of love, see Pichon 157-158, Prop. 1.1.7, 1.4.11, 1.5.3 and cf. Virg. *Ecl.* 10.60 where Gallus attempts hunting as a cure for the *furor* of his love (cf. *Ecl.* 10.22 *Galle, quid insanis*?, 10.44-45 *insanus amor ... me ... / ... detinet*). In view of Sulpicia's warning at **19-22** for him to remain chaste during the hunt, a reference to such love-madness cannot be excluded here. For *mens* as a furious mood, equivalent to anger, cf. Hor. *Carm.* 1.16.22 *compesce mentem* (with N-H 213 ad loc.), *Epist.* 1.2.59-60 *... qui non moderabitur irae / infectum uolet esse dolor quod suaserit et mens*. At Cat. 15.14 *mala mens furorque uecors* the idea is emphasised by the epithet *mala*; cf. Virg. *Aen.* 2.519 (Hecuba to Priam) *quae mens tam dira*?

densos ... colles: i.e. hills thickly planted with trees. For *densus* in this context cf. Sen. *Phaed.* 506 *nemoris alti densa ... loca*, *Thy.* 413 *saltus ... densos*. In view of *teneras ... manus* (see **8n.** below) and the contrast between *duro ... fune* and *teneras ... manus* quoted there in Prop. 3.7.48, it seems possible that *densos* here could be used metapoetically of 'epic/tragic' boar hunting being unsuitable for the 'elegiac' (*teneras*) hands of Cerinthus. On metapoetic *tener* referring to elegy and love poetry see Ingleheart (2010) 294 on Ov. *Trist.* 2.361-362 and on metapoetic *densus* referring to epic/tragedy (as an antonym of *tenuis*), see Robinson (2011) 202 on Ov. *Fast.* 2.253 and cf. the mention of Tragedy's *densum caesarie ... caput* in Ov. *Am.* 3.1.32.

7-8 indagine ... / claudentem: For the practice of closing off quarry by means of a circle (*indagine*) of nets cf. Xen. *Cyneg.* 10.7; Virg. *Aen.* 4.121 *saltusque indagine cingunt*; Ov. *Met.* 7.766 (Cephalus) *latos indagine cinximus agros*; Lucan 6.42 *et siluas uastaque feras indagine cingunt*; Stat. *Theb.* 2.553-554 *ut clausas indagine profert / in medium uox prima feras* and see Bréguet (1946) 166-167. Hubbard [(2004) 192] compares Tib. 1.4.49 *uelit insidiis altas si claudere ualles*.

8 teneras laedere ... manus: cf. Tib. 2.3.10 *laederet et teneras pussula rupta manus*; Prop. 3.3.34 *exercent teneras in sua dona manus*, 7.48 *et duro teneras laedere fune manus*; Ov. *Fast.* 4.774 *mollis et ad teneras quamlibet apta manus*, and **12.2** below. The adj. could suggest that Cerinthus, like his namesake at Hor. *Serm.* 1.2.81 is a *puer delicatus*. On the frequency of this adj. in elegy see Bréguet [(1946) 158-161] and cf. especially (see **9-10n.** below) Virg. *Ecl.* 10.49 (Gallus to Lycoris) *a tibi ne teneras glacies secet aspera plantas*. Hubbard [(2004) 192] compares, in a similar hunting context, Tib. 1.4.48 *insuetas atteruisse manus* in a didactic poem on attracting young boys. On the possible metapoetic significance of *tener* in all these passages (= 'suitable for elegy') and its probable contrast with *densos* (= 'suitable for epic') in **7** see **n.** above.

9-10 The couplet contains no less than three reminiscences from the beginning of Ovid's *Metamorphoses*, suggesting that Ovid's work served as the model for the author here: for *iuuat ... latebras intrare ferarum* **9**, cf. *Met.* 1.475-476 (of Daphne fleeing Apollo) *siluarum latebris captiuarumque ferarum / exuuiis gaudens*; the hexameter ending *latebras intrare ferarum* **9** = *Met.* 1.593 (Jupiter to Io) *quod si sola times latebras intrare ferarum*; for *hamatis crura notare rubis* **10**, cf. *Met.* 1.508-509 (Apollo to Daphne) *ne ... / crura notent sentes*.

quidue iuuat: cf. **3.17-18** and **5.19**. Fabre-Serris [(2009) 158-159] compares Prop. 2.19.17-18 (Propertius will go hunting) *ipse ego uenabor: iam nunc me sacra Dianae / suscipere et Veneri ponere uota iuuat*, and Phaedra to Hippolytus at Ov. *Her.* 4.87-88 *quid iuuat incinctae studia exercere Dianae / et Veneri numeros eripuisse suos*?, and argues for a Gallan model behind those two passages and the present couplet.

furtim: the adv. is normally used in elegy of secret erotic activity (see **8.8.n.**), as at **21** below, and cf. Tib. 1.2.10, 1.5.65 etc. Tib. combines it with a hunting metaphor at 1.6.5-6 *nam mihi tenduntur cases; iam Delia furtim / nescioquem tacita callida nocte fauet*. As is made obvious there from the juxtaposition of *Delia* and *furtim*, so here too with *Delia* in **5** and *furtim* in **9** there may be a play *e contrario* on ideas of openness and secrecy implicit in their meanings ('Delia' in Greek implying 'bright', 'open'), a theme which runs through poems **8-18**, see **8.8.n**. Again there is a change of focus between the two halves of the poem, with *furtim* here used of Cerinthus' stealthy approach to his prey and in **21** of the imagined stealthy approach of a girl to Cerinthus.

latebras ... ferarum: in addition to Ov. *Met.* 1.475 and 1.593 (quoted above) cf. Lucr. 6.766 *ducere de latebris serpentia saecla ferarum*; Lucan 2.153 *nec populum latebrae cepere ferarum*. Given the context of Ov. *Met.* 1.593 (in which Jupiter is about to rape Io) there may be a suggestion here of erotic danger for Cerinthus, see **20** below.

10 candida ... crura: the adj. emphasises Cerinthus' tender youth, as with *candida ... colla* of Bacchus at Prop. 3.17.29; elsewhere in elegy it is normally applied to the neck and arms of the mistress, e.g. Prop. 2.9.10 *candida ... ora*, 2.16B.24 *candida ... bracchia*; Ov. *Am.* 1.5.10 *candida ... colla*, *Ars* 2.457 *candida ... colla*. For the implied white/ red colour contrast in *candida ... rubis* see **4.34n.** and cf. *seu uirides rubrum / dimouere lacertae*, where the green lizards on the red brambles pose another source of fear for the timid fawn in Hor. *Carm.* 1.23.6-7.

hamatis crura notare rubis: cf. Prop. 4.4.28 (of Tarpeia) *rettulit hirsutis bracchia secta rubis*; Ov. *Met.* 1.509 *crura notent sentes*; Sen. *Phaed.* 1103 *acutis asperi uepres rubis*. For *hamatus* in this context cf. Ov. *Met.* 2.799 *tangit et hamatis praecordia sentibus implet*. Bréguet [(1946) 185] compares the simile at Colum. *Rust.* 7.3.10 *rubis quibus uelut hamis inuncata lana pascentium tergoribus auellitur*.

11-18 The inspiration for this central section in which Sulpicia expresses the wish to accompany Cerinthus on the hunt seems to come from Phaedra's letter to Hippolytus at Ov. *Her.* 4.41-44 *in nemus ire libet pressisque in retia ceruis / hortari celeris per iuga summa canes / aut tremulum excusso iaculum uibrare lacerto / aut in graminea ponere corpus humo*. The theme goes back to Phaedra's speech at Eur. *Hipp.* 215-222 πέμπετέ μ' εἰς ὄρος· εἶμι πρὸς ὕλαν / καὶ παρὰ πεύκας, ἵνα θηροφόνοι / στείβουσι κύνες / βαλιαῖς ἐλάφοις ἐγχριμπτόμεναι. / πρὸς θεῶν, ἔραμαι κυσὶ θωύξαι / καὶ παρὰ χαίταν ξανθὰν ῥῖψαι / Θεσσαλὸν ὅρπακ', ἐπίλογχον ἔχουσ' / ἐν χειρὶ βέλος ["send me to the mountain; I am going to the wood, to the pine wood, where hounds that kill beasts tread, pursuing close the dappled deer. By the gods how I would love to shout at the hounds and to throw a Thessalian javelin past my golden hair, holding a barbed weapon in my hand"], and occurs again in Latin in Phaedra's soliloquy at Sen. *Phaed.* 112-114 *quo tendis, anime? quid furens saltus amas? / fatale miserae matris agnosco malum; / peccare noster nouit in siluis amor.* Also at play is the myth of Venus following her lover Adonis on the hunt at Ov. *Met.* 10.533-541 which was alluded to in the opening couplet.

11 sed tamen: i.e. despite the discomforts of the hunt mentioned in **7-10**. The strong adversative introduces the change of focus in the second half of the poem, mentioned in the **headnote** above from the rejection of hunting in **1-10** to a willingness to take part in it for the sake of love in **11-20**.

ut tecum liceat: For *ut* + subjunctive here introducing a limiting clause with the meaning 'on the understanding that', 'with the proviso that' see *OLD ut* 31. For the sentiment and expression, cf. Sil. 6.501-503 *hoc unum, coniunx ... / ... oro liceat tecum quoscumque ferentem / terrarum pelagique pati caelique labores.*

Cerinthe: named first here. On the significance of the name see Gen. Intro., section 3.4. The name, like that of Vertumnus in **8.13**, opens the central couplet of the poem.

uagari: the word occurs at the line-end also in Lucr. 4.53, 127, 129, 724; Lucan 8.182, 10.300; Sil. 7.369; Stat. *Ach.* 1.358. In a hunting context it is used of Venus following Adonis at Ov. *Met.* 10.535 *per iuga, per siluas, dumosaque saxa uagatur* (an important intertext for the present poem, see **headnote** and **1n.** above). Here Sulpicia's willingness to roam the hills with Cerinthus illustrates the change of heart that she undergoes in this central couplet of the poem.

12-14 The hunting activities Sulpicia is presented as willing to take part in echo those described by Ovid in his narrative of the Calydonian boar hunt at *Met.* 8.331-333 *... pars retia tendunt, / uincula pars adimunt canibus, pars pressa sequuntur / signa pedum.*

12-13 ipsa ego ... / ipsa ego: also found at the line-opening in Virg. *Georg.* 4.401; Ov. *Her.* 8.79, 12.97; Val. Fl. 4.363; Stat. *Theb.* 5.623. In the same context Propertius discloses his own intention to hunt at 2.19.17

with the words *ipse ego uenabor*, cf. Phaedra at Ov. *Her.* 4.40 *Delia, iudicium subsequor ipsa tuum*.

12 per montes: cf. Phaedra in pursuit of Hippolytus at Sen. *Phaed.* 235 *sequi per alta nemora, per montes placet* and Apollo in pursuit of Hyacinthus at Ov. *Met.* 10.172-173 (quoted below).

retia torta: cf. Calp. *Ecl.* 7.53-54 *auro quoque torta refulgent / retia*. The verb is used frequently of cables (e.g. Ov. *Met.* 15.696 *torta coronatae soluunt retinacula nauis*) ropes and woollen threads (e.g. *stamina torta* Tib. 1.6.78), though here it may refer to the 'rolling up' of the nets to make them easier to carry. With personal objects it is most commonly used in elegy of the torture experienced by the lover, e.g. Tib. 2.6.17-18 *tu miserum torques, tu me mihi dira precari / cogis* of Love torturing Tib., cf. **10.11** and **20.4** below. Here in the central couplet of the elegy it could also be taken as nom. fem. sing. with the subject (Sulpicia) = 'changed' describing her change of heart in regard to hunting, as discussed in the **headnote** above. For one word to have two possible meanings in the same sentence ('double entendre') is of course common in Latin poetry (e.g. *arma* in *Sulpicia Cycle* **8.4** with **n.** above) as elsewhere, and for the use of this verb of changing character or outlook cf. Cic. *Cael.* 6.13 *uersare suam naturam et regere ad tempus atque huc et illuc torquere et flectere*. The same double meaning may also be operative in **10.11** and **20.4** below, see **nn.** ad loc. Our author uses three words for 'nets' in this poem with no particular technical distinction: *retia* here and **20**, *plaga* **16** and *casses* **17**.

retia ... feram: the carrying of hunting nets, a task usually performed by slaves, becomes a standard example of *obsequium amoris*, going back to the myth of Milanion, who won over the huntress Atalanta by carrying her nets, cf. Ov. *Ars* 2.189 *saepe tulit iusso fallacia retia collo*. Fabre-Serris [(2009) 158], following Ross [(1975) 61-65], argues that the Milanion *exemplum* in Latin poetry, as attested e.g. in Prop. 1.1.9-16, goes back to Gallus. For the same idea cf. Virg. *Ecl.* 3.75 *dum tu sectaris apros, ego retia seruo*; Tib. 1.4.49-50 (as a way of winning over boys, especially relevant if we are to see Cerinthus as a *puer delicatus*) *nec, uelit insidiis altas si claudere ualles, / dum placeas, umeri retia ferre negent*; Ov. *Her.* 4.41-42 (Phaedra to Hippolytus) *in nemus ire libet, pressisque in retia ceruis / hortari celeris per iuga summa canes*, *Met.* 10.171-173 (Apollo wooing Hyacinthus) *immemor ipse sui non retia ferre recusat, / non tenuisse canes, non per iuga montis iniqui / ire comes*. On the use of nets in hunting, see Xen. *Cyneg.* 2.4-9; Gratt. *Cyneg.* 25-33. On metaphorical uses of *retia* in elegy see Pichon 253.

13 uelocis ... cerui: for the epithet cf. Virg. *Aen.* 5.253 *uelocis iaculo ceruos ... fatigat* and *celeris uestigia ceruae* at Cat. 64.341.

quaeram uestigia: for tracking as an essential part of the hunt cf. Lucr. 4.705 *canes ... uestigia quaerunt*; Ov. *Met.* 8.332-333 (quoted in **12-14n.** above); [Ov.] *Hal.* 78 (sc. *canes*) *demisso quaerunt uestigia rostro*. For the phrase *uestigia quaeram* cf. Stat. *Theb.* 11.689 *inmitis domini uestigia quaeram*.

uestigia cerui: Like Venus in her pursuit of Adonis at Ov. *Met.* 10. 537-539 *tutaeque animalia praedae, / aut pronos lepores aut celsum in cornua ceruum / aut agitat dammas; a fortibus abstinet apris*, Sulpicia chooses to hunt deer rather than the dangerous boar. For the verse-ending cf. *uestigia ceruae* at Cat. 64.341; Ov. *Trist.* 5.9.27; Stat. *Silu.* 2.3.22.

14 demam celeri ... uincla cani: cf. Ov. *Met.* 8.332 *uincula pars adimunt canibus*. For the phrase *demere uincla* cf. Liv. 9.11.13 *i, lictor, deme uincula Romanis*; Ov. *Met.* 3.168 *uincla ... pedibus demunt*. It may be significant that the phrase *mea uincla leua* occurs in the same line (**14**) of poem **11**, where Sulpicia asks Venus to lighten her bonds of love if Cerinthus does not reciprocate her feelings.

celeri ... cani: cf. Phaedra's mention of *celeris ... canes* at Ov. *Her.* 4.42 (quoted in **11-18n.** and **12n.** above); here the collective singular is used.

ferrea: like *durus* (see **3n.** above) the adj. can be used of those who reject elegiac values, see **2.1-2n.** above and Pichon 146.

15-17 tunc mihi, tunc ... / ... / tunc: gemination of *tunc* is rare, see Wills (1996) 109 and cf. Pers. 1.11-12 *tunc tunc – ignoscite ... / ... cachinno*; Stat. *Ach.* 1.835 *tum uero, tum praecipue manifestus Achilles*.

15 tunc ... si: for *tum / tunc* as a correlative to a conditional *si* clause see H-Sz 659, K-S II 2.387, McKeown III 344 on Ov. *Am.* 2.16.19 *tum mihi, si premerem ... Alpes* and cf. Ov. *Am.* 2.11.27-29 *quod si ... Triton exasperet undas / ... / tum generosa uoces ... sidera*. It may, as McKeown points out, have been characteristic of Gallus' style, as it occurs twice in his account of Lycoris' Alpine expedition at Virg. *Ecl.* 10.33-34 *tum quam molliter ossa quiescant, / uestra ... si fistula dicat amores* and 10.38 *quid tum, si fuscus Amyntas*, but is rare elsewhere in the Augustan period.

placeant siluae: cf. Virg. *Ecl.* 2.62 (Corydon) *nobis placeant ante omnia siluae*. See **6n.** above on the contrast with *pereant siluae* there. Cf. the author's wish at **19.9** to withdraw to *secretis ... siluis* (on which see **6n.** above). Both the present passage and **19.9** may have been influenced by Cephalus' words to Aura at Ov. *Met.* 7.819 *tu facis ut siluas ut amem loca sola*, see Gen. Intro., section 1.3 and **headnote** above.

lux mea: this endearment, which is attested already in Cic. *Fam.* 14.2.2 (to Terentia), is usually addressed in elegy by a male lover to his mistress, so Cat. 68.132, 160; Prop. 2.14.29, 28.59, 29A.1; Ov. *Am.* 1.4.25 (with McKeown II 88 ad loc.), 2.17.23, *Trist.* 3.3.52 (Ovid to his wife), but it is used of Cerinthus here and at *Sulpicia* **18.1** and by Tecmessa of Ajax at Ov. *Ars* 3.524. The phrase is not used by Tibullus himself.

16 arguar: a legal term, frequent in Cicero, but rare in poetry: Plaut. *Mil.* 190, 244; Ov. *Her.* 20.79, 224, *Ars* 1.733, 3.803, *Pont.* 4.6.50; Gratt. *Cyneg.* 236; Sen. *Medea* 501, *Phaed.* 721; [Sen.] *Oct.* 865. The verb 'I shall be proved' to have slept, etc. suggest a public scandal, recalling the capture of Venus and Mars in Vulcan's net. Hinds [(1987) 35] suggests that while Sulpicia continues to be identified with Venus, Cerinthus is recast here from Adonis (see **1n.** above) to Mars. On the important theme of scandal and reputation in the *Sulpicia* poems themselves, cf. **13.1-2, 9-10, 16.1-6** below, and see the closural *rumor... tace* at the end of the collection **20.4**. An important intertext here is probably also the tale of Cephalus and Procris at the end of Ov. *Met.* 7 (see **headnote** and **15n.** above), where news of Cephalus' supposed adultery with Aura while out hunting is reported back to his wife Procris, with disastrous results: *Met.* 7.823-825 *nympham mihi credit amare. / criminis extemplo ficti temerarius iudex / Procrin adit linguaque refert audita susurra.*

concubuisse: the verb normally implies sexual intercourse, cf. Tib. 1.8.35 *at Venus inuenit puero concumbere furtim*; Prop. 2.15.16 *dicitur* (sc. *Endymion*) *... nudus concubuisse deae*. In all its ten instances in the elegiac poetry of Ovid it occurs in the form *concubuisse* in penultimate position in the pentameter, as here: *Am.* 2.17.18, *Her.* 16.204, *Ars* 2.632, 3.522, *Fast.* 4.32, 172, 5.86, 6.574, *Pont.* 4.10.14, see further McKeown III 373 on *Am.* 2.17.17-18. For the theme of sleeping during the course of the hunt cf. Phaedra's words at Eur. *Hipp.* 210-211 and Ov. *Her.* 4.44 (quoted in **11-18n.** above). Fabre-Serris [(2009) 159-160] suggests that a pause for love-making during the hunt may have originated in Gallus' account of the Milanion /Atalanta myth in his *Amores*. Phaedra gives three examples of the theme in her letter to Hippolytus at Ov. *Her.* 4.93ff.: Cephalus and Aurora (93-96), Venus and Adonis (97-98) and Milanion and Atalanta (99-100), while Sappho mentions the same idea in her letter to Phaon at Ov. *Her*. 15.143-145 *inuenio siluam, quae saepe cubilia nobis / praebuit et multa texit opaca coma.*

plagas: 'nets' for catching game; see *OLD plaga* (2) 4. For their use in a boar hunt cf. Hor. *Carm*. 1.1.28 *seu rupit ... aper plagas* (with N-H), *Epod*. 2.32 (sc. *trudit*) *apros in obstantis plagas* (with Mankin). The word is absent from Tib. and Prop., but occurs five times in Ov., see Bréguet (1946) 167-168. Like *retia* **12** and *casses* **17** the word is normally used of metaphorical 'snares' in elegy, see Pichon 234.

17-18 ueniat ... / ... Veneris: for the possible etymological word-play see **8.2n.** *ipse ueni* above. The mention in the same couplet of *casses* may also suggests a second etymology of Venus from *uincio*, see **11.13-14n.** below.

17 casses: 'nets' set up on forked props into which the prey was driven by the hounds; full details in Mynors (1990) 236 on Virg. *Georg*. 3.371-372. As with *retia* **12** and *plagas* **16**, the word can be used in hunting metaphors in elegy, see Tib. 1.6.5, Ov. *Ars* 1.392, Pichon 100.

inlaesus: in poetry after Naev. *Trag*. 18 *alte iubatos angues inlaesae gerunt* not until Ovid (*Her*. 15.168, *Met*. 2.826, 12.489, *Fast*. 6.499) then Lucan, Silius Italicus, Statius, and Martial; in prose first in Pliny the Elder. Whereas in **4** it was Cerinthus whose safety Sulpicia was praying for (*incolumem*) now, in a comic turn of the tables, it is the boar who is imagined as going 'unharmed'.

abibit: the change of mood from subjunctive to future serves to bring the imagined scene to life.

18 Veneris cupidae: although Venus is frequently associated with *cupido / Cupido* (personified as her son), the adj. *cupidus* is not applied to her elsewhere. In fact it more commonly applies to the male partner in love elegy, cf. Ov. *Am*. 2.5.26 *cupido ... uiro*; **[Tib.] 3.4.52** etc.

Veneris ... gaudia: this combination occurs also at Ov. *Am*. 2.3.2, *Ars* 2.459, 3.805; *Lydia* 162; Petr. 132.15.5; Mart. 11.26.5, but never in Tib. or Prop. Tränkle [270 ad loc.] may be correct in seeing a connection between the present line and **13.5-6** *exsoluit promissa Venus. mea gaudia narret / dicetur si quis non habuisse sua*, see further ad loc. below. Fabre-Serris [(2009) 163] sees in the word *gaudia* a connection between Sappho's letter to Phaon, Ov. *Her*. 15, and the *Sulpicia Cycle/ Sulpicia* poems, quoting Ov. *Her*. 15.109 *cum mihi nescio quis 'fugiunt tua gaudia' dixit*. For *gaudia* used specifically of the joys of love and even 'orgasm' see Maltby

(2002) 251 on Tib. 1.5.39-40, Pichon 159, Bréguet (1946) 44 and cf. Ov. *Met.* 7.736 (Procris to the disguised Cephalus) *uni mea gaudia seruo*, **3.7n.** above. Hinds [(1987) 35] sees in the phrase *Veneris cupidae gaudia* in the context of a copulating couple in the vicinity of nets a hint at the well-known myth of the adultery of Mars and Venus, see **8.3n.** and **9.16n.** above, referring back to a possible erotic connection between Sulpicia and Mars suggested in **8.1-3**.

gaudia turbet: cf. Lucan 6.284 *ire uel in clades properat dum gaudia turbet.*

19 nunc: 'as it is', introducing a fact as opposed to a previous wish, see *OLD nunc* 11; here, returning to the real world after the dream-world wishes of **11-17**.

sine me sit nulla Venus: the hypothetical *Veneris ... gaudia* of **17** where Sulpicia dreams of accompanying her lover are to be replaced by no love at all in the real world in which Cerinthus hunts alone. The line may also suggest the continued association of Sulpicia with Venus. For *nulla Venus* cf. Virg. *Georg.* 4.516. For metonymic *Venus* here see **19.4n.** below.

lege Dianae: for *lex* used of the powers of deities cf. Ov. *Am.* 1.1.10 *lege pharetratae Virginis arua coli* with McKeown II 18 ad loc. and see *ThLL* 7(2).1249.37-1250.33. For the contrast between Venus and Diana, chaste goddess of the hunt, cf. Prop. 2.19.17-18 *ipse ego uenabor: iam nunc me sacra Dianae / suscipere et Veneris ponere uota iuuat*; Ov. *Her.* 4.87-88 (Phaedra) *quid iuuat incinctae studia exercere Dianae / et Veneri numeros eripuisse suos, Rem.* 199-200 *uel tu uenandi studium cole: saepe recessit / turpiter a Phoebi uicta sorore Venus.*

20 puer: here a term of endearment, an object of love like *puella*, which need not imply extreme youth, cf. Prop. 2.4.17-18 *hostis si quis erit nobis, amet ille puellas; / gaudeat in puero, si quis amicus erit* and see *OLD puella* 2, *puer* 3; youth and inexperience, however, may be hinted at, as in the reference to *teneras ... manus* **8**, *candida ... crura* **10** and *parenti*, possibly a father **23**.

casta ... manu: a common combination in Ovid (*Her.* 2.116, 20.10, *Fast.* 4.260, 324, 6.290), cf. also Varro *Men.* 27.1; Sen. *Phoen.* 222; *Il. Lat.* 78. For the repetition of the adj. with two different nouns *caste puer, casta ... manu* cf. *laetus* referring to Apollo and then to Sulpicia and Cerinthus in **10.23-24** below.

tange manu: cf. Plaut. *Trin.* 288 *manu non queunt tangere*; Ov. *Am.* 1.4.27 *tange manu mensam*, *Ars* 1.662 *uda lumina tange manu*; Val. Fl. 1.787 *manu tangens ... cornua tauri*.

21 meo ... amori: 'my lover'; for *amor* as the object of one's love (less frequent in this sense than the pl. *amores*) cf. Prop. 2.8.36 *tantus in erepto saeuit amore dolor*; Ov. *Am.* 3.9.32 (of Tibullus' Nemesis and Delia) *altera cura recens, altera primus amor* and see *OLD amor* 3d.

furtim subrepit: the adv., as often, strengthens the sense latent in the *sub*-verbal compound, cf. Sen. *Contr.* 1 pr. 24.4 *ut quod aures offensurum esset si palam diceretur, id oblique et furtim subreperet* and see **8.8** (with **n**. ad loc.) *furtim subsequiturque*. On the erotic implications of *furtim* see **8.8n.** and **9.9n.** above. Here the stealthy behaviour of the putative rival, creeping up on Cerinthus, reflects his earlier behaviour (**9**) in stealthily approaching wild beasts' lairs. In a turn of the tables characteristic of this group of poems, the wild beasts, which were to be his prey, are to become her killers.

22 incidat in ... feras: for the use of this verb of falling into dangerous situations see *OLD incido*[1] (4) and cf. Liv. 25.39.4 *incidunt inermes inter cateruas armatorum*; Juv. 10.314 *ut in laqueos numquam incidat*.

saeuas ... feras: a common combination, perhaps first at Tib. 1.10.6, then Ov. *Her.* 4.38, 7.38, *Met.* 4.404, 7.387; Sen. *Troad.* 845, *Herc. Oet.* 1327; [Sen.] *Oct.* 515, 637; Stat. *Ach.* 1.132-133.

diripienda: cf., in the same *sedes*, **6.28** *diripienda ferant*. For the predicative use of the gerundive cf. **12.4** *staret ... ante tuos conspicienda focos*.

23 at: for the use of this particle in a return at the end of an elegy to a person addressed earlier see Fedeli (1985) 492 on Prop. 3.15.43 and cf. Tib. 1.3.83, 1.8.77. For its use with the imperat. *adnue* see **8.3** above.

at tu uenandi studium: cf. Ov. *Rem.* 199 *uel tu uenandi studium cole*, where hunting is seen as a cure for love, see **19n.** *lege Dianae* above. Here *uenandi studium* picks up *uenandi ... cura* of the opening (**5**).

concede parenti: the phrase is found in the same *sedes* at Lucan 3.744 and Stat. *Theb.* 10.705.

parenti: it is impossible to know who is meant here; the easiest interpretation would be to take it as a reference to Cerinthus' father. There may be another echo here of Horace's Chloe Ode, *Carm.* 1.23. At the end of that poem Chloe is asked to leave her mother for a man 11-12 *tandem desine matrem / tempestiua sequi uiro*. Here Cerinthus is asked to leave hunting to his relative/father and return to Sulpicia's embrace. On the possible connection between the Horace passage and the present poem see **14.6** *tempestiuae ... uiae* below.

24 in nostros ... recurre sinus: cf. Prop. 3.20.10 *in nostros curre, puella, toros*. There could well be an allusion here to Sulpicia's words about Cerinthus at **13.3-4** *... illum Cytherea ... / attulit in nostrum deposuitque sinum*. Fabre-Serris [(2009) 165] points to a similarity with Ov. *Her.* 15.95 *huc ades inque sinus, formose, relabere nostros*.

Poem 10

The poem takes the form of an address to Apollo, in his function as a healing deity, on the occasion of Sulpicia's illness. The anonymous observer, one of the masks assumed by the author of **book 3**, speaks in his own voice.

The poem's contents, based on the assumption that lines 21-22 need to be placed between lines 16 and 17, may be analysed as follows:

1-8 A direct address to Apollo, in the form of a kletic hymn, asking the god to come and lay his healing hands on the sick girl and drive away her illness.

9-14 Repeat the appeal and introduce the figure of her lover Cerinthus, who fears his girl may die.

15-16, 21-22, 17-18, An address to Cerinthus, whose love alone will save his girl, assuring him that she loves him.

19-20, 23-26 A concluding address to Apollo, pointing out the praise he will receive from the thankful couple and his fellow deities should he save the girl's life.

As with poems **8** and **9** of this group a change is effected in the middle of the poem at **13-14**, describing Cerinthus' ambiguous reaction to his mistress' illness, sometimes making vows and sometimes cursing the gods. The second half of the poem, beginning *pone metum* **15**, moves in a new direction, provided he continues to love her, Sulpicia will be safe. The god who does not harm lovers in **15** (*deus*) is not named, and could suggest *Amor*, since his role involves saving lovers, though Apollo himself is not without expertise in this area, as his erotodidaxis in **4.43-80** shows. The final section **19-26** provides the poem with a neat ring structure, by returning to the theme of Apollo as healer. As with *torta* in poem **9.12**, the use of the verb *torque* here at **11** has a double meaning in this case 'torture' and 'change' picking up the theme of change emphasised in the opening poem of this group by the appearance of Vertumnus (**8.13-14**), see further **12n.** below.

For the theme of the mistress's illness in elegy cf. Tib. 1.5.9-18; Prop. 2.9.25-28, 2.28; Ov. *Am.* 2.13 (with McKeown III 276 headnote) and 2.14 (Corinna's abortion), *Her.* 20 and 21, *Ars* 2.315ff.; **[Tib.] 3.17** (*Sulpicia*), and see N-H II 272 on Hor. *Carm.* 2.17 (headnote). The present poem anticipates poem **17** on Sulpicia's illness. As with the hunting theme in poem **9**, the author here plays with the literal and metaphorical meanings of disease *morbus*, both as a physical illness and as lovesickness see **9 headnote** on the possible background to this and cf. **2n., 5n.** and **16n.** below. Fredericks (1976) sees the poem as experimental in its objective treatment of elegiac themes, and suggests some ambiguity about the speakers, with the section **15-22** possibly spoken in the voice of Apollo. On the whole it seems more reasonable to take the anonymous observer as the speaker throughout. Three addresses to deities are strategically placed at the beginning of the first (Mars), middle (Apollo) and last (Juno) poems in the *Sulpicia Cycle* poems **8, 10** and **12** respectively, reflecting the careful construction of this group of five poem in which all the poems spoken in the anonymous poet's own voice begin with an address to a god/goddess.

1-2 Huc ades ... / huc ades: for this type of repetition in a kletic hymn cf. Virg. *Georg.* 2.4-7 *huc pater o Lenaee ... / ... / ... / huc pater o Lenaee ueni* and see Wills (1996) 110 and n. 48. For the terminology of the kletic hymn see **7.131n., 8.2n.** and cf. **3.33-34n.** and **6.1n** above. For the combination of *ades* here and *faue* (**19**) in a kletic context see McKeown III 289 on Ov. *Am.* 2.13.21-22. For *huc ades* at the beginning of the verse, often in a kletic context, cf. Virg. *Ecl.* 2.45, 7.9, 9.39, 43; Tib. 1.7.49, 2.1.35; Ov. *Am.* 1.6.54, 2.12.16, 3.2.46, *Her.* 15.95, *Trist.* 5.3.43; Manil. 3.36; Petr. 133.3.5; Sil. 7.78; Stat. *Theb.* 1.81, *Silu.* 3.1.28; *Priap.* 81.2,. Apollo is here addressed in his function as healer, Apollo Medicus, who had had a temple in Rome since 431 BC. Tib. mentions the loss of Apollo's medical skills occasioned by his love for Admetus at 2.3.13-14

Book Three of the Corpus Tibullianum:
Introduction, Text, Translation and Commentary

nec potuit curas sanare salubribus herbis: / *quidquid erat medicae uicerat artis amor*. Apollo wards off diseases as early as Homer, and for his role as a healing god in later Greece see Strabo 14.1.6 Ἀπόλλωνα καλοῦσι ... ὑγιαστικὸν καὶ παιωνικόν ["They call upon Apollo ... as a god of health and healing"].

1 tenerae ... puellae: a common combination, cf. Tib. 1.3.63, 10.64, 2.1.61; Prop. 2.25.41; Ov. *Am*. 2.1.33, 14.73, 3.1.27, 3.25, 4.1, 7.53, *Her*. 14.87, 19.7, 127, *Med. Fac. Fem*. 17, *Ars* 1.403, 2.533, 3.31, *Fast*. 3.815; *Copa* 33; *Eleg. in Maec*. 1.71, Mart. 1.109.16, 3.65,1, 14.149.1. It is used of Sulpicia again at **12.2**. The adj. here suggests emotional vulnerability and susceptibility to the pains of love, cf. Fredericks [(1976) 765] who contrasts it with the elegiac *durus* 'insensitivity to love', comparing Tib. 1.8.50-51 *in ueteres esto dura, puella, senes*. / *parce, precor, tenero*; see further Bréguet (1946) 158-161.

morbos expelle: cf. Cat. 44.7 ... *malam ... pectore expuli tussim*, Hor. *Epist*. 2.2.137 *expulit helleboro morbum*; Quint. *Decl. Mai*. 14.6.24 *morbos infusis medicaminibus expellere*. The normal expression in medical prose is *morbum depellere*, e.g. Cels. 3.20.4 *ad morbum ipsum depellendum* (also found at Caes. *BG* 6.17. *Apollinem morbos depellere* and Virg. *Aen*. 9.328 ... *non ... potuit depellere pestem*). Ov. prefers the uncompounded form: *Rem*. 115 *pellere morbos*, *Fast*. 3.827 *morbos qui pellitis*. On the plural *morbos* see **17.3n**. below.

2 intonsa Phoebe superbe coma: for Apollo's unshorn locks see **4.27n**. and cf. Tib. 1.4.38 *intonsus crinis*, 2.5.121 *intonsi ... capilli* and cf. his Homeric epithet ἀκερσεκόμης (*Il*. 20.39 etc.). *Phoebe superbe* occurs in the same *sedes* at **8.22**, see **n**. ad loc. on its meaning. For the phrase *intonsa coma* of Apollo cf. Tib. 2.3.12 *nec cithara intonsae profueruntue comae*; the *iunctura* is found elsewhere at Acc. *Trag*. 674; Varro *Men*. 123.3; Sen. *Phaed*. 754 (of Bacchus); Sil. 4.203-204, 16.525; Stat. *Theb*. 6.587. For the pentameter ending *superbe coma* cf. Prop. 2.1.8 (of his mistress) *gaudet laudatis ire superba comis*. Fredericks [(1976) 764-765] suggests this part of Apollo's description associates him with love, poets and poetry, rather than medicine, which comes to the fore in *medicas ... manus* (**4**). Sulpicia's disease may to some extent be amatory (perhaps as a result of her psychological turmoil described in poem **9**), a field in which Apollo is also expert, as is shown by his erotodidaxis at **4.43-80**.

3 crede mihi: a colloquial expression lending emphasis, common in this initial position in Prop. [(7) (not in book four)] and, especially, Ov. (30), but not found in Hor., Virg. or elsewhere in the *Corp. Tib.* For its use to reinforce an imperative, as here, cf. Ov. *Am.* 3.4.11 *desine, crede mihi, uitia irritare uetando*. The phrase is slightly more colloquial in tone than *mihi crede* [Ov. (14), Hor. *Serm.* (3), but not in Tib., Virg., or Prop.] and is restricted in Cicero to the letters, whereas the more formal *mihi crede* is also found in the speeches; see further Bréguet (1946) 137-138, Tränkle (1960) 9-10, Citroni on Mart. 1.3.4, McKeown on Ov. *Am.* 1.8.62, Ingleheart on Ov. *Trist.* 2.353-354.

4 formosae: see **1.7n.** above and for its substantival use see Bréguet (1946) 156-157 and Fedeli (1980) 341 on Prop. 1.15.8. Sulpicia's beauty adds urgency to the appeal for a cure, as at Prop. 2.28.1-2 *Iuppiter, affectae tandem miserere puellae: / tam formosa tuum mortua crimen erit*.

medicas applicuisse manus: recalls Virg. *Georg.* 3.455-456 *dum medicas adhibere manus ad uulnera pastor / abnegat*, which is also the first adjectival use of *medicus* (before Tib. 2.3.14 *medicae ... artis* and Ov. *Am.* 2.9.8 *medica ... ope*). The combination of *medica* with *manus* occurs elsewhere at Virg. *Aen.* 12.402-403 *multa manu medica Phoebique potentibus herbis / nequiquam trepidat*; Plin. *Nat.* 8.58; Stat. *Silu.* 5.5.42-43 *medicasque manus ... quaero / uulneribus*; Serenus *Med.* 48.898 *ni medicas adhibere manus discamus*. Here the reference is to a therapeutic laying on of hands, see Bréguet [(1946) 168-169)], rather than to surgery as is implied in Virg. *Georg.* For *manus applicare* (not in a medical sense) cf. Quint. *Decl. Mai.* 1.11 *manum cruentam parieti adplicat*.

5 effice: apart from Lucr. 1.29, the use of this form in initial line-position is restricted to, and frequent in, Ovid: *Her.* 12.82, 14.54, 19.155, *Ars* 2.312, 3.802, *Rem.* 31, *Fast.* 3.683, 6.380, *Trist.* 1.8.49, 5.5.57, *Pont.* 1.3.45, 3.3.63, 4.12.41.

ne macies pallentes occupet artus: for the expression cf. Hor. *Carm.* 3.27.53-54 *antequam turpis macies decentis / occupet malas*, and for the idea cf. Sen. *Herc. Oet.* 119 *nos turpis macies et lacrimae tenent*. Here *pallentes* describes a negative feature, the pallor of disease, while the positive sense of Horace's *decentes* is brought out by the conjecture *candida* in the pentameter, see **6n.** *candida*. The language of the couplet with *notet* and *candida* in **6** is close to **9.10** *candidaque hamatis crura notare rubis* describing the disfigurement Sulpicia fears for Cerinthus as a result of his hunting. We may also see in *pallentes* here a transference of Cerinthus' qualities to Sulpicia (from the yellow pallor of 'wax' κηρίον, one of the elements of his name – see Gen. Intro., section 3.4). For its use in the context of pale limbs, cf. Ov. *Pont.* 1.10.27-28 *paruus in exiles sucus mihi peruenit artus / membraque sunt cera pallidiora noua.* Both *macies* and *pallor* can be signs of physical illness and lovesickness. For physical illness, cf. Cels. 1.8.2 *stomachum autem infirmum indicant pallor, macies.* For *macies* of lovesickness see Pichon 193 and cf. Prop. 4.3.27; Ov. *Ars* 1.733, *Met.* 9.536, 11.793, and for *pallor* and related terms of lovesickness see Maltby (2002) 307 on Tib. 1.8.17-18 and cf. Theocr. *Id.* 2.88-89; Hor. *Carm.* 1.13.5-6; Prop. 1.9.17; Ov. *Am.* 2.7.10, *Ars* 1.729. The close connection here with Cerinthus through reference to his name suggests that Sulpicia's illness is in fact lovesickness, hence the emphasis in **16** on Cerinthus' continued love for her as a source of a cure.

occupet artus: the very similar line-ending *occupat artus* is found at Virg. *Georg.* 4.190, *Aen.* 7.446, 11.424; Ov. *Met.* 3.40, 14.757, 15.166; Lucan 1.246; Sil. 6.409; Stat. *Ach.* 1.930.

6 notet informis candida membra color: There may be an echo here of the warning to Cerinthus about disfiguring his pale legs on the red brambles in the previous poem **9.10** *candidaque hamatis crura notare rubis.* Male and female suffering are compared and contrasted as part of the Vertumnan theme of change which dominates the *Sulpicia Cycle.* For *notet* in this context = 'disfigure' as well as **9.10** cf. Prop. 1.6.16 *Cynthia et insanis ora notet manibus*; Ov. *Am.* 3.6.78 *desint famosus quae notet ora pudor*; Mart. 7.18.2 *cum corpus nulla litura notet.* For the general expression cf. Prop. 1.5.16 *timor informem ducet in ore notam* (of the effect of Cynthia's wrath on Gallus). For *informis* = 'unsightly', contrasting with *formosae* (**4**), cf. Virg. *Ecl.* 2.25 (Corydon) *nec sum adeo informis* (Calp. *Ecl.* 2.84 *num ... informis uideor tibi), Georg.* 3.354-355 *iacet aggeribus niueis informis ... / terra*; Prop. 1.5.16 (quoted above), 2.8.33 *uiderat informem ... Patroclon* (the body of Patroclus); Lucan 6.225 *informis facies.*

candida: a reading found in the Roman edition of 1475. *pallida* of the manuscripts can hardly be correct after the close, but not identical, *pallentes* in **5**. Guietus suggests *tabida* 'wasting', but, in view of *decentis* in Hor. *Carm.* 3.27.53-54 quoted in **5n.** above, as well as the intertext with **9.10**, *candida* is perhaps to be preferred. An unsightly colour disfigures her beautiful body. On the possible reference in this adj. to Sulpicia's style as well as to her beauty see **8.12n.** above. For the literary associations of *color* see **1.18n.** and **4.30n.** above; the suggestion here could be that a bad *color* brought on by disease could have damaging effects on her style, but the text is too uncertain to press the point here.

7-8 It was common Roman religious practice to submerge things of evil omen beneath the purifying sea, cf. Tib. 2.5.79-80 ... *sed tu iam mitis, Apollo, / prodigia indomitis merge sub aequoribus* with Maltby (2002) 455-456 ad loc. and Tib. 1.9.50 quoted on **8** below. Given the prevalence of Callimachean imagery elsewhere in the cycle, it seems likely that the present couplet could contain an echo of Callimachus' metapoetic words at the end of his Hymn to Apollo, Call. *Hymn* 2.108-109 Ἀσσυρίου ποταμοῖο μέγας ῥόος, ἀλλὰ τὰ πολλὰ / λύματα γῆς καὶ πολλὸν ἐφ' ὕδατι συρφετὸν ἕλκει ["Great is the stream of the Assyrian river (i.e. the Euphrates), but it carries in its waters much filth of the earth and much rubbish"]. The reference there is to the muddy waters of epic. But here, as with the reference to the Tiber in Virg. *Aen.* 7.30-32 *hunc inter fluuio Tiberinus amoeno / uerticibus rapidis et multa flauus harena / in mare prorumpit*, this Callimachean imagery is reversed, so that the river washes away, rather than brings with it, the negative elements connected with Sulpicia's disease in **7**; see on this reversal in the Virgilian passage Kyriakidis (1998) 147- 152. The opening address to Apollo and the use of the Greek loan-word *pelagus* (**8**) serves to confirm the Callimachean context here, and the echo in *rapidis* (**8**) of the same word at *Aen.* 7.31 acknowledges the important Virgilian intertext.

7 quodcumque mali est et quicquid triste: the use of *quodcumque* + gen. may have been familiar in tone. In Cicero it is restricted to the letters (*Fam.* 5.19.1, *Att.* 8.12a.4), but it occurs occasionally in the elegists (Tib. 1.1.13; Prop. 1.4.3; Ov. *Fast.* 2.579, 6.381). For the combination with *quidquid* cf. Cat. 39.6-7 ... *quidquid est, ubicumquest / quodcumque agit*; Prop. 2.1.15 *seu quidquid fecit, siue est quodcumque locuta*.

8 pelagus: this Greek loan-word occurs only here in the whole *Corp. Tib.*, once in Prop. at 4.6.17, but no less than 37 times in Ov. [*Am.* (2), *Her.* (9), *Met.* (18), *Fast.* (1), *Trist.* (6), *Pont.* (1)]. Elsewhere in verse it is mainly restricted to epic and didactic, e.g. Lucr. (3), Virg. *Georg.* (4), *Aen.* (44), Lucan (68), Manil. (33); see further Bréguet (1946) 207-208.

rapidis ... aquis: for the common *iunctura* see Cat. 70.4; Ov. *Am.* 1.15.10, 2.4.8, 3.6.80, *Ibis* 514; Sil. 4.596; Mart. 10.103.2. or the manuscript confusion found here between the epithets *rabidus* and *rapidus* applied to the sea see **7.72n.** above.

euehat amnis aquis: for the verse-ending cf. especially Tib. 1.9.50 *et liquida deleat amnis aqua* (of his verses to Marathus) and Ov. *Ars* 3.386 *nec Tuscus placida deuehit amnis aqua*. Other combinations of *amnis* (penultimate) with various cases of *aqua* (final) occur at Tib. 1.4.66; Ov. *Ars* 2.344, *Fast*. 1.292, 3.652 and *Ibis* 78.

9 sancte, ueni: the same verse opening, in this case addressed to Cupid, is found at Tib. 2.1.81. The same voc. is addressed to Cerinthus' birthday Genius, in this case in the voice of Sulpicia, at **11.12** below and at **12.7** Juno is addressed as *sancta*. For the kletic injunction, *ueni*, see **8.2n.** above.

ueni ... feras: for the alternation between imperative and jussive subjunctive see Pinkster (2015) 499 and cf. Liv. 3.48.4 *primum ignosce patrio dolori ... deinde sinas hic coram uirgine nutricem percontari*.

sapores: for its use in a concrete sense of a strongly perfumed mixture or liquid cf. Virg. *Georg.* 4.62-63 *huc tu iussos asperge sapores, / trita melisphylla et cerinthae ignobile gramen*, 267 *tunsum gallae admiscere saporem*; Tib. 1.7.35 *iucundos ... sapores* (of wine). Interestingly the use of *sapores* in *Georg.* 4.62 is followed in 4.63 by mention of the plant *cerintha*, from which Sulpicia's lover's name Cerinthus could have been derived. For the use of such potions in healing cf. *sucus amarus* at Ov. *Am.* 3.11.8 (quoted in **12n.** below).

10 cantus: incantation was an important element in ancient cures, cf. Tib. 1.5.11-12 (of Delia's illness) *ipseque te circum lustraui sulpure puro / carmine cum magico praecinuisset anus* and see further Maltby (2002) 245 ad loc.; also Zell (1829) 119-120, Wille (1967) 42, 443-446 and cf. examples in Cato *Agr.* 160; Varro *Rust.* 1.2.27. As god of music and poetry as well as of healing Apollo would have been expert in this aspect of the cure.

corpora fessa: the same phrase is used of Sulpicia's fevered body at **17.2** below *quod mea nunc uexat corpora fessa calor*. For other examples of the phrase in verse see **17.2n.** below. For *fessus* and equivalents used in the context of illness cf. Hor. *Carm. Saec.* 63-64 (of Apollo as healer) *qui salutari leuat arte fessos / corporis artus*, Tib. 1.5.9 (quoted in **12n.** below), Ov. *Am.* 2.13.2 *in dubio uitae lassa Corinna iacet*, 3.11.8 *saepe tulit lassis sucus amarus opem*. The only word for 'tired' used in the whole *Corp. Tib.* is *fessus*, whereas Prop. and Ov. use both *fessus* and the less elevated *lassus*; full figures and discussion in McKeown II 36 on Ov. *Am.* 1.2.4.

11-12 Cerinthus' obvious concern for Sulpicia here in her sickness, as reflected in *metuit qui fata puellae* (**11**) and *uota ... uix numeranda facit*

(12) contrasts with Sulpicia's fears about his possible lack of *pia cura* concerning her illness at **17.1**; see Batstone (2018) 105-106. Again there is a marked contrast in the attitudes of the lovers between the *Sulpicia Cycle* and the *Sulpicia* poems (cf. **9.5n.** *abducit* above).

11 neu iuuenem torque: echoes Tib. 1.8.49 *neu Marathum torque*. On the use of *toqueo* of the tortures of unrequited love, see McKeown III 423 on Ov. *Am.* 2.19.33-34. Here, as in **9.12** above, the word *torqueo* has a double meaning, both 'torture' and 'change'. At one level Apollo is asked not to torture Cerinthus with fear for his mistress' health, at another he is asked not to 'change' Cerinthus' present behaviour of making vows to the gods **(12)**, since he is inclined to curse the gods **(14)** as her condition deteriorates *quod langueat illa* **(13)**.

metuit: contrast *pone metum* **(15)**, introducing the second half of the poem in which Cerinthus is asked to lay aside his fear since his love can keep his mistress safe. These are the only occurrences of *metuo* and *metus* in **[Tib.] 3**. Tib. himself avoids the archaising *metuo* and has only one occurrence of *metus* (Tib. 1.6.75). Elsewhere in the *Corp. Tib. timeo* and *timor* are the rule; on the relative distribution of *timeo /timor* and *metuo/metus* see Ernout (1957) 7-56, Adams (2016) 51-52 and *ThLL* 8. 901-902.

fata: = 'death', cf. **5.18** above and see *OLD fatum* 4, 6.

puellae: probably genitive, but *timeo* can also be constructed + acc. + dat.; examples in McKeown III 236 on Ov. *Am.* 2.11.9-10.

12 uotaque ... facit: *uota* were promises made to a god, to be fulfilled if one's prayer was answered, see **4.53n.** They occur commonly in elegy in this context of a mistress's illness, cf. Tib. 1.5.9-10 (of Delia) *cum tristi morbo defessa iaceres, / te dicor uotis eripuisse meis*; Prop. 2.9.25 *haec mihi uota tuam propter suscepta salutem*, 2.28.43, 61; Ov. *Am.* 2.13.23, *Ars* 2.327 (quoted below). For the expression *uota facere* cf. Cic. *Att.* 8.16.1 *illo aegroto uota faciebant*; Prop. 4.1.101; Ov. *Pont.* 2.7.56.

uota ... uix numeranda: a possible reference to Ovid's advice to the lover whose mistress is sick at *Ars* 2.327 *multa uoue, sed cuncta palam*.

domina: see **4.74n.** Elsewhere in the *Corp. Tib.* it is used with reference to *seruitium amoris*, see **6.14, 19.22.**

uix numeranda: apart from Prop. 4.8.72 the use of *uix* + gerundive is restricted in elegy to Ovid (*Her.* 7.143, 16.178, 18.8, *Fast.* 1.556, *Trist.*

3.3.22, 3.4.42, *Pont.* 1.4.28, 1.8.12). The gerundive *numerandus* occurs here only in elegy. It is mainly prosaic (e.g. Cic. 12) and is found elsewhere in verse only at Hor. *Serm.* 2.3.150; Ov. *Met.* 15.45; [Ov.] *Epiced. Drusi* 448; Manil. 2.622, 3.105; Sil. 15.747; Mart. 1.39.1, 4.40.2.

13 interdum ... interdum: repeated *interdum* is rare in verse. It is not found elsewhere in elegy, but occurs in Ov. at *Met.* 8.736-737 and 12.518-520.

uouet: Ovid advises the lover to make vows for her safety in the case of a mistress's illness as an indication of devotion *Ars* 2.327 *multa uoue, sed cuncta palam.*

quod langueat illa: for *langueo* in the sense of 'be sick, unwell' see **5.28n.** above, *OLD langueo* 1b. and cf. the description of Cydippe's pain as *languor* at Ov. *Her.* 20.3 *discedat sic corpore languor ab isto.* For the subjunctive in a causal *quod* clause, see Pinkster (2015) 646-650. This is the only example in the *Corp. Tib.* where the verb in the main clause is in the indicative; at Tib. 2.3.9 the verb in the main clause *quererer* is subjunctive. All other causal *quod* clauses in the *Corp. Tib.* have their verbs in the indicative.

14 dicit in aeternos aspera uerba deos: very close in expression to Tib. 1.3.52 *non dicta in sanctos impia uerba deos*, where the sick Tib. asks Jupiter to spare him on the grounds that he has not spoken impious words to the gods. No mention is made here of the possible consequences of Cerinthus' blasphemous words. The phrase *aeternos ... deos* is found in the same *sedes* at Tib. 2.3.30; Ov. *Rem.* 688, *Fast.* 3.804, 4.954, 6.322. Cf. *aeterno ... Olympo* at. **8.13**, as here in the central couplet of the poem. The combination *aspera uerba* occurs in the same *sedes* at Ov. *Pont.* 2.7.56 and Sil. 10.272 and in a different line-position at Ov. *Pont.* 2.6.8.

15 pone metum: a favourite phrase with Ovid (16), of which 10 are found at the verse-opening as here; cf. especially Ov. *Her.* 20.1 (Acontius to Cydippe) *pone metum, nihil hic iterum iurabis amanti*, just before the mention of Cydippe's *languor* (see **13n.** above). The phrase is avoided by Tib. and Prop.; see further Bréguet (1946) 138-139.

deus non laedit amantes: contrast Ov. *Am.* 2.9.3-4 (to Cupid) *quid me, qui miles numquam tua signa reliqui, / laedis?* For the inviolability of lovers, cf. Tib. 1.2.29-30 *quisquis amore tenetur eat tutusque sacerque / qualibet; insidias non timuisse decet* [with further examples in Maltby

(2002) 162-163 ad loc.]; Prop. 3.16.11 *nec tamen est quisquam sacros qui laedat amantes.*

16 tu modo semper ama: for *tu modo* + imperat. see **4.64n.** above and cf. Ov. *Pont.* 3.6.59-60 *tu modo* ... / ... *ama.* For the expression cf. also Ov. *Her.* 17.254 *tu, Pari, semper ama.* The combination in elegy of *semper* with *amo* is frequent (Prop. 2.13.52, 2.22.18; Ov. *Am.* 1.3.2, 2.4.10, *Her.* 15.80, 17.254). For the emphasis on the perpetuity of affection as a common feature of marriage songs see G. Williams (1958), L. C.Watson (2003) 465 and cf. *semper habendus* at **11.2** below. The fact that Sulpicia's illness can be cured by Cerinthus' continued love, suggests the illness is in part of an amatory nature, see Fredericks (1976) 764-765.

salua puella: cf. Prop. 2.28.44 (in the context of Cynthia's illness) *PER MAGNVM EST SALVA PVELLA IOVEM.* Also of recovery from illness at Tib. 1.5.19 *si salua fuisses.* The adj. can also imply 'chaste', 'safe' from the attentions of rival lovers, as at Prop. 2.9.3-4 *Penelope poterat bis denos salua per annos / uiuere,* a sense emphasised here at **17-18** below.

tibi est: a common pentameter ending in Ov., cf. *Her.* 9.52, 21.120, *Ars* 3.52, *Fast.* 1.480, *Trist.* 5.7.10, 14.42, *Pont.* 2.10.10.

21-22 It is clear that this distich has been transmitted in the wrong position, since it would be inappropriate after the address to Phoebus in **19-20** and *at* in *at nunc tota tua est* **17** would not make sense after *salua puella tibi est* **16**. Both difficulties are removed by its transposition to a position after **16**.

21 nil opus est fletu: tears are not required as Sulpicia will soon be well again **(16)** and is devoted to Cerinthus **(17-18)**. Again (cf. **13n.** above) Ovid recommends tears as a sign of devotion when the mistress is ill: *Ars* 2.325-326 *et uideat flentem* ... / *et sicco lacrimas conbibat ore tuas.* Elsewhere in elegy male tears are mentioned mostly in the context of unrequited love (cf. Tib. 1.2.78 *cum fletu nox uigilanda uenit,* 8.68 *et tua iam fletu lumina fessa tument,* 2.6.35; Prop. 1.6.24, 18.6). *opus est* is common in prose, but rare in Augustan poetry outside Hor. *Serm.* and Ov. It is constructed with the abl. in Hor. *Serm.* (8 times); Tib. 1.6.33; Virg. *Aen.* 6.261, 9.148-149 and Ov. (13 times). For *nil opus est* at the line-opening cf. Lucr. 5.263; Ov. *Am.* 1.2.21 (with McKeown. II 44 ad loc.), *Her.* 20.185, *Ars* 1.137, 2.162, *Met.* 10.565, *Fast.* 4.813, 926, *Pont.* 1.2.92, 4.15.12.

erit aptius uti: the construction *aptius est* + inf. is common in prose from Cic. *Fin.* 3.74 on, but is rare elsewhere in verse outside Ovid (cf. *Am.* 1.7.41, 2.3.17, *Ars* 3.226); see further Bréguet (1946) 139-140.

22 tristior: here, as often in elegy, the adj. means 'ill-humoured, cross', see *OLD tristis* 3 and cf. Plaut. *Cas.* 230 *heia, mea Iuno, non decet esse te tam tristem tuo Ioui*; Tib. 1.6.2 *post tamen es misero tristis et asper, Amor*; Prop. 1.6.9-10 *illa minatur / quae solet ingrato tristis amica uiro*, 14.16 *nulla mihi tristi praemia sint Venere* with Fedeli (1980) 329 ad loc.; Ov. *Ars* 1.363 *tum, cum tristis erat, defensa est Ilios armis*; see further Bréguet (1946) 188-191.

17 at nunc tota tua est: the phrase *at nunc* introduces the contrast between *tristior* and *tota tua*; it is a common line-opening in Ovid (10). For the combination *tota tua* cf. Cat. 62.62 *uirginitas non tota tua est*; Mart. 2.2.6 *laurea tota tua est*.

candida: here in the transferred sense of 'without guile', 'chaste', as used, in a similar context, of the faithful Penelope at Ov. *Am.* 2.18.29 *candida Penelope signum cognouit Vlixis*; see *OLD candidus* 8b and cf. Apul. *Met* 8.30 *pudore illo candido*. The use of the adj. in this sense is rare elsewhere in poetry, but its occurrence in Cicero's letters and Horace *Serm., Epod.* and *Epist.* suggests it belongs to an elevated colloquial register, a register characteristic of our poet as Sulpicia in poems **13-18**; see further Bréguet (1946) 177-180.

17-18 secum / cogitat: outside Enn. *Trag.* 308 Jocelyn *ibi quid agat secum cogitat*, the phrase is restricted to prose writers, e.g. Cic. *Fin.* 2.69 *iubebat eos ... secum ipsos cogitare*. Virg. makes use of a more elevated equivalent at *Aen.* 1.50 *talia ... secum ... corde uolutans*.

credula turba: an Ovidian reference. At *Rem.* 685-686 the phrase is used, as here, of rejected lovers who continue to believe in the possibility of being loved: *desinimus tarde, quia nos speramus amari; / dum sibi quisque placet, credula turba sumus*. For *credula turba* in the same *sedes* cf. also Ov. *Fast.* 2.716 (of a crowd misunderstanding an oracle) and 4.312 (of a crowd's inclination to believe the worst in regard to sexual morals). The Romans derived the term *turba* from θορυβεῖν (see *LALE* 626) and connected it with noisy, unruly behaviour. Manilius uses the word in a similar way at 2.138 *nec in turba nec turbae carmina condam*: see Kyriakidis (2016) 142, where he relates *turba* with the πλῆθος of the Stoic Cleanthes; see above **3.19-20**. In Tib. it is normally used of slaves, children and noisy crowds (1.2.97, 1.5.63, 2.1.23, 2.1.85), but more positive instances are found, e.g. 1.4.80 the *sedula turba* 'sedulous youth' who will listen to advice of a *magister amoris* or 1.3.32 and 2.1.16 of religious processions. It is possible that the term has Callimachean implications here, derived from Call. *Epigr*. 28.4 σικχαίνω πάντα τὰ δημόσια ["I hate all common things"] and *Aetia* 1 fr. 1.25-28 Pf., referring to everything that is 'epic, pompous and unartistic', see **3.19-20n.** above, and **19.7n.** below. For these Callimachean implications of the *turba* see Heyworth [(1994) 71], who compares Prop. 3.1.11-12 and 3.3.23-24, and Ingleheart (2010) 114 on Ov. *Trist*. 2.87-88. It is unclear why this potentially pejorative term is applied to the gods later in the poem, see **25n.** below.

frustra ... sedet: the would-be rivals sit in vain in Sulpicia's house, waiting for news of her recovery. The regular verb used in this context of attending on a sick person is *adsideo*. In Ov. *Her*. 20.133-136 Acontius fears her betrothed will sit in this way at sick Cydippe's bed: *me miserum, quod non medicorum iussa ministro, / effingoque manus, adsideoque toro. / et rursus miserum, quod me procul inde remoto, / quem minime uellem, forsitan alter adest*, but is reassured by Cydippe's words at *Her*. 21.191-192 *adsidet ille quidem, quantum permittitur, ipse / sed meminit nostrum uirginis esse torum*. A doctor is praised at Sen. *Ben*. 6.16.4 for not only prescribing remedies but also for sitting at a patient's bedside: *inter sollicitos adsedit*.

19 Phoebe, faue: the same line-opening is found at Tib. 2.5.1; cf. *Il. Lat.* 1070 *tuque faue ... Phoebe.*

laus magna tibi tribuetur: cf. Cic. *Off*. 3.64.1 *huic nec laus magna tribuenda nec gratia est*. Elsewhere in Cicero the combination *magna laus* (always in this order) is common (10). In verse it occurs only here and at Ov. *Pont*. 4.13.48 *laus ... est tibi magna*. The construction *laus est* (*tribuitur* etc.) + inf. (*restituisse* 20) is found from the time of Plaut. *Mil.* 703-704 *... laus est ... / liberos homines educare*. For *tribuere laudem* cf. Prop. 3.24.3 *noster amor tales tribuit tibi, Cynthia, laudes.*

19-20 in uno / corpore seruato restituisse duos: the sentiment is common in the context of the illness of the beloved, cf. Prop. 2.28.41-42 (addressed to Jupiter during Cynthia's illness) *si non unius, quaeso, miserere duorum: / uiuam, si uiuet; si cadet illa, cadam*; Ov. *Am*. 2.13.15-16 (addressed to Isis in the context of Corinna's abortion) *huc adhibe uultus, et in una parce duobus. / nam uitam dominae tu dabis, illa mihi.*

This concept of the joint existence of the lover and his beloved occurs twice elsewhere in Ovid, both close in expression to the present couplet: *Her*. 11.60 *uiue nec unius corpore perde duos*, *Met*. 11.388 *animasque duas ut seruet in una*; cf. similar expressions at Ov. *Her*. 20.233-234, *Met*. 4.373-375 (on the embrace of Salmacis and Hermaphroditus); also *Fast*. 3.683 (of Mars and Minerva) *effice, di studio similes coeamus in unum*. The idea that each person is half of an original being and searches forever for his complimentary half goes back to Plato's *Symposium* ἕκαστος οὖν ἡμῶν ἐστιν ἀνθρώπου σύμβολον, ἅτε τετμημένος ὥσπερ αἱ ψῆτται, ἐξ ἑνὸς δύο· ζητεῖ δὴ ἀεὶ τὸ αὑτοῦ ἕκαστος σύμβολον. (Plat. Symp. 191d) ("Then each of us is a symbol of a human, since we have been cleaved just like flatfish, two generated from one. So each person forever searches for the symbol of himself", trnsl. Struck [2004] 79), and a similar idea is found in Aristotle *De gen. anim*. 722b. It is possible that Ovid and others were aware of the Old Testament works in Greek translation. If this were true of our author, the passage could possibly contain a reference to a phrase used in a wedding context at *Genesis* 2.24 καὶ ἔσονται οἱ δύο εἰς σάρκα μίαν ["and the two shall be one in the flesh"]. It may also be possible to see in *corpore* a reference to a body of poetic work, see **2.17n**. and **7.196n.**; for *corpus* as a body of literary work cf. Cic. *Att*. 5.12.4; Vitr. 5 pr. 5.7, and for *seruare* of keeping books in a library cf. Serv. *Aen*. 6.72. Exactly what the significance of 'restoring two [poets] or poetic works/collections by saving one body of work' would be here is unclear, but there could be some reference to Apollo, as the god of poetry, preserving the poems of two poets, e.g. Tibullus and [Tibullus] or two poetic collections (e.g. *Sulpicia Cycle* and the *Sulpicia poems*) in a single volume at some stage in the development of the *Corp. Tib*. Even if, as seems likely, the author of **8-12** is the same as the author of **13-18**, and in fact of the whole collection, the reference could support the impression he wishes to give that two authors were at work in this section of the *Corp. Tib*. In view of the importance of Vertumnus, the god of change, for this collection (see **8.13-14n**. above) it could be significant that Propertius' poem in which Vertumnus speaks begins with the words *qui mirare meas tot in uno corpore formas, / accipe Vertumni signa paterna dei* (4.2.1-2). The god who 'in a single body' contains so many shapes is surely relevant to the author of this collection. This idea of multiplicity within a single unified work is also emphasised in the last line of the epigram which ends Prop.'s Vertumnus poem: 4.2.64 *unum opus est, operi non datur unus honos*. For *restituisse* in the same *sedes* cf. Ov. *Pont*. 3.6.35-36 *exstinctos ... / nulla potest iterum restituisse dies*. Ovid is the only other elegist to use this medical technical term, see Bréguet (1946) 169-170.

23 celeber: 'honoured', 'celebrated', for its use of deities cf. Hor. *Carm.* 2.12.20 *Dianae celebris die*; Tib. 2.1.83 (of Amor) *uos celebrem cantate deum* (in a passage beginning *sancte, ueni* already imitated in **9** above); Ov. *Met.* 1.747 (of Isis) *nunc dea linigera colitur celeberrima turba*.

laetus eris: the god will be pleased at the couple's repayment of their vows (*debita reddet*), just as the couple will be pleased to repay them (*laetus uterque* **24**). There is no difficulty in the repetition of the adj. in adjacent lines with two different references, cf. **9.20** above *caste puer, casta retia tange manu*.

debita reddet: *debita* here stands for *debita uota* or *debita munera*; the use of the participle without further definition is rare, but cf. Ov. *Fast.* 5.596 *uoti debita soluit*. For the use of *debita reddere* in the context of recovery from illness, cf. Prop. 2.28.59-60 (addressed to Cynthia) *tu, quoniam es, mea lux, magno dimissa periclo, / munera Dianae debita redde choros*.

24 certatim: a common line-opening, especially in epic, e.g. Virg. *Aen.* (9); Sil. (8).

sanctis ... focis: found in the same *sedes* at Tib. 1.2.84, 8.70; Ov. *Fast.* 3.734, 4.296, *Pont.* 2.1.32; Mart. 9.31.6.

laetus uterque: the phrase is found also at Sil. 9.453. On the repetition of *laetus* from **23**, see **23n**. For *laetus* = 'happy and grateful' in the context of fulfilling vows cf. Virg. *Aen.* 5.235-237 *di, quibus imperium est pelagi ... / uobis laetus ego hoc candentem in litore taurum / constituam ante aras uoti reus* and the formula *uotum soluit laetus libens* on inscriptions (*ILS* III 2 p. 759).

25 pia turba: the combination occurs elsewhere at Prop. 3.13.18; Ov. *Fast.* 2.507, *Trist.* 5.3.47; [Ov.] *Epiced. Drusi* 296; Lucan 8.79; Val. Fl. 1.750; Sil. 10.952; Mart. 7.32.3, 8.38.13. It is normally used of crowds of worshippers rather than of the gods. For *pius* applied to gods who recognise an obligation cf. Virg. *Aen.* 4.382 (in Dido's prayer for vengeance) *si quid pia numina possunt*; Ov. *Ars* 3.347 *pia numina uatum*.

turba deorum: the same hexameter ending occurs at *Aetna* 62; Juv. 13.46; for the phrase cf. also Ov. *Fast.* 2.667-668, *Trist.* 4.1.53-54; Sen. *Thy.* 843; Stat. *Silu.* 3.1.108-109. The repetition of *turba* from **18** cannot be fortuitous; there the pejorative tone is clear (see above). Here, though mitigated by *pia*, some of this deprecatory nuance must rub off on the gods, who in this case display envy towards Apollo; cf. the far from reverent treatment of Mars in **8.1-4**.

26 optabunt artes: the gods will envy Apollo's skill at healing, just as Athena praises the skill of the Muses at Ov. *Met.* 5.267-268 *felicesque uocat pariter studioque locoque / Mnemonidas*, and cf. the reaction of the Muse at 271 *merito ... probas artesque locumque*.

optabunt ... quisque: the *constructio ad sensum* of the plural verb with the singular subject *quisque* is not found in Tib. or Prop., but cf. Virg. *Aen.* 11.185-186 *huc corpora quisque suorum / more tulere patrum*; Ov. *Ars* 1.109 *respiciunt ... sibi quisque puellam, Rem.* 74 *uindictae quisque fauete suae*; the same construction with *genus* occurs at **4.9-10** (above) *hominum genus omina noctis / farre pio placant*; see further Bréguet (1946) 247-248.

Poem 11

The genethliakon, or birthday poem, is a favourite of the *Corp. Tib.*, cf. Tib. 1.7 (for Messalla), 2.2 (for Cornutus), **[Tib.] 3.11** (for Cerinthus), **[Tib.] 3.12** (for Sulpicia), **[Tib.] 3.14** and **[Tib.] 3.15** (Sulpicia's birthday). It is found also in Prop. 3.10 (for Cynthia); Hor. *Carm.* 4.11 (for Maecenas); Ov. *Trist.* 3.13 (his own), 5.5 (his wife's) and Stat. *Silu.* 2.7 (for Lucan ten years after his death). In Greek it occurs only at the end of the first century BC in the epigrams of the Greek grammarian Crinagoras, who lived for a time in Rome: *AP* 6.227, 261, 345. The term genethliakon is not used in Greek of this kind of poem and occurs for the first time in Latin at Stat. *Silu.* 2 *praef.* On the generic background see Cairns (1972) 112-113 and on Roman birthday celebrations see Balsdon (1969) 121-122. Hubbard [(2004) 183-184] is instructive on the influence of Tib.'s poem 2.2 on the birthday poems **11, 12, 14** and **15**, and possible links between Cornutus and Cerinthus. Of course, since the *Sulpicia Cycle* and the *Sulpicia* poems seem to have been written later than Ovid's *Ars* (see Gen. Intro., sections 2.2.3 and 2.2.4), a real chronological connection between the Cornutus of Tib. 2.2 and Cerinthus would be impossible, since Tibullus died in 19 or 18 BC [see Maltby (2010) 336], a good twenty years before the *Ars* was published.

The present poem in the mask of the anonymous observer speaking as Sulpicia (see **8 headnote**) on Cerinthus' birthday, forms a pair with **12** in the mask of the observer in his own voice on Sulpicia's birthday and these two poems anticipate the two short epigrams on Sulpicia's birthday in the *Sulpicia* poems **14** and **15**. All these poems are in my view written by the unitary author of **book 3**, either in the mask of the anonymous observer in **11** (as Sulpicia) and **(12)**, or in the mask of Sulpicia (in **14** and **15**), see Gen. Intro., sections 2.2.3 and 2.2.4. Parker (1994), Hallett (2002), Dronke (2003) and Fabre-Serris (2009) argue that this poem, like **9**, is by Sulpicia herself. For convincing arguments against this view, based mainly on stylisitic grounds, see Hubbard (2004) 189-192. Pairs of poems on related themes appear first in Hellenistic Greek epigram (e.g. Meleager *AP* 5.136 and 137, 151 and 152, 172 and 173, 12.82 and 83) and then, in Latin, in Catullus (e.g. 2 and 3, 5 and 7, 37 and 39, 70 and 72, 107 and 109); Propertius 1.7 and 9, 3.4 and 5; Ovid *Amores* 1.11 and 12, 2.2 and 3, 2.11 and 12, 2.13 and 14; see further Jäger (1967), Davis (1977) and McKeown II 309-10.

Like Tib. 1.7 and 2.2, the poems **[Tib.] 3.11** and **3.12** reflect the cult practice of Roman birthdays and share a number of common features, such as the offering of incense to the birthday spirit (**11.9** *cape tura libens* and **12.1** *cape turis aceruos*), the formation of wishes by the celebrant, either secretly (**11.17** *tectius optat*, cf. **12.16** *tacita ... mente rogat*), or openly (**12.8** *quaeso* **12.15** *quod optet*) and a request for the spirit to grant them *adnue* (**11.20, 12.13**). As in Tib. 2.2 these wishes concern the celebrants' hopes for love and here again the two poems share a number of common themes: mutual love in **11.6** *mutuus ignis*, **7** *mutuus ... amor*, **13-14** *... uel seruiat aeque / uinctus uterque* occurs again at **12.8** *sed iuueni, quaeso, mutua uincla para*; indissoluble union in **11.16** *nulla queat posthac quam soluisse dies*, cf. **12.7** *neu quis diuellat amantes*. In both poems Sulpicia experiences the fires of love, **11.5** *uror ... uror*, cf. **12.17** *uritur ut celeres urunt altaria flammae*, and in both she is happy to suffer in this way, **11.5** *iuuat ... quod uror*, cf. **12.18** *nec liceat quamuis sana fuisse uelit*.

The contents of poem **11** may be summarised as follows:

1-8 Your birthday, Cerinthus, will always be sacred for me; the fates gave you sovereignty over girls and over me in particular, who will always burn for you, provided our love is mutual.

9-12 Genius, I will sacrifice to you provided Cerinthus loves no other but me, but if he longs for another you must leave his house.

13-18 Venus, make our love equal; I know my young man prays for the same as I, though secretly.

19-20 Natalis, grant his prayers, no matter if he does not speak them aloud.

Again the central couplet **9-10** introduces a change of direction, with the birthday wishes being made conditional upon Cerinthus' remaining faithful to Sulpicia alone.

Fulkerson [(2017) 255] points out that evidence from Martial (8.64, 9.52, 10.24, 12.60) suggests that, at least in his time, birthdays were celebrated on their respective Kalends, a fact which provides a link between these two birthday poems **11** and **12** and *Lygd.* 1 and the *Sulpicia Cycle* **8**. The theme of secrecy and openness, as reflected at the end of this poem in *tectius* **17**, *palam* **18** and in *clamne palamne* **20**, is a recurrent motif in the *Sulpicia Cycle* and in the *Sulpicia* poems; see Prolegomena p. 83 and **8.8.n.** above; see also **7n.** below.

1-2 The stately opening recalls in its content Hor. *Carm.* 4.11.15-20 (on Maecenas' birthday) *qui dies mensem Veneris marinae / findit Aprilem, / iure sollemnis mihi sanctiorque / paene natali proprio, quod ex hac / luce Maecenas meus adfluentes / ordinat annos.*

1 Qui mihi te … dies dedit: for the expression cf. Mart. 7.21.1-2 *haec est illa dies … quae … / Lucanum … tibi, Polla, dedit.*

sanctus: also used of a birthday at Hor. *Carm.* 4.11.17 *sanctior* (quoted above) and, of feast days in general, at Afran. *Tog.* 141 *ut degerem sanctum diem Dianae*; Cic. *Verr.* 2.4.151 *cum diem festum ludorum de fastis suis sustulisset celeberrimum et sanctissimum.*

2 inter festos … habendus: the normal prose expression is *inter festos referri*, cf. Suet. *Claud.* 11.3.9 *diem tamen necis … uetuit inter festos referri*; Tac. *Ann.* 13.41.21 *ut … inter festos referretur dies.*

semper: stressing the perpetuity of her relationship with Cerinthus, a marriage theme, see **10.16n.** above.

habendus erit: the same pentameter ending occurs at Ov. *Rem.* 376, 564, 630; cf. also *Her.* 20.230 *habendus erat.* The whole construction is Ovidian in character and has no parallel in the other elegists: cf. Ov. *Am.* 1.11.2 *docta neque ancillas inter habenda Nape, Fast.* 5.347-348 *non est / illa coturnatas inter habenda deas.*

3-4 te … / … tibi: for the pronoun framing the couplet in this way see Wills (1996) 430-431 and n. 75.

nouum ... / seruitium: cf. Val. Fl. 2.180-181 *nouis ... / seruitiis*. In the elegiac theme of *seruitium amoris* the reference elsewhere is normally to the servitude of the lover to his mistress, cf. Tib. 1.1.55, with Maltby (2002) 142 ad loc., 2.4.1-6; Prop. 1.5.19-20, 3.15.9-10; Ov. *Am.* 1.3.5-6, with McKeown II 64-5 ad loc., and see Copley (1947), Lyne (1979) and Murgatroyd (1981); what is *nouum* 'new' or 'strange' here is the idea of women's erotic slavery to a man, although this had been the norm in earlier Greek poetry, for which there are examples in N-H 374-375 on Hor. *Carm.* 1.33.14, and is found in Latin elegy at Prop. 2.26A.21-22 *nunc admirentur quod tam mihi pulchra puella / seruiat et tota dicar in urbe potens.*

3 te nascente: the idea that the Fates predicted a child's future at the moment of his birth is found only in Roman poetry; cf. Tib. 1.7.1-2, Ov. *Trist.* 5.3.25-26 (quoted below) and *CLE* 1533.3-4 *terminus hicc est, / quem mihi nascenti quondam Parcae cecinere*. In Greek literature this usually took place at the marriage of the child's parents cf. Aristoph. *Aues* 1731 and the Fates' song at the wedding of Achilles' parents, Peleus and Thetis, at Cat. 64.320ff.

Parcae: originally in the singular *Parca* was a Roman goddess of childbirth, her name being derived from *partus* – see *LALE* 450. Later, through a false etymology from *pars*, the *Parcae* became plural, equivalent to the Greek Fates (Μοῖραι); see further above **3.35n.** *tristesque sorores* and cf. De Melo (2019) II 855.

Parcae cecinere: an echo of the opening of Tib.'s birthday poem for Messalla, 1.7.1-2 *hunc cecinere diem Parcae fatalia nentes / stamina*. For the use of *cano* in this context to mean 'foretell' see **4.77n.** above, Maltby (2002) 282 on Tib. 1.7.1-2 and cf. Serv. *Aen.* 8.656 *canebat: quasi praediuinabat, nam canere et dicere et diuinare significat*, *ThLL* 3.272.57. The phrase *Parcae cecinere* occurs in Ovid's account of Bacchus' double birth at *Trist.* 5.3.25-26 *scilicet hanc legem nentes fatalia Parcae / stamina bis genito bis cecinere tibi*; cf. also Cat. 64.383 *cecinerunt ... Parcae* (the fates predict the future felicity of Peleus on the day of his marriage to Thetis); Hor. *Carm. Saec.* 25 *uosque ueraces cecinisse, Parcae, CLE* 1533.3-4 (quoted above).

4. dedĕrunt: this archaising use of the short vowel in the 3rd person plural perfect ending is rare in Tib. (2.3.12 *profuĕrunt*) and Prop. (2.3.25 *contulĕrunt)*, but more common in Ov.; see examples in Platnauer 53 and n.1.

regna superba: an echo of the erotic use of *regna* at Tib. 1.9.80 *et geret in regno regna superba tuo*; cf. Hor. *Carm.* 4.1.3-4 *bonae / sub regno Cinarae*; Prop. 2.16B.28 *et subito felix* (sc. *barbarus*) *nunc mea regna tenet*, 34.57 *ut regnem mixtas inter conuiua puellas*, 3.10.18 (to Cynthia on her birthday) *inque meum semper* (sc. *pete ut*) *stent tua regna caput*, 4.7.50 *longa mea in libris regna fuere tuis*; Ov. *Rem.* 15 *at si quis male fert indignae regna puellae*. In other contexts the phrase *regna superba* is found at Prop. 4.1B.88 and Mart. 12.48.16. Bréguet [(1946) 172-173] argues that *superba* here has more positive connotations than at Tib. 1.9.80, see **8.22n.** above.

5 uror ... uror: for line-framing of this type see Wills (1996) 427-428. For *uror* with reference to the flames of love at the line-opening cf. Hor. *Carm.* 1.13.9; Tib. 2.4.6; Ov. *Am.* 1.2.26, 2.4.12, *Her.* 7.23, 15.9, *Met.* 3.464, *Fast.* 3.682; Calp. *Ecl.* 3.8, and, in other line-positions, at Cat. 72.5; Ov. *Her.* 18.167. Within the *seruitium amoris* image, as here and Tib. 2.4.6, the verb may also suggest punishment by branding. For the image of love as fire cf. Sappho frs. 38-40 *PLF*; Meleager *AP* 5.57; Asclepiades *AP* 5.210; Virg. *Ecl.* 2.68, and see *calet* at **10** below, *urit* repeated of Sulpicia at **8.11-12** and *uritur* of Sulpicia at **12.17**; see further Mankin on Hor. *Epod.* 11.4, N-H on Hor. *Carm.* 1.13.9-10 and 1.33.6; Pease on Virg. *Aen.* 4.2 and McKeown II 27 on Ov. *Am.* 1.1.25-26. Whereas at **8.11-12** Sulpicia caused others to burn, here and at **12.17** it is Sulpicia herself who burns. Fabre-Serris [(2009) 155] compares the double *urimur* of Phaedra in her letter to Hippolytus at Ov. *Her.* 4.19-20 and [(2009) 163] Sappho's *uror* in initial line-position at Ov. *Her.* 15. 9.

ante alias: for this comparative use of *ante* cf. **4.93** *ante alias ... mitissima mater* with **n.** ad loc. and **19.16** *sola ante alios ... magna.*

iuuat ... quod uror: for the construction cf. Ov. *Pont.* 2.8.55 *nos ... uestra iuuat quod ... ora uidemus*. For the idea of not wishing to be cured of love's pains cf. Tib. 2.5.110 *et faueo morbo* (sc. *amoris*), *cum iuuat ipse dolor*, **[Tib.] 3.** *Sulpicia Cycle* **12.18** (of Sulpicia) *nec liceat quamuis sana fuisse, uelit* with **12.17-18nn.** and **18n.** below. With *iuuat* contrast its use with reference to Cerinthus' hunting at **9.9** *quid iuuat?* and compare its use by Sulpicia herself of her love for Cerinthus at **13.9** *sed pecasse iuuat*.

6 de nobis: i.e. 'concerning me', cf. **16.1-2** *... multum quod iam tibi de me / permittis*.

mutuus ignis: on the theme of *mutuus amor* in elegy and other contexts, suggesting a permanent marriage-like union, see **1.19n.** and cf. **7** *mutuus ... amor* and **13-16** below, and *mutua uincla para* at **12.8** (also with reference to Cerinthus). The metaphorical use of *ignis* of the fires of love is frequent in Cat., Prop. and Ov., but is found only here in the *Corp. Tib.*; full references in Bréguet (1946) 153-155, N-H on Hor. *Carm.* 1.19.5; also Heyworth and Morwood (2011) 155 on Prop. 3.6.39-40. Hallett [(2002b) 147] compares the *ignis* that burns Acme with love for Septimius at Cat. 45.16 where the image is combined with that of *mutuus amor* at 20 *mutuis animis amant amantur*. Particularly close in sense is Prop. 3.6.39 *me quoque consimili imposito torrerier igni* (in a message from Prop. to Cynthia to be delivered by Lygdamus) and Ov. *Her.* 19.5 *urimur igne pari*. For the combination *mutuus ignis* cf. Sen. *Phaed.* 415 *amare discat, mutuos ignes ferat*, making the connection with Phaedra, suggested above **5n.**, seem more likely.

7 mutuus ... amor: repeats and emphasises the theme of mutual love introduced in **6** (see **n.** on *mutuus ignis* above). For the combination cf. Cic. *Fam.* 13.50.2; Hor. *Epod.* 15.10; Tib. 1.2.65, 6.76; *Catal.* 4.12; Sen. *Contr.* 2.7.7, *Epist.* 9.52. Particularly close in context is *Catal.* 4.11-12 *quare illud satis est, si te permittis amari: / nam contra ut sit amor mutuus, unde mihi?*

per te dulcissima furta: the separation of the preposition from its substantive in prayers and oaths, on the model of Greek πρός + gen., is absent from Classical prose, but relatively frequent in verse, cf. Plaut. *Bacch.* 905-906 *per te, ere, opsecro / deos immortalis*; Tib. 1.5.7-8 *... per te furtiui foedera lecti / per Venerem quaeso*, **[Tib.] 3.1.15-16** with **n.** above, and see further examples at Jocelyn (1967) 169 on Enn. *Trag.* 3-4 Jocelyn, K-S II 1.584. For *dulcia furta* with reference to secret love-making cf. Virg. *Georg.* 4.346 *Martisque dolos et dulcia furta*; Prop. 2.30.28 *dulcia furta Iouis*; Ov. *Met.* 9.558 *dulcia fraterno sub nomine furta tegemus*; Stat. *Ach.* 1.938 *o dulcia furta dolique*. On the theme of secrecy in the *Sulpicia Cycle* see Prolegomena p. 83 and **8.8n.** and cf. *tectius* **17**, *palam* **18** and *clamne palamne* **20** below. On the relation between *furta* and secrecy, cf. Tib. 1.2.36 *celari uult sua furta Venus*.

8 perque tuos oculos: the same pentameter opening is found at Ov. *Am.* 3.11.48 *perque tuos oculos, qui rapuere meos*. For swearing by the eyes in Latin and Greek poetry, see **6.47-49n.** above.

Book Three of the Corpus Tibullianum: 493
Introduction, Text, Translation and Commentary

per Geniumque rogo: the Genius was a Roman's guardian spirit, who was born with him and protected him during his life, cf. Hor. *Epist.* 2.2.187-189 *scit Genius, natale comes qui temperat astrum, / naturae deus humanae, mortalis in unum / quodque caput*. According to Censorinus *De Die Natali* 3 he was identified with the household Lar (cf. *relinque focos* **12**). Honours and offerings to him (cf. *cape tura libens* **9**) were particularly appropriate on a man's birthday [cf. Tib. 1.7.49-54 (Messalla's), 2.2.5-8 (Cornutus')], which the Genius was invited to attend [Tib. 1.7.49, 53, 2.2.5]. Possibly his image was carried in procession from the Lararium to the scene of the birthday ceremonies. Here he could grant requests made to him (cf. 2.2.9-10 *adnuat* ... / ... *adnuit*, **20** below *adnue*). In the present poem the Genius is addressed at **9-12** and **19-20**. Tränkle [285 ad loc.] points out that slaves in particular prayed to and swore by their master's Genius, cf. Prop. 4.8.69 (of Prop.'s slave Lygdamus praying for protection from Cynthia by the *genius* of his master) *geniumque meum prostratus adorat* with Hutchinson (2006) 201-202 ad loc.; Sen. *Epist.* 12.2 (of the *uilicus*) *iurat per genium meum*, so that 'Sulpicia''s request by Cerinthus' Genius here could place her in the role of a slave as foreshadowed in the *seruitium amoris* image at **4** above.

9 magne Geni: so Scaliger (*ex libris*) for *mane Geni* of the MSS. The use of the archaic *manus* (for which cf. Varro *Ling.* 6.4 *bonum antiqui dicebant manum*) would be unique in Latin verse, its occurrences elsewhere being restricted to archaic or archaising inscriptions and to technical grammatical works. The epithet *magnus*, on the other hand, is well attested in verse with gods' names, cf. **8.1** above, *Mars magne*, and see **4.16n.** For the use of *magnus* with *Genius* cf. *CIL* X 1576 (first century AD) *deo magno Genio coloniae Puteolanorum*. The MSS reading could possibly be retained with the meaning 'in the morning', cf. the early morning laughter of the Camenae standing before Propertius' bed on Cynthia's birthday at Prop. 3.10.1 *mirabar quidnam risissent mane Camenae*.

cape tura libens: on the meaning of *tus* see **3.2n.** above. For the use of incense in honouring the Genius at a birthday cf. Tib. 2.2.3-5 (Cornutus' birthday); Prop. 3.10.19-20 (with Fedeli 347 ad loc.) and cf. the offerings to *Natalis Iuno* at **12.1** *cape turis aceruos*. The participle *libens* is relatively rare in elegy: Prop. 1.2.28, 2.24B.27; Ov. *Her.* 21.240.

uotisque faueto: common in requests to deities to grant prayers, cf. **3.33** *timidis faueas, Saturnia, uotis* (with **3.33-34n.** above), **12.7** (addressed to *Natalis Iuno*) *at tu, sancta, faue*; Sen. *Phaed.* 423 *faue uotis, dea, Phoen.*

633-634 *fauisse fac uotis deos / omnes tuis*. On *uota*, see **3.1n.** above. For the birthday request as a standard feature of the ritual, cf Tib. 2.2.9-10; **[Tib.] 3.12.16, 19-20** with Hubbard (2004) 184. For *uota* as an integral part of the address to the birthday Genius, see Argetsinger (1992) 181-183.

10 de me cogitat: the construction is mainly prosaic, but cf. Ov. *Ars* 2.686 *siccaque de lana cogitat ipsa sua*.

ille: common in this position in the pentameter in Tib. (34 examples).

calet: the metaphorical use 'to be hot with passion' (cf. *OLD caleo* 6) is found in Hor. e.g. *Carm.* 1.4.19 *nec tenerum Lycidan mirabere, quo calet iuuentus* and Ov. e.g. *Ars* 1.526 (*Liber*) *flammae, qua calet ipse, fauet*, but not with an erotic sense in Tib. (1.5.22, 1.10.53) or Prop. (4.3.62). Apart from here, the verb in this sense is always accompanied by a qualifying ablative; further examples in Bréguet (1946) 155-156.

11 quod si: on the distribution of this phrase in poetry see **4.77n.**, cf. also **7.201** above. For *quod si forte* at the beginning of the hexameter at Prop. 1.5.9, 2.14.31, 26A.13, 28.25; Ov. *Her.* 12.83, 183 see Bréguet (1946) 140.

alios ... suspiret amores: clearly inspired by Tib. 1.6.35 *te tenet, absentes alios suspirat amores*. For the verse-ending cf. also Lucr. 4.1192 *ficto suspirat amore*; [Virgil] *Lydia* 3 *nostrum suspirat amorem*. The word *amores* occurs in consecutive line ends at Virg. *Ecl.* 10.53-54 with reference to Gallus's love, and also probably to the title of his poetic composition the *Amores,* see Harrison (2007) 69-70. The theme of jealousy, first introduced in the mask of the anonymous poet at **9.19-22**, echoes the mood of poem **16**; jealousy is experienced by Sulpicia but never by Cerinthus.

iam nunc: suggesting the affair is at an early stage. For the phrase cf. Tib. 1.3.53, 1.6.77, 2.3.3; Prop. 2.19.17, 4.11.93; Ov. *Am.* 3.1.64, *Her.* 2.83, 4.108, 17.147, *Ars* 1.212, 3.59, *Met.* 13.19, 14.175, 203, *Pont.* 2.1.61.

12 The image of Cerinthus' Genius would have been kept in the Lararium by the hearth. As he was also Genius of the bed, Sulpicia may see any infidelity on Cerinthus' part with respect to the *dulcissima furta* (**7**) he enjoyed with another as a sin against the Genius, which Sulpicia asks him to punish by leaving Cerinthus' faithless hearth. The theme of gods leaving their sphere of activity in reaction to the wickedness of men occurs first in Hes. *Op.* 197f., and is taken over into Latin by Virg. *Ecl.* 5.35 *ipsa*

Pales agros atque ipse reliquit Apollo. The wording of the line here is close to Tib. 2.3.64 *tu quoque deuotos, Bacche, relinque lacus,* where Bacchus is asked to leave his country wine-vats, when Nemesis is held in the country far from the poet.

sancte: the epithet is used in Sulpicia's address to Apollo at **10.9** above, and is found frequently on inscriptions referring to birthdays and the birthday Genius, see **1n.** above and **12.7n.** on *sancta* addressed to Sulpicia's *Natalis Iuno.*

13-16 A return to the theme of *mutuus amor* introduced in **6-8** above and recurring at **12.8** below. On this theme see further **1.19n.**, Fedeli 83 on Prop. 1.1.25, N-H 195 on Hor. *Carm.* 2.12.15-16, N-R 137 on Hor. *Carm.* 3.9.13-14 and cf. Ter. *Eun.* 91ff.; Cat. 45.20 *mutuis animis amant amantur* (of Septimius and Acme), 76.23ff.; Hor. *Carm.* 4.1.30, *Epod.* 15.10; Ov. *Met.* 14.25.

13 nec tu sis iniusta, Venus: normally it is Venus who upholds the laws of lovers, cf. Tib. 1.5.58 *saeuit et iniusta lege relicta Venus,* **[Tib.] 3.19.24** *haec* (sc. *Venus*) *notat iniustos supplicibusque fauet.* For Prop. it is the mistress, not Venus, who is unjust: 1.7.11-12 *me laudet ... / ... iniustas saepe tulisse minas* (sc. *puellae*), 2.5.14 (in a self-address) *iniusto subtrahe colla iugo.*

13-14 Venus ... / uinctus: Venus was linked etymologically with *uincio,* see *LALE* 635 sv *Venus,* Michalopoulos (2001) 169, 171, Hinds (2006) 2-15 and cf. Varro *Ling.* 5.61-62. For the possible etymological play here cf. **19.23** below *Veneris sanctae considam uinctus ad aras.* For *uinctus* connected with the bonds of love cf. Tib. 1.1.55 *me retinent uinctum formosae uincla puellae,* 1.9.79 *cum me uinctum puer alter habebit*; Ov. *Her.* 20.86 (Acontius to Cydippe) *seruabor firmo uinctus amore tui* with Kenney [(1996) 195] who, following Murgatroyd [(1981) 596], sees the theme as Tibullan. The idea of binding is suggested by the figure of servitude to Venus, first attested in Tibullus, cf. 1.2.99-100 *at mihi parce Venus. semper tibi dedita seruit / mens mea,* 2.3.33-34 *felices olim, Veneri cum fertur aperte / seruire aeternos non puduisse deos.* The idea of joint servitude to Amor occurs earlier in Cat. 45.14 (of Septimius and Acme) *huic uni domino usque seruiamus.*

14 uinctus ... uincla: Like Venus, *uinclum* is associated etymologically with *uincio,* see *LALE* 646 sv *uinculum* and Michalopoulos (2001) 177. For a similar play on this link, in the context of *seruitium amoris* cf. Tib.

1.1.55 and **1.9.79** (quoted in **13-14n.** above). For the use of *uincula* (= marriage bonds) in the context of Cornutus' birthday wishes, cf. Tib. 2.2.18-19 *coniugio uincula portet Amor, / uincula quae maneant semper* with Maltby (2002) 392 ad loc. and Hubbard (2004) 184.

uincla leua: for the idea of loosening the bonds of love cf. Tib. 2.4.4. *et numquam misero uincla remittit Amor*. For the expression cf. Virg. *Aen.* 2.146-147 *uiro ... manicas atque arta leuari / uincla iubet Priamus*.

14-15 uterque ... / ... uterque: the repetition underlines the theme of *mutuus amor*. In **14** the emphasis is on each lover's bond with Venus, while in **15** the bond is with each other.

15 ualida ... catena: cf. Tib. 2.6.25 *ualida ... compede*.

teneamur ... catena: another possible etymological play (cf. **7.117-118n.** above). It is found earlier in the context of *seruitium amoris* at Tib. 2.4.3 *seruitium sed triste datur, teneorque catenis*; cf. also Hor. *Carm.* 3.11.43-45 *nec te feriam neque intra / claustra tenebo. / me pater saeuis oneret catenis*, and Ov. *Met.* 4.175-178 (Vulcan's reaction on hearing of Venus' adultery with Mars) *et mens et quod opus fabrilis dextra tenebat / excidit: extemplo graciles ex aere catenas / retiaque et laqueos ... / elimat*. For *catena* used elsewhere of the bonds of love cf. Prop. 2.15.25-26 *atque utinam haerentes sic nos uincire catena / uelles, ut numquam solueret ulla dies* (where the pentameter is echoed in **16** here); Ov. *Her.* 20.85-86 *sed neque compedibus nec me compesce catenis – / seruabor firmo uinctus amore tui, Met.* 4.678-679 (Perseus on prisoners' and lovers' chains) *... non istis digna catenis, / sed quibus inter se cupidi iunguntur amantes*; Stat. *Silu.* 5.1.43-44 (in the context of marriage) *uos collato pectore mixtos / iunxit inabrupta concordia longa catena*; see further Syndikus (2006) 278 n. 107 and, for Greek examples in the *AP*, N-H 177 on Hor. *Carm.* 1.13.18.

16 nulla queat ... soluisse dies: cf. Hor. *Carm.* 1.13.18-20 *nec malis / diuulsus querimoniis / suprema citius soluet amor die* and Prop. 2.15.26 quoted on **15** above. For this wish for insoluble bonds in the birthday context cf. Sulpicia's words at **12.7** *neu quis diuellat amantes*. Hubbard [(2004) 184] sees both the *Sulpicia Cycle* examples (**11.16** and **12.7**) as renewing in some way Cornutus' birthday wish for a happy marriage at Tib. 2.2.11-12. Certainly Tib.'s poem must have influenced poems **11** and **12**, but Cerinthus cannot simply be identified with Cornutus (see Gen. Intro., section 3.4).

posthac: the adv. occurs here only in the *Corp. Tib.* and is not found in Prop. or Ov. In Cat. it is found at 24.3, 65.9, 11, 99.16.

17 The verse is close in expression, but reverses the male and female roles of Ov. *Ars* 1.276 *uir male dissimulat: tectius illa cupit*; see Hinds (1987a) 40-41. This is the only other verse passage in which the comparative adv. *tectius* appears, so that a link between the two seems likely. Elsewhere the adverb occurs only in Cicero: *tecte* at *Orator* 2.28.14 and *Att.* 1.14.4; *tectius* at *Fam.* 9.22.2 and 10.8.5. For a similar reticence on Sulpicia's part in making birthday requests cf. **12.16** *tacita ... mente rogat*, and of her secret amatory desires **12.6** *occulte ... placuisse uelit*. For the shyness of young men in amatory situations cf. Cat. 61.169-171 *illi non minus ac tibi / pectore urit in intimo / flamma, sed penite magis*; Tib. 1.4.13-14 *at illi / uirgineus teneras stat pudor ante genas* (but this is of a young boy who is the object of male erotic attention). On the theme of secrecy in general in this group of poems see Prolegomena p. 83 and **8.8n.** above and cf. **18** and **20** below. Here in **17-18** Cerinthus, in keeping his wishes secret, does what Sulpicia herself is ashamed of doing in **13.1-2, 9-10** and **18.6**; see Batstone (2018) 107.

optat ... optat: for the line-framing repetition see Wills (1996) 430 and cf. **7.166** here and **5** above. For the use of this verb of the framing of birthday wishes cf. **12.15** (of Sulpicia) *quod optet*.

optat idem iuuenis: for the line-opening, cf. Ov. *Trist.* 5.11.27 *optat idem populus*.

18 The situation recalls Tib. 2.2.9-10 in which the birthday celebrant, Cornutus, is asked to make a wish in the presence of the Genius: *adnuat* (sc. *Genius*) *et, Cornute, tibi quodcumque rogabis. / en age, quid cessas? adnuit ille – roga*. For this traditional feature of the genethliakon see Cairns (1972) 113 and Fedeli 345 on Prop. 3.10.17. The expression is inspired by another Tibullan passage, in which celebrants at a country festival are asked to call for love for their flocks or even for themselves: 2.1.83-86 *uos celebrem cantate deum* (sc. *Amorem*) *pecorique uocate: / uoce palam pecori, clam sibi quisque uocet, / aut etiam sibi quisque palam, nam turba iocosa / obstrepit*. On the theme of secrecy and openness in the *Sulpicia Cycle* see Prolegomena p. 83 and **8.8n.** above and cf. **20** below *clamne palamne*. The theme also has an important role to play in the *Sulpicia* poems, as in **13.1-2** and **9-10** where 'Sulpicia' is no longer willing to hide her love and **18.6** where she had wished to keep it secret; it recurs in the closing two poems of the collection at **19.8-10**

where the wise man keeps his love to himself, and where the poet's *garrula lingua* **19.20** is at the root of his problems, and in poem **20** where *rumor* is asked to be silent *tace* **4**. This suggests that, as we shall see below, poems **19** and **20** are well integrated thematically with the two *Sulpicia* groups **8-12** and **13-18** and the whole of the collection.

hic: i.e. at the birthday celebration, where wishes of this kind were expected to be spoken out loud (*palam*).

dicere uerba palam: for the pentameter ending cf. Tib. 2.5.94 *dicere uerba senem*.

19 at tu, Natalis: the same words open the final distich of Tibullus' birthday poem to Messalla, 1.7.63. The adj. *Natalis* is used to designate a man's Genius on the occasion of his birthday (cf. also Tib. 2.2.1, 2.2.21; Ov. *Trist.* 3.13.2), just as *Natalis Iuno* (*Sulpicia Cycle* **12.1**) designates the birthday spirit of a woman.

quoniam deus omnia sentis: very close in expression to Ov. *Pont.* 1.2.71 *nescit enim Caesar, quamuis deus omnia norit*. For the omniscience of the gods cf. e.g. Hes. *Op.* 267 πάντα ἰδὼν Διὸς ὀφθαλμὸς καὶ πάντα νοήσας ["the eye of Zeus sees all and knows all"]. For the concept used of the birthday spirit cf. Tib. 2.2.11-12 *auguror uxoris fidos optabis amores; / iam reor hoc ipsos edidicisse deos*. The conjunction *quoniam* is found only here in the *Corp. Tib.*, but is relatively common elsewhere in Augustan poetry [Hor. *Serm.* (4), *Epist.* (1); Prop. (14); Virg. *Ecl.* (5), *Georg.* (3), *Aen.* (7); Ov. *Am.* (1), *Her.* (6), *Ars* (4), *Rem.* (2), *Met.* (30), *Fast.* (2), *Trist.* (14), *Pont.* (15), *Ibis* (1)].

20 adnue: at the beginning of the verse also at Tib. 2.5.121, addressed to Apollo, in the final distich of the poem. For *adnuere* with the Genius as subject in a birthday context see Tib. 2.2.9-10, the birthday of Cornutus, sometimes associated with Cerinthus [Hubbard (2004) 183-184 quoted on **18** above], and cf. **12.13** *adnue* addressed to Sulpicia's birthday Juno. The verb, which comes from the same root as *numen* [see **4.53n**. and cf. *LALE* 416, De Melo (2019) II 1000], usually has a god as subject, see *Laud. Mess.* **7.133** with **n**. above (of Jupiter) and cf. Ov. *Pont.* 2.8.51 *adnuite o timidis, mitissima numina, uotis*.

quid refert clamne palamne roget?: the use of *ne ... ne* 'whether ... or' to introduce alternative indirect questions occurs occasionally in prose, e.g. Caes. *BG* 7.14 *nihil interesse dicit ipsosne interficiant impedimentisne exuant*, but is mainly poetic, e.g. Hor. *Epist.* 1.15.15, *AP*

117; Virg. *Aen.* 1.308, 5.95, 702, 12.321; Ov. *Met.* 3.256, 13.912, *Fast.* 2.782; see K-S II 2. 528. On the thematic significance of *clamne palamne* see **8.8n. above**. Since the birthday spirit is omniscient it makes no difference whether Cerinthus speaks his wish out loud or not.

Poem 12

This poem in celebration of Sulpicia's birthday forms a pair with *Sulpicia Cycle* **11** on Cerinthus' birthday and shares with it a number of common themes. On the links between the two, their relation to the genethliakon tradition and their anticipation of *Sulpicia* **14** and **15** see **11 headnote**. The form returns to that of a third person narrative in the mask of the anonymous observer with addresses to Juno at **1-6** and **7-14**. The contents may be summarised as follows:

1-6 accept offerings of incense, Juno, on the birthday of an educated girl, who has bathed and dressed today openly for you and secretly for her lover.

7-14 holy one, let no one split up these lovers, but make sure they burn with mutual passion; give your assent and accept offerings of cake and wine.

15-20 the girl ignores her mother's advice and makes her own prayers; she burns with love and wishes for no cure; may she please her young man and may their love last long as a result of her vows.

There are particularly striking echoes of the first poem of the *Sulpicia Cycle,* **8**, clearly giving a recognisable ring-structure to the five poems of this group **(8-12)**. This, together with important stylistic differences between **8-12** and **13-18**, would suggests that the poems **8-12** were conceived as a separate unit from **13-18**, despite being linked by the theme of Sulpicia's love for Cerinthus. So *compsit* **12.3** picks up *compsit* **8.10** (both combining literal and metapoetic meanings); *conspicienda* **12.4** echoes the request to Mars *spectatum ... ueni* at **8.2**; the active metaphorical *urit* at **8.11** and **8.12**, is picked up by the passive metaphorical *uritur* (of Sulpicia) and the active literal *urunt* of the flames on the altar at **12.17**; the *Tyria ... palla* of Sulpicia at **8.11** is reflected in Juno's *purpurea ... palla* at **12.13** and whereas Sulpicia is *candida* **8.12**, Juno is *perlucida* **12.13** (clearly suggesting parallels between the girl and the goddess); the *mille ... ornatus* of Vertumnus at **8.14** are echoed in the *uias mille* suggested by Amor in **12.12**; Sulpicia who is *digna* at **8.15** and *dignior* at **8.24** is *dignior* again at **12.10** (a term taken form marriage contexts). Finally the rite of the Matronalia to be celebrated *multos ... in annos* **8.23**, is echoed in the birthday celebration to be celebrated *ueniet cum proximus annus* at **12.19**. The two poems are further linked by the goddess Juno who both presided over the Matronalia (the setting of poem 8) and over the birthday of women (the occasion of poem 12).

1 Natalis Iuno: the female equivalent of a man's birthday Genius was her Natalis Iuno, which was worshipped in the same way. For women swearing by Juno as their patron goddess cf. **6.48** with **47-49n.** above and **19.15**.

sanctos cape turis aceruos: cf. Tib. 2.2.3-4 (Cornutus' birthday) *urantur pia tura focis*; **[Tib.]** 3.11.9 *magne Geni, cape tura libens*. Offerings of incense are also mentioned in the context of Cynthia's birthday at Prop. 3.10.19 *inde coronatas ubi ture piaueris aras*, see Fedeli 347 ad loc. The hexameter ending *turis aceruos* occurs also at Ov. *Met.* 5.131; Stat. *Theb.* 11.222, *Silu.* 2.1.21; Mart. 7.54.5.

2 tenera ... manu: cf. the same *iunctura* applied to Cerinthus at **9.8**.

docta puella: on the use of this epithet to refer to poets and Muses see **4.45n.** *doctaeque sorores*. On its use to hint at a mistress's literary expertise cf. e.g. Cat. 35.16-17 *Sapphica puella / Musa doctior*; Prop. 2.11.6 (of Cynthia, in the same metrical *sedes* as here) *cinis hic docta puella fuit*. In the present context the adj. may refer to what are to be regarded as Sulpicia's poetic compositions, i.e. poems **13-18** of **book 3**.

3 lota tibi est hodie: the conjecture *lota* in place of *tota* of the MSS is first found in the margin of the ed. Plant. 1569. In view of **5-6** below it is clear that Sulpicia is not devoting herself entirely, *tota*, to Juno, whereas *lota* would well suit ritual washing in a religious context, cf. Tib. 1.3.25-26 ... *pie dum sacra colis, pureque lauari / te memini,* and a similar care for washing and self-adornment is mentioned in the context of Cynthia's birthday at Prop. 3.10.13-14 *ac primum pura somnum tibi discute lympha, / et nitidas presso pollice finge comas*. For the form *lota* in place of *lauta* in verse cf. Prop. 4.1B.86; *Culex* 62; Sen. *Phaed.* 750; Lucan 1.600; Pers. 5.86; Juv. 6.464; Mart. 4.28.3, 6.53.1, 10.11.6, 30.70, 11.58.11, 12.70.6, 14.163.2. For a similar misreading of *lotam* as *totam* in the MSS cf. Petr. 40.7. In our passage the reading *tota* could have been influenced by **10.17** above, *at nunc tota tua est*.

se ... compsit: for *comere* with a personal object cf. Ov. *Am.* 2.8.2 *comere sed solas digna, Cypassi, deas* (with McKeown III 158 ad loc.) and see *ThLL* 3.1991.43-63. The mention here of Sulpicia adorning herself for a festival recalls the opening of the first poem of the *Sulpicia Cycle*, **8.1** *Sulpicia est tibi culta tuis, Mars magne, Kalendis*. As with *culta* there, so *compsit* here could have metapoetic associations of well-polished verse, see **1.14n.** *comptum ... opus*, **8.10n.** *comptis ... comis* and cf. **5n.** *ornandi causas* below. Juno's association with the Matronalia perhaps also serves to link the present poem with poem **8** as well as with poem **1**.

laetissima: used at Virg. *Aen.* 4.687 *cum te gremio accipiet laetissima Dido*, of Dido, taking on her lap Ascanius, who will inspire her with love for Aeneas. For the possible association of Sulpicia and Dido in poems **13-18** and the relevance of Virgil's line here see **13.3-4n.** below.

4 ante tuos ... focos: the phrase in this line-position is used elsewhere of animal sacrifices, cf. Prop. 4.5.66 *ante tuos guttura secta focos*, 4.6.2 *ante meos icta iuuenca focos*.

conspicienda: 'for all to see'; the gerundive here approaches the adjectival sense of 'admirable', cf. Sen. *De Ira* 2.5.5 *magnificum quiddam conspiciendumque*. For the sense cf. Tib. 2.3.52 (of Nemesis) *incedat donis conspicienda meis*; Ov. *Am.* 2.4.42 *Leda fuit nigra conspicienda coma*, *Fast.* 2.310 (of Omphale) *aurato conspicienda sinu*. It is particularly frequent in Ovid and occurs elsewhere in the same *sedes* at Tib. 1.2.70; Ov. *Ars* 3.308, 780, *Rem.* 680, *Fast.* 5.28, 118, 170, 552, *Trist.* 2.114, *Pont.* 1.8.42, 4.13.16. For other gerundives in this position cf. **9.22** *diripienda*, **10.12** *numeranda*, **11.2** *habendus*. On a possible link with the request to Mars in *Sulpicia Cycle* **8.2** *spectatum ... ueni* to see Sulpicia at the Matronalia, see **12 headnote**.

5-6 The couplet is close in sense to Tib. 1.9.71 *non tibi sed iuueni cuidam uult bella uideri*; a similar idea lies behind Prop. 4.8.16 (of Cynthia driving off in a chariot) *causa fuit Iuno, sed mage causa Venus*. Here our author dissembles Sulpicia's real reason for her dressing up, continuing the theme of openness and secrecy, which characterises the whole collection; see also **6n.** *occulte* below.

5 ornandi causas: cf. the common use in Cicero of *ornandi causa* referring to rhetorical embellishment, e.g. *De Oratore* 2.80, 341, 352, 3.39, 167, *Brutus* 82, *Topica* 100, which makes a metapoetic meaning seem likely here; see **3n.** *se ... compsit* above and cf. Ov. *Trist.* 1.1.9 *felices ornent haec instrumenta libellos.*

relegat: the use of this verb + dat. in the sense of shifting responsibility onto someone else occurs first here in verse and is mainly prosaic, see *OLD relego*¹ 3b and Bréguet (1946) 141-142.

6 occulte: for the theme of secret desires in general in this *Cycle* see **8.8n.** above, and, in the context of birthday wishes, cf. **11.17** (of Cerinthus) *sed tectius optat* and *tacita ... mente rogat* (of Sulpicia) at **16** below. The adv. occurs only here in the *Corp. Tib.*, is avoided by Prop. and is rare in Ov. (*Am.* 1.8.49, *Her.* 17.153, *Ars* 2.708).

placuisse uelit: on the metrical convenience of perfect infinitives in Augustan poetry, see Maltby (2002) 132-133 on Tib. 1.1.29-30 and Perotti (1989). For *placuisse* in this *sedes* cf. Ov. *Her.* 21.34 *et placuisse nocet* and *Fast.* 2.612 *tum placuisse deo.* The combination with *uelit* here recalls its use in Early Latin prohibitions of the type *ne quis fecisse uelit.*

7 sancta: the same adj. is used in the address to Cerinthus' Genius at 11.12. For *sancte* elsewhere in addresses to gods in elegy cf. Tib. 2.1.81 (Amor); Prop. 4.9.71 (of Sancus), 10.9 (Apollo).

faue: the same request is made of Cerinthus' Genius at **11.9**, see further **n.** ad loc. on *uotisque faueto*. Juno, goddess of marriage, addressed as Saturnia, is asked to favour his relationship with Neaera by Lygdamus at **3.33**, see **33-34n.** Here Juno's marriage role may hint at a future marriage between Sulpicia and Cerinthus. For *faue* addressed to Phoebus cf. Tib. 2.5.1; [Tib.] 3.10.19.

neu quis diuellat amantes: cf. **11.16** *nulla queat posthac quam* (sc. *catenam amoris*) *soluisse dies.* For this figurative use of *diuellere* = 'to separate' see *OLD diuello* 3 and cf. Hor. *Carm.* 1.13.17-20 *felices ter et amplius, / quos inrupta tenet copula nec malis / diuulsus querimoniis / suprema citius soluet amor die.* The verb is found elsewhere in elegy only at Ov. *Trist.* 3.9.27-28 of Medea's dismemberment of her brother ... *diuellit diuulsaque membra per agros / dissipat.* For Juno's role in joining rather than separating lovers, see **9n.** below.

8 iuueni: of Cerinthus also at **9.1, 10.11, 11.17**.

mutua uincla: for the theme of *mutuus amor* in a birthday poem see **11.6n.** *mutuus ignis* above and cf. **11.7** *mutuus ... amor* and **11.13-14** ...

uel seruiat aeque / uinctus uterque tibi. For the significance of *uincla* in this context see **11.13-14n., 14n.,** and **15n.** (on *catena*) above.

9-10 The central couplet of the poem stresses how well suited the couple are to one another.

9 bene compones: for *compono* in the sense of 'matching' a pair of lovers etc. see *OLD compono* 3b, Bréguet (1946) 180-181 and cf. Ov. *Ars* 2.385 (of deception in love) *hoc bene compositos, hoc firmos soluit amores*, *Fast.* 3.484 (Bacchus cheating Ariadne) *tam bene compositum sollicitare torum*; [Ov.] *Epiced. Drusi* 301-302 (of a married couple) *par bene compositum: iuuenum fortissimus alter, / altera tam forti mutua cura uiro*. It is not found in this sense in Tib., Prop. or elsewhere in the *Corp. Tib.* For Juno's role in joining lovers in matrimony, cf. Paul. Fest. 92 L *ara Iunonis Iugae, quam putabant matrimonia iungere*.

ullae: a unique example of this form (if correctly transmitted) of the dat. pron. in place of the regular *ulli*. Cf. Prop. 1.20.35 *nullae* for *nulli* (if this reading is correct; Heyworth prints the early conjecture *nulli*) of which the only other example occurs at Coel. Antipat. ap. Prisc. *GL* 2.198.4 – see Fedeli 478 on Prop. 1.20.35-36. Other isolated examples of analogous forms occur in Early Latin, e.g. Plaut. *Mil.* 356 *solae*, 438 *eae*, *Truc.* 790 *istae*, and in Classical prose at Cic. *Diu.* 2.30 *aliae*. The fact that most of them are feminine could be significant, although cf. *toto* at Prop. 3.11.57 (again Heyworth prints an early correction to *toti*); see further Bréguet (1946) 142-143, Tränkle (1960) 36-37. The effect may be of an archaism, appropriate for the language of a prayer.

ullae non: equivalent of *nullae* (*-i*).

10 seruire ... dignior: for the theme of *seruitium amoris* see **11.3-4n.** The use of *dignior* perhaps anticipates Sulpicia's own words at **13.10** *cum digno digna fuisse ferar*. On its importance with relation to Sulpicia, its association with well-suited marriage partners, and its possible Gallan connections, see **1.8n., 8.15n., 24n.** (see **headnote** above on other links between the present poem and poem **8**), **13.10**. For *dignus* + inf. cf. Cat. 68.131-132 *cui tum concedere digna / lux mea*; Tib. 2.6.43 *nec ... oculos digna est foedare*; Ov. *Am.* 2.8.2 *comere ... digna... deas*, 2.14.6 *militia fuerat digna perire sua* (*Her.* 4.86) etc.

11-12 For the theme of divine help and guidance to lovers cf. Tib. 1.8.55-56 *poterat custodia uinci; / ipse dedit cupidis fallere posse deus*, 1.2.16-24 (of Venus), 2.1.73-78 (of Amor); Ov. *Am.* 1.6.7-8 *ille* (sc. *Amor*) *per* *excubias custodum leniter ire / monstrat*: *inoffensos derigit ille pedes*. The theme again anticipates Sulpicia's words at **13.3-4** *illum Cytherea ... / attulit in nostrum deposuitque sinum*. The mention of the *custos* (**11**) and the use of the verb *fallo* (*fallendi* **12**) suggests an illicit relationship of some kind; perhaps one not sanctioned by Sulpicia's parents, cf. the role of her mother at **15-16** below.

cupidos: for the substantival use cf. Tib. 1.8.56 (quoted above, in the same context); Ov. *Ars* 3.674 *prona uenit cupidis in sua uota fides*. Substantival *cupidus* is absent from Prop. and does not occur in any Latin writer before Tib. and, apart from here, after Ov.; see Bréguet (1946) 157-158.

deprendere: of catching lovers in the act at Ov. *Am.* 1.9.39 (of Mars with Venus), *Ars* 2.557 (lovers should avoid catching their girls with rivals); see Pichon 127.

custos: the role of the 'guard' in elegy was to bar the lover's access to his mistress, cf. Tib. 1.2.5, 15; Prop. 1.11.15 and the address to the *custos* Bagoas at Ov. *Am.* 2.2 and see Pichon 121. For Amor as *custos* in the different sense of 'guardian', 'protector' see **9.4** above.

uias mille: for the phrase cf. Tib. 1.3.50; Virg. *Aen.* 5.590, 12.753; Val. Fl. 5.316. Given the links between the present poem and poem **8** mentioned in the **headnote** above, it is possible that there is an intentional echo here of Vertumnus' *mille ... ornatus* at **8.14**. In an important intertext (see Gen. Intro., section 1.3) at Ov. *Met.* 7.726 the disguised Cephalus uses *mille dolos* to gain access to his wife: *uix aditus per mille dolos ad Erecthida factus*.

ministret amor: cf. Tib. 1.10.57 *Amor rixae mala uerba ministrat*. Given the possible influence on Cerinthus of Tib.'s Cornutus it may be significant that the verb occurs in the birthday poem to Cornutus at Tib. 2.2.21 requesting his Genius to provide him and his wife with children.

13 adnue: the same word is used of the assent of the birthday spirit at **11.20** (see **n**. ad loc.). Here Sulpicia has not expressed her wishes, but the author assumes they will resemble those mentioned in **7-12**.

purpureaque ... palla: on the long robe or *palla* appropriate for deities and for women on festive occasions, see **4.35n**. and cf. the description of Sulpicia in a purple *palla* at **8.11** *seu Tyria uoluit procedere palla* with **n**. ad loc. For gods and heroes wearing such a purple robe cf. Prop. 4.9.47; Ov. *Met.* 11.166 (Apollo); Sen. *Phaed.* 330 (Hercules); Stat. *Ach.* 2.5

(Achilles). Most relevant to our context is the offering of a purple robe interwoven with gold made by the Spartan women to the chaste goddess *castae ... diuae* Juno at Stat. *Theb.* 10.56-60, quoted in **14n.** below. For the poet giving directions as to the clothing in which a deity should appear cf. Cat. 61.6-10 (to Hymenaeus) *cinge tempora floribus / suaue olentis amaraci, / flammeum cape, laetus huc / huc ueni niueo gerens / luteum pede soccum*; Tib. 1.7.45-47 (to Osiris-Bacchus) *sed uarii flores et frons redimita corymbis, / fusa sed ad teneros lutea palla pedes*, 2.2.6 (to the Genius) *cui decorent sanctas mollia serta comas*, 2.5.7-8 (to Apollo) ... *nunc indue uestem / sepositam, longas nunc bene pecte comas.*

perlucida: 'bright', 'radiant' as in *OLD perlucidus* 2, suggesting divine beauty, cf. Tib. 2.5.7 (to Apollo) *nunc nitidus pulcherque ueni* and **4.36** with **n.** ad loc., where Apollo wears a *palla* on his *nitido corpore*. The adj. *perlucidus* is not found in Prop., Tib. or elsewhere in the *Corp. Tib.* and in its four occurrences in Ovid it has the meaning of 'transparent' (*Her.* 21.157, *Met.* 2.856, 3.161, 10.733); see further Bréguet (1946) 148-151. As with the purple *palla* used of Juno here and of Sulpicia at **8.11**, so the description of Juno here as *perlucida* picks up the epithet *candida* used of Sulpicia at **8.12**. The intention is clearly to suggest parallels between the girl and the goddess, see **headnote** to the poem above.

14 ter: the only mention of a triple offering in the context of birthday celebrations. On the magic significance of the odd numbers see Tupet (1986) 2600, and on the number three, in particular, see Usener (1903) and cf. Tib. 1.2.56 [with Maltby (2002) 169-170], 3.11 and 5.14. A triple libation to Oceanus by Cyrene is mentioned at Virg. *Georg.* 4.384 *ter liquido ardentem perfundit nectare Vestam.*

ter tibi fit libo ter, ... mero: for the offering of cake and wine to the birthday spirit cf. Tib. 2.2.8 (Cornutus' birthday) *atque satur libo sit madeatque mero* (with *libo* and *mero* in the same *sedes*). On *libum* a cake made from cheese, flour and eggs (Cato *Agr.* 75), an offering particularly associated with birthday ceremonies and other religious occasions, see Maltby (2002) on Tib. 1.7.53-54, McKeown II 249 on Ov. *Am.* 1.8.94, Robinson (2011) on Ov. *Fast.* 2.643-644 and cf. Ov. *Ars* 1.429, *Trist.* 3.13.17, 4.10.12; Mart. 10.24.4. For *fit* = *sacrum fit, facio* = *sacrum facio* + abl. of the thing offered, an example of religious technical language, cf. Plaut *Stich.* 251 *quot agnis fecerat*; Virg. *Ecl.* 3.77 *cum faciam uitula pro frugibus* (with Clausen 111); Varro *Ling.* 6.16 *agna Ioui facit* (sc. *flamen Dialis*), Varro ap. Non. p. 246 L. *dis Semonibus lacte fit, non uino* and see H-Sz 121, K-S II 1.385, Bréguet (1946) 164-165.

dea casta: since Juno Lucina was seen as a defender of marital fidelity *genialis tori ... / custos* (Sen. *Medea* 1-2), see **4.13n.** above, the epithet could be appropriate here in a poem where Sulpicia is wishing for a marriage with Cerinthus, see **10n.** above. At Virg. *Ecl.* 4.10 *casta ... Lucina* refers not to Juno, but to Diana, with whom this epithet is more usual. Ov. *Am.* 3.13.3 mentions a chaste festival for Juno: *casta sacerdotes Iunoni festa parabant*. Especially relevant to our passage, however, is the offering of a purple robe (see **13** above), woven by Spartan women (none of whom was barren or divorced from her husband) and offered in supplication for the return of their loved ones to the chaste goddess *castae ... diuae*, Juno, at Stat. *Theb.* 10.56-60 *peplum etiam dono, cuius mirabile textum / nulla manus sterilis nec dissociata marito / uersarat, calathis castae uelamina diuae / haud spernenda ferunt, uariis ubi plurima floret / purpura picta modis mixtoque incenditur auro*.

15-16 The equivalent in Sulpicia's case of the couplet **11.17-18** relating to Cerinthus. In both cases the young pair are unwilling to speak their real wishes concerning their love for one another out loud. Here, although her mother tells her what to wish for, Sulpicia is now her own mistress *iam sua*, and knows what to ask for secretly *tacita ... mente*.

15 et: to be taken closely with *mater*. The author has suggested in **7-12** what Sulpicia should wish for, and (**15** *et*) her mother also has suggestions to make, although these do not correspond with her daughter's secret wishes (**16**).

mater: the only mention of Sulpicia's mother in the *Sulpicia Cycle* or *Sulpicia* poems. The theme of a parent's wishes being resisted suggests a marriage context, cf. Cat. 62.60-61 *non aequumst pugnare, pater cui tradidit ipse, / ipse pater cum matre, quibus parere necessest*.

studiosa: i.e. 'concerned', 'anxious' about her daughter's future, perhaps connected with Sulpicia's reference to Messalla as *nimium ... mei studiose* in **14.5**, see **n.** ad loc. The mother would naturally be concerned that her daughter should make a good marriage.

quid optet: indirect question 'what she should pray for', a correction of the *recentiores* for *quod optat* 'a thing she wants' of A+.

16 tacita ... mente: cf. *tectius* of Cerinthus at **11.17** above. The theme of secrecy and openness runs through the *Sulpicia* poems, see Prolegomena p. 83 and **8.8n**. The phrase is used first of the secret desires of unmarried girls in Cat.'s wedding hymn, 62.37 *quid tum, si carpunt, tacita quem* *mente requirunt*? and is frequent in Ov. *Am.* 1.4.23 with McKeown II 87, 3.7.63, *Ars* 1.602, *Met.* 5.427, 15.26, *Fast.* 3.634; cf. Manil. 2.60; Lucan 9.564; Stat. *Theb.* 2.331. As McKeown points out, loc. cit., such phrases are mostly equivalent to adverbs, cf. Virg. *Aen.* 4.105 *simulata mente*; Ov. *Am.* 2.15.3 *laeta mente,* 3.2.10 *forti mente, Met.* 8.634 *iniqua mente*; **[Tib.] 3.6.34** *tristi ... mente,* and passed into Romance with that function, e.g. *Gloss. Reich. singulariter: solamente*; see further Väänänen (1967) 98-99, Bauer (2010), and Pinkster (2015) 871 with full bibliography in n. 86.

iam sua: 'now her own mistress', 'now independent'. Originally used of free men as opposed to slaves, e.g. Plaut. *Pers.* 472 *ita ancilla mea quae fuit hodie, sua nunc est*, the possessive adj. *suus* came to be applied to those who were their own master, e.g. Stat. *Silu.* 2.6.52-53 *... tecum tristisque hilarisque nec umquam / ille suus uultumque tuo sumebat ab ore*. This usage is absent from Tib. and Prop., but Bréguet [(1946) 141] compares Ov. *Met.* 8.35 *uix sua*, 14.166 *iam suus*. For a similar expression in Sulpicia with reference to her dependence on Messalla, cf. **14.8** *arbitrio quamuis non sinis esse meo* with **n.** ad loc.

mente rogat: the same pentameter ending occurs in Tib.'s dedication to Venus at 1.9.84 *... grata sis, dea, mente rogat*.

17-18 uritur ... / ... uelit: applies the same imagery of the flames of love and makes the same point about not wishing to be cured as had been used of Sulpicia at **11.5** *uror ego ante alias; iuuat hoc, Cerinthe, quod uror*. On *uror* in this context and its combination of the fires of love with the imagery of *seruitium amoris*, see *Sulpicia Cycle* **11.5n.** Whereas in **8.11** and **12** it was Sulpicia who actively inspired love (*urit .... / urit*), here it is she who is burned *uritur* with love, see **headnote** to this poem above.

17 celeres ... flammae: the combination occurs also at Lucr. 2.192, 6.224; Ov. *Trist.* 1.2.45.

altaria: burnt-offerings placed on an altar (found only in the plural), see *OLD altaria* 2. The word occurs only here in the *Corp. Tib.*

18 nec ... sana fuisse uelit: for the idea cf. Tib. 1.2.66 *... nec te posse carere uelim,* 2.5.110 *et faueo morbo* (sc. *amoris*), *cum iuuat ipse dolor*. On the common image of love as a disease (implied in *sana fuisse*) see above **6.3n**. For the contrast between *uritur* **17** and *sana fuisse* cf. Cat. 83.3-6 *si* (sc. Lesbia) *nostri oblita taceret, / sana esset: nunc quod gannit ... / ... / iratast. hoc est, uritur et loquitur*. The adj. *sanus*, though common in Prop. and Ov., occurs only here in the *Corp. Tib.*

19-20 The text and meaning of the final couplet are disputed. In **19** I print *sis* (a reading found in F) for A's *si* at the line opening and *Iuno* (Gruppe) for A's *iuueni*; an address by the poet to *Natalis Iuno* of the opening would conform with the structure of other genethliaka in which the birthday spirit is asked for favour in the final couplet, cf. Tib. 1.7.63-64 and 2.2.21-22, and **[Tib.] 3.** (*Sulpicia* Cycle) **11.8**. Mention of the young man (Cerinthus) at this point would, by contrast, be out of place in a birthday poem for Sulpicia, while, if Juno is addressed, she needs to be named at this point after three verses **16-18** referring to Sulpicia. *grata ac* (Lipsius, Gruppe) for A's *grata* avoids an awkward *breuis in arsi*; in **20** G^{ac}'s *extet* improves upon the meaningless *esset* or *adsit* of the rest of the tradition. The form in which I print the final couplet is, then, conjectural, but would at least be in line with the generic norms of the genethliakon.

19 grata: for the sense here, closer to 'pleasing', 'favourable' than to 'grateful', cf. Tib.'s dedication to Venus at 1.9.83-84 *hanc tibi fallaci resolutus amore Tibullus / dedicat et grata sis dea mente rogat.*

proximus annus: a reference to the annual celebration of Sulpicia's birthday, cf. Tib. 1.7.63 (Messalla's birthday) ... *Natalis, multos celebrande per annos*. Again there appears to be an echo here of the annual celebration of the Matronalia ceremony mentioned at **8.23** *hoc sollemne sacrum multos celebretur in annos*; see **headnote** to this poem above.

20 uotis: on such vows made in the hope of divine favour see above **3.1n**. For *uota* addressed to the Genius as a traditional part of the birthday ceremony, see **11.9n**.

uetus ... amor: used (in the plural *ueteres amores*) of long-standing amatory relationships ended only by death at Cat. 96.3 and Tib. 2.4.47. The wish for long-lasting marriage bonds occurs at the end of the birthday poem for Cornutus at Tib. 2.2.18-19 *flauaque coniugio uincula portet Amor, / uincula quae maneant semper.*

Poems in the Mask of Sulpicia 3.13-3.18

Poem 13

The epigram serves as an introduction to Sulpicia's poems **14-18**, which are arranged to give a chronological narrative. Its dramatic date would best be imagined as immediately after the events described in the final poem **18**, see Santirocco (1979) 234. The willingness to give open expression *nudasse* (**2**) to her love in publically available literary form rather than in private letters *signatis ... tabellis* (**7**) contrasts with her wish in **18.6** to keep her passion secret *ardorem cupiens dissimulare meum*. This first poem of the *Sulpicia* poems, differs from **14-18** in not being in the form of a verse letter, but rather serves as a link between **8-12** and **14-18**. In poem **13** she is being open about her relationship, whereas poems **14-18** can be seen as *signatae ... tabellae* addressed to Cerinthus; see Luck (1961) 104, Hooper (1975) 132, Wyke (1994) 114 and Holzberg (1998) 186-187. This theme of openness and secrecy in the first and last poems gives a thematic ring structure to this six-poem group. On the metrical, lexical and stylistic differences between the *Sulpicia Cycle* **8-12** and the *Sulpicia* poems see Santirocco (1979) 235-237, Lowe (1988) 197-205, Hinds (1987) 44, Hubbard (2004) 189-192 and Maltby (2010) 332. This can be seen in particular by contrasting the dramatic monologues put in her mouth by our author (as the anonymous observer) in poems **9** and **11**, and the epistolary letters **14-18**. The *Sulpicia* poems use for the most part the language of polite conversational prose as found in, for example, Cicero's letters. They are closer in some ways, particularly in length, to the aristocratic epigrams of earlier writers such as Lutatius Catulus, and Porcius Licinus, and seem to follow the advice of Ovid at *Ars* 3.479-482 regarding the plain style to be followed by women in writing letters to their lovers; see Hooper (1975) 121, Holzberg (1998) 187. Propertius gives an example of such a letter from Cynthia at 3.23.11-16, quoted by Holzberg (1998) 187; its similarity to the style of the *Sulpicia* poems was first noted by Hooper (1975) 142-143. None of this evidence can be used for or against the theory that the poet was a historically identifiable Sulpicia, but links between the various sections of the collection suggest a single author, taking on different masks [Lygdamus in **1-6**, the young Tibullus **7, 19** and **20** the anonymous observer **8-12** and Sulpicia in **13-18**; see Gen. Intro., section 1.2].

The contents of this first poem of the *Sulpicia* group is as follows:

1-5 Venus, in response to my poems, has at last brought me a love that I am not ashamed to speak of.

5-8 The message I send is not a secret for my lover alone but is for all to read, especially those who have no love of their own.

9-10 I am happy to sin and tired of hiding my feelings through shame; I shall be spoken of as one who has met her match.

510   Commentary

This is the only poem in the collection without a specific addressee, and it could either be taken as a dramatic monologue or as an address to the reader of the whole collection. The emphasis on revelation in **2** *nudasse alicui*, **5** *mea gaudia narret*, **10** *ferar*, and especially the imagery of the rejection of the sealed message of **7-8** suggests at a metapoetic level a poem introducing a publication; so Hinds (1987) 43, Lyne (2007) 343. In this sense it resembles the opening poems of the *Lygd.* group **1** and the *Sulpicia Cycle* **8**. Her love is to be revealed to all through publication, even to those who have no love of their own (**5-6**). However, the details of the object of her affections are kept intentionally vague: *illum* **3**, *meus* **8**. Cerinthus is not in fact named until poem **14**. The theme of openness and secrecy, which played an important role in the *Sulpicia Cycle* (see **8.8n.** above) remains a key feature of the *Sulpicia* poems themselves. Santirocco [(1979) 234-235] is instructive on the amount of indirect discourse in the poem reflecting the poem's concern with revelation and reputation, both at the oral, *fama* (**2**), *narret* (**5**), *ferar* (**10**), and at the written *signatis ... tabellis* (**7**) level. Hardie [(2012) 368-373] is helpful on the way in which Sulpicia's embrace of *fama* and rejection of *pudor* in this opening poem reverses Ovid's instruction to his mistress in the penultimate poem of his *Amores* to throw a veil of *pudor* over her indiscretions in order to preserve her good name *fama* (see **1-2n.**, **7n.**, **9-10n.** below).

The poem displays a considerable amount of literary sophistication, see especially Merriam (2005), with possible allusions (in addition to those to Ov. *Am.* 3.14) to Homer (**3-4n.**), Sappho [see Tränkle 304 on **3-4** and cf. **3-4n.** below], the *Fragmentum Grenfellianum* [see Cozzolino (1992)], Catullus [see Fabre-Serris (2009) 155-156 and **3-4n.** below], Virgil [see Keith (1997) and **3-4n.**], Gallus [see Fabre-Serris (2009) 150 and **1-2n.** *tandem uenit amor*] and Ovid *Her.* 4 (Phaerda to Hippolytus – see **n.** **1-2** *tandem uenit amor*) and *Her.* 15 (Sappho to Phaon); on the latter two see Fabre-Serris (2009).

1-2 The text and interpretation of the opening couplet are in doubt. The MSS. offer a choice between *pudori*, predicative dative, and *pudore*, instrumental ablative. In the first case the translation would be 'the reputation (*fama*) that I had concealed it (*texisse*) would be a greater cause of shame (*pudori ... sit ... magis*)'. In the second the infinitive would be the subject: 'which it would disgrace me more (*mihi fama magis*) to hide (*texisse*) out of shame (*pudore*) than to reveal to anyone', and *fama* would have the unusual but not unprecedented meaning of *infamia*, see **n.** on **sit mihi fama** below. I print *pudore* believing that this version makes better sense, since Sulpicia has not hidden her love and the word order *nudasse*

... *sit mihi fama magis* would be more straightforward. There would then be some parallel between *texisse pudore* of the opening and *componere* ... / *taedet* of the closing couplet. However, the different meaning of *fama* in **2** and **9** is somewhat awkward in this interpretation, although the double meaning of *fama* in this poem perhaps reflects a concern with the Vertumnan theme of the multifaceted nature of reality, as hinted at in **8.13-14** and reflected both in the *Sulpicia Cycle* and in the *Sulpicia* poems themselves. For similar discussions of *pudor* and *fama* from women addressing their lovers in letters Fabre-Serris [(2009) 152-153 and 165] compares Phaedra to Hippolytus at Ov. *Her.* 4.9-10 and 17-20 and Sappho to Phaon at Ov. *Her.* 15. 133-134. Hardie [(2012) 368-373] aptly contrasts Ov. *Am.* 3.14.3-4 *nec te nostra iubet fieri censura pudicam, / sed tamen, ut temptes dissimulare, rogat*, where the poet asks his mistress to try to hide her misdemeanours for the sake of her good name, cf. **11** *tu tua prostitues famae peccata sinistrae*. Just as the opening poem of the *Lygd.* group at the beginning of **book 3, 1.1**, with its mention of *Martis Romani* echoes the mock-epic opening of Ovid's *Amores* 1.1.1 *arma graui numero*, so the opening poem of the *Sulpicia* poems at the end of the book echoes the theme of *Am.* 3.14 at the end of Ovid's *Amores* collection.

Tandem uenit amor: the adv. *tandem* is unusual, and probably unparalleled, as the opening word of this poetic group. However, see Heyworth [(1995) 125] on *tandem* as a key word in prologues and endings. The *tandem* at Gallus fr. 2.6-7 (Courtney = 145.6-7 Hollis) ... *tandem fecerunt carmina Musae / quae possem domina deicere digna mea* is either part of a prefatory poem (Courtney 266 ad loc.) or, more likely, of a triumphant epilogue (Courtney 266 = Hollis 246 ad loc.); its mention of the Muses (cf. **3** below) and the use of the adj. *digna* (cf. **10** below) may connect this fragment in some way with the present poem. The whole phrase could serve to link the opening of this poem with the close of poem **12**, *iam uetus extet amor*. Beginnings and endings of poems would be most susceptible to change at a late editorial stage of a poetry book's arrangement. On literary play with beginnings, middles and endings of poems and collections and their appropriate emblems see Zetzel (1983) 261, Fowler (1989) 101 n. 39 and (1997), Dunn and Cole (eds) (1992), Roberts, Dunn and Fowler (eds) (1997) 20, Kyriakidis (ed.) (2004). For a similar case of closural material in an opening poem, see **1.17n.** above. For the phrase *uenit amor* cf. Ov. *Am.* 1.6.13 *nec mora, uenit amor*, *Her.* 4.19 (Phaedra to Hippolytus) *uenit amor grauius, quo serius* (itself influenced by Prop. 1.7.26 *saepe uenit magno faenore tardus amor* (codd.: *honos* Heyworth). Fabre-Serris [(2009) 153] sees Ovid as our author's imitator here, but the opposite direction of influence seems more likely. Because of

Camenae (**2**) and *digna* (**10**) some have seen in *tandem* a connection with Gallus fr. 2.6-7 (Courtney = 145.6-7 Hollis) quoted above. If so, the echo of Gallus in the opening of *Sulpicia*'s collection here would be parallelled in the opening poem of the *Sulpicia Cycle* (see **8.15n.**) and of the *Lygd.* group (see **1.8n.**). Futhermore Fabre-Serris [(2009) 149] connects the opening phrase *tandem uenit amor* with the possibly Gallan *omnia uincit amor* at Virg. *Ecl.* 10.69 (generally thought to be echoing Gallus' lost *Amores*). For *tandem uenit* of a deity cf. Tib. 2.5.46 *tandem ... diua superba uenit*. In the present poem there is ambiguity as to whether the reference here is simply to 'love' or to the god Amor. The use of *uenit* suggests that love's arrival could have been the outcome of a kletic hymn introduced by *ueni*, cf. **8.2** (to Mars) *spectatum ... ipse ueni* with **n.** ad loc.; see further **7.131n.**, Lyne (2007) 351. For a possible echo of *uenit* at Virg. *Ecl.* 8.109, see **3-4n.** *Camenis* below. At any rate, we learn at **3-4** below, that poems addressed by Sulpicia to Venus had resulted in the arrival of love / a lover (*illum* **3**). In **8.2n.** (*ipse ueni*) above it was suggested that the opening of the first poem the *Sulpicia* group here associates the coming of love specifically with Venus through the etymological connection between Venus (named in **5**) and the verb *uenire* (**1**). Our author at **8**, in the opening of the *Sulpicia Cycle* **8-12** refers specifically to this connection here by allowing the role of Venus to be usurped in that poem by Mars; see Hinds (2006) 18-25, 31.

qualem: object of the two perfect infinitives dependent on *sit mihi fama* complicates the syntax after an initial clear and unambiguous statement, *tandem uenit amor*. The exact implications of *qualem* are not made clear. It could refer to a type of love that is suitable for publication [so Milnor (2002) 271], or perhaps simply that her lover is suited to her and is socially acceptable (cf. **10** below *cum digno digna*).

texisse ... / ... nudasse: Lyne [(2007) 351] suggests a pun on *nudus amor* (for which see Prop. 1.2.8; Ov. *Am.* 1.10.15), with *tegere* 'to cover', being the opposite of *nudare* 'to bare'. McKeown III 87 on Ov. *Am.* 2.5.5 *non mihi deceptae nudant tua facta tabellae* comments on the appropriateness of the verb *nudare* in a sexual context. The combination of *nudant* with *tabellae* (cf. *tabellis* **7** below) here suggests that *Am.* 2.5 is an important intertext for the present poem, cf. also *pecasse* (*Am.* 2.5.3 and **9** below, *gaudia Am.* 2.5.29 and **5** below) and see Batstone (2018) 90-91. The importance of the theme of openness and secrecy in the *Sulpicia Cycle* and the *Sulpicia* poems is discussed at Prolegomena p. 83 and **8.8n.** above. The verb *texisse* here looks forward to *dissimulare* in the last line (**6**) of poem **18** and provides a link between the opening and closing poems of the *Sulpicia* poems, based on the central theme of disclosure and secrecy. If poem **13** is imagined as having a later dramatic date than poem **18**, there is a movement from secrecy in **18** to openness in **13**; see further **18.6n**. For the combination of *nudare* with *retego* 'to reveal', cf. the words of Sychaeus' ghost revealing his murder to Dido at Virg. *Aen.* 1.355-356 *crudelis aras traiectaque pectora ferro / nudauit, caecumque domus scelus omne retexit* (with Serv. ad 356 '*nudauit*' *indicauit*). The plethora of dependent infinitives in this poem [*texisse* (**1**), *nudasse* (**2**), *habuisse* (**6**), *mandare* (**7**), *pecasse* (**9**), *componere* (**9**), *fuisse* (**10**)] is reminiscent of Catullus' epigrammatic style, cf. Cat. 73.1-2 *desine de quoquam quicquam bene uelle mereri / aut aliquem fieri posse putare pium*.

pudore: 'shame' is one of the typical opponents of *amor*, e.g. Ov. *Am.* 1.2.32 *et Pudor et castris quidquid Amoris obest*; cf. Prop. 1.2.24 *illis ampla nimis forma pudicitiae*. Keith [(1997) 295-310] points out that the theme of *pudor* and the dangers of *fama* 'evil reputation' which are key themes in this poem, as in poem **18**, may well echo similar themes in the Dido episode of book 4 of the *Aeneid*. The author further emphasises the Virgilian context of this poem by the use of *Cytherea* for Venus and *Camenae* for the Muses (**3**), see **3-4n**. below.

nudasse alicui: elision is very rare in *Sulpicia* poems; only here and **14.4** *atque Aretino*, **16.5** *dolori est*. None at all in poems **15**, **17** and **18**.

alicui: prosaic in tone, see McKeown III 100 on Ov. *Am.* 2.5.41; elsewhere in elegy only at Ov. *Ars* 2.289, *Trist.* 4.7.7. The pronoun is intentionally vague, perhaps referring to a hypothetical reader of the collection the poem is intended to introduce (see **headnote** above).

sit mihi fama: for *fama* in the sense of *infamia* see examples in *OLD fama* 6b and cf. Cic. *Planc.* 72 *an fuisse* (sc. *putes*) *in eis aliquem aut famae metum aut poenae*; Non., p. 475 L *fama est rursus infamia*. For the construction nom. + *esse* + dat. in place of a predicative dative cf. Enn. *Trag.* 61 Jocelyn *eum esse exitium Troiae, pestem Pergamo*; Lucr. 3.897-898 *non poteris factis florentibus esse tuisque / praesidium*; Sulpicia **18.1** *ne tibi sim ... cura* and see Löfstedt (1956) I^2 194-199.

3-4 Tränkle [304 ad loc.] sees in this couplet a reference to Sappho's first poem (fr. 1 *PLF*) in which the poetess asks again, as she has in the past, for Aphrodite's help in procuring the love of a young girl; see also Fabre-Serris (2009) 150. Sappho had considerable influence on Latin love poetry from Catullus on, (e.g. his translation of Sappho fr. 31 in poem 51 and the naming of his mistress Lesbia); cf. Hor. *Carm*. 2.13.24f., 4.9.9-12, *Epist*. 1.19.38; Prop. 2.3.19; Ov. *Rem*. 761, *Trist*. 2.362. Sappho was specially recommended to cultured female readers by Ovid, cf. *Ars* 3.331 *nota sit et Sappho –quid enim lasciuius illa*? Merriam [(2005) 167] and Lyne [(2007) 352] compare Hom. *Il* 3.380-382 where Aphrodite rescues Paris from the battlefield and brings him eventually to an assignation with Helen. Closer perhaps to the truth is Keith's idea [(1997) 295-310] that the inspiration could have come from Virgil's description of Venus persuading Cupid, disguised as Ascanius, to sit in Dido's lap and so inspire her love for Aeneas, see *Cytherea* **n.** below.

exorata: for the sense here = 'win over', 'prevail upon' see *ThLL* 5.1585.42. The verb is not found elsewhere in the *Corp. Tib.*, but occurs twice in Prop. and ten times in Ov. in prayers to gods or men. Close to the present context is Ov. *Trist*. 2.22 *exorant magnos carmina saepe deos*. For *exorare* of erotic 'wooing' cf. Ov. *Fast*. 4.111 *eloquiumque fuit duram exorare puellam* and see Pichon 139.

illum: refers to the man who will later (**14.2**) be revealed as Cerinthus, but the word simultaneously looks back to *amor* (**1**). For such delaying tactics in the revelation of information in elegy, see Cairns (1979) 144-145. This use of *ille* referring to a known person, whom the author has no need (or wish) to name is common in Cicero's letters, e.g. *Att.* 13.42 *uenit ille ad me* (of Q. Cicero), but rare in verse. This is another example, like *alicui* (**2**), of our poet's language in the *Sulpicia* poems being closer in places to that of polite conversation. The reluctance to reveal her lover's name at this stage is perhaps intended as an inducement to the reader to proceed further into the collection; so Lyne (2007) 350.

Cytherea: a common epithet for Aphrodite in Greek literature from Hom. *Od.* (e.g. 8.288, 18.193) on; it connected her with the island of Cythera where she was born from the sea foam and where she had a famous cult (Hes. *Theog*. 198). However, the ancient etymology of *Cytherea* from κεύθειν 'to hide', Schol. in Hes. *Theog*. 196, Schol. in Hom. *Il*. 5.422, Schol. in Hom. *Od*. 288.6, 7-9 [cf. Paschalis (1997) 50, 52; Ziogas (2014) 328-330], must be relevant here to the theme of hiding and revealing in the opening couplet; while Cytherea represents the earlier emotional stage of hiding one's love, in her appearance as Venus she represents its revelation (**5-6** *exoluit promissa Venus, mea gaudia narret,* / *... siquis* etc.). In Latin the adj. is found from the 20s of the first century BC in Hor. (*Carm*. 3.12.4 etc.), Prop. (2.14.25), Virg. (*Aen*. 1.257 etc.) and Ov. (*Am*. 1.3.4 etc.). In the *Corp. Tib.* it occurs only here; see further *ThLL Onomast.* 2.811.29-50,

Bréguet (1946) 46, Pichon 121, and, on the prosody, Austin 59-60 on Virg. *Aen.* 4.128. Keith (1997) sees in the use of this epithet here a specific reference to Virgil, who uses the term no less than six times (*Aen.* 1.257, 657, 4.128, 5.800, 8.523, 615). One of these six, significantly, is at *Aen.* 1.657 where Venus Cytherea tells Cupid to disguise himself as Aeneas' son, Ascanius, so that when Dido takes him in her lap (685 *cum te gremio accipiet laetissima Dido*) he will inspire her with love for Aeneas (688 *occultum inspires ignem*); this reference is clearly picked up by *in nostrum deposuitque sinum* below **(4)**. Ov. puts Cytherea in a similar role of providing a partner at *Her.* 16.20 (Paris to Helen) *pollicita est thalamo te Cytherea meo*. Fabre-Serris [(2009) 150] sees in *Cytherea* a possible reference to Gallus' mistress Lycoris, who in real life was the mime-actress Cytheris. Flaschenriem [(1999) 40] sees in the juxtaposition of Greek *Cytherea* with Roman *Camenis* a reference to the fact that our author here is making use of both Greek and Roman poetic traditions. The same point could be made of the alternation between Greek *Cytherea* **(3)** and Roman *Venus* **(5)**.

Camenis: for the *Camenae* and for this metonymic use = 'verses', occurring again first in the 20s BC, see **7.24n.** and cf. **7.192** above. However, as *ThLL Onomast.* 2.117.55-118.12 points out, it is sometimes difficult to distinguish between persons and verses. The verses in question could refer to the poems of the *Sulpicia* group that follow, namely **14-18**. The statement could also have inspired our poet at **8-12** to compose poems **9** and **11** in Sulpicia's voice to provide the poems referred to here, especially **11.13-18** where she specifically asks Venus to foster her love; so Hinds (1987a) 42. Hinds sees the *amicus Sulpiciae* group (as he terms them i.e. **8-12**) as coming later than the poems of the *Sulpicia* group. In my view, however [see Gen. Intro., section 1.2 and cf. Holzberg (1998) 186], the same author wrote both the *Sulpicia Cycle* **8-12** and the *Sulpicia* poems **13-18**. For the role of the Muses in bringing back a lover, Lyne [(2007) 352] compares the refrain of Alphesiboeus in Virg. *Ecl.* 8.68 *ducite ab urbe domum, mea carmina, ducite Daphnim*, which is changed in the last line (109) to *parcite, ab urbe uenit, iam parcite carmina, Daphnis*, with the author perhaps echoing *uenit* there in line **1** of this poem. Again poet's use of *Camenae* here, like *Cytherea* above, could constitute a clear reference to Virgil, who, at *Ecl.* 3.59 *alternis dicetis*: *amant alterna Camenae* was the first to re-introduce this term since the time of Livius Andronicus and Naevius. Horace makes an elegant reference to this fact at *Serm.* 1.10.44-45 ... *molle atque facetum / Vergilio adnuerunt gaudentes rure Camenae*. The *Camenae* are absent from Tib. and occur elsewhere in elegy only at Prop. 3.10.1 (where they announce

Cynthia's birthday to Prop.) and Ov. *Pont.* 4.13.13; see further **7.24n.**, Bréguet (1946) 46-47. They are more frequent in Mart. (6). For *meis ... Camenis* cf. Calp. Sic. 3.42 (*meas*), 4.46 (*nostras*); Stat. *Silu.* 4.7.21 (*nostris*); Mart. 7.68.1 (*meas*).

in ... sinum: for the use of *sinus* in the erotic sense of 'embrace', cf. Tib. 1.1.46 *et dominam tenero continuisse sinu*, 8.30; Ov. *Ars* 2.360, *Her.* 3.164, 13.157, 16.266, *Met.* 4. 396, and misunderstood as such at Ov. *Met.* 7.814 (Cephalus to Aura) *intresque sinus, gratissima, nostros* etc. For the Virgilian context of this phrase, see *Cytherea* **n.** above. The present verse seems to be linked with **9.24** (Sulpicia to Cerinthus) *celer in nostros ipse recurre sinus*. The normal construction with *affero* would be *ad* + acc., and with *depono in* + abl. Here *in* + acc. = 'into' is appropriate for both verbs; cf. in a similar context Cat. 68.132 *lux mea se nostrum contulit in gremium*.

5 exsoluit promissa: the suggestion is that Venus had promised Sulpicia success in love with Cerinthus and had fulfilled her promise. For *exsoluere* in the sense of 'to fulfil' a promise see *OLD exsoluo* 4 and cf. Cic. *Off.* 3.7 *nec exsoluit id quod promiserat*; Tac. *Dial.* 27.1 *exsolue promissum*. The relationship between Sulpicia and Venus is similar to that between Sappho and Aphrodite in Sappho fr. 1 *PLF* see 3-4n. above.

5-6 mea gaudia ... / ... habuisse sua: These lines in the view of Hinds [(1987) 42] could have inspired a separate author of the *Sulpicia Cycle* **8-12** to write about and expand upon *Sulpicia* poems, **13-17**. In my view a single author of the whole collection could refer back to himself, both as author of **8-12** and in another persona as Lygdamus of poems **1-6** (neither of whom had any *gaudia* of their own); see also Holzberg (1998) 186. In its immediate context our author probably meant Sulpicia to indicate that she does not care what others without love (presumably *senes seueriores* as in Cat. 5.2) say about her successful affair. Such a carefree attitude to what detractors may say goes well with what follows in **7-8**; see Lyne (2007) 353. On the sense of *gaudia* here see **9.18n.** above. Fabre-Serris [(2009) 163] connects *gaudia* and *si quis* in this couplet with Sappho's words at Ov. *Her.* 15.109-110 *cum mihi nescio quis "fugiunt tua gaudia" dixit, / nec me flere diu nec potuisse loqui.*

si quis: the gender here is not made clear, see Flaschenriem (1999) 41, Batstone (2018) 92.

6 sua: one of three occasions in *Sulpicia* poems where the pentameter ends in a short open syllable, also at **16.4** *Sulpicia* and **17.6** *mala*. Examples are found in Tib.'s second book, but not in Ovid; see Tränkle 301.

7-8 Since Sulpicia is unconcerned about what others may say, she does not wish to send messages under seal which no one could read before her lover. At a metapoetic level she could be referring to the publication of her collection of poems for anyone to read, see Lyne (2007) 349-350.

7 signatis ... tabellis: 'sealed tablets', used for the transmission of confidential information. The boards of the wax tablets were fastened together, melted wax applied and a mark with a signet ring was made to identify the sender. On the theme of openness and secrecy in these poems see Prolegomena p. 83 and **8.8n.** above. For the expression cf. Plaut. *Bacch*. 924 *aequomst tabellis consignatis credere*, *Bell. Afr.* 3.4 *tabellas signatas dederat*; Cic. *Att*. 11.1.1 *accepi a te signatum labellum*; Hor. *Epist*. 1.13.2 *Augusto reddes signata uolumina*. The line perhaps has some relation to Prop. 3.23 which refers to tablets in line 11 *forsitan haec illis fuerunt mandata tabellis* and to the fact that they were not signed in 4 *qui non signatas iussit habere fidem*. The reference is to the tablets with which Propertius and Cynthia communicated. The contents of specimen letters from Cynthia in lines 12-14 and 15-16 of Propertius' poem are very reminiscent of the contents of *Sulpicia*'s epistolary epigrams **14-16**. Lyne (2007) argues for the priority of *Sulpicia* here. More significant, however, seems to be Ov. *Am*. 3.14.31 *cur totiens uideo mitti recipique tabellas?*, in a poem in which Ovid argues for secrecy and discretion on the part of his mistress, a type of behaviour which is rejected here by Sulpicia, almost certainly in reaction to Ovid's poem (see **headnote** and **1-2n.** above and **9-10n.** below).

8 ne ... nemo: the double negative is used for emotional emphasis, cf. Prop. 2.19.32 *absenti nemo non nocuisse uelit*. Although the double negative is more common in comedy [e.g. Plaut. *Rud*. 359 *nec te aleator nullus est sapientior* with further examples in Fordyce on Cat. 73.3 and Löfstedt (1956) ii 210], it is not restricted to colloquial contexts, cf. Enn. *Trag*. 140 *quos non miseret neminis* with Jocelyn 282 ad loc., Cic. *Verr*. 2.2.60 *debebat Epicrates nummum nullum nemini*; see above on *nulla nec* at **7.127n.** and **7.164n.**

nemō: rare in the higher styles of poetry and restricted to speeches in Ov. *Am*. (Dipsas at 1.8.43 and 100) and Virg. *Aen*. (Aeneas at 5.305 and 349, Dares at 5.383 and Iris at 9.6). Uncertainty over the length of the final *-o* may have contributed to its rarity; so Axelson (1945) 77, n. 61. In Augustan poetry it is short at Ov. *Am.* 1.8.43 (see McKeown II 223 ad loc.), *Fast.* 6.324, *Trist.* 2.348 and *Pont.* 2.3.16 but long at Prop. 2.19.32 (quoted above); Ov. *Am.* 1.8.100, *Trist.* 1.9b.8, *Pont.* 3.6.58, and here.

quam ... ante: for the word order cf. Lucr. 3.973 *quam nascimur ante*, 4.884 *quam mens prouidit quid uelit ante*; Mart. 9.35.6 *uictricem laurum quam uenit ante uides*, and in prose only Varro *Ling.* 8.13 *de eorum declinatione quam de uerborum ante dicam*.

meus: used in the sense of 'my lover', cf. Prisc. *GL* 3.173.27-174.12 K *frequenter tamen etiam sine nomine licet huiuscemodi possessiua proferre ... et omnibus maritis mos est de uxoribus suis dicere 'mea' et inuicem uxoribus de suis maritis dicere 'meus' per defectionem nominis*. For obvious reasons *mea* is more common in elegy, but for *meus* in this sense cf. Ov. *Ars* 1.322 *ite, placete meo*. This is a colloquial feature which became part of the language of elegy, see Bréguet (1946) 44-45.

9-10 sed ... / taedet: Sulpicia's openness and unwillingness to dissimulate reverses the advice given by Ovid to his mistress at *Am.* 3.14.27-28 *indue cum tunicis metuentem crimina uultum, / et pudor obscenum diffiteatur opus*.

9 peccasse: here, as often, the reference is to sexual transgression, cf. Hor. *Serm.* 1.2.63; Tib. 1.6.16, 71, 9.23; Ov. *Am.* 2.5.3, 3.14.1 (an important intertext for the present poem); **[Tib.] 3.20.1** below and see Pichon 227-228.

iuuat: cf. **11.5** *iuuat hoc, Cerinthe, quod uror*. Fabre-Serris [(2009) 165] sees a connection with Sappho's words at Ov. *Her.* 15.133-134 *ulteriora pudet narrare, sed omnia fiunt / et iuuat*.

uultus componere famae: the phrase *uultum (-us) componere* means to 'put on' or 'compose' an expression; see *ThLL* 3(2).2114.49-58 and cf. Polyphemus composing his expression in the sea's reflection at Ov. *Met.* 13.767 *et spectare feros in aqua et componere uultus* and Tac. *Ann.* 1.7.2-3 *uultuque composito* 'his expression adjusted'. Unusual here is the dat. *famae* 'to adjust my expression for the sake of reputation'. On the difference between a man's *fama* which depends upon his achievements and a woman's which depends upon her chastity and how she is seen and talked about see Batstone (2018) 88. For erotic activity damaging a girl's *fama* cf. Prop. 1.16.11-12; Ov. *Am.* 3.14.36. On the difference in meaning between *fama* here and in **2** above, see **1-2n.**

10 cum digno digna: proverbial in tone, cf. Plaut. *Poen.* 1270 *eueniunt digna dignis* and see Otto 252. For this type of adjectival polyptoton see Wills (1996) 230 and cf. Enn. *Trag.* 128 Jocelyn *cur talem inuitam inuitum cogis linquere?* (in a marriage context); **[Tib.] 3**. *Sulpicia Cycle* **9.20** *caste puer, casta retia tange manu.* Catullus uses it of an insalubrious coupling at 78.3-4 *Gallus homost bellus*: *nam dulces iungit amores, / cum puero ut bello bella puella cubet.* Sulpicia's reference here to herself as *digna* has its parallel in **12.9** (*non*) *cuiquam dignior illa uiro*, cf. **8.15** and **24**. For the possible Gallan associations of the adj. *dignus* see **1.8n**. and **8.15n**. above. Hubbard [(2004) 185] sees the phrase as a conventional part of a marriage ceremony, citing Virg. *Ecl.* 8.32 *o digno coniuncta uiro* (in a bitter reference to the marriage of Nysa and Mopsus), echoed in Ausonius *Cento Nuptialis* (6.70 Prete); further examples of *dignus* in this context at **8.15n**. above. Keith [(1997) 302] connects it with Virg. *Aen.* 4.191-192 (also relevant to a marriage context) *uenisse Aenean Troiano sanguine cretum, / cui se pulchra uiro dignetur iungere Dido.*

cum digno ... fuisse: the euphemism *esse cum* for 'sleeping with' someone is a colloquialism found in Early Latin, e.g. Plaut. *Amph.* 817 *quid ego tibi deliqui, si cui nupta sum tecum fui?*, *Bacch.* 891, *Truc.* 688; Ter. *Hec.* 156, but was perhaps found rather old-fashioned by Varro *Ling.* 6.80 *potius cum muliere fuisse quam concubuisse dicebant*, though later examples occur at Cic. *Fat.* 30; Ov. *Am.* 2.8.27, *Ars* 3.664 and *Priap.* 14.3, see Adams (1982) 177.

ferar: 'I shall be spoken of'; again our author has Sulpicia refer to the publication of her work, as suggested by other uses of this and similar future verbs with reference to literary works at Hor. *Carm*.2.20.1-2 *non usitata nec tenui ferar / penna*, 3.30.10 *dicar qua uiolens obstrepit Aufidus*; Prop. 1.7.22 *tunc ego Romanis praeferar ingeniis*; Ov. *Am.* 3.15.8 *Paelignae dicar gloria gentis ego, Trist.* 3.7.51-52 *dumque ... orbem / prospiciet domitum Martia Roma, legar*; further examples in Lyne (2007) 350. These parallels suggest the verb here is future rather than subjunctive. Flaschenriem [(1999) 44-45] argues that the verb is appropriate for epitaphs, citing Prop. 4.11.36 *uni nupta fuisse legar.*

Poem 14

The poem forms a pair with **15** on the subject of a birthday. In **15.2** the mss. reading *tuo* would mean that Cerinthus' birthday was being discussed there, whereas the wording of **1-2** in the present poem suggest the birthday is Sulpicia's. Most editors now accept that the two poems must refer to

Sulpicia's birthday and emend *tuo* in **15.2** to *suo* or *meo* in order to solve this problem. On the genethliakon, or birthday poem, in the *Corp. Tib.* and on its generic background, particularly in relation to Tib.'s birthday poem for Cornutus at Tib. 2.2, see **11 headnote**. In the present poem, in place of the usual celebration of another's birthday, Sulpicia laments the fact that her own birthday will have to be spent away from Rome and her lover at her relative's country estate. The vague *illum* and *meus* of **13.3** and **8** are now replaced by a named lover, Cerinthus **2**, and a new character in the narrative, her relative Messalla **5**, is introduced. In the following poem **15** Sulpicia celebrates the fact that the birthday can after all be spent with her friends in Rome. For pairs of poems on related themes, see **12 headnote**. Santirocco [(1979) 231-231] discusses Sulpicia's two birthday poems **14** and **15**, showing how, despite verbal similarities *tristis* (**14.2** / **15.1**), *natalis* (**14.1** / **15.2**), *animus* (**14.7** / **15.1**), the tone of the two poems is different, with poem **14** purporting to be an exercise in juvenile rhetoric and **15** a more simple outburst of joy, reflecting the efficacy the earlier poem's argument. Stock rhetorical themes he identifies in the present poem include: the pathetic fallacy *rure molesto* **1**, *dulcius urbe quid est* **3**, *frigidus amnis* **4**; the contrast of city and country **1-4**; the generalisation about the unsuitability of travel **6**, and the rather exaggerated idea of leaving one's heart and soul in a different place from the body **7**. The poem is the first of a group of verse letters **14-18**, which differ in style from the poems in Sulpicia's voice at **9** and **11** and from **13**. They cannot be the letters of Tibullus, referred to in the Suetonian *Vita Tibulli*: *epistolae quoque eius amatoriae, quamquam breues, omnino subtiles sunt*, as suggested by Hubbard [(2004) 185-188], since they were written probably after Ovid's *Ars*, which was published a good twenty years after Tib.'s death; see Maltby (2010) 336.

1 Inuisus natalis: the reference is to Sulpicia's birthday, which is hateful to her because it has to be spent without Cerinthus **2**, though, in a poem addressed to Messalla **5**, who has invited her for the occasion to his country estate (*rure* **1**), she gives prominence to other reasons **3-4**, namely her hatred of the country and her preference for the city. This hatred of her own birthday reverses the theme of the celebration of the mistress's birthday in elegy, e.g. Prop. 3.10. Here, poems **14** and **15** on Sulpicia's birthday are anticipated in the *Sulpicia Cycle* by the pair of poems on the birthday of Cerinthus **11** and Sulpicia **12**.

rure: here, as often, the word refers (like *uilla* **3**) to a country estate, cf. Tib. 2.3.1 quoted on **3n.** below; see *OLD rus* 2 and Cic. *S. Rosc.* 133 *habet ... rus amoenum et suburbanum*.

molesto: the adj. is frequent in comedy, but is avoided in the higher genres (absent from Virg.; restricted in Hor. to *Serm.* and *Epist.* and in Ov. to *Am.* and *Ars*; twice only in Prop. 1.5.1, 3.14.28 and absent from Tib.); see further Axelson (1945) 60 and Fedeli 154 on Prop. 1.5.1. Its colloquial flavour sets the tone for the whole poem. For its use in this context see Cic. *Leg.* 3.19.2 quoted in **2-3n.** below. On the pathetic fallacy implicit in *molesto* see **headnote** above.

2-3 tristis ... / dulcius: Lyne [(2007) 355] compares the turn from *tristis* to *dulcis* in Gallus fr. 2.1-2 (Courtney = 145.1-2 Hollis) *tristia nequit*[*ia fact*]*a, Lycori, tua. / fata mihi, Caesar, tum erunt mea dulcia ...* On the pathetic fallacy implied in *dulcius* see **headnote** above. For its use in this context, cf. Cic. *Leg.* 3.19.2 *nihil erit eis urbe, nihil domo sua dulcius, nec laboriosius molestiusque prouincia.*

agendus: of 'spending' a birthday also at Cic. *Fin.* 2.101 *ad diem agendum natalem*, Hor. *Carm.* 4.11.14 *Idus tibi sunt agendae* (of the Ides of April, Maecenas' birthday) and **15.3** below; see *OLD ago* 30.

3 urbe ... uilla: the standard city and country contrast gains significance from its reversal of Tib. 2.3.1-2 (addressed to Cornutus whom some identify with Cerinthus): *rura meam, Cornute, tenent uillaeque puellam: / ferreus est, eheu, quisquis in urbe manet.* This is the only other occurrence of *uilla* in the *Corp. Tib.* The city rather than the country is the normal setting for elegy in Propertius and Ovid, cf. **19.3n. in urbe** below. In Tib. the setting for his affair with Delia in book 1 is an idealised countryside, whereas this is rejected in book 2 for his urban affair with Nemesis, see Maltby (2004). Hallett [(1989) 70] draws attention to similarities between this passage and Ovid's advice to potential lovers at *Ars* 1.61-66 that the city of Rome is the best place to find girls. Heyworth [(2018) 83] points to similarities with Prop. 1.8B.31-32 *illi carus ego, et per me carissima Roma / dicitur, et sine me dulcia regna negat*, with Sulpicia's *sine Cerintho* (**2**) recalling this model.

puellae: Sulpicia is presented as referring to herself with this word in this line-position also at **15.1** and **17.1**, setting herself firmly in the tradition of the elegiac mistress.

4 Arretino frigidus amnis agro: the reference is to the river Arno in the region of Arezzo, which was Maecenas' home town. There is no other reference to Messalla having a villa in this region, but Cicero's friend Atticus certainly did: Nepos *Att.* 14.3 *nullos habuit hortos, nullam* *suburbanam aut maritimam sumptuosam uillam, neque in Italia, praeter Arretinum et Nomentanum, rusticum praedium.* For its connection with the Sulpicii see Fatucchi (1976). As Tränkle [307 ad loc.] points out, the region was famous in antiquity for its beauty and rich grain and wine production (Plin. *Nat.* 14.36, 18.87, 26.87). The river was cold as it flowed down from the Tuscan Appenines. For *frigidus* in this context cf. Virg. *Ecl.* 5.24-25 *pastos ... egere ... / frigida ... boues ad flumina.* On the pathetic fallacy implied in the word, see **headnote** above. For *frigus / frigidus* in elegy implying lovelessness / rejection of love see Maltby (2002) 217 on Tib. 1.4.5-6, and 310 on Tib. 1.8.30, and Pinotti on Ov. *Rem.* 492. Sulpicia, by contrast, is on fire with love, **17.2**, cf. **12.17** *uritur.* The phrase *Arretino ... agro* is also found in Sall. *Cat.* 36.1 *sed ipse paucos dies commoratus apud C. Flaminium in agro Arretino.* Heyworth [(2018) 80] is tempted by Heinsius' suggestion of *Arnus* for *amnis* on the grounds that river names are often replaced by the gloss *amnis* in MSS.

5 Messalla: his identification as a relation or uncle of Sulpicia could simply be the invention of our author, see **6n**. *propinque* below. The fact that he is addressed here as live and well, serves to lend the *Sulpicia* poems a dramatic date before Ovid's exile in AD 8, which Messalla's death appears to have antedated (Ov. *Pont.* 1.7.27-30). On Messalla as Tib.'s patron, the addressee of Tib. 1.7, *Laud. Mess.* 3.7 and Sulpicia's guardian here see Gen. Intro., section 3. For the theme of the interfering uncle Santirocco [(1979) 232] compares Hor. *Carm.* 3.12.1-3 *miserarum est neque amori dare ludum neque dulci / mala uino lauere, aut exanimari metuentis / patruae uerbera linguae.*

mei studiose: 'worried about me', a feature of elevated colloquial language, cf. Cic. *Att.* 3.22.4 *mei studiosos habeo Dyrrachinos.* The adj. is used of Sulpicia's mother at **12.15**, see **n**. ad loc.

quiescas: for this absolute use = 'do nothing, relax', another colloquial feature, see *OLD quiesco* 4 and cf. Hor. *Serm.* 2.1.4-5 *'Trebati, / quid faciam praescribe'. 'quiescas'.*

6 non tempestiuae saepe... uiae: 'journeys are often ill-timed'. The text of this line is uncertain. The reading *non* is found in some later MSS for *neu* of A+, which would form an awkward connection with the preceding line. The adj. *tempestiuus* 'timely' occurs only here in elegy, and in Ov. is restricted to *Met.* (5.550, 14.585). For its use in Hor. *Carm.* 1.23.11-12 in an address to Chloe, for whom it is time to leave her mother for a man *tandem desine matrem / tempestiua sequi uiro* see **9.23n**. Heyworth

[(2018) 79-80], following a suggestion by Lenz, thinks *intempestiuae* (an adj. found 8 times in Ovid) may be preferable to *non tempestiuae*, but goes on to conjecture *intempestiua est ista, propinque, uia.* The theme of rejecting family relations in favour of a lover could be relevant here. For the phrase *tempestiua uia* cf. Apul. *Met.* 8.21 *qui requisitum comitem tempestiuae uiae commonefactum reduceret.* The reference must be to Sulpicia's proposed journey to her uncle's estate. For the use of *uiae* = 'travel' in Tib. to represent one of the hardships of military life that separated male lovers from their girls cf. Tib. 1.1.26, 52 with Maltby (2002) 131 and 140 ad loc., Tib. 1.3.35-36, and, recalling Tib., Ov. *Am.* 2.16.15-18. In a reversal of this elegiac theme here the mistress's travel would separate her from her lover.

propinque: This vocative is not found elsewhere in the singular. The uncertainty of the text means we cannot lay too much weight on this word, which may not be the original reading. If correctly transmitted, the vocative 'kinsman' could refer to the fact that Sulpicia is presented as the daughter of the famous jurist Servius Sulpicius Rufus (cf. **16.4** *Serui filia Sulpicia*), who had married a sister of Messalla (Jerome *Adu. Iouinian.* 1.46). Others, however, for example Holzberg [(1998) 184], think her character and relationship with Messalla were simply invented by the anonymous author of the collection, a view which seems to be correct (see Gen. Intro., sections 3.3 and 3.5).

7 animum sensusque: for the use of these quasi-synonyms in the sense 'mind and soul', cf. Cic. *Sest.* 47 *animos hominum sensusque morte restingui*, *De Orat.* 1.222 *ita peragrat per animos, ita sensus hominum mentisque pertractat ut ...,* 3.67 *omne animi sensusque iudicium*; Virg. *Aen.* 4.22-23 *inflexit sensus animumque labantem / impulit*; Ov. *Met.* 14.177-178 *nisi si timor abstulit omnem / sensum animumque.* For the idea of having one's mind in a different place from one's body Lyne [(2007) 356] compares Cic. *Ad M. Brutum* 1.3 *te uelim habere cognitum, meum quidem animum in acie esse* and Smith 510 cites several passages from Plautus, e.g. *Aul.* 181 *nam egomet sum hic, animus domi est* (*Amph.* 1081, *Cist.* 211, *Merc.* 585); cf. Lutatius Catulus fr. 1.1-2 *aufugit mi animus*; *credo, ut solet, ad Theotimum / deuenit. sic est, perfugium illud habet* and see further examples in N-H 82 on Hor. *Carm.* 2.5.5.

abducta: a strong word in the circumstances, often used of the forcible abduction of a mistress or wife; see *OLD abduco* 5 and cf. Cat. 68.103-104 *ne Paris abducta gauisus libera moecha / otia ... degeret*; Prop. 2.20.1 *quid fles abducta grauius Briseide?*; Tac. *Ann.* 1.10 *abducta Neroni uxor.*

Lyne [(2007) 356] sees some humour in this exaggeration. Batstone [(2018) 104-105] compares the way Delia (= Diana) leads Cerinthus off to the country in **9.5** *procul abducit uenandi Delia cura*.

8 arbitrio ... esse meo: 'to be my own master'; for abl. *arbitrio* (*suo, meo* etc.) with active verbs of doing something 'on one's own initiative' see *OLD arbitrium* 4c and cf. Liv. 25.21.1 *spes haud dubia suo id arbitrio ubi uellent facturos*. Other examples of *arbitrio* with *esse* do not occur until the second century AD; Tränkle [310 ad loc.], compares Afric. *Dig.* 23.5.11 *si* (*fundus*) *arbitrio mariti sit, contra esse* and Ulp. *Dig.* 30.34.14 *duo esse legata et arbitrio eius esse, an uelit*. The phrase may have been anticipated in *iam sua* of Sulpicia, at **12.16**. Here the reference is to the fact that Sulpicia is under Messalla's tutelage.

quamuis non sinis: addressed to Messalla, 'although you do not allow me'. For *quamuis* + indicative, on the analogy of *quamquam*, see **6.29n** and cf. K-S II 2.334 and Virg. *Ecl.* 3.84 *Pollio amat nostram, quamuis est rustica, Musam*, *Aen.* 5.542 *quamuis solus auem caelo deiecit ab alto*. The construction is common in Ovid; see examples in McKeown II 400 on *Am.* 1.15.14 *quamuis ingenio non ualet, arte ualet*. Heyworth [(2018) 79] may be right in rejecting the concessive *quamuis* as out of place here; he suggests *quam tu non sinis* 'I whom you do not allow'.

Poem 15

The poem forms a pair with poem **14**. On such pairs in elegy, see **11 headnote** above. The journey to Messalla's villa on Sulpicia's birthday has been cancelled. The reader assumes that the poem is addressed to the unnamed Cerinthus in her joy at being able to celebrate her birthday with him and her friends in Rome. The joy of this poem contrasts with the gloom of **14**, as the joy of Prop. 1.8B contrasts with the gloom of Prop. 1.8A, when Cynthia first proposes and then cancels a voyage to Illyria. On the contrast in style between **14** and **15** see Santirocco [(1979), 231-232], who argues that the rhetoric of **14** is presented as procuring the success of **15**, in the same way that the *Sulpicia* poems in **13.3-4** are said to have been effective in bringing Cerinthus to her embrace.

1 Scis: an informal opening, conveying immediacy, occurring at the line-opening also in Prop. 2.22.1 and 2; Ov. *Am.* 1.8.23, where McKeown II 213 ad loc. compares, for the conversational tone; Petr. 13.2 and Plin. *Epist.* 7.24.6.

iter ... sublatum: again, conversational in tone, cf. Cic. *Att.* 16.4.4 *iter illud Brundisium de quo dubitabam sublatum uidetur*.

iter ... triste: picks up *natalis ... / ... tristis* of **14.1-2** and refers to the journey proposed in that poem to Messalla's villa. The combination occurs also at Ov. *Trist.* 3.9.32 *triste retardet iter*; Sen. *Herc. F.* 1136, *Oed.* 657; Mart. *Spect.* 12.6.

ex animo sublatum ... puellae: 'lifted from your girl's heart'; for the image cf. Plaut. *Cas.* 23 *eicite ex animo curam atque alienum aes*; Hor. *Epist.* 1.5.18 (sc. *uinum*) *sollicitis animis onus eximit*. For *tollo* in the sense of 'take away' see *OLD tollo* 10 and cf. Cic. *Att.* 16.4.4. (quoted above), *Imp. Cn. Pomp.* 30 *bellum aduentu* (sc. *Pompei*) *sublatum*, *S. Rosc.* 110 *si sublata sit uenditio bonorum*.

puellae: see **14.3n.** above and cf. **17.1**.

2 Romae: on the importance of the urban setting for Sulpicia's affair, see **14.3n.** above. The city is named frequently in Prop. (30), but rarely in elegy elsewhere [Tib. (2); Ov. *Am.* (3), *Ars* (5)].

iam licet: an oblique reference to Messalla's authority and casual permission, see Batstone (2018) 95.

suo: corrected in the Aldine edition of 1502 from *tuo* of A+ and F. In view of the clear connection with **14**, the birthday referred to must be that of Sulpicia (who is already presented as referring to herself in the third person *puellae* in line **1** above and not that of Cerinthus.

3 omnibus ... nobis: all Sulpicia's friends will now be present, including Cerinthus.

ille dies: singular *dies* is normally masculine, except in Prop.; see Fedeli 167 on Prop. 3.4.12 *illa dies*. In [**Tib.**] **3** the masc. sing. is found at **11.1** and the fem. sing. at **6.32, 7.205** and **11.16**.

agatur: optative subjunctive. For the verb in this context, cf. **14.2** above.

4 necopinanti: what was unexpected for Cerinthus was not the birthday itself but the fact that it would be celebrated in Rome. The form *necopinans* (or *nec opinans*, word divisions were not preserved in ancient MSS) is found in prose in Cicero, *Bell. Hisp.*; Sen. *Dial.*; Apul. *Apol.* and Suet. *Aug.*, and in verse at Ter. *And.* 180, *Heaut.* 186, *Hec.* 362; Lucil.

526   Commentary

4.779 M.; Lucr. 3.959, 5.1320, 6.402; Phaedr. *Fab. Aesop.* 5.7.8. The word is not found elsewhere in elegy.

forte: a true ablative 'by chance', rather than the adverb 'perhaps'.

Poem 16

The poem, whose language reflects the colloquial tone of Cicero's letters, allows an element of jealousy to enter for the first time into Sulpicia's relations with Cerinthus. Exaggeration and rhetorical point make it difficult to gauge how seriously we are to take Sulpicia's characterisation of her rival as a whore who spins. Perhaps it is simply that the rival is not as noble as Sulpicia herself, whose high-born connections are stated clearly in **4**, with the punning reference to herself as *Serui filia*, and are hinted at in **5-6** with the reference to those who are concerned about her choice of partner, suggesting perhaps that her social status is higher than that of Cerinthus. An important intertext is probably Prop. 3.16, where Cynthia's direct speech to the slave Lygdamus accuses Propertius of an affair with a prostitute. Unlike Sulpicia, who is presented as using the word *scortum* of her rival, Cynthia uses a euphemism to avoid such a specific reference: Prop. 3.6.21-22 *ille potest nullo miseram me linquere facto, / et qualem nolo dicere habere domi?* (see Gen. Intro., section 3.1). Such direct speech by the mistress, like the letter of Cynthia at Prop. 3.23.11-16, could have provided the author of the *Sulpicia* poems with their inspiration.

1 Gratum est ... quod: 'I am grateful that', here used ironically. The phrase is most common in Cicero's letters (see the more than thirty examples quoted in *ThLL* 6(3). 2261.35-50, with *quod* as a conjunction, normally in the order *quod ... gratum est* e.g. *Fam.* 7.25.1 *quod autem me mones, gratum est,* 16.17.2 *Cuspio quod operam dedisti mihi gratum est, Att.* 14.16.4 *quod ad Xenonem scripsisti, ualde mihi gratum est,* except for the elliptical *gratum quod mihi epistulas* at *Att.* 15.7.1.

securus: connected etymologically with *sine cura* (see *LALE* 555 and **2n.** below) and used in the *Lygd.* poems of freedom from care about a mistress's fidelity at **3.32** and **4.54**. But *cura* in elegy can also stand for the 'love' or 'affection' experienced by a couple for one another, e.g. **1.19** *sit nostri mutua cura,* **6.29** *quamuis nulla mei superest tibi cura, Neaera,* **18.1** *feruida cura* (of Cerinthus for Sulpicia), with the possible suggestion here that Cerinthus is 'without love' for Sulpicia. His 'love' *cura* **3** has been transferred to a prostitute (see further **3n.** below *cura togae*), whereas his *pia cura* towards Sulpicia in her illness at **17.1** below is questioned; see Batstone (2018) 99-102. The opening lines of the last three poems in the *Sulpicia* group thus all question Cerinthus' *cura* for Sulpicia (**16.1** *securus*, **17.1** *pia cura*, **18.1** *feruida cura*).

de me: two monosyllables at the end of the hexameter in elegiac poetry are extremely rare except in Propertius (32 examples), elsewhere occurring only at Gallus fr. 2.2 (Courtney = 145.2 Hollis) *quom tu*; Tib. 1.4.63 *ni sint*, and here at **17.5**; see further Norden (1927) 448 and Lyne (2007) 364. For the meaning 'concerning me' *in me* would be more common, but cf. Cic. *Att.* 12.27.2 *ipsi permittam de tempore*.

1-2 multum ... tibi de me / permittis: 'you allow yourself much (leeway) in my regard'. *tibi* in H and Y (also conjectured by Heinsius) must be correct here for *mihi* in A+. For *permitto* + dat. 'to allow', 'grant something to someone', see Cic. *Att.* 12.27.2 quoted in **1n.** above, OLD *permitto* 6 and Tränkle [314 and n. 9] for a long list of parallels; particularly relevant are the reflexive uses at Ov. *Her.* 7.39 *quem sibi permisit, genero concedet amorem*, *Trist.* 2.356 (sc. *carmen nostrum*) *plus sibi permisit compositore suo*.

2 subito ne ... cadam: Lee (1975) takes the clause as dependent on *securus* 'unconcerned that I should suddenly fall (sc. for some other man)' on the model of Liv. 39.16.6 *ne quis ... errore labatur ... non sum securus*. More probable [with Smith 512, Tränkle 314-315 and Lyne (2007) 360], is that *ne cadam* is to be taken as an ironic 'pseudo-final' clause with *permittis*, expressing as his intention what is actually the consequence of Cerinthus' unfaithfulness, namely, that she should not suddenly fall into the disgrace of marrying him, a man whom her friends in **5-6** characterise as too low-born for her. For this type of ironic final clause Tränkle [315 n.10] compares Ov. *Met.* 9.735-736 *ne non tamen omnia Crete / monstra ferat, taurum dilexit filia Solis*. The verb *cado* means 'to fall into disgrace', 'be ruined' OLD *cado* 11 rather than 'commit a sexual misdemeanour' (for which the term would be *pecco*), the sense required if *ne* were dependent on *securus*. A connection with *turpiter arma cadant* of the weapons of Mars in **8.4** cannot be ruled out [see Batstone (2018) 104], though the god's disgrace would be trivial compared with hers.

male inepta: for *male* as a colloquial intensifier of the pejorative *inepta* cf. Cat. 10.33 *insulsa male* (with Fordyce ad loc.); Hor. *Serm.* 1.3.45 *male paruus*, 4.66 *rauci male*; on this colloquial usage see further Hofmann (1926) 74.

3 cura togae: 'love for a toga.' The phrase refers by metonymy to love for a prostitute or other woman of low esteem who wore a toga since the long *stola* of the respectable married woman (*matrona*) would be denied her. It may be significant for the construction of Cerinthus' character that both uses of *puella togata* for a prostitute in Horace occur in a poem addressed to a *puer delicatus* named Cerinthus (see Gen. Intro., section 3.4): Hor. *Serm.* 1.2.62-63 *quid inter- / est in matrona, ancilla peccesne togata*?, cf. ibid. 80-82 *nec magis huic, inter niueos uiridisque lapillos / sit licet, hoc, Cerinthe, tuo tenerum est femur aut crus / rectius, atque etiam melius persaepe togatae est*. As Hinds [(1987) 45] points out, the first half of the line *sit tibi cura togae potior*, before the mention of the *pressum ... quasillo / scortum*, would most naturally have referred to Cerinthus' concern for his own Roman citizen's toga, in other words, for his own dignity. The associations of the toga as worn by a man are completely reversed when worn by a woman, cf. Cic. *Phil.* 2.44 (of Antony) *sumpsisti uirilem quam statim muliebrem togam reddidisti*. As it is, Cerinthus' 'love' *cura* for a prostitute is contrasted with his lack of concern *securus* **1** for Sulpicia. For *cura* = 'love' see **1.19n.** and for *securus* etymologised by the Romans as 'lack of *cura*' see **1n.** above *securus, LALE* 555 and **3.32n.** Hubbard [(2004) 186-187] sees in the reference to love for a slave girl a traditional theme of the marriage poem or epithalamium, in which the bridegroom is asked to put aside his previous affairs. In Cat. 61.119-143, for example, the bridegroom is asked to put aside his interest in a slave boy. For the Greek background to this epithalamic topos see Fedeli (1985) 96-97.

3-4 pressum quasillo / scortum: 'a strumpet weighed down by a wool basket'. Spinning was the occupation of the lowliest of slave girls. On *pressum ... scortum* as nominative, in apposition to *cura*, instead of genitive, dependent on *cura* and parallel with *togae*, as normal syntax would demand, see Tränkle [317 ad loc.] with parallels. The word *quasillum* is prosaic and occurs elsewhere in verse only at Prop. 4.7.41 *et grauiora rependit iniquis pensa quasillis* (spoken by Cynthia of the new mistress, Chloris, in Prop.'s house, in which Lygdamus is a slave, punishing slave girls who praise the now dead Cynthia for her beauty, see Gen. Intro., section 3.1). Both here and in Prop. 4.7.41 the word is spoken by a woman and Porphyrio, commenting on *qualum* at Hor. *Carm.* 3.12.4-5, sees it as characteristic of female speech: '*qualum' metonymicos pro lanifico dixit. sed mulieres per deminutionem uasculum hoc usurpant, quasillum dicentes*. Poetry prefers its Greek equivalent *calathus* (Prop., Virg., Ov., Calp., Stat., Juv., Mart., Sil.). For *scortum* as a prostitute, often used of hired dancing girls invited to symposia, see *OLD scortum* 2 and

Lyne (1980) 197-198. Adams [(1983) 324-327] argues the term is more pejorative than the less emotive *meretrix*. Again the word is un-poetic (though not vulgar or obscene, common, e.g., in Cicero's speeches) and, apart from its occurrence here, is absent from elegy. Frequent in Plautus and Terence, its use in later verse is extremely limited [Cat. 6.5 again in the context of love for a slave-girl; Lucr. 4.1274; Hor. *Carm.* 2.11.21 (with N-H 177 ad loc.), *Epist.* 1.18.34]. Sulpicia's characterisation of her rival as a lowly prostitute engaged in spinning no doubt displays some rhetorical exaggeration. More important is the literary ancestry in Prop. 3.6.21-22 and 4.7.41 For the love of slave girls as a poetic theme in Hellenistic and Augustan verse see N-H 66-67 in their introduction to Hor. *Carm.* 2.4 and cf. Prop. 1.9.4 (to Ponticus) *et tibi nunc quiduis imperat empta modo*, 3.6.22 (Cynthia of Propertius), where Cynthia uses the euphemism *qualem nolo dicere* for Sulpicia's more direct *scortum* (see **headnote** above). This unmentionable rival for Cynthia, is probably the same Chloris, mentioned above, who replaces Cynthia in Prop.'s affections after her death.

4 Serui filia Sulpicia: Sulpicia is presented as giving her poetic signature (*sphragis*) at the most humiliating point of her erotic narrative, where she sees herself as rejected in favour of a common prostitute. The *sphragis* occurs in the mid couplet of the poem, cf. **5.17-18**. At the surface level the phrase emphasises her noble birth, possibly as daughter of Servius Sulpicius Rufus, himself the son of a patrician jurist of the same name, cos. 51 BC. As to whether this relationship was 'real' or a poetic invention see **14.6n.** above. In my view it is clearly an invention. Again (as with *togae* above) the word *Serui* could contain a double meaning 'daughter of Servius' but also 'daughter of a slave', a play on words familiar to Romans from the discussion of the servile origins of the early king Servius Tullius; see Hinds (1987) 44-45. This is the only non-disyllabic pentameter ending in the *Sulpicia* poems. For the short open syllable at the pentameter end see above **13.6n.** *sua* and cf. below **17.6** *mala*.

5 solliciti sunt pro nobis: the care of Sulpicia's friends contrasts with the unconcern of Cerinthus *securus* 1. The reference is more likely to be to family members who care for her (cf. **15.3** *omnibus ... nobis*) than to rivals of Cerinthus. The construction of *sollicitus* with *pro* seems to be restricted elsewhere to prose, e.g. Cic. *Amic.* 45 *ne necesse sit unum sollicitum esse pro pluribus*; Liv. 22.59.16, 38.9.4. The adj. occurs in the *Lygd.* poems with reference to the cares of love at **4.20, 6.36** and **6.61**.

6 ne cedam: the reading *ne* of some later MSS for *nec* of A+, and Statius' *cedam* for *credam* of the MSS are necessary to restore sense to the line.

For *cedo* in the sense of 'fall to' 'become the property of', see *OLD cedo* 15.

ignoto ... toro: must refer, again with some rhetorical exaggeration, to Cerinthus, as an 'obscure' or 'ignoble' partner, at least in comparison with Sulpicia daughter of Servius, with a possible play on his name as a lowly plant, see Gen. Intro., section 3.4. For this metonymy of *torus* = 'partner' [cf. Ov. *Her.* 8.26; Val. Fl. 5.444] and for the phrase *ignotum ... torum* in the vicinity of *sollicitus* cf. **6.59-61** *non ego, si fugit nostrae conuiuia mensae / ignotum cupiens uana puella torum / sollicitus repetam tota suspiria nocte* above with **n.** ad loc., an important link between these two sections of the book.

maxima causa: to be taken with the relative clause *quibus illa dolori est* (**5**) 'to whom it is the greatest source of pain'. For the construction with the dat. *dolori* cf. Ov. *Rem.* 322 *haec odio uenit maxima causa meo*. The gen. after *maxima causa* is more common, cf. Prop. 1.16.35 *tu* (sc. *ianua*) *maxima causa doloris*; Ov. *Rem.* 768, *Trist.* 5.12.46; *Catalepton* 9.12; *Aetna* 399.

Poem 17

This poem on her own illness and Cerinthus' possible reactions is a variation on the well-known elegiac theme of the mistress's illness, for which see **10 headnote**. The present poem is related to poem **10** as it attempts the same theme from two different angles. Whereas traditional elegies on the subject pray for the mistress's recovery, here Sulpicia wishes to be cured only if such a cure would be welcome to Cerinthus. On the links between this poem and Ov. *Ars* 2.319-336 see Yardley (1990). The poem is linked to **18** by the theme of the lover's silence. Neither of the questions posed to Cerinthus here in **1-2** and **5-6** receives an answer, just as in **18** Sulpicia regrets her own silence about her true passion for her lover; see further Batstone (2018) 100-102.

1 Estne: a rare verse opening outside comedy (Plaut. 18, Ter. 2), only Cat. 66.15 *estne nouis nuptis odio Venus?*; Sen. *Herc. F.* 621, 697; Stat. *Theb.* 10.238. In Cicero it commonly opens sentences in the speeches (8) and philosophical works (4), but is less frequent in the letters (2). The effect here is perhaps prosaic rather than colloquial.

pia cura: a conjectural reading for the nonsensical *placitura* of the MSS (emended to *placiture* in G^{pc} and V^{pc}). The phrase can be paralleled in the same *sedes* at Ov. *Am.* 2.16.47 *si qua mei tamen est pia cura relicti* (addressed by Ovid to his girl while alone in Sulmo) and *Her.* 8.15 (Hermione to Orestes) *at tu, cura mei si te pia tangit, Oreste.* For the sense of 'dutiful care', 'dutiful love' to be shown to a sick mistress, cf. Ov. *Ars* 2.321 *tunc amor et pietas tua sit manifesta puellae*; see further McKeown III 363 on Ov. *Am.* 2.16.47-48 and Yardley (1990). Here *cura* recalls the complex *securus / cura / solliciti* of 16.1-5. For *pietas* in the context of an erotic relationship cf. Cat. 76.1-2 *siqua recordanti benefacta priora uoluptas / est homini, cum se cogitat esse pium.*

cura puellae: the phrase occurs in this position also at Prop. 3.21.3; Ov. *Am.* 1.9.43, *Her.* 21.59, *Med. Fac. Fem.* 1, *Ars* 2.295, 3.631, *Rem.* 205, 311, 681 and cf. Tib. 2.3.31 *cura puella est.*

2 uexat corpora: the only parallel for this phrase in verse is Ov. *Trist.* 5.2.3-5 *corpus ... / ... / ... ipso uexatum induruit usu*; in prose Lyne [(2007) 363] compares Liv. 45.39.19 *uexatum corpus*; Cic. *Tusc.* 4.18.10 *cum uexatione corporis*; Sen. *Epist.* 78.10.3 *in uexatione corporis*; Colum. *Rust.* 6.2.11 *corporis uexationem*; to these should be added Cic. *Phil.* 11.8.5 *corpore lacerando et uexando*; Liv. 7.10.11 *corpus ... ab uexatione intactum*; Cels. 5.27.2d *infirmum corpus in aqua frigida vexatum*, 7.26.5a *si ualens corpus est neque magnopere uexatum*; Curt. 7.9.13 *uexationem inualidi corporis pati non poterat*; Tac. *Hist.* 1.49 *Galbae corpus ... ludibriis uexatum*; Just. *Dig.* 47.12.3, 50.5.2, 50.6.6. pr. 5. For *uexo* of the infliction of suffering by disease cf. Suet. *Cal.* 50.2 *puer comitiali morbo uexatus.* Again *Sulpicia*'s idiom is closer to that of prose than to that of elegiac verse.

corpora fessa: in the same *sedes* at **10.10**, see **n**. ad loc. above. The phrase occurs elsewhere in verse at Cat. 64.189; Lucr. 4.848; Virg. *Aen.* 4.522-523; Ov. *Met.* 11.624-625; Gratt. *Cyneg.* 473; Lucan 4.623 (and in prose in Liv. and Tac. *Ann.*). Cf. *morbo defessa* in Tib. 1.5.9 quoted on **3** below.

calor: common in technical medical writers of 'fever', e.g. 20 examples in Cels. In verse in this sense only Juv. 12.98-99 *sentire calorem / si coepit locuples Gallitta.* As Santirocco [(1979) 233] suggests, there could be some ambiguity here between real 'fever' and the metaphorical 'heat' of passion; on the latter see **12.17-18n**. and on love as a disease see **12.18n**.

3-4 aliter ... / ... quam: common in Ovid *Her.* (2), *Met.* (15), *Fast.* (1), *Trist.* (4), *Pont.* (1), but absent from *Am.* and *Ars* and the elegies of Tib. and Prop.

3 a, ego: see **4.82n.** above. These are the only two occurrences of the phrase in elegy. This is the only example of hiatus in the *Sulpicia* poems.

tristes ... morbos: for the phrase cf. Tib. 1.5.9 *ille ego, cum tristi morbo defessa iaceres*, a line perhaps also echoed in *ego* (**3**) and *fessa* (**2**) here. The combination is found also at Virg. *Aen.* 4.252 and Ov. *Met.* 7.601. For the plural *morbos* here, at **10.1** above, and at **5** below = *febrim* see K-S II 1.85 and cf. *morbos* at Ov. *Rem.* 115, *Fast.* 3.827, and *pestes* at Cic. *Tusc.* 2.21. As in poem **10** there is some ambiguity in this poem as to whether Sulpicia's illness is to be conceived as physical or whether it is metaphorical love sickness; see **10 headnote**, and **10.2n.**, **5n.** and **16n.** above.

euincere morbos: another phrase taken from the technical language of medical prose, elsewhere only Cels. 3.22.8; Colum. *Rust.* 6.5.2; *Mulomedicina Chironis* 4.3.6.

4 optarim: elsewhere in elegy at Tib. 1.6.74 *optarim non habuisse manus*; Ov. *Her.* 17.109 *optarim fieri tua Troica coniunx*.

te si quoque: for this rare hyperbaton of *quoque* Tränkle [321 ad loc.] compares Lucr. 2.216 *illud in his quoque te rebus cognoscere auemus*, 581, 5.192-193, 6.317, 577; Ov. *Met.* 6.403-404 *tamen haec quoque dicitur unus / flesse Pelpos*; Mart. 9.8.10 *infantes te quoque, Caesar, amant*.

5-6 Simply recapitulates the idea of the previous couplet in slightly different terms.

5 si tu: for two monosyllables at the end of the hexameter, see **16.1n.** above. *si* here is a necessary correction in G^{pc} and V^{pc} for *quid* of A+.

6 lento pectore: for *lentus* here in the sense of 'unfeeling', 'unemotional' see *OLD lentus* 8 and cf. Cic. *De Orat.* 3.205 *nimium patiens et lentus existimor*; Prop. 1.6.12 *a pereat, si quis lentus amare potest*, 3.8.20 *hostibus eueniat lenta puella meis*. For the phrase *lento pectore* cf. Ov. *Her.* 15.169-170 *amor tetigit lentissima Pyrrhae / pectora*.

mala: for the pentameter ending in a short open syllable, see **13.6n.** *sua* and cf. **16.4**.

Poem 18

The poem is composed in a single six-line sentence, reminiscent of Catullan epigrams 75, 81, 82, 96, 102, and 103. The hexameter-opening *si quicquam* **3** is also Catullan: 96.1, 102.1, 107.1. The syntax of the whole poem is shown by Lowe [(1988) 198] and Lyne [(2007) 364-365] to contain a high concentration of features for which the *Sulpicia* poems have an idiosyncratic fondness: love of subordinate clauses; comparative constructions *aeque ... ac* **1-2**, *magis ... quam* **4-5**, cf. **13.1-2, 16.3-4, 17.3-4**; *quod* noun- clause **5**, cf. **16.1, 17.2**; perfect infinitives as penultimate words in the pentameter **2, 4,** cf. **13.6, 10**. Two of its adj. /noun combinations can be paralleled elsewhere in verse only from the late first century AD, namely *paucos ... dies* **2** and *tota ... iuuenta* **3**. In its expression of regret at leaving her lover (unnamed) on the previous night for fear of revealing her passion the poem provides the *Sulpicia* group **13-18** with a neat ring-structure. The regret at hiding her passion in the concluding poem **18** echoes her willingness finally to reveal her love in the introductory **13**. The positioning of this poem in the mss. tradition varies; most often it is connected to **17**, but sometimes it occurs after **16**.

1-3 Ne tibi sim ... / ... / si: the construction, like *gratum est... quod* in **16.1f.**, belongs to the language of polite conversational prose. *OLD ne* 4 gives in addition to the present occurrence the following examples, all from Cicero's letters: Cic. *Att.* 4.17.5 *ne uiuam, si scio*, 12.3.1 *ne uiuam, mi Attice, si...,* 16.13a.1 *ne sim saluus, si aliter scribo ac sentio, Fam.* 7.23.4 *ne uiuam, si tibi concedo*. See further K-S II 1.190-191, Lyne (2007) 365.

1-2 aeque ... / ac: on comparative constructions of this type as typical of the style of the *Sulpicia* poems, see **headnote** above. The phrase *aeque ... ac* occurs only here in the *Corp. Tib.* and is restricted mainly to prose (Cic., Liv., Cels., Plin. *Nat.*, Suet., Tac.), except for single occurrences in Early Latin verse in Plaut., Ter., Lucil., Acc., Afran. Its eight occurrences in Cicero's letters show it is at home in polite conversation. On *atque* or *ac* in place of *quam* after comparative adjs or advs see L. C. Watson (2003) 409 on Hor. *Epod.* 12.14 *minus ac* and cf. *Epod.* 15.5 *artius atque, Serm.* 1.2.22 *peius ... atque*; Suet. *Caes.* 14 *grauius atque*.

1 ne tibi sim ... cura: for the construction nom. *cura + esse +* dat. in place of the more common predicative dative *curae esse +* dat. see **13.1-2** with **n**. *sit mihi fama* and cf. Cic. *Att.* 10.8.4 *naualis apparatus ei semper antiquissima cura fuit*; [Ov.] *Epiced. Drusi* 196 *nos erimus magno maxima* *cura Ioui*. The fact that *cura* here is used metonymically = 'object of love', as at **16.3**, makes the construction more natural. The noun is a key concept in the *Sulpician* collection, see **16.3**, **17.1** with **nn.** ad loc., and the present occurrence echoes in particular the opening line of poem **17**.

mea lux: this term of endearment was addressed by Cicero to his wife, Terentia, at *Fam.* 14.2.2, and was obviously at home in polite conversation. In elegy *mea lux* or *lux mea* is normally applied to the mistress; examples in **9.15n.** above, of particular relevance here is Prop. 2.29.1 (quoted in **5n.** below). It is used of a male beloved elsewhere at Ov. *Ars* 3.524 (Tecmessa to Ajax) and **9.15** (also of Cerinthus).

feruida cura: the combination is found only here, but cf. Hor. *Carm.* 1.30.5 *feruidus puer* of Cupid. The adj. may look forward to *ardorem* in the last line (**6**) of the poem. On *cura* here and its relation to *securus* **16.1** and *pia cura* **17.1** see **16.1n.** *securus* above.

2 uideor: continues the theme of appearance and reality, revealing and hiding, introduced in poem **13** with *texisse* **1**, *nudasse* **2**, and *uultus componere* **9** and picked up in this final *Sulpicia* poem here and in *dissimulare* at **6** below. The verb form *uideor* occurs only here in the *Corp. Tib.*, twice in Prop. (2.21.3, 22.21), but no fewer that 27 times in Ov.

paucos ante ... dies: the phrase occurs here for the first time in verse (Plaut. *Truc.* 348 has *cis dies paucos*) and is restricted mainly to prose, especially Livy who has 14 examples. It occurs only once in Cicero at *Att.* 9.8.1. The combination *paucos ... dies* is rare in verse, occurring at Juv. 13.160 and, in the same *sedes* as here, at Mart. 1.15.4.

fuisse: all three pentameters in this poem have an inf. in this penultimate position (*paenituisse* **4**, *dissimulare* **6**). On perfect infinitives in verse see **3.2n.** above.

3 si quicquam: a common hexameter opening in Catullus, cf. 96.1, 102.1, 107.1. Particularly close to the couplet **3-4** here is Cat. 102.1-2 *si quicquam tacito commissumst fido ab amico, / cuius sit penitus nota fides animi.* Other verse occurrences at the line-opening at Ter. *And.* 863; Hor. *Serm.* 2.6.55; Lucan 6.613.

tota ... iuuenta: also, in the same *sedes*, at Val. Fl. 3.682 *sit satis et tota pelagus lustrasse iuuenta*; cf. Prop. 3.11.7 *praeterita ... iuuenta*; Virg. *Aen.* 4.32 *perpetua ... iuuenta*. The expression need not imply, as Tränkle

300 states, that the time of her youth is as good as over, but simply refers to the whole period of her youth so far. The form *iuuenta* (never *iuuentas*) is used by Prop. and Ov., whereas Tib. uses only *iuuentas* (1.4.37, 8.41). Both forms are found in Hor. *Carm.*; see further Bréguet (1946) 47. The adj. *totus* is used commonly in other ablative expressions of time, e.g. Cat. 109.5 *tota ... uita*; Ov. *Am.* 1.6.68 *tota ... nocte, Fast.* 1.49 *toto ... die* and cf. *Lygd.* **6.61n.** above on *tota ... nocte.*

stulta: cf. *male inepta* in **16.2**; in both cases the reference is to incompetence in amatory matters, as also with *stulte* at **19.18**. For the philosophical implications of the word see **19.8n.** *stulte* below.

4 paenituisse: this perf. inf. is found five times in this position in Ovid (*Am.* 3.7.46, *Her.* 17.32, *Ars* 2.592, *Trist.* 4.9.4, *Pont.* 1.1.58) but this form does not occur in Tib. or Prop. On the metrical convenience of perfect infinitives, see **3.2n.**

magis: on *Sulpicia*'s love of comparative constructions see **headnote** above.

5 hesterna ... nocte: for other poetic examples of this phrase see **4.2n.** above. Of particular note here is its use in the same *sedes* at Prop. 2.29A.1 with its combination with *mea lux* (cf. **1** above): *hesterna, mea lux, cum potus nocte uagarer.*

te solum ... reliqui: there may, as Lyne [(2007) 367] suggests, be a hint of gender reversal here. It is normally the heroine who is abandoned alone by her lover, e.g. Cat. 64.200 *quali solam Theseus me mente reliquit*; Prop. 2.24B.46 (of Medea) *sola relicta*; **[Tib.] 3.6.40** (of Ariadne) *fleuisti ignoto sola relicta mari.*

6 ardorem: for its use of the fire of love, cf. Lucr. 4.1077 (with Brown ad loc.), 1086 etc.; Cat. 2.28, 62.29; Prop. 1.3.13, 7.24 etc.; Ov. *Am.* 2.16.12 (with McKeown III 339 ad loc.), *Her.* 16.311 etc. Tib. uses *ardere*, but not the corresponding noun. There may be a reference here back to *feruida cura* of **1**.

cupiens dissimulare: cf. Cic. *S. Rosc.* 102.2 *si dissimulare omnes cuperent se scire, Verr.* 1.1.21 *cupiebam dissimulare me id molestum ferre.*

dissimulare: the verb is inordinately frequent in Ovid (50), occurring in this line-position at *Am.* 2.2.18, *Her.* 9.122. It is absent from Prop. and occurs twice in Tib. 1.8.7 and 44; see further McKeown III 38 on Ov. *Am.* 2.2.17-18. It occurs, significantly, in Ovid's advice to his mistress at *Am.* 3.14.3-4 *nec te nostra iubet fieri censura pudicam, / sed tamen, ut temptes dissimulare, rogat*. On the way in which Sulpicia appears to reverse the advice of this poem see **13 headnote** above. The verb recalls *texisse* and *nudasse* of the opening couplet of the *Sulpicia* group (see **13.1-2n.**). If poem **13**, as seems likely, represents a time later than the dramatic date of poem **18** (see **13 headnote** and **13.1-2n.**), there has been a movement in the course of the affair from dissimulation to revelation. The echoing of *texisse* **13.1** in *dissimulare* here provides the six poem group **13-18** with a neat ring-structure.

An Elegy in the Mask of Tibullus

Poem 19

The poet of this elegy names himself apparently as Tibullus (**13**), and of the poems of **book 3** this one was longest considered to be a genuine work of that author. Heyne, for example, was happy to describe it as a *carmen uere Albianum*, and there are still those today who would defend that attribution. However, there are a number of serious objections to seeing this as anything but a product of a Tibullus *personatus*. Its length at 24 lines is shorter than any genuine Tibullan poem except 2.2, the birthday poem to Cornutus (22 lines) and much closer to the five poems of the *Sulpicia Cycle* at 24, 24, 26, 20 and 20 lines each. It certainly shows a number of close connections verbally and thematically with that group: see **7n.** on links with **10.18** and **21**; **8n.** on links with **8.2**; **8n.**, **9n.** and **20n.** on links with **8.8**; **19n.** on links with **8.11-12**, **11.5** and **12.17**; **23n.** on links with **11.13-14**. If **19** did belong to that *Cycle* it would mean that the *Sulpicia Cycle*, like the *Lygd.* group (**1-6**) and the *Sulpicia* poems (**13-18**), would consist of six poems (**8-12 + 19**). These groups, as I have argued, need not have been written by different people. A substantial argument in favour of a unitary author for all these groups could be based on the intertextuality between the first of the *Lygd.* group and the two final poems of our collection with the Cephalus and Procris episode at the end of Ov. *Met.* 7. The important points of similarity are set out in the Gen. Intro., section 1.3, **1 headnote** and in the individual notes on **1.19**, **25** and **26**. The same episode appears to be echoed in the last two poems of our collection at **19.2**, **11-12** and **13-14** as well as at **20.3** below (see individual notes ad loc.). Such echoes are unlikely to be coincidental and argue for a unitary author for the whole collection who wished to connect the first and last poems of **[Tib.] 3** and thus provide a ring structure for the whole book. Further links with the opening poem of *Lygdamus*, the beginning of the *Laudes Messallae* and the first poems of the *Sulpicia Cycle* and the *Sulpicia* group are provided by the Callimachean imagery and poetics discussed in **nn. 6, 7, 9** and **10** below. Wiseman [(1985) 183], backed up his claim that the Catullan collection as we now have it, was made up originally of three books (1-60, 61-64 and 65-116), by pointing out that each of these books began with poems which exploited his audience's knowledge of Callimachus' *Aetia*. Could our author have linked the different sections of his work by using a similar device? Certainly Catullus is named as an important predecessor in the last of the *Lygdamus* poems (**6.4**), just as his influence was acknowledged in the reference to the gift of a *libellus* of poems in the first, *Lygd.* **1.9** and **17**. This Catullan influence was carried through into the opening of the *Laud. Mess.* **7**, with its thematic use of Cat.'s translation of Callimachus *Coma Berenices* (Cat. 66, see **7 headnote, 7.9-11n.** and **7.18n.** above) and his influence resurfaces in these last two poems, see **19.2n., 4n., 5n., 21n., 22n., 23n.** and **20.1n.**

The importance of Vertumnus, the god of change, for the whole of the book is discussed above in the notes on **8.13-14** and there are clear links in the present poem to this god's wooing of Pomona at Ov. *Met.* 14.641ff., see **4n., 8n., 12n.** below, suggesting this unifying theme is intentionally picked up in this concluding elegy. In fact poems **19** and **20** act as a conclusion not simply to the *Sulpicia* poems **8-18** but to the whole collection. Given our assumption that the author of these final two poems is the same as that of the *Lygd.* **1-6** and indeed of the whole book, we could perhaps be justified in seeing in these final poems hints that the meaning of the names Lygdamus and Neaera, with which the book opened (for which see Gen. Intro., sections 3.1 and 3.2), are no longer appropriate at the end. The elements of 'publicising' his sorrows, present in the δᾶμος ('people') and λύζω / λυγμός ('to sob'/ 'a sob') elements of Lygdamus' name would be negated here by the recognition of the pain caused by a *garrula lingua* at **19.20** as it would by the closural *tace* addressed to *rumor* in **20.4**. Lygdamus, the former publiciser, is now replaced by a character who closes his ears (**20.2** *surdis ... auribus*) to such revelations and who wants to enjoy his love *secretis ... siluis* (**19.9**). Similarly Neaera, the *nea era* (or *noua domina*) of the opening poems, has now been replaced by a *notae ...dominae* (**19.22**) as the poet has acquired a true understanding of female behaviour over the course of the book (cf. Cat. 72.5 *nunc te cognoui*). The rejection of the significance of these two names from the beginning of the book to the end of the whole collection could be seen as a closural marker. Both names are now annulled and the author takes up explicitly the mask of Tibullus, an identity he had hinted at in the *Laud. Mess.*(see **7 headnote**). Just as Tibullus' second book, where the mistress is the 'dark' figure of Nemesis, can be seen to reverse in many instances the themes of the first book based on the 'bright' Delia, so espousal of secrecy in this poem reverses the themes of openness and revelation which characterised the earlier *Lygd.* and *Sulpicia* poems. Our poet, in the mask of Tibullus, adopts an important structural element from his Augustan model.

The verse technique of the poem, with its short, simple sentences and its use of disyllabic pentameter endings in all but one case (**22** *dominae*) is inconsistent with an early Tibullan composition date and is closer to that of Ovid and the other poems of **[Tib.] 3**. Furthermore the clear and simple structure of the poem, with its six groups of four lines, would also argue against Tibullan technique with its structural complexity [on which see Murgatroyd (1984) 283-291, Mutschler (1985), Maltby (2002) 31-32]. Similarities with other works of Ovid, apart from *Met.* 7, namely with *Remedia* and *Tristia*, at **9** and **11-12** appear less suited to their context here than they do in Ovid, suggesting Ovid as the originator and our poet as the imitator (see **9n.** and **11-12n.** below), and similarities with Propertius in almost every couplet (see individual notes below) are far more frequent than in the poems of the genuine Tibullus. Finally, its frequent reminiscences of the genuine Tibullan poems are intended to strengthen his adoption of a persona, and such self-reference would not be as frequent in Tibullus himself. The poem, then, is unlikely to have been written before Ovid's *Tristia* and so cannot have been composed by the real Tibullus. Tibullan authorship was argued for by Lenz (1932), Hanslik (1952) 32-33, and Eisenhut (1977); for the more convincing arguments against Tibullan authorship see Knoche (1956), Lee (1963), Wimmel (1968) 257-259, Hooper (1975) 145-151, Tränkle 323-334, and Holzberg (1998) 170.

The poem's contents may be summarised as follows:

1-4 no other girl will please me as much as you.

5-8 would that you pleased me alone. I wish you would displease your other admirers but my jealousy must be avoided and private joys kept silent.

Book Three of the Corpus Tibullianum: 539
Introduction, Text, Translation and Commentary

9-12 with you, who are all to me, I could live happily in woodland seclusion.

13-16 I swear by Juno I would reject any girl sent from heaven for me, Tibullus, in favour of you.

17-20 alas such pledges are foolish, my loose talk has freed you from fear and given you confidence to torture me more boldly.

21-24 but whatever you do I will remain true to your service and sit chained at Venus' altars, for she favours suppliants and punishes the guilty.

1 Nulla ... lectum: the wording is close to Prop. 1.8B.45 *nec mihi riualis certos subducet amores*. The difference here is that the author is speaking not of a male rival stealing his love, but of another woman *femina* stealing him away from his mistress as at Prop. 2.6.41-42 *nos uxor numquam, numquam diducet amica: / semper amica mihi, semper et uxor eris*. Such reversal of typical elegiac gender roles is characteristic of the **[Tib.] 3** as a whole, see **6.49-50n., 18.5n.** above.

subducet: for the use of this verb in the sense 'remove', 'steal away from' + dat. see *OLD subduco* 7 and cf. Prop. 1.8.45 (quoted above); Ov. *Am.* 3.4.39 *at si uenturo se subduxisset amanti*. The verb is relatively common in Prop. (3) and Ov. (17): *Am.* (3), *Her.* (2), *Ars* (1), *Met.* (5), *Fast.* (3), *Trist.* (2), *Pont.* (1) but does not occur elsewhere in the *Corp. Tib.* S. J. Heyworth, in an as yet unpublished lecture, and Fulkerson [(2017) 295 ad loc.] see a possible connection with Hom. *Od.* 23.177-204, the description of Odysseus' bed which was built into the house and could not be stolen away.

femina: see **4.61-62n.** above.

lectum: 'bed', used metaphorically of a sexual relationship, as at Tib. 1.5.7 and Prop. 3.20.21 quoted in **2n.** below; see Pichon 185-186.

2 For the idea of the bed as the basis of an agreement or bond (*foedus*) of love, divinely sanctioned by Venus cf. Tib. 1.5.7-8 *parce tamen, per te furtiui foedera lecti, / per Venerem quaeso compositumque caput* with further examples in Maltby (2002) 244 ad loc. The concept begins in Catullus: 64.335, 373 (with reference to the marriage of Peleus and Thetis) 76.3-4, 87.3 and 109.6 (with reference to his relationship with Lesbia), before being taken up by the elegists. Also close in sense is Prop. 3.20.21-

22 *namque ubi non certo uincitur foedere lectus, / non habet ultores nox uigilata deos*. On *foedus* in this contexts see Pichon 152; for its presence in the important *Met.* 7 intertext (discussed in the **headnote** above), cf. Procris' oath *per nostri foedera lecti* at Ov. *Met.* 7.852, picking up her husband Cephalus' reference to their first union at *Met.* 7.710 *primaque deserti referebam foedera lecti*.

iuncta ... Venus: the phrase *Venerem iungere* is used to refer to the sexual act, cf. Tib. 1.9.76; Ov. *Ars* 2.679, *Rem.* 407, *Ibis* 351. Venus is derived etymologically from *uincire* (Varro *Ling.* 5.61) and the use of its synonym *iungere* here obviously contains a pun on her name. Other such puns on Venus' name, involving in these cases the verb *uenire*, had occurred at the beginning of the *Lygdamus poems* (see **1.1n. uenere**) and of the *Sulpicia Cycle* (see **8.2n. ipse ueni**). For the use of *Venus* metonymically see **14n.** below. The mention of Venus here in the first couplet is picked up in the final couplet (**24**) by *Veneris ... aras*, suggesting poem **19** is a complete poem with intentional ring-structure. The veneration of Venus as a protector of lovers is a typically Tibullan theme, see Maltby [(2004) 119-120] and cf. **14n.** below, and so her mention at the beginning, middle and end of the poem is a good choice for a poet acting as a *Tibullus personatus*. For Venus in Juno's role as protector of the marriage bed cf. Manil. 2.924-926 *propria est haec reddita parti / uis, ut conubia et thalamos taedasque gubernet: / haec tutela decet Venerem*. For *iungere* of joining in marriage, cf. the important intertext Ov. *Met.* 7.697-698 (Cephalus of his marriage to Procris) *pater hanc mihi iunxit ... / hanc mihi iunxit amor*.

3 tu mihi sola places: the same phrase occurs in the same *sedes* at Prop. 2.7.19 *tu mihi sola places*; *placeam tibi, Cynthia, solus*. It also occurs in a passage of Ov. *Ars* on seeking for girls in the city, which has other similarities with the present poem: *Ars* 1.42-44 *elige cui dicas 'tu mihi sola places.' / haec tibi non tenues ueniet delapsa per auras* (cf. **13** below): / *quaerenda est oculis apta puella tuis* (cf. **4** below).

iam: the significance of the adverb is uncertain. The suggestion may be that the poet used to find other girls attractive, but now, since meeting his current girl, he does not.

te praeter: the preposition is not found in Tib. or Prop. but is used freely by Hor. and Ov., and occurs elsewhere in the *Corp. Tib.* at **7.5**. For the anastrophe cf. *te propter* at Tib. 1.6.57, 65, 7.25, 2.6.35 and possibly *te praeter* at **7.5**, see **n.** ad loc.

in urbe: cf. Ovid's insistence on Rome as the place to meet girls at *Ars* 1.55-60. On Sulpicia's preference for an urban setting for her affair with Cerinthus, as contrasted with the idyllic rural setting desired by Tib. for his affair with Delia, see **14.3n.** above. There is a contrast in the present poem between *in urbe* here and the rural retreat contemplated in **9-10** below. For *in urbe* at the verse-end, cf. Prop. 4.4.75; Ov. *Am.* 3.1.21, *Her.* 2.76, *Rem.* 291, *Met.* 8.7, 15.35, 801, *Fast.* 5.553, *Trist.* 5.9.5, *Pont.* 3.2.101, 4.3.39.

4 formosa ... oculis ... meis: For the general sentiment cf. Cat. 86.1-5 *Quintia formosast multis ... / ... / totum illud 'formosa' nego ... / .../ Lesbia formosast*, and for the wording cf. Ov. *Ars* 1.44 (quoted in **3n.** above), *Met.* 9.476 *ille quidem est oculis quamuis formosus iniquis*; even closer is Prop. 4.4.32 *et formosa oculis arma Sabina meis*. This is the first of a number of apparent references to the wooing of Pomona by Vertumnus, disguised as an old woman, at Ov. *Met.* 14.641ff. (see Gen. Intro., p. 82, 89). At *Met.* 14.681-682 the old woman tells Pomona of how Vertumnus does not fall in love with every girl he sees: *nec, uti pars magna procorum, / quam modo uidit, amat.* Further echoes of this story at **8** *qui sapit* and **12** *solis ... locis* suggests perhaps that our author wishes, in his Tibullan mask here, to be associated with this master of disguises in his final poem, as elsewhere in his work, see *Sulpicia Cycle* **8.13-14n.** above.

formosa: see **1.7n.**

ulla puella: occurs in the same *sedes* at Tib. 1.1.52.

5 atque utinam: a common line-opening in Prop. (8) and Ov. (21), but the phrase is not found in Tib. (who has *o utinam* at 1.3.2). It occurs elsewhere in the *Corp. Tib.* only at *Lygd.* **5.27**, see **n.** ad loc.

uni mihi: occurs in the same *sedes* at Tib. 1.2.9; Ov. *Her.* 1.51 and *Nux* 127.

bella uideri: the same line-ending is found at Tib. 1.9.71 *iuueni cuidam uult bella uideri*; for the phrase cf. Cat. 8.16 *cui uideberis bella?* On the colloquial tone of *bellus* and its occurrences elsewhere in Catullus and elegy, see **4.51-52n.** above on *bella puella*. The verb *uideri* anticipates the use of *inuidia* in its etymological sense at **7** below, see **n.** ad loc.

6 displiceas aliis: cf. Prop. 4.5.49 *nec tibi displiceat miles non factus amori*. The verb occurs elsewhere in elegy only at Tib. 1.8.75; Ov. *Her.*13.46, *Trist.* 1.1.50, 2.1.140.

sic ego: see **9n**. below.

tutus ero: the same pentameter-ending is found at Prop. 2.13.14 *nam domina iudice tutus ero*; in Ov. *tutus eris* is found in this position at *Ars* 1.752, 2.58, *Rem*. 144, 650, *Fast*. 3.432, *Trist*. 1.1.38. The adj., like *securus*, indicates in elegy a state of freedom from concern about rivals. At *Rem*. 580 (quoted in **12n**. below) it is used of freedom from the cares of love. This phrase, together with the reference to *inuidia* and *gloria uulgi* in 7, recalls Ovid's account of Romulus' provision of the temple of Veiovis as a refuge for the ancient Romans, a primitive race, free from envy: *Fast*. 3.431-434 *Romulus ut saxo lucum circumdedit alto, / 'quilibet huc' inquit 'confuge, tutus eris.' / o quam de tenui Romanus origine creuit*! */ turba uetus quam non inuidiosa fuit*! The Callimachean language in this passage (*tenuis, origo, turba,* and *inuidia*) is discussed in detail in Heyworth (2019) 168-169 ad loc. Our author's wish for safety here, in the absence of *inuidia* and the *uulgus* **7**, with his retreat into trackless woodland **9**, where his mistress is the only *turba*, carries with it similar Callimachean ideals.

7 nil opus inuidia est: cf. Lucr. 5.263 *nil opus est uerbis*; **[Tib.] 3.10.21** *nil opus est fletu*; the phrase *nil opus est* is a common hexameter-opening in Ovid: *Am*. 1.2.21, *Her*. 20.185, *Ars* 1.137, 2.162, *Met*. 10.565, *Fast*. 4.813, 926, *Pont*. 1.2.92, 4.15.12. For *inuidia* and its connection with the *uulgus* as a Greek Stoic and Callimachean theme (cf. *Hymn*. 2.105-113 discussed below), see *Lygd*. **3.19-20** *in illis / inuidia est. falso plurima uulgus amat* with **n**. ad loc. and cf. **10.17-18n**. above. For the combination of envy and the crowd, cf. Call. *Aet*. 1 fr. 1.17 Pf. ἔλλετε Βασκανίης ὀλοὸν γένος ["be gone, destructive race of Envy"] and Prop. 3.1.21 *inuida turba*. For the theme of envy in Ovid, see McKeown I 389-390 on *Liuor edax* at *Am*. 1.15.1 and cf. the role of *liuor* in *Rem*. 361-398. For a discussion of the role of *inuidia* in Roman society in general see Kaster (2005) 84-103. Our author will avoid *inuidia* in its literal sense of 'being looked at' by retreating to the woods, where no human will tread; see **9-10** below.

procul absit gloria uulgi: The reference is to the 'boasting' *gloria* of the 'common crowd' *uulgi* about their erotic conquests, which would occasion the kind of 'envy' *inuidia* in others that the author is anxious to avoid; cf. Tib. 1.5.2 *at mihi nunc longe gloria fortis abest* where again the reference is to boastful language, as is clear from the preceding *bene discidium me ferre loquebar*. A link with the *credula turba* of **10.18** cannot be ruled out (see on *nil opus inuidia est* above). For the rejection of the common mob as a Callimachean theme, see **3.19-20n., 10.17-18n**. and cf. *Catal*. 9.64 *pingui nil mihi cum populo*. The combination of *procul* with *absum* is characteristically Tibullan: Tib. 1.6.39, 1.9.51, 2.1.11, but goes back ultimately to the traditional call for the sinful to be absent from the ceremony at Call. *Hymn* 2.2 (to Apollo) ἑκὰς ἑκὰς ὅστις ἀλιτρός ["away, away, he that is sinful"]. Significantly this is a poem which ends (2.105-113) with Apollo's dismissal of Envy Φθόνος (*inuidia*), whom he urges to avoid the muddy stream of the many and to cultivate the pure, undefiled stream.

8 qui sapit: on the implications of the phrase and on its colloquial tone, see **8.2n.** *si sapis*. Whereas at **8.2** 'being wise' involves Mars appearing in public before Sulpicia at the Matronalia, here, by contrast, the wise man keeps his amatory success to himself. It may be significant that Vertumnus, disguised as an old woman, addresses Pomona with this phrase at Ov. *Met.* 14.675 *sed tu si sapies*, since this *Met.* passage about Vertumnus appears to be echoed elsewhere in the poem, see **3-4n., 12n.** below. For *sapiens* in a philosophical sense ('sage') as opposed to *stultus* ('unphilosophical') see **18n.** below on *stulte*.

in tacito gaudeat ille sinu: proverbial in tone (see Otto 324) and close in expression to Cic. *Tusc.* 3.51 *in sinu gaudeant, gloriose loqui desinant*; Sen. *Epist.* 105.3 *inuidiam effugies, ... si bona tua non iactaueris, si scieris in sinu gaudere*. Joys should be kept to one's self, for boasting in an erotic context could be dangerous, cf. Prop. 2.25.29-32 *tu tamen interea, quamuis te diligat illa, / in tacito cohibe gaudia clausa sinu. / [namque in amore suo semper sua maxima cuique / nescioquo pacto uerba nocere solent]*, (lines 31-32 are printed at the end of the poem separately in Heyworth). Ov. *Ars* 1.741-742 *ei mihi, non tutum est quod ames laudare sodali; / cum tibi laudanti credidit, ipse subit*. The phrase *tacito ... sinu* is found also at Prop. 3.21.31-32 (in the same *sedes*) in the opposite context of keeping quiet about the sufferings of love: *aut spatia annorum et longa interualla profundi / lenibunt tacito uulnera nostra sinu*. Here *in tacito ... sinu* continues the theme of secrecy and revelation which runs through the whole collection, especially in the *Sulpicia Cycle* and *Sulpicia* poems; see *Sulpicia Cycle* **8.8n.** *furtim subsequitur*.

9. sic ego: always at the line-opening in Tib. 1.4.7, 1.10.43; Prop. 1.16.47, 2.29B.41, 3.15.1 and **[Tib.] 3.2.26**; frequently so in Ov. (24), as opposed to (3) in Ov. in other line-positions, as at **6** above.

sic ... possim bene uiuere: as Heyne points out, some such protasis as *si tecum esse liceat* must be understood. It is clear from **12** *et in solis tu mihi turba locis* that the good life envisaged in the deserted woods is to be shared with his mistress. For *bene uiuere* of living a good life in simple surroundings, cf. Tib. 1.3.35 *quam bene Saturno uiuebant rege*. It is used of the Epicurean life at Cic. *Fin.* 1.45, and is frequent in philosophical contexts: Cic. *Parad.* 1.15; Hor. *Epist.* 1.11.29, 15.45, 17.10; Sen. *Ben.* 3.31, *Epist.* 17.6, 28.6, 70.4; Apul. *De Deo Socr.* 22.1-3. Particularly close to the present context is Ovid's combination of living well with withdrawal from life at *Trist.* 3.4a.25 *bene qui latuit bene uixit*. In Greek the concept of 'living well' goes back to Plato: *Rep.* 353e ff. ["The just soul and the just man will live well, the unjust will live badly ... But the man who lives well is blessed and fortunate, he who does not is the opposite."]

secretis ... siluis: contrasting with *in urbe* (3) and linking with the theme of secrecy and revelation mentioned in **8n.** above. For the seclusion of the country as a more appropriate location for the poet (in contrast to the bustle of the town) cf. Hor. *Epist.* 2.2.77 *scriptorum chorus omnis amat nemus et fugit urbem*, *Carm.* 1.1.30-32 ... *me gelidum nemus / nympharumque leues cum Satyris chori / secernunt populo*, *Ars Poetica* 298 (sc. *bona pars poetarum*) *secreta petit loca* (with Brink [1971], 331 ad loc.). The phrase here recalls Horace's question to Albius (who must be Tibullus) at *Epist.* 1.4.1-4 *Albi, ... / quid nunc te dicam facere in regione Pedana? / scribere ... / an tacitum siluas inter reptare salubris*. For the philosopher's retreat into solitude far from the follies of men we may compare the Epicurean ideal of living inconspicuously λάθε βιώσας [Usener (1887) 551], cf. Lucr. 2.7-13 with Fowler (2002) 48-66 ad loc.; Hor. *Epist.* 1.17.10; Ov. *Trist.* 3.4.25 (quoted above); Plutarch also wrote a work on the subject [*Moralia* 1128A: *an recte dictum sit latenter esse uiuendum*]. The phrase *secretae ... siluae* occurs in the same line-position in a passage of Ov. *Rem.* where the author advises those who are unhappy in their love to avoid such lonely places: *Rem.* 591 *quid nisi secretae laeserunt Phyllida siluae*; cf. *siluarum secreta* at Manil. 2.23 and Lucan 2.602, and *secreta ... silua* at Ov. *Met.* 7.75; Mart. 12.18.23. For *secretis* cf. earlier in the *Rem.* passage 581-582 *non tibi secretis (augent secreta furores) / est opus: auxilio turba futura tibi est*. On the relevance of the *Rem.* passages to the present poem see Lee (1963) 8. Another passage in the author's mind here (cf. Gen. Intro., section 1.3, and **11-12n.**, **12n.**, **13n.** below) is clearly Ov. *Met.* 7.819 Cephalus to *Aura: tu facis ut siluas ut amem loca sola*. Fulkerson [(2017) 297 ad loc.] points to a possible intertext with Call. *Aet.* fr. 73 Pf. (Acontius carving the name of Cydippe on the bark of trees as he hides in the woods), a theme picked up in relation to Gallus at Virg. *Ecl.* 10.50-54, where *siluis* 52 acts as a metonymic term for pastoral verse; see Harrison (2007) 31, 70-71. As at the end of the *Lygd.* group (**6**), where a move from elegy to lyric is suggested, and at the end of the *Eclogues* where there is an attempt to include the Gallan genre of elegy within pastoral (see above **6 headnote**), so here at the end of the whole collection there may be a suggestion of a move towards pastoral.

10 qua nulla ... pede: for this expression in a metapoetic context of original composition, cf. Lucr. 1.926-927 *auia ... peragro loca nullius ante / trita solo*. The literary doctrine that the well-trodden road of poetic composition should be avoided is Callimachean (*Aet.* fr. 1.25-28 Pf.). Here the reference seems to be to a more literal withdrawal from society or, continuing the theme of *bene uiuere* in **9**, to a secluded philosophical life, see **9n.** above (admittedly in this case in the presence of the mistress); cf. Sen. *Vit. Beat.* 1.2, *Epist.* 122.9.

humano: the adj. occurs only here and at **4.26** in the *Corp. Tib.* The combination with *pes* is restricted elsewhere to prose (Plin. *Nat.* 8.70; Suet. *Iul.* 61.1; Apul. *Met.* 11.11; Fest. 230.10 L.).

uia trita: for the phrase cf. Cic. *Orat.* 11; Prop. 3.18.22 *cunctis ista terenda uia*; Ov. *Ars* 1.52 *nec tibi ... longa terenda uia est*; Plin. *Nat.* pr. 14; Sen. *Epist.* 91.5, 122.9; Sil. 2.356-357; cf. Lucr. 1.926-927 *auia Pieridum peragro loca nullius ante / trita solo*, where Lucretius, like our poet here, aligns himself with the Callimachean precept that the poet should follow the untrodden path at Call. *Aet.* 1.1.27-28.

11-12 tu mihi ... tu ... / ... tu mihi: the central couplet of the poem emphasises the importance of his mistress to the author. The anaphora of the second person pronoun belongs to a long poetic tradition emphasising the importance of a person to the speaker, going back to Hom. *Il.* 6.429-430 (quoted above on **4.51-52**) and seen in elegy at Prop. 1.11.21-23 (quoted above on **4.51-52**); cf. also Ov. *Her.* 3.52 (Briseis to Achilles) *tu dominus, tu uir, tu mihi frater eras*. On the IE background to the use of this figure in prayers see West (2007) 310-311. The author replaces the traditional mention of family members with the more abstract concepts *curarum requies, lumen* and *turba*. For the first, rest from care, one can compare Ovid's reference to his Muse as *tu curae requies* at *Trist.* 4.10.118, to sleep as *requies curarum* at *Pont.* 3.3.7, and, more to the point, Cephalus' words about *Aura* at *Met.* 7.812 *auram expectabam, requies erat illa labori* (a passage clearly in our author's mind here, cf. **headnote** above, **2n., 9n., 12n., 13n.** and see the repeated *tu* in his address to Aura a little later at 7.817-819 *tu mihi magna uoluptas / ... tu me* *reficisque fouesque,* / *tu facis ut siluas ut amem loca sola*). At Lucr. 1.51 (sc. *animum*) *semotum a curis adhibe ueram ad rationem* and 2.18-19 *mente fruatur* (sc. *natura*) / *iucundo sensu cura semota metuque* freedom from care is the prerequisite for the Epicurean philosopher's search for truth. The second two, *lumen* and *turba*, may have originated, as Lee [(1963) 8] suggests, in the same passage of Ov. *Rem.* quoted in **9n.** above, advising those unhappy in love to avoid lonely places *loca sola* (579) and the night-time where no sociable *turba* can relieve his grief: 585-586 (quoted in **11n.** below); cf. *Rem.* 582 quoted on **9n.** above. For our author his mistress will lighten the dark night [for *lumen*, like *lux*, as a term of endearment cf. Mart. 1.68.6 *Naeuia lux, ... Naeuia lumen, aue*; Apul. *Met.* 5.13.5 (Psyche to Cupid) *teneo te, meum lumen*]. In this she may represent a parallel with Tib.'s Delia ('bright' in Greek) and the antithesis Tib.'s urban Nemesis, who in mythology is daughter of Night. Furthermore she will provide company enough for him (*in solis ... turba locis*) in his loneliness. As Lee points out, *turba*, usually a noisy crowd, is more appropriate to Ovid's context than to that of our author, who thus reveals himself as post-Ovidian, a fact which casts doubt on his reference to himself as Tibullus in **13**.

11 nocte ... atra: the phrase in the abl. occurs also at Hor. *Epod.* 10.9; Virg. *Aen.* 4.570; Ov. *Met.* 5.71; Manil. 2.46-47, 5.725; Sen. *Herc. F.* 282, *Herc. Oet.* 1294, and in the same *sedes* at Sil. 7.126; Stat. *Theb.* 8.69. In Tib. the adj. is applied to death at 1.3.5 and 10.33. This is the only use of *ater* in [**Tib.**] **3**, where the normal word for black is *niger*. On the distinction between the two, with *ater* being the more emotive term, denoting sinister objects, see Marouzeau (1949) 67-68, and (1962) 166. For night as a difficult time for lovers wishing to forget their mistress cf. Ov. *Rem.* 585-586 *tristior idcirco nox est quam tempora Phoebi*: / *quae releuet luctus turba sodalis abest*.

12 solis ... locis: the phrase occurs in the same *sedes* at Ov. *Her.* 11.84 and *Fast.* 4.514; cf. also Plaut. *Rud.* 205; Cic. *Diu.* 1.59; Plin. *Nat.* 18.282. For *loca sola* in a similar context, see Ov. *Met.* 7.819 quoted on **9n.** above. Eisenhut [(1977) 213] and Lee [(1963) 8] stress the importance of Ov. *Rem.* 579-580 *quisquis amas, loca sola nocent, loca sola caueto.* / *quo fugis? in populo tutior esse potes* as an influence here. In view of the importance of Vertumnus in this poem (see **3-4n.** and **8n.** above) the following words of Vertumnus, disguised as an old woman and describing himself to Pomona at Ov. *Met.* 14.681 *haec loca sola colit* may be relevant here.

turba: for the use of the term in this context cf. Ov. *Met*. 1.355 *nos duo turba sumus* (of Deucalion and Pyrrha after the flood), 6.200 *Latonae turbam* (of Apollo and Diana). At Ov. *Rem*. 586 (quoted in **11n.** above) the presence of a *turba sodalis* helps the lover forget his mistress. As Lee [(1963) 8] points out the meaning of 'distracting crowd' in Ov. *Rem*. is more common than the sense of 'company' required here, an indication perhaps of the priority of Ovid. The word is common in elegy, especially Ovid: Tib. (14); Prop. (25), Ov. (elegiac works) (143); [**Tib.**] 3 (3); The whole of this line is found in a late inscription at *CIL* 10.378.

13 e caelo mittatur amica: the reference is to a 'gift from heaven', in this case a girl of perfect beauty, who would nevertheless not divert the Tibullus of the poem from his chosen mistress. Cf. Ov. *Ars* 1.43 *haec* (i.e. a suitable girl) *tibi non tenues ueniet delapsa per auras* in a passage which has other connections with the present poem, see **3n.** and **4n.** above and cf. Lee (1963) 7. Lact. *Inst*. 1.11.55, quoted by Tränkle [330 ad loc.], gives two meanings for the idea conveyed in 'fallen from heaven'; (1) those whom we admire, and (2) those who arrive unexpectedly: *Saturnum ... caeli filium dictum, quod solemus eos, quorum uirtutem miremur, aut eos, qui repentino aduenerint, de caelo cecidisse dicere*. The first is clearly appropriate here, whereas the passage of Tibullus which inspired it belongs to the second category, describing Tib.'s imagined unexpected return to Delia from absence abroad, where he had been sick in Corcyra on military campaign: Tib. 1.3.90 *sed uidear caelo missus adesse tibi*. For the gender reversal here, cf. **19.1n.** above. For the idea here of not being tempted by divine beauty cf. Ov. *Met*. 7.802-803 (Cephalus of his young bride Procris, in an important intertext already echoed above, see **headnote** above, and **2n., 9n., 11-12n., 12n.**) *nec me quae caperet, non si Venus ipsa ueniret, / ulla erat* (sc. *alia*).

amica: of the mistress only here in the *Corp. Tib.* Tib. himself avoided it, perhaps because of its colloquial connotations [in Hor. only in *Serm*. and *Epist*. and avoided by Ov. in *Met*.; see Adams (1983) 348-350], though it is used commonly in this sense in Cat. (4), Prop. (3) and Ovid's elegiac works (8).

Tibullo: this verse in which the author names himself as Tibullus is ironically the least Tibullan in style. Self-naming is restricted in Tib. to the two embedded epigrams 1.3.55 and 9.83. It is far commoner in the other elegists in this more open context. Prop. (8); Ov. [Naso] (49). Here and in the use of *amica* our author again is closer to Propertius and Ovid than to Tibullus. On self-naming as an assertion of a person's status or authority, here giving emphasis to his oath in **15-16**, see L. C. Watson [(2003) 463 on Hor. *Epod.* 15.12], who gives as other examples Hom. *Il.* 1.240 (Achilles), Virg. *Aen.* 11.440-442 (Turnus). On the author's adoption of a Tibullan mask here and its relevance to the structure of the whole book see **headnote** above. On the positioning of the name Tibullus here (line **13** of a 24 line poem) which is parallel with the naming of Vertumnus at **8.13** see **8.13-14n.** above.

14 deficietque Venus: clearly modelled on Tib. 1.5.39-40 *saepe aliam tenui: sed iam cum gaudia adirem, / admonuit dominae deseruitque Venus.* On the theme of impotence as central to Horace's *Epodes* see L. C. Watson (1995), Harrison (2007) 129 and Grassmann (1966) 30, n. 23 on Hor. *Epod.* 12.16; see further Tränkle [345-347 on *Priap.* 2] and cf. Prop. 4.8.27ff., Ov. *Am.* 3.7. For *deficio* in **[Tib.] 3** see **4.20, 7.4, 7.191, 9.6**. An important intertext here and for **[Tib.] 3** as a whole is Prop. 3.6 where at 34 Cynthia (via the slave Lygdamus) threatens Propertius with impotence as a punishment for his supposed infidelity with a prostitute: *noctibus illorum* (i.e. of Prop. and his prostitute) *dormiet ipsa Venus*, see Gen. Intro., section 3.1. For *Venus* used as a metonymy for the sexual act, cf. **2n.** above and **9.19**. Some editors print both with a small *u*, but this distinction would have been less clear-cut for the ancients, and impossible to indicate in a majuscule text.

15 hoc ... Iunonis numina iuro: for *iuro* with double accusative cf. Cic. *Fam.* 7.12.2 *Iouem lapidem iurare*; Virg. *Aen.* 12.197 *haec eadem ... terram mare sidera iuro.* For *iurare numen* cf. Virg. *Aen.* 6.324 *di cuius iurare timent et fallere numen* and on *numen* see **4.53n.**above. For swearing by Juno as the patron goddess of women, see **6.47-49n.** above. The echo in this final poem of the final poem of the *Lygd.* group is unlikely to be a co-incidence (see **17n.** *quid facio demens*? and **20n.** *garrula lingua* below). Whereas in poem **6** the mistress swears falsely by Juno, here the poet's true oath is the cause of his mistress's cruelty (**19**). There may also be a reference to Lygdamus' oath of loyalty to Neaera at **1.25** *teque suis iurat caram magis esse medullis*, linking the first and last poems of **[Tib.] 3**. For Juno's role in 'joining' lovers see **3.33-34n., 12.9n.** A woman's Juno was equivalent to a man's Genius (see **12.1n.**), and just as slaves swore by the Genius of their master (see **11.8**) so they swore by the Juno of their mistress, a fact which places the author here, like Sulpicia in **11.8**, in the role of a slave of his love, cf. *seruitium* **22**. On the importance of Juno in **[Tib.] 3** overall see *Lygd.* **6.48**, *Sulpicia Cycle* **12.1**, both final poems in their cycles.

sancta ... numina: the combination occurs first in Lucr. 2.434, 5.309, 6.70 and then in Virg. at *Aen.* 3.543, 8.389. Elsewhere in verse only at *Il. Lat.* 922. Cf. Serv. auct. *Aen.* 8.383 *'numen' ergo 'sanctum' ut 'leges sanctas' dicimus, id est firmos, a sanciendo.*

16 sola ante alios ... magna: for the pleonastic expression cf. Liv. 1.9.12 *unam longe ante alias ... insignem*; Virg. *Aen.* 3.321 *felix una ante alias uirgo*, 11.821 *fida ante alias quae sola Camillae*; [Tib.] 3.4.93 *longe ante alias omnes mitissima mater.* For this colloquial use of *ante* in comparative and superlative expressions see above **4.93n.** and cf. **11.5** *uror ego ante alias.* For *sola* cf. the emphatic *tu mihi sola* places of **3** above.

magna: a common epithet of gods and goddesses (see above **4.16n., 8.1n.**), applied to Juno in Helenus' injunction to Aeneas at Virg. *Aen.* 3.437 *Iunonis magnae primum prece numen adora.*

17 quid facio demens?: See **6.27n.** above and cf. Ov. *Met.* 3.641 *quid facis, o demens?* and *Pont.* 4.3.29 *quid facis, a demens?* The expression, referring to the madness of love, provides another connection between this final poem and the final poem of the *Lygd.* group.

heu heu: repeated *heu* is characteristic of Tibullus (1.4.81, 6.10, 2.3.2, 49, 5.108). Cf. *ei mihi* in a similar context of admitting one's feelings at Ov. *Her.* 21.204 (Acontius to Cydippe) *ei mihi, quod sensus sum tibi fassa meos.*

mea pignora cedo: for *cedo* in the sense of 'yield', 'surrender' + acc. obj. see *OLD cedo* 13. It appears from the context of **18** *proderat iste timor* that the pledges he had given concerned being faithful to her alone. Once these pledges had been given, her fear of being betrayed, which had been to his advantage, disappeared. For *pignora* in the more concrete sense of written pledges of love, causing fear (cf. **18** here) and unhappy servitude (cf. **22** here) in a mistress if given to a new lover, cf. Ov. *Ars* 3.485-490: 485 *ancillae puerique manu perarate tabellas,* / 486 *pignora nec puero credite uestra nouo* / 489 *perfidus ille quidem, qui talia pignora seruat,* / 490 *sed tamen Aetnaei fulminis instar habent:* / 487 *uidi ego pallentes isto terrore puellas* / 488 *seruitium miseras tempus in omne pati* with Lee (1963) 8-9. For *pignora* elsewhere as pledges of love, cf. Prop. 3.20.16-17 *et scribenda mihi lex in amore nouo.* / *haec Amor ipse suo constringet pignora signo*; Ov. *Her.* 4.100 *illa* (sc. *Atalanta*) *ferae spolium pignus amoris habet.*

550   Commentary

18 stulte: Tib.'s only use of the adv. occurs in a similar context at 1.9.45 *tum miser interii, stulte confisus amari*. The context, lack of experience in an amatory situation, recalls **18.3** *stulta*, see **n**. ad loc. Cairns [(2004) 307 and n.39] discusses a passage of Propertius in a similar context of amatory jealousy and fear at Prop. 2.34.19-20 *ipse meae solus, quod nil est, aemulor umbrae, / stultus, quod falso saepe timore tremo* and points out that *stultus* and *sapiens* (as with *stulte* here and *qui sapit* at **8** above) are often used in philosophical contexts to contrast philosophical and unphilosophical approaches to life (e.g. Cic. *Parad. Stoic.* 2.29, *Fin.* 1.57, 1.61, 3.60, *Tusc.* 4.14, 5.54; Hor. *Epist.* 1.1.41-42).

iste timor: cf. *isto terrore* in a similar context at Ov. *Ars* 3.491 quoted on **17n.** above. Similar in wording but different in context is Call. *Aet.* 3 fr. 74 Pf. where Acontius reproaches himself for the oath he made Cydippe swear, that she would marry him, which now causes her to fear Artemis' retribution: λιρὸς ἐγώ, τί δέ σοι τόνδ' ἐπέθηκα φόβον; ["I am shameless – why have I imposed this fear upon you?"]. For fear as a constant companion of lovers cf. Cephalus' words at Ov. *Met.* 7.719 (an important intertext here and elsewhere) *sed cuncta timemus amantes*.

19 fortis ... audacius: the girl's added confidence will enable her to dominate her lover. At Tib. 1.4.13 such boldness is seen as attractive in boys: *hic, quia fortis adest audacia, cepit*. Here it simply increases the girl's capacity for inflicting pain. Another example of gender reversal?

ures: the verb is appropriate for inflicting pain in the context of the fires of love. It also suggests slave punishment, looking forward to *seruitium* in **22**. Cf. Tib. 1.5.5-6 *ure ferum et torque, libeat ne dicere quicquam / magnificum posthac*, 2.4.3-6 *seruitium sed triste datur ... / et numquam misero uincla remittit Amor, / et seu quid merui seu nil peccauimus, urit. / uror: io remoue, saeua puella, faces*. The verb is used frequently of Sulpicia, either in the active sense of inflicting the flames of love at *Sulpicia Cycle* **8.11** and **12**, or in the passive sense of suffering them at **11.5** and **12.17**.

20 misero: see **20.4n.** below.

garrula lingua: the phrase is used in the same *sedes* of Tantalus, whose garrulous tongue got him into trouble at Ov. *Am.* 2.2.44 *hoc illi garrula lingua dedit*. The sentiment links this poem with the themes of openness and secrecy, hiding and revealing that have such an important role to play in the whole collection starting with *Lygd.* **2.27-28**, especially in the

Sulpicia Cycle and *Sulpicia* poems, see Prolegomena, p. 83, also **8.8n.** and here **8n.** and **9n.** above and picked up in the last word *tace* of the closing epigram **20.4**. See also **2.7n.** above on the contrast between Lygdamus' free speech there and the rejection of it here with its concomitant acceptance of *seruitium amoris* in **21-24** below. Manilius 4.574-576 mentions *garrulitas* along with a slanderous tongue as the gift of the star sign Pisces, in a passage which links the themes of **19** here with those of *rumor* in **20**: *garrulitas odiosa datur linguaeque uenenum / uerba maligna nouas mutantis semper ad aures / criminaque ad populum populi ferre ore bilingui*. On the dangers of saying too much cf. Prop. 2.28.13-14 *semper, formosae, non nostis parcere uerbis. / hoc tibi lingua nocens, hoc tibi forma dedit*, 4.7.41-42 of Cynthia's replacement Chloris, who punishes the slave girls who praise their former mistress's beauty (cf. **16.3n.** and **4n.** above) *et grauiora rependit iniquis pensa quasillis / garrula de facie si qua locuta mea est*; Ov. *Met.* 2.540 of the raven which informed Apollo of Coronis' infidelity *lingua fuit damno*. The phrase may recall Lygdamus' denial of committing blasphemy with a *lingua inpia* at **4.16** and the *sordida lingua* of girls who swear false loyalty at **6.46**, another connection with the final poem of the *Lygd.* group. The adj. *garrulus* is found in Tib. at 1.5.26, 2.5.30 and **[Tib.] 3.** *Lygd.* **4.38**. At 3.23.17-18 Propertius describes Cynthia as a *puella / garrula* in the context of the letters she exchanged with the poet on tablets. The phrase *garrula lingua* occurs also at Val. Max. 7.2 ext. 1 and, in the same *sedes* as here, Mart. 13.71.2; see further McKeown III 47 on Ov. *Am.* 2.2.43-44, a poem which also has similarities with **21** below.

21 iam facias quodcumque uoles: for the sentiment cf. Cat. 75.4 *nec desistere amare, omnia si facias* and Ovid's words about the powers of a persuasive wife over her husband at *Am.* 2.2.33-34 *cum bene uir traxit uultum rugasque coegit, / quod uoluit fieri blanda puella, facit*, a poem also echoed in **20** above. *facias* is Müller's correction for *faciam* of the *codd.* and makes for a more forceful depiction of the author's servitude.

22 fugiam: the *vox propria* for a fleeing slave, see *OLD fugio* 5.

notae seruitium dominae: for the use of *domina* of the mistress in the context of *seruitium amoris* see **4.74n.** above and cf. Tib. 2.4.1 *sic mihi seruitium uideo dominamque paratam*. On the elegiac theme of *seruitium amoris* see **11.3-4n.** above. Cairns [(2006) 190-191], on the basis of Gallus fr. 2.7 (Courtney = 145.7 Hollis) *quae possem domina deicere digna mea*, thinks this use of *domina* and its association with *seruitium amoris* could have started with Gallus. The adj. *notae* refers to servitude to a

552   Commentary

mistress the author has become accustomed to, cf. Prop. 1.4.3-4 (to Bassus, who tries to persuade him to change his mistress) *quid me non pateris uitae quodcumque sequetur / hoc magis assueto ducere seruitio*? Again Cairns [loc. cit.] sees a possible reference in *notae* to Gallus, given the use of the adj. of Gallus and his mistress Lycoris at Ov. *Am.* 1.15.29-30 *Gallus et Hesperiis et Gallus notus Eois, / et sua cum Gallo nota Lycoris erit*. If such an echo exists, then the meaning of *notae* here would have to be something like 'well-known' or even 'notorious', perhaps as a result of our author's poems about her. The new mistress, Neaera, of the opening of **[Tib.] 3**, has then been replaced at the end of the collection by a mistress who has become 'known', as a result of the experiences examined in the third book (see Gen. Intro., pp. 83, 90, 111 and the **headnote** above). As mentioned above, Cat. 72 is close in sentiment, where the mention of the *uulgus* suggests it may have influenced the present poem: 72.3-6 *dilexi tum te non tantum ut uulgus amicam / sed pater ut gnatos diligit et generos. / nunc te cognoui: quare etsi impensius uror, / multo mi tamen es uilior et leuior*. Lines **3-4** were of course echoed in Apollo's description of Lygdamus' attitude to Neaera at **4.51-52** above. On the trisyllabic pentameter ending *dominae*, the only one in this poem, see Cairns (2006) 190-191 and Maltby (2010) 337.

23 Veneris sanctae: the combination is not found elsewhere in elegy, but cf. Cat. 36.3-4 *nam sanctae Veneri Cupidinique / uouit*, 68.5 *sancta Venus*; Sen. *Phaedr.* 211 *sancta ... Venus*. For the same adj. applied to Juno see **15n.** above. For Tib.'s particular veneration for Venus in his first book, reversed in 2.4.23-26, see Maltby (2002) 422 on Tib. 2.4.23-26 and cf. **2n.** above. The mention of Venus in the final couplet looks back to Venus in **2** above, and provides the poem with a clear ring-structure.

uinctus: the image of being bound in chains at Venus' altar continues the *seruitium amoris* theme of **22**, but *uinctus* also suggests the bonds of love, as at *Sulpicia Cycle* **11.13-14** *nec tu sis iniusta, Venus: uel seruiat aeque / uinctus uterque tibi*. On the theme of servitude to Venus and on the supposed etymological connection between *uincio* and *Venus* see **11.13-14n.** and cf. Tib.1.2.91-92 *uidi ego, qui iuuenum miseros lusisset amores, / post Veneris uinclis subdere colla senem*.

24 notat iniustos: given the *seruitium* theme, the verb could suggest punishment by branding. The phrase serves as a warning to his mistress not to incur Venus' wrath by mistreating him. Fulkerson [(2017) ad loc.] sees a pun on *notae ... dominae* in **22** above. For Venus' ferocity in her protection of wronged lovers, cf. Tib. 1.5.57-58 *sunt numina amanti, /*

saeuit et iniusta lege relicta Venus, 1.8.28 *persequitur poenis tristia facta Venus,* 1.9.20 *asperaque est illi* (i.e. the man who accepts money for love) *difficilisque Venus.*

supplicibusque fauet: cf. Tib. 1.4.71-72 *blanditiis uult esse locum Venus: illa querellis / supplicibus, miseris fletibus illa fauet.* As Tränkle points out [334 ad loc.], the mention of Venus in the final couplet is typical of Tibullus, cf.1.2.99-100, 1.9.81-84. The elegiac lover commonly poses as a suppliant, cf. Tib. 1.2.14; Prop. 1.9.3, Ov. *Am.* 1.7.61, *Ars* 2.527 and see Pichon 271.

Epigram to Rumour

Poem 20

This is an elegant and well-constructed four-line epigram, with the opening *rumor* picked up by *rumor* in the last line. The closural *tace* at the end is appropriate for the position of the poem at the end of the book. This polished structure argues against its being a fragment of a longer poem. The fact that it is an epigram rather than an elegy is in line with our unitary author's love of exploring his themes within different generic frameworks (elegy, hexameter panegyric, epigram). On the importance of *surdis auribus* **2** and *tace* **4** for the structure of the whole book see **19 headnote** above. Ovid treats the same theme on the scale of a full elegy at *Am.* 3.14, whose opening couplet sums up the idea behind both poems: *non ego, ne pecces, cum sis formosa, recuso, / sed ne sit misero scire necesse mihi.* On the importance of Ov. *Am.* 3.14 for the *Sulpicia* group see **13 headnote** above and for its influence on the present poem see **2n.** and **3n.** below. Similar themes occur in Propertius, and many of the poem's closest parallels are to be found in that author (see individual notes below). As Heyne argues, the *lepor* and *urbanitas* of the poem are worthy of Tibullus, but in the end he confesses himself uncertain about the authorship *an Tibullum auctorem habeat, credere licet et non licet.* On the whole the evidence would argue in favour of a post-Tibullan and post-Ovidian date which would be in line with the late first century AD date posited for the unitary author of the whole book.

The poem's central concern with rumour provides a suitable conclusion to the whole collection in which questions of openness and secrecy and the public and private nature of elegiac verse have played a key role. The theme of jealousy connects this poem with **19** (see especially **19.5**); see Hozberg (1998) 172. Although no name is provided for this final epigram, I would suggest it continues the Tibullan mask of **19**. An important intertext connecting this last poem with both poem **19** and also poem **1** is the Cephalus and Procris episode at the end of Ov. *Met.* 7.796-862; see **1 headnote** and **19 headnote** above. The *dolor* caused to Procris by the false report of her husband's *crimen* (unfaithfulness) with Aura, is exactly paralleled by that caused to our author by accusations, *crimina*, about his mistress: Ov. *Met.* 7.824-827 *criminis extemplo ficti temerarius iudex / Procrin adit linguaque refert audita susurra. / credula res amor est; subito conlapsa dolore, / ... cecidit*; cf. **20.3** *crimina non haec sunt nostro sine facta dolore*. It is important to note that the mention of *dolor* here recalls the etymology of Lygdamus' name (see Gen. Intro., section 3.1). Such an intentional echo between the first and last two poems of our collection adds weight to the argument for a single unitary author for the whole **[Tib.] 3**.

1 Rumor ait: the phrase is found also at Prop. 4.4.47 *cras, ut rumor ait, tota potabitur urbe*, and, in the same *sedes*, and introducing an acc. + inf. clause, at Mart. 3.80.2 *rumor ait linguae te tamen esse malae*. For the personification of *rumor* and similar words relating to gossip as the subject of verbs of speaking Tränkle [335 ad loc.] compares Cat. 78.10 *qui sis, fama loquetur anus*, on which see Feeney (2012) 45; Hardie (2012) 325. A reference to Catullus in the final poem of the book would recall the Catullan references in the opening and closing poems of the *Lygd.* group (see **19 headnote** above) and would perhaps echo Ovid's naming of Catullus in the final poem of his *Amores*: 3.15.7-8 *Mantua Virgilio gaudet, Verona Catullo; / Paelignae dicar gloria gentis ego*. Other examples of personified *rumor* or *fama* speaking occur at Prop. 2.18.37 *credam ego narranti ... famae*; Mart. 3.87.1 *narrat te rumor, Chione, numquam esse fututam* and, close in content to the present line; Prop. 2.32.23-24 *nuper enim de te nostras manauit ad aures / rumor, et in tota non bonus urbe fuit*.

crebro: the adv. is rare in elegy; elsewhere only at Tib. 1.5.72; Prop. 3.8.15; Ov. *Her.* 20.129, *Rem.* 223.

peccare puellam: for the phrase at the line-end, cf. Prop. 2.32.51 *peccare puellae*. On *peccare* in an elegiac context see **13.9n.**

2 surdis auribus: a common combination in poetry from Ter. *Heaut.* 330 onward. Particularly close in context is Prop. 2.20.13 *de te quodcumque, ad surdas mihi dicitur aures*, and, in the same *sedes*, and Prop. 2.16B.36 *turpis amor surdis auribus esse solet*. Contrast the *suspensis auribus* 'with

Book Three of the Corpus Tibullianum: 555
Introduction, Text, Translation and Commentary

ears held poised' with which Prop. will drink in news of Cynthia's actions from his slave Lygdamus at Prop. 3.6.8. For *aures* in the context of slander cf. Manil. 4.575 quoted in **19.20n.** above. For the general sentiment of the lover wishing to remain ignorant of his mistress's infidelity, see Ov. *Am.* 3.14, an important intertext for the *Sulpicia* group (see **13 headnote**) and one likely, by its position, to have influenced this final epigram in the [Tib.] 3 collection (see further **3n.** below). On the significance of these words for the structure of the whole book see **19 headnote** above.

3 For the pains caused to the lover by knowledge of his mistress's infidelity, cf. Ov. *Am.* 3.14.37-38 *mens abit et morior, quotiens peccasse fateris, / perque meos artus frigida gutta fluit.* On the importance of this poem for themes of openness and secrecy in the opening *Sulpicia* poem see **13 headnote** above. On Ov. *Met.* 7.824-828 as an important intertext here, with its foreshadowing of *crimina* and *dolore* see **20 headnote** above, where the Ovid passage is quoted in full. For the structural significance of Ovid's Cephalus and Procris episode as linking poem **1** of the collection and poems **19** and **20** see **1 headnote** and **19 headnote** above.

crimina ... facta: Tränkle [335 ad loc.] finds Lachmann's parallels for this phrase at Cic. *Flacc.* 33 *crimen sibi ipsum facere, in quo crimen esset nullum* and Prop. 4.4.43 *quantum ego sum Ausoniis crimen factura puellis* in the sense 'make a reproach against' unsatisfactory and prints the humanist conjecture *crimina ... iacta* (for which cf. Cic. *Q. Rosc.* 25). However, Lachmann's parallels do not seem far enough away from the sense required here of 'accusations have been made' to warrant departing from the reading of the MSS. On *crimina* in an elegiac context see **4.84n.**; cf. further Ov. *Met.* 7.824 quoted in the introduction above, where *criminis ... ficti* would perhaps lend support to the reading *crimina .... facta* here and Manil. 4.576 quoted in **19.20n.** above.

dolore: used here, as often, with reference to the sorrows of love, see **2.3n.** and **29n.** above, cf. Ov. *Met.* 7.826 quoted in the **headnote** above. The word may suggest in this final poem the etymology of the name Lygdamus (see Gen. Intro., section 3.1).

4 miserum torques: the phrase occurs in the same *sedes* at Tib. 2.6.17-18 *tu miserum torques, tu me mihi dira precari / cogis.* For *miser* referring to a lover made wretched by reports of his mistress's infidelity, as here, cf. **19.20** above, Ov. *Am.* 2.2.54 *siue amat* (sc. *maritus*), *officio fit miser ille tuo* (with McKeown III 52 ad loc.), 3.14.1-2 *non ego, ne pecces, cum sis* *formosa, recuso, / sed ne sit misero scire necesse mihi, Met.* 7.828 (Procris hearing of Cephalus' suspected unfaithfulness) *se miseram, se fati dixit iniqui*. The adj. is common with reference to the misery of the elegiac lover [see Quinn on Cat. 8.1, Pichon 202-203, Hinds (1988) 29-34], but is absent from *Lygdamus, Sulpicia Cycle* and *Sulpicia* poems. For *torqueo* with the meaning of the tortures of (unrequited) love see **10.11n.** above. As in *Sulpicia Cycle* **9.12** and **10.11**, the verb could contain an additional meaning of 'change', an important theme running thrugh the whole book. The author asks why the painful changes which have characterised the lover's state throughout the book should continue. This question together with the closural *tace* act as a sign that these changes are now over. The movement involved in the dispatch of the volume in poem **1**, and the necessity for the poet in poems **1** and **2** to make public his grief, is replaced at the end of the book by a request for stillness and silence.

rumor acerbe: returns neatly to the personification of *rumor* with which the poem opened. The adj. *acerbus* is applied elsewhere in elegy to the cruelty of Venus (Tib. 1.2.100, 1.6.84) and to the bitterness of hatreds occasioned by love (Prop. 2.8.3). It also forms part of the closural line Tib. 2.6.41 quoted below.

tace: a suitable closural verb with which to end the collection, see **19 headnote** above and cf. *sit satis* at Tib. 1.10.61, 62, 63 and *desino* at Tib. 2.6.41 *desino, ne dominae luctus renouentur acerbi*. Fulkerson 2017 301-2, without positing a unitary author, still sees *tace* as possibly closural for the whole collection. For *taceo* at the line-end cf. Ov. *Fast*. 2.572 *sacra facit Tacitae uix tamen ipsa tacet* (of a gossiping old woman). On silence as the cure for pain cf. also (with reference to the pain of his exile) Ov. *Pont*. 2.2.57-59 *uulneris id genus est quod cum sanabile non sit / non contrectari tutius esse puto. / lingua sile, non est ultra narrabile quicquam*.

Epitaph of Tibullus attributed to Domitius Marsus

This epigram, transmitted at the end of **book 3** in A+, and attributed to Domitius Marsus in F and the *Excerpta Petrei* of 1528, concerns the death of Tibullus which it tells us occurred shortly after that of Virgil (21 September 19 BC). We know little about the life of Marsus. He is often mentioned by Martial as his predecessor in epigram (Mart. 1 pr.12, 2.71.3, 75.5, 4.29.8, 5.5.6, 7.99.7, 8.55.24) and Ovid names him in a list of contemporary poets (*Pont*. 4.16.5), together with the epic poets Rabirius, Macer and Pedo, who were active in the late Augustan and early Tiberian period. Perhaps Ovid is here thinking of Marsus' epic poem *Amazonis*, also mentioned by Martial (4.29.8). He was probably a protégé of Maecenas (see Mart. 7.29.7-8 *et Maecenati Maro cum cantaret Alexin / nota tamen Marsi fusca Melaenis erat*, 8.55.23-24 *ergo ero Vergilius, si munera Maecenatis / des mihi? Vergilius non ero, Marsus ero*). His satirical poem *Cicuta*, fr. 1 (Courtney = fr. 174 Hollis), attacks one Bavius, an adversary of Virgil mentioned in *Ecl.* 3.90, while fr. 3 (Courtney = fr. 176 Hollis) mentions Q. Caecilius Epirota, who set up a school for talented young poets shortly after the death of Cornelius Gallus in 27/26 BC. Quintilian 3.1.18 mentions his receiving a letter from the rhetorician Apollodorus of Pergamum, who included among his pupils the poet Valgius Rufus and the young Octavian. Domitius' treatise *De urbanitate* is discussed with approval by Quintilian (*Inst.* 6.3.102-12), who describes its author as *homo eruditissimus* (6.3.108). From the above it appears that Domitius may have begun his poetic activity with epigram in the 30s BC and turned to epic late in his career, perhaps in the early first century AD. The present epigram is discussed as fr. 7 (Courtney = fr. 180 Hollis).

At a more speculative level we could note that the attribution of this epitaph to Domitius Marsus is not beyond doubt. The epitaph and the *Vita* are transmitted together at the end of **book 3**, but we do not know if the epitaph had originally been attached to the end of the two books of the genuine Tibullus. Both these pieces could be said to be more relevant to **book 3**. Is it possible that after concluding his collection with the closural **20** our author could have added an epitaph on Tibullus' death, a poet who had served as his inspiration for the book and whom our author had himself impersonated in **7** as well as in **19** and **20**? The phrase *te quoque* with which it begins has Callimachean connections (*Hec.* fr. 253.3 Pf. = 40.3, Hollis) and marks the middle of Virgil's *Aeneid* (7.1 *tu quoque* – in a funerary context addressed to Caieta) and his *Georgics* (3.1 *te quoque, magna Pales, ... canemus* – opening a hymn to Pales) could mark the fact that the book just completed contained both Callimachean and, in the *Laud. Mess.*, Virgilian epic elements. For a detailed discussion of *tu quoque* and its metapoetic and transitional significance in Virgil see Kyriakidis (1998) 79-86; also Hinds (1998) 108-109. Similarly the *Life* which follows this epigram could be part of the outer frame of **book 3**. Like the epigram, its provenance is uncertain. The information it contains on Tibullus is particularly relevant to the third book. The mention of Messalla and the Aquitanian war (lines **2** and **3**) brings to mind Tib. 1.7 which was the inspiration for the central poem **7** the *Laud. Mess.*, his primacy in elegy (lines **4-5**) reflects the elegies of the *Lygd.* group **1-6** and the *Sulpicia Cycle* **8-12,** while the short subtle amatory letters would be a perfect description of the short elegies attributed to Sulpicia herself in the *Sulpicia* poems **13-18**. Whether the writer of this life was the author of **book 3**, or a later scholar who wished to associate himself with the collection can perhaps never be known. It could be that in composing an epitaph for Tibullus while impersonating that very poet our author was writing about his own death, as he had in the mask of *Lygdamus* in the second poem of the collection. One cannot ignore, however, the possibility that both the epitaph and the *Life* were written after the composition of **book 3** and were added at the end to give credence to the book's strong Tibullan connections. Even if they were derived from earlier sources such as Domitius Marsus and Suetonius, their positioning here at the end of **book 3** serves to honour the poet who was its chief inspiration.

1 Te quoque: for the Callimachean and Virgilian associations of this phrase and their relevance to **book 3** see **headnote** to the epitaph above. For its use in funerary epigram Courtney [ad loc.] compares 'Anacreon' *AP* 7.263.1 καὶ σέ, Κληνορίδη, πόθος ὤλεσε πατρίδος αἴης ["and you too, Clenorides, were killed by desire for your homeland"]. Ovid uses the phrase in an enumeration of shades who will meet Tibullus in the underworld at *Am.* 3.9.63-64 (a funeral poem for Tibullus) *tu quoque ... / ... Galle*.

Vergilio comitem: cf. Ov. *Am.* 3.9.65 *his comes umbra tua est*, of Tibullus' shade being a companion to those of Calvus, Catullus and Gallus in Elysium. For the death of Tibullus following shortly after that of Virgil in September 19 BC, see McGann (1970). Interestingly Virgil is not mentioned in Ovid's poem on Tibullus' death, but only his predecessors in love poetry.

non aequa: Tibullus' death is seen as unfair because he was carried off while still a young man (*iuuenis* **2**).

2 iuuenem: the term can refer to a young man of any age below forty. The last sentence of the *Vita* also mentions Tibullus' death at a young age: *obiit adulescens*.

campos misit ad Elysios: cf. Tib. 1.3.58, where the poet imagines his death while sick on the island of Corcyra: *ipsa Venus campos ducet in Elysios*. This is the third point of contact with Ovid's poem *Am.* 3.9, cf. 3.9.60 *in Elysia ualle Tibullus erit*. Marsus here, unlike Ovid, employs Tib.'s polysyllabic pentameter ending which was going out of fashion at around the time of Tibullus' death.

3 ne foret: death is presented as deliberately robbing Latin poetry of the leaders of elegy and epic.

elegis: it was conventional in an epitaph of this type for the death of a poet to signify the death of the genre in which he wrote; Courtney compares [Moschus] *Epist. Bionis* 11-12 where Doric song is said to die with the death of Bion, and Hollis compares, on the death of Cicero, Sextilius Ena fr. 202 Hollis *deflendus Cicero Latiaeque silentia linguae* and Cornelius Severus fr. 219.11 Hollis *conticuit Latiae tristis facundia linguae*. The fact that the famous elegists Propertius and Ovid survived Tibullus is conveniently ignored.

molles qui fleret amores: the adj. *mollis* is used to describe elegy, just as *durus* describes epic; see Cairns (1979) 102. The verb *fleret* is also appropriate for a genre that concentrates on the unhappy aspects of love, cf. Hor. *Epod.* 14.11 (of Anacreon) *qui persaepe caua testudine fleuit amorem*. The related adj. *flebilis* becomes elegy's standing epithet, cf. Hor. *Carm.* 2.9.9-10 of Valgius' poem, no doubt in elegiacs, on the death of his lover Mystes *tu semper urges flebilibus modis / Mysten ademptum*. Cf. Horace's mention of the *miserabiles / ...elegos* of Albius (Tibullus) at *Carm.* 1.33.2-3.

4 forti ... pede: the epic hexameter. In fact the death of Virgil probably left few epic poets active. Varius Rufus was very likely composing tragedies by then; Cornelius Severus, Rabirius and Pedo were yet to begin their epics, and Marsus' own *Amazonis* was also still in the future.

regia bella: kings and wars were the defining subject matter of epic, cf. Virg. *Ecl.* 6.3 *cum canerem reges et proelia*; Hor. *AP* 73-74 *res gestae regumque ducumque et tristia bella / quo scribi possent numero monstrauit Homerus*; Prop. 3.3.3 *reges, Alba, tuos et regum facta tuorum*.

Life of Tibullus [derived from Suetonius ?]

The *Vita* is transmitted at the end of A+. It probably contains extracts from a lost work of Suetonius entitled *De poetis*; see Rostagni (1935), (1944), Avery (1960).

This work would have been written more than a century after the death of Tibullus and it is impossible to tell how much of the *Vita* is taken from Suetonius. Lee [(1990) 163] quotes the following Suetonian parallels: *Nero* 20.3 *insignes ... coma* (cf. *insignis forma* 1); *Iulius* 45.3

cultu notabilem (cf. *cultu ... obseruabilis* **1-2**); 50.2 *ante alias dilexit* (cf. *ante alios ... dilexit* **2-3**); 42.1 *contubernalis* (cf. *contubernalis* **3**); *Augustus* 8.1 *militaribus donis ... donatus est* (cf. *militaribus donis donatus est* **3-4**); *De grammaticis* 23.1 *principem locum inter grammaticos tenuit* (cf. *principem inter elegiographos optinet locum* **4-5**); 18 *mimographos* (cf. *elegiographos* **5**); *Nero* 57.1 *obiit* (cf. *obiit* **6**); *De grammaticis* 16 *quod etiam uersiculus Domiti Marsi indicat* (cf. *ut indicat epigramma supra scriptum* **6-7**). Information available in the *Vita* that is not to be found in the works of Tibullus himself or in the two poems of Horace addressed to Albius, now generally believed to be Tibullus, *Carm.* 1.33 and *Epist.* 1.4, includes the following: Messalla's *nomen, Coruinus* **2**; the fact that Tibullus was Messalla's *contubernalis* in the Aquitanian campaign and received military decorations for his participation **3**; the fact that many regarded Tibullus as the foremost of the elegists **4-5** and that he had the status of a Roman knight **1**. On the possibility that this piece was written specifically for its place at the end of **book 3**, or, like the epitaph, was derived from earlier sources but deliberately placed there in order to give weight to the book's Tibullan connections, see **headnote** to the epitaph above.

References are to the line-numbers of the text as printed in this edition.

1. Albius Tibullus: the *nomen* Albius is attached to Tibullus in most MSS, as well as in Porphyrio and Pseudacron on Hor. *Carm.* 1.33.1 *Albi, ne doleas plus nimio* (cf. Porph. ad loc. *Albium Tibullum adloquitur elegiorum poetam*) and *Epist.* 1.4 *Albi, nostrorum sermonum candide iudex* (cf. Pseudacron ad loc. *hac epistola Albium Tibullum elegorum scriptorem alloquitur*) and Diom. *GL* 1.484.27-28 *Horatius ... ad Albium Tibullum elegiarum auctorem scribens*.

eques Romanus: the reading of P *eques Ro.* (= *Romanus*) reveals the truth behind *eques regalis* of A+. The *Vita* is the only source which speaks of Tibullus' status as a knight. This would be unsurprising as the other Roman elegists Propertius and Ovid were probably also *equites*; see Taylor (1968). The fact that all three complain of lack of money is not to be taken at face value [see Maltby (2002) 40], since to qualify as a knight a minimum property qualification of 400,000 sesterces was required. However, Baerhens conjectures *e Gabis* 'from Gabii' for *regalis*, as Gabii is an ancient city of Latium, which would be consistent with Horace's description of Tibullus at *Epist.* 1.4.2 as being *in regione Pedana*.

1-2 insignis forma cultuque corporis obseruabilis: cf. Hor. *Epist.* 1.4.6-7 *non tu corpus eras sine pectore: di tibi formam ... / ... dederunt*; Suet. *Nero* 20.3 *insignes* (sc. *adulescentuli*) *pinguissima coma et excellentissimo cultu*, *Iul.* 45.3 *etiam cultu notabilem ferunt*.

2-3 ante alios ... dilexit: cf. Suet. *Iul.* 50.2 *sed ante alias dilexit Marci Bruti matrem Seruillam*.

2 Coruinum Messallam oratorem: on Messalla's achievements as an orator see **7.45-47n.** above. On his keen eye for Latin style cf. Sen. *Contr.* 2.4 *Latini utique sermonis obseruator diligentissimus*.

3 contubernalis: literally 'one who shares the same tent'. The term is applied to a young man attached for training to the staff of a general; see *OLD contubernalis* 1b and cf. Cic. *Planc.* 27 *fuit in Creta ... contubernalis Saturnini*; Suet. *Iul.* 42.1 *neu qui senatoris filius contubernalis aut comes magistratus peregre proficisceretur*.

Aquitanico bello: Messalla's Aquitanian campaign, for which he was awarded a triumph 25 September 27 BC, is one of the subjects of Tib. 1.7, where Tibullus' own participation in the campaign is hinted at by the words 1.7.9 *non sine me est tibi partus honos*.

3-4 militaribus donis donatus est: this is our only reference to Tibullus' receiving military honours for service in Messalla's campaign. *dona militaria* were awarded to soldiers for distinguished service; see *OLD donum* 2b and cf. Cic. *Mur.* 11 *donis militaribus triumphum patris decorare*, Suet. *Aug.* 8.1 *militaribus donis ... donatus est*.

4-5 multorum iudicio principem ... locum: for Tibullus' high rank among the Roman elegists cf. Quint. *Inst.* 10.1.93 *elegia quoque Graecos prouocamus, cuius mihi tersus atque elegans maxime uidetur auctor Tibullus. sunt qui Propertium malint. Ouidius utroque lasciuior, sicut durior Gallus.* For *principem ... locum* in a similar context cf. Suet. *De gramm.* 23.1 *principem locum inter grammaticos tenuit*.

5 elegiographos: here only; cf. the parallel formation *mimographos* at Suet. *De gramm.* 18.

epistolae ... amatoriae: often taken to refer to the *Sulpicia Cycle* **8-12**, but echoes in these of late Ovid mean they could not have been written by Tibullus; see Gen. Intro., section 2.2.3 above and Fuchs (1947). These poems are in any case not strictly letters. If, as argued in the **headnote** to the epitaph above, the *Life* was written specifically for its place at the end of **book 3**, the most obvious reference would be to the small elegiac letters *Sulpicia* **13-18**.

6 subtiles: a persuasive conjecture by Rostagni from the meaningless *utiles* of A+.

obiit adulescens: for Tibullus' young death cf. *Epigr. Domiti Marsi* 2 *iuuenem*. The verb *obiit* is the one used most frequently of dying in Suetonius: *Aug.* 4.1, 63.1, 100.1, *Tib.* 4.3, 73.1, *Cal.* 1.2, 2.1, *Cl.* 1.3, 46.1, *Nero* 3.2, 57.1, *Gal.* 3.4, *Vit.* 2.2, *Vesp.* 1.3, *De poetis* 40.66.

6-7 ut indicat epigramma supra scriptum: shows that this was the relative position of the *Epigram* and *Vita* at the end of the MSS in A+. Verses from Domitius Marsus are quoted by Suetonius in *De gramm.* 9.3 *ut et Horatius significat ... et Domitius Marsus scribens 'si quos Orbilius ferula scuticaque cecidit'* fr. 4 (Courtney = fr. 177 Hollis) and 16.3 *quod etiam uersiculus Domiti Marsi indicat: 'Epirota tenellorum nutricula uatum'* fr. 3 (Courtney = fr. 176 Hollis). But this does not prove the Suetonian origin of the *Life*.

Appendix

Important Intertexts for the Understanding of [Tibullus] 3

1. Lygdamus

(a) Horace *Epodes* 15

Nox erat et caelo fulgebat luna sereno
    inter minora sidera,
cum tu, magnorum numen laesura deorum,
    in uerba iurabas mea,
artius atque hedera procera adstringitur ilex
    lentis adhaerens bracchiis,
dum pecori lupus et nautis infestus Orion
    turbaret hibernum mare
intonsosque agitaret Apollinis aura capillos,
    fore hunc amorem mutuum.   10
o dolitura mea multum uirtute Neaera,
    nam si quid in Flacco uiri est,
non feret adsiduas potiori te dare noctes,
    et quaeret iratus parem,
nec semel offensae cedet constantia formae,
    si certus intrarit dolor.
et tu, quicumque es felicior atque meo nunc
    superbus incedis malo,
sis pecore et multa diues tellure licebit
    tibique Pactolus fluat,   20
nec te Pythagorae fallant arcana renati,
    formaque uincas Nirea,
heu heu, translatos alio maerebis amores.
    ast ego uicissim risero.

(b) Propertius 3.6

Dic mihi de nostra quae sensti uera puella:
    sic tibi sint dominae, Lygdame, dempta iuga. 2
omnis enim debet sine uano nuntius esse, 5
    maioremque metu seruus habere fidem.
nunc mihi, si qua tenes, ab origine dicere prima
    incipe: suspensis auribus ista bibam.
sic illam incomptis uidisti flere capillis?
    illius ex oculis multa cadebat aqua? 10
nec speculum in strato uidisti, Lygdame, lecto?
    ornabat niueas nullane gemma manus? 12
num me laetitia tumefactum fallis inani, 3
    haec referens quae me credere uelle putas? 4
< '. . . . . >
    < . . . . >
et maestam teneris uestem pendere lacertis, 13
    scriniaque ad lecti clausa iacere pedes.
tristis erat domus, et tristes sua pensa ministrae 15
    carpebant, medio nebat et ipsa loco,
umidaque impressa siccabat lumina lana,
    rettulit et querulo iurgia uestra sono:
"haec te teste mihi promissa est, Lygdame, merces?
    est poena et seruo rumpere teste fidem. 20
ille potest nullo miseram me linquere facto,
    et qualem nolo dicere habere domi?
gaudet me uacuo solam tabescere lecto?
    si placet, insultet, Lygdame, morte mea.
non me moribus illa, sed herbis improba uicit: 25
    staminea rhombi ducitur ille rota;
illum turgentis sanie portenta rubetae
    et lecta exsucis anguibus ossa trahunt,
et strigis inuentae per busta recentia plumae
    raptaque funesto lanea uitta toro. 30
si non uana cadunt mea somnia, Lygdame, testor,
    poena erit ante meos sera sed ampla pedes:
putris et in uacuo texetur aranea lecto:
    noctibus illorum dormiet ipsa Venus."
quae tibi si ueris animis est questa puella, 35
    hac eadem rursus, Lygdame, curre uia,
et mea cum multis lacrimis mandata reporta:

iram, non fraudes, esse in amore meo.
me quoque consimili impositum torrerier igni
    iurabo, bis sex integer esse dies.   40
quod mihi si tanto felix concordia bello
    exstiterit, per me, Lygdame, liber eris.

(c) Propertius 4.7. 35-48

'Lygdamus uratur; candescat lamina uernae: 35
    sensi ego cum insidiis pallida uina bibi;
ut Nomas arcanas tollat uersuta saliuas,
    dicet damnatas ignea testa manus.
quae modo per uiles inspecta est publica noctes,
    haec nunc aurata cyclade signat humum;   40
et grauiora rependit iniquis pensa quasillis
    garrula de facie si qua locuta mea est;
nostraque quod Petale tulit ad monumenta coronas,
    codicis immundi uincula sentit anus.
caeditur et Lalage tortis suspensa capillis,   45
    per nomen quoniam est ausa rogare meum.
te patiente meae conflauit imaginis aurum,
    ardente e nostro dotem habitura rogo.'

(d) Propertius 4.8.37-38

Lygdamus ad cyathos uitrique aestiua supellex
    et Methymnaei grata saliua meri.

Propertius 4.8.68-70

Lygdamus ad plutei fulcra sinistra latens
eruitur, geniumque meum prostratus adorat.
Lygdame, nil potui: tecum ego captus eram.

Propertius 4.8.79-80 (spoken by Cynthia)

'Lygdamus in primis, omnis mihi causa querelae,
    ueneat, et pedibus uincula bina trahat'.

2. Neaera

(a) Licinius Imbrex (fr. 1.1 Ribbeck$^{2\text{-}3}$ 1898, 39-40 = Gell. 13.23.16)

Imbrex, uetus comoediarum scriptor, in fabula quae *Neaera* scripta est, ita scripsit:

>nolo ego Neaeram te uocent, set Nerienem,
>cum quidem Mauorti es in conubium data.

(b) Virg. *Ecl.* 3.3-5

>   ipse Neaeram
>dum fouet ac ne me sibi praeferat illa ueretur,
>hic alienus ouis custos bis mulget in hora.

(c) Hor. *Carm.* 3.14.21-25

>dic et argutae properet Neaerae
>murreum nodo cohibere crinem;
>si per inuisum mora ianitorem
>   fiet abito.

>lenit albescens animos capillus.

(d) Hor. *Epod.* 15.11

>o dolitura mea multum uirtute Neaera!

(e) Ov. *Am.* 3.6.27-28

>nondum Troia fuit lustris obsessa duobus,
>   cum rapuit uultus, Xanthe, Neaera tuos.

3. Messalla

(a) *Catalepton* 9. 13-20

pauca tua in nostras uenerunt carmina chartas,   13
  carmina cum lingua tum sale Cecropia,
carmina quae Phrygium, saeclis accepta futuris,
  carmina quae Pylium uincere digna senem.
molliter hic uiridi patulae sub tegmine quercus

Moeris pastores et Meliboeus erant,
  dulcia iactantes alterno carmina uersu,
  qualia Trinacriae doctus amat iuuenis.   20

(b) Tibullus 1.7

Hunc cecinere diem Parcae, fatalia nentes
  stamina non ulli dissoluenda deo,
hunc fore Aquitanas posset qui fundere gentes,
  quem tremeret forti milite uictus Atur.
euenere: nouos pubes Romana triumphos   5
  uidit et euinctos bracchia capta duces;
at te uictrices lauros, Messalla, gerentem
  portabat nitidis currus eburnus equis.
non sine me est tibi partus honos: Tarbella Pyrene
  testis et Oceani litora Santonici,   10
testis Arar Rhodanusque celer magnusque Garunna,
  Carnutis et flaui caerula lympha Liger.
an te, Cydne, canam, tacitis qui leniter undis
  caeruleus palcidis per uada serpis aquis?
quantus et aetherio contingens uertice nubes   15
  frigidus intonsos Taurus alat Cilicas?
quid referam ut uolitet crebras intacta per urbes
  alba Palaestino sancta columba Syro?
utque maris uastum prospectat turribus aequor
  prima ratem uentis credere docta Tyros?   20
qualis et, arentes cum findit Sirius agros,
  fertilis aestiua Nilus abundet aqua?
Nile pater, quanam possim te dicere causa
  aut quibus in terris occuluisse caput?
te propter nullos tellus tua postulat imbres,   25
  arida nec pluuio supplicat herba Ioui.
te canit atque suum pubes miratur Osirim
  barbara, Memphitem plangere docta bouem.
primus aratra manu sollerti fecit Osiris
  et teneram ferro sollicitauit humum.   30
primus inexpertae commisit semina terrae
  pomaque non notis legit ab arboribus.
hic docuit teneram palis adiungere uitem,
  hic uiridem dura caedere falce comam.
illi iuncundos primum matura sapores   35

expressa incultis uua dedit pedibus.
ille liquor docuit uoces inflectere cantu,
    mouit et ad certos nescia membra modos.
Bacchus et agricolae magno confecta labore
    pectora tristitiae dissoluenda dedit.   40
Bacchus et afflictis requiem mortalibus affert,
    crura licet dura compede pulsa sonent.
non tibi sunt tristes curae nec luctus, Osiri,
    sed chorus et cantus et leuis aptus amor,
sed uarii flores et frons redimita corymbis,   45
    fusa sed ad teneros lutea palla pedes
et Tyriae uestes et dulcis tibia cantu
    et leuis occultis conscia cista sacris.
huc ades et Genium ludis Geniumque choreis
    concelebra et multo tempora funde mero.   50
illius et nitido stillent unguenta capillo,
    et capite et collo mollia serta gerat.
sic, uenias, hodierne: tibi dem turis honores,
    liba et Mopsopio dulcia melle feram.
at tibi succrescat proles quae facta parentis   55
    augeat et circum stet ueneranda senem.
nec taceat monumenta uiae quem Tuscula tellus
    candidaque antiquo detinet Alba Lare.
namque opibus congesta tuis hic glarea dura
    sternitur, hic apta iungitur arte silex.   60
te canat agricola a magna cum uenerit urbe
    serus inoffensum rettuleritque pedem.
at tu, Natalis, multos celebrande per annos,
    candidior semper candidiorque ueni.

(c) echoes of Callimachean epinicion in Tib. 1.7:

1.7.21-22   qualis et, arentes cum findit Sirius agros,
                fertilis aestiua Nilus abundet aqua?

Call. fr. 384.27 Pf. (for Sosibius) θηλύτατον καὶ Νεῖλο[ς ἄ]γων ἐνιαύσιον ὕδωρ
                'As the Nile brings each year its most fertile water'

1.7.23-24   Nile pater, quanam possim te dicere causa
                aut quibus in terris occuluisse caput?

Call. fr. 384.31-32 Pf. (for Sosibius) ... ὃν οὐδ' ὅθεν οἶδεν ὁδεύω / θνητὸς ἀνήρ

'And no mortal man knows whence I flow'

1.7.27-28   te canit atque suum pubes miratur Osirim
            barbara, Memphitem plangere docta bouem

Call. fr. 383.16 Pf. εἰδυῖαι φαλιὸν ταῦρον ἰηλεμίσαι
            '(the maidens) knowing how to lament the white-blazed bull'

4. Cerinthus

(a) Horace Serm. 1.2.80-82

> nec magis huic, inter niueos uiridisque lapillos
>   sit licet, hoc, Cerinthe, tuo tenerum est femur aut crus
> rectius, atque etiam melius persaepe togatae est.

Porph. ad loc. Cerinthus nomine prostitutus dicitur fuisse insigni specie atque candore.

(b) Tibullus 2.2

> dicamus bona uerba; uenit Natalis ad aras:
>   quisquis ades, lingua uir mulierque faue.
> urantur pia tura focis, urantur odores
>   quos tener e terra diuite mittit Arabs.
> ipse suos genius adsit uisurus honores,   5
>   cui decorent sanctas mollia serta comas.
> illius puro destillent tempora nardo,
>   atque satur libo sit madeatque mero.
> adnuat et, Cornute, tibi quodcumque rogabis,
>   en age, quid cessas? adnuit ille: roga.   10
> auguror, uxoris fidos optabis amores:
>   iam reor hoc ipsos edidicisse deos.
> nec tibi malueris totum quaecumque per orbem
>   fortis arat ualido rusticus arua boue,
> nec tibi gemmarum quidquid felicibus Indis   15
>   nascitur, Eoi qua maris unda rubet.

uota cadunt. utinam strepitantibus aduolet alis
    flauaque coniugio uincula portet Amor.
uincula quae maneant semper, dum tarda senectus
    inducat rugas inficiatque comas.   20
hic ueniat Natalis auis prolemque ministret,
    ludat et ante tuos turba nouella pedes.

5. Sulpicia

(a) Ovid *Ars Amatoria* 3.479-482

munda sed e medio consuetaque uerba, puellae,
    scribite: sermonis publica forma placet.
a, quotiens dubius scriptis exarsit amator
    et nocuit formae barbara lingua bonae.

(b) Propertius 3.23.11-16

forsitan haec illis fuerunt mandata tabellis:
    'irascor quoniam es, lente, moratus heri:
an tibi nescioquae uisa est formosior? an tu
    non bene de nobis crimina ficta iacis?'
aut dixit: 'uenias hodie, cessabimus una: 15
    hospitium tota nocte parauit Amor.'

(c) Martial 10.35

omnes Sulpiciam legant puellae
uni quae cupiunt uiro placere;
omnes Sulpiciam legant mariti
uni qui cupiunt placere nuptae.
non haec Colchidos asserit furorem,   5
diri prandia nec refert Thyestae;
Scyllam, Byblida nec fuisse credit:
sed castos docet et pios amores,
lusus, delicias facetiasque.
cuius carmina qui bene aestimarit,   10
nullam dixerit esse nequiorem
nullam dixerit esse sanctiorem.
tales Egeriae iocos fuisse
udo crediderim Numae sub antro.

hac condiscipula uel hac magistra 15
esses doctior et pudica, Sappho:
sed tecum pariter simulque uisam
durus Sulpiciam Phaon amaret.
frustra: namque ea nec Tonantis uxor
nec Bacchi nec Apollinis puella 20
erepto sibi uiueret Caleno.

(d) Martial 10. 38

o molles tibi quindecim, Calene,
quos cum Sulpicia tua iugales
indulsit deus et peregit annos.
o nox omnis et hora, quae notata est
caris litoris Indici lapillis. 5
o quae proelia, quas utriumque pugnas
felix lectulus et lucerna uidit
nimbis ebria Nicerotianis.
uixisti tribus, o Calene, lustris:
aetas haec tibi tota computatur 10
et solos numeras dies mariti.
ex illis tibi si diu rogatam
lucem redderet Atropos uel unam
malles quam Pyliam quarter senectam.

BIBLIOGRAPHY

1. Works referred to by abbreviations only

AP *Anthologia Palatina*
ANRW H. Temporini and W. Haase (eds), *Aufstieg und Niedergang der römischen Welt*, Berlin and New York (1972-).
CHCL *Cambridge History of Classical Literature. II Latin Literature*, Cambridge (1982).
CIL Th. Mommsen and W. Henzen (eds), *Corpus Inscriptionum Latinarum*, Berlin (1863-).
CLE F. Bücheler and E. Lommatzsch (eds), *Carmina Latina Epigraphica. I-III*, Leipzig (1894-1926).
FLP S.M. Goldberg, and G. Manuwaldt G. (2018) *Fragmentary Latin Poetry. I*, Ennius. Cambridge MA – London. R.
FGrHist F. Jacoby (ed.), *Die Fragmente der griechischen Historiker*, Berlin (1923).
GL H. Keil (ed.), *Grammatici Latini. I-VII*, Leipzig (1857-1870), repr. (1961).
G-P A. S. F. Gow and D. L. Page (eds), *The Greek anthology: Hellenistic epigrams*, Cambridge (1965).
GRF H. Funaioli (ed.) *Grammaticae Romanae Fragmenta*, Leipzig (1907), repr. Stuttgart (1969).
H-Sz J. B. Hofmann and A. Szantyr, *Lateinische Grammatik II. Syntax und Stylistik*, Munich (1965).
ILS H. Dessau (ed.), *Inscriptiones Latinae Selectae*, Berlin (1892-1916).
K-S R. Kühner and C. Stegmann, *Ausführliche Grammatik der lateinischen Sprache. I-II.* (ed. 3) Auflage A. Thierfelder, Leverkusen (1955).
LALE R. Maltby, *A Lexicon of Ancient Latin Etymologies*, Leeds (1991).
L-H-S M. Leumann, J. B. Hofmann, A. Szantyr, *I: Lateinische Laut- und Formlehre* von Leumann, M., (1926-1928), neuarbeitet (1977). *II: Lateinische Syntax und Stylistik* von Hofmann, J. B., neuarbeitet von Szantyr, A. Munich (1965).
LIMC *Lexicon Iconographicum Mythologiae Classicae*, Zurich – Munich (1981).

Book Three of the Corpus Tibullianum: 573
Introduction, Text, Translation and Commentary

LSJ⁹ H. G. Liddell, R. Scott and H. S. Jones, *A Greek-English Lexicon*, Oxford (1940), with revised supplement ed. by P. G. W. Glare, Oxford (1996).
N-A F. Navarro Antolín, *Lygdamus: Corpus Tibullianum iii 1-6* (*Mnemosyne Suppl.* 154), Leiden (1996).
N-H R. G. M. Nisbet and M. Hubbard, *A Commentary on Horace Odes Book I*, Oxford (1970). *A Commentary on Horace Odes Book II*, Oxford (1978).
N-R R. G. M. Nisbet and N. Rudd, *A Commentary on Horace Odes Book III*, Oxford (2004).
OLD P. G. W. Glare (ed.), *Oxford Latin Dictionary*, Oxford (1982).
PLF E. Lobel and D. L. Page (eds), *Poetarum Lesbiorum Fragmenta*, Oxford (1955).
PMG D. L. Page (ed.), *Poetae Melici Graeci*, Oxford (1962).
RAC *Reallexikon für Antike und Christentum*
RE *Real-Encyclopädie der classischen Altertumswissenschaft*, Stuttgart (1893-1978).
SH H. Lloyd-Jones and P. Parsons (eds), *Supplementum Hellenisticum*, Berlin – New York (1983).
ThLL *Thesaurus Linguae Latinae*, Leipzig-Stuttgart (1900-).

Periodicals are abbreviated as in *L'Année Philologique*

2. Texts and Commentaries

Apart from the commonly cited editions and commentaries referred to under abbreviations above (**Bibliography 1**), the following texts used as the source of quotations in the commentary should be noted:

Charisius   Barwick (1925) = B
Ennius' tragedies   Jocelyn (1967)
Ennius' *Annales*   Skutsch (1985)
Festus and Paul the Deacon   Lindsay (1913) = L
Fragmentary Latin Poetry   Morel (1927), Courtney (1993),
                                    Hollis (2007)
Fragmentary Republican Drama   Ribbeck (1897-1898) = R
Lucilius   Marx (1904-1905) = M
Lucretius   Bailey (1947)
Martial   Shackleton-Bailey (1993)
Nonius Marcellus   Lindsay (1903) = L
Ovid *Metamorphoses*   Tarrant (2004)

Ovid *Tristia*   Hall (1995)
Plautus   De Melo (2011-2013)
Propertius   Heyworth (2007)
Roman Grammarians (not Charisius)   Keil (1857-1880)
Servius (Virgil Commentaries)   Thilo and Hagen (1881-1887)
Statius *Thebaid* and *Achilleid*   Hall (2007)
Terence   Barsby (2001)
Varro   De Melo (2019)

Full references for each of these works, as for the other standard editions cited, are to be found below in **Bibliography 3** under the name of the editor.

3. Alphabetical list of works cited

Abdale, J. R. (2019) *The great Illyrian revolt: Rome's forgotten war in the Balkans, AD 6-9*, Barnsley.
Acosta-Hughes, B., Lehnus, L. and Stephens, S. (eds) (2011) *Brill's Companion to Callimachus*, Leiden.
Adams, J. N. (1972) "Latin words for 'woman' and 'wife'", *Glotta* 50, 243-255. Adams, J. N. (1982) *The Latin sexual vocabulary*, London.
Adams, J. N. (1983) *Words for 'prostitute' in Latin*, *RhM* 126, 321-358.
Adams, J. N. (2016) *An anthology of informal Latin 200 BC – AD 900*, Cambridge.
Adams, J. N. and R. Mayer (eds) (1999) *Aspects of the language of Latin poetry*, 377-398, London.
Adams, J. N. and Vincent, N. (eds) (2016) *Early and late Latin: Continuity or change?*, Cambridge.
Amden, B., Flensted-Jansen, P., Nielsen, T. H., Schwartz, A., Tortzen, C. G. (eds) (2002) *Noctes Atticae: 34 articles on Greco-Roman antiquity and its Nachleben: Studies presented to Jorgen Mejer on his sixtieth birthday, March 18, 2002*, Copenhagen.
Anderson, J. K. (1961) *Ancient Greek Horsemanship*, Berkeley.
Anderson, J. K. (1985) *Hunting in the ancient world*, Berkeley.
André, J. (1949) *Études sur les termes de couleur dans la langue latine*, Paris.
Andreae, B. (1977) *Römische Kunst*, ed. 3, Freiburg – Breisgau.
Argetsinger, K. (1992) "Birthday rituals: friends and patrons in Roman poetry and Cult", *CA* 11, 179-193.
Armstrong, D., Fish, J., Johnson, P.A., Skinner, M. B. (eds) (2004) *Virgil, Philodemus, and the Augustans*, Austin.

Asmis, E. (1995) "Philodemus on Censorship, Moral Utility and Formalism in Poetry", in D. Obbink (ed.), 148-177.
Augoustakis, A. (ed.) (2014) *Flavian Poetry and its Greek Past*, Mnem. Suppl. 366, Leiden – Boston.
Austin, R. G. (1968) *"Ille ego qui quondam ..."*, *CQ* 18, 107-115.
Austin, R. G. (1971) *P. Vergili Maronis Aeneidos liber primus*, Oxford.
Austin, R. G. (1977) *P. Vergili Maronis Aeneidos liber sextus*, Oxford.
Avery, W. T. (1960) "The Latin love elegy. George Luck", *CPh* 55, 285-286.
Axelson, B. (1945) *Unpoetische Wörter: Ein Beitrag zur Kenntnis der lateinischen Dichtersprache*, Lund.
Axelson, B. (1948) "Die Synonyme *adulescens* und *iuuenis*", in *Mélanges offertes à J. Marouzeau*, 7-17, Paris.
Axelson, B. (1960a) "Lygdamus und Ovid. Zur Methodik der literarischen Prioritätsbestimmung", *Eranos* 58, 93-111.
Axelson, B. (1960b) "Das Geburtsjahr des Lygdamus: ein Rätsel der römischen Elegien-dichtung", *Eranos* 58, 281-297.
Bailey, C. *Titi Lucreti Cari De Rerum Natura Libri Sex*, 3 vols, Oxford.
Baligan, G. (1948) "Il libro terzo del *Corpus Tibullianum*", *SIFC* 1, 1-35.
Balsdon, J. P. V. D. (1969) *Life and leisure in ancient Rome*, London.
Barchiesi, A. (2005) *Ovidio Metamorfosi, volume I, libri I-II* (trad. L. Koch), Roma.
Barchiesi, A. (2011) "Roman Callimachus", in B. Acosta-Hughes, L. Lehnus and S. Stephens (eds), *Brill's Companion to Callimachus*, 511-533.
Barsby, J. (2001) *Terence*, 2 vols, Cambridge, MA - London.
Barwick, K. (1925) *Flavii Sosipatri Charisii Artis grammaticae libri V*, Leipzig.
Batstone, W. W. (2018) "Sulpicia and the Speech of Men", in S. Frangoulidis and S. J. Harrison, 85-100.
Bauer, B. L. M. (2010) "Forerunners of Romance *-mente* adverbs in Latin prose and poetry", in E. Dickey and A. Chahoud (eds), 339-353.
Bernabé, A. (2004) *Orphicorum et Orphicis similium testimonia et fragmenta. Poetae epici Graeci. Pars II, Fasc. I*, Munich – Leipzig.
Bessone, F. (2003) "Saffo, la lirica, l'elegia: su Ovidio, *Heroides* 15", *MD* 51, 209-243.
Bickel, E. (1960) "Die Lygdamus-Elegien: Lygda appellativisch *seruus amoris*, Messalla Messsalinus als Verfasser der Elegien", *RhM*, 103, 97-109.
Billerbeck, M. (1999) *Seneca: Hercules Furens*, Leiden – Boston.

Blümner, H. (1899) "Über die Farbenbezeichnungen bei den römischen Dichtern", *Philologus* 2, 142-67.
Blümner, H. (1911) *Die römische Privataltertümer*, Munich.
Blümner, H. (1916) "*Umbilicus* und *cornua*", *Philologus* 73, 426-445.
Bo, Dominicus (1965/ 1966) *Lexicon Horatianum* (2 vols), Hildesheim.
Bolle, L. (1872) *De Lygdami carminibus*, Detmold.
Bömer, F. (1957-1958) *P. Ovidius Naso: Die Fasten*, Heidelberg.
Bömer, F. (1969-1986) *P. Ovidius Naso: Metamorphosen*, Heidelberg.
Booth, J. and Maltby, R. (2005) "*Light and dark*: play on candidus and related concepts in the elegies of Tibullus", *Mnemosyne* 58, 124-131.
Boucher, J. P. (1976) "A propos de Cérinthus et de quelques autres pseudonyms dans la poésie augustéenne", *Latomus* 35, 504-519.
Boyle, A. J. (2003) *Ovid and the monuments: A poet's Rome*, Bendigo.
Boyle, A. J. and Dominik, W. J. (eds) (2003) *Flavian Rome: Culture, Image, Text*, Boston – Leiden.
Bréguet, E. (1946) *Le roman de Sulpicia: élégies IV, 2-12 du 'Corpus Tibullianum'*, Geneva.
Bréguet, E. (1962) "Le thème *alius... ego* chez les poètes latins", *REL* 40, 128-136.
Bright, D. F. (1971) "A Tibullan Odyssey", *Arethusa* 4, 197-214.
Bright, D. F. (1978) *'Haec mihi Fingebam'. Tibullus in his World*, Leiden.
Bright, D. F. (1984) "The Role of Odysseus in *Panegyricus Messallae*", *Quaderni Urbinati di Cultura Classica* 17.2, 143-154.
Brink, C. O. (1971) *Horace on Poetry: The* Ars Poetica, Cambridge.
Brink, C. O. (1982) *Horace on Poetry:* Epistles *Book 2*, Cambridge.
Brown, R. D. (1987) *Lucretius on love and sex: a commentary on De rerum natura IV. 1030-1287*, Leiden.
Büchner, K. (1965) "Die Elegien des Lygdamus", *Hermes* 93, 65-112, 503-508.
Büchner, K. (1976) *Die römische Lyrik. Texte, Übersetzungen, Interpretationen, Geschichte*, Stuttgart.
Bürger, R. (1903) "Eine Elegie des Gallus", *Hermes* 38, 19-27.
Bürger, R. (1905) "Studien zu Lygdamus und den Sulpiciagedichten", *Hermes* 40, 321-335.
Burkert, W. (1985) *Greek religion, archaic and classical*, Oxford. (= translation of *Griechische Religion der archäischen und klassischen Epoche*, 1977).
Butrica, J. L. (1992) Review of H. Tränkle (1990), *CR* 42, 45-47.
Butrica, J. L. (1993) "Lygdamus, nephew of Messalla", *LCM* 18, 51-53.
Butterfiled, D. J. (2008) "The poetic treatment of *atque* from Catullus to Juvenal", *Mnemosyne* 61, 386-413.

Cairns, D. L. (ed.) (2005) *Body language in the Greek and Roman worlds*, Swansea.
Cairns, F. (1969) "Catullus I", *Mnemosyne* 22, 154.
Cairns, F. (1972) *Generic composition in Greek and Roman poetry*, Edinburgh.
Cairns, F. (1979) *Tibullus: a Hellenistic poet at Rome*, Cambridge.
Cairns, F. (1984) "Propertius and the battle of Actium (4.6)", in A. J. Woodman and D. West (eds), 129-168, 229-236.
Cairns, F. (1996) "Ancient etymology and Tibullus: on the classification of etymologies and on etymological markers", *PCPhS* 42, 24-59.
Cairns, F. (2004) "Varius and Virgil: Two pupils of Philodemus in Propertius 2.34?", in D. Armstrong, J. Fish, P. A. Johnson and M. B. Skinner (eds), 299-321.
Cairns, F. (2005) "Lavinia's blush: Virgil *Aeneid* 12.64-70", in D. L. Cairns (ed.), 195-213.
Cairns, F. (2006) *Sextus Propertius. The Augustan elegist*, Cambridge.
Cameron, A. (1995) *Callimachus and his critics*, Princeton.
Carcopino, J (1929) "Épitaphe en vers de la lectrice Pétalè, découverte à Rome", *Bulletin de la société Nationale des Antiquitaires de France*, 84-86.
Cartault, A. (1909) *Tibulle et les auteurs du Corpus Tibullianum*, Paris.
Christensen, D. (2000) *Plautus* Amphitruo, Cambridge.
Christensen, H. (1908) "*Que- que-* bei den römischen Hexametrikern", *ALL* 15, 164-211.
Churchill, L. J., Brown, P. R. and Jeffrey, J. E. (eds) (2002) *Women writing Latin: From Roman antiquity to early modern Europe*, New York.
Citroni, M. (1975) *M. Valerii Martialis epigrammaton liber primus*, Florence.
Clausen, W. V. (1994) *A commentary on Virgil, Eclogues*, Oxford.
Coleman, K. M. (1988) *Statius, Siluae IV*, Oxford.
Coleman, R. G. G. (1977) *Virgil: Eclogues*, Cambridge.
Conte, G. B. (1986) *The rhetoric of imitation*, Ithaca, NY.
Copley, F. O. (1947) "*Servitium amoris* in the Roman elegists", *TAPhA* 78, 285-300.
Copley, F. O. (1951) "Catullus, c.1", *TAPhA* 82, 201-202.
Costa, C. D. N. (1973) *Seneca: Medea*, Oxford.
Courtney, E. (1993) *The fragmentary Latin poets*, Oxford (= Courtney).
Courtney, E. (2003-2004) "The 'Greek' accusative", *CJ* 99, 425-431.
Cowan, R. (2014) "Fingering Cestos: Martial's Catullus' Callimachus", in A. Augoustakis (ed.), 345-371.

Cozzoli, A.-T. (2011) "The Poet as a Child", in B. Acosta-Hughes, L. Lehnus and S. Stephens (eds), 407-428.
Cozzolino, A (1992) "Il carme III 13 del *Corpus Tibullianum* e il Fragmentum Grenfellianum", *Athenaeum* 80, 475-478.
Cucchiarelli, A. (2012) *Le Bucoliche. Introduzione e commento*, trad. di Alfonso Traina, Roma.
Currie, H. M. (1983) "The poems of Sulpicia", *ANRW* 2.30.3, 1751-64.
Davies, C. (1973) "Poetry in the circle of Messalla", *Greece and Rome* 20, 25-35.
Davis, G. (1983) *The death of Procris*: Amor *and the hunt in Ovid's* Metamorphoses, Oxford.
Davis, J. T. (1977) *Dramatic pairings in the elegies of Propertius and Ovid* (*Noctes Romanae* 15), Bern – Stuttgart.
De Luca, E. (2009) *Corpus Tibullianum III 7*: *Panegyricus Messallae*, Rubbettino.
De Melo, W. D. C. (2011-2013) *Plautus*, 5 vols, Cambridge, MA – London.
De Melo, W. D. C (2019) *Varro* De Lingua Latina: *Introduction, Text, Translation and Commentary,* 2 vols, Cambridge.
Della Corte, F. (1964) "Aspetti sociali del III libro del 'Corpus Tibullianum'', in *Synteleia V. Arangio-Ruiz*, 690-695, Naples = *Opuscula III* (1972), 191-196.
Deroux C. (ed.) (1986) *Studies in Latin literature and Roman history IV*, Brussels.
Dickey, E. (2002) *Latin forms of address*: *from Plautus to Apuleius*, Oxford.
Dickey, E. and Chahoud, A. (eds) (2010) *Colloquial and Literary Latin*, Cambridge.
Diggle, J. (1970) *Euripides*: Phaethon, Cambridge.
Diggle, J. (1980) "Notes on Ovid's *Tristia*, Books I-II", *CQ* 30, 401-419.
Dirichlet, G. L. (1914) *De ueterum macarismis* (*Religionsgeschichtliche Versuche und Vorarbeiten* 14,4), Giessen.
Dissen, L. (1835) *Albii Tibulli carmina ex recensione Car. Lachmanni passim Mutata*, Göttingen.
Dodds, E. R. (1960) *Euripides*: Bacchae, ed. 2, Oxford.
Doncieux, D. (1888) "Sur la personnalité de Lygdamus", *RPh* 12, 129-134.
Dronke, P. (2003) "Alcune osservazioni sulle poésie di Sulpicia", *Giornate filologiche Francesco Della Corte* 3, 81-99.
Dunn, F. M. and Cole, T. (eds) (1992) *Beginnings in Classical literature. Yale Classical Studies XXIX*, Cambridge.

Du Quesnay, I. M. (2012) "Three problems in poem 66", in I. M. Du Quesnay and A. Woodman (eds), 153-183.
Du Quesnay, I. M. and A. Woodman (eds) (2012) *Catullus*: *Poems, books, readers*, Cambridge.
Du Quesnay, I. M. (2017) "Contextualising Catullus: A re-examination of 66.1-14", in A. Woodman and J. Wisse (eds), 13-42.
Duret, L. (1983) "Dans l'ombre des plus grands: poètes et prosateurs mal connus de l'époque augustéenne, in *ANRW* II 30.3.1447-1560.
Ehrengrüber, S. (1889-1899) *De carmine panegyrico Messalae Ps. Tibulliano*. Prog. Kremsmüster I 1889; II 1890; III 1891; IV 1892; V 1894; VI 1895; VII 1896; VIII 1897; IX 1898; X 1899.
Ehrwald, R. (1889) *Ad historiam carminum Ovidianorum recensionemque symbolae*, Gotha.
Ehrwald, R. (1901) "Zu Lygdamus c.I", *Philologus* 1, 572-578.
Eisenhut, W. (1973) *Virtus Romana*, Munich.
Eisenhut, W. (1977) "Die Autorschaft der Elegie 3.19 im Corpus Tibullianum", *Hermes* 105, 209-223.
Eisenhut, W. (ed.) (1970) *Antike Lyrik*, Darmstadt.
Elder, T. P. (1966) "Catullus I, his poetic creed and Nepos", *HSCP* 71, 143-149.
Enk, P. J. (1911) *Ad Propertii carmina commentarius criticus*, Zutphen.
Erath, W. (1971) *Die Dichtung des Lygdamus*, Inaugural Dissertation, Erlangen.
Ernout, A. (1947) "B. Axelson. *Unpoetische Wörter*", *RPh* 21, 55-70.
Evans, R. (2003) "Containment and corruption: the discourse of Flavian empire", in J. Boyle and W. J. Dominik (eds), 255-276.
Fabre-Serris, J (2009) "Sulpicia: An/other female voice in Ovid's *Heroides*: A new reading of *Heroides* 4 and 15", *Helios* 36, 149-173.
Fain, G. L. (2008) *Writing epigrams*: *The art of composition in Catullus*, Brussels.
Fantham, E. (1998) *Ovid: Fasti, Book 4*, Cambridge.
Fantham, E. (2019) *Senenca's* Troades, Princeton.
Fatucchi, A. (1976) 'Le ferie aretine di Sulpicia (Nota topografica)', *Orpheus* 23, 145-160.
Fedeli, P. (1965) *Properzio: elegie: libro IV*, Bari.
Fedeli, P. (1980) *Sesto Properzio: il primo libro delle elegie*, Florence.
Fedeli, P. (1985) *Properzio: il libro terzo delle elegie*, Bari.
Fedeli, P. (2005) *Properzio: elegie libro II*, Cambridge (= Fedeli).
Feddern, S. (2013) *Die Suasorien des älteren Seneca: Einleitung, Text und Kommentar*, Berlin - Boston.

Feeney, D. (1992) "*Si licet et fas est*: Ovid's *Fasti* and the problem of free speech under the Principate", in A. Powell (ed.) 1-25, London [repr. in P. E. Knox (ed.) (2006) 464-488].
Feeney, D. (2012) "Representation and the materiality of the book in the polymetrics", in I. M. Du Quesnay and A. Woodman (eds), 29-47.
Fitch, J. G. (1987) *Seneca's* Hercules Furens, Ithaca NY.
Flaschenriem, B. (1999) "Sulpicia and the rhetoric of disclosure", *CP* 94, 36-54.
Fontenrose, J. E. (1940) "Apollo and the sun-god in Ovid", *AJP* 61, 429-444.
Forbes, R. J. (1964) *Studies in ancient technology, vol. 4*, ed. 2, Leiden.
Fordyce, C. J. (1961) *Catullus*, Oxford (= Fordyce).
Fowler, D. (1989) "First thoughts on closure: Problems and prospects, *MD* 22, 75-122.
Fowler, D. (2002) *Lucretius on atomic motion: A commentary on De rerum natura 2.1-332*, Oxford.
Fraenkel, E. (1917) "Das Geschlecht von *dies*", *Glotta* 8, 24-69.
Fraenkel, E. and Fränkel, H. (eds) (1931) *Festschrift Richard Reitzenstein, zum 2 April 1931 dargebracht*, Leipzig – Berlin.
Fraenkel, E. (1950) *Aeschylus Agamemnon*, 2 vols, Oxford.
Frangoulidis, S. and Harrison, S. J. (eds) (2018) *Life, Love and Death in Latin Poetry* Studies in Honor of Theodore Papanghelis, Trends in Classics 61, Berlin – Boston.
Fraser, P. M. and Matthews, E. (1987-) *A lexicon of Greek personal names*, Oxford.
Fredericks, S. C. (1976) "A poetic experiment in the Garland of Sulpicia (*Corpus Tibullianum* 3.10)", *Latomus* 35, 761-782.
Fuchs, H. (1947) "Besprechung L. Alfonsi *Albio Tibullo e gli autori del Corpus Tibullianum*", *Erasmus* 1, 340-343.
Fulkerson, L. (2017) *A literary commentary on the elegies of the Appendix Tibulliana*, Oxford.
Gagé, J. (1963) *Matronalia*: *Essai sur les devotions et les organisations culturelles des femmes dans l'ancienne Rome*, Brussels.
Gale, M. (2012) "Putting on the yoke of necessity: myth, intertextuality and moral agency in Catullus 68", in I. M. Du Quesnay and A. Woodman (eds), 184-211.
Giangrande, G. (1967) "Sympotic literature and epigram", in *L'Épigramme grecque*: *Fondation Hardt Entretiens* 14, 97-134, Geneva.
Giangrande, G. (1990) "Symptoms of love in Theocritus and Ovid", *Analecta Malacitana* 13.1, 121-123.
Gibson, R. K. (2003) *Ovid*: *Ars Amatoria book 3*, Cambridge.

Gold, B. K. (ed.) (2012) *A Companion to Roman Love Elegy*, Malden, MA.
Gransden, K. W. (1991) *Virgil: Aeneid book XI*, Cambridge.
Grassmann, V. (1966) *Die erotische Epoden des Horaz. Literarischer Hintergrund und sprachliche Tradition* (= Zetemata 39), Munich.
Green, R. P. H. (1991) *The Works of Ausonius*. Oxford.
Greene, E. (ed.) (2005) *Women poets in ancient Greece and Rome*, Norman.
Griffin, J. (1976) "Augustan poetry and the life of luxury", *JRS* 66, 87-105.
Griffin, J. (1985) *Latin poets and Roman life*, London.
Gruppe, O. F. (1838) *Die römische Elegie, I*, Leipzig.
Gow, A. S. F. (1952) *Theocritus vols I and II*. ed. 2, Cambridge. (= Gow).
Günther, H-C. (ed.) (2006) *Brill's Companion to Propertius*, Leiden.
Günther, H-C. (ed.) (2018) *A Short Companion to Tibullus* (= *Classica et Mediaevalia*, Band 22), 135-160, Nordhausen.
Gutzwiller, K. (2012) "Catullus and the *Garland* of Meleager", in I. M. Du Quesnay and Woodman (eds), 79-111.
Haase, F. (1837) Review of Dissen (1835), *Jahrbuch für wissenschafliche Kritik, herausgegeben von der Societät für wissenschafliche Kritik zu Berlin*, 2-5, Berlin.
Hagen, B. (1954) *Stil und Abfassungszeit der Lygdamusgedichte*, Diss. Hamburg.
Hall, J. B. (1995) *Ovidius: Tristia*, Stuttgart – Leipzig.
Hall, J. B. (2007) *P. Papinius Statius: Thebaid and Achilleid*, 2 vols, Newcastle.
Halla-aho, H. (2009) *The non-literary Latin letters: A study of their syntax and pragmatics*, Helsinki.
Hallett, J. P. (1989) "Women as *Same* and *Other* in Classical Roman elite", *Helios* 19, 59-78.
Hallett, J. P. (1992) "Heeding our native informants: The uses of Latin literary texts in recovering elite Roman attitudes towards age, gender and social status", *EMC* 36, 333-355.
Hallet, J. P. (2002a) "The eleven elegies of the Augustan poet Sulpicia" in L. J. Churchill, P. R. Brown, and J. E. Jeffrey (eds), vol. I, 45-65, New York.
Hallet, J. P. (2002b) "Sulpicia and the Valerii: family ties and poetic unity", in B. Amden, P. Flensted-Jansen, T. H. Nielsen, A. Schwartz, C. G. Tortzen (eds), 141-149.
Hallet, J. P. and Skinner, M. B. (eds) *Roman sexualities*, Princeton.

Hammer, J. (1925) *Prolegomena to an edition of the Panegyricus Messallae*, New York.
Hanslik, R. (1952) "Der Dichterkreis des Messalla", *Anzeiger d. Öst Akad. D. Wiss. Phil. Hist. Kl.* 89, 22-38.
Hanslik, R. (1955) *Valerius Messalla Corvinus*, *RE* 15.2, 131-157.
Harder, M. A., Regtuit, R. F. and Wakker, G. C. (eds) (1993) *Hellenistica Groningana* I: *Callimachus*, Groningen.
Harder, M. A., Regtuit, R. F. and Wakker, G. C. (eds) (2009) *Nature and science in Hellenistic poetry*, *Colloquia Hellenistica* 8, Leuven.
Harder, M. A. (2012) *Callimachus: Aetia*, 2 vols, Oxford.
Hardie, A. (2003) "The *Georgics*, the mysteries and the Muses at Rome", *PCPS* 48, 175-208.
Hardie, A. (2010) "An Augustan hymn to the Muses: Horace *Odes* 3.4", *PLLS* 14, 191-318.
Hardie, P. R. (1986) *Virgil's* Aeneid: *Cosmos and imperium*, Oxford.
Hardie, P. R. (1989) "Flavian epicists on Virgil's epic technique", *Ramus* 18, 3-12.
Hardie, P. R. (1992) "Augustan Poets and the Mutability of Rome", in A. Powell (ed.), 59-82.
Hardie, P. R. (1994) *Virgil. Aeneid. book IX*, Cambridge.
Hardie, P. R. (2009) *Lucretian receptions: History, the sublime, knowledge*, Cambridge.
Hardie, P. R. (2012a) *Rumour and Renown: Representations of* Fama *in Western literature*, Cambridge.
Hardie, P. R. (2012b) "Virgil's Catullan plots", in I. M. Du Quesnay and A. Woodman (eds), 212-238.
Hardie, P. R. (2015) *Ovidio Metamorfosi*, vol. vi, libri xiii-xv, Roma.
Harich-Schwarzbauer, H. (ed.) (2015) *Weben und Gewebe in der Antike / Texts and Textiles in the Ancient World*, Oxford and Philadelphia.
Harrison, S. J. (2007) *Generic enrichment in Vergil and Horace*, Oxford.
Harrison, S. J. (2017) *Horace: Odes book 2*, Cambridge.
Harrison, S. J. (ed.) (1995) *Homage to Horace: A bi-millenary celebration*, Oxford.
Hartung, H. (1880) *De panegyrico ad Messallam pseudo-Tibulliano*, Diss. Inaug. Halle.
Haupt, M. (1871) "Varia LXII", *Hermes* 5.502-503 = *Opuscula* 3 (Leipzig 1876), 502-504.
Hauser, E. (2016) "*Optima tu proprii nominis auctor*: The semantics of female authorship in ancient Rome, from Sulpicia to Proba", *EuGeStA* 151-186.

Hellegouarc'h, J. (1989) "*Parce precor* ... ou Tibulle et la prière: étude stylistique", *ICS* 14, 49-68.
Helzle, M. (1989) *Publii Ovidii Nasonis Epistularum ex Ponto Liber IV. A commentary on poems 1-7 and 16*, Hildesheim – Zurich– New York.
Hermann, L. (1951) *L' âge d'argent doré*, Paris.
Herter, H. (1957) "Dirne", in *RAC* iii 1154-1213.
Heyne, C. G. (1777) *Albii Tibulli carmina, libri tres cum libro quarto Sulpiciae et Aliorum*, ed. IV, Leipzig.
Heyne, C. G. and Wunderlich, E. C. F. (1817) *Albii Tibulli carmina*, Leizig. repr. 1975 Hildesheim.
Heyworth, S. J. (1994) "Some allusions to Callimachus in Latin poetry", *MD* 33, 51-79.
Heyworth, S. J. (1995) "Dividing Poems", in O. Pecere and M.D. Reeve (eds.), 117-48.
Heyworth, S. J. (2007a) *Sexti Properti Elegos, critico aparatu instruxit et edidit*, Oxford.
Heyworth, S. J. (2007b) *Cynthia: a companion to the text of Propertius*, Oxford.
Heyworth, S. J. and Morwood, J. H. W. (2011) *A commentary on Propertius book 3*, Oxford.
Heyworth, S. J. (2018) "Place and Meaning in Tibullus, Lygdamus and Sulpicia" in S. Frangoulidis and S. Harrison (eds), 69-84.
Heyworth, S. J. (2019) *Ovid* Fasti *book III*, Cambridge.
Hill, T. (2004) *Ambitiusa mors: Suicide and self in Roman thought and literature*, New York.
Hinds, S. (1983) "*Carmina digna*. Gallus *P Qasr Ibrim* Metamorphosed", *PCPS* 31, 13-32.
Hinds, S. (1987a) "The poetess and the reader: further steps towards Sulpicia", *Hermathena* 143, 29-46.
Hinds, S. (1987b) *The metamorphosis of Persephone: Ovid and the self-conscious Muse*, Cambridge.
Hinds, S. (1998) *Allusion and intertext: Dynamics of appropriation in Roman Poetry*, Cambridge.
Hinds, S. (2006) "Varro, Venus and the *vates*: towards the limits of etymologising", *Dictynna* (on line) 3. URL: http://journals.openedition.org/dictynna/206
Hofmann, J. B. (1926) *Lateinische Umgangssprache*, Heidelberg.
Hollis, A. S. (1970) *Ovid. Metamorphoses Book VIII*, Oxford.
Hollis, A. S. (1977) *Ovid. Ars Amatoria Book I*, Oxford.
Hollis, A. S. (1990) *Callimachus: Hecale,* Oxford.
Hollis, A. S. (2007) *Fragments of Roman poetry*, Oxford. (= Hollis).

Holzberg, N. (1990) *Die römische Liebeselegie: Eine Einfürung*, Darmstadt.
Holzberg, N. (1998) "Four poets and a poetess or a portrait of the poet as a young man? Thoughts on book 3 of the *Corpus Tibullianum*", *CJ* 94, 169-191.
Holzberg, N. (2004) "Impersonating Young Virgil: The author of the *Catalepton* and his *libellus*", *MD* 52, 29-40.
Holzenthal, E. (1967) *Das Krankheitsmotiv in der römischen Elegie*, Diss Cologne.
Hooper, R. W. (1975) *A stylistic investigation into the third and fourth books of the Corpus Tibullianum*, Diss., Yale.
Hope, V. M. and Huskinson, J. (eds) (2011) *Memory and Mourning: Studies on Roman death*, Oxford.
Hopkinson, N. (1989) *A Hellenistic anthology*, Cambridge.
Horsfall, N. M. (1990) "Virgil and the illusory footnote", *PLLS* 6, 49-63.
Horsfall, N. M. (1999) *Virgil* Aeneid 7: *A commentary*, Leiden.
Houghton, L. B. T. (2011) "Death ritual and burial practice in the Latin love elegists", in V. M. Hope and J. Huskinson (eds), 61-77.
Housman, A. E. (1937) *M. Manilii Astronomicon libri I-V.* ed. 2, 5 vols, Cambridge.
Hubbard, T. K. (1983) "The Catullan *libelli*", *Philologus* 127, 221-222.
Hubbard, T. K. (2004) "The invention of Sulpicia", *CJ* 100, 177-194.
Hunter, R. L. (2006) *The Shadow of Callimachus*, Cambridge.
Hutchinson, G. O. (2006) *Propertius: elegies Book IV*, Cambridge.
Hutchinson, G. O. (2012) "Booking lovers: desire and design in Catullus", in I. M. Du Quesnay and A. Woodman (eds), 48-78.
Ingleheart, J. (2010) *A commentary on Ovid* Tristia, *Book 2*, Oxford.
Jäger, K. (1967) *Zweigliedrige Gedichte und Gedichtspaare bei Properz und in Ovids Amores*, Diss. Tübingen.
Jeffreys, R. (1994) "Corpus Tibullianum 3.7 (4.1).142", *Phoenix* 48, 68-72.
Jocelyn, H. D. (1967) *The tragedies of Ennius*, Cambridge.
Jordan, H. (1860) *M. Catonis praetor librum de re rustica quae extant*, Leipzig.
Kaibel, G. (1878) *Epigrammata Graeca ex lapidibus conlecta*, Berlin.
Kaster, R. A. (2005) *Emotion, restraint and community in ancient Rome*, Oxford.
Kayachev, B. (2016a) *Allusion and allegory: Studies in the Ciris*, Berlin – Boston.
Kayachev, B. (2016b) "Catalepton 9", *CQ* 66, 180-204.

Kayachev, B. (2020) "[Tibullus] 3.7.175: an emendation", *CQ* 70 (2020), online pre-print.
Keith, A. M. (1997) *"Tandem venit amor*: a Roman woman speaks of love", in J. P. Hallet and M. B. Skinner (eds), *Roman sexualities,* 295-311, Princeton.
Keith, A. M. (ed.) (2011) *Latin Elegy and Hellenistic Epigram: a tale of two genres at Rome*, Newcastle.
Kennedy, D. (1982) "Gallus and the *Culex*", *CQ* 32, 371-389.
Kennedy, G. (1989) "Hellenistic literary and philosophical scholarship", in G. Kennedy (ed.), 200-214.
Kennedy G. (ed.) (1989) *The Cambridge history of literary criticism, vol. I,* Cambridge.
Kenney, E. J. (1959) "Notes on Ovid: II", *CQ* 9, 240-260.
Kenney, E. J. (1971) *Lucretius: De Rerum Natura book III,* Cambridge.
Kenney, E. J. (1982) "Books and readers in the Roman world", in *CHCL* II 3-32, Cambridge.
Kenney, E. J. (1990) *Apuleius Cupid and Psyche*, Cambridge.
Kenney, E. J. (1996) *Ovid* Heroides *XVI-XXI*, Cambridge.
Kershaw, A. (1980) "Emendation and usage: two readings of Propertius", *CPh* 75, 71-72.
Kershaw, A. (1983) "*A!* and the elegists: more observations", *CPh* 78, 232-233.
Kidd, I. G. (1972) *Posidonius: Vol. I The Fragments*, Cambridge.
Kleingünther, A. (1933) ΠΡΩΤΟΣ ΕΥΡΕΤΗΣ: *Untersuchungen zur Geschichte einer Fragestellung (Philologus Suppl.* 26.1), Leipzig.
Kneppers, H. (1904) *De Lygdami carminibus*, Jena.
Knoche, U. (1956) "Tibulls früheste Liebeselegie? (Tibull III 19)", in *Navicula Chiloniensis. Studia philologica Felici Jacoby professori Chiloniensi emerito octogenario oblata*, Leiden; repr. (1970) in W. Eisenhut (ed.) 340-358, Darmstadt.
Knox, P. (1995) *Ovid* Heroides: *Selected epistles*, Cambridge.
Knox, P. (2006) "Propertius and the neoterics", in H-C. Günther (ed.), 127-146.
Knox, P. (2018) "The Corpus Tibullianum", in H-C Günther (ed.), 135-160.
Knox, P. (ed.) (2006) *Oxford Readingss in Classical Studies,* Oxford.
Kost, K. (1971) *Musaios: Hero und Leander (= Abhandlungen zur Kunst-, Musik-und Literaturwissenschaft* 88), Bonn.
Krafft, P. and Tscheidel, H. J. (eds) (1986) *Concentus exachordus*, Regensburg.

Krevans, N. (1993) "Fighting against Antimachus: The *Lyde* and the *Aetia* Reconsidered", in M. A. Harder, R. F. Regtuit and G. C. Wakker (eds), 149-160.
Kroll, W. (1924) *Studien zum Verständnis der römischen Literatur*, Stuttgart.
Kroll (1959) *C. Valerius Catullus*, ed. 3, Stuttgart.
Kyriakidis, S. (1998) *Narrative structure and poetics in the Aeneid: The frame of book 6*, Bari.
Kyriakidis, S. (2002) "*Georgics* 4.559-566. The Vergilian sphragis" *Kleos* 7, 275-285.
Kyriakidis, S. (2013) "The poet's afterlife: Ovid between epic and elegy", in Th. Papanghelis, S. J. Harrison, S. Frangoulidis (eds), 351-366.
Kyriakidis, S. (2016) "The universe as audience: Manilius' poetic ambitions", in S. Kyriakidis (ed.), 111-143.
Kyriakidis, S. (ed.) (2016) Libera fama: *an endless journey*, Pierides VI, Newcastle.
Kyriakidis, S. and De Martino, F. (eds) (2004) *Middles in Latin Poetry*, Bari.
Lachmann, K. (1829) *Albii Tibulli libri quattuor*, Berlin.
Laguna, G. (1992) *Estacio: Silvas III*, Madrid.
Lammert, F. (1950) "Das Kriegswesen im Panegyricus auf Messalla, Vers 82-105", *Symbolae Osloenses* 28, 44-65.
La Penna, A. (1951) "Note sul linguaggio erotico dell' elegia Latina", *Maia* 4, 187-209.
La Penna, A. (1991) "Dal *Panegyricus Messallae* alla *Laus Pisonis*. Transformazione di modelli etici", in M. Pani (ed.), 167-188.
La Penna, A. (1995) "Towards a history of the poetic catalogue of philosophical themes", in S. J. Harrison (ed.), 314-328.
Latte, K. (1960) *Römische Religionsgeschicte = Handbuch der Altertumswissenschaft* 5, Munich.
Lattimore, R. (1942) *Themes in Greek and Latin epitaphs*, Urbana.
Lausberg, H. (1995) *Handbook of literary rhetoric: A foundation for literary study*, trnsl. by A. Jansen, M. T. Bliss and D. F. Orton (D. F. Orton and R. D. Anderson (eds), Leiden – Boston – Cologne.
Lee, A. G. (1958-1959) "The date of Lygdamus and his relationship to Ovidius", *PCPS* 5, 15-23.
Lee, A. G. (1963) "On Tibullus III 19 (IV 13)", *PCPS* 9, 4-10.
Lee, A. G. (1974) "Tibulliana", *PCPS* 20, 53-57.
Lee, A. G. (1990^3) *Tibullus: Elegies. Introduction, text, translation and notes*, Leeds.

Lefèvre, E. (ed.) (1975) *Monumentum Chiloniense: Studien zur augusteischen Zeit: Kieler Festschrift für E. Burck*, Amsterdam.
Lenz, F. W. (1932) "Ein Liebeselegie Tibulls (*IV 13*) ?" *SIFC* 10, 125-145; repr. (1970) in W. Eisenhut (ed.), 321-339.
Leo, F. (1912) *Plautinische Forschungen. Zur Kritik und Geschichte der Komödie*, Berlin.
Leonotti, E. (1990) "Semantica di *durus* in Tibullo", *Prometheus* 16, 22-47.
Levine, P. (1969) "Catullus c. 1. A playful dedication", *CSCA* 2, 201.
Lieberg, G. (1962) Puella Divina: *Die Gestalt der göttlichen Geliebten bei Catull im Zusammenhang der antiken Dichtung*, Amsterdam.
Lieberg, G. (1980) "Le Muse in Tibullo e nel *Corpus Tibullianum*", *Prometheus* 6, 29-55, 138-152.
Lightfoot, J. L. (1999) *Parthenius of Nicaea*, Oxford.
Lindsay, W. M. (1903) *Nonii Marcelli de Compendiosa Doctrina*, 3 vols., Leipzig.
Lindsay, W. M. (1913) *Sexti Pompei Festi: De uerborum significatu quae supersunt cum Pauli epitome*, Oxford.
Löfstedt, E. (1911) *Philologischer Kommentar zur Peregrinatio Aetheriae*, Uppsala.
Löfstedt, E. (1942) *Syntactica*, 2 vols, Lund.
Lowe, N. J. (1988) "Sulpicia's syntax", *CQ* 38, 193-205.
Luck, G. (1959) *The Latin love elegy*, London.
Luck, G. (1967) *P. Ovidius Naso* Tristia, *vol. I*, Heidelberg.
Luck, G. (1977) *P. Ovidius Naso* Tristia, *vol. II*, Heidelberg.
Luck, G. (1983) "Lavinia's blush: Virgil *Aeneid* 12.64-70", *Greece and Rome* 30, 55-64.
Luck, G. (1988) *Albii Tibulli aliorumque carmina*, Stuttgart.
Luck, G. (1994) Review of Tränkle (1990) *Göttingische Gelehrte Anzeigen* 246, 70-86.
Lyne, R. O. A. M. (1979) "*Servitium amoris*", *CQ* 29, 117-130.
Lyne, R. O. A. M. (1980) *The Latin love poets from Catullus to Horace*, Oxford.
Lyne, R. O. A. M. (1995) *Horace: Behind the public poetry*, New Haven, CT.
Lyne, R. O. A. M. (2007) *Collected papers on Latin poetry*, Oxford.
Mass, E. (1895) *Orpheus*, Munich.
Maltby, R. (1999a) "Tibullus and the language of Latin elegy", in J. N. Adams and R. Mayer (eds), 377-398.
Maltby, R. (1999b) "Technical language in Tibullus", *Emerita* 67, 231-249.

Maltby, R. (2002) *Tibullus elegies*, Cambridge.
Maltby, R. (2004) "The wheel of Fortune, Nemesis and the central poems of Tibullus I and II", in S. Kyriakidis and F. De Martino (eds), 103-122.
Maltby, R. (2010) "The unity of Corpus Tibullianum Book 3: some stylistic and metrical considerations", *Papers of the Langford Latin Seminar* 14, 319-340.
Maltby, R. (2011) "The influence of Hellenistic epigram on Tibullus", in A. Keith (ed.). 87-98.
Maltby, R. (2016) "Analytic and synthetic forms of the comparative and superlative from early to late Latin", in J. N. Adams and N. Vincent (eds), 340-366.
Maltby, R. (2018) "The language, style and metre of Tibullus", in H-C Günther (ed.), 111-134.
Mankin, D. (1995) *Horace: Epodes*, Cambridge.
Marouzeau, J. (1949) *L'ordre des mots dans la phrase latine* III, Paris.
Marx, F. (1904-1905) *C. Lucili carminum reliquiae*, 2 vols, Leipzig.
Massimilla, G. (2010) *Callimacho: Aetia libro terzo e quarto*, Rome.
Matthews, V. J. (1996) *Antimachus of Clophon*, Leiden.
Mayer, R. (1994) *Horace: Epistles book 1*, Cambridge.
Mayer, R. (2012) *Horace: Odes book 1*, Cambridge
Mayor, J. (1886-1889) *Thirteen Satires of Juvenal*, ed. 4, London.
McDonnell, M. (2006) *Roman manliness*: Virtus *and the Roman Republic,* Cambridge.
McEnerney, J. I. (1978) "*Panegyricus Messallae* 36, a suggested emendation", *L' Antiquite Classique* 47.1, 188-189.
McGann, M. J. (1970) "The date of Tibullus' death", *Latomus* 29, 774-780.
McKeown, J. C. (1987) *Ovid: Amores. Vol. I. Text and prolegomena*, Liverpool.
McKeown, J. C. (1989) *Ovid: Amores. Vol. II. A commentary on Book One*, Leeds.
McKeown, J. C. (1998) *Ovid: Amores. Vol. III. A commentary on Book Two*, Leeds. (= McKeown).
Merriam, C. U. (2005) "Sulpicia and the art of literary allusion: [Tibullus] 3.13", in E. Greene (ed.), 158-168.
Michalopoulos, A. (2001) *Ancient etymologies in Ovid's Metamorphoses: A commented Lexicon*, Leeds.
Michalopoulos, A. (2006) *Ovid: Heroides 16 and 17: introduction text and Commentary*, Cambridge.

Michalopoulos, A. (2016) "*famaque cum domino fugit ab urbe* suo: aspects of *fama* in Ovid's exile poetry", in S. Kyriakidis (ed.), 94-110.
Miguet, T. (1980) "Une élégie plus virgilienne que Virgile dans l'*Appendix Virgiliana*", in A. Thill (ed.), 245-260.
Miller, J. I. (1969) *The spice trade of the Roman Empire*, Oxford.
Milnor, K. (2002) "Sulpicia's (corpo)reality: Elegy, authorship and the body in [Tib.] 3.13", *CA* 21, 259-282.
Mills, D. H. (1974) "Tibullus and Phaeacia: a reinterpretation of Tib. 1.3", *CJ* 69, 226-233.
Miralles Maldonado, J. C. (1990) "La lengua de Sulpicia: *Corpus Tibullianum* 4.7-12", *Habis* 21, 101-120.
Momigliano, A. (1950) "*Panegyricus Messallae* and *Panegyricus Vespasiani*. Two references to Britain", *JRS* 40, 39-42.
Monteil, P. (1964) *Beau et laid en Latin*, Paris.
Morel, W. (ed.) (1927) *Fragmenta poetarum latinorum epicorum et lyricorum, praeter Ennium et Lucilium*, ed. 2, Stuttgart.
Morgan, J. D. (1992) "The origin of Molorc(h)us", *CQ* 42, 533-538.
Moritz, L. (1958) *Grain mills and flour in classical antiquity*, Oxford.
Muecke, F. (1993) *Horace: Satires II*, Warminster.
Müller, R. (1952) *Motivkatalog der römischen Elegie: Eine Untersuchung zur Poetik der Römer*, Zurich.
Mulder, H. M. (1954) *P. Papinii Statii Thebaidos liber secundus commentario exegetico aestheticoque instructus*, Groningen.
Murgatroyd, P. (1975) "*Militia amoris* and the Roman elegists", *Latomus* 34, 59-79.
Murgatroyd, P. (1980) *Tibullus I: A commentary on the first book of the elegies of Albius Tibullus*, Pietermaritzburg.
Murgatroyd, P. (1981) "*Servitium amoris* and the Roman elegists", *Latomus* 40, 589-606.
Murgatroyd, P. (1984) "Amatory hunting fishing and fowling", *Latomus* 43, 362-368.
Murgatroyd, P. (1994) *Tibullus: Elegies II*, Oxford.
Mutschler, F. H. (1985) *Die poetische Kunst Tibulls. Studien zur klassischen Philolgie* 18, Franfurt a.M.
Myers K.S. (1996) "The poet and the procuress: The *lena* in Latin love elegy", *JRS* 86, 1-21.
Myers, K. S. (2012) "Catullan contexts in Ovid's *Metamorphoses*", in I. M. Du Quesnay and A. Woodman (eds), 239-254.
Mynors, R. A. B. (1990) *Virgil: Georgics*, Oxford. (= Mynors).
Nelis, D. P. (2012) "Callimachus in Verona: Catullus and Alexandrian poetry", in I. M. Du Quesnay and A. Woodman (eds), 1-28.

Némethy, G. (1905) *Albii Tibulli carmina*, Budapest. (= Némethy).
Neumeister, K. (1983) *Die Überwindung der elegischen Liebe bei Properz (Buch I-III)*. *Studien zur Klassischen Philologie* 9, Frankfurt a.M. – Bern.
Newlands, C. E. (1980) *Criticism of wealth in Tibullus, Propertius and Ovid's Amores*, Diss. Columbia.
Nielson, H. S. (1997) "Interpreting epithets in Roman epitaphs", in B. Rawson and P. Weaver (eds), 169-204
Nisbet, R. G. M., and Hubbard M. (1970) *A commentary on Horace: Odes, Book I*, Oxford.
Nisbet, R. G. M., and Hubbard M. (1978) *A commentary on Horace: Odes, Book II*, Oxford.
Nisbet, R. G. M., and Rudd, N. (2004) *A commentary on Horace: Odes, Book III*, Oxford.
Norden, E. (1913) *Agnostos Theos. Untersuchungen zur Formengeschichte religiöser Rede*, Leipzig – Berlin.
Norden, E. (1927) *P. Vergilius Maro: Aeneis Buch VI*, ed. 3, Berlin.
Nordera, R. (1969) "I virgilianismi in Valerio Flacco", in A. Traina et al. (eds), *Contributi à tre poeti latini*, 1-92.
Oakley, S. P. (1997) *A Commentary on Livy Books VI-X*, Oxford.
Obbink, D. (ed.) (1995) *Philodemus and Poetry: Poetic theory and practice in Lucretius, Philodemus and Horace*, Oxford.
Oebeke, Fr. (1831) "De uero elegiarum auctore quae tertio Tibulli libro uulgo continentur", in *Jaresbericht über das Königl. Gymn. Zu Aachen für das Schuljahr von Michaelis* iii-xv, Aachen.
Otto, A (1890) *Die Sprichwörter und sprichwörtlichen Redensarten der Römer*, Leipzig; with *Nachträge* (ed.) R. Hässler (1968), Darmstadt (= Otto).
Pani, M. (ed.) (1991) *Continuità e trasformazione tra repubblica e principato. Istituzioni, politica, società*, Bari.
Paoli, U. E. (1953) *Die Geschichte der Neaira*, Bern.
Papanghelis, Th., Harrison, S. J. and Frangoulidis, S. (eds) (2013) *Generic Interfaces in Latin Literature*, Trends in Classics 20, Berlin – Boston.
Papke, R. (1986) "*Panegyricus Messallae* und *Catalepton* 9: Form und gegenseitige Bezug", in P. Krafft and H. J.Tscheidel (eds), 123-168, Regensburg.
Parca, M. (1986) "The position of Lygdamus in Augustan poetry", in C. Deroux (ed.), 461-474.
Parker, H. N. (1994) "Sulpicia, the *auctor de Sulpicia*, and the authorship of 3.9 and 3.11", *Helios* 21, 39-62.
Parsons, P. J. (1977) "Callimachus: *Victoria Berenices*", *ZPE* 25, 1-50.

Paschalis, M. (1997) *Virgil's* Aeneid: *Semantic relations and proper names*, Oxford.
Pease, A. S. (1935) *Publi Vergili Maronis Aeneidos liber quartus*, Cambridge, Mass.
Pease, A. S. (1955) *M. Tulli Ciceronis De natura deorum*, Cambridge, Mass.
Pecere, O. and Reeve, M.D. (eds) (1995) *Formative Stages of Classical Traditions: Latin texts from Antiquity to the Renaissance*, Spoleto.
Peirano, Irene (2012) *The rhetoric of the Roman fake. Latin pseudepigrapha in context*, Cambridge.
Peraki-Kyriakidou, E. (2010) "Ο Διόνυσος στην υπηρεσία τους βουκολιικής ποιητικής του Βιργιλίου", in S. Tsitsirides (ed.), 555-579.
Peraki-Kyriakidou, E. (2016) "The Ovidian Leuconoe: Vision, Speech and Narration", in S. Kyriakidis (ed.), 71-93.
Perotti, P. A. (1989) "L'infinito perfetto in Tibullo e nel *Corpus Tibullianum*", *Orpheus* 10, 141-149.
Pfeiffer, R. (1949 and 1953) *Callimachus Vols I and II*, Oxford. (= Pf.)
Philip, J. A. (1966) *Pythagoras and early Pythagoreanism* (*Phoenix* Suppl. 7), Toronto.
Pichon, R. (1902) *De sermone amatorio apud latinos elegiarum scriptores*, Diss. Paris. 75-303; repr. 1966 *Index uerborum amatorium*, Hildesheim. (= Pichon).
Pieri, M.-P. (1982) "L'omaggio del libro in Ligdamo", *QILL* 4, 57-59.
Pinkster, H. (2015) *The Oxford Latin syntax. Vol. 1. The simple clause*, Oxford.
Pinotti, P. (1988) *P. Ovidio Nasone*: *Remedia Amoris*, Bologna.
Plantinga, M. (2007) "Hospitality and rhetoric: The Circe episode in Apollonius Rhodius' *Argonautica*", *CQ* 57, 543-564.
Platnauer, M. (1951) *Latin elegiac verse. A study of the metrical usages of Tibullus, Propertius & Ovid*, Cambridge. (= Platnauer).
Possanza, D. M. (1994) "*Cornua* and *frontes* in [Tibullus] 3.1.13", *CQ* 44, 281-282.
Postgate, J. P. (1905 / 1915[2]) *Tibulli aliorumque carminum libri tres*, Oxford. (= Postgate).
Postgate, J. P. (1914) "*Neaera* as a common name", *CQ* 8, 121-122.
Postgate, J. P. (1922[2]) *Selections from Tibullus and others*, London.
Powell, A. (ed.) (1992) *Roman Poetry and Propaganda in the Age of Augustus*, Bristol.
Powell, J. G. F. (1988) *Cicero*: *Cato maior de senectute*, Cambridge.
Powell, J. G. F. (2010) "Horace, Scythia and the East", *PLLS* 14, 137-190.
Powell, J. U. (1925) *Collectanea Alexandrina*, Oxford.

Privitera, G. A. (1970) *Dionysus in Omero e nella poesia greca arcaica*, Rome.
Probst, S., and Probst, V. (1992) "Frauendichtung in Rom: die Elegien der Sulpicia", *Der altsprachliche Unterricht* 35, 19-36.
Quinn, K. (1973) *Catullus: The Poems*, ed. 2, London.
Race, W. H. (1982) *The classical priamel from Homer to Boethius*, Leiden.
Ramsby, T. R. (2007) *Textual permanence: Roman elegists and the epigraphic Tradition*, London.
Rawson, B. and Weaver, P. (eds) (1997) *The Roman family in Italy: status, sentiment, space*, Oxford.
Rawson, E. (1985) *Intellectual life in the late Roman Republic*, London.
Reinhold, M. (1970) *History of purple as a status symbol in antiquity*, Brussels.
Reitzenstein, E. (1931) "Zur Stiltheorie des Kallimachos", in E. Fraenkel and H. Fränkel (eds), 23-69.
Reynolds, J. (1982) *Aphrodisias and Rome: Documents from the excavation of the theatre at Aphordisias* (*Journal of Roman Studies* Monographs 1), London.
Reynolds, L. D. (ed.) (1983) *Texts and transmission: a survey of the Latin classics*, Oxford.
Ribbeck, O. (ed.) (1897) *Scaenicae Romanorum poesis fragmenta. Vol. I. Tragicorum romanorum fragmenta.* ed. 3, Leipzig.
Ribbeck, O. (1898) *Scaenicae Romanorum poesis fragmenta*: Vol. II, *Comicorum Romanorum praeter Plautum et Terentium fragmenta*, ed. 3, Leipzig.
Roberts, D. H., Dunn, F. M. and Fowler, D. (eds) (1997) *Classical closure: Reading the end in Greek and Latin literature*, Princeton.
Robinson, M. (2011) *A commentary on Ovid's* Fasti, *Book 2*, Oxford.
Roche, P. (ed.) (2011) *Pliny's praise: the Panegyricus in the Roman World*, Cambridge.
Roessel, D. (1990) "The significance of the name Cerinthus in the poems of Sulpicia", *TAPhA* 120, 243-50.
Roman, Luke (2014) *Poetic Autonomy in Ancient Rome*, Oxford.
Romano, A. J. (2011) "Callimachus and contemporary criticism", in B. Acosta-Hughes, L. Lehnus and S. Stephens (eds), 309-328.
Ross, D. O. (1969) *Style and tradition in Catullus*, Cambridge.
Ross, D. O. (1975) *Backgrounds to Augustan Poetry: Gallus, Elegy and Rome*, Cambridge.
Rossi, L. E. (1971) "I generi letterari e le loro leggi scritte e non scritte nelle letterature classiche", *BICS* 18, 69-94.

Rostagni, A. (1935) "La vita svetoniana di Tibullo e la costituzione del *Corpus Tibullianum*", *RF* 13, 20-51.
Rostagni, A. (1944) *Svetonio 'De Poetis' e biografi minori*, Turin.
Rostagni, A. (1959) "Il Panegirico di Messalla e i componimenti a Messalla dedicati nell' Appendice Virgiliana", *RAL* 14, 349-355.
Rouse, R. H., and Reeve, M. D. (1983) "Tibullus", in L. D. Reynolds (ed.), 420-425.
Rudd, N. (1989) *Horace: Epistles book 2 and Epistle to the Pisones (Ars Poetica)*, Cambridge.
Ruiz Sánchez, M. (1996) "Poetica y simbolo en el ciclo de Sulpicia (*Corpus Tibullianum* 3.8-12 y 3.13-18", *Helmantica* 47, 379-413.
Russell, D. A. and Wilson, N. G. (1981) *Menander Rhetor*, Oxford.
Salvatore, A. (1949) "De Laudibus Pisonis cum Panegyrico Messallae atque Calpurni Bucolicis comparatis", *RFC* 27, 177-190.
Sandbach, F. H. (1952) "Guilty men? – Lygdamus 5.7", *CR* 2, 6-7.
Santirocco, M. (1979) "Sulpicia reconsidered", *CJ* 74, 229-235.
Scaliger, J. J. (1577) *Castigationes in Catullum, Tibullum, Propertium*, Paris.
Scheidegger Lämmle, C. (2015) "Einige Pendenzen. Weben und Text in der antiken Literatur", in Harich-Schwarzbauer, H. (ed.), 165-208.
Schmidt, V. (1985) "*Hic ego qui iaceo*: die lateinischen Elegiker und ihre Grabschrift", *Mnemosyne* 38, 307-333.
Schöffel, C. (2002) *Martial Buch* 8, Stuttgart.
Schoonhaven, H. (1983) "The *Panegyricus Messallae*: date and relations with *Catalepton* 9", *ANRW* II 30.3, 1681-1707.
Schrijvers, P. H. (2009) "In praise of Messalla: Hellenistic geography in three panegyric Roman poems, in M. A. Harder, R. F. Regtuit and G. C. Wakker (eds), 149-176.
Schuster, M. (1930, repr. 1968) *Tibull-Studien*, Vienna (repr. Hildesheim).
Scullard, H. H. (1981) *Festivals and Ceremonies of the Roman Republic*, Ithaca.
Segal, C. (2005) "Il corpo e l' io nelle 'Metamorfosi' di Ovidio", in A. Barchiesi *Ovidio, Metamorfosi, vol. I, libri I-II*, Roma, xvii-ci.
Seibel, F. (1909) *Quibus artificiis poetae Latini numerorum uocabula difficilia euitauerint,* Diss. Munich.
Shackleton Bailey, D. R. (1956) *Propertiana*, Cambridge.
Shackleton-Bailey, D. R. (1993) *Martial Epigrams*, 3 vols, Cambridge, MA - London.
Sharrock, A. (1994) *Seduction and repetition in Ovid's* Ars Amatoria *II*, Oxford.

Sider, D. (1997) *The Epigrams of Philodemos. Introduction, text, and commentary*, Oxford.
Skempis, M. and Ziogas, I. (eds) (2014) *Geography, Topography, Landscape*: *Configurations of Space in Greek and Roman Epic*, Trends in Classics 22, Göttingen.
Skiadas, A. D. (1975) "*Periuria amantum*. Zur Geschichte und Interpretation eines Motivs des augusteischen Liebesdichtung", in E. Lefèvre (ed.), 400-418.
Skoie, M. (2002) *Reading Sulpicia: Commentaries 1475 – 1990*, Oxford.
Skoie, M. (2012) "Corpus Tibullianum, Book 3", in B. K. Gold (ed.), 86-100.
Skutsch, O. (1956) "Zu Virgils Eklogen", *RhM* 99, 193-200.
Skutsch, O. (1959) "Cum cecidit fato consul uerque pari", *Philologus*103, 152-154.
Skutsch, O. (1966) "Zur Datierung des Lygdamus", *Philologus* 110, 142-146.
Skutsch, O. (1985) *The Annals of Q. Ennius*, Oxford.
Smith, K. F. (1913) *The elegies of Albius Tibullus*, New York; repr. 1985 Darmstadt. (= Smith).
Snyder, J. M. (1989) *The woman and the lyre: Women writers in Classical Greece and Rome*, Carbondale.
Solodow, J. B. (1986) "*Raucae, tua cura, palumbes*: a study of poetic word-order", *HSPh* 90, 129-153.
Solodow, J. B. (1989) "Forms of literary criticsm in Catullus: polymetric vs. epigram", *CP* 84, 312-319.
Somerville, T. P. (2006) *Ovid and the tradition of exile elegy,* Diss., Harvard.
Spengel, L. (1853-1856) *Rheotores Graeci*, 3 vols, Leipzig.
Spies, A. (1930) *Militat omnis amans. Ein Beitrag zur Bildersprache der antiken Erotik*, Diss. Tübingen.
Stroh, W. (1971) *Die römische Liebeselegie als werbende Dichtung*, Amsterdam.
Struck, P.T. (2004) *The birth of the symbol: Ancient readers at the limits of their Texts*, Oxford-Princeton.
Sweet, F. (1972) "Propertius and political panegyric", *Arethusa* 5, 169-175.
Swoboda, A. (1889) *P. Nigidi Figuli operum reliquiae*, Vienna.
Syme, R. (1986) *The Augustan aristocracy*, Oxford.
Syndikus, H. P. (2006) "The second book", in H-C. Günther (ed.) *Brill's companion to Propertius*, 245-318, Leiden.
Talbert, R. J. A. (1984) *The senate of imperial Rome*, Princeton.

Tansey, P. (2007) "Messalla Corvinus and the *bellum Siculum*", *Latomus* 66, 882-890.
Tarrant, R. J. (1976) *Seneca Agamemnon*, Cambridge.
Tarrant, R. J. (2004) *P. Ovidi Nasonis Metamorphoses recognouit breuique adnotatione critica instruxit*, Oxford.
Tarrant, R. J. (1976) *Seneca Agamemnon*, Cambridge.
Tarrant, R. J. (2012) *Virgil: Aeneid book XII*, Cambridge.
Taylor, L. R. (1968) "Republican and Augustan writers enrolled in the equestrian Centuries", *TAPhA* 99, 469-486.
Thesleff, H. (1965) *Pythagorean Pseudepigrapha - Holger Thesleff: The Pythagorean Texts of the Hellenistic Period collected and edited*. (Acta Academiae Aboensis, ser. A, vol. 30, nr. 1.) Pp. vii+266. Åbo: Akademi, 1965. Paper, Fmk. 50.
Thill, A. (ed.) (1980) *L'élégie romaine. Enracinement. Thèmes. Diffusion*, Paris.
Thilo, G and Hagen, H. (eds) (1881-1887) *Servii grammatici qui feruntur in Virgilii carmina commentarii*, 3 vols, Leipzid – Berlin [reprinted Cambridge 2011]
Thom, J. C. (2005) *Cleanthes' Hymn to Zeus*, Tübingen.
Thomas, O. (2020) *The Homeric Hymn to Hermes*, Cambridge.
Thomas, R. F. (1988) *Virgil. Georgics. Vols I and II*, Cambridge.
Thomas, R. F. (2008) "Callimachus, the *Victoria Berenices*, and Roman poetry", in K. Volk (ed.), 189-224.
Thomas, R. F. (2009) *Lands and peoples in Roman poetry: The ethnographical Tradition* (Cambridge Philological Supplement 7), Cambridge.
Thomas, R. F. (2011) *Horace: Odes book 4 and Carmen Saeculare*, Cambridge.
Thorsen, Th. (ed.) (2013) *The Cambridge Companion to Latin Love Elegy. Cambridge companions to literature*, Cambridge – New York.
Tissol, G. (2014) *Ovid* Epistulae ex Ponto. *Book 1*, Cambridge.
Toynbee, J. M. C. (1971) *Death and burial in the Roman world*, London.
Tränkle, H. (1960) *Die Sprachkunst des Properz und die Tradition der lateinischen Dichtersprache* (Hermes Einzelschr. 15), Wiesbaden.
Tränkle, H. (1990) *Appendix Tibulliana*, Berlin (= Tränkle).
Traina, A., Nordera, R., Bertotti, T., Bezzi, L., Pianezzola, E. and Lunelli, L. (eds) (1969) *Contributi à tre poeti latini*, Bologna.
Treggiari, S. (1991) *Roman marriage: iusti coniuges from the time of Cicero to the time of Ulpian*, Oxford.
Tsitsirides, S. (ed.) (2010) Παραχορήγημα. Μελετήματα προς Τιμήν του Καθηγητή Γρηγόρη Μ. Σηφάκη, Ηράκλειο.

Tupet, A.-M. (1986) "Rites magiques dans l'antiquité romaine", *ANRW* II 16.3, 2591-2675.
Ullman, B. L. (1915) "Some type-names in the *Odes* of Horace", *CQ* 9, 27-30.
Unger, R. (1848) *De C. Valgii Rufi poematis commentatio*, Halle.
Usener, H. (1887) (1963) *Epicurea*. Leizpig.
Usener, H. (1903) "Dreiheit", *RhM* 58, 1-47, 161-208, 321-362.
Väänänen, V. (1967) *Introduction au latin vulgaire*, Paris.
Vahlen, J. (1908) *Opuscula academica I-II*, Leipzig.
Valvo, A. (1983) "M. Valerio Messalla Corvino negli studi più recenti", *ANRW* II 30.3, 1663-1680.
Vergados, A. (2013) *The Homeric Hymn to Hermes: Introduction, Text and Commentary*, Berlin – Boston.
Volk, K. (ed.) (2008) *Oxford readings in Classical studies: Vergil's Georgics*, Oxford.
Voss, J. H. (1811) *Tibull und Lygdamus nach den Handschriften berichtiget, mit Anmerk. P. Burmanns und den Konjecturen Schraders*, Heidelberg.
Wagenvoort, H. (1917) "De Lygdamo poeta deque eius sodalicio", *Mnemosyne* 45, 103-122.
Watson, L. C. (1995) "Horace's *Epodes*: The impotence of Iambos?", in S. J. Harrison, (ed.), 188-202, Oxford.
Watson, L. C. (2003) *A Commentary on Horace's Epodes*, Oxford.
Watson, P. (1983) "*Puella* and *uirgo*", *Glotta* 61, 119-143.
Watson, P. (1985) "Axelson revisited: the selection of vocabulary in Latin poetry", *CQ* 35, 430-448.
West, D. (1995) *Horace: Odes I, Carpe Diem*, Oxford.
West, M. L. (1966) *Hesiod: Theogony*, Oxford.
West, M. L. (1971, 1972) *Iambi et elegi Graeci ante Alexandrum cantati.* Vols. *I* and II, Oxford.
West, M. L. (1978) *Hesiod: Works and Days*, Oxford.
West, M. L. (1997) *The East face of Helicon*, Oxford.
West, M. L. (2007) *Indo-European poetry and myth*, Oxford.
West, M. L. (2011) *The making of the Iliad: Disquisition and analytical commentary*, Oxford.
Whitcomb, K. (2018) "Vergil, Octavian and Erigone: Admiration and admonition in the proem to *Georgics* I", *CJ* 113, 411-426.
Wilamowitz-Moellendorff, U. von (1916) *Vitae Homeri et Hesiodi in usum scholarum*, Bonn.
Wille, G. (1967) *Musica Romana: die Bedeutung der Musik im Leben der Römer*, Amsterdam.

Williams, Gareth (1994) *Banished voices: Readings in Ovid's exile poetry*, Cambridge.
Wilkinson, L. P. (1963) *Golden Latin artistry*, Cambridge.
Williams, F. (1978) *Callimachus: hymn to Apollo*, Oxford.
Williams, G. (1958) "Some aspects of Roman marriage ceremonies and ideals", *JRS* 48, 16-29.
Williams, G. (1968) *Tradition and originality in Roman poetry*, Oxford.
Williams, G. D. (1992) "Representation of the book-roll in Latin poetry: Ovid, *Tr.* 1.1.3-14 and the related texts", *Mnemosyne* 45, 178-189.
Wills, J. (1996) *Repetition in Latin poetry*, Oxford.
Wimmel, W. (1960) *Kallimachos im Rom. Die Nachfolge seines apologetischen Dichtens in der Augusteerzeit* (Hermes *Einzelschriften* 16), Wiesbaden.
Wimmel, W. (1968) *Der frühe Tibull*, Munich.
Wiseman, T. P. (1969) *Catullan Questions*, Leicester.
Wiseman, T. P. (1974) *Cinna the poet and other Roman essays*, Leicester.
Wiseman, T. P. (1985) *Catullus and his World*, Cambridge.
Wölfflin, E. (1879) *Lateinische und romanische Komparation*, Erlangen.
Woodman, A. J. (1977) *Velleius Paterculus: The Tiberian narrative* (2.94-131), Cambridge.
Woodman, A. J. and Martin, R. H. (1996) *The Annals of Tacitus: Book 3*, Cambridge.
Woodman, A. J. (2012a) *From poetry to history: Selected papers*, Oxford.
Woodman, A. J. (2012b) "A covering letter: poem 65", in I. Du Quesnay and A. Woodman (eds), 130-152.
Woodman, A. J. and Kraus, C. S. (2014) *Tacitus: Agricola*, Cambridge.
Woodman, A. J. (2017) *The Annals of Tacitus books 5 and 6*, Cambridge.
Woodman, A. J. (2018) *The Annals of Tacitus book 4*, Cambridge.
Woodman, A. J. (forthcoming) *Horace Odes book 3*, Cambridge.
Woodman, A. J. and West, D. (eds) (1984) *Poetry and politics in the age of Augustus*, Cambridge.
Woodman, A. and Wisse, J. (eds) (2017) *Word and context in Latin poetry: Studies in honour of David West* (Cambridge Classical Journal Supplements), Cambridge.
Wyke, M. (1994) "Taking the woman's part: Engendering Roman love elegy", *Ramus* 23, 110-128, (rev. 2002, 155-178).
Wyke, M. (2002) *The Roman mistress: Ancient and Modern Representations,* Oxford.
Yardley, J. C. (1990) "Cerinthus' *pia cura* ([Tibullus] 3.17.1-2)", *CQ* 40, 568-570.

Zagagi, N. (1987) "Amatory gifts and payments: a note on *munus, donum, data* in Plautus", *Glotta* 65, 129-132.
Zell, K. (1829) "Über die Volkslieder der alten Römer", *Ferienschriften* 2.99-125, Freiburg.
Zetzel, J. E. G. (1983) "Catullus, Ennius and the poetics of allusion", *ICS* 8, 251-266.
Zetzel, J. E. G. (1996) "Poetic baldness and its cure", *MD* 36, 73-100.
Ziogas, I. (2014) "The Topography of Epic Narrative in Ovid's *Metamorphoses*", in M. Skempis and I. Ziogas (eds), 325-348.
Zissos, A. (2008) *Valerius Flaccus'* Argonautica *Book 1*, Oxford.

INDEX 1

GENERAL INDEX

Numbers in Italics refer to pages of the Prolegomena and General Introduction, non-italic to poem and line numbers in the commentary

ablative: spatial, 5.1, 7.68
accusative: exclamatory, 3.25-26; internal/'Greek'/retained, 7.57, 7.172
Actium, *101*, *121*, 7 *headnote*
addressee, 13 *headnote*
adjective: in place of gen. subst., 7.56, 7.58, 7.196
Admetus, 4.67-72, 4.67
Adonis, 9 *headnote*, 9.1, 9.11-18, 9.11, 9.13
Aedituus, Valerius, *106-107*
Aetna, 7.196
Agave, 6.24
agriculture, 7. 169-174, 169, 170
Alcides (= Hercules), 7.12
Alcinous, 7.54-78
alternative poet: topos of, 7.177-180
amaranth, 4.33-34
ambiguity (of speakers), 10 *headnote*
Amor, 6 *headnote*, 6.4, 6.13-17, 6.13
anadiplosis, 5.1-2
anaphora, 2.5-6, 3.1, 5.9, 6.1-2, 8.9-12, 19.11-12
anastrophe, 7.5-6, 19.3
ancestors: praise of, 7.28-32
Antarctic, 7.153-157
Antiphates, 7.59-60
Antipodes, 7.150

Apollo: *99*, *103*, *114*, *117*, *118*, 1.15-16, 7.178, 8 *headnote*, 9.5, 10 *headnote*, 10.1, 10.10; Citharoedus, 4 *headnote*, 4.23-42, 4.23, 4.24, 4.35. 4.43-44; Phoebus 4.21, 7.8-9, 7.8, 7.66, 8.21-24, 10.2
apostrophe: of characters, 6.39
apotropaic formulae, 4.1, 4.95-96
apposition, 7.14
Aqua Marcia, 6.58
Aquitania, 7 *headnote*, 7.29, 7.137-138
Arabs, 2.24, 8.17-18
archaism, 12.9
archery, 7.89
Archilochus, *119*
Arctic, 7.153-157
Arethusa, 1 *headnote*
Ariadne, 6.39-42, 6.42
Armenian: tigresses, 6.15
Arno: river, 14.4
ars desultoria, 7.114
Artacie: spring, 7.60
Arupini, 7.110
asyndeton, 3.38, 7.3-4
Atalanta, 9.7-10, 9.16
Atticus, 14.4
auersio, 2.5-6, 5.7-14, 5.7, 5.9-10, 5.10, 5.12, 6.25-26, 6.59
authorship of book 3: unitary, *80*, *83*, *86-90*, *91*, *94*, *106*, *110*, *111*,

1 *headnote*; multiple, *84-86*; possibly female *82*
Bacchus, 2.19, 4.43-44, 4.45-48, 4.45, 6.1-2, 6.1, 6.2, 6.4, 6.5, 6.11, 6.13-17, 6.13, 6.15, 6.17-18, 6.28, 6.57, 7.9-11, 7.57, 11.12
Baiae, 5.3
bathos, 7.196, 9.2
battle formations, 7.101-102, 7. 103-105
bees: and poetry, *124*
Berenice: lock of, 7 *headnote*, 7.9-11, 7.12-13
birthday: theme of, *84, 88, 105, 106, 126*; spirit, 11 *headnote*, 12.14; wishes 11.18, 12.20; Roman, 11 *headnote*, 12 *headnote*, 14 *headnote*, 15 *headnote*
blasphemy, 5.12, 5.13-14, 10.14
blush, 4.31-32
boar hunting, 9.1, 9.3, 9.5, 9.6, 9.7-10
Bona Dea, 5.7-8, 5.8
book: as present, 1 *headnote*, 1.5, 7.7; burning of, 7.196; production of, 1.9-14; roll 1.9-14
Bootes, 7.9-11
branding (of slaves), 19.24
Britain, *102*, 7.149
bucolic diaeresis, 6.7

Caesar, Julius, 7.149
calendar: old Roman, 1.2; Julian, 1.1
Calenus, *127*
Callimachus: *81*, *87-88*, *123*, 4.43-44, 4.45-48, 4.50, 6.57, 19.9; *Aetia*, 1 *headnote*; dialogue with Muses in, 1 *headnote*; epinicia of, 7 *headnote*; myths in, 7.8-15, 7.12, 7.13; poetics of, 81, *87-88*, *122*, 1 *headnote*, 1.9-14, 4 *headnote*, 7 *headnote*, 7.4, 7.7,
7.16, 7.177-180, 7.196, 8.1, 10.7-8, 10.11-24, 19.7, 19.9; programmatic elements in, 1 *headnote*
Calypso, 7.77
Camenae, 7.24, 7.179
camp sites: positioning of, 7.85, 7.87
Castalian spring, 1.15-16
Catalepton 9, *101*, *121*, 7 *headnote*
catalogues, 7.137-146, 7.151-174
catasterism, 7.9-11
cattle (of the sun), 7.76
Catullus: influence of, *81, 82, 86, 89, 100, 106-108, 127*, 1.9-14, 1.9, 4.51-60, 4.51-52, 4.65, 4.85-89, 6.41, 18 *headnote*, 19 *headnote*, 19.2, 19.5
Catulus, Q. Lutatius, *107-108*
causa mortis: on epitaphs, 2.27, 2.29
Cephalus and Procris, *80, 90-93, 110*, 1 *headnote*, 19 *headnote*, 20 *headnote*
Cerberus, 4.87, 4.88
Cerinthus: *81-84, 88, 89, 95, 102-109, 123-126*, 8 *headnote*, 8.1, 8.15, 8.19-20, 9 *headnote*, 9.1, 9.11, 10 *headnote*, 10.5, 10.6, 10.9, 11 *headnote*, 11.2, 13 *headnote*, 14 *headnote*, 15 *headnote*, 15.4; name of, *124*; social status of, 16 *headnote*, 16.2, 16.6
change: theme of, *80-82, 88, 90, 93-94, 110, 114-115, 129*, 2.26, 8 *headnote*, 10 *headnote*, 10.6, 13.1-2
chaos, 7.158-164
Charon, 3.10
Charybdis, 7.70, 7.70-75, 7.73-75, 7.74, 7.75
Chimaera, 4.86
Chloris, *81*, *116*, *117*
Choaspes (river), 7.140

chronological periphrasis, 4 *headnote*, 4.17-24, 4.17-18, 4.55
Cicones, 7.54
Cimmerians, 5.24, 7.64, 7.65-66
Cinna, 7.7
Circe, 7.61, 7.62,
Ciris: influence of, 7.202, 7.211
Citharoedus, see Apollo: Citharoedus
Claudian, *102*
climate (temperate), 7. 168, 7.169-174
Clio, 1 *headnote*
Clodius Pulcher, P., 5.7-8, 5.8
closural features, 1.17, 6.63, 13.1-2, 13.1-2, 20 *headnote*, 20.4
colloquialism, *107-108*
comparative: analytic, 1.25
constructio ad sensum, 10.26
Cornutus, *84, 104-106, 125-126*, 8 *headnote* 8.19-20, 11 *headnote*, 11.14, 11.16, 12.11-12, 14 *headnote*, 14.3
cosmology, 7.18-27, 7.19-23, 7.19, 7.20, 7.21-22, 7.23, 7.65-66, 7.151-174
Crete, 7.8-9
Crinagoras, 11 *headnote*
Croesus, 3.29, 7.198-199
Culex: influence of, 1.15-16, 5.1, 5.24
curse formula, 9.6
Cyclops, 7.56
Cynthia (in Propertius), 9.7-10
Cynthus, Mount, 4.50
Cyrene, 7.139
Cyrus the Great, 7.140, 7.141
Cytherea, 13.3-4
Cytheris, 13.3-4

Dalmatia, 7.1-2, 7.114
date (of Corp. Tib. III), *85-86*, 7.66
dative: of agent, 5.29
death: pallor of, 1.27-28, 5.32; blackness of, 5.5; as cure for love, 1.27-28; of the poet, 2

headnote, 2.4, 3 *headnote*, 3.7-10, 3.35-38
deification (of mistress), 8.10
delay (in exposition), 13.3-4
Delia (= Diana), 9.5,
Delia (in Tibullus), 9.9-10, 19.11-12
Delian (Apollo), 4.79
Delos, 9.5
Delphi, 7.8-9
Demophoon, 1 *headnote*
deriuatio, 2.19
desert zone, 7.158-164
Diana, 4.13-14, 4.29, 9 *headnote*, 9.5, 9.19
Dido, *108*, 12.3, 13.1-2, 13.3-4, 13.10
digression, 7.8-15
Dis (= Gk. Pluto), 1.27-28, 3.38, 5.33-34
diues amator, 8.15-20
divine invocation, 10 *headnote*
divine protection: for poets, 4.43-44; for lovers, 12.11-12
docta puella, 1.7
dog star, see Sirius
dogs: hunting, 9.6
Domitius Marsus, *Ep. Tib. headnote*, *Vit. Tib.* 6-7
double meaning, 16.4
double negatives, 7.126, 7.164, 13.8
dreams, 4 *headnote*, 4.1, 4.2, 4.7-8, 4.13-14, 4.17-24
drinking competitions, 6.11

-*erunt* (short vowel perfect), 11.4
ekphrasis, 4 *headnote*
elegy: seriousness of, 6 *headnote*, 6.33-36; etymology of, *113*, 6.51-52; development in Lygdamus, *98*, *99*; rejection of for lyric, 6.51-52, 6.53
Eleusis: mysteries of, 5.7-8, 6.1-2
elision, 2.4, 4.14, 4.49, 4.72, 6.27-28, 6.40, 13.1-2
Elysium, 5.23
Empedocles, 7.196

endings and beginnings (of poems), *99*
Ennius, *108*
envy, 3.19-20, 10.25, 19.7
epanalepsis, 5.1-2
epic: simile, 4 *headnote*; style, 7.130-134
Epicurean philosophy, 19.9
epigram, *106-107*
epinician poetry, *68*
epitaph: of the poet, 2 *headnote*, 2.9-30, 2.27-30, 2.27, 2.29-30; inscriptions on, 5.19, 5.30
epithalamium, 16.2
equestrian training, 7.91-87
Er-Stil, 6.13-17
Eratosthenes, *123*, 7 *headnote*, 7.9-11, 7.79-81, 7.151-174, 7.165-168
Erigone, *87, 123*, 7 *headnote*, 7.9-11, 7.151-174
erotodidaxis, 4.61-62, 4.64, 4.65
Etna, 7.56
Etruria, 5 *headnote*, 5.1
etymology, *83, 112, 113, 119*, 2.1-2, 4.74, 5.1-2, 5.3, 6.51-52, 7.61, 7.72, 7.79, 7.113, 7.117-118, 8.2, 8.3, 8.10, 8.12, 8.13-14, 9.17-18, 10.17-18, 11.3, 11.13-14, 11.14, 11.15, 1.20, 13.1-2, 13.3-4, 16.1, 19.23
eyes (of beloved), 8.5-6

Falernian wine, 6.6
fates, 3.35, 11.3
father (of mistress), 4.94
female impersonation, 8.1
final clause (ironic), 16.2
first inventor, 2.1-8
fives zones (of earth), 7.9-11, 7.151-174
Fortuna, 7.182
four element theory, 7.18-27
funeral (of the poet), 2 *headnote*, 2.9-30, 2.11-143.8,
future (indefinite), 4.11-12

future works topos, 7.16-17
Gallus: influence of, 1.8, 1.19, 1.27-28, 4 *headnote*, 4.19-20, 4.43-44, 4.51-52, 4.56, 4.57-58, 4.71, 4.76, 5.13, 6 *headnote*, 6.3, 6.7, 6.8, 7.106, 7.136, 8.15, 8.24, 9 *headnote*, 9.1, 9.3, 9.7-10, 9.7, 9.8, 9.12, 9.15, 9.16, 12.10, 13.1-2, 13.3-4, 13.10, 14.2-3, 19.9, 19.22
Gaul, 7.137-138
gender roles: reversal of, 6.49-50, 18.5, 19.1, 19.13, 19.19
generic ambiguity, 6.33-36, 8.1, 8.4
genethliacon, 11 *headnote*, 12 *headnote*, 12.19-20, 14 *headnote*
Genius, 11 *headnote*, 11.12
geography (Hellenistic), 7 *headnote*
gerundives, 12.4
Getae, 7.146
gnomic perfect, 2.1-2, 2.3-4, 7.14
go-between (in elegy), 1.23-28
golden age, 7.169-174
golden horns (on sacrifice), 7.14-15, 7.15
golden line (*uersus aureus*), 3.5, 7.13, 7.38, 7.57, 7.76, 7.112, 7.117, 7.124, 7.125, 7.144, 7.155, 7.164
Gylippus, 7.199

Hades, 3.38
hair, 1.20, 2.11-12, 8.9, 8.10
haruspicy, 4.5-6, 4.7-8
Hecale (of Callimachus), 7.8-10
Hecate, 4.13-14
Helicon, 1.5, 1.15-16, 4 *headnote*
Hercules, 7.9-11, 7.12-13
Herodotus: influence of, 7.144-145
hexameter endings (monosyllabic), 16.1, 17.5
hiatus, 2.17-18, 4.82, 17.3
Hippocrene, 1.15-16

Homer: comparison with, 7.180, 7.200
Horace: influence of, 9 *headnote*, 9.23, 11.1-2, 14.6
hospitality, 7.8-10
humour, 7 *headnote*
hunting, *91*, *93*, *124*, 9 *headnote*
hyperbaton, 17.4
hysteron-proteron, 7.130-131

iambic shortening, 4.64, 5.20
Iapydians, 7.108, 7.110
Icarus/Icarius/Ikarios, 7.9-11
illness: theme of, *88*, *103*, *105*, *106*, *109*, *108*, 5 *headnote*, 5.7-14, 10 *headnote*, 17 *headnote*
Illyrian campaigns, *101*, *122*, *123*, 7.106-117, 7.108, 7.108-109
immature grapes (image), 5.19
impotence, 19.14
inadequacy (of poet), 7.2, 7.3-4, 7.5-6, 7.177-180
inauguration (of consuls), 7.118-134, 7.121, 7.122, 7.123, 7.130-134, 7.134
incantation (as cure), 10.10
incense, 2.24, 3.2, 12.1
India, 7.145
insensitivity: theme of, 4.85-89
insomnia (of lover), 4.19-20
interrogatives: accumulation of, 6.23
inviolability (of lovers), 10.15
invocation, 9 *headnote*, 9.1-2
Isles of the Blessed, 5.23
Ithaca, 7.49
ivy, 6.2

jealousy: theme of, *91*, *93*, *105*, *108*, 11.11, 16 *headnote*, 20 *headnote*
Juno: *103*, 3.33-34, 8.11, 12 *headnote*, 12.1, 12.7, 12.13, 12.19-20, 19.15; in women's oaths, 6.47-49
Juno Lucina, *134*, 1.1-4, 4.13-14, 8.1, 12.14

Jupiter: 4.47-48, 7.130-134;
Capitoline temple of, 7.130-134

Kalends, 11 *headnote*
Kalends (of March), 1.1-4, 1.1, 8.1
kletik hymn, 3.33, 6.1, 7.131, 8.2, 10 *headnote*, 10.1, 10.9

Laestrygonians, 7.59-60
Lararium, 11.12
Latona (Leto), 4.29, 4.72
Laudes Messallae, *82*, *84*, *85*, *87*, *94*, *100-102*, *122*
laurel (Apollo's symbol), 4.23
Laus Pisonis, *122*, *129*, 7 *headnote*
lena, 4.61-62, 8.15-20
Lenaea (festival), 6.38
Lenaeus (= Bacchus), 6.38
Lethe, 1.27-28
lexical *uariatio*, 6.33-36
Liber (= Bacchus), 6.1
Licinus, Porcius, *106*, *107*
links: between consecutive poems, 2 *headnote*, 3 *headnote*, 4.1, 6 *headnote*; between first and last poems of a cycle, 6.29, 6.56, 12 *headnote*, 12.11-12, 3.13.1-2, 3.18.6; between Lygd. and *Laud. Mess.*, 1 *headnote*, 1.15-16, 1.24, 2.26; between Lygd. and *Sulpicia Cycle*, 1 *headnote*, 1.1-4, 1.1, 1.2, 1.8, 1.14, 1.17, 2.26, 4.37-38, 8 *headnote*, 8.22, 12.3; between Lygd. and Sulpicia, 1.8, 1.17, 6.60, 13.1-2, 16.6; between *Sulpicia Cycle* and Sulpicia, 8 *headnote*, 8.8, 10 *headnote*, 10.10, 11 *headnote*, 11.18, 12.2, 12.3, 12.11-12, 12.15, 12.16,13.1-2, 13.3-4, 13.10, 14.8; between Lygd. and 3.19:19.17; between *Sulpicia Cycle* and 3.19: 8.8, 8.11-12, 11.18, 19 *headnote*, 19.8, 19.15, 19.18; between *Sulpicia Cycle*

and 3.20: 20.4; between Sulpicia
and 3.19: 19.8, 19.18, 19.19
lions, 6.15-16
Livius Andronicus, *108*
locus amoenus, 9 *headnote*
love: as a disease, 4.19-20, 6
 headnote, 6.3, 10.2, 10.5, 10.16,
 12.18, 17.2, 17.3; as fire, 8.5-6,
 8.11-12, 11 *headnote*, 11.5,
 11.6, 12.17-18, 17.2, 18.6;
 cruelty of, 4.65, 4.73, 8.5-6
lover: as suppliant, 19.24
Lucan, *102*
Lucina, see Juno Lucina
Lucretius: influence of 4.85, 4.86,
 4.89, 6.32, 7.18, 7.20, 7.130,
 7.161, 7.211
Lyaeus (= Bacchus), 2.19
Lycotas, 1 *headnote*
Lydia, 7.198-199
Lygdamus: *80-90, 96-100, 111-117,
 119* 1 *headnote*, 2.10, 2.29; and
 earlier elegy, *98-99*; colour
 combinations in, 1.9, 2.10, 2.18,
 5.4, 5.15; date of, 5.12-18, 6.41
 name of *83, 112, 119*, 3.3.75;
 pleonasm in, 2.15, 3.4, 3.9,
 4.47-48, 4.93, 6.55
Lynceus, 1 *headnote*
lyre (of Apollo), 4.37, 4.39
lyric: playfulness of, 6 *headnote*,
 6.33-36

madness, 5.13, 6.27, 19.17
Maecenas, 4.4
Maenalus, 9.7-10
magister amoris, 6.43
magister bibendi, 6.10, 6.11
Magyni, 7.146
makarismos, 3.26
malaria, 5.27, 5.28
manuscript tradition (of Tibullus),
 128-129
Marathus, *84, 95, 103*, 1 *headnote*
marble, 3.3, 3.13, 3.14, 3.16,
Maro (in Homer), 7.57

Maronea, 7.57
marriage, *83, 89, 98, 99, 113, 114,
 120, 125*, 1.9, 4 *headnote*, 4.79,
 4.93, 8 *headnote*, 8.1, 8.15,
 8.21-24, 11.16, 12.7, 12.14,
 12.20, 16.213.10
married love, 1.26. 3.7-10
Mars, *89, 103*, 1.1, 8.1, 8.3, 8.4,
 9.16, 9.18
Marsus, Domitius, *96*
Martial: influence of, 1 *headnote*,
 1.19, 1.21-22, 4.57, 6.21, 6.26,
 6.43
masks (of the poet), *94-110*
Matronalia, *89, 103, 125*, 1.1-4,
 4.13-14, 8 *headnote*, 8.1, 8.21-
 24, 12 *headnote*
Melampus, 7.120
Meles (river), 7.200
Messalla Corvinus: *80-82, 85, 87,
 120-123*, 7 *headnote*, 14
 headnote, 14.5, 15 *headnote;* as
 orator, 7.45-47, 7.54-79, 7.81;
 future victories of, 7.135-176; as
 patron of Ovid, 7.197-200; style
 of, 8.12
Messallinus, Catullus, *85*
Messallinus, Marcus Valerius
 (eldest son of Messalla
 Corvinus), *97*. 7.197-200
Messallinus, Lucius Valerius
 (second son of Messalla
 Corvinus), *97*
metamorphosis, *91, 93*
metaphor 9 *headnote,* 10 *headnote*,
 11.6, 17.3, 19.1
metapoetic signals/terminology,
 4.29-34, 4.67-72, 4.67, 4.75, 6
 headnote, 6.4, 6.37, 6.38, 6.57,
 6.52, 7.4, 7.16, 7.196, 8
 headnote, 8.1, 8.8, 8.10, 8.12,
 9.7, 9.8, 12.4, 12.15, 13
 headnote, 13.7-8, 19.10
metonymy, 2.13, 2.19, 3.1, 3.8,
 3.17, 3.25, 4.74, 6.5, 6.8, 6.57,
 7.57, 7.58, 7.66, 18.1

Milanion, 9.7-10, 9.12, 9.16
military exercises, 7.88, 7.89-97
militia amoris, 1.7, 4.65, 4.76
misogyny, 4.61-62
Molorcus/Molorchus/Molorkos, *87, 123*, 7 *headnote*, 7.9-11, 7.12-13
moods, verbal: mixture of, 1.19-20, 5.32
moon, 4.29
mother (of mistress), 2.13, 4.93, 12.15
Muses: 1.17, 1.18, 1.23-28, 4 *headnote*, 8 *headnote*; dialogue with, *87*, 1 *headnote*, 1.5
mutuus amor, *80, 81, 114, 115, 116*, 1.19, 11 *headnote*, 11.6, 11.7, 11.13-16, 12.8
myrrh, 4.28
mythological *exempla*, 7 *headnote*

Naevius, *87*
Naiads, 1.15-16, 6.57
nard, 6.63
Neaera: *118-200, 80, 81, 89, 90, 97, 114, 118-120*, 1 *headnote*, 1.23, 1.26, 3.1, 5 *headnote*, 19.22; name of, *83, 90, 93, 119*
negatives, double, see double negatives
Nekyia, 7.67-68
Nemean games, 7.9-11
Nemesis, 8.15-20, 11.12, 19.11-12,
Neoboule, *119*
Nereus, 7.58
Nestor, 5.26, 7.48-49, 7.50-51, 7.112
nets, hunting, 9.12, 9.16, 9.17
Night: horses of, 4.17-18; chariot of, 4.17-18
Nile, 7 *headnote*, 7.140

oaths: by eyes, 6.47-49; lovers', 6.49-50
obsequium, 4.63-76
Ocean: 7.53, 7.135-176, 7.147; as a river, 4.17-18

Octavian, *100, 101, 102, 120, 121, 122*, 7 *headnote*, 7.9-11, 7.149
Odysseus, 7.48-49
offerings, of milk, 2.20
offspring, 5.26
Ogygia, 7.77
old age: love in, 3.7-10; pallor of, 5.25
Old Testament, 10.19-20
Olympus, 8.13
omniscience (of gods), 11.19
-on (Gk. gen. pl.), 7.64
oracles, 4.77
Orcus, 3.38
Osiris, 7.9-11
ossilegium, 2.15-25, 2.17-18
otium, of poet, 7.181
Ovid: addresses to wife in, 1.26; exile poetry, 1 *headnote*, 1.26; *Heroides*, *82*; influence of, *82, 103, 108, 126*, 1.1, 1.9-14, 1.10, 4 *headnote*, 3.4, 4.1, 4.16, 4.33-34, 4.34, 4.45, 4.47-48, 4.65-66, 4.96, 5.15-20, 5.16, 5.17-18, 5.19-20, 6.21, 6.26, 6.47-49, 6.49-50, 7.206, 7.206-210, 9 *headnote*, 10.17-18, 10.19-20, 11.2, 11.17, 13.1-2, 13.7, 13.9, 19 *headnote*, 19.3, 19.9, 19.11-12, 19.12, 19.13, 19.17, 19.20, 19.21, 20 *headnote*, 20.2
oxymoron, 6.11

Pactolus (river), 3.29
Padaei, 7.144-145
pairs (of poems), 11 *headnote*, 14 *headnote*, 15 *headnote*
pallor: of lover, *112, 124*; see also old age, death
Panchaia, 2.23
panegyric: 7 *headnote*; ambiguity in, 7.137-146; *amplificatio* in, 7.118-134; competition in, 7.37; digressions in, 7.54-78, 7.89-97, 7.151-174; elegiac themes in, 7.91, 7.137, 7.192-200;

ethnography in, 7. 106-117,
7.137-146; hyperbole in, 7.48-
49; mythology in, 7.48-49
Panegyricus Messallae (as title),
101, see also *Laudes Messallae*
Panthus, 1 *headnote*
parallel half-lines, 2.14
parataxis, with *rogo*, 1.24
Pannonians, 7.108-109
Parcae (fates), 3.35
Parnassus, 1.15-16
parody, 7.8-15, 7.54-78, 7.81
pathetic fallacy, 14 *headnote*, 14.1,
14.2-3, 14.4
pearls, 3.17-18, 8.19-20
pentameter endings, 13.6, 16.4,
17.6,19 *headnote*, 19.22
Pentheus, 6.23-24, 6.24
perfect infinitives, 7.48, 12.6, 18.2,
18.4
Permensis, Cassius, *97*
Persephone, 5 *headnote*, 5.5, 5.7-8
personification, 20.1
Petale, *116-117*
Phaecia, 7.78
Phaedra/Hippolytus, 9 *headnote*,
9.1, 9.7, 9.9-10, 9.11-18, 9.16,
11.5, 11.6
Phoebus (= sun), 7.66, see also
Apollo
Pholoe, 1 *headnote*
Pieria, 1.15.16
Pierian spring, 1.15-16
Pierides, 1 *headnote*, 1.5, 1.15-16,
1.17, 8.21
pietas, 17.1
Pimplean spring, 1.15-16
plectrum, 4.39
ploughing, 7.170
pluperfect, for perfect, 7.184-185
poisoning, 5.9-10, 7.61
Pollio, 7.205-206
Pomona, *82, 89*
popular values, rejection of, 3.19-20
Poseidon, 7.56

postponed particles, 1.9, 1.10, 4.91,
5.28, 6.19, 6.55, 7.34, 4.43-44,
4.91, 5.28, 7.34, 7.20, 7.22,
7.42, 7.58, 7.61, 7.110, 7.144,
7.154, 7.168
poverty (of poet), 3 *headnote*, 3.23-
24, 7.183-189, 7.188-189
present participles, 4.39, 4.46
priamel, 2.1-8, 7.18
prodigy, 7.118-134
propemptikon, 3.27, 5.31, 7.193-196
Propertius: influence of, *81, 84, 85,
87, 89, 90, 94, 100, 103, 105,
113, 115, 117, 126*, 19
headnote, 19.3, 19.4, 19.6, 20
headnote, 20.1, 20.2
prophesy, by Apollo, 4.45-48
prostitute, 16.3-4
proverbial expressions, 19.8
pseudepigraphy, *122, 126, 127, 129*
pseudonyms, *84, 96, 97, 100, 104,
111, 112,115, 120, 123, 124*, 1
headnote, 8.1
publication (literary), 13 *headnote*
puer delicatus, 124-125
pumice, 1.9-14, 1.10
purple dye (Tyrian purple), 3.17-18,
3.18, 8.15-16n.
purple robe, 12.13
Pythagorean philosophy, *80, 82, 88,
114, 129*, 7.206-210

-*que* (postponed), 3.4

recusatio, 7.18, 7.24, 7.35, 7.177-
180
re-incarnation (of poet), 7.206-210
reputation (*fama*), 9.16, 13 *headnote*
revelation: theme of, *55, 63, 70-71,
76, 83, 96, 103, 114*, 13
headnote, 13.1-2, 13.3-4, 18.2,
18.6, 19.8, 19.9, 19.20, 20
headnote, 20.3
rhyme, internal, 1.2
ring-composition, 2.29-30, 4
headnote, 4.95-96, 5.29-34,

6.57-58, 6.63, 7 *headnote*, 10
headnote, 12 *headnote*, 13
headnote, 18 *headnote*, 18.6,
19.2, 19.23
rivers (in triumphal procession),
7.137-146
Rome, 15.2
roof beams: gilded, 3.16
rumour, 20 *headnote*, 20.1

Sabine women, 1.1-4
sacral language, 6.13-17
sacrifice: modest, 7.14-15, 7.14;
poetry as, 7.14-15
sacrilege, 4.15-16, 5.7-14, 5.12,
Salassi, 7.106-117
Sappho, 13.3-4
Saturn: age of, 3.33-34
Saturnalia, 1 *headnote*, 1.1-4
Scopas, 4 *headnote*, 4.23-42
Scylla, 4.89, 7.70, 7.70-75, 7.71-72,
7.71, 7.72
Scythia, 4.91
seafaring, 7.169-174
sealed tablets, 13.7
seasons, 7.169
secrecy: theme of, *70-71*, *76*, *83*, *93*,
95, *96*, *110*, *111*, *113*, 8.8, 11
headnote, 11.17, 11.18, 12.5-6,
12.6, 12.16, 13 *headnote*, 13.1-
2, 18.2, 18.613.3-4, 19.8, 19.9.
19.20, 20 *headnote*, 20.3
self-naming (by poet), 2.29
Semele, 4.45
senex amator, 3.7-10
seruitium amoris, *81*, *111*, *112*, *115*,
117, 4.66, 4.73, 4.74, 6.14,
10.12, 11.3-4, 11.5, 11.13-14,
11.14, 12.10, 19.15, 19.22,
19.23, 19.24
Servius Sulpicius Rufus, *126*, 14.6,
16.4
shame (*pudor*), 13 *headnote*
shell (of Venus), 3.33-34
Sicily, 7.56
silence of nature (topos), 7.124-129

Sirens, 7.69
Sirius (dog star), 5.1-2, 7.9-11
slave girls (in elegy), 16.3-4
slave names, *100*, *117*
Sleep: personified, 4.19-20; cloak
of, 4.55
small stature (of poet), 7.196
Sosibius, 7 *headnote*
Spain, 7.138
speaking names, *111*
sphragis, *86*, *97*, *118*, *124*, 5.17-18,
16.4
spinning: 16.3-4; of fates, 3.36
Statius, *98*, *101*, *102*
Stoic: polemic, 3.19-20; philosophy
(cosmology), 7.18-27, 7.21-22,
7.23, 19.7, 19.9
story-telling (by old men), 5.26
stylistic: elevation 8.5-6; variety, *82*
Styx, 3.37
subjunctive: iterative, 7.98-99;
optative, 15.3; potential, 4.83
Suetonius, *Vit. Tib. headnote*
suicide, 2 *headnote*
Sulpicia: *104-119*, *126-128*, 8
headnote, 8.1, 9 *headnote*;
analysis of emotion in *105-106*;
colloquial style of, *106*-108, 16
headnote, 18 *headnote*; dramatic
date of poems, 14.5; social
status of, 16 *headnote*, 16.2,
16.6
Sulpicia Cycle, *102-104*, *Vit. Tib.* 5
Sulpicius, Servius *97*
supine of purpose, 8.2
surprise: poetic technique of, 6.13
suspense, 4.51-60
symposium, *81*, *99*, *117*, *119*, 6
headnote, 6.7, 6.31-32
sympotic themes, 6.25
synonyms, 7.160
Syria, 7 *headnote*
Syrtes, 4.91

Tagus (river), 3.29
Thalia, 1 *headnote*

Theseus. 6.39-40, 6.39, 6.42
three (as magic number), 12.14
Tibullus: impersonation of, *82, 83, 84, 87, 88, 90, 94, 101, 110,* 7 *headnote*, 7.5-6, 7.14-15, 7.16-17, 7.52, 7.78, 7.137-146, 7.137, 7.165-168, 7.183-189, 7.187, 7.196, 7.197-200, 7.211, 19 *headnote* 19.17; influence of, *81, 83, 95, 96-97, 103, 104, 105, 112*; *Vita, 96*; *Epitaph, 96*
tigers, 6.15-16
Tigris, 7.140, 7.141
Titan (= the sun), 7.51, 7.113,
toga praetexta, 7.118-134, 7.121
Tomyris (Tamyris), 7.143
tortoiseshell inlay, 4.3
towns: building of, 7.169-174
transmigration of souls, 7.206-210
triumph, 7.187
triumphal procession, 7.137-146
Tyrian purple, see purple dye

underworld: gods of, 5 *headnote*, 5.33-34, 5.33
unfaithfulness (of lover), 1.23-28, 4.13-14. 6.12
unripe fruit (image), 5.19-20
unshorn locks (of Apollo), 4.27
urban/rural contrast, 9.2, 9.5, 14 *headnote*, 14.3, 15.2, 19.3, 19.9

Valgius (C.Valgius Rufus), 81, 7.180
Varus, *102*
Venus, 3.33-34, 6.47-49, 8.1, 8.2, 8.3, 9 *headnote*, 9.1, 9.11-18, 9.11, 9.13, 9.16, 9.17-18, 9.18, 9.19, 11.13, 11.13-14, 19.23, 19.24
uersus aureus, see golden line
Vertumnus, *81-82, 88, 89, 90, 93, 94, 115, 129,* 2.26, 8 *headnote*, 8.1, 8.13-14, 8.13, 8.14, 9 *headnote*, 13.1-2, 19 *headnote*
Virgo (constellation), 7.9-11
viticulture: invention of, 7 *headnote*, 7.9-11, 7.187,
vowel lengthening, (*in arsi*) 8.3
uotorum nuncupatio, 7.130-134

washing, ritual, 2.16, 12.3
wealth: rejection of, 3 *headnote*, 3.3, 3.11-19, 3.13-16, 3.23-24, 3.29, 3.30; love preferable to, 3.23-24, 3.30
weather (compared to fate), 6.32
weaving (metaphor), 7.5-6
wine (and love), 6 *headnote*
winds (in curses), 6.27-28, 6.49-50
word order: in adj. and noun pairs, 1.3-4; prepositional, 1.15-16, 7.185
word play, 16.4

INDEX 2

INDEX OF LATIN AND GREEK WORDS

Numbers in Italics refer to pages of the Prolegomena and General Introduction, non-italic to poem and line numbers in the commentary

(a) Latin

a (interj.), 4.61-62
ab (*metri causa*), 7.42
abduco, 14.7
acerbus, 20.4
acuo, 9.3
adeo, -ire (in kletic hymns), 3.33-34, 6.1, 10.1-2
adnuo, 7.133, 11.20, 12.13
agmen quadratum (military), 7.101-102
adhibeo, 4.75
aeque ac, 18.1-2
aequora ponti, 4.85
Aetnaeus, 7.56
Alcides, 7.10
ales (= 'omen'), 6.8
alludo, 4.35
altaria, 12.17
alter: (= 'rival'), 4.58; (= *alius*) 7.18
amabilis, 4.94
amarantus, 4.33-34
amica, 19.13
Amythaonius, 7.120
annosus, 2.19, 6.58,
ante (in comparative/superlative expressions), 4.93, 11.5, 19.16
arbitrio esse, 14.8
arbitrium, 6.14
ardor, *107*, *109*, 18.6

arguo, 9.16
arma, 8.4
assuetus, 7.125
Assyria, 2.24
Assyrius, 2.24
at tu, 8.3
atque utinam, 5.27, 19.5
audio, 7.24
auena, 4.71
aurifer, 3.29
ausim, 7.193
autem, 5.3
auus, 1.2

bellus, 4.51-52, 19.5
benignus, 3.6
blanditia, 4.75-76, 4.75
blandus, 3.2

Cadmeus, 6.24
cado, 3.8, 16.2
caelum (= 'gods'), 3.1
caeruleus, 4.17-18
calor, *107*, 17.2
Camenae, *108-109*, 1.5, 7.24, 13.3-4
candens (of the sun), 7.65
candidus, 2.10, 3.25, 6.1, 6.30, 8.12, 9.10, 10.17

candor (rhetorical), 4.29-34, 4.29
cani (= 'white hairs'), 5.15
cano (= 'prophesy'), 4.77, 11.3
capillus, 2.11-12
carbaseus, 2.21-22
carmen, 1.7, 2.28
carus, 1.6, 3.32
cassis, 9.17
Castalius, 1.15-16
castus, 1.23, 4.43-44, (of Juno) 12.14
catena, 11.15
caueo (+ abl.), 6.44
celeber, 2.22, 10.23
cerintha, 10.9
cerno (= *decerno*), 7.103
certo (+ dat.), 7.120
cerui (military), 7.84
charta, 7.200
Cimmerius, 5.24
Circe, 7.61
clarus, 3.4
Cnosia (= Ariadne), 6.39
colo, 6.20, 9.2
color (rhetorical), 1.18, 4.30, 10.6, 4.29-34, 4.30
coma, 2.11-12, 8.9
comes, 6.10
como, 12.3
compono, 2.26, 6.35-36, 8.8, 12.9
comptus, 1.4, 8.10, 12.3
concha, 3.17, 3.33-34
conclamatio, 2.15
concumbo, 9.16
conditor, 7.4
confinia mortis, 7.70
confluo, 7.20
coniugium, *76*, *114*, 4.74, 4.79
coniunx, *98-99*, *114*, 1 headnote, 1.26, 4.74
conspiciendus, 12.4
conspicuus, 3.4
contendo, 7.31
contrarius, 4.83
contundo, 6.13-14
cornua, 1.13

corpora fessa, *104*
corpus (= 'body of work'), 2.7, 7.196, 10.20, 10.19-20
crede mihi / mihi crede, 10.3
crimen (amatory), 4.84, 20.3
crinis, 2.11-12, 8.9
crudelis (= 'insensitive'), 4.61-62
cultus, 1.17, 4.92
cupidus, 4.51-52, 7.35
cura, 1.19, 2.29, 4.43-44, 7.197, 9.5, 16.1, 17.1, 18.1
custos, 9.4, 12.11-12
Cytherea, *108*, 13.3-4
Cynthius / -a, 4.50
Cypria (of Venus), 3.33-34

decenter, 8.14
decido, 1.20
decor, 8.8
decus, 7.32
deduco: of marriage, 4.31; metapoetic, 4.29-34
deficio: 7.1, 9.6, 19.14; (+ ad) 7.185; (medical + inf.) 7.191
defluo, 1.18, 4.81
defungor, 3.9
Delius, 4.79
demonstro, 2.27
densus, 9.7
depugnatio obliqua (military), 7.103-105
desideo, 7.19
desine (+ inf.), 4.80
deuius, 9.2
dico, 7.18
dignus, 1.8, 8.15, 8.24, 12.10, 13.10
Dis, 1.27-28
discedo, 6.37
discurro, 1.3-4
dissimulo, 18.6
diuersus, 7.45
dixit et, 4.81
doctus, 4.45, 6.41, 7.206-210
dolor, *112*, *113*, 2.3, 2.29, 6.3, 20.3
dolus, 6.12
domina, 4.75, 6.14, 10.12, 19.22

domus (= 'grave'), 2.21-22
dubito, 4.75
durus, 2.3, 4.76, 4.92, 9.3

edo, 4.42
ei mihi, 6.33
Elysii campi, 5.23
emetior, 4.17-18
Eoos, 2.24
equus, 7.91
ergo, 2.9
eripio, 2.1-2
erumpo, 7.86
Erythraeus, 3.17, 8.19-20
esse cum, *107*, 13.3-4
estne (verse opening), 17.1
etenim, 1.14
Etruscus, 5.1
etsi, 6.47-48
ex aequo, 6.19
exoriens, 1.2
exoro, 13.3-4
expello (for *depello*), 10.1
exta, 4.5-6

fabula ficta, 4.48
fallo, 1.6, 4.61-62, 6.12
falso, 3.19-20
fama: *108*; (= *infamia*), 13.1-2
far, 4.10
fatum (= 'day of death'), 5.18
faueo, 3.33-34
felix (rhetorical), 4.40
femina, 4.61-62
ferar, 13.10
ferox, 6.13-14
ferreus, 9.14
fessus/lassus, 10.10
flecto, 4.63
findo, 3.12
firmus, 2.5-6
fit (= *sacrum fit*), 12.14
foedo, 7.57
foedus (amatory), *99*, 19.2
formosus, 1.7
fortuna, 3.21-22

frater (= 'friend'), 1.23
fraudo, 5.19
frigidus, 14.4
frons, 2.28
frontes, 1.13
fruor, 3.32
funda (military), 7.97
fundo (of libations), 6.6
furor, 9.9-10
furtim, 8.8, 9.9-10, 9.21

garrulus, *90*, *117*, 4.38
gaudium, 3.7, 9.18
geminus, 8.6
gemma (= 'pearl'), 8.19-20
gener, *99*, *114*
generosus, 6.5
genus, 7.62
gloria, 7.29
gyrus, 7.94

habendus est, 11.2
hac ... illac, 7.96
haec ... et maiora, 6.17
hominum genus, 4.9
hora: of death, 5.5; = 'season', 7.51
horrendus, 4.91
humilis, 7.4

iamdudum (closural), 6.63
ignauus, 4.81
ignis (of love), *107*, 11.6
ignotus torus, 6.60, 16.5-6
ille ego, 4.72
ille ... ille, 7.50-52
immitis, 4.74
impleo, 3.1
in ore, 7.202
inaequatus, 7.43
incipio, 7.3, 7.136
inconstantia, 7.45
indago, 9.7
index, 730
indomitus, 6.16
inerro, 7.202
inesse, 4.84

infelix, 6.37
inficio, 4.32
ingratus, 6.42
ingenium, 2.5-6
insisto (+ dat.), 7.135
interiaceo, 7.150
interruptus, 7.74
intonsus, 10.2
inuidia, 3.19-20, 19.7
is, 4.94
ite ... ite (pastoral feature), 6.7
iucundus, 3.23-24
iuuat, 11.5
iuuenis, 2.1-2, 4.31, 5.6
iuuenta/iuuentas, 18.3

kalendae, 1.1

labor, 4.65, 7.16
lacus: = 'spring', 1.15-16; = 'underworld waters', 5.24
laedo, 4.16, 5.15
lampas, 8.6
Latona, 4.29
Latonius, 4.29
leaena, 4.90
lentus, 5.30
Lethaeus, 3.10
libellus, 1.9
littera (= 'label, 'inscription'), 1.12, 2.27
longe, 4.93
Lucina, 4.13-14
lumen (term of endearment), 19.11-12
lumina (= 'eyes'), 4.22
luridus, 3.38
lux: = 'life', 3.9; = 'day', 3.25, 7.160; as term of endearment, 88, *104*, 9.19, 18.1
Lyaeus, 2.19
lympha, 5.3

macies, 10.5
madeo, 6.5
maereo (+ abl.), 2.14

maestus, 2.11-12
magis (in analytic comparatives), 1.25
magnus: of gods, 4.16, 8.1; as official title, 7.176
male (as intensifier), 108, 16.2
malum, 4.33-34
maritus, 4.31
marmoreus, 3.3
medicus, 10.4
meditor, 4.71
medullae, 1.25
Meleteus, 7.200
mens, 9.9-10
merum, 5.34
meto, 8.17-18
meus/mea, 13.8
mica, 7.14
mille (indefinite number), 3.12, 12.11-12
ministro, 12.11-12
Minoi (voc.), 6.41
miser, 19.20, 20.4
mitto (= 'export'), 2.23
mixtus, 5.34
modulor, 4.39
molestus, 14.1
mollis, 4.76
Molorceus, 7.13
moneo (in erotodidaxis), 6.43
mora, 7.137-146, 7.147
mortifer, 5.9
mulier, 4.61-62
mundus, 7.150
munera parua, 7.7
Musae, 1.5
mutabilis (= 'flexible'), 4.63
mutuus amor, *114*
mysticus, 6.1-2

nam, 4.43-44
namque, 4.36
natalis/Natalis, 5.17, 11.19
nato, 7.43
ne (+ imperative), 4.75
neaera, *119*

Book Three of the Corpus Tibullianum: 613
Introduction, Text, Translation and Commentary

neco, 7.168
necopinans, *107*, 15.4
nemo, 13.8
nemus, 3.15
nequiquam, 5.27
niger, 3.37, 5.5
nitidus, 4.36
niueus, 1.9, 3.25, 4.30, 6.8
nobilis (of springs), 7.60
non alius, 7.46
non ego, 5.7-14, 5.7
nostro nomine, 4.78
noto, 19.24
notus, 19.22
nouo, 7.188
nouus, 7.79-81, 7.80, 11.3-4
nudo, 13.1-2
nudus, 3.10
numen, 4.53
numerandus, 10.12
nuntius, 4.5-6
nupta (= 'wife'), *99*, 4.60

obnoxius (+ dat.), 4.15
occulte, 12.6
ocellus, 6.47-48
olim ... cum (with future reference), 5.23-25
omen (= 'dream'), 4.9
oportet, 1.14
opus: = 'literary work', 1.14; = 'statue' 4.26
opus est: + subjunct., 7.101; + abl., 10.21
orbis (= 'orbit'), 7.159
ornatus, *94*
orno, 12.5
ortus (= 'sun's disk'), 4.21, 7.65
ossilegium, 2.15-25, 2.17-18

palla, 4.35, 8.11, 12.13
pallens, 10.5
pallor, 10.5
Panchaia, 2.23
Parcae, 11.3
parce, -ite (+ inf.), 5.6

parceo, 5.21, 9.1-2, 9.1
parma (military), 7.95
paruulus, 7.197
paruus (metapoetic), 1.24, 7.196
pascuum, 9.1-2
patera, 6.3
patientia, 2.5-6
paupertas, 3.23-24
pectus, 4.76
pelagus, 10.7-8, 10.8
pendeo (of embraces), 6.45
per (in imprecations), 1.15-16
pereo, 2.29
perlabor / prolabor, 7.155
perlucens, 4.71
perlucidus, 12.13
pertimeo, 4.14
pes, 4.24, 7.36
Phoebus (= the sun), 7.66
pia cura, *107*, *109*
Pierides, 1.5
Pierius, 1.15-16
pignus, 19.17
pilum (military), 7.90
pinguis, 3.12
plaga, 9.16
pompa, 1.3-4
pomum, 5.20
pone metum, 10.15
pono, 2.26
pontus, 7.20
posthac, 11.16
praeconium, 7.177
preces, 4.75-76
pretium, 1.7
primo, 5.17
primus, 2.1-2
probo, 4.5-6
procul, 9.5
prodest, 3.1
proles, 4.45
propero (transitive), 7.205
propositum, 6.9
pudor, *108*, 2.7
pudor est (+ inf.), 2.7

puella, 1.26, 2.1-2, 6.51-52, 6.60, 14.3
purpureus: 5.4; rhetorical, 4.29-34, 4.30
purus, 7.10
Pylius, 7.112

qualiter, 7.84
quam (comparative), *109*
quam uellem, 6.53
quamuis (+ indic.), 6.29, 14.8
quare, 4.49
quasillum, *105*, *116*, 16.3-4
-que: disjunctive, 2.1-2; *-que* position of, 8.8; *-que ... et*, 3.38, 7.87, 7.91-92, 7.167; *-que ... -que*, 1.3-4, 6.47-48, 7.11; *-que ... uel*, 7.63
quidcumque (+ gen.), 10.7
quidquid, 8.7, 10.7
quies, 4.22
quiesco, *107*
quis (= *quibus*), 7.65
quod causal (+ subjunct.), 10.13
quod (with noun clause), *107*, *108*
quod si, 4.77
quondam, 4.67, 6.39
quoniam, 11.19
quoquo, 8.7

rabidus, 7.72
recipio, 7.210
recuso, 4.73
regnum (erotic), 11.4
relego (+ dat.), 12.5
remitto, 5.4
remoror, 7.137-138
respuo, 7.8
rete, 9.12
rogus, 2.11-12
Roma, 15.2
ros (of perfumes), 4.28
Ruber, 3.17, 8.19-20
rugosus, 5.25
rumor, *93*, 20.1
rus, 14.1

sacrilegus, 5.11
sal, 4.10
salue, 4.43-44
sanctus, 11.2, 12.7
sapor, 10.9
Saturnia (of Juno), 3.33-34
scis, 15.1
scortum, *105*, *108*, 16.3-4
securus, 3.32, 16.1
sed, 2.13
senecta, 3.8
sentio (= 'feel to one's cost'), 6.26
serpo, 7.72
seruitium amoris, *112*
seu ... seu, 8.8-12, 9.1-2
si ... an ... an, 1.19-20
si modo (+ subjunctive), 7.198
si quicquam 18 headnote, 18.3
si quis (+imperative), 9.1-2
si sapis, 8.2
sic (+ optative subjunctive), 6.1-2
siccus, 6.18
Sidonius, 3.18
siue, 1.26
siue ... seu, 5.32
sollicitus (+ *pro*), 16.5
sonorus, 4.69
sonus (= 'voice'), 1.21-22
soror (= 'friend'), 1.23
sortior, 5.22
sperata (= 'betrothed'), 1.27-28
studiosus, *107*, 12.15, 14.5
subditus, 7.67
submissus, 1.21-22
subsequor, 8.8
subsisto, 7.2
subtexo, 7.211
sucus, 5.9
sudes (military), 7.89
superbus, 8.22, 11.4
supra, 2.10
suus, 12.16
Syrius, 2.24, 4.28

taceo, 20.4
tacita ... mente, 12.16

Book Three of the Corpus Tibullianum: 615
Introduction, Text, Translation and Commentary

taedia uitae, 2.7-8
talis, 8.13
tamen, 1.6, 6.56
tandem, 13.1-2
tantum ... quantum, 4.51-52
tecte/tectius, 11.17
temerarius, 4.7-10, 5.7, 6.27-28
temero, 5.7
tempestiuus, 14.6
teneo, 11.15
tener (metapoetic), 9.7, 9.8, 10.1
teneo, 5.1
tenuis (metapoetic), 1.11-12, 2.9, 9.7
ter quini, 5.28
tertia regna, 5.22
testis, 123, 7.107-110
Titan (= the sun), 7.51
toga, 16.2
torqueo, 9.12, 10.11, 20.4
torus, 6.19, 16.6
tota nocte, 6.61
tu modo + (imperat.), 4.64
tu quoque, 96, Ep. Tib., headnote, Ep. Tib. 1
turba, 10.17-18, 10.25, 19.11-12, 19.12
turpis, 6.37
tus, 3.2

Tuscus (= *Etruscus*), 4.5-6, 5.1
tutus, 196

uastus, 3.37, 4.85
uates, 4.49
-ue ... -ue, 7.39
uel (disjunctive), 7.202
uela (= 'cloth'), 2.21-22
uenerandus, 8.10
uenia, 8.3
uenio, 1.1, 4.39, 8.2
Venus, 8.2, 8.3, 11.13-14
uerbera (in *seruitium amoris*), 4.66
uerto, 2.26
uestigium, 8.8
uideor, 18.2
uilla, 14.3
uinclum, 117, 9.14, 11.14, 12.8
uinco, 4.76, 11.13-14, 19.23
uir, 99
uirgo, 4.31
uirtus, 7.1
uis/uires, 7.2, 8.3
uix (+gerundive), 10.12
ullae (= *ulli* f.), 12.9
umbilicus, 1.13
unda, 5.1-2, 7.155
uotum, 3.1, 4.53, 10.12
uro, 8.11-12, 11.5, 12.17-18, 19.19

(b) Greek

ἄγνοια, 3.19-20
ἄγριος, 4.65
ἀείδω, 7 headnote
ἄελλα, 4.96
αἰθήρ, 7.124-129
ἀκερσεκόμης, 4.27, 10.2
ἀλιτρός, 4.3, 19.7
ἀμάρτυρος, *123*, 7.106
ἀνανεοῦσθαι, 7.113
ἁπαλός, 4.31-34
Ἀπόλλων, 4.23-42, 4.49, 7.14-15, 7.178, 10.1-2

ἀποπομπή, 6.25-26
ἀρειμάνιοι, 7.108
αὔξησις, 7.118-134
αὐλός, 4.71

βαρύς, 4.65
Βασκανίη, 19.7

γένος, 7.62

δᾶμος, δῆμος, *113*
δεινός, 4.65

Δήλιος / Δήλια, 9.5
δῆλος, 113
δημόσιος / δημόσια, 2.29, 3.19-20, 7.17-18
διαυγής, 4.71
δόναξ, 4.71
δόξα, 3.19.20
δῶρα Διονύσου, 6.17-18

εἱμαρμένος (νόμος), 4.47-48
ἑκάς, 4.3
ἐπαινή (for Persephone), 5.7-8
ἐσθλός, 4.43-44

Ζυγία (Ἥρα), 3.33-34

θαῦμα, 3.19-20
θορυβεῖν, 10.17-18

ἴσος Ἔρως, 1.19

καθαρή ... λιβάς, 3.19-20
κατανεύω, 7.113
κήρινθος, 124
κηρίον / κηρός, 10.5
κισσοφόρος (παῖς), 6.2
κόγχη, 3.33-34
κόραι, 7.57
κυλίνδομαι, 5.1-2
κῦμα, 5.1-2, 7.124-129
Κύπρις /Κυπρογενής / Κυπρογένεια, 3.33-34

λάθε βιώσας, 19.9
λέαινα, 4.90
λεπταλέος, 1.11-12
λεπτός, 4.71, 7.16
ληνός, 6.38
Λητώ, 4.29
λιρός, 19.18
λύγδην, 112
λυγμός, 112
λύζω, 112

μακαρισμός, 3.26, 6.43-44
μελάνιππος (νύξ), 4.17-18

μελιηδής (νόστος), 3.27
μέλισσαι, 3.19-20
μικρός, see *parua* ... *mica* 7.14-15
Μοῖραι, 3.35, 11.3
μύστης, 6.1

νέα – era, *90, 119*
νιφάς, 7.48-49
νόμος, 4.47-48
νόστος, 3.27
νύμφη (= 'water'), 5.3

οἶνος, 6.5
ὄμμα, 7.57, 8.5-6,
ὅρκος, 4.79, 6.49
οὔλιος, 4.65
οὐρανίωνες, 7.14
οὐρανός, 7.23

πάντα ῥεῖ, 8 *headnote*
παρειά, 4.31-34, 4.32
πέπλος, 4.35
πλῆθος, 3.19-20
πόνος, *87*, 1.14, 7.16, 7.181
πόντος, 3.19-20, 7.20
ποταμός, 7.17-18
πρός (+ gen.), 11.7
πρῶτος εὑρετής, 2.1-8

ῥόος, 3.19-20, 10.7-8

σαφήνεια, 7.48-49
σίδηρος, 2.1-2 2.1-2
σιδηρόφρων, 2.1-2
σικχαίνω, 3.19-20, 7.17-18
σκύλαξ, 4.89, 7.72
σοφός, 3.19-20, 6.41,
σῦριγξ, 4.71
σχέτλιος, 4.65

ὕδωρ, 3.19-20, 7.140, 7.155
Ὕπνος, 4.19-20

φάρμακα, 7.62-63
Φθόνος, 19.7
φιλόσοφος λόγος, 3.19-20

Φοῖβος, 4.27

χαλεπός, 4.65
Χρυσορρόας, 3.29

ψόγος πλούτου, 3 headnote

Ὠκεανός, 4.17-18
ὠκύς, 7.91
ὥρα, 7.51
ὠφελεῖν, 3.1

INDEX 3

INDEX LOCORUM

Numbers in Italics refer to pages of the Prolegomena and General Introduction, non-italic to poem and line numbers in the commentary

Accius (Ribbeck³)
Praetext. 36-37: 7.55
Trag. 37: 3.25
Trag. 174: 6.13-14
Trag. 288: 7.45-47
Trag. 297: 7.72
Trag. 331: 8.6
Trag. 394: 7.155
Trag. 397: 7.75
Trag. 399: 7.20
Trag. 570: 5.1-2
Trag. 670: 8.6
Trag. 674: 10.2
Trag. 687-688: 6.1-2

Achilles Tatius
4.5.1: 7.145

Aeschines
2.153: 6.47-49

Aeschylus
Ag. 1573: 6.25-26
Choeph. 660-661: 4.17-18
Eumen. 17-18: 4.45-48
Eumen. 19: 4.47-48
fr. 69.5-6R: 4.17-18

[Aeschylus]
Prom. 7-8: 2.1-8
Prom. 242: 2.1-2

Aëtius
3.13.1: 7.151-174
Afranius (Ribbeck³)
6: 6.55
141: 11.1
289-290: 6.19

Alcaeus
346.3-4 (*PLF*): 6 *headnote*
356: 6 *headnote*
362.2: 6.5

Alcuin
Carm. 1.1090: 7.191

Ampelius
2.6: 7.9-11
13.1: 7.143

Anacreon
16 (*PMG*): 3 *headnote*
356: 6 *headnote*, 6.5
396: 6 *headnote*

Anthologia Latina
236.1: 7.139
762.54: 7.91

Anthologia Palatina (*AP*) –see also individual authors
5.26.1-3: 8.9
5.101: 1 *headnote*

9.15: 8.5-6
12.155: I *headnote*

Antigonus
AP 9.406.3: 5.3

Antipater of Sidon
AP 7.8.3: 7.124
AP 7.8.4: 7.126
AP 9.93.2-3: 7.14-15

Antiphanes
AP 9.258: 5.3

Apollodorus
2.4.12: 7.12
2.5.1: 4.87
3.10.44: 4.67-72
3.14.7: 7.9-11

Apollonius Rhodius
1.26-27: 7.125
3.297: 4.32
3.297-298: 4.31-34
3.297: 4.65
3.744f.: 4.19-20
3.1078: 4.65
4.357ff.: 6.39
4.445: 4.65

Appian
3.16.48: 7.110
3.18.52: 7.108
3.22.64: 7.108-109
3.23: 7.108-109
3.24: 7.108-109
3.25.71ff: 7.116

Apuleius
De Deo Socr. 22.1-3: 19.9
Flor. 6.11: 8.19-20
Flor. 15: 4.39
Flor. 17: 4.71
Flor. 20: 7.35
Met. 1.4: 4.65
Met. 4.6: 9.2

Met. 4.7: 5.16
Met. 4.11: 7.196
Met. 4.33: 4.65
Met. 5.13: 19.11-12
Met. 8.21: 14.6
Met. 8.30: 10.17
Met. 9.34: 4.53
Met. 10.22: 4.28
Met. 11.14: 2.10
Met. 11.26.1: 7.93
Plat. 2.20: 4.47-48

Aratus
Phaen. 1: 7.3
Phaen. 227-332: 7.9-11

Archilochus
19 (West): 3 *headnote*, 3.29

Aristophanes
Acharn. 491: 2.1-2
Aues 778: 7.124, 7.126
Aues 1731: 11.3
Lys. 155-156: 8.4
Plut. 558-561: 3 *headnote*
Thesm. 43-48: 7.124-129

Aristotle
Meteor. 2.5 p. 362a32-b30 Bekker: 7.151-174
fr. 76 (Rose): 7.200

Arnobius
Nat. 5.24: 7.196

Asclepiades
AP 5.210: 11.5
AP 7.11.1: 7.16
AP 12.50: 6 *headnote*

Atta (Ribbeck[3])
Com. 18: 1.2

Augustine
Ciu. 6.9: 8.3

Augustus
Res Gestae 19: 4.23-42

Ausonius
Cento Nuptialis 6.70: 13.10
Cento Nuptialis 10.9-10: *127*
Cupid. 14: 7.189
Epig. 54.1: 7.121
Epig. 399.3: 1.15-16
Prec. Kal. Ian. 3-4: 7.123

Avienus
Arat. 399-340: 7.172
Arat. 1208: 7.189
Arat. 1348: 7.150
Orb. Terr. 335: 7.155
Orb. Terr. 680-681: 7.155

Bellum Africum
3.4: 13.7

Bellum Alexandrinum
17.4.5: 7.87

Caecilius (Ribbeck[3])
Com. 262: 6.3
Com. 290: 7.7

Caesar
BC 2.24: 7.93
BG 1.28: 9.1
BG 1.205: 1.24
BG 3.21: 7.128
BG 3.25: 7.87
BG 4.20: 5.23
BG 4.38: 7.128
BG 5.14: 4.31
BG 6.17: 10.1
BG 7.14: 11.20

Callimachus
Aet. fr. 1 Pf.: 7.18-27, 7.177-180
Aet. fr. 1.5: 1.24, 7.16
Aet. fr. 1.5-6: *87*
Aet. fr. 1.9: 7.196
Aet. fr. 1.21-24: 7.14-15

Aet. fr. 1.21ff.: 4 *headnote*
Aet. fr. 1.24: 1.11-12
Aet. fr. 1.25-28: 10.17-18, 19.10
Aet. fr. 1.25f.: 3.19-20
Aet. fr. 54-59: 7.12-13
Aet. fr. 59.16: 7.13
Aet. fr. 67.6: 4.50
Aet. fr. 73: 19.9
Aet. fr. 74.2: 19.18
Aet. fr. 75.23: 5.24
Aet. fr. 75.26-27: 4.79
Aet. fr. 75.44-48: 3.23-24
Aet. fr. 75.49: 4.65
Aet. fr. 79.45: 8.6
Aet. fr. 110.64: 7 *headnote*
Aet. fr. 178.3: 7.9-11
Aet. fr. 178.4: 7.9-11
Iamb. fr. 191.7-8: 4.43-44
Epig. 5: 3.33-34
Epig. 6.1-2: *87*, 7.16
Epig. 7: 4.43-44
Epig. 8: 4.43-44
Epig. 25.3-4: 6.49-50
Epig. 28.1ff.: 3.19-20
Epig. 28.4: 10.17-18
fr. 383.16ff.: 7 *headnote*
fr. 383.27:7 *headnote*
fr. 383.31-32: 7 *headnote*
fr. 612: *123*, 7.106, 7.107-110
Hecale: 7.8-10
Hecale 90.1-2 (Hollis): 7.72
Hymn. 1.40: 7.58
Hymn. 1.55-57: 7 *headnote*
Hymn. 2.2: 4.3
Hymn. 2.9: 4.43-44
Hymn. 2.32-42: 4 *headnote*, 4.23-42
Hymn. 2.32: 4.35, 4.37
Hymn. 2.36: 4.23, 4.26, 4.33-34
Hymn. 2.38: 4.28
Hymn. 2.47-48: 4.67-72
Hymn. 2.47: 4.67
Hymn. 2.48: 4.67-72
Hymn. 2.68-69: 4.45-48
Hymn. 2.68: 4.49
Hymn. 2.106: 3.19-20
Hymn. 2.108-112: 3.19-20

Hymn. 2.108-109: 10.7-8
Hymn. 2.185: 4.39
Hymn. 3.145: 7.12
Hymn. 4.10: 4.50
Hymn. 4.165-170: 7.135-176
Hymn. 4.269: 9.5
SH fr. 254-269: 7 *headnote*, 7.9-11
SH fr. 257-268: 7.12-13
SH fr. 265.16: 7.13

Calpurnius Siculus
Ecl. 1.77-78: 7.10
Ecl. 2.11: 7.209
Ecl. 2.15: 7.125
Ecl. 2.16-17: 7.124
Ecl. 2.55: 6.7
Ecl. 2.84: 10.6
Ecl. 3.8: 11.5
Ecl. 3.42: 13.3-4
Ecl. 3.72: 7.171
Ecl. 3.75: 4.75
Ecl. 4.46: 13.3-4
Ecl. 4.78: 7.136
Ecl. 4.84: 7.79
Ecl. 4.93: 7.130
Ecl. 4.121: 7.161
Ecl. 4.142: 7.206
Ecl. 5.45: 7.45-47
Ecl. 5.98: 7.136
Ecl. 5.102-103: 5.23-25
Ecl. 6.43: 7.44
Ecl. 7.53-54: 9.12
Ecl. 7.68: 7.60

Calvus
fr. 15 (Courtney = 27 Hollis): 2.9

Carmina Latina Epigraphica (*CLE*)
14.2: 2.17
55.1-2: 2.21-22
55.7: 5.5
251.4: 7.68
367.1: 5.5
369.11: 7.196
373.1: 5.31
389.2: 5.5

400.3: 5.5
434.15: 2.21-22
461: 2.29
522.5: 5.23
542.7: 3.32
661.1: 7.177
931: 6.6
965.7: 3.32
1038.5: 2.26
1141.16: 3.36
1165.4: 5.23
1200.6: 5.23
1247.1: 2.17
1430.3: 2.7-8
1515.9: 5.23
1533.3-4: 11.3
1970.1-2: 5.23
2075.1-2: 3.37
2155.4: 7.68

Cassiodorus
Chron. Min. II 130: 1.2

Cassius Dio
49.35.4: 7.108
49.36.2: 7.110
49.37.2ff.: 7. 108-109
49.38.2: 7.149
49.38.3: 7.106-117
51.21.5: 7.116
53.22.5: 7.149
53.25.2: 7.149
67.6.2: 7.146

Cato
Agr. 75: 12.14
Agr. 160: 10.10
Mil. fr.10 (Jord.): 7.101-102

Catullus
1: 1 *headnote*, 1.9
1.1: *86*, 1.5
1.1.1-2: 1.9-14, 7.7
1.8: 1.9
2 and 3: 11 *headnote*
2.28: 18.6

3.14: 4.29
5.2: 13.5-6
5 and 7: 11 *headnote*
6.5: 16.3-4
8.1: 20.4
8.3: 3.25, 6.8, 6.30
8.5: 4.51-52
8.16: 4.51-52, 19.5
9.8: 7.182
10.33: *107*, 16.2
11.1-4: 7.193-197
11.10: 7.176
11.11-12: 7.149
11.21-22: 6.4
12.2: 6.34
12.5: 6.29
14: *132*, 1 *headnote*
15.14: 9.7
16: 5-6: 4.43-44
17.5-7: 6.1-2
22.6-8: 1.9-14
23.10: 6.42
24.3: 11.16
27: 6 *headnote*
27.1: 6.5, 6.55
27.3: 6.10
27.5-7: 6.21
29.4: 7.149
29.19: 3.29
30.2: 6.9
30.4: 6.42
30.9-10: 4.96, 6.27-28
30.10: 6.49-50
32: 6.54
34.5-6: 4.29
34.13-14: 4.13-14
34.15-16: 4.29
35.7: 8.2
35.8: 4.29
35.16-17: 12.2
36.3-4: 19.23
37.11-14: 4.51-60
36.11: 7.20
37.12: 4.51-52
37 and 39: 11 *headnote*
39.6-7: 10.7

39.11: 5.1
44.7: 10.1
45.14: 11.13-14
45.16: 11.6
45.20: 11.13-16
45.21-22: 7.197-200
50.1-2: 7.181
50.21: 8.3
51: 13.3-4
51.9: 1.9
55.2: 2.27
60.1-3: 4.85-94, 4.90, 4.92
60.2: 4.89, 7.62
61.6-10: 12.13
61.9-10: 1.9
61.15: 4.31
61.28-30: 7.60
61.54-55: 4.31
61.61-63: 3.23-24
61.91: 4.31
61.102-103: 7.171
61.119-143: 16.2
61.185-188: 4.31-34
61.186: 4.32
62.5: 6.1
62.29: 18.6
62.37: 12.16
62.60-61: 12.15
62.62: 10.17
63.8: 4.30
63.15: 6.10
63.40: 7.207
63.48: 4.85
63.92: 6.25
63.92-93: 6.25-26
64.2: 7.123
64.6: 7.69
64.23: 7.62
64.30: 7.53, 7.147
64.52-264: 6.39-42
64.54: 7.34
64.57: 6.40
64.58-59: 6.39
64.59: 4.96, 6.49-50
64.60: 6.39-42, 6.41
64: 66-67: 4.35

Book Three of the Corpus Tibullianum: 623
Introduction, Text, Translation and Commentary

64.111: 5.27
64.132-135: 6.39
64.132-133: 6.40
64.135: 6.39, 6.39-42
64.136-137: 4.63
64.136: 4.61-62
64.142: 4.96, 6.27-28, 6.49-50
64.154-157: 4.85-94
64.156: 4.89, 4.91
64.159: 5.26
64.164: 6.51-52
64.169: *88*
64.172: 7.69
64.179: 7.20
64.183: 5.30
64.189: 17.2
64.192: 5.7-8
64.193-194: 4.87
64.193: 4.87
64.200: 18.5
64.204ff.: 7.130-134
64.204-206: 7.133
64.215: 4.93
64.254: 5.3
64.266: 4.55
64.271: 7.76
64.282: 4.96
64.306-310: 3.36
64.311-314: 3.36
64.318-319: 8.15-16
64.320ff.: 11.3
64.323: 7.32
64.332: 6.45
64.335: 19.2
64.341: 9.13
64.357: 7.107-110
64.364: 4.30
64.373: 19.2
64.374: 4.51-52
64.383: 11.3
64.384: 4.60
65.2: 4.45
65.4: 4.82
65.5-6: 5.1
65.5: 3.10

65.9: 11.16
65.10: 4.94
65.11: 11.16
65.13: 7.154
65.17-18: 4.96
66: *87*
66.1: 7.18
66.10: 4.64
66.15: 17.1
66.24-25: 1.20
66.46: 7.70
66.48: 7.64
66.55-66: 7.9-11
66.64: 7 *headnote*
67: *131-132*, 1 *headnote*
67.25-26: 5.32
67.25: 4.59
68.5: 19.23
68.68: 4.74
68.81-83: 6.53
68.84: 2.4
68.100: 7.53
68.103-104: 14.7
68.106-107: 2.4
68.110: 3.12
68.131-132: 12.10
68.132: *88*, 9.15, 13.3-4
68.136: 4.74
68.140: *88*
68.143: 4.31
68.144: 2.24
68.147-148: 3.25
68.152: 7.17
68.155: 6.30
68.156: 4.74
68.160: 9.15
69.8: 4.51-52
70.2-3: 4.96
70 and 72: 11 *headnote*
70.4: 7.72, 10.8
72.3-4: 4.51-52, 6.49-50
72.5: *90*, 11.5
73: *107*
73.1-4: 13.1-2
73.3: 13.8
75: *106*, 18 *headnote*

76: *109*
76.1-2: 17.1
76.3-4: 19.2
76.3: *99*
76.5: 7.210
76.13-14: 6.33-34
76.23ff.: 11.13-16
76.25: 6.3
78.4: 4.51-52
78.10: 20.1
81: 18 *headnote*
82: 18 *headnote*
83.3-6: 12.18
85: 106
86: 1.7
87.1-2: 4.51-52
87.3: *99*
88.1-2: 6.54
95.7f.: 3.19-20
95.9-10: 7.7
96: 18 *headnote*
96.1: 18 *headnote*, 18.3
96.3: 12.20
99.16: 11.16
100.8: 6.30
101.3: 1.21-22
102: 18 *headnote*
102.1-2: 18.3
102.1: 18 *headnote*, 18.3
103: 18 *headnote*
104.2: 1.25
107.1: 18 *headnote*, 18.3
107.3-6: 6.55
107.6: 3.25
107 and 109: 11 *headnote*
109.5-6: 6.61
109.5: 18.3
109.6: *99*, 19.2
115.3: 3.29
116.2: *88*

Celsus
Praef. 36: 1.19-20
1 pr.22: 7.84
1 pr.23.2: 4.75
1.3.14: 6.18

1.8.2: 10.5
2.16.10: 5.5
2.18.6: 5.20
3.18.22: 1.19-20
3.20.4: 10.1
3.21.8: 1.19-20
3.22.8: 17.3
5.27.2d: 17.2
7.26.5a: 17.2

Censorinus
De Die Natali 3: 11.8

Charisius
258.3 (Barwick): 6.47-49

Chrysippus
SVF II 649: 7.151-174

Cicero
Ad M. Brut. 1.3: 14.7
Amic. 9.2: 4.51-52
Amic. 45: 16.5
Amic. 90.5: 6.9
Arat. 4: 7.13
Arat. 23: 7.20
Arat. 47-48: 7.72
Arat. 59: 7.153
Arat. 68: 17.2
Arat. 82: 4.2
Arat. 97-98: 7.165-168
Arat. 100: 7.124, 7.165-168
Arat. 111: 7.86
Arat. 126: 7.155
Arat. 133: 7.69
Arat. 299: 7.147
Arat. 326: 4.86
Arat. 343: 7.51
Arat. 396: 7.155
Att. 1.13.5: 5.22
Att. 3.15.4: 4.51-52
Att. 3.22.4: 14.5
Att. 4.14.2: 1.24
Att. 4.17.5: 18.1-3
Att. 5.12.4: 7.196
Att. 5.18a.2: 4.93

Book Three of the Corpus Tibullianum: Introduction, Text, Translation and Commentary

Att. 7.8.1: 4.94
Att. 8.12a.4: 10.7
Att. 8.16.1: 10.12
Att. 9.8.1: 18.2
Att. 10.8.4: 18.1
Att. 11.1.1: 13.7
Att. 12.3.1: 18.1-3
Att. 12.15.1: 7.128
Att. 12.27.2: 16.1
Att. 13.42: 13.3-4
Att. 14.16.4: 16.1
Att. 15.7.1: 16.1
Att. 16.4.4: 15.1
Att. 16.12.1: 6.17
Att. 16.13a.1: 18.1-3
Brut. 40: 7.48-49
Brut. 82: 12.5
Brut. 297: 6.23
Caec. 8: 4.15
Cael. 6.13: 9.12
Catil. 1.31: 5.27
De Orat. 1.53: 7.46-47
De Orat. 1.222: 14.7
De Orat. 1.192: 7.34
De Orat. 1.261: 7.151
De Orat. 2.76: 4.26
De Orat. 2.80: 12.5
De Orat. 2.203: 7.72
De Orat. 2.252: 12.5
De Orat. 2.341: 12.5
De Orat. 3.39: 12.5
De Orat. 3.67: 14.7
De Orat. 3.85: 6.23
De Orat. 3.116: 7.115
De Orat. 3.137: 4.46
De Orat. 3.153: 4.45
De Orat. 3.167: 12.5
De Orat. 3.184: 7.36
De Orat. 3.205: 17.6
Diu. 1.20: 1.1
Diu. 1.29: 4.47-48
Diu. 1.59: 19.12
Diu. 2.30: 12.9
Diu. 2.63: 7.15
Diu. In Caec. 57: 7.61
Dom. 4: 7.45-47

Fam. 1.7.6: 4.46
Fam. 4.2.2: 9.15
Fam. 5.13: 1.20
Fam. 5.19.1: 10.7
Fam. 6.6.3: 4.5-6
Fam. 7.12.2: 19.15
Fam. 7.23.4: 18.1-3
Fam. 7.25.1: 16.1
Fam. 8.4.2: 4.46
Fam. 9.14.4: 4.51-52
Fam. 13.50.2: 11.7
Fam. 14.2.2-3: 1.26
Fam. 14.2.2: 18.1
Fam. 14.7.1: 1.25
Fam. 16.17.2: 16.1
Fat. 30: 13.10
Epist. fr. 6.3: 7.1
Fin. 1.45: 19.9
Fin. 2.5: 3.1
Fin. 2.69: 10.17-18
Fin. 2.101: 14.2-3
Fin. 3.45: 3.29
Fin. 3.74: 10.21
Fin. 5.5: 7.13
Flacc. 32: 7.107-110
Flacc. 33: 20.3
Flacc. 66: 1.21-22
Flacc. 92: 6.11
Font. 42.4: 7.1
Harusp. 26.14: 4.59
Harusp. 57: 5.8
Harusp. 63: 7.46-47
Imp. Cn. Pomp. 30: 15.1
Inu. 2.77: 4.15
Leg. 1.8: 7.16
Leg. 2.35.58: 2.11-12
Leg. 3.19.2: 14.1, 14.2-3
Lig. 18: 7.113
Manil. 30.1-7: 7.107-110
Marc. 4: 7.3-4
Mil. 8: 4.68
Mur. 11: *Vit. Tib.* 3-4
Nat. Deor. 1.24: 7.151-174
Nat. Deor. 1.26: 7.19
Nat. Deor. 1.43: 7.45-47
Nat. Deor. 2.53.6: 7.169

Nat. Deor. 2.66: 1.27-28
Nat. Deor. 2.68: 4.13-14
Nat. Deor. 2.69: 8.2
Nat. Deor. 2.109.5: 7.13
Nat. Deor. 3.71: 5.13
Off. 3.7: 13.5
Off. 3.64: 10.19
Orat. 11: 19.10
Orat. 27: 7.36
Orat. 76: 7.4
Parad. 1.15: 19.9
Parad. 13: 3.3
Parad. 49: 3.16
Part. Or. 71: 7.118-134
Part. Or. 73: 7.118-134
Part. Or. 74: 7.28-32
Phil. 2.44: 16.3
Phil. 2.108: 7.101-102
Phil. 3.31: 7.13
Phil. 5.1: 7.11
Phil. 5.20: 7.101-102
Phil. 8.9.9: 4.1
Phil. 10.5.3: 4.1
Phil. 11.8.5: 17.2
Phil. 11.21: 7.3-4
Phil. 13.18: 7.101-102
Phil. 13.22: 7.169
Phil. 14.28.7: 1.27-28
Planc. 22: 4.49
Planc. 27: *Vit. Tib.* 3
Planc. 72: 13.1-2
Planc. 89.14: 7.175
Poet. fr. (Morel) 30.9: 7.138
Poet. fr. (Morel): 43.4: 7.91
Progn. 3.7: 7.75
Q. Rosc. 25: 20.3
Quinct. 40.5: 7.169
Rep. 1.65: 7.46
Rep. 2.19: 4.68
Rep. 6.24: 7.169
S. Rosc. 102: 18.6
S. Rosc. 110: 15.1
S. Rosc. 133: 14.1
Sen. 18.62: 5.15

Sen. 31: 7.50-51

Sen. 47.6: 4.1
Sen. 71: 5.19-20, 5.20
Sest. 47: 14.7
Somn. Scip. 20-22: 7.135-176
Somn. Scip. 21: 7.151-174
Tim. 43: 4.47-48
Topica 100: 12.5
Tusc. 1.10: 4.88
Tusc. 1.30: 2.14
Tusc. 1.53: 8.13
Tusc. 1.71: 5.9
Tusc. 1.116: 4.46
Tusc. 2.21: 17.3
Tusc. 2.212: 4.91
Tusc. 3.51: 19.8
Tusc. 4.18: 17.2
Verr. 1.1.21: 18.6
Verr. 2.1.47: 4.79
Verr. 2.2.60: 13.8
Verr. 2.3.149: 7.107-110
Verr. 2.3.182: 4.68
Verr. 2.4.95: 7.2
Verr. 2.4.151: 11.1
Verr. 2.5.28: 6.10
Verr. 2.5.30: 2.21-22
Verr. 2.5.80: 2.21-22
Verr. 2.5.86: 8.11-12
Verr. 2.5.146: 7.56

Cinna
fr. 11.3 (Courtney =13.3 Hollis):
   1.9-14

Claudian
Carm. 5.325: 4.55
Carm. 34.15: 4.39
Carm. Min. 27.54: 7.206
Carm. Min. 27.70-71: 7.70
Carm. Min. 30.49: 7.138
Carm. Min. app. 2.19: 4.23
Paneg. Cons. Hon. 357: 7.109
Paneg. Cons. Olybrio et Probino 1f.
   : 7.123
Paneg. Cons. Olybrio et Probino 6-7: 7.122
Rapt. Proserp. 1.277: 7.181

Claudius Quadrigarius
Fr. 81 P.: 5.11

Cleanthes
fr. 4 (Powell): 3.19-20
SVF I 535: 7.21-22

Columella
Arb. 7.1: 7.84
Rust. 1.4.6: 7.84
Rust. 2.9.10: 4.87
Rust. 2.20.1: 5.1-2
Rust. 3.13.3: 3.9
Rust. 6.2.11: 17.2
Rust. 6.5.2: 17.3
Rust. 6.13.2: 7.65
Rust. 6.29.2: 4.27
Rust. 6.32.1: 7.65
Rust. 7.3.10: 9.10
Rust. 7.10.5: 4.87
Rust. 9.11.1: 7.86
Rust. 9.14.14: 2.10
Rust. 10.3: 6.17-18
Rust. 10.14: 7.128
Rust. 10.84: 7.161
Rust. 10.175: 4.33-34
Rust. 10.256-257: 5.4
Rust. 10.274: 7.67
Rust. 10.354: 2.10
Rust. 10.430: 6.38
Rust. 10.435: 2.1-2
Rust. 11.3.65: 7.84

Corippus
Ioh. 1.544-545: 7.94
Ioh. 3.200: 7.99
Ioh. 6.239: 7.99

Corpus Inscriptionum Latinorum
  (*CIL*)
I 2231: 5.33
VI 2174.4: 2.29
VI 53272.2: 2.29
X 1576: 11.9
XV 1418-1419: 2.29

Crates
fr. 34a (Mette): 7.152

Curtius Rufus
3.3.18: 4.35
5.1.19: 7.101-102
5.2.9: 7.140
5.12.11: 4.47-48
6.9.1: 4.29
7.7.35: 7.92
7.9.13: 7.92, 17.2
8.14.6: 7.92
9.1.20: 7.45-47
9.3.5: 4.59
10.2.13: 8.7

[Demosthenes]
Or. 59: *119*

Digesta
Iust. *Dig.* 7.8.10.2: 4.92
Iust. *Dig.* 12.1.9.8: 4.78
Iust. *Dig.* 19.2.60: 4.92
Iust. *Dig.* 36.1.4.2: 4.78
Iust. *Dig.* 47.11.4 pr.3: 5.19
Iust. *Dig.* 47.12.3: 17.2
Iust. *Dig.* 50.5.2: 17.2
Iust. *Dig.* 50.6.6. pr. 5: 17.2
Paul. *Dig.* 2.13.12: 4.42
Ulp. *Dig.* 14.4.1.3: 2.5-6
Ulp. *Dig.* 15.1.3: 5.11
Ulp. *Dig.* 39.4.16.7: 2.21-22
Ulp. *Dig.* 48.5.30 *Praef.* 4: 2.5-6
Ulp. *Dig.* 49.5.13: 6.12

Dio Chrysostom
36.4: 7.146

Diodorus Siculus
1.2.5: 7.137-146
4.5.1: 6.38

Diogenes Laertius
7.137 (= *SVF* II 580): 7.22

Donatus
Vit. Verg. 147: 7.196
Vit. Verg. 153-154: 7.196

Ecl. Einsid.
1.17: 4.50
1.71: 10.1
1.47: 4.55
2.27: 7.174

Elegia in Maecenatem
1.6: 3.37
1.15: 4.39
1.30: 7.97
1.117: 8.23

Ennius
Ann. 2-11 (Skutsch): 7.206-210
Ann. 3: 4.24
Ann. 14: 7.149
Ann. 54: 3.33-34
Ann. 124: 9.1
Ann. 185: 7.103
Ann. 190: 4.16
Ann. 217: 7.20
Ann. 264: 9.2
Ann. 327-328: 4.65
Ann. 385-386: 6.13-14
Ann. 445: 3.33-34
Ann. 520-521: 6.13-14
Ann. 537: 9.1
Ann. 582: 7.90
Op. Inc. 1 (Skutsch): 5.23
Sat. 6 (*FRL*): 7.107-110
Trag. 3-4 (Jocelyn): 11.7
Trag. 23: 3.33-34
Trag. 33: 1.23
Trag. 50-51: 4.24
Trag. 50: 5.1-2
Trag. 58-59: 4.42
Trag. 61: 13.1-2
Trag. 90-91: 3.16
Trag. 96-97: 4.17-18
Trag. 109: 2.1-2
Trag. 120-121: 2.19
Trag. 120: 6.38

Trag. 128: 13.10
Trag. 140: 13.8
Trag. 152: 3.37
Trag. 208: 3.15
Trag. 213: 7.15
Trag. 216: 4.65
Trag. 280: 7.65
Trag. 308: 10.17-18
Trag. 314: 5.9
Trag. 394: 5.16
Trag. 399: 7.57
Trag. 415: 4.87
Trag. xxxiv: 1.27-28
Trag. lxxiii: 7.124-129
Spur. 10 (Skutsch): 4.93
Var. 78 (Skutsch): 1.27-28, 3.38

Ephorus
fr. 1 (Jacoby): 7.200

Epicurus
Ep. 3.130: 3 *headnote*

Eratosthenes
Cat. 14 p. 79: 7.9-11
Hermes fr. 16 (Powell): 7.151-174
Hermes fr. 16. 15-18: 7.165-168

Euripides
Alcest. 8: 4.67-72, 4.67
Andr. 629-631: 8.4
Bacch. 773: 6 *headnote*
Bacch. 988-990: 4.85-94
Bacch. 990: 4.90
Bacch. 1084-1085: 7.124, 7.124-129
Cycl. 20ff.: 7.56
Cycl. 104: 7.62
Cycl. 130: 7.56
Cycl. 298: 756
Cycl. 366: 7.56
Cycl. 463: 7.57
Cycl. 470: 7.57
Cycl. 510: 7.57
Hel. 569-570: 4.13-14
Heracl. 219: 7.107-110
Heracl. 351: 4.39

Heracl. 611: 4.87
Hipp. 35: 6.3
Hipp. 210-211: 9.16
Hipp. 283: 6.3
Hipp. 394: 6.3
Ion 94ff.: 1.15-16
Ion 1150-1151: 4.17-18
Ion 1150: 4.55
Med. 21-23: 6.49-50
Med. 21ff.: 6.39
Med. 160-163: 6.49-50
Med. 208-209: 6.49-50
Med. 492-498: 6.49-50
Med. 492: 6.39
Med. 1342-1343: 4.90
Or. 146: 4.71
Or. 1287: 8.4
Phaeth. 224-225: 7.66
Phoen. 225-226: 1.15-16
Phrixus fr. 1.7: 5.1-2
Suppl. 1155: 4.96
Trachin. 419: 4.96
Trachin. 454: 4.96

Festus
131 (Lindsay): 1.1.4
136: 1.2
198-200 1.1
474.31ff.: 5.34

FGrHist (*Fragmente der griechischen Historiker*)
63: 2.23

Frontinus
Aqu. 91.5: 6.58
Strateg. 2.3.17: 7.84
Strateg. 2.5.26: 7.85
Strateg. 2.5.31: 7.92

Fronto
Epist. 2.7.19: 1.27-28

Fulgentius
Virg. cont. p. 104.13: 4.29

Gaius
Inst. 3.195: 5.11
Inst. 4.81: 4.78
Inst. 4.153: 4.78

Gallus
fr. 2.1-2 (Courtney = 145.1-2 Hollis): 14.2-3
fr. 2.2 (Courtney = 145.2 Hollis): 16.1
fr. 2.6-7 (Courtney = 145.6-7 Hollis): 1.8, 8.15, 13.1-2
fr. 2.7 (Courtney =145.7 Hollis): 19.22
fr, 2.8 (Courtney = 145.8 Hollis): 7.136

Gellius
1.26.7: 6.51-52
2.1.2: 4.21
3.16.9f.: 3.35
14.6.3: 7.79-81

Germanicus
Arat. 2: 1.15-16
Arat. 91: 6.17-18
Arat. 260: 7.191
Arat. 314: 7.156
Arat. 340: 4.21
Arat. 480: 7.65
Arat. 569: 7.209
Arat. fr. 3.14: 7.156

Grammaticorum Romanorum Fragmenta (*GRF* ed.Funaioli)
482ff.: 7.180

Grattius
7-8: 7.102
25-33: 9.12
150-153: 9.6
236: 9.16
405: 7.62-62, 7.63
473: 17.2
534: 7.130

Gregory of Tours
Hist. Franc. 6.22: 1.19-20

Hedylus
2.5: 7.141

Herodotus
1.185: 7.142
1.188: 7.140
1.189ff.: 7.141
1.205-214: 7.143
2.32.2: 4.91
3.99: 7.144-145
4.150-158: 7.139
5.101: 3.29

Hesiod
Op. 1: 1.5, 1.15-16
Op. 167ff.: 5.23
Op. 197: 11.12
Op. 267: 11.19
Op. 417: 5.1-2
Op. 614: 6.17-18
Scut. 203: 4.37
Scut. 206: 1.5
Theog. 1: 1.15-16
Theog. 66-68: 4.45-48
Theog. 198: 13.3-4
Theog. 311-312: 4.87
Theog. 311: 4.87
Theog. 319f.: 4.86
Theog. 768: 5.7-8
Theog. 771-773: 4.87
Theog. 904-906: 3.35
Theog. 933-937: 8.3
fr. 54 (M-W): 4.67-72
fr. 124: 6.49-50

Hipponax
fr. 13.2 (West): 6.5

Hirtius
BG 8.1: 7.211
BG 8.8.4: 7.101-102
BG 8.8.42: 7.148

Homer
Il. 1.128: 3.26
Il. 1.247-249: 7.48-49
Il. 1.250ff.: 7.50-51
Il. 1.526-527: 7.133
Il. 2.335: 7.48-49
Il. 2.484-492: 1.5
Il. 2.538: 123
Il. 2.767: 4.67
Il. 3.221-223: 7.48-49
Il. 3.380-382: 13.3-4
Il. 4.141-147: 4.30, 4.32
Il. 6.179-182: 4.86
Il. 6.429-430: 4.51-52, 19.11-12
Il. 6.454: 4.19-20
Il. 8.41ff.: 7.130-134
Il. 8.438-439: 7.130-134
Il. 8.836: 4.87
Il. 9.57f.: 7.50-51
Il. 9.378-391: 2.1-8
Il. 9.457: 5.7-8
Il. 10.294: 7.15
Il. 11.416: 9.3
Il. 13.474-475
Il. 14.233ff.: 4.19-20
Il. 14.245: 4.17-18
Il. 15.187-196: 5.22
Il. 16.33-35: 4.85-94
Il. 16.245: 7.98
Il. 20.39: 4.27, 10.2
Il. 22.26-31: 5.1-2
Il. 23.595: 1.20
Il. 24.607-608: 5.13-14
Od. 1.1-2: 7.52
Od. 1.3: 7.52
Od. 1.52: 7.77
Od. 1.71-73: 7.56
Od. 3.245: 7.50-51
Od. 3.338: 7.15
Od. 3.426: 7.15
Od. 3.437: 7.15
Od. 4.561-569: 5.23
Od. 4.563ff.: 5.23
Od. 4.605f.: 7.49
Od. 5.63-73: 7.77
Od. 5.135: 7.77

Book Three of the Corpus Tibullianum: 631
Introduction, Text, Translation and Commentary

Od. 5.306: 3.26
Od. 7.245: 7.77
Od. 7.256: 7.77
Od. 8.267-366: 8.3
Od. 8.288: 13.3-4
Od. 8.408-409: 4.96, 6.27-28
Od. 8.488: 7.178
Od. 9.36-61: 7.54
Od. 9.37-38: 7.81
Od. 9.82-104: 7.55
Od. 9.193: 13.1-2
Od. 9.196-201: 7.57
Od. 10.47: 7.58
Od. 10.105-108: 7.59-60
Od. 10.106: 7.59
Od. 10.136: 7.62-63
Od. 10.138: 7.62
Od. 10.221: 7.62-63
Od. 10.254: 7.62-63
Od. 10.327: 7.61, 7.62-63
Od. 10.491: 5.7-8
Od. 10.495: 7.67-68, 7.68
Od. 11.14-19: 5.24
Od. 11.14-15: 7.64
Od. 11.15-18: 7.65-66
Od. 11.369: 4.17-18
Od. 11.427: 4.61-62
Od. 11.456: 4.61-62
Od. 11.568-631: 7.67-68
Od. 11.568: 7.67-68
Od. 11.576: 7.67-68
Od. 11.582: 7.67-68
Od. 11.630: 7.67-68
Od. 11.631: 7.67-68, 7.68
Od. 12.85-86: 4.89
Od. 12.85-100: 4.89
Od. 12.85-92: 7.71-72
Od. 12.85-87: 7.72
Od. 12.91-92: 7.71
Od. 12.93: 7.72
Od. 12.105-106: 73-75
Od. 12.107-110: 4.89
Od. 12.133: *119*
Od. 12.165-200: 7.69
Od. 12.166-167: 7.69
Od. 12.222-259: 7.70-75

Od. 12.235ff.: 7.73-75
Od. 12.238-239: 7.74
Od. 12.242-243: 7.75
Od. 12.245-246: 4.89
Od. 12.450: 7.77
Od. 12.353-402: 7.76
Od. 13.6: 7.81
Od. 13.70-95: 7.78
Od. 13.243: 7.49
Od. 15.225: 7.120
Od. 19.562-567: 4.1
Od. 19.564-565: 4.7-8
Od. 21.295: 6 headnote
Od. 23.177-204: 19.1
Od. 23.310: 7.54
Od. 23.350-353: 7.81

Homeric Hymns
Aphrodite 89: 4.29
Apollo 388ff.: 7.8-9
Apollo 441-442: 4.29
Apollo 509: 7.8-9
Demeter 27ff.: 7.130-134
Hermes 41-54: 4.37
Hermes 242: 4.37
Hermes 419-451: 4.23-42
Hermes 462: 4.49
Hermes 471-472: 4.47-48
Hermes 499: 4.38
Hermes 534-539: 4.47-48
Hermes 545: 4.49

Horace
AP 10: 7.24
AP 39: 4.73, 7.2
AP 61: 7.111
AP 73-74: *Ep. Tib.* 4
AP 105-106: 6.38
AP 105-107: 6.51-52
AP 117: 11.20
AP 145: 4.89
AP 275: 7.24
AP 285: 7.43
AP 302: 7.51
AP 333: 3.1
AP 395: 6.46

AP 464-466: 7.196
Carm. 1.1: 2.1-8
Carm. 1.1.11-12: 3.12
Carm. 1.1.25-26: 9.5
Carm. 1.1.28: 9.16
Carm. 1.1.29: 3.23-24, 6.41
Carm. 1.1.29ff.: 3.19-20
Carm. 1.1.35: 4.49
Carm. 1.2.31-32: 4.29
Carm. 1.2.32: 4.45-48
Carm. 1.2.41-43: 7.206
Carm. 1.2.50-52: 6.10
Carm. 1.3.12: 2.1-8
Carm. 1.4.1: 5.4
Carm. 1.4.10: 5.4
Carm. 1.4.16: 3.37
Carm. 1.4.18: 6.10
Carm. 1.4.19: 11.10
Carm. 1.6.1-2: 7.180
Carm. 1.6.1-4: 7.177-180
Carm. 1.6: 7.18-27
Carm. 1.6.5-9: 7.54-78
Carm. 1.6.5: 7.18
Carm. 1.6.9-12: 7.2
Carm. 1.7.10: 3.23-24
Carm. 1.7.17-19: 6.7
Carm. 1.7.20-21: 7.154
Carm. 1.7.28-29: 4.79
Carm. 1.10.5-6: 7.1
Carm. 1.12.9-10: 7.125
Carm. 1.12.10: 7.124
Carm. 1.12.15-16: 7.51
Carm. 1.12.39: 7.24
Carm. 1.12.50: 7.176
Carm. 1.13.5-6: 10.5
Carm. 1.13.9: 11.5
Carm. 1.13.14: 4.66
Carm. 1.13.17-20: 12.7
Carm. 1.13.17-18: 3.26
Carm. 1.13.18-20: 11.16
Carm. 1.13.18: 11.15
Carm. 1.16.22: 9.7
Carm. 1.17.13-14: 4.43-44
Carm. 1.17.17-18: 5.1-2
Carm. 1.17.22: 4.45
Carm. 1.18.3: 6.21

Carm. 1.18.4: 6 *headnote*
Carm. 1.18.6: 6.38
Carm. 1.18.11: 6.1
Carm. 1.19.2: 4.45
Carm. 1.19.5-7: 8.11-12
Carm. 1.21.1: 7.18
Carm. 1.21.2: 4.27
Carm. 1.21.13: 6.25-26
Carm. 1.21.22: 4.50
Carm. 1.22.5: 4.91
Carm. 1.23: 9 *headnote*
Carm. 1.23.2: 9.2
Carm. 1.23.3-4: 9.6
Carm. 1.23.6-7: 9.10
Carm. 1.23.11-12: 9.23, 14.6
Carm. 1.25.7-8: 6.53
Carm. 1.26.1-3: 4.96
Carm. 1.26.2: 6.27-28
Carm. 1.26.9-12: 3.23-24
Carm. 1.27.23-24: 4.86
Carm. 1.28.3-4: 1.24, 7.7
Carm. 1.28.17: 6.19
Carm. 1.28.19-20: 5.5
Carm. 1.28.25-26: 6.23
Carm. 1.29.8: 6.5
Carm. 1.30: 6.1
Carm. 1.30.5: 18.1
Carm. 1.31.1-3: 6.6
Carm. 1.31.15: 7.8-10
Carm. 1.33: *Vit. Tib. headnote*
Carm. 1.33.1: *Vit. Tib.* 1
Carm. 1.33.2: 4.74
Carm. 1.33.6: 11.5
Carm. 1.33.10-12: *125*
Carm. 1.33.14: 11.3-4
Carm. 1.34.9: 7.143
Carm. 1.35.31-32: 7.150
Carm. 1.38.1-8: 6.5
Carm. 1.38.1: 3.29, 6.5
Carm. 2.3.12: 5.3
Carm. 2.3.13-16: 6 *headnote*
Carm. 2.3.14: 6.5
Carm. 2.3.15: 3.35
Carm. 2.4: 16.3-4
Carm. 2.5.5: 14.7
Carm. 2.5.9-10: 4.74, 5.19

Book Three of the Corpus Tibullianum: 633
Introduction, Text, Translation and Commentary

Carm. 2.5.12: 4.30
Carm. 2.5.18-20: 4.29
Carm. 2.6.1: 7.193-196
Carm. 2.6.3: 4.91
Carm. 2.6.6: 3.8
Carm. 2.6.22-24: 2.25
Carm. 2.7.2: 7.116
Carm. 2.7.8: 4.28
Carm. 2.7.25-26: 6.10
Carm. 2.8.13: 6.47-49, 6.49-50
Carm. 2.9.1: 6.32
Carm. 2.9.9-10: *Ep. Tib.* 3
Carm. 2.9.9-16: 4.43-44
Carm. 2.9.13: 7.50-51
Carm. 2.9.18: 7.180
Carm. 2.11.3-4: 4.1
Carm. 2.11.13-17: 6.63
Carm. 2.11.13-15: 6.64
Carm. 2.11.13-14: 6 *headnote*
Carm. 2.11.14-15: 6.64
Carm. 2.11.16: 2.24, 4.28, 6.63
Carm. 2.11.18: 6.5
Carm. 2.11.19: 6.57-58
Carm. 2.11.21: 16.3-4
Carm. 2.12.8: 3.4
Carm. 2.12.9.12: 7.177-180
Carm. 2.12.15-16: 11.13-16
Carm. 2.12.20: 10.23
Carm. 2.12.21: 3 *headnote*
Carm. 2.12.21-24: 7.197-200
Carm. 2.12.21-28: 3.23-24
Carm. 2.13.23: 5.23
Carm. 2.13.24f.: 13.3-4
Carm. 2.14.17-18: 3.37, 3.38
Carm. 2.15.14-16: 3.13-16
Carm. 2.16.35-37: 8.15-16
Carm. 2.16.39ff.: 3.19-20
Carm. 2.17: 10 *headnote*
Carm. 2.17.13: 4.86
Carm. 2.18: 3 *headnote*
Carm. 2.18.1-2: 3.18
Carm. 2.18.1-6: 3.13-16
Carm. 2.18.9-10: 3.23-24
Carm. 2.18.30: 3.38
Carm. 2.19.1-2: 4.43-44
Carm. 2.19.7-8: 9.1-2

Carm. 2.19.31-32: 4.88
Carm. 2.20.1-5: 7.206-210
Carm. 2.20.1-2: 7.209, 13.10
Carm. 2.20.2: 7.209
Carm. 2.20.13: 7.56
Carm. 2.20.21-22: 6.37
Carm. 3.1.41-43: 3.13
Carm. 3.1.42: 3.18
Carm. 3.2.26-27: 5.7-8
Carm. 3.3.13-14: 6.15
Carm. 3.3.13: 6.38
Carm. 3.4.15-16: 3.12
Carm. 3.4.18-19: 4.23
Carm. 3.4.61: 1.15-16
Carm. 3.4.74-75: 3.38
Carm. 3.5.2-4: 7.149
Carm. 3.7.9: 6.61
Carm. 3.7.25: 7.94
Carm. 3.8.1: 1.1-4
Carm. 3.9: 1 *headnote*
Carm. 3.9.1-4: 3.23-24, 7.197-200
Carm. 3.9.2-3: 7.199
Carm. 3.9.13-14: 11.13-16
Carm. 3.9.24: 3.7-8
Carm. 310.5-6: 3.15
Carm. 3.11.5: 4.38
Carm. 3.11.17-18: 4.87
Carm. 3.11.20: 4.88
Carm. 3.11.44-45: 7.117-118
Carm. 3.11.45: 11.15
Carm. 3.11.51-52: 2.25
Carm. 3.12.1-3: 14.5
Carm. 3.12.4: *108*,13.3-4
Carm. 3.13.9-10: 5.1-2
Carm. 3.13.9: 7.51
Carm. 3.14.17: 6.5
Carm. 3.14.21-24: *119*
Carm. 3.14.22: 4.28
Carm. 3.16.19: 3.4
Carm. 3.19.20: 4.38
Carm. 3.20.9: 7.89
Carm. 3.21.14-16: 6.20
Carm. 3.23.17-20: 7.14-15
Carm. 3.23.19-20: 4.10
Carm. 3.23.19: 7.14
Carm. 3.23.20: 7.14

Carm. 3.25.1-3: 4.43-44
Carm. 3.25.14-15: 6.57
Carm. 3.25.19: 6.38
Carm. 3.26.12: 7.97
Carm. 3.27.13-14: 5.31, 6.30
Carm. 3.27.39-42: 4.7-8
Carm. 3.27.40-42: 4.56
Carm. 3.27.40: 4.7-8
Carm. 3.27.50-51: 9.1-2
Carm. 3.27.53-54: 10.4, 10.6
Carm. 3.29.14: 3.23-24
Carm. 3.30.6-7: 2.17
Carm. 3.30.10: 13.10
Carm. 3.30.16: 6.64
Carm. 4.1.8: 6.46
Carm. 4.1.30: 11.13-16
Carm. 4.2.15-16: 4.86
Carm. 4.2.27-32: *124*
Carm. 4.2.31-32: 1.24
Carm. 4.2.33-34: 7.177-180
Carm. 4.4.38-41: 7.107-110
Carm. 4.4.41: 2.1-2
Carm. 4.5.7-8: 7.123
Carm. 4.5.18: 7.163
Carm. 4.5.21: 4.60
Carm. 4.5.33: 3.2
Carm. 4.5.38-40: 6.18
Carm. 4.6.27: 7.24
Carm. 4.6.37: 4.72
Carm. 4.7.27-28: 3.10
Carm. 4.9.4: 4.70
Carm. 4.9.8: 7.24
Carm. 4.9.9-12: 13.3-4
Carm. 4.9.21: 7.18
Carm. 4.11: 11 *headnote*
Carm. 4.11.15-20: 11.1-2
Carm. 4.11.17: 11.1
Carm. 4.11.34-35: 4.70
Carm. 4.14.41-52: 7.137-146
Carm. 4.14.46: 7.140, 7.141
Carm. 4.14.47-48: 7.149
Carm. 4.14.49-50: 7.137-138, 7.138
Carm. 4.14.51-52: 7.148
Carm. 4.15.9-10: 7.102
Carm. 4.15.26: 6.20
Carm. Saec. 13-16: 4.13-14

Carm. Saec. 25: 11.3
Carm. Saec. 61: 4.45-48
Carm. Saec. 63-64: 10.10
Epist. 1.1.1: 7.24
Epist. 1.1.20: 6.53
Epist. 1.2.6-16: 7.54-78
Epist. 1.2.12: 7.165-168
Epist. 1.2.17-31: 7.54-78
Epist. 1.2.23: 7.61
Epist. 1.2.59-60: 9.7
Epist. 1.2.64-65: 7.207-208
Epist. 1.4: *Vit. Tib.* headnote
Epist. 1.4.1-4: 19.9
Epist. 1.4.6-7: *Vit. Tib.* 1-2
Epist. 1.5: 7.137-138
Epist. 1.5.18: 15.1
Epist. 1.6.45-46: 7.187
Epist. 1.7.12: 6.9
Epist. 1.7.16: 8.3
Epist. 1.7.25-26: 5.15
Epist. 1.7.71: 6.62
Epist. 1.10.22: 3.13, 3.15
Epist. 1.10.26: 3.18
Epist. 1.11.29: 19.9
Epist. 1.13.2: 13.7
Epist. 1.13.18: 3.2
Epist. 1.14.3: *97*
Epist. 1.14.7: 2.14
Epist. 1.14.17: 7.210
Epist. 1.14.34: 6.62
Epist. 1.15.4: 7.60
Epist. 1.15.5: 11.20
Epist. 1.15.13: 7.202
Epist. 1.15.18-20: 6.13-17
Epist. 1.15.18: 6.5
Epist. 1.15.45: 19.9
Epist. 1.16.16: 7.51
Epist. 1.16.26: 7.18
Epist. 1.16.58: 7.210
Epist. 1.18.5: 4.59
Epist. 1.18.34: 16.3-4
Epist. 1.18.40ff.: 9.1
Epist. 1.18.73: 3.3
Epist. 1.19.1ff.: 4.43-44
Epist. 1.19.5: 7.24
Epist. 1.19.8: 7.18

Book Three of the Corpus Tibullianum: 635
Introduction, Text, Translation and Commentary

Epist. 1.19.37ff.: 3.19-20
Epist. 1.19.38: 13.3-4
Epist. 1.20.1-2: 1.9-14
Epist. 1.20.4f.: 3.19-20
Epist. 2.1.21-22: 3.9
Epist. 2.1.50: 7.180
Epist. 2.1.64f.: 3.19-20
Epist. 2.1.225: 1.11-12
Epist. 2.1.257-258: 1.24
Epist. 2.1.258-259: 7.24
Epist. 2.1.529: 4.73
Epist. 2.2.50-51: 7.183-189
Epist. 2.2.51f.: 3.23-24
Epist. 2.2.55: 4.54
Epist. 2.2.137: 10.1
Epist. 2.2.175-176: 5.1-2
Epist. 2.2.185: 4.21
Epist. 2.2.187-189: 11.8
Epod. 1.11-12: 7.193-196
Epod. 1.25-34: 3 *headnote*
Epod. 1.29: 7.183
Epod. 2.2: 5.26
Epod. 2.29-36: 9.1
Epod. 2.32: 9.16
Epod. 3.9: 4.29
Epod. 4.17-18: 3.11
Epod. 5.22: 2.23
Epod. 7.15: 4.32
Epod. 9.7-8: 7.56
Epod. 9.14: 2.25
Epod. 9.31: 4.91
Epod. 9.33: 6.5
Epod. 9.37-38: 2.19
Epod. 10.9: 19.11
Epod. 11.4: 11.5
Epod. 11.16: 4.96
Epod. 12.9: 6.16
Epod. 12.16: 19.14
Epod. 12.21: 8.15-16
Epod. 13.13: 7.149
Epod. 14.11: *Ep. Tib.* 3
Epod. 15: I *headnote*, 3 *headnote*, 7 *headnote*
Epod. 15. 1-10: 6.47-49
Epod. 15.1-2: *114*, 6.47-49
Epod. 15.3: *114*

Epod. 15.3: *114*, 4.16
Epod. 15.8: 6.26
Epod. 15.10: *80*, *113*, 11.7, 11.13-16
Epod. 15.11: *119*
Epod. 15.13: 6.53
Epod. 15.16: *114*
Epod. 15.20: *114*, 3.29, 7.198-199
Epod. 15.21: *80*, *82*, *114*, 7.206-210
Epod. 15. 23-24: *123*
Epod. 15.23: *80*, *82*, *114*, 1 *headnote* 1.23, 2.14
Epod. 15.29: 4.27
Epod. 16.29: 7.79-80
Epod. 16.35-36: 3.27
Epod. 16.41-42: 5.23
Serm. 1.1.5: 4.65
Serm. 1.1.22: 7.132
Serm. 1.1.38-119: 3 *headnote*
Serm. 1.1.45: 7.113
Serm. 1.2.13: 3.11-12
Serm. 1.2.62-63: 16.2
Serm. 1.2.63: 13.9
Serm. 1.2.68-69: 4.82
Serm. 1.2.80-82: *124-125*
Serm. 1.3.45: *108*, 16.2
Serm. 1.3.69: 6.9
Serm. 1.3.87: 1.1
Serm. 1.3.139-140: 6.9
Serm. 1.4.8: 7.17
Serm. 1.4.43-44: 4.40
Serm. 1.4.66: *108*, 16.2
Serm. 1.4.71ff.: 3.19-20
Serm. 1.4.85: 8.3
Serm. 1.4.118-119: 9.4
Serm. 1.4.132: 7.210
Serm. 1.5.42: 4.94
Serm. 1.5.104: 7.78
Serm. 1.6.83: 2.1-2
Serm. 1.7.11-12: 7.165-168
Serm. 1.7.25-26: 5.1-2
Serm. 1.7.33: 4.16
Serm. 1.8.28-29: 2.15
Serm. 1.8.33: 4.13-14
Serm. 1.10.32-33: 4.24
Serm. 1.10.32: 4.17-24
Serm. 1.10.44: *109*, 13.3-4

Serm. 1.10.73ff.: 3.19-20
Serm. 1.10.81-82: 7.180
Serm. 1.10.85-86: *126*
Serm. 1.10.85: 7.180
Serm. 2.1.4-5: 14.5
Serm. 2.1.10-11: 7.24
Serm. 2.1.11: 7.18
Serm. 2.1.26: 4.60
Serm. 2.2.88: 5.16
Serm. 2.2.123: 6.11
Serm. 2.3.150: 10.12
Serm. 2.5.64: 7.176
Serm. 2.6.55: 18.3
Serm. 2.6.67ff.: 6.10
Serm. 2.6.68-70: 6.12
Serm. 2.6.68: 6.18
Serm. 2.6.101-102: 7.13
Serm. 2.6.114: 7.183
Serm. 2.7.108: 4.73

Hyginus
Astr. 2.4.2-6: 7.9-11
Astr. 2.4: 7.9-11
Fab. pr. 39.2: 4.89
Fab. 4.33.13: 7.69
Fab. 130: 7.9-11
Fab. 151.1: 4.87
Fab. 167.2: 4.45
Fab. 191: 3.29
Fab. 224.1: 4.45

Hymni Orphici
50.5: 6.38
52.2: 6.38

Ilias Latina
66: 7.64
78: 9.20
120: 7.209
231: 7.183
267: 7.54
388: 7.105
607-608: 7.127
654: 9.2
851: 8.3
867: 4.21

876: 7.174
891: 4.87
1070: 10.19

Incerta Tragica (Ribbeck[3])
136: 7.161

Inscriptiones Graecae (*IG*)
14.769: 5.19.20

Isidore
Etym. 2.17.3: 7.4
Etym. 5.22.9: 7.117-118
Etym. 5.36.2: 7.113
Etym. 6.11.4: 1.9
Etym. 8.11.76: 8.3
Etym. 10.56: 1.14, 8.10
Etym. 10.134: 3.19-20
Etym. 11.1.118: 5.12
Etym. 15.33: 5.1-2
Etym. 16.2.3: 4.10
Etym. 18.8.1: 7.89
Nat. 4.2: 1.2
Nat. 37.4: 5.4

Isocrates
Paneg. 13: 7.5-6

Jerome
Adu. Iouin. 1.46: 14.6

Justinus
4.4-5: 7.199
4.4.7: 7.199
14.4.12: 5.3

Juvenal
1.19: 7.207
2.64: 4.77
2.67: 3.19-20
3.26: 5.16
3.163: 6.64
3.318: 5.31
4.125: 7.175
6.89: 7.197
6.329: 7.182

6.464: 12.3
6.610: 7.63
6.629: 6.43
7.242: 7.169
8.74-76: 7.32
9.53: 1.1-4
9.131-132: 7.35-36
9.144: 7.135
10.103: 6.51-52
10.248-249: 7.50-51
10.275: 3.7
10.295: 7.112a
10.313-314: 8.3
10.314: 9.22
10.340: 7.197
11.13: 4.71
12.5: 6.25
12.65: 3.36
12.98-99: 17.2
12.233-234: 5.33
13.46: 10.25
14.157: 7.112a
14.161: 7.111
14.205: 7.202
15.131-132: 6.16

Juvenal Scholia
9.53: 1.1-4

Laberius (Ribbeck[3])
Mim. 122: 7.168

Lactantius
Inst. 1.11.55: 19.13

Laevius
fr. 7.13 (Courtney): 7.50-51
fr. 11.2 (Courtney): 7.20
fr. 32.1 (Courtney): 7.76

Laus Pisonis
32-34: 7.28-32
37: 7.175
38: 7.185
43-56: 7.45-47
44-48: 7.46-47

51: 7.92
61-64: 7.48-49, 7.54-78
68-71: 7.118-134
72-80: 7.2
91: 7.107-110
97-98: 7.1
153: 6.59
158: 7.39
159: 3.26
168: 7.178
211: 7.112a
214-215: 7.7
219: 3.11
221-223: 7.37
232: 7.180
248-249: 7.34
260-261: 7.2

Licinius Imbrex (Ribbeck[3])
fr. 1.1: *119*

Limenius
8: 7.124
9-10: 7.126

Livius Andronicus
Od. 1.1: 7.24
Od. 21.1: 4.72

Livy
fr. 60: 2.7-8
1.9.12: 19.16
1.15.8: 4.93
1.20.5: 4.77
1.21.1: 4.53
2.42.10: 4.19-20
2.63.4: 4.14
3.3.3: 4.14
3.27.7: 4.46
3.48.4: 10.9
4.52.8: 6.37
5.15.11: 4.5-6
5.39.3: 7.52
5.45.4: 1.27-28
6.4.6: 7.189
7.2.11: 7.5-6

7.7.3: 7.3-4
7.10.11: 17.2
7.29.6: 7.101-102
7.36.9: 7.3-4
8.4.8: 4.78
8.6.5: 4.53
9.11.13: 9.14
10.23.12: 7.130-134
10.31.12: 4.76
21.41.16: 4.59
21.63.7: 7.118-134
21.63.8: 8.23
22.59.16: 16.5
23.5.1: 4.74
23.48.1: 7.161
24.26.10: 3.28
24.34.15: 7.87
25.6.18: 7.46-47
25.12.13: 7.15
25.21.1: 14.8
25.39.4: 9.22
26.3.6: 4.14
26.13.9: 4.65
26.13.13: 5.7
26.35.7: 7.45-47, 7.46
26.45.8: 7.75
26.51.3-8: 7.88
26.51.4: 7.90
27.5.6: 4.53
27.43.2: 4.17-18
27.48.10: 6.7
29.37.16: 7.45-47
30.28.11: 4.9
31.96.6: 7.85
32.23.7: 7.87
34.32.20: 5.6
35.31.37: 4.14
37.20.10: 7.92
37.39.9: 7.102
38.9.4: 16.5
38.28.8: 4.14
39.16.6: 16.2
39.18.8: 8.23
39.30.10: 7.75
41.23.18: 4.14
41.28.8: 7.30

44.26.11: 8.7
45.8.6: 4.46
45.39.19: 17.2
Perioch. 131: 7.116

Lucan
1.6-7: 7.90
1.17: 5.4
1.63-65: 4.53
1.183: 7.109
1.221-222: 5.30
1.246: 10.5
1.287: 4.23
1.439: 7.126
1.457: 3.7, 7.112a
1.472: 7.177
1.582: 7.60
1.600: 12.3
1.668: 8.23
1.669: 3.1
2.86: 7.42
2.153: 9.9-10
2.213: 7.75
2.228: 7.152
2.399-400: 7.53
2.535: 7.109
2.570: 7.60
2.585: 7.60
2.602: 19.9
2.610: 7.139
2.665: 7.53
2.723: 7.10
3.15: 8.6
3.38: 4.
3.230: 7.152
3.269: 7.91
3.336: 7.149
3.407: 7.135
3.362-363: 7.128
3.667: 6.45
3.744: 9.23
4.13: 7.126
4.45: 7.83
4.53: 7.10
4.58-59: 7.41
4.107: 7.10

4.134: 7.149	8.232: 6.19
4.161: 9.2	8.244: 7.207
4.164: 7.100	8.275: 7.152
4.170: 3.4	8.391: 7.152
4.244: 7.174	8.392-393: 4.91
4.404: 7.53	8.625: 3.7, 7.112a
4.441: 7.8-9	9.57: 8.5
4.501: 7.5-6	9.87: 5.5
4.553-555: 7.62-63	9.107: 7.130
4.623: 17.2	9.115: 4.83
4.733: 7.207	9.149: 7.194
4.813: 7.177	9.217: 7.45-4
5.214f.: 4.32	9.233: 7.112a
5.218: 7.129	9.335: 7.75
5.234: 7.75	9.383: 5.1
5.265-266: 7.138	9.440: 4.91
5.357: 6.37	9.465: 7.44
5.415: 7.45-47	9.474: 7.130
5.463-464: 2.30	9.543: 7.23
5.484-485: 4.91	9.564: 12.16
5.491: 6.51-52	9.568: 7.112a, 7.210
5.734: 4.2	9.696-697: 7.77
6.31: 7.85	9.861: 4.91
6.42: 9.7-8	9.865: 7.5-6
6.97: 4.97	10.114: 7.183
6.135: 8.6	10.126: 7.182
6.205: 7.128	10.300: 9.11
6.225: 10.6	10.157: 7.152
6.284: 9.18	10.408: 5.3
6.414-415: 4.59	10.434-435: 4.21
6.492: 7.62-63	10.477: 4.91
6.613: 18.3	10.492: 8.6
6.664-665: 4.87	10.543: 7.185
6.830: 7.154	
6.836: 7.135	Lucian
7.21-22: 4.9	*Dial. Marin.* 15.3: 3.33-34
7.80: 7.207	
7.129: 7.202	Lucilius (Marx)
7.205: 7.152	237: 7.182
7.266: 7.35	275: 5.31
7.813: 7.75	390: 7.194
8.74: 7.112	430: 5.25
8.79: 10.25	456: 7.202
8.129: 7.152	557: 5.25
8.182: 9.11	588f.: 3.19-20
8.209: 9.2	779: 15.4

1044: 7.173
1278: 7.127

Lucretius
1.2-7: 8.2
1.12: 7.127
1.49: 6.35-36
1.55: 7.3
1.83: 6.42
1.108-109: 7.2
1.115: 3.37
1.117-119: 1.5
1.121: 7.34
1.229: 7.161
1.558-559: 7.111
1.605: 7.17
1.722: 7.56
1.813: 7.17
1.926 (= 4.1): 1.5, 19.10
1.938: 7.86
1.986-987: 7.20
1.1040-1041: 7.191
1.1079: 7.2
2.20-61: 3 *headnote*
2.20-36: 3.3
2.24-28: 3.13-16, 4.83
2.25: 8.6
2.34: 3.18
2.66: 7.132
2.159-160: 5.1-2
2.192: 12.17
2.216: 17.4
2.236: 7.2
2.332: 7.151
2.339: 7.202
2.417: 2.23
2.501f.: 3.18
2.581: 17.4
2.596-597: 7.161
2.602: 7.151
2.651: 6.35-36
2.705: 4.86
2.776: 7.17
2.996: 7.161
2.1096: 7.115
2.1110: 7.183

2.1144: 7.18
3.2: 2.1-2
3.4: 7.13
3.307: 4.9
3.403: 6.29
3.486: 4.47-48
3.665-666: 6.32
3.859: 7.150
3.897-898: 13.1-2
3.900-901: 7.188
3.959: 15.4
3.973: 13.8
3.990: 2.3
3.1011: 3.37
3.1037-1038: 1.5
4.23: 7.86
4.53: 9.11
4.54: 7.3
4.94: 7.31
4.127: 9.11
4.129: 9.11
4.342-343: 4.24
4.410-411: 4.85
4.412: 7.150
4.421: 7.72
4.603-605: 6.32
4.705: 9.13
4.724: 9.11
4.764: 4.3
4.848: 17.2
4.884: 13.8
4.981: 4.38
4.993: 7.127
4.1031: 7.205
4.1057: 7.129
4.1077: 18.6
4.1086: 18.6
4.1106: 3.7
4.1127: 3.18
4.1192: 11.11
4.1274: 16.3-4
5.14-15: 7.163
5.52-53: 5.33
5.62-63: 4.7-8
5.62: 4.56
5.95-96: 6.32

5.158: 7.18
5.192-193: 17.4
5.263: 10.21, 19.7
5.298-299: 5.1-2
5.306: 7.42
5.387: 7.75
5.433: 7.18
5.496-497: 7.20
5.501: 7.127
5.503: 7.17
5.506-507: 7.22
5.545: 7.18
5.654-655: 7.65-66
5.764: 7.127
5.772: 7.18
5.890-924: 4.85-94
5.892-893: 4.89, 7.72
5.901: 6.15
5.904-906: 4.86
5.925ff.: 7.169-174
5.944: 4.9
5.985: 2.1-2
5.991: 7.161
5.1000-1001: 4.85
5.1007-1008: 5.28
5.1064: 9.3
5.1087: 7.129
5.1204: 7.18
5.1274: 9.1
5.1285: 7.79
5.1318: 4.90
5.1320: 15.4
5.1383: 4.71
5.1423f.: 3.18
5.1430: 4.9
6.1: 4.9
6.42: 7.211
6.51: 4.7-8
6.224: 12.17
6.317: 17.4
6.400-401: 7.10
6.402: 15.4
6.459: 7.131
6.493: 7.18
6.506-507: 2.21-22
6.515: 7.18

6.577: 17.4
6.627-628: 2.21-22
6.691: 4.86
6.766: 9.9-10
6.797: 5.28
6.906: 7.3
6.994: 7.96
6.1092: 4.87
6.1171: 7.153
6.1177-1178: 17.2
6.1197: 7.65
6.1221: 5.28

Lutatius Catulus
fr. 1.1-2: 14.7

Lycophron
45.669: 7.72

Macrobius
Sat. 1.18: 4.45-48

Maecenas
fr. 3.1-2 (Courtney = 186.1-2
   Hollis):1.25
fr. 5.1 (Courtney = 188.1 Hollis):
   6.1

Maecius
AP 5.133.4: 6.49-50

Manilius
1.17: 7.18
1.89: 7.82
1.153: 7.130
1.159: 7.19
1.166: 4.85
1.176: 7.130
1.196: 7.13
1.200: 7.130
1.232: 7.159
1.247: 7.18
1.283: 7.18, 7.130
1.286: 3.11
1.296: 7.32
1.367: 7.12

1.381: 7.10
1.422-423: 4.16
1.472: 7.10
1.491: 7.206
1.516: 7.169
1.574: 7.152
1.669: 8.8
1.743: 7.125
1.764-765: 7.50-51
1.809: 7.3
1.815: 7.209
1.827: 7.157
1.846: 8.6
1.855: 5.1
2.20-21: 7.163
2.23: 19.9
2.46-47: 19.11
2.49: 4.45
2.60: 12.16
2.137: 3.19-20
2.138: 10.17-18
2.149: 4.47-48
2.217: 7.150
2.410: 7.99
2.471: 7.99
2.517: 7.17
2.558: 7.163
2.578: 7.99
2.622: 10.12
2.643: 7.135
2.742: 7.10
2.836: 4.17-18
2.850: 7.112a
2.893: 7.112a
2.941: 7.60
3.1: 7.2
3.27: 5.1
3.30: 7.32
3.36: 10.1-2
3.105: 10.12
3.152-153: 7.163
3.159: 7.135
3.227: 7.102
3.305: 7.41
3.307: 7.102
3.319: 7.102

3.433: 7.41
3.554: 7.169
3.560: 7.112a
3.576: 5.28
4.142-143: 7.170
4.157: 7.180
4.204: 6.17-18
4.207: 2.1-2
4.247: 8.5
4.268: 7.80
4.512: 7.52
4.527: 4.42
4.548: 7.41
4.562: 7.64
4.590: 7.130
4.591: 4.21
4.600: 4.91
4.602: 7.59-60
4.649: 4.85
4.678-679: 4.85
4.776: 7.18
4.814: 4.83
4.828: 7.77
5.16: 3.11
5.73: 7.130
5.192: 4.91
5.204: 9.5
5.207-208: 5.1-2
5.330: 4.38
5.332: 4.40
5.419: 7.127
5.430: 7.23
5.443: 7.123
5.653: 7.13
5.666: 4.32
5.698: 4.2
5.725: 19.11

Martial
1 *praef.*: 1.9
1.3.4: 10.3
1.27.1: 4.2
1.39.1: 10.12
1.61.1: 6.41
1.68.1-2: 8.7
1.68.6: 19.11-12

Book Three of the Corpus Tibullianum: 643
Introduction, Text, Translation and Commentary

1.70.15: 4.45
1.82.10: 4.43-44
1.88.1-2: 5.19
1.109.16: 10.1
1.117.16: 1.9-4
2.2.6: 10.17
2.4.3: 1.23
2.91.3: 4.16
3.2.7-11: 1.9-14
3.2.9: 1.9-14, 13
3.2.10: 1.9-14, 11-12
3.2.11: 1.9-14, 11-12
3.20: 1 *headnote*
3.53.3-4: 1.10
3.65.1: 10.1
3.65.5: 8.17-18
3.65.6: 2.24
3.67.8: 7.126
3.80.2: 20.1
3.87.1: 20.1
3.93.26: 4.31
4.1.3: 7.112
4.1.4: 7.123
4.10.1-2: 1.9-14
4.14.1: 1.15-16
4.28.1: 12.3
4.40.2: 10.12
4.45.7: 4.23
4.57: 5 *headnote*
4.57.1: 5.1
4.57.7-8: 5.3
4.57.9-10: 5.1-2
4.78.3: 1.3-4
4.87.4: 6.51-52
4.89.1-2: 1.13
5.2.7: 4.32
5.7.6: 8.3
5.20.1-2: 4.54
5.37.4: 3.17
5.65.9: 3.11
5.79.5: 4.49
5.84.10-12: 1.1-4
6.13.2: 4.37
6.42.1-2: 5.1
6.42.7: 5.3
6.42.11-13: 3.14

6.43.8: 4.14
6.53.1: 12.3
6.58.7-8: 3.36
6.59.3: 7.160
6.64.25: 7.152
6.64.29-30: 7.12-13
6.73.6: 8.4
6.79.1: 8.3
7.6.10: 8.2
7.12.5: 3.1
7.12.10: 1.15-16
7.15.2: 6.57
7.18.12: 10.6
7.21.1-2: 11.1
7.30.40: 8.19-20
7.32.3: 10.25
7.40.5: 5.19
7.47.2: 1.2
7.54.1-6: 4.10
7.54.5: 12.1
7.64.6: 6.37
7.68.1: 13.3-4
7.72.4: 1.2
7.88.4: 4.51-52
7.99.7: 6.41
8.2.7: 7.112
8.3: 1 *headnote*
8.3.17: 6.21
8.28.14: 8.19-20
8.33.15: 1.3-4
8.38.13: 10.25
8.39.1: 6.59
8.39.4: 5.34
8.39.6: 8.2
8.45.3: 6.6
8.50.14: 4.40
8.64: 11 *headnote*
8.68.4: 6.17-18, 7.153
8.72.1-3: 1.17
8.72.1-2: 1.9-14
8.72.9: 6.53
8.73.4: 6.41
8.75.11: 1.21-22
8.76.7: 6.51-52
8.77.3: 2.24
9 *praef.* 7: 7.32

9.8.10: 17.4
9.22.16: 6.51-52
9.29.2: 1.27-28, 3.38
9.31.6: 10.24
9.33.1: 6.5
9.35.6: 13.8
9.42.3: 4.45
9.43.13: 7.12-13
9.52: 11 *headnote*
9.75.7-9: 3.14
9.90.13-18: 1.1-4
9.90.15: 1.1
9.93.1: 6.57, 6.62
9.94.1-2: 6.3
10.2.12: 4.46
10.4.12: 7.4
10.10.7: 4.73
10.11.6: 12.3
10.13.9: 1.19
10.17.5: 8.19-20
10.18.2: 10.6
10.19.17: 7.200
10.20: 1 *headnote*
10.24: 11 *headnote*, 12.14
10.30.70: 12.3
10.31.3: 6.35-36
10.33.7: 7.31
10.35: *127*
10.37: 7.123
10.38: *127*
10.38.4: 7.112
10.72.1: 8.3
10.94.5-6: 5.20
10.98.1: 6.57
10.103.2: 10.8
10.107: 1.13
11.1.1-2: 1.9-14, 1.17
11.26.5: 9.18
11.36.5-6: 6.57
11.57.6: 6.51-52
11.58.11: 12.3
11.70.3-4: 4.75
11.80.1-2: 5.1-2, 5.3
11.102.7: 8.3
11.107.1: 1.9-14
12.11: 1 *headnote*, 1.21-22

12.11.6: 1.21-22
12.18.23: 19.9
12.48.16: 11.4
12.59.1-3: 4.51-52
12.60.8-9: 6.62, 11 *headnote*
12.70.6: 12.3
13.71.2: 19.20
14.47.1: 4.3
14.54.1: 6.45
14.54.2: 4.38
14.100.1: 6.41
14.149.1: 10.1
14.152.1: 6.41
14.163.2: 12.3
14.169.1: 4.38
14.170.7: 6.62
Spect. 12.6: 15.1
Spect. 16.2: 4.37
Spect. 26.7: 7.123

Maximianus
3.39: 2.3
5.77f.: 8.4

Mela
1.46: 4.50
2.42: 4.26
3.57: 7.153-157
3.79: 8.17-18

Meleager
AP 4.1.1: 1.5
AP 5.8.5: 6.49-50
AP 5.57: 4.65, 11.5
AP 5.96: 8.5-6
AP 5.136 and 137: 11 *headnote*
AP 5.151-152: 11 *headnote*
AP 5.172 and 173: 11 *headnote*
AP 5.176.1-2: 4.65
AP 5.199: 7.141
AP 12.49: 6 *headnote*
AP 12.49.1: 6.62
AP 12. 82 and 83: 11 *headnote*

Menander
Dysk. 41-44: 9.1

Book Three of the Corpus Tibullianum: 645
Introduction, Text, Translation and Commentary

Menander Rhetor (Spengel)
368.4: 7.118-134
369.11: 7.196, 7.197-200
370.11f.: 7.28-32
372.21-25: 7.48-49
372.25: 7.39
373.17ff.: 7.89-97, 7.106-117
378.10-12: 7.123
378.21-23: 7.123
381.16-18: 7.123
398.26ff.: 5.31

Mesomedes
Hymn. 2.2: 7.124, 7.126
Hymn. 2.4: 7.127

Minucius Felix
36.2: 4.47-48

Mulomedicina Chironis
4.3.6: 17.3

Musaeus
314: 5.1-2

Naevius (Ribbeck[3])
Trag. 18: 9.17

Nemesianus
Cyn. 44: 7.61
Ecl. 1.5: 4.43-44
Ecl. 1.24: 7.178
Ecl. 2.28: 6.3
Ecl. 2.46: 7.127
Ecl. 2.54: 7.178
Ecl. 3.39: 7.172

Nepos
Ag. 4.4.: 7.169
Att. 14.3: 14.3-4
ex. fr. 2.P.: 2.7-8
ex. fr. 24 P.: 3.14
fr. 27.3: 8.15-16

Nigidius Figulus
fr. 93 (Swoboda): 7.12-13

Nonius Marcellus (Lindsay)
446: 12.14
706: 1.27-28

Nonnus
1.32: 7.9-11
47.389: 6.39

Orosius
2.14: 7.199

Orphicorum fragmenta (Bernabé)
fr. 338: 7.206-210

Ovid
Am. Epigr. 1.1: 1.9
Am. 1.1: *89*, 7.18-27
Am. 1.1.1-2:1.1
Am. 1.1.5: 4.65
Am. 1.1.10: 9.19
Am. 1.1.11-12: 2.11-12
Am. 1.1.20: 8.9, 8.10,
Am. 1.1.25-26: 8.11-12
Am. 1.2.1-4: 4.19-20
Am. 1.2.4: 10.10
Am. 1.2.8: 4.65
Am. 1.2.17-18: 8.6
Am. 1.2.18: 4.66
Am. 1.2.21: 10.21, 19.7
Am. 1.2.26: 11.5
Am. 1.2.32: 13.1-2
Am. 1.2.47-48: 6.15
Am. 1.2.50: 5.6
Am. 1.2.54: 4.17-18
Am. 1.3.1: 4.39
Am. 1.3.2: 10.16
Am. 1.3.4: 13.3-4
Am. 1.3.5-6: 4.66, 11.3-4
Am. 1.3.9-10: 3.23-24
Am. 1.3.11: 4.43-44
Am. 1.3.13: 4.39
Am. 1.3.16: 4.43-44
Am. 1.3.19: 4.40
Am. 1.4.3: 6.51-52
Am. 1.4.11-12: 4.96, 6.27-28
Am. 1.4.11: 6.5

Am. 1.4.12: 4.96
Am. 1.4.23: 12.16
Am. 1.4.25: 9.15
Am. 1.4.27: 9.20
Am. 1.4.29: 7.210
Am. 1.4.51: 1.24
Am. 1.4.52: 6.62
Am. 1.4.61: 2.11-12
Am. 1.5: 6.54
Am. 1.5.8: 7.152
Am. 1.5.9-10: 4.39
Am. 1.5.10: 4.29, 7.72, 8.9, 9.10
Am. 1.5.11: 1.7
Am. 1.5.28: 4.92
Am. 1.5.56: 6.5
Am. 1.6.7-8: 12.11-12
Am. 1.6.13: 13.1-2
Am. 1.6.21: 6.51-52
Am. 1.6.24: 4.54
Am. 1.6.27: 2.1-2, 5.27
Am. 1.6.33.34
Am. 1.6.34: 4.65
Am. 1.6.38: 6.63
Am. 1.6.49: 1.6
Am. 1.6.52: 6.33
Am. 1.6.54: 10.1-2
Am. 1.6.68: 6.61, 18.3
Am. 1.7.1-2: 9.1-2
Am. 1.7.6: 7.202
Am. 1.7.11: 6.51-52
Am. 1.7.15: 6.39
Am. 1.7.40: 4.29, 5.15
Am. 1.7.41: 10.21
Am. 1.7.56: 4.96
Am. 1.7.61: 19.24
Am. 1.7.63-64: 4.75
Am. 1.8: 4.61-62
Am. 1.8.19: 5.7
Am. 1.8.23: 15.1
Am. 1.8.43: 13.8
Am. 1.8.49: 12.6
Am. 1.8.59: 4.35
Am. 1.8.60: 4.37
Am. 1.8.62: 10.3
Am. 1.8.85-86: 6.49-50
Am. 1.8.94: 12.14

Am. 1.8.95: 8.3
Am. 1.8.100: 13.8
Am. 1.9.1ff.: 4.65
Am. 1.9.4: 3.7-10
Am. 1.9.6: 4.51-52
Am. 1.9.16: 7.156
Am. 1.9.26: 8.4
Am. 1.9.39: 6.26, 12.11-12
Am. 1.9.43: 17.1
Am. 1.10: 1.7
Am. 1.10.9-10: 4.19-20, 6.3
Am. 1.10.14: 5.15
Am. 1.10.15: 13.1-2
Am. 1.10.29-30: 4.61-62
Am. 1.10.33-34: 6.19
Am. 1.10.47: 1.7
Am. 1.10.57: 8.13
Am. 1.10.59-60: 4.57
Am. 1.10.64: 4.80
Am. 1.11 and 1.12: 11 *headnote*
Am. 1.11.2: 11.2
Am. 1.11.11: 6.26
Am. 1.11.27: 2.29
Am. 1.12.22-24: 4.76
Am. 1.13.17-18: 3.7-10, 3.7-8
Am. 1.13.25: 2.7-8
Am. 1.14: 8.9
Am. 1.14.6: 2.21-22
Am. 1.14.31-32: 4.27
Am. 1.14.32: 4.84
Am. 1.14.33-34: 4.67
Am. 1.14.39: 5.15
Am. 1.15.10: 10.8
Am. 1.15.14: 14.8
Am. 1.15.29-30: 19.22
Am. 1.15.33-34: 3.29
Am. 1.15.35-36: 1.15-16
Am. 1.15.35: 3.19-20
Am. 1.15.38: 4.19-20
Am. 1.15.41-42: 2.17
Am. 2.1: 7.18
Am. 2.1.2: 4.72
Am. 2.1.11: 7.24
Am. 2.1.22: 4.76
Am. 2.1.33-34: 1.9
Am. 2.1.33: 10.1

Am. 2.2: 12.11-12
Am. 2.2 and 2.3: 11 *headnote*
Am. 2.2.9: 8.2
Am. 2.2.17-18: 18.6
Am. 2.2.33-34: 19.21
Am. 2.2.42: 7.117
Am. 2.2.44: 19.20
Am. 2.2.54: 20.4
Am. 2.2.63-64: 5.7-14
Am. 2.2.64: 5.12
Am. 2.2.65: 5.10
Am. 2.2.66: 4.76
Am. 2.3.2: 1.19, 9.18
Am. 2.3.3-4: 1.1-2
Am. 2.3.17: 10.21
Am. 2.4.1: 7.193
Am. 2.4.8: 7.72, 10.8
Am. 2.4.10: 10.16
Am. 2.4.11-12: 8.9-12
Am. 2.4.12: 11.5
Am. 2.4.17: 4.37
Am. 2.4.41-43: 8.9
Am. 2.4.42: 12.4
Am. 2.5.5: 13.1-2
Am. 2.5.9: 3.26
Am. 2.5.26: 4.51-52, 9.18
Am. 2.5.33-37: 4.31-34
Am. 2.5.41: 13.1-2
Am. 2.5.43-44: 8.7-14, 8.8, 8.14,
Am. 2.5.46: 4.32
Am. 2.5.47: 8.4
Am. 2.6.4: 4.32
Am. 2.6.8: 4.75
Am. 2.6.11: 7.209
Am. 2.6.20: 7.208
Am. 2.6.37: 4.33-34
Am. 2.6.44: 6.27-28
Am. 2.6.59: 7.204
Am. 2.6.59-60: 2.28
Am. 2.6.61-62: 2.27-30
Am. 2.7.1: 6.51-52
Am. 2.7.4: 10.5
Am. 2.7.19: 4.1
Am. 2.8.2: 12.3, 12.10
Am. 2.8.18: 6.22
Am. 2.8.19-20: 4.96, 6.49-50

Am. 2.8.20: 4.96
Am. 2.8.27: 13.10
Am. 2.9.2: 4.82
Am. 2.9.3-4: 10.15
Am. 2.9.7: 4.82
Am. 2.9.8: 10.4
Am. 2.9.11: 6.26
Am. 2.9.39: 6.61
Am. 2.10: *104*
Am. 2.10.7-8: 1.7
Am. 2.10.9: 7.124
Am. 2.10.13: 7.10
Am. 2.10.15-16: 6.25-26
Am. 2.10.19: 4.65
Am. 2.10.29: 1.19
Am. 2.11 and 2.12: 11 *headnote*
Am. 2.11.3-4: 3.4
Am. 2.11.5: 4.82
Am. 2.11.7-8: 6.59
Am. 2.11.7: 6.60
Am. 2.11.9-10: 10.11
Am. 2.11.13: 3.17
Am. 2.11.18: 4.89
Am. 2.11.27-29: 9.15
Am. 2.11.30: 5.1
Am. 2.11.37: 5.31
Am. 2.12: *104*
Am. 2.12.1: 4.23
Am. 2.12.2: 9.24
Am. 2.12.13: 6.10, 7.116
Am. 2.12.15-16: 7.182
Am. 2.12.16: 10.1-2
Am. 2.12.25-26: 4.67
Am. 2.13 and 2.14: 11 *headnote*
Am. 2.13: *105*, 10 *headnote*
Am. 2.13.2: 10.10
Am. 2.13.11-12: 1.15-16, 2.29, 6.1-2
Am. 2.13.13: 7.116
Am. 2.13.15-16: 10.19-20
Am. 2.13.21-22: 10.1-2
Am. 2.13.23: 10.12
Am. 2.13.25: 2.29
Am. 2.14: 10 *headnote*
Am. 2.14.6: 12.10
Am. 2.14.17: 5.7
Am. 2.14.23-24: *98*, 5.19-20

Am. 2.14.23: 5.19
Am. 2.14.24: 5.20
Am. 2.14.25: 5.20
Am. 2.14.31-32: 2.27
Am. 2.14.35: 6.15
Am. 2.14.73: 10.1
Am. 2.15.3: 12.16
Am. 2.15.9: 4.82
Am. 2.16: *105*
Am. 2.16.1: 5.1
Am. 2.16.4-6: 4.96
Am. 2.16.4: 7.9-11
Am. 2.16.11-15: *109*
Am. 2.16.12: *107*, 18.6
Am. 2.16.15-18: *109*
Am. 2.16.19: 9.15
Am. 2.16.19-39: 7.193-196
Am. 2.16.21: 7.193
Am. 2.16.43-46: 6.47-49
Am. 2.16.45-46: 6.49-50
Am. 2.16.47: *109*, 17.1
Am. 2.16.48: 7.136
Am. 2.17.10: 8.8
Am. 2.17.17-18: 9.16
Am. 2.17.18: 9.16
Am. 2.17.23: 9.15
Am. 2.17.27: 4.40
Am. 2.18.4: 7.24
Am. 2.18.29: 10.17
Am. 2.19.1-2: 4.80
Am. 2.19.2: 5.16
Am. 2.19.21-22: 6.53
Am. 2.19.25-26: 2.7
Am. 2.19.33-34: 10.11
Am. 2.19.34: 6.43
Am. 2.19.38: 7.136
Am. 2.19.39: 7.136
Am. 2.19.44: 6.12
Am. 2.19.57: 2.5-6
Am. 2.19.59-60: 2.5-6
Am. 2.26.15-18: 14.6
Am. 2.26.25-26: 7.73-75
Am. 2.29.37: 3.32
Am. 3.1: 7.18-27
Am. 3.1.11: 4.39
Am. 3.1.16: 4.82

Am. 3.1.17: 4.39
Am. 3.1.20: 4.65
Am. 3.1.21: 19.3
Am. 3.1.27: 10.1
Am. 3.1.32: 9.7
Am. 3.1.34: 1.6
Am. 3.1.43-44: 8.2
Am. 3.1.64: 1.21-22, 11.11
Am. 3.2.8: 6.51-52
Am. 3.2.10: 12.16
Am. 3.2.42: 4.30
Am. 3.2.46: 10.1-2
Am. 3.2.71: 6.37
Am. 3.2.76: 9.24
Am. 3.3.1: 6.55
Am. 3.3.4: 6.26
Am. 3.3.5-6: 4.30
Am. 3.3.5: 4.29
Am. 3.3.9-14: 6.47-49
Am. 3.3.9: 6.47-48
Am. 3.3.25: 10.1
Am. 3.3.34: 4.84
Am. 3.3.41-42: 3.1
Am. 3.3.41: 6.37
Am. 3.4.1: 10.1
Am. 3.4.11: 10.3
Am. 3.4.39: 19.1
Am. 3.4.43: 8.2
Am. 3.3.43-44: 6.35-36
Am. 3.5: 4 *headnote*
Am. 3.5.31-33: 4.56
Am. 3.5.31-32: 4.7-8
Am. 3.5.40: 4.61-62
*Am.*3.6.27-28: *119*
Am. 3.6.28: 1.23
Am. 3.6.51: 7.72
Am. 3.6.73: 4.82
Am. 3.6.77: 7.147
Am. 3.6.78: 10.6
Am. 3.6.80: 7.72, 10.8
Am. 3.6.87: 1.19
Am. 3.6.95: 7.125
Am. 3.7: 19.14
Am. 3.7.8: 4.29
Am. 3.7.45-46: 4.16
Am. 3.7.46: 18.4

Book Three of the Corpus Tibullianum: 649
Introduction, Text, Translation and Commentary

Am. 3.7.53: 10.1
Am. 3.7.63: 12.16
Am. 3.7.80: 4.58
Am. 3.8.23: 4.72
Am. 3.9.1-4: 2.11-14
Am. 3.9.12: 4.40
Am. 3.9.17: 4.43-44
Am. 3.9.32: 9.21
Am. 3.9.47: 7.78
Am. 3.9.60: 5.23, *Ep. Tib.* 2
Am. 3.9.62: 6.41
Am. 3.9.65: *Ep. Tib.* 1
Am. 3.9.66: 4.92
Am. 3.10.13: 7.170
Am. 3.10.19: 7.8-9
Am. 3.10.37: 7.113, 7.122
Am. 3.10.43: 7.210
Am. 3.11.8: 10.9, 10.10
Am. 3.11.9-12: 4.66
Am. 3.11.9: 6.51-52
Am. 3.11.11: 6.51-52
Am. 3.11.47: 6.22
Am. 3.11.48: 11.8
Am. 3.12.1-2: 6.8
Am. 3.12.7: 1.6
Am. 3.12.9: 7.177
Am. 3.12.26: 4.88
Am. 3.13.1: 1.26
Am. 3.13.3: 12.14
Am. 3.13.7: 7.169
Am. 3.13.8: 4.84
Am. 3.13.23: 4.39
Am. 3.13.26: 8.11
Am. 3.13.30: 8.8
Am. 3.14.1-2: 3.20, 20.4
Am. 3.14.1: 13.9
Am. 3.14.7: 9.7
Am. 3.14.50: 6.47-48
Am. 3.15.8: 13.10
Am. 3.17.3: 4.82
Ars 1.4: 7.130
Ars 1.9: 4.65
Ars 1.12: 6.13-14
Ars 1.30: 4.77
Ars 1.42-44: 19.3
Ars 1.43: 19.13

Ars 1.44: 19.4
Ars 1.52: 19.10
Ars 1.53: 8.19-20
Ars 1.54: 4.51-52
Ars 1.55-60: 19.3
Ars 1.61: 5.19
Ars 1.67: 4.64
Ars 1.97: 2.28
Ars 1.99: 8.2
Ars 1.109: 10.26
Ars 1.117-218: 7 *headnote*
Ars 1.137: 10.21, 19.7
Ars 1.142: 7.201
Ars 1.206: 4.40
Ars 1.209: 7.18
Ars 1.212: 11.11
Ars 1.219ff.: 7.137-146
Ars 1.226: 4.37
Ars 1.229-244: 6 *headnote*
Ars 1.231-232: 6.4
Ars 1.245-246: 4.7-8
Ars 1.255-262: 5.3
Ars 1.270: 4.64
Ars 1.290: 7.208
Ars 1.293: 6.39
Ars 1.310: 4.61-62
Ars 1.322: 13.8
Ars 1.343: 4.75
Ars 1.351-398: 4.61-62
Ars 1.363: 10.22
Ars 1.387: 6.43
Ars 1.392: 9.17
Ars 1.403: 10.1
Ars 1.425: 8.23
Ars 1.429: 12.14
Ars 1.455-456: 1.19-20
Ars 1.459: 6.43
Ars 1.480: 4.64
Ars 1.501: 6.14
Ars 1.516: 7.44
Ars 1.525: 4.43-44
Ars 1.526: 11.10
Ars 1.531: 4.61-62
Ars 1.532: 4.32
Ars 1.545: 6.15
Ars 1.550: 6.15

Ars 1.559: 6.15
Ars 1.565: 6.17-18
Ars 1.591: 8.3
Ars 1.594: 7.97
Ars 1.602: 12.16
Ars 1.612: 4.4
Ars 1.623: 7.177
Ars 1.631-632: 6.49-50
Ars 1.633-634: 4.96
Ars 1.662: 9.20
Ars 1.682: 4.51-52
Ars 1.710: 6.46
Ars 1.729: 10.5
Ars 1.733: 9.16, 10.5
Ars 1.735-736: 4.19-20
Ars 1.741-742: 19.8
Ars 1.752: 19.6
Ars 2.14: 4.37
Ars 2.28: 4.47-48
Ars 2.58: 19.6
Ars 2.96: 7.204
Ars 2.108: 7.201
Ars 2.124: 3.17
Ars 2.162: 10.21, 19.7
Ars 2.183: 6.15-16
Ars 2.189: 9.12
Ars 2.212: 4.32
Ars 2.213: 2.23
Ars 2.233-250: 4.65
Ars 2.233: 6.37
Ars 2.239: 4.50, 4.67
Ars 2.239-241: 4.67-72
Ars 2.239-240:4.65, 4.65-66, 4.67
Ars 2.256: 1.24
Ars 2.272: 4.61-62
Ars 2.289: 13.1-2
Ars 2.295: 17.1
Ars 2.297-298: 8.7-14, 8.9-12
Ars 2.312: 10.5
Ars 2.315ff.: 10 *headnote*
Ars 2.321: 17.1
Ars 2.325-326: 10.21
Ars 2.327: 10.12, 10.13
Ars 2.340: 2.5-6
Ars 2.344: 10.8
Ars 2.373-374: 7.71-72

Ars 2.374: 7.72
Ars 2.385: 12.9
Ars 2.388: 4.1
Ars 2.418: 2.19, 6.58
Ars 2.419: 5.1
Ars 2.458: 3.8
Ars 2.475: 9.10
Ars 2.493-510: 4 *headnote*
Ars 2.493-497: 4.39
Ars 2.494: 4.37
Ars 2.495: 9.18
Ars 2.496: 4.49
Ars 2.527: 19.24
Ars 2.533: 10.1
Ars 2.535: 7.147
Ars 2.557: 12.11-12
Ars 2.592: 18.4
Ars 2.601: 5.7-8
Ars 2.632: 9.16
Ars 2.670: 5.16
Ars 2.671: 3.12, 7.173
Ars 2.679: 19.2
Ars 2.686: 11.10
Ars 2.708: 12.6
Ars 2.744: 2.29
Ars 3.31-32: 6.39-42, 10.1
Ars 3.35-36: 6.39, 6.39-42, 6.40
Ars 3.40: 2.27
Ars 3.52: 10.16
Ars 3.59: 11.11
Ars 3.79-80: 8.4
Ars 3.88: 4.51-52
Ars 3.121-122: 2.1-8
Ars 3.130: 8.19-20
Ars 3.133-168: 8.9, 8.10
Ars 3.135: 8.10
Ars 3.141-143: 8.10
Ars 3.141: 8.9
Ars 3.153: 8.9
Ars 3.165: 8.11
Ars 3.170: 3.18, 8.15-16
Ars 3.172: 9.7
Ars 3.203: 2.7
Ars 3.226: 10.21
Ars 3.227: 7.202
Ars 3.258: 4.46

Book Three of the Corpus Tibullianum: 651
Introduction, Text, Translation and Commentary

Ars 3.273: 8.3
Ars 3.308: 12.4
Ars 3.312-320: 4.39
Ars 3.322: 4.88
Ars 3.331: 13.3-4
Ars 3.347: 10.25
Ars 3.347-348: 4.43-44
Ars 3.353: 6.43
Ars 3.386: 10.8
Ars 3.404: 7.16
Ars 3.455: 6.43-44
Ars 3.457-460: 6.39-42
Ars 3.457: 6.39
Ars 3.479-482: *127*
Ars 3.484: 4.61-62
Ars 3.485-490: 19.17
Ars 3.491: 19.18
Ars 3.522: 9.16
Ars 3.524: 9.15, 18.1
Ars 3.535: 1.8, 7.177
Ars 3.539-550: 4.43-44
Ars 3.548: 4.43-44
Ars 3.551: 1.7
Ars 3.568: 4.32
Ars 3.631: 17.1
Ars 3.664: 13.10
Ars 3.673-678: 5.8
Ars 3.674: 4.51-52
Ars 3.683-746: *91*
Ars 3.703: 5.15
Ars 3.714: 4.43-44
Ars 3.723: 2.9
Ars 3.733-784: 8.9
Ars 3.735: 6.37
Ars 3.780: 12.4
Ars 3.789-790: 4.43-44
Ars 3.790: 4.77
Ars 3.801: 8.3
Ars 3.802: 10.5
Ars 3.803: 9.16
Ars 3.805: 9.18
Ars 3.812: 2.29
Fast. 1.27-28:1.2
Fast. 1.39: 1.2
Fast. 1.49: 18.3
Fast. 1.75ff.: 7.118-134

Fast. 1.81: 7.121
Fast. 1.137: 3.3
Fast. 1.185: 5.25
Fast. 1.186: 8.12
Fast. 1.197: 5.26
Fast. 1.205: 2.7
Fast. 1.209: 7.123
Fast. 1.215: 7.42
Fast. 1.244: 9.1
Fast. 1.268: 4.37
Fast. 1.292: 10.8
Fast. 1.302: 4.65
Fast. 1.320: 7.15
Fast. 1.337-338: 7.14-15
Fast. 1.468: 6.9
Fast. 1.480: 10.16
Fast. 1.495-496: 6.32
Fast. 1.507: 7.135
Fast. 1.515: 1.6
Fast. 1.527: 4.40
Fast. 1.544: 4.17-18
Fast. 1.556: 10.12
Fast. 1.621-622: 6.42
Fast. 1.631: 9.1-2
Fast. 1.637: 4.29
Fast. 2.4: 1.14
Fast. 2.17: 3.33-34
Fast. 2.24: 7.14
Fast. 2.38: 6.42
Fast. 2.41: 7.130
Fast. 2.45: 4.61-62
Fast. 2.55-66: 4.13-14
Fast. 2.64: 1.19
Fast. 2.73: 7.51
Fast. 2.107: 4.35, 8.15-16
Fast. 2.119: 1.21-22
Fast. 2.123: 7.2
Fast. 2.175: 7.80
Fast. 2.248: 4.24
Fast. 2.253: 9.7
Fast. 2.269: 1.5
Fast. 2.273-276: 7.107-110
Fast. 2.285: 1.3-4
Fast. 2.287: 7.32
Fast. 2.305: 7.12
Fast. 2.310: 12.4

Fast. 2.336: 8.8
Fast. 2.445: 6.51-52
Fast. 2.451: 6.51-52
Fast. 2.499: 6.25
Fast. 2.503: 4.25, 4.26
Fast. 2.507: 10.25
Fast. 2.519f.: 4.10
Fast. 2.523: 2.10
Fast. 2.533-535: 1.24
Fast. 2.534-535: 7.7
Fast. 2.553: 1.3-4
Fast. 2.557: 6.51-52
Fast. 2.572: 20.4
Fast. 2.579: 10.7
Fast. 2.606: 6.57
Fast. 2.612: 12.6
Fast. 2.623: 4.3
Fast. 2.641-644: 9.1-2
Fast. 2.643-644: 12.14
Fast. 2.667-668: 10.25
Fast. 2.716: 10.17-18
Fast. 2.723-724: 7.181
Fast. 2.729-730: 1.19
Fast. 2.754: 7.153
Fast. 2.767: 4.40
Fast. 2.782: 11.20
Fast. 2.810: 6.51-52
Fast. 2.841: 1.15-16
Fast. 2.850: 5.12
Fast. 2.853: 1.6
Fast. 3.1-4: 8.1
Fast. 3.135-136: 1.1, 1.2
Fast. 3.145: 1.2
Fast. 3.169-170: 1.1, 8.1
Fast. 3.173: 4.19-20
Fast. 3.229-232: 1.1-4, 1.1
Fast. 3.233-234: 1.1
Fast. 3.245-248: 1.1-4
Fast. 3.249: 7.147
Fast. 3.255: 4.13-14
Fast. 3.346: 4.50
Fast. 3.353: 4.50
Fast. 3.361: 4.21
Fast. 3.432: 19.6
Fast. 3.461: 6.39
Fast. 3.462: 6.42

Fast. 3.470: 4.42
Fast. 3.473: 6.39
Fast. 3.484: 12.9
Fast. 3.497: 6.39
Fast. 3.525: 7.109
Fast. 3.549-550: 2.27-30, 2.27
Fast. 3.561: 2.23-25
Fast. 3.591-592: 7.75
Fast. 3.593: 7.115
Fast. 3.634: 4.46, 12.16
Fast. 3.639-640: 4.24
Fast. 3.641: 4.75
Fast. 3.652: 10.8
Fast. 3.682: 11.5
Fast. 3.683: 10.5, 10.19-20
Fast. 3.689: 4.31
Fast. 3.699: 4.75
Fast. 3.707: 7.107-110
Fast. 3.714: 4.43-44
Fast. 3.721: 6.24
Fast. 3.734: 10.24
Fast. 3.767-770: 6.2
Fast. 3.772: 4.29, 6.1
Fast. 3.783: 4.68
Fast. 3.804: 8.13, 10.14
Fast. 3.815: 10.1
Fast. 3.827: 10.1, 17.3
Fast. 4.13-14: 8.2
Fast. 4.32: 9.16
Fast. 4.69: 7.107-110
Fast. 4.103: 6.15-16
Fast. 4.111: 13.3-4
Fast. 4.116: 6.25
Fast. 4.126: 5.4
Fast. 4.151: 2.20
Fast. 4.172: 9.16
Fast. 4.180: 7.51
Fast. 4.193: 4.31
Fast. 4.202-204: 5.6, 7.107-110
Fast. 4.296: 10.24
Fast. 4.231: 6.57
Fast. 4.240: 4.61-62
Fast. 4.241: 4.61-62
Fast. 4.260: 9.20
Fast. 4.312: 10.17-18
Fast. 4.324: 9.20

Book Three of the Corpus Tibullianum: 653
Introduction, Text, Translation and Commentary

Fast. 4.344: 7.107-110
Fast. 4.365: 6.37
Fast. 4.403: 7.170
Fast. 4.409-412: 7.14
Fast. 4.439: 4.33-34
Fast. 4.442: 4.33-34
Fast. 4.476: 9.1
Fast. 4.493: 8.6
Fast. 4.496: 5.1-2
Fast. 4.507-560: 7.8-10
Fast. 4.514: 19.12
Fast. 4.515: 7.43
Fast. 4.528: 8.8
Fast. 4.569: 2.24
Fast. 4.584: 5.22
Fast. 4.601-602: 4.63
Fast. 4.664: 4.42
Fast. 4.671: 7.113
Fast. 4.774: 9.8
Fast. 4.780: 5.34
Fast. 4.813: 10.21, 19.7
Fast. 4.825-826: 4.67
Fast. 4.831: 7.210
Fast. 4.865: 5.29
Fast. 4.910: 4.42
Fast. 4.926: 10.21
Fast. 4.939: 7.9-11
Fast. 4.954: 8.13, 10.14
Fast. 5.13: 7.19
Fast. 5.28: 12.4
Fast. 5.33: 8.23
Fast. 5.38: 4.16
Fast. 5.58: 5.25
Fast. 5.86: 9.16
Fast. 5.104: 4.37
Fast. 5.118: 12.4
Fast. 5.153: 5.8
Fast. 5.160: 8.6
Fast. 5.170: 12.4
Fast. 5.178: 6.24
Fast. 5.219-20: 6.64
Fast. 5.243: 7.138
Fast. 5.345: 6.57
Fast. 5.347-348: 11.2
Fast. 5.374: 5.1-2
Fast. 5.424: 7.122

Fast. 5.427: 7.32
Fast. 5.434: 7.68
Fast. 5.435: 2.16
Fast. 5.480: 2.26
Fast. 5.499-534: 7.8-9
Fast. 5.532: 2.7
Fast. 5.537: 9.5
Fast. 5.549: 1.6
Fast. 5.550: 8.2
Fast. 5.552: 12.4
Fast. 5.553: 19.3
Fast. 5.596: 10.23
Fast. 5.626: 4.78
Fast. 5.637: 7.123
Fast. 5.640: 7.185
Fast. 5.704: 5.18
Fast. 6.22: 7.24
Fast. 6.108: 5.27
Fast. 6.290: 9.20
Fast. 6.322: 8.13, 10.14
Fast. 6.324: 13.8
Fast. 6.380: 10.5
Fast. 6.381: 10.7
Fast. 6.408: 6.35-36
Fast. 6.412: 5.1-2
Fast. 6.426: 4.50, 4.70
Fast. 6.450: 5.1-2
Fast. 6.474: 8.19-20
Fast. 6.483: 6.2
Fast. 6.499: 9.17
Fast. 6.503: 4.45
Fast. 6.539-540: 4.26
Fast. 6.574: 9.16
Fast. 6.662: 4.37
Fast. 6.679: 6.57
Fast. 6.699: 7.123
Fast. 6.709: 1.15-16
Fast. 6.765: 7.107-110
Fast. 6.772: 7.91
Fast. 6.775: 5.29
Fast. 6.799: 1.5
Fast. 6.799-811: 1 *headnote*
Fast. 6.811: 4.45, 6.41
Her. 1.2: 8.2
Her. 1.8: 4.54
Her. 1.12: 4.19-20

Her. 1.20: 7.188
Her. 1.41: 6.21
Her. 1.51: 19.5
Her. 1.59: 7.69
Her. 2.39-41: 6.47-49
Her. 2.42: 6.1-2
Her. 2.72: 3.37
Her. 2.76: 19.3
Her. 2.83: 11.11
Her. 2.103: 6.27, 6.37
Her. 2.105: 1.20
Her. 2.116: 9.20
Her. 2.142: 6.64
Her. 2.147-148: 2.27-30
Her. 2.158: 2.27
Her. 3.5: 4.74
Her. 3.30: 6.46
Her. 3.52: 19.11-12
Her. 3.61: 8.3
Her. 3.125: 4.1
Her. 3.164: 13.3-4
Her. 4: *103, 9 headnote*, 9.5
Her. 4.2: 4.51-52
Her. 4.8: 7.90
Her. 4.9-10: 13.1-2
Her. 4.17-20: 13.1-2
Her. 4.19-20: 11.5
Her. 4.19: 13.1-2
Her. 4.38: 9.22
Her. 4.39-42: 9.5
Her. 4.40: 8.8, 9.5, 9.12-13
Her. 4.41-42: 9.12
Her. 4.41-44: 9.11-18
Her. 4.42: 9.14
Her. 4.44: 9.16
Her. 4.45: 7.130
Her. 4.59: 6.39
Her. 4.70: 4.65, 8.6
Her. 4.79-84: 8.7-14
Her. 4.86: 12.10
Her. 4.87-88: 9.9-10, 9.19
Her. 4.93-96: 9.16
Her. 4.97-98: 9.16
Her. 4.99-100: 9.16
Her. 4.100: 19.17
Her. 4.103-104: 9.1

Her. 4.108: 11.11
Her. 4.131: 4.47-48
Her. 4.148: 9.1
Her. 4.153-154: 4.64
Her. 4.162: 9.1
Her. 4.165: 6.13-14
Her. 4.167: 9.1
Her. 5.13: 6.53
Her. 5.28: 5.25
Her. 5.59: 2.9
Her. 5.96: 7.210
Her. 5.151: 4.67
Her. 5.151-152: 4.67
Her. 6.7: 7.194
Her. 6.17: 6.37
Her. 6.21: 7.194
Her. 6.28: 3.37
Her. 6.44: 6.2
Her. 6.71: 7.194
Her. 6.124: 4.46
Her. 7.1: 3.37
Her. 7.3: 4.64
Her. 7.23: 11.5
Her. 7.28: 9.22
Her. 7.37-39: 4.85-94
Her. 7.39: 16.1-2
Her. 7.43: 7.201
Her. 7.51: 4.63
Her. 7.67: 6.39
Her. 7.84: 6.40
Her. 7.118: 7.201
Her. 7.143: 10.12
Her. 7.157-163: 4.51-60
Her. 7.182: 4.61-62
Her. 7.195-196: 2.27-30, 2.27
Her. 7.217-218: 4.84
Her. 8.15: 17.1
Her. 8.24: 8.2
Her. 8.26: 16.6
Her. 8.39: 16.1-2
Her. 8.79: 9.12-13
Her. 9.13-14: 7.53
Her. 9.14: 7.58
Her. 9.22: 18.6
Her. 9.39-40: 4.9
Her. 9.52: 10.16

Her. 9.64: 7.97
Her. 9.94: 4.87
Her. 10.76: 1.15-16, 6.39
Her. 10.83: 7.96
Her. 10.99-100: 6.42
Her. 10.111: 4.95-96
Her. 10.131-132: 4.85-94
Her. 11.60: 10.19-20
Her. 11.76: 4.96
Her. 11.84: 19.12
Her. 11.120: 2.9
Her. 11.125: 5.31
Her. 12.34: 4.16
Her. 12.79: 9.12-13
Her. 12.82: 10.5
Her. 12.83: 11.11
Her. 12.84: 3.28
Her. 12.94: 3.12
Her. 12.124: 6.42
Her. 12.133: 4.89
Her. 12.138: 8.6
Her. 12.148: 6.34
Her. 12.165: 7.61
Her. 12.167: 7.62-63
Her. 12.169: 4.19-20
Her. 12.181-182: 5.9
Her. 12.183: 11.11
Her. 13.46: 19.6
Her. 13.65: 8.3
Her. 13.78: 3.8
Her. 13.94: 2.1-2
Her. 13.107: 4.11-12
Her. 13.108: 6.33
Her. 13.139: 4.31
Her. 13.157: 13.3-4
Her. 14.16: 5.12
Her. 14.25: 8.6
Her. 14.54: 10.5
Her. 14.66: 7.97
Her. 14.87: 10.1
Her. 14.93: 6.37
Her. 14.106: 6.10
Her. 14.125-126: 3.9
Her. 14.129-130: 2.27-30
Her. 15.5-8: 6.33-36
Her. 15.9: 11.5

Her. 15.79: 6.16
Her. 15.80: 10.16
Her. 15.91-92: 8.3
Her. 15.95: 9.24, 10.1-2
Her. 15.109-110: 13.5-6
Her. 15.109: 9.18
Her. 15.112: 7.153
Her. 15.133-134: 13.1-2, 13.10
Her. 15.143-145: 9.16
Her. 15.168: 9.17
Her. 15.169-170: 17.6
Her. 16.20: 13.3-4
Her. 16.53-54: 9.2
Her. 16.141: 7.177
Her. 16.143: 4.21
Her. 16.167: 6.45
Her. 16.174: 8.4
Her. 16.176: 1.2
Her. 16.178: 10.12
Her. 16.185: 7.185
Her. 16.204: 9.16
Her. 16.253-254: 8.4
Her. 16.266: 13.3-4
Her. 16.311: 18.6
Her. 16.320: 3.25, 6.30
Her. 17.15: 7.202
Her. 17.30: 4.1
Her. 17.32: 18.4
Her. 17.52: 3.4
Her. 17.91-92: 4.63
Her. 17.109: 17.4
Her. 17.147: 11.11
Her. 17.153: 12.6
Her. 17.195: 7.107-110
Her. 17.207: 7.177
Her. 17.226: 5.1
Her. 17.254: 10.16
Her. 18.2: 7.53
Her. 18.7: 7.194
Her. 18.8: 10.12
Her. 18.23: 7.97
Her. 18.55: 4.36
Her. 18.61: 4.29
Her. 18.75: 4.59
Her. 18.166: 7.91
Her. 18.167: 11.5

Her. 18.196: 4.19-20
Her. 18.200: 2.27
Her. 19.5: 11.6
Her. 19.7: 10.1
Her. 19.12: 7.91
Her. 19.72: 4.2
Her. 19.92: 7.58
Her. 19.105: 4.61-62
Her. 19.114: 5.18
Her. 19.127: 10.1
Her. 19.155: 10.5
Her. 19.164: 4.61-62
Her. 19.191-200: 4.17-24
Her. 19.191: 4.17-18
Her. 19.193-202: 4 *headnote*
Her. 19.193: 4.2
Her. 19.195-196: 4.2
Her. 19.196: 4.1
Her. 19.199-200: 4.23
Her. 19.200: 4.24
Her. 20.1: 10.15
Her. 20.3: 10.13
Her. 20: 10 *headnote*
Her. 20.10: 9.20
Her. 20.46: 3.8
Her. 20.55-56: 8.5-6
Her. 20.71-72: 3.31-32
Her. 20.72: 3.32
Her. 20.77-78: 4.66
Her. 20.79: 9.16
Her. 20.83: 2.7-8
Her. 20.85-86: 11.15
Her. 20.86: 11.13-14
Her. 20.95: 9.5
Her. 20.129: 20.1
Her. 20.131: 8.8
Her. 20.132: 7.96
Her. 20.134-136: 10.17-18
Her. 20.181: 4.53
Her. 20.185: 10.21, 19.7
Her. 20.188: 1.20
Her. 20.224: 9.16
Her. 20.233-234: 10.19-20
Her. 20.236: 3.18
Her. 21: 10 *headnote*
Her. 21.34: 12.6

Her. 21.45-46: 5.5
Her. 21.59: 17.1
Her. 21.72: 6.27
Her. 21.88: 8.10
Her. 21.120: 10.16
Her. 21.133: 3.1
Her. 21.157: 12.13
Her. 21.161: 4.28
Her. 21.164: 4.35
Her. 21.170: 3.11
Her. 21.191-192: 10.17-18
Her. 21.204: 19.17
Her. 21.232: 4.77
Her. 21.238: 4.16
Her. 21.240: 11.9
Ibis 2: 4.1
Ibis 29: 8.3
Ibis 78: 10.8
Ibis 94: 4.16
Ibis 141: 2.9
Ibis 278: 4.45
Ibis 318: 2.27
Ibis 351: 19.2
Ibis 425: 7.63, 7.206
Ibis 431: 6.59
Ibis 478: 5.1-2
Ibis 512: 7.72
Ibis 514: 10.8
Ibis 609ff.: 7.9-11
Ibis 613: 3.3
Med. Fac. Fem. 1: 17.1
Med. Fac. Fem. 17: 10.1
Med. Fac. Fem. 91: 8.17-18
Met. 1.1: 7.18
Met. 1.8-12: 7.158-164
Met. 1.12: 7.19, 7.151
Met. 1.36-37: 7.20, 7.194
Met. 1.45-51: 7.151-174
Met. 1.95: 7.123
Met. 1.99-100: 7.181
Met. 1.116-124: 7.169
Met. 1.165: 6.59
Met. 1.168: 8.3
Met. 1.181: 5.14
Met. 1.286: 5.7-8
Met. 1.355: 19.12

Book Three of the Corpus Tibullianum:
Introduction, Text, Translation and Commentary

Met. 1.380: 4.93
Met. 1.381: 6.37
Met. 1.414: 6.7
Met. 1.452-567: 4.23
Met. 1.454: 4.79
Met. 1.475-476: 9.9-10
Met. 1.498-499: 8.5-6
Met. 1.508-509: 9.9-10
Met. 1.509: 9.10
Met. 1.517-518: 4.45-48
Met. 1.557-559: 4.23
Met. 1.564: 4.27
Met. 1.574: 7.206
Met. 1.593: 9.9-10
Met. 1.607-608: 1.6
Met. 1.637: 4.42
Met. 1.677: 4.71
Met. 1.678: 7.56
Met. 1.708: 4.70
Met. 1.747: 10.23
Met. 1.762: 6.45
Met. 2.101: 4.75
Met. 2.112: 4.21
Met. 2.125: 6.61
Met. 2.145-146: 4.63
Met. 2.150: 7.130
Met. 2.307: 7.138
Met. 2.327: 2.29
Met. 2.464: 4.3
Met. 2.506: 7.130
Met. 2.540: 19.20
Met. 2.589: 3.1
Met. 2.662: 7.207
Met. 2.681-682: 4.67-72
Met. 2.683: 4.71
Met. 2.709: 9.9-10
Met. 2.737-738: 4.37
Met. 2.799: 9.10
Met. 2.826: 9.17
Met. 2.856: 12.13
Met. 2.871: 7.13
Met. 2.872: 4.85
Met. 3.8: 4.45-48
Met. 3.14: 1.15-16
Met. 3.17: 8.8
Met. 3.37: 7.123

Met. 3.40: 10.5
Met. 3.75-76: 5.9
Met. 3.104: 7.161
Met. 3.114: 4.24
Met. 3.146: 9.2
Met. 3.161: 12.13
Met. 3.168: 9.14
Met. 3.256: 11.20
Met. 3.261: 5.14
Met. 3.274: 4.45
Met. 3.275-277: 5.15-16
Met. 3.278: 4.45
Met. 3.284-285: 6.23
Met. 3.336-338: 4.47-48
Met. 3.342: 7.125
Met. 3.375-376: 4.75-76
Met. 3.376: 4.75, 4.76
Met. 3.389: 6.45
Met. 3.401: 1.21-22
Met. 3.420-423: 4.23-42
Met. 3.421: 4.27
Met. 3.423: 4.30
Met. 3.464: 11.5
Met. 3.469: 7.112a
Met. 3.473: 10.19-20
Met. 3.477-478: 4.61-62
Met. 3.482-485: 4.23-42
Met. 3.483-484: 4.33-34
Met. 3.484-485: 4.33-34
Met. 3.485: 4.30
Met. 3.494: 6.56
Met. 3.511-733: 6.24
Met. 3.520: 4.45
Met. 3.531: 9.7
Met. 3.607: 4.89
Met. 3.641: 19.17
Met. 3.668: 6.15
Met. 4.10: 7.62
Met. 4.11-17: 2.19
Met. 4.49: 7.62-63
Met. 4.102: 4.90
Met. 4.109: 7.112a
Met. 4.127: 4.30
Met. 4.175-178: 11.15
Met. 4.175-176: 7.117-118
Met. 4.205: 7.61

Met. 4.214: 7.76, 9.1
Met. 4.223: 6.37
Met. 4.261: 2.11-12
Met. 4.317-319: 8.8
Met. 4.329-322: 4.33-34
Met. 4.342-348: 4.35
Met. 4.360: 7.96
Met. 4.373-375: 10.19-20
Met. 4.380: 7.123
Met. 4.396: 13.3-4
Met. 4.403: 8.6
Met. 4.404: 9.22
Met. 4.428-430: 6.24
Met. 4.433: 7.129
Met. 4.434: 3.38
Met. 4.451: 4.88
Met. 4.538: 3.33-34
Met. 4.556: 7.53
Met. 4.621: 7.124
Met. 4.667: 7.209
Met. 4.673-675: 4.26
Met. 4.678-679: 11.15
Met. 4.700: 7.127
Met. 4.765: 6.5
Met. 5.5-10: 2.4
Met. 5.43: 3.3
Met. 5.52-53: 4.28
Met. 5.71: 19.11
Met. 5.105-106: 4.42
Met. 5.112: 4.41
Met. 5.131: 12.1
Met. 5.146: 4.47-48
Met. 5.175-176: 4.64
Met. 5.206: 7.202
Met. 5.234-235: 1.21-22
Met. 5.255: 4.45
Met. 5.266-267: 10.26
Met. 5.271: 10.26
Met. 5.294-317: 1.5
Met. 5.302: 3.38
Met. 5.329: 4.45
Met. 5.335: 4.75
Met. 5.367: 7.89
Met. 5.427: 12.16
Met. 5.428: 6.22
Met. 5.433: 7.60

Met. 5.549: 4.5-6
Met. 5.550: 14.6
Met. 5.558: 7.135
Met. 5.639: 9.5
Met. 5.645: 7.130
Met. 5.663-678: 1.5
Met. 6.49: 4.21
Met. 6.62: 2.9
Met. 6.118: 4.93
Met. 6.200: 19.12
Met. 6.222: 8.15-16
Met. 6.225-226: 7.91-97
Met. 6.315: 6.22
Met. 6.325: 2.10
Met. 6.403-404: 17.4
Met. 6.453: 6.57
Met. 6.554: 7.210
Met. 6.591-592: 6.1-2
Met. 6.622-623: 8.15-16
Met. 6.681: 4.80
Met. 6.705: 4.35
Met. 7.6: 7.72
Met. 7.32-33: 4.85-94
Met. 7.37: 4.1
Met. 7.53: 4.91
Met. 7.59-60: 3.30
Met. 7.62-65: 4.89
Met. 7.63: 7.73-75
Met. 7.64-65: 4.89
Met. 7.75: 19.9
Met. 7.90: 1.21-22
Met. 7.98: 7.62-63
Met. 7.118: 3.11
Met. 7.161-162: 7.15
Met. 7.177: 7.113
Met. 7.184: 7.129
Met. 7.195-196: 7.62-63
Met. 7.222: 7.206
Met. 7.244-250: 5.33-34
Met. 7.246-247: 5.34
Met. 7.354: 7.209
Met. 7.387: 9.22
Met. 7.394: 4.31
Met. 7.413: 4.88
Met. 7.428: 3.1
Met. 7.446-447: 7.156

Met. 7.626: 5.25
Met. 7.661-682: *80, 90-93*
Met. 7.689: *92*
Met. 7.691-692: *92*
Met. 7.692: 3.32
Met. 7. 697: *92*
Met. 7.697-698: 19.2
Met. 7.698: *92*
Met. 7.705: *92*
Met. 7. 707: *92*
Met. 7.708: 7.202
Met. 7. 709: *93*
Met. 7.710: *92*, 19.2
Met. 7.722: *92*
Met. 7. 724-725: *92*
Met. 7.726: *93*
Met. 7.733: *93*
Met. 7.736: *93*
Met. 7.759-792: *80, 93*
Met. 7.766: *93*, 9.7-8
Met. 7.799: 1 *headnote*, 1.26-27
Met. 7.800: 1 *headnote*, 1.19
Met. 7.802-803: *92*, 1 *headnote*, 19.13
Met. 7.805: 8.2
Met. 7.812: 19.11-12
Met. 7.814: *93*
Met. 7.817-819: *92*, 1 *headnote*, 19.11-12
Met. 7.819: 19.9, 19.12
Met. 7.821: 7.132
Met. 7.822: 19.13-14
Met. 7.825-827: *92*, 1 *headnote*, 20 *headnote*, 20.3
Met. 7.847: *92*, 1 *headnote*, 1.25
Met. 7.852: *92*, 1 *headnote*, 19.2
Met. 7.855: *93*, 2.27
Met. 7.861: 7.202
Met. 8.7: 19.3
Met. 8.15-16: 4.37
Met. 8.20: 7.98
Met. 8.25-27: 8.7-14, 8.9-12,
Met. 8.28: 7.90
Met. 8.35: 12.16
Met. 8.52: 7.135
Met. 8.120-125: 4.85-94

Met. 8.120-121: 4.91
Met. 8.120: 4.91
Met. 8.121: 6.15
Met. 8.159: 4.37
Met. 8.223-224: 4.55
Met. 8.331-333: 9.12-14
Met. 8.332-333: 9.13
Met. 8.332: 9.14
Met. 8.334-338: 9.2
Met. 8.380: 7.89
Met. 8.448: 2.18
Met. 8.460-461: 5.11
Met. 8.469: 5.25
Met. 8.488-489: 2.15
Met. 8.533: 4.40
Met. 8.595-596: 5.19
Met. 8.628-629: 8.14
Met. 8.629-720: 7.8-9
Met. 8.634: 12.16
Met. 8.674: 5.25, 5.34
Met. 8.694: 7.13
Met. 8.724: 4.43-44
Met. 8.736-737: 10.13
Met. 8.754: 4.42
Met. 8.801: 7.202
Met. 8.858: 6.1-2
Met. 8.879: 7.147
Met. 9.90: 8.9
Met. 9.104: 7.72
Met. 9.121: 8.3
Met. 9.147: 6.51-52
Met. 9.169: 7.166
Met. 9.269-270: 4.26
Met. 9.299: 8.3
Met. 9.321: 4.59
Met. 9. 322: 6.35-36
Met. 9.333: 4.80
Met. 9.381: 3.32
Met. 9.425: 7.113
Met. 9.459: 6.45
Met. 9.461: 4.45
Met. 9.474-475: 4.1
Met. 9.476: 19.4
Met. 9. 497: 4.1
Met. 9.504: 2.19
Met. 9.509: 6.37

Met. 9.536: 10.5
Met. 9.546: 3.33-34
Met. 9.558: 11.7
Met. 9.605: 6.45
Met. 9.613-615: 4.85-94
Met. 9.622: 7.126
Met. 9.647-649: 4.86
Met. 9.657: 6.57
Met. 9.682: 4.53
Met. 9.698: 4.75
Met. 9.735-736: 16.2
Met. 9.743-744: 7.61
Met. 9.787: 7.202
Met. 10.22: 4.88
Met. 10.24: 5.19
Met. 10.30: 3.37
Met. 10.38-39: 3.35
Met. 10.53: 7.129
Met. 10.56: 19.7
Met. 10.64: 6.46
Met. 10.66-67: 4.88
Met. 10.71: 4.73
Met. 10.75: 2.29
Met. 10.171-173: 9.12
Met. 10.172-173: 9.12
Met. 10.178: 7.127
Met. 10.204: 7.202
Met. 10.209: 4.50
Met. 10.213: 4.30
Met. 10.254-255: 1.19-20
Met. 10.260: 3.17
Met. 10.307-309: 2.23
Met. 10.336: 6.37
Met. 10.351: 8.3
Met. 10.380: 2.27
Met. 10.422: 4.80
Met. 10.432: 8.12
Met. 10.450: 7.9-11
Met. 10.451: 7.11
Met. 10.462: 4.31
Met. 10.482: 2.7-8
Met. 10.503-739: 9 *headnote*
Met. 10.533-541: 9.11-18
Met. 10.535: 9.11
Met. 10.537-539: 9.13
Met. 10.545: 5.6, 9.1

Met. 10.565: 10.21
Met. 10.588: 3.8
Met. 10.624-625: 2.7-8
Met. 10.633-634: 3.35
Met. 10.642: 3.2
Met. 10.717: 7.130
Met. 10.733: 12.13
Met. 11.68: 4.38
Met. 11.116: 7.123
Met. 11.132: 6.38
Met. 11.134-145: 3.29
Met. 11.134: 6.11
Met. 11.165-171: 4.23-42
Met. 11.166: 4.35, 12.13
Met. 11.167-168: 4.39
Met. 11.177: 4.47-48
Met. 11.194: 7.209
Met. 11.266: 4.80
Met. 11.364: 7.53
Met. 11.388: 10.19-20
Met. 11.492-645: 4.19-20
Met. 11.496: 5.1-2
Met. 11.500: 3.37
Met. 11.544: 7.202
Met. 11.562: 7.202
Met. 11.592-593: 5.24
Met. 11.593: 4.81
Met. 11.594-595: 7.65-66
Met. 11.624-625: 17.2
Met. 11.624: 4.19-20
Met. 11.706: 2.27
Met. 11.732: 7.209
Met. 11.747: 7.53
Met. 11.793: 4.27, 10.5
Met. 12.28: 7.46-47
Met. 12.187-188: 7.50-51
Met. 12.216: 4.31
Met. 12.222: 6.59
Met. 12.223: 4.31
Met. 12.247: 8.6
Met. 12.251: 7.202
Met. 12.301: 6.63
Met. 12.359: 6.25
Met. 12.398: 5.3
Met. 12.468: 7.91-97
Met. 12.489: 9.17

Book Three of the Corpus Tibullianum: 661
Introduction, Text, Translation and Commentary

Met. 12.518-520: 10.13
Met. 12.556-558: 4.47-48
Met. 12.573: 7.177
Met. 12.585: 4.27
Met. 12.586: 4.93
Met. 13.19: 11.11
Met. 13.44: 7.64
Met. 13.63: 7.48-49
Met. 13.113: 7.201
Met. 13.132: 3.35
Met. 13.196: 7.64
Met. 13.289-290: 4.37
Met. 13.292: 7.10
Met. 13.316: 4.65
Met. 13.380: 5.31
Met. 13.390: 4.37
Met. 13.531: 7.147
Met. 13.535: 7.123
Met. 13.585: 8.3
Met. 13.639: 6.62
Met. 13.641: 1.6
Met. 13.646: 7.45-47
Met. 13.669: 6.38
Met. 13.687: 2.11-12
Met. 13.730-731: 4.89, 7.73-75
Met. 13.732-734: 4.89
Met. 13.739: 6.61
Met. 13.767: 13.9
Met. 13.770: 7.56
Met. 13.775-776: 4.5-6
Met. 13.804: 4.74
Met. 13.899: 7.126
Met. 13.912: 11.20
Met. 13.968: 7.61
Met. 14.10: 7.62
Met. 14.18: 2.7
Met. 14.25: 11.13-16
Met. 14.59-60: 4.89
Met. 14.75: 4.89
Met. 14.96: 5.25
Met. 14.98-99: 6.39
Met. 14.111-112: 5.23
Met. 14.127: 7.127
Met. 14.160: 7.56
Met. 14.166: 12.16
Met. 14.175: 11.11

Met. 14.177-178: 14.7
Met. 14.203: 11.11
Met. 14.215: 7.35
Met. 14.247: 7.61
Met. 14.254: 3.3
Met. 14.301: 4.83
Met. 14.337: 4.37
Met. 14.343: 7.24
Met. 14.349-50: 8.4
Met. 14.403: 5.9
Met. 14.419: 1.3-4
Met. 14.481: 4.36
Met. 14.489: 5.3
Met. 14.585: 14.6
Met. 14.622-771: 8.13-14
Met. 14.633: 7.60
Met. 14.641-642: *82*, 8.13, 19
   headnote
Met. 14.654: 4.23
Met. 14.659: 5.16
Met. 14.675: 8.2, 19.8
Met. 14.680: 7.152
Met. 14.681-682: 19.4, 19.12
Met. 14.684-685: 8.13-14, 8.14
Met. 14.693: 4.76
Met. 14.716-717: 2.3
Met. 14.730: 5.31
Met. 14.744-745: 4.42
Met. 14.757: 10.5
Met. 14.825: 7.97
Met. 14.843-844
Met. 14.939: 4.30
Met. 15.26: 12.16
Met. 15.35: 19.3
Met. 15.45: 10.12
Met. 15.55-56: 7.204
Met. 15.67: 7.18
Met. 15.86: 6.15
Met. 15.96: 7.111
Met. 15.106: 5.17
Met. 15.135: 7.123
Met. 15.153ff.: 7.206-210
Met. 15.158-159: 7.210
Met. 15.166: 10.5
Met. 15.170: 7.184-185
Met. 15.177: 7.152

Met. 15.181: 5.1-2
Met. 15.234: 5.25
Met. 15.310: 7.60
Met. 15.325: 7.120
Met. 15.335: 7.17
Met. 15.374: 7.206
Met. 15.456ff.: 7.206-210
Met. 15.482: 4.80, 7.24
Met. 15.488: 7.128
Met. 15.618: 7.161
Met. 15.619: 4.21
Met. 15.663-664: 4.81
Met. 15.672: 3.16
Met. 15.696: 9.12
Met. 15.721: 7.34
Met. 15.801: 19.3
Met. 15.808-809: 3.35
Met. 15.838: 7.112
Met. 15.875-876: 2.17
Met. 15.878: 7.112
Pont. 1.1.58: 18.4
Pont. 1.2.15: 2.27
Pont. 1.2.50: 1.6
Pont. 1.2.71: 11.19
Pont. 1.2.80: 7.91
Pont. 1.2.92: 10.21, 19.7
Pont. 1.2.136: 4.60
Pont. 1.3.32: 6.16
Pont. 1.3.45: 10.5
Pont. 1.4.2: 5.25
Pont. 1.4.10: 7.50-51
Pont. 1.4.28: 10.12
Pont. 1.4.29: 4.21
Pont. 1.4.44: 6.26
Pont. 1.6.10: 4.65
Pont. 1.6.15: 4.19-20
Pont. 1.6.26: 4.16
Pont. 1.7: 7.106-117
Pont. 1.7.27-30: 14.5
Pont. 1.7.45-50: 7.48-49
Pont. 1.7.57: 7.166
Pont. 1.8.12: 10.12
Pont. 1.8.31: 6.9
Pont. 1.8.32: 1.6, 3.32
Pont. 1.8.42: 12.4
Pont. 1.8.53: 7.135

Pont. 1.8.65: 7.154
Pont. 1.9.31: 2.7-8
Pont. 1.9.53: 2.23-25
Pont. 1.10.27-28: 10.5
Pont. 2.1.32: 10.24
Pont. 2.1.39: 7.137-146
Pont. 2.1.61-62: 7.39
Pont. 2.1.61: 11.11
Pont. 2.2: 7.106-117
Pont. 2.2.9-14: 5.7-14
Pont. 2.2.9: 5.7
Pont. 2.2.11: 5.13
Pont. 2.2.13: 5.7
Pont. 2.2.30: 7.106
Pont. 2.2.49: 8.12
Pont. 2.2.77: 7.117
Pont. 2.2.80: 6.2
Pont. 2.2.113: 7.56
Pont. 2.3.16: 13.8
Pont. 2.3.75: 7.81
Pont. 2.3.77-78: *121*, 7.197-200
Pont. 2.4.23-24: 1.20
Pont. 2.4.30: 6.30
Pont. 2.5.28-29: 7.24
Pont. 2.5.50: 8.19-20
Pont. 2.5.75: 7.115
Pont. 2.7.3: 8.8
Pont. 2.7.23: 4.50
Pont. 2.7.56: 10.12, 10.14
Pont. 2.7.79: 7.46-47
Pont. 2.7.80: 9.6
Pont. 2.8.11: 5.1
Pont. 2.8.21: 1.6
Pont. 2.8.41: 7.112
Pont. 2.8.51: 3.33-34, 11.20
Pont. 2.9.2: 4.56
Pont. 2.9.30-31: 7.163
Pont. 2.9.35: 4.16
Pont. 2.9.41: 7.59
Pont. 2.9.67-72: 5.7-14
Pont. 2.9.67: 5.7, 5.12
Pont. 2.9.68: 5.10
Pont. 2.10.10: 10.16
Pont. 2.10.13: 7.180
Pont. 2.10.33: 7.196
Pont. 2.11.2: 7.4

Book Three of the Corpus Tibullianum: 663
Introduction, Text, Translation and Commentary

Pont. 3.1.13: 4.77
Pont. 3.1.26: 3.18, 5.9
Pont. 3.1.118: 8.15
Pont. 3.1.127: 4.21
Pont. 3.1.149-150: 1.21-22
Pont. 3.1.161: 4.16
Pont. 3.2.29: 7.112a
Pont. 3.2.49: 3.13
Pont. 3.2.83: 7.15
Pont. 3.2.101: 19.3
Pont. 3.2.103: 6.13
Pont. 3.3: 4 *headnote*
Pont. 3.3.7: 19.11-12
Pont. 3.3.16: 8.10, 6.35-36
Pont. 3.3.60: 8.6
Pont. 3.3.63: 10.5
Pont. 3.3.83: 7.46-47
Pont. 3.3.93-94: 4.81
Pont. 3.3.106: 3.18
Pont. 3.4.13: 7.1-2, 7.2
Pont. 3.4.45: 4.71
Pont. 3.4.79-82: 7.14-15
Pont. 3.4.79: 7.7
Pont. 3.4.83-84: 7.2
Pont. 3.4.113: 4.47-48
Pont. 3.5.53: 4.61-62
Pont. 3.6.21: 4.53
Pont. 3.6.35-36: 10.19-20
Pont. 3.6.45: 5.17
Pont. 3.6.58: 13.8
Pont. 3.6.59-60: 10.16
Pont. 4.2: 7 *headnote*
Pont. 4.4.23-24: 7.122
Pont. 4.4.25: 7.121
Pont. 4.4.27ff: 7.118-134
Pont. 4.3.29: 6.27, 19.17
Pont. 4.3.39: 19.3
Pont. 4.6.11: 2.27
Pont. 4.6.47: 6.31-32
Pont. 4.6.50: 9.16
Pont. 4.7.12: 2.27
Pont. 4.7.40: 4.65, 8.6
Pont. 4.7.41-42: 7.48-49
Pont. 4.8.39-44: 7.14-15
Pont. 4.8.45: 7.177
Pont. 4.8.65-66: 7.26-27

Pont. 4.8.89-90: 4.53
Pont. 4.9.26: 7.121
Pont. 4.9.31-32: 7.130-134
Pont. 4.9.42: 7.121
Pont. 4.9.53-54: 7.134
Pont. 4.9.59-60: 7.122
Pont. 4.10.14: 9.16
Pont. 4.10.17: 6.35-36
Pont. 4.10.25: 4.89
Pont. 4.11.22: 4.80
Pont. 4.12.27: 7.200
Pont. 4.12.41: 10.5
Pont. 4.13.13: 7.24, 13.3-4
Pont. 4.13.16: 12.4
Pont. 4.13.23: 7.18
Pont. 4.13.48: 10.19
Pont. 4.15.12: 10.21, 19.7
Pont. 4.16.16: 7.205
Pont. 4.16.23: 7.18
Pont. 4.16.35: 6.57
Rem. 26: 5.9
Rem. 31: 10.5
Rem. 74: 10.26
Rem. 81: 6.3
Rem. 109-10: 4.19-20
Rem. 115: 6.3, 10.1, 17.3
Rem. 119: 9.23
Rem. 144: 19.6
Rem. 181: 4.39
Rem. 199-206: 9.7-10
Rem. 199-200: 9.19
Rem. 205: 17.1
Rem. 223: 20.1
Rem. 249: 7.161
Rem. 260: 6.4
Rem. 286: 4.96
Rem. 291: 19.3
Rem. 311: 17.1
Rem. 314: 8.4
Rem. 315: 7.135
Rem. 322: 16.6
Rem. 359: 2.7
Rem. 372: 8.2
Rem. 376: 11.2
Rem. 381: 7.18
Rem. 407: 19.2

Rem. 439: 4.1
Rem. 443: 1.3-4
Rem. 461: 7.147
Rem. 462: 6.4
Rem. 477: 8.2
Rem. 485-486: 4.19-20
Rem. 492: 14.3-4
Rem. 497: 6.33
Rem. 526: 8.14
Rem. 537-538: 6.54
Rem. 552: 8.6
Rem. 554: 4.51-52
Rem. 555-576: 4 *headnote*
Rem. 557: 4.19-20
Rem. 564: 11.2
Rem. 579: 8.3, 19.11-12
Rem. 579-580: 19.12
Rem. 580: 19.6
Rem. 581-582: 19.9
Rem. 582: 19.11-12
Rem. 585-586: 4.4, 19.11-12, 19.11
Rem. 586: 19.12
Rem. 591: 19.9
Rem. 608: 4.51-52
Rem. 613: 9.1-2
Rem. 630: 11.2
Rem. 650: 19.6
Rem. 681: 17.1
Rem. 685-686: 10.17-18
Rem. 688: 8.13, 10.14
Rem. 689: 8.3
Rem. 697: 2.5-6
Rem. 704: 6.1
Rem. 740: 7.73-75
Rem. 761: 13.3-4
Rem. 768: 16.6
Rem. 772: 4.58
Rem. 780: 8.4
Rem. 788: 7.91
Rem. 805-806: 6 *headnote*
Rem. 808: 7.168
Trist. 1.1.5-14: 1.9-14
Trist. 1.1.7: 1.11-12
Trist. 1.1.8: 1.13
Trist. 1.1.9: 12.5
Trist. 1.1.11: 1.13

Trist. 1.1.11-12: 1.10
Trist. 1.1.38: 19.6
Trist. 1.1.50: 19.6
Trist. 1.1.87: 2.9
Trist. 1.1.117-118: 7.196
Trist. 1.1.117: 5.28
Trist. 1.2.26: 7.53
Trist. 1.2.27: 4.21
Trist. 1.2.37-44: 1.26
Trist. 1.2.45: 12.17
Trist. 1.2.53: 5.18
Trist. 1.2.107: 1.6
Trist. 1.3.17-18: 1.26
Trist. 1.3.23: 2.14
Trist. 1.3.41-46: 1.26
Trist. 1.3.63-64: 1.26
Trist. 1.3.79-102: 1.26
Trist. 1.3.80: 6.38
Trist. 1.4.18: 5.1-2
Trist. 1.5a.39: 7.54
Trist. 1.5b.12: 7.2
Trist. 1.5b.40: 6.26
Trist. 1.6: 1.26
Trist. 1.7.1: 9.1-2
Trist. 1.7.19-20: 7.196
Trist. 1.7.38: 7.196
Trist. 1.8.35: 4.96
Trist. 1.8.37-44: 4.85-94
Trist. 1.8.38: 5.1-2
Trist. 1.8.39-40: 4.91
Trist. 1.8.40: 4.85-94
Trist. 1.8.49: 10.5
Trist. 1.9a.3: 4.53
Trist. 1.9a.25: 4.94
Trist. 1.9b.8: 13.8
Trist. 1.9b.9: 7.123
Trist. 2.1.140: 19.6
Trist. 2.4: 1.7
Trist. 2.11-12: 7.16
Trist. 2.13: 4.45, 8.2
Trist. 2.15-18: 4.51-60
Trist. 2.16: 4.24
Trist. 2.22: 4.16, 13.3-4
Trist. 2.27: 4.93
Trist. 2.53: 5.22
Trist. 2.73-74: 7.2

Book Three of the Corpus Tibullianum: 665
Introduction, Text, Translation and Commentary

Trist. 2.75-76: 7.14-15
Trist. 2.77-78: 4.61-62
Trist. 2.87-88: 10.17-18
Trist. 2.114: 12.4
Trist. 2.123-124: 4.94
Trist. 2.133: 6.38
Trist. 2.142: 4.54, 6.32
Trist. 2.159-160: 6.1-2
Trist. 2.162: 8.15
Trist. 2.184: 4.16
Trist. 2.195-196: 7.151-174
Trist. 2.196: 7.53, 7.155-156
Trist. 2.199: 7.146
Trist. 2.224: 7.181
Trist. 2.225: 7.106-117
Trist. 2.235: 7.181
Trist. 2.236: 13.3-4
Trist. 2.241-242: 1.13
Trist. 2.284: 4.51-52
Trist. 2.291-292: 4.13-14
Trist. 2.307-308: 1.23
Trist. 2.321-322: 7.16
Trist. 2.327-328: 1.14
Trist. 2.332: 1.24
Trist. 2.334: 7.18
Trist. 2.335-336: 7.4
Trist. 2.337: 7.24
Trist. 2.348: 13.8
Trist. 2.353-354: 10.3
Trist. 2.355-356: 1.14
Trist. 2.356: 16.1-2
Trist. 2.361-362: 9.7
Trist. 2.371-374: 7.54-78
Trist. 2.375-380: 7.54-78
Trist. 2.416: 7.4
Trist. 2.441-442: *126*
Trist. 2.445: 4.57
Trist. 2.461-462: 4.61-62
Trist. 2.490: 6.62
Trist. 2.503-504: 5.7
Trist. 2.527: 8.9
Trist. 2.529-530: 4.40
Trist. 2.529-532: 7.2
Trist. 2.532: 3.4
Trist. 2.575: 5.23-25
Trist. 3.1.43-48: 1.26

Trist. 3.1.57-66: 1.26
Trist. 3.1.57: 7.210
Trist. 3.1.60: 4.27
Trist. 3.1.70: 5.1-2
Trist. 3.3: 1.26
Trist. 3.3.22: 10.12
Trist. 3.3.23: 4.74
Trist. 3.3.52: 9.15
Trist. 3.3.57: 2.5-6
Trist. 3.3.69: 2.23-25
Trist. 3.3.73-76: 2.27-30
Trist. 3.3.83: 2.9
Trist. 3.3.88: 7.201
Trist. 3.4a.34: 6.30
Trist. 3.4a.42: 10.12
Trist. 3.4b.1-2: 5.1
Trist. 3.4b.7: 3.32
Trist. 3.4b.7-16: 1.26
Trist. 3.5.15: 6.45
Trist. 3.7.1: 8.2
Trist. 3.7.34: 5.25
Trist. 3.7.51-52: 13.10
Trist. 3.8.7-10:1.26
Trist. 3.8.19-20: 5.23-25
Trist. 3.8.25: 4.19-20
Trist. 3.9.27-28: 12.7
Trist. 3.9.32: 15.1
Trist. 3.10.2: 4.27
Trist. 3.10.54: 7.91
Trist. 3.10.76: 5.1-2
Trist. 3.11.3-4: 4.85-94
Trist. 3.11.7: 4.91
Trist. 3.11.15-16: 1.26
Trist. 3.11.15: 1.6
Trist. 3.11.59: 2.7-8
Trist. 3.13: 11 *headnote*
Trist. 3.13.2: 11.19
Trist. 3.13.7: 12.14
Trist. 3.14.19-20: 7.196
Trist. 4.1: 7.106-117
Trist. 4.1.40: 3.4
Trist. 4.1.53-54: 10.25
Trist. 4.2: 7 *headnote*
Trist. 4.2.27: 3.18
Trist. 4.2.37: 7.137-146
Trist. 4.2.41-42: 7.137-146

Trist. 4.3: 1.26
Trist. 4.3.40: 6.40
Trist. 4.4: 7.106-117
Trist. 4.4a.27-30: *121*
Trist. 4.4a.29-30: 7.197-200
Trist. 4.4a.47-48: 5.23-25
Trist. 4.4b.29: 7.18
Trist. 4.6.24: 7.91
Trist. 4.6.45-46: 1.26
Trist. 4.7.7: 13.1-2
Trist. 4.7.12: 4.87
Trist. 4.7.13: 4.86, 4.89
Trist. 4.7.16: 4.88
Trist. 4.8.2: 5.15
Trist. 4.8.5-12: 1.26
Trist. 4.8.11-12: 3.7-10
Trist. 4.8.11: 3.8
Trist. 4.8.23: 5.16
Trist. 4.9.4: 18.4
Trist. 4.9.19: 7.177
Trist. 4.10.3: 7.60
Trist. 4.10.5-6: *86, 94, 97, 118,*
    5.15-20, 5.17-18, 5.17
Trist. 4.10.6: 5.18
Trist. 4.10.12: 12.14
Trist. 4.10.51-52: *97*
Trist. 4.10.65-66: 6.16
Trist. 4.10.73-74: 1.26
Trist. 4.10.118: 19.11-12
Trist. 5.1.10: 7.4
Trist. 5.1.17-19: 6.41
Trist. 5.1.17: 7.97
Trist. 5.1.18: 7.97
Trist. 5.1.19: 7.177
Trist. 5.1.39-40: 1.26
Trist. 5.1.39: 1.6
Trist. 5.2: 1.26
Trist. 5.2.3-5: 17.2
Trist. 5.2.31: 4.91
Trist. 5.2.73-75: 7.196
Trist. 5.3.1: 4.43-44
Trist. 5.3.21ff.: 6.15
Trist. 5.3.24: 8.19-20
Trist. 5.3.25-26: 3.36, 11.3
Trist. 5.3.35-36: 6.1-2
Trist. 5.3.43: 10.1-2

Trist. 5.3.47: 10.25
Trist. 5.3.50: 5.34
Trist. 5.5: 1.26, 11 *headnote*
Trist. 5.5.57: 10.5
Trist. 5.5.62: 7.112
Trist. 5.7.4: 6.30
Trist. 5.7.10: 10.16
Trist. 5.8.25: 4.21
Trist. 5.8.28: 6.16
Trist. 5.9.12: 4.16
Trist. 5.9.24: 7.16
Trist. 5.9.27: 9.13
Trist. 5.10.2: 7.53
Trist. 5.10.21: 6.27
Trist. 5.10.25: 4.71
Trist. 5.11: 1.26
Trist. 5.11.23-24: 7.2
Trist. 5.12.31: 2.5-6
Trist. 5.12.46: 16.6
Trist. 5.14: 1.26
Trist. 5.14.42: 10.16

[Ovid]
Epiced. Drusi
73-74: 2.21-22
130: 4.16
196: 18.1
273: 7.117
296: 10.25
301-302: 12.9
327: 6.40
334: 6.2
385-391: 7.107-110
390: 7.108-109
395: 4.19-20:
407: 7.152
415: 4.47-48
424: 6.46
448: 10.12
459: 4.23

Halieut.
49: 7.128, 7.164
50: 4.14
78: 9.13
131: 4.30

Nux
93: 7.172
127: 19.5
152: 3.7
159: 2.7-8

Pacuvius (Ribbeck³)
Trag. 2: 7.128
Trag. 37: 6.19
Trag. 112: 4.1
Trag. 268: 7.182

Parthenius
Erotika Pathemata 18: *119*

Paulus' epitome of Festus (Lindsay)
38: 7.24
45: 3.33-34
55: 3.33-34
92: 3.33-34
107: 5.3
407: 7.89
501: 5.7

Paulus Silentiarius
AP 5.260: 8.7-14

Pausanias
2.7.7: 7.8-9
10.8.9: 1.15-16
10.38.1: 7.9-11

Persius
Sat. 1.11-12: 9.15-17
Sat. 1.26: 5.25
Sat. 3.113: 7.202
Sat. 5.23: 6.9
Sat. 5.86: 12.3

Petronius
1.30.4: 8.4
5.1.10: 7.139
9.3.4: 1.23
13.2: 15.1
15.6.15: 2.21-22
18.5: 5.30

25.4: 6.47-49
26.5: 5.30
40.7: 12.3
63.7: 5.20
65.5: 4.74
71.7: 2.21-22
83.8: 7.4
89.117: 4.7-8
108.14.1: 9.7
118.1: 7.5-6
122.132-133: 7.143
124.282: 7.86
128.6-12: 4.7-8
132.155: 9.18
133.1: 5.10
133.3.5: 10.1-2
133.3.6-9: 5.11
138.2: 5.30
fr. 30.1: 4.7-8

Phaedrus
Fab. Aes. 1 pr.7: 4.68
Fab. Aes. 2.6.10: 3.11
Fab. Aes. 3.15.19: 2.27
Fab. Aes. 4.9.6: 7.86
Fab. Aes. 5.7.8: 15.4
Fab. App. 7.16: 2.27
Fab. App. 28.9: 2.27

Philemon
fr. 49 (Kassel-Austin): *119*

Philodemus
AP 5.4.5 (=7.5 Sider): 1.26
AP 5.46 (=20 Sider): 1 *headnote*
AP 5.120.1 (=27.1 Sider): 3 *headnote*

Pindar
fr. 130: 3.38
Isth. 6.22ff.: 7.135-176
Isth. 6.49-51: 7.118-134
Nem. 5.24: 4.39
Nem. 8.37-38: 3.11-12
Ol. 1.75: 3.33-34

Ol. 2.27: 6.2
Ol. 13.90: 4.86
Paean 6.6-9: 1.15-16
Pyth. 1.1: 4.37
Pyth. 4.4-23: 7.139
Pyth. 4.64: 5.4
Pyth. 9.64: 4.67

Plato
Alc. 2.149b-c: 7.14-15
Phaedr. 261b-c: 7.48-49
Phileb. 65c: 6.49-50
Rep. 9.588c: 4.85-94, 4.87

Plautus
Amph. 246: 7.57
Amph. 605: 5.20
Amph. 738-740: 4.10
Amph. 817: 13.10
Amph. 1081: 14.7
Asin.: 3.7-10
Asin. 655: 7.32
Asin. 691: 7.32
Asin. 753: 6.54
Asin. 858: 4.93
Asin. 892: 7.32
Asin. 917-918: 3.32
Asin. 944: 2.5-6
Aul. 72-73: 6.54
Aul. 181: 14.7
Aul. 692: 4.13-14
Aul. 872: 6.61
Bacch.: 3.7-10
Bacch. 262a: 4.1
Bacch. 325: 7.55
Bacch. 905: 1.15-16, 11.7
Bacch. 924: 13.7
Capt. 516: 5.32
Cas.: 3.7-10
Cas. 23: 15.1
Cas. 230: 10.22
Cas. 780: 4.31
Cas. 782: 4.31
Cas. 796: 8.6
Cas. 813: 4.1
Cas. 840: 8.6

Cas. 859: 4.31
Cas. 881: 4.31
Cist.: 3.7-10
Cist. 71: 6.3
Cist. 211: 14.7
Cist. 472: 6.49-50
Cist. 696: 7.97
Curc. 211: 3.29
Curc. 672: 6.57
Epid. 135: 1.19, 4.43-44
Men. 841: 8.6
Men. 906: 7.182
Men. 1060: 6.47-48
Merc.: 3.7-10
Merc. 225-226: 4.7-8
Merc. 285: 4.1
Merc. 585: 14.7
Merc. 861: 4.65
Merc. 923: 6.21
Merc. 972-973: 2.1-2
Merc. 1004: 7.101
Mil. 190: 9.16
Mil. 244: 9.16
Mil. 356: 12.9
Mil. 389: 4.24
Mil. 438: 12.9
Mil. 703-704: 10.19
Mil. 814: 2.1-2
Mil. 1123: 4.64
Mil. 1272: 6.3
Most. 680: 1.24
Pers. 313: 5.20
Pers. 361: 6.23
Pers. 472: 12.16
Pers. 634: 1.24
Poen. 96: 2.20
Poen. 857: 7.42
Poen. 1107: 6.53
Poen. 1270: 13.10
Poen. 1400: 4.1
Pseud. 94-95: 2.4
Pseud. 240: 4.54
Pseud. 315: 4.1
Pseud. 941: 5.13
Rud. 102: 4.71
Rud. 198: 5.12

Book Three of the Corpus Tibullianum: 669
Introduction, Text, Translation and Commentary

Rud. 205: 19.12
Rud. 359: 13.8
Rud. 488-490: 4.24
Rud. 513: 7.161
Rud. 704: 3.33-34
Rud. 828: 6.44
Stich.: 3.7-10
Stich. 251: 12.14
Stich. 700: 6.62
Trin. 288: 9.20
Trin. 523-524: 5.23-25
Trin. 824: 4.93
Truc. 16: 7.182
Truc. 348: 18.1
Truc. 476: 4.13-14
Truc. 517: 7.32
Truc. 539-540: 2.24
Truc. 790: 12.9

Pliny the Elder
Nat. 1.1.14: 7.199
Nat. 2.172: 7.151-174, 7.152, 7.153-157, 7.164, 7.165-168
Nat. 2.186: 7.153-157
Nat. 2.235: 7.142
Nat. 2.237: 7.142
Nat. 3.96: 7.77
Nat. 4.77: 7.93
Nat. 5.14: 7.128
Nat. 5.28: 7.64
Nat. 5.110: 3.29
Nat. 5.118.3: 7.200
Nat. 7.147: 7.34
Nat. 7.186: 2.7-8
Nat. 8.58: 10.4
Nat. 8.65: 6.15
Nat. 8.66: 6.15
Nat. 9.11: 4.37
Nat. 9.106-124: 3.17
Nat. 9.106: 8.19-20
Nat. 9.124-135: 8.15-16
Nat. 9.125-141: 3.18
Nat. 10.37: 9.6
Nat. 10.94: 4.26
Nat. 11.17: *124*
Nat. 12.42: 6.63

Nat. 12.47: 9.2
Nat. 12.51: 2.24
Nat. 12.54: 8.17-18
Nat. 12.70: 3.17
Nat. 13.7: 1.18
Nat. 13.22: 7.84
Nat. 13.78: 1.9
Nat. pr. 14: 19.10
Nat. 14.10ff.: 7.171
Nat. 14.36: 14.3-4
Nat. 14.53: 7.57
Nat. 14.62: 6.6
Nat. 14.119: 5.34
Nat. 18.2: 9.3
Nat. 18.87: 14.3-4
Nat. 18.190.2: 7.60
Nat. 18.270: 5.1-2
Nat. 18.277: 7.65
Nat. 18.282: 19.12
Nat. 19.19: 2.10
Nat. 21.46: 1.9
Nat. 21.47: 4.33-34
Nat. 21.70: *124*
Nat. 23.40.10: 6.58
Nat. 25.4: 7.180
Nat. 26.87: 14.3-4
Nat. 27.2: 4.26
Nat. 27.146: 5.10
Nat. 31.2: 7.168
Nat. 31.35: 7.140
Nat. 31.41: 6.58
Nat. 33.39: 7.15
Nat. 35.150: 2.21-22
Nat. 35.157: 7.130-134
Nat. 35.179: 7.142
Nat. 36.121: 6.58
Nat. 36.135: 3.14
Nat. 36.156: 6.11
Nat. 36.158: 3.14

Pliny the Younger
Epist. 2.14.13: 7.36
Epist. 5.6.10: 7.161
Epist. 5.6.39: 7.171
Epist. 6.11.3: 3.25
Epist. 7.9.14: 7.36

Epist. 7.19.7: 8.10
Epist. 7.24.6: 15.1
Paneg. 26.4.1: 1.27-28
Paneg. 68.2: 4.54
Paneg. 95.3: 6.9

Plutarch
Cic. 28: 5.7-8
Mor. 761e: 4.67-72
Mor. 44b: 3.19-20
Rom. 21.1: 1.1-4
Sept. Sap. 147f.: 5.3

Porcius Licinius
fr. 7 (Courtney): 8.5-6

Porphyrio
Hor. Carm. 3.22.2-3: 4.13-14
Hor. Epist. 1.17.55: 7.117-118
Hor. Epod. 3.9: 4.68

Porphyry
Abst. 2.15: 7.14-15
Abst. 2.15ff.: 7.8-9

Posidonius
fr. 49 (Kidd): 7.151-174

Pratinas
fr. 14 (Page): 6.57

Priapea
14.3: 13.10
16.6: 4.51-52
33.1: 6.57
47.3-4: 6.12
81.2: 10.1-2

Priscian
GL 2.36.22: 5.3
GL 2.198.4: 12.9
GL 3.173.27-174.12: 13.8
GL 3.268.20: 3.19-20
GL 3.407.2: 5.3
Periheg. 375: 7.64

Propertius
1.1.1: 1.7, 8.1
1.1.5-6: 4.65
1.1.7: 9.7
1.1.8: 5.14
1.1.9-16: 4.65-66, 9.12
1.1.10: 6.13-14
1.1.12: 9.7-10
1.1.16: 4.75-76
1.1.23-24: 4.83
1.1.25: 11.13-16
1.1.31: 3.28
1.1.33: 4.19-20
1.2.1-5: 4.51-60
1.2.1: 2.11-12, 8.10, 8.11
1.2.8: 13.1-2
1.2.17-18: 4.67
1.2.17: 6.27-28
1.2.24: 13.1-2
1.2.28: 11.9
1.2.32: 2.7-8
1.3.1-2: 6.39-42
1.3.1-8: 8.13
1.3.2: 6.39
1.3.13: 18.6
1.3.14: 6 *headnote*
1.3.17-18: 5.13
1.3.19: 13.3-4
1.3.35-46: *115*
1.3.35: 6.43
1.3.36: 4.58
1.3.39: 4.82
1.3.45: 4.55
1.3.46: 2.13
1.4.1-4: 4.66
1.4.3-4: 19.22
1.4.3: 10.7
1.4.7: 4.25-26
1.4.11: 3.29, 9.7
1.4.13: 8.8
1.4.15: 7.31
1.5.1: 5.13, 14.1
1.5.9: 4.83, 11.11
1.5.16: 10.6
1.5.19-20: 11.3-4
1.5.24: 4.56

1.5.28: 6.3
1.5.31-32: 4.49
1.6.1-18: 7.193-196
1.6.9-10: 6.42, 10.22
1.6.12: 17.6
1.6.13: 5.23
1.6.16: 10.6
1.6.24: 10.21
1.6.30: 5.32
1.7 and 1.9: 11 *headnote*
1.7.1: 7.18
1.7.3: 7.120
1.7.11-12: 11.13
1.7.11: 6.41
1.7.19: 7.17
1.7.21: 7.4
1.7.22: 13.10
1.7.24: 18.6
1.7.26: 13.1-2
1.8A and 8B: *105*, 15 *headnote*
1.8A.9: 4.82
1.8A.16: 4.61-62
1.8A.23: 7.100
1.8B.29: 6.33
1.8B.32: 3.29
1.8B.33-36: 3.23-24
1.8B.33-34: 6.53
1.8B.36-37: 7.197-200
1.8B.38: 6.59
1.8B.39-40: 3.23-24, 4.63
1.8B.39: 3.17
1.8B.42: 4.37
1.8B.44: 5.32
1.8B.45: 19.1
1.9.3: 19.24
1.9.4: 16.3-4
1.9.9: 3.1, 7.18
1.9.17: 10.5
1.9.19: 6.15
1.9.21: 6.26
1.9.24: 4.63
1.9.33: 4.49
1.10.17: 4.22
1.10.18: 6.3
1.10.20: 6.17
1.10.23: 8.2

1.10.25: 6.19
1.11.3: 7.67
1.11: 5 *headnote*, 5.31
1.11.11-12: 5.30
1.11.12: 5.30
1.11.15: 12.11-12
1.11.16: 6.55
1.11.18: 5.3
1.11.21-23: 4.51-52, 19.11-12
1.11.25-26: 2.27
1.11.27-28: 5.3
1.11.29: 7.184-185
1.11.30: 4.61-62, 4.84
1.12.13-14: 6.53
1.12.15-20: 2.1-8
1.12.20: 2.14
1.13.33-36: 6.47-49
1.13.35-36: 2.27-30
1.14: 3 *headnote*, 3.23-24
1.14.6: 10.22
1.14.12: 3.17, 8.19-20
1.14.14: 5.32
1.14.15-16: 3.23-24
1.14.23-24: 3.23-24, 3.29
1.15.8: 10.4
1.15.15: 1.26
1.15.21: 1.26
1.15.33: 6.47-48
1.15.41: 6.43
1.16: *115*
1.16.12: 4.61-62
1.16.27: 4.82
1.16.34: 4.96
1.16.35: 16.6
1.16.43: 6.55
1.16.46: 6.8
1.16.47: 19.9
1.17.9: 4.95-96
1.17.13-14: 2.1-8
1.17.13: 4.61-62
1.17.16: 4.37
1.17.19-24: *94*, 2 *headnote*
1.17.22: 2.26
1.18.6: 10.21
1.18.11: 7.166
1.18.29: 7.24

1.19.7: 1.26
1.19.9: 7.35
1.20.2: 7.201
1.20.13-14: 9.3
1.20.13: 9.3
1.20.15: 7.78
1.20.35-36: 12.9
1.20.42: 4.56
1.20.51: 6.43
2.1.5: 8.12
2.1.7-8: 8.9
2.1.8: 10.2
2.1.15: 10.7
2.1.27-38: 7 *headnote*
2.1.33: 7.117
2.1.35: 7.22
2.1.71: 7.210
2.1.74: 6.27-28
2.1.78: 2.30
2.1.8: 8.22
2.1.15-16: 8.7-14, 8.7, 8.9-12
2.1.58: 6.3
2.1.76: 7.149
2.2.8: 7.13
2.2.16: 6.47-48
2.3.2: 6.4
2.3.9-12: 4.30
2.3.10-12: 4.33-34
2.3.13: 4.27
2.3.14: 8.5-6, 8.6
2.3.25: 11.4
2.3.43-44: 8.9-12
2.3.49-50: 6.13-14
2.3.51: 7.120
2.4.1: 4.60
2.4.5: 5.27
2.4.17-18: 9.20
2.5.3: 6.55
2.5.14: 11.13
2.5.18: 5.6
2.6.21: 6.40
2.6.23: 1.26
2.6.28: 4.60
2.6.41-42: 19.1
2.7.19: 19.3
2.8: 2 *headnote*

2.8.1: 1.6, 2.1-2, 2.4
2.8.3: 20.4
2.8.5: 4.58
2.8.12: 2.1-2
2.8.13: 4.7-8
2.8.15: 4.66
2.8.17-28: 2.9-30
2.8.17-18: 2.4
2.8.19-20: 2 *headnote*
2.8.25-28: 2 *headnote*
2.8.29: 1.26, 2.1-2, 2.4,
2.8.30: 2.1-2
2.8.33: 10.6
2.8.36: 9.21
2.9.2: 4.58
2.9.3-4: 10.16
2.9.5: 1.26
2.9.10: 9.10
2.9.25-28: 10 *headnote*
2.9.25: 10.12
2.9.28: 6.55
2.9.31-32: 4.61-62
2.9.45: 7.13
2.10.4: 7.18
2.10.5-6: 7.2, 7.7, 7.24
2.10.13-18: 7 *headnote*
2.10.17: 7.53, 7.149
2.11.6: 12.2
2.12.20: 2.9
2.12.23: 1.26
2.13-14: 19.6
2.13.13f.: 3.19-20
2.13.17-58: *94*, 2 *headnote*
2.13.17-36: 2.9-30
2.13.17: 2.9-30, 7.210
2.13.19-32: 2.9-30
2.13.26: 5.5
2.13.33-36: 2.9-30
2.13.35-36: 2 *headnote*
2.13.44: 3.35
2.13.45: 5.5
2.13.46: 7.50-51
2.13.52: 10.16
2.13.53: 4.30
2.14: *104*
2.14.16: 6.3

Book Three of the Corpus Tibullianum: 673
Introduction, Text, Translation and Commentary

2.14.21: 4.58
2.14.25: *108*, 13.3-4
2.14.27: 2.29
2.14.28: 6.61
2.14.29: 9.15
2.14.31: 11.11
2.15.1: 3.25
2.15.16: 9.16
2.15.25-26: 11.15
2.15.26: 11.16
2.15.31: 7.172
2.15.35: 2.3
2.16A.6: 6.61
2.16A.7: 4.49, 8.2
2.16B.24: 9.10
2.16B.28: 11.4
2.16B.36: 20.2
2.16B.39: 1.19-20
2.16B.47-56: 6.49-50
2.16B.55: 3.18
2.17.3-4: 4.19-20
2.17.14: 5.10
2.18.11: 7.145
2.18.19: 6.55
2.18.20: 5.16, 7.11
2.18.37: 20.1
2.19.1: 6.47-48
2.19.2: 9.2
2.19.3: 9.2
2.19.5: 7.127
2.19.17-26: 9 *headnote*, 9.7-10
2.19.17-18: 9.9-10, 9.19
2.19.17: 9.12-13, 11.11
2.19.30: 7.143
2.19.32: 13.8
2.20.1: 14.7
2.20.13: 20.2
2.20.14: 4.75
2.20.20: 6.11
2.21: *120*, 1 *headnote*
2.21.3: 18.1
2.21.11-16: 6.39-42
2.21.16: 6.43-44
2.21.17: 4.58
2.22: *120*, 1 *headnote*
2.22.1-2: 15.1

2.22.18: 10.16
2.22.21: 18.1
2.22.24: 6.61
2.23.4: 13.7
2.23.7-8: 4.65
2.23.10: 6.61
2.23.11: 7.169, 13.7
2.23.27: 4.61-62
2.24.1-2: *89*, 8.1
2.24.15: 4.61-62
2.24B.27: 11.9
2.24B.29: 4.65
2.24B.34: 5.5
2.24B.35: 2.26
2.24B.46: 6.40, 18.5
2.24B.50: 2.17-18
2.25.1: 2.29
2.25.9-10: 3.7-10
2.25.22: 4.61-62
2.25.29-32: 19.8
2.25.41: 10.1
2.26A: 4 *headnote*
2.26A.13: 11.11
2.26A.21-22: 11.3-4
2.26A.23: 3.29
2.26B.35: 2.7-8
2.26B.40: 6.40
2.26B.53-54: 7.73-75
2.26B.53: 4.89
2.27.5: 7.149
2.28: *105*, 10 *headnote*
2.28.1-2: 10.4
2.28.5-8: 6.49-50
2.28.9-14: 5.13-14
2.28.10: 4.96
2.28.13-14: 19.20
2.28.27: 4.45
2.28.33:1.26, 8.3
2.28.35: 11.11
2.28.41-42: 10.19-20
2.28.42: 3.8
2.28.43: 10.12
2.28.44: 10.16
2.28.47-48: 5.5
2.28.48: 1.26
2.28.59: 9.15

2.28.59-60: 10.23
2.28.61: 10.12
2.29A.1: 4.2, 9.15, 18.5
2.29B.27: 8.2
2.29B.27-28: 4.13-14
2.29B.31-38: *115*
2.29B.41: 19.9
2.30.1: 6.27
2.30.7-9: 9.4
2.30.8: 7.117
2.30.9: 4.65, 8.6
2.30.19: 7.193
2.30.24: 4.84
2.30.28: 11.7
2.30.37f.: 4.43-44
2.31.5: 4.25-26
2.31.5-6: 4.23-42, 4.35
2.31.15-16: 4.23-42
2.31.15: 7.165-168
2.31.16: 4.35
2.32.15: 7.152
2.32.23-24: 20.1
2.32.48: 4.24
2.33A.3: 4.82
2.33A.12: 4.61-62
2.33B.29: 7.9-11
2.33B.31: 4.89
2.33B.39: 6.5, 6.6
2.34: *120*, 1 *headnote*
2.34.43: 7.136
2.34.46: 4.16
2.34.51: 7.18
2.34.51ff.: 7.18-27
2.34.51-54: 7.19-23
2.34.57: 11.4
2.34.60: 7.97
2.34.61-62: 7.177-180
2.34.62: 7.18
2.34.84: 4.50
3.1.5: 1.11-12
3.1.8: 1.9-14, 1.10, 1.11-12
3.1.11-12: 10.17-18
3.2.3-4: 7.125
3.2.9: 4.43-44
3.2.11-13: 3.13-16
3.2.11: 3.14

3.2.12: 3.16
3.2.14: 6.58
3.2.15: 4.43-44
3.2.17: 4.57
3.3: 4 *headnote*, 7.18-27
3.3.1: 1.15-16, 4.24
3.3.3: *Ep. Tib.* 4
3.3.13: 1.15-16
3.3.14: 4.37
3.3.18: 1.24
3.3.23-24: 10.17-18
3.3.27-38: 1.15-16
3.3.27: 1.15-16
3.3.31: 7.141
3.3.32: 1.15-16
3.3.34: 9.8
3.3.41-42: 9.3
3.4 and 3.5: 11 *headnote*
3.5.1: 8.10
3.5.3-5: 3.11-12
3.5.5: 3.12
3.5.14: 3.10
3.5.20: 6.64
3.5.23-25: 5.23-25
3.5.24: 5.15
3.5.25: 5.23
3.5.43: 4.88
3.5.45: 4.68
3.6: *81, 87, 90, 94, 100, 112, 113, 115, 116, 129*, 1.17, 2.29
3.6.8: *81, 116*, 7.136
3.6.9: *116*
3.6.19-34: *115, 118*
3.6.21-34: *81, 116*
3.6.21-30: *94*
3.6.21-22: *116*
3.6.22: *117*
3.6.31: *115*
3.6.34: *81, 116*
3.6.39: *81, 115*, 6.40
3.6.41-42: *116*
3.7.3: 7.161
3.7.48: 9.8
3.8.7: 8.5
3.8.15: 20.1
3.8.20: 17.6

Book Three of the Corpus Tibullianum: 675
Introduction, Text, Translation and Commentary

3.9.29: 2.9
3.10: *104-105*, 11 *headnote*, 14.1
3.10.1: 7.24, 13.3-4
3.10.1-4: 4 *headnote*
3.10.13-13: 12.3
3.10.18: 11.4
3.10.19: 12.1
3.10.19-20: 7.134, 11.9
3.11.7: 18.3
3.11.8: 6.43-44
3.11.31: 1.26
3.11.51: 7.143
3.11.57: 12.9
3.12.15: 3.26
3.12.16: 1.26
3.12.22: 6.45
3.12.26: 7.57
3.12.28: 4.89, 7.73-75
3.13.3-4: 9.24
2.13.5-8: 3.17-18
3.13.5: 2.23
3.13.6: 3.17
3.13.8: 8.17-18
3.13.17: 5.9
3.13.20: 2.7
3.13.22-24: 7.127
3.13.23-24: 4.61-62
3.13.52: 4.27
3.13.64: 7.72
3.14.28: 14.1
3.15.1: 19.9
3.15.9-10: 11.3-4
3.15.20: 2.7-8
3.15.43: 9.23
3.16.11: 10.15
3.16.15: 2.27
3.16.24: 4.46
3.16.25-26: 2.28
3.17: 4.43-46, 6 *headnote*
3.17.1-2: 6.38
3.17.3-4: 6.3
3.17.23: 5.25
3.17.31-32: 4.23-42
3.17.32: 4.35
3.17.42: 7.57
3.18.22: 19.10

3.18.23: 4.88
3.18.28: 3.29
3.18.29: 9.10
3.19.15: 3.8
3.19.27: 3.38
3.19.28: 6.19
3.20.10: 9.24
3.20.16-17: 19.17
3.20.21-22: 19.2
3.20.21: 19.1
3.20.30: 4.46
3.21.3: 17.1
3.21.31-32: 19.8
3.22.15: 6.27-28
3.22.24: 6.58
3.22.42: 1.26
3.23.4: *127*
3.23.11-16: *127*
3.23.18: 6.12
3.23.23: 6.62
3.24.3: 10.19
3.24.17f.: 4.19-20, 6.3
3.25.14: 5.25
4.1A.24: 4.5-6
4.1A.58: 1.21-22, 1.24
4.1A.59-60: 7.26-27
4.1A.64: *87*, 1 *headnote*
4.1B.71-150: *115*
4.1B.86: 12.3
4.1B.88: 11.4
4.1B.101: 10.12
4.1B.104: 4.5-6
4.1B.120: 7.13
4.1B.127: 2.17-18
4.1B.128-130: 7.183-189
4.1B.133: 7.178
4.1B.139: 7.16
4.1B.143: 6.14
4.1B.147: 7.202
4.2: *82*, *115*, 8.13-14
4.2.2: 4.49
4.2.3: 8.13-14
4.2.13ff.: 8.13-14
4.2.21-22: 8.13-14
4.2.22: 8.14
4.2.45-46: 8.14

4.3: *82, 103, 120,* 1 *headnote*, 1.26,
4.3.10: 8.19-20
4.3.27: 10.5
4.3.29: 4.19-20
4.3.49: 1.26
4.3.62: 11.10
4.3.72: 4.51-52
4.4.3: 20.3
4.4.21-22: 8.4
4.4.28: 9.10
4.4.32: 19.4
4.4.39-40: 7.72
4.4.47: 20.1
4.4.75: 19.3
4.5.40: 4.58
4.5.49: 19.6
4.5.66: 12.4
4.6: 7 *headnote*
4.6.2: 12.4
4.6.4: 7 *headnote*
4.6.5: 3.2
4.6.9: 4.3
4.6.17: 10.8
4.6.22: 8.4
4.6.31: 8.9
4.6.32: 4.37, 8.22
4.6.73: 6.6
4.6.75-76: 4.43-44
4.6.85: 6.3
4.7: *81, 82, 87, 90, 94, 100, 105, 112, 113, 115, 126,* 2.29, 4 *headnote*
4.7.3: 4.24
4.7.13-94: *115*
4.7.16: 6.12
4.7.21-22: 6.27-28
4.7.21: 4.96
4.7.27-28: 2.18
4.7.34: 2.19
4.7.35-46: *116*
4.7.39: *117*
4.7.41-42: *81, 108, 117*
4.7.41: *116, 125,* 16.3-4
4.7.50: 11.4
4.7.52: 4.88
4.7.83-84: 2.28

4.7.85-86: 2.27-30
4.8: *81, 87, 90, 94, 100, 112, 113, 115, 117, 126,* 2.29
4.8.16: 12.5-6
4.8.27ff.: 19.14
4.8.37-38: *116, 117*
4.8.53: 8.4
4.8.68: 4.46
4.8.69: *81, 117*, 11.8
4.8.72: 10.12
4.8.73-80: *118*
4.8.74: 4.49
4.8.79-80: *81, 117*
4.9.2: 4.82
4.9.20: 9.1
4.9.23: 6.25
4.9.25-26: 5.8
4.9.47: 12.13
4.9.63: 4.41
4.9.71: 12.7
4.9.72: 4.84
4.10.35: 7.207
4.11: *82, 103*
4.11.11: 1.26
4.11.13: 3.35
4.11.15: 3.38
4.11.36: 13.10
4.11.64: 3.8
4.11.87: 1.26, 4.74
4.11.93: 11.11

Publilius Syrus
15: 2.21-22

Quintilian
Decl. Mai. 1.7.11: 7.13
Decl. Mai. 1.11: 10.4
Decl. Mai. 2.16: 4.74
Decl. Mai. 13.2: 3.1
Decl. Mai. 14.6.24: 10.1
Decl. Min. 260.12: 4.78
Decl. Min. 306.11: 7.111
Decl. Min. 314.13: 7.111
Decl. Min. 323.5: 5.11
Inst. 1.11.19: 8.8
Inst. 3.1.4: 7.86

Book Three of the Corpus Tibullianum: 677
Introduction, Text, Translation and Commentary

Inst. 3.1.18: 7.180
Inst. 4.3.12: 7.8-15, 7.151-174
Inst. 6.2: 7.46-47
Inst. 6.3.69: 7.64
Inst. 8.3.26: 4.45
Inst. 8.3.42: 1.14
Inst. 9.2.39: 5.7-14
Inst. 9.4.19: 7.36
Inst. 9.4.27: 4.40
Inst. 10.1.93: *Vit. Tib.* 4-5
Inst. 10.1.113: 7.5-6, 8.12
Inst. 12.1.36: 7.111
Inst. 12.3.5f.: 7.82-117

Rhetorica ad Alexandrum
31 p. 1425b 36: 7.118-134

Rhetorica ad Herennium
3.6.11: 7.5-6
3.6.12: 7.5-6
3.7.13: 7.28-32
4.31: 7.135-176
4.54: 7.17
4.60: 4.35

Rhianus
fr. 10 (Powell): 4.67-72

(Rufus) Festus
10.1: 7.145

Sallust
Cat. 36.1: 14.3-4
Cat. 52.12: 6.19
Cat. 52.21: 4.15
Cat. 60.2: 7.99
Iug. 19.3.2: 7.139
Iug. 25.9: 7.105
Iug. 85.31: 4.15
Iug. 100.1: 7.101-102

Sappho
1 *PLF*: 13.3-4, 13.5
31: 13.3-4
38-40: 11.5
94.7-8: 5.31

96.6-8: 4.29
112: 4.31-34
114: 1 *headnote*
137: 1 *headnote*
140a: 1 *headnote*

Scriptores Historiae Augustae
Aurel. 41.6.1: 6.34

Seneca the Elder
Contr. 1 *praef.* 22: 7.211
Contr. 1 *praef.* 24.4: 9.21
Contr. 2.4: *Vit. Tib.* 2
Contr. 2.4.8: 7.5-6
Contr. 2.7.1: 2.5-6
Contr. 2.7.7: 11.7
Contr. 7.5.7: 7.22
Contr. 9.2.16: 4.15
Suas. 3.1: 4.54
Suas. 6.5: 4.26
Suas. 6.17: 2.7-8
Suas. 6.22: 7.5-6

Seneca the Younger
Ag. 14: 4.88
Ag. 94: 7.154
Ag. 198: 6.57
Ag. 263: 4.74
Apoc. 4.1.2: 7.112a
Apoc. 4.1.21: 7.112a
Apoc. 7: 7.125
Apoc. 12.3.19-20: 7.117
Apoc. 12.13ff.: 7.135-176
Apoc. 12.13-14: 7.149
Ben. fr. 14 (*Haase*): 3.1
Ben. 1.14.2: 7.91
Ben. 3.31: 19.9
Ben. 6.7.4: 7.100
Ben. 6.16.410.17-18
Ben. 7.2.5: 6.40
Ben. 7.27.3: 5.25
Clem. 1.7.2: 6.13
Clem. 1.25.1: 6.13
De Ira 2.5.5: 12.4
De Ira 3.21.1-5: 7.141
De Vita Beata 1.2: 19.10

De Vita Beata 2.4: 3.19-20
De Vita Beata 25.1: 7.100
Dial. 1.6.3: 4.7-8
Dial. 2.9.4: 6.9
Dial. 2.26.3: 6.14
Dial. 3.1.6: 9.3
Dial. 4.10.5: 6.13
Dial. 4.15.3: 6.13
Dial. 4.31.6: 7.170
Dial. 5.10.4: 4.93
Dial. 5.22.4: 6.13
Dial. 7.2.4: 3.19-20
Dial. 10.16.3: 4.54
Dial. 12.16: 6.35-36
Epist. 8.8.22: 6.14
Epist. 9.52: 11.7
Epist. 10.8.25: 4.54
Epist. 12.2: 11.8
Epist. 17.6: 19.9
Epist. 24.18: 3.37
Epist. 28.6: 19.9
Epist. 59.7: 7.101-102
Epist. 60.4: 2.21-22, 3.3
Epist. 70.4: 19.9
Epist. 70.11: 5.5
Epist. 78.10.3: 17.2
Epist. 88.7: 7.79-81
Epist. 88.19: 7.89-97
Epist. 90.41: 3 *headnote*
Epist. 91.5: 19.10
Epist. 94.45: 1.14
Epist. 99.10: 3.9
Epist. 105.3: 19.8
Epist. 107.8-9: 6.32
Epist. 110.7: 4.24
Epist. 114.24: 7.196
Epist. 120.14: 4.9
Epist. 122.9: 19.10
Herc. F. 19-20: 7.139
Herc. F. 137-138: 4.59
Herc. F. 181: 3.35
Herc. F. 282: 19.11
Herc. F. 396: 3.37
Herc. F. 415: 4.67
Herc. F. 573: 7.125
Herc. F. 599: 5.22

Herc. F. 609: 5.22
Herc. F. 621: 17.1
Herc. F. 663: 7.128
Herc. F. 666: 3.37
Herc. F. 686: 3.38
Herc. F. 697: 17.1
Herc. F. 785: 4.88
Herc. F. 796: 4.88
Herc. F. 829: 7.3-4
Herc. F. 849: 5.16
Herc. F. 850: 7.112a
Herc. F. 867: 7.205
Herc. F. 909-911: 8.17-18
Herc. F. 956: 7.67
Herc. F. 1014: 6.46
Herc. F. 1136: 15.1
Herc. F. 1249: 3.8
Herc. F. 1280: 4.74
Herc. Oet. 3-4: 7.53
Herc. Oet. 119: 10.5
Herc. Oet. 143: 4.91
Herc. Oet. 143-146: 4.85-94
Herc. Oet. 144: 4.90
Herc. Oet. 793: 8.17-18
Herc. Oet. 1036-1039: 7.125
Herc. Oet. 1202: 4.88
Herc. Oet. 1294: 19.11
Herc. Oet. 1327: 9.22
Herc. Oet. 1991: 7.79
Medea 1-2: 4.13-14, 12.14
Medea 20: 7.52
Medea 46-47: 4.59
Medea 61: 4.30
Medea 227: 7.68
Medea 271: 4.53
Medea 318-319: 4.85
Medea 408: 4.89
Medea 501: 9.16
Medea 597-598: 5.22
Medea 605: 8.3
Medea 609: 7.154
Medea 627: 7.124, 7.125
Medea 717-719: 5.9
Medea 792: 7.91
Medea 797-798: 8.23
Medea 846: 3.2

Medea 850: 4.65
Medea 878: 7.122
Medea 930: 6.27
Medea 940-941: 7.124
Medea 1023-1024: 7.170
Oed. 135: 7.97
Oed. 230: 4.49
Oed. 266-267: 4.35
Oed. 269: 4.49
Oed. 405-407: 6.1
Oed. 413-416: 6.2
Oed. 419: 6.33
Oed. 430: 4.23
Oed. 495: 2.19
Oed. 508: 6.1
Oed. 563-567: 5.33-34
Oed. 558-559: 5.34
Oed. 562=563: 7.68
Oed. 581: 4.88
Oed. 657: 15.1
Oed. 700-701: 4.14
Oed. 712-713: 1.15-16
Oed. 780: 5.18
Oed. 787: 5.18
Oed. 801-802: 6.37
Oed. 1006: 6.24
Phaed. 112: 9.7
Phaed. 112-114: 9.11-18
Phaed. 118: 6.16
Phaed. 166: 4.91
Phaed. 230: 4.61-62
Phaed. 235: 9.12
Phaed. 272-273: 4.74
Phaed. 296-298: 4.67-72
Phaed. 298: 4.67
Phaed. 330: 12.13
Phaed. 333-334: 4.17-18
Phaed. 346-347: 9.3
Phaed. 362: 5.27
Phaed. 375-376: 4.30
Phaed. 378: 4.36
Phaed. 408: 4.95-96
Phaed. 412: 6.1
Phaed. 415: 11.6
Phaed. 423: 11.9
Phaed. 424: 8.23

Phaed. 506: 9.7
Phaed. 636: 4.7-8
Phaed. 687: 4.61-62
Phaed. 721: 9.16
Phaed. 750: 12.3
Phaed. 754: 10.2
Phaed. 815: 7.8-9
Phaed. 1006: 7.92
Phaed. 1055: 7.91
Phaed. 1082: 4.7-8
Phaed. 1088: 7.130
Phaed. 1103: 9.10
Phaed. 1136-1137: 7.131
Phaed. 1149: 8.10
Phaed. 1162-1163: 7.53
Phoen. 222: 9.20
Phoen. 316: 7.148
Phoen. 633-634: 11.9
Quaest. Nat. 1 pr. 3: 4.47-48
Quaest. Nat. 1.13.11: 7.44
Quaest. Nat. 3.26.3: 7.125
Quaest. Nat. 4a.2.7: 8.23
Quaest. Nat. 4.11.5: 7.131
Quaest. Nat. 6.16.2: 7.22
Thy. 126: 3.4
Thy. 156-157: 4.35
Thy. 347: 3.16
Thy. 372: 8.19-20
Thy. 413: 9.7
Thy. 523-524: 6.45
Thy. 581: 7.73-75
Thy. 646-647: 3.16
Thy. 665-666: 3.37
Thy. 843: 10.25
Thy. 858: 7.41
Troad. 185: 8.3
Troad. 321: 4.39
Troad. 470: 3.26
Troad. 491: 3.11
Troad. 511: 3.35
Troad. 778: 8.23
Troad. 845: 9.22
Troad. 1019-1021: 3.11-12
[Seneca the Younger]
Oct. 74: 5.16
Oct. 116-117: 4.22

Oct. 177: 4.74
Oct. 225-226: 4.59
Oct. 356-357: 7.53
Oct. 515: 9.22
Oct. 522: 7.68
Oct. 544: 8.15
Oct. 564: 6.4
Oct. 637: 9.22
Oct. 797: 4.91
Oct. 820: 5.30
Oct. 865: 9.16

Serenus
Med. 5.69: 7.53
Med. 48.898: 10.4
Med. 49.915: 7.41

Servius
Aen. 1.47: 6.61
Aen. 1.147: 7.127
Aen. 1.269: 7.113
Aen. 1.446: 4.77
Aen. 3.12: 4.16
Aen. 3.118: 5.33
Aen. 3.171: 7.77
Aen. 3.357: 2.21-22
Aen. 4.166: 3.33-34
Aen. 4.200: 4.77
Aen. 4.692: 4.47-48
Aen. 5.85: 7.78
Aen. 5.760: 3.33-34
Aen. 6.156: 6.34
Aen. 6.244: 6.6
Aen. 7.198: 4.17-18
Aen. 8.64: 3.1
Aen. 8.72: 3.33-34
Aen. 8.656: 4.77, 11.3
Aen. 11.185: 2.11-12
Ecl. 6.3: 4.50
Ecl. 8.82: 4.10
Georg. 1.146: 3.23-24
Georg. 1.469: 4.85
Georg. 2.194: 4.5-6
Gerog. 3.2: 4.67-72
Georg. 4.62-63: *124*

Servius auctus
Aen. 1.394: 7.22
Aen. 1.720: 8.3
Aen. 2.374: 3.32
Aen. 3.35: 1.1
Aen. 4.511: 4.13-14
Aen. 11.619: 7.95
Aen. 12.121: 7.101-102
Ecl. 5.56-57: 4.29
Georg. 1.33: 7.9-11
Georg. 2.389: 7.9-11

Sextus Empiricus
Pyrrh. Hyp. 130: 3.14

Sidonius Apollinaris
9.261-262: *127*

Silius Italicus
1.97: 7.130
1.107: 3.35
1.116: 7.92
1.135: 7.22
1.157-158: 3.29
1.197: 7.75
1.225: 7.205
1.281: 3.35
1.408: 4.91
1.503-504: 5.28
1.638-639: 4.85-94
2.63: 4.91
2.93: 7.8-9
2.136: 7.153
2.285: 4.77
2.289: 7.10
2.356-357: 19.10
2.551: 4.88
2.572: 4.85
2.620: 2.7-8
3.111-112: 7.191
3.131-132: 4.19-20
3.213: 7.174
3.233-234: 6.12
3.288-289: 6.16
3.351: 7.161
3.410: 7.127

3.671: 7.12	7.476: 7.10
3.678: 4.77	7.697: 7.92
4.8: 7.130	8.118: 4.19-20
4.22: 7.11	8.239: 7.118
4.45: 5.26	8.267: 7.117
4.80: 4.85	8.368-369: 7.60, 7.146
4.113: 4.21	8.418: 7.159
4.136: 7.130	8.587: 7.202
4.203-204: 10.2	8.641: 4.7-8
4.448: 7.72	9.136: 7.98
4.475: 6.5	9.207: 7.60
4.476: 7.5-6	9.250-251: 1.27-28
4.508: 3.37	9.250: 5.21
4.539: 4.86	9.298: 7.169
4.581: 7.17	9.337: 7.97
4.587: 7.123	9.453: 10.24
4.596: 10.8	9.634: 7.117
4.731: 4.16	9.645-646: 7.94
5.36: 4.55	10.151: 7.97
5.269: 3.10	10.261: 7.92
5.399: 7.138	10.272: 10.14
5.480: 7.171	10.275: 5.28
5.494: 7.17	10.317-318: 4.86
5.659: 7.185	10.363: 7.60
5.671: 7.88	10.410: 7.83
6.10: 7.100	10.412-413: 7.84
6.67: 4.42	10.518-519: 2.5-6
6.397-398: 7.13	10.952: 10.25
6.409: 10.5	11.40-41: 8.15-16
6.440: 4.85	11.117: 7.117
6.476: 5.32	11.180: 7.165-168
6.501-503: 9.11	11.271: 7.144
6.505: 7.117	11.285: 6.17-18
6.533: 7.152	11.293: 7.68
6.561-562: 4.53	11.418: 5.28
6.573: 6.5	11.461: 7.10
6.617: 7.39	11.579: 4.40
7.13-14: 7.203	12.44: 7.64
7.32: 7.117	12.92: 7.152
7.41-42: 7.137	12.117: 7.75
7.72: 7.117	12.132: 5.24
7.78: 10.1-2	12.333: 7.15
7.126: 19.11	12.440: 7.75
7.161: 7.133-134	12.613: 4.55
7.254-255: 7.123	13.339: 4.59
7.369: 9.11	13.395: 2.15

13.404-406: 5.33
13.441: 7.31
13.571-573: 3.37, 3.38
13.574: 4.88
13.758: 7.152
13.774-776: 7.121-123
14.39: 7.8-9
14.46-47: 7.174
14.160: 7.44
14.244: 7.130
14.459: 9.6
14.474: 4.89
14.527: 7.56
14.571: 7.91
15.33: 9.7
15.285: 4.55
15.416: 7.31
15.440: 7.98
15.455: 5.14
15.456: 7.112
15.537: 8.5
15.747: 10.12
15.765: 7.154
15.823: 7.98
16.203: 7.98
16.223: 2.27
16.355: 7.102
16.380: 7.91, 7.102
16.502: 3.19-20
16.525: 10.2
17.207-208: 7.124
17.314: 7.60
17.341-342: 6.27-28
17.475: 7.183
17.630: 7.117
17.634: 4.91

Simonides *PMG*
575: 4.65

Sophocles
fr. 742 (Nauck): 6.49-50

Statius
Ach. 1.57: 7.126
Ach. 1.132-133: 9.22

Ach. 1.161-162: 4.30, 4.31-34
Ach. 1.161: 7.202
Ach. 1.231: 7.152
Ach. 1.237: 6.5
Ach. 1.252: 6.5
Ach. 1.259: 6.57
Ach. 1.262: 4.35
Ach. 1.358: 9.11
Ach. 1.361-362: 4.61-62
Ach. 1.386: 6.30
Ach. 1.395: 7.44
Ach. 1.409: 6.25
Ach. 1.411: 7.53
Ach. 1.582: 2.27
Ach. 1.640: 7.154
Ach. 1.835: 9.15-17
Ach. 1.930: 10.5
Ach. 1.938: 11.7
Ach. 2.5: 12.13
Ach. 2.23: 2.13
Ach. 2.101: 7.163
Ach. 2.155: 3.35
Ach. 2.157-158: 4.39
Ach. 2.158: 7.31
Silu. 1 *Praef.*: 1.9
Silu. 1.2.6: 5.1
Silu. 1.2.85-87: 8.11-12
Silu. 1.2.85: 7.35
Silu. 1.2.117-118: 3.33-34
Silu. 1.2.145: 7.183
Silu. 1.2.148-149: 3.14
Silu. 1.2.220: 4.45
Silu. 1.2.244-245: 4.31-34
Silu. 1.3.21: 7.72
Silu. 1.3.35-37: 3.16
Silu. 1.4.127-131: 7.14-15
Silu. 1.5.2: 4.43-44
Silu. 1.5.4: 4.69
Silu. 1.5.6: 6.57
Silu. 1.5.26-27: 6.58
Silu. 1.5.34: 3.14
Silu. 1.5.51: 4.17-18
Silu. 1.6.87: 7.154
Silu. 1.8.25: 7.207
Silu. 2 *praef.*: 11 *headnote*
Silu. 2.1.21: 12.1

Book Three of the Corpus Tibullianum: 683
Introduction, Text, Translation and Commentary

Silu. 2.1.41: 4.30
Silu. 2.1.45: 4.75
Silu. 2.1.54: 5.5
Silu. 2.1.81: 7.48
Silu. 2.1.87: 7.48
Silu. 2.1.147: 5.5
Silu. 2.2.11: 7.35
Silu. 2.2.85-93: 3.14
Silu. 2.2.107: 6.30
Silu. 2.3.22: 9.13
Silu. 2.4.11: 4.37
Silu. 2.6.22: 7.202
Silu. 2.6.52-53: 12.16
Silu. 2.7: 11 *headnote*
Silu. 2.7.21-22: 7.36
Silu. 2.7.34: 7.200
Silu. 2.7.84: 3.33-34
Silu. 3.1.28: 10.1-2
Silu. 3.1.29: 7.12-13
Silu. 3.1.82: 4.77
Silu. 3.1.108: 10.25
Silu. 3.2.14: 5.22
Silu. 3.2.82: 5.30
Silu. 3.2.84-85: 7.72
Silu. 3.2.85-86: 4.89, 7.73-75
Silu. 3.2.86: 4.89
Silu. 3.2.92: 5.24
Silu. 3.3.21: 3.35
Silu. 3.3.34-35: 8.17-18
Silu. 3.3.58: 4.67-72
Silu. 3.3.88: 7.18
Silu. 3.3.110: 7.48
Silu. 3.3.156: 5.16
Silu. 3.3.203: 7.112a
Silu. 3.4.5: 3.33-34
Silu. 3.4.8: 4.27
Silu. 3.4.32: 7.64
Silu. 3.4.39: 7.152
Silu. 3.4.56: 4.31-34
Silu. 3.4.60: 6.5
Silu. 3.4.103: 7.112
Silu. 3.5.83: 7.169
Silu. 4.1.1: 7.121
Silu. 4.1.2-3: 7.122
Silu. 4.1.18-19: 7.122
Silu. 4.1.22: 7.121

Silu. 4.1.23-24: 7.134
Silu. 4.1.45-47: 7.130-134
Silu. 4.2.15: 4.43-44
Silu. 4.2.26-29: 3.14
Silu. 4.2.34: 7.163
Silu. 4.2.38: 3.13
Silu. 4.2.40: 7.35
Silu. 4.3.149-150: 7.169
Silu. 4.3.156: 7.150
Silu. 4.4.10-11: 1.21-22
Silu. 4.4.80: 4.86
Silu. 4.5.29-30: 4.91
Silu. 4.6.18: 3.17
Silu. 4.6.51: 7.12-13
Silu. 4.7.21: 13.3-4
Silu. 4.8.11: 7.31
Silu. 5.1.25-26: 4.43-44
Silu. 5.1.43-44: 11.15
Silu. 5.1.205: 7.112a
Silu. 5.1.212: 8.17-18
Silu. 5.1.225: 3.18
Silu. 5.1.228: 7.11
Silu. 5.1.241: 7.10
Silu. 5.2.30-60: 7.28-32
Silu. 5.2.46: 4.91
Silu. 5.3.41-43: 3.12
Silu. 5.3.43: 8.17-18
Silu. 5.3.76: 7.9-11
Silu. 5.3.114f.: 7.48-49
Silu. 5.3.139-140: 7.94
Silu. 5.3.255: 7.112
Silu. 5.4.9: 8.6
Silu. 5.5.2-4: 1.15-16
Silu. 5.5.31-33: 4.40
Silu. 5.5.42: 10.4
Silu. 5.5.79: 6.5
Theb. 1.81: 10.1-2
Theb. 1.212-213: 3.11
Theb. 1.263: 2.24
Theb. 1.271: 7.136
Theb. 1.294: 7.209
Theb. 1.357: 7.60
Theb. 1.698: 1.15-16
Theb. 1.705-708: 4.45-48
Theb. 2.101: 6.17-18
Theb. 2.176-177: 4.59, 7.177

Theb. 2.213: 9.7
Theb. 2.231: 4.30, 4.31-34
Theb. 2.287-288: 8.8
Theb. 2.331: 12.16
Theb. 2.397: 7.52
Theb. 2.497: 7.128
Theb. 2.553-554: 9.7-8
Theb. 2.646: 8.3
Theb. 2.681: 8.15-16
Theb. 3.322: 7.64
Theb. 3.392-393: 4.22
Theb. 3.415-416: 4.55
Theb. 3.452-453: 7.120
Theb. 3.487: 7.135
Theb. 3.606-607: 7.45-47
Theb. 4.125: 7.195
Theb. 4.160-164: 7.12-13
Theb. 4.419: 5.16
Theb. 4.536: 3.8
Theb. 4.565: 6.24
Theb. 4.615: 7.70
Theb. 5.173: 7.149
Theb. 5.217: 6.45
Theb. 5.248-249: 9.2
Theb. 5.274: 3.35
Theb. 5.366-367: 6.27-28
Theb. 5.397: 8.4
Theb. 5.524: 7.209
Theb. 5.623: 9.12-13
Theb. 5.670: 1.2
Theb. 5.685: 5.11
Theb. 5.751: 7.112
Theb. 6.1-2: 7.127
Theb. 6.108: 7.123
Theb. 6.211-212: 2.20
Theb. 6.284: 7.44
Theb. 6.353: 9.2
Theb. 6.376: 3.35
Theb. 6.397: 4.40
Theb. 6.587: 10.2
Theb. 6.589: 5.28
Theb. 6.609: 7.149
Theb. 6.620: 7.31
Theb. 6.710: 7.130
Theb. 6.716-718: 7.56
Theb. 6.841: 7.44

Theb. 7.3: 7.130-134
Theb. 7.38-39: 4.35
Theb. 7.45: 4.35
Theb. 7.143: 7.75
Theb. 7.264: 2.7-8
Theb. 7.338: 7.97
Theb. 7.352: 7.63
Theb. 7.415: 7.207
Theb. 7.566: 3.17
Theb. 7.579: 7.97
Theb. 7.602: 4.45
Theb. 7.656: 7.121
Theb. 7.782-783: 3.38
Theb. 7.783: 4.88
Theb. 8.43: 7.35
Theb. 8.87: 7.202
Theb. 8.175-176: 1.15-16
Theb. 8.235: 4.31
Theb. 8.333-334: 4.5-6
Theb. 8.416: 7.97
Theb. 8.643-644: 7.202
Theb. 8.691: 19.11
Theb. 8.728: 7.35
Theb. 9.37: 7.1
Theb. 9.137: 4.45
Theb. 9.269: 7.171
Theb. 9.336: 4.35
Theb. 9.379: 7.53
Theb. 9.447: 7.60
Theb. 9.626-627: 4.13-14
Theb. 9.877: 9.2
Theb. 10.56-60: 12.13, 12.14
Theb. 10.91-92: 7.129
Theb. 10.145: 7.10
Theb. 10.238: 17.1
Theb. 10.457: 7.35
Theb. 10.533: 7.130
Theb. 10.545: 7.96, 7.97
Theb. 10.603: 2.27
Theb. 10.629: 7.202
Theb. 10.705: 9.23
Theb. 10.857: 7.115
Theb. 11.151: 7.97
Theb. 11.214: 7.126
Theb. 11.222: 12.1
Theb. 11.329: 9.7

Theb. 11.358: 7.64
Theb. 11.400: 4.35
Theb. 11.524: 7.100
Theb. 11.533: 4.40
Theb. 11.604: 7.129
Theb. 11.686: 7.35
Theb. 11.688: 7.136
Theb. 11.689: 9.13
Theb. 12.138-139: 4.28
Theb. 12.220: 2.27
Theb. 12.312: 4.35
Theb. 12.336: 6.37

Strabo
4.6.10: 7.108
5.2.9: 5.1
7.3.11: 7.146
7.5.4: 7.108, 7.110
13.4.5: 3.29
14.1.6: 10.1-2
16.1.4: 7.142
31.1.23: 3.29

Suetonius
Aug. 8.1: *Vit. Tib.* 3-4
Aug. 29: 4.23-42
Aug. 94.4: 8.23
Calig. 20.1.5: 7.35
Calig. 37.3: 7.169
Calig. 50.2: 17.2
Claud. 11.3.9: 11.2
De gramm. 6: 7.196
De gramm. 9.3: *Vit. Tib.* 6-7
De gramm. 16.3: *Vit. Tib.* 6-7
De gramm. 18: *Vit. Tib.* 5
De gramm. 23.1: *Vit. Tib.* 4-5
Iul. 42.1: *Vit. Tib.* 3
Iul. 45.3: *Vit. Tib.* 1-2
Iul. 50.2: *Vit. Tib.* 2-3
Iul. 68.3: 7.89
Nero 20.3: *Vit. Tib.* 1-2
Nero 34: 5.7-8
Tit. 3.1: 7.82
Vesp. 19.1: 1.1-4

Symphosius (*PLM* 4)
211: 7.93

Tabulae Vindolandiae
II 310: 1.23

Tacitus
Agric. 2.3: 7.111
Agric. 36.3: 7.100
Ann. 1.7.2-3: 13.9
Ann. 1.10: 14.7
Ann. 1.24: 6.33
Ann. 1.34: 5.16
Ann. 1.55.11: 5.18
Ann. 3.2.2: 2.18
Ann. 13.41.21: 11.2
Ann. 13.45.11: 4.29
Ann. 14.1: 5.13
Dial. 16.5: 7.48-49
Dial. 18.2: 7.5-6
Dial. 27.1: 13.5
Dial. 31.1: 7.46-47
Dial. 36.3-4: 7.88
Hist. 1.41-42: 5.17-18
Hist. 1.49: 17.2
Hist. 2.4.36: 8.11-12
Hist. 2.42.11: 7.100

Terence
Ad. 487: 4.13-14
Ad. 532: 6.53
Ad. 751: 4.31
Ad. 867: 4.82
Ad. 907: 8.6
Ad. 938: 4.31
And. 180: 15.4
And. 326: 6.53
And. 343: 6.57
And. 473: 4.13-14
And. 492-493: 6.12
And. 863: 18.3
And. 956: 3.26
Eun. 91: 1.19, 11.13-16
Eun. 193: 6.54
Eun. 649: 6.55
Eun. 733: 6 *headnote*

Heaut. 185: 6.53
Heaut. 186: 15.4
Heaut. 230: 20.2
Hec. 362: 15.4
Phorm. 165: 3.32
Phorm. 203: 2.5-6

Tertullian
Anima 48.1: 4.17-24
Idol. 14: 1.1-4
Idol. 14.6: 1.3-4
Pud. 13: 4.47-48
Spect. 22.1: 7.43

Theocritus
Id. 1.29-30: 5.1-2
Id. 1.120-121: 2.27-30
Id. 2.85-90: 6.3
Id. 2.88-89: 10.5
Id. 3.15-16: 4.85-94, 4.90
Id. 3.15: 4.73

Id. 4.41-43: 6.32
Id. 5.7: 4.71
Id. 6.22: 6.47-49
Id. 6.43: 4.71
Id. 7.55: 8.11-12
Id. 7.148: 1.15-16
Id. 8.53-56: 3.23-24
Id. 10.34: 4.71
Id. 11.1ff.: 6.3
Id. 16: 3.23-24
Id. 17.13-33: 7.28-32
Id. 17.71-73: 7.118-134
Id. 22.167: 4.96
Id. 24.75: 6.47-49

[Theocrtitus]
Id. 23.16-48: 2 *headnote*
Id. 23.19-20: 4.85-94
Id. 23.19: 4.90
Id. 23.47-48: 2.27-30

Theognis
83-86: 3 *headnote*
227-232: 3 *headnote*

523-524: 3 *headnote*
879-833: 6 *headnote*
1155: 3 *headnote*
1168: 4.96
1231: 4.65, 8.6

Tibullus
1.1: 3 *headnote*
1.1.1-6: *84*, 2.1-8
1.1.1-5: 3.31
1.1.1-2: 3.11-12
1.1.3-4: 7.137
1.1.3: 4.65
1.1.5: 3 *headnote*, 3.23-24
1.1.13: 10.7
1.1.19-22: *101*, 7 *headnote*, 7.183-189
1.1.26: *109*, 14.6
1.1.27: 5.1-2
1.1.33-42: *101*
1.1.33-34: 7.187
1.1.33: 6.47-48, 7.187
1.1.34: 5.21
1.1.37: 3.33-34
1.1.40: 8.8
1.1.41-44: 7.188-189
1.1.41-42: 7 *headnote*, 7.183-189
1.1.43-46: 6.53
1.1.44: 6.60
1.1.46: 13.3-4
1.1.48: 3.32
1.1.51: 4.61-62
1.1.52: 14.6, 19.4
1.1.55: 4.66, 11.3-4, 11.13-14, 11.14
1.1.56: 2.3
1.1.59: 3.7-10, 5.5
1.1.59-68: *94*, 2 *headnote*, 2.9-30
1.1.64: 4.85-94
1.1.67-68: 2.11-12
1.1.69: 3.7, 3.35
1.1.71-72: 3.7-10
1.1.75-76: 4.3
1.1.77-78: 3.32
1.2: *100*
1.2.1: 6.62
1.2.1-6: 6 *headnote*

1.2.2: 6.3, 7.57
1.2.3: 7.57
1.2.5: 12.11-12
1.2.9: 19.5
1.2.10: 9.9-10
1.2.11: 2.13
1.2.14: 19.24
1.2.15: 12.11-12
1.2.16-24: 12.11-12
1.2.17-18: 9.1-2
1.2.17-22: 6.13-17
1.2.19-20: 4.24
1.2.29-30: 10.15
1.2.33: 4.65
1.2.36: 11.7
1.2.43: 1.26
1.2.53-56: 7.62-63
1.2.54: 4.13-14
1.2.56: 6.40, 12.14
1.2.62: 7.62-63
1.2.65: 1.19, 11.7
1.2.66: 12.18
1.2.67: 2.1-2
1.2.70: 3.4, 12.4
1.2.72: 2.4, 7.91
1.2.73: 9.5
1.2.77-78: 3.1, 3.23-24
1.2.78: 10.21
1.2.81: 4.16
1.2.81-82: 5.13-14
1.2.81-88: 4.14-16
1.2.82: 5.14
1.2.84: 10.24
1.2.89: 8.3
1.2.91-92: 19.23
1.2.92-98: 3.7-10
1.2.95: 1.6
1.2.99-100: 11.13-14, 19.24
1.2.100: 20.4
1.3: *100*, *105*, 5 *headnote*
1.3.2: 4.82, 5.31
1.3.3: 5.1, 6.40, 7.75, 7.78
1.3.4: 3.37
1.3.5: 19.11
1.3.5-9: 2.13
1.3.5-6: 2.17-18

1.3.5-10: *94*, 2 *headnote*, 2.9-30,
1.3.7: 2.23-25, 4.28
1.3.8: 2.11-12
1.3.11: 7.166, 12.14
1.3.33-34: *94*
1.3.35: 19.9
1.3.35-36: 7.169-174, 14.6
1.3.35-48: 3.33-34, 7.165-168
1.3.36: *109*, 4.14
1.3.50: 3.12, 12.11-12
1.3.51-52: 5.7-14
1.3.51: 5.21
1.3.52: 5.13-14, 5.14, 10.14
1.3.53: 11.11
1.3.55-56: *111*, 2.9-30, 2.27-30
1.3.55: 2.29, 19.13
1.3.57-66: 5.23
1.3.58: 5.23, *Ep. Tib.* 2
1.3.63: 10.1
1.3.66: 4.28
1.3.71: 4.87
1.3.79: 4.16, 4.45
1.3.80: 3.10
1.3.83: 1.23, 9.23
1.3.90: 19.13
1.3.91: 2.11-12
1.3.93-94: 2.10, 3.25,
1.4: 1 *headnote*, 4 *headnote*
1.4.1-6: 6.1-2
1.4.5-6: 14.3-4
1.4.6: 5.1-2
1.4.7: 4.45, 19.9
1.4.11: 7.91, 7.91-97
1.4.12: 4.30, 4.76, 5.30
1.4.13: 19.19
1.4.14: 4.32
1.4.16: 2.7-8
1.4.21-22: 4.96, 6.27-28
1.4.21-26: 6.49-50
1.4.25-26: 1.3-4
1.4.29: 4.30
1.4.37: 18.3
1.4.37-38: 4.27
1.4.38: 4.27, 10.2
1.4.41: 6.29
1.4.42: 5.1-2

1.4.43: 6.29
1.4.45: 7.193
1.4.46: 4.65
1.4.47: 4.65
1.4.48: 9.8
1.4.49-50: 9.12
1.4.49: 9.7-8
1.4.53-54: 8.10
1.4.56: 6.64
1.4.59-60: 2.1-8
1.4.61-62: 1.5, 1.7
1.4.61: 6.41
1.4.63: 16.1
1.4.66: 10.8
1.4.71-72: 4.75, 4.75-76, 19.24
1.4.73: 4.42
1.4.74: 1.26
1.4.81: 19.17
1.4.83: 9.6, 15.21
1.5: *105*, 6.13
1.5.2: 4.93, 19.7
1.5.4: 7.125
1.5.5-6: 6.13-14, 19.19
1.5.7: 19.1
1.5.7-8: 11.7, 19.2
1.5.9-18: 10 *headnote*
1.5.9-10: 4.72, 10.12
1.5.9: 10.10, 17.2, 17.3
1.5.11-12: 10.10
1.5.13-14: 4.2, 4.10
1.5.14: 12.14
1.5.17: 3.32, 4.58
1.5.19: 10.16
1.5.21: 9.5
1.5.22: 11.10
1.5.26: 19.20
1.5.33: 8.3
1.5.35-36: 4.96, 6.27-29
1.5.37-38: 2.29, 6 *headnote*, 6.3
1.5.39-40: 3.7, 9.18, 19.14
1.5.45-46: 4.678.13
1.5.47-58: 4.61-62
1.5.47-48: 8.15-20
1.5.47: 1.1
1.5.57-58: 19.24
1.5.58: 11. 13

1.5.60: 6.4
1.5.65: 9.9-10
1.5.72: 20.1
1.6.2: 10.22
1.6.3: 4.65
1.6.5-6: 9.9-10
1.6.5: 9.17
1.6.10: 19.17
1.6.15: 1.26, 6.51-52
1.6.16: 13.9
1.6.17: 8.3
1.6.18: 4.76
1.6.22: 5.1-2, 5.7-8
1.6.24: 9.3
1.6.31-32: 4.72
1.6.31: 2.7
1.6.32: 6.61
1.6.33: 1.26, 10.21
1.6.34: 4.84
1.6.35: 11.11
1.6.37-38: 4.66, 4.73
1.6.39: 19.7
1.6.41: 4.84
1.6.49: 4.76
1.6.51-52: 9.4
1.6.54: 6.27-28
1.6.57-58: 4.93
1.6.57: 19.3
1.6.58: 2.13
1.6.63-66: 4.93
1.6.65: 19.3
1.6.67-68: 6.29
1.6.67: 1.23
1.6.71: 13.9
1.6.72: 5.6
1.6.74: 17.4
1.6.75: 1.23
1.6.76: 9.4, 11.7
1.6.77: 11.11
1.6.78: 3.36, 9.12
1.6.83-84: 8.13
1.6.84: 20.4
1.6.85: 7.190
1.7: *97*, *101*, *104*, 7 headnote, 7.9-11, 11 *headnote*, 14.5
1.7.1-2: 3.35, 3.36, 11.3

1.7.1-4: *123*
1.7.3: *123*
1.7.5-8: *122*
1.7.7-9: *122*
1.7.9-22: 7.135-176, 7.137-146
1.7.9-12: *123*, 7.107-110
1.7.9: *Vit. Tib.* 3
1.7.11-12: 7.137-146
1.7.12: 5.3
1.7.13: 7.1
1.7.13-22: *122*
1.7.19: 4.85
1.7.19f.: 2.1-8
1.7.21: *123*, 5.1-2
1.7.22-48: *123*
1.7.23-26: *122*
1.7.25: 19.3
1.7.27-28: 7 *headnote*
1.7.29f.: 2.1-8
1.7.33-42: 7.9-11
1.7.35: 7.9, 10.9
1.7.40: 4.76
1.7.45-47: 12.13
1.7.46-47: 8.11
1.7.46: 1.9, 4.35
1.7.49-54: 11.8
1.7.49: 6.1, 10.1-2
1.7.51: 4.28
1.7.53: 12.14
1.7.55-56: 5.26
1.7.56: 8.10
1.7.58: 2.10
1.7.63-64: 12.19-20
1.7.63: 8.23, 11.19, 12.19
1.8: 1 *headnote*
1.8.3: 4.5-6
1.8.5: 4.47-48
1.8.7: 8.6, 18.6
1.8.9-10: 8.9
1.8.9: 3.1
1.8.13-16: 8.7-14
1.8.15-16: 8.9
1.8.15: 6.29
1.8.17-20: 7.62-63
1.8.17-18: 10.5
1.8.30: 13.3-4, 14.3-4

1.8.31-32: 8.17
1.8.33-34: 3.23-24
1.8.35: 9.16
1.8.41: 18.3
1.8.44: 18.6
1.8.48: 5.16
1.8.49: 10.11
1.8.50-51: 10.1
1.8.51: 5.21
1.8.55-56: *95*, 12.11-12
1.8.56: 4.47-48, 51-52
1.8.63: 1.9, 6.55
1.8.68: 10.21
1.8.69: 6.43
1.8.70: 3.2, 10.24
1.8.74: 4.51-52
1.8.75: 19.6
1.8.77: 8.22, 9.23
1.9.1-6: 6.49-50
1.9.6: 6.26
1.9.23: 13.9
1.9.24: 6.12
1.9.25-26: 4.42
1.9.28-30: 8.10
1.9.31-32: 3.11
1.9.34: 4.43-44, 6.6
1.9.37: 4.61-62
1.9.45: 19.18
1.9.50: 10.7-8, 10.8
1.9.51: 19.7
1.9.53-54: 6.12
1.9.58: 4.51-52
1.9.71: 4.51-52, 12.5-6, 19.5
1.9.73-74: 3.7-10
1.9.74: 4.92
1.9.76: 19.2
1.9.79: 11.13-14
1.9.79-81: 11.14
1.9.80: 8.22, 11.4
1.9.81-84: 19.24
1.9.83: 2.29, 19.13
1.9.83-84: *111*, 12.19
1.9.84: 12.16
1.10.1: 2.1-2, 4.91
1.10.1f.: 2.1-8
1.10.1-6: 4.74

1.10.2: 2.1-2
1.10.6: 9.22
1.10.7: 3.11
1.10.9-24: 3.33-34
1.10.10: 3.32
1.10.13: 8.3
1.10.17: 5.26
1.10.18: 4.24
1.10.19: 3.31
1.10.21-22: 9.1-2
1.10.33: 9.7, 19.11
1.10.38: 1.27-28, 5.24
1.10.39-42: 3.31
1.10.43: 5.15, 19.9
1.10.44: 5.26
1.10.45f.: 2.1-8
1.10.53: 11.10
1.10.54: 6.51-52
1.10.55: 4.32
1.10.57: 12.11-12
1.10.59-60: 4.61-62
1.10.61-62: 20.4
1.10.63-64: 3.26
1.10.64: 10.1
1.10.65-66: 7.89
2.1.2: 1.2
2.1.3-4: 7.163
2.1.5: 3.25
2.1.8: 12.7
2.1.11-12: 4.3, 19.7
2.1.12: 3.7, 4.2
2.1.13-14: 2.16
2.1.25: 4.47-48
2.1.25-26: 4.5-6
2.1.26: 4.5-6
2.1.27: 6.6
2.1.29-30: *6.5*
2.1.33-34: 7.29
2.1.35: 10.1-2
2.1.37f.: 2.1-8
2.1.41: 7.48
2.1.46: 5.3, 5.34
2.1.48: 7.172
2.1.53: 4.71
2.1.53-54: 4.39
2.1.61: 10.1

2.1.67-68: 6.16
2.1.68: 8.15-16
2.1.73-75: 6.13-17
2.1.73-78: 12.11-12
2.1.76: 2.1-2
2.1.81: 10.9
2.1.83: 10.23
2.1.84: 7.166
2.1.87: 4.17-18
2.1.89-90: 4.19-20, 4.55
2.2: *104*, *125*, 8 *headnote*, 11, 14 *headnote*
2.2.1: 11.19
2.2.2: 4.61-62
2.2.3-4: *125*, 2.23, 2.24, 8.17-18, 12.1
2.2.3-5: 11.9
2.2.5: 3.33-34, 8.3
2.2.5-8: 11.8
2.2.6: 12.13
2.2.7: 4.28, 6.63
2.2.8: *125*, 6.5, 12.14
2.2.9-10: *125*, 11.8, 11.9, 11.20
2.2.10-16: 3.23-24
2.2.10: 6.57
2.2.11-16: 7.199-200
2.2.11-12: 11.16, 11.19
2.2.13-16: 3 *headnote*
2.2.15-16: *126*, 8.19-20
2.2.16: 7.53
2.2.18-19: *125*, 11.14, 12.20
2.2.18: 1.26
2.2.19-20: 3.7-10, 5,15-16, 5.25
2.2.19: 5.16
2.2.21-22: 12.19-20
2.2.21: 11.19, 12.11-12
2.3: *104*, *105*, *125*
2.3.1-2: 14.3
2.3.1: 5.1, 14.1
2.3.2: 2.1-2, 19.17
2.3.3: 11.11
2.3.5: 4.82
2.3.6: 3.12
2.3.9: 10.13
2.3.10: 5.15, 9.8
2.3.11-32: 4.67-72

Book Three of the Corpus Tibullianum: Introduction, Text, Translation and Commentary

2.3.11: 4.25, 4.67
2.3.12: 4.27, 4.67-72, 10.2, 11.4
2.3.13-14: 4.19-20, 6.3, 10.1-2
2.3.14: 10.4
2.3.14b-c: 8.10
2.3.15: 4.67
2.3.21: 4.67
2.3.23: 4.67-72
2.3.25-26: 8.9
2.3.27: 4.72
2.3.30: 8.13, 10.14
2.3.31: 4.68, 17.1
2.3.33-34: 11.13-14
2.3.35-36: 3.13-16
2.3.36: 6.38
2.3.41: 7.139
2.3.44: 3.12
2.3.49: 19.17
2.3.52: 3.4, 12.4
2.3.63: 7.9, 7.163
2.3.64: 11.12
2.3.79-80: 4.66
2.3.79: 4.74, 6.14
2.4.1-6: 4.66, 11.3-4
2.4.1: 4.74, 19.22
2.4.3-6: 19.19
2.4.3: 1.9, 7.118-119, 11.15
2.4.4: 11.14
2.4.6: 11.5
2.4.7: 4.82
2.4.9: 7.202
2.4.10: 7.53
2.4.11: 4.19-20
2.4.14: 7.178
2.4.15: 1.17, 4.3
2.4.17-18: 7.18-27, 7.19-23
2.4.19: 1.7, 7.87
2.4.20: 4.3
2.4.23-26: 19.23
2.4.26: 5.11
2.4.27-30: 3. 17-18, 8.15-20
2.4.27: 4.61-62
2.4.28: 3.18
2.4.30: 3.17
2.4.31: 3.19-20
2.4.35-36: 1.7

2.4.45: 7.61
2.4.47: 12.20
2.4.51: 4.5-6, 6.43
2.4.53: 4.24
2.4.57: 6.13-14
2.4.60: 3.12
2.5.1: 3.33-34, 10.19, 12.7
2.5.1-10: 4 *headnote*, 4.23-42, 4.25-26
2.5.5: 4.23, 6.2
2.5.6: 8.2
2.5.7-8: 4.35, 12.13
2.5.7: 2.13, 4.36, 12.13
2.5.11-12: 4.44-45
2.5.11: 4.47-48
2.5.14: 4.5-6
2.5.29-30: 4.38
2.5.30: 19.20
2.5.38: 8.12
2.5.46: 2.11-12, 8.22, 13.1-2
2.5.54: 8.4
2.5.60: 4.17-18
2.5.63: 4.23, 4.77
2.5.79-80: 10.7-8
2.5.79: 7.184-185
2.5.86: 9.6
2.5.87: 6.5
2.5.93-94: 5.26
2.5.108: 19.17
2.5.110: 6.3, 12.18
2.5.121-122: 6.1-2
2.5.121: 4.27, 10.2, 11.20
2.6.5: 6.13-14
2.6.11: 8.10
2.6.15: 4.65, 8.6
2.6.17-18: 5.13-14, 9.12, 20.4
2.6.18: 5.13
2.6.19: 2.7-8
2.6.25: 11.15
2.6.35: 10.21, 19.3
2.6.37: 4.2
2.6.40: 5.24
2.6.41: 20.4
2.6.43-54: 4.61-62
2.6.43: 12.10

Timocles
fr. 25-26 (Kassel-Austin): *119*

Turpilius (Ribbeck³)
Com. 193: 5.23-25

Valerius Flaccus
1.37: 4.85
1.150: 1.3-4
1.260: 6.5
1.278: 4.23
1.300: 6.4
1.315-316: 2.5-6
1.385: 4.35
1.424: 7.91
1.497: 7.19
1.580: 4.91
1.616-617: 7.23
1.616: 7.22
1.750: 10.25
1.766: 2.3
1.783: 7.67
1.787: 9.20
2.98: 7.153
2.180-181: 11.3-4
2.218: 4.77
2.230: 4.61-62
2.517: 7.23
2.600: 2.16
3.316: 2.4
3.469: 7.135
3.481: 4.29, 7.67
3.718: 4.35
4.53: 6.5
4.73: 7.63
4.104ff.: 7.56
4.257: 7.129
4.334: 4.23
4.363: 9.12-13
4.388: 4.22
4.445: 4.49
4.490-491: 5.25
4.603-604: 6.23
4.606-607: 4.91
4.697: 7.92
5.140: 4.2

5.215-216: 7.163
5.316: 12.11-12
5.350: 7.60
5.444: 16.6
5.689: 7.54
5.694: 6.57
6.62: 7.11
6.148: 4.90
6.161-162: 7.114
6.193: 7.97
6.355: 7.72
6.518: 1.2
6.563: 7.169
6.674: 7.202
6.726: 3.1
6.740: 7.54
7.36: 9.7
7.86: 4.91
7.138: 7.193
7.437: 6.27, 7.79
7.562: 7.63
7.607-608: 3.12
8.231: 7.56
8.234: 7.121
8.408-409: 4.14

Valerius Maximus
7.3 (ext.) 1: 19.20
9.2.9: 4.37
9.10 (ext.) 1: 7.143

Valgius Rufus
fr. 1 (Courtney = 165 Hollis): 5.25
fr. 2 (Courtney = 166 Hollis): 7.180
fr. 3 (Courtney = 167 Hollis): 7.180
fr. 4 (Courtney = 168 Hollis): 7.180
fr. 5 (C0urtney = 169 Hollis): 7.180

Varro
Ling. 5.46: 8.13-14
Ling. 5.61-62: 11.13-14
Ling. 5.69: 4.13-14
Ling. 5.100: 6.15
Ling. 6.4: 11.9
Ling. 6.16: 12.14
Ling. 6.33: 1.2, 7.32

Ling. 6.46: 5.12
Ling. 6.80: 13.10
Ling. 7.2: 7.36
Ling. 7.19.1: 6.1-2
Ling. 7.81: 3.3
Ling. 7.85: 5.3
Ling. 8.13: 13.8
Ling. 8.63: 4.2
Ling. 9.10.5: 4.24
Men. 27.1: 9.20
Men. 36-13: 3.21-22
Men. 123.3: 10.2
Men. 382: 3.17
Men. 471.1: 7.194
Rust. 1.2.27: 10.10
Rust. 1.7.10: 9.1
Rust. 1.9.1: 9.1
Rust. 1.65: 6.6
Rust. 2.4.9: 4.31
Rust. 2.5.7: 4.27
Rust. 2.9.4: 4.27

Varro Atacinus
fr. 17 (Courtney = fr. 112 Hollis):
 7.151-174, 7.153

Vegetius
Mil. 1.15: 7.89
Mil. 1.22: 7.86
Mil. 2.15: 7.90
Mil. 2.23: 7.89
Mil. 3.2: 7.86, 7.88
Mil. 3.8.3: 7.86, 7.87
Mil. 3.20.6-8: 7.103-105
Mil. 3.26.18: 7.101-102

Velleius Paterculus
1.14.1: 7.211
2.5.3: 7.210
2.46.1: 7.135-176
2.103.1: 1.27-28
2.125.5: 7.39
2.127: 5.3
3.131.1: 1.1

Vetus Latina
Luc. 12.27: 3.36
Matth. 6.28: 3.36

Virgil
Aen. 1.1: 6.41
Aen. 1.8: 1.5, 4.16, 6.26
Aen. 1.18: 3.35
Aen. 1.25-26: 1.20
Aen. 1.35: 7.173
Aen. 1.39: 8.5
Aen. 1.50: 10.17-18
Aen. 1.62-63: 7.91
Aen. 1.63: 4.69
Aen. 1.94-95: 3.26
Aen. 1.95: 7.65
Aen. 1.127: 7.123
Aen. 1.139-40: 5.21
Aen. 1.147: 7.127
Aen. 1.151-153: 7.44
Aen. 1.158: 7.31
Aen. 1.187: 7.89
Aen. 1.198: 1.23
Aen. 1.210: 7.179
Aen. 1.239: 4.83
Aen. 1.257: 13.3-4
Aen. 1.263-264: 6.13-14
Aen. 1.308: 11.20
Aen. 1.330: 6.30
Aen. 1.334: 7.15
Aen. 1.355-356: 13.1-2
Aen. 1.374: 4.93
Aen. 1.392: 6.60
Aen. 1.398: 4.40
Aen. 1.404: 4.35
Aen. 1.440: 5.29
Aen. 1.446: 3.18
Aen. 1.603: 4.53
Aen. 1.613: 3.18
Aen. 1.639: 4.37
Aen. 1.657: *108*, 13.3-4
Aen. 1.683-684: 6.12
Aen. 1.685: 13.3-4
Aen. 1.688: 13.3-4
Aen. 1.715: 6.45
Aen. 1.743: 4.4-9

Aen. 2.13: 7.3
Aen. 2.17: 4.94
Aen. 2.146-147: 11.14
Aen. 2.160: 6.9
Aen. 2.183: 4.16
Aen. 2.268: 4.9
Aen. 2.270-271: 4.24
Aen. 2.325-326: 5.32
Aen. 2.337: 3.35
Aen. 2.364-365:1.3-4
Aen. 2.396: 3.28
Aen. 2.416: 7.194
Aen. 2.448: 3.16
Aen. 2.450: 7.185
Aen. 2.519: 9.7
Aen. 2.591-592: 6.23
Aen. 2.623: 6.22
Aen. 2.644: 6.37
Aen. 2.738: 2.4
Aen. 2.772-773: 4.26
Aen. 3.12: 4.16
Aen. 3.41-42: 5.6
Aen. 3.42: 2.16
Aen. 3.81: 4.23
Aen. 3.119: 4.25
Aen. 3.120: 5.33
Aen. 3.251-252: 4.47-48
Aen. 3.252-252: 4.45-48
Aen. 3.264: 6.22
Aen. 3.302: 2.11-12
Aen. 3.303-304: 2.15
Aen. 3.316: 4.75-76
Aen. 3.321: 4.93, 19.16
Aen. 3.330-331: 2.4
Aen. 3.420ff: 7.73-75
Aen. 3.420-421: 4.89
Aen. 3.432: 7.72
Aen. 3.456-457: 4.77
Aen. 3.476: 4.43-44
Aen. 3.483: 7.121
Aen. 3.493: 5.31
Aen. 3.559: 4.91
Aen. 3.605: 4.85
Aen. 3.637: 8.6
Aen. 3.641-642: 6.23
Aen. 3.678: 7.56

Aen. 3.684-686: 7.70
Aen. 3.684: 4.89
Aen. 3.693-694: 4.25
Aen. 4.2: 8.11-12, 11.5
Aen. 4.6: 8.6
Aen. 4.22-23: 14.7
Aen. 4.32: 18.3
Aen. 4.41: 4.91
Aen. 4.58: 6.38
Aen. 4.88: 7.75
Aen. 4.91: 3.32
Aen. 4.121: 9.7-8
Aen. 4.128: 13.3-4
Aen. 4.141: 4.93
Aen. 4.147-148: 4.27
Aen. 4.166-168: 3.33-34
Aen. 4.183: 4.40
Aen. 4.191-192: 13.10
Aen. 4.216: 6.63
Aen. 4.262: 8.15-16
Aen. 4.314: 1.15-16
Aen. 4.325: 7.147
Aen. 4.365-367: 4.85-94
Aen. 4.367: 6.15
Aen. 4.382: 10.25
Aen. 4.412: 4.65
Aen. 4.419-420: 2.3
Aen. 4.425-426: 5.7-14
Aen. 4.425: 5.7
Aen. 4.517: 2.16
Aen. 4.522-523: 17.2
Aen. 4.522f.: 4.19-20
Aen. 4.569-570: 4.61-62, 4.63
Aen. 4.578: 7.10
Aen. 4.596: 6.42
Aen. 4.628-629: 4.83
Aen. 4.685: 12.3, 13.3-4
Aen. 4.698-699: 5.5
Aen. 5.27: 6.63
Aen. 5.95: 11.20
Aen. 5.191-192: 5.22
Aen. 5.235-237: 10.24
Aen. 5.246: 4.23
Aen. 5.269: 6.2
Aen. 5.305: 13.8
Aen. 5.349: 13.8

Book Three of the Corpus Tibullianum: 695
Introduction, Text, Translation and Commentary

Aen. 5.383: 13.8
Aen. 5.397: 7.184-185
Aen. 5.485: 7.89
Aen. 5.498-499: 4.65
Aen. 5.520: 7.127
Aen. 5.539: 4.23
Aen. 5.542: 14.8
Aen. 5.590: 12.11-12
Aen. 5.702: 11.20
Aen. 5.721: 4.17-18
Aen. 5.724-725: 1.25
Aen. 5.729: 2.5-6
Aen. 5.736: 5.33
Aen. 5.790: 7.23
Aen. 5.791: 7.58
Aen. 5.800: 13.3-4
Aen. 5.859: 7.123
Aen. 6.7-8: 7.141
Aen. 6.11-12: 4.45-48
Aen. 6.12: 4.49
Aen. 6.49-50: 4.26
Aen. 6.82: 4.50
Aen. 6.123: 7.12
Aen. 6.132: 3.37
Aen. 6.134-135: 3.37
Aen. 6.134: 5.24
Aen. 6.147: 3.37
Aen. 6.153: 5.33
Aen. 6.166: 7.184-185
Aen. 6.202: 7.209
Aen. 6.227: 2.19
Aen. 6.261: 10.21
Aen. 6.279: 5.9
Aen. 6.288: 4.86
Aen. 6.306: 3.9
Aen. 6.322: 7.68
Aen. 6.324: 19.15
Aen. 6.343-344: 4.49
Aen. 6.429: 5.5
Aen. 6.442: 4.65
Aen. 6.448-449: 7.63
Aen. 6.464: 2.3
Aen. 6.477-478: 7.145
Aen. 6.513-514: 6.33
Aen. 6.528: 7.147
Aen. 6.533: 7.182

Aen. 6.535: 4.17-18
Aen. 6.539: 4.61-62
Aen. 6.540-543: 5.23
Aen. 6.566: 5.22
Aen. 6.587: 8.6
Aen. 6.633-634: 6.22
Aen. 6.638ff.: 5.23
Aen. 6.647: 4.39
Aen. 6.697: 6.22
Aen. 6.705: 7.61
Aen. 6.726-727: 4.59
Aen. 6.735ff.: 7.206-210
Aen. 6.791: 7.48-49
Aen. 6.796: 7.150
Aen. 6.805: 6.15
Aen. 6.840: 5.7
Aen. 6.881: 7.91-97
Aen. 6.893-901: 4.1
Aen. 6.896: 4.7-8
Aen. 7.26: 4.17-18
Aen. 7.30-31: 10.7-8
Aen. 7.31: 10.7-8
Aen. 7.56: 1.2
Aen. 7.59-60: 4.23
Aen. 7.65: 7.209
Aen. 7.148: 8.6
Aen. 7.194: 4.42
Aen. 7.263-265: 6.9
Aen. 7.293-294: 4.83
Aen. 7.302-303: 4.91
Aen. 7.302: 4.89
Aen. 7.310-311: 6.22
Aen. 7.327: 6.38
Aen. 7.389-390: 8.15
Aen. 7.416-417: 5.25
Aen. 7.446: 10.5
Aen. 7.505: 7.128
Aen. 7.566: 7.43
Aen. 7.646: 7.127
Aen. 7.704-705: 6.27-28
Aen. 7.717: 4.61-62
Aen. 7.757-758: 7.62-63
Aen. 8.30: 4.22
Aen. 8.33: 4.55
Aen. 8.64: 4.17-18
Aen. 8.134: 4.50

Aen. 8.286: 6.2
Aen. 8.287-288: 7.3-4
Aen. 8.303: 4.57
Aen. 8.339: 7.31
Aen. 8.355: 7.174
Aen. 8.369: 4.55
Aen. 8.377: 3.32
Aen. 8.444: 7.56
Aen. 8.508: 5.16
Aen. 8.523: 13.3-4
Aen. 8.547-549: 4.5-6
Aen. 8.581: 6.5
Aen. 8.615: 13.3-4
Aen. 8.627: 4.47-48
Aen. 8.628-630: 8.11-12
Aen. 8.643: 4.78
Aen. 8.679: 4.16
Aen. 8.686: 8.19-20
Aen. 8.720: 4.29
Aen. 9.6: 13.8
Aen. 9.115: 8.5
Aen. 9.138: 2.4
Aen. 9.141-142: 4.61-62
Aen. 9.148-149: 10.21
Aen. 9.186-187: 4.59
Aen. 9.239: 7.75
Aen. 9.312-313: 4.96
Aen. 9.328: 10.1
Aen. 9.401: 7.205
Aen. 9.426: 2.3
Aen. 9.442: 7.202
Aen. 9.480: 3.1
Aen. 9.535: 8.6
Aen. 9.590: 7.89
Aen. 9.593-594: 8.17
Aen. 9.603:6.7
Aen. 9.610: 5.16
Aen. 9.618: 4.40
Aen. 9.627: 7.15
Aen. 9.680: 7.79-80
Aen. 9.741: 7.136
Aen. 9.788: 7.185
Aen. 10.90: 2.30
Aen. 10.92: 6.10
Aen. 10.101: 7.183
Aen. 10.103: 7.124, 7.126

Aen. 10.115: 7.130-134
Aen. 10.158: 7.23
Aen. 10.232: 7.202
Aen. 10.268: 7.69
Aen. 10.273-275: 5.1-2
Aen. 10.274: 4.9
Aen. 10.356: 7.124
Aen. 10.471-472: 3.37
Aen. 10.501: 4.5-6
Aen. 10.613: 7.184-185
Aen. 10.642: 4.7-8
Aen. 10.652: 4.96
Aen. 10.681-683: 1.19-20
Aen. 10.691-692: 5.1-2
Aen. 10.764: 7.58
Aen. 10.881: 7.17
Aen. 10.882-887: 7.91-97
Aen. 11.28: 5.5
Aen. 11.94: 4.41
Aen. 11.96-97: 3.37
Aen. 11.165-166: 3.8
Aen. 11.182: 4.9
Aen. 11.185-186: 10.26
Aen. 11.244: 4.17-18
Aen. 11.263: 7.56
Aen. 11.301: 2.15
Aen. 11.389: 6.57
Aen. 11.424: 10.5
Aen. 11.456-457: 4.87
Aen. 11.524: 7.43
Aen. 11.642: 7.75
Aen. 11.650: 7.90
Aen. 11.779: 7.79-80
Aen. 11.795: 4.96
Aen. 11.818-819: 4.30
Aen. 11.821: 19.15, 19.16
Aen. 12.56-60: 1.15-16
Aen. 12.67-68: 4.30, 4.32, 4.33-34
Aen. 12.67-69: 4.31-34
Aen. 12.73: 7.98
Aen. 12.97-100: 4.28
Aen. 12.120: 6.2
Aen. 12.139: 4.69
Aen. 12.197: 19.15
Aen. 12.199: 5.22
Aen. 12.321: 11.20

Book Three of the Corpus Tibullianum: 697
Introduction, Text, Translation and Commentary

Aen. 12. 392: 4.65, 8.6
Aen. 12.394: 7.89
Aen. 12.402-403: 10.4
Aen. 12.487: 4.59
Aen. 12.489: 7.90
Aen. 12.546: 7.183
Aen. 12.709: 7.103
Aen. 12.712: 4.69
Aen. 12.725: 7.130
Aen. 12.753: 12.11-12
Aen. 12.771: 7.207
Aen. 12.790: 7.98
Aen. 12.802: 4.42
Aen. 12.819: 4.47-48
Aen. 12.845-847: 4.90
Aen. 12.850: 4.9
Aen. 12.873-874: 3.9
Ecl. 1.2: 4.71
Ecl. 1.6-9: 6.12
Ecl. 1.10: 4.71
Ecl. 1.24: 7.123
Ecl. 1.57: 7.141
Ecl. 1.66: 7.149
Ecl. 1.70-72: 7.183-189
Ecl. 2.20: 2.20
Ecl. 2.21: 3.12
Ecl. 2.25: 10.6
Ecl. 2.29: 9.1
Ecl. 2.34: 4.71
Ecl. 2.36: 4.71
Ecl. 2.37: 4.71
Ecl. 2.42-45: 3.18
Ecl. 2.45: 10.1-2
Ecl. 2.48: 8.17-18
Ecl. 2.60: 6.27
Ecl. 2.62: 9.15
Ecl. 2.68: 11.5
Ecl. 3.3-4: *119*, 1.23
Ecl. 3.22: 4.71
Ecl. 3.25: 4.71
Ecl. 3.27: 4.71
Ecl. 3.38: 7.171
Ecl. 3.58: 7.136
Ecl. 3.59: *108*, 13.3-4
Ecl. 3.67: 9.5
Ecl. 3.72-73: 6.49-50

Ecl. 3.75: 9.12
Ecl. 3.77: 12.14
Ecl. 3.78: 4.93
Ecl. 3.84: 14.8
Ecl. 3.94: 5.6
Ecl. 4.9: 7.150
Ecl. 4.10: 4.13-14, 12.14
Ecl. 4.25: 2.24
Ecl. 4.28: 7.184-185
Ecl. 4.32-33: 7.174
Ecl. 4.48: 7.135-136
Ecl. 4.53: 3.7, 7.112a
Ecl. 4.53-55: 7.205-206
Ecl. 4.55: 7.211
Ecl. 4.56-57:4.25
Ecl. 4.60: 7.136
Ecl. 4.62: 7.136
Ecl. 5.2: 4.71
Ecl. 5.8: 7.120
Ecl. 5.10: 7.136
Ecl. 5.12: 7.136
Ecl. 5.24-25: 14.3-4
Ecl. 5.25: 7.127
Ecl. 5.29-30: 6.15
Ecl. 5.33: 3.12
Ecl. 5.35: 11.12
Ecl. 5.40-41: 5.4
Ecl. 5.43-44: 2.27-30
Ecl. 5.48: 4.71
Ecl. 5.56-57: 4.29
Ecl. 5.60-61: 5.13
Ecl. 5.76: 9.2
Ecl. 6.3-5: 7.18-27
Ecl. 6.3-4: 4.50
Ecl. 6.3: *Ep. Tib.* 4
Ecl. 6.4-5: 7.178
Ecl. 6.6-7: 7.177-180
Ecl. 6.8: 4.71
Ecl. 6.19-20: 5.1-2
Ecl. 6.46: 4.67
Ecl. 6.53: 4.30
Ecl. 6.64: 7.106
Ecl. 6.66: 8.24
Ecl. 6.69: 4.71
Ecl. 6.74-75: 4.89
Ecl. 6.82-83: 4.71

Ecl. 7.9: 10.1-2
Ecl. 7.22-23: 5.3
Ecl. 7.24: 4.71
Ecl. 7.29-36: 7.14-15
Ecl. 7.29: 9.5
Ecl. 7.40: *109*
Ecl. 7.44: 6.7
Ecl. 7.61: 7.12
Ecl. 8.3-4: 7.124-129
Ecl. 8.4: 7.125
Ecl. 8.19: 6.49-50
Ecl. 8.20: 5.5
Ecl. 8.21: 4.71, 7.136
Ecl. 8.25: 4.71
Ecl. 8.32: 13.10
Ecl. 8.33: 4.71
Ecl. 8.43-45: 4.85-94
Ecl. 8.43: 4.73
Ecl. 8.47-48: 4.65
Ecl. 8.49-50: 8.6
Ecl. 8.49: 4.65
Ecl. 8.63:1.5
Ecl. 8.68: 13.3-4
Ecl. 8.70: 7.62-63
Ecl. 8.85: 4.71
Ecl. 8.109: 13.1-2, 13.3-4
Ecl. 9.2-6: 7.183-189
Ecl. 9.25: 8.3
Ecl. 9.33-34: 4.49
Ecl. 9.39: 10.1-2
Ecl. 9.40: 5.4
Ecl. 9.42: 7.171
Ecl. 9.43: 10.1-2
Ecl. 10.1: 7.16
Ecl. 10.6: 4.19-20
Ecl. 10.21-23: 4 *headnote*, 4.55-58
Ecl. 10.21: 4.39
Ecl. 10.22: 1.19, 4.43-44, 5.13, 6.7, 9.5
Ecl. 10.24: 4.39
Ecl. 10.26: 4.39
Ecl. 10.29-30: 4.65, 8.6
Ecl. 10.33-34: 9.15
Ecl. 10.34: 4.71
Ecl. 10.38: 9.15
Ecl. 10.40: 7.171

Ecl. 10.44-45: 5.13
Ecl. 10.46-48: 9.3
Ecl. 10.46: 9.3, 9.5
Ecl. 10.49: 9.8
Ecl. 10.50-51: 4.71
Ecl. 10.51: 4.39
Ecl. 10.55-57: 9.1, 9.3
Ecl. 10.55-60: 9.7-10
Ecl. 10.60: 9.7
Ecl. 10.64: 6.3, 6.7
Ecl. 10.69: 2.5-6, 4.76, 6.4, 13.1-2
Ecl. 10.70-77: 1.17
Ecl. 10.71-72: 5.1-2
Ecl. 10.73-74: 4.51-52
Ecl. 10.77: 6.7
Georg. 1.5: 7.3
Georg. 1.8: 3.12
Georg. 1.15: 4.67
Georg. 1.16-18: 7.131
Georg. 1.24-47: *122*, 7 *headnote*
Georg. 1.32-35: 7.9-11
Georg. 1.33: 7.9-11
Georg. 1.38: 5.23
Georg. 1.45: 7.161
Georg. 1.56-57: 2.23
Georg. 1.63: 6.7
Georg. 1.64: 3.12
Georg. 1.71: 7.172
Georg. 1.86: 7.161
Georg. 1.105: 3.12
Georg. 1.152: 7.128
Georg. 1.166: 6.1-2
Georg. 1.218: 7.9-11
Georg. 1.229: 7.9-11
Georg. 1.233-251: 7.151-174
Georg. 1.237: 4.9
Georg. 1.238-239: 7.150
Georg. 1.243: 3.37
Georg. 1.265: 7.171
Georg. 1.276-277: 3.26
Georg. 1.290: 7.3-4, 7.172
Georg. 1.293-294: 3.36
Georg. 1.316: 7.184-185
Georg. 1.333: 7.156
Georg. 1.337: 7.159
Georg. 1.342: 7.154

Georg. 1.349: 4.23
Georg. 1.404: 7.209
Georg. 1.469: 4.85
Georg. 1.472-473: 4.86
Georg. 1.511: 7.152
Georg. 2.2: 7.1
Georg. 2.4-7: 10.1-2
Georg. 2.4: 6.38
Georg. 2.7: 6.38
Georg. 2.11-12: 7.125
Georg. 2.17: 7.128
Georg. 2.68: 4.82
Georg. 2.92: 3.12
Georg. 2.115: 2.24
Georg. 2.128: 5.9
Georg. 2.139: 2.23, 2.24, 3.12
Georg. 2.180: 1.11-12
Georg. 2.184: 3.12
Georg. 2.198-199: 7.185
Georg. 2.203: 3.12
Georg. 2.221: 7.202
Georg. 2.243: 5.1
Georg. 2.248: 2.12
Georg. 2.274: 2.12
Georg. 2.341: 7.123
Georg. 2.342: 7.10
Georg. 2.353: 5.1-2
Georg. 2.378-379: 9.3
Georg. 2.458-467: 3.13-16
Georg. 2.461-466: 3.3
Georg. 2.461: 7.183
Georg. 2.463: 4.37
Georg. 2.465: 3.18
Georg. 2.475-482: 7.18-27, 7.19-23
Georg. 2.490-493: 2.1-8
Georg. 2.523: 6.45
Georg. 2.524: 4.60
Georg. 2.592: 6.38
Georg. 3.1-2: 4.67-72
Georg. 3.1: 7.1
Georg. 3.9: 5.7-8
Georg. 3.19-20: 7 *headnote*
Georg. 3.19: 7.9-11, 7.12-13
Georg. 3.21-22: 7.8-9
Georg. 3.46-47: 7.179
Georg. 3.66: 4.9

Georg. 3.73-74: 4.64
Georg. 3.113-122: 7.91-97
Georg. 3.114: 7.135
Georg. 3.167-168: 7.117
Georg. 3.172: 7.13
Georg. 3.190-208: 7.91-97
Georg. 3.203: 5.1
Georg. 3.204: 7.202
Georg. 3.225: 9.3
Georg. 3.245-246: 4.90
Georg. 3.259: 4.65
Georg. 3.291-293: 1.15-16
Georg. 3.294: 4.40
Georg. 3.350: 7.120
Georg. 3.354-355: 10.6
Georg. 3.359: 4.17-18
Georg. 3.371: 9.17
Georg. 3.384: 7.128
Georg. 3.407-408: 7.187
Georg. 3.455-456: 10.4
Georg. 3.458: 7.128
Georg. 3.518: 2.14
Georg. 3.526-527: 6.17-18
Georg. 4.6: 7.16
Georg. 4.62-63: *124*, 10.9
Georg. 4.105: 7.44
Georg. 4.118: 2.12
Georg. 4.190: 10.5
Georg. 4.233: 4.17-18
Georg. 4.252: 5.28
Georg. 4.267: 10.9
Georg. 4.278: 7.125
Georg. 4.281ff.: 2.1-8
Georg. 4.332: 2.7-8
Georg. 4.346: 11.7
Georg. 4.352: 7.123
Georg. 4.384: 12.14
Georg. 4.385-386: 7.134
Georg. 4.397: 2.23
Georg. 4.401: 9.12-13
Georg. 4.408: 6.15
Georg. 4.430: 4.85
Georg. 4.453: 5.1-2
Georg. 4.472: 2.9
Georg. 4.475: 3.9
Georg. 4.483: 4.88

Georg. 4.487: 4.36
Georg. 4.495-496: 3.37
Georg. 4.506: 7.70
Georg. 4.517: 7.146
Georg. 4.560: 7.176
Georg. 4.563-566: *124*, 7.181

[Virgil]
Aen. 1a-1b: 4.71

Aetna
2: 4.86
4: 1.15-16
62: 10.25
77-79: 5.21
94-95: 7.53
104: 7.19
339: 4.53
399: 16.6
583-584: 6.39
636: 3.26

Catalepton
4.1: 7.112a
4.11-12: 11.7
4.12: 11.7
9: 7 *headnote*
9.1: 4.29, 4.30
9.3-4: 7 *headnote*
9.3: 7.32
9.4: 7.53
9.6: 7.48-49
9.8: 8.24
9.10: 7.2
9.12: 16.6
9.13-20: 7.25
9.13: 7.26-27, 7.211
9.16: 7.48-49
9.43: 7.39
9.47-49: 7.193-195
9.49: 7.194, 7.196
9.51-54: 7.137-146
9.53-54: 7.135-176
9.55-56: 7.5-6
9.56-60: 7.178
9.59-60: 4.43-44

9.60: 4.50
9.61-64: 7 *headnote*
9.61ff.: 3.19-20
9.61: 7.4
15.2: 7.180

Ciris
7: 7.18
9: 7.211
27: 3.26
39: 7.5-6, 7.211
62: 7.200
82: 4.14
100: 7.34
133: 4.65
135-136: 4.65, 6.12, 6.15
144: 4.35
151: 4.35
185: 6.27
222: 3.3
247-248: 4.82
250: 4.55
269: 1.5
287: 3.8
291: 4.65
314: 3.8
356-357: 7.202
357: 7.202
387: 3.18
404: 7.124
455: 4.82
473: 4.93
499: 7.197
504: 5.30
541: 7.209

Copa
33: 10.1
34: 4.61-62
35: 8.17-18

Culex
12: 1.15-16
12-19: 1.15-16
12-18: 1.15-16
16: 1.13

62: 12.3
87: 2.23
102: 4.17-18
108: 7.154
111: 6.24
117-118: 7.125
148: 5.1
157: 7.154
202: 4.17-18
212: 7.130
220-221: 4.87
231-232: 5.24
248: 7.194
278: 7.125
281: 4.69
331: 4.89332: 7.56
333: 1.27-28
349: 7.52
372-373: 3.3, 5.248
374: 3.37
406: 4.33-34
411-412: 2.27, 2.28

De Rosa Nascente
43: 7.210

Dirae
8-9: 6.42
21: 4.30, 5.4
53: 4.91
61: 8.3

67: 7.143

Lydia
3: 11.11
113: 7.13
162: 9.18

Moretum
90: 7.134

Vita Homeri (Wilamowitz)
p. 25.10: 7.200
p. 28.10: 7.200

Vitruvius
1.6.2: 7.98-99
5 *pr.* 5: 7.196
8.3.15: 5.9
9 *pr.* 16: 7.192

Xenophanes
fr. 1 (West): 6 *headnote*

Xenophon
Cyneg. 2.4-9: 9.12
Cyneg. 10.6: 9.2, 9.6
Cyneg. 10.7: 9.7-8

Zeno
SVF I 115: 7.23